Sociology

A Comprehensive South African Introduction

Second edition

Paul Stewart & Johan Zaaiman (editors)

JUTA

Sociology: A Comprehensive South African Introduction

First published 2014
Revised reprint 2015
Second edition 2020

Juta and Company (Pty) Ltd
PO Box 14373, Lansdowne, 7779, Cape Town, South Africa
1st Floor, Sunclare Building, 21 Dreyer Street, Claremont 7708
www.juta.co.za

ISBN 978 1 48513 033 8
WebPDF 978 1 4851 3034 5

Production Specialist: Mmakasa Ramoshaba
Editor: Wendy Priilaid
Proofreader: Wendy Priilaid
Typesetter: Lebone Publishing Services
Cover designer: DragandDrop
Indexer: Kobie Ferreira

Typeset in Frutiger LT Std 9/13

Table of contents

About the authors

Tapiwa Chagonda DLitt et Phil (Sociology) is an Associate Professor of Sociology at the University of Johannesburg in South Africa. His research interests mainly centre on Zimbabwe's socio-economic and socio-political challenges since 2000. He has published numerous articles on Zimbabwe's crises in journals such as the *Review of African Political Economy* and the *Journal of Contemporary African Studies* and popular media such as *The Conversation*. Tapiwa is a member of the South African Sociological Association (SASA), the International Sociological Association (ISA) and the Council for the Development of Social Science Research in Africa (CODESRIA).

Elsa Crause is a sociologist with a doctorate in Sociology and Industrial Psychology. She has taught at various South African universities including Port Elizabeth (now NMMU), University of the Free State, University of the North, and is currently the QwaQwa Campus Vice Principal: Academic and Research, University of the Free State. Her interests and activities are in research on youth, social business, social inclusion and empowerment in the development field.

Gretchen du Plessis is Professor of Development Studies at the University of South Africa. Her work centres on social policy, population and identity, gender and human security, and social research methodology. She is interested in questions relating to identity, social policy, critical social theory, and the development of new approaches to seemingly intractable social problems.

Ran Greenstein is an Associate Professor of Sociology at the University of the Witwatersrand. He has published and edited *Genealogies of Conflict: Class, Identity and State in Palestine/Israel and South Africa to 1948* (Wesleyan University Press 1995), *Comparative Perspectives on South Africa* (Macmillan 1998), and *Zionism and its Discontents: A Century of Radical Dissent in Israel/Palestine* (Pluto Press 2014). His most recent publication is *Identity, Nationalism, and Race: Anti-Colonial Resistance in South Africa and Israel/Palestine* (Routledge 2021).

Cornie Groenewald (DPhil) is Professor Emeritus and former Chair of the Department of Sociology and Social Anthropology at Stellenbosch University. He started his career as a social researcher and lecturer in Sociology at the University of the Western Cape. He subsequently moved to the University of Port Elizabeth (now NMU) and to Stellenbosch, his alma mater. He retired from his office at Stellenbosch in 2005 and since then has intermittently taught at Stellenbosch, Walter Sisulu University, North-West University (Mafikeng Campus), and the Cornerstone Institute. He wrote the Sociology curriculum for the restructured Huguenot College. He has published in the fields of history of (South African) sociology, population studies, community development, urbanisation, social development and evaluation research. He consults as a sociologist.

Phephani Gumbi is a Doctor of Philosophy. His research interest and publications are mainly on language planning, policy implementation and literacy development of African languages. He championed the establishment of the isiZulu Discipline/Department as a head and a lecturer between 2012 and 2015 at the University of Free State, QwaQwa Campus. He serves on various academic boards, including editorial boards, and has chaired numerous research proposal review boards. He also chaired a conference plenary during a Yale University conference. He is currently a lecturer at the University of KwaZulu-Natal (UKZN) Edgewood Campus, a UKZN language champion in Bilingual Education within the School of Education and a Bilingual Tutoring Programme Champion within the UKZN language board. His contribution to the National Institute of Human Social Sciences (NIHSS) has been in the catalytic project, investigating the role of African languages in developing isiZulu literacy.

Kirk Helliker is a Research Professor in the Department of Sociology at Rhodes University in Makhanda. He established and heads the Unit of Zimbabwean Studies in the department, including supervising a large number of Zimbabwean PhD students on a diverse array of themes. He writes extensively on Zimbabwean history and society. His two most recent books are co-edited collections, both published by Routledge Press in 2018: *Politics at a Distance from the State (Radical and African Perspectives)* and *The Political Economy of Livelihoods in Contemporary Zimbabwe*.

Shandre Hoffmann-Habib is a Mandela Rhodes scholar currently completing her Master's degree in Industrial Sociology at the University of Johannesburg. She graduated with a BA Honours in Industrial Sociology (cum laude) in 2018 after completing her undergraduate degree in BA Psychology (cum laude) in 2017. At the 2018 SASA Congress, she co-presented working research titled 'Graduate employability: Examining the career paths of former Sociology students' and chaired a PhD session on precarious labour. Her research interests include education and student activist movements, gender, the sociology of work and the Fourth Industrial Revolution.

Khosi Kubeka (PhD) is currently working as a Senior Lecturer in the Department of Social Development at the University of Cape Town. Her areas of research interest are youth developmental wellbeing, family and work and social development. She teaches courses in social research methodology, social work and social development, and youth development. She has previously taught introduction to sociology, sociology of youth and crime, social problems and sociology of education.

Grey Magaiza (PhD) is a lecturer in Sociology at the University of the Free State, QwaQwa Campus. He has diverse interests in Sociology including, among others, research methods, sociological theory, media and society, community development and youth sociology. His special focus is on applied, transformative and enabling social research that has livelihood outcomes.

Prishani Naidoo is director of the Society, Work and Politics Institute at the University of the Witwatersrand. Her research interests include questions related to political subjectivity, resistance, social movements, labour, poverty, neoliberalism and higher education.

Kiran Odhav is a Senior lecturer at Mafikeng campus, North-West University, and he is the current Vice President of the Youth Research Committee (Sub-Saharan Africa). He has researched on sport, higher education and AIDS. He is currently working on the Sociology of BRICS and on Social Justice and Inequality in BRICS. His interests include labour, cultural activities, international and regional collaborations.

Engela Pretorius is Professor Emeritus and former Chair of the Department of Sociology at the University of the Free State (UFS). After having served a five-year stint as vice-dean of the Faculty of the Humanities at the UFS, she retired in 2009. Currently, she is a research fellow at the UFS. Her fields of specialisation are gender studies, and health and healthcare.

Marlize Rabe is a Professor in the Department of Sociology at the University of the Western Cape.. Her key research interests are in the construction of masculinities within the family context and intergenerational relations. She has published on a wide range of topics including fatherhood among mineworkers, academics leaving academic careers for the private sector and power dynamics within qualitative research. She is an associate editor of the *Journal of Family Studies.*

Jacques Rothmann is a Senior Lecturer in Sociology at the North-West University, Potchefstroom campus. His key research interests include gender and sexuality studies, with a particular focus on lesbian and gay studies and queer theory. He has published on a number of gender and sexuality foci including gay masculinity and sexual identity in higher education. He established and convened the Lesbian, Gay and Queer Studies working group for the South African Sociological Association (SASA) and currently serves as member of the South African Association for Gender Studies (SAAGS) steering committee.

Pragna Rugunanan is an Associate Professor and current Head of Department of Sociology at the University of Johannesburg. Her research focuses on the construction of African and South Asian migrant communities to South Africa and migration in the Global South. She has been involved in NRF-funded research projects on Family, Well-Being and Resilience, and Social Capital and Citizenship. Her research interests include the sociology of migration, labour studies, changing patterns of work, social networks and community studies. She has published on migration, gender, xenophobia, education and citizenship. Pragna has served on the executive of the South African Sociological Association, was a council member and is currently a working group convener for the Industrial and Economic Group.

Babalwa Sishuta is a lecturer in the Department of Sociology at Rhodes University, Makhanda (Grahamstown). Research interests include violence and crime; the environment and society; the sociology of development with a focus on agricultural and rural development; teaching and learning in higher education; and student activism. She is an active member of the South African Sociological Association.

Muhammed Suleman (PhD) is a lecturer in the Department of Sociology at the University of Johannesburg (South Africa). He recently completed his doctoral research that focuses on the views of Muslim religious leaders regarding domestic violence experienced by married Muslim women. His research and teaching interests are in religion, crime, clinical sociology, sport, social justice, family sociology, gender studies, population dynamics, and conflict studies. He has worked as a sessional lecturer at Monash SA. Suleman is active in community organisations, particularly with the Azaadville Health and Wellness Association and the South African National Zakaah Fund. A recent publication is a 2016 co-authored article (with S Rasool) entitled 'Muslim women overcoming marital violence: Breaking through "structural and cultural prisons'". He recently co-authored a chapter titled 'women, children & families in southern Africa: Sub-narratives and interventions' with Prof Kammila Naidoo and Dr Nalego Indongo (in *Clinical Sociology for Southern Africa,* edited by Prof Tina Uys and Prof Jan Marie Fritz and published by Juta).

Shannon Morreira is Senior Lecturer in the Humanities Education Development Unit at the University of Cape Town. Her research centres on the impact of coloniality on knowledge systems, including human rights law and alternative forms of justice; land use; migration; and higher education. She is a member of the executive council of Anthropology Southern Africa, and an editor of the journal *Critical African Studies.*

Paul Stewart (editor) is an Associate Professor at the University of Zululand. He is orienting towards Rural Sociology after having taught in the Sociology Department at the University of the Witwatersrand for over 20 years. He continues to publish on mine worker health and safety, and hopes to publish his 2012 PhD, Labour time in South African gold mines: 1886–2006, as a book.

Christopher G Thomas has been teaching in the Department of Sociology at the University of South Africa since the mid-1980s. His research interests include the sociology of developing countries, poverty and social inequality; industrial restructuring in South African firms; social and economic rights; housing rights and land protests; and youth development.

Johan Zaaiman (editor) is an Associate Professor at the North-West University, Potchefstroom campus. He has taught first-year sociology for 21 years, first at the Huguenot College in Wellington, and at the North-West University. His research interests include political sociology, social theory and research methodology.

Glossary

A

absolutist view that something is beyond questioning or is not subject to interpretation; in moral reasoning, certain acts are unquestionably right or wrong

absolute poverty the condition of not being able to satisfy basic needs such as food, clothing and shelter as measured against a universal baseline

achieved identity one that is acquired from our interaction with and perceptions of our observed reality

acid mine drainage highly acidic and toxic underground water flowing in large quantities from derelict and or defunct mining areas usually containing high concentrations of heavy metals, salts and radioactive particles polluting surface water (and ultimately into streams and rivers) endangering other ecosystems and the health of communities

action research method of social investigation where researchers and respondents identify a problem, investigate it, repeatedly if necessary, act on and submit their method and findings for evaluation by other scientists; also known as participatory research and collaborative inquiry, among other names

acupuncture the insertion and manipulation of fine needles into specific points on the body to relieve pain or treat ailments; in its classical form it is a characteristic component of traditional Chinese medicine, one of the oldest healing practices in the world (see **Chinese medicine**)

advocacy/participatory knowledge claims reject the notion of value freedom and suggests that all research is value-driven or political; associated with critical perspective

aetiology the origin of or set of factors that cause disease

affectual social action for Weber, intentional or conscious human behaviours or doings arising out of emotional attachments, concerns or values

affirmative action policies or programmes designed to redress historic injustices against racial, ethnic or class groups; sometimes referred to as positive discrimination

affordance a concept borrowed from the psychology of perception which suggests that social action takes place within an environment of possibilities which are both perceived and real

agency the individual's capacity to actively and independently make choices, decisions and plans

agents of socialisation people, groups of people and institutions that affect the self-concept, attitudes or other orientations toward life of the individual

age-specific fertility rate (ASFR) calculated for 5-year age categories, for example for women aged from 15 to 19 years, 20 to 24 years, etc up to women from 45 to 49 years of age

agrarian society in which land is central with most people engaging in horticulture, animal husbandry and agriculture; also referred to as agricultural societies

AIDS (acquired immunodeficiency syndrome) an immune system disease due to infection with HIV (see **HIV**)

alienation Marx's term describing the separation experienced by workers under capitalism: from the product, the work process, from fellow workers and from self

allopathic a term used to refer to Western medicine based on biomedical science (see **complementary and alternative medicine**)

alter-globalisation movement/anti-globalisation movement terms referring to the global movement of people organising against the various effects of neoliberal policies; movements of international scope seeking to create a world free of inequality and oppression reproduced by contemporary capitalism

alternative medicine (see **complementary and alternative medicine**)

altruistic suicide individual taking own life due to overly high level of social integration

anarchists people who oppose the state because they believe it constrains the individual; people who hold that individual freedom is the highest good, individuality is valuable in itself, but which needs a new kind of society to be realised

ancestral related to deceased forbears

ancestral ecological knowledge familiarity with ancient wisdom and practices regarding the environment

androgynous an individual manifesting or expressing characteristics associated with both masculinity and femininity

anomic suicide individual taking own life due to low level of social regulation

animal husbandry farming with and care of animals

anomie Durkheim's term for a social condition characterised by a breakdown in the norms governing society; the personal experience of dislocation in the absence of rules or when the individual falls outside existing social rules

anthropocentrism the supremacy of humans as a species and the ideology that nature exists primarily for human use

antibiotic a substance that kills or inactivates bacteria

apartheid a political system in South Africa that distinguished people according to their race, as defined by law; came to an end in 1994 with new non-racial democratic dispensation

Arab Spring a series of mass uprisings beginning in December 2010 in Tunisia, followed by Egypt, Libya, Syria and other countries across the Arab world, characterised by collective demands for an end to authoritarian forms of rule and corrupt leadership

artificial intelligence the capacity of a computing machine to simulate human thought

artisan skilled working person due to apprenticeship, internship or learnership in a particular craft or trade

ascetic/asceticism renounces material comforts; refers to a life of strict self-discipline and contemplation, often an act of religious devotion

ascribed identity the inherited features of identity, especially sex, race and religion

assembly line a technique of manufacturing production where a complex product, such as a motor vehicle or television, moves on a conveyor-driven belt or moving work station along which workers are positioned; product assembled by each worker repeatedly adding a designated piece to the moving product

assisted families households with paid workers such as live-in domestic workers, nurses or nannies responsible for child or frail care

associational society a society characterised by a complex division of labour, formal social units (producer groups, organisations and corporations), an economy based on manufacturing and related activities, high technology, bureaucratic structures, complex stratification, strong emphasis on rationality and less on spirituality

assumptions statements taken for granted as being true; can be either implicit or explicit

asymmetrical a lack of proportion, harmony, balance and correspondence; applied to social groups with widely diverging resources

asymptomatic regarding disease, being a carrier without manifesting signs or symptoms of disease

austerity programmes the World Bank's prescribed policies to countries defaulting on their debt requiring the reduction of social spending on healthcare, education, pensions and wage increases

autonomous Marxism also referred to a workerist communism, autonomism or operaismo, has independent human and worker action and freedom as focus, including from ideological control by trade unions and political parties

autonomy the capacity for individual or collective self-determination; in political science, the extent to which the state is characterised by self-government and specific interest groups in society are not subject to determination by any force, but are free to express their own goals

B

Bantu Education System an inferior system of education designed under apartheid to massify the production of a basic skilled African workforce and a small intellectual elite

Bantustan ethnically and linguistically defined, geographically fragmented territory under apartheid, also called 'homeland'

basic needs food, shelter and clothing to ensure survival

bedside manner a medical doctor's way of talking to and dealing with patients in an either sympathetic or unsympathetic manner

behaviourism a system of thought, philosophy and research practice based on the observation and measurement of animal and human conduct; generally considered by practitioners to establish the empirical basis of social science

behaviourist person orientation or attitude related to behaviourism

biocentrism emphasises the intrinsic value of all natural life forms informed by their equality where none is prioritised above the other, but explained by their intricate network of relationships

biodiversity the variety of life on earth including the genetic composition of organisms

biological determinism the tendency to prioritise biological aspects at the expense of social and cultural influences

biological fatherhood procreation of children by males

biomedical model (of disability) assumes that disability stems solely from forces within the individual mind or body, rather than from constraints built into the environment or into social attitudes

biomedical model (of health and disease) a specific way of thinking about and explaining disease based on biological factors

biomedicine employs the principles of biology, biochemistry, physiology and other basic natural sciences to solve problems in clinical medicine

biosphere the totality of ecosystems on the planet

bisexual person sexually attracted to both men and women

Black Consciousness philosophy of Steve Biko stressing reassertion of dignity, pride and self-assertion of black people; has psychological liberation from racial discrimination as key focus

bourgeoisie the townspeople, urban entrepreneurial class or burghers; used by Marx to denote the social class of owners of capital, generally referred to as the middle class

breadwinner the individual who earns the money used for the upkeep of the household; generally refers to wage or salaried individuals who do not own the primary economic resources in capitalist societies

bureaucracy an impersonal system of administration, management and/or governance characterised by hierarchical structuring, rigidity, top-down organisation, written rules defining separate tasks and duties and the employment of impartial officials; social system designed to achieve greatest possible efficiency in complex societies; applies to all formal organisations in complex industrial and earlier forms of society

bureaucratisation process whereby the application of formal rules and administrative procedures increasingly dominate human affairs

C

calling strong inner impulse towards a particular course in life requiring dedication and sustained commitment, especially under the conviction of a divine influence

capital an asset owned by an individual as wealth eg a sum of money, financial investments, stocks and shares; for classical economics, capital can be anything serving as an income or potential income; for Marx, more specifically, capital is not a thing, but a set of social production relations historically specific to a society dominated by capitalism

capitalised rural farming areas, generally white-owned, dominated by mechanised agriculture

capitalism an economic system based on private ownership of the means of production, wage-labour and commodity production for sale, exchange and profit

caste an internally complex hierarchical system of social stratification characterised by hereditary membership and endogamy (marriage within a social group or class) which orders the lives of Indian Hindus

cause force or action responsible for an identifiable effect

census a comprehensive count of all the inhabitants of a well-defined area at a specific time to render information on the total size, territorial distribution, composition and key socio-economic attributes of a population

central business district or area concentration of business, commercial and administrative buildings forming the hub of a city or large town; also sometimes known as 'downtown' or 'inner city'

centralised planning state or political command over economic policy direction, organisation and regulation attempting to dispense with market mechanisms; key economic policy implemented by state capitalist/communist regimes

charisma refers, especially for Weber, to leaders who disrupt tradition, transcend bureaucracy and are imbued with exceptional qualities or powers; ordinary people can be elevated to and maintain positions of charismatic authority due to social support; generally unstable and temporary phenomenon

charismatic (Christians) members of various denominations who seek direct ecstatic religious experiences inspired by the Holy Spirit in the theological doctrine of the Trinity; often practise glossolalia (speaking in tongues)

charter company companies that originated in the colonial metropoles provided with state support and which generally established monopoly control over rights, trade and the imposition of taxes in colonised territories

chiefdom a socio-economic organisation in which power is exercised by a single person over many; generally refers to pre-industrial societies, but still exists in parts of South Africa

child abuse the active maltreatment of children physically, sexually or emotionally

child neglect ignoring the needs of children

child or under-five mortality rate the number of children under five years of age who die in a year, per 1 000 live births during the year

child-headed household a household with no adult members and usually where older siblings take care of younger siblings with or without external support from other kin or community members

Chinese medicine one of the oldest healing systems in the world, dating back 5 000 years, one of the healing systems being practised and recognised in South Africa; comprises a full philosophy of healthcare and combination of therapies, with acupuncture the predominating component

chiropractic both in South Africa and globally, the most widely accepted and most 'mainstream' of the CAM (complementary and alternative medicine) modalities; manipulations are applied to any muscle or joint in the body for the relief of musculoskeletal pain and restoration of mobility

Christian-centric society dominated by values, beliefs and practices associated with Christian religion

chronic poverty a hopeless situation where it appears impossible to move out of poverty because the poverty sustains itself

church formal, hierarchical, bureaucratically organised religious organisation that accommodates all the members of a particular, generally Christian, congregation or denomination

cisgender person whose biological sex matches their gender identity

city a relatively large and permanent settlement, usually bigger than 100 000 inhabitants

civil religion set of secular or sacred beliefs, attitudes and rituals related to the nation, that tie people of a political community together

civil society communities of citizens with shared interests independent of government and the state, such as non-governmental organisations, social movements, clubs and societies

class consciousness the sense of collective awareness – potentially leading to social action or defence of interests; the self-understanding a group of people with shared economic interests have of themselves

class experience the way in which people perceive an identity of interests among themselves and against others as a result of common interests rooted in their shared access or lack thereof to economic resources

class for Marx, a social group standing in a relation of ownership or non-ownership of the means of production; for Weber, a social group sharing similar life chances and opportunities in relation to the market. A collective term to signal a specific position in a social stratification system

class differentiation division of society into groups according to access to socio economic resources

class formation the way in which social groups – defined in terms of access to economic resources – come into being

class fractions segments of a larger class with different economic activities and ideologies

class interests that which serves the purposes – increased material wealth, political power or advancement of certain values and principles – relevant to a group of people of the same class

class situation for Weber, ultimately the same as the market situation – the life chances, income, the access to goods and services, the external living conditions and personal life experiences of a certain group of people

class structure the way in which society is organised or ordered in terms of social groups which are defined in terms of access to economic resources

class struggle for Marx, the conflict between two fundamentally opposing social classes; the driving force of social change

classical economics first modern school of thought of economists in the 18th and 19th centuries

closed questions compel a respondent to choose between a limited number of predefined answers

cognition the mental process and ability to think, understand and know

cohesion (social) factors binding society together

cohort (in population studies) a group of persons who enter some stage of the life cycle simultaneously; eg a birth cohort consists of all the males, females, or both, who were born in a given year; a marriage cohort consists of all the men, women or both who were married in a given year

collective agency capacity of institution, government, corporation or social movement to actively make choices, decisions and plans

collective conscience set of shared norms, values and beliefs regulating social behaviour

collective effervescence shared sense of enthusiasm and excitement and related actions

collective representations set of norms, values and beliefs shared by members of a particular group in society

colonial division of labour the geographic separation of work and production between the extraction of raw materials in the global south for processing and manufacture in the global north

colonial encounter the meeting and continued interaction of native or indigenous people and a foreign conquering nation with far reaching effects

colonial rural term used to describe open agrarian areas beyond town and city prior to political independence

colonialism a policy and practice according to which one power expands its territory through control or governance over a dependent area or people; generally refers to process of expansion of European economic and political forces into other parts of the world

coloniality the global power structure, including its epistemological design, which continues to live on beyond colonialism

colonisation ruling of a territory and people by a foreign nation, generally by force; domination of a territory by a foreign nation

commercialisation the trend and pressure for ever-increasing kinds of non-economic activities, organisations and institutions to become financially self-supporting, make a profit and not rely on state funding

commercialised where the methods of manufacture and consumption are applied to personal and social matters and subject to market forces, e.g. parents pay to send children to a nursery school or creche` which assumes the responsibility of child care previously located in the family

commodification a process whereby goods, a person or even an idea is turned into or treated as a commodity and an article of trade

communal action collective social or political behaviour or action taken by a social group, who feel they share certain norms and values, to advance their interests

communal rural area largely coinciding with previous apartheid homelands falling under the jurisdiction of traditional leadership arrangements

communal society type of society that features personalised relationships, an economy based on resources in the local habitat, low levels of technology, non-bureaucratic institutions, limited stratification and a rich ceremonial life

communism for Marx, a classless society; a future society free of domination and exploitation characterised by co-operation and equality

co-morbidity the simultaneous co-existence of two chronic diseases or conditions

compensatory theory a theory in psychology to account for ways in which various personal inadequacies are masked by adopting alternative courses of action and behaviour

complementary and alternative medicine approaches to healthcare that are outside the sphere of conventional allopathic (biomedical) medicine

composition or structure (of a population) characteristic patterns of a population in terms of sex, age, ethnic characteristics, educational attainment and economic activity

comprador bourgeoisie the ruling elites in government and business in postcolonial territories that serve as intermediaries of foreign capitalist interests and their domination of the postcolonial economy

concentration (social concentration) concept for describing a process, whether self-propelled or engineered, of centralising urban functions and facilities into a single urban space

concept abstract component of cognition expressed as a word which picks out, isolates or identifies some aspect or phenomenon; important aspect of abstract contents of the human mind

conceptual analysis ideas expressed as words used to understand and explain some aspect of reality

conflict perspective the view that society is characterised by fundamentally antagonistic and opposing socio-economic classes; the continual dynamic tension between major social groups is considered as the source of social change

consensus establishing agreement between all parties in a discussion despite differing views

consensus theory sociological perspective focusing primarily on agreement, joint action, regularity and routine as central feature of society

conservative elitism the view that privileged or superior minority groups, i.e. elites, are inevitable

conservative inclined to preserve existing conditions, institutions and state of affairs or aims to restore traditional ones and limit or resist change

conspicuous consumption public display or open flaunting of wealth in commodities to gain prestige and social status

contingent dependent on or subject to certain circumstances

contradictions conflicting opposites; irreconcilable tension; signals falsity when it appears as a clash between premises in an argument

contradictory class locations term used by Eric Olin Wright to refer to intermediate class locations between the bourgeoisie and proletariat that are neither capitalist exploiters or exploited working class, but share aspects of both, eg foremen

conurbation a single urban area resulting from the merging of towns and cities; closely related to megalopolis and metropolis

core economies the industrial capitalist countries of Europe, North America and Japan that, until recently, dominated the global economy

credentialism excessive or overreliance on the educational or academic qualifications particularly in hiring practices and for promotion; an origin of the idea of social superiority and inferiority

credit borrowing money or capital to be repaid at a future date generally with interest added

criminal capacity the ability to know the difference between right and wrong and to act in accordance with that knowledge

criminal justice system the system of law enforcement, the bar, the judiciary, correctional services and probation directly involved in the apprehension, prosecution, defence, sentencing, incarceration, and supervision of those suspected of or charged with criminal offences

criminal trajectories the term referring to continuity and change in the nature and pattern of criminality over time, including its onset or initiation, termination or desistence and duration or career length of offending

critical social science seeks to uncover the underlying causes which explain the surface appearances of social phenomena

critical sociology adopting a questioning and reflexive attitude and practice when studying the social world, including questioning the role and place of the discipline itself

critical theory an examination and critique of society associated with the Frankfurt Schule

'crony capitalism' description of an economy where business success depends on close, personal and hence often corrupt relationships with politicians and state officials

cults groups without fixed religious doctrines but tend to be esoteric and individualistic and with limited organisation

cultural capital for Pierre Bourdieu, the accumulation of assets such as skills, education and knowledge that contribute to social mobility in a stratified society

cultural hegemony the philosophic and sociological concept, originated by the Marxist philosopher Antonio Gramsci, that a culturally diverse society can be ruled or dominated by one of its social classes

cultural lag a condition where social problems emerge because a society's institutions do not keep pace with technological change

culturally postulated something assumed as evident within a culture

culture industry a term used to refer to commercial organisations involved in the production and distribution of mainly entertainment products

culture of consumption entails the meaning-making processes by which consumer goods and services are created, bought and used

culture-related syndromes these refer to 'diseases of African people' – ukufa kwabantu in IsiZulu – understood only by Africans only treatable by African traditional healers (see **personalistic explanations**)

D

data collection techniques methods or tools and/or instruments (such as a questionnaire or thematic list), to gather information, facts and statistics

data information, facts or statistics attained through observation and/or research; here with specific reference to sociological research

data mining exploring large sets, repositories or banks of information to discover patterns or generate new information from such sources

data profiling exploring large sets, repositories or banks of information to collect statistics or summaries of the information in such sources

dataveillance recently coined term combining data and surveillance; refers to the systematic tracking and monitoring of personal online communication and behaviour of internet users

decennial lasting ten years or recurring every ten years

decent work a popularised term originated by the International Labour Organisation to refer to employment opportunities providing productive work performed for a fair income, security in the workplace and social protection under conditions of freedom, equity and dignity

decolonial imaginations the many unique individual ways resulting from reconceptualising the sociological imagination in terms of decoloniality

decolonial thinking taking one's own personal social position (in terms of gender race and class and geographical location) as the starting point of thought and understanding

decoloniality a political and epistemological movement aimed at liberation of (ex-) colonised peoples from coloniality; a way of thinking, knowing and doing taking personal social position and geographical location as the starting point of thought

decolonisation politically, the process whereby a colonial power relinquishes control over another territory; an epistemic, political and cultural project for decolonial theorists

deconcentration a concept for describing a process, self-propelled or engineered, of decentralising urban functions and facilities away from existing urban centres

deconstructed exposed or dismantled the existing structures in a system or organisation

deconstruction the accepted meanings and use of terms are critically dismantled and analysed

deduction conclusion made from general premises to specific conclusion which must follow from the premises

demand the amount of goods and services buyers are willing to purchase (or produce) at a given price; an economic model proposing how the relation between the two determines the prices of goods and services on the market

demedicalisation the process by means of which a condition or behaviour becomes defined as a natural condition or process rather than by an illness or as defined by medical science

democracy rule of and by the people

demographic surveillance systems any method of tracking well-defined entities or primary subjects (individuals, households, and residential units) in population studies within a clearly circumscribed geographical area

denomination group of religious congregations united under a common faith, name and a common hierarchical structure

depersonalisation the process by means of which an individual comes to feel less than fully human or comes to be viewed by others as less than fully human

deprivation a lack of basic economic and social supports of human existence such as food

deregulated free from control; does not have to follow set rules

deregulation relaxing or removing state controls over market-related activities

desacralised people's actions not directed by religious beliefs but by secular goals

deskilling the erosion and breaking up of craft and artisanal skill into semi-skilled and unskilled tasks

despotism exercise of absolute power in an oppressive manner

deterritorialisation for Gilles Deleuze and Felix Guattari, the separation of established control, culture and practices from the territory where they originated – and that are geographically re-established or reterritorialised elsewhere; globalisation, of Western origin, can be seen as deterritorialisation

descriptive research noting what has been observed; exercise generally conducted prior to analysis

developmentalism economic theory applying to less-developed societies recommending integrated local markets and high import tariffs

dialectics (dialectical analysis) a form of logic and theorising about social change identifying contradictions or tensions in a prevailing situation and their resolution in a changed situation

dictatorship autocratic rule of individual, usually supported by military force

difference the condition or quality of dissimilarity, divergence or unlikeness; distinction between people in post-modern thought

differential association in criminology, the process whereby the attitudes, values and techniques of criminal groups are learned

differentiation an evolutionary process in the specialisation of society's institutions

diffuse spread freely in different fields or applications

diffusion copying, adopting or importing cultural features, values and institutions, technology or financial resources from one society to another; spread freely in different fields of applications

digital citizenship regular, effective and responsible use of information technology, generally the internet and computers, to engage with society

digital culture social norms and practices associated with the use of information technology, for example cell phone use behaviour

direct action a public, confrontational, disruptive (and sometimes illegal) attempt to elicit an immediate change in a social system

discourse language and its structure and functions and how it is used

disembeddedness social contact and access in economic, political and cultural affairs becomes distant and is no longer linked to people's immediate local experience

disenchantment Weber's term for the experience of the loss of wonder and awe

diverse the whole made up of different types, allowing for variety

divinities supernatural entities or beings

division of labour continuous specialisation in productive tasks in pursuit of increased efficiency of individual tasks designed to increase productive output; the structured separation of work into various forms or occupations

doctrine of specific aetiology the idea that a single agent causes a single type of disease and that a specific therapy can be used to treat that disease

dogma set of opinions, beliefs or doctrine held strongly, often expressed authoritatively and arrogantly

domestic production the creation of economic wealth taking place within a household, country or nation

domestic violence harmful behaviours, between intimates or previously related persons, such as emotional, verbal, psychological, physical, sexual and economic abuse; including intimidation, harassment, stalking, damage to property or entry into a residence without consent.

dominant ideology tendency of subordinate classes and minority groups to accept their disadvantaged condition because the ideas and culture are largely controlled by powerful, superordinate social groups

dominant sports generally team-based competitive physical games that are universally popular, highly organised globally and subject to established and evolving rules and regulations

dysfunctional deviating from the normal and expected function; adversely affecting the whole

E

earth-centred cosmologies understandings, knowledge, wisdom and practices employed in environmental management; generally refers to indigenous knowledge systems

ecology the scientific study of the structure, patterns and processes of interrelationships between living organisms and their natural habitat

economic fatherhood financial contributions to the raising of children by male family member

economic growth a positive change or rate of improvement in the level of production or service providing activity

economic sanctions the use of political and administrative mechanisms preventing or constraining economic trade and activity of a country in order to compel it to effect political change

economic surplus the difference (or profit) between production and consumption

economism the view that the form and shape of society is due solely or can be reduced to the development of its (economic) productive forces

ecosystem a dynamic system of plant, animal and micro-organism communities and their non-living environment interacting as a functional unit

education literally, to lead out of ignorance; generally refers to a formal social institution that plays a decisive role in society by transmitting society's values and morals, shaping its views, upholding traditions, regulating individual and social behaviour and bringing about increase in knowledge and ideally contributing to positive social change

egoistic suicide individual taking own life due to low level of social integration

elite a minority privileged or superior group excluding the majority, usually due to exercise of power and access to resources

embodiment the concrete expression of an idea or principle; in gender studies, refers to the way in which individuals incorporate cultural ideals of gender which are given expression in their bodies

embourgeoisiement the process of becoming middle class; process whereby segments of the working class adopt and assimilate the values and lifestyles of the middle class

emerging economies a term used to describe middle income economies in the developing world

emphasised femininity an exaggerated form or display of femininity

empirical pertains to observable and measurable evidence and which hence can be positively demonstrated; widely considered to be the basis of all science

empiricism philosophy and research practice based on the view that only observable and measurable phenomena are real; opposite of rationalism

empiricist see empiricism

enclave economy an area in which production for export in one country is dominated by another country; the domination of non-local or foreign capital in an export producing region or locale

enculturation the process whereby an individual acquires, absorbs and is shaped by the norms, values and practices in a social environment, occurring especially in the processes of socialisation

endogamy marrying within one's own social group or community

endogenous social change driven by cultural or structural factors internal to a society

Enlightenment a body of thought based on rational, secular and scientific explanations developed in the 18th century, which challenged explanations of the world based on religion or superstition

enumeration areas (EAs) geographical units into which a country is divided for census enumeration and which one enumerator can carry out; typically contains between 100 and 250 households

environment the full totality of the surroundings within which humans exist, including the land, water and atmosphere of the earth; micro-organisms, plant and animal life or combination or interrelationships among and between them

environmental justice a rights-based and people-centred discourse focusing on how marginalised and powerless communities bear the brunt of risks and hazards due to the actions of powerful elites in society, including governments and multinational corporations

environmental management care and custodianship of the environment

environmental racism institutionalised racial discrimination in environmental policy, regulation and practices which deliberately locates toxic waste sites and industrial facilities in poor minority neighbourhoods

environmentalism an ideology and an action-oriented political programme designed to bring about desired social change or a new social order which will improve society–environment relationships

epistemic adequacy sufficient for knowledge; contemporary term replacing that of truth

epistemic derived from the Greek word for knowledge; in sociology what on rational and evidential grounds is worth believing

epistemology the study of the conditions required for establishing knowledge

equality similar and fair treatment of individuals irrespective of social difference relating to circumstances of birth, sex, age, race, class, gender or any other form of social differentiation; the state of being equal

estate generally refers to the form of social hierarchy of post-feudal states of continental Europe

ethics in social science, the obligation of professional conduct in the use of scientific method

ethnic identity a sense of identity determined by acquired hereditary characteristics

ethnocentric to see one's own culture as superior to others or to use it as a benchmark to evaluate the culture of outsiders

ethnography descriptive research strategy of living in the time and space of informants to understand their cultural habits, customs and differences and share their experience and perspectives of social reality

eurocentrism an attitude that regards European culture and way of life as superior to those whose origins lie elsewhere

evaluative research type of applied research usually undertaken to measure in some way the impact or changes a particular programme may have made

evolution gradual development, adaptation and change of biological species in relation to the natural environment and hence ensuring their survival over time

evolutionary universals principles repeatedly encountered deemed to further the evolution of human society

exclusion generally refers to processes in contemporary global capitalism where the periphery has become less important as a supplier of inputs for the industrial capitalist core regions

exhurb a settlement that lies outside a city and beyond its suburbs

existential related to or dealing with human experience and life

exogamy marrying outside one's own social group or community

exogenous social change driven by factors external to a society

experiential knowledge based on personal observation and familiarity

explanations to account for or provide sound reasons for the occurrence of phenomena

exploitation for Marx, the technical term describing the expropriation of economic value from the expenditure of workers' labour power

extended family at least three generations of a family who live together in one household or in polygamous marriages where more than two marriage partners share a household

external areas in Immanuel Wallerstein's world-systems theory these are structurally defined locations not yet part of the capitalist system

externalisation the process whereby human beings imprint or express their ideas on the outside world; for Peter Berger and Thomas Luckman, the social construction of reality is the dialectic between externalisation and its opposite, namely internalisation

F

fact that which has demonstrated and been proven, whether a material or non-material social fact as construed by Durkheim

fake news false information put out purposively to deceive and distributed by others often unintentionally

false consciousness for Marx, the failure to be aware, have a collective sense of or recognise what is in the interests of the working class, objectively defined (as a class 'in-itself')

family households comprising group living together bound by bonds of blood, sexual mating or legal ties; husband, wife, children and grandparents

fatalistic suicide individual taking own life due to overly high level of social regulation

feminisation of poverty the majority of poor people being women

feminism the view that men and women should have equal rights

fertility the number of births or the reproductive performance of an individual or population

feudalism historical period prior to capitalism, characterised by political and economic obligations between peasant serfs and lords controlling the land; social arrangements regulating relations between chiefs and ordinary people can be construed as feudal

fidelity being committed to a sexually exclusive union

financial speculation engaging in generally risky investment in the money market for high short-term gain

financialisation term describing the increasing and significant social power and influence wielded by banks and institutions that loan money to investors and the public

First World the advanced capitalist industrialised economies of the capitalist world system

focus group a group with a limited number of people brought together to discuss a topic under guidance of a facilitator

forced removals eviction from places of abode accompanied by physical coercion

forces of production for Marx, the physical tools, instruments and technologies employed in production, including new forms of energy, developments in machinery and the labour process, the education of the proletariat and science

Fordism term used to identify the widespread transformation of work and society in the 20th century characterised by mass production and mass consumption

foreign exchange the amount of money in an economy which has its origin in another country

formal economy the organised sector; the result of productive, trade and financial activity occurring within and between legally registered business firms, companies and corporations

formal rationality achieving calculated goals or ends by using rules and regulations established by reason

Foucauldian relating to or characteristic of the philosophy of Michel Foucault (1926–1984)

Fourth Industrial Revolution the combined impact on society of digitisation, robotisation, artificial intelligence and related innovations (such as 3D printing and fingerprint, ocular and facial recognition) that often obscure the boundaries between the digital, physical and biological spheres or domains

franchise business economic enterprise operating and trading a branded product or service or using a trademark under licence

'free enterprise' popular ideological term for permitting open and unfettered financial transactions and exchanges on the market

functional flexibility the combination of multi-skilling and multi-tasking; the redistribution and re-organisation of skills and/or tasks among workers by way of job rotation

functional prerequisites the conditions that a society must meet to sustain itself

functional specialisation the process whereby increasing forms of work and different kinds of jobs results in greater social stratification

functionalist perspective theoretical framework in which society is viewed as composed of various parts, each with a function that, when fulfilled, contributes to society's equilibrium

functionalism sociological theory focusing primarily on how the various parts of society perform specific tasks and work together as a whole

functionalist theory a view of society as composed of different but related parts, each of which serves a particular purpose in relation to the whole

fundamentalism religious movement or point of view that strictly holds to non-negotiable principles and is hostile to alternative views

G

Gemeinschaft (German) a homogeneous and regulated community enjoying close, emotional and face-to-face ties and relationships

gender the social construction of what it means to be male or female

generalisation broad, widely applicable and valid statement about particular phenomena, whether natural or social

genre a term for a type of artistic or cultural composition made up of generally recognisable conventions

gentrification renewal of inner city areas to accommodate more well-to-do citizens, young families and single persons

germ theory (see **doctrine of specific aetiology**)

Gesellschaft (German) a heterogeneous society associated with urbanism, industrialism and impersonal social relations

ghetto usually a poor section of a city inhabited by a minority group, characterised by high rates of unemployment, crime and a decayedbuilt environment

gig-based economy economic activity dependent on electronic technologies

Gini coefficient a widely accepted measure of inequality using housing, income, and security as key indices

global economy the sum total under capitalism of all productive, trade and financial activity in the world

globalisation the multiplicity of linkages, interconnections and interdependencies that transcend nation-states comprising the modern world system and which affect most of the world's inhabitants

gospel four books in the Christian New Testament; colloquially refers to human salvation

government a group of people in the legislature, parliament and executive who have the power to make and enforce laws for a country or territorial area

governmentality for Michel Foucault, combining government and rationality, refers to how government aims to guide and shape human behaviour and conduct of citizens

grace unconditional salvation granted by monotheistic God

great transformation term used by Karl Polanyi for understanding the deep social and historical changes in social structure linked to industrialisation

gross domestic product (GDP) the total value of all goods and services a country produces in a year, but excluding income from outside a country

gross national product (GNP) the total value of all goods and services a country produces in a year, including income from investments outside a country

ground rent monies payable in exchange for the right to use land

guilds associations of independent self-employed craftsmen organised by occupation to serve common interests, for mutual support and to regulate standards and conditions of work

H

hegemonic masculinity the predominance of the expectation that men are competitive, dominant and aggressive and manifest attitudes, occupy roles and forms of dress that display physical process and power in society

hegemony a concept initially used by the Marxist theorist Antonio Gramsci to describe how a ruling class maintains power not only by economic authority, but also by exercising its intellectual, moral and ideological influence in civil society in order to persuade the people of its economic and cultural legitimacy

herd immunity regarding disease in groups of people, the process of becoming immune

heterogenous diverse or different in kind or nature; displaying completely different characteristics

heteronormativity the belief that heterosexual behaviour is and should be the norm

heterosexual person sexually attracted to the opposite sex

heuristic related to making a discovery; generally applied to the learning experience and process

hidden agenda intentions underlying a particular course or programme of action not made explicit, but which have attitudinal and behavioural effects

hidden curriculum usually the behaviour or attitudes that are learnt at schools that are not part of the formal curriculum

hierarchy an arrangement or system of steps, grades, orders or classes relating to power or rule, generally organised institutionally from top to bottom and relating to an organised body of persons or things; originally with reference to the gods and religious orders

historical materialism for Marx, the science of society based on the study of real, physical events, processes and conditions determining human actions over time

historicism a view that maintains human history has a discernible pattern, an almost law-like movement towards some predictable type of social structural arrangements

HIV (human immunodeficiency virus) the virus that causes AIDS

homelands (see **Bantustan**)

homo duplex for Durkheim, the tension between individual desire and social obligation; a characteristic of modern individuality

homoeopathy a complementary disease treatment system in which a patient is given minute doses of natural drugs that in larger doses or at full strength would produce similar symptoms to a given disease

homogeneous, of the same kind or nature, sameness, alike, similar

homonormative the privileging or imposing of heterosexual constructs on homosexuals; based on the assumption that homosexuals should emulate heterosexual norms and values, thereby reinforcing the dominance of heterosexuality

homophobia the fear of and discrimination and violence against persons attracted to the same sex

homosexual person sexually attracted to the same sex

household economy productive, service and financial activity occurring within the home

household generally, a related group of people living in one dwelling and sharing food and other necessities

human capital attributes such as skill, training and education, including personal and social knowledge, essential for productive economic activity

human development approaches ways of understanding poverty by integrating notions of economic and social advancement and upliftment

Human Development Index a poverty measurement that incorporates changes in life expectancy, educational attainment and per capita income

hybrid a concept sometimes used to refer to multiculturalism, or the mixing of cultures, and the questions this raises about identity

hybrid identity a sense of identity that is influenced by exposure to various cultures, beliefs and lifestyle as a result of globalisation

hybridity see hybrid; the condition, state or result of

hydraulic fracturing a mining process which involves a deep drilling technique at high pressure in order to break the shale underground rock structure using a mixture of water, sand and an elaborate mix of toxic chemicals creating wells to release and access the natural gas or oil trapped in rock formations (also called fracking)

hypermasculinities forms of expression that are associated with stereotypical male behaviour generally relating to physical prowess and strength

hysterectomy the removal of the uterus disabling females from bearing children

I

iatrogenesis the harmful consequences of medical intervention; disease contracted in hospitals; literally meaning harm caused by doctors

ideal type Weber's specialised cognitive and conceptual tool designed to describe and evaluate social phenomena; an abstract model used as a standard of comparison

idealism sociological approaches that focus on the meaning, ideas, values and beliefs behind social interaction; philosophy stressing the priority of ideas in social explanation

ideas complex mental pictures or mental image of something, generally expressible in words, concepts or theories

identity a disputed term in sociology; generally refers to one's sense of self; who you are, where you come from and the various factors impacting on self-understanding and self-definition

identity formation the process whereby the individual is established as unique resulting from interaction with a wide variety of inter-personal, social and other material factors and forces

ideology a set of ideas based on an interpretation of selected evidence, generally referring to the politics of organisations especially political parties

illness (behaviour) the subjective experience of having a disease

illusion the condition of being deceived by a false image or representation of what is real

imperialism the rule, spirit and practice/s of an emperor or empire, especially when despotic

implosion literally, bursting inwards; technical term used by Ankie Hoogvelt of the contemporary trend in the capitalist world system where core regions prefer to intensify capital and trade linkages among themselves

import substitution a post-Second World War development strategy popular in developing countries whereby local manufacturing is supported through imposing high tariffs and quotas on competing imported goods

impression management attempt or effort to present oneself in a particular light to others

independent churches church organisations not formally aligned with established denominations or mainline church institutions

indigenised adaptations for use of artefacts or products foreign to local culture and customs

indigenous games play-related and sporting activities specific to a particular place or environment

indigenous occurring in, specific or original to a particular place or environment; native

indirect rule form of governance of a conquered people via their own traditional leadership arrangements

individualism prioritisation of the individual over the social group

induction interrogating and inferring from particular observations or data in a systematic way to derive generalisations in order to lead to a theory that explains the findings

industrial capitalism the phase of capitalism beginning in the late 18th century characterised by factory-based production using machinery and increasing the division of labour and specialisation of tasks to produce commodities for resale and making a profit

Industrial Revolution the emergence in England in the 19th century of machines which transformed production, the economy and society, generally driven by steam and electrical power

industrialisation the emergence and establishment of machine-based manufacturing processes in economic development

infant mortality rate (IMR) the number of children younger than one year of age who die in a year, per 1 000 live births during that year

infectious diseases diseases capable of being passed from one person to another

inflation a sustained increase in the cost of services and goods in an economy, with a resultant overall increase in the cost of living; purchasing power falls as a result of inflation

informal economy the unorganised market sector; the result of productive, trade and financial activity occurring outside the ambit of legally registered business firms, companies and corporations

informalisation the increase in subcontracted, outsourced and temporary, piece work or home-based forms of work

information society the explosion and dominance of media and communications technology and attendant creation, distribution and manipulation of data – or information; society based on a knowledge economy; stands in contrast to agrarian/agricultural or industrial societies

institutional homophobia oppression of and discrimination towards homosexuality embedded in formal, mainstream and established forms of social organisation

institutional racism also referred to as systemic racism, racial discrimination embedded as normal practice in organisations or society

institutional violence also referred to structural violence, refers to the impairing or preventing people meeting their basic needs that can result in harm and death

institutions established or structured sets or forms of social arrangements; variously subject to change over time

instrumental rationality reason devoted to achieving a goal or end

instrumentalism in political theory, the view that capitalists intervene directly in the state in the interests of capitalism

integrated development the recognition and practice of combining and coordinating a wide range of institutional activities to advance social progress

interactionism taking communication and relations between people as central when studying society

interest money earned from making a loan or investing money in a bank or financial institution generally at a predetermined rate or proportion of the money loaned or invested

intergenerational equity emphasises the idea that the environment needs to be conserved for future generations

internalisation the process whereby human beings absorb, adopt or accept a set of norms, values and practices through socialisation; the opposite of externalisation

internalised homophobia self-hatred of one's own homosexuality

interpretations the different ways in which individuals independently understand phenomena or occurrences

interpretivism an approach in the social sciences, sociology in particular, derived from Weber and which stresses the capacity of human agents to make meaning, understand and deliver independent judgements about the world

intersectionality the way in which different social identities/categories/relationships intertwine/overlap/interact; often used in the social sciences to account for the inter-relationships between race, class and gender

intersex people who have biological characteristics of both sexes – previously referred to as hermaphrodites

inter-subjectivity the result of the relation between two or more individuals pertaining to personal perspectives, beliefs, feelings or desires

interventionist state a state which has or plays a proactive role and involvement in the economy

investment the use or outlay of money in anticipation of making a profit

'invisible hand' the term, first used by classical economist Adam Smith (1723–1790), to describe the self-regulating effect of the market in which everyone is free to sell or buy goods and services

iridology a diagnostic method used by CAM practitioners; refers to the study of the iris of the eye; the iris reveals changing conditions of every part and organ of the body

J

jobless economic growth the positive change or rate of improvement in the level of productive or service providing activity, but which does not result in increased employment

justification the provision and acceptance of valid reasons in the making of a claim to knowledge or truth; establishing the grounds for epistemic adequacy

K

Keynesianism economic policies adopted from John Maynard Keynes' views that government spending should increase during times of recession and high unemployment and reduce during times of full employment and inflation

Kinsey scale influential method to chart sexual attraction

knowledge claims the epistemic statements made by theorists who hold, generally on the presentation of evidence and argument, that what they say is thereby defensible or even true (theorists differ in their definition of what knowledge is)

knowledge economy where the production of goods and services depends on the quantity, quality and accessibility of knowledge-based information; economy in which growth and employment depends on knowledge-intensive activity and skills

knowledge information that is viewed as specific and certain; that which is backed up with evidence, but is provisional and open to revision

L

labour hard work or toil performed under coercion; also used as a collective name for workers

labour market a generalised concept denoting the exchange of work for money; the interaction of supply of and demand for labour; sites where workers find paying work and employers find willing workers

labour power the capacity to work or labour

labour process the purposive activity of work, the objects or raw materials and the instruments or technologies employed which, when combined, creates useful products or provides services

labour reserves areas from which generally low waged workers can readily be drawn

labour time the duration of work measured in minutes, hours, days, months and years

laissez *faire* the unfettered, unregulated and free activity of trading on the market; normally associated with and applied to an economic system manifesting these characteristics

legal authority for Weber, the power of law accepted as legitimate

legitimise making something legal, acceptable or correct

leisure relates to free time, (re)creational activity, for knowledge or skills, for its own sake or even for spiritual involvement.

level of urbanisation the proportion of a population living in urban settlements, expressed as a percentage

liberation movement organisation seeking overthrow of colonial or national government by popular mobilisation of an oppressed people

life expectancy the average number of years individuals born in a given year can expect to live in a particular population

life-chances the opportunities and possibilities available to individuals or groups of people – closely related to access to material resources for Weber

Likert scale series of options open to questionnaire respondents listed in terms of weighted categories such as 'strongly agree', 'agree', 'undecided' or 'neutral', 'disagree' and 'strongly disagree'

liquidity the availability of money, generally in the form of cash, to spend or invest

living customary law actually existing traditional normative practices

logical reasoning in argument comprising premises that adhere to established rules to ensure the conclusion follows from the premises

lockdown imposed closure of and prevention or limiting movement of citizens

logical deductions what one is compelled to accept as the conclusion follows from the premises according to established rules of rational thinking

logical fallacy a form of argument where the conclusion does not follow from its premises

longitudinal when the same group of people or the same area is studied over a period (in contrast with cross-sectional studies that focus on a specified point in time)

lumpen-proletariat for Marx a subordinate class not in wage labour; the lowest social level of the working class made up of the unemployed, indigent and criminal elements

M

mainline the principal or a well-established position in society

manual labour physical work done by hand performed by 'blue collar' workers

manufacturing industries economic sector responsible for the production of the majority of goods and commodities available in a society

marginalised status or position of a group living on the periphery of society

marginality the experience of social groups separated from the mainstream in society or from society in general

market economy the unplanned system in which investment, production and distribution of goods and services results in a technically free price system; does not exist in a pure form

Marxian theoretical and political perspectives influenced by, but not necessarily strictly following the thought of Karl Marx

Marxism theoretical and political perspectives arising from the thought of Karl Marx

masculinist attitudes and behaviours associated with boys and men; can also mean antifeminist attitudes and behaviour

mass media forms of communication designed to reach large audiences without face-to-face contact between those conveying and those receiving the messages

massification making available to the broader population or the masses; regarding education, ensuring open access by all to institutions of learning

master status the social position of an individual which overshadows all other social positions

material inequalities the disparity between individuals or social groups in access to goods and services necessary for sustaining life

material social fact for Durkheim, physical or real phenomena peculiar to social science to be treated as things and which are external, general and exercise coercive influence over human agents and of which they are generally unaware

materialism philosophy stressing the priority of actual, physical and real phenomena in social explanation

materialist conception of history Karl Marx's sociological approach that ultimately explains history in terms of the production and reproduction of real life

materialist dialectics Marx's method of thinking and investigating history and society; the unification, synthesis or resolution of contradictions or opposites occurring in actual states of affairs

maternal deaths those that occur while the woman is pregnant or within 42 days of the termination of a pregnancy

maternal mortality ratio (MMR) the number of maternal deaths per 100 000 live births in a 12-month period

means of production for Marx, the physical tools, instruments and technologies employed in production

mechanical metaphor in medicine, the idea that doctors can act like engineers to mend that which is dysfunctional

mechanical solidarity for Durkheim, the form of social cohesion arising from a shared set of common values, norms and beliefs, generally encountered in primitive or simple pre-industrial societies

mechanisation the use of machines in production, generally replacing human labour

mediator a person who facilitates contact and agreement between opposing parties

medicalisation concept used to describe the tendency for biomedicine to increasingly extend its influence and scope over areas of life previously not considered to be medical

megalopolis very large functionally interconnected system of cities and suburbs; closely related to metropolis and conurbation

membership taking part in an organisation or institution

mental labour cognitive work performed by 'white collar' workers

mercantile imperialism economic policy in 16th to 18th century Europe associated with seeking to maximise economic trade to augment state power, central to the early development and spread of merchant capitalism

meritocracy generally refers to an educational system where individuals are rewarded on the basis of their level of ability and personal achievements

meritocratic related to meritocracy

metaphysics the study of what is real and what exists; assumes vastly contrasting forms such as empiricism (things are real) and idealism (ideas are real)

metatheoretical choices the options open and the capacity to make decisions about which theory, theories or conceptual paradigms to accept over and above others

methodological individualism the view, generally associated with Max Weber, that the motives behind the social action of individuals are vital to understanding social structures and processes

methodological practices a body of practices, procedures and rules used by scientists in a discipline to engage in an inquiry; a set of working methods

methodologies different or alternative ways of working or doing things

metrosexual heterosexual male who uses products and services, stereotypically associated with women or gay men, to improve their physical appearance

migrant labour system a form of organising labour by separating work and home further than commuting distance

migration the geographical movement of people from one location to another

Millennium Development Goals (MDGs) eight development goals which were agreed upon at the United Nations' Millennium Summit in 2000 as a plan to improve the quality of life in developing countries with a target achievement date of 2015

Millennium Development Goal 4 (MDG 4) a target of reducing, by two-thirds, the mortality rate for children under five years of age by 2015

Millennium Development Goal 5 (MDG 5) a target of reducing, by three-quarters, the maternal mortality ratio between 1990 and 2015

mind/body dualism in the medieval church the view that the mind and matter cannot be reduced to one another; that body and soul are distinguishable but inseparable

mini-system for Immanuel Wallerstein, an early social form of organisation with a self-contained division of labour and economies based on reciprocal exchange such as hunting and gathering societies

missionary a representative of a religious organisation or faith community sent to expand and extend its membership

mixed economy the combination of aspects of regulation and planning and unplanned, market-type systems producing goods and services; the feature of most economies

mixed methods the combined use of quantitative and qualitative research instruments aimed at providing robust degrees of validity

mode of production for Marx, the way successive societies throughout history organise the necessities of life with available technologies and accompanying forms of social relations, idea systems and social institutions

modernism a contemporary or modern quality of thought; expression or use of terms characteristic of being modern

modernity a general term to describe the various processes associated with industrialisation, urbanisation, and bureaucratisation emerging in late 19th and 20th century society in Europe

modified extended families signifies biologically related groups of people living in different households between which goods and services are regularly exchanged

modified extended family household members who live apart, but who exchange services and goods on a regular basis

monarchy the absolute rule of a single sovereign over society; generally hereditary

monetary policy the process whereby the amount of money or money supply in an economy is controlled by the relevant authorities

money metric approaches measuring poverty by income levels or shortfalls in a predetermined income level

money the symbolic repository of wealth

monogamy the practice of having a single sexual partner over a period of time, generally in marriage

monopoly capitalism a stage of capitalism commencing towards the end of the 19th century characterised by large-scale corporations

monopoly relates to a market with a single dominant supplier of a good or service

monosexual attraction to one sex or gender only

monotheism the belief in and worshipping of one supreme being or god

moral socially acceptable correct behaviour

moral development the gradual process by which an individual develops attitudes and behaviours towards others, generally involving an understanding of right and wrong, based on social and cultural norms and values

moral judgement an evaluation or assessment and decision about some or other human behaviour or action based on norms and values considered authoritative

mortality the death rate (in terms of demographic processes); deaths occurring in a population

multiskilling the capacity to perform or exercise a range of different competencies in the workplace

multi-spatial household shared living arrangements in different places of abode

multitasking the capacity to perform or exercise a range of different elements of a job in the workplace

mystical relating to paranormal, supernatural, spiritual or transcendent religious experience

N

narrative a description or account of a sequence of events and experiences; often refers to a person's biography or historical story

national democratic revolution definitionally contested, but involving radical or reformist restructuring of society through the mobilisation of and rule by the people, whether popular, bourgeois or proletarian in style of politics; assumes the form of liberal constitutional democracy in South Africa

nationalisation the process of transferring private ownership of economic resources into public ownership, generally to be owned and operated by the state; opposite of privatisation

nationalism attitudes, sentiments, views and practices reflecting and generally propagating the consciousness and political aspirations of a group of people who feel themselves united by a common language, shared customs, traditions and beliefs in a geographical location or nation-state

nation-states cohesive institutional political structures and defined geographical boundaries at the level of individual countries

natural religion socially binding view of the world and related practices based on or emerging from a force or forces of nature

natural science the establishment of the fact or state of knowing regarding inanimate, physical and non-human phenomena; systematic investigation and research relying on evidence and rational thought resulting in knowledge of the material world

naturalism philosophical view with real world settings and common sense as its focus

naturopathy a CAM therapy that holds that healing depends on a vital curative force within the human organism which under proper conditions is capable of healing itself

negative punishment in behavioural psychology, when something which is desired is removed as a result of a certain behaviour, the action of which is designed to decrease the frequency of such behaviour

negative reinforcement the removal of something which is unpleasant when the desired behaviour occurs thereby supporting the desired behaviour

negative socialisation teaching or inculcation of behaviour through punishment, harsh criticism, anger or some degree of force

neoclassical economics approach focusing on supply and demand on the market as the primary principle to determine what is produced, services to be delivered and the prices of goods and services

neocolonial the continuation of especially economic dominance and control after political independence

neoliberalism the policy and practice advocating free trade and open markets, deregulation (including labour market deregulation), fiscal prudence, privatisation and the reduction of the public sector

network society a term coined by Manuel Castells to describe a globalised world as linked and interconnected by cultural, social, political and economic associations and relationships

new fatherhood implies more than just financial contributions to children by including an emotional and caring relationship with a child by the male parent or caregiver

new petty bourgeoisie the class of artisans, engineers and supervisory workers in the era of monopoly capitalism who earn wages, but do not produce surplus value

nobility in traditional or feudal societies, linked to or the ruling elite related by family or blood ties

nomothetic law making; law applying to everything

non-core assets resources not directly connected to the main economic activity of a business

non-family households group living together not bound by blood or legal ties, e.g. student commune

non-material or immaterial social facts for Durkheim, non-physical or abstract phenomena peculiar to social science to be treated as things and which are external, general and exercise coercive influence over human agents and of which they are generally unaware

non-probability sample a selection of cases where it is unknown which will be selected and where some cases have a zero chance of being selected

non-racialism a state wherein people's racial categories do not determine group relations and distribution of resources in society

norms generally accepted standards or rules of life

nuclear family two adult members living with their dependent biological or adopted children in one household

numerical flexibility the practice of increasing or decreasing the number of jobs in a company to suit changing production demands

nuptiality marriage rate

O

objectification human agents realise their creative intentions and produce an artefact or thing or object, e.g. writing an essay, baking a cake; the act or process whereby persons are treated as objects. e.g slavery.

objective (noun) a goal; (adjective) to be unbiased; without prejudice; not permitting the intrusion of personal judgements

objectivity dispassionate assessment; absence of bias and prejudice resulting in general agreement about the nature of some phenomenon

occupy movement a mobilisation of people against social injustice, inequality and the lack of substantive democracy which targets the undue influence of the financial services sector over government in particular

oligarchy rule by the few, generally a small elite

open market the site or sites in which the unregulated and free sale and purchase of goods and commodities takes place

open question respondents participating in research inquiry invited to supply their own answers in their own wording

open-access (or open-source) journal regular publication or magazine in popular or academic format posted on the internet for ready access

organic solidarity for Durkheim, the form of social cohesion arising from interdependence in the division of labour of complex industrial societies

organisation a formal, goal-orientated structure with clearly defined rules and principles that determine the engagement of members and the operations of the collective

organised labour workers who are members of a trade union of staff association

oscillating migrancy constant movement of people, generally between rural and urban areas, for purposes of maintaining employment

outsourcing business practice of contracting out aspects or parts of work, generally done internally, to a third, external party

P

pandemic a disease infecting people across a whole country or the world

pansexual attraction to people regardless of their sex

paradigm a model or whole way of thinking, often with a distinctive set of concepts; fundamentally conflicting ways of thinking are incommensurable (cannot be compared)

parastatal institutions business concerns owned partly or predominantly by the state; referred to as state-owned enterprises when fully-owned by the state

parity in population studies, the number of births a woman has had up to the point of investigation (women who have never given birth are referred to as nulliparous)

parsimony a methodological principle stressing the criterion of simplicity in theory construction

participatory approach a subjectivist approach to producing knowledge where poor people themselves participate in the conceptualisation, definition and measurement of poverty

party for Weber, membership of political group, association or affiliation

patriarchy within the family context it refers to the power of men over women and children, especially when men have control over the family's resources

patrimonialism for Weber, a form of political domination; rule by a traditional military master or household via the exercise of personal and bureaucratic power; applies to certain traditional African and Oriental societies

peasant member of the peasantry

peasantry historically, a class of people who worked the land as poor, rent-paying agricultural labourers or small landowners; independent small-scale agricultural producers

perception the capacity and action of the senses and the mind in apprehending and appropriating some or other phenomenon or phenomena; a condition for any form of knowledge

peri-urban areas areas on the outskirts of existing urban centres, often not under local government control and regulations for land use

personalistic explanations assume that the cause of disease is a direct result of the influence of human or non-human, supernatural agents

petty bourgeoisie for Marx, a subordinate class comprising traders, shopkeepers, teachers, lawyers, doctors, accountants, etc

phenomenology the philosophy that especially studies the essence of perception and consciousness of people with the view that these phenomena can be grasped and understood as they really are

planned economy an economic system which is generally centrally organised and controlled by the state; opposite of market economy. There is no pure form of either of these types of economy

platform capitalism economic activity in which transnational high-tech companies set up software and hardware operating systems for other people and generally smaller businesses, e.g. Google, Apple, Uber

pluralism a theoretical perspective which argues that the state in capitalist society acts as broker between the interests of all groups in capitalist society

plurality many or various

pluriversal term popularised and used (but not clearly defined) by Walter Mignolo; aims to signal the end of universalism in knowledge; knowledge is 'multiple', has many sources; is an 'entanglement'; is in contrast to universal, but does not, for Mignolo, signal relativism in knowledge

political action collective behaviour or action taken by a group or some of its members to realise their goals whether of an ideal or material nature

political franchise eligibility to vote

politics of production the role and power of the state and the agency of workers in shaping the social relations between classes interacting in the economy

polyamorous engaging in multiple intimate relationships with mutual consent of all partners

polyandry one woman being married to several husbands at the same time

polygamy a sanctioned marriage between one person and several partners of the opposite sex at the same time

polygyny one man being married to several wives at the same time

polymorphous occurring in several different forms

polytheist the belief in and worshipping of multiple gods

population estimation mathematical computations on the size and composition of a population

population projection the calculation of future changes in population numbers, given certain assumptions about future trends in fertility, mortality, and migration rates

positive punishment a negative consequence follows an undesired behaviour is manifested in order to decrease the frequency of that behaviour

positive reinforcement involves the addition of something of value to the individual as a consequence of certain behaviour in order to stimulate the desired behaviour

positivism the philosophy responsible for establishing criteria for knowledge; the rules and criteria focused on empirical evidence required for any statement to constitute knowledge, i.e. representivity, replicability, reliability and elimination of reactivity

positivist the approach that sees knowledge relying solely on what can be directly experienced verified through scientific experiments

post-truth situation in which the acceptance of ideas is based on emotion rather than facts

post-colonial after political liberation from colonialism; thinking from the perspective of the post-colony (see **Achille Mbembe**)

post-colonial rural agrarian/agricultural areas generally remaining unchanged after political independence, with key exceptions, such as *ujamaa* (socialist village co-operatives) in Tanzania

post-colonialism articulates perspectives and experience of colonised peoples as opposed to those of the coloniser

post-enumeration survey (PES) a special kind of survey designed to measure census coverage and content error

post-industrial a society characterised by manufacturing industries losing significance to service industries, the prominence of knowledge in production, the increasing power of a managerial strata and the diminution of class conflict between producers and capitalists

post-modern usually refers to broad-ranging developments in the 1970s across literature, the arts and philosophy which subjected the aims of the Enlightenment to critique and introduced historical and cultural relativism as a guiding motif

postmodernity the era replacing modernity and its characteristic belief in rationality, progress, and truth

post-structuralism broad-based interdisciplinary perspective showing that words and signs represent an autonomous system independently of reference to reality or the social world, e.g. language has or is an autonomous structure with its own independent, internal rules which refers to its use; can further apply to discrete philosophies, ideologies and sciences, e.g. the terms, practice and logic of traditional African or Chinese medicine is discrete and fundamentally different from allopathic biomedicine

post-truth beliefs based on emotions instead of facts

poverty a state or condition in which especially material and cultural resources are lacking; the condition in which basic needs of clothing, food and shelter are not met

poverty eradication social structural reforms and changes to end poverty

poverty reduction policies and strategies to reduce the levels of poverty

power the ability to influence the views, choices and actions of others, often against their will

pragmatism in philosophy and social science the stress on prioritising what is practical as defining the course of thought and action

precariat a social group of unprotected, temporary and hence vulnerable workers whose livelihoods are fragile due to little or no job security or established employment rights

predatory journal publication of a selection of academic articles posing as academic scholarly works yet without adhering to academic standards and quality, often requiring payment to publish; not recognised by formal academic institutions

predestination a Christian doctrine based on the belief that God has elected certain souls to eternal salvation and others not

prescribed identity often imposed; a family or communal expectation an individual will adopt or follow a specific course or procedure, e.g. a doctor imposes the career choice of a doctor for a son or daughter

primary sector the agriculture, forestry and mining activities and areas of an economy

primary socialisation the process whereby individuals learn to become members of society in the home

primitive accumulation for Marx, the historical process of accumulating wealth by plunder and force, principally by divesting peasants of their land; a necessary process prior to capital accumulation; the process whereby capitalism itself is established

primordial the beginning or origin, when first created or emerged, such as earliest forms of life, e.g. amoeba

private enterprise business for profit not owned or controlled by the state; alternative term for 'free enterprise' system

private property entitlement by law to sole proprietorship, ownership or use of land or commodities

privatised when public or state-owned business enterprises and economic resources are transferred into private hands; the opposite of nationalisation

production the economic process within which the basic material and all other conditions for human life are realised or created

profane non-religious focus, marked by negation of or even contempt for that which is deemed sacred by others

proletarianisation the process whereby independent, self-employed or subsistent peasant producers lose access to the land and are compelled to move into urban areas to sell their labour power and become a social class relying solely on waged labour

proletariat term used by Marx for the working class; the class which survives by selling their ability to perform work (labour power) in return for wages

pro-natalist policies actively encourage women and couples to have many children and discourage them from limiting their number of offspring; the opposite of anti-natalist policies

prophets people chosen and authorised to speak for a deity or god, or self-selected by divine inspiration

propositions statements that can be true or false, which confirm or deny something

protective factors enhance the likelihood of positive outcomes and lessen the likelihood of negative consequences from exposure to risk

psychopathology the scientific study of mental disorders

public enterprise business or economic activity or resources partly or fully owned by the state

public interest a generally vague term that contrasts general welfare of the majority with the selfish interests of the minority (claimed generally by governments in matters of state secrecy and confidentiality)

public sociology extends the discipline beyond the university to citizens, for Michael Burawoy, the mirror of conscience of society

purity the condition or state of being or acting unblemished

push-pull model a theoretical model to explain migration and urbanisation according to forces pushing people out of their sending areas and pulling them toward their receiving areas

Q

qualitative research that focuses on gathering in-depth, experiential and testimonial evidence for thematic analysis

quantification process of counting and measurement presented in numbers and statistics

quantify to determine or measure the amount of something numerically

quantitative gathers numerical data for statistical analyses for the identification and analysis of correlative indices

queer acceptance of open and diverse sexual identities and intimate relationships

R

race a social construct based on biological differences; has no basis in science; humans belong to a single race.

racial order social system organised in terms of race

racial segregation policy and/or practice of the separation of groups of people distinguished by real, but non-essential characteristics such as skin colour

racism discrimination of the grounds of biological characteristics

racist attitude, behaviour, act or practice which discriminates against a person on the basis of their biological characteristics

radical elitism a theoretical perspective which argues that a dominant power elite exists in capitalist society and that the state serves the specific interests of this power elite

random probability sample the selection of a limited number of cases, where all cases have an equal chance of being selected

rational based on appropriate reasons

rationalisation for Weber, the increasingly intensified application in complex societies of legal and administrative mechanisms instituted on reasonable grounds designed to regulate social affairs

rationalism the view that reason and its role in thinking should receive priority over views based on sensory experience

rationality exercising reason or an approach that is agreeable to reason

realist perspective all views of the world are seen as grounded in a particular perspective and all knowledge is partial and incomplete with no possibility of attaining a single understanding of the world independent of a particular viewpoint

reason to think, argue or discuss in a connected, sensible logical manner; to think something through in a critical and questioning manner

rebundled when previously integrated parts or divisions of a business enterprise are merged or restructured, possibly including new acquisitions

reconstituted or joint family divorced, widowed or never married parent marries or cohabits with a new partner

records compilations; list of activities; in sport, the setting of new time performances

reductionism the attempt to explain a range of phenomena in terms of a single concept or idea

reflexivity the capacity of the social analyst to critically reflect on his/her own role, social position, attitudes, bias and preferences when conducting social research

reflexology originating in Chinese traditional medicine, a form of massage in which pressure is applied to certain parts of the feet and hands so as to promote relaxation and healing elsewhere in the body

regionalisation extension of economic activity into geographical environments beyond established local areas to establish new markets

regulations state control over market-related activities

relative autonomy for Louis Althusser, the partial or temporary independence of the political state from the influence of the capitalist economy; the political is only determined by the economic 'in the last instance'

relative deprivation the perception of an unfair socio-economic disparity between one's own position and that of those of others in our environment

relativism the concept or philosophy that no point of view can claim absolute knowledge or truth; all views are particular and subjective and none is to be prioritised above another

reliability principle of positivism establishing the dependability of social scientific research findings

religiosity the quality of being religious, which comprises various aspects

Renaissance the revival of art and literature in Europe from the 14th to 16th centuries; generally, a revival of interest in something

repressive a legal system, generally informal or traditional, which metes out punishment

repressive apparatus for Louis Althusser, term to describe the combined forces of the police, military and prisons under capitalism

reproduction the process of copying or replicating something, including biological and social phenomena

Republicans members of a political party in a state not ruled by a king; members of a major political party in the United States of America

research a systematic investigative process employed to increase or revise current knowledge and understanding

research design reasoning and planning how a study will be conducted

research problem the question posed on the issue to be investigated

resocialisation changing by force or the voluntary learning of new norms, values designed to change social behaviour; takes place within a controlled environment with the goal of changing a person's behaviour

restitutive a legal system, generally formal, which remedies or compensates for loss

retrenchment the process of reducing expenditure (usually by a company) in order to improve its financial stability involving the reduction of the number of employees

retroduction a form of argument proposing an explanation of an observed series of incidents or facts based on similarity or simultaneous occurrence with a separate series of incidents or facts

revolution major socio-political upheaval resulting in significant social change

risk factor something which increases susceptibility

risk society a term coined by Ulrich Beck to describe modernity as seeking to assess and insure against the unintended social and environmental consequences of industrialisation

risk taking making decisions or acting in dangerous or hazardous ways which may result in loss, damage or harm

rites of passage cultural ceremonies that mark decisive transitions in a person's life

ritual established formal patterns of behaviour associated with the sacred

roles playing a part or assuming a social function or functions, often simultaneously, such as daughter, mother and teacher

rural development facilitating and enabling people in rural areas to make sustainable improvements to all aspects of their lives

rural sociology focus on human activities and societies where agrarian, agricultural and natural environments predominate

rural space literally means 'open' space; generally less populated than urban areas

rurality the condition of being in or of the rural; the human and nature co-created environment, including managed geographical spaces such as nature reserves

rural–urban transition a major transformation in human history impacting on all aspects of life, geographically, economically, socially, psychologically and culturally

S

sacred set apart, venerated or subject to devotion, relating to religious practices; opposite of profane

salary remuneration for undertaking 'white collar' employment, generally paid monthly

salient identity a dominant part of identity which is expressed in specific situations

same-sex families are constituted by same-sex couples with children from previous relationships, adopted children or children born with the help of in-vitro techniques

scepticism philosophical position which questions and doubts everything, at least until compelling evidence is advanced and presented, thereby dispelling the questioning and doubtful attitude

science the establishment of the fact or state of knowing; systematic investigation and research relying on evidence and rational thought resulting in knowledge

scientific evidence is collected in a systematic and repeatable way

scientific management also referred to as Taylorism; the application of rational, scientific principles in managing business enterprises, especially the workplace behaviour of employees

scientific observations made in a systematic, methodical and rigorous manner and refer to a body of techniques for investigating and acquiring new knowledge

Second World the planned, industrialised socialist economies of the former Soviet bloc

secondary sector the manufacturing industries and activities in an economy

secondary socialisation learning how to become members of society in the schooling environment

sect a distinct group of people breaking away from a larger, usually religious, group to follow a different set of rules or establish different values

secular non-religious

semantic differential scale question a method of rating responses during research designed to measure connotative meanings of concepts, objects and events by noting where respondents' preferences lie when confronted with two polar opposites

semiotics the study of signs and sign systems, e.g. language is a system or structure of signs.

semi-proletarianised describes wage labourers who retain access to productive forces such as land and livestock

serfdom an unfree social system in which a quasi-independent labouring peasantry performs the work ruled by chiefs or lords

serial monogamy being married more than once, but with one partner at a time

service work work performed in the tertiary sector of the economy

sex the biological features of being male or female

sexism discrimination on the grounds of gender

sexist attitude, behaviour, act or practice which discriminates against a person on the basis of their gender

sexology the study of sex

sexual orientation a person's emotional, psychological and physical attraction to another person

sexuality sexual behaviour reflecting deeply embedded rules, regulations and patterned behaviour prescribed by particular cultural expectations and social institutions

shamanic labour work or labour performed under the direction of a traditional medical healer, visionary seer, a 'priest-doctor' or 'witch doctor'

sharecropper a partially independent, itinerant or semi-autonomous agriculturalist who works on the land and divides their produce with a landowner

shareholders owners of shares in the stock of companies or corporations, especially enterprises listed on the Securities Exchange (Stock Exchange)

sick role the position occupied by the ill used in functionalist theory to outline the privileges and expectations associated with being legitimately sick

sign a process, event or thing standing for or indicating something else

significant others parents, relatives, siblings or important individuals whose primary and sustained interactions with the individual are especially influential

single-parent family single parent who lives with dependent children in a household

single-parent household one parent living with dependent children in a household

sinner a transgressor of a specified religious conduct

slavery an economic and social system in which labour is performed as a result of non-economic compulsion or force

social action for Max Weber, when subjects engage in a particular choice of action because of the meaning it holds for them

social behaviourism for GH Mead, the approach, analysis and view that the nature of human conduct and personality is derived solely from interaction and association with others and in which language, symbols and communication are primary factors

social capital shared living and working relationships and networks enabling society to function effectively

social closure first formulated by Max Weber, refers to various strategies of preserving privilege by restricting access of others to resources and rewards

social cohesion the condition, varying in degrees of strength or weakness, of being linked and bound together into a group of individuals; interchangeably used with solidarity

social construction the socially created nature of social life, i.e what does not occur naturally but is humanly created e.g notions of femininity and masculinity differ as they are due to different modes of socialisation (see **socially constructed**)

social contract unwritten agreement between the state and it's citizens expressing the rights and duties of each whereby political relations in society will be organised and regulated

social differentiation distinctions between social groups

social division of labour the specialisation of tasks that produces interdependence and social solidarity

social exclusion the complete or partial exclusion of people from full participation in the society in which they live

social facts for Durkheim, range of phenomena peculiar to social science to be treated as things and which are external, general and exercise coercive influence over human agents and of which they are generally unaware

social fatherhood various roles men play in children's lives such as nurturing, teaching and playing

social grants regular income paid by the state to different categories of vulnerable members of society

social honour the social status people are acknowledged to have based on their economic resources and political influence

social identity how one is viewed or seen by others in society; a person's self-concept of who they are based on their perceptions of their membership of a group or position in society

social inequality extent of difference in socio-economic and social status between members of society; generally indicated by race, gender and class

social integration bonds and links between people; solidarity between people; occurs in different degrees in social groups

social mobility the movement between different, generally vertical hierarchical social ranks

social model of health and disease also referred to as psycho-socio-environmental model, emphasises people's behaviour and social context in determining health and disease outcomes

social movement organisation a formal collective organisation which has specific identifiable goals it seeks to implement through mobilisation, direct action or legal means

social movements opinions and beliefs collectively held that reflect a desire for change in some elements of the social order, generally including the reward and distribution structure of society

social relations interactions between people; can assume many forms

social relations of production for Marx, in order to produce, people must relate to and co-operate with one another, the sum total of such interactions being the structural and real basis for the economy of any society

social science the establishment of the fact or state of knowing regarding social phenomena; systematic investigation and research relying on evidence and rational thought resulting in social knowledge

social solidarity the different types and degrees of social cohesion in traditional and modern society

social stratification the hierarchy of different layers of unequal social classes in society; levels of social distinction or social difference

social structure routinised pattern of events; generally deemed to influence or exercise force over human agents

social system a systems theory notion of human society being analogous to a biological organism with specialised and interdependent parts that make up the whole

social theory abstract conceptual ideas about human affairs; construction or explanation of the nature of human affairs or some aspect of it

social wage the subsidised or free benefits and services provided by state budgets which supplement the earnings of citizens, such as housing, education and healthcare

social welfare range of services and assistance rendered to vulnerable members of society

socialisation the process by which people learn the characteristics of their group: the attitudes, values, and actions thought appropriate for them; learning to become members of society

socialism a future transitional form of society based on freedom, equality and co-operation and the absence of exploitation, domination and oppression

socially constructed the result of the human interactions, events and processes creating a powerful structural constraining force over individuals in society; humanly created circumstances manifesting influential impact on individual and collective behaviour

societal action collective social or political behaviour or action consciously and rationally motivated to advance the interests of a particular group

sociological competence the common-sense capacity to negotiate and manage the social world

sociological imagination ability to place and link personal life processes within and relate them to the broader social and historical context

sociological realism an approach that inclines or is directed towards literal truth, pragmatism and the mind-independent character of social reality and social structures

sociological research methods the scientific study of society using conventionally accepted ways of investigating the social sphere of life

sociological theory abstract conceptual construction or explanation of the nature of human affairs or some aspect of it based on evidence

sociologist social scientist who studies human social behaviour and the affairs and development of human society

sociology *in* medicine an approach to the sociological study of health, disease and healthcare to answer research questions of interest to doctors

sociology of knowledge an approach showing how ideas and theories reflect the society in which they are formulated

sociology *of* medicine an approach that critically analyses matters of health, disease and care to answer research questions of interest to sociologists in general, often

relating to power and power relationships within the healthcare domain

solidarity the cohesive force that binds people together in a society

Southern Theory expression of systematic views, sustained narratives or formal descriptions or explanations emanating from previously colonised societies; conceptual perspectives grounded in and expressing interests of developing societies

spatial dimension the extent, in terms of width-breadth and length of an area, generally of a lived-in or working environment

spatial practice activities invested with meaning taking place in a living environment; for Henri Lefebvre, conceptualised as lived space (in which one lives), perceived space (how the immediate environment is seen) and conceived space (how an environment can be imagined as different)

specialisation in the division of labour, productive tasks continuously dividing into more varied and discrete tasks; regarding work, focusing exclusively on a specific field or function and limiting options

speculation akin to gambling, but based on some or other kind of information or even evidence but which remains uncertain; relates particularly to investing money in fluctuating financial markets in the hope of reward or profit

state a form of political association which subsumes all other such forms; sovereign political entities; the totality of infrastructure government, judiciary and the executive, including all departments, ministries employed to implement policies and programmes which regulate society

state-form different forms of state ranging from liberal democracy states to fascist and authoritarian states

status the regard, attitude and prestige in which individuals or social groups are held due to their social position and standing, referred to as 'honour' by Weber

step-families partners living together with children from previous relationships, including with children from a current union; also referred to as reconstituted families

stigma a characteristic that discredits or prevents a person's claim to a 'normal' identity or full acceptance in a particular situation

stigmatised to label or characterise someone or something as socially undesirable or unacceptable

stratification a model of social difference, variation and structured inequality in the organisation of society (which appeals to the striations or 'layers' in geological rock formations); divides and defines people into social 'layers' by rank, social status, class or any other such division

stretched households joint financial commitment of a particular group of related individual family members unable to share the same dwelling on a regular basis

Structural Adjustment Programmes macro-economic reforms implemented in developing countries by the International Monetary Fund and World Bank in the 1980s

structural differentiation in structural functionalism, the development of increasing complexity of societies or sub-systems within a society, e.g societies from simple hunter-gatherer to complex industrial ones can be distinguished; sub-systems such as family, education, occupation in complex functional social systems

structuralism any view, approach or perspective in the social sciences which prioritises social structure over individual action or agency; structures can be identified lying behind appearances of social reality

structural functionalism a sociological perspective established by Talcott Parsons stressing the way society is ordered by patterned regularities in the way in which the parts of the whole work together; often employs a biological analogy of how the constituent parts of an organic whole work towards maintaining the whole organism

structuration for Anthony Giddens, the mutually reinforcing interaction between social structure and individual human agency

structure mechanism, system or institution which regularises or routinises a pattern of events, e.g timetable at school or university

subjective a personal or single view or perspective, belief, feeling or desire pertaining to and not valid as knowledge beyond the individual concerned; opposite of objective

subjectivity the state of being subjective; the self-conscious perspective of the individual

subsistence economy variously defined, the collective activity of producing only enough, generally in agriculture, for one's own family or community use, generally from day to day

suburbs residential areas of a city or large town, with their own social identity, but normally included under the city government

supernatural relates to phenomena or beings said to exist outside the natural observable world

superstructure for Marx, the range of social institutions arising from the economic base of society

surplus value Marx's concept regarding the value created by wage labourers over and above the value of their wages and costs of reproduction

surrogate families unrelated individuals providing support for each another

survey investigation conducted by means of a standardised questionnaire in which all respondents are asked the same questions and designed to arrive at statistical results

survival kinship networks dependent children sent to relatives to ensure better opportunities

sustainable development defined by the World Commission on Environment and Development (WCED) as development that meets the needs of the present without compromising the ability of future generations to meet their own needs

symbol some thing or act which stands for or represents something else, e.g The South African flag stands for or represents the South African people or nation

symbolic capital the resources of honour and prestige, reputation and recognition available to an individual

symbolic interactionism emphasises the micro scale interaction of humans and their process of creating meanings

syncretism the combining of different beliefs and practices from different sources, usually in religious practise

syphilis a potentially fatal sexually transmitted disease

T

tables, graphs and illustrations visual ways of presenting research findings

tariff barriers duties or taxes imposed on goods and commodities imported into a country

tax monies levied by the state on businesses and all individuals earning above a specified income

TBVC states (Transkei, Bophuthatswana, Venda and Ciskei) abbreviation for tribally defined settlement of Africans under apartheid dismantled in 1994

teleological explanations see teleology

teleology the study of ultimate causes; sociological explanation of processes as moving towards identifiable end states

temporal flexibility the allocation of time in the workplace by way of part-time or seasonal work, shift work or flexi-time working time arrangements

tenderpreneurship recent local South African term referring to favoured, politically connected business people securing work put out to public tender by the state

tertiary sector the service sector of the economy; wholesale, retail, hospitality, entertainment

theological stage for Comte, a long period in human history in which religious belief was both primary and necessary

theology the systematic and rational study of concepts and ideas about religious questions, truth and God

theory abstract conceptual construction serving to explain some or other social phenomenon or phenomena

Third World the poor, undeveloped, unindustrialised, less industrialied or developing societies

tithes a proportion of income or earnings given to the church

tolerance a fair, open and accommodating attitude to those holding different opinions and views

total fertility rate (TFR) the average number of children born alive during a woman's childbearing years conforming to the age-specific fertility rates of a given year

total institutions places in which the lives of large numbers of like-situated persons are controlled in all aspects

totalising system of thought capturing everything under its ambit; term used in post-modernism and post-structuralism

totalitarianism highly centralised political and social system in which the state is in complete control and absolute authority is exercised over citizens

totemism a natural object taken as the emblem of a clan with which the members have a kinship or mythical relationship

townships (also called locations) a special name under apartheid for African residential areas

trade liberalisation the relaxation or removal of rules, regulations or restraints (such as tariffs, import duties and taxes) over buying, selling or trading in the market; opening the market to competition

trade unions organisations established in workplaces representing interests of workers – especially in respect of wages and working conditions – in negotiations with employers

traditional action for Weber, something done intentionally based on established ways of doing things

traditional leaders a historically hereditary governance structure, constitutionally recognised under democracy, comprising the kingship or chieftaincy (*amakhosi*) and its deputies (*izinduna*)

tragedy of the commons destructive behaviour in which a public-owned common natural resource is overused and degraded

transactional sex the sustained exchange of sex for money or other desired goods and services

transcendence that which surpasses human knowledge or natural experience

transcendental idealism philosophy based on the view that the perception of objects are shaped or conditioned by the mind; things themselves cannot be known; formulated by Immanuel Kant

transformation the process of completely changing something

transgender includes transsexual people but also refers to other people who are cross-dressers and/or express themselves in ways that are beyond socially stipulated gender norms

transnational communication communication across national borders and boundaries

transnational corporate finance relating to the money owned and managed by large global business enterprises

transnational corporations global companies, normally with a home base in one country and subsidiary companies in other countries

transnational elite term used to describe the contemporary minority global social grouping enjoying disproportionate political and economic power exercised seemingly independently of generally respected national or international legal norms and rules

transsexual person who feels that their body that does not match their gender identity

triangulation a research method involving two or more research methods providing different kinds of evidence requiring integration

tuberculosis an infectious, airborne disease caused by the bacillus *Mycobacterium tuberculosis*; attacks and destroys lung tissue and can be fatal if not treated

U

unbundled when a large corporation is broken up, generally for purposes of greater efficiency; a business dismantled into core and non-core divisions, departments or activities

underemployment not having enough paid work or not using one's full set of skills and competencies while employed

unemployment joblessness; occurs when workers have no work despite being active job seekers

unintended consequences social actions or occurrences which are not foreseen by their agents

universal laws laws that apply to all places at all times

universalism the pursuit of universal knowledge; often used to refer to the dominance of Western knowledge

urban centres a metropole, city, town or village, defined according to size of population, form of government and services available

urban growth the growth in the urban population expressed in absolute numbers or in a growth rate

urban hierarchy a gradation between the largest and the smallest urban centres in a country, forming a continuum

urbanisation the increasing proportion of a population living in settlements defined as urban areas or centres

urbanism patterns and styles of life associated with the densification of human populations in towns and cities

urban–rural linkages a concept used to refer to linkages between towns and cities and agricultural settlements

usurpation to take over, infringe or seize control; generally illegally by force

V

validity the question whether research is measuring what it claims to measure and results in the measurement or concept being well founded thereby accurately corresponding to the real world

value neutrality lack of bias; not being influenced by values

value statements human questions on values and on how things should be

value worth; for Marx, that which is embodied in commodities due to human labour expended in their creation

value-rational for Weber, actions motivated by reason derived to achieve a goal or end considered worthwhile

vanguard political party for Vladimir Lenin, the group at the head of working class revolution

variables concepts with a value that changes from case to case; can be viewed as independent or dependent

verification the attempt to establish criteria for truth and falsity; the provision of empirical evidence to enable the belief that a statement is true

Verstehen for Weber, the approach to the interpretation or meanings individuals give to parts of or their subjective experience, or understanding of the social world

virtual reality perception and experience derived solely from, within and dependent on electronic media

W

wage flexibility the use in workplaces of various forms of performance-based pay, incentive schemes and productivity bonuses

wage remuneration for undertaking 'blue collar' employment, generally paid weekly

'Washington consensus' originally a set of conservative prescriptions for economic development in South America; used commonly as pejorative term synonymous with neoliberalism and globalisation

weblining tracking of internet use for purposes of attaining personal data generally in order to market goods and services to specific profiles of users

women's rights movements a general type of social movement fighting for specific rights for women in various contexts

work purposive productive activity undertaken with tools, generally with the expectation of a reward

working class traditionally used to describe the social class performing physical and much practical cognitive work in capitalist societies, but who do not own or control economic resources

workplace flexibility the re-arrangement, re-allocation and re-distribution of tasks, skills and jobs among and between workers

world economy a common division of labour made up of units characterised by different cultures and no single overarching political structure and the economic surplus is distributed by market forces

world empires civilisations which had a common, unified, centralised political system reigning over an extended geographical territory

world-systems theory for Wallerstein, a multidisciplinary approach stressing that the current global social arrangement should be the primary, but not exclusive unit of social analysis

X

xenophobia fear and/or hatred of strangers

Introduction

Why are you reading this book?

If you are reading this book, the chances are you are young and one of the elite, or at least potential elite, in South African society. You are one of the few to put it plainly. Is that the way you think of yourself – as a member of the elitè? If you do not think of yourself in this way, there may be some surprises in store for you if you continue to read thoroughly. As you have probably just registered for a diploma or a degree at a tertiary institution, that already puts you in the top 12 per cent of all young people in South Africa.

You have just had the opportunity to test an educated guess, bordering on a prediction, namely that you are young and privileged. If you have started lectures, you are already well on your way to becoming a sociologist. In fact, the sociologist, Charles Lemert, persuasively argued that all normally functioning human beings, even prior to adulthood, possess 'sociological competence'. In short, most people can negotiate their way in and around their social environment. You do not have to go to sociology lectures to be able to do so. Well, you might ask, if I am already sociologically competent, why am I reading this book?

You might well be reading this book because it is a prescribed text book. There are different attitudes you can have towards being compelled to do so. If you just want to get your academic qualification you are being *instrumental* about your studies. Generally, that is thought not to be such a good thing. It means you are only reading right now because you need to pass this course. If you are reading these words now, because you are curious and believe that education is valuable and may even be a little excited, then you are exercising what the great European sociologist, Max Weber, called **value rationality**. By the way, let us note quickly, you can accept this concept (or not) without betraying your commitment to Africanism – the view that Africans should develop and pursue a perspective which emerges out of and expresses African values, beliefs and traditions. We will address this issue, as well as the guiding

idea of **decolonial thinking** behind the 2015 and 2016 #RhodesMustFall and #FeesMustFall student protests at previously advantaged, well-resourced universities in the first chapter of this book.

We have, in the three paragraphs above, already started *doing* sociology beyond the level of everyday sociological competence. The social group under the spotlight has been tertiary education students. You may already even have started to see yourself as a member of this group – and even probably disagreed that you are part of the elite group in society, especially if you are the first of your family to study at a college or university, like one of the editors of this book. This is, in fact, one of the most remarkable things about taking sociology seriously. The more you learn about society, the more we learn about ourselves. It is something nobody can ever take away from us. The study of society is empowering. At least that is what we editors think, otherwise we would not have spent our time teaching, researching and writing as fulltime academics. We hope to have started to convince you that reading this book may be your time well spent.

You are reading this textbook because it aims to address many uniquely South African issues, large and small, everyday and global – seemingly obvious ones and tough, difficult ones. This means developing the analytical and thinking skills necessary to understand the social forces and factors that shape our individual identities, influence the form which families and the schooling system takes and impacts on the world of work, alongside many other social topics. What, for instance, impedes or advances social and economic progress? How can South Africa's young democracy be further entrenched? What prevents this society of ours from achieving a better life for all South Africans?

The opportunities any society presents to its people cannot be taken for granted. Its challenges cannot be ignored. In any society, how opportunities are grasped and how challenges are met depends on the people and those they elect to represent them. Or, as you will well know if you come from a rural area, the fortunes of communities depend on how well traditional leaders, who are not elected, enjoy local support where they have influence to allocate land and adjudicate disputes. More than we realise, our individual fortunes depend significantly on those in leadership positions in politics and the economy, the way in which a society is ordered and structured, the involvement of its citizens and a range of other social factors and forces. These factors and forces and a range of social processes can both hinder and help a society in its quest to function at its best. Much also depends on global economic and political forces beyond the control of the people of any society. The overall result of this complex set of individual actions, as well as local and global social forces, can be a social environment in which there is opportunity for some, but which remains beset with social problems. It is these kinds of issues that this textbook will tackle in a systematic manner.

South Africa is a developing country, often referred to as an emerging market society. The development of a country is not only dependent on its people and their leaders and how it is organised. Development also involves the place a country or society occupies in an increasingly and rapidly globalising world. Global, cultural and technological developments are increasingly determining the way people work, their styles of life, their patterns of consumption and their life opportunities in societies across the world. Global politics and economics powerfully shape the possibilities of local political and economic developments. Global tendencies have a powerful impact on national stability in many countries. Such tendencies include issues of regional political and economic power, ethnic and religious fervour and rivalries and an increasingly interconnected world. How does South Africa fare in all of this? What is the impact of these complex sets of factors and forces on you as an individual? This book addresses these kinds of questions and many more in a rigorous and scholarly manner. This goes well beyond the everyday sociological competence of which Charles Lemert speaks.

Sociology: A Comprehensive South African Introduction, was written by sociology lecturers who teach at South African universities. It was specifically designed for first year students registered at university and tertiary educational institutions. But because it is such an extensive textbook, it will also serve all undergraduate students in the social sciences and sociology in particular. Postgraduate students in sociology have found previous editions useful. This is because it is a comprehensive compendium of the themes that form the basis for a sociological understanding of South African society and beyond.

Taken seriously, this textbook will provide you with a solid grounding in the social sciences in general and sociology in particular. The intention of the book is to equip tertiary education students with the conceptual and theoretical foundation on which to build sound reasoning skills in the social sciences. Through such skills you will be able to grasp and understand how South African society works, what its challenges and possibilities are and how it fits into the global village of which we are all part. The plight of marginalised people for instance, is central to how well or poorly any society meets the needs of its citizens. Learning how to think sociologically enables those of us privileged to be educated to play a more active role and thereby contribute positively to society, in this case South African society in particular. How, you might ask, can the study of sociology help in understanding the world around us and enable this kind of empowerment? This book begins by giving you an example of the way in which sociologists think about and explain one aspect of the social world with which you will be very familiar. You will have already noted words in **bold** type which you will find explained in the Glossary at the front of this book. Don't be surprised if you have to consult a word more than once. You are already beginning to study sociology!

Thinking sociologically

Why do you feel lost without your cell phone? Sociology has a series of responses. One classical sociologist, Emile Durkheim, whose theories you will encounter, would say cell phones contribute to social cohesion – they help link and bind people and social groups together. A cell keeps us connected. We are in immediate contact with our friends and family. When we are out of contact, because we find ourselves without our cell phone for some reason, we feel anxious. What if we missed an important event? We experience a loss of being linked with our immediate social group. The social relationships we maintain through being connected have been disrupted and so we feel dislocated.

Another influential classical thinker, Karl Marx, whom you will also learn about, starts his social analysis with the everyday things of life – its material basis in other words. He would explain how this late 20th century technology cellular telephony has powerfully shaped the form and quality of our social relations which have arisen out of an advanced industrialised capitalist society. This thinker, who died in the late 19th century, would be interested in how the global economy has developed the material basis for the production of over 5 billion cell phones, on a planet of 7 789 billion people (7 789 000 000 plus people) as of May

2020 – and growing literally by the second – has defined our awareness and consciousness of ourselves and how much we depend on this contemporary technology in our everyday lives (see https://www.worldometers.info>world-population). By the way, there are 500 million more people on this planet than when this book was first published in 2014. Go straight to the chapter on the environment (Chapter 26) if the implications of this startling figure make you wonder. Work though it slowly. Some parts you might find alarming as to what is happening to global society.

But to get back to having lost your cell. One leading sociologist, Manuell Castells, would explain our sense of being lost in terms of the network society in which we live. Another sociologist, Ulrich Beck, argued that we feel a greater sense of being at risk without our cell phones. What if something happened to us? What if we could not contact anybody? It boils down to the social fact that we live in a risk society, he would explain. You will almost definitely find it intriguing to see how sociological theories are used to arrive at understandings and explanations about all manner of aspects of the social world, not merely 'ordinary' experiences such as missing cell phones. But let us, briefly, look at what sociology is in a more systematic and formal manner.

What is sociology?

Sociology involves the scientific study of human social interaction and the social forces which shape much of human behaviour. Sociology studies the patterns, trends and forms of collective social action and the social processes and structures in society which arise out of the way human beings act in the world. We suggest you go over those two sentences again – and then come back to them at the end of your course before exams and you might be pleasantly surprised at how much your perspective has changed and your understanding has grown. Hopefully you have started on a life-long learning process as there is always something new when society is the object of your study.

The following paragraphs explain the two sentences you re-read. Here is one brief definitional overview of sociology. Do take it slowly and needless to say, strive to be disciplined and look up words unfamiliar to you. Do also check the words in **bold** in the Glossary!

- The term 'sociology' comes from the French word *sociologie*, which means the science of companions. Sociology is therefore a combination of two words. The first part 'socio'- derives from the Latin *socius* meaning 'companion'. The second part '-logy' stems from the Latin *logia* meaning 'sayings'. The Latin was derived from the Greek word *logos*, which means 'word', and *legein*, which means 'to speak'. In sociology, therefore, its researchers speak about the social aspects of life.

- The social features sociology studies include the wide variety of social actions of people and the social patterns, organisations and institutions arising from our collective social action. Such a variation can range from fleeting encounters of individuals on the street to global social processes. Sometimes students of sociology distinguish these social contexts by referring to micro-, meso- or macro-sociology. This implies that the micro will focus on individual relationships, the meso on groups or communities, and the macro on national and global social processes. The point is that sociology has to deal with a very wide variety of social aspects in society, such as those of the following themes:

  Ageing, agriculture, armed forces, arts, childhood, communication, conflict, deviance, disasters, economy, education, environment, ethnicity, families, gender, health, housing, illness, labour, language, law, leisure, migration, organisation, politics, political elites, poverty, racism, religion, social classes, social movements, sport, stratification, welfare, women, work and youth.

  Where humans interact, social relations between people emerge which sociology can study. As this applies to every person, the study of sociology is immediate, interesting and relevant to who we are as individuals and how we have become who we are.

- Crucially, sociology involves *scientific* study. This means that knowledge in sociology is obtained by specific methodologies or ways and rules of social investigation. To give an example of what methodology is, if rugby players were invited to play in a soccer match, they would be expected to play according to the rules of soccer. Similarly, sociologists are expected to abide by the rules of scientific study. This means that sociological inquiry must fulfil certain requirements.

  - Sociological arguments and conclusions must be **logical**.
    You will learn quickly that any assertions or argument in sociology must be internally logically coherent. A sociological account must fit together as a consistent whole. This means the account must be based on **logical deductions** or inferences, **generalisations** or **interpretations** of observations or of other assertions. Through such a logical **discourse**, sociology is therefore 'playing' *within the rules* of **rational** deduction and generalised ideas relating to social phenomena.

- Sociological knowledge must provide **explanations** of social reality.

  Explanations – especially *social* explanations – illuminate and empower. The sociological knowledge in which such explanations are embedded must ultimately be **justified** and **verified**. **Reasons** must, in other words, be given and must be supported for the knowledge claims that sociology makes.

- Sociology must strive for **objectivity**.

  It should be clear that the sociological knowledge is *not* based on **subjective** bias. The reasons given through explanations should be based on thorough research. Sufficient objectivity is attained by demonstrating that the findings on which the knowledge is based were verified through acknowledged procedures of **empirical** observation and techniques of inquiry.

- Sociology must strive against making **moral judgements**.

  A characteristic of scientific knowledge is not to make ethical or moral judgements on what is good or bad. Social scientific knowledge rather presents things as they are. However, it will be clear from the Chapter 1 on sociological theory that in many cases sociologists are forced to make **ethical** assessments and moral choices.

- Sociological knowledge is *not final*.

  It is important to note that scientific knowledge should not be seen as final. Sociological knowledge does not consist of **absolute** and unchanging truths, but is provisional. This means that the knowledge can change as knowledge develops. Continuous peer reviewing and new research contributes to broaden sociological knowledge.

- Scientific knowledge is based on **theory**.

  Sociology describes and explains social phenomena (things) through **reasoned** arguments. This is what 'theoretical' means. Such forms of reasoning are built up by means of **concepts** which pick out phenomena. Concepts are imaginable mental phenomena, such as age, racism and compassion. Sociologists can, of course, and *do* differ in how they imagine these phenomena. They can, therefore, define the *same* concepts *differently*. As you progress in sociology, you may find that the definitions of some of these concepts are a contested terrain and that defining social phenomena is not always straightforward.

To repeat, do turn to these paragraphs again in a while. This is advisable as you may have already struggled somewhat!

You will then be pleasantly surprised at how much you have learned. When you begin to understand sociology in the systematic way as described above, you already will have learned that sociologists have specific *approaches* and *perspectives* on how they study society. This introduction now focuses on one typical sociological approach to society. If missing cell phones was a fun example, this is a serious one. Unemployment, especially among the youth, is one of the direst challenges South African society faces currently.

The sociological imagination

Imagine you are the only one of your friends in your community who is unemployed. Think about this for a moment. Being unemployed has a dramatic effect on your personal circumstances. Not having a job or having lost your job may lead to low or no income, and this makes you feel excluded from the mainstream of social life and society. This condition thus creates personal troubles for you. You are held responsible and might be blamed for being incompetent or lazy.

Imagine that you and quite a number of your friends in your community are unemployed and that is the case in South Africa as a whole. You do not just all have *personal troubles*. You all share a *social problem*. Unemployment is a social issue. Your shared unemployment is a feature of a dislocated place in society, which you experience collectively. The situation of your unemployment thus can no longer be seen solely as your personal trouble. It is a product of social strife. Under such circumstances, *you are not personally responsible for this situation*. Nobody can blame you for not pulling your weight.

The two situations are quite different. According to your first imagination you were on your own. In the second imagination you found yourself together with others in a shared social situation. In the first case you *personally* had to shoulder the responsibility and blame. In the second case neither you nor your friends could be blamed for being unemployed when youth unemployment has soared. You all still had a personal problem, but your lack of a job must be seen as the result of the pressing state of the local economy, as well as broader regional and global economic processes. In this sense, your personal circumstances form part of a bigger social problem. Some good news is that, despite high youth unemployment rates, the unemployment rate among college graduates in South Africa has hovered about 7 per cent over the past two years. There will be regional differences, so Google the latest statistics! To understand that your shared unemployment is linked to broader social events and circumstances, however, is to display a

sociological imagination. To exercise this sociological imagination means to be able to link and understand your own situation in the light of what is happening in broader society.

This notion of the sociological imagination was used by C Wright Mills (1916–1962) to describe the approach by which people could discern what affects them adversely in life. It links the two poles of social understanding and analysis – the individual and society. This insight shaped much of sociology as we know it today. So powerful is this insight that you will find it expressed near the beginning of most sociology textbooks. This is because, by using the sociological imagination, people could begin to understand the *underlying issues* and *social factors and forces* that impact on their lives. This gives them the insight to deal with these matters and thereby contributes to potentially improving both their own situation and that of society.

From a personal perspective, one focuses only on one's own life, private troubles and experience – one's own individual biography. One does not take into account that these troubles may form part of a larger social issue. This insight that the sociological imagination provides enables individuals to see their troubles, not as a result of lacking personal abilities, but by understanding them in the light of the bigger social picture. Once they do this, then they can view their life as part of a larger history that operates *independently* of the individual. This leads people to understand that their personal troubles are related to broader social issues. Adopting this view enables us to look beyond our personal circumstances and see how our lives fit into a larger social framework. That can be very empowering.

Viewed through a sociological imagination, ordinary social phenomena are not accepted at face value. This might at first be tricky to understand. This is because people tend to internalise social patterns and rules, and make them their own. For the most part, people are therefore totally unaware of the underlying social aspects that **structure** human thought, experience and behaviour. People's lives are to a large extent already patterned – they live according to patterns that they have acquired through learning. People's ways of thinking, feeling and acting may thus be what other people and external social forces (such as unemployment) imposed on them. *This is the core insight of sociology.*

To see how social factors largely have made individual human beings who they are, read and study the chapter on socialisation and identity (Chapter 6). Some of the most important factors which impact on us as people are our culture and language, our gender, our ethnicity and race, class and what work people do, as well as our socio-

economic background. You will see how these social factors powerfully influence our lives and that can each be taken in turn and then considered as a whole to better understand the huge changes our lives underwent during the Covid-19 pandemic and how it affected people different social groups in very different ways depending on the access to resources and profile of each social group across these factors.

Sociology thus aims to lay bare the issues that cause personal troubles for people. In this way, people develop their sociological imagination and are thereby able to answer the question on what effect social issues have on their own life. In sociology, it is therefore important to broaden one's imagination with the help of scientific knowledge.

Sociology consequently does not shy away from studying controversial topics. This fact makes sociology an exciting discipline and one that evokes debate. Sociology can therefore contribute to the unveiling of social issues like oppression, domination, exploitation, racism, sexism and other social influences and forces that limit people's freedom and impact on their sense of themselves. By enabling this unveiling of external issues, the discipline of sociology can promote the improvement of society. However, the extent to which sociology should indeed improve society is a controversial matter. Some sociologists prefer merely to study society solely in a strictly scientific way. Others believe that sociologists should also be involved politically and participate directly in processes that may help better society. For C Wright Mills, private issues must be turned into public issues and play an illuminating and transformative role in society. As can be expected, there is a huge debate about this view of sociology. This boils down to the question: who or what does sociology serve?

Once your *sociological imagination* or, as you will see, our individual *decolonial imaginations*, begin to develop, the question arises: what do we do with the powerful insights gained? Is such an imagination only applicable to a scientific discourse? The brief answer is no. In the early 20th century sociologists following the **conflict perspective** in particular argued that sociology should also contribute directly to positive social change. The classroom is therefore not only a place in which to present academic scientific knowledge, but also a springboard from which active students can be equipped to participate in positive social change. In this way it is argued that sociology should steer away from being a typical conservative, **bourgeois** practice, which functions in the service of the status quo.

This idea of a critical sociology was developed strongly in the 1950s in Germany by a prominent group of social analysts and thinkers called the *Frankfurter Schule* (The

Frankfurt School). Their names might not mean a lot to you right now, but any serious student will come across them in studies both in and well beyond sociology. The main collaborators were influential scholars whose great body of work – critical sociology – is still keenly studied today such as Theodor Adorno, Lucien Goldmann, Jürgen Habermas, Harry Hoefnagels, Max Horkheimer, Robert S Lynd, Serge Mallet, Herbert Marcuse, Karlheinz Messelken, Herman Milikowsky and C Wright Mills.

Proponents of critical sociology initially promoted the idea of a society in which all members will be fully included. It was soon realised, however, that a scarcity of economic means makes this ideal impossible. In time, Habermas began to dominate the debate. He pleaded rather for a dominant free dialogue of sensible people. Such a dialogue could help people to develop a **consensus** on the general goals and means of a new society. In such an ideal society the social processes are consciously directed towards a more desirable and humane society. It is important for a developing society such as South Africa to make social progress, which may be achieved if greater consensus could be found on how to embed human-oriented aims more deeply into the social fabric of South African society.

However, currently the engagement of sociology with society is argued differently. In 1990, one of the world's leading sociologists, Michael Burawoy, attended the Association for Sociology in Southern Africa (ASSA) congress. He was impressed by what he referred to as public sociology in South Africa. He saw sociologists actively engaged in society. When he became president of the American Sociological Association in 2004, he argued strongly in his presidential address for the involvement of sociology in public life. This form of public sociology implies an approach in which the discipline engages with the public. Burawoy contrasted this kind of sociology with professional sociology – an academic discipline that mainly addresses other professional sociologists – and which can be dry, technical and difficult to follow.

Burawoy argued that the idea of public sociology encourages adherents of the discipline to engage in debates about political activism, public policy, the institutions of civil society and the purposes of social movements (Burawoy 2005). Public sociology therefore sought to renew the discipline by applying its theoretical insights and empirical methods to engage in debates. These debates did not only cover what society is or was, but also what it could become. The question was thus put to sociologists: to what extent can one only study the subject as an academic? Should sociologists not be involved in public debates and controversies that are related to the improvement of human

social conditions? Burawoy's analysis of sociology in South Africa sparked a huge international debate about the nature and status of the discipline. Do Google 'public sociology' to see just how far the debate raged and what the arguments for and against this view of sociology were.

This debate, in fact, continues. In a leading international sociology journal, *Current Sociology*. 2018, 66(1): 92–109, Alberto Lozano has shown that Michael Burawoy was in effect 'naming' what some South African sociologists were doing, namely *engaging critically* in society, or as he puts it, engaging in a more 'collaborative and decolonial praxis' when doing sociology. This means choosing sides when doing sociology, which is not without its risks. This is clearly expressed in the title of a chapter by Emeritus Professor Edward Webster entitled 'Choosing sides: The promise and pitfalls of a critically engaged sociology in apartheid South Africa'. Look out for a book edited by three South African sociologists, Sonwabile Mnwana, Andries Bezuidenhout and Karl von Holdt, provisionally named *Critically Engaging Public Sociology: Towards a South–North Dialogue.*

When following a critical approach, however, sociologists can appear to be finding fault all the time. Critical sociologists criticise not only the interpretations of society of their peers, as we have just seen, but also the role and place of sociology in society as well. Precisely this critical position of sociology causes economic and political leaders to query the discipline's contribution to the improvement of society. Prominent leaders in the political and economic spheres do not always receive constructive critique from sociologists. They mostly have to handle penetrating critique of the social processes and structures underlying society.

Yet governments worldwide, South Africa included, need and use social scientific studies to formulate their own policy. Sociologists therefore need to be fair in their critique on society. It is important that they ask two questions:

1. What is the factual state of affairs and the consequences or results of this?
2. What can be done to change the present state of affairs and bring about a new condition that realises definite goals, ideals and values?

The prerequisite for answering this second question is that sociologists must state the goals, ideals and values which they would like society to realise. In many cases, sociologists do *not* separate the two questions mentioned above, hence they are *not* clear about their personal preferences for society. Such preferences stem from the value system of individual sociologists. It is therefore crucial for a sociologist to be specific on what goals, ideals and values are under consideration, who is supporting them and who will be affected if they are implemented. It is also important that sociologists work within interest groups, but remain scientists. This means that, in studying society, a sociologist must adhere to certain scientific standards and act as an analyst whose study reveals social reality as fully as possible, yet in a way which acknowledges the *preliminary nature* of knowledge. This means also being aware of the context from which we as sociologists write. Sociologists must consequently keep in mind that further analysis may prove their initial analysis as lacking or even wrong!

When you study this textbook, it should become clear that sociology originated – and took shape as a discipline – out of conditions that demanded urgent social change. This was not much more than a century ago. In light of these pressing events, the discipline developed with the aim of giving answers to the social challenges of the time. The social challenges of the past and present thus demand a scientific application of the sociological imagination.

Thinkers and theorists have always reflected on society. Sociology has deep historical roots, the fascinating story of which will be briefly told below. The discipline stands on the shoulders of the intellectual giants who figure in this story of how human beings have attempted to understand their world and themselves. Most of these people were, of course, great philosophers. These thinkers, for over 2 000 years, turned their gaze onto the social world around them.

Origins of sociology

The origins of sociology lie in the thoughts of great thinkers of the past. The following is a brief overview of early social thought that preceded sociology. This is followed by an exposition of the social conditions that demanded such a science.

Usually the origins of Western sociology are traced back to Auguste Comte who, in 1838, conceptualised sociology as a scientific discipline. However, from ancient times, thinkers were approaching and to some extent successfully formulating the main problems that sociology as science faces theoretically and methodologically. These early thinkers also analysed – albeit often in a rudimentary way – the social factors that are the subject of sociological inquiry. Cover 2 500 years of social thinking in a few pages! It is unlikely your lecturer will include this in any examination. Gaining a sense of the great evolution of social thought will, however, help you understand the task that sociology as a science currently faces.

Ancient times

Long before sociology developed as a science, people thought about how society worked. This early reflection was caught up in views concerning two issues in particular:

- What do the gods or the godhead expect of a particular society?
- What are the codes of conduct of the ruling powers – kings, chiefs, emperors, religious leaders, tyrants and councils?

Reflection on society in those ancient times was mostly aimed at explaining but also justifying the existing state of affairs of the particular society.

A 'deeper reality' below the surface of the world

The ancient Greek Empire (800–300 BCE) was characterised by the diminishing influence of religious and undemocratic powers that had dominated society for a long time. This gave thinkers the opportunity to begin reflecting independently about social affairs within the empire. They envisaged a deeper reality 'beyond' the things that people saw and experienced. The thinkers spent all their time trying to discover what the substance in the existing order was that remains constant – when all else seemed to keep on changing. Such an underlying element, they thought, could explain the foundation of reality as such and provide the basis on which society functions. The early theorists focused on different 'candidates' for such a 'deeper reality', as can be seen below. Eventually their focus shifted to trying to understand this deeper reality that informed their society.

The underlying structure of the logos

Heraclitus (540–480 BCE), for instance, proposed that there is an underlying structure (logos) according to which the surrounding world functioned. If this structure could be comprehended, he thought, this would help one to lead a true and wise life. This has much in common with the notion of social imagination discussed above. Heraclitus also reflected on change in terms of this structure underlying the nature of the world. The structure is not static, but consists of opposing forces (opposites) in an eternal war that continually creates new forms. Heraclitus himself focused on social forces that clashed within his society in the city of Ephesus. Here can be found some of the earliest concepts of the conflict theory you will encounter as a major theoretical theme in this book – *negative energy* is essential for change in society.

In terms of South African society, what are called social service delivery protests come to mind. Conflicting interests between the ruling party's political aims and the collective aspirations of citizens can create such negative energy – which can have positive effects as they can lead to improved social conditions.

The guiding power of Mind

Anaxagoras (500–428 BCE) introduced new scientific thought patterns – those relating to speculative research. This way of thinking began asking questions about the composition of the world and the functioning of society as the ancient Greeks knew it. For Anaxagoras, all of the disorderly parts in the world are combined and structured in an orderly manner through some sort of force, which he named Mind or the Nous. The development of the underlying force – the Nous – was responsible for all movement towards a new integration in society. Anaxagoras expressed this principle by his credo *The Nous rules the world*. It is extremely important to grasp this motif of an overarching Mind that creates and orders the world of objects. This idea is particularly important for understanding German Idealism and theoretical **rationalism** of the 18th century that influenced Karl Marx. Herein also lies the rudimentary view of a rational ordering of society, which reached its peak in the emergence of the system of organisations and the **bureaucracy** that dominates much of the contemporary social landscape.

What can we know?

The thinkers of the 5th century BCE contradicted one another in their theoretical designs of reality. This confused ordinary people. 'What can one really know of the surrounding world?', they asked. The Sophists were 'wisdom teachers' who facilitated the mental attitude that 'man is the measure for all truth and sure knowledge'. Truth is thus relative (see **relativism**) to the concrete situation of each individual. This already indicates the embryo of the phenomenological or **interpretive** perspectives in sociology that you will encounter in Chapter 1 and throughout this textbook. This way of thinking is also applicable to the qualitative research methodology explained in Chapter 2.

The idea of justice

Together with the insight of the Sophists, another transformation occurred in Greek thinking, which was linked to political upheaval and social turmoil due to war. Philosophers began to ask deeper questions about an ideal and just society. Socrates (469–399 BCE) is known for his method of investigation through dialogue (later called dialectics). He did not accept social matters at face value, but asked searching questions. Socrates did not only describe the existing order. Through his dialogue he also informed society and infuriated its autocratic leaders. He refused to be coerced and prescribed to by local authorities. Legend depicts him ending his own life by taking poison in a public display guided by an inner orientation of what is right.

The ideal society

These informal teachings were followed by teaching institutions where there was thorough reflection on reality and especially on the relationship between the comprehensive world structure (cosmos) and the social functioning of society. Plato (427–347 BCE) founded the first Western 'university' in Athens. There he developed Socrates' discourse technique of dialectics into a fully-fledged research method. Through this method, rational dialogue was used to investigate deeper reality – the reality beyond the things people see around them. Plato began by investigating the different forms of political organisation as he saw them in the city state of Athens. He viewed the actual society or existing reality as a reflection of an ideal society that exists eternally. Thus, the present society is not the ideal one, but strives to reach the highest ideal – utopia (a perfected state).

The main point is that such a state is actually unattainable and cannot be established concretely. The idea merely serves as a guiding principle that entices citizens to strive towards better social integration. In the same sense, the ideal post-apartheid democratic society in South Africa is depicted by images of a deeper reality, such as 'the rainbow nation' ascribed to Archbishop Emeritus Desmond Tutu. Such an ideal image helps guide the drive for actual nation building in our society.

Plato argued that the alluring idea of such a society (which could not be reached in this life) encourages people never to be satisfied with their current political dispensation. Here we already encounter strains of the progressive thinking typical of the 19th century. These methods of thought aim to apply rational means to explain certain general laws that steer human history towards an ideal final purpose.

Aristotle (384–322 BCE) was a pupil of Plato, and corrected the weak points in Plato's rational design.

If one wants to envisage an ideal reality 'beyond' existing things, one must separate the ideal state in one's mind from the current factual one. Only then can one reach the new unity again in one's mind. Aristotle did not separate things from the idea about those things. He rather viewed the idea as an inherent potential which could be transformed into the thing – just like a block of marble is potentially a statue. The idea only needed an external force or movement to become factual or actualised. This motif of inner forces bearing down on a distinct purpose is crucial to understanding modern theorists' analysis of society. Through applied science, society can be understood and that knowledge used to the benefit of the citizens of society.

The centrality of law

In the Roman Empire which followed, the philosophers had a more practical and legalistic disposition. They focused on the application of law. During this time Lucretius (99–55 BCE) contributed to an evolutionary view of society. Already over 2 000 years ago, he demonstrated how social relationships were becoming more complex in relation to an evolving society. According to Lucretius, society progresses to the extent that human beings strive to improve their lives and to stay clear of unnecessary complexities. This early theorising is in line with the **functionalist perspective** that you will find explained in this book. The different aspects of society have a positive function that results in society developing in an ordered and evolutionary manner.

Viewpoint of the early church and the Middle Ages

Society as natural

In the times of the Early Christian Church, the church fathers helped establish the idea that society is a natural phenomenon, thus it requires a ruling authority to control humankind's crimes and vices. For them, poverty was an unalterable part of society. One could not therefore place too much emphasis on social development and social institutions because of the coming judgement that would end society. Ask yourself whether the idea still exists that **poverty** is natural and cannot be eliminated.

Parallel modes of social being

Aurelius Augustine (354–430) was an influential church father in Hippo, Algeria – the Roman province in Africa. He used a basic social analysis to explain the disintegration of the Roman Empire – and the seemingly inevitable takeover of society by ungodly heathen powers. According to his design, society unfolds dynamically into two parallel cities that exist simultaneously. These are the earthly or worldly city and the spiritual City of God. This analysis implied two opposing cultures or ways of life – that of good and

evil. These two opposing cultures had divergent futures: the good represented fulfilment in contrast to evil, which represented total destruction. This analysis also dissuaded his fellow believers from participating in political affairs. By contrasting and explaining the world in terms of good and evil, this understanding informed them of their choice – to concentrate on the spiritual realm, in light of its outcome, as against that of the worldly realm.

The king as God's representative

In the Middle Ages, this line of thought was carried further. The Roman Catholic priest, Thomas Aquinas (1225–1275), was the key thinker in this regard. According to his social analysis, society should be seen as the realm in which humans, by nature, seek their own interests. A superior power, God, Aquinas argued, is needed to direct society to benefit all people. Aquinas' social analysis helped to provide theological legitimacy for the **monarchy**, which was the form of government at that time. A monarch, he thought, was the ideal form of society. The king was seen as God's representative on earth, which offered the best model for organising the affairs of humanity. This view is still held by significant numbers of South Africans today.

The state and external social factors

In Africa, another early contribution to social thought was that of Ibn-Khaldun (1332–1406). He indicated the important role the state had in maintaining order. He also showed that different societies went through different stages of development that related to psychological and environmental factors. We will study his work.

Age of Enlightenment

The power of reason

The Age of Enlightenment was an intellectual movement of the 17th and 18th centuries. During this period, human reason was strongly promoted as a source of knowledge over tradition and faith. Scientific thought, intellectual interchange and **scepticism** were advanced as the new pursuit of intellectuals over religious intolerance, superstition and intolerance.

In this way the dominating role of the church within society – and the king as its head – were increasingly questioned. The eventual rediscovery of the ancient philosophies and reinstatement of Roman law increasingly posited the supreme authority of the state (see Chapter 16 on politics and governance) above that of the church.

In addition, the intellectuals of the day began examining the existing state of affairs critically and envisaged an improved society. They began to see human rationality as a noble force that could make a difference to their world. All that was needed was for thinking people to apply their minds to societal problems. Through abstract theoretical analysis they could posit the perfect society in which all could live free and content.

The social contract

The focus then shifted away from blindly accepting authority to a relationship of collaboration in creating such a just and free society. As a consequence of this development in thought, from the 1600s onwards, the theme of the social contract between rulers and citizens became prominent. The English philosopher, Thomas Hobbes (1588–1679), departed from earlier viewpoints that humankind lived and cared for each other. Hobbes typified humans as being self-centred and therefore people rather lived in fear of each other, somewhat like a pack of wolves. A social contract was therefore necessary as a basis for peaceful co-existence. He argued that citizens should agree to surrender their freedom willingly in exchange for recognising structures of state control. This would establish a society in which citizens' natural rights would be guaranteed. Such a social contract, however, would also empower citizens to discard the rulers if they did not comply with the agreement.

Another English philosopher, John Locke (1632–1704), took this notion further: a social contract establishes a society that functions *independently* of government. Government thus should act as an independent institution to which society delegates political control. This conceptualisation provided the possibility for monarchies and **dictatorships** to be overthrown in favour of the emerging **nation-states** during the following three centuries.

I think therefore I am

Most researchers trace this intellectual approach to the world back to the method of systematic scepticism of the French natural science philosopher, René Descartes (1596–1650). According to Descartes' method, one should keep on doubting until one finds a clear principle that cannot be doubted. The only thing that one cannot doubt is the fact that you are the one who is performing the doubting. From this follows his famous statement: *I think, therefore I am.* Thus the point of departure for scientific knowledge is: I can think for myself. This notion was a great breakthrough in social thought, which eventually resulted in the idea of individual human rights.

Enlightenment

Building on this principle, thinkers dared to be critical and even to question facts in society which they had always accepted on the higher authority of the church or state. In light of this development these philosophers named their 'movement' the Enlightenment – in German, *Aufklärung*. This meant that people were free to think and investigate things for themselves. They began to register contradictions in society that differed from how they thought reality ought to be. This attitude connected with the scientific insight (eg of physics and mathematics) about general laws that control the movement of social phenomena. The philosophers proposed such universal laws 'beyond' the phenomena that people observe in the economy, politics and culture. When a mental image can be formed of these laws, they contended, people can understand the different processes in all areas of life, giving them another view on the existing society.

Metaphysics

What this means is that intellectuals began to see social problems as existing issues that contradicted their ideal – the deeper reality – of how society ought to be organised. Such speculative reflecting on a deeper reality became known as the science of metaphysics (*meta* means 'outside' or 'beyond'). The question was whether this mental speculation was truly science. The problem was that it could only point out contradictions among facts, but did not deliver true knowledge about the facts themselves.

This is where the speculative philosophy of Immanuel Kant (1724–1804) produced an impressive rational construct. Kant attempted to find answers to the problem: human reason itself conceptualises universal laws (values) of a deeper reality that imports meaning to the world of phenomena (facts). The question that arose, however, was how that could be possible. How can universal law be formulated without – or even *before* – experiencing the phenomena directly and have it tested through experimentation? For this was the criterion for true science at that time. Kant proposed the correction: the thinking self should understand and except the limitations to its reasoning. We cannot *know* the phenomena as they are *beyond* what we can *experience*. Our impressions of the phenomena around us are mediated and filtered through our mind. Our mind acts as a mental 'processing plant' that orders these impressions into understandable units (perceptions) and then processes them by applying mental structures (or ideas of how things ought to be). Kant's conceptual construction is difficult to understand and remains much discussed and debated to this day.

The creative mind

This Kantian form of knowledge implies a unique relationship between our mind and the things around us. The human mind interacts with the phenomena it observes, but not merely in the manner of a student taking 'notes'. It is rather like a judge asking the right questions to give the correct judgment, thus the things that people observe are relative to the angle or position of the observer. The person or self who observes any phenomenon imports meaning to their perceptions from a certain perspective or 'point of view'. You will quickly see that sociology embodies this idea – there are many 'perspectives' and different approaches in the discipline.

For Kant, the world of objective facts 'appears' to the human mind if and when the mind perceives each of these facts. This is what is meant by 'my perception of the facts'. I, as thinking self, do not accept facts on account of a higher authority, such as the church or respected scientific institutions. I reserve the right to interpret things surrounding me, to import new meaning to those things in accordance with my position as examiner. On the other hand, however, this means I can only perceive those things that 'appear' to me. With this design of the relationship between the observing mind and phenomena, Kant paved the way theoretically for the later development of phenomenology as we know it today.

The rational world

After Kant's theorising, a debate flared up among German intellectuals of the 19th century. They took the basic principles of the Enlightenment further. Their analyses focused critically on society in order to understand forces which underlie the development of new social and political dispensations. Instead of following Kant's cue about the limits of human reason (the boundaries of the mind that can only perceive things that appear to it), Johann Gottlieb Fichte (1762–1814) created a grand design. Reason, he thought, is not only a mental faculty (mind), but the whole of reality, in itself, is rational. All of humanity, nature and society are driven by an underlying process of reason, which unfolds progressively. In this process, everything that does not fit into the rational design (called 'inner contradictions') is made rational and becomes part of a harmonious rational whole.

Inner 'logic' of transformations

Georg Wilhelm Friedrich Hegel (1770–1831) built on German Idealism's idea of such an underlying rational structure that steers the existing society towards an ideal and free outcome. Hegel envisages the cultural development of societies through the ages as the life cycle of a single World-Spirit – *Weltgeist* in German. This Spirit inevitably drove human history on towards the ideal society – for Hegel, German social integration. According to Hegel's design, this World-Spirit took on a concrete shape in external structures, such as nature, politics and economics during consecutive stages in human history. By examining the processes of these stages closely, Hegel finds a certain 'logic' that governs the transformations in society. The dialectical tension between the existing and emerging stages unleashes masses of creative energy. This tension is carried over in social transformations. In this way the World-Spirit develops through the different stages on its way to the total rational and free society.

Idealists wanted to prescribe through their lofty ideas (**values**) how the society of their time ought to function (**facts**). However, in stark contrast to their magnificent mental designs of the ideal society, the undeniable reality of the suffering of the people of that period stood out sharply. These people were in a very vulnerable position, particularly in the face of famine, epidemics and exploitation.

Change the world!

The philosophy of rational ideals, by being turned upside down, laid the foundation for Karl Marx's well-known critique of society. It should be clear that Marx's applied social analysis cannot be understood outside of this framework of the complex debate among the idealist theorists, such as his teacher Hegel and others, on how to establish the ideal society within the existing order. This theorising reaches back to the speculative impulse of Heraclitus on social analysis, then to the grand absolutist rational social theories of the speculative 'masters'. Inevitably the question arose whether one can merely describe society by uncovering the underlying structure (general laws), or whether thought and ideas can impact on society and actually change it,

The priority of facts

Marx moved from social theory to social analysis through his critique on Hegel's 'spiritualistic' interpretation of the struggle between historical stages in human development. The idealist philosophers, Hegel in particular, had developed complex rational solutions which were the products of thinking alone. These ideas of the mind had, as their goal, the social integration of society by means of political arrangements or dispensations. Marx thought such ideas should be based on concrete social facts. Marx hence did not only examine the ideas about the world, but focused on the material basis of production in society – as you will see in Chapter 1.

However, it took Marx some time to reflect on and wrestle with the huge and difficult philosophy of Hegel before he reached this point of view. He only found his master key after applying the method of Ludwig Feuerbach (1804–1872), a young follower who critiqued Hegel's idealist approach. In the end, Marx's analysis of the economic, material 'base of society' was in many ways equivalent to Hegel's mental construct, but turned onto its head or, rather, the right way up – as far as Marx was concerned. Marx's overtly materialist approach to science was born out of the poor living conditions created by the age of revolution and industrialisation. The social context out of which Marx wrote will be dealt with in the following section.

A summary of this trajectory of human thought about the social world, which, as noted above, covered a period of over 2 500 years, first needs to be made. Table 1 gives an overview of the development of Western social thought throughout the centuries and how it informed later social perspectives in sociology.

Table 1 Introduction

Social theorist	Social perspectives that originated from the theorist
Heraclitus (540–480 BCE)	Social imagination; the suggestion of conflict theory
Anaxagoras (500–428 BCE)	Rational ordering of society
Sophists (5th century BCE)	Phenomenological or interpretative perspective
Plato (427–347 BCE)	Idealism; emphasises the importance of theory
Socrates (469–399 BCE)	Investigative theory informing society
Aristotle (384–322 BCE)	Applied science; the beginning of social theory
Lucretius (99–55 BCE)	Functionalism; the evolutionary development of society
Augustine (354–430)	Social analysis explaining the status quo
Thomas Aquinas (1225–1275)	Social analysis legitimising the status quo
Ibn-Khaldun (1332–1406)	Functionalism; the evolutionary development of society
Thomas Hobbes (1588–1679)	Social theory on political power
John Locke (1632–1704)	Social theory on governance
Immanuel Kant (1724–1804)	Interpretative perspective
Johann Gottlieb Fichte (1762–1814)	Meta-theory (absolutism)
Georg Wilhelm Friedrich Hegel (1770–1831)	Idealism; meta-theory (rational design); social theory

Age of revolution and industrialisation and the need for sociology

The domination of Western thought
It may be frustrating to South African students that sociology seems to be so deeply embedded in Western thought, yet it is against the history of ideas, traced above and to be further expounded in the following section, that the discipline must be understood. This Western connection is evident in all the chapters of the book and even applies to the final chapter, which focuses entirely on the history of sociology in South Africa. The simple reason is that Western thought and philosophy dominated the discourse of not only sociologists, but also provides sociology's intellectual heritage in general. This needs reconsideration at university level. Only recently have sociologists – as well as other social thinkers – begun to try to develop ideas and analyses *outside* the scope of Western sociology. They pose the question whether a non-Western sociology – or African sociology in our case – is indeed possible. For that reason, these sociologists are starting to look for old and new theories on society that may exist in their respective cultures, not only in South Africa, but elsewhere in the world. But the fact remains that, even though the father of sociology was African, it has come down to us as of Western origin.

Enlightenment and revolution

There are two main reasons why Western sociology is dominant. Firstly, the Enlightenment created the condition for sociology to flourish. The rational approach of the Enlightenment later became acceptable to the rest of the world and the related critical view of society which then developed, meant an adoption of Western thought about society. Secondly, the question with which sociology grappled, when it took form in Western society, is common to all societies. The question was how social order in society was established or could be recovered.

In South Africa's transition to democracy after apartheid in 1994 the road to social disintegration was avoided. Ask your parents or community elders about this time. In Europe, in the age of revolution, this was not the case. The whole social order was turned upside down. This led to massive social dislocation and human suffering. The drive for individual human rights was thus born in the ferment and social upheaval of revolutionary periods.

Social conditions give birth to sociology

The immediate conditions of Western sociology were created by the age of revolution and industrialisation in Europe. The age of revolution refers to the French Revolution (1789–1799), which led to widespread social and political instability and upheaval in Europe that continued until 1945. This revolution comprised an uprising against the rule of the Bourbon monarchy with King Louis XVI at that time. The revolution was a result of several causes, the main one being the inability of the ruling classes of nobility, bourgeoisie and clergy to deal properly with the problems of the state. This occurred in the period leading up to the storming of the Bastille by the masses in France in 1789.

There were other factors as well. The monarch was indecisive by nature, the peasantry was exorbitantly taxed and the workers were exploited and impoverished. In addition, the age of Enlightenment produced a fundamental critique of this state of affairs in French society, and the American War of Independence created an example that the Republicans, who articulated the aspirations of a downtrodden people in France, could follow.

Liberty, Equality and Fraternity

This uprising eventually resulted in the public beheading on the guillotine of the king and his wife, Marie Antoinette, as well as of the champions of the monarchy and certain church leaders. About 8 000 people were sent to the guillotine in this manner. In total, approximately 18 000 people were executed. The age of revolution, however, changed European and world society irreversibly. The driving force and positive development resulting from this revolutionary period was the establishment of a society in France, which embodied the watchwords 'Liberty, Equality, Fraternity'. Among a whole slew of dramatic social changes, these new principles guiding society meant the abolition of serfdom, as well as the elimination of the feudal privileges of the nobles, and feudal dues and tithes. The principle of equal liability to taxation was introduced. Feudal estates were broken up. This redistribution of wealth and land tenure made France the European country with the largest proportion of independent small landowners.

Dictatorship

The uprising, however, did not immediately deliver a stable leadership for the new society. Faction fighting made the republican struggle an ugly process with continuous changes of power and with previous revolutionary leaders being put on trial. The defeat of the monarchy in France caused other monarchies in Europe to act against the new republic. To deal with this threat, France had to reply with military force. During this time of instability, the hugely successful general Napoleon Bonaparte seized power and established the Napoleonic Empire (1799–1814). He consequently ravaged Europe through wars in order to extend his sphere of influence – until his abdication in 1814. From 1814 to 1830 the Bourbon monarchy was reinstated. France proclaimed another Napoleonic Empire from 1848 to 1870.

Sociology as solution

This brief historical overview is meant to show the degree of political instability that France experienced during this period of revolution and industrialisation. In terms of progressive ideas, European society went *backwards*. Little remained of the Enlightenment thinkers' rational designs promoting hope and expectations of idealised human progress. France experienced discord and overt conflict. Within this unstable social context in France, but also in the rest of Europe, in 1838 Auguste Comte specifically began to promote sociology, putting it forward as a scientific way to create an intellectual, moral and political reorganisation of the social order.

It was not, however, only the political volatility that called for a new answer to social stability. The economy had also been utterly transformed. These social conditions were due to the **Industrial Revolution** that extended from approximately 1760 to 1840. This revolution dramatically changed the **mode of production** – the way in which the economy and the social classes supporting and making up production was organised. This new industrial economy was driven by the introduction of steam-powered machinery and tools, as well as developments in metallurgy, chemicals, textile manufacture, gas lighting and glass making. This industrial revolution, while starting in Britain, rapidly extended to Germany and the United States. France was also affected by the restructuring of society. Britain as an empire had the advantage of international markets available for their mass-produced goods. This revolution initially delivered the most significant economic results for Britain. Early technological advancements in the cotton industry gave Britain the economic edge. When it could no longer supply its own needs, Britain colonised India, which has been producing cotton for thousands of years.

Improved means of production

The Industrial Revolution itself was largely triggered by James Watt's improvement of the steam engine in the period 1763–1775. As he modified the engine it became suitable for driving factory machinery, which speeded up the Industrial Revolution by multiplying the production of goods. At the height of this technological revolution, steam power was used on the railways. The first public railway utilising steam locomotives was introduced between Liverpool and Manchester in Britain in 1830. In the 1840s, Britain had already constructed about 10 000 km of railway, the German states 6 000 and France 3 000. By 1850 the United States had constructed 15 000 km of railway and a decade later 48 000 km. The employment opportunities for manual **labour** generated by this industry were manifold. In contrast, South Africa as a colony had, by the end of the 1860s, constructed railway line of only 72 km from Cape Town to Wellington. This major development of the railway system in the industrialising countries allowed the mass transportation of iron ore and coal for production purposes and opened up markets for mass-produced goods. This process accelerated the Industrial Revolution further and also concluded it.

Capitalist industrialisation

The development in steam power helped transform people's economic activity as a whole. The new capitalist mode of production transformed a previously agricultural society into an industrial one. Society changed completely. The Industrial Revolution soon created new and problematic labour relationships. The means of production, namely the machines and factories, were owned by the employers, which meant that the workers were separated from the products which they made. They were thus only viewed

in terms of their contribution to production. The pace of production was set by machines, which created **assembly line** production, making simple tasks and set routines as the norm in the workplace. This also made it possible to employ cheap labour – which at that time consisted of women and child workers. In a short span of time people were exposed to a totally new dispensation of labour in which manual labour was replaced by mechanised production (see **mechanisation**).

Owing to this sudden upsurge in production and increased technological development, capital and new enterprises were necessary. This new mode of production required organised management. Industrial management and organisation therefore became paramount and later were key study areas for sociologists, as a discussion on the discovery of diamonds and gold in South Africa in Chapter 14 will show. Finance and insurance were needed by the capitalists, thus the banking sector and insurance companies grew. To enhance production and profit, continual technological advancements were invented, and managerial techniques developed. In this way the cost of labour could be minimised, which led to desperate conditions for the labourers.

Urbanisation

People flocked from the rural areas to the cities, seeking employment in the factories. City planners had never before experienced such an influx and did not know how to deal with it. To make matters worse, during the time of the revolution the population of Britain doubled. Terrible housing conditions were the result of poverty and overpopulation. Sewers were uncovered, water supplies contaminated and dampness was prevalent. The outbreak of epidemics, such as tuberculosis, cholera and typhoid, were common. Lung diseases tormented the miners.

Ironically, this surplus of labourers made it possible for Britain to abolish slavery at that time. At the end of the revolution, industrial unrest led to the introduction of the first labour laws in history, which limited the working hours of children in 1847. Further labour legislation followed. Eventually the conditions of the workers began to improve. However, this was also because a large percentage of the poor emigrated to the colonies and to America.

Political struggles

The mechanisation brought about by the Industrial Revolution also led to new methods of political control. Thereafter the formation of nation-states became possible and caused widespread political disruptions. Conflicting ideas about the ideal state became an important source of contention. This concerned in particular the struggle between monarchy, **democracy** and totalitarianism.

The changing face of society was dramatic. The power of monarchies diminished, with no clarity being reached on alternative political models. The church's powers declined. The new capitalist industrial mode of production created pressing socio-economic problems and new forms of political power. These conditions created a radically new society and for the people of that time, an unknown one.

The need for social order

From within these taxing social, political and economic circumstances sociology as a field of study originated mainly to answer the question: 'How is order and stability possible in society?' There simply was no knowledge to provide people with direction on how such a society should be established and developed. The ongoing struggles, tensions, conflicts and wars at that time underlined the need for a discipline like sociology to provide direction to society.

Sociology as discipline

The idea of sociology developed over time and became more refined when it was applied as an analytical science and an academic discipline. The earliest use of the concept 'sociology' appears in the unpublished writings of the Frenchman Emmanuel Josef Sieyès (1748–1836), dated 1780. At that time sociology was, however, not yet connected to a field of study. It was left to another Frenchman, Auguste Comte (1798–1857), who conceptualised the discipline of 'sociology' in 1838 and thereby placed the name of the discipline in general use. The main early contributors to sociology were Auguste Comte and Karl Marx (1818–1883), who both developed scientifically justified systems with which to interpret society. Their analytical systems were very influential, especially that of Marx. An early popular sociologist was Herbert Spencer (1820–1903), who advocated a **laissez faire** style of government, but this was before formal sociology was introduced into universities.

Formal academic status

Formal academic sociology was first established in France by Emile Durkheim (1858–1917). Academic sociology was introduced in the United States in 1875 and in Britain in 1902. This was because of a preference for social anthropology in the academic circles of both countries. Full undergraduate sociology was introduced in South Africa in 1933.

After its establishment as an academic discipline, sociology progressed rapidly. As theory and methodology, the discipline developed and resulted in profound social insight.

Sociology in this form also exerted a huge influence on the way people thought about and analysed societies. This gave new impetus to the creation of new ideologies governments used to control their subjects. Sometimes the control was to the benefit of those societies, but many times also to their detriment! The complexity of people's social existence and the multifaceted nature of societies resulted in sociology developing into an extended and intricate discipline.

As a fully-fledged discipline, sociology is at the same time stimulating, interesting and constantly posing challenges. Sociology entails a field of study that covers a wide variety of elements, forms, levels and interrelations. Some sociologists aim to identify relationships and order in this field of study, while others place more emphasis on the dynamics, activity and fluidity of people's social existence.

Because much of contemporary sociology is based on the sociological imagination, extensive investigation has gone into exploring the relation between the individual and society. This function of sociology is often not appreciated by authoritarian regimes. For that reason, sociology was banned in China from 1952 until 1979. The Union of Soviet Socialist Republics allowed only Marxist sociology from the 1930s until 1966. In contrast, South Africa's apartheid regime banned or restricted Marxist literature from the 1950s until 1990. However, currently sociology is practised as an academic discipline in most countries throughout the world.

Networking and association

Sociologists globally also maintain extensive formal and informal networks among each other. Many countries have established sociological associations. The largest association is that of the USA, consisting of approximately 21 000 members (founded in 1905). In comparison, the South African Sociological Association (SASA) has a small membership (founded in 1993 out of previous associations). However, SASA is active and presents its own sociology congresses each year. Website of the South African Sociological Association (SASA): http://www.sociology.africa/

The discipline is served internationally by the International Sociological Association (ISA), founded in 1949. Website of the International Sociological Association (ISA): https://www.isa-sociology.org/en

Different perspectives

While reading this book it is important that you understand that sociology is a discipline characterised by diverse perspectives on society. You need to keep in mind that even sociologists differ on the contribution sociology can make to society. As was mentioned in the previous section, sociology developed in disruptive times as an attempt to give a scientific answer on whether order is possible in society. It can rightly be asked whether sociology could indeed contribute to such an order. The answer to this question is yes and no:

- Yes, sociology did contribute, for instance, to the development of organisations. It contributed to understanding how goal-orientated organisations operate and how they can be managed even more effectively. The critical thought of sociology also helped create a theory for democracy in modern times and address exploitation on different levels in society. Sociology laid bare the inequalities between people and the exploitation of certain sections of society. Such analyses helped to establish government policies aimed at addressing these issues. For this reason, the disciplines of sociology and social work developed side by side in some countries. In this sense, sociology did indeed assist with the logical restructuring of society and helped improve people's living conditions.
- No, the use of sociology led to the more effective functioning of military forces. The reason is that the earliest sociological theories provided a new focus on power and the mobilising of people around extended self-interest. Sociology also researched the methods to exercise power through coercion and manipulation. This in turn eventually led to a situation where wars could be waged more efficiently. The far-reaching theoretical differences among sociologists on how society ought to be structured also led to fierce ideological debates, which flared into conflict that did not benefit people directly. In addition, the enormous growth of the world population caused large-scale inequalities and tensions which are difficult to address by science alone. This state of affairs limits the contribution that sociology can make in society if political acceptance of its recommendations is not forthcoming.

Even if the contribution of sociological knowledge may in some instances be limited, its 'knowhow' can assist in improving society. Sociology is therefore useful for students and scholars in sensitising us to the dynamics of society and how it functions, and what positive contributions we can make in this regard.

In the chapters throughout this book you as a student will be confronted with different theories that interpret the same subject differently. You will also be exposed to different, contrasting and conflicting perspectives. This can be disconcerting if you are looking for clear-cut answers. This does not mean that sociology is merely **subjective** as some might argue. It may even seem to you that sociology does not provide 'real' answers to social problems. The fact is that social phenomena are complicated, because people interpret their conditions uniquely and act according to their own unique interpretations. It is important hence to understand this fact early on in the study of sociology and to realise the usefulness such diverse insights into the complexities of society potentially holds for us all.

Sociology as social science

The broad field of sciences

In the broad field of sciences, the divisions of natural and social sciences and the humanities can be distinguished.

- The natural sciences deal with natural phenomena. Examples of such study fields are physics, chemistry, biology and zoology.
- The formal sciences include philosophy and mathematics.
- The humanities deal with aspects such as languages, music and art.
- The social sciences developed during the time of the Industrial Revolution and the French Revolution (as was shown). During that time of upheaval and in response to the empirical successes of the natural sciences and the speculations of metaphysics, scholars attempted to develop applicable disciplines. Such disciplines had to deal scientifically with the social challenges of the time. Through this process the social sciences came into being.

In a wider sense, social sciences can be viewed in terms of a variety of fields of study, such as: anthropology, communication studies, economics, education, geography, history, law, linguistics, political science, psychology, public administration and sociology.

Pure social sciences

Currently the pure social sciences are viewed in terms of anthropology, economics, political science, psychology and sociology. Of these, the oldest field of social scientific study is economics, with its origin traced back to the publication of Adam Smith's *The Wealth of Nations* in 1776. As noted above, sociology as a scientific discipline was popularised by Comte's use of the term in 1838. Within the broad encyclopaedia of sciences, sociology can therefore be viewed, in particular, as the discipline with the *broadest* focus of *all* the social sciences. Where the other social sciences focus on specific areas of social life, sociology attempts more. This discipline makes the whole of society its field of study. Sociology therefore develops good general social interpreting skills among those who take it seriously.

Careers and sociology

As can be seen above, sociology develops people's sociological imagination. With such a skill one can have a deeper understanding of how society functions, and also how people can be at the mercy of social processes and structures. Students can profitably apply the theoretical skills learnt in sociology in a variety of professions. Sociology is therefore a very useful discipline in many careers due to its insights that can aid people in diverse occupations. Such occupations can include the following: project managers, labour relations negotiators, town planners and developers, managers, impact assessment researchers, communication scientists, population scientists, community developers, public servants, human resource managers, political officials, psychologists and social workers. Sociology may be very helpful in all of these careers. With postgraduate qualifications in sociology, specific careers can also be followed: academic sociologists, social researchers, social analysts and social project evaluators. This book wishes to present you, as a student of society, with the first steps to develop the social analysis skills you may need in your future career.

Structure of the book

The aim of this textbook is to present you with an introduction to general sociological knowledge, but with a specific South African focus. To realise this aim, the book is divided into five parts:

Part 1 presents the foundations of sociology.
- The foundations refer to the core-elements of sociology. As was shown in the definition of sociology, this discipline involves the use of theory. You are introduced to classic sociological theories in Chapter 1 (sociological theory) as well as a critical assessment of them in the light of our present intellectual moment of decoloniality. It was also pointed out that sociology is a scientific discipline, which means that it functions according to certain methodologies. This is introduced and much is explained in greater detail than you might need now, but will later need, in Chapter 2 (research methodology). The focus of the book then moves on to the key complex issue within which social life is expressed, namely culture (Chapter 3), yet which like all else in society, is continually subject to social change (Chapter 4).
- For society to exist, however, there must be people. How populations are constituted is hence elucidated in Chapter 5 (population).

Part 2 deals with the individual and society.
- In this part of this textbook you will learn how social processes and structures impact on the lives of individuals. Having been introduced to the dynamism of the role of culture in people's lives, you will see this cannot be separated from how the socialisation process and the formation of individual identities are formed which we will examine in Chapter 6, socialisation and identity. Individual identity formation in our country is, as elsewhere, powerfully shaped by our gender (Chapter 7) which leads to an area becoming ever more prominent in the social sciences, sexualities (Chapter 8), which, along with virtually all other aspects of our lives, have powerfully been shaped, in South Africa particularly, by race (Chapter 9) and class (Chapter 10).

Part 3 focuses on the Institutions in society.
- Institutions are the established practices in society that are executed by means of organisations. Where the previous part dealt with more dynamic aspects of society, this part is concerned with the more static elements of societies. However, major upheavals can also occur in institutions. All societies have institutions which are common to all contemporary societies. The institutions discussed in this start with family and households (Chapter 11), with which we are all familiar, before moving on to education (Chapter 12), religion (Chapter 13), work (Chapter 14), the economy (Chapter 15) and politics and governance (Chapter 16). Much of the way in which these institutions in society function and change can be seen in the chapter on organisation, bureaucracy and social movements (Chapter 17) and of which we know largely through the media and technology (Chapter 18). This part of the textbook ends with a focus on what too often only becomes important when we are injured or ill, namely medicine and health (Chapter 19) or simply enjoy without thinking about it too much, sport and society (Chapter 20).

Part 4 presents the challenges for society.

- The main challenges facing South African society especially, are social inequality, discussed in Chapter 21, poverty (Chapter 22) and crime and deviance (Chapter 23). These challenges for society are framed by the broader processes of urbanisation (Chapter 24) and rurality and rural development (Chapter 25) which are, in turn intimately implicated in the environment (Chapter 26).

Part 5 concludes with placing the discipline of sociology in its context and presents A brief history of sociology in South Africa.

Features of the book
This book includes standard features for each chapter that students will find helpful. They include an introductory synopsis, case studies, key themes, guides for further reading, detailed reference lists at the end of each chapter, bold key words in the text (for which explanations are provided in the Glossary), a review of the chapter, additional sources to consult and selected bibliographic references. These features assist lecturers when presenting the chapters and help equip students with tools to master the chapters.

Supplements to the book
The following supplements are available for prescribing instructors and students:

- For instructors
  Contact Juta for access to multiple choice questions, short paragraph questions, long questions with memoranda and PowerPoint presentations. They are provided for each chapter.
- For students
  Students can access the Glossary or online on a mobile-friendly web page at www.jutaacademic.co.za/pages/sociology-glossary.

Acknowledgements
This book would not have been possible without the continuing effort of the publisher, Corina Pelser from Juta. We are much obliged to her for her perseverance and patience. The editing contributions of Wendy Priilaid and Mmakasa Ramoshaba from Juta are also acknowledged with great appreciation. We also especially thank Ken Jubber and Louise Hagemeier and two anonymous referees for their reviews. Last, but not least, our gratitude is extended to all the writers of the chapters for their excellent contributions. They are: Babalwa Sishuta, Christopher

Thomas, Cornie Groenewald, Elsa Crause, Engela Pretorius, Gretchen du Plessis, Grey Magaiza, Jacques Rothmann, Khosi Kubeka, Kiran Odhav, Kirk Helliker, Marlize Rabe, Phephani Gumbi, Pragna Rugunanan, Prishani Naidoo, Ran Greenstein, Shandré Hoffmann-Habib, Shannon Morreira, Tapiwa Chagonda, Muhammed Suleman. Each contribution is highly appreciated. The end-product offers students of the discipline a publication that stems from the heart of the broad sociological academic community in South Africa.

The Editors

Copyright acknowledgements
The authors and publisher gratefully acknowledge permission to reproduce copyright material in this book. Every effort has been made to trace copyright holders, but if any copyright infringements have been made, the publisher would be grateful for information that would enable any omissions or errors to be corrected in subsequent impressions.

- Figure 1.2 Auguste Comte, Figure 1.3: Karl Marx and Figure 1.5: Max Weber, courtesy of Granger/INPRA
- Figure 1.5 Émile Durkheim, courtesy of Corbis Images
- Figure 5.1 Bar graph depicting the years it took (and would take) to add another billion to the world population courtesy of United Nations Population Division. 2009. *World Population Prospects, the 2008 Revision*. Washington DC: Population Reference Bureau.
- Figure 5.2 Population growth in billions, 1950–2050 in more and less developed countries courtesy of United Nations. 2005. *World Population Prospects: The 2004 Revision (medium scenario)*. Washington DC: Population Reference Bureau.
- Case study 5.2 Can African countries reap the demographic dividend?, courtesy of Lori S Ashford and the Population Reference Bureau (PRB)
- Case study 5.3 Setting the scene: migration and urbanisation in South Africa, courtesy of Sally Perberdy
- Table 5.2 Indices of mortality and health in selected world regions, 2010, courtesy of WHO, UNICEF, UNFPA and the World Bank. *Trends in Maternal Mortality in 1990–2008*. WHO: Geneva
- Case study 4.1 Comparing livelihoods. 'Herders and hunters: the Khoikhoi and San in the south-west of the subcontinent', courtesy of Oxford University Press, UK
- Case study 4.1 Comparing livelihoods. 'Pastoralism and settled agriculturalists: the Nguni in the interior of southern Africa', courtesy of Croom Helm, UK

- Case study 4.2 Globalisation, class struggle and social change in post-apartheid South Africa/'Cosatu strike will damage SA, say analysts', courtesy of Times Media
- Figure 6.1 Xhosa circumcision initiate (*Umkhweta*) photo of *kwekudee* courtesy of Kopano Ratele
- Case study 6.1 Isolation (Genie's story), courtesy of Curtiss, S. 1977. *Genie: A Psycholinguistic Study of a Modern-day 'Wild Child'*. Boston: Academic Press
- Case study 6.1 Isolation (Saturday Mthiyane), courtesy of *Mail&Guardian*
- Case studies 7.1 Gender issues in South Africa, and 7.2 Tsietsi Mashinini, courtesy of South African History Archive (SAHA)
- Case study 7.3 Nwabisa Ngcukana, courtesy of SAPA
- Table 10.1 The structure of employment and unemployment in Soweto (all Sowetans aged 16 and over), courtesy of UKZN Press
- Case study 11.1 A grandmother, courtesy of Professor Tinyiko Maluleke (Deputy Registrar, Unisa)
- Figure 11.1 Extended family, courtesy of the extended Pheiffer family
- Figure 11.2 Socialisation of children, courtesy of the Kelderman family
- Case study 12.1 Just one bag, courtesy of www.mediaclubsouthafrica.com, a Brand South Africa website
- Case study 12.2 The textbook saga, courtesy of Chisholm L. 2012. 'The textbook saga and corruption in education' in *Southern African Review of Education*, 19(1): 7–22
- Case study 12.3 Kliptown hero, courtesy of SA – the Good News (www.sagoodnews.co.za).
- Figure 12.1 Hector Pieterson photo epitomising the 1976 Soweto uprising, courtesy BrandSouthAfrica.com;
- Figure 12.2 Framework for education, courtesy of Professor Kobus Maree;
- Figure 12.3 #FeesMustFall reminiscent of the 1976 Soweto Uprising protests, courtesy of Christian I de Witt)
- Figure 13.1 National celebration – depicting civil religion?;
- Case study 19.1 Stephen Hawking opening photograph
- Case study 17.3, courtesy of Mark Schefermann
- Case study 22.2 South Africa: Inequality not so black and white, courtesy of IRIN News (www.irinnews.org)
- Table 21.4 Racial composition of top occupational categories, 2001, courtesy of Seekings J. 2005. *Race, Class and Inequality in South Africa*. New Haven: Yale University Press
- Table 23.1 Categories of crimes committed, courtesy of Department of Correctional Services, Republic of South Africa
- Box 24.2 The gentrification of central cities, courtesy of Steinberg J, Van Zyl P, Bond P. 1992. 'Contradictions in the transition from urban apartheid: Barriers to gentrification in Johannesburg' in *The Apartheid City and Beyond: Urbanisation and Social Change in South Africa*. Smith DM (ed). London: Routledge.

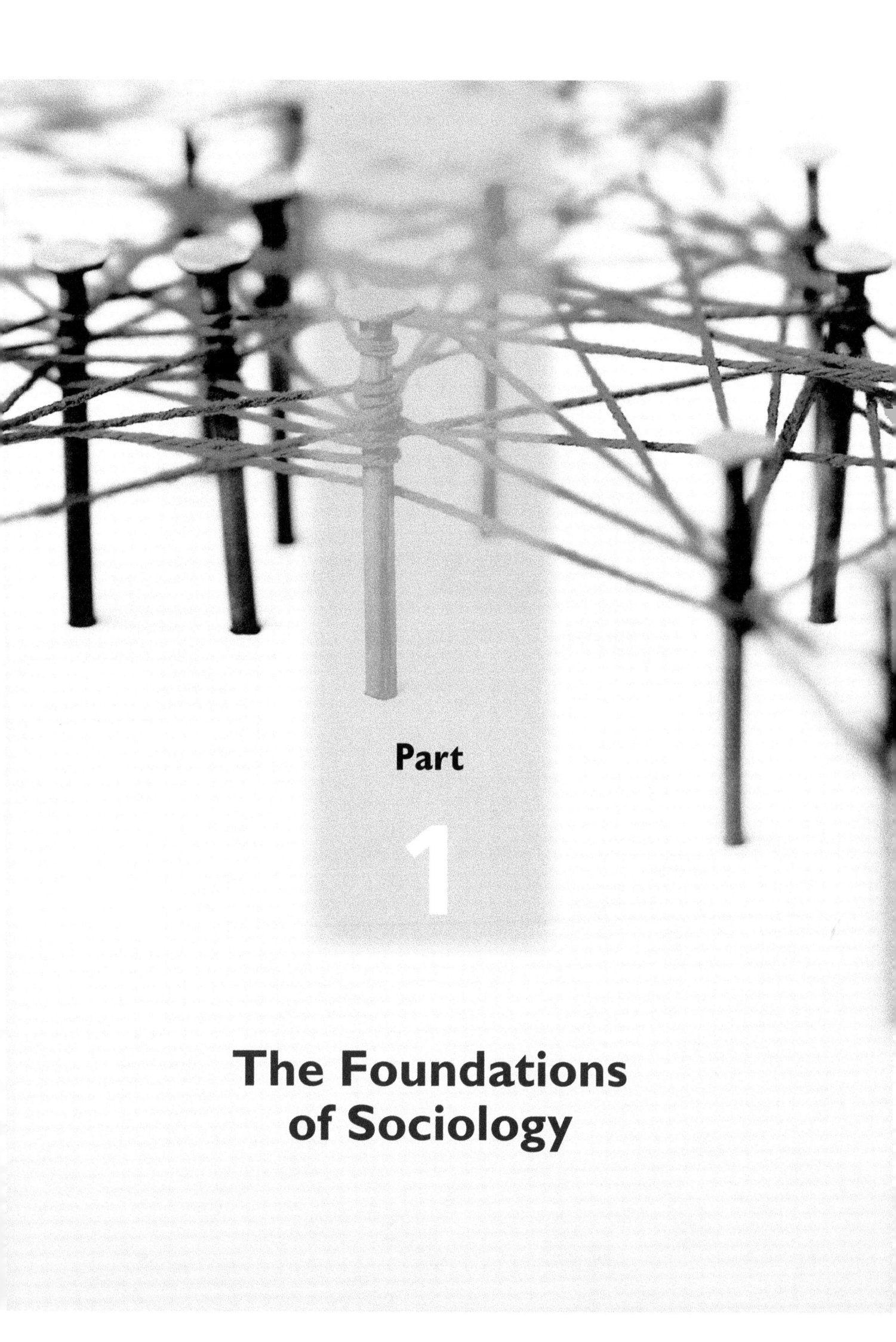

Part

1

The Foundations of Sociology

Sociological theory

Paul Stewart

Thinking is a mental activity in which every normal person engages. Theory is likewise a mental activity to which none of us are strangers. We all have ideas and 'theories' about something or other. This has occurred ever since the mental or cognitive powers of human beings developed as we as *homo sapiens* engaged with our immediate environment, and forms of social organisation emerged. Normal thinking and everyday 'theories' lie at the basis of the ideas and social theories we saw traced over the past 2 500 years in the introduction of this book. These ideas and theories in turn lie at the basis of the more systematic attempt of sociological theory which, based on evidence, seeks to describe and explain some aspects of the world of human experience.

Thinking sociologically and sociological theory are based on normal ordinary thinking and the way in which thinkers have tried to understand the social world around them. Sociological theory attempts to understand and explain – and even sometimes predict – social events in a more systematic, scientific way than ordinary normal thinking. Sociological theory then is one kind of social scientific theory. Political science, psychology and economics develop other types of social scientific theory.

This opening chapter starts by showing how sociological theory is distinguished from ordinary theorising about the social world, as well as the great social thinkers of the past. You will find the origin of the word 'theory' to be surprisingly familiar.

The chapter goes on to lay the foundations of the thinking and theory that lie behind much of what follows in this textbook. What you will quickly discover is that there is no one single way of sociological thinking and theorising. The reason for this is that the foundational pillars of the discipline are based on different ways of approaching systematic thinking about society. The works of key thinkers traditionally associated with having established the theoretical foundations of the discipline are introduced in this chapter. The three main perspectives in sociological theory can be attributed to their intellectual work and the theories and analyses they produced. Because sociological theory does not rest on one single idea, approach or perspective, this is what makes it both challenging and interesting.

What is probably the most interesting about the three main perspectives in sociological theory is that each is intimately tied to the approach they adopt when examining society. In this way they direct themselves to the social world in an attempt to understand our own role within society, how society is ordered and how it changes, and even how to improve and change society in the interests of its members.

South African society continues to go through turbulent times and must continually confront issues of social order and social change as its young democracy establishes itself. How, for instance, is a society like South Africa to be understood, developed and improved for its citizens? How must a society like South Africa transform itself? What is the place of decolonising the mind in this much-needed process? One of the major theoretical approaches in sociological theory addresses how social order and stability are achieved. Another of the major sociological approaches focuses on the extent of social changes manifesting themselves in society. The third major approach in sociological theory powerfully alerts us to the different ways in which people act and how what happens in society is subject to differing interpretations. Sociological theory is founded on these three perspectives, but they are not inclusive of its range and scope. Decolonial theory challenges all three of these perspectives. All of this can only be introduced in this textbook.

While theoretical issues are abstract and intellectual, the effects of sociological theory are often very practical. The ways in which sociological theory is used means that sociology becomes part of the social world it studies. International institutions use the results of sociological theorising and research in regulating global socio-political and economic developments. Governments employ sociologists and sociological theories in the formulation of policy. Companies use sociological research to improve their organisations, survive and make bigger profits. Sociological theories and methodologies are used in market research. Advertising uses its ideas to convince us to buy certain products. Trade unions use sociologists and their theoretical skills to assess how well they are serving their members. Political party strategists use sociological thinking to win more votes. Student activism often takes sociological theory for granted when mobilising for changes to the curriculum. In short, sociological theories and methodologies inform and shape much of the rapidly changing and complex world in which we live. For sociologists to be able to engage in providing ideas and analyses in such a wide variety of activities means having strong intellectual foundations.

This chapter makes a start in being able to understand and meaningfully engage in applying sociological theories and knowledge in social life. Before we improve and change the world around us for the better, we need to understand our role within the much bigger picture of the social world and understand contemporary developments in the society of which we are part. This requires developing a sociological and theoretical imagination.

Like any intellectual activity, it is best to take this slowly and carefully, working through the chapter in a methodical manner.

This is not something you should feel you have to learn because there is an examination at the end of your course. Engage with sociological theory, rather, because you have the opportunity to develop your own mind. You will find that the subsequent chapters open up your understanding much more clearly if you do so. Prepare to advance and even perhaps change the way you think. You will soon be thinking and talking in new ways which will surprise those around you. Sociological theory is a living and vibrant intellectual activity, and this will happen before you know it.

To see just how much things do change in sociological theory, the final part of the chapter very briefly traces major shifts in thinking from the classical theorists through to introducing some key concepts lying behind the calls for decolonisation. Do not expect to cover all of this in lectures in your first year of studying sociology. By the end of this brief story about theory itself, you will find theory which explicitly puts you at the very centre of sociological thinking and theorising.

Case study 1.1 Student protests in democratic South Africa

South Africa has a long history of student protests going way back to the anti-apartheid marches that predated South Africa's democracy. Since 1994, when democracy was established, South African students had their own struggles, and in recent years, there has been a wave of student protest action.

One development is that as protests have increased so too has police brutality towards the students. Protesters often come up against heavily armed police leading to tragic outcomes.

The major demands by protesting students across the country are similar. However, the main one has been more financial support from the National Student Financial Aid Scheme (NSFAS). NSFAS is the South African government's student loan and bursary scheme, which provides loans and bursaries to students at all 25 public universities and 50 public Further Education and Training (FET) colleges throughout South Africa.

(Source: Adapted from South African History Online 2019)

Questions

1. What theory or theories lay behind students' action and mobilisation in the #RhodesMustFall (starting March 2015) and #FeesMustFall (starting October 2015) campaigns?
2. Were these ideas born of experience only or were they informed by previous learning?
3. How can sociological theory take these actions and ideas forward practically?

Bear these questions and your own in mind as you begin your study of the social sciences.

Key themes

- Concepts and how they combine to form theories
- The criteria of a good theory
- The difference between social and sociological theories
- Choosing between different sociological concepts and theories
- The importance of identifying assumptions
- The difference between natural and social science
- The three main theoretical perspectives in the discipline
- Auguste Comte, positivism and the criteria for knowledge

- Introduction to positivist social science and key concepts of Émile Durkheim
- Introduction to critical social science and key concepts of Karl Marx
- Introduction to interpretive social science and key concepts of Max Weber
- Critiques of classical sociological theory
- Surveying decolonial theory.

1.1 Introduction

This chapter introduces the activity of engaging in theory and thinking sociologically. It does so by noting the interesting origin of the word 'theory'. When we think and theorise, we use concepts. According to one of the founders of sociology, Max Weber, the concept is 'one of the great tools of all scientific knowledge' (Gerth & Mills 1974: 141). Concepts are basic to all theory.

Some issues introduced in this chapter are: the prevalence of assumptions (that which we take for granted) and how they underlie any theory; the criteria (the standards by which to judge something) of a good theory; the difference between social theory and sociological theory, and the need to make conceptual and theoretical choices. It is helpful to know from the outset that some of these issues relate to intellectual activities in which all normal people engage. We all think and exercise our cognition – our capacity to think, understand and know things. You hae already seen that, according to one sociological thinker, people possess a degree of **sociological competence**. Our starting point will therefore be more familiar than you might have thought. Once this basic groundwork is laid, the chapter will introduce key concepts and theories of the three major foundational thinkers in the discipline of sociology.

Learning changes people. When you learn something, you are not quite the same person as before. This book seeks not only to build on what you already know. The aim of education, a term that is derived from the Latin word *educere*, is 'to lead out of' (of ignorance, in this case). You can (and perhaps should) test this claim for yourself by re-reading this chapter when you have worked through the whole textbook. Thinking sociologically can potentially change our outlook on the world around us, how we understand ourselves within it and even how we behave. This can even contribute to understanding who we are.

Exploring ideas and studying social and sociological theories will introduce you to new ways of seeing and understanding. What you took for granted will sometimes come into view in a startling manner. You may never again be able to look at the world in the way you do right now, but to gain such insights and learn new ways of seeing is not always easy. The reason for this is that in the social sciences we are part of what we study. Because we are familiar with our immediate social environment, it is not easy to be neutral and adopt a more 'objective' perspective in relation to the object of our study, namely the social world in which we live and our position within it. Some theorists think being objective is impossible and that we need to choose between competing theories and pursue the one we think provides the best explanation of the world. Whichever route you take, it is a major objective of this chapter and the primary objective of this textbook to facilitate the process of learning about society and the place of human agents within it, ourselves included.

1.2 The origin and meaning of 'theory'

The word 'theory' comes from *theos*, the Greek word for 'god'. Over 3 000 years ago the ancient Greeks and Romans worshipped many gods and hence had many 'theories' about the world. They made sense of and offered explanations for what happened in the world in terms of the gods they believed in. Poseidon was, for instance, the Greek god of the sea, while Ares was honoured as the god of war and Cupid held sway over all matters of love. For the ancient Romans these gods were Neptune, Mars and Eros.

What changed this many-sided view of the world was a more powerful theoretical idea which came out of Africa. An early form of monotheism (the belief in one God) gradually emerged from around 3200 BCE. This idea challenged the idea of 'many gods'. The one-god 'theory' came to dominate and shape Egyptian society as the pharaoh ruled over society as a sole godlike sovereign, served by the architecture of the pyramids and the social ritual of embalming to preserve his immortal status. Around the same time, monotheism has been traced to Zoroastrianism and Judaism.

One proposed explanation for this early conception of *theos* emerging in early Egypt was that no life was possible without the daily rising and setting of the sun, which gave light, warmth and growth, enabling a population to settle and develop agriculture, irrigation systems and some of humankind's earliest inventions. This natural force was worthy of worship. The dominance of the sun and the regular pattern of the forces of nature in this ancient geographical area gave birth to the idea that there was one god. This was a natural religion, a powerful prompt and a universal development in the thinking in humankind. This particular development was a theoretical revolution in the ancient world. For the first time the unifying idea of one *theos* explained everything and in the light of this, Egyptian society was organised.

The idea of one god, and the concept of unity which it expresses, is a foundational concept. It is perhaps not surprising that the concept of zero originated in Arabic thought in the same geographical region where the monotheism of Judaism, Christianity and Islam developed.

Millennia later, the majority of South Africans, including a Zoroastrian community around Durban, claim to adhere to a form of monotheism. Were you and your parents, grandparents, forebears and ancestors influenced by this idea? Whatever the case, do consult Chapter 13 on religion in this textbook.

1.2.1 Theory and the criterion of simplicity

A 'one-god' theory was a simpler idea than the 'many gods' one. To this day, simplicity (or what philosophers term **parsimony**) is a criterion for choosing between scientific theories. In the natural sciences of astronomy, physics and chemistry, for example, when it comes to choosing between competing scientific theories with the same explanatory power, the simple theory is preferred, accepted and used. Incidentally, the Greek philosopher Aristotle (AD 384–322), whose intellectual influence remains strong and alive, had already arrived at this criterion for what makes a good theory.

1.2.2 Concepts as the building blocks of theory

We can usefully start to understand theory as a 'story', a narrative, an account, a detailed mental picture or as a linked set of concepts about the world around us. Concepts exist only in our heads. To put it another way, concepts are

an integral part of the contents of our minds. Concepts are abstract mental constructs that we express in words and language. A good story or theory is made up of a range of concepts that explain, in the minds of those who hold them, why things are the way they are. Theories are built out of concepts.

What a concept does is pick out, isolate or identify something or a phenomenon in the world around us. Think about that for a moment. We are, for instance, all familiar with simple concepts, such as the concept of a chair. A chair is something to sit on. We understand this concept because we recognise what a chair is, even though chairs are of different shapes and sizes, and made of many different materials. Let us compare two other familiar, simple concepts. Take the concept of a bush and the concept of a tree. We can be confronted by an herbaceous plant and not know whether it is a bush or a tree. A botanist would presumably have two specialised definitions, one for the concept of a bush and another for the concept of a tree and easily solve our untutored quandary. To take another example, when you look under the bonnet of a motor vehicle, what do you see? You do not see or understand much unless you already know something of the theory behind the internal combustion engine and what each component does. The relation between the spark plugs, the high-tension leads and the cylinder head means nothing unless you can identify these mechanical components in the first place.

In a similar way, specialised sociological concepts pick out, isolate or identify a particular social phenomenon and other social phenomena in the world. Sociological concepts immediately direct us to some aspect of social life. Sociological concepts connect our thinking minds to the social world around us. Carefully linked together, they provide us with a theory that explains some aspect of social life.

1.2.3 All normally functioning people are sociologically competent

Theories, then, are built, made up of and formed out of linking concepts coherently together to create a 'picture' or explanation of an aspect of the world we observe around us. The concept of 'coherence' simply means fitting logically and rationally together without any sense of mental discomfort or awkwardness. By integrating theories of ever larger scope, we develop more complex descriptions and more powerful explanations.

We all have such 'theories' that shape the opinions and views about the world in which we live. All normal and healthy human beings possess, without even knowing it, what the sociologist Charles Lemert (1993) calls sociological competence. We are familiar with and competently negotiate our way around our own neighbourhood. Since childhood, our primary caregivers – our parents and teachers – named things for us, explained how things worked, told us what to do, where we could go, what not to do, and had preferences about our friends. They perhaps did not like some of our friends because we learned things of which they did not approve. They wanted us to learn particular sets of norms, values and behaviours so we would fit into our community and broader society. This is what sociologists mean by the concept of socialisation. The processes of socialisation have enabled us to competently manage the immediate world around us. We connect concepts with our environment and social life without even thinking about it. We hence all have views about the world and are able to use concepts and have theories about aspects of the social world which we inhabit. The task of sociological theory, however, is to elevate this common-sense and everyday practical sociological competence into theoretically informed practices of social scientific inquiry and investigation that result in knowledge.

1.2.4 Distinguishing between social theory and sociological theory

We all have theories about the world in much the same way as ancient civilisations developed theories about the social and physical world, whether in Europe or Africa or elsewhere. In fact, this is what Ibn Khaldun did 600 years ago and is rightly called the first sociologist, as you will see. As Ibn Khaldun developed a sociologically informed explanation of the historical process, so can our social theories, it could then be said, provide explanations for the multitude of things and complexity and even mystery and wonder of the world around us. Most of us ask questions and are curious about life. Why is there poverty and wealth? Why is crime worse in some societies than in others? Why is there conflict in the world? How is social order achieved? Why do people disagree about what is beautiful? In short, human beings have always, either implicitly (without stating as much) or explicitly (actually being able to express as much) thought about these things, developed theories about them and continue to ask questions about what happens around them.

Ancient philosophers and great writers considered such issues and are the subject of the great literatures of the world, but no definitive answers to some of these questions could be given or theoretical disputes resolved until the emergence of science – modern science in particular. With science, where theories conflicted with one another, one of the criteria for choosing a theory was to ask which

one depended on the strongest evidence. Were there any observations or facts to support the theory? Could the facts be measured? *Evidence* for theories emerged as crucial.

If you cannot provide evidence for your theory about the world, you are probably thinking in the realm of social theory. If you can provide evidence for your theory about social matters, then you have a sociological theory – one that explicitly rests on the evidence of facts informed by the theory. With the emergence of modern science, this reliance on evidence became central in human understanding, knowledge and even the never-ending quest for 'truth' – or epistemic adequacy, as contemporary philosophers prefer to say.

Following Ibn Khaldun centuries later, four of the thinkers who were foundational to the academic discipline of sociology – Comte, Marx, Weber and Durkheim, to be introduced shortly – all sought evidence for their theories. This made the work of these theorists not just social theories, but sociological ones. In different ways and even with different concepts of science, they carefully observed what happened in society and sought to develop a scientific analysis of society. But what precisely, you might ask, is science and scientific analysis?

1.2.5 Theoretical predictions

The question of what science is immediately becomes complex because the very identification and recognition of observable facts depends, in turn, on theory. For example, some natural scientific theories predict facts we cannot see or that have not yet been established. Light was thought to travel in straight lines until Albert Einstein (1879–1955) made the theoretical prediction that light could bend. His mathematically based theory was later proved correct by evidence from a practical scientific experiment. Even in the natural sciences, however, making accurate predictions is not a common occurrence. Just think of how the weather bureau often gets predictions wrong. It is even more difficult to make predictions in the social sciences, although the social analyses of some great sociological thinkers stand the test of time and are as appropriate today as when they were written. Sociological and social scientific theories consequently generally confine themselves to identifying, describing and analysing patterns, regularities and trends in social life instead of trying to predict what will happen.

Capturing all the relevant facts under the umbrella of a single theory hence remains the challenge of science in general.

For not only these reasons, the relation between theory and facts is complex. What constitutes science and knowledge has consequently occupied the greatest of minds throughout human history. This is the issue with which we now have engaged – the challenge of exercising our theoretical imaginations in a rigorous social scientific manner.

1.2.6 The power of theory

What is even more fascinating is what happens when we do exercise our theoretical imaginations. Very few ideas are genuinely original. When we grapple with ideas and concepts, we find we are generally thinking thoughts which themselves have a history and were originally the thoughts of some or other individual mind. We all know the earth moves around the sun and that the planet is not flat. This was not obvious before the emergence of a scientific world view. The 'flat-earth theory' dominated human thought until Copernicus (1473–1543) taught us otherwise. We now know this and we are all, in some sense, Copernicans. We share his theory. In fact, so strong is the evidence that we believe it and can even say, 'I know the world is round'. Like the good scientist he was, Copernicus also thought a theory must agree with the facts and that a simple theory must be preferred over a complex one. Copernicus's simple helio-centric theory put the sun and not the earth at the centre of the universe and replaced the earlier geometrical model of the ancient Greek astronomer and thinker Ptolemy (AD 90–168), which described how the planets move in space.

Sociological theories are similar in striving for evidence-based accuracy and simplicity – although one might not think so sometimes! And most sociological theorising stands on the shoulders of great thinkers of the past. We have inherited much of the contents of our own minds from the theories of such thinkers who began to analyse society in a scientific manner.

1.2.7 The nature of conceptual analysis

Conceptual analysis is like a knife. The process of thinking and analysis, expressed in words, makes sense of the world by cutting it up into concepts in order to develop our understanding of it. The mental exercise of cutting and dividing up the world is what is meant by conceptual analysis – using concepts to identify phenomena, name or attach concepts to things and draw conceptual distinctions. Concepts are grouped into clusters of concepts or distinct conceptual categories. Categories are the most fundamental division of any subject matter. A colour has no sound, for instance. Colours and sounds are different conceptual categories. What is living and animate on the one hand and

non-living and inanimate on the other are clearly different categories of things.

Conceptual analysis by its very abstract nature, however, rarely captures the full complexity of what exists. When analysing some aspect of the social world, there are limits to the concepts we use. Take note in this chapter and in Chapter 10 on class how differently Karl Marx and Max Weber define and use the same concept. The concepts we use are limited because they only pick out the social phenomena informed by the theories within which they have been formulated and defined. In addition, when concepts are not defined sufficiently clearly, they will not accurately identify and isolate the social phenomenon at which they are directed. The findings about the social world derived from conceptual analysis and hence our knowledge about the social world is always provisional, but not only for this reason.

In trying to understand something about the social world, conceptual analysis requires that concepts must continually be tested against the **empirical** evidence to construct better, more accurate theories – ones that more accurately reflect what we are trying to explain and understand. An idea or concept is empirically based if it is based on experience and evidence gleaned from the five human senses of sight, hearing, touch, taste and smell, or can be observed or measured by instruments.

Social scientific theories are hence constrained or limited by their lack of conceptual clarity (or lack of definition) on the one hand and the degree to which they are based on empirical evidence on the other. Depending on what we are studying and how our concepts are defined, theories will be different in scope. The sociological theories, to be discussed below, deal mainly with large macroscopic social issues – explaining the nature of society as a whole. Less ambitious, middle-range theories are often called meso-level theories. It is useful when you start out conducting your own social research, however, to engage with a research question that is more manageable and so pose your theoretical question at a more immediate or micro-sociological level.

By selecting concepts carefully in terms of scope, defining them to achieve maximum clarity and closely interrogating the evidence they illuminate, the accuracy and reliability of your conceptual analysis and sociological theorising will be enhanced. But how, you might ask, does one start this process?

1.2.8 Making conceptual and theoretical choices in sociological inquiry

When we embark on examining some feature of society, it will almost inevitably be something that is of interest to us born out of our life's experience. There will be a range of concepts and theories to choose from which have tackled the self-same subject. For this reason, we are going to have to choose which concepts, theory and method of inquiry to adopt. How to do this can be illustrated by looking at a real example.

We all know that under apartheid South Africans were separated by race in virtually all aspects of their lives. With few exceptions, there was a stark division between mainly well-resourced, rich, white and inadequately resourced, poor, black people. Since 1994 when South Africa achieved its non-racial democratic transition, everyone, including sociologists, agrees that there has been significant social change, but there are different sociological theories about the extent of it. One political sociological theory says the extent of social change in South African society is significant because now we all have the vote and apartheid legislation has been abolished. Another economic sociology theory says the extent of social change is not so significant because there is still social and economic inequality despite the demise of apartheid. This is a highly relevant issue, and involves big theoretical and empirical questions about the extent of social change.

If you wanted to investigate this issue, you would clearly need firstly to narrow the scope of your inquiry. Let us say you limited your study to particular groups of South Africans and their perceptions and experience of social change since 1994. This is a manageable exercise. Perceptions and experience are good indicators of social change. Such a study would illuminate the theoretical question about the significance of social change. What concepts would we choose to begin such a sociological study? Would the inquiry be best conducted by using the concept of peer group – defined as those of similar age? Or should one use the concept of social class – defined as a social group sharing similar socioeconomic conditions? Would Marx's concept of class do – defined as ownership or non-ownership of productive economic wealth? Would it be best to use Weber's concept of class, which is defined in terms of one's life opportunities available in the market? Or would you choose the concept of ethnicity – defined as sharing linguistic, cultural and racial attributes? What social phenomenon would each concept pick out in your neighbourhood? What evidence could be marshalled to support these concepts or others you might choose? Which concept or concepts would best answer your sociological question about social change in South Africa today? In order to begin answering these questions it is always important to try to identify the assumptions underlying the concepts or theories we might want to use.

1.2.9 What is an assumption?

Assumptions are important when we think, conceptualise and develop theories. An assumption is something we take for granted. If you are reading this book now, we can correctly assume you are a breathing, living human being, but we cannot assume you are a student registered at a South African university required to study the subject of sociology. Your mother or father or brother or sister or friend might be reading it to see what you are studying. You might correctly assume that if you do not read this textbook carefully you might fail your sociology exam! Assumptions define not only thought, but human behaviour as well. Watch out for the assumptions made by your friends in any discussion or those of politicians when they speak. Identifying the assumptions people make often reveals a lot about the strength of the argument being made.

Also watch out for the assumptions made by the theorists we are about to discuss. They are often very difficult to uncover, but once you do, the theorist's perspective on the social world makes a great deal more sense. We will assume you will be watching out for the underlying assumptions in what you read as we get into deeper theoretical waters.

Identifying assumptions

To make a start, what are the assumptions sociologists make when they employ the concepts of nation and that of social class? First, we assume these are useful concepts and that they will help us illuminate something about society. Secondly, we assume they refer to social groups of people. Thirdly, both concepts assume similarity and difference among human beings. Both concepts pick out different characteristics and features of human and social life. The shared similarities of one group of people distinguish them from those shared by other social groups. Being South African, Nigerian or Brazilian means belonging to nations from different geographical areas of the world. Language is often a defining feature. The concept of social class also assumes similarity and difference, but more particularly of a socioeconomic character, highlighting poverty and wealth and social status in particular.

Let us assume the concepts of nation and social class are important and meaningful in distinguishing between social groups. How would you rank the relative importance of the two concepts – nation and social class? What theoretical assumptions do we get caught up in when using these concepts? The concept of nation might be more familiar to you. If so, check whether this is still the case once you have studied this textbook.

How do we understand the human species inhabiting this global village of ours in the 21st century? This will depend on the theoretical assumptions that we make. Does the world comprise a host of nations or over seven and a half billion people divided by poverty and wealth? In short, the concepts we use to understand the social world and the theories in which they are often embedded has implications for how we end up understanding the society around us.

Box 1.1 Exercising your theoretical imagination

Has your race had a greater influence on your identity as a person or has your social class (socioeconomic) position more powerfully shaped your life chances and personal identity?

QUESTIONS

1. Decide on your choice of concept, list the reasons for your choice and then go and ask your parents (or someone their age) and two of your friends what they think.
2. Can you explain the different responses you got?
3. Write down your explanation of the different answers your older and peer respondents gave.

Once you have worked through this textbook, especially by reading Chapter 9 on race and the section in this chapter on Marx, check whether you still agree with your explanation. Our assumptions lie deeply embedded in our own specific social context. Can we make the assumption that you are a serious student and did the practical exercise in the application box and have already identified some of your assumptions? If you did, you might have noticed that the responses both you and your respondents gave were powerfully influenced by individual biography and life experience. Indeed, if one of the tasks of a good theory is to be able to make predictions, then our theoretical prediction is that the responses you received were reflections of the social experience and position in society which shaped your respondents (and yourself) in important ways. Social phenomena or events can be interpreted very differently depending on the social context in which they occur.

1.2.10 The importance of social context

Sociological theories are often reflections of the society from which they emerged. Strong sociological theories will be applicable more widely and transcend the social context from which they emerged. Strong sociological theories will apply to societies very different from those of the theorist who developed them. As new social situations emerge,

developments take place and society changes, and even strong theories change as they attempt to grasp and explain what is happening in society. In short, sociological theories change or give way to others in the light of new experience and evidence in changing social contexts.

Part of the power of sociological theories is that they also guide how we see things. If taken seriously, theory can shape our behaviour and our actions, for theories and ideas contribute to changing society. No further reason need be given for making sure we get our theory right! In fact, a study of sociological theories, even if they have been proven wrong, can still tell us much about the way the social world was at the time the theory was developed, because our ideas, thoughts and behaviour are the product of social and sociological theories – as well as other social scientific theories – developed in the past. Such theories can, in addition, also tell us much about the social position of the thinkers who came up with them in the first place. Social and sociological theory itself is a product of social life. This is a peculiar characteristic of sociology and one which has significant implications for social scientific knowledge. For if sociology is itself a social product, what makes it scientific? Is objectivity then even possible in social science?

1.2.11 Can sociology be a science?

If it is true that sociologists are influenced by their immediate social context – their social position or if they have been insufficiently critical of their own intellectual culture – the question of **objectivity** arises. Related to this question is whether sociology is or can be science. A strong definition of science refers to a neutral and objective assessment of the facts based on empirical evidence and which results in a law that can be confirmed by other scientists under different conditions and over time. The natural sciences strive to be **nomothetic** (law making). The law of gravity is such a scientific law. This law applies to all people and things, but when it comes to social science and the behaviour of people – and not just things – lawlike behaviour generally does not apply. However, you will encounter one stunning example below where laws do appear to apply to collective human behaviour. In brief, the nature and status of science and knowledge have been and remain topics of debate. Whether the social sciences constitute science in terms of the strict hard definition is especially complicated. Sociologists study society, but are part of society itself. Sociologists therefore have no privileged *external* position from which to observe and analyse the object of their investigation. How can we achieve any objective distance and standpoint apart from what we study if that is the case?

Many contemporary sociologists would argue that individual identity, as well as social scientific **knowledge**, is **socially constructed**. Humans have *constructed* the world in which we live, where we are shaped by the complex, socially constructed realm of language, traditions, rituals, norms and values that served previous generations well. Some theorists would say we cannot tear ourselves away from these social moorings and be objective and neutral. Out of this social matrix we form our own individual ideas and learn to express our own independent **agency**. We generally have a personal interest in what we study. We study sociology not just because it is fascinating, but because we have an interest in getting a university degree! We have interests and so, as you will see Max Weber would say, we might prioritise our capacity for instrumental action (action performed with a goal in mind) of getting a degree above the hard task of striving to be as objective and neutral as possible in asking the difficult questions of **epistemology**. Yet we need to strive for objectivity as our very assumptions and the implicit theories we hold usually reflect our upbringing (our **primary** and **secondary socialisation**) and the **structure** of the society we inhabit. These are social forces that can prevent us from being objective. Because the theories we propound are born out of and often reflect the society from which they emerge, we need to contrast natural and social science.

The difference between natural and social science

The natural sciences – such as physics and chemistry – study the physical world, the world of inanimate, non-living things. Physicists and chemists stand in a clear *external* and objective position in relation to the objects of their study. Physical phenomena being studied or chemical processes being measured do not change their properties or chemical composition simply because the natural scientist is observing and measuring them – except at the quantum level, apparently (Wolf 1981) – but only explore that if you are really interested! For our purposes, water always boils at the same temperature at the same altitude and this can be clearly observed, measured and repeated time and time again by other natural scientists. Laws can be formulated about boiling water and other forces of nature, and the hard definition of science can be applied.

The social sciences – such as history, sociology, anthropology and political science – study the social world, the world of human, animate, living beings. Social scientists cannot stand outside or in an external position to the objects

of their investigation. The behaviour and social actions of human subjects is not readily captured in strict laws, and the hard definition of science cannot be applied. Note that this distinction between the natural and social sciences has been cut with a sharp analytical knife. Biology, for instance, studies living things and falls somewhere in between. This immediately suggests that clear-cut analytical distinctions seldom capture the complexity of issues, which is one of the many intellectual challenges of the sciences in general.

Reflexivity in the social sciences

To overcome the power of context and the fact that we are part of what we study, we need to develop a special awareness of what it is we are doing by critically reflecting on our own thinking activity, our own social context and the role of our own thinking. Theorists call this **reflexivity** and to be reflexive is generally understood to be sound social scientific theoretical practice. The importance of this epistemological issue and these questions lie at the foundation of the discipline of sociology. The word *epistemic* means that which is related to knowing and to knowledge. Epistemology asks the question: *How* do we *know*? What it is to acquire knowledge has, of course, occupied the minds of thinkers since the beginning of time, the importance of which will soon become evident. To claim to know something in the social sciences means stripping the veil off our own socialised learning and practices. You might find it useful to know that your lecturers and sociologists in general struggle with these timeless issues and even reflect on how to introduce social theory in the best possible way to undergraduates such as the majority of you reading this textbook (see Stewart 2003). This is because sociology cannot be separated from the constant awareness of how we are caught up in the object of our study, our reflections on what it is we are doing and how best to conduct practical social research. This points to the importance of **methodology** in the social sciences, which is the topic of the next chapter in this book.

1.2.12 The dominance of 'Western' sociological theory

In this chapter and textbook, the theories of society are still largely, but not exclusively, associated with Western thought. The reason for this is that Western thinkers remain widely accepted as the founders of the still young modern academic discipline of sociology – established only around a century ago. Under the influence of the European Enlightenment (1650–1800) and the French Revolution (1879), the three foundational thinkers of sociology all tried to explain the massive shifts that occurred in human society with the invention of machines which, from the 1830s, ushered in the Industrial Revolution. The capacity to exercise control over society developed in a way which had not been possible before. New ideas and sociological theories based on evidence sought to conceptualise this radically new phenomenon as human beings gained a newfound sense of themselves and their power to respond to and create the social world around them. We face very similar issues today as these ideas have developed and been challenged. This matter will be addressed at the end of this chapter.

Box 1.2 Ideas, values norms and traditions

Read the following statement and answer the three questions below:

As Africans, we may hold a set of ideas, values, norms and traditions which do not entirely fit with the dominant 'Western' or, for that matter, 'Eastern' views of the social world.

QUESTIONS

1. What are the key ideas, values, norms and traditions of Africanism?
2. Do you think we can escape the traditions of Western thought and culture?
3. Add to your initial thoughts as you study. This is a longer-term intellectual project.

1.3 Major perspectives or approaches in sociology

How one identifies the main foundational thinkers and major perspectives in sociology is controversial. After briefly introducing two such thinkers, Ibn Khaldun and Auguste Comte, the three major theoretical perspectives, approaches or paradigms that have been widely accepted as foundational to sociology will be discussed. Despite much deserved criticism of the intellectual tradition sociology has inherited, the writings of Émile Durkheim (1858–1917), Karl Marx (1818–1883) and Max Weber (1864–1920) will be the focus. This textbook will certainly present evidence of this claim to their continuing relevance, although by no means uncritically, as you will soon discover.

Modern science and the prospect that certainty in knowledge could be achieved had captured the human imagination when these thinkers wrote, and impacted on the way they thought. The great hope was that science would solve many human and social problems. Marx, Weber

and Durkheim were influenced by this hope. In their case it was the age of **modernity** that followed the period of the **Enlightenment** in Europe when a great flowering of the arts and knowledge accompanied the emergence of modern science. This exciting period in human development also massively influenced intellectual giants such as Charles Darwin (1809–1882), who developed the scientific theory about the origin of the human species, Sigmund Freud (1856–1939) the father of modern psychology, and many others. Such was the impact of the Enlightenment – also referred to as the Age of **Reason** – that it had its echo in the idea of the African **Renaissance** as articulated by former president of South Africa, Thabo Mbeki. He wished Africa would emulate this powerful artistic, cultural and scientific movement and work towards it, but do so by adopting a purely African stance and perspective, one located in Africa.

Of the three key foundational thinkers in sociology, Émile Durkheim, has been associated with the view that sociology can be a science modelled on the strict definition of science. He thought that the criteria that lay the epistemological foundations for knowledge in the natural sciences can and must apply to the social sciences. The criteria for knowledge were laid down in the philosophy of positivism.

Max Weber strenuously disagreed with this view. Science as defined by natural science, which examined physical objects and natural forces, could simply not, he thought, be applied to the complexity of what it was to be human. Owing to the fact that human beings have free will and that many interpretations of the same phenomena or social events can be encountered, any study of human affairs was subject to the capacity of interpretation of which human beings are capable. Human beings continually interpret the world around them and so Max Weber is associated with the approach of interpretive sociology.

While Karl Marx wrote earlier than both Durkheim and Weber, theorists who have taken their lead from his voluminous writings adopt the perspective that both Durkheim's and Weber's theories essentially express and represent the views and thinking of the ruling and the economically and politically powerful social class in any society. The origin of this view is that the task of philosophy, Marx thought, was not merely to interpret and *understand* the world, but to *change* it. For Marx, this meant changing **capitalist** society. The critical perspective in social science has consequently been based on and associated with his complex theoretical works spanning philosophy, politics and economics.

Each of these theorists will be introduced and their influence will be found throughout this textbook and virtually any other good sociology textbook you might consult. Test yourself to see whether you can identify the assumptions of these three major perspectives. In fact, the theorists of decoloniality, introduced at the end of this chapter, do just that. It is with the original 'father' of sociology, Ibn Khaldun, we will, however, begin.

Figure 1.1 Abdul al-Rahman ibn Khaldun
(Source: Image courtesy of Wikimedia)

1.3.1 Abdul al-Rahman ibn Khaldun

Ibn Khaldun (1332–1406) 'received a careful education', schooled by his father and 'scholars teaching in the mosques and schools of Tunis' in the 14th century in North Africa where he lived. He studied the Qur'an, the Word of God for Muslims as 'revealed through the prophet Muhammed'; the Hadith, the 'traditions of what the Prophet had said and done, jurisprudence, the science of law – as based on the Qur'an and Hadith, the Arabic language and the rational sciences, mathematics, logic and philosophy' (Hourani 1991: 1). North African students have long been taught that the scholar Ibn Khaldun was the first sociologist. This recognition has only fairly recently been rediscovered in the West (Ritzer 2000). Many of his ideas prefigure those of other thinkers in the discipline, whose ideas and theories will also be discussed.

Standing out in history when compared to his peers, living when the dominant idea was that everything had already been discovered, and anticipating Comte, Ibn Khaldun considered himself as the founder of a new 'science',

the 'science of human association' (Wardi 1950: 265). This would be 'a new and independent science of society and culture which he called *ilm al-'umran* – literally translated to mean "sociology" – whose subject matter and objects of study would be human society and social organisations, and whose primary concerns would be explaining the conditions that often inform social change and the essence of civilisation' (Abdullahi & Salawu, citing Ibn Khaldun 1967: 38–39). Ibn Khaldun has consequently been thought to be the only writer in Islam at the time who recognised 'the importance of preconceptions and categories of thought in the settling of intellectual debate' (Wardi 1950: 261). He set out to discover a logic based on the actual events of human society as his data, which he referred to as a 'scientific tool'. He sought to distinguish between what was true and false when examining historical data – and formulated social laws to verify the validity of such data (Ibn Khaldun, *Al-Muqaddimah*, cited in Wardi 1950: 264). In doing so, Ibn Khaldun has the distinction of being the 'only writer in medieval Islam' – free of 'idealistic' orientation (Wardi 1950: 81).

What is hugely controversial even today is that Ibn Khaldun 'can rightly be considered as the first thinker in Islam' who was prepared to analyse the sacred tradition of his religion by putting it 'on the dissection-table of time and place' (Wardi 1950: 101). His work, thought by some to be opaque, yet by others very clear, distinguished itself from the traditional thinking and the historiography of the time. These ideas relied on commonly held traditional views and 'idealistic preconceptions and classical rules of thinking' (Wardi 1950: viii). The varied responses to Ibn Khaldun's work stem directly from the context in which it was written. No one could go against the religious **absolutism** of the accepted and orthodox dogma of the day. Wardi argues that Ibn Khaldun consequently had a dilemma in presenting his realist and materialist perspective in the face of the idealistic absolutist orientation of the dominant religious culture and the learned men of his day (1950: 86ff). Independent thinkers have often faced this dilemma. In order not to be condemned, he 'superficially supported' his **secular** theory with traditional religious sayings that would have been acceptable to his readers, but who in any case ignored his realist orientation and his focus on the doings of ordinary people (1950: 86ff). This has led commentators astray when interpreting Ibn Khaldun's work, the theoretical orientation of which is 'relativistic, temporalistic and materialistic' (Wardi 1950: 88). Do go and check what **relativism** and **materialism** mean if you are not sure.

Al-Muqaddimah (Introduction or Prolegomena)

Ibn Khaldun's theoretical orientation is developed in what is an early universal view of history and society. His central text is the *Muqaddimah* (Introduction or Prolegomena). The *Muqaddimah* explicitly developed a distinctly sociological perspective to understand history informed by sociological concepts. This laid the basis for his Universal History in which his historiography, cultural history and philosophy of history found expression. A modern scholar assessed Ibn Khaldun's work as rational, analytical and encyclopaedic, and which presented not only history, but an **explanation** of history (Rosenthal 1967). Anticipating Weber and the importance of understanding, *verstehen*, Ibn Khaldun penetrated deeply into what other people thought and their value systems (Wardi 1950: 404). This was a novel and highly original achievement for the 14th century.

It is not surprising Ibn Khaldun was highly critical of the intellectual culture and attitudes and suspicions of his day. The uncritical acceptance of ideas apparently particularly irked him and he took this to task. He was instead concerned with the clear definition of specialised concepts, such as existed in the natural sciences at the time, needed for 'the purpose of explaining, clarifying, and understanding the phenomenon under investigation' (Abdullahi & Salawu 2012: 28). In a thoroughly modern vein, Ibn Khaldun wrote about 'actual happenings of society and customary ways of life' (Wardi 1950: 269). Because he did not deal with what were considered to be the important issues, namely the eternal ideas of the sacred, his contemporaries missed the importance of his work. In a society shaped by a religious world view and the strict separation of good and evil, the eternal and sacred belonged to what was *good*. The ordinary affairs of the world were associated with evil. Ibn Khaldun rejected this *binary* way of thinking.

For Ibn Khaldun the actual happenings of society were inescapable and permanent. He hence sought to trace the pattern which ordinary everyday events followed. He observed how the common people acted according to custom, inherited manners and beliefs, and considered this to be natural and valid. In the minds of these common pre-modern people there was no distinction between ideal and real as the logicians and philosophers of the day held. Anticipating Marx, as you will see, Ibn Khaldun was of the view that 'the human mind is a product of the environment and man is the child of his habits and customs' (*Muqadimmah*, cited by Wardi 1950: 271). Consequently, for Ibn Khaldun, one cannot get to know or understand ideas for which one has no 'mental preparedness' (Wardi 1950: 271). Today this is clearly obvious to us. In the 14th century, to the logicians of his day, who were attempting to get ordinary people to change their ways, Ibn Khaldun advocated they leave their 'ivory towers' and 'go along with the multitude' (Wardi 1950: 277). It is not surprising that Ibn Khaldun's work has been thought to have a remarkably modern feel about it.

Asabiyyah and cyclical social change

Prefiguring Émile Durkheim, Ibn Khaldun can be interpreted as having the notion of *asabiyyah* as his central organising concept. Translated from Arabic, *asabiyyah* means social solidarity, group cohesion or group consciousness (Abdullahi & Salawu 2012: 31). *Asabiyyah* has also been rendered as 'a corporate spirit orientated towards obtaining and keeping power' (Hourani 1991: 2). This meant that strong degrees of integration and identification needed to be established and maintained within nomadic tribes, whom Ibn Khaldun greatly admired for their independence and strength in comparison to those who lived in the towns on the fringes of the desert. Any leader who had a sufficiently strong and cohesive following manifesting *asabiyyah* could establish himself as the authoritative ruler of a dynasty or what today we would call a state. Once such rule was firmly within grasp: 'populous cities would grow up and in them there would be specialised crafts, luxurious ways of living and high culture' (Hourani 1991: 2).

Such was the importance of *asabiyyah* that it lay at the heart of how Ibn Khaldun thought dynasties followed each other in cyclical fashion. He observed how nomadic tribes living on the fringes of great dynasties or empires, who manifested stronger degrees of *asabiyyah* than those of the dynasties, would come to replace them in regular cycles. As the *asabiyyah* of the dynasties loosened over time within a cycle, they became less disciplined and lax. Such dynasties were weakened as a result of political infighting, factionalism and individualism. The dynasties would become weakened as a political unit and unable to resist challenges from beyond their borders in a time when there was no distinction between religious and political power, and force and might were accepted as right.

The concept of *asabiyyah* was hence central to his understanding of social change. *Asabiyyah* would 'play itself out' within a dynasty, with those displaying stronger forms of social cohesion taking their place. These cycles, Ibn Khaldun suggested, would repeat themselves every four generations. He argued that they further applied to other pre-modern civilisations in China, India, Persia and Europe. In each of these instances the religions and world views of the invaders would take root, whether it was Islam in the

East or Roman-Greco culture and Christianity in the West. From his learning, Ibn Khaldun would have studied the march of history and how the great empires of the Greeks and the Persians had been replaced by the Arabs, who in turn had been replaced by Berbers in Spain in the west and by Turks in the east.

These historical cycles were inevitable, Ibn Khaldun thought. He held that 'the future and past run on the same pattern and according to the same laws and so both future and past can be observed in the present', hence his concern with studying the routines of everyday life (Wardi 1950: 85). This orientation led him to accept the inevitable march of history and have social order as his focus. He consequently disparaged the campaigns of those 'troublemakers' whose actions tried to change society, as disruptions to the social order would weaken *asabiyyah* in the process (Wardi 1950: 277).

Range and scope of Khaldunian sociology

You might like to Google Ibn Khaldun to appreciate the range and scope of his work. A number of ideas across the social science disciplines are attributed to him: a conflict theory based on the struggle between 'town' and 'desert'; the originator of a labour theory of value adopted by Marx; notions that would later only be encountered in the work of luminary thinkers such as Georg Hegel, Marx and Friedrich Nietzsche in the 19th century and Arnold Toynbee in the 20th century; comparisons to some of the views of the influential economist John Maynard Keynes; and the Khaldun-Laffer curve principle used, intriguingly, in both economics and solid-state physics and chemistry as well as Islamic theology and psychology. Let us end this brief review, however, with Ibn Khaldun's explanation of a matter of critical importance for us today.

Explaining racial difference

Couched within 'the principles of general sociology' (Bin Syed Agil 2008, cited by Abdullahi & Salawu 2012: 29), Ibn Khaldun addressed a range of issues of his day, including that of difference of **race**. His explanation, again, was modern and makes good scientific sense 600 years later. Ibn Khaldun explained the biological differences evident among different peoples in terms of the interaction of different groups of people with the biological conditions of their **environment**. Personality traits of particular groups were not determined by innate differences, but were instead environmentally and socially conditioned (Abdullahi & Salawu 2012). Ibn Khaldun also argued that the differentiating national characteristics of the Arabs and the Jews are not based on innate differences but on culture, experience and historical exigencies (Abdullahi & Salawu 2012: 29).

Figure 1.2 Auguste Comte
(Source: Image courtesy of INPRA)

1.3.2 Comte and positivism

Auguste Comte (1798–1857) is important not simply because he first conceptualised sociology as a discipline, which he initially referred to as 'social physics.' Comte was important due to being generally recognised as the first thinker to clearly articulate the rules of method in the natural sciences. His concern was to lay the foundations for certainty regarding knowledge. Positivism provides strict epistemological criteria and rules for scientific method and is based on limiting theory to the evidence collected. Comte's strict interpretation of positivism has been formally discredited philosophically, simply because human and social affairs are too complex to be treated as mere empirical data. Positivist principles relating to the role of evidence, however, remain in practice in powerful ways within both the natural and social sciences. In short, if there is no evidence to support a statement, that statement does not represent an item of knowledge. Here is a quick example of which Comte would have approved as there is plenty of evidence for the statement: Many tertiary education students cannot afford university fees.

Auguste Comte's theory of three stages

For Auguste Comte, ideas govern the world, but because these ideas could not be proved in a way which every reasonable and rational person would be forced to accept, everyone expressed their own views and opinions, and fruitlessly argued with anyone who disagreed. For Comte, this explained why there was disorder in the world. There was simply no yardstick to assess different arguments or which was the better one, for people behave according to, and social groups act on, their preferred beliefs. There was no way for protagonists of different arguments to resolve their differences and arrive at any degree of certainty. Society consequently manifested, Comte thought, aspects of disorder due to competing arguments. Overall agreement between people was therefore not possible.

Comte attempted to resolve this matter once and for all. Society needed science to be properly ordered and a solid foundation for agreement. He developed a theory of how human intelligence went through three stages, each being a grand conception about life and the world in general. Somewhat controversially, he thought these three stages applied not only to the development of human intelligence in general down the ages, but also that the development of the mind of every individual, both yours and mine, followed these three stages.

To use our definition of what a concept does, these three stages, he postulated, picked out or identified three stages of both historical and individual human development. This 'three stages' theory both described the social world and prescribed how disorder could be overcome. Do pay close attention if you want to understand the recent university students' struggles around decolonising the curriculum!

The theological stage

The first stage was the *theological stage* or what he also called the 'fictitious' stage. Comte argued that this stage was a necessary stage of development; in other words, it *had* to have occurred. Its role was to release the mind from the circular trap in which human thinking found itself. This circular trap can be described as follows. We need concepts and theory to guide our thinking in order to make sense of what we perceive (see **perception**) when we observe things, but we cannot *perceive* things without having a concept to isolate them from the rest of the world in which they are placed. This is the trap Comte thought early human thinking encountered. He put it this way in his work *The Positive Philosophy* (1832):

Between the necessity of observing facts in order to form a theory, and having a theory in order to observe facts, the human mind would have been entangled in a vicious circle, but for the natural opening afforded by theological conceptions (Thompson & Tunstall 1971: 20).

The belief in gods and then later the unifying idea of a single divine being (monotheism) satisfied the questions the human mind posed in its attempt to understand the world and find answers about the origin and purpose of human existence. This theological stage culminates in one grand conception of a divine being and represents **absolute** knowledge.

The philosophical stage

The next stage in the development of the human mind is the metaphysical, *philosophical*, *abstract* or '*speculative*' stage. This stage, Comte's theory says, is a development of the theological stage and is a *transitional* or bridging stage. As the human mind develops, it begins to think more abstractly and deeply about the physical world, hence the meaning of the term *metaphysics* – thinking about physics. Humans begin to reason and think about the abstract forces of nature. Once observed and noticed, the power of nature – the seasons, the sea, the wind, fire and the fertile character of the earth – provides a more immediate and more reasonable *explanation* for human experience than that of an unseen god. Human life is subject to the abstract forces such as the weather and the forces of human instincts and human passions. The mind could make reference to these forces, but not yet properly understand them prior to the advent of science. This metaphysical (see **metaphysics**) stage also culminates in one grand conception, that of nature, which is understood to be the cause of all phenomena.

The scientific stage

In the final, positive or *scientific stage* the mind comes to the realisation that absolute knowledge is not possible and that metaphysical speculation must be substituted by a form of knowledge that provides real certainty. Reason and observation together finally enable us to rely on facts and evidence. The mind has reached what Comte thought was its final flowering – the end state of knowledge, namely positivism. Such knowledge is scientific. It is based on *scientific observations*, and is open to question and debate. It is subject to the power of reason and logic in the light of the emergence of new facts and theories, and is hence progressive. But for *whom* – which social groups – is it progressive, you might ask, in the South African intellectual climate today?

Static and dynamic social analysis

There are two aspects in Comte's theory of the three stages. We observe both order and progress in social affairs. We hence need a static or stable conceptual aspect in our theory as well as a conception of dynamism and change in order to grasp the relation between the parts of society and society as a whole. The static aspect focused on and accounted for the evidence of stability in society, while the dynamic aspect focused on social change. Comte's theory of society constituted a whole – ie statics and dynamics must be integrated in social analysis. From these two aspects of Comte's theory, much of sociological theorising followed.

Comte's theory was sufficiently sophisticated to recognise that one stage leads to the next, not in a neat linear fashion, but rather as a complex series of dynamic changes and that all three stages could co-exist. One stage would influence successive ones. He was clear, however, that confusion and disorder arise when all three exist together, for then no agreement can be achieved. For this to occur and an ordered society to arise, the final scientific stage had to be reached. Only the power of rational thought, relying on evidence, would secure an ordered society. Comte certainly intended that his ideas and theory would shape others' ideas and powerfully influence human thinking and action.

Each thinking individual was to develop through these stages to attain the final stage of positive knowledge – *science*. If a person's intellectual development has not gone through these stages, Comte thought, they have immature minds as they are not prepared to base beliefs on evidence and facts.

Box 1.3 Order and progress

The Brazilian flag has the motto of Comte – *Order and Progress* – emblazoned on it.

QUESTION

Would Comte's motto be appropriate for South African society today? What would this mean?

Comte's influence

From having been able to explain disorder in society and how order (and social progress) can be achieved, a range of influential theories followed, such as **functionalist** and **consensus** theories. Examples of these theoretical orientations are to be found throughout this textbook. *Functionalist theories* examine how different parts of society work and how they fit together. *Consensus theories* examine how agreement occurs in society, and stresses the need for social cohesion via the attainment of agreement between people of different views and persuasions. Not only did Comtean sociology emerge as a serious attempt to solve the problem of disorder, but here was a social scientific approach comprising *both theory and methodology* providing certainty regarding knowledge! This would serve, Comte thought, as an arbiter between competing theories and contribute to a more ordered society. What goes for science and how knowledge is constituted are, however, our contemporary questions.

1.3.3 The vast scope of sociology

Sociology was consequently to *observe* and *examine* all manner of human, social and historical events, processes and procedures – hence the vast scope of the discipline and the *broad reach* of its theories. Sociology was to examine all social interaction in relation to the whole of society and to take account of past and future development. Comte even foresaw and warned of the danger of 'the action of Man upon his environment' (Thompson & Tunstall 1971: 27) and automation when he wrote in the first decades of the 19th century. He observed the increasing division of labour and saw once multiskilled artisans relegated to the simple task of making pinheads, which so horrified the economist Adam Smith (1723–1790) in the late 18th century and which Karl Marx sought to explain. One can only wonder what he would have thought of the **Fourth Industrial Revolution!** Comte would certainly have been aghast at how knowledge was to become so specialised that academics have virtually been forced, by the astounding growth of it, to study only one thing or topic, often losing sight of the whole. This is perhaps not surprising. For despite its dynamic aspect and much subsequent criticism of it, Comte's theory assumed the power of ideas and prescribing what should happen. It was not very good in predicting and explaining social change. Sociology remains stuck with poor prediction, but has achieved sound *explanations* of social events and processes.

There was one social thinker, however, who was to focus not on social order, but on social change.

1.3.4 Marx and critical social science

When *social change* comes into focus, **conflict perspectives** and theories are developed. *Conflict theories* observe competing interests in society. Such theories reveal the dynamism that develops as different social classes of people interact and come into conflict. They argue that conflict provides the impetus for social change.

Figure 1.3 Karl Marx
(Source: Image courtesy of INPRA)

Karl Marx was the pre-eminent conflict theorist. He rejected Comte's focus on ideas that could change the world. Like Comte, however, he thought there were laws of human development, but that, contrary to Comte, they were to be found by examining the *material forces* of history. If Comte had an evolutionary view, Marx propounded a *revolutionary* one based on a theoretical approach he called **historical materialism**. Even more so than Comte's work, Marx's theories have been the subject of much debate and criticism.

The starting point of materialist social analysis

For Marx, it had to be recognised that human beings first had to *produce* their basic material needs before doing anything else. Each society at different stages of development had to collectively organise how to satisfy these needs. The manner in which things were produced, or what Marx called society's **mode of production**, was therefore central not only to social life and the social relations of production, but also to social analysis. His theory consequently stressed the importance of what happened at the economic *base* of society and out of which the **superstructure** (law, politics, religion, education and art) of society emerged.

Except for the most primitive societies where everything was shared, Marx theorised that as human society developed, in every form of social and economic organisation there were those who owned and controlled the resources society had at its disposal and those who performed the labour with the means of production – the tools and materials needed to produce what society needed. Society was hence divided into opposing social classes. This division gave rise to conflict between these classes, and would shape society and social development. This was for Marx the 'motor' of social change. History, for Marx, is a succession of developments in which different societies are characterised by their mode of production. History is driven by **class struggle** between two basic social groups – the 'haves' and 'have-nots', the rich and the poor, the oppressor and the oppressed or, when it comes to modern capitalist society, between the **proletariat** (the labouring working class) and the **bourgeoisie** (the owners of the means of production). Apart from these two major or fundamental social classes, Marx's **stratification** of society into social classes also included the **petty bourgeoisie** (small-business owners, teachers, lawyers and other professionals) and the **lumpen-proletariat** (the unemployed and other vulnerable and socially marginalised people). How the economy or the mode of production was organised was based on these simple facts. With the rise of capitalism especially, the mode of production was characterised by fundamental *antagonism* and *conflict* between the two basic and opposing social classes. It is hence no surprise that the concepts of **labour**, **work** and **production** and the need for every society to produce a *surplus* (**surplus value** under capitalism) are centrally critical concepts for Marx, as later chapters in this textbook will show.

Exploitation and revolutionary theory

Marx thought capitalist society was based on **exploitation**. This was not a moral but a technical issue for him. Simply put, exploitation occurs in the capitalist mode of production as the wages workers earn are worth less than the economic value they produce. Under capitalism, exploitation results in the experience of **alienation**, which occurs in a number of ways. Workers, those actively engaged in the economic base of society, were *alienated* from their own work as they exercised little or no control over it. They were *alienated* from each other as they had to compete with other workers. They were *alienated* from what they produced as they did not own their own product. Finally, they were *alienated* from themselves as individuals as they were unable to realise their own human potential. Workers had to learn that this was the situation in which they found themselves. Marx sought to provide them with a social analysis of **revolution** and practical ideas to overcome their exploitative situation. He wanted his ideas to be weapons in the struggle between the proletarian workers and the bourgeois capitalist class. It is quite clear whose side Marx was on.

Historical materialism and materialist dialectics

In order to develop these ideas, Marx had to confront the dominant philosophy and teaching of his day. The method he used to articulate his historical materialist perspective he took from the idealist German philosopher Georg Wilhelm Friedrich Hegel (1770–1831), namely **dialectics**. There is no easy way of defining dialectics in a sentence or two, not least because the philosophy of Hegel is renowned for its difficult and abstract language. Hegelian dialectics rests on the idea or thesis that all logic and world history itself is characterised by internal **contradictions**. It is hence subject to change, but confronts resistance or an antithesis to change that transcends or resolves the contradictions. This results in a synthesis that is the accommodating resolution of the contradictory sets of forces, but which sets in motion new sets of contradictions requiring resolution.

Marx challenged the Hegelian notion that the world could be explained in terms of ideas interacting with nature or the world external to the human mind. For Marx, the driving forces were fundamentally material ones. **Capital**, for instance, faces its contradictory opposite, labour (who demand higher wages), resolves the contradiction (by introducing machines), but which gives rise to new contractions (the machinists demand higher wages), which themselves must be resolved (by automating production). Like Hegel, however, the Marxist theory of historical materialism, combined with his method of materialist dialectics, results in a grand, overarching theory of history and society. Some have called this a 'totalising narrative', capturing everything under its complex matrix of concepts and interlocking theories. This grand theoretical framework explains what some Marxist theorists call 'the combined and uneven development' of society on a global scale – how and why development and underdevelopment (or developed and developing societies) are inextricably linked together in a complex, global capitalist economic system. Many critics, such as postmodern thinkers discussed in Chapter 3 on culture, *do not* think such grand conceptual schemes can explain our highly complex modern world – so keep an eye out for this discussion!

Human consciousness

Marx thus begins with *the everyday* – the need to produce our material needs of existence and what we do on a daily basis. The existing tools and technology with which we do this powerfully frame our very thinking and consciousness. To take an extreme example, a pre-industrial peasant farmer obviously cannot share the world view of scientists formulating the physics required of the Square Kilometre Array (SKA) (partly built in the Northern province of South Africa) or the Large Hadron Collider (built underground in Europe). Both of these technologies – the one exploring the stars and the other exploring subatomic matter – are the biggest machines ever to be built by human beings. The minds and knowledge of the scientists responsible for these astonishing endeavours are light years away from the pre-industrial experience and consciousness shaped by working with primitive hand-held tools. Yet as humans grasped and shaped their world with increasingly sophisticated tools, so did our knowledge, consciousness and sense of ourselves and our world develop.

Human consciousness then, for Marx, arises out of materially rooted social experiences and the social structuring of life appropriate to each of the stages or modes of production that characterise human history. As Marx famously wrote in 1859 in the preface to *A Contribution to the Critique of Political Economy*: 'It is not the consciousness of men that determines their being, but on the contrary, their social being determines their consciousness' (see Bottomore & Rubel 1963: 67–70). Human beings naturally struggle to assert their collective agency against these socially structuring influences as they construct their world, yet are compelled to do so within the context of the influence of the past. As Marx put it in *The Eighteenth Brumaire of Louis Bonaparte* in 1852: 'Men make their own history, but they do not make it just as they please … but under circumstances directly found, given and transmitted from the past' (Tucker 1978: 595). The point is that as we mould and change the world to satisfy our wants and needs, while we face the weight of past traditions and circumstances, we transform ourselves, including the way we think and become aware of things.

Social classes and the mode of production

Like us, Marx wanted to understand and explain his own society and the emergence of capitalism in particular. From the 1830s onwards, the Industrial Revolution in Britain had utterly transformed the previous slow-moving feudal society based on agriculture. Two new social classes had arisen and had replaced the aristocratic lords and peasant serfs (see **serfdom**) of feudal society (see **feudalism**). In an African agriculturally dominated society, we would refer to chiefs or traditional leaders overseeing the lives and work of those who work the fields. Marx noted, with considerable admiration, that the new social class – the townspeople or bourgeoisie who had replaced the aristocracy dominating the previous feudal mode of production – was a progressive one. In society, as Marx was to proclaim in the *Manifesto of the Communist Party* of 1848, '[t]he bourgeoisie, historically, has played a most revolutionary part' (Tucker 1978: 475). This new bourgeoisie often had no inherited land and wealth, and was the first entrepreneurial class. They organised the making of things they sold for a profit, thereby transforming the ancient agriculturally dominated economy into the greatest, most powerful and productive industrial economy and society the world had ever seen.

Analysing capitalism

Marx conceptualised this achievement as the capitalist mode of production, but to do this, he needed to define money and capital. He did so in his book *Capital: Critique of Political Economy* in 1867. Where did this fabulous wealth and profit come from? Previous classical economists, Adam Smith and David Ricardo (1772–1823), had given answers to this question – labour. The purposeful application of human energy at work was labour in other words. Labour created things, artefacts and commodities for sale on the market. Labour, Marx argued, was the source of all economic value and wealth. However, neither Smith nor Ricardo had properly explained profit and this Marx set out to do with both far-reaching conceptual and politically revolutionary consequences. He invented new concepts to pick out, isolate and identify new social phenomena, such as **labour-power** (the capacity to work) and explained the role of private property. He developed new understandings of old concepts such as labour and the **division of labour**.

Challenging the dominant ideas of the ruling class

For Marx, the dominant ideas of the day – the ideas of the ruling class – constituted the **ideology** (set of ideas) that provided the **justification** for cooperation in the capitalist mode of production. These ideas provided the social cohesion in a capitalist society underpinned by class conflict and class struggle. Marx was seeking a deeper explanation for the bourgeois ideology that held to the theory that the driving force in society was the 'equal exchange' on the market between buyers and sellers. This exchange also, however, included a particular commodity he called *labour-power* – the human capacity to work and produce. Once he had identified the social phenomenon of labour-power, conceptualised it and developed a theory of profit based on the economic surplus workers created, he believed he had discovered the secret of bourgeois production.

The secret of labour-power

The 'equal exchange' between the sellers (workers) and buyers (employers) of human labour-power masked the potentially explosive productive power of this capacity that lay at the basis of the creation of economic value. For the wage agreed to on the market between the employer and the worker was worth far less than the capacity of labour-power to create untold wealth – once harnessed with materials and tools to produce commodities. Herein also lay the fundamental conflict at the base of capitalist society, for the wages of workers are a *cost* for the bourgeois employer, but are the sole source of *life* for the working proletariat. For many, these two social classes – the bourgeois owners of the means of production and the working proletariat who owned only their own labour-power – would forever clash as long as capitalism survived.

The concept of class

Class, for Marx, was defined in terms of ownership and non-ownership of the means of production. Class was not just a concept, but an objective reality. Social class defines the subjective experience of its members. To get the idea across to the proletariat, namely that they were exploited by the bourgeoisie, who did not pay them the full value of the commodities they produced and that they suffered alienation under capitalism as a result, a revolution was needed and for that a revolutionary political working-class party was required. If workers failed to understand this, they would forever suffer from what Marx called '**false consciousness**' – the belief that if they worked hard under capitalism they would prosper. Evidence that hard work is not enough to prosper is the existence of the 'working poor' – workers who, though employed, remain poor. Does one of Marx's theories – the 'immiseration thesis', the theory that the working class will become ever poorer formulated 150 years ago – come close to establishing itself as a social scientific law, at least as it pertains to an increasingly marginalised population in the global South? Can this theory be tested?

Revolutionary politics

Marx was not a passive social analyst. He took sides instead of standing back seeking objectivity. Together with his lifelong collaborator Friedrich Engels (1820–1895), they co-authored the Communist Manifesto to get the new revolutionary ideas of historical materialism across to the new proletarian industrial working class. Marx and Engels wanted to create an international revolutionary working-class political party and indeed initiated its formation – the First Working Men's International Association (First International) in 1864. The collective agency of the working class would be needed to accelerate the contradictory structural tendency of capitalism to sow the seeds of its own destruction. Marx thought that as a social and economic system, capitalism had deeply embedded and fatally contradictory flaws.

Box 1.4 A political party

Find friends and colleagues who are serious about rigorous and fair intellectual debate based on the provision of evidence and then do this exercise.

Marx and Engels wanted to create a revolutionary working-class political party and indeed initiated one – the First Working Men's International Association (First International) in 1864.

QUESTION

Is there such a political party in South Africa today? Discuss this in your group and give reasons for your answer.

The contradiction in capitalism

To this day, Marx's economics, the slew of sociological concepts he invented and the theories he developed to define capital and capitalist society, are controversial. For Marx, capital was the crystallisation of the labour-power expended and expropriated from previous generations of the working class. His economic theory, however, predicted that there was an inherent tendency in capitalism for the rate of profit – not the absolute amount of profit – to decline. This happens when an entrepreneur invents and introduces a new product to the market and ideally makes a lot of money, but which attracts other entrepreneurs who enter the market and dent the high profits the inventor was first making. The inventor must drop his prices, improve his product or invent something else, or go out of business. Marx thought this never-ending process, whereby money was made and capital was accumulated, was a structural and unavoidable feature of capitalism. This in-built logic of capitalism, Marx theorised, was responsible for the series of crises capitalism has subsequently faced throughout its history and would be a key factor contributing to its eventual demise. The logic of the structural contradictions within the capitalist economy, combined with fundamentally antagonistic social relations within capitalism as a whole, pointed to the emergence of new forms of society – **socialism** and **communism**. Once the social class of the bourgeoisie had been replaced by the proletariat, much in the same way as the bourgeoisie had replaced the aristocracy in their own **national democratic revolution**, the means of production created under capitalism would fall under the control of its working-class producers.

Dictatorship

When workers replaced the employers, there would need to be a political arrangement that Marx called the dictatorship of the proletariat. This was envisioned as a collective democratic **dictatorship**, not the rule of a single person represented by the Nazi Adolph Hitler (1889–1945) or the person who would exercise complete despotic control over society shortly after the Russian Bolshevik revolution, Joseph Stalin (1878–1953). Marx's vision was that socialism would be a society where people were put before profits and that this form of society would be a transitional social arrangement. This, he thought, would lead to communism – a classless society where everybody had a say and were different, but equal. History, as we all know, has so far turned out somewhat differently and regarding which a welter of social theories and explanations continue into the present.

The idealistic vision of Marx

Despite the materialist basis for Marx's thought and complex interlocking set of theories based on an extraordinary range of concepts applying to the widest possible range of phenomena and issues, there is a powerful **idealism** embedded in his theoretical accomplishment. He certainly assumed – correctly or incorrectly – that human nature would change if social conditions improved. He provided a majestic vision that society would improve for the better, but understandably and wisely did not sketch what society would look like in a future transitional socialist and then finally in the classless communist society he predicted. It is virtually impossible to think what human society will be like in 100, 500, 1 000 or 2 000 years' time. Will the state 'wither away' as a communist society is established as Marx predicted? Is a classless society in which people are free of exploitation and oppression possible? Will humanity look back on the astounding technological achievements of the 20th and early 21st century as remarkable, yet be appalled by our current lack of moral substance and the continuation of poverty and social inequality in the context of fabulous wealth under capitalism? Or will humanity on earth have destroyed itself and be living in space? These are questions which evidently appear to go beyond science when the social world falls under the analytical gaze. A text on social theory has, for instance, pointed to this characteristic of sociology. The sociology of two great American sociologists, C Wright Mills and Robert Bellah, has been described as 'moral sociology' (Seidman 2004: 97–113).

The emergence of ethical and moral questions in sociology

While a sociology aspiring to be a science is required to stick to the **facts** as best it can, given the best theories it can advance, the discipline of sociology is peculiar in that it readily spills over to asking the bigger, ultimate questions about life. When the fact of poverty is observed, the immediate **moral** response is that it is wrong. What undeniably exists – the extent of poverty in the context of great wealth – begs the question of whether it ought to be different. Facts and **norms** can quickly become confused. Sociology engenders thoughts about ethics (how to behave well) and morality (what is right and wrong). Science and belief appear to become intertwined. Perhaps much of sociology is ultimately a set of beliefs born out of a particular perspective and is well described as a secular religion – as has economics (see Nelson 2001) – and cannot be a science at all. However, this matter cannot be entertained here and is noted to indicate the complexity of important issues in the social sciences which remain unresolved. The point is that as Comte wished for order in society to be realised, the idealist element in Marx has encouraged thought about the social world that stretches well beyond what can be justified empirically – the hallmark of science as we have been discussing.

The relevance of Marx for developing societies

To conclude this brief introduction on Marx, it should be noted that he thought a proletarian revolution would break out in the advanced capitalist societies where the forces of production were fully developed. It did not. It broke out in Russia, the poor cousin of economically advanced and developed European society. The role of the political party of the working class, the Bolsheviks, led by Vladimir Ilyich Lenin (1870–1924), was crucial. Despite the minute size of the working class, Lenin argued that its objective power, or what Marx called a class 'in itself', could be transformed into a class 'for itself' – a social class which had (like the bourgeoisie) become aware and conscious of its historic role to change human society. The significance of the fact that a revolution occurred in an economically backward country inspired by Marx's ideas and led by Lenin was not lost on developing societies elsewhere in the world.

This signals the historical relevance of Marx's theory of society in Africa and elsewhere in the developing world. The importance of African slavery and the slave trade for economic and social development in North America and Europe cannot be underestimated. Slaves were owned body and soul, and had nothing of their own. Some

Marxist sociologists would argue that workers are really not much more than wage slaves. Low wages and very poor working and living conditions characterised most workers under **colonialism**. Notions of social class, born in European struggles between contending social groups, were imported into a society where race radically dissolved such social cleavages by virtue of all African, Asian and Latin American people becoming subjugated as workers and forced into subservience to Europeans, no matter their social class position. What was a matter of social class in Europe was overlaid by race in Africa and elsewhere. There was the emergence, for instance, of an African proletariat in the South African mining industry. The struggles of these workers and others against white employers under colonialism, segregation and apartheid have repeated themselves under employers of all stripes under democracy. These developments have both confirmed and seriously challenged Marxist analyses based on concepts and theories developed 150 years ago on another continent. They remain wide open for reconceptualisation by a new generation of sociologists – such as those reading this introductory text. A keen student might like to go and find the article by Sarah Chiumbu (2016), which uses Marxist theory to develop a decolonial analysis of how the media represented workers at Marikana in 2012.

This chapter started out by discussing knowledge, science and society and has ended up noting ethics, morality and what a future society might look like, but it is to the strict or hard definition of science that it must again return.

1.3.5 Durkheim and positivist social science

Émile Durkheim was a follower of Auguste Comte. He thought sociology could establish itself as a value-neutral and objective science (see Noble 2000: 145ff) and spent his life attempting to achieve this aim, starting by becoming the very first professor of sociology. His first task was to distinguish sociology from psychology and philosophy. To do this, his theoretical work defined a realm of distinctly **social facts**.

Social facts

The way in which Durkheim defined social facts was broader than the way facts were defined in psychology and philosophy. What psychology construes as facts applies to the individual and the individual psyche. While philosophy has much to say about facts and the way in which concepts refer to the external world, in empiricism especially, a fact is generally understood to be an actual state of affairs. Durkheim went further and argued that social facts should be treated as external 'things' in the same way as facts were treated in the natural sciences. Social facts, Durkheim was to show, played a central socially structuring role in society. The concept *social fact* hence did not just refer to some social phenomenon, but was, for Durkheim, not only a real thing – an identifiable social phenomenon – but played a social role in relation to human agency.

Figure 1.4 Émile Durkheim
(Source: Image courtesy of Corbis Images)

Social facts played a socially structuring role due to their characteristics. First, social facts were general as they were in evidence everywhere. Secondly, they were *external* to human agency. Thirdly, they exercised a *coercive force* over people, and fourthly, people were *generally unaware* of their existence and the coercive power they had over them. These characteristics of social facts were a central aspect of Durkheim's positivist perspective. Some theorists do not think there are such things as social facts and it is not easy at first to grasp this concept. Social facts, however, can be neatly illustrated by looking at one of Durkheim's major works entitled *Suicide*, published in 1897.

Studying suicide
Suicide is a gloomy topic but an instructive one to study, which is what the French government was doing at the time Durkheim lived. Much statistical data was being collected, but establishing the cause of suicide proved to be elusive.

Durkheim came up with a remarkable finding, thereby establishing sociology as an academic discipline as well as establishing his own reputation, which endures to this day.

Committing suicide is probably the most deeply intimate and personal thing an individual can do. Despite this, Durkheim established that there were different *rates* of suicide among different groups of people. This strongly suggested that broader social factors were at work beyond the personality of the individuals who committed suicide. These different rates of suicide, Durkheim positively showed, were directly related to the degree of **social cohesion** within different social groups. The concept of social cohesion – also referred to as **social solidarity** or **social integration** by many sociologists – refers to the bonds, links and ties keeping a social group together. Social cohesion can be considered as the social 'glue' that keeps a community or group of people together in an ordered manner. Where individuals were not closely tied to a community or social group, suicide rates were higher than where there were close bonds of shared norms and values which regulated people's lives. For Durkheim, this finding was akin to that of the laws in the natural sciences. Sociology was shown to be **nomothetic** (law making) and hence mirrored the natural sciences and resulted in real scientific knowledge.

Durkheim argued that incidence and the rates of suicide were closely related to levels of social cohesion. He distinguished between **egoistic suicide** and **anomic suicide**, which occurred when individuals detached themselves or were dislocated from social bonds. **Fatalistic suicide** and **altruistic suicide** occurred in overly highly regulated environments. Anomic suicide occurs during times of economic hardship or where individuals experience becoming separated and dislocated from their social group – such as failing matric. Where religious or nationalistic bonds are overly regulated, suicide is clearly a social affair. Japanese *kamikaze* fighter pilots in World War II, contemporary Muslim suicide bombers and the Tibetan monks who have immolated (set fire to) themselves in opposition to Chinese occupation of their country would be examples of altruistic suicide. All types of suicide occurred then when social cohesion was either very weak or oppressively strong. Durkheim hence proved that committing suicide was more than simply an individual and personal decision.

Social cohesion
Durkheim made a very strong case for the powerful force of social cohesion to qualify as a social fact. The phenomenon met the criteria of his fourfold definition of a social fact. Social cohesion was *general* in society – no group could do

without some form of social cohesion. Social cohesion is *external* to the individual as it is a characteristic of the social group as a whole. It exercises different degrees of *coercion* over people and is hence a social force of which people are *generally unaware*. Interestingly, as so often happens, the concept of social cohesion, like other sociological concepts, has found its way into popular language.

Box 1.5 Social cohesion and discipline

When this textbook first appeared in 2014, politicians were calling for a greater degree of *social cohesion* in South African society. Three years later, they were calling for *discipline* within the African National Congress ruling party. Now the ruling party appears internally *divided*, which suggests a lack of both *social cohesion* and party *discipline*.

QUESTION

Discuss what this might mean.

Functionalism and structuralism

The surprising finding of Durkheim's study on suicide lies in the explanatory power of Durkheim's concepts and theoretical work. His studies resulted in what is probably the most coherent explicitly sociological theory of society – leading to sociological strains of thought such as **functionalism** and **structuralism**, which you will find expressed in different ways throughout this textbook. Of the many basic concepts emerging from theories founded on Durkheim's work, a few more will now be introduced.

The division of labour

Society rapidly became considerably more complex in the transition from a rural/agrarian to an urban/industrialised society. Durkheim spells this out in his celebrated text *The Division of Labour in Society*, published in 1893 (see Durkheim 1964). At the heart of this transition was the increasing division of labour in modern industrialised society and its socially destabilising effects. As a result of both population increases and density, a considerably more complex **division of labour** – the distribution of work tasks in society – increased interaction between people in their struggle over scarce resources. The form of social cohesion changed. In societies where there was little distinction between people and they consequently shared common traditions and values due to the division of labour being simple, relationships between them were defined by what Durkheim referred to as **mechanical solidarity**.

Mechanical solidarity

Mechanical solidarity was marked by and reinforced through shared social rituals in which it was obligatory to participate. Anyone who did not do so was punished by the law of the clan or tribe. Law was consequently **repressive** in societies dominated by mechanical solidarity. In modern society, which was no longer **homogeneous** (similar) but **heterogeneous** (different) due to the increasing division of labour separating into a host of occupations and professions to perform society's many tasks, a new form of **organic solidarity** developed.

Organic solidarity

We trust strangers with our lives when we climb into a taxi. To enforce such trust, complex regulations are formulated and new laws are passed. If these are not adhered to and you suffer loss due to the illegal actions of others, you can institute a claim against the offender. Law is no longer repressive in a modern society dominated by organic solidarity, but has become **restitutive**. Clearly, whether repressive or restitutive, these ways of ensuring social solidarity and compliance with social norms powerfully shapes individual identity. It is a social fact that the social structuring power of the law has a material influence over us as individuals. Smokers are prohibited, for instance, from smoking in most buildings. Such a social fact is a **material social fact** for Durkheim. The fact that there are norms and values by which we must abide shapes our conscience, and would be examples of **non-material social facts** as defined in Durkheim's sociological theory.

Box 1.6 Social theory and social research are two sides of the same coin

Read the following paragraph and then think about how you would answer the question below.

We trust people with things that are important to us, even our lives. We trust that lecturers will mark examination scripts fairly; that doctors will provide proper treatment in hospitals; that the cell phone company will bill our contract correctly, to name a few examples of organic solidarity. We know that if regulations and laws covering such relationships are not adhered to and we suffer a loss, a legal claim can be instituted.

QUESTION

Do we live in a society in which trust will continue to be a source of social cohesion or one in which we are likely to increasingly resort to litigation (the law) in the event that we suffer damage or loss?

Norms and morality

Durkheim was primarily a sociologist of morality. He thought society, at its very base, was governed by **norms**, from which the word 'normal' is derived. Trust is such a norm. People are generally more trusting than they realise. Durkheim illustrated, for example, how even impersonal economic transactions or dry legal contracts assume a level of trust. There had to be, in other words, an underlying moral stance adopted by members of society characterised by organic solidarity. When the norm is broken, social disorder occurs. It is normal to drive a vehicle courteously and to stop at red traffic lights. Serious social consequences follow when such norms are not adhered to and many South Africans are critical of some members of our local taxi industry who are regularly seen to flout them. A consequence of such behaviour is a breakdown of law and order in society. There are social effects – injuries, fatalities and suffering as a result – not to mention enormous and unnecessary financial costs to society. Individuals are deeply affected, and lives are lost and changed forever. Social attitudes change. All taxi drivers, even good and responsible ones, become **stigmatised** as a result. Other motorists' driving behaviour changes, the phenomenon of road rage asserts itself, and so on. Breaking norms and socially sanctioned rules of behaviour clearly has serious social consequences.

Anomie

Durkheim goes further and says that when you break a norm, you cannot deny the pain you feel. If you do not feel seriously bad and traumatised after having been responsible for killing someone in a car accident, that is abnormal. The breaking of norms then has both individual and social consequences and effects. When such a lack of social integration occurs on too large a scale, **anomie** (the absence of norms) is experienced. Much of modern society, characterised by organic solidarity, Durkheim concluded, is marked by the lack of social cohesion and anomie resulting in individual and social dislocation and suffering. This threatens social order which, like Comte, was his particular theoretical interest. With so many competing interests in complex societies, how indeed does society hold itself together?

Order and social conflict

Like both Comte and Marx and much of sociology today, Durkheim was preoccupied with the tension between social order and social conflict. Like Comte, he thought social order was a critical issue, as opposed to Marx who analysed society chiefly in terms of social conflict. In the social context of a violent liberation struggle to destroy apartheid, Marxian theories came to the fore. Now that our young democracy needs to establish a new social order, will we see a resurgence of Durkheimian theory? Durkheim developed a range of concepts to explain how this tension between order and conflict in society – and hence in sociological theory – powerfully influences how individuals experience social life itself.

The cult of the individual and homo duplex

In contrast to the strong bonds and tight social cohesion of pre-industrial, agriculturally based communities, modern urban, industrially based societies in Europe encouraged what Durkheim called 'the cult of the individual'. As South African society has become increasingly modernised the importance of *ubuntu* – the idea that to be an individual means being integrated into the social group – has largely given way to egoistic individualism. The importance of the social group has increasingly been replaced by the glorification of the individual as it has in fully developed industrialised societies. As a local example of how this cult manifests itself, just think of the T-shirts with the faces of political leaders prominently displayed. While Durkheim approved of individualism occurring within the bounds of social norms, he did not approve of egoism that glorifies the individual at the expense of the social group. Durkheim would approve of good role models, but would disdain the vain mimicry of celebrities or egoistic politicians.

Most people have been successfully socialised to follow society's norms and values, yet often insist on going their own, potentially harmful individualistic way. Yet, as individuals, we cannot escape the tension between following social norms and following our own mind. Human agents hence experience this tension of being pulled in two directions, the experience Durkheim called **homo duplex** – the competing, dual forces characterising modern social life. Human beings are constituted of body, desire and passion, but are also socialised personalities (see Coser 1977: 132–136). These two aspects of the human experience are at war with one another. Everybody has experienced the tension between following their own individual desires and feeling constrained by generally accepted social norms, obligations and values. Durkheim's theory did go to the heart of how we as individuals actually often feel, but explained these feelings as originating within the normative structure of our society, rather than merely from our own unique experiences or perspectives. He therefore provided a *social explanation* for the individual experience of being conflicted within ourselves.

Society is normative

Despite Durkheim's insistence that the methods of natural science should also apply to the social sciences, society, for Durkheim, is normative. Without values, rules and norms, it falls apart. In this respect, he was a conservative thinker. Anomie is the result when the regulatory norms required by society are broken.

Where conflict occurs, much of this too is normal and, within certain socially defined bounds, can have positive effects. Individual members of society and social groups with competing interests are bound to come into conflict. Where such conflicts are resolved *within* the broader normative framework of society, however, the result is a positive one. Similarities and differences can be recognised, procedures can be put in place to deal with social conflict, and society can be regularly ordered by new sets of institutional norms with which we can in the future be expected to abide.

The collective conscience

The division of labour and the forms of legal regulation that accompany it result in what Durkheim identifies as a further non-material social fact – that of a **collective conscience**. This collective conscience could also be termed a 'common conscience' that encompasses the individual consciences that constitute it. The collective conscience is more marked in a society characterised by mechanical solidarity, yet is still a feature of modern societies in which the individual refers to what others do in order to assess the morality or correctness of their own actions. Durkheim later used the more specific concepts of **collective representations** and **collective effervescence** to identify the way in which certain norms and values are shared and the way they are expressed. Executing a 'Mexican wave' at a large sports gathering is an example of collective effervescence – coming together in thought and action – in which individuals get caught up as in a current in the ocean. Collective representations can be seen as aspects of the collective conscience as more specifically manifested in communities or institutions in society such as the family, the work environment or church and state. The unique character of any specific institution and the ways its norms and values are expressed or represented cannot be explained by reference to an individual, but are represented

by the collective. Put simply, we share ways of thinking and feeling with those with whom we are part of the same social group. Think of the rivalry between two schools, how this is collectively expressed and how their different collective representations have shaped our own individual identities. This is a powerful non-material social fact that is general, external, coercive and of which, as Durkheim argues, we are generally unaware.

Social cohesion as the function of religion

Take religion as an example of another way collective representations are expressed. The original Latin verb – *religare* – means to bind. Belonging to a specific religion, whether we go to a church, mosque, shul or temple, represents something important about who we are as a definable social group. Religion is the primary force of social cohesion in society for Durkheim. Religions codify, systematise and develop society's many different representations or 'pictures' of the world. Durkheim argues that religions divide the world into what is **sacred** and what is **profane**. Religion encourages a set of beliefs about the sacred which is entrenched by a set of rituals – or forms of mechanical solidarity – which are sustained by a community, and what is profane – that which is ordinary or mundane and of no special significance. The source of religion, for Durkheim, emerges out of the collective conscience or representations in a society. This can be understood as our 'evolving collective social experience' out of which all our ideas, including our religious beliefs, have their source (Noble 2000: 168). In Durkheim's view, religion must be understood as a creation of society itself – a necessary social construction reflecting human norms, values and needs, which has its ancient source in the closest and most immediate collective social experience of the social group. As Durkheim put it in 1912 in his seminal text, *The Elementary Forms of the Religious Life*, '[r]eligious force is nothing other than the collective and anonymous force of the clan' (Bellah 1982: 184). It is generally believed that this force has diminished in modern societies marked by organic solidarity, but its role continues through other institutions and events. Is this the case in South Africa today? For more on this topic, see Chapter 13 on religion in this book.

Applying Durkheim

A major event in 2010 in South Africa can be usefully viewed using Durkheim's perspective and approach. Many South Africans got caught up in what could be described as an outpouring of national pride during the hosting of the soccer World Cup. A great many South Africans across all social classes were gripped by the collective effervescent excitement and sense of togetherness it engendered, which the rest of the world was able to witness. Some social commentators suggested this sense of a collective South African identity was not developed. Ways could have been found to regularise or ritualise the rather short-lived phenomenon that briefly seemed to bind together and unite our heterogeneous, unequal, multicultural and still very racially divided society.

On a darker note, does collective effervescence apply to the outbreaks of xenophobia in South African society?

1.3.6 Weber and interpretive social science

Weber is, for many, the foremost sociological theorist of the 20th century. Weber's sociology influenced developments in law and disciplines in the social sciences such as economics, political science and religious studies. His historical investigations proved to be very detailed and highly technical. His sociological insights embedded in these writings are exceedingly rich and complex, and have been subject to numerous interpretations. This is the reason we still study and attempt to understand them today.

The 'bourgeois Marx'

Max Weber was an outspoken public intellectual, even during the time of war. During World War I in Germany in 1917, he campaigned for the right of all to vote and an empowered parliament. Unsuccessful in his brief foray into formal politics, Weber turned to scholarly work and, like Marx and Durkheim, attempted to identify and understand the social forces responsible for driving the changes of a rapidly evolving industrialising modern-world economy and society. He was also an intellectual child of the European Enlightenment. His work has been described as one in constant dialogue with the work and ideas that cast a long shadow over the world – those of Karl Marx. He has even been referred to as 'the bourgeois Marx' and was a conceptually radical social thinker – if radical is understood as getting to the root of an issue.

Bridging 'either/or' social explanations

Sociology has, as a core theoretical theme, made the attempt to try to understand the many influences that have impacted on us as individuals. As we have seen, this occurs especially via the key socialising institutions of family and schooling and then of work, more of which you will find in Chapter 6 on socialisation and identity. Yet Weber thought we could not easily explain society by means of either materialist theoretical conceptual categories following

Marx or by employing idealist ones by following Comte and Durkheim. Weber insisted that his historical sociology was neither an idealist interpretation of history (like Comte) nor a case of historical materialism (like Marx). One can infer from his work that, for Weber, these 'either/or' options were philosophical positions, the concepts of which did not analyse society sufficiently accurately.

Human actions and interactions could not be grasped by explaining them solely in terms of the social circumstances or social structures that caused them. Weber's sociology was hence not a structural sociology that explained the actions of the individual by seeing them primarily as a function of, or as powerfully influenced by, the broader social context within which they took place. Given the stress on the power of social structure in the works treated thus far in this chapter, you might have wondered how you are to manage the structuring influence of the educational process you are undergoing at tertiary level. How is your own intellectual capacity and agency to be developed in this context? On this last point, Weber had something to say to university lecturers that you may find interesting.

Values, objectivity and teaching

In his essay *Science as a vocation*, Weber was very clear that 'politics is out of place in the lecture-room' (Gerth & Mills 1974: 145). Students should never be able to discover the politics of their lecturers from their lectures. Weber valued **objectivity** highly and so thought that lecturers should be able to present social analyses without giving away what they really thought, both personally and politically. Only objectively determined facts, not personal values, were to be transmitted in the classroom. Weber's epistemology was hence not focused on the distinction between natural and social science, but on *objectivity*. By now you know that Marxists would say objectivity is a 'bourgeois concept' as 'facts' and the 'values' learned in the context of being a member of a specific social class cannot be separated. You also know that Durkheim thought that the realm of social facts was external to us as human beings. Weber, however, avoided this debate by stressing how we could win through to an objective stance in relation to the social world. Weber wanted sociologists to engage in sober empirical analysis on which sociological arguments should be based.

Differentiating sociology from other disciplines

If Durkheim differentiated sociology from psychology and philosophy, Weber distinguished the new discipline of sociology from the established field of history. History examined individual events and their broader cultural significance. While sociology had to be rooted in a close empirical examination of historical events, it sought to formulate types of human interaction. Sociology was to identify generalised uniformities emerging from a close empirical study of historical events. He thought that theories could only be formulated after having conducted detailed substantive empirical studies of particular social phenomena. In such studies he was concerned 'with using generalised conceptions in order to understand society as subject to lawful regularities' (Gerth & Mills 1974: 60). This is not the same as saying human affairs are subject to cast-iron laws.

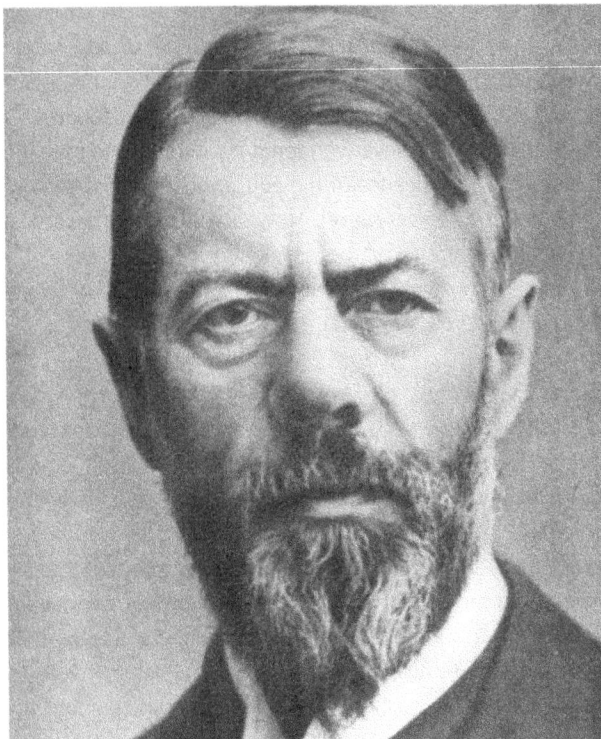

Figure 1.5 Max Weber
(Source: Image courtesy of INPRA)

Instead of searching for laws or establishing sociology as a social science, Weber immersed himself in detailed empirical studies. In the debate about whether there are laws of history and society, which both Marx and Durkheim, albeit differently, thought existed, Weber's empirical studies led him to believe and argue that there were no such laws regulating history and the economy and society. Sociology could also not establish social laws – in other words, be nomothetic. Weber's criticism of theoretical sociological perspectives was subtle. Weber did not think there was only one sociology. Being consistent, he even held that his own sociology was but one type of sociology among others. Bear this in mind in the final section of this chapter, which deals

with criticisms of the classical sociological tradition of Marx, Weber and Durkheim.

Instead of making comparisons between different events to establish the causes for them, it was more important to try to *understand* events that had taken place in the social world rather than formulating abstract ideas into which the world was thought to fit or laws with which it complied.

Understanding society
Weber consequently developed the notion of **Verstehen** into a methodological tool to analyse how individuals make sense of their world. *Verstehen* is similar in meaning to the Afrikaans word *verstaan* – to understand. If the natural sciences are widely considered to be the strong and epistemically 'hard' sciences, and social sciences are the 'soft' ones, we could say the truly 'hard' or difficult science is the science of understanding or *Verstehen* for Weber. Because, as we will shortly see, human beings all try to understand the world in their own unique ways, it should not be surprising that there have been multiple interpretations of *Verstehen* and this is why Weber assumes such a central role in sociology (see Ritzer 2000: 112–113).

Weber's explicit assumption
Weber wanted to get to the very basis, to the root of social life. To do this his main unit of analysis was not the social group like most sociologists, but the individual and individual action. Individualism was hence Weber's central and explicit assumption. This is because it is individuals who act in the social world.

For Weber, as individuals we all *interpret* the world around us. We seek meaning in our lives. In fact, Weber thought human beings were 'meaning-making' animals and that we did so in different ways. Individual meaningful action is central for Weber. What he thought needed to be understood, above all, was why individuals act in the way they do.

Individual action as the basic unit of social analysis
In Weber's interpretive sociology, the basic unit of social analysis was the individual and individual social action. Weber explicitly noted in his 1922 work *The Nature of Social Action* that sociology is:

the science whose object is to interpret the meaning of social action and thereby give a causal explanation of the way in which the action proceeds and the effects which it produces (Runciman 1991: 7).

Individual action for Weber, it should immediately be noted, is social. The concept of action is to be distinguished from behaviour. Behaviour is a response to a stimulus, an almost automatic and instinctual doing, with no intervening thought process or interpretation – like taking our hand away from a flame. Weber's concept of individual action is not just something we do out of our socialised habits or instinct. An act is imbued with intention and importantly, for Weber, is performed for a reason. An act has *significance* or *meaning* behind it. This explains why human agents engage in social action in the first place. Social action results from the independent agency of individuals. Such social action is not passive, but active and reactive. The action is social because it is directed at other human agents. In acting we generally take account of the social context within which we act and the reactions of others around us. In other words, social action is reciprocal.

For Weber, to understand society we must understand how we subjectively create meaning and how we act based on the meanings we attach to situations, events and others' actions. What is significant about Weber's emphasis on social action is his focus on the individual acting in institutional settings. Even when examining larger social groupings such as institutions or organisations, we cannot understand social phenomena without recognising that it is the social actions of individuals that compose them. As Weber puts it in his 1922 work *The Theory of Social and Economic Organisation*, only people act and 'for sociological purposes there is no such thing as a collective personality which "acts"' (Gerth & Mills 1974: 135). For Weber, institutions and organisations are, however, 'collective personalities' that have a meaning for individuals. We become fond of our university and may even get nostalgic for our old school. Such institutions actually exist and possess normative authority and we 'orient' our action in relation to them (see Gerth & Mills 1974: 135f). This is difficult to understand as we must both grasp how we as individuals *create* meaning, how we act based on the meanings we attach to situations and events, and combine this with the many social actions of others across society.

Social action is the basis and cause of human interaction and social events. This even applies to when we want to understand collective concepts such as 'state' and 'feudalism'. Such broader conceptual categories of human interaction were to be understood as the combined actions of individuals. This view immediately combines two seemingly polar opposites that are both essential to incorporate into social analysis – the individual and history, the individual and society, or the individual agent and social structure. Weber's interpretation of the social world, his

sociological imagination – how the actions of the individual and large-scale social structures are linked – is consequently a complex one. So how did Weber view collective concepts and social structure?

Three basic types of social structure

Weber thought we could only understand society if we understood social structure in terms of his central concept of social action. With social action as primary intellectual focus, Weberian interpretive sociology gets to the heart of explaining cause and effect in the social sphere. Individual social actions and interactions possess causal force and have organisational effects. **Social structure** must be explained in terms of meaningful *social action*. Society is hence not comprised of 'things' (material and non-material social facts) as it is for Durkheim, but must rather be understood as a web of meaningful beliefs and practices born out of social actions.

Weber divided the social world analytically into three basic social structures – association, community and (modern) society to which different forms of social action were linked. It should be noted that methodologically, in Weber's work, the three concepts and related forms of social action were derived from examining historical processes out of which these generalised concepts were derived.

Association and affectual social action

People come together and associate with one another when feelings or sentiments are shared. This is **affectual social action**. We associate with those with whom we feel we have an affinity. Some of our first friendships are formed in this way before we properly think about why and who we associate with socially. This is a very rudimentary and basic form of social interaction, yet modern society continues to be characterised by such associations and affectual (feeling) action. Weber, for instance, criticised the widely held view that American society was just a nation of atomised individuals. He pointed out the vast array of active voluntary associational groups of like-minded citizens in American society who share something in common. Weber was not too concerned, however, about this particular form of social action, but in its two other forms.

Community and traditional social action

Weber was interested in what he termed **traditional action**. This kind of social action is found in any close-knit social group going back to ancient times. Such social groups were originally simple and the actions and interactions between individuals within the social group were defined by habit and tradition. Where habit and tradition predominate, actions do not demand much prior thought and are generally unreflective. One does things in a certain way because that is always the way things have been done. This form of social action continues today. This is not to confuse traditional social action with instinctual behaviour. We do many things because we were taught that way and so traditional action was for Weber a primary type of social action.

Society and rational social action

This form of social action introduces Weber's most important distinction: many of our actions are rational, while others are not. When human interactions become more regular as populations become denser, and social organisation more complex, society becomes increasingly characterised by rational social action. Unlike affectual and traditional forms of social action, many of our social actions have an aim or goal. We can provide a reason or rationale for acting the way we did. These are rational actions of which, for Weber, there are two types.

We can act in a way that is a means towards a specific end. We study hard in order to pass exams. This is what Weber called **instrumental rationality** or instrumental social action. However, sometimes we act because of certain values that are important to us. We do household chores because we love our parents and want to help or meet our obligations. For Weber, this was **value-rational** action.

The limits of conceptual analysis (again)

This is not to say this analytical typology – dividing actions into types or kinds – can always be neatly and separately identified. We go off to university or work partly as that has become our routine – traditional action – as well as because we want to get a certificate or earn money – instrumental rational action. We also value education or work that introduces an element of value rationality into our action.

When rational forms of action predominate, we can speak of the collective form of rational actions as a whole and this, for Weber, was designated by his concept of **formal rationality**. Institutions, for instance, which operate to achieve calculated goals or ends by using universally applied rules and regulations, would constitute formal rationality. The law itself and **bureaucracy**, which we all especially encountered to register at university, would be examples. The collective form of the sum total of the value-rational actions of individuals, on the other hand, would constitute an instance of substantive rationality. Institutions that operate to achieve value-driven goals or

ends using calculated rational means to do so, such as social movements or religious organisations, which embody and promote a set of values and corresponding actions by their members, would be instances of substantive rationality.

Rationalisation in society

This brings us to Weber's key insight that modern society is marked by increasing **rationalisation**, both in individual actions and in social institutions. The process of rationalisation then is one in which individual actions are increasingly instrumentally rational and where formal rationality is institutionalised in the very structure of society. In arriving at this analysis of modern society, Weber asked the question as to why a rational capitalist economy emerged with modern society in the West. Both Chinese and Indian societies were, for instance, considerably more advanced than European society. Weber gave an important, if controversial, answer to this question.

Box 1.7 Testing Weber's 'spirit of capitalism' thesis

In explaining the triumph of capitalism, Max Weber argued that hard work, thrift, living a frugal life and saving and investing were values common to both the spirit of capitalism and Protestantism.

QUESTIONS

1. Which churches are the Protestant churches?
2. In your view, are the values of early capitalism and Protestantism the kind of values needed in South Africa today to ensure social, political and economic prosperity?
3. List the arguments – and note the evidence – for and against Weber's thesis.

The spirit of capitalism and religion

Weber addressed the question of why capitalism arose in the West in one of his most important works, *The Protestant Ethic and the Spirit of Capitalism* published in 1904. In this work Weber adopted a multicausal analysis of this large-scale socio-historical phenomenon. His focus was considerably broader than that of Marx, who centred his analysis on capital and capital accumulation in a capitalist economy.

Economic factors, such as the market, the money economy, a formally free labour force and increasingly complex accounting and banking institutions, featured strongly in Weber's analysis of capitalism. Political factors, such as the **nation-state** and government, and legal factors, such as laws governing private property, as well as the role of science and technology, all contributed to the emergence of a modern capitalist society in his view. More than these obviously structural features, what needed most especially to be factored into a comprehensive analysis of the emergence of Western capitalism was the cultural system of norms, values and beliefs regulating the conduct and actions of people.

The foundation of this cultural system, for Weber, was religion. In Weberian terms, capitalism can be defined as an economic system based on the pursuit of profit through exchange in the market, and the accumulation of wealth. In addition, the spirit of capitalism was the system of ideas, attitudes and beliefs, and related actions required for capitalism in the first place. For Weber, the entrepreneurial spirit of early capitalism was remarkably similar to the religious ethic of the Protestant churches in western Europe. In particular, Weber identified a clear correspondence between the values and norms of Calvinism and those of the early entrepreneurial capitalists. Hard work, thrift, living a frugal life and saving and investing were values that were common to both the spirit of capitalism and the Protestant faith. There was a distinct similarity, Weber argued, between the two sets of values that permitted capitalists to aggressively pursue wealth and yet see it as a duty. This strict religious ethic also provided motivation to a labour force that was disciplined, sober and hard working. Even more importantly, inequality was justified as a special dispensation from God in the Calvinist-inspired Protestant religious tradition. The reason is clear. If you followed the values of thrift and hard work, and lived a modest lifestyle, you were rewarded with wealth. What happened, according to Weber's theory, was that capitalism took root. His theory thereby attempted to explain the rise of capitalism in Europe and why it did not emerge elsewhere.

Class, status and party

It is clear that, for Weber, social class alone did not define the nature of social groupings in capitalist society. His analysis of **social stratification** is complex and multidimensional. For instance, the complex ways in which modern capitalist society was divided into social groups or 'layers', for instance, needed a more sophisticated theory to describe and explain social stratification. Weber defined class by reference to the market. Class, in Weberian terms, signals the opportunities or life chances available to an individual in a society dominated by the market where goods, services and commodities are bought and sold. If you do not think the market has an influence over how you feel and what your life chances are, just think about the difference in your

attitude to life at the beginning of a weekend depending on whether you have money or not – or whether you have *enough* money for all your plans if you are from a wealthy family! Note immediately that the *same* concept – class – picks out a different set of social phenomena from that of Marx's definition. Concepts and the way in which we define them analytically pick out social phenomena in different ways. Weber would say we *interpret* the world in different and unique ways, depending on the conceptual and theoretical lenses we employ.

Because Marx's conceptual dichotomy between the bourgeoisie and the proletariat was too crude a conceptual construction for Weber, he introduced the concept of status into his analysis of social stratification. Social status lies at the heart of how individuals construct meaning out of their lives. A plumber might earn more than a university lecturer, but the latter has greater social status. When combined with the concept of social class, a greater degree of accuracy can be achieved when examining how social groups are stratified. In addition, the group or political party to which you belonged was a further conceptual distinction which Weber applied in his study of similarities and differences central to investigating social stratification or **social differentiation**. Membership of the ruling party in South Africa, as elsewhere, has always played an important role in defining the life chances of individuals. This is equally true of the National Party under apartheid or the African National Congress under democracy.

Weber's typology of social stratification – **class**, **status** and **party** – is an example of how his central concept of social action enables the analysis of social structure. Weber has given weight to the motivating force of how individuals seek meaning and status in presenting this explanation of social stratification. You must admit that it is trickier to analyse different social groups in terms of Weber's three concepts as opposed to Marx's one concept of class. It is, arguably, however, a sharper analytical knife.

Ideal types

This brings us to the much-discussed **heuristic** device of Weber's ideal type for which he is famous in sociology. The **ideal type** is a logically constructed conceptual tool developed by the social scientist. It is hence a mental construct. However, unlike a concept which is a single knifelike tool, an ideal type is more like a mental toolbox. Weber constructed a range of ideal types to study history, society, social structures and social action. Of the ideal type Weber says, 'it cannot be found empirically anywhere in reality' (Shils & Finch 1949: 90) or in social life. Commentators have referred to the ideal type as a 'measuring tool' or 'yardstick' by which actual social phenomena can be evaluated (see Ritzer 2000: 115). Any social phenomenon will diverge from its ideal typical features and is best illustrated by way of Weber's own example – namely that of bureaucracy. Examining bureaucracy also serves the purpose of demonstrating the extent of the process of the increasing rationalisation of modern industrial society.

The continuing dominance of bureaucracy

Everyone is familiar with bureaucracy. Weber defined the ideal typical features of a bureaucracy as a rational form of social organisation that has a specific aim, consists of a continuous organisation of official functions, is hierarchical, has written rules and procedures, and its officials are technically trained servants who perform their duty in an impartial and unbiased manner. Bureaucracies were not, however, only established and organised in a rational manner, but also had **legal authority**. Do you recognise these features of a bureaucracy as a description of what happened when you last went to the local licensing office, government department or large financial institution? If not, you can fruitfully compare your actual experience with Weber's ideal type. When you do so you will quickly see how your experience with any actual bureaucracy diverges from the ideal type. The ideal type, the conceptual construct, not only serves as a tool to describe and analyse a specific social phenomenon, but in addition enables a prescription of how a bureaucratically organised institution could potentially function more efficiently.

Weber's study of bureaucracy showed how, as society becomes more complex, rationalisation increasingly occurs across ever-widening spheres of social life and impresses its legal authority over our social actions. This has implications and serious consequences for how we experience modern life.

Disenchantment

Sociologists can be a depressing lot. For Marx, capitalism is dominated by alienation. For Durkheim, society is characterised by anomie. For Weber, individuals are caught up in 'the iron cage' of increasingly powerful bureaucracies and ever tighter rules and regulations that constrain individuals' free and voluntary social actions, leaving them in a state of **disenchantment** with modern life. The enchanting wonder and mystery of the world has been eroded by the need to constantly have to make decisions in order to survive. We have become locked up in a mesh of bureaucratic regulations, rules, laws and procedures.

The reason for this, according to Weber, is because there is no other way in which a complex industrial society can be regulated. Today Weber might say that we only rediscover that it is indeed still an enchanting world when we manage to escape the iron cage when we go on holiday, can chill, smell the coffee again and do not have to think and make any decisions!

Weber's view of socialism

If Marx was critical of capitalism, so was Weber, but unlike Marx, Weber was not a revolutionary, nor did he think socialism would initiate and mark the end of capitalism and the bureaucratic state. Weber fundamentally disagreed with the view of a socialist society envisioned to run on more participative and democratic lines once political and economic power had been seized by the proletariat. On the contrary, when viewed historically over the past century, Weber seems to have better predicted that any society attempting to move towards socialism and be subject to greater conscious planning, independently of the organised chaos of the marketplace, would require more bureaucracy. Weber argued that no modern, complex industrial society could work without institutions being organised along bureaucratic lines. His reason was clear. Bureaucracy, for all its pitfalls when actually implemented, was the only and most rational way of organising complex societies.

Traditional and legal authority

Part of having been snared in the iron cage of an increasingly bureaucratic and rationalised society is the rational legal authority which accompanies it. This is the most efficient form of social regulation and organisation, and dominates modern society. This form of authority – or legitimate domination – replaced the traditional authority of previous, less complex societies based on kinship, **patriarchy** (rule by men) and **patrimonialism** (rule by a traditional military master). The ideal typical bureaucracy is useful to describe, explain and compare the workings of such societies with our more familiar one. Instead of a rational aim regulating society, there is the dictate of the traditional leader. Instead of written rules, there is the whim and interests of the patriarch. Instead of formal training, there are traditional customs which can be oppressive. Instead of impersonal bias, there is a feared and autocratic personality to confront.

Traditional authority and legal bureaucratic authority were for Weber, however, not the only forms of authority or domination.

Charisma and revolutionary leadership

From time to time on the stage of human history, members of social groups have reasons for elevating an individual who is seen or believed to have special, extraordinary and often superhuman powers. This is the leader imbued with **charisma** and charismatic authority. Such a person cuts through the 'red tape' of bureaucracy, can get things done, is a beacon of light in a disenchanted world and is treated with godlike status. Weber said this can happen to quite ordinary people, but that if members of a group imbue a person with these attributes, the process by which this happens can encourage such a person to manifest extraordinary qualities and become the personification of *charisma*.

Charisma is a force for revolution and for changing things. Charisma has the capacity to change how people view themselves and the world around them, and to shape it according to their own will. Such collective power finds its expression in the charismatic authority of the leader. When this happens, the re-enchantment of the world again seems possible, but to sustain this powerful, potentially socially revolutionary force it needs to be routinised for it to survive and realise the ambitious aims its members have for it. Does this Weberian image ring any bells and possess any analytical power to understand South African society since democracy in 1994? If the first part of the question is a resounding 'yes', how would you go about using this heuristic device to explain our current macro-situation in South Africa from a Weberian interpretive perspective?

Box 1.8 Meet the challenge of how sociology encourages social action and social change

It does not require much research to find some information – an anecdote, a saying, an event, an achievement or one of many stories – about Nelson Rolihlahla Mandela, widely and affectionately known as Madiba.

QUESTIONS

1. What evidence of charisma was displayed in the piece of information you found?
2. How might the lesson in charisma be routinised into the fabric of South African social life?
3. Who captures your imagination as charismatic in the Weberian sense? Explain!

Applying Weber to an everyday action

To provide an example from micro-sociology, we both create and embody meaning when we lift our hand to make a taxi

stop for us. How we ensure we get to university and not go to town is part of a wider social structure of meaning of how to catch a taxi in South Africa. The various meanings of our meaningful symbolic hand signs are foreign to any non-South African and have to be learned. In his work, Weber examined how these and other actions are *regularised* and *patterned* in the social structures of institutions and organisations in society. If particularly modern society is, as Weber argued, chiefly characterised by the increasing dominance of rational actions, especially instrumental rational actions, it has become part of us to learn such things and make our way in the world. As we do this, there are new theoretical challenges to confront.

1.4 Developments and challenges to classical sociological theory

As you would expect, there have been major developments, criticisms and challenges to classical sociological theory over the past century and longer. One such major challenge in South Africa today is the call for **decolonisation** made during student protests across South African universities in 2015 and 2016. A key question is how did theorising about society get from classical sociological theory to thinking about **decoloniality**? What follows here can only begin to answer this question. This section briefly outlines how the classical tradition emerged, was interrogated, developed and was criticised. By placing a few steppingstones in the flow of theoretical developments in social thought, this exercise begins to reveal the roots of decolonial thinking, or *decoloniality*. As Weber taught, you know this will be an interpretation and can be neither systematic nor complete. In doing so, however, the names and key ideas of a few of the sociologists discussed in this textbook will also be mentioned.

1.4.1 The sociology of knowledge

Recall the importance of the social context – the specific time and place – in which theory develops. To examine how social context impacts on knowledge, whether knowledge is *produced* or results from *discovery*, means to engage in the sociology of knowledge. The **sociology of knowledge** is a theory or approach to talk about *how* knowledge itself emerges in specific social contexts. For one theorist, this applies to all ideas, theories and knowledge, including natural scientific theories (Bloor 1976). It certainly applies to the sociological theories we have been discussing as well as to the call for decolonisation. The object of investigation is hence the origin and circumstances of the emergence of social and sociological theories themselves. While this approach to understanding theory can be traced back to Georg Lucàcs – inspired by Marx and who was a friend of Weber – this idea is strongly associated with Karl Mannheim (1893–1947). Mannheim was influenced by Marx, but was also a friend of Weber and Lucàcs, and was opposed to a positivist perspective. For Mannheim, social theories and the assumptions underlying them are bound to particular times and places. He thought that theory should seek to understand what people think about society and not try to develop hypotheses to explain society. More than that, Mannheim considered all thought to further *reflect* the social position of its thinker. A person's class position, membership of a status group and generation (age) *locates* an individual in a specific social and historical time and place that will shape much of how they think.

This final section of the chapter adopts a sociology of knowledge approach by locating thinkers in their time and place. It will enable us to move from the classical sociological theoretical tradition of Marx, Weber and Durkheim to noting a few key paradigmatic shifts in social thought. We will end with some key concepts and ideas of contemporary theorists of decoloniality, the Latin Americans Anibal Quijano and Walter Mignolo, and the South African-based decolonial thinker, Sabelo J Ndlovu-Gatsheni.

1.4.2 The assumptions flowing from the social context of classical sociological theory

Let us start by making *explicit* the assumptions of the classical theorists. Remember that an assumption is something we take for granted, is generally *implicit* and is not easy to detect. In fact, it is often only in the light of a new perspective and experience that the assumptions of previous thinkers can be identified. What were the shared assumptions of Marx, Weber and Durkheim born of their social context? In brief, their social thought emerged out of and was an expression of the social context of **modernity** – the period from the late 18th century in Europe onwards. This was the period characterised by the industrial revolutions and the emergence of democracy along with the modern nation state. It was a period of momentous social change, crucially marked by the shift from a rural agricultural society to an urban industrial one. This historical context, importantly, gave birth to sociology as a discipline, which came to 'find a place *within*' and '*reflect* upon' this 'project of modernity' (Smart 2000: 447).

As you know, for Marx, this period signalled the rise of the proletariat who would usher in *progress* to a classless society. For Durkheim, modernity signalled the end of mechanical solidarity, the rise of the individual and

a more complex division of labour, heralding *progress* in human affairs. For Weber, it would be the emergence and institutionalisation of bureaucracy and increasing *rationalisation* and efficiency that had come to dominate industrial society. From the standpoint of our time and place as South African sociologists – and our respective class, status and generational positions – it is worth continually asking: Do these key conclusions help explain or express what is happening in our society – both historically and in the present?

In reflecting their social and historical context, the classical tradition had mainly two assumptions in common. They shared a belief in progress, both in human and social affairs and especially in technology. Despite significant differences, they also shared a commitment to scientific rationality and some form of universalism. Society would progress, Durkheim thought, as science was based on facts and so was value neutral and objective. Subjective bias could be eliminated, and social science could discover universal laws of human behaviour. Marx thought his historical materialist approach revealed the laws of development and progress in human affairs as different modes of production succeeded one another. Facts and values were intertwined as values were reflected in the class one occupied during these unfolding historical periods. Weber, as you now know of course, did not think natural scientific models of thinking applied to human society, nor that there were strict laws of historical development. However, he did think objectivity and value neutrality could be achieved by rational thinking and a careful empirical, historically sensitive study of society that would lead to progress. In short, these three 'founders' of the classical sociological theoretical 'canon' shared the belief in progress and scientific rationality. Much social, sociological and social scientific thinking would share these fundamental assumptions, which would also come to be seriously challenged.

1.4.3 Applying the sociology of knowledge to sociological theory

Fashions change, not only regarding the clothing we wear, but in sociological theory as well. As thinkers try to keep abreast of changing social circumstances, they often reflect the key concerns of their social milieu as their theories express what is happening in society. When many sociologists followed Durkheim in seeing themselves engaged in sociology as science in the strict sense, Charles Cooley (1864–1929) formulated the idea of the 'looking-glass self'. The individual's sense of self is like a mirror as we see ourselves as others see us. This idea remains contemporary as we worry about what others think of us and so we adapt what we say and do accordingly. Who we are is, in an important sense, an expression of our own time and place. The same idea, but reflecting social experience differently, can be found in the work of the great American thinker, sociologist and social reformer, WEB Du Bois (1868–1963). Du Bois formulated the idea of 'double consciousness' to articulate the perspectives of African Americans. Admired by Max Weber, Du Bois wrote that:

> ... it is a peculiar sensation, this double-consciousness, this sense of always looking at one's self through the eyes of others, of measuring one's soul by the tape of a world that looks on in amused contempt and pity. One feels this twoness – an American, a negro: two souls, two thoughts, two unreconciled strivings; two warring ideals in one dark body, whose dogged strength keeps it from being torn asunder (cited in Scott & Marshall 2005: 170).

WEB Du Bois clearly deepened Durkheim's notion of *homo duplex* and also followed his view of sociology as a strict science. Written in the time of 'the golden age in the sociology of blacks in America' (Ladner 1973: 3), this perspective would be drowned out in the formal academic sociological tradition that later came to be dominated by the **structural functionalism** of Talcott Parsons (1902–1979). Parsons sought to combine the stress Weber laid on the individual and the science of Durkheim that aimed at an overarching holism – a unified and universal theory that explained society as a whole. Parsons thought that individuals generally followed accepted rules and norms, and shared the values of the community and society to which they belonged. He assumed a shared set of **values** and **norms** in American society. WEB Du Bois showed this was problematic in a racially discriminatory society.

Parsons' sociological theory nevertheless dominated America and much of sociology more broadly, as his theory *reflected* the stability of American society after World War II, but major social events occurred that had a significant impact on social theory in general and on sociological theory in particular. Some of these are only fully appreciated in retrospect, and the Algerian national liberation struggle (1954–1962) is one such example. Franz Fanon was 'totally immersed in it personally, intellectually and politically' (Neocosmos 2016: 114). Fanon's work prefigured the challenge to the **structuralist** orientation of much of European and North American social theorising.

Parsonian structural functionalism was, for instance, unable to explain the challenges to Western society in the 1960s. American society was shaken by the Vietnam war. European society was convulsed in May 1968 when a million workers and students took to the streets. In the same year the mass musical event that was Woodstock captured the imagination of the new hippie generation – tragically followed by the shooting of students on university campuses in the United States in 1971. New social and sociological theorising flowed from these events and signalled major shifts in the self-understanding and social theorising of both Europeans and Americans as they needed to find new theories to understand and explain massive social change. It was in this context that C Wright Mills introduced Marx's work into the sociological theoretical 'canon' – in direct response to the 'radicalisation of metropolitan university students' (Connell 2007: 23) even though a conflict perspective had been introduced to sociology in the United States in the late 19th century.

In American society in the decade to follow, 'many assumptions of the academic world were challenged' (Blauner & Wellman 1973: 310). In South Africa, the mass strikes of workers in Durban in 1973 and the June 1976 uprising of high-school students in Soweto had a similar impact on apartheid society, the struggle for political liberation and on social and political theory, such as writing 'history from below', which impacted powerfully on university social science curricula.

When confronted with fresh social conditions and changing social contexts, social theorists must go back to the past or forge ahead and develop new theories. While Marx's work came to the fore in the 1960s in the United States and in South Africa in the 1970s, other thinkers, in Europe particularly, sought new theoretical horizons in response to their social context. What seemed increasingly clear to many was that the search for a single and unified epistemic project and way of understanding the world could not be realised. The assumptions of scientific rationality and progress could no longer be taken for granted. The modernist project seemed to have failed. The reason for this was clear as 'the construction of modernity produced untold suffering and misery for its victims, ranging from the peasantry, proletariat, and artisans oppressed by capitalist industrialisation to the exclusion of women from the public sphere, to the genocide of imperialist domination' (Best & Kellner 1991: 3). A new theoretical paradigm in social theory now conceived of society as having entered a *postmodern* age.

In response to this major shift in social thinking, in the 1980s George Ritzer, the writer of a well-known textbook, *Sociological Theory* (2000), introduced Georg Simmel (1858–1918) alongside Marx, Durkheim and Weber as part of the classical theoretical sociological tradition. Simmel engaged in micro-sociological studies and influenced **symbolic interactionism**, which you will encounter later in this book. While writing over a century ago, the flavour of Simmel's work is even 'post' modern. As you will now see, postmodernism holds that there is no overarching universal idea or theoretical approach that adequately captures and understands the totality of the complexity and unpredictable consequences of modernity itself.

Postmodernism and poststructuralism

Postmodern thinking fundamentally challenged the assumptions of progress and scientific thinking. Influenced by rapid modernisation after World War II, in France especially, postmodern thinking proper emerged out of experimentation in art and culture in Europe in the 1960s. These cultural innovations were a response to 'the high-tech media society, emergent processes of change and transformation' (Best & Kellner 1991: 3). An emphasis on **plurality**, **diversity** and **difference** replaced the modernist aim of attempting to accurately represent the world through carefully defined universal and abstract concepts. Any single or absolute universal 'truth' or grand overarching narrative, which tried to capture the totality of what was happening in society, was no longer deemed possible. 'Truth' increasingly came to be seen as subjective, and knowledge appeared to be relative to social position, stance, standpoint and perspective. **Relativism** in knowledge hence asserted itself powerfully. Two central theorists in this wide-ranging and multidisciplinary endeavour were the philosopher Jean-Francois Lyotard (1924–1998) and the sociologist and philosopher, Jean Baudrillard (1929–2007). Among many other prominent theorists, Michel Foucault (1926–1984) significantly influenced both postmodern and poststructuralist thought, but refused to be pinned down by these labels.

The idea that the world had entered a postmodern age relied on three main claims. The first was that the ideas of progress, rationality and scientific progress were no longer adequate as they did not and could not explain cultural differences. The second was that 'high' culture – including abstract sociological theorising – could no longer be held to be superior to so-called 'low' or popular culture – which would soon include indigenous knowledge, African philosophy, Latin American theories of liberation and other

'Third World' or developing society perspectives. Thirdly, in a social context in which technologies were becoming increasingly dominant with the emergence of *virtual reality* – not nearly as seemingly real as it is now – it was 'no longer possible securely to separate the "real" from the "copy", or the "natural" from the "artificial"' (During 1993: 170).

This resulted in a major critique of the modernist project. With the shared assumptions of modernism rejected, the result was huge disagreement, debate and 'disputes, even wars, between liberals, conservatives and leftists' (Lyotard 1993: 172). Major arguments ensued as to who precisely had been 'truly victimised by the lack of development – whether it was the poor, the worker, the illiterate' (Lyotard 1993: 172). For Lyotard, one thing was clear – that 'all parties concurred in the belief that enterprises, discoveries and institutions are legitimate only insofar as they contribute to the emancipation of mankind' (Lyotard 1993: 172).

Around the same time as the emergence of postmodernism, another train of thought was articulated – poststructuralism. This challenge to modernist classical theory was not the work of a sociologist, but a semiologist – Ferdinand Saussure (1857–1913). We cannot go into the interesting matter that Saussure was the grandfather of structuralism and yet his work was reinterpreted as the origin of poststructuralism! In brief, the theoretical work of semiologists such as Saussure is to interpret the meaning and significance of **signs** and **symbols**. Systems of signs and symbols – such as the specific mother languages we all speak – have their *own* rules, criteria and methods that are internal to them. You can speak a language other than your mother tongue, but only *truly* understand it when you grasp its many subtle nuances and inflections that belong to it alone. Each language and form of speech grasp and understand reality in their own very specific and sometimes very different ways. If you speak more than one language – which very many South Africans do – only a moment's thought will convince you of this. In short, we do not and are not able, as the classical tradition assumed, to unproblematically represent reality with carefully defined concepts which then represent or picture the world accurately. Our concepts do not simply name or stand for the things which they aim to represent in thought. Words and signs can have meaning without referring to things in the world, and only make sense within the rules of how our respective languages and forms of speech are used and understood. That simply means there is no universal or single way of understanding the world. Even if you have grasped this – as you probably have if you have thought about it – this is tough theoretical stuff and will not be part of your first-year exams, but here is a quick example which may make you smile.

Many years ago, under apartheid, a South African Sotho language university lecturer went to Lesotho and saw a road sign which read: *Butle*! What? Bootle, he thought! This lecturer did not understand a word in his own language. *Butle* in Sesotho means 'slowly'. He did not understand the road sign as the word *butle* occurred in a context outside his own South African Sesotho linguistic tradition. He could be forgiven as there are still no road signs in South Africa in an indigenous African language. The point is that the road sign – the word *butle* – only made immediate sense to Sesotho speakers in Lesotho. The Sesotho lecturer, of course, figured this out after much astonishment and huge merriment, and shared his experience with his students. Language is an *autonomous* system of linking all signs (written words themselves and road signs as an example) with the mental image associated with them. Every language has its own internal structure that goes far beyond the life and death of the individuals who use it.

The point is this: you simply need to note the massive challenge to the assumptions of classical theory to which postmodern thinking gave rise. Simply put, the challenge of postmodernism and poststructuralism is that the shared assumptions of modernist thought – including the classical sociological tradition – were no longer tenable. Despite raging debate, which continues, note this important point: It enables us to take a further step towards our theoretical present.

Anticolonialism and postcolonialism
Postcolonial theory emerged out of the social context of struggles against colonialism and anticolonial frames of thought. A South African sociologist, Windsor Leroke (1998: 54), succinctly summarised the key thinkers of anticolonial discourses, and differentiates between anticolonial and postcolonial perspectives:

Anti-colonial discourses were put forth, in Africa, for example, by diverse writers/activists such as Frantz Fanon (psychiatrist) [see 1967; 2004], Leopold Dedar Senghor (poet) [see 1964], Cheikh Anta Diop (historian) [see 1974], Albert Memmi [see 1990], Amical Cabral [see 1973; 1980], Aime Cesaire (poet) [see 1972], Walter Rodney (historian) [see 1972]. The focus of their critique was colonialism and its effects on the lives of the colonised. Thus, their critique tended to be external; it was directed at the colonialists. It is on this

point that post-colonialism differs from anti-colonial discourses, in that their criticism is largely internal.

Leroke (1998: 54) goes on to define postcolonialism and notes key postcolonial thinkers:

Post-colonialism is a reflection on the post-colonial situation in Africa. Thus, it locates its critique inside the internal conditions of the independent countries. Its proponents include diverse writers such as Ngugi wa Thiong'o [see 1981; 1993], Valentine Mudimbe [see 1988], Anthony Kwame Appiah [see 1992], Edward Said [see 1993], Homi Bhabha [see 1994], Christopher Miller [see 1985], Trinh T, Minh-ha [see 1989], Gayatri Spivak [see 1991; 1993] and Pauline Houtoundji [see 1983]. As such, post-colonialism means different things to different writers. However, what all have in common is a critical rethinking of present Third World conditions. In this sense, post-colonialism becomes a reconstructive exercise.

These thinkers articulated the experience of life and the struggles of African people, and contributed to political liberation in Africa and across the global South. Central to anticolonial struggles, resistance to colonialism and postcolonial thinking was both Marxism and a framework of ideas emanating from postmodern and poststructuralist theoretical perspectives. The multidisciplinary academic discipline of postcolonialism or postcolonial studies expresses, in different degrees and contrasts, these two major influences. The Marxist orientation emphasises the economic dominance of the North over the South. The postmodern and poststructuralist orientation places special value on the human dimension – the importance of language and culture. Both theoretical orientations stress how the colonial encounter resulted in the division between coloniser and the colonised. Of particular significance is how black scholarship challenged the assumptions born out of Euro-North American social theory.

Black scholarship
Sociology only became closely connected to the black Afro-American people in the social context of emancipation and the end of slavery (Ellison 1973). Objectivity and value neutrality then still dominated social scientific thinking and scientific method, but instead of failing to treat the experience of black Americans objectively in the name of science, sociology had justified 'anti-democratic and unscientific racial attitudes and practices' (Ellison 1973:

84). This was only debunked by Gunnar Myrdal's study on race relations, *The American Dilemma*, in 1944, which showed that the values social scientists took for granted could not be assumed, but had to be made explicit. In the late 1940s a black American sociologist, E Franklin Fraser (1894–1962), pointed out the importance of social context for social theorising. Prefiguring a decolonial perspective, in comparing African and African American intellectuals, Franklin Fraser argued as early as 1962 that 'all African intellectuals begin with the fact of the *colonial experience* of the African' (Franklin Fraser 1962: 57) (author's emphasis). He did not think that Afro-American scholars took their own experience of racial discrimination seriously.

Franklin Fraser was writing when there were very few black students in American universities – still under two per cent at college level in 1969 (Wilhelm 1973: 136). The social context of the civil rights movement would change this – as well as the university curriculum – and challenge white-dominated sociology. Black students of sociology and other social sciences started asking: 'Why should we study classical sociological theory and be taught nothing about the history of Black sociological thought?' (Ladner 1973: xxv). Tough questions were asked about formal sociological theory. From the standpoint and location of Afro-American students, one postgraduate asked: 'What kind of graduate training or socialisation do Black students majoring in sociology receive?' (Davidson 1973: 23). The short answer was that while the objective situation is the same, 'the subjective state is actually quite different for black and white students', with black students facing racism and what Davidson refers to as 'internal colonialism' – which he defined as 'the social and cultural expression of racism' (Davidson 1973: 24). Chapter 9 on race and its discussion of colonialism, **Eurocentrism** and the 'colonial encounter' will permit the framing of this experience and how these questions are mirrored in South African universities today.

During these years of the early 1970s, here at home, Frantz Fanon's *The Wretched of the Earth* ([1963] 2004) was being circulated at the University of Natal by Steve Biko in his dormitory to 'friends and comrades – writers, activists, community workers, actors, students ...' – described as 'the intellectual centre of the Black Consciousness movement' (Bhabha 2004: xxviii–xxix). Fanon was one of the 20th century's most important theorists of revolution, colonialism and racial difference. According to Homi Bhabha, Fanon extended the 'economistic theories of Marxism towards a greater emphasis on the importance of psychological and cultural liberation' (Bhabha 2004: xxix). This is central to understanding Steve Biko's analysis of apartheid society

and the experience of black South Africans as expressed in his philosophy of **Black Consciousness**. Social theorising cannot simply be an abstract theoretical intellectual exercise. This theoretical point is an important one. The cold intellect and its abstract formulations had to be supplemented by the warm heart of psychological awareness.

In 1978, when Steve Biko's seminal text, *I Write What I Like* (2006), was first published, the legitimate representatives of the majority of South Africans were either banned, banished, imprisoned or in exile. While fully recognising these leaders, Biko was critical of their analysis of apartheid society, whether coming from a Marxist-inspired critique or an Africanist one. Biko was an extraordinarily subtle and nuanced philosopher, social theorist and political thinker. Prefiguring contemporary decolonial thinking, Biko's starting point was the immediate *lived experience* of being black in a racially discriminatory white-dominated colonial society. In explaining the philosophy of Black Consciousness adopted in the policy manifesto of the organisation he founded in December 1971, the South African Students Organisation (SASO), he 'defined blacks as those who are by law or tradition politically, economically and socially discriminated against as a group in South African society and identifying themselves as a unit in the struggle towards the realisation of their aspirations' (Biko 2006: 52). Clear theoretical thinking is required to align this definition with the next sentence in *I Write What I Like*:

This definition illustrates to us a number of things:

1. *Being black is not a matter of pigmentation – being black is a reflection of a mental attitude.*

2. *Merely by describing yourself as black you have started on a road towards emancipation you have committed yourself to fight against all forces that seek to use your blackness as a stamp that marks you as a subservient being* (Biko 2006: 52).

In the following three pages of his book, Biko succinctly distinguishes between non-white and black, and further defines Black Consciousness (BC) as that 'which seeks to infuse the black community with a new-found pride in themselves, their efforts, their value systems, their culture, their religion and their outlook to life' (2006: 53). The aim of Black Consciousness is 'to completely transform the system' and show what 'liberation' and the 'free self' entails (2006: 53). Biko goes on to criticise Marxian 'Class Theory' (2006: 54), and identifies 'white racism' (2006: 54) as the central target of Black Consciousness. Sociologically astute, Biko points out that despite there being a 'few good whites' and a 'few bad blacks' (2006: 55), his concern is with 'group attitudes and group politics' (2006: 55). Biko explains the relation between them and the resolution for the future (yet to be attained) in terms of Hegelian **dialectics** (Biko 2006: 52–55). To note only one point in his rich text, Biko employs a sociology of knowledge approach. He argues that it was the political independence of 'so many African states within so short a time' and not 'the American "Negro" movement' which was responsible for the 'growth of awareness among South African blacks' (Biko 2006: 75). Biko thereby points to the immediate and familiar experience of black South Africans as the social basis for his own philosophy and political practice – a rare feat among social theorists. In having his own and his black compatriots as his starting point, Biko's work anticipates decolonial theory.

Decolonial theory

Figure 1.6 Sabelo Ndlovu-Gatsheni

These few steppingstones have brought us to today's intellectual and political moment. Our grasp of this must be theoretical and intellectual, political and practical. Clearly, we can only make a start.

To grasp what the call for decolonisation means, we need to define and distinguish **colonialism** and **decolonisation** from **coloniality** and **decoloniality**. The key insight is that the legacies of colonialism, in South Africa for instance, continue to live on after the departure of the colonial powers (Jansen 2017: 157). Coloniality is a global power structure (Maldonado-Torres 2007). Coloniality is also an 'epochal condition' and an 'epistemological design' (Ndlovu-Gatsheni 2013: 11). Coloniality is thus different

from and survives beyond colonialism (Maldonado-Torres 2007: 243). Maldonado-Torres (cited in Ndlovu-Gatsheni 2015c: 487) explains how this happens:

Coloniality ... refers to long-standing patterns of power that emerged as a result of colonialism, but that define culture, labour, inter-subjectivity relations, and knowledge-production well beyond the strict limits of colonial administrations.

Recall that knowledge reflects not only the social context and position of its thinkers, but that significant social events, liberation wars, workers' strikes and popular uprisings often have an especially marked effect on social thought. University students' call for decolonisation did this in our context in 2015 and 2016, even if this process had started during the apartheid era. Crucially, the call for decolonisation, most especially decolonising the mind, thinking and the curriculum, is not only political, but also represents a serious epistemic challenge **postcolonial** societies face.

The concept of decolonisation initially referred to the process of *political emancipation* from colonial rule – in Africa, starting with Ghana in 1957 and ending in South Africa in 1994. Decoloniality, however, refers primarily to an epistemic and political project (Mignolo 2009). It is best to work through this issue historically and look at the history of colonisation from the standpoint of our current geographical location, namely South Africa.

The decolonial scholar Sabelo J Ndlovu-Gatsheni asks where one must start when examining the 'long interaction of Africa with outside world' – one which goes back to before Europe existed (2015: 17). Colonial invasions of Egypt occurred before the emergence of the Greek civilisation over 2 500 years ago. North Africa was also subject to invasions before it became part of the Roman Empire by 147 BCE and was later colonised by the Arabs in the seventh century. It is only in the 15th century, however, with the arrival of Christopher Columbus in North America in 1492, that we can speak of a 'Euro-North American-centric modernity'. Citing a range of decolonial scholars, Grosfoguel especially (2011), Ndlovu-Gatsheni (2015: 17) describes the emergence of this global phenomenon as follows:

[T]he dawn of Euro-North American-centric modernity gave birth to a modern world- system that decolonial theorists understood as constitutively racially **hierarchised, patriarchal, sexist, imperial, colonial, capitalist,** *Christian-centric,* **hetero-normative,** *asymmetrical and modernist ...*

Check the Glossary at the beginning of this book for the meanings of these terms and concepts in order to grasp the extent of what the formulation 'Euro-North American-centric modernity' means. There is much to take in here.

The **colonisation** of Africa (and elsewhere) defined Africans (and other colonised peoples) as an uncivilised *anthropos* – a biological species – to be differentiated from a supposedly civilised *humanitas* – the sacrosanct personhood of collective humanity. In the mind of the Euro-North American, shaped by a totalising universalist epistemic framework, this justified '[e]nslavement, conquest, colonisation, dispossession, domination, repression and exploitation [which] characterised the dragging of Africa into Euro-North American-centric civilisation' (Ndlovu-Gatsheni 2015: 19).

In short, there was one set of rules for white Euro-North Americans who considered themselves superior to Africans and other colonised societies, and another for those subjected to domination and enslavement whose labour and lives were forced to serve Euro-North American society and its conception, belief and consequent attempts at 'human progress and promised emancipation, civilisation and development' (Ndlovu-Gatsheni 2015: 19).

Even after *political* decolonisation in Africa in the 20th century, most importantly for understanding key concepts, both the *effects* and *practices* of colonialism and colonisation remained – continued to live on, in other words. What remained and survived was *coloniality*. In the name of the 'civilising mission, emancipation and development' of Eurocentrism, the **hidden agenda** of coloniality 'enabled racial classification of human population, enslavement of non-European people, primitive accumulation, imperialism, colonialism, apartheid and neo-colonialism' (Ndlovu-Gatsheni 2015: 19). To 'decolonise the mind', as Ngugi wa Thiong'o first put it (wa Thiong'o 1981), means to understand both the self and the world from the perspective and point of view of those who have been subject to these forces. This means taking on the epistemic project of decoloniality. For if a society is colonised, and what justifies this is a totalising epistemic framework, which by definition negates and erases the possibility of any other views, then this means that knowledge itself is also colonised. If this occurs, there is the need to *decolonise knowledge*. This entails a fundamental epistemic challenge to the way in which Euro-North American thought and practice 'described, conceptualised and ranked' the world, as Walter Mignolo expressed it (cited in Ndlovu-Gatsheni 2015: 20). Ndlovu-Gatsheni (2015b: 22) provides the reason for this need to *rethink* dominant social scientific theories:

Epistemologically and theoretically speaking, dominant social science theories (structuralism, post-structuralism, post-modernism and post-colonialism) are experiencing an epistemic limit.

The question arises: how does one go beyond the epistemic limits of classical sociological thinking and its subsequent development?

Decolonial thinking

How is one to engage in decolonial thinking? There are two aspects which need to be taken seriously, both of which Euro-North American thought ignored, passed over in silence or simply assumed. For Mignolo (2009) this means taking seriously one's own geographical location (that of colonised peoples) and one's own body politics (being colonised, oppressed, disadvantaged, black) as the *starting point* of thinking and theorising. Mignolo directly challenges what he calls the 'zero point' of the dominant hegemonic epistemology of Euro-North American people and society. Think of Mignolo's notion of the 'zero point' as the European philosopher in his armchair engaged in thought, but taking his own privileged position for granted. Intellectual work that results from this location and social context all too often neglects to consider the power of social context and circumstances that shape thought and knowledge. We need to take our own context and position seriously to move beyond this framing limit of thought. This requires decolonial thinking – decoloniality to be precise. Ndlovu-Gatsheni (2015: 485c) spells out what the concept of decoloniality refers to:

Decoloniality is not only a longstanding political and epistemological movement aimed at liberation of (ex-)colonised peoples from coloniality but also a way of thinking, knowing and doing.

Further, 'Decoloniality exposes the "hidden script" [or hidden agenda] of modernity known as coloniality' (Ndlovu-Gatsheni 2015: 19).

There are three major aspects to decolonial thinking, knowing and doing. Leaning on Ndlovu-Gatsheni (see 2015c: 490), there are three key concepts or units of analysis to be taken into account. The first is the *coloniality of power*. This concept permits analysis of the classical Euro-American universalist dominant epistemologically rooted power structure. It 'enables delving deeper' into how the world was divided by binary thinking (either/or; good/evil; owner/slave; black/white) expressed socially and globally as the beneficiaries of imperialism, colonialism and apartheid (*humanitas*/allegedly civilised) and its victims (*anthropos*/supposedly uncivilised).

The second concept or unit of analysis is the *coloniality of knowledge*. This refers to examining epistemological issues and the production of knowledge and whose purposes and interests the dominant global epistemic framework serves. It further permits examining how the indigenous knowledge of oppressed peoples was marginalised and thereby disempowered.

The third unit of analysis is the *coloniality of being*. This unit of analysis explores how what it is to be human was disfigured by colonialism, how the construction of modern human subjectivity was skewed and how especially Afro-American and African scholars started looking at the world afresh. Notions of 'negritude' and the 'African personality' reasserted and restored self-pride and dignity in the context of a 'dehumanising colonialism' by way of 'the "**objectification**/thingification/**commodification**" of Africans' (Ndlovu-Gatsheni 2015c: 490).

In short: 'Decoloniality announces the broad 'decolonial turn' that involves the 'task of the very decolonisation of knowledge, power and being, including institutions such as the university' (Maldonado-Torres 2011, cited by Ndlovu-Gatsheni 2015c: 490).

Not to be simplistic, however, it needs to be understood that decolonisation is itself a social science construct born of its social context. Decolonisation theory assumes a number of perspectives, namely as the decentring of European knowledge (shifting the centralised perspective of Euro-American epistemology and practice) and the Africanisation of knowledge (adopting an African perspective). Decolonisation can be taken as additive-inclusive knowledge; as critical engagement with settled knowledge; as encounters with entangled knowledges; and as the repatriation of occupied knowledge (and society) (see Jansen 2017: 156–163).

Box 1.9 Decolonising the postcolonial university

New theories and new thinking present surprises. In his lecture, 'Decolonising the postcolonial university', delivered at the University of Cape Town on 22 August 2017, the renowned African scholar and global decolonisation theorist, Mahmood Mamdani, said Afrikaans 'represents the most successful decolonising initiative on the African continent'.

(Source: *Mail&Guardian Online* 2017)

QUESTIONS

Discuss the following questions with a fellow sociology student:
1. Is Mamdani talking here about political decolonisation or the epistemic and cultural project of decoloniality?
2. Do you find this statement surprising? If so, why? If not, what reasons do you have for holding this view?
3. Did you find contrasting and conflicting interpretations of South African society and history coming into your discussion? If so, can you relate them to the theories in this chapter?

Decolonial imaginations

One way in which decolonial thinking can be thought of is as *specifying*, *localising* and *contextualising* and thereby *deepening* the 'sociological imagination' first proposed by C Wright Mills. Remember that the sociological imagination requires *linking* our own *personal biography* with our own *social and historical context*. Doing this enables us to see *how what we think and how we act* are powerfully influenced by the limits and constraints our *socialised upbringing* impose on us, but which also reveal the possibilities our own independent agency and capacity for action can achieve. Walter Mignolo's injunction to start with *the material basis of our own body politics and own geographical location* can be seen as *concretely specifying* our perspective by making explicit and taking our *race, class, gender and location* as the *starting point* of thinking and theory.

Adopting this standpoint both builds on yet breaks with traditional classical thinking as it takes our own time, place and situation seriously. It also means that there is not a single universal decolonial imagination, but many **decolonial imaginations**. How the development of such a **pluriversal** epistemic reconstruction of society will cohere and unfold in the future may well be largely up to the generation of readers of this textbook. In short, this is only the start of new understanding and the realisation of the theoretical task ahead. The age-old ambitions of social and sociological thinking and practice to achieve emancipation failed. It is now necessary in our social context to develop a locally contextualised epistemic for broader liberation in society to come to fruition.

Finally, an important point of departure of this introduction to sociology is that theoretical thinking does not lie in burning theoretical bridges. For ill or good, all thinkers inherit a socialised and particular geographically located epistemic paradigm from within which thinking must start. This book presents sociological theories and views with Western origins as steppingstones to understand social phenomena. Its objective is to empower you, the student of sociology, in developing your own sociological, and indeed decolonial imagination, not to impose or subordinate your views to any particular theory or epistemic framework. Recall how thinkers such as Frantz Fanon and Steve Biko used Western knowledge to confront Western forces. Can you similarly apply theory and write it from the vantage point of where you are sitting now?

Summary

- Sociological concepts and theory provide the intellectual basis for social scientific investigation and social research. Socialised by significant social others in society and powerfully shaped by such and other social contexts, social analysts nevertheless strive to understand society in a way that transcends common sense, the results of which qualify as social scientific knowledge, however provisional such knowledge, by its very nature in our contemporary times, happens to be.
- The criteria of a good social scientific theory in general and sociological theories in particular are simplicity, logical coherence and factual evidence. This distinguishes them from social theories and ideology.
- Identifying assumptions underlying theories is instructive. Nothing can be taken for granted regarding knowledge in general, but especially in the social sciences where the social analyst is intimately implicated in the object of their study, ie the social interactions and affairs and goings-on of social life.
- The difference between natural and social science, and whether sociology needs to adhere to the methodological canons of the natural sciences, demarcates the social scientific perspectives that lie at the basis of sociology. Questions about science, knowledge and how all human endeavours are humanly created social constructions lie at the basis of all sociology and constitute its primary epistemological challenge.
- The chapter introduced the generally accepted, three main theoretical perspectives of sociology as its foundations, yet which are not exhaustive of a young discipline that is required to keep up with a rapidly changing social world.
- The contribution of the classical theorist, Auguste Comte, and his formulation of the naming of the discipline of sociology and the criteria for natural scientific knowledge that he formulated remains in practice, it was suggested, to be the basis of what constitutes knowledge and social science.
- Positivist social science, combined with evidence of the manner in which some key concepts of Émile Durkheim treat social reality, continues to stand as a challenge that the aim of certainty in knowledge, uniquely combined with the view that society is normative, is an epistemic endeavour worth pursuing in the social sciences.
- Introducing critical social science and a few of the key concepts of Karl Marx clearly showed that a grand theoretical story of human social life remains relevant to understanding contemporary social issues such as wealth, poverty and social inequality, and the resulting social dislocation and marginalisation of a significant proportion of the world's population and which predominate as features of social life in developing societies such as the one to which this textbook directly applies.
- An introduction to interpretive social science and the key concepts of Max Weber merely intimated that complex, multicausal and multidimensional social explanations are required to understand contemporary society, both locally and globally. The centrality of the individual and the irrepressible capacity to interpret social life and the conceptual foregrounding of the concept of social action implied that social science stands to realise its position as the conceptual framework to understand our current social situation.
- Introduction to the epistemic challenge to modernist sociological theory via decolonial thinking requires taking one's own body politics and geographical location as the starting point of thinking seriously.

1. What is sociological theory?
2. Did any sociological concept or theory prompt you to change your view of some aspect of social life? Explain this to someone else studying sociology.
3. Whose theoretical ideas in the classical tradition did you find of greatest explanatory force – those of Comte, Marx, Durkheim or Weber? Why? Express your view to both a social science and a non-social science student.
4. What is decolonial thinking and how is decolonisation related to, but distinguished from, decoloniality?
5. Does Steve Biko's philosophy of Black Consciousness prefigure those of the decolonial thinker Walter Mignolo? If so, how?

More sources to consult

Berger P. 1963. *An Invitation to Sociology*. New York: Doubleday.

Freire P. 2017 [1970]. *Pedagogy of the Oppressed*. Penguin Books. Modern Classics. South Africa: Penguin Random House.

Giddens A. 1971. *Capitalism and Modern Social Theory: An analysis of the Writings of Marx, Durkheim and Max Weber*. Cambridge: Cambridge University Press.

Lukes S. 1977. *Émile Durkheim*. New York: Penguin.

McLellan D. 1985. *Karl Marx*. New York: Harper Colophon.

Noble T. 2000. *Social Theory and Social Change*. Hampshire: Palgrave.

Pickering M. 1993. *Auguste Comte*. Cambridge: Cambridge University Press.

Ritzer G. 2000. *Sociological Theory*. 5th ed. New York: McGraw-Hill.

Ritzer G. 2006. *The Blackwell Companion to Major Classical Social Theorists*. Malden, MA: Blackwell Publishing.

Seidman S. 2004. *Contested Knowledge: Social Theory Today*. 3rd ed. Oxford: Blackwell Publishers.

More advanced reading

Bhambra GK. 2007. *Rethinking Modernity: Postcolonialism and the Sociological Imagination*. Hampshire: Palgrave Macmillan.

Erasmus Z. 2017. *Race Otherwise: Forging a New Humanism for South Africa*. Johannesburg: University of the Witwatersrand Press.

Mbembe A. 2015 [2000]. *On the Postcolony*. Johannesburg: University of the Witwatersrand Press.

Turner BS. 2000. *The Blackwell Companion to Social Theory*. 2nd ed. Oxford: Blackwell Publishers.

References

Abdullahi AA, Salawu B. 2012. 'Ibn Khaldun: A forgotten sociologist?' *South African Review of Sociology*, 43(3): 24–40.

Appiah AK. 1992. *In My Father's House*. New York: Methuen.

Bellah RN. 1982. *Émile Durkheim: On Morality and Society: Selected Writings*. Chicago: University of Chicago Press.

Berger P. 1963. *An Invitation to Sociology*. New York: Doubleday.

Best S, Kellner D. 1991. *Postmodern Theory: Critical Interrogations*. Hampshire: Macmillan.

Bhabha HK. 1994. *The Location of Culture*. London: Routledge.

Bhabha HK. 2004. 'Foreword: framing Fanon' in *The Wretched of the Earth*. Fanon F. New York: Grove Press.

Biko S. 2006. *I Write What I Like*. Johannesburg: Picador Africa.

Blauner R, Wellman D. 1973. 'Toward the decolonisation of social research' in *The Death of White Sociology*. Ladner JA (ed). New York: Random House.

Bloor D. 1976. *Knowledge and Social Imagery*. Chicago: University of Chicago Press (1991).

Bottomore TB, Rubel M. 1963. *Marx: Selected Writings in Sociology & Social Philosophy*. Harmondsworth: Penguin.

Cabral A. 1973. *Return to the Source: Selected Speeches of Amilcar Gibral*. New York: Monthly Review Press.

Cabral A. 1980. *Unity and Struggle*. London: Heinemann.

Cesaire A. 1972. *Discourse on Colonialism*. New York: Monthly Review Press.

Connell R. 2007. *Southern Theory: The Global Dynamics of Knowledge in Social Science*. Cambridge: Polity Press.

Coser LA. 1977. *Masters of Sociological Thought: Ideas in Historical and Social Context*. 2nd ed. Fort Worth, TX: Brace Jovanovich.

Davidson D. 1973. 'The furious passage of the black graduate student' in *The Death of White Sociology*. Ladner JA (ed). New York: Random House.

Diop CA. 1974. *The African Origin of Civilisation: Myth or Reality?* New York: L Hill.

During S (ed). 1993. *The Cultural Studies Reader*. London: Routledge.

Durkheim E. 1964. *The Division of Labour in Society* (translated by Simpson G). (First published 1893.) New York: Free Press.

Ellison R. 1973 [1964]. 'An American dilemma: A review' in *The Death of White Sociology*. Ladner JA (ed). New York: Random House.

Fanon F. 1967 [1952]. *Black Skin, White Masks*. New York: Grove Press.

Fanon F. 2004 [1963]. *The Wretched of the Earth*. New York: Grove Press.

Franklin Fraser E. 1962. 'The failure of the Negro intellectual' in *The Death of White Sociology*. Ladner JA (ed). New York: Random House (1973).

Gerth HH, Mills CW (eds). 1974. *From Max Weber: Essays in Sociology*. London: Routledge.

Giddens A. 1971. *Capitalism and Modern Social Theory: An Analysis of the Writings of Marx, Durkheim and Max Weber*. Cambridge: Cambridge University Press.

Grosfoguel R. 2011. 'Decolonising post-colonial studies and paradigms of political economy: Transmodernity, decolonial thinking, and global coloniality'. *Transmodernity: Journal of Peripheral Cultural Production of the Luso-Hispanic World*, 1(1): 1–25.

Hourani A. 1991. *A History of the Arab Peoples*. London: Faber & Faber.

Houtoundji P. 1983. *African Philosophy: Myth and Reality*. Bloomington: Indiana Press.

Houtoundji P. 1995. 'Producing knowledge in Africa today: The second Bashorun MKO Abiola distinguished lecture'. *African Studies Review*, 38(3): 1–10.

Ibn Khaldun-Kassus. *Wikimedia commons*. Wikimedia. org. 11 July 2007. [Online] Available at: https://upload.wikimedia.org/wikipedia/commons/0/[Online], Available at: 0a/Ibn_khaldoun-kassus.jpg [Accessed 4 January 2018].

Jansen J. 2017. *As by Fire*. Cape Town: Tafelberg.

Ladner JA. 1973. *The Death of White Sociology*. New York: Random House.

Lemert C. 1993. *Social Theory: The Multicultural and Classical Readings*. Boulder, CO: Westview Press.

Leroke WS. 1998. 'Post-colonialism In South African social science', in *Theory and Method in South African Human Sciences Research: Advances and Innovations*. Mouton J, Muller J (eds), in conjunction with Franks P, Sono T. Pretoria: Human Sciences Research Council.

Lukes S. 1977. *Émile Durkheim*. New York: Penguin.

Lyotard J-P. 1993. 'Defining the postmodern' in *The Cultural Studies Reader*. During S (ed). London: Routledge.

Mail&Guardian Online. 2017. 'Post-colonial universities are trapped by their past'. 31 August. [Online] Available at: https://mg.co.za/article/2017-08-31-00-post-colonial-universities-are-trapped-by-their-past/

Maldonado-Torres N. 2007. 'On the coloniality of being: Contributions to the development of a concept'. *Cultural Studies*, 21(2–3): 240–270.

Maldonado-Torres N. 2011. 'Thinking through the decolonial turn: Post-continental interventions in theory, philosophy, and critique – An introduction'. *Transmodernity: Journal of Peripheral Cultural Production in the Luso-Hispanic World*, 1(2): Fall.

McLellan D. 1985. *Karl Marx*. New York: Harper Colophon.

Memmi A. 1990. *The Coloniser and the Colonised*. London: Earthscan.

Mignolo W. 2009. 'Epistemic disobedience, independent thought and freedom'. *Theory, Culture, Society*, 26(7–8): 159–181.

Miller C. 1985. *Blank Darkness: Africanist Discourse in French*. Chicago: University of Chicago Press.

Minh-ha TT. 1989. *Woman, Native, Other: Writing Postcoloniality and Feminism*. Bloomington: Indiana University Press.

Mudimbe V. 1988. *The Invention of Africa: Gnosis, Philosophy and the Order of Knowledge*. London: James Currey.

Ndlovu-Gatsheni SJ. 2013. 'Why decoloniality in the 21st Century?'. *The Thinker*, 48: 11–15.

Ndlovu-Gatsheni SJ. 2015a. 'Genealogies of coloniality and implications for Africa's development'. *Africa Development*, XL(3): 13–40.

Ndlovu-Gatsheni SJ. 2015b. 'Decoloniality in Africa: A continuing search for a new world order'. *The Australasian Review of African Studies*, 36(2): 22–50.

Ndlovu-Gatsheni SJ. 2015c. 'Decoloniality as the Future of Africa'. *History Compass*, 13(10): 485–496.

Nelson RH. 2001. *Economics as Religion: From Samuelson to Chicago and Beyond*. University Park, PA: Pennsylvania State University Press.

Neocosmos M. 2016. *Thinking Freedom in Africa: Toward a Theory of Emancipatory Politics*. Johannesburg: Wits University Press.

Noble T. 2000. *Social Theory and Social Change*. Hampshire: Palgrave.

Pickering M. 1993. *Auguste Comte*. Cambridge: Cambridge University Press.

Ritzer G. 2000. *Sociological Theory*. 5th ed. New York: McGraw-Hill.

Rodney W. 1972. *How Europe Underdeveloped Africa*. Harare: Zimbabwe Publishing House.

Rosenthal F. 1967 [2015]. 'Introduction', in *The Muqaddimah: An Introduction to History* (abridged edition). Khaldun I (translated and introduced by Franz Rosenthal). Princeton: University of Princeton Press.

Runciman WG. 1991. *Weber: Selections in Translation*. Cambridge: Cambridge University Press.

Said E. 1993. *Orientalism*. London: Routledge & Kegan Paul.

Scott J, Marshall G. 2005. *Oxford Dictionary of Sociology*. 3rd ed. Oxford: Oxford University Press.

Senghor LS. 1964. *Liberti I: Negritude et Humanisme*. Paris: Le Seuil.

Shils E, Finch H (eds). 1949. *The Methodology of the Social Sciences*. New York: Free Press.

Smart B. 2000. 'Postmodern social theory', in *The Blackwell Companion to Social Theory*. Turner B (ed). Oxford, MA: Blackwell.

South African History Online. 2019. Available at: https://www.sahistory.org.za/article/student-protests-democratic-south-africa

Spivak G. 1991. *The Post-colonial Critic: Interviews, Strategies, Dialogues*. London: Routledge.

Spivak G. 1993. *Outside the Teaching Machine*. London: Routledge.

Stewart P. 2003. 'Introducing social theory to first-year students phonetically'. *Society in Transition*, 34(1): 149–158.

Thompson K, Tunstall J (eds). 1971. *Sociological Perspectives: Selected Readings*. Harmondsworth: Penguin Education.

Tucker RC. 1978. *The Marx-Engels Reader*. 2nd ed. New York: WW Norton & Co.

Wardi AH. 1950. 'A sociological analysis of Ibn Khaldun's theory: A study in the sociology of knowledge'. PhD dissertation, Faculty of the Graduate School, University of Texas.

wa Thiong'o N. 1981. *Decolonising the Mind: The Politics of Language in African Literature*. Oxford: James Curry.

wa Thiong'o N. 1993. *Moving the Centre: The Struggle for Cultural Freedom*. London: James Currey.

Weber M. 1978. *Economy and Society: An Outline of Interpretive Sociology*. California: University of California Press.

Wilhelm SM. 1973. 'Equality: America's racist ideology' in *The Death of White Sociology*. Lader JA (ed). New York: Random House.

Research methodology

Elsa Crause

When you go on a journey, the kind of transport you use will influence what you see and how and when you arrive at your destination. The way you do things, the *method* you employ, will shape its outcome. This chapter describes the theoretically guided steps that sociologists follow in the social sciences to ensure the results of their research qualify as objective and scientifically reputable and reliable.

Method and theory in sociology are intimately linked. The extent to which theory and research are closely related is evident from the following: it is one thing to have ideas and even clearly defined concepts and an exciting theory, *but* sociology also demands that such abstract theorising needs to be tested against the social reality it purports to describe and explain. This is where method plays its generally hidden but critical role in the knowledge claims sociology makes. You will recognise the three main approaches to sociology, though they are expressed in a different way to that of the previous chapter. Theory powerfully defines which methodologies will be adopted in any inquiry. Method, in turn, powerfully impacts on the theoretical stance adopted and the nature and quality of the research findings that result from testing and applying theories in the social world. To successfully achieve this interplay of theory and method requires learning about the strategies and techniques of social research, so it is important to get to know and understand how to assess different methodologies and their respective purposes.

If the way you go about investigating society does not conform to certain rules and procedures, the result is likely to fall short of the stringent requirements of what constitutes rigorous social scientific inquiry resulting in knowledge. Informed by the approach adopted in sociological theory, this chapter deals with how sociologists (and social scientists more broadly) select a variety of different methods in collecting the information and data to confirm, renew or even jettison their preferred theories. Only social research can advance social scientific knowledge. This chapter teaches how to go about producing or discovering knowledge by *doing* sociology. When you go and investigate some aspect of social reality for the first time, whether in your undergraduate or graduate years of study or perhaps even in your first job, only then will you truly discover the value of the contents of this chapter. That is a prediction. Test it!

Everybody reading this book has done things that achieved goals and had results. Achieving results in the realm of social scientific knowledge is a special activity and requires a special set of characteristics and frame of mind. Honesty, objectivity and scepticism, as this chapter will note, are the key characteristics required of a sociologist and are goals worthy of the aspirations of any human being. In doing sociology we do not just learn about society from an academic point of view, but may need to learn about ourselves and change the way we think if knowledge is our objective.

This chapter is a neat and concise reading of method in the social sciences. In saying this, an evaluative statement is made. This chapter shows that this kind of statement is not what sociological knowledge is based on. Its knowledge statements are rather directed towards providing a sound account of the facts of the social matter under inquiry and how to go about implementing the idea with which the social investigator set out. It deals with observations – the hallmark of all science – the steps in the research process and how sociological theory in research is related to the different approaches sociologists can adopt. The ways in which positivist (or 'scientific' sociology), interpretive (or social constructionist) and critical (or advocacy/

participatory) approaches prefer different methods are then discussed. The chapter goes on to discuss an approach not dealt with in the previous chapter, which is the realist or pragmatist approach. The pragmatists argue that what needs to be of primary concern in sociology are the solutions to social problems. In order to respond directly to what society needs, pragmatists use a combination of social research methods. This way of conducting social research has become increasingly popular.

A mixed methods strategy combines research instruments usually associated with the two primary methods of data gathering in sociology and the social sciences more widely. As its name suggests, quantitative research presents its findings in terms of statistics, generally by means of a survey administered across a sample or proportion of a population whose views are being canvassed. To argue against the results that this form of social research delivers, you need statistical skills. In contrast, also as its name suggests, qualitative research digs more deeply into how respondents experience the quality of their human experience, generally by means of in-depth one-to-one interviews and focus groups. Both forms of research strategies and instruments have their advantages and disadvantages and are often combined in what is called a triangulated research strategy – a two-pronged approach focusing on the point of investigation, thereby forming a triangle and hence the name. How these research strategies work, how they are related to the theoretical approaches which traditionally adopt different methodologies and the results each obtain, are discussed in close detail.

As always, your detailed attention is required. If you first encounter this chapter in the lecture hall setting of the university, separated from the social world beyond its halls, take it seriously. You will need to understand the knowledge claims sociology makes and the steps and structure of its procedures, as real life is vibrant and confusing. The way sociologists make sense of this world is through abstractions such as theories and concepts, which allow us to order our observations. This is why you will consult the chapter when out in the open and often chaotic field of live social research – which is where sociology (and its practitioners) truly comes alive. The topic of decolonising knowledge is also pertinent here as our theoretical approach then speaks directly to the knowledge claims we make (Connell 2014; Beck & Stolterman 2016):

'Method' has to do, first of all, with how to ask and answer questions with some assurance that the answers are more or less durable. "Theory" has to do, above all, with paying close attention to the words one is using, especially their degree of generality and their logical relations. The primary purpose of both is clarity of conception and economy of procedure, and most importantly just now, the release rather than the restriction of the sociological imagination (Mills 1961).

Case study 2.1 Innovative research

Thabo: Hey love the story.bt u shuld wach ur splng.bt all in all its a grt stry jst hve 2 mke it nt dat cmplt at sme point.

Textspeaker criticising spelling? Indeed, yes!

With the advent of new phone apps such as Twitter, the SMS-based local social network Mxit and all its intellectual rights were given to an independent public benefit organisation, The Reach Trust, with programs such as 'move up' (a reading program), which to this day provides cost effective mobile solutions that improve South African lives (The Reach Trust 2019).

The Mxit space published short cell phone stories (ie m-novels) that were available on mobi and Mxit. This was done around 2010 up until 2013, Today this initiative still lives on through The Reach Trust. Now the reading is integrated with schools and teachers, but when it started it was hip, interactive and free. Users read the chapters and left comments, and entered writing competitions. Each main story was a series, and chapters were published daily. Picture this: soap operas on your phone.

Unintended spelling errors slipped into one chapter and drew immediate responses, much the same as the one quoted above. Remember that this is *generation* txt, who supposedly cannot spell or write properly. This may seem true based on the txtspk example above, but it is clearly evident that when they read, they know their spelling from their 'splng'.

➡

It is well known that one of the contributors to the low-literacy levels of South African learners is that not enough reading and writing happen at schools and at home. This was known to Steve Vosloo, who initiated the novel reading idea (Vosloo 2010) after realising that although leisure books were seldom found in poor households, those teens were actually reading and writing on their cell phones via platforms like Mxit and today's WhatsApp.

He must have thought about how to use this reading to their advantage, instead of lamenting changing times.

Vosloo developed a pilot research project that led to the Mxit novels, a wonderfully South African approach to support student learning. One can generate hypotheses or ideas about relationships between social concepts that you may want to test through Deduction or, in the case of new knowledge, Retroduction. Accordingly, retroduction explains the imaginative leap taken to account for observed phenomena. We can thus claim that he used his sociological imagination to analyse and understand the world in which teens live. He saw individuals engaged in behaviour that transcends the individual to become a social phenomenon. Instead of viewing cell phone texting as detrimental to literacy and spelling, he read reports and realised that relatively little research has been done on this in South Africa. He then created a creative research project to establish the possibilities of using the mobi environment to draw young people towards reading.

Analysing the world we live in and exercising our sociological imagination are all part of the exciting world of how sociologists do research to grow in theoretical and practical understanding of the world. Here we go…

Key themes

- Why and when a particular choice about methodology and method needs to be made in research
- The context available for social research in South Africa and to encourage student socialisation into the discipline
- Characteristics of scientific research and how it differs from knowledge from sources such as tradition or common sense
- Validity and reliability in research
- Steps in the research process
- The advantages of theory in research
- The four knowledge claims of sociological theory

- The link between the three methodologies and particular research questions
- Quantitative and qualitative research designs and some methods of data gathering
- The characteristics of mixed methods methodology
- Quantitative and qualitative data – how they are presented and analysed
- Types of samples and the application of each within the quantitative and qualitative methodologies
- Ethics in social research and avoiding plagiarism through quoting, paraphrasing and summarising
- Dimensions of research.

2.1 Introduction

In this chapter you will find a general overview of the steps in research, major theoretical paradigms behind current debates within the field of sociology, and a sense of how they are translated into concrete research. As you have learnt in Chapter 1, sociologists study society and social interaction. This is achieved by using **sociological research methods**. Such methods in sociology always have two parts: **theory** and **research**. **Sociologists** are constantly striving to uncover and develop insight about the social world and to understand the way it works. Believe it or not, studying people is much more challenging than studying lifeless objects! This is why innovation in research design such as displayed in the opening case study is to be welcomed. Every time we throw a stone in the air, it will come down, no matter how often we do it. However, if we slap someone, the reaction may not be the same with every person – one may hit us back, another may burst into tears, yet another may simply ignore us. Thus, people as complex beings require various ways to study them. This is why the social sciences have an abundance of theories supporting our view of the world and the types of research we do.

The social enterprise is never practised in a vacuum. Worldwide sociologists have also practised different sociologies, depending on the dominant perspectives and power structures that influence society. Following the dominant American positivism of the 1900s especially, South African universities were divided between those who practised the large-scale studies and who were viewed by liberal universities of the time as supportive of the status quo, and the more liberal universities who practised a more **critical or social science**, wishing to support social change. Today, South African sociologists are less bound by these stereotypes, and more likely to contemplate a wider variety of theoretical and **methodological practices** (Webster 2004).

In moving with the times and dominant ideas, South Africa is engaged in understanding and researching themes such as uses of southern and postcolonial perspectives in applied social science in areas ranging from education to urban planning (Connell 2014). Nothing about the methodologies that we are about to study is inherently good or bad, wrong or correct. Indeed, as you will see later, sociology cannot answer moral questions, but to this day the theories and the methods at the sociologists' disposal will emphasise the factors that a particular theory highlights, while paying less attention to other dimensions of society that are also real but not the focus of the particular theory. After more than a century of adhering to this limiting practice of an either/or approach, sociology worldwide is growing towards what some would call the **realist perspective**, both in its theories and in its methodological practices (Pawson 2006).

Box 2.1 The South African Sociological Association (SASA)

In South Africa we are privileged to have a well-organised sociology association to which academics, practitioners and students belong. Each year they hold a conference where research and analysis of socially relevant topics are disseminated. The association is the result of an amalgamation of two different associations that put aside their differences in 1993, prior to the democratisation in South Africa.

The goals of the Association are to:

- promote the discipline and the profession of sociology
- promote research, teaching and debate about society
- promote cooperation at the national, regional and international level among persons engaged in the study of society.

The name of the official journal of the South African Sociological Association is *South African Review of Sociology (SARS)*. See Chapter 27 for more information.

2.2 Characteristics and limitations of scientific research

Before we start with how we study the social world, let us begin with what makes a good sociologist. Sociologists are special people in that they bind themselves to a code of honour. (See section 2.10 on ethics at the end of this chapter.) They strive to pursue knowledge in a way that is **objective**, honest, sceptical and open. This means that they try to leave their personal judgements aside when studying the social world and do not let their idea of what should be unduly influence their results (they use *objectivity*). They are honest in their studies and do not lie about results they did not really find. They also do not claim that someone else's work is actually their own (*honesty*). They do not believe everything they read and hear, and will only do so when it has been scientifically verified (*scepticism*). They are open to new ideas and suggestions, and are not afraid to change or adjust their theories if a better explanation is proposed (*critical thinking*). As you can see, being a scientist takes a certain frame of mind that pursues knowledge and answers in an honourable manner for honourable purposes. As a science of human social facts and groupings, sociology strives to understand and explain the impact of society on human thinking. It studies how we perpetuate or change society and social behaviour through the meanings we create. The wide variety of sociology's applications makes it a major force in contemporary research in the humanities and social sciences.

We will now look at the characteristics that support sociological research as an important force, keeping in mind that a researcher has a great responsibility towards telling it as it is, to present the data professionally and not to overclaim what the research means, while clearly stating the premises of the research.

2.3 Scientific observation – and value statements

Everybody observes, experiences, hears of and reads about things and make **deductions** or generalisations on which to base their opinions. This may be viewed as their **experiential knowledge** base from casual observation. Examples of this order of knowledge would be arguments presented in a convincing manner, based on the opinions of friends or on traditions and urban legends. **Scientific observations** are made in a systematic, methodical and rigorous manner, and refer to a body of techniques for investigating and acquiring new knowledge. The scientific approach sets researched knowledge apart from other forms of knowledge and generalisations. **Scientific evidence** is generally critically appraised with regard to being collected in a systematic, repeatable and scrutinised way.

The scientific attitude is a key element in valid and reliable research data as all research carries a risk that it may be wrong or may not yield usable results. How data is gathered speaks to the twin concepts of *validity* and *reliability*. **Validity** refers to the question of whether the research is measuring what it claims to measure (Neuman 2014). For example, if research claims to report on the attitudes of girls towards premarital sex, but the questionnaires were distributed to be answered by their aunts, the research cannot be valid as it only includes data on what aunts believe girls' attitudes are. The research does not measure what it is supposed to measure. Thus, a scientific attitude ensures transparency on how the data was gathered to help determine if the research really captures the information the researcher claims it does.

Reliability refers mostly to the possibility that the method of data gathering leads to consistent results. Does the method always measure the same thing no matter in what context it is used? When we hear that a detective is investigating a crime, we accept that the process will be logical, systematic and able to lead to strong evidence. We expect the evidence to lead to findings on the crime and point out the perpetrators, as this will have to stand up in a court of law.

Detectives often do a preliminary investigation on a crime and the crime scene, and assimilate what they see into a theory of what had occurred and who to look at as a potential suspect. Detectives then look for evidence that will connect that person to the crime, unless new evidence starts redirecting them to change their theory about what happened. Similarly, the sociological investigator will be systematic in gathering data (information or evidence) and be directed by sociological theory to support interpretation of evidence. It is important to realise that sociological research cannot provide answers to all human questions. Researchers consciously try to avoid mistakes that can bedevil findings and their applicability. This is part of their professional responsibility.

Some of the common errors researchers make include inaccurate observations, making sweeping generalisations (overgeneralising) and making selective observations (Babbie 2010).

The topic of interest to a researcher may present itself as a value statement that will need to be reformulated and made researchable. **Value statements** are human questions that research cannot answer – for instance the

difference between good and bad. The researcher can provide answers to what respondents consider to be good or bad, or how they come to make the distinction, but cannot give an answer as to whether they are correct or wrong in their beliefs because that involves a moral question. This means that theory cannot settle debates on values and on how things *should* be.

When the initial statement of a **research problem** is phrased like a value statement, it needs to be 'translated' and reformulated into a researchable statement, for instance: 'examinations are bad for learning' or 'sexism is a problem in Africa'. If we look at the second example on sexism, can you turn it into a researchable statement? Some possibilities could be that sexism is illustrated by the rates of aggressive sexuality when compared to other continents, by the rates and types of crimes against women, or by the subjective feelings and beliefs of males and females about themselves and the opposite sex. For the researcher to be able to investigate the matter, each value statement needs to be turned into a researchable one.

This chapter will now consider the steps in the research process, and then explore the role of sociological theory in research.

Box 2.2 Information on search engines, databases and scientific journals

The explosion of information and the daily growth of its availability on internet platforms such as Google can make it difficult to determine if information is real and of value, or part of advertising campaigns, or even so-called false or fake news distributed to wilfully distort the information people have at their disposal to influence their opinions. When you start researching a topic, it helps if you know where to go to for information and to recognise the difference between some of the different sources. By now you know that there are many academic books that you can refer to. You have also read earlier that sociologists should publish their research in journals. How does a journal differ from a magazine, and what other ways are available to access information on sociological research? It is important that you are able to distinguish between a peer-reviewed journal article, a database and a search engine.

➠

An academic journal is *peer reviewed*, which means that a draft of the journal article was critically assessed and evaluated by other established scholars who are also in the author's field of specialisation before it is published. It is important to note that a peer-reviewed journal article always systematically cites its sources using in-text references and footnotes, and includes a full reference list or bibliography at the end.

This will be required from you when you write for an academic department. The review process is a way or method of guaranteeing that published journal articles reflect solid scholarship in their particular field of study.

Table 2.1 Platforms and sources of information for research

Search engine	Database	Journal
Google Yahoo Ananzi	JSTOR Juta e-Publications EBSCO SAGE	*Agenda Development Southern Africa Social Work* *South African Journal of Economic & Management Sciences* *South African Review of Sociology (SARS)*

2.4 The steps in the research process

If you want to do research, these are the typical steps you would take. Remember that the steps actually flow into one another. That is why, if you start with a question that you want to answer, at the end of the process you will go right back to see if you actually answer it. For this reason, research is a cyclical process and we identify the steps only to create a form of order to the process. These steps should be described if you write a research proposal or when you write a report on research. The information provided in the rest of this chapter is embedded in the steps and will ensure that as you read, your ability to expand your understanding of each step increases. In the same way that the steps create order to a process, sociological theory also helps us order and analyse our data. Remember that science is a systematic process. Whether you follow a **qualitative**, **quantitative** or **mixed methods** strategy or methodology,

all are rigorous and can be checked or verified by another sociologist. It is a prerequisite that the steps in the research process are followed and documented. This means that with any findings you read about, you should be able to go to the researcher and ask how he/she came to this finding. The researcher should be able to show you step by step how the findings and conclusion were reached, but if he/she cannot, it is not solid, scientific research.

2.4.1 Getting to a topic, research question and the nature of evidence you will seek

This involves deciding what you will investigate, and involves several steps (Leedy & Ormrod 2018).

- Identify and develop your topic: reading and personal interest impact on the topic you decide to investigate. You have to briefly state the research problem and explain your reasons for selecting it.
- Reviewing literature: this not only reveals what others have done, but may also indicate areas that may be under-researched or not yet resolved, and could lead to ideas about how to do the research.
- Describe the research question(s): the description of the problem means you have to specify what you want to learn, and what your subproblems or aims are. This will also require that you describe the theory you want to build or test and within what group or community you will do the study. Do you plan to replicate earlier studies in a different setting or extend the use of a theory to an area not investigated before? You may also want to apply a theory to a new group or community.
- Identify the nature of the evidence: this and the involvement that you will have to attain to satisfy your research question(s) need to be identified. Choose between the natural science positivist approach, an interpretive (or social constructionist) approach, a critical (advocacy/participatory) approach or the emergent realist views in social science.

2.4.2 Decide on a research methodology and create or choose a research design

This step involves deciding and planning how you will do the study. Guided by the nature of the evidence needed to answer your research questions, you would need to choose between **quantitative**, **qualitative** and **mixed methods** depending on what type of data and researcher involvement your research problem requires. You must first choose or develop a research design and then develop a time frame and plan of action for the project. The **research design** is viewed as a roadmap of how the study will be conducted. This involves much more that the selection of a methodology as it includes the plan, structure and execution of the research. It also includes:

- an explanation of the data-gathering methods or techniques (such as a questionnaire or thematic list) according to the data required
- specification of the type of sample or case selection
- a description of the process of dealing with ethical matters
- a schematic outline of the project, showing how it is designed to maximise the validity of findings.

The goal is to give readers sufficient information to allow them to successfully evaluate your proposed or reported project and the analysis and conclusions which you will present later. The work plan is specified and described.

2.4.3 Data collection, analysis and conclusions

Data-collection techniques or methods can be quantitative or qualitative. Quantitative research is where a researcher gathers data so that statistical analyses can be performed. Qualitative research focuses on in-depth subjective data that will be analysed to lay bare themes, topics or other patterns for understanding. Mixed methods of data gathering may also be adopted, which may also allow the researcher to triangulate results (ie gather different types of evidence or data on the topic). Your findings are subjected to your sociological imagination, critical analysis and critical reflection compared with other theories, and presented in a manner that illustrates the relevance to the research question. The necessary evidence and the conclusions based upon it should be clearly stated. It is here that you will present most of your **tables, graphs** and **illustrations**. Your main objective must be to communicate clearly.

Meticulous attention should be paid to each reference used and the references in the text. The bibliography should be done according to accepted procedures such as the Harvard method – this applies to your tables as well as to your sentences.

All research should have a conclusion, which may begin with a summary of the findings showing how they confirm or reject the hypotheses with which you started or achieve answers for the research questions. It also includes a re-visitation of the theories from which your research originated, and new knowledge claims that you may make. Your own criticism of the research indicating the shortcomings and limits to generalisation of findings should also be included. Lastly, the report should identify further questions raised by the findings and additional research that is needed.

2.4.4 Dissemination of results

Sharing the results involves writing a report and possibly publishing the results, thus making the research available for replication or critical scrutiny. Dissemination may also involve attending a conference and reading a paper, and publishing it in a journal after peer review. There are also **predatory journals** that are scams and money-making schemes, through extravagant page money for instance. Based on the important notion that knowledge should be free, a number of **open-source journals** have also developed. It is important to always ensure that the information you use is from reputable sources. Libraries can often assist with such information.

2.5 The guiding role of sociological theory in research

As we can see from the steps in the research process, research is about gathering the appropriate information and data from people or other sources. Such data would be impossible to analyse and understand without the aid of sociological theory to guide us.

Sociologists rely on theory to support our understanding of how and why evidence is related. First, theory tells us how and why data may be related. Secondly, it provides a way to organise the data in a systematic way and helps explain the findings. Thirdly, sociologists develop and test theories to explain social phenomena (Handlechner 2008).

Theory often starts as a proposed relationship between two or more concepts. Using untested common sense to base decisions on is riskier than using science to plan activities. As an example, we may take supposed knowledge about female and male dating behaviour. In adolescence and early adulthood, humans gain personal experience and try to make sense of it. Much of the planning and thinking about how to approach a date centres on how to control the situation so that it is a positive experience for all concerned. We may call on our own past experience and that of friends, perhaps those who seem to be successful in their dates, to provide us with advice. This wisdom we seek from them is not scientific and is probably based on sweeping generalisations and selective observation. If a scientist wishes to research female and male dating behaviour, the first thing to do is to read up on other studies about the topic, and especially to search for theories applicable to it. The theory and other studies will help point the way to things not yet established, such as how the sexes understand a particular situation (create meaning). The theory may also support our ability to make a problem statement or a research question on the topic of our interest.

Kurt Levin, a German social scientist, said that there is nothing as practical as a good theory. What he meant is that the theory may help us to decide what our concepts will mean and how we will expect them to be related (Sanderson 2009:11).

Let us take the following example as our theoretical statement, remembering that the statement would follow only after extensive reading and would be designed to make the topic researchable:

Both sexes reported higher rates of having a good time on a date when it involved cooperative games such as cards or board games and lower satisfaction when they only talked to one another. As a result, theorists can propose that taking cooperative roles during a date is associated with positive feelings about the date by both sexes.

This 'theory' would then need further testing against other applicable theory, existing research and different audiences. Our 'theory' above consists of two elements: the data stating the correlation between outcomes, gender, date activities and levels of satisfaction, and the proposed relationship. Data by itself is not informative beyond the facts themselves, but to understand the social world around us, theory draws the connections between what may seem to be unrelated aspects of it.

2.6 Sociological theory knowledge claims and sociological research

The often-repeated words of C Wright Mills indicate the important role that theory plays in sociological research. He said: 'Empirical data are blind without theory, and theory is empty without data' (Mills 1961).

Sociologists have different traditions of theory that view society from different vantage points and explain social life from different perspectives. The three main historical perspectives of sociology represent distinctive ways to approach reality, and thus also to do research. Sociology is richer because of the multiple views on society.

Let us illustrate how different perspectives could exist at the same time. A well-known and successful photographer, Kevin Connolly, was born without legs (Connolly 2009). He started roller-skating, which provided him with a means to move from place to place, but also afforded him a unique viewpoint from which to witness and photograph people. His perspective would be the same as that of a young child, as he has to look upwards at people. From this perspective he has done a photo essay of faces from all over the world,

all photographed from his angle or perspective. He calls it the rolling exhibition in which he tried to capture the faces of people as they glance or stare at him, or ignore him. The resultant exhibition documents individuals' reactions to his physical uniqueness. He claims that people need to make sense of his difference – being without legs – by creating a narrative based on their own life exposures. If he travelled to Mozambique or Angola, he may be asked if he stepped on a landmine. If he moves around at a taxi rank in Johannesburg, people may wonder if he lost his legs in a collision or accident. Thus, in the exhibition he addresses a very interesting sociological phenomenon about how we make sense of the world around us.

Our understanding and interpretation of Connolly's situation vary greatly, and may well be thought of as different theoretical perspectives. Let us now assume that the particular view that Connolly has from the skateboard represents a particular theory of society. From this perspective, one may view a face dominated by the underside of the chin and nose on a foreshortened face. It is a good perspective from below and provides us with fairly accurate data about that angle that we can analyse, compare and seek explanations or patterns about. However, if you wish to study the head (society) from a level perspective or from the top, this view becomes much less useful. It does not, for instance, provide an accurate rendition of the length of the face or any useful data about the top of the head. This is the very same dilemma that the sociological researcher faces. Which theoretical perspective or combination of perspectives will best shed light on the phenomena that will be studied? Of necessity, one approach (view) enhances some aspects but obscures others.

One of the most enduring gifts generations of previous sociologists bestowed on current practitioners through the three early perspectives and their current representations resides in the differences they display with regard to what can be considered good evidence.

The differences represent different sociological practices and reside in the different **knowledge claims** each follow. Knowledge claims refer to what the researcher will view as good evidence, and what types of information he/she will accept. Though there are many ways to categorise and compare differences in the foundational theories of sociology, the differences in the definition of knowledge or knowledge claims will support your understanding of the choices sociological researchers make. The different knowledge claims refer to researchers starting their research with assumptions of how and what they will learn during an inquiry (Matthews & Kostelis 2011). These are called respectively 'scientific sociology' or 'positivist knowledge claims'; 'interpretive' or 'socially constructed knowledge claims'; 'critical' or **advocacy/participatory knowledge claims**; and 'realist' or **pragmatic knowledge claims'**. You must understand that identifying these knowledge claims aids our understanding, but real cases will often not be as clearly identifiable as the categories imply. The knowledge claims have their roots in the three early dominant theories of sociology. An important newer insight comes from Southern Theory – the notion that societies in the southern hemisphere have different world experiences that have high relevance in the postcolonial world (Connell 2014). The range of knowledges does not change and remains enmeshed with the notion of how one comes to knowledge of society, what is viewed as good evidence, how to collect it, and what the role of the sociologist should be with regard to social knowledge and society (Neuman 2014).

Let us now look at the different knowledge claims and what each means for the practice of sociological research and especially for decisions on the methodology of a particular study or research question.

2.6.1 Positivism or 'scientific' sociology

This tradition of sociology is one of the oldest and started as an application of the natural science methods to society. The emphasis is on systematic observation of social behaviour, based on emphasising the existence of social structures, independent from individuals. Thus, society is viewed as 'out there' and as an objective reality that shapes our behaviour. The view emphasises social systems that exist independently of individuals and create forces that influence and shape our individual behavioural choices. For this reason, research will focus on how social structures that are real but cannot be seen have effects that can be empirically observed. Theorists such as Comte and Durkheim viewed society as organic, with the institutions of society as functional for the continuation of society (Comte 1998). Later, Talcott Parsons and Robert Merton expanded the use of functionalism (Steinmetz 2005). Scientific sociology focuses on society as real in its consequences that can be observed and recorded as objective facts.

The reason to do research is to learn more about how our world that is built upon the natural world works. People are viewed as self-interested and rational. People operate on the basis of external causes that affect individuals in similar ways. That is why we can learn more about people by observing and analysing patterns in their external behaviour – that which is seen rather than subjective reality.

This view is mechanical, with human behaviour caused by external forces. Knowledge for positivists consists of identifying how and why people behave as they do and making connections between different facts to produce theories that explain behaviour. Emphasis is on repeatedly finding similar patterns to lay lawlike rules bare. The knowledge that develops through the positivist lens is based on careful observation and measurement of the objective reality that exists 'out there' in the world, exposed in studies involving hundreds and sometimes thousands of respondents. To maintain objectivity and minimise influence on respondents' behaviour, researchers should not interact with the people they are studying. Though objectivity is difficult to obtain, it is viewed as a desirable characteristic of research worth aspiring to. **Data** is collected on mental constructs or concepts, and analysed to find relationships between **variables**. Statistical concepts such as averages are used to simplify description. Variables may be viewed as independent, tracking how values on a second dependent variable change, for example how the age at which respondents start drinking relates to how much they consume. Surveys with predeveloped instruments that yield statistical data are dominant. The knowledge resulting from such research is abstracted and far removed from 'common sense' notions. Proponents would predominantly prefer the quantitative methodology to research, as this allows for the collection of numerical data. A quantitative methodology is one that uses positivist claims for developing knowledge, variables, measurement and observation to test theories. Today this type of research is, for instance, important to track social indicators of poverty and other mass indicators for policy and planning, as social patterns are constantly changing across place and over time (Neuman 2014).

2.6.2 Interpretivism or social constructionist knowledge claims

Interpretive sociology does not just record behaviour, but also attempts to determine the meanings actors attach to their behaviour and the behaviour of others. Weber's concept of *Verstehen* or 'understanding' provides the foundation for interpretive sociology influenced by phenomenology and the critique of positivism in the social sciences (Tucker 1965). Typically for sociology, this view represents an almost polar opposite from the positivists, claiming that objective reality only seems real. Realists would claim that reality would probably display both. Reality is seen as something constructed by people, and only qualitative information gathered in interaction with people allows us to best understand how they make sense of their everyday world. People's common-sense notions are collected and studied as valid understanding of their reality. Multiple 'knowledges' can coexist when equally competent (or trusted) interpreters disagree (Denzin & Lincoln 2005). The interpretivist paradigm views theory as an aid to understanding. This means theory may not have strong predictive power and is of limited generality. The interpretative approach stresses the importance of getting to know the inside interpretations of the subject. It relies on three principles: we are aware of both ourselves and our relationship with others; people make deliberate choices on how to behave in different situations; and behaviour is unpredictable and should not be studied 'from the outside'. Society does not exist in an objective, observable form (Given 2008). Rather, we create a 'sense of social system' on a daily basis through meanings. The social world is different from the natural world and cannot force us – only other people can force us. When studying behaviour, it is best to describe and explain it from the point of view of those involved. Knowledge is relative to context, as one person's interpretation is as valid as the next person's. Facts about behaviour can be established, but they will always be context bound and may not apply to different persons in the same situation. If behaviour is conditioned by the way people interpret and understand their world, causal relations cannot be empirically established because there are far too many variables involved in the social construction of reality. Understanding social behaviour means understanding how people, individually and collectively, define and interpret their particular social situation or how they construct 'social realities'. The methods employed by a researcher have to reflect the fact that people consciously and unconsciously construct their own sense of social reality. The goal of research is to rely as much as possible on the participants' view on what is being studied. These meanings are often constructed in interaction with others, which means that they are not imprinted on individuals but are socially and historically negotiated (Denzin & Lincoln 2005). Researchers realise that their own background in turn shapes their interpretation, and they have to consciously 'position themselves' in the research to acknowledge their interpretation while making sense and interpreting the meanings of others. (Beck & Stolterman 2016) Proponents would mostly prefer the qualitative methodology to research as it allows for deep understanding and rich descriptions. Rather than starting with theory, researchers often generate a theory or pattern of meaning based on their findings.

2.6.3 Critical or advocacy/participatory knowledge claims

Critical sociology rejects the notion of value freedom and suggests that all research is value driven or political. Like Karl Marx, the founder of critical theory, contemporary critical theorists attempt to change the social world in the direction of democracy and social justice.

Critical approach research arose in the 1980s and 1990s from individuals reacting to the positivist structural laws and theories that did not adequately address marginalised individuals and groups or issues of social justice. Writers drew from the works of Marx, Marcuse and Habermas. In general, these practitioners felt that the constructivist stance did not go far enough in advocating for an action agenda to help marginalised people (Creswell 2017).

The approach assumes that the researcher and his/her knowledge is but one version, no more or less important than that of the marginalised where the research is conducted. The approach supports advocacy roles and that the researcher will act collaboratively not to marginalise participants through the research. Examples of theories with this knowledge claim would include feminist perspectives and critical theory. Some key features of advocacy or participatory forms of inquiry are the advancement of an action agenda and to promote political debate and discussion. Proponents would favour the qualitative methodology, linked to particular research designs such as **action research**.

2.6.4 Realist or pragmatist knowledge claims

Pragmatism derives from the works of George Herbert Mead and John Dewey. Pragmatists are not committed to any one system or philosophy and reality (Creswell 2017). They believe that sociology needs to stop asking questions about reality and/or the laws of nature. The applications and solutions to problems are what should be of concern. Instead of methods being important, the problem is the most important, and researchers use multiple approaches to understand it. Individual researchers have the freedom to choose procedures that best suit their purpose. The pragmatists or realists would prefer an approach called mixed methods, which constitutes elements from both quantitative and qualitative methodologies.

2.7 The link between methodologies and types of research problems

We now know that sociologists use various theories to analyse society, and that when we do research, the knowledge claims of our theoretical position will influence whether we use quantitative, qualitative or mixed methods methodology. Some research problems have clear links to the preferred methodology, but this is not always true. The word 'methodology' has many meanings, but here we use it to refer to the principles and practices that underlie the research and that determine what research tools are deployed and how evidence is interpreted. In this chapter we identified three methodologies. Let us practise a few examples of the methodology and research-problem linkup. If the problem is to identify the strongest factors associated with early school dropout rates, a quantitative methodology would be appropriate.

On the other hand, if the particular factors are not known, have not been investigated in a particular group or community, or existing theories do not apply to the group, a qualitative methodology may be more appropriate as qualitative research is often exploratory and useful if little is known about the topic, group or theory application. Whereas researchers in the previous century often contrasted, debated and defended the two methodologies, the mixed methods approach has done much to relieve this tension. It is currently more accepted that most research does not fall squarely within one methodology, but may be situated on a continuum between the two extremes, and that the nature of the problem may indicate the use of mixed methods.

2.8 The three methodologies and data gathering methods

2.8.1 Quantitative research methodology and methods

The major characteristics of quantitative research are a focus on deduction, confirmation of theory or hypothesis testing, prediction, standardised data collection and statistical analysis. The data is often used for descriptive as well as market studies. Quantitative studies begin with measures and end with generalisations – getting the 'facts', finding patterns and making extrapolations to other applicable units. The two methods used are either experiments or surveys, but sociologists predominantly use **surveys** (Neuman 2014). During a survey, questionnaires are distributed to collect data from respondents, and answers are statistically analysed. The answers on the questionnaire are called raw data and once entered into the computer, statistical analysis can be done. The answers are generally provided and the respondent chooses between them (**closed questions**). In a survey, respondents are systematically asked the same questions to record and analyse the answers. Mostly closed questions

are used, and the respondent chooses between available answers. The advantage of using quantitative methods (where questionnaires and structured, questionnaire-driven interviews are used) is that they can attain a high level of objectivity and reliability. They also tend to provide valid results and are quick to administer. One can reach a large number of people in a short space of time through a census, for example. The problem with a survey is that the data you receive is only as good as the questions you ask. If you did not ask something, you will have no data on it. Variables such as social class can be measured in many ways, for example by using an indicator such as education, income, work type and even types of holidays taken. Measurement is thus often arbitrary. This is why researchers tend to do a pilot study (smaller-scale test run) before using questionnaires in a large-scale survey. Furthermore, unless open questions (where the answers are not provided, and the respondent can answer in his/her own words) are included, one cannot gain an understanding of the lifeworld of a respondent. There are many ways to ask questions.

The questions provided in Box 2.3 are all examples of categorical questions. Respondents are requested to categorise themselves in the first question. Question 2 is an example of a Likert scale question where respondents are asked to express their attitude or other response in terms of ordinal level categories (eg agree, disagree and ranked on a continuum of 5). Question 3 is an example of a **semantic differential scale question** in which people are presented with a topic or object and a list of many polar opposites' adverbs or adjectives. They indicate their feelings by marking one of several spaces between adverbs. Question 4 is an example of an open question where respondents can supply their own answers (Fink 2003). This kind of question helps to gain some understanding of respondents' motivation.

Box 2.3 Examples of different types of questions in a survey

1. Sex
2. To what extent do you agree or disagree with the following statements?
3. If early school leavers can become apprentices to skilled workers, for 'on the job training', generally speaking, where would you place your view on the following scale?
4. Please describe in your own words why you gave the answer above.

There are a number of ways that questionnaires may be presented to the respondents, and each has advantages and disadvantages. You may use this as an exercise and try to generate some questions around each type. Examples are house-to-house surveys with the interviewer completing the questionnaire based on the answers the respondents provide. Telephone and group-administered surveys where the respondents are in one place are other examples. Computer surveys via email are also gaining popularity.

Quantitative data analysis and presentation
Remember that statistics are a 'language of concepts' that we use to understand data better. There are many visual ways of presenting statistical information. Figure 2.1 is an example of a simple pie chart.

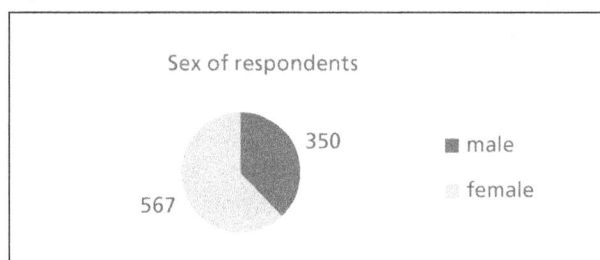

Figure 2.1 A pie chart

In quantitative studies, statistical formulae are applied to the data to deduct patterns. The findings in such a study are abstracted to a different (statistical) level of explanation.

2.8.2 Qualitative research methodology, research designs and the methods
As we have said, qualitative researchers firstly reject positivism (Johnson & Onwuegbuzie 2004: 15) and rather argue for increased attention to be given to the way people construct and interpret their reality. They emphasise the importance of space, social context and time. The major characteristics of traditional qualitative research are **induction**, discovery, exploration and theory or hypothesis generation. The researcher is the primary 'instrument' of data collection and qualitative analysis. Qualitative research is **naturalistic** – with a focus on real-world settings. Sampling is generally based on non-probability sampling such as snowball or data saturation. Credibility and trustworthiness are important, and results are deemed reliable if they are consistent with data collected with valid deductions from data illustrating trustworthiness. Symbolic interactionism inspired by interpretivism proposes that there are multiple rather than single realities of phenomena, and that these

realities can differ across time and place. Unlike quantitative research, there is no overarching framework for how qualitative research should be conducted; rather, each type of qualitative research is guided by particular philosophical stances that are taken in relation to each phenomenon. Qualitative methods generate a high volume of data as they emphasise understanding from the point of view of the respondent (Given 2008). The three main methods are:
1. Interviewing (such as **focus group** or in-depth interviews) where respondents verbally describe their experiences
2. Written descriptions asked from respondents
3. Observation, where researchers make descriptive observations of verbal and non-verbal behaviour.

Qualitative data analysis and presentation
The data of qualitative research is very often in the format of language. This is why the analysis of such data uses different tools from those interested in statistics. Many specialised ways have been developed that can accurately map the actions of the researcher with the data. Programs such as ATLAS.ti and NVivo support researchers in working with the data after recordings of conversations have been transcribed into the program. Certain programs can translate spoken words into typing to assist this type of research. Classification of answers can be made and one can even see the distribution of predominance of certain responses. Analysis is made on a detailed level and results in 'dense' descriptions (much detail).

In qualitative work, the data gathering and data analysis are much more closely linked than in quantitative research. Very often one can only abstractly distinguish between the processes of gathering data, analysis and reflexivity. Two examples of such reflexive analysis are explored here:
1. **Thematic content analysis** is the preferred technique for analysing semi-structured interviews. Content analysis establishes themes and subthemes. Analysis progresses quickly but can be 'dirty' and easily marred by analyst bias. Focus group and narrative data content analysis is a good beginning but often needs to be supplemented with other methods (Denzin & Lincoln 2005).
2. **Narrative summary analysis** was invented by Carol Gilligan in response to the movement in literature and history called **deconstruction**. Gilligan reminded us that after taking our data apart to get at essences, we also could gain valuable insights by putting the data back together, not in its raw form, but in reordered form to tell stories from the points of view of different

participants. Narrative summary analysis technique is also called 'threading' (Gilligan 2009).

2.8.3 The mixed methods methodology and methods

Mixed methods are a response to a research problem that is of such a nature that the best research design to answer the problem should involve the use of many methods. This research is formally defined as 'the class of research where the researcher mixes or combines quantitative and qualitative research techniques, methods, approaches, concepts or language into a single study' (Johnson & Onwuegbuzie 2004: 17). A key feature of mixed methods research is its methodological pluralism and these results are sometimes deemed superior or better research results as compared to a single method research (Johnson & Onwuegbuzie 2004: 14). The goal of mixed methods research is not to replace either the quantitative or qualitative approach, but rather to draw from strengths and minimise the weaknesses of both in a single research study. Mixed methods may mean adopting a research strategy employing more than one type of research method. The methods may be a mix of qualitative and quantitative methods, or of quantitative methods or qualitative methods. Mixed methods study designs can be created from scratch to enable answering the research question, or may use strategies such as ethnography and action research or particular examples of case study strategies that may also employ more than one method (Creswell 2017).

Box 2.4 An example of a mixed methods study design

A multi-sequenced design: the life transitions to work or livelihoods of selected unemployed youths

Method 1: in an ongoing study of the life transitions of unemployed youth, a survey was carried out in several villages mainly to identify three types of unemployment (looking for work, no longer looking for work, cash earners in alternative ventures).

Method 2: the survey was followed by semi-structured interviews with managers at the Department of Labour, skills development training centres and the Department of Social Development in order to examine the context in which an entry to careers can develop.

⏵

Method 3: next, a purposive sample of different youths was selected to represent the range of unemployed youths, while biographical methods were used to capture these youths' experiences of gaining work over the life course.

Method 4: a follow-up telephone survey was carried out to ascertain changes in the work careers of survey respondents.

The one consequence of using many methods is that it may often entail working with different types of data. This lends itself to team research where the research team members may be from different subjects. This methodology is often practised in larger research projects that make use of researchers in teams from multiple disciplines. Mixed methods research is often referred to as multi-strategy research since a number of different research strategies are applied to address the complex range of research questions and a complex research design (Brannen 2006). On the other hand, mixed methods may form part of a long-term strategy (several years), as in the case of the example in the box above.

Brannen (2006) identifies a number of advantages in the use of mixed methods. These include opportunities for *skills enhancement* by different researchers, enhancing lifelong learning, fostering 'thinking outside the box' due to contact and conversation with academics from other theoretical traditions, more focus on strategic and practically oriented research and the dissemination of knowledge.

We will now briefly look at how researchers identify their respondents.

2.9 Sampling in sociological research

2.9.1 Quantitative sampling methods

Because surveys can be used in large-scale operations, they can become prohibitively expensive, so there is a need to take a few samples to represent the many cases. These samples are called **random probability samples** and are a 'representative' part of a larger whole that mimics the population from which it is drawn. Samples must be randomly selected to accurately generalise to the population, which means that each potential respondent in the population must have an equal chance to all others of getting selected. The process must be objective, and no human or subjective interference should occur in the completely random selection procedure. The basic form is a simple random sample, and other forms are variations used under certain circumstances to still attain random samples. To draw a simple random sample, one needs a complete and up-to-date sample frame with a number for each element. The lottery uses such principles.

2.9.2   Qualitative sampling methods

Sampling in qualitative research does not need randomness as a characteristic. If you want to do research on retired couples, you will not find them evenly distributed in the population. Many congregate in retirement facilities and there may also be some couples at clubs for retirees. They are also likely to congregate in one place on days when the Department of Social Development pays out pensions. Depending on your target group, you will find that each of these examples will constitute retired couples from different social strata. Your interest in their lived-in worlds means that one will not generalise findings. **Non-probability sample methods** can be used in testing an instrument

such as a questionnaire, but it is especially important to understand lived realities. In a survey one may have noticed that respondents who classify themselves as liberal or conservative also classify themselves as very religious. One will not be able to account for this pattern, without in-depth information on how respondents came to their particular positions. This is information and understanding that can only be accessed through qualitative methods. The sampling types used are ways of accessing respondents that are not randomly distributed. Examples of types are convenience and quota samples where you may take the first 30 persons in a doctor's rooms, or a particular type of person, say mothers, up to a quota of 10. Another example is the snowball sample, used when one has difficulty in identifying the respondents. If you start with one person, you may ask that respondent to introduce you to two others and then repeat this referral system until you have the number that you need (Babbie 2010; Neuman 2014).

Case study 2.2   Descriptions of a day in the life of rural youths who are not employed, in education or in training (NEET)

'I don't do much from wake up until bed time so there is not much to tell. First thing when I wake up is to make a small prayer, brush my teeth and after that start preparing breakfast for two, for myself and my little baby girl who is 11 months old. It is only the two of us because the others are at school and my mother is a domestic worker. Every day is the same unless maybe for going somewhere like clinic or to town for shopping. I sleep, listen to music or watch the TV. Last Wednesday was different because I did shopping for the whole family I am living with. It is not easy to go to town, because I must find someone to look after the baby. Sometimes my grandmother who is my mother's big sister [thus an aunt] who lives close will agree. I then had the one chance for shopping.'

'Wednesday I woke up about eleven, made my bed and then washed up. Afterwards to see my friends to catch up about men's stuff, that is girls and most of the time soccer. By four I went for soccer practice, then went back home to eat supper and watch television until late.'

'Saturday is like any other day but everything changes in the afternoon, when I meet with my guys at a local tavern and booze and smoke till Sunday morning.'

'Saturday I woke up in the morning and cleaned my room. After cleaning I washed myself and ate a full meal because it's Saturday. In our village everybody drinks on weekends. Me too.'

Young people who have left school without a Grade 12 certificate and who are unemployed are excluded from opportunities to fully develop their potential and contribute to their families and society through the activities of learning and work (RSA NYC 2009; Rushby nd).

There is a high level of unemployment and poverty generally in South Africa, but with the youth constituting 70 per cent of the total unemployed, the problem of unemployment has primarily become a youth problem (State of the Youth Report (SYR) 2004 in WCYC 2008).

The SYR indicates that two-thirds of all youth are unemployed and the majority have never had a job. The current state of youth exclusion in South Africa would be filled with the 'public issues' of an unequal social structure, lasting personal and family poverty, death and deprivation, failing in and leaving school, unemployment and geographical remoteness (Mills & Etzioni 2000). These are all factors that contribute to exclusion and intergenerational poverty. The discontinuities that contribute to such a 'toxic state' that many young people find themselves in is the backdrop to the personal hardship of individuals caught up in a particular social context, and transcends from being personal problems to becoming social issues of public debate and action.

QUESTIONS

1. Do you think studying youth should best be approached from an individual micro- or a societal macro-perspective? How would each of the perspectives approach this matter?
2. Should such problems in society be addressed by policy and top-down strategies, or by a bottom-up approach?
3. What theories can you identify that may assist you in deciding what information should be gathered and in the analysis of your findings?
4. What potential research problems can you generate from the application?
5. How would the different knowledge claims approach the topic?
6. What are the kinds of information you may need to address each research problem you identified?
7. What other sources of information on NEET youth is available and how can one tell if it is accurate?
8. How will you identify potential respondents?
9. What type of sampling will you use?
10. How should you gather information from respondents?
11. What are the advantages and disadvantages of your approach?
12. How will you determine how far your findings may be generalised?
13. How would you present descriptive information?

2.10 Ethics in research

When a sociologist decides to do research their first concern is for their subject. After all, wanting to know more about society and its people, or wanting to plan for the future or to influence and support a more just society is rooted in respect. Sociologists should thus be respectful of the respondents and societies where they do research. If sociologists wish to study the experiences of families who are caring for dying members, they have to be sensitive and realise that their questions are an intrusion on the lives of the family and this may open painful wounds. This realisation has led social scientists to bind themselves to a code of ethics when doing research. In practice, it is important to protect respondents and ensure that they are not harmed physically or psychologically through abuse, loss of self-esteem or stress. They must also be protected against legal harm and deception. Enough information should be provided so that respondents can make an informed judgement of whether they are willing to take part in the research or not. Once respondents take part, their right to remain anonymous should be respected and their privacy must be ensured. Only the researcher should have access to information linked to a particular respondent, thus ensuring confidentiality as well (The SRA nd). The researcher has very serious responsibilities with regard to how to conduct the capturing, interpretation and reporting of data. This thus requires the researcher to respect the evidence, tell as it is and, importantly, to know the boundaries of what they know and especially of what they do not know (limit generalisations to what may safely be claimed, based on the data they have and how they selected respondents).

A South African example of a code of ethics is the one used by the Human Sciences Research Council of South Africa (HSRC). The HSRC is South Africa's statutory research agency doing critical and independent research on all aspects of human and social development (www.hsrc.ac.za).

Box 2.5 Information: ethics, plagiarism and referencing

When you start reading other people's research, you will come across things that you wish you had said or could have presented so eloquently. You may feel that the author summarised salient issues that you agree or disagree with.

In academic writing you are expected to confirm or illustrate your views by referring to those of other researchers.

Referencing is an important part of learning to write academically and involves how you identify the arguments and views of other authors in your own writing. The method most widely used by sociologists is called the Harvard method. It is a very serious offence to use parts of an article from a book, journal or the web without proper referencing to the real author. It is a crime against the actual author, as well as a transgression of the ethical code of honesty.

In this era of cyber information and the possibility to cut and paste material, being honest is very important for the development of your own integrity as a social scientist.

Avoiding plagiarism requires you to either select a quote from the work you want to use, summarise the points made, or paraphrase the content. It also requires you to present your own argument, which you may illustrate as supportive or different from the point of view of the referred to authors. What you may not do under any circumstances, no matter how applicable the work you come across, is to cut and paste sections and claim that it is your work.

2.11 Types of research dimensions that can vary

Research can vary with regard to the type of knowledge sought. In this section we will discuss two examples of research to illustrate some of the possible variations.

Research is done for many reasons, and takes many forms, but to familiarise you with some of the variations, we will discuss the example of primary and applied research, and descriptive and explanatory research (Neuman 2014).

2.11.1 Primary and applied research

Some research is done strictly to increase knowledge and is called primary research. The types of research undertaken to address particular problems is known as applied research. It is seldom that research conforms completely to one of the types. Applied research has supported theoretical insights, and likewise basic research has been used to provide solutions to problems. **Evaluative research** may be viewed as a type of applied research as it is usually undertaken to measure in some way the impact or changes a particular programme may have made in a community, organisation or other social unit that was targeted.

2.11.2 Descriptive and explanatory research

Research may also vary in that it may describe what is going on or attempt to explain particular phenomena. The way in which researchers develop research designs is fundamentally affected by whether the research question is descriptive or explanatory. It affects what information is collected. Social researchers ask two types of research questions: what is going on (descriptive research) and why is it going on (explanatory research)?

Descriptive research informs us of the shape and nature of our society. The 2011 census is an example of essential descriptive research. The census is normally held every five years.

Generally, descriptive studies provide statistics about the characteristics of the study area, and/or will provide rich information based on observations and in-depth interviews with the study population. An example would be looking at the unemployment rates in a country, describing the distribution and comparing it to other African nations. Explanatory research focuses on the 'why' questions. If one wants to develop explanations about why the unemployment rate is as high as it is, or why unemployment is increasing among youth in particular, this kind of research would be useful. For example, if we want to explain why some people are more likely to be unemployed and excluded, we need to have an idea or a theory about why this is so. We may have many ideas and will need to collect information that enables us to see which is best supported empirically while also testing the theoretical premises that were stated.

Summary

- Sociological research cannot be separated from its theory. The data gathered in research is interpreted and provided with meaning by the theory.
- Scientific observation has validity and reliability, and is different from common-sense generalisations due to the rigorous discipline imposed by the steps in the research method.
- The steps in research are identifying and developing the topic; deciding on the methodology; creating the research design; collecting the data; analysing the conclusion; and then disseminating the results.
- Sociological theory has a number of advantages in research and the choice of methodology is directed by the knowledge claims inherent to the positivist, interpretive, critical and realist approaches to society. The methodologies of quantitative and qualitative methods and mixed methods are linked via the research questions and accepted knowledge claims to research designs that are created to provide the highest level of validity possible.
- The methodologies used by sociology are traditionally linked with certain methods of sampling and data presentation. Sampling for quantitative research is called probability sampling. Samples are randomly selected to enable generalisation. Qualitative samples are not representative and cannot readily be generalised. For this reason, samples are selected with a view to describe and thus are not representative.
- Both quantitative and qualitative researchers use empirical observations to address their respective research questions. They describe their data, construct explanatory arguments from it and speculate about why the outcomes they observed happened as they did.
- Remember that good scholarship is not just the result of a specific method but the result of how one employs, cross-checks, collates and analyses the data that methods assist one in collecting. Research should be judged on how its constituent parts logically link together.
- Ethics is important to the sociological research undertaking and includes the obligation towards professional conduct and the use of appropriate methods.
- Sociological research may take various forms and has many cross-cutting dichotomies that result in examples such as primary and applied research, or descriptive and explanatory research.

ARE YOU ON TRACK?

1. Can you think of some advantages of scientific observation?
2. Generate four advantages of theory in research.
3. Can you identify and describe the different steps in the research process?
4. 'Men are more aggressive than women'. This is a value statement. How will you make the statement researchable? How many ways can you formulate?
5. We have identified different ways of approaching society and knowledge (positivist, interpretive/constructionist, critical/participatory and realist). Can you explain the main knowledge claim of each, what they believe about society and what type of evidence one would value and expect if they do research?
6. Can you identify and explain the difference between the quantitative, qualitative and mixed methods methodologies of research, and why a given theoretical view on society or a particular knowledge claim would prefer any one methodology in particular?
7. We have identified different methodologies. Can you name and describe them?
8. Can you explain why there are different ways to attain samples in the quantitative and qualitative methodologies, and which ways each find useful?
9. Which ethical matters should researchers be aware of protecting when they request respondents to be part of their research?

More sources to consult

Kevin Connolly photos (www.therollingexhibition.com/)
Examples and exercises that show you how to quote, paraphrase or summarise your sources, to avoid plagiarism (http://owl.english.purdue.edu/owl/owlprint/563/).

Universities and academic departments often have money available to support research. In South Africa, the most important body that supports research in the social sciences is called the National Research Foundation (NRF). You can learn more about the various programmes from their website: www.nrf.ac.za/funding_overview.php

Websites

Campus France. This website introduces all sociology study programmes in France and showcases the contribution of French sociologists. www.campusfrance.org

Human Sciences Research Council. www.hsrc.ac.za (a government research and think tank)

National Research Foundation (NRF). Universities and academic departments often have money available to support research. In South Africa the most important body that supports research in the social sciences is called the National Research Foundation (NRF). You can learn more about the various programmes from their website: www.nrf.ac.za/funding_overview.php

OWL Purdue. This website has examples and exercises that show you how to quote, paraphrase or summarise your sources to avoid plagiarism. http://owl.english.purdue.edu/owl/owlprint/563/

The South African Sociological Association (SASA) has student members. SASA maintains useful links to all South African universities, research organisations and other relevant sites, and has a blog where one can read about previous and coming conferences, the history of the association and many more useful features. http://www.sasaonline.org.za/

References

Babbie ER. 2010. *The Practice of Social Research.* Ohio: Cengage Learning.

Beck J, Stolterman E. 2016. 'Examining the types of knowledge claims made in design research'. *She Ji: The Journal of Design, Economics, and Innovation*, 2(3): 199–214.

Brannen J. 2006. 'Mixed methods research: A discussion paper.' Swindon: ESRC.

Comte A. 1998. *Auguste Comte and Positivism: The Essential Writings.* Chicago: Transaction Publishers.

Connolly K. 2009. 'The Rolling Exhibition'. [Online] Available at: http://www.therollingexhibition.com/ [Accessed 5 February 2019].

Connell R. 2014. 'Using southern theory: Decolonizing social thought in theory, research and application'. *Planning Theory,* 13(2): 210. Available at: https://journals.sagepub.com/doi/pdf/10.1177/1473095213499216 [Accessed 2 February 2019].

Creswell JW. 2017. *Research Design: Qualitative, Quantitative, and Mixed Methods Approaches.* London: SAGE.

Denzin NK, Lincoln YS. 2011. *The SAGE Handbook of Qualitative Research.* London: SAGE.

Fink A. 2003. *The Survey Kit.* London: SAGE.

Gilligan C. 2009. *In a Different Voice.* Boston: Harvard University Press.

Given L. 2008. *The SAGE Encyclopaedia of Qualitative Research Method.* London: SAGE.

Handlechner M. 2008. *An Investigation into Seasonality – How to Increase Overnight Stays in the Shoulder Season: A Case Study in Austria.* Austria: GRIN Verlag.

HSRC. nd. [Online] Available at: www.hsrc.ac.za/en/ [Accessed 25 February 2019].

Johnson RB, Onwuegbuzie AJ. 2004. 'Mixed Methods Research: A Research Paradigm Whose Time Has Come'. *Educ. Res.* 33:14–26.

Leedy PD, Ormrod JE. 2018. 'Practical Research: Planning and Design Plus' in *My Education Lab with Pearson EText. Access card package.* 12th ed. Pearson USA.

Matthews TD, Kostelis KT. 2011. *Designing and Conducting Research in Health and Human Performance.* New Jersey: John Wiley & Sons.

Mills CW. 1961. *The Sociological Imagination.* 1st Evergreen ed, 8th ed. New York: Grove Press.

Mills CW, Etzioni A. 2000. *Sociological Imagination.* United States: OUP.

Neuman WL. 2014. *Basics of Social Research: Qualitative and Quantitative Approaches.* New Jersey: Harlow Pearson.

Pawson R. 2006. *Evidence-Based Policy: A Realist Perspective.* London: SAGE.

Rushby L. nd. LibGuides. 'Youth: Government Sources. South Africa: Provincial and Local'. [Online] Available at: http://libguides.lib.uct.ac.za/GovtPubs/Youth/South Africa/Policies [Accessed 27 February 2019].

Sanderson CA. 2009. *Social Psychology.* New Jersey: John Wiley & Sons.

Steinmetz G. 2005. *The Politics of Method in the Human Sciences: Positivism and Its Epistemological Others.* North Carolina: Duke University Press.

The SRA. nd. 'Ethics guidelines'. [Online] http://the-sra.org.uk/sra_resources/research-ethics/ethics-guidelines/ [Accessed 6 February 2018].

Tucker WT. 1965. Max Weber's 'Verstehen'. *Sociology Quarterly.* 6: 157–165.

The Reach Project. 2013. [Online] Available at: http://www.thereachtrust.org/ [Accessed 25 February 2019].

Webster E. 2004. 'Sociology in South Africa: Its past, present and future'. *Social Transition,* 35: 27–41.

Culture

Shannon Morreira

If human beings are in essence social beings, their sociality is expressed by, through and within a specific inherited and learned set of beliefs, knowledge, skills and practices. The food we eat, the words we speak, the gestures we make, the behaviours we enact and the social actions in which we engage – and how we do so – are all *culturally* defined. This is but one way of trying to describe what culture is. There are many more possible descriptions, understandings and analyses of the concept of culture. This is due to the social phenomenon it designates encompassing so wide a range of ways of being and shared forms of social life. As this chapter explains right at the beginning, there is much debate about how best to use the word, term or concept of culture. If nothing else, however, culture refers to our immediately lived experience and its very many forms and styles expressed in the language we speak – itself a cultural product.

You will already have discovered that defining terms in sociology and the social sciences more broadly is seldom a clear-cut exercise. How to define the term 'culture' is especially tricky and you will be surprised at how many attempts have been made in advancing a definition of the concept of culture. The reason is that our very lives are culturally defined. Even families living in the same neighbourhood will do things slightly differently. Culture is intimately part of our immediate daily experience and so culture can be described, analysed and sociologically explained in many different ways. Sometimes one has to simply choose a working definition and work with it. This is what this chapter does and so returns to the definition in the course of the discussion. This is not the end of the matter and you are encouraged to define for yourself what culture is. This means that not all the intellectual work has been done for you, partly because no prescriptions are available. There are hence many avenues you can go down in exploring what is meant by the concept of culture. Consider yourself to have been challenged to make the concept and reality of culture, which is so much part of our lives and who we are, real and meaningful for yourself. Incidentally, this is a perfect opportunity to develop your sociological imagination. Discuss with a fellow sociologist how they understand the concept from their particular vantage point. Such a discussion is potentially the beginning of developing a series of decolonial imaginations. How does one engage in this exercise and find the necessary distance in order to be objective in your thinking and analysis if you are going to understand something important about a 'culture' which is foreign or strange to you? If you do manage to do this, however, you will see both how practical sociology can be and how it can lend itself to analysis of cultural experiences which are very different from your own. To be able to view the world and the life experiences of others and be able to understand the world from their point of view is critical to social analysis and understanding.

Consider this chapter as your introduction to the world of micro-sociology, which has its focus on small, seemingly unimportant things. This is the sociology of the everyday. It is also the sociology in terms of which the larger, more expansive issues must always be explained. The chapters on race, class and gender, each in their own way, *presuppose* this cultural bedrock discussed in this chapter. This discussion on culture means that it refers back to the theoretical ideas of the classics already introduced and points to sociological ideas and theories you will encounter in chapters to follow.

One more note is appropriate. There is not a series of facts to learn here. The exercise is cognitive and intellectual. Consider this chapter an opportunity to apply sociological concepts to your own lived reality. To modify a current phrase, take this chapter seriously and it could turn out to be a conceptual 'game changer' in your life and you might never view the world again in quite the same way. Reading and taking to heart what follows could acculturate you into sociology for life.

Case study 3.1 Fast food

The fast food or take-out phenomenon is a global trend that began with eating out or away from home. It has much to do with our increased mobility, cooking, entertaining guests and experiencing new cultural activities.

The changing patterns of how we eat and what we eat are partly explained by what we want to do with our time, but are also partly dictated to us by the way our world is organised. We know that take-out began in the USA in the early 20th century with the transformation of franchise restaurants into drive-in eateries. This was both a process of standardisation (same menu everywhere) and mobility (cars and public transport). It may also have had something to do with leisure time, changing family values, changing tastes and the commercialisation of everyday life.

When we step into a fast food outlet, we step into a sophisticated collection of processes that sociologists find very interesting. For example, the food we are going to eat will taste almost the same as the last time we had it because it is pre-prepared according to a formula, and the place where it is cooked looks more like a production line than a kitchen. In addition, there are no chefs or cooks preparing to excite our taste buds. More than likely, this outlet is part of a vast chain of outlets all over the world, making money, providing jobs, using state-of-the-art technology and meeting a lot of people's needs to eat and run. It is quick and it becomes a platform for eating and doing other things. We can contrast it with the 'slow food' movement which suggests we spend more time over our food, taking care over the nutritional value and conviviality of time spent sharing this basic human pleasure of eating.

Fast food is popular. It is a competitive industry, so we will see and hear a lot of marketing and advertising telling us how clever we are and how tasty it all is. How a picnic is just not the same without it. How it brings families together and tramples the lines between rich and poor. Of course, there are debates about the nutritional value of many fast foods, debates about the lifestyles associated with fast foods, and concerns about the displacement of long-held beliefs and practices regarding eating.

Spend a few minutes on the Internet and check out the backstory on this apparently simple and convenient phenomenon – fast food.

Key themes

- Culture as ordinary lived experiences
- Defining culture
- Theoretical perspectives on culture
- Structural functionalism
- Symbolic interactionism

- Conflict perspectives
- Post-colonial perspectives
- Elements of culture
- Cultural diversity
- Culture, socialisation and identity.

3.1 Introduction

From the moment that we wake up in the morning to the moment we go to sleep at night, everything we do is influenced by the cultural patterns of the society in which we live. It is not just the food we eat, the clothes we wear, how we interact and behave that define our specific learned style of life or culture. In fact, even when we sleep we do so in a culturally specific way. For example, the average number of hours of sleep a person gets each night varies in different cultural contexts, as do the expectations of whether adults and children in a family will sleep together or alone. Whatever we are doing, then, humans are cultural beings. Awake or asleep, we are constantly immersed in the patterns of our culture.

Human beings are quintessentially cultural beings as all of our actions are situated within the social contexts in which we live. Human beings are social animals. We are also capable of learning. We learn far more over the course of our lifetimes than we are formally taught in schools and universities. Throughout our lives, we are taught particular ways of doing things and ways of being in the world. In other words, we are constantly taught and learn how to live within the patterns and routines of a specific culture. Some of these things will be explicitly told to us – for example respect your elders – while other things will be implicit and unspoken, but learned nonetheless. For example, the personal space that you feel comfortable having between you and another person is something that is specific to your cultural context. No one ever told you what the right distance for personal space was, but nonetheless everyone within your cultural context will know what the comfortable boundaries of personal space are. You can test this by standing a little closer to a friend than you ordinarily would when you are talking to them. The chances are they will take a small step away from you, possibly without even being aware of having done so. If you move closer once more, they will move away again. Do it often enough and you will get an odd look from them, because you are stepping outside of the unwritten and unspoken code of your culture with regard to personal space. There are thousands of these spoken and unspoken rules that we all use each and every day. Some are more permanent than others. These ways of being and ways of doing *constitute* culture.

In the social sciences, culture as a unit of study was originally seen to be the realm of anthropologists, academics who left their places of origin to do fieldwork to discover more about the cultures and traditions of others. It is because of this history that we sometimes think of culture as something 'exotic'. But the examples above illustrate that culture is something we all embody. Our *culture* is part of who we are. The social reality of culture does not lie in the realm of the exotic, but is in fact in the realm of every person's ordinary daily existence. This is not to say that everyone is the same. There are, of course, a multitude of different ways in which people experience 'ordinary' life. The point, rather, is that everyone experiences their own culture as *ordinary*.

In the social sciences today, the concept of culture is used across academic disciplines. Indeed, new disciplines such as Cultural Studies have emerged that take notions of culture as central to their analysis of the social world. The concept of culture is therefore an analytic category used by social scientists across the globe. But it is important for us as South African sociologists and anthropologists in particular to situate global ideas within our South African context. We need to understand the origin and history of these ideas and the ways in which the local and the global interact in the present.

In South Africa, the concept of culture has a tumultuous past. This is partly because of the academic history of the study of the *exotic*. Cultural difference was seen as an object of academic interest. Africa in particular was one of the places in which exotic difference could be found and studied. But it is also because of the political history of colonisation. During colonialism, cultural and racial differences were used as the basis for oppression. The 'civilising mission' that accompanied colonialism was one in which direct attempts were made to change indigenous cultural patterns in order to make 'the natives' behave more like the coloniser. The assumption here was that the culture of the coloniser was somehow better than or superior to that of indigenous colonised populations. These attempts at shifting people's cultural patterns were sometimes named and justified as contributing to 'modernising' people. The assumption was that equality would accompany modernity. This turned out to be false. In reality, of course, the project of colonialism was a deeply damaging one. Modernity, as experienced both in the past and in the present, has not been an equalising process. Modern culture introduced with colonialism instead created and maintained social hierarchies very different from the societies on which they were imposed.

In South Africa, culture was a tool used by the apartheid government as a way of justifying and maintaining separation between groups. The apartheid apparatus of 'separate development' was predicated on the idea that different racialised cultural groups did things differently and so they should be kept geographically and socially separate to 'develop' at their own pace. It was for this reason that different tribes were allocated to different Bantustans. For the same sorts of reasons as have been outlined for the concept of culture, the idea of 'tribe' is also a problematic one in South Africa. While the rhetoric employed during apartheid was one of separate development, in reality this was a political justification for the economic and social oppression of the majority of South Africans. Given the role of the idea of separate cultures in our history then, the very concept of culture is rightly a contentious one in our social context.

Despite the way in which the concept of different cultures was introduced locally, this does not mean that the idea, concept or use of the term 'culture' has been discarded by ordinary South Africans. In fact, the opposite has happened. The concept of culture has taken a strong hold in the popular imagination. Most South Africans will carry some form of cultural identity they hold as important to them. Garuba and Raditlaho (2010) argue that it is precisely because of our tricky history that this is the case. These theorists argue that, because people were oppressed on the basis of culture, culture has been a site for resistance and struggle against oppression, marginalisation and domination. This has also occurred in response to globalisation. People have held onto their cultural differences in the face of global forces which push towards homogenisation. Culture, then, is very much present in South African thought and daily experience.

With this context in mind, this chapter explores how culture can be defined and looks at the different theoretical perspectives on culture used by sociologists and anthropologists. The chapter then moves to ideas of cultural diversity and how they might play out in a 'multicultural' setting – and, indeed, what the idea of 'multiculturalism' might tell us about how people imagine similarity and difference in a time of globalisation. The chapter also explores how cultures change over time. It concludes by returning to a consideration of South Africa in particular, in order to think through how culture could contribute to addressing some of the social problems that exist in our country today.

3.2 Defining culture

Sociologists define culture as *the patterns that we have for living: the beliefs we hold about how to live in the social world and the practices, behaviours and material objects that accompany them*. While culture is dynamic, in that it changes over time, it also has elements of continuity with the past. For whether we are aware of it or not, we all carry beliefs, practices and patterns of behaviour across the generations. While the specific patterns of any culture will

vary from place to place and across time, all human societies assume some or other form of culture. Culture consists of both the symbols with which we think – for example our languages or our religions – and the material things that accompany our thinking – for example libraries, books or mosques and churches.

It is worth thinking a little bit about how sociologists and anthropologists have come to this present-day definition of culture. Understanding culture as a set of material and non-material patterns that are learned and are dynamic can help us grasp the relationship between sociological theories about how society works and sociological definitions of the different elements of society.

There have been a great many definitions of culture put forward over time. This reflects both how tricky it is to define something as diverse as culture and how our understandings of what culture is has changed as our views of what society is and how society works have changed. As long ago as 1952, when two academics did a review of definitions of culture, they found that there were 164 different definitions of culture being used by anthropologists at the time (Kroeber & Kluckholm 1952). The situation has not improved today. So how did we come to the definition we are using in this textbook? Let us begin by looking at the history of culture as an academic concept. Then we can think a little more about the concise definition given above in relation to the South African context in which we live and work.

The anthropologist Susan Wright (Wright 1998) has examined the ways in which the concept of culture has been used. Wright differentiated between what she calls 'old' and 'new' ideas of culture. The 'old' ideas of culture tended to see culture as a bounded whole, with a checklist of defined attributes. These attributes or characteristics were self-reproducing and stable over time and led to groups of homogeneous individuals who shared an underlying system of meanings. The patterns of life, what beliefs were held and their impact on behaviour and the practices of daily social life sharing common material resources, what we have called culture in other words, was similarly experienced by all in a similar way. In this version of culture, being a Zulu person would mean that you came from a particular geographical place, spoke the same inherited language and shared the same norms and values with all other Zulu people. You would go on to have Zulu children who all shared those same cultural attributes.

If we pause, even for a moment, however, and consider contemporary South African society, it becomes evident that this definition is not entirely satisfactory. Are you only a Zulu person if you were born in KwaZulu-Natal? Of course not! Many people who ascribe to a Zulu identity come from elsewhere in South Africa and from beyond the country's borders. Is Zulu culture unchanging and stable? No! For to be Zulu today carries a different set of meanings than it did 100 years ago. And is Zulu culture homogeneous? No! There have been debates, for instance, over something like *Ukweshwana* (first fruit ceremony), which reveal many diverse views within this single societal grouping. Do Zulu people only marry other Zulu people and have Zulu children? Of course not! The point is that the world cannot be so easily divided into separate cultural groups as was once imagined.

Box 3.1 Cultural change and internal variation as seen through *Ukweshwana*

Umkhosi Ukweshwana, or the festival of the first fruits, is a festival that was revived by King Goodwill Zwelethini kaBhekuzulu in the mid-2000s. *Ukweshwana* had not been practised since the colonial period when it was outlawed. The Zulu king revived it in keeping with a move to reinstate pre-colonial practices in the post-colonial period. However, one element of the festival, in which young men kill a bull, came under severe public scrutiny and led to a great deal of debate in South Africa, including being the subject of a court case. Proponents for the killing of the bull argued that the festival should be as true to the original as possible.

Others argued that animal rights should be taken into account. The example shows that culture changes over time and that views on cultural rituals and practices are not homogeneous: there is room for debate. (For more on *Ukweshwana*, see Boonzaier & Spiegel 2008; Rautenbach 2011.)

South African theorist Robert Thornton has thus argued that the problem with the use of the concept of culture in South Africa in the past was to do with the idea of seeing cultures as separate ways of being in the world, rather than thinking about culture as a set of resources to which people had varying degrees of access. 'The problem,' writes Thornton, 'is the little s that makes cultures from culture' (Thornton 1988: 18). By this, he meant that the modes of thinking instilled in the academy by colonialism and apartheid insisted in creating and maintaining the idea of separate, bounded cultures. This was a dangerous idea that detracted from the realities of similarity and instead had difference as its key focus.

Box 3.2 Fluidity between cultural groups

So-called separate cultures are not as separate as we might think. The anthropologist David Webster (1991) conducted research that showed that women living in a KwaZulu border region during apartheid identified as Zulu in some contexts and Thonga in others.

Women presented themselves as Zulu in relation to the apartheid state, regarding pension payouts and in their dealings with the Inkatha Freedom Party. But they identified as Thonga when it came to marriage. This was because Zulu rules of *hlonipha* (respect) were more patriarchal and allowed women less autonomy in marriage than did Thonga practices. As such, women embraced the Zulu parts of their heritage at some times and Thonga at others.

This example shows us that we are not stuck in a single cultural category but that our cultural affiliation can change according to context. It also shows us that categorisations and power relations within a group – in this instance, those of gender – can influence our views on cultural practices (see Webster 1991; Boonzaier & Spiegel 2008).

You can thus see that even the act of defining what we mean by culture is fraught with conceptual difficulties when analysing complex sets of beliefs and practices, not only when comparing cultures, but when doing so within a specific cultural environment. If we define a culture as a way of life distinctive to a particular group of people, then we are faced with the dilemma of deciding who is included and who is excluded from that particular group and on what grounds we do so. We also have to decide what the substance of that culture is – what practices are 'authentically' Zulu, and what are not. Because of issues like this, definitions of culture have become considerably more nuanced, or complex.

According to Wright, these new definitions of culture share the following features:
- Culture is seen as an active process of meaning making within which there is room for debate and contestation.
- The sites of culture are not bounded by geography – people draw on local, national and global links in making culture.
- People are situated differently within society and will use the resources of their culture differently.

When we define culture as *the patterns that we have for living: the beliefs we hold about how to live in the social world, and the practices, behaviours and material objects that accompany them*, we therefore understand that these patterns shift over time. There may be different views on the patterns of behaviour within any society. We can therefore think about these cultural patterns as a set of resources people draw on for various purposes.

Ideas of culture thus differ depending upon time, period, place and theoretical perspective. This is because when social scientists try to understand the phenomenon of culture, they do so through the lens of varied *theoretical approaches or paradigms*. The influences of these paradigms have, in turn, shifted over time and place. It is these perspectives which now become our focus.

3.3 Theoretical perspectives on culture

3.3.1 Ideas of culture in structural functionalism

Functionalism was a school of thought that was seen most prominently in sociological theory in the work of Auguste Comte, Herbert Spencer and, after Comte's death, Émile Durkheim (see Chapter 1 on sociological theory). The central idea behind functionalism as a social theory was the notion that society is comprised of a number of institutions that *function* as part of an interrelated whole. The different parts of society – for example the family, political structure, economic structure – were all seen as working together to create and maintain order and stability. Society was seen as composed of a series of social structures, all of which worked together towards establishing societal equilibrium. Through this theoretical lens society was seen as fairly orderly and stable.

In functionalism, culture was seen as a stabilising mechanism. The elements of culture that received most attention were the *values and norms* of any given society. These values and norms were held to shape the everyday and bring together the members of society to work towards common goals. We can define values as the standards people have about what is considered good and what is considered bad. Norms are the behaviours that accompany the value system: the rules about what is the normal or correct way in which we do things. In structural functionalist thinking, cultural practices were thus seen as part and parcel of the interrelated whole that was society. Our learned behaviours and values were seen as linked to the core structures that made society function.

Structural functionalism also proposed the idea of cultural universals: cultural traits that exist in every culture. While the way we do things might differ across contexts, all cultures have to deal with similar problems. For example, the kinship network, or family, would be considered a cultural

universal: all societies organise themselves in terms of some formalised idea of how its members are related to one another by descent or marriage. In the last half of the 20th century in the West, the nuclear family (some version of biological mother, father and children) has become marked as the norm, while the extended family (encompassing more than two or more generations and involving cousins, aunts and uncles as well as mothers and fathers) is more likely to be the norm in most rural areas across southern Africa. In southern Africa, ancestors also play a prominent role in ideas of family organisation as they did in ancient Greece over 3 000 years ago, while currently in Western societies this is no longer the case. However, despite these differences, the concept of family is still a universal one, in that the two different versions of family both organise their societal contexts in such a way that society is able to function smoothly. Whether this is achieved through a nuclear family or an extended one and whether it includes only the living or the living and the living-dead, in a functionalist view the family always works to provide a means of socialising the next generation.

As in most theoretical frameworks, approaches or paradigms, some elements of structural functionalist thinking have continued to carry weight in academia. For example, most sociologists would agree that it is heuristically useful for purposes of analysis to break down society into its component parts or institutions, such as the family, the economy, political organisations and so forth. Other elements of structural-functionalist theory are seen as simplistic or outdated. For example, structural-functionalist views of culture have been subject to critique for their emphasis on cultural stability, which limits this theoretical approach from being able to explain social change, especially major structural transformation, when it does occur. Furthermore, an underlying assumption of this view of culture is that everyone within the society embraces its norms and values with equal enthusiasm. If we are to think of Wright's taxonomy of 'old' and 'new' ideas of culture, as mentioned above, a structural-functionalist analysis would be situated as an 'old' one that does not adequately account for power differentials, conflict and the fluidity of culture over time.

3.3.2 Symbolic interactionism

While the theory of structural functionalism is concerned with large-scale structure, the theoretical perspective of symbolic interactionism falls under the umbrella of 'micro-sociology' in that it is concerned with individuals and the everyday. The symbolic interactionist perspective sees society as primarily a space of meaning making. A symbol is any shared cultural representation of reality. Language, for example, is a symbolic system, in that words come to stand for objects or behaviours or places. Clothes can also be symbols, in that they carry meaning for the person wearing them and the people looking at the person wearing them. In symbolic interactionism then, our social world is composed of the ways in which we make meaning and interact with one another. It is through these everyday acts of interacting with one another that society gets made.

In the words of the symbolic anthropologist Clifford Geertz,

> [m]an is an animal suspended in webs of significance he himself has spun. I take culture to be those webs, and the analysis of it not to be an experimental one in search of law but an interpretive one in search of meaning (Geertz 1975: 5).

In this view, culture is not seen as interesting or worthy of study because of the ways in which it contributes towards the smooth functioning of society, as it is in structural functionalism. Culture is rather viewed as a way in which humans create meaning and make sense of their social world. For example, where a funeral rite from a functionalist perspective might be seen as something that is done in order to make sure that grief is dealt with in such a way that society continues to function uninterrupted, a symbolic interpretation of a funeral rite would focus on the ways in which the different cultural elements within the funeral work to create meaning for people as they deal with their grief. The focus is on the people and the way in which they make and find meaning in their social world through the shared symbols that constitute culture.

In terms of Wright's (1998) taxonomy, the ideas of culture used in symbolic interactionism can be seen as a mixture of the 'old' and the 'new'. While culture is not necessarily seen as a bounded or homogeneous whole, there is nonetheless the idea that culture consists of a set of underlying meanings everybody shares. Furthermore, there is more room for change than in a theory such as structuralism. Meanings are interpreted by people and those interpretations can easily and inevitably do change over time. There is further a recognition of the power differentials between people in society. Not everyone has the same access to symbols of meaning making or is able to draw on symbols in the same way. For example, a symbolic interactionist analysis of gender in a patriarchal society would argue that the symbols and meanings associated with

women and femininity carry a different set of entitlements than those associated with men and masculinity. As symbolic interactionism emphasises the meanings people attach to their own behaviour, as well as the meanings other people ascribe or impose on them regarding their own behaviour, there is thus the recognition of change and of power. Despite having been powerfully influenced by Weber, who has strong emphases on economic class and domination, it is perhaps surprising that the role of power is fairly covert in symbolic interactionist perspectives. It has been largely left to another theoretical perspective on culture in which power plays a central role: the conflict perspective. It is to that approach which we now turn.

3.3.3 Conflict perspectives on culture

In contrast to the ideas of stability contained in structural functionalist thinking, or the focus on the ways in which people make meaning in symbolic interactionism, conflict perspectives have focused on the power tussles in society. Conflict theories see society as composed of different groups who have fundamentally different interests and who thus are either covertly or openly in opposition with one another. Some of the interests that might lie behind social groups clashing in any society are those of different social classes, genders, nationalities, sexualities and age groups. The conflict paradigm emphasises that society is composed of groups with starkly different means of access to or little or no access to social power. Marxism (with its focus on class), feminism (with its focus on gender), queer theory (with its focus on sexual orientation), black scholarship (with being black as a key focus), post-colonial theories (which have race and the colonised as key foci) and decolonial theory (with body politics and geographical location as starting points), are all conflict perspectives. A conflict perspective assumes that the composition of society is not equal, but rather that social structures generally privilege some groups over others.

Unfortunately, given South Africa's history and its present position as one of the most unequal countries in the world, it is all too easy, in one sense, for us as South African sociologists and students to understand conflict theories. Apartheid was a system that wrote differential access to power and resources into law on the basis of race. While the laws may have changed, we are still living with their after-effects in the present. A great many of our cultural repertoires – or our ordinary ways of thinking and acting – are influenced by this history. This is particularly the case as apartheid was a system that conflated race and culture. Being designated black or white meant it was also assumed you carried with you particular ways of acting and doing (Erasmus 2008). Neville Alexander (2013: 160) hence argued that we still have a 'racial habitus' ingrained in our behaviours in South Africa. By this Alexander meant that our very habits, reactions, thoughts and attitudes are unconsciously or consciously affected by race and the social hierarchies we associate with different racial groups.

One way in which we can think about this is through the notion of *cultural hegemony*, an idea that stems from the conflict perspective. Cultural hegemony is the idea that despite societies being composed of diverse interest groups, one way of being, or one set of interests, comes to be held as more important than others. This results in the values and interests of one group of people being imposed on and considered to be the norm, in other words, the universally valid way of doing things. South African social intellectual Steve Bantu Biko was speaking out against notions of white hegemony in South Africa in the 1970s, for example, when he argued that black is beautiful. The idea that lay behind Black Consciousness was that centuries of oppression during colonialism and into apartheid had resulted in black people internalising a cultural identity which devalued their own blackness and held whiteness in high esteem. Biko wrote that, 'the African child learns to hate his heritage in his days at school. So negative is the image presented to him, that he tends to find solace only in close identification with the white society' (Biko 1978: 29). Black Consciousness was a political philosophy that set out to change this by challenging the cultural hegemony of apartheid society by celebrating elements of black South African culture.

Contemporary South African political theorist Thiven Reddy has argued that South Africa has seen a resurgence in ideas of Black Consciousness in popular rhetoric in the last decade or so. He argues that this is because social inequality has remained a key feature of South African society (Reddy 2008). Archbishop Desmond Tutu had this same notion in mind when he said in 2006 that, 'We still depressingly do not respect each other. Black Consciousness did not finish the work it set out to do' (Tutu 2006). Within this viewpoint, practices such as people straightening their hair are seen as due to centuries of oppression in which straight hair was seen as more respectable than kinky hair because straight hair was associated with whiteness while kinky hair was associated with blackness (Erasmus 2000). A social conflict perspective of culture would see the resurgence of Biko's ideas in contemporary South Africa as a direct result of our society being composed of social groups with differing access to power. At present, young black people in particular use cultural symbols, such as clothing and hairstyles, to challenge what they see as the continuation of a dominant white cultural hegemony in democratic South Africa.

3.3.4 Post-colonial perspectives on culture

One form of conflict perspective that is particularly pertinent to democratic South Africa is post-colonial theory. Broadly speaking, post-colonial theory is concerned with analysing the social realities of spaces that were colonised during the imperialist expansion of Europe. Post-colonial theory has undergone a number of permutations since its inception, but all have involved a focus on culture.

The first wave of post-colonial theory drew attention to the fact that the society and culture or ways of life of colonised people had been positioned as inferior by colonising societies. As with Biko, who prefigured decolonial theory given his emphasis on body politics, theorists from this school showed that the cultural hegemony of imperialism impacted upon the way in which colonised people thought about themselves and their culture. Post-colonial theory showed the ways in which culture in colonised and previously colonised spaces worked to maintain hierarchies of privilege. The work of the Palestinian-American scholar Edward Said, for example, showed the patronising ways in which 'the East' or 'the Orient' was represented by 'the West'. During the 19th and early 20th centuries, 'the Orient' was used as shorthand for the many middle-Eastern and Asian countries and cultures that lay to the east of Europe and were perceived as particularly 'exotic' in relation to Europe. Said (1978) did a very detailed textual analysis of European literature to show that the cultures of 'the Orient' were not only portrayed as exotic, but also as static and unchanging and as less advanced than those of imperial Europe.

Building on this foundation, the next step taken by post-colonial theorists with regard to culture was the recognition that people in post-colonial settings needed to strive to reclaim cultural autonomy. In other words, people should make their own decisions about what is valuable and celebrate their ways of doing things and ways of being in the world. This in turn led to a recognition that post-colonial spaces were generally hybrid ones where a great deal of mixing of cultural forms takes places. For example, most South Africans are comfortable consulting both biomedical practitioners and traditional healers to deal with illness. Homi Bhabha's (1994) idea of **hybridity** sees the mixtures of cultural forms used by previously colonised people as a subversive way of challenging the dominant narratives of imperialism.

3.4 Elements of culture

We can see from all the different theoretical perspectives presented above that culture has been a concept which has engendered much critical engagement by sociologists and other social scientists. While the perspectives may differ, at their core is a concern to analyse and understand people's ways of being in the world.

We can summarise the key elements of the complex concept of culture from the theoretical perspectives:

* Cultural forms vary hugely, yet culture itself contains universals which will exist in all cultural settings – family or kinship structures, political arrangements, economic structures, language, symbols, norms, beliefs and values, as well as material culture (food, clothing and shelter and time for work among others). The specific form these cultural attributes take will vary, but all cultures are composed of similar sets of institutions and practices that help to organise society.
* Culture can be divided into non-material and material forms for the purpose of analysis. Non-material culture refers to the symbols and behaviours that we use in our daily lives. Material culture refers to the 'things' that accompany these practices. Sociologists analyse both material and non-material culture. Furthermore, within any one cultural setting, the forms taken by non-material and material culture will be linked. For example, a capitalist society is founded on a particular economic system. How the economy is organised is an example of non-material culture. But it leads to particular forms of material culture. A shopping mall, for example, or the fashionable clothing it houses, is a form of material culture intimately linked to the capitalist economy.
* Culture does not stay still; it changes. It provides us with a link to the past, a shifting template for the present, and a map to the future.

Box 3.3 *Amakrwala*, material culture and hybridity

The formal clothing worn by *amakrwala* – Xhosa men who have been through initiation rites – for six months after they have finished initiation school is a form of material culture. *Amakrwala* are expected to wear a particular style of smart Western clothing. The (material) clothing acts as a marker for the (non-material) shift between childhood and manhood that happens during initiation. The formal clothing worn by *amakrwala* also gives us an example of hybridity as discussed above, as 'Western' clothing of a particular form is being used to mark an African practice. The clothing brand

➡

maxhosa (www.maxhosa.com) takes this a step further by designing *amakrwala*-styles with traditional Xhosa patterns and iconography on them.

3.5 Cultural diversity

A core thread running through this chapter so far has been the idea that all around the world people do ordinary life slightly differently to one another. Even within any one geographical setting, there will often be groups and sub-groups who perform daily life in slightly different ways. They might speak different languages, ascribe to different religions, or hold slightly (or very) different norms and values to one another. Sociologists refer to this as *cultural diversity*. Cultural diversity, or multiculturalism, has been exacerbated by the rise in migration (people moving between places) and urbanisation (people from all over the country or world settling in towns and cities).

It is worth bearing in mind, however, that even without migration, no single culture is homogeneous. Even if people do speak the same language, follow the same religion and manifest many of the same behaviours, they do so from differing perspectives. We could also argue that the very idea of multiculturalism – many cultures in one place – comes from the 'old' idea of culture (Wright 1998) which assumes bounded cultures are linked to geography.

Nonetheless, the concepts of cultural diversity and multiculturalism can allow us to analyse how the structures of society work with regard to culture. The notion of *dominant culture* refers to the group within society that carries the most social power or is the most influential. If we think back to the idea of cultural hegemony above, we can see the two concepts are linked – a dominant culture would be the one that was considered 'normal' within society, with people who belong to other minority cultures – or *subcultures* – seen as doing things in a way that is somewhat different from the norm. A *subculture*, then, is that segment of the population who follow slightly different cultural patterns to the dominant culture. A *counter-culture* refers to a segment of the population who ascribe to ways of doing and ways of being that directly oppose those which are widely accepted within society. The Numbers Gangs, which originated within South African prisons, and operate both within and outside prisons, are an example of a local counter-culture. The gangs are highly ritualised, and operate according to a strict code of conduct. It is an extremely violent code of conduct, however, and one that goes against many of the usual norms of social life in South Africa. For a vivid, yet balanced, ethnographic account of prison gangs the work of Jonny Steinberg (2004) is worth tracking down.

It is common in today's globalised societies to regularly encounter difference. The challenge for people is to avoid ethnocentrism. *Ethnocentrism* refers to evaluating other ways of being and doing from the viewpoint of your own cultural setting, rather than understanding them as part and parcel of a different set of norms. An example of ethnocentric thinking would be if a Christian South African from an own viewpoint unreflexively disapproved of polygamous marriage (having multiple wives, as practised by multiple social groups in South Africa) instead of recognising it as a legitimate different cultural form.

The concept of *cultural relativism* is in some ways the opposite of ethnocentrism. The central tenet of cultural relativism is the idea that a culture can only be judged within its own terms. In other words, cultural relativism maintains that things like morality, values and beliefs can only be judged in relation to the culture in which they originate. From within a Christian cultural and moral ethic it is immoral to have more than one wife. Within certain traditional African and Islamic communities polygamy is a socially accepted normative practice. There is no external arbiter to pronounce on the moral status of either of these marital practices. A cultural relativist stance is not a morally neutral one. Such a position does not distinguish between good and evil. It is not an amoral position which takes neither morality nor immorality into account. Cultural relativism simply maintains that the measure of good or bad can only be decided by the standards of the culture within which a practice takes place. This idea, in a certain sense, reflects the 'old' version of culture as it assumes homogeneity within a cultural group. The 'new' stance regarding culture, unsurprisingly in a heterogeneous context in which there is often a great deal of debate and contestation over morality in society, nevertheless tends to favour the powerful whose moral norms are advantaged over those of other social groups.

Box 3.4 Legislating for difference. The South African Constitutional Court and culture

Article 30 of South Africa's Constitution protects every person's right to participate in the cultural life of their choice – but with the caveat that no one can exercise this right in a manner that is inconsistent with other rights protected by the Constitution.

South African law thus constitutes a balancing act between validating the legitimacy of different cultural practices. This has meant a number of cases have come to the Constitutional Court with regard to culture.

For example, in 2007, the Court heard a case in which a Hindu learner's family argued that it was her cultural right to wear a nose stud to school. The case first went to the Equality Court, which found the school had not discriminated against the girl. The case then went to the High Court, which overturned the Equality Court's decision. The case finally went to the Constitutional Court, which upheld the High Court's decision.

Chief Justice Langa argued that even though the practice was voluntary, the school still had an obligation to reasonably accommodate cultural differences (*MEC for Education: KwaZulu-Natal and Others v Pillay* 2007).

Another challenge faced in contemporary South African society is that of xenophobia. *Xenophobia* refers to an unreasonable fear or distrust of strangers or foreigners. In South Africa, xenophobic attitudes are extremely common. The derogatory term *makwerekwere* has been coined to refer to black African foreigners and ostensibly stems from the unintelligibility of non-South African African languages to South African ears. Xenophobia has also been attributed to the competition over scarce resources – justified on economic grounds that foreigners are 'stealing' jobs from South Africans. Research done by social scientists has shown, however, that migration (whether legal or illegal) contributes to a stronger economy (Peberdy 2016). In other words, 'foreigners' are creating jobs rather than stealing them. It is also worth noting that the boundaries of contemporary nation-states in Africa stem from colonialism and the great deal of shared cultural continuity between South Africa and neighbouring countries. In some ways, xenophobia in South Africa is an example of prejudice working to create ideas of cultural difference that are exaggerated.

Xenophobia can and does lead to violence. In its worst guise, disregard for cultural difference can lead to *genocide*: the mass slaughter of a large group of people on the basis of their cultural or ethnic affiliation. Africa has seen numerous genocides, from the lesser known genocide of the Herero people in Namibia carried out by Germany in the 1900s, through to the well-documented genocide in Rwanda in the 1990s. Here, 'culture' is used as a marker of social difference, and intolerance of difference is so great that death is the result.

3.6 Culture, socialisation and identity

Sociologists and other social scientists often break down society into different aspects, themes or conceptual categories in order to make sense of and analyse the social world. While conceptually distinct, social phenomena are often entangled and linked in terms of how they actually operate or are lived in practice. It is perhaps useful to see how sociological concepts are linked and related when attempting to grasp the complex phenomena of social life.

Chapter 6 in this textbook examined the relation between socialisation and identity. These two concepts are closely linked to the hazardous concept of culture. It is consequently worth concluding this chapter by considering the connections, links and relationships between culture, socialisation and identity. The explicit concern here is to explore briefly how social science in general and sociology in particular can help understand our society in order to address some of the problems and issues it faces.

Culture is intimately bound up with and inextricable from the processes of socialisation. The processes of socialisation must assume some or other cultural form and content. Socialisation can also be understood as the process of enculturation – becoming familiar with, acclimatising to and internalising norms and values when learning how to live within a set of practices and traditions. No human being is socialised in the abstract. There must be a context to the processes of socialisation. We learn from those around us and we belong to many different social groups who socialise us into different norms and values for different contexts. We can hence substitute the word 'enculturation' for socialisation, which gives a better sense of the link between the two concepts.

If we go back to our definition of culture as *the patterns that we have for living: the beliefs we hold about how to live in the social world, and the practices, behaviours and material objects that accompany them*, then we can see that we are socialised into many different patterns, practices and behaviours across our lifetime and in different social contexts. The culture of our homes is thus likely to be different to the culture of our primary or high schools; and this in turn will be different to the culture of college or university or the workplace. Within all those spaces or aspects of social life we will also encounter dominant and minority ways of acting and thinking. Socialisation or enculturation is hence a lifelong process and assumes multiple forms.

It is worth pausing here for a moment to think a little about how social life has changed or shifted in different historical eras. There is a debate at present, for example, as to whether global society can be said to have moved from a modern to a postmodern era. This may be true of some societies, but not others. In social science, modernity refers both to a particular period of time, as well as the trends and sociocultural norms that accompany that historical period.

In terms of time frames, modernity, or the modern era, is said to have begun with the European Renaissance in the 1600s. In terms of the norms that accompany it, modernity marks a period in time where the authority provided by tradition came to be questioned and where individualism came to be prioritised over collectivism (Giddens 1998) – and when sociology itself emerged as a discipline which permits us to reflect on the world we make as human agents. In addition, modernity saw the rise of a belief in science and progress and a move towards industrialisation and the rise of global capitalism. Of particular relevance for us as southern African social scientists and scholars is that for many parts of the world modernity was accompanied by colonialism. Colonialism carried with it two main projects, both of which were part and parcel of modernity: the so-called civilising mission, and the economic mission. The civilising mission sought to 'improve' peoples' cultures, while the economic thrust of colonialism brought Africa more closely into an unequal system of global capitalism. Decolonial theorists, therefore, consider modernity to be a deeply hierarchical and oppressive system (see Mignolo 2011; Ndlovu-Gatsheni 2013).

Other elements of modernity that have been examined by sociologists focus on the way society is organised and the effects this has upon how we view culture. Stephen Crook, Jan Pakulski and Malcolm Waters (1992, cited in Haralambos & Holborn 2004), for example, argue that modern culture consists of three main characteristics: differentiation, rationalisation and commodification.

Differentiation refers to the ways in which society is split into separate parts, such that the economic, political and social spheres come to be viewed as separate from one another in ways that they were not in pre-modern societies. One element of differentiation was that some of the products of culture – like music and art – came to be seen as distinct from other elements of life, and came to be labelled as high culture and valued more highly. A distinction was therefore made between 'popular culture' – the things that everybody did – and 'high culture' – the things that were produced by specialist individuals, trained in specialist institutions to be artists or musicians.

Following Weber, for Crook et al, modern culture is also shaped by *rationalisation*, the process whereby systems are made more efficient and rational. For material culture like music or art, this has happened through the rise of technology which allows for mass production and reproduction.

Rationalisation leads to the third element of modern culture: *commodification*. With the rise of global capitalism, everything becomes a commodity which can be bought and sold. Culture does not escape this process. Cultural forms become part of commodity chains.

Crook et al argue that we have entered into a new historical era, the postmodern. These theorists see post-modernity as intensifying some of the processes of modernity, such that we enter an era of hyper-differentiation, hyper-rationalisation and hyper-commodification. In short, these processes are taken to their extreme limit.

We see *hyper-differentiation* in that there is a huge variety of cultural forms available for people. Rather than just having a few styles of music to choose from, there are multiple genres and subgenres available to us.

Hyper-rationalisation means that the rise of technology allows for cultural forms to become more widespread and easily shared. People can become more individual in their consumption of cultural forms, through having individual music players or televisions or computers through which to make their choices.

Hyper-commodification refers to the fact that all aspects of social life become a commodity. Previously private aspects of social life are also turned into commodities. The rise of reality television is a good example of this. Advertising also enters into our private spheres, so that we are always immersed into the capitalist market in ways that we previously were not.

Post-modern culture, in other words, leads to a process of fragmentation in which we have a great deal more choices open to us, many of which are commodified. This brings us to the notion of identity and its relation to culture and socialisation. With the possibility of virtually unlimited choice available to us, we can engage in the self-formation of our individual identities in ways which were previously inconceivable. Identities are therefore not fixed. People can change their lifestyles and the identities that accompany them multiple times. Taste is no longer dictated by one's background. Whilst Crook et al argue that processes of post-modernity are clearly under way, other social theorists such as Giddens (1998) see the present as a new phase of modernity, as the underlying norms of the modern moment are not significantly changed, but are rather just speeding up.

Whether we categorise our contemporary condition as *post-modernity* (Crooks et al 1992) or *high modernity* (Giddens 1998), there is little doubt that the world has undergone qualitatively significant shifts and changes in the last century. These external changes and attendant cultural forces have had an immense impact on both individual and collective cultural identities and identity formation. It is increasingly clear to sociologists that our cultures give us identities – in the plural – to draw on. Expressed differently, we are socialised into *multiple identities* across our lifetimes and in different contexts. Yet socialisation or enculturation is not something which simply happens to us. Human agents are capable of choice and self-formation. Do look at George Herbert Mead in Chapter 6 on Socialisation and identity if this crucial point is not crystal clear.

The close links between culture, socialisation and identity can now be seen more clearly if we turn to the example given in Box 3.2. Women identified in some contexts as Zulu and in others as Thonga. This is not an unusual case. We all identify differently in different social situations all the time. Sometimes you are a daughter and sometimes you are a student. Cultural identities are fluid and shift according to context and are often subject to individual choice. While we think of South Africa as multicultural because of our different linguistic, ethnic, tribal, national or indeed our cultural origins into which we have been socialised, every society is in some important sense multicultural, especially in our era of globalisation. We step in and out of different social roles and the practices that accompany them in different contexts.

Culture, then, has led to being the subject of some contention and contestation in South Africa. Go back to the debates around *Ukweshwana* in Box 3.1 to the Constitutional Court cases noted in Box 3.4.

Our various cultures are, however, also an important resource we can use to address the social problems we face as South Africans and as global citizens. There has been a recent push in the social sciences from the global South in particular to ensure that social science is harnessed for the good of local communities (Tuhiwai Smith 1999; Connell 2007; Zeleza 1997) rather than simply to analyse the social world for the sake of analysis. Sociology and its ever developing – albeit often contested – understandings of culture is well poised to explore solutions to South African problems by drawing on our widely varied cultural resources. For example, non-adherence to treatment regimes for illnesses such as TB has been posed as a social problem. Social scientists have emphasised that if we take culture and cultural understandings into account such problems might not be intractable. Social scientists in Ghana, for instance, have explored the ways in which beliefs in witchcraft impacted on adherence to allopathic TB treatment (Danso et al 2015). This piece of social science could therefore allow us to find ways to adjust pre-treatment counselling to fit the cultural context in Ghana.

Social sciences such as anthropology and sociology, with their grasp on the nuances of culture, are thus well positioned to bring about positive social change. No one has all the answers, let alone sociology. Yet if we continue with trends in the discipline that push towards culturally sensitive problem-based research, address issues of power and grapple meaningfully with that complex interaction between social structure and individual agency which assumes cultural forms of expression; the next generation of social scientists, such as those of you reading this book, might be able to seriously contribute to addressing the pressing problems society faces today.

Summary

- Human beings are quintessentially cultural beings as all of our actions are situated within the social contexts in which we live. Throughout our lives, we are taught particular ways of doing things and ways of being in the world. In other words, we are constantly taught and learn how to live within the patterns and routines of a specific culture.
- In South Africa, the concept of culture has a tumultuous past. This is partly because of the academic history of the study of the exotic. Cultural difference was seen as an object of academic interest. Africa in particular was one of the places in which that exotic difference could be found and studied. But it is also because of the political history of colonisation. During colonialism, cultural and racial differences were used as the basis for oppression.
- Despite the way in which the concept of different cultures was introduced locally, this does not mean that the idea, concept or use of the term 'culture' has been discarded by ordinary South Africans. In fact, the opposite has happened. The concept of culture has taken a strong hold in the popular imagination. Most South Africans will carry some form of cultural identity they hold as important to them.

- Sociologists define culture as *the patterns that we have for living: the beliefs we hold about how to live in the social world and the practices, behaviours and material objects that accompany them*. However, these patterns shift over time, and there may be different views on the patterns of behaviour within any society. We can therefore think about these cultural patterns as a set of resources people draw on for various purposes.
- There have been many theoretical perspectives on culture. We have discussed structural functionalism (in which culture acts as a stabilising function to keep society in equilibrium/order); symbolic interactionalism (where culture is seen as a way of meaning making through symbols); conflict perspectives (which emphasise the power struggles within society between different groups); post-colonial and decolonial perspectives (which recognise culture imperialism and the struggle for cultural autonomy in post-colonial settings); and postmodern perspectives (which recognise that in society at present, people have many cultural options open to them, many of which are commodified).

ARE YOU ON TRACK?

1. What is culture? Does it stay the same or change over time?
2. Is culture something we are born with or something we learn?
3. What theoretical perspective on culture do you think carries the best explanatory capacity?

4. Do you find Wright's (1994) taxonomy of 'old' versus 'new' ideas of how culture works to be a useful one?
5. Does where a theory originates from matter to how it explains culture? Might some theories better fit 'the West' and other theories better fit 'the rest', for example?

References

Alexander N. 2013. *Thoughts on the New South Africa.* Johannesburg: Jacana.

Bhabha HK. 1994. *The Location of Culture.* London: Routledge.

Biko S. 1978. *I Write What I Like.* Johannesburg: Picador Africa.

Boonzaier E, Spiegel AD. 2008. 'Tradition' in *The New South African Keywords.* Shepherd N, Robins S (eds). Johannesburg: Jacana/Athens: Ohio University Press.

Connell R. 2007. *Southern Theory. The Global Dynamics of Knowledge in Social Science.* Sydney: Allen & Unwin.

Danso E, Yeboah Addo I, Gyamfuah Ampomah I. 2015. 'Patients' compliance with tuberculosis medication in Ghana: Evidence from a periurban community.' *Advances in Public Health*, doi:10.1155/2015/948487.

Erasmus Z. 2000. 'Hair politics' in *Senses of Culture*. Nuttall S, Michael C (eds). Cape Town: Oxford University Press.

Erasmus Z. 2008. 'Race' in *The New South African Keywords*. Shepherd N, Robins S (eds). Johannesburg: Jacana/Athens: Johannesburg: Jacana/Athens: Ohio University Press.

Garuba H, Raditlaho S. 2008. 'Culture' in *The New South African Keywords*. Shepherd N, Robins S (eds). Johannesburg: Jacana/Athens: Ohio University Press.

Geertz C. 1975. *The Interpretation of Cultures*. New York: Basic Books.

Giddens A. 1998. *Conversations with Anthony Giddens: Making Sense of Modernity*. Stanford, CA: Stanford University Press.

Haralambos M, Holborn M. 2004. *Sociology: Themes and Perspectives*. London: Harper Collins.

Kroeber AL, Kluckhohn C. 1952. 'Culture. A Critical Review of Concepts and Definitions'. Cambridge, MA. Papers of the Peabody Museum XLVII: 1.

MEC for Education: *KwaZulu-Natal and Others v Pillay* (CCT 51/06) [2007] ZACC 21; 2008 (1) SA 474 (CC); 2008 (2) BCLR 99 (CC) (5 October 2007).

Mignolo W. 2011. *The Darker side of Western modernity. Global Futures, Decolonial Options*. Durham, NC: Duke University Press.

Ndlovu-Gatsheni S. 2013. *Empire, Global Coloniality and African Subjectivity*. New York: Berghahn Books.

Peberdy S. 2016. 'International migrants in Johannesburg's informal economy'. SAMP Migration Policy Series No. 71. SAMP: Waterloo and Cape Town.

Reddy T. 2008. 'Black Consciousness in contemporary South African politics' in *State of the Nation: South Africa*. Kagwanja P, Kondlo K (eds). Cape Town: HSRC Press.

Said E. 1978. *Orientalism*. New York: Pantheon.

Steinberg J. 2004. *The Number: One Man's Search for Identity in the Cape Underworld and Prison Gangs*. Johannesburg: Jonathan Ball.

Thornton R. 1988. 'Culture: A contemporary definition' in *South African Keywords. The Uses and Abuses of Political Concepts*. Boonzaier E, Sharp J (eds). Cape Town: David Philip.

Tuhiwai Smith L. 1999. *Decolonizing Methodologies: Research and Indigenous Peoples*. London: Zed Books.

Tutu D. 2006. 'The Annual Steve Biko Memorial Lecture'. Cape Town: University of Cape Town.

Webster D. 1991. 'Abafazi bathonga bafihlakala: Ethnicity and gender in a KwaZulu border community' in *Tradition and Transition in Southern Africa*. Spiegel AD, McAllister PA (eds). Johannesburg: University of Witwatersrand Press.

Wright S. 1998. 'The Politicization of "Culture"'. *Anthropology Today*, 14(1): 7–15.

Zeleza P. 1997. *Manufacturing African Studies and Crises*. Dakar: CODESRIA.

Social change

Christopher Thomas

Human beings act according to social patterns. This may give the impression that society is stable and constant. However, human self-awareness and social action make it possible for human beings to continuously surpass the social patterns they create. In addition, population and natural changes cause people to adjust their social patterns. We can therefore say that if anything is true, it is that the only constant in life is change. This does not only refer to physical and biological life, but personal and social life as well. The study of social change is a demanding and extremely challenging topic for the social sciences in general and sociology in particular. In fact, visiting scholars to South Africa are amazed by the extent of the social change the country continues to experience. It is no exaggeration to say that our society is changing before our very eyes and at a rate with which it is difficult to keep up.

True to its topic of investigation, this is a fast-moving chapter which encompasses a wide-ranging set of concepts, ideas and supporting evidence focusing on the development and nature of South African society. In the past, except for natural cataclysms, social change was, as far as we know, exceptionally gradual. You may be familiar with the stories from the past in the opening case study, but do not be deceived. By the time you reach the end of the chapter, you will marvel at the extent of social change with this southern tip of Africa as its empirical basis. The Covid-19 pandemic has simply accelerated this process.

Any good sociological account, of which there are many, is informed by sociological theory. This chapter well illustrates the abiding relevance of the classical theorists – Marx, Weber and Durkheim. In tackling the topic of social change, you will find a number of the theoretical ideas of the classical founders are embedded in well-known sociological theories of social development, modernisation theory and dependency theory in particular. Other more contemporary theories are discussed where classical ideas are not as readily identifiable. The chapter hence looks both to the past and present theoretical work to understand the extent and impact of social change. Do not be surprised if you find references and some intriguing details to a range of societies beyond South Africa when being introduced to how our own society has changed.

The material presented here is a neat synthesis of history, theory and empirical data. Towards the end of the chapter you will find that the evidence cited pertains to both economics and politics. You might conceptualise this as an exercise in **political economy**. You might further be unfamiliar with some of the specific references noted in the discussion. A good number of the theoretical points do, however, elaborate on references that have already appeared in the chapters thus far.

You will find, in addition, that many of the empirical details, especially those describing the foundational role of the South African economy, will provide you with valuable items of knowledge you will need as you work through this textbook. You will *recognise* them as you read and study further. The careful reader will hence immediately note how this chapter, focusing on social change, builds on what has gone before. It does so by opening up the theoretical perspectives introduced in Chapter 1 and further enables making sense of new conceptual perspectives and views introduced in later chapters. Bear this in mind when you start encountering some facts and figures presented in this chapter. Do not, however, lose sight of the topic and intention of the chapter as a whole. Sociology requires flexible minds. We are, after all, trying to grasp the notion of social change and attempting to grasp something in motion – society itself.

The theoretical orientations with which the chapter started out and the empirical evidence cited is presented in this chapter with the sole purpose of illustrating the extent of social change over the past 150 years in the trajectory of South African society. It strongly articulates a critical social scientific perspective of not only how social change is framed by economic policy changes post-1994, but by implying that social change continues as our society has become even more globally connected since the emergence of capitalism in the 16th century (CE), while certain social forces seek alternatives to the dominant trends. This chapter, exemplifying the vast scope of sociology, takes us on a conceptual journey of social change from the San to contemporary South Africa.

Case study 4.1 Comparing livelihoods

Read the two case studies and answer the questions that follow.

Herders and hunters: The Khoikhoi and San in the south-west of the subcontinent

The hunters and collectors described by the early travellers and settlers inhabited the mountains and sea-shore. They had no domestic animals except the dog and lived off game, of which there were enormous herds in southern Africa; wild roots and berries, commonly called veldkos; caterpillars, termites, and locusts; wild honey; and fish. One of the early references to the hunters in the Cape mountains describes them as living by shooting dassie (Hyrax capensis) 'with bow and arrow which they use with remarkable skill', and their dogs were trained 'to drag these animals out of their holes' (Wilson 1969: 47–48).

The Khoikhoi herders had large flocks of fat-tailed sheep and herds of cattle, and milk was their staple food, men drinking cow's milk only, women and children that of ewes. The Nama alone, who were trading with the goat people – the Sotho-speaking Thlaping – had goats. The cattle were the long-horned type, ancestral to the modern Afrikander strain, and they were numerous in proportion to men. Van Riebeeck speaks of a camp of 'Saldanha men' with fifteen huts and a population of about two-hundred-and-fifty men, women, and children, with fifteen or sixteen hundred cattle, and sheep besides – six head of cattle per person ... The women milked, as they typically do among a people who are primarily pastoral and depend little, if at all, on agriculture, and life was geared to the need for pasture. Each group or horde was nomadic, moving on a regular beat which Herry, the interpreter to van Riebeeck, could predict (Wilson 1969: 55).

Pastoralism and settled agriculturalists: the Nguni in the interior of southern Africa

By the nineteenth century the southern Nguni comprised five main groupings: the Xhosa, Thembu, Mpondo, Mpondomise and Bomvana ... [I]t is possible to provide a fuller picture of southern Nguni economic behaviour in the two centuries before the difaqane. The accounts of shipwrecked travellers from the sixteenth century show that this economy was firmly based on cultivation and herding. The evidence suggests that a wide range of agricultural products were grown in various parts of southern Nguni territory at different times. The basic crop was sorghum and its cultivation seems to have been widespread. Maize was known to be grown in the mid-Transkei by 1635. This was not an indigenous crop, probably spreading into Nguni territory from the east coast of Africa.

Further fragments of evidence reveal that other products were cultivated during this era in a few or more areas occupied by the southern Nguni. These products included calabashes, watermelons, gourds, beans, pumpkins, potatoes, bananas, sugar, tobacco and dagga. Cattle-keeping was general practice. There is also evidence that some groups domesticated sheep, goats, dogs or poultry in limited numbers. However, the southern Nguni did not generate a food supply only by domesticating plants and animals. Like the San and Khoikhoi they also resorted to hunting and the gathering of wild plants (Maylam 1986: 33).

QUESTIONS

QUESTIONS

1. Name or list the different types of societies mentioned in the extracts.
2. Have these types of livelihoods completely disappeared from our society?
3. What types of livelihoods do you think would have replaced these?
4. What features would you say describe 'traditional society'?

Key themes

- The phenomenon of social change and sociological theorists' approaches to understanding social change
- Social change in South Africa
- The development of industrial capitalism in South Africa
- Traditional, pre-capitalist and modern society
- Modernity and modernisation
- Modes of production

- Industrialisation and capitalism
- The division of labour
- Urbanisation
- Socialism
- Knowledge-based economy
- Technological determinism
- Social change and development.

4.1 Introduction

The issue of 'social change' has been an area of concern from the inception of classical sociological theory, and stimulated its growth. This chapter is an introduction to the subfield of social change. It aims to help you understand social change processes in South Africa through sociological theories. While not attempting to explain all social changes, it does attempt to argue what the key forces are that underlay explanations and characterisations of social changes. The chapter discusses the evolutionary development of social change in terms of mainstream characterisations of the development of types of human societies, but gives particular attention to the modern era shaped by the emergence of **industrial capitalism** in 16th-century Europe and its global social change impact. Considerable attention is given to the structure of modern industrial capitalism, its global expansion, the component elements of the structure of a global economy, and the historical unfolding of South Africa's incorporation into and location in that global economy.

To say that present-day South Africa is characterised largely by two types of society, namely traditional and modern, is a broad sweeping description of a society's complex nature and the changes it has undergone. Nevertheless, the categories 'traditional' and 'modern' are foundational concepts in sociological theories of social change. Under, particularly British, colonial rule, two forms of authority system prevailed in South Africa. In the course of its industrial 'take-off', both black and white inhabitants in the emerging towns and cities were ruled by ideas

of individualism and codes of modern citizenship rights associated with European modernity, while black inhabitants in rural areas were subjected to ideas of communal solidarity and traditional forms of authority. It was important for the colonial rulers' strategy of dividing the colonised peoples' opposition to colonial rule by reviving the latter forms of tribal communal identities and solidarities because black urban elites drew on modern European citizenship ideas in the course of their opposition to colonial rule in their quest for equality between the colonisers and the colonised people (see Mamdani 1996: 18, 92). Interestingly, the post-apartheid Constitution accommodates the influence of Western ideas of individual rights and citizenship (see Chapters 1 and 2 of the Constitution), while recognising traditional leaders and customary law as an ancillary form of authority (see Chapter 12 of the Constitution). How should we make sense of or attempt to characterise South Africa? The two case studies above describe and explore the widespread human settlement and interaction among various peoples in southern Africa several centuries before the arrival and impact of European settlement from the mid-17th century. This was in a land that conservative or pro-apartheid white historians chose to characterise as an 'empty land' (or *terra nullius*, in legal terms). The extracts rely on archaeological evidence and European settlers and travellers' depictions of some aspects of the livelihoods and social organisation of these indigenous inhabitants upon which European colonial territorial conquest, followed by white control of industrial capitalism, would effect profound social changes.

4.2 Conceptualising, defining and theorising about social change

The professionalisation of the discipline of sociology and the growth of new theories of social change made advances on Karl Marx, Émile Durkheim and Max Weber's foundational studies of the social changes associated with the emergence of modern industrial capitalist society. Sociologists have offered several definitions of this area of sociological theory, such as:

- 'variations over time in the relationships among individuals, groups, cultures, and societies' (Kammeyer, Ritzer & Yetman 1990: 643)
- 'any modification in the social organisation of a society in any of its social institutions or social roles' (Tischler 1996: 616)
- 'relatively long-term and permanent alterations in the components of culture, social structure, and social behaviour' (Sullivan 2001: 572)
- 'alteration of social interactions, institutions, stratification systems, and elements of culture over time' (Andersen & Taylor 2011: 418).

Terms such as 'variation', 'modification' and 'alteration' are synonyms for change. In addition, there is reference to changes occurring at different levels and spheres of social interaction, namely individuals, groups, cultures, societies, social roles, cultures and institutions. Given this range of areas of focus, we should understand why there are a large number of theories of social change and not just one, as the following sections elaborate.

4.2.1 Illustrating micro-, middle and macro-levels of social change

Courting practices and marriage as a social institution is about relations between individuals and has witnessed change from one generation to the next. Compare the views and experiences of somebody who is about 50 years older than you to learn about past accepted ways of initiating courting and whether marriage was the expected outcome. Does the older generation's experience fit in with present-day trends such as being involved in a series of relationships without ever contemplating marriage, cohabitation without marriage plans, several children out of wedlock and with little concern for public censure?

Another sphere of social interaction may be between groups. Strict segregationist policies of the apartheid era restricted interracial contact and the friendship circles that schoolchildren formed. Scrapping apartheid laws accelerated the integration of schools and means that in many schools the present generation of schoolchildren find themselves in circumstances where they have racially mixed friendship circles. We may also look at issues such as the incorporation of women into the workforce, changing fatherhood roles from one generation to the next, changes in culture or beliefs and different attitudes towards gender identities, among many others, as the subject matter of theories of social change.

Changes are also apparent at the level of interaction between societies in a world system of nation-states. Apartheid-era South Africa had little, if any, trading, cultural and political interaction with Russia, the People's Republic of China, India, most African countries, and Arabic and Islamic countries in the Middle East. However, South Africa's trade, cultural and political interactions with these nations, particularly after the political transition of 1994, are overt and have grown tremendously.

4.2.2 Metatheoretical choices in constructing theories of social change

An additional factor contributing to the abundance of theories of social change is the underlying **metatheoretical choices**. These distinguish different theories or categories of theories (Noble 2000). One of the first choices that theorists make is between accounting for change due to factors that are **endogenous** or **exogenous** to a social system. The question is whether change is driven by cultural or structural forces internal to a social system. Conversely, external forces such as adapting to contact with other cultures or invasion may be another choice of explanation. Then there is the choice between portraying *change as inevitable or contingent*. One of the dominant Enlightenment approaches was to argue that human history has a discernible pattern: despite the confused flurry of events there is an almost law-like movement towards some predictable type of social structural arrangements given the pursuit to find those social structural arrangements that best facilitate the realisation of human nature. Critics of the latter position label it '**historicism**' and find fault with such **teleological explanations** of past and present events as leading to a particular future.

Sociologists sometimes prefer to explain social processes by focusing on the meaning that individual actors attach to their actions or they may prefer to explain individuals as products of the society, culture, social class, or social era that has shaped them. This is called the choice between *methodological individualism* versus *sociological* realism. The latter is closely related to another way of making sense of the social world, that is, the choices between **materialism** and idealism. Materialist approaches begin with understanding the conflicts and co-operative social arrangements among people to produce things necessary for the continuation of human life, to meet human needs and desires, and the resources at their disposal. Idealist approaches focus on the meaning, ideas, values and beliefs behind social interaction. There are strains of all these choices in different theories of social change, however, it appears that most materialist approaches are closer to **sociological realism** and idealist approaches are closer to **methodological individualism**.

Then there are the choices about the character of theorists' explanations. Sociologists who see theories as *objectively neutral science* and are concerned with explaining order and control in society are seen as having a politically conservative commitment by others who contend that ideological thinking is unavoidable. Their explanations are part of their *commitment to liberation* from the oppressive and exploitative nature of capitalist society. *Rationalist types of explanations* contend that satisfactory explanations of events or observations must be based on logically deducing the principles of a system and how events are a result thereof. On the other hand, the **empiricist** types of explanations contend that satisfactory explanations build theories based on observations and experience.

4.2.3 Developmentalism, progress, historicism and agency

Later in the chapter you will encounter summaries of three foundational theorists of social change, namely, Karl Marx, Émile Durkheim and Max Weber. They illustrate four other key elements characteristic of theories of social change (Sztompka 1993). First, there is the idea of **developmentalism**, which is closely connected to the second, namely progress. The idea of progress in theories of social change entails the view that society is moving towards improved and better conditions from those that preceded it. Interestingly, despite integrating the theme of progress into their theories, the three abovementioned theorists also expressed a sense of disenchantment with the modern industrial society. The developmentalism aspect in these theories entails seeing human society as moving towards greater differentiation and complexity, similar to the evolution of biological species from simple to complex forms of life. Third, the **historicism** element in theorising about human society and social change entails society having different rhythms and stages, but nonetheless its own logic, and is moving on some predetermined path towards a particular end state. Fourth, the **agency** trend in theorising about social change attempts to transcend depictions of

history and social change as some dominant structure along which humans are carried in its inevitable path towards a predetermined end state. Agency theories focus on humans as actors in various collectivities – classes, ethnic groups, etc – act as agents with knowledge and purposes producing social changes, sometimes with intended consequences and sometimes with unintended outcomes.

4.3 Some foundational theories of the change to modern industrial capitalism

In Chapter 1 you will have seen that Karl Marx, Émile Durkheim, and Max Weber offer foundational sociological theories explaining social changes induced by the Industrial Revolution in Europe and the American and French political revolutions through the 18th and 19th centuries. These foundational theories in different words and measures bear elements of optimism about the emergence of modern industrial capitalism – it was accompanied by reason, new technological developments, advances in science, an efficiently operating modern state, a highly productive capitalist form of production, and a sense of progress and order. However, they also wrote about their **disenchantment** with modern industrial capitalism (see Sztompka 1993: 78–81). The latter events had further global social change consequences once industrialised European countries intensified their colonisation of Africa, Asia and the Americas which had already begun in the 16th century. These changes saw people moving out of rural areas and away from the types of self-sufficient livelihoods they had maintained for centuries. Increasing urbanisation and the growth of larger cities emerged with new production methods based in urban factories. Large numbers of people without land converged on cities because they became dependent on working in factories for wages. There was a decline of authority structures where monarchs and aristocrats dominated. Centralised modern nation-states were formed that exercised authority over territory within fixed borders and the role of religion and the church in society declined.

4.3.1 Émile Durkheim

Émile Durkheim's premier study of social change, *The Division of Labour in Society*, is about social cohesion or **social solidarity**, that is, how society is held together, in two types of society, how the change is induced and one type of solidarity replaces another. Each type of society has discernible forms of dependence and mechanisms generating social order or harmony. The isolated villages and other settlements which make up segments of 'primitive', 'simple' and 'traditional' society have a common religion which is the basis of value systems and norms. These form the moral basis of individual conduct in settlements with a restricted division of labour, the forerunners to modern society. The growth of population size in urban complexes increases the density of social interactions, or the number of people that one has social interactions with, and prompts the growth of the division of labour in society. This increases the **specialisation** of tasks that people perform and prompts the specialisation of societies' organisations performing law making, education, defence, production tasks, among others, in a process of **differentiation**. The consequence is the change from traditional to modern society. In modern societies religion is a less dominant force and individuals' personalities grow in complexity. The declining significance of religion causes a loss of common values and norms producing a situation called **anomie**. Durkheim's sense of disenchantment with modern society, anomie, is also discussed in Chapter 1.

4.3.2 Karl Marx

Karl Marx in *The German Ideology* and in *Capital* argues that social change or human history is a succession of stages or **modes of production**. He explains the emergence of and nature of the stage of modern society characterised by industrial capitalism. The change from one mode of production to another is driven by conflicts between social classes over the control of nature's resources. It is also driven by conflict over the ownership and control of tools and machinery used in the production of goods, the collective organisation of the production of goods to meet human needs, and struggles over the distribution of these goods among society's members. The dominant social classes in these conflicting relations (or class struggle) are seen to use the modern state as an instrument to protect its position. The leading normative view of the state has been that it should be a neutral force in society. Class-based societies emerge along with evolving idea systems and social institutions that protect the institution of private property and worsen a condition Marx called **alienation**, the distortion of the essential co-operative nature of human beings. Modern industrial capitalist society represents the highest form of alienation, or his sense of disenchantment with modern society (see also Chapter 1). Marx's theory (called a **materialist conception of history**) has an enduring influence in how contemporary sociologists understand the emergence of present day capitalist society, the changes it

undergoes, and the likelihood of a new type of social order, socialism, succeeding capitalism.

4.3.3 Max Weber

Max Weber supplemented Marx's materialist theory with his concern about why industrial capitalism first emerged in Western Europe and not in any of the other societies with very complex social orders such as India, Persia or China. Weber felt Marx's emphasis on the material base of society must be complemented by an analysis of the idea systems, values, and norms that rationalise particular types of social action and which have **unintended consequences**. He felt that societies adopt such idea systems in an uneven manner. For Weber, industrial capitalism first emerged in Western Europe because the types of rationalisation found here were different to that in other societies. His premier study of such idea systems and rationalisation processes, *The Protestant Ethic and the Spirit of Capitalism*, shows how people's religious beliefs influenced social action or a mode of economic behaviour that had the unintended consequence of stimulating the growth of industrial capitalism. His analysis of the modern state elaborates on how it secures its legitimation, develops modern bureaucratic institutions for administration within the boundaries of a specific geographic territory and to legitimately use violence. Although he asserted rationalism was the dominant force underlying the transition to modern society, Weber recognised it was also 'the source of irrationalities, unfreedom and the retreat of ultimate values from practical life' (Abrams 1982: 85). Hence he termed his sense of disenchantment about the negative consequences of rationalisation in the political sphere as the 'the iron cage of bureaucracy'.

Following these classical foundations, the growth of sociological studies began to look at the rise of industrial capitalism into different countries and the emergence of a capital-owning bourgeoisie and proletariat dependent on a wage income. Modern industrial capitalism first emerged in Britain and Western Europe. It is an expansionist type of economic organisation and since the 16th century has accelerated the global interconnectedness of most human society and their adoption of the institutions of a capitalist market economy. The modern nation-state also emerged in Europe. Factors such as European colonial expansion, the modernisation of the impoverished former colonial territories and the current globalisation of the capitalist liberal democratic form of the modern nation-state shaped the forms of state in territories outside of Europe. Sociologists see all other changes as effected by the aforementioned two thrusts. Poverty, class and gender-based social inequality, race and ethnic relations and conflict, urbanisation, population and demographic changes, crime, changes in family and marriage patterns and changes in education trends all include the rise of industrial capitalism and the emergence of the modern nation-state in their

explanations. The essence of this chapter is to provide a foundation for your understanding of the emergence of and changes in industrial capitalism and the modern nation-state in South Africa.

Case study 4.2 BRICS: South Africa in the current global order

Read the case study and answer the questions that follow.

The world's four main emerging economic powers, known by the acronym BRIC – standing for Brazil, Russia, India and China – now refer to themselves as BRICS.

The capital 'S' in BRICS stands for South Africa, which formally joined the four on Dec. 24 [2010], bringing Africa into this important organization of rising global powers from Asia, Latin America and Europe.

This is a development of geopolitical significance, and it has doubtless intensified frustrations in Washington. The US has been concerned about the growing economic and political strength of the BRIC countries for several years: The whole international system – as constructed following WWII – will be revolutionized. Not only will new players – Brazil, Russia, India and China – have a seat at the international high table, they will bring new stakes and rules of the game.

The BRICS countries, by their very existence, their rapid economic growth and degree of independence from Washington, are contributing to the transformation of today's unipolar word order – still led exclusively by the United States – into a multipolar system where several countries and blocs share global leadership.

The addition of South Africa was a deft political move that further enhances BRICS' power and status. The new member possesses Africa's largest economy, but as number 31 in global GDP economies it is far behind its new partners, nearly 20-1 in China's case. It's also behind such other emerging countries as Turkey, Mexico and South Korea – but African credentials are important geopolitically giving BRICS four-continent breadth, influence and opportunities. China is South Africa's largest trading partner and India wants to increase commercial ties to Africa.

The U.S. seeks to forestall the development of a genuine multipolar system by making limited concessions to the emerging nations that will leave Washington in charge for many years.

(Source: Smith 2011)

***

Much excitement surrounded the 10th BRICS Summit that took place in Johannesburg 4 years ago. How does South Africa rank in terms of population and economy?

The BRICS countries make up a sizeable portion of the world's population. The five BRICS countries are home to just over 3 billion people (42% of the global population). South Africa contributes only 1,8% of the total BRICS population [57.7 million people].

China is the economic powerhouse in the BRICS bloc. The country was responsible for producing 67c of every dollar created by the five countries in 2016. South Africa is the smallest economy in the club, producing 2c for every dollar created.

The economic influence of the BRICS bloc on the world stage should not be underestimated. The five countries had a combined GDP of US16,8 trillion in 2016, comprising 22% of global economic activity. China is ranked as the second largest economy in the world after the United States. India is ranked at 7, Brazil at 9, Russia at 13, and South Africa at 38.

(Source: Statistics SA 2018)

***

Brics has become a forum for greater global equality, and to push forward the developmental agenda of the global South.

The progressive BRICS agenda has become more relevant that the criticism from some quarters of civil society that BRICS is pushing global capitalism, is only interested in resource extraction, corporate investment, and market access. BRICS is a collective pushing for the industrialisation of the developing south, agricultural diversification, beneficiation, infrastructure investment, and digitisation. These goals have long been what developing countries have aspired to achieve, but without the necessary funding and development of South-South institutions, their realisation has been difficult.

For Africa in particular, due to the infrastructure gap, it has been largely unable to unlock its growth potential. One of the most remarkable achievements of BRICS to date has been the establishment of the New Development Bank (NDB), and its ability to fund large development projects.

(Source: Ebrahim 2017)

***

Chinese officials and their African allies like to call their growing relationship a win-win proposition, a rising tide that lifts all boats in China's ever-widening sea of influence.

This year China pledged $20 billion to finance trade and infrastructure across the continent over the next three years. In Zambia alone, China plans to invest $800 million in the next few years.

But China is also exporting huge volumes of finished, manufactured goods – T-shirts, flashlights, radios and socks, just to name a few – to those same countries, hampering Africa's ability to make its own products and develop healthy, diverse economies.

Across Africa, and especially in the robust economies of southern Africa, there are clear winners and losers. Textile mills and other factories here in Zambia have suffered and even closed as cheap Chinese goods flood the world market, eliminating jobs in a country that sorely needs them.

'Their interest is exploiting us, just like everyone who came before … They have simply come to take the place of the West as the new colonizers of Africa.'

China's growing presence in global trade is wiping out thousands of jobs in countries with fledgling manufacturing sectors like Zambia and South Africa.

(Source: Polgreen & French 2007)

QUESTIONS

1. What sociological concepts have been used to describe the trends in the current global order to exclude the global South from investment finance from the rich developed north countries?
2. What have been the leading international financial institutions since the end of WWII?.
3. China and India improved their economic competitiveness by paying low wages. What would follow if SA also used this development strategy? Why?
4. What is the left-wing civil society activists' criticism of BRICS?
5. What industries in Africa would benefit from BRICS loans?
6. Write an essay about your views on the consequences of China's role in Africa as a leading member of BRICS with its agenda and the role of China as a trading partner in African countries.

4.4 The global expansion of industrial capitalism and social change

All theories of social change offer some type of periodisation of societies where there is transition between different stages with discernibly different structural features, forms of division of labour, differences in the extent of specialisation and differentiation of social institutions.

4.4.1 Mainstream approaches to the development of human societies

Sociologists generally place the evolution of human societies into *pre-modern societies* and *modern societies* (Haralambos, Holborn & Heald 2004: xi). Pre-modern societies include hunting and gathering societies, pastoral and settled agrarian societies, and non-industrial civilisations usually centred around a major city and with a large component of a literate population. The 'modern' era is associated with Europe's capitalist industrialisation and its conquest and colonisation of territories on other continents. In this evolutionary schema the first types of societies were *hunter gatherers* which existed about 50 000 years before the Christian Era (BCE) until about 10 000 BCE when other types of social organisation emerged. Hunter gatherer societies were made up of small bands of about 30 persons, living a subsistence life where they produced enough to meet their basic survival needs. They were constantly roving over large territories, surviving by gathering edible nuts, berries and plants, hunting animals and sometimes fishing. Such social units are noted for low levels of social inequality and being co-operative in a **division of labour** based mainly on sex lines. Only a small proportion of the world's population still live as hunter gatherers in parts of Africa and South America. They are on the decline and have different measures of frequent contact with and influence by modern industrial society.

Pastoral and *settled agrarian societies* emerged between about 20 000 and 12 000 years BCE. Pastoral societies engage in some measure of hunting but mainly keep livestock such as sheep, cattle, goats and pigs which provide meat and milk. Often they move about in nomadic fashion. Because some individuals may own large numbers of animals, there tends to be some inequality in such societies. Pastoral societies still survive fairly well in parts of present day Africa and Asia.

Agrarian societies are settled in specific locations where they make a living through a cycle of planting and harvesting crops. Ownership of large crop harvests permits high levels of social inequality. Even today in some countries large sections of the population live as agriculturalists, however, these societies do have considerable interaction with modern industrial societies.

Giddens and Sutton's (2017: 116–117) typology of different types of societies includes *"traditional societies"*. They emerged around 6 000 BCE and cities such as Rome, Jerusalem and Cairo fit this typology. These cities had fairly complex systems of writing, scientific practices, and sophisticated cultural development in spheres such as painting, sculpture, music and theatre. These cities traded with outside pastoral and agrarian cities and other cities. Traditional societies are further characterised by networks of isolated villages, each village being relatively self-sufficient and with low levels of division of labour, thus tasks are easily interchangeable among the members of each household and village (see Durkheim's characterisation of traditional society in Chapter 1).

From around 1600, *industrial economies* began to emerge along with European modernity. As we have seen from the foregoing discussion of Émile Durkheim, the broad category 'traditional' often emerges in characterisations of societies which have not adopted the key features of 'modern' society. These features include:

- industrial based economies with a large manufacturing sector and the incorporation of technology that allows mass production
- capitalist social relations where the institution of private property protects the private ownership of enterprises run on a profitmaking basis and which employ labourers who work for wages
- centralised states, often with a government formed on the basis of a blend of ideologies of liberalism and democracy, which have control over armies and police and legitimate authority to use violence.

These are some of the social institutions which make up an era also called modernity.

The characterisation of societies as **First World**, **Third World** and **Second World** relates to the global spread of European capitalism and the major role the United States of America assumed as a First World economy in the global economy from the mid-20th century. The transnational corporations (TNCs) originating in the First World were criticised for their exploitation and underdevelopment of the former colonised territories which made up most of the Third World. From the beginning of the 20th century the Soviet Union emerged as a model of industrial modernisation along socialist lines and several of its allies, mainly in

Eastern Europe, comprised the 'Second World' grouping of countries which offered the Third World an alternative model of 'development', a term that became synonymous with 'social change'.

In the post-World War II period, the governments of Third World countries and the United Nations became preoccupied with the 'ideology of developmentalism'. This was a deliberate social change project synonymous with a transition to the industrial economy and social and political institutions that emerged with Western Europe's industrial revolution. Debate about the status of different societies on a preconceived trajectory to a state of development spurred a classification of various stages, for instance, 'undeveloped', 'underdeveloped', 'less developed' and 'developed'. The terminologies in this debate were about deliberate strategies to effect social change, or development, in the Third World but have been contested at different points. Former president of Zaire, Mobutu Sese Seko argued:

all countries are in a state of perpetual development and as such no country, not even the most developed of the so-called developed countries of Europe and America, has stopped developing; therefore they also logically qualify as 'developing' countries (Mkandiwire 2005: 166).

The first European and North American societies to industrialise since the 19th century continued to develop in ways that prompted new characterisations by the 1960s. Technological developments have a profound impact on social change. The invention of the first computer during World War II, the later widespread use of computers, the restructuring of work and professions, and the dependence upon 'knowledge work', prompted suggestions by the 1960s that the advanced industrial societies had become **post-industrial** societies. Some theorists contended that class conflict is no longer a distinguishing feature of the age of information driven societies. These are societies where the producers of knowledge are a new dominant elite rather than owners of the means of production.

By the late 1970s certain sociologists contended that the global interconnectedness of societies had reached a new stage and changed the character of institutions. Sovereign states, for instance, were subordinated to the power of international institutions such as transnational corporations, international financing and trading treaties, and international governing bodies. This era of accelerated globalisation saw societies also adopt the rationalisation processes associated with bureaucracies, as well as the assembly line organisation of the mass production of commodities in other social spheres. American sociologist George Ritzer uses the fast food chain store McDonalds, which has franchises across the globe, as his reference point and calls this the 'McDonaldization of society'. It is 'the process by which the principles of the fast-food restaurant are coming to dominate more and more sectors of American society as well as the rest of the world' (Ritzer 1996: 1). Modern society has been overwhelmed by the process of rationalisation and the efficiencies derived from bureaucracy as a form of social organisation, particularly Max Weber's conceptualisation of it, and the assembly line mass production methods of the Ford motor company since the early 20th century. These are apparent in the production of consumer commodities, and the provision of social goods such as housing, healthcare and education.

Characterising the present has also been the preoccupation of proponents of the notion of postmodernity. Many take their cue from new trends and developments in cultural practices that depicted a sense of the times – art, architecture, films, novels, poetry, and music, all suggested that the contemporary world had moved beyond the modern age and contend that we now live in an age that it would be appropriate to call **postmodernity**.

The 'End of History' approach, spelled with a capital 'H', takes up the challenge spurred by Immanuel Kant's philosophy of History, namely, that the task of historians should be to uncover the final form of social institutions that humankind seeks. This is a teleological view of social change. Since the rise of industrial capitalism in the 19th century, socialism was a vibrant idea of an alternative society. Marxists contended that the class struggle was the human agency that would take humankind towards socialist and communist forms of social institutions. Some form of socialism (or communism) was practised for about 80 years in several countries (Russia, Eastern Europe, China, Vietnam, Cuba, Angola, Ethiopia) with vastly different degrees of industrialisation. However, by the mid-1980s, there were signs that 'socialism/communism had failed'. Francis Fukuyama emerged as the leading theorist proclaiming that alternatives such as communism, fascism, and theocracy (rule by religious leaders), which were also driven by a pursuit of economic modernisation, were incompatible with the rationalisation processes demanded by modern science and technology. In addition, consistent with his philosophical sense of human nature, he contended that the future towards which societies would develop would be some model of free market economies and liberal democratic political systems, or 'capitalist liberal democracy'.

4.5 Social change in the Third World

European and North American societies were the first to industrialise their economies and to have most of their populations located in urban areas. Other features of their modern development included centralised political systems or states, and most of them practised a liberal democratic form of government. Furthermore, the class conflict that characterised modern industrial society inspired socialist visions of an alternative to capitalist industrialisation. The rivalry between these two approaches continued through the 20th century. Following the end of 'The Great War' (WWI, 1914–1918) and later WWII (1939–1945), several territories that had been colonised by the industrial nations during the 18th and 19th centuries attained political independence and were starkly undeveloped in comparison with their erstwhile colonial rulers. French demographer Alfred Sauvy called the poor, undeveloped, less industrialised societies, most of which were former colonies, the 'Third World'. Prospects for their industrial development has been the subject of several theories of social change prompted by the notion of 'development' or the 'ideology of developmentalism'. Deliberate government policies, informed by a range of social science disciplines, sought to emulate the social changes that accompanied industrialisation in western Europe. After WWII, Third World governments, state bureaucracies and aid agencies all spoke of some dimension of development, such as, 'development programmes', 'industrial development', 'economic development', 'social development' or 'political development'. All had in mind a reproduction in Africa, Asia, and South America the social, political and economic institutions that emerged in Western industrial nations. In the Cold War rivalry between the US-led Western bloc of capitalist nations and the Russian-led Communist bloc of nations the 'Third World' was proffered two development paths – repeat the capitalist development of the West or emulate the centrally planned economy model of the Communist bloc. Such was the optimism that development would transpire rapidly in the formerly colonised territories that the United Nations called the 1960s the 'Development Decade' (Elliot 1994: 5). This post-WWII 'development project' (see McMichael 2012: 25–109) in the mostly formerly colonised territories was dominated by the US and its influence over pro-capitalist industrialisation institutions in organisations conceptualised in meetings at Bretton Woods, New Hampshire, USA. The World Bank, the International Monetary Fund, the United Nations, and the International Trade Organisation (which was replaced by the General Agreement on Tariffs and Trade, or GATT) (Edwards 1999: 33) would be key agents of diffusing Western finance and technology, and 'modernising' the Third World.

4.5.1 Marx and Lenin on the worldwide expansion of industrial capitalism

Marx understood capitalism to be necessarily expansionist. European **mercantile imperialism** from the 16th century allowed explorers and traders to plunder wealth in Africa, Asia, and the 'New World' of the Americas. Primary accumulation of wealth in Europe made investments in industries possible and saw the rise of industrial capitalism. Europe's industries required cheap raw materials and this economic stimulus was behind the European **colonisation** of territories and installation of settler colonial administrations on other continents during the 19th century. Colonisation secured control over markets, protecting the supply of resources and exploiting labour supplies. Marx studied imperialism during the competitive phase of capitalism. Imperialism was a way of dealing with the contradictions inherent in capitalism, the periodic crises of overproduction and under-consumption of commodities. Marx's **dialectical analysis** of imperialism acknowledged that imperialism and colonial rule was destructively brutal in dealing with long existing economic institutions, social relations and political structures in colonies. It was also regenerative by introducing advanced forces of production in order to facilitate its exploitation of the non-capitalist territories. Railroad systems had to be introduced and maintained in order to facilitate colonial exploitation. This stimulated the development of local industries, making further industrial development possible. The development of these industries changed the indigenous class structure. A bourgeoisie emerged along with a wage labour proletariat. Through the course of time, the struggle and conflict between these two classes placed them in a similar position to their counterparts in Western Europe. Socialism appears to be a possible option to resolve the class struggle. Socialist revolutions, Marx predicted, would begin in Western Europe where capitalism was most advanced and these revolutions would assist the immature working class that was still developing in the colonial territories.

Russian revolutionary Vladimir Ilyich Ulyanov ('Lenin') complemented Marx's study of imperialism. Russian revolutionaries debated whether a society with neither full blown capitalism nor a high level of development of the **forces of production** was ripe for socialist transformation. In addition, they pondered over whether capitalist development itself was possible in predominantly agrarian Russia with a huge peasant class. Lenin (1956) systematically investigated the development of capitalism in 'backward' nations. He argued that capitalism was well established in Russia by the late 19th century and he explains why the development of capitalism in Russia was slower when compared to other nations. Three factors accounted for this:

- the Russian bourgeoisie was weak as an agent to develop capitalism
- competition from Western Europe hampered the growth of industries in Russia
- the traditional structures had a very resilient capacity to survive.

Foreign capital had an ambiguous presence in Russia. In the first instance, it accelerated the industrialisation of Russia. Second, it was a crutch upon which the weak Russian bourgeoisie was dependent. Lenin saw Russia as a 'late' industrialiser; its industrial sector was still at the level of traditional artisanal manufacture, while other countries had progressed to more efficient industrial methods. The traditional sectors survived because they were really involved in a complex interaction with the modern industrial sector. He concluded that nascent capitalism does not simply uproot traditional structures, but articulates with these in ways which still benefit capitalist industry.

Lenin's study of imperialism during the monopoly phase of capitalism gives primacy to economic factors in accounting for imperialism. Lenin's dialectical analysis argued that imperialism is a consequence of a profitability crisis during its monopoly capitalism phase. Because capitalism grew through industrialisation and mechanisation, a profitability crisis emerged – the levels of profit could not be maintained as new investments in capital were being made. There was a tendency for the rate of profit to fall. The tendency could be offset by reducing the cost of machinery or increasing labour productivity through cutting wages and getting workers to work longer hours. Lenin argued that another way to keep up the rate of profit was for capitalism to expand overseas and secure control over a global market, to use cheaper foreign labour, and to get cheaper raw materials abroad. His analysis of the relationship between capitalism and imperialism contains four propositions:

1. to maintain profitability, capitalist enterprises in advanced countries exported capital to the colonies assisted by the political and military strength of European governments
2. this made it possible to obtain raw materials in the colonies on very favourable terms
3. it also meant that capital was needed in the colonies to build railways, roads and ports to service the capitalist penetration
4. these developments led to a concentration and centralisation of capital by large transnational firms.

Lenin acknowledged that imperialism had destructive and disruptive effects on the non-capitalist societies it plundered and exploited. It had a constructive effect in the sense that it introduced advanced forces of production and altered the social structure giving birth to a bourgeoisie and proletariat who were in an antagonistic and conflictual relationship. Thus it laid the foundation of a more progressive society – the capitalist precursor to socialism.

4.5.2 Modernisation theory

Following the Russian revolution of 1917, the new communist controlled government's organisation of a centrally planned economy and the rapid industrialisation that resulted after about four decades, the Third World was offered an alternative to capitalist industrialisation. The West responded and sought the allegiance of the Third World through a range of development aid and advice programmes associated with a broader approach about social change in the Third World called 'modernisation theory'. Modernisation theory drew its influences from Émile Durkheim, Max Weber and their distinctions between 'traditional' and 'modern' societies. The Americans Talcott Parsons and Walt W Rostow added intermediate stages between the latter two polar opposites. Parsons's theory was **ethnocentric** and conservative because his theory depicted industrial capitalist America as the highest stage of the evolution of human social development. Samuel Eisenstadt (cited in Webster 1990: 53) defined modernisation thus:

Historically, modernisation is the process of change towards those types of social, economic and political systems that have developed in Western Europe and North America from the seventeenth to the nineteenth centuries.

Modernisation theorists argued there was a particular logic by which European development occurred. They argued that there was a structural correspondence between advanced economic institutions like money, markets, occupational specialisation, profit maximisation, and the modern political, social and cultural institutions of Western Europe. The type of political, social, and cultural institutions which developed in Western Europe were seen as necessary prerequisites for economic development. Modernisation theorists developed from Parson's ideas the view that social actions in the undeveloped countries must make a transition influenced by modern values such as achievement, universalism, self-orientation, specificity and affective neutrality. Drawing from Durkheim they elaborated on the need for specialisation and differentiation of tasks and organisations in undeveloped countries. Drawing from Weber they elaborated on the need for the adoption of a rationality that overcomes the superstition and fatalism of traditional society, as well as the adoption of rational bureaucracies that realise greater efficiency.

Wilbert E Moore argued that all social changes, like the extension of education to all, required financial resources that had to be funded by economic growth. However, factory-based industrial production was not a practical option for the undeveloped countries since their economies were predominantly agricultural. To modernise their economies undeveloped countries must increase their agricultural efficiency and outputs through the use of 'industrial products' – often purchased from other countries. Undeveloped societies needed to adopt four 'structural prerequisites' in order to facilitate their industrialisation. First, they need to shift to modern values like achievement and universalism and move away from kinship related values like ascription and universalism. Second, they must adopt economic institutions that allow the free movement of labour, individual property rights and freedom to sell property, and institutions which allow for the rational and efficient exchange of money, goods and services. Third, they must adopt specialised organisations and bureaucracies for the conducting of business and government affairs. the motivation or an achievement orientation where the workforce is committed to economic goals and entrepreneurs are stimulated to be innovative.

WW Rostow discerned five stages in the modern economic history of a variety of countries that became modern industrial nations, namely the *traditional society*, the *preconditions for take-off*, the *take-off*, the *drive to maturity*, and the *age of high mass consumption*. In each stage he identifies the structure and role of particular sectors of the economy and how these grew, as well as the common strategic choices these societies made about the use of their resources. They are strategic choices because often the social decisions or government policies that drove them were contrary to the logic of market processes. His generalisation entails observing and describing certain facts about the sequence of the stages. He argues each stage has an inner logic and continuity. This is the basis of his analysis of the structure of each stage in combination with a dynamic theory of production that examines the investment choices made in each stage and in the different sectors of the economy. His theory appears to emphasise economic factors as primary factors driving the change, but he insists

that there is a complex interplay with social, political and cultural factors.

National elites would be the main agents leading the development and social change process in undeveloped societies. Elites were to adopt capitalist economies and democratic political systems that allowed for the inclusion and participation of the masses thereby bringing allegiance to the system and political stability to undeveloped countries. Sustained interaction between the advanced Western countries and the undeveloped countries exposes the latter to the institutions, values, cultural patterns, financial aid and loans, knowledge, skills, and transfer of technology that will help them develop. This is referred to as 'modernisation by diffusion'. Recruiting foreign experts as advisors, getting financial loans from banks in the rich industrial nations, and the buying of sophisticated technology from corporations in developed countries, would speed up the **diffusion** process. If an undeveloped country persists in lagging behind with its modernisation process, then it can only blame itself for not adapting. Modernisation theorists referred to a society's failure to adapt its non-material culture to changes experienced in its material culture as **cultural lag**.

4.5.3 Dependency theory
Dependency theory emerged in the 1960s as a fundamental critique of modernisation theory and its solutions to Third World developmental problems. Dependency theorists criticised modernisation theorists' failure to recognise the exploitative nature of imperialism and colonialism the expansion of capitalism (Webster 1990: 61–62). André Gunder Frank popularised the notion of dependency used by Latin American scholars and the United Nations Economic Commission for Latin America's (ECLA). ECLA contended that an unequal, exploitative relationship existed between industrialised, capitalist countries and Latin America in an international capitalist system characterised by an international division of labour wherein Latin America supplied low value food and raw materials to the industrialised countries and bought high value industrial goods from the latter which constrained domestic capital accumulation in Latin America. Theotonio dos Santos (2003: 278) defined 'dependency' thus: 'By dependence we mean a situation in which the economy of certain countries is conditioned by the development and expansion of another economy to which the former is subjected.' ECLA encouraged Latin American countries to adopt **import substitution** industrialisation and internal market protection despite these strategies being contrary to those advocated by modernisation theorists.

Frank criticised modernisation theorists' view that: underdeveloped countries were not shifting to the modern society ideal types of pattern variables as identified by Talcott Parsons; and, they clung to traditional society pattern types which signalled the 'gap' they had to bridge in order to become developed. Frank demonstrated how, contrarily, modern industrial societies in the metropolis still adhered to traditional society pattern variables. He criticised Rostow for ignoring the fact of several hundreds of years of exploitative relations between the underdeveloped and developed countries. Furthermore, Rostow's stages did not accurately depict the history of the underdeveloped countries. They were presented as having no stages prior to the underdeveloped status in the 20th century. Modernisation theorists saw the prevailing underdevelopment in the satellite countries as similar to the 'original' or the 'traditional' and 'preconditions for take off' stages of the developed metropole societies. Frank's alternative understanding of history asserted that they have been rendered into that state over a drawn out history of interaction where there has never been any beneficial diffusion from the dominant metropoles, they have been *underdeveloped*. Another central critique Frank levels against modernisation theory is about how a process of diffusion of values, institutions and capital will allow capital to enter the underdeveloped countries and propel their development. He argues that contrary evidence shows the relationship between the metropole and satellite countries is one of a history of the flow of capital or economic surplus out of the satellite countries to the metropole countries.

Dependency theory revised classical Marxist theory. They rejected Marx and Lenin's analysis of imperialism and predictions that full blown capitalism would emerge in the colonised territories. Dependency theorist's analysis of imperialism's impact on the social change prospects of the less developed countries discerns three distinct phases to imperialism. They contend that a dialectical relationship occurs between the two poles of imperialist interaction – meaning that there is a two-way causal connection between two poles. At the one polar end are the developed core or First World countries that reached a developed status because of their domination and exploitation of the less developed periphery or Third World. At the other polar end are the poor, unindustrialised periphery countries that have been actively *under*developed through centuries of interaction with the core countries. Frank (1966: 31) expresses the point thus:

[U]nderdevelopment is not due to the survival of archaic institutions and the existence of capital shortage in regions that have remained isolated from the stream of world history. On the contrary, underdevelopment was and still is generated by the very same historical process which also generated economic development: the development of capitalism itself.

Interchangeably used terms such as 'core', 'metropole', 'centre', 'First World', 'North' signify the advanced industrialised areas, while 'periphery', 'satellite', 'Third World' and 'South' signify their polar opposite, the undeveloped areas.

Dependency theorists view the development prospects of the Third World far more pessimistically than the classical Marxists' prediction that imperialism would stir the development of full blown capitalism in the colonies. The introduction of capitalism into Third World countries led to their underdevelopment and associated poverty, debt and general social and economic decline. Europe's transition to industrial capitalism was not only about the creation of a wage labour proletariat but was helped along by the plunder of wealth outside of Europe, the **primitive accumulation** of capital. This plunder of wealth occurs through three historical phases of imperialism, incorporating different territories, at different times either as core or periphery areas. Dependency theorists refer to an 'economic surplus' (Frank 1967: 6–9) as an actual economic surplus arising from a current cycle which can be saved or invested. However, because of a monopoly structure in society and the economy that appropriates the surplus, this potentially investible surplus is not made available to society – it is used on luxury consumption or invested elsewhere. In the different phases of imperialism an external monopoly, the metropolis centres, expropriates the economic surplus out of underdeveloped or periphery satellite countries. Periphery satellites remain underdeveloped because of lack of control over their **economic surplus**. Economic development of the metropolis centre is only possible because it is simultaneously linked to the underdevelopment of the periphery satellites.

The first phase of imperialism, the *mercantile phase of capitalism* (the 16th century to late 18th century), entails the accumulation of wealth in core regions through a system of unfair trade and plunder with other parts of the world and was facilitated by the technological and military advantage of the European nations. The three-cornered system of exchange between three zones of the Atlantic seaboard – Europe, Africa, and the American mainland and Caribbean Islands (the 'New World' as it was dubbed by European explorers) – illustrates the simultaneous accumulation of wealth and underdevelopment. At each stage of the triangular trade, profits were made which found their way back to the European core and contributed to the accumulation of wealth there. European explorers had seen tremendous wealth in the Americas and set off a chain of events that brought wealth to Europe but underdevelopment and dependence to the African, Asian and American periphery. More than 100 million slaves were taken from Africa to work on sugar, cotton and tobacco plantations in the 'New World'; once the slave ships were emptied of their slaves they were reloaded with the harvests from plantations owned by colonists in the 'New World' and taken to European port cities where emerging industries used these as inputs for the manufacture of a range of commodities sold on domestic and colonial markets. Mercantilism established the range of raw materials that Africa, Asia and the Americas should provide for Europe. The mercantilist accumulation of wealth had provided vital inputs for European industrialisation in its port cities and a rivalry amongst the European nations for lucrative areas of supply ensued by the late 19th century. The solution to the rivalries was to secure control over the territories as colonial annexes.

In the *colonisation phase* (1850 to early 1900) European powers took direct political, legal and administrative control of periphery regions, accompanied by a military and settler population. Europeans increased their profits through introducing more efficient farming and mining strategies along with increased control over the local labour force. Once some form of colonial authority was established along with administrative structures in place, the capitalist **charter companies** from the colonial power did the real work of colonial conquest and the extraction of wealth from the colonised periphery areas. Charter companies were monopolies with sole rights over vast areas. Charter companies could enter the territories, extract minerals (gold, copper, iron etc.), clear land for 'cash crop' plantations (tea, coffee, cocoa, sugar etc.), collect taxes, recruit labour, and perform colonial administrative tasks. Long existing land tenure practices of indigenous people were disrupted by the presence of the charter companies. Charter companies sought the type of agricultural produce required by European markets. Gradually, agricultural production for local self-sufficiency was impaired; the local population lost their land and resorted to wage labour employment on charter company plantations and mines and settler colonists' farms. Traditional crops were no longer produced and 'cash crops' were produced for export. The long-term poverty and underdevelopment of the colonised territories has its roots in the imposition of an agricultural system that did not

balance the mixture of goods produced for consumption by the local market and goods produced for the export market (Webster 1990: 78). Colonial authorities imposed taxes that forced many local people to seek cash paying jobs. A wage labour proletariat emerged in the rural and urban areas of the colonies. Many people were displaced from land ownership, lost the means of a livelihood that generations of their ancestors had practised, and, consequently, resorted to patterns of migrant labour. Local authorities were not entirely destroyed in the transition to colonial rule but they were sufficiently co-opted and brought under the control of the colonial administration. Local chiefs and other elites became agents implementing colonial rule. European legal systems were grafted onto the customary law institutions of indigenous people to effectively 'pacify' and subordinate them in ways that facilitated foreign control of tax-paying subjects and labourers for their enterprises.

The neocolonial period (after 1945 to the early 1970s) entails the granting of political independence to the colonies after years of resistance and violent national liberation struggles. Political rule by the European powers was no longer necessary because the internal social structures and economies of erstwhile colonies had been transformed and external socio-economic domination persisted through a system of a range of international laws, regulations and agreements on property, trade, commodity pricing, banking and financing, as well as the control of production in the periphery by the subsidiary companies of transnational corporations which extracted **economic surplus** from the periphery. Ghana's president, Kwame Nkrumah (quoted in Offiong 1982: 122, 123) said:

the process of handing independence over to the African people with one hand, only to take it away with the other hand ... the practice of granting a sort of independence by the metropolitan power, with the concealed intention of making the liberated country a client-state and controlling it effectively by means other than political ones.

Under neocolonialism, the economic systems and political policies of independent territories are managed and manipulated from outside, by monopoly finance capital in league with the indigenous bourgeoisie ...

Transnational corporations (or multinational corporations – MNCs) emanating from the United States, then later Europe and Japan, secured lucrative niches in countries across the whole world. The core areas now included Europe, North America (the United States of America and Canada), and

Japan. TNCs controlled production from the extraction of raw materials in the periphery satellites, through the manufacturing stage, and the retail stages too. Production of commodities worldwide is concentrated in the hands of a number of TNCs that own about two-thirds of fixed assets of the entire global economy (Webster 1990: 80). Many TNCS grew from small 19th century family-owned businesses. Their power and influence in the world economy is built on their ownership and control of knowledge, the technology of production, marketing systems, and financial systems. They dominate in vehicle manufacturing, office and business machines, electronics, to mention but a few industries vital to any modernising economy. Almost all the world's patents are held by TNCs. By the 1980s TNCs had investments and subsidiary branches in almost every Third World country. TNCs take surplus out of the Third World mainly by sending profits back to their head offices in the First World. Economic surplus is extracted through intra-firm trade across the globe: machinery is sold to subsidiaries at deliberately inflated prices. TNCs add in the costs of patents they in fact own when goods are transferred between branches. They thus integrated their activities on a worldwide scale and continued a relationship that exploited the economic surplus produced in the periphery and siphoned off these profits to the headquarters and economies of the core areas thereby retarding industrial development and related social changes in the periphery. In addition, the internal elite that administered the postcolonial societies is unable to take the leading role in the management of the economies and is instrumental in securing the interests of the TNCs. This elite is called the **comprador bourgeoisie**.

Contrary to modernisation theorists' views about financial diffusion assisting Third World development, loans from First World banks, the International Bank for Reconstruction and Development (IBRD or the World Bank) and the International Monetary Fund (IMF) worsened dependence since governments found it difficult to repay the interest on loans. Repaying or servicing debts is a huge burden on the gross domestic product of Third World countries; servicing of debt is done by earnings made from exports thus limiting financial resources for domestic investment. Since the mid-1980s the world has episodically faced the issue of the Third World's inability to meet payments and the IMF imposed unpopular austerity programmes upon Third World governments as a concession to reschedule debt obligations and to revive their economies and meet debt obligations. The conditions of these **austerity programmes** entailed freezes on wage increases, prohibitions on strikes, reduced government

spending on social welfare (healthcare, education, pensions), devaluation of currencies, and removing of tariffs on imports. This conditionality worsened the incidence of strikes, food riots, unemployment, rising infant and child mortality and growing poverty. All these factors contributed to the persistent political instability in Third World countries since the mid-1980s.

4.5.4 World-systems theory
World-systems theory emerged in the early 1970s with Immanuel Wallerstein as its premier exponent. These theorists felt dependency theory was limited in its capacity to explain new developments in the capitalist world-system. For instance, certain South East Asian countries, referred to as the 'four tigers' (Hong Kong, Singapore, South Korea and Taiwan) began to show significant economic growth, to the extent that 'these East Asian industrial states had begun to challenge the economic superiority of the United States' (So 1990: 170; also see Kiely 1995: 85). The crisis experienced by socialist states and their gradual incorporation into the capitalist world-system also contributed to the emergence of the world-systems perspective (So 1990: 170). The crisis in socialist states represented, for many theorists, a crisis in Marxist theory itself, and its utility as a model for development was questioned. World-systems theory was also influenced by the crisis in US capitalism, and the decline of America's international political and economic dominance. World-systems theorists felt that none of these developments could be explained by existing theories.

World-systems theory incorporates certain ideas and concepts of dependency theory, for example exploitative core/periphery relations and unequal exchange (So 1990: 171), and dependency theorists' critique of classical Marxist and modernisation notions of development (So 1990: 172). World-systems theory also incorporates aspects of the French Annales school, which concentrates on 'total' or 'global' history (So 1990: 172). The focus here is not on history as the 'uniqueness of events' but on its cyclic or recurring nature (Kaye, in So 1990: 172). World systems theorists have attempted to focus on 'big' issues like the world system, and to trace its history, dynamics and evolution.

World-systems theory focuses on the emergence of the capitalist world system or world economy, which was facilitated by the growth of trade, the efficient organisation of production, and a structure of unequal nation-states (Kiely 1995: 45). While dependency theorists focused on nation-states, world-systems theory focuses on the total 'social system', of which the capitalist world economy is one (Wallerstein 1979a: 53–54). Systems theorists see the social world as a whole made up of interconnected and interdependent parts and analyse the division of labour among the components. Wallerstein (1979a: 5) writes:

The defining characteristic of a social system [is] the existence within it of a [single] division of labor, such that the various sectors or areas within are dependent upon economic exchange with others for the smooth and continuous provisioning of the needs of the area. Such economic exchange can clearly exist without a common political structure and even more obviously without sharing the same culture.

Wallerstein contends different types of social systems have occurred historically. In this evolutionary approach, the first type of social system is the **mini-system**. All societies were once mini-systems. At the time when this type of social system occurred, the world consisted of relatively autonomous, economically self-sufficient societies or mini-systems with a 'self-contained division of labor' (Wallerstein 1979a: 5) with economies based on reciprocal exchange. An example of a mini-system would be hunting and gathering societies. Mini-systems no longer exist today. Even in the past there were fewer than most people would think because once a such a community came under the domination of an empire and had to pay a form of tribute for 'protection', it ceased to be a self-contained division of labour.

The next development was the emergence of **world systems**. Two types have emerged, one with a common political system and one without a common political system (Wallerstein 1974: 390). The first type is the **world empires** of the ancient Egyptian, Roman and Chinese civilisations which had a common political system reigning over the empire's territory. In this type of social system a society had a unified or centralised political structure with a single division of labour. During a process of expansion, when other territories were brought under the control of the empire, political power did not decentralise. This means that the incorporated territories fell under the political domination of the empire's political system. In the case of the world empire, economic domination and/or exploitation depended on centralised political domination, and the ability of the polity to maintain that dominance. World empires were a constraint on the economic dynamism of their domain because a great proportion of their economic surplus was used to maintain their extensive bureaucracies.

The second type of world-system Wallerstein identifies is the **world economy**. So far only one world economy

has emerged, namely the capitalist world economy which emerged in the 16th century. Capitalism as a world system is economically unified, has a single division of labour, but is politically diverse, with many nation-states. The capitalist world economy thrives despite different cultures, and no single dominant political centre, as long as the peculiar division of labour of the system persists and market exchange relations actively cause an unequal distribution of the economic surplus among the system's different parts:

The 'world economy' is a fundamentally different kind of social system from a 'world empire' and a fortiori from a mini-system – both in formal structure and as a mode of production. As a formal structure, a world economy is defined as a single division of labor within which are located multiple cultures – hence it is a world-system like the world-empire – but it has no overarching political structure. Without a political structure to redistribute the appropriated surplus, the surplus can only be redistributed via the 'market', however frequently states located within the world economy intervene to distort the market. Hence the mode of production is capitalist (Wallerstein 1979a: 159).

Capitalism transcended the political boundaries of individual nation-states. Its single division of labour is an *international division of labour*. It succeeded as a world economy because new transportation enabled reliable access to distant markets and Europeans' military technology imposed favourable terms of trade. Capitalists flourished because they were not burdened with the costs of maintaining a unified empire and they successfully opposed Europe's royal families' attempts to consolidate the emerging world economy into a world empire.

The division of labour occurs among the components or structural locations of a system Wallerstein calls the core and periphery. From its emergence in the 16th century in Europe, the capitalist world economy always had this feature of three levels or structural locations that all try to improve on their position in the hierarchy. The different locations depend on economic exchange with each other for the smooth functioning of the whole, and there is no need for the parts to have a common political structure or similar culture. The development of 'strong' state mechanisms that first emerged in Western Europe is partly why Western Europe became a core area. By contrast the periphery is characterised by weak state mechanisms (Wallerstein 1979a: 18).

The core, historically, first emerged in Western Europe due to historical, ecological, and geographic circumstances in the 16th century that allowed Western Europe to diversify its agricultural specialisation and well-developed towns emerged (textile, shipbuilding and metal industries), their agriculture sectors were technologically advanced, investment was high, and the labour force was skilled and relatively well paid. Expansion of the core regions was possible due to the extraction of surplus from periphery regions in Eastern Europe. The periphery in 16th century Eastern Europe used lots of slave labour, and specialised in the export of grains, bullion, wood, cotton, and sugar. The semi-periphery emerged in Mediterranean Europe where lots of share-cropping was used in its agricultural sector, and it specialised in high-cost industrial products like silks. By 1640 these three structural locations were stabilised. Wallerstein also identifies the external areas as regions that are not (yet) part of the world system. By its expansionary nature, the inner logic of capitalism, where strong states with considerable military strength also play a part, capitalism has a tendency to draw these *external areas* into its sphere of influence and to peripheralise them. Eventually, given the dynamic nature of the system, external areas potentially move upwards to become periphery areas. This conception of capitalism, with three structural positions plus an external area, enables Wallerstein to deal with the dynamics of capitalism as a world system. For example, he introduces the notion of (potential) mobility within the international division of labour: states can move from the external area to the periphery, upwards from the periphery to the semi-periphery, or downwards from the core to the semi-periphery. Differences in the strength of state structures means there is an '... operation of 'unequal exchange' which strong core states enforce on weak peripheral ones, hence, 'capitalism involves not only appropriation of the surplus value by an owner from a labourer, but an appropriation of surplus of the whole world-economy by core areas' (Wallerstein 1979a: 18–19). The core dominates the world-economy and exploits the other locations in the system which provides it with raw materials. He makes another point about the development of state mechanisms in relation to a structural position within the international division of labour: while strong state mechanisms may initially have developed by accident, long-term structural positions within the international division of labour have to be explained in terms of 'the operations of the world-market forces which accentuate the differences, [and] institutionalize them' (Wallerstein 1979a: 21.)

The semi-periphery falls between the (exploiting) core and the (exploited) periphery. The relation between the 'core' and 'periphery' cannot be fully understood without analysing a third structural position in the international division of labour, the semi-periphery. Wallerstein felt that a bipolar model of the world system did not account for nations that did not fit either core or periphery characteristics. Semi-peripheries occupy, in terms describing the extent of their economic activity and not in terms of their geographic location, an intermediate status between the level of development of the economies of the core and periphery. The economies of semi-periphery countries are dominated by the core countries, but semi-periphery economies have significant industrial development and the capacity to dominate and exploit periphery countries. The range and types of economic production taking place in the semi-periphery is more diversified than in the periphery, but less so than in the core. Another distinguishing characteristic of the semi-periphery is that its wage levels and profit margins fall between the core's high-wage products and the periphery's low-wage products, which are a result of different levels of technology. When higher wages are paid to workers, the capitalists' profit margins will be lower. In instances where workers are **semi-proletarianised**, the wage levels can be lower than those of fully proletarianised workers. Higher levels of technology generally require higher levels of skill and this pushes up wages. Greater degrees of union organisation can also push up wages. Furthermore, in semi-periphery countries the state is more likely to interfere in its international and national markets than either periphery or core states. Finally, semi-peripheries trade with both the core and periphery.

The economic status of the semi-periphery is less important than its political function. The semi-periphery contributes to the stability of a social system, the capitalist world economy, which is inherently exploitative, and has an unequal distribution of wealth. An exploitative social system polarised between a core and periphery would be inherently unstable, with the core facing large-scale opposition from the periphery. Thus the semi-periphery plays an important role in stabilising the exploitative capitalist world-system. During the 16th century Spain fulfilled the role of semi-periphery keeping control over the periphery in Latin America. But Spain declined to the rank of periphery during the 17th and 18th centuries. Sweden fulfilled the role of semi-periphery keeping control over Poland during the 17th and 18th centuries. In Latin America during the late 20th century, Brazil played the role of semi-periphery, and, following the colonisation of Africa, in southern Africa

South Africa fulfilled the function of semi-periphery from the mid-20th century.

4.5.5 Globalisation: implosion of the core and exclusion of the periphery

Industrial capitalism is a geographically expansionist type of social organisation and a key force behind the growing interconnectedness of different parts of the globe, incorporating the economic activities of different parts of the world, regardless of whether the outcomes were development, or dependency and underdevelopment. Modernisation, dependency and world system theories emerged at a time when thinking about social change and development in the Third World had a national economic development type of focus often entailing industrialisation strategies through import-substitution and tariffs on imported goods.

Transnational corporations (TNCs), major players in the economy, were pushing for a shift in the economic nationalism project associated with the development thinking of the 1960s and 1970s, and advocating for a global free market (see McMichael 2012: 126–127, 136–138). The formation of the World Trade Organisation (WTO) in 1995 was an important step in the consolidation of a new phase of the dominance of an interconnected global economy by TNCs and the industrialised developed nations of the global North. WTO member states are under pressure to comply with the shift from nation-focused development to global free markets and open trade.

Globalisation theories emerged in the latter context and offer explanations of social change and development dynamics in an interconnected world at the beginning of the 21st century. Globalisation theories sensitise us to the fact that events and processes we associate with social change in our immediate environments have some form of connection to distant events and processes. Anthony Giddens asserts that globalisation is not only nor primarily an economic phenomenon. Rather, it is about the transformation of time and space where 'action at a distance' is possible (Giddens 1994: 4, 1998: 30). He calls his theory of globalisation 'time/space distanciation'. Compared to two centuries back, in recent decades, the time involved in human travel or the transport of material commodities from one point of the globe to another has shrunk tremendously Electronic telecommunications such as news broadcasts on CNN, the internet and social media exchanges in today's world can inform people in one part of the globe of events in another in a very short space of time. The 'global village' of today has overcome space through the mastery of time. It is now possible to have organised social and community relations regardless of how far apart from each other peoples' immediate locations may be.

Ankie Hoogvelt (1997) accepts 'global babble' as a recent important current in sociology and the debate signifies that capitalism is undergoing a transformation. Old patterns of technological use and economic organisation and related cultural, ideological and political forms have become undermined and a variety of labels, such as postmodernist, post-Fordist, post-materialist, post-industrial, suggest that society has shifted away from one type of social order to another as yet not fully formed order. However, Hoogvelt questions some of these interpretations and the issue of whether there is such a process as globalisation at all. Her questioning of the globalisation thesis is based on an examination of changes in industrial capitalism and related institutions, practices and cultures in recent decades. Hoogvelt argues that industrial capitalism is undergoing a reorganisation that questions certain arguments about global interdependence. The periphery is becoming less significant to capitalism and her concepts of **implosion** and **exclusion** characterise contemporary trends.

Her concept of implosion is based on an examination of statistical data which reveal the transformations in world trade, foreign direct investment, the growth of transnational corporations and world capital flows since the 1970s and Hoogvelt (1997: 75) concludes:

> The conclusion to be drawn from these figures is that the record of world trade can neither be summoned to testify to 'the increasing interconnectedness which characterises our world economy', nor to evidence of 'the deepening and widening penetration by the core of the periphery'. Rather, it stands as evidence of a modestly thickening network of economic exchanges within the core, a significant redistribution of trade participation within the core, the graduation of a small number of peripheral nations with a comparatively small population base to 'core' status, but above all to a declining economic interaction between core and periphery, both relative to aggregate world trade and relative to total populations participating in the thickening network.

Her examination of historical data on the growth of world trade in relation to world output since the 19th century contends that the peak period of the growth of world trade was between 1880 and 1913 and has not been surpassed (Hoogvelt 1997: 70). Foreign trade in the 1990s did not surpass the 1913 peak.

A closer focus on the participation of core and periphery regions in world trade shows that the percentage share of the industrial areas has increased (68.9 per cent in 1953 to 71.9 per cent in 1990) while that of the non-industrial areas has decreased (26.3 per cent in 1953 to 20.0 per cent in 1990). There has been a tremendous increase of trade amongst the industrialised group of countries; as a percentage of world trade, trade between this group of countries stood at 37.1 per cent in 1953 but has increased to 55 per cent in 1990. Foreign direct investment in the Third World has been shrinking since the 1960s. From the colonial period up to 1960 half of the world's total direct investment flows went to the Third World, but by 1988 to 1989 the percentage had dropped to 16.9 (Hoogvelt 1997: 77).

Statistical data form the basis of her thesis of 'imploding capitalism' or the contraction of the core. By this Hoogvelt (1997: 84) means that trade and capital linkages within the core of the world capitalist system have intensified, and that there has been a relative and selective withdrawal of such linkages with the periphery areas of the world capitalist system. As this implosion was taking place, the difference in shares of the core and the periphery in world income also increased significantly. In the global expansion of industrial capitalism many regions at some stage have played an important role in an international division of labour whereby they were exploited for certain raw materials and other commodities. Technological developments at the end of the 20th century make it possible to replace a variety of raw materials that had been supplied by periphery regions, consequently, these regions are now 'structurally irrelevant' to the production requirements of a transformed capitalism. In dependency and world systems theories of the geographic expansion of industrial capitalism, the 'core' and 'periphery' referred to hierarchical relations between geographic regions of the world. Today, however, an international division of labour has emerged such that 'core' and 'periphery' are now social relationships amongst the labour force in both the traditional core and periphery (Hoogvelt 1997: 135–138). Hoogvelt's explanation of these outcomes of a globalised world focuses on three areas: the integration into a global cultural subsystem or the global acceptance of a market discipline; the new trends in the global division of labour; the deepening of financial flows between the core regions.

Developments such as the emergence of BRICS (see Case study 4.2), an alliance of 'middle-income' states, suggest that there are counter movements to the phenomenon of implosion and the Western nations' control of major organisations influencing the global economy

such as WTO (McMichael 2012: 229–237). BRICS has set up its own New Development Bank (NDB) that makes funds available for infrastructure development. China is the major economy in BRICS and, other than contributing to the NDB's funds, also enters into bilateral loan agreements with states in Africa and the global South for funding infrastructural development.

4.5.6 Sustainability, human development theory and post-development theory

An underlying issue in the foregoing 'development theories' was a concern about improving human living standards across all countries. While a vast archive of reports spanning decades about the different indicators and measurements of such improvements show that a considerable number of people's lives have improved, contrarily there has been considerable deterioration of the environment (McMichael 2012). The globalisation project of free trade and open markets has increased access to natural resources across the globe and their depletion as well as deterioration of the natural resources indigenous people had access to. Some of the counter movements to neoliberal globalisation include sustainable development thinking and its concerns about the impact on the environment of development projects and the use of natural resources in a sustainable manner that considers the needs of future generations. Human development thinking attempts to shift the focus away from economic indicators of growth and increased consumption towards improvement in health, education, the enhancement of people's subjective sense of their well-being and their life experiences, and the capability of people to choose a life that they value.

The emergence of post-development theory signifies a vast spectrum of thinking in opposition to the domination of Western thought about 'development', critique of the Western model of life of as good and desirable, appreciation for indigenous technologies, modes of organising economic activity and producing to meet basic needs and cosmologies about humans' relationship with the natural environment (Matthews 2010).

4.6 Social change and the development debate in South Africa

South Africa's incorporation as a periphery of the expanding capitalist world system commenced with European settlement at the Cape Town area (Table Bay) from the mid-17th century and the colonial territorial conquest over the next two centuries. This subordinated and brought the demise of the nomadic, hunter-gatherer, pastoralist and settled agriculturalist livelihoods and the social organisation of the indigenous peoples you were familiarised with in the case studies at the beginning of this chapter. Four factors contributed to South Africa's progressive emergence as a semi-periphery in the world capitalist system:

- South Africa's location in the temperate climate zone encouraged settler colonialism and the development of a racial order; European settlers became a bourgeoisie with an interest in developing the local economy and they attracted capital from the metropoles (core/centre)
- South Africa had gold and diamonds and these stimulated the development of local industries
- the state played a prominent role in organising and controlling labour as well as developing an Afrikaner bourgeoisie
- a shift in the exports economy such that, besides earnings made from the export of raw materials, local manufacturing industries made goods for export particularly to neighbouring periphery regions in southern Africa.

This section is an overview of the development of industrial capitalism in South Africa to the contemporary reincorporation into the global economy dominated by neo-liberal economic thinking and practices.

4.6.1 South Africa as a periphery in the capitalist world system

The Dutch settlers brought slaves into the Cape to cultivate crops on farms that were close to the harbour. A system of anti-vagrancy laws was used to tie the indigenous inhabitants into labour services to the white settler farmers. The market in fresh produce and livestock was limited to visiting ships, thus there was limited export potential. Cape wines were initially not attractive to potential consumers. Dutch and later French settlers sought to expand their production of agricultural products that they used to trade with, thus they progressively displaced the Khoikhoi from the land in the Cape forcing many Khoikhoi and San out of the expanding colonial borders. Later the British took control of the Cape. British rule disrupted the order established by Dutch settlers and prompted them to move ('trek') into the interior of southern Africa. Trek farmers through conquest, claimed more land where more communities of indigenous Bantu-speaking black peoples were encountered. Afrikaner nationalist historians would later claim this interior was an 'empty land' into which northbound trek farmers and the southward migrating Bantu arrived around the same time. White settlers occupied land used by the Bantu-speaking

peoples who lived off crop production and livestock herding in fixed areas. Trek farmers used conquered black pastoralist communities as labourers on the farms they set up in the interior. The trek farmers sold their agricultural surpluses on the market in the Cape and obtained more guns and supplies to fuel their expanded conquest of the interior. Over time the colonial authorities installed a 'pass document' system to tie indigenous peoples to labour to the services of white farmers.

During the 1820s the British colonial powers introduced merino sheep into the colony and encouraged more British to settle in the expanding borders of the Cape colony. Wool became the colony's first major export to Europe. By 1860 wool comprised about 75 per cent of the colony's export income. Larger parts of the interior were conquered by settlers who increased commercial agricultural activity. The exploration and commercialisation of the interior necessitated more metropolitan (European colonial) capital investment in a transport infrastructure and the support of a military force. The extent of profits made from commercial agriculture did not warrant a large investment in the transport infrastructure. However, the discovery of diamonds (1867) and gold (1886) encouraged the colonial powers to spend more on the infrastructure and the military force. The mineral discoveries also stimulated the growth of towns and urban markets for agricultural produce. Despite colonial conquest many indigenous African communities still controlled land and expanded their production to supply the growing urban population and a prosperous African peasantry emerged. Many subsistence peasants had an alternative to wage labour employment in the mines and towns and in later decades settlers complained of a 'labour shortage'.

4.6.2 Mineral discoveries and the industrial take-off

Diamond and gold discoveries made South Africa an important destination for metropolitan investment. Capital investment in mining started off as British but later became mostly 'South African'. Good profits accelerated incorporation into the expanding world capitalist system. But further profitmaking required a systematic incorporation of the indigenous black people into wage labour relations in a society organised along the lines of a race hierarchy with the European settlers at the top. Greater profits could be made by a system of cheap labour (semi-proletarianised) migrant labour thus necessitating greater state involvement in organising the migrant labour system and dealing with the 'labour shortage'. More black migrant labour was recruited in Portuguese and British colonies in southern Africa. British domination of the economy clashed with Afrikaners (Dutch settler descendants) and white labour. From 1924 a Pact government gave greater attention to: nurturing the interests of a (white settler) national bourgeoisie – particularly the development of an Afrikaner bourgeoisie; decreasing metropolitan control over the economy; and protecting the interests of a white working class. Import substitution policies nurtured the development of local industries. For example, by imposing high tariffs on imported explosives, the local explosives manufacturing firms grew and supplied explosives to the mining companies, and, by setting up parastatal companies like the Iron and Steel Corporation (ISCOR). Anglo-American emerged as a South African mining company but gained stature as a transnational corporation with multifaceted investments beyond South Africa. By the 1970s South Africa supplied 80 per cent of the capitalist world's gold.

After the 1948 elections the victorious National Party (NP) began the era of *apartheid* rule and **embourgeoisiement** of the Afrikaners was a pronounced policy. Afrikaner enterprises effectively mobilised for and received state support, but never exceeded the assets of traditionally English capital. State support came through joint ventures between the state and the Afrikaner private sector, pricing policies to protect industries, and tax and tariff concessions. Soon two Afrikaner business giants emerged – Sanlam and Rembrandt Tobacco. During colonialism, **charter companies** had uncovered the extensive mineral and agricultural potential of southern Africa and TNCs continued the exploitation of this potential. Most TNCs preferred to base their operations in South Africa and their presence provided business opportunities for the settler bourgeoisie. More South African companies grew to TNC status and often with operations in neighbouring southern Africa states, for example De Beers (diamonds), Huletts (sugar), Johannesburg Consolidated Investments (mining), Barlows (electronics), SA Mutual (insurance). After the black urban revolt of 1976, the NP and white business leaders in the Urban Foundation agreed to support the growth of a pro-capitalist black business elite as a means of undermining the radical political inclinations of the black political leadership.

4.6.3 South Africa as a semi-periphery

In 1898 South Africa sent 97.5 per cent of its exports to Britain, but by the mid-20th century South Africa had to diversify its trading partners. The metropolitan markets were becoming harder to compete in, and, because of the skewed wealth between South African whites and blacks, the local black consumer market was too small. More markets were sought in neighbouring African countries. Despite international condemnation of apartheid policies, many African countries traded with South Africa. By the mid-1980s South Africa had fixed trading relations with 19 African countries and a trade surplus with all the neighbouring states of southern Africa. The neighbouring states were linked to South Africa through a South African-owned transport network (roads, rail and seaports), their governments benefited from tax revenues from citizens who worked in South African mines as migrant workers. South Africa's trade surplus with Africa came from exports of machinery, metals and metal products, vegetable products, animal products, plastic and rubber products, chemicals and chemical products, animal and vegetable fats and oils, wood by-products like paper and pulp, vehicles and transport equipment, and prepared food products.

In 1979 Angola, Botswana, Lesotho, Malawi, Mozambique, Swaziland, Tanzania, Zambia and Zimbabwe formed the Southern African Development Coordinating Conference (SADCC) to organise their mutual development support and to minimise their dependency on SA's regional economic dominance. The apartheid government responded by broadening its 'Total Strategy' of containing internal black trade union militancy and township revolt with a destabilisation campaign that disrupted many of the SADCC countries' economic development projects and supported armed groups that opposed SADCC governments. In an era of open trading between a post-apartheid South Africa and the rest of Africa, South Africa's dominance is still apparent. Kenya has accused South Africa of loading cheap goods onto its markets and imposing trade barriers such as tariffs on Kenyan exports to South Africa; in 2002 South African exports to Kenya amounted to almost $2.3 billion, while Kenyan exports to South Africa amounted to about $110 million (Esipisu 2003).

Despite South Africa's emergence as a dominant semi-periphery power in southern Africa, it is important to understand that there were nevertheless crises simmering in the structure of its economy, and these worsened as class tensions unfolded in the form of a revival of black trade unions involved in strikes over working conditions as well as broader political issues, the activities of liberation movements, protest campaigns against various apartheid measures and attempts to repress black opposition. The social inequality and race hierarchy patterns nurtured by apartheid policies of low wages for blacks and higher incomes for the other groups in supervisory and managerial positions created a small market for the consumer goods produced by local manufacturing industries: it was mostly white with a small proportion of the coloured and Indian sectors of the population capable of living consumerist lifestyles. An international campaign to isolate the apartheid regime economically, diplomatically and culturally mounted since the 1960s and inhibited the ability of local manufacturers to access overseas markets and to source spares to maintain machinery. To a measure the apartheid state was successful in repressing opposition up to the 1960s. However, the revival of black trade unions that aligned themselves with political campaigns since 1973, youth movements protesting apartheid education policies since 1976, new waves of exiles that joined the military wings of liberation movements which stepped up their internal military attacks, and sustained internal opposition to the National Party's reforms which did not create a political dispensation of equal franchise rights, forced the contending sides to agree to a negotiated political transition. The negotiations through the late 1980s and early 1990s culminated in racially inclusive elections in 1994 and the African National Congress (ANC) came into power as the new majority party in the national assembly. Representatives from the different parties in the national assembly drafted a new constitution which was adopted in 1996.

4.6.4 Political transition in 1994 and the new elite's shift to neoliberal capitalism

It is widely acknowledged (Bond 2000; Lodge 2002; Marais 2011; Terreblanche 2002) that the ANC inherited a semi-industrial, semi-periphery economy that was handicapped by symptoms of a structural crisis that had been lingering since the early 1970s. This was made worse by international economic isolation. The ANC would have to restructure the economy while re-integrating into the international economy in a context of the global triumph of neoliberal economic policies which forced the decline of welfare state social spending. Since the mid-1970s, big business corporations and other organised business associations, acknowledged that there were pressures to change the economy to a capital-intensive, high-wage, high-productivity accumulation strategy, and were adapting their respective firms accordingly. A build-up of several factors was the most prominent symptom of the crisis, these included:
- increasing black resistance to the cheap labour system since the early 1970s
- episodic labour unrest linked to community political struggles

- declining productivity in the rural reserve areas that apartheid laws set aside for blacks, which threatened the basis of the cheap migrant labour system
- the inflation rate that fuelled black protest, decreased manufacturing output and earnings from mineral exports
- decreased foreign exchange reserves
- international economic sanctions that hindered the replacement of machinery and spare parts.

The *Freedom Charter* adopted in 1955 was the ANC's core policy orientation on post-apartheid social, political and economic reconstruction containing radical demands for a welfare type of state, sharing of the country's wealth and resources, control of banks and industries by the people, freedom of trade and for the movement of labour, land redistribution. Nonetheless, in exile, ANC leaders were adamant that the party was not a socialist one (Mbeki 1984). Its leaders steered clear of Marxist rhetoric and calls for the nationalisation of banks, mines and other productive assets while drifting towards the notion of a 'mixed economy'. The trade union movement allies of the ANC played a major role in drafting the ANC government's first major policy-making orientation, the *Reconstruction and Development Programme* (RDP) which was released before the 1994 elections and adopted by the post-elections government of national unity. The RDP acknowledged weaknesses of both market-led and centrally-planned economies as models to address the revival of the economy and undo a legacy of inequality in delivery of services such as healthcare, education and housing. The RDP veered towards notions of 'people-centred' development strategies and Keynesian ideas of the state playing a major role in employment creation. Growth and development were seen as the products of a policy that emphasised reconstruction and redistribution. The economy's performance is crucial to the state's acquisition of social spending resources. The RDP acknowledged that demand for raw material and mineral exports central to the apartheid economy did not guarantee a significant income in a global economy with pressures for free trade and competition in manufactured goods. It also recognised that demand for such goods stagnated and domestic manufacturers faced international competition in the production of manufactured goods (ANC 1994). The new government was championing implementing social democratic welfare state types of policies and institutions (see Seekings & Natrass 2016), but the resources and tax revenues for welfare state spending would be dependent on sound consistent economic growth.

In 1995 the ANC contended that the economy's growth rate of three per cent made it difficult for government to deliver on RDP promises. This contextual factor abetted the struggle elite's drift from state interventionism to a convergence with the old white elite's own drift to neo-liberal policies. ANC leaders began advocating neo-liberal ideas about local firms achieving international competitiveness and announced in Parliament in 1996 the adoption of its new macro-economic policy framework, *Growth, Employment and Redistribution: a Macroeconomic Strategy* (GEAR), which the ANC elite leadership claimed was still intended to realise RDP objectives. Effectively, the ANC's elite leadership followed the advice of big business sector think-tanks and elite beneficiaries of black economic empowerment ventures. The ANC converged with the principles of the NP's reform period neoliberal paradigm evident in *The Key Issues in the Normative Economic Model* of 1993, as well as a document by the Macro-Economic Research Group which advised against state spending. The ANC followed models developed by big business associations, the Development Bank of South Africa, the Bureau of Economic Research, the World Bank, and the South African Reserve Bank. The GEAR document recognised the population was growing faster than the economy's growth rate (GDP grew by 1.3 per cent in 1993, 2.7 per cent in 1994, and 3.5 per cent in 1995), and the unemployment rate at GEAR's inception was between 38 to 40 per cent (ANC 1997: 6, 10). Emphasis was placed on 'a competitive fast-growing economy which creates sufficient jobs for all work seekers', thereby achieving 'a redistribution of income and opportunities in favour of the poor' (ANC 1996). GEAR shifted to an export oriented economy that attracted investment and created jobs as a means of effecting redistribution. The lofty expectations of GEAR's policy package were: an average growth rate increase of 4.2 per cent for four years, then by six per cent by 2000; creating 1.35 million jobs or 400 000 jobs per annum by 2000; increasing exports by an average of 8.4 per cent per annum, and improving infrastructure. GEAR promised a shift away from reliance on raw materials exports by promoting exports of manufactured goods and an end to tariff protection of local industries, thus forcing them into restructuring for international competitiveness (ANC 1996: Appendix 1). GEAR's plan to put the economy into a new growth path through restructuring industries and increasing their openness to international competitiveness was expected to have long-term benefits of increasing employment opportunities, and with some later redistribution gains through wages. GEAR's critics

(see Marais 2010, 2011, Terreblanche 2002 and Bond 2000) pointed out that it contrarily produced an upsurge in unemployment, poverty and inequality, which is behind the considerable growth in protest actions. The political transition had nonetheless facilitated the acquisition of tremendous wealth through Black Economic Empowerment (BEE) deals by the well-connected black struggle elite. Without abandoning the basic neoliberal principles of GEAR, the ANC government announced new development strategies to turn around unemployment and poverty. The *Employment Strategy Framework* of 1998 did not veer from the neoliberal paradigm in its hope to create jobs and fight poverty. The adoption of the *Accelerated and Shared Growth Initiative for South Africa* (AsgiSA) in February 2006 promised to halve poverty and unemployment by 2014. Achieving that goal proved out of reach given an economic growth rate of 2.5 per cent for 2012 as reported by the then Finance Minister Pravin Gordhan. The unemployment rate for 2012 hardly changed from its 25 per cent rate through 2011. The *New Growth Path* (NGP) mooted by the ANC in 2010 continued the rhetoric of creating jobs, reducing inequality and economic growth but for its critics, especially in the trade unions, it was still not a departure from GEAR's neoliberal orientation; the party leadership subsequently abandoned NGP. The *National Development Plan* 2030 adopted in 2012 acknowledges the same structural problems as its predecessor guiding documents for post-apartheid policymaking with its own promises to address poverty, have sustained job creation, reduce inequality, and the need to transform the economy in order to do so. Nonetheless, there is little reversal of these three major structural problems: the economy's growth rate in the fourth quarter of 2018 was at 1.4 per cent and the overall growth rate for the same year of 2018 was 0.8 per cent (StatsSA 2019); quarterly labour force surveys persistently report on increases in unemployment – that is, 27.2 per cent or 6.1 million people in 2018 (StatsSA 2018: 1).

The NDP includes its perspective on globalisation, how countries are dependent on external capital flows in this environment, and what South Africa should do. Despite seeking an alliance with China, the world's fastest growing economy, in BRICS, the impact of trade relations with China on South Africa's industries, as well those of other African countries, is the source of considerable industrial decline and job losses (see Polgreen & French 2007). China's economy contributes 70 per cent of BRICS' gross economic output and is regarded as having veto power over any BRICS initiatives (see Rothkopf 2009). It appears that SA has aligned itself with a new imperial power in Africa, and with the new underdevelopment consequences of China's presence in Africa.

Summary

- This chapter provided an overview of the evolutionary development of human societies through to social changes that accompanied the emergence of modern industrial society and its global impact on social change.
- The discussion was presented by first conceptualising and defining what sociologists understand by social change and illustrating changes at micro-, middle- and macro-levels of social interaction.
- A summary of the metatheoretical choices that underlay theorists' construction of theories of social change was also provided. Generally these are choices between opposite ends of a spectrum although some theories attempt to synthesise both ends of a spectrum. Émile Durkheim, Karl Marx and Max Weber were presented as foundational thinkers on the origins, nature of, and consequences of industrial capitalism upon which subsequent theories have expanded.
- The rise of industrial capitalism and modern nation-states are treated as the two main social developments which are central to understanding several other social phenomena today.
- Industrial capitalism created a globally connected world and the chapter discerns different locations which have emerged, namely, First World, Second World and Third World. The Third World represented the least industrialised and its prospects for industrial development were dealt with in a number of theories from classical Marxism, modernisation theory, dependency theory, world systems theory, and theories of globalisation.
- South Africa's incorporation in the global capitalist system was sketched with reference to hunter, gatherer, pastoralist and settled agricultural societies that preceded colonial conquest and the transition to a periphery of the world capitalist system that emerged in the 16th century.
- The late 19th century mineral discoveries enabled an industrial take-off and by the mid-20th century South Africa became a semi-periphery economy that dominated southern Africa.
- The system of apartheid racial domination in a capitalist economy endured for some decades until internal social conflict and structural problems in the economy contributed to a political settlement against the backdrop of a new era of globalisation.
- The leadership elite of the anti-apartheid liberation movements were progressively won over to implementing neoliberal capitalism ideas that have been dominant in this era of globalisation.
- Social inequality and class conflict have considerably increased in the era of a racially inclusivist political transition.

ARE YOU ON TRACK?

1. What insights do notions of 'class struggle' offer you to understanding the rise and decline of apartheid rule?
2. What insights do notions of 'class struggle' offer you to understand events in post-1994 South Africa?
3. What are the prospects of post-1994 South Africa shifting between the structural locations of core, semi-periphery and core in the contemporary capitalist world economy?

More sources to consult

Terreblanche S (Solomon Johannes). 2002. *A History of Inequality in South Africa, 1652–2002*. Pietermaritzburg: University of Natal Press.

References

Abrams P. 1982. *Historical Sociology*. Ithaca, NY: Cornell University.

African National Congress. 1994. *The Reconstruction and Development Programme. A Policy Framework*. Johannesburg: Umanyano.

African National Congress. 1996. 'Growth, Employment and Redistribution. A macroeconomic strategy'. [Online] Available at: http://www.polity.org.za/html/govdocs/policy/gear-02.html [Accessed 14 June 2013].

ANC. 1997. 'Understanding GEAR. Growth, Employment and Redistribution. The government's new economic strategy'. [Online] Available at: http://www.anc.org.za/ancdocs/pubs/gear.htm [Accessed 30 May 2013].

Andersen ML, Taylor HF. 2011. *Sociology. The essentials.* 6th ed. Wadsworth: Cengage.

Beinart W, Dubow S (eds). 1995. *Segregation and Apartheid in Twentieth Century South Africa.* London: Routledge.

Benjamin C. 2006. 'COSATU strike will damage SA, say analysts.' *Business Day*, 18 May.

Boddy-Evans A. 2018. *The Mfecane in South Africa.* https://www.thoughtco.com/what was the mfecane- 43374 [Accessed 15 January 2020].

Bond P. 2000. *Elite Transition. From Apartheid to Neo-liberalism in South Africa.* London: Pluto Press.

Bundy C. 1979. *The Rise and Fall of the South African Peasantry.* London: Heinemann.

Congress of South African Trade Unions (COSATU). nd. 'Government's New Growth Path Framework: one step forward, two steps backward'. [Online] Available at: http://www.cosatu.org.za/show.php?ID=4459 [Accessed 16 September 2013].

Department of Labour. 1998. 'Create jobs, fighting poverty: an employment strategy framework'. [Online] Available at: http://www.info.gov.za/otherdocs/1998/jobs_poverty.htm. [Accessed 5 August 2013].

Dos Santos T. 2003. 'The structure of dependence' in *Development and Underdevelopment: The Political Economy of Global Inequality.* Seligson MA, Passé Smith JT. 3rd ed. Boulder, CO: Lynne Rienner Publishers.

Ebrahim S. 2017. BRICS building a new order. *The Star*, 8 September: 10.

Edwards M. 1999. *Future Positive: International Co-operation in the 21st Century.* London: Earthscan.

Ehrensaft P. 1985. 'Phases in the development of South African capitalism: From settlement to crises', in *The Political Economy of Contemporary Africa.* Gutkind PCW, Wallerstein I (eds). Beverly Hills: SAGE.

Elliot JA. 1994. *An Introduction to Sustainable Development: The Developing World.* London: Routledge.

Esipisu 2003. 'Kenya calls on South Africa to lower its tariffs'. *The Star, Business Report.* 7 August: 7.

Frank AG. 1981. *Crisis: In the Third World.* New York: Holmes & Meier.

Frank AG. 1983. 'Crisis and transformation of dependency in the world system', in *Theories of Development. Mode of Production or Dependency?* Chilcote RH & Johnson D (eds). London: SAGE.

Frank AG. 1995. 'The development of underdevelopment', in *Development Studies: A Reader.* Corbridge S (ed). London: Edward Arnold.

Frank AG. 1998. *ReOrient: Global Economy in the Asian Age.* Berkeley: University of California Press.

Frank AG. 1967. 2010. 'Sociology of development and underdevelopment of sociology', in *Theory and Methodology of World Development: The Writings of André Gunder Frank* by Chew SC, Lauderdale P (eds). New York: Palgrave Macmillan.

Fukuyama F. 1989. 'The end of history?' *The National Interest*, Summer, 16(3): 18.

Fukuyama F. 1992. *The End of History and the Last Man.* New York: The Free Press.

Giddens A. 1986. *Sociology: A Brief and Critical Introduction.* 2nd ed. London: Macmillan.

Giddens A.1994. *Beyond Left and Right: The Future of Radical Politics.* Cambridge: Polity.

Giddens A. 1998. *The Third Way: The Renewal of Social Democracy.* Oxford: Polity.

Ginsburg D. 1996. 'The democratisation of South Africa: transition theory tested'. *Transformation*, 29: 74–102.

Hall S, Gieben B (eds). 1992. *Formations of Modernity.* Milton Keynes: The Open University.

Haralambos M, Holborn M, Heald R. 2004. *Sociology. Themes and Perspectives.* 6th ed. London: Collins.

Hoogvelt AMM. 1997. *Globalisation and the Postcolonial World: The New Political Economy of Development.* London: MacMillan.

Kammeyer KCW, Ritzer G, Yetman NR. 1990. *Sociology: Experiencing Changing Societies.* Boston: Allyn & Bacon.

Kiely R. 1995. *Sociology and Development: The Impasse and Beyond.* London: UCL Press.

Lenin VI. 1956. *The Development of Capitalism in Russia: The Process of the Formation of a Home Market for Large-scale Industry.* Moscow: Foreign Languages Publishing House.

Lenin VI. 1975. *Imperialism, the Highest Stage of Capitalism.* Peking: Foreign Languages Press.

Libby T. 1987. 'Transnational corporations and the national bourgeoisie: Regional expansion and party realignment in South Africa', in *Studies in Power and Class in Africa.* Markowitz IL (ed). New York: Oxford University Press.

Lodge T. 2002. *Politics in South Africa. From Mandela to Mbeki.* Cape Town: David Philip.

Mamdani M. 1996. *Citizen and Subject. Contemporary Africa and the Legacy of Late Colonialism.* Princeton, NJ: Princeton University Press.

Marais H. 2010. *Limits to Change: New Views on the Political Economy of South Africa's Transition.* London: Zed Books.

Marais H. 2011. *South Africa Pushed to the Limit: The Political Economy of Change.* London: Zed Books.

Marks S. 1980. 'South Africa: The myth of the empty land'. *History Today*, 30(1): 7–12.

Matthews SJ. 2010. *Post-development theory.* Oxford Research Encyclopedia of International Studies. http://oxfordre.com/internationalstudies/view/10.1093/acrefore/9780190846626.001.0001/acrefore-9780190846626-e-39?print=pdf

Maylam P. 1986. *A History of the African People of South Africa: From the Early Iron Age to the 1970s.* London: Croom Helm.

Mbeki T. 1984. 'The Fatton thesis: A rejoinder'. *Canadian Journal of African Studies*, 18(3): 609–612.

McMichael P. 2012. *Development and Social Change. A Global Perspective.* Los Angeles: SAGE.

Mkandiwire T (ed). 2005. *African Intellectuals. Rethinking Politics, Language, Gender and Development.* Pretoria: Unisa Press.

Muthien Y. 'Imperialism and underdevelopment', in *Development is for People.* Coetzee JK (ed). 2nd ed. Johannesburg: Southern.

Noble T. 2000. *Social Theory and Social Change.* London: Macmillan.

Offiong DA. 1982. *Imperialism and Dependency. Obstacles to African Development.* Washington, DC: Howard University Press.

Padayachee V (ed). 2006. *The Development Decade? Economic and Social Change in South Africa, 1994–2004.* Cape Town: HSRC Press.

Palma G. 1978. 'Dependency: A formal theory of underdevelopment or a methodology for the analysis of concrete situations of underdevelopment?' *World Development*, Vol 6.

Polgreen L, French HW. 2007. China's trade in Africa carries a price tag. *New York Times*, 21 August.

Republic of South Africa. 1996. The Constitution of the Republic of South Africa. Act 108 of 1996.

Republic of South Africa, National Planning Commission. 2012. *National Development Plan 2030. Our future – make it work. Executive Summary.* https://www.gov.za/sites/default/files/Executive%20Summary-NDP%20 2030%20-%20Our%20future%20-%20make%20it%20work.pdf

Republic of South Africa. sa nd. 'Accelerated and Shared Growth Initiative for South Africa (AsgiSA)'. [Online] Available at: http://www.info.gov.za/asgisa [Accessed 19 June 2013].

Ritzer G. 1996. *Sociological Theory.* 4th ed. New York: McGraw-Hill Companies Inc.

Ritzer G. 1996a. *The McDonaldization of Society. An Investigation into the Changing Character of Contemporary Social Life.* (Revised edition). Thousand Oaks, CA: Pine Forge Press.

Rostow WW. 1960. *The Stages of Economic Growth: A Non-communist Manifesto.* Cambridge: Cambridge University Press.

Rothkopf D. 2009. *The BRICS and what the BRICS would be without China ...* http://rothkopf.foreignpolicy.com/posts/2009/06/15/the_brics_and_what_the_brics_woul... [Accessed 9 April 2014].

Saul JS, Gelb S. 1986. *The Crisis in South Africa.* (Revised edition). London: Zed Books.

Schlemmer L, Webster E. 1978. *Change, Reform and Economic Growth in South Africa.* Johannesburg: Ravan Press.

Seekings J, Natrass N. 2016. *Poverty, Politics & policy in South Africa. Why has Poverty Persisted after Apartheid?* Johannesburg: Jacana.

Smith JA. 2011. *BRIC becomes BRICS: changes on the geopolitical chessboard.* http://www.foregin policyjournal.com/2011/01/21/bric-becomes-brics-changes-on-the-geo [Accessed 9 April 2014].

Statistics SA. 2011. *Quarterly Labour Force Survey.* Quarter 3, 1 November.

Statistics SA. 2018. *BRICS: Where does South Africa rank?* http://www.statssa.gov.za/?p=11355 [Accessed 6 August 2018].

Statistics SA. 2018. *Quarterly Labour Force Survey.* Quarter 2: 2018.

Statistics SA. 2019. *Economy edges up by 0,8% in 2018.* http://www.statssa.gov.za/?p=11969 [Accessed 6 March 2018].

So AY. 1990. *Social Change and Development: Modernisation, Dependency and World-systems Theories.* Newbury Park, California: SAGE.

Sztompka P. 1993. *The Sociology of Social Change.* Oxford: Blackwell.

Sullivan TJ. 2001. *Sociology. Concepts and Applications in a Diverse World.* 5th ed. Boston: Allyn & Bacon.

Terreblanche S. 2002. *A History of Inequality in South Africa, 1652–2002.* Pietermaritzburg: University of Natal Press.

Tilly C. 1984. *Big Structures, Large Processes, Huge Comparisons*. New York: Russell Sage Foundation.

Tischler HL. 1996. *Introduction to Sociology*. 5th ed. Fort Worth, TX: Harcourt Brace.

Turok B. 2008. *From the Freedom Charter to Polokwane. The Evolution of ANC Economic Policy.* Cape Town: New Agenda.

Uzodike UO. 2016. South Africa and BRICS: Path to a new African hegemony?, in *State of the Nation. South Africa 2016: Who is in Charge?* Plaatjies D, Chitiga-Mabugu M, Hongoro C, Meyiwa T, Nkondo M, Nyamnjoh F (eds). Cape Town: HSRC Press.

Yudelman D. 1975. 'Industrialization, race relations, and change in South Africa: An ideological and academic debate'. *African Affairs*, (294): 82–96.

Wallerstein I. 1974. 'The rise and demise of the world capitalist system: Concepts for comparative analysis'. *Comparative studies in society and history*, 16(4). September.

Wallerstein I. 1979. *The Capitalist World Economy.* Cambridge: Cambridge University Press.

Wallerstein I. 1979a. 'A world-system perspective on the social sciences', in *The Capitalist World Economy: Essays by Immanuel Wallerstein*. Cambridge: Cambridge University Press.

Webster D. 1990. *Introduction to the Sociology of Development*. 2nd ed. London: Macmillan.

Wilson M. 1969. 'The hunters and herders', in *The Oxford history of South Africa: South Africa to 1870*. Wilson M, Thompson L (eds). Oxford: Oxford University Press.

Wolpe H. 1995. 'Capitalism and cheap labour power in South Africa: From segregation to apartheid', in *Segregation and Apartheid in Twentieth-century South Africa*. Beinart W, Dubow S (eds). London: Routledge.

Population

Gretchen du Plessis

This chapter is given early prominence in the first part of the book because population is a prerequisite for all social action. There is no society without people. If sociology has as its central concern the study of people and especially what groups of people do, the concept of population is important. The role of the collective concept of population is to conceptually capture everyone in our global society in its ambit. The study of population, also referred to as demography, hence importantly defines, in the broadest possible way, the very object of sociological inquiry.

Population is not only a requirement for social action, but it also shapes social action. The study of populations, whether at a global or local level, consequently frames all social analysis. The size and density of a population give us a good idea of the form and shape of the society we can expect to find. Society itself is going to look very different, for instance, depending on the number and density of its population or whether it is rural or urban. Human interactions and what people do depend heavily on whether the population is small and spread over a sparsely inhabited geographical area or large and concentrated in high-rise city apartment blocks. The rate of births and deaths and the relation between the two, central to population studies, signal whether the population is growing or not. This can in turn suggest the degree of stability or extent of social change in a society and often indicates whether it is a well- or less-developed one. Whether a population is mainly elderly or youthful not only tells us much about the state of a society, but also has very different implications for its challenges and its future. The migratory patterns of movement of people within a country, region or across the globe are important indicators of social change and affect the life chances of individuals, and so on. These are some of the issues with which this chapter concerns itself.

This chapter illustrates very clearly how sociological concepts work. The definitions of some key concepts used in population studies listed in Information Box 5.1 gives a clear conceptual picture of how populations are analysed. While important in all social science, you will notice how many of them relate to measuring features of a population. Measurement hence features prominently as an issue in this chapter. When you consider that the idea of the global population represents over seven billion people, the thought is an astounding one and challenges the imagination. South Africa had a population of 57.73 million people in 2018. It is hard to imagine what it would be like to live in either India or China, which both have populations exceeding one billion people or 1 000 million. There were 1 415 045 928 people in China and 1 354 051 854 people in India in 2018 (OECD Stats nd). At a broad conceptual level, thinking in terms of population numbers and sex and age structures aids our understanding of social change.

To make the exercise manageable, more so than in other areas of sociology, we need to make use of numbers, which in this case tell a story of their own. There is inevitably some use of technical terms in population studies which it is useful to work through carefully. While the use of statistics is crucial to demography, this is kept to a minimum in this chapter. A few relatively simple formulae are introduced, but are well worth learning. They are not difficult to apply and result in extremely rewarding mental pictures of what society looks like once grasped through a demographic lens. For instance, when breaking up the population according to age, as you will see in this chapter, startling graphic representations result when a country with a zero population growth is compared to one where either young people or the aged comprise a significant proportion of the population.

A key way of collecting population data is by the familiar means of a census. The way in which a census is conducted and some of the social scientific challenges in enumerating and analysing census data since 1994 in South Africa is explained in a straightforward manner in this chapter. You may be surprised to find out how 'youthful' South African society is. Moreover, this chapter locates the demographic profile of South Africa in the context of sub-Saharan Africa and the globe on a number of different variables. In fact, careful study of this chapter provides an opportunity to see a fascinatingly clear picture of a range of aspects of South African society.

You may also be interested to know that there are currently very few demographers in South Africa and that the demand for those qualified in that field is consequently high. If you follow through with population studies and master demography, one thing is certain – not only will you have learned to look at and understand society in a way that combines conceptual breadth and depth based on hard empirical evidence, but you will also almost definitely walk straight into an important and intellectually stimulating job after you graduate!

Case study 5.1 Population events

Gita (22) lived in Port Elizabeth. She shared a home with her mother, grandmother, sister and one-year-old son. When she was 28 weeks' pregnant with her second child, she developed blinding headaches and blurred vision. She went to the public hospital seeking treatment. She was told that she had hypertension and should be admitted to hospital. However, she asked to be discharged after one day, because she feared that she would be dismissed from her job. Because she was the only adult in her household earning an income, this would have been devastating. A week later, Gita's baby girl was born prematurely. What should have been a happy occasion for Gita and her family turned into a tragedy as Gita died in childbirth.

What happened to Gita and her family unfolds at the micro-level of societal analysis. We all experience births, deaths and marriages, and we are likely to change residences or migrate. Taken together (or aggregated), all these events produce the trends in fertility, mortality and migration that can be studied over time and weighed against different regions. Each year, many women die due to childbirth and pregnancy-related complications. Such deaths, referred to as the maternal mortality ratio, can be expressed as deaths per 100 000 live births (World Health Organization 2018). In 2015, for every 100 000 babies born, 138 South African mothers died (World Health Organization 2018). South Africa used to have a very high rate of maternal deaths if compared with rates in other countries with similar socioeconomic characteristics, but since 2009 these deaths have been steadily declining (Moodley & Pattison 2018). Maternal deaths are preventable, so South Africa addressed this problem by introducing antiretroviral treatment for pregnant mothers with HIV and other measures to bring down this number. Death due to hypertension (as illustrated in the case study above) remains high in South Africa, and the figure of 138 maternal deaths for every 100 000 live births is still higher than the international target set for this. The point is that maternal mortality ratios are seen as sentinel events that tell us something about the state of healthcare services and development in a country. One of the Sustainable Development Goals (SDGs), particularly SDG3 entitled 'Ensuring healthy lives and promoting well-being for all at all ages', is to drastically reduce the deaths of mothers to below 70 per 100 000 live births by 2030 (World Health Organization 2015).

QUESTIONS

1. How do sociologists measure population events such as births, deaths and movements across borders?
2. What are the sources of information on population events and how can one tell that they are accurate?
3. How are population events related to development?
4. What specific challenges do population growth, change and characteristics pose for development?

Key themes

- Why sociologists study population
- The dynamic and the structural elements of a population and how these interact
- Population size, growth and change as important sources of social change
- Past and current trends in world population processes in terms of age structures, size and composition

- Urbanisation as a major variable in the social dynamics of societies
- Demographic data sources
- Published demographic data and errors in population data
- Sustainable Development Goals (SDGs) and their link to the study of population
- The interplay between fertility, mortality and migration in the population equation.

5.1 Introduction: Why study population?

What does the word 'population' mean to you? Do you imagine a crowd of people, like spectators at a soccer match? Do you think of the number of people in a country? Do you associate population with environmental or other social problems such as mass migration, poverty or **HIV/AIDS**? Perhaps you associate the word 'population' with numerical

or political strength. Sociologists and demographers define a population as a collection of persons alive at a specific time who meet certain criteria, for example the population of South Africa on 1 March 2019.

Population has both a spatial (referring to geographical place such as South Africa) and a time dimension (Feeney & Lutz 1990).

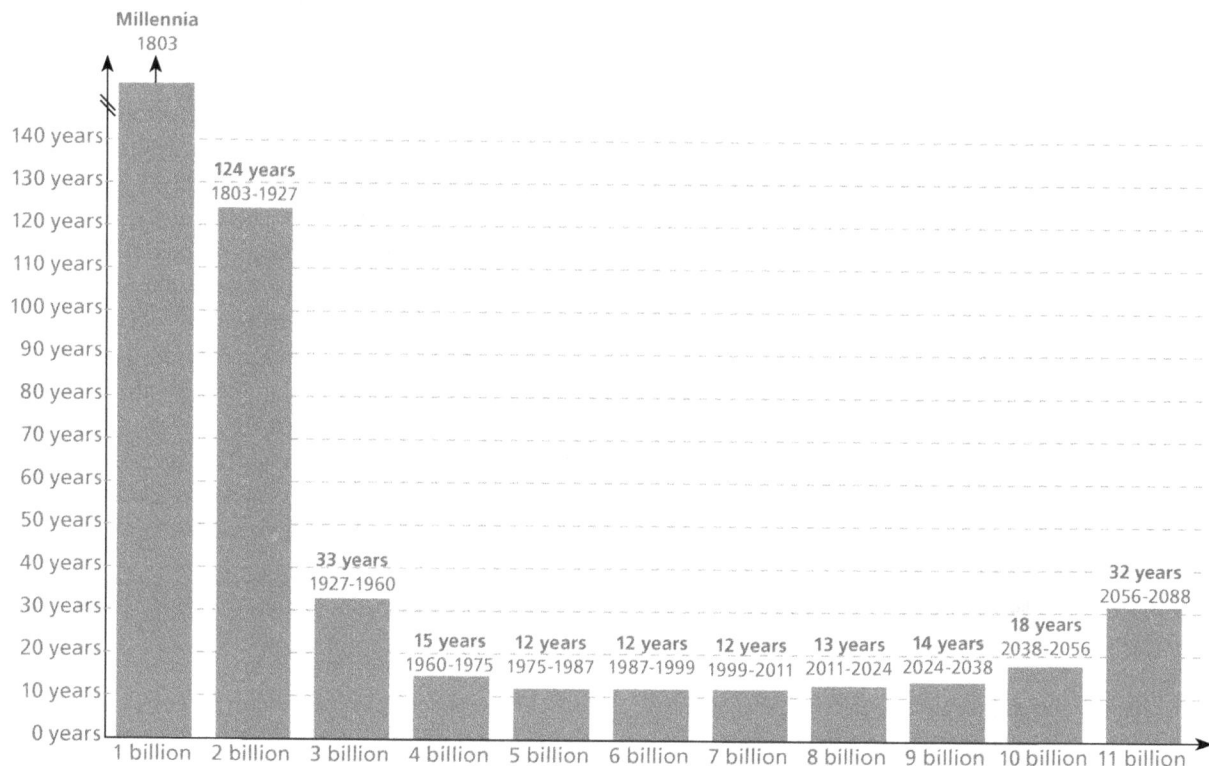

Figure 5.1 Bar graph depicting the years it took (and would take) to add another billion to the world's population

(Source: Our World in Data nd)

The formal study of population (also referred to as demography) is concerned with many issues that we may associate with the word 'population'. These include the size, spatial distribution, **composition**, **structure** and characteristics. There are three main population processes, namely **fertility**, mortality and **migration**. The study of population is also concerned with the question of how population processes and structures affect a nation's economy, healthcare and general way of life.

Populations have *structural* and *dynamic* elements. The *dynamic* elements are those things that continually change, such as births, deaths and migration streams. In other words, dynamic elements are fertility (people are added to the population by birth), mortality (people are subtracted from the population due to death) and migration (people can be added due to in-migration or immigration, or subtracted due to out-migration or emigration).

The *structural* elements result from past trends in births, deaths and migration streams. This is the given structure of the population at a given moment, such as how many men and women there are and their ages. *Structural* aspects include characteristics such as the composition of the population by age, sex, marital status or economic characteristics. In turn, a given population structure enables and facilitates current and future trends in births, deaths and migration. For example, a high birth rate may indicate a population with many babies and young people, which could encourage out-migration (due to competition for jobs) and continued high levels of births as the younger people reach their own childbearing years.

The study of population presents sociologists with techniques and theories that can help us understand that the demographic story is quite different depending on the parts of the world in which it is experienced. This is despite the fact that it deals with seemingly universal human experiences. Thus, the answer to the question of why the study of population is important lies in the fact that births, deaths and population movements affect the shape of a population, which in turn enables or restricts trends in births, deaths and population movements. In addition, population change is an important force in broader societal change (Weeks 2015). In the following sections we expand on the three ways population change affects our lives. First, we argue that in terms of sheer numbers, the world population is a force to be reckoned with. Second, we argue that the world population is becoming older and that the age structure of populations has particular significance for socioeconomic development. Third, we present arguments concerning population, human livelihoods and ecology.

5.2 Population growth and change as an important source of social change

In November 2018 the world population reached 7.7 billion people. The rate of increase of the world population during the second half of the 20th century was faster than at any other point in history. Figure 5.1 shows how quickly the next billion people were added to the world population until 1927, then the rate slowed down, but is projected to pick up slightly by 2024.

For most of human history, our ancestors eked out an insecure existence as hunters and gatherers. Owing to the hardships they faced and the scarcity of food, their numbers were small. The world population expanded to about 300 million by the 1st century AD, and continued to grow at a slow rate. Rapid population increase is therefore a contemporary issue and a major variable in development. This is dramatically illustrated in Figure 5.1.

The reason why scientists paid special attention to the 'six billion' milestone in world population during 1999 goes beyond the mere number of humans on the planet. It is the shortest period in human history that a next billion mark was reached (ie the time period between five and six billion was a mere 12 years). The world population increased from one billion to six billion in less than 200 years. Human population entered the 20th century with 1.6 billion people and left it with 6.1 billion. It is likely to reach 11 billion by the end of the projected period shown in Figure 5.1.

To help you understand the notions of population size, growth and change, you need to consider that there are two ways in which a person can enter a population, namely by birth or by in-migration or immigration. There are also two ways in which a person can exit a population, namely through death or by out-migration or emigration. This balance between the elements can be expressed in a simple formula known as the demographic balancing equation, namely:

Population change = (Births − Deaths) + (Immigrants − Emigrants)

Now let us elaborate on the notion of 'population change' as consisting of two parts, namely the initial population or Po (eg the population of South Africa in 2001) and the population after some time has passed or Pt (eg the population of South Africa in 2018), so that we can now say:

Pt − Po = (Births − Deaths) + (Immigrants − Emigrants)

The 'Births − Deaths' component of the demographic balancing equation is known as *natural increase* and the

'Immigrants – Emigrants' component is known as *net migration*. Natural increase is often called natural growth, or for populations in which the deaths are more than the number of births, natural decrease. For population change over time, natural increase plays an important role (and often the largest one) for most populations. Of course, when talking about growth in the world population, only natural increase is considered.

For pre-modern societies, their hunter-gatherer existence required them to live in small, mobile family units. Often, the ailing and old were left behind when the group moved to a new area, and food scarcity coincided with infanticide. There was high mortality due to infectious diseases and malnutrition. High levels of mortality also implied that women did not survive to complete their reproductive years and have the maximum number of pregnancies. At the time of the Agricultural Revolution, the world population was estimated to be four million. In terms of the demographic balancing equation, a growth to this level means that births were exceeding the number of deaths. The introduction of agriculture made it possible to support more people on the available resources. Domestication of animals implied a more intensive use of resources and a sustainable food supply. Although farming activities introduced new infectious diseases (animal-borne disease, sanitation problems and the aiding of communicable disease due to high-density settlements),

the availability of plant foods implied better diets. Improved nutrition and settlement in more stable living arrangements meant that women's fecundity improved. This raised the birth rate as birth intervals shortened due to smaller periods of breastfeeding (infants weaned sooner, because other softer foodstuffs became available).

Some sociologists believe that the acceleration in numbers took off after the Industrial Revolution in the 18th century, because living standards increased and widespread famines and epidemics diminished in some regions. They also claim that during this period, advances in technology meant that foodstuffs could be produced in bulk and that preservation methods were found to keep food fresh for longer. Although living standards in the early industrial towns were poor, growth in medical science and knowledge and public health measures eventually led to a decrease in the death rate and added numbers to the population base. Other sociologists see the increase in population numbers at the time of the Agricultural Revolution as the reason for (and not as the consequence of) the Industrial Revolution. Whether the Industrial Revolution was initiated by a rise in population or whether it started one is a matter of theoretical interpretation. The fact is that the world population increased to about 760 million in 1750 and reached one billion by 1800.

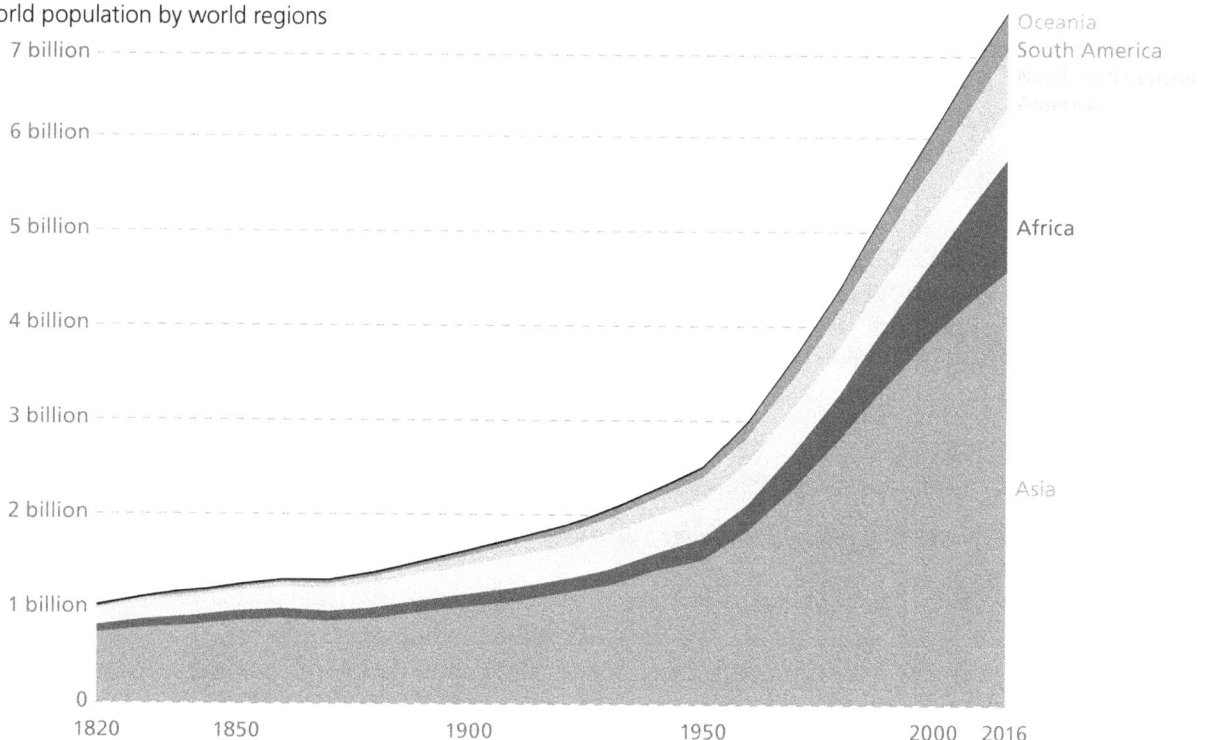

Figure 5.2 Population growth in billions, 1820–2016 by different regions of the world
(Source: Our World in Data nd)

The early processes of accelerated growth in the world population therefore occurred gradually as public healthcare interventions not only became known, but also were implemented through efforts on the part of public healthcare reformers. Throughout the early 20th century, infectious disease as a leading cause of death was brought under control due to improvements in medical technology, which led to the control of such diseases as tuberculosis, smallpox and cholera. The next spike in the growth of the world population occurred after World War II, when the population of the least-developed countries began to increase dramatically. Rapid population growth is therefore a recent phenomenon.

5.3 The age structure of populations and its impact on social issues

The growth rates and compositions of populations differ considerably between countries and regions of the world. The changing composition of populations is as striking a feature as its sheer size. The most obvious changes in the composition of the contemporary populations are the age structure and the distributions of populations over rural areas and cities.

The age structure and rural/urban distributions of population differ between different world regions. Although these are much-contested labels, the United Nations Economic and Social Council analysts often differentiate between more developed countries (the so-called MDCs) and least developed countries (the so-called LDCs). The MDCs regions include the major developed economies or G7, which are Canada, Japan, France, Germany, Italy, the UK and the US, and they are home to about 751 million people, or 10 per cent of the world population (United Nations Population Division 2017). Population growth rates in these regions are low, as birth rates and death rates have stabilised. The LDCs include 34 countries in Africa, 14 in Asia and one in Latin America. These LDCs are among the poorest nations in the world with very low per capita (ie per person) incomes – well below those of the MDCs. The population of the LDCs is estimated at around 880 million

people or 12 per cent of the world population. In addition, the largest proportion of the world population growth takes place in the LDCs.

These differences in the dynamics of populations of the MDCs and LDCs translate into differences in the static compositions of their populations. Countries with high rates of population growth have high birth rates and a large proportion of young people. Those with low rates have low birth rates, long life expectancies and many elderly people. Such differences have a range of social, economic and political consequences. For example, countries with a large number of babies and young people have great needs in terms of housing, education, health services and jobs. Countries with a large number of elderly people have a greater need for an efficient healthcare system.

To help you understand the differences in the age structures of populations and regions, we will introduce you to three ways in which the age structure can be summarised, namely head counts and percentage distributions of the population for different age categories, the age dependency ratio and population pyramids. Usually, data on the age structure of a population is reported in age categories of five-year intervals. This method, however, is rather cumbersome. Instead we use the following three functional age categories:

- *Dependent children* from birth to the age of 14 years (they are financially dependent on adults)
- The *potentially economically* active population between the ages of 15 and 64 years
- The *aged* or people aged 65 years and older (generally people who have retired).

These classifications may not conform to the realities in a given population. Individuals within the second functional age category may never have been employed and while some individuals may retire earlier, others continue to work after 65 years of age. Although functional age categories are in some instances flawed, they enable comparison of the population structures across different countries and time frames.

Case study 5.2 Can South Africa reap any benefits from demographic dividends?

Watch the videoclip produced by Population Reference Bureau at: http://www.prb.org/Multimedia/Video/2015/national-transfer-accounts.aspx
Then read the section below. Questions testing your understanding follow.

A demographic dividend is when changes in a population's age structure imply possible economic or developmental gains for the affected country. Oosthuizen (2018) suggests that there are two types of demographic dividends. ➡

The first happens when children survive for longer and birth rates fall so that the proportion of people of working age increases relative to the total population. Household resources previously used to sustain many dependent children are then freed up so that the average living standard of the household improves. This, however, can only pay off if the working population is gainfully employed and inflation is under control. The second demographic dividend is possible when the large number of working-age people survive for many years (in other words, longevity improves) and they are able to invest in savings or pensions so that they can remain financially independent. Again, this potential is afforded to a country because shifts in its population's age structure can only be realised if these aging adults were able to accumulate economic and human capital. Oosthuizen (2018) concludes that South Africa was unable to reap benefits from the first demographic dividend because of a fall in life expectancy between 1990 and 2011 due to HIV/AIDS and also due to stagnation in job creation. Because HIV/AIDS wreaked havoc on the key potential income earners (adult women between the ages of 20 and 40 years, and adult men between the ages of 30 and 44 years), the dependency ratios (number of earners versus numbers of non-earning consumers) remained high. In addition, the labour market could not absorb the large number of potential income earners.

For many South Africans, old-age pensions are used for the benefit of many dependants, not only the elderly (Klasen & Woolard 2009). This brings us to the missed opportunity of the second demographic dividend. Oosthuizen (2018) notes that although South Africa invests in human capital, persistent inequalities in educational and healthcare provision even in post-apartheid years would mean that the ability of an ageing population to invest and save will remain constrained.

QUESTIONS

1. Can the demographic dividends be proclaimed as a positive outcome of population dynamics and development in South Africa?
2. What will South Africa have to do in order to cash in on these dividends?
3. Is the South African population ageing? What would be needed to ensure productive, positive and successful ageing?

It is not a given that countries can use their demographic dividends to effect economic development. Certain factors must be addressed, such as the labour supply, savings and human capital. The large number of potential jobseekers implies a potential oversupply of labour that can lead to rising and protracted unemployment, competition for jobs, low wages and insecure livelihoods. To maximise the demographic dividend, there should be enough jobs created, and couples should practise family planning so that women, relieved of the care burden of children, can also enter the labour market. Potentially more working-age people in a population implies greater numbers who save and produce more (if compared with the youth and the elderly, who potentially consume more than they can produce). Finally, maximising the demographic dividend implies an investment in human capital. Declining birth rates and lower youth age dependency ratios encourage parents to invest more in the education of their children. At the same time, however, governments should provide quality and accessible educational, healthcare and social services, and look into ways to stimulate sustainable job growth or for households to secure livelihoods through entrepreneurship or agriculture. These population concerns become much more complex in the current socio-political context of the Fourth Industrial Revolution and sustained global environmental degradation (Szreter 2018).

Box 5.1 Demographic definitions

- The **demographic dividend** occurs when declining birth rates changes the age distribution of a population so that youth age dependency requires less investment (Oosthuizen 2018; Van der Ven & Smits 2011).
- A **histogram** is a bar chart.
- A **population pyramid** is a detailed picture of the age–sex structure of a population.
- **Gradient** refers to the slope of line of the pyramid. If you trace your finger along the South African population pyramid (Figure 5.3) from the left-hand bottom side, right to the top and down the right-hand side to the bottom again, you would have traced the gradient or slope of the population pyramid.
- **Population characteristics** describe a population in terms of variables such as level of education, income, occupation, race and ethnicity, language, religious affiliation, and so on.
- **Population distribution** refers to where people are located and why.
- **Population processes** refers to levels and trends in fertility, mortality and migration.

- **Population size** refers to how many people are in a given place at a given time.
- **Population structure** refers to how many males and females there are in each age group.
- **Symmetry** refers to the correspondence and balance between sides. Compare the right-hand and the left-hand sides of the South African population pyramid (Figure 5.3) – can you see that the sides are not completely symmetrical?

- The **age dependency ratio** describes the variations in the proportions of dependent children, aged persons, and persons of working age.
- **Youth dependency** describes the number of children (birth to age 14 years) that are economically dependent on the working-age population (those aged 15 to 64 years).
- **Old-age dependency describes** the number of individuals aged 65 and older per 100 people of aged 15 to 64 years.

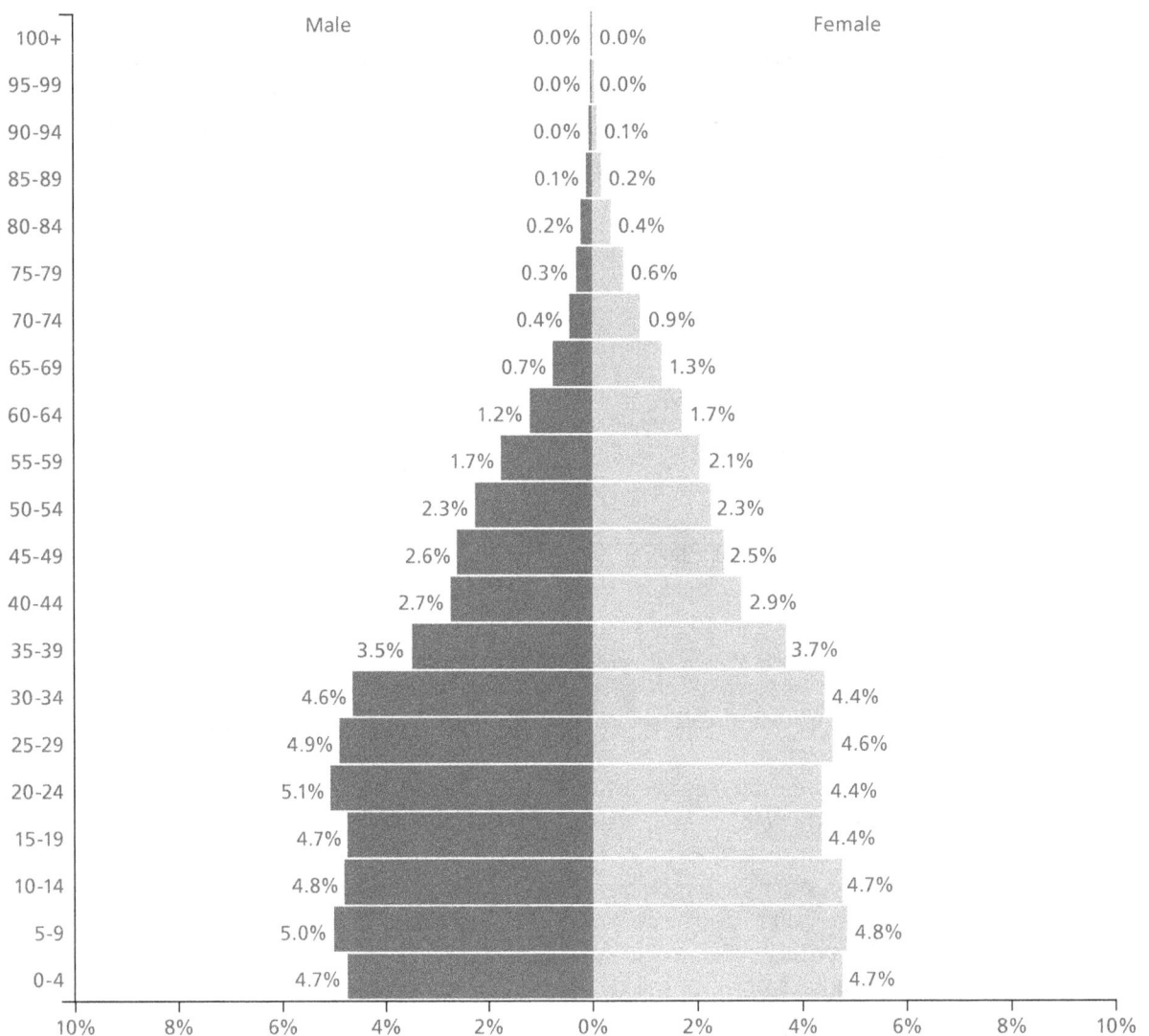

Age	Male	Female
100+	0.0%	0.0%
95-99	0.0%	0.0%
90-94	0.0%	0.1%
85-89	0.1%	0.2%
80-84	0.2%	0.4%
75-79	0.3%	0.6%
70-74	0.4%	0.9%
65-69	0.7%	1.3%
60-64	1.2%	1.7%
55-59	1.7%	2.1%
50-54	2.3%	2.3%
45-49	2.6%	2.5%
40-44	2.7%	2.9%
35-39	3.5%	3.7%
30-34	4.6%	4.4%
25-29	4.9%	4.6%
20-24	5.1%	4.4%
15-19	4.7%	4.4%
10-14	4.8%	4.7%
5-9	5.0%	4.8%
0-4	4.7%	4.7%

South Africa – 2018
Population: 55 866 711

Figure 5.3 South African population pyramid for 2018
(Source: PopulatonPyramid.net 2018)

The age structure of a population can also be depicted by means of a population pyramid (see Figure 5.3). Age categories are demarcated on a vertical axis, usually in five-year intervals, with the lowest category at the bottom and the highest at the top of the graph. Age categories are arranged in ascending order. Sex categories are demarcated by a division on the horizontal axis of the graph. Males are represented on the left-hand side and females on the right-hand side of the central vertical axis of the graph. When you look at a population pyramid, focus on two key features:

1. *Symmetry:* this gives an indication of the extent to which the sexes constitute equal or different proportions of a population. When you look at the symmetry of a population pyramid, you are in fact making a horizontal comparison between the two halves that represent males and females.

2. *Gradient:* the age categories of the pyramid can also be compared vertically. This gives an indication of the proportions of the population in the functional age categories. The gradient of the pyramid reflects the impact of population growth over time (Hobbs 2004).

Can you see that the population structure of South Africa in Figure 5.3 is shaped like a pyramid? Look at the age categories from the bottom to the top: can you see how the youngest age category has proportionately fewer members than the subsequent one?

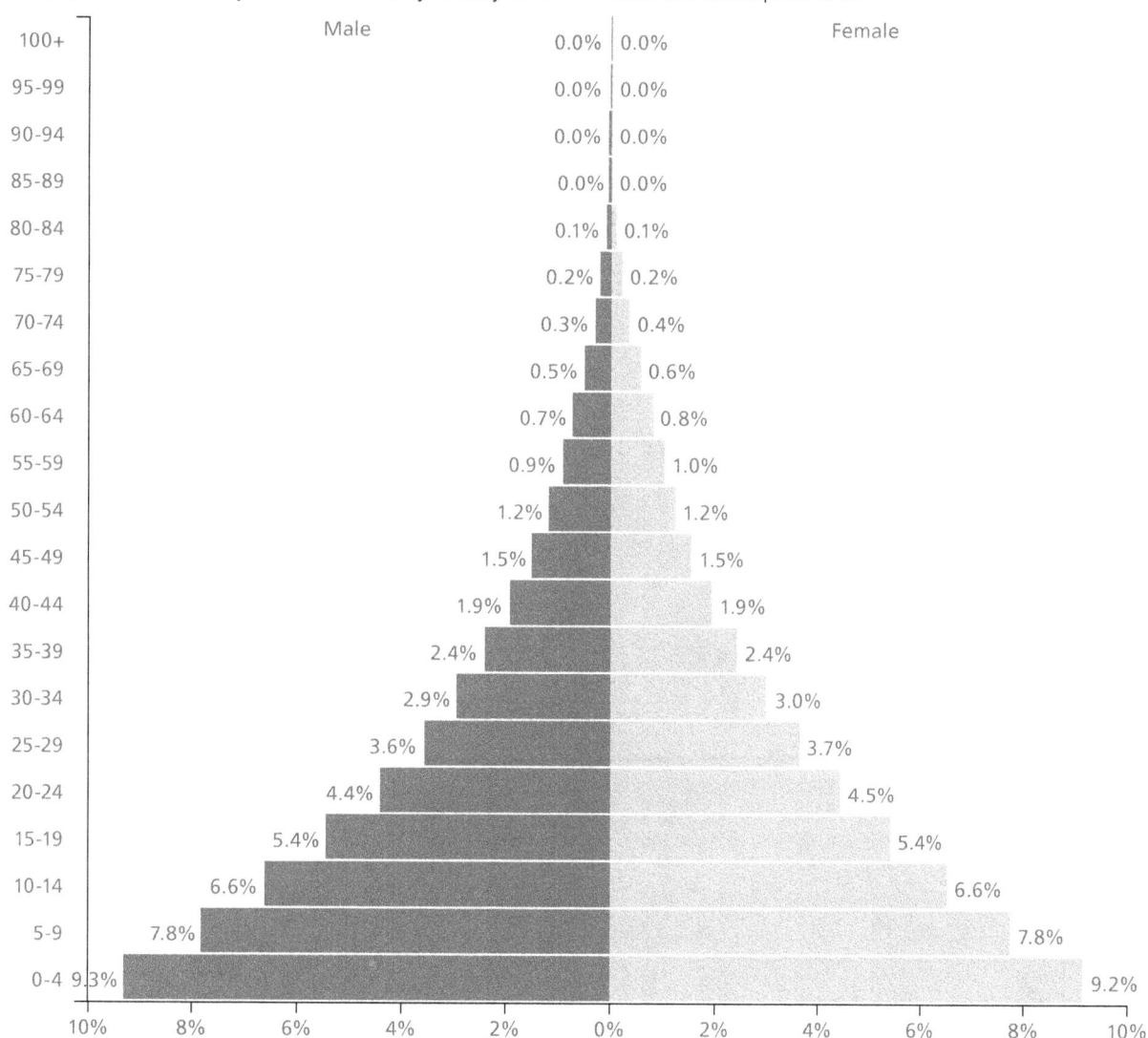

Angola – 2018
Population: 27 497 645

Figure 5.4 Population pyramid for Angola 2018
(Source: PopulatonPyramid.net 2018)

This narrowing base suggests a decline in fertility. The rate of fertility has an impact on the initial size of an age category. The narrowing of successive categories as you look upwards in particular reflects the impact of mortality. Now compare the two sides of the pyramid – the male and the female sides. Can you see that in the higher age categories the population represented on the female side increasingly outnumbers the population represented on the corresponding male side? This can be attributed to lower mortality among women than men. The effect of this differential mortality is more pronounced at the highest age categories.

Go to: http://www.statssa.gov.za/census/census_2011/census_products/Provinces%20at%20a%20glance%2016%20Nov%202012%20corrected.pdf for the breakdown of the age-and-sex pyramids for the 2011 census of South Africa by province.

If you look at these figures, you will notice that:
- Eastern Cape, Northern Cape, KwaZulu-Natal, North West, Mpumalanga and Limpopo all have youthful pyramids
- Gauteng and Western Cape have narrowing bases with large proportions of people in the 20- to 34-year age groups.

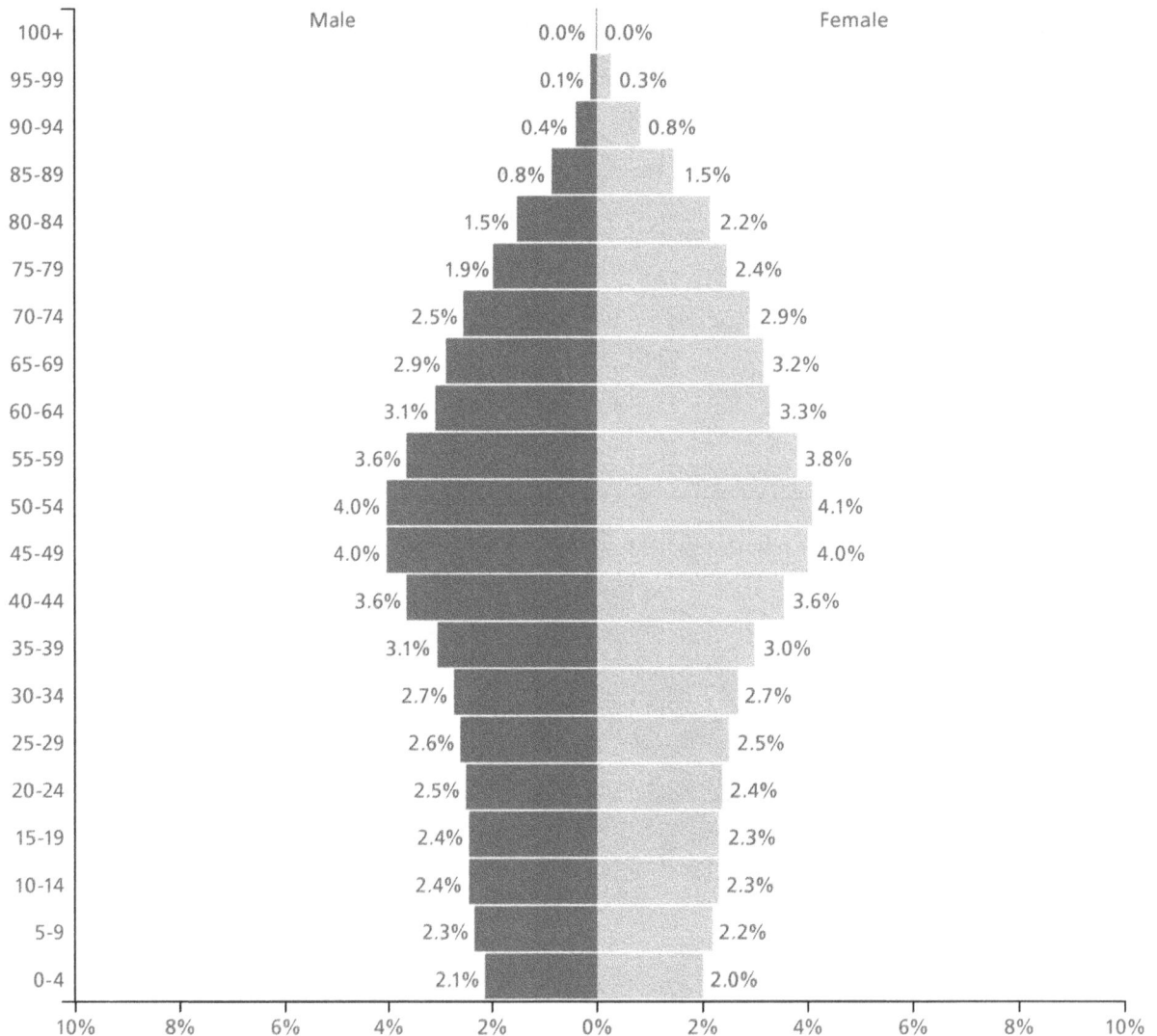

Italy – 2018
Population: 59 788 104

Figure 5.5 Population pyramid for Italy 2018
(Source: PopulatonPyramid.net 2018)

When you look at the population pyramid of an LDC such as Angola (see Figure 5.4), you will see that it shows a large youth population typical of the rapid growth pattern. In general, about 60 per cent of the population in LDCs is under the age of 25 years. Compare this with the population pyramid of an MDC like Italy (see Figure 5.5).

Can you see that Italy's population pyramid reflects the barrel shape of zero population growth? Can you see that on the right-hand side of Italy's population pyramid, the older age groups show more females than males? This phenomenon is known as the feminisation of old age.

At the discussion of the age dependency ratio, we introduced you to the idea of a demographic dividend. It is important to note that the dividend is a precursor for population ageing, which is the process by which persons in the older age categories represent a proportionally larger share of the total population. Look at the population pyramid of Italy in Figure 5.5 again – can you see that proportionally, the older ages represent a larger segment of the population?

To understand the drivers of population ageing, you should keep the demographic balancing equation in mind. The size of each age category (or the steps on the population pyramid) is determined by the births (fertility), deaths (infant mortality for the lower steps and age-specific mortality for the others) and migration occurring in that age category. The main driver of population ageing is a sustained decline in fertility. Fertility plays a key role in determining the proportionate size of a first age category in relation to subsequent ones. Where fertility increases or remains high, the base of a population pyramid is broad. The converse, a narrowing base of a population pyramid, reflects declining fertility.

Declines in death rates also affect the age structure of populations. The exact impact of declining mortality depends on which age categories are affected. You should bear in mind that population ageing depends on a shifting distribution of the population across age categories. If all age categories benefit equally by a decline in mortality, there will be no change in the age structure of a population. Declines in under-five mortality are attributed to better sanitation, housing, nutrition and control over infectious disease. Such declines in the mortality of babies and infants broaden the base of the population pyramid.

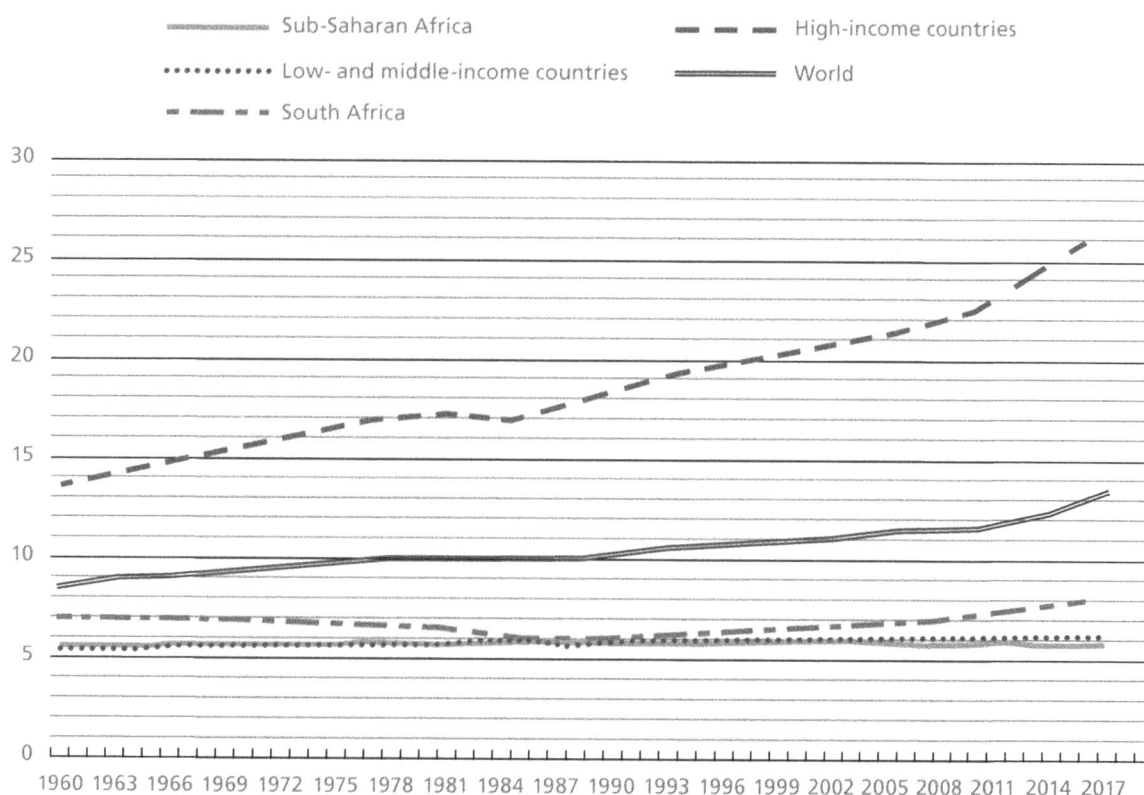

Figure 5.6 Old-age dependency ratios* for selected countries and regions from 1960–2017
(Source: World Bank nd)

* The old-age dependency ratio expresses people aged 64 years and older in terms of those aged 15 to 64 years.

High mortality due to famine, epidemics and war can have a noticeable impact on the age structure of a population for many years. Migration usually occurs among the economically active population, and this will impact on the proportionate size of age categories depending on the extent of such migration.

Whereas ageing is occurring in all populations, it is more advanced in the MDCs. Population ageing holds particular consequences for the countries in which it occurs. To understand this, you have to keep the three functional age groups (the youth, the working-age group and the elderly) in mind and consider how ageing will affect the proportional representation in a population of these three groups. Look at Figure 5.6. Can you see that in 2017 there were almost six elderly people in sub-Saharan Africa for every person aged between 15 and 64? Now look at the ratios for the high-income countries where the old-age dependency ratio is 26.6 for 2017. Globally, the numbers of working-age people able to support the elderly declined over time as the proportion of elderly increased. Now read Case study 5.2 again. We can deduce that the burden of care for the elderly would increase globally, but due to inequality, only the elderly in the higher income countries are likely to be able to invest in retirement, savings, private pensions and other financial asset instruments to assist them in sustaining their lifestyles for longer periods.

5.4 Human settlement, overurbanisation and ecological pressures

The final compositional feature of a population we focus on in this chapter is the composition of the population according to urban and rural residency, and what human settlement and livelihoods imply for the environment, and vice versa. Other chapters in this book deal with migration and urbanisation in greater detail, but in this section we merely wish to point out that the world is becoming increasingly urbanised. In addition, climate change and ecological pressures have become matters that will burden policymakers, planners, demographers and social scientists for the next millennia.

> ### Box 5.2 Urban vs rural settlement, overurbanisation and ecology
>
> The definitions of *urban* and *rural* differ considerably in the literature, and remain a contentious matter in South Africa. Many of South Africa's administrative borders were artificially and arbitrarily set around political ideals. Since 1994, there has been much discussion about the definition of geographical areas in this country.

Statistics South Africa (StatsSA) distinguishes between the following residential types:

Table 5.1 Types of settlements used by StatsSA for population enumeration

Type of residential area	Population size
Metro	500 000 and more
Large city	350 000 to 499 999
Medium city	200 000 to 349 999
Small city	100 000 to 199 999
Large town	50 000 to 99 999
Medium town	20 000 to 49 999
Small town	10 000 to 19 999
Large village	5 000 to 9 999
Small village	1 000 to 4 999
Settlement	Up to 999
Rural	Varies
Informal settlement	Varies

(Source: Medani 2016)

Urban areas grow due to natural increases in births, rural-to-urban migration, or even rural areas being reclassified as urban areas. Internationally, scholars are increasingly questioning the urban/rural dichotomy and instead regard them as parts of a continuum. Generally speaking, an urban area would have:

- the majority of the labour force working in non-agricultural jobs
- a high population density, or
- formal residential areas with tarred roads, commercial enterprises, educational, healthcare, and other services.

Nationally, the racialised, forced settlement patterns of apartheid made the classification of urban and rural more complex, thereby introducing notions such as semi-urban or even peri-urban areas (Statistics South Africa 2006a).

Globally, urbanisation has reached such levels that over- or hyper-urbanisation are used as terms to describe situations where urban population growth has outstripped the promises and possibilities of the socioeconomic prospects usually associated with cities. Many sub-Saharan countries face crises of overurbanisation, with core or primate cities forming that further impoverish the secondary urban areas (such as urban slums) they feed on. Moreover, human resettlement patterns exacerbate the depletion of environmental resources, making ecological factors a major concern for developmental planning for the future. In this regard, acid rain; deforestation; overfishing; overgrazing; overreliance on fossil fuels leading to global warming; the generation of nuclear, plastic and toxic waste; and the pollution and damming of water have all created irreversible environmental damage.

Case study 5.3 Setting the scene: Migration and urbanisation in South Africa

Read the following extract.

Urbanisation is an important but contested process because of its far-reaching social, economic and environmental implications. The paper explores the relationship between urbanisation and living conditions in South Africa over the last decade. The central question addressed is whether population growth in the main cities has been accompanied by improved living standards, housing and public services. One finding is that employment growth has tended to coincide with demographic trends, which is necessary to reduce poverty. In addition, the provision of urban infrastructure has outstripped population growth, resulting in better access to essential services and reduced backlogs. In contrast, the provision of affordable housing has not kept pace with household growth, so more people than ever are living in shacks. A more comprehensive assessment is required before one can be sure that urbanisation is on a sustainable trajectory.

(Source: Turok & Borel-Saladin 2014)

QUESTIONS

1. What are the social, economic and environmental consequences of increased urbanisation for South Africa?
2. Why would sociologists study urbanisation

5.5 Sources of population data

Obtaining the data to describe a population and how it changes is a challenging task. Sociologists devote a great amount of time and effort ensuring that the information collected is complete and accurate. In this chapter, we introduce you to the following sources of population data:

- The population censuses
- Administrative data
- Demographic sample surveys
- Population estimation and projections
- Qualitative sources.

5.5.1 Census

StatsSA is the agency responsible for running the census and related surveys in this country. It collects social and economic data needed for policy, planning and service delivery by government.

The earliest documented censuses were conducted by basic governments of ancient civilisations. These censuses collected information useful to authorities for levying tax or determining military conscription. With the emergence of modern nation-states in Europe in the 18th century, a demand emerged for information on the population within a circumscribed area. The United Nations played a key role in promoting censuses from the mid-20th century (Weeks 2015).

What role have censuses played in South Africa? Historical records reveal several instances where the population within administrative regions were counted for official purposes. The earliest official documented counting of the population in South Africa occurred in the Cape Colony during the 17th century. The first census of the total area comprising the current boundaries of South Africa was undertaken in 1904. Several national censuses conducted before 1904 enumerated white people only. The censuses of 1911, 1921, 1936, 1946, 1951, 1960 and 1970 enumerated the whole population of the region. The areas known as the **TBVC states** were excluded from the 1980, 1985 and 1991 censuses for South Africa with the granting of independence to several erstwhile 'homelands' from the mid-1970s. Legislation passed after 1994 initially required five-yearly censuses in South Africa. A review of the costs and benefits of this, however, led to the decision to have decennial census in South Africa. Three censuses were conducted in the new democratic dispensation of South Africa, namely in 1996, 2001 and 2011. Although a census was planned for 2006, it could not take place and in 2007 was replaced by the Community Survey 2007. The latest South African census is the 2011 census (Mostert et al 1998; Statistics South Africa 2011).

Because a census strives to provide a complete enumeration of a population in a defined geographical area, it is the most challenging single data-gathering exercise that can be undertaken. The census provides government and business with key information on the size, distribution and characteristics of a population. Such demographic, economic and social information is vital for planning infrastructure, delivering services, the allocation of resources and budgetary allocations.

The United Nations encourages its member-states to enumerate their populations at regular intervals. In addition, the United Nations publishes guidelines to help countries standardise the topics covered in census questionnaires and to encourage uniformity in the collection and presentation of data. This contributed towards an increase in the number of censuses conducted, as well as to an improvement of the quality of the data collected (Weeks 2015). Such guidelines are as follows:

- Definition of the geographical areas in which the population will be enumerated. A census should cover the whole country.
- National sponsorship by the government. Generally speaking, a national government has the authority and resources to support such a grand venture as a national population census.
- Encouragement of participation in the census.
- Publication of the data gathered by the national population census. The United Nations emphasises the importance of disseminating and publishing aggregate data from censuses.

In addition to these guidelines, the United Nations specifies four basic features of a successful population census:

1. Individual enumeration requires that information about the characteristics of each person in the population be recorded separately.
2. Universality within a defined territory requires that all individuals within the population in the defined territory be enumerated once. Duplication (over-enumeration) or omission (under-enumeration) should be avoided. This principle of universalism deals with the issue of coverage.
3. Simultaneity requires that the enumeration of individuals be linked to a particular date. The official date of a census is usually proclaimed by government. For the 2011 census in South Africa, the proclaimed census date (or reference point) was midnight on 9–10 October 2011. Setting a precise reference point for an enumeration is important so that over- and under-counts can be kept to a minimum.
4. Defined periodicity requires that censuses should be conducted at fixed intervals. The United Nations recommends **decennial** censuses. The guidelines suggest that when a census is conducted every 10 years, it should be scheduled for a calendar year ending with a zero. Obtaining data on population size and composition at regular intervals helps analysts to make comparisons (Statistics South Africa 2011).

5.5.2 The phases of a census

A census typically has three main phases, namely the *pre-enumeration phase*, the *enumeration phase* and the *post-enumeration phase*. In the pre-enumeration phase, preparation work for the census is done. This includes planning, seeing to legal requirements, budgeting, mapping and demarcation, determining of the items to be included in the census questionnaire, the training of fieldworkers, publicly marketing the census, and printing census material. For the 2011 census in South Africa, StatsSA employed more than 160 000 staff to supervise, coordinate and conduct fieldwork to collect information from individuals and households on census night. The country was divided into about 120 000 **enumeration areas (EAs)** (Statistics South Africa 2011).

Some of the important decisions that should be taken in the pre-enumeration phase of a census are the following:

- A census questionnaire should be constructed so that important population data can be gathered.
- Key variables should be defined such as 'household' or 'usual residence'. Without clear definitions of important concepts, it is not possible to compare data obtained from different censuses.
- The geographical area should be demarcated, and enumeration areas (EAs) should be defined.
- The procedure of enumeration should be decided on. Here the decision should be made whether the population should be enumerated on a *de facto* or a *de jure* basis. When the enumeration is according to the *de jure* system, persons are enumerated at their usual place of residence irrespective of where they were on the night of the census. When the enumeration is according to the *de facto* system, persons are enumerated at

the places where they are physically present on the night of the census (Weeks 2015). The 2011 South Africa population census was a *de facto* enumeration. Everyone who was in the country at midnight on the census night was counted (Statistics South Africa 2011).

- The method of enumeration should be determined. There are two major methods, namely the direct census interview and the self-enumeration method. Some countries, like the US, post the census questionnaire to people and each household completes its questionnaire without the presence of a census taker. The 2011 South African census used both methods, namely face-to-face interviews and self-enumeration questionnaires that were hand-delivered to respondents who were able to complete the questionnaire in their own time.
- An awareness campaign should be run to encourage the public to participate in the census. To ensure cooperation, information about the census is publicised beforehand. In this media campaign, reasons for collecting information and the benefit of participating are explained to communities. Confidentiality of individual information is emphasised to allay fears that information provided may be used against individuals. The South African census in 2011 was run under the logo: 'You count!'
- Decisions should be made on how to code, capture and tabulate the census data.
- Staff should be recruited and trained for the various tasks of the census.

In the enumeration phase of a census, enumerators visit the households and individuals in their assigned areas. Each census enumerator is assigned to a specific area and responsible for collecting data within it. Checks on the accuracy of the data and of the demarcation method take place while the enumerators are still in the field.

During the post-enumeration phase, the agency responsible for the census should process the data. Data processing involves checking, coding, capturing and tabulating data. Data capturing is the process of transferring answers from completed questionnaires to a database on a computer. Checks on data quality are implemented during this phase. One of the most important checks of the coverage of a census is done by carrying out a **post-enumeration survey (PES)**.

After all the above-mentioned steps, the agency responsible for the census will produce draft tables of the data. These tables of census data are then carefully scrutinised and reviewed before the final publication of the census results.

Three kinds of errors can befall census data: coverage, content and sampling errors. Coverage errors occur when people are missed (under-enumeration) or counted more than once (over-enumeration) in a census. Content errors arise when there are mistakes made in the recording of information on the census questionnaire, such as inaccurate recording of a person's age or sex. Sampling errors occur when part of the census is done as a sample survey and where the sample is not fully representative of the population it is intended to represent.

Box 5.3 Test your understanding of population enumerations

1. In each of the following examples, say whether it represents content or a coverage error:
   a) A household forgets to mention a new-born baby to the enumerator.
   b) Undocumented migrants hide from enumerators on census night.
   c) When completing the census questionnaire, the enumerator accidentally checks the wrong option for an answer given.
2. Are the following statements regarding *de facto* and *de jure* population enumerations true or false?
   a) The main advantage of a *de facto* population enumeration is that it provides a count of the permanent population.
   b) The main advantage of a *de jure* population enumeration is that it addresses the problem of coverage error through over- and under-counts much better than the *de facto* system.
   c) Both the *de facto* and the *de jure* systems of population enumeration should yield the same population totals but would differ significantly at the subnational or provincial levels.
3. Are the following statements regarding self-enumeration and the direct census interview technique true or false?
   a) When the chosen method of enumeration is self-enumeration, the principle of simultaneity can be met.
   b) Self-enumeration is better suited to a *de jure* population census.
   c) The direct census interview is better suited where the level of literacy of the population to be enumerated is low.
   d) Direct census interviewing eliminates all content errors arising from response error.

5.6 Administrative data and vital registration data

Many countries have registration systems for vital events. Do you have a birth certificate or an identity document? Do you have a marriage certificate? These all document vital events. The recorded data serves both administrative and statistical purposes. The United Nations collects annual information from countries about their vital statistics and publishes the results in the *United Nations Demographic Yearbook*.

Registration systems are legally mandated, and usually an official certification is issued. The Department of Home Affairs (DHA) runs a registration system in South Africa that collects particulars of each resident in the country. The DHA keeps information about your citizenship, surname, forenames, date of birth, sex, marital status, occupation, and residential and postal address. The DHA issues you with an identity document (ID). Without an ID, you cannot obtain a driver's licence, open a bank account, register for an election, legally execute an estate or access certain services you may qualify for, such as state grants or pensions.

As a source of demographic information, vital registration systems have advantages and disadvantages. The first advantage is that vital event registration can provide complete and accurate data on births, deaths, marriages, divorces, immigration, emigration and abortions occurring in a population. There is, however, an important condition that has to be met: for vital event registration to be accurate and complete, the registration needs to happen as soon as these events occur. This, however, only occurs in an ideal world. This would mean that the data would be potentially more accurate than, for example, data on births and deaths obtained from a census or a population sample survey. A second advantage of vital event registration is related to its dual function as a source of statistics and to issue legal records on vital events. Because the public relies on legal documentation of vital events, the continual availability of the data is assured.

The disadvantages related to administrative data as sources for population data relate to the accuracy, coverage and completeness of reporting. When the prompt and universal registration of vital events cannot be assured, this data source will be of limited value. Also, keep in mind that, because vital records are legal documents, the amount of information that can be collected is limited. In addition, registration systems rely on those persons who report such events: health practitioners, funeral directors, the police, clergy, court officials and individual members of the public. Part of the problem with registration systems is that other duties may seem more pressing than recording events.

Moreover, the administrative capacity to collect and process these records is crucial. Where administrative infrastructure or capacity is deficient, the underreporting of vital events is greater.

Setel et al (2007) comment as follows on vital registration in Africa and Asia:

Most people in Africa and Asia are born and die without leaving a trace in any legal record or official statistic. Absence of reliable data for births, deaths, and causes of death are at the root of this scandal of invisibility, which renders most of the world's poor as unseen, uncountable, and hence uncounted. This situation has arisen because, in some countries, civil registration systems that log crucial statistics have stagnated over the past 30 years. Net of debt relief, official development assistance reached US$80 billion in 2004. Yet because of the weakness in recording vital statistics, we have little authoritative evidence that these funds have their desired effects on either mortality or poverty reduction. Sound recording of vital statistics and cause of death data are public goods that enable progress towards Millennium Development Goals and other development objectives that need to be measured, not only modelled. Vital statistics are most effectively generated by comprehensive civil registration.

Another problem related to vital event registration is that such official documentation can be used by political authorities or groups to oppress minorities. An example of this is the passbook system, In South Africa under apartheid and as a means of institutionalised racism, this system was used to fix minorities' identities and to oppress them by restricting their movements. A further example is the use of Tutsi identity cards as a tool in the Rwandan genocide (Longman 2001).

There is an important connection between census data and administrative population data which you should take note of. Registration systems provide information on population processes (such as how many births, deaths, marriages, divorces, abortions, immigrations or emigrations are taking place). Census data provides cross-sectional data on a population at a specified time. What you should note is that many demographic measures require both cross-sectional (such as census or survey data) and continuous data (such as births or deaths per year).

One of the most pressing problems regarding the accuracy of administrative data is the quality and accuracy of cause-of-death data. South Africa, as a member state, reports its cause-of-death data to the World Health Organization (WHO). Like other WHO member states, South Africa uses the 10th revision of the *International Statistical Classification of Diseases and Related Health Problems* (ICD-10) to code the cause of death. However, South African cause-of-death data is regarded as low quality due to the low reporting of causes and the large number of deaths that are ill defined (Statistics South Africa 2006b). To understand where errors in death reporting can come from, you need to consider that:

- there may be a difference between the immediate and the underlying causes of a death (eg the immediate cause may be tuberculosis, but the underlying cause may be HIV infection)
- 'unnatural deaths' are particularly problematic as the specific manner of death is rarely recorded on the death notification forms (DNFs). To help address this, the National Injury Mortality Surveillance System (NIMSS) was introduced (Bradshaw et al 2010).

The persons completing the DNFs may find it difficult to give the correct clinical diagnosis. In addition, errors may occur in the statistical coding and data processing of the DNFs. Non-governmental organisations (NGOs) and charities may also keep records of the services they deliver. When sociologists use administrative data, they should keep in mind that – just as with vital registration data – such data was collected for purposes other than demographic analysis. They should therefore pay special attention to the definition of variables, the accuracy and the completeness of the data. The keeping of administrative records depends on an administrative infrastructure and on officials who are trained and motivated to keep such records.

5.7 Demographic sample surveys

Demographic sample surveys are carried out to fill gaps in population information that cannot be solved through the analyses of data from censuses and vital registration systems. Sample surveys are studies collecting data from a representative sample of the universe (a collection of all cases). The representativeness of a sample implies that the sample resembles the characteristics of the universe (the entire group of persons being studied). You will recall that this chapter already made mention of the post-enumeration survey that is carried out after a census to check the accuracy and the problems of coverage error in a census.

Large population sample surveys are often initiated by large international bodies such as the United Nations Population Fund (UNFPA), and conducted in various countries. A leading example is the Demographic and Health Surveys (DHS) conducted in various developing countries (Draper & Howell 2006). Another important demographic sample survey conducted on a regular basis in South Africa by StatsSA is the October Household Survey (OHS).

The strengths of sample surveys as sources of demographic data lie in their unique ability to provide detailed information with a wide diversity. Can you remember in our discussion of the census and vital registration systems that the variety of information that can be asked is limited by costs (for a census) and administrative demands (for vital event registration)? A demographic sample survey, being more manageable, allows greater flexibility. Because sampling allows for a smaller-scale study, information that is more detailed can be collected. For instance, it is possible in survey research to move beyond factual questions and to seek opinions.

Sample surveys in population studies are not without problems or errors. They are also subject to sampling and content errors, lack of clarity in the definition of variables, inconsistency in responses and methodological inaccuracies. However, in countries where good-quality census or vital registration data is lacking, demographic sample surveys can be used to obtain information on population size and structure, and trends in fertility, mortality and migration.

In some countries, continuous demographic research projects are concentrated in chosen sites. Such projects are referred to as **demographic surveillance systems (DSSs)**. More than 30 DSS sites have been created in Africa, Asia and the Americas, such as the one researching pneumococcal vaccines in Basse, Gambia; a maternal mortality surveillance site at Matlab, Bangladesh; a research site for non-communicable diseases in Filabavi in Vietnam; and a HIV/STIs site in Rakai, Uganda.

In South Africa, the Agincourt Health and Socio-Demographic Surveillance System (AHSDSS, see https://wwww.agincourt.co.za/); the Africa Centre for Population Health, established by the University of Natal; the Wellcome Trust; and the South African Medical Research Council do DSS work related to HIV and TB. Demographic surveillance systems are useful for:

- difficult-to-access populations (such as deep rural areas or those with a high influx of migrants)
- events that are often underreported in censuses or vital registration (such as migration or the incidence of HIV/AIDS)
- measuring events that can change rapidly between two censuses, such as family and household formation or migration status
- describing the long-term (**longitudinal**) history of the population under study.

5.8 Population estimation and population projections

Over the years, advanced methods have been developed to adjust incomplete data obtained from sources such as those mentioned in the previous section. By using **population estimation** methods, demographers can estimate past, current or future population sizes and trends.

Population projection refers to the prediction of future population trends. Such projections depend on a set of assumptions about trends within population processes such as fertility, mortality and migration.

Population estimates are done for the past, while projections are based on assumptions about future demographic trends. To prepare population estimates, one would use existing data collected from various sources. To do projections, however, one must assume what demographic trends will be like in the future, hence there is a distinct difference between the two.

The accuracy of projections depends on the following:

- The projection period: the further into the future the projection is made, the greater the degree of speculation and error.
- The quality of the data from which projections are made: if the data is incomplete or inaccurate, the projection will be too.
- The development of demographic theory and methods (Mosley & Chen 1984).

Population projections have been undertaken in South Africa since 1950. StatsSA annually publishes population estimates for the nine provinces and the country as a whole. StatsSA compares its estimates to those done by other institutions such as the Actuarial Society of South Africa, the Human Sciences Research Council and the Bureau for Market Research.

5.9 Qualitative population information

Since the 1970s, sociologists begun to realise the value of qualitative data in enhancing the discipline's ability to connect the demographic decisions and actions of people to their social and cultural contexts. Draper and Howell (2006) undertook an ethnographic study of the demographic regimes of the !Kung in Botswana. This was important with regard to advancing the approach known as demographic microanalysis.

5.10 Population processes: Trends in the world, sub-Saharan Africa and South Africa

In this final section of the chapter, you are introduced to the sources of information of and trends in the three main population processes, namely fertility, mortality and migration. In each of the subsections, we highlight the sources of information on that particular population process, possible sources of error in the information, key measures, key theories and major trends.

5.10.1 Births

Fertility refers to the births or the reproductive performance in a population. Some demographic texts might refer to the birth performance statistics of a population as natality data. In contrast to the notions of fertility and natality, the notion 'fecundity' refers to the physiological ability to produce a live birth.

Birth statistics differ from mortality statistics in two important ways. First, births are multiple events in an individual woman's life, whereas death occurs once. Second, individual mortality is less suitable to individual choice and decision making than births, which can, to some extent, be planned and manipulated by individuals. The most important source of fertility data is vital registrations of births. A second important source is population sample surveys. Irrespective of the source of birth statistics, sociologists are concerned with at least five possible sources of error in birth data. These are expanded on in the next section.

Inaccuracies in defining births

There are a few aspects to be considered, such as whether it was a live birth, the gestation period, evidence of life, foetal deaths, stillbirths, abortions and miscarriages. The United Nations recommends that only live births should be included in birth statistics. This, however, does not account for babies who were alive at birth but died soon after. As not all countries share the same rules regarding the registration of births, babies who die soon after birth might not be registered. In Algeria, French Guinea, Taiwan and Syria, parents are not required to register a birth if the baby died within a specified time after birth.

Incomplete birth registration

Most of you would probably recognise this as a problem in the LDCs, but birth registration is incomplete for most countries. Even with better birth registration in the MDCs, incomplete coverage of birth events among certain subpopulations such as foreigners or labour migrants occurs.

Inaccuracies in registering of the place of birth

There is a tendency towards an urban bias in birth registration in the LDCs because of the urban bias in the availability of maternity services at clinics and hospitals in these countries. When births are recorded according to the place of confinement (where the mother gave birth), these are called occurrence birth data. Such data is valuable to provide an overview of the caseloads of women attending maternity service points. Fertility data where births are recorded by the usual residence of the mother are de jure data. Such residence fertility data is useful when the analyst wants to relate it to the socioeconomic and other characteristics in the area of residence.

Inaccuracies in registering the time of birth

In the LDCs, there might be a difference between births registered for the year in which such births actually occurred and those registered for the year in which births were actually registered. Not all registration systems would automatically adjust the birth to its correct year of occurrence.

Inaccuracies in classification of births according to demographic and background characteristics of the parents

In this respect, the area of residence, marital status of the parents, their ethnicity, occupational status, educational attainment, religion or income might be important additional information that is often not recorded in birth registration. Data on the birth order of the child, the spacing in terms of the last and the current birth, the age of the mother and her **parity** status is additional information that can only be gauged through population sample surveys (Udjo 1993).

Different types of measures of fertility performance in a population

There are two types of fertility measures, namely period measures and cohort measures. Period measures are snapshot or cross-sectional measures of fertility, whereas cohort measures are longitudinal ones. Period measures are the more commonly used direct measures of fertility. The reason for this is that snapshot demographic data is more readily available than longitudinal demographic data. There is, however, one important weakness in relying solely on period measures of fertility, and that is that they express the fertility experience for a given period of time.

Large fluctuations in the fertility trends in a population can, however, mean that we draw incorrect conclusions from our data. The main weakness of period measures of fertility is therefore that they distort (or hide) the changes

and fluctuations in birth rates within the childbearing age range. We might, for example, notice that the **age-specific fertility rate (ASFR)** for women aged 20 to 35 is around and below 2.1 for two consecutive periods, say 2000 and 2001. From this we might conclude that women in their prime childbearing years in this population have low fertility. Yet hypothetically it might happen that these women dramatically change their childbearing behaviour in the next two years and start having more, closely spaced children. Reasons for this might be an upswing in the economy, greater hope for the future, active encouragement of childbearing through **pronatalist policies**, restrictions on contraceptive services, and elective abortion or specific cultural value attached to a given year (eg many women wanting to give birth to a millennium baby). This means that these women were not stopping their childbearing, but instead postponing it until a later date. Our conclusions from our period measures would therefore have been misleading for this population and we might find that, when we analyse the average number of children ever born to these women when they reach the end of their childbearing years, that they have had on average just as many or even larger numbers of births than their mothers and grandmothers.

Owing to the paucity of cohort data on fertility, demographers often use period data to set up a synthetic cohort. This means they treat the different age-specific fertility rates for the various age groups as cohort data. The **total fertility rate (TFR)** is a prime example of a synthetic fertility measurement because it does not refer to the fertility experiences of any actual woman, but instead expresses the average number of births a woman would have if she were to live through her reproductive years (which are ages 15 to 49 years) and bear children at each age at the rates measured for women in a population for a particular calendar year.

Considering the difference between period and cohort fertility measures brings us to the distinction between the quantum and the tempo of fertility. The quantum of fertility refers to the average number of children that would be born to a woman in a given cohort and relies on period measures of fertility to describe these trends. The tempo of fertility refers to the timing of births by the age of the mother in the cohort – in other words, it refers to the average age of the mother when giving birth to her first, second and subsequent children. Should there be no changes in the fertility behaviour of the cohort of women over time, the period measures of fertility would accurately describe the quantum of fertility in a population and would also accurately predict the tempo of fertility. The tempo effect of fertility refers to distortions in the timing of childbearing over time. In discussing the weaknesses of period measures of fertility, we mentioned that these may underestimate the real fertility in a population if changes in the spacing of children and the ages at which women give birth should occur. It is important to understand that a change in the rate at which women are bearing children in a calendar year is not an indication of change in the number of children they will bear altogether in their reproductive years (Frejka & Calot 2001; Kohler & Ortega 2001). The cohort measures of fertility express the birth trends of a group of women as they proceed through their childbearing years. A generational cohort refers to a group of individuals who live through the same event within a certain time interval – such as *Baby Boomers, Generation Xs, Generation Ys, Madiba Babies, Millennials* or *Generation Zs*.

When analysing cohort fertility, a demographer can detect if a current generation of women of childbearing age (or a cohort) is matching, exceeding or falling below the fertility levels of previous generations or cohorts.

When industrial development and urbanisation began in the MDCs in the 19th century, fertility rates began to decline and this trend continued throughout the 20th century. The same trend was observed in other countries in the 20th century. This process is known as a fertility transition and there are various explanations for it:

- *The supply–demand theories* of Richard Easterlin (1966) and Gary Becker (1960) postulate that fertility levels in a society are determined by parents within their domestic and cultural context. Parents try to maintain a balance between the potential supply (births) of children and the demand. If it is their perception that the cost of having children would be too high in terms of factors such as time spent on education, family finances, the social **stigma** of a large family, the desire for a high standard of living and ideals regarding more and better opportunities for their children, they could rationally decide to halt or restrict the demand for more children through fertility control.
- *The innovation/diffusion and 'cultural' perspective* on fertility transition argues that the desire for a smaller family, like other trendy ideas, begins with a few influential people and groups, usually the upper classes, with the rest of the population following suit later on. However, the decline in birth rates depends on the assumption that individuals believe that it is within their power to restrict the number of children they will have and apply fertility control. As the population's values and norms on an ideal family size begin to change,

increased fertility control becomes the norm and part of a society's culture.

Countries with very high total fertility rates (TFRs) in 2018 were Niger (TFR = 7.153), Somalia (TFR = 6.123), the Democratic Republic of Congo (TFR = 5.963), Mali (TFR = 5.922) and Chad (TFR = 5.797). In contrast, extremely low levels of fertility were measured for countries such as Singapore (TFR = 0.83), Macau (TFR = 0.95), Taiwan (TFR = 1.13), Hong Kong (TFR = 1.19) and Puerto Rico (TFR = 1.22) (Population Reference Bureau 2018).

South Africa has also experienced declines in fertility and, in 2018, the TFR was 2.40 (Statistics South Africa 2018). In interpreting these TFRs, take the notion of replacement fertility into account. Replacement fertility refers to a birth rate that is at a level that would ensure that the population merely replaces itself in the next generation and thus stagnates or approaches zero population growth. Replacement fertility is set as a TFR of between 2.1 and 2.3 depending on the mortality rates in a country (thus some women might die before giving birth to two babies). Can you see from this that South African fertility is close to replacement level?

5.10.2 Deaths

Mortality refers to the nature and extent (number) of deaths in a population. We can distinguish between the biological and social dimensions of mortality. The biological aspect relates to lifespan and longevity. Lifespan refers to potential length of life. Cases have been recorded where people have lived to be 122 and even 137 years old, but this is the exception. The normal expectation is that people will not live longer than 80 to 90 years, or in exceptional cases, 100. Longevity refers to length of life, or in other words the ability to go on living from one year to the next. In statistics, the longevity of populations is measured according to life expectancy at birth, which is the statistical average length of time that one could expect a certain category of people to live. In many countries that have been severely affected by HIV and AIDS, the life expectancy at birth has declined.

Differences in life expectancies for various categories of people (eg men and women or urban and rural residents) are related to the social dimension of mortality, namely socioeconomic and political factors, and to differences in lifestyle that influence the risk of dying.

In this chapter you have already been introduced to some of the sources of information about deaths and also to sources of error, especially in the recording of the causes of deaths. In terms of key measures of mortality, you have also been introduced to the CDR. Other important measures are the **infant mortality rate (IMR)** and the **maternal mortality ratio (MMR)**.

Besides the direct and underlying causes of death as discussed above, sociologists also study social, economic, political and cultural factors that *indirectly* cause deaths. Unemployment, poverty, malnutrition, environmental pollution, political discrimination and persecution, for example, create conditions in which tuberculosis, cholera and malaria flourish, thus indirectly causing deaths.

The two measures of mortality, namely the IMR and the MMR, are regarded as key surveillance measures for the health status of a country. Monitoring trends in the IMR in low-income countries has become a target for the third Sustainable Development Goal (SDG3). In Table 5.2 the following trends can be seen:

- Improvements in reducing childhood deaths since 1994 are astounding, but the IMR for low-income countries is still more than 10 times higher than what is reported in 2017 for the high-income countries. SDG3 sets a target of fewer than 12 neonatal deaths per 1 000 live births by 2030. This would imply further efforts in South

Africa, sub-Saharan Africa and low-income countries to achieve this target.

- Maternal survival rates also showed marked improvements over the years, with a strange anomaly for South Africa. The apparent increase in the MMR was due to the impact of HIV/AIDS on pregnant mothers, but these rates have shown marked improvements since the introduction of antiretroviral therapy (ART).
- Overall, females live longer than males, but the differences in life expectancy at birth is less pronounced in the poorer regions of the world.
- The percentage of the adult population living with HIV has also declined for the regions indicated in Table 5.2 between 1994 and the latest available data, but for South Africa, that accounts for 0.7 per cent of the world population, but 17 per cent of the global HIV infection burden, the epidemic is still a force to be reckoned with (Mayosi & Benatar 2014). Eaton et al (2014) found that for the 2009 to 2014 period, HIV infection rates declined for pregnant women in the 15 to 30 age group, but the incidence increased among South African women in the 35 to 49 age group.

Table 5.2 Indices of mortality and health in selected world regions in 1994 and 2015–2017*

Region and dates	Infant mortality rate	Maternal mortality ratio	Life expectancy at birth (in years)			% of the adult population living with HIV	
			Total	**Male**	**Female**	**Male**	**Female**
World 1994 2015/6/7	61.3 29.4	372 216	66.1 72.0	63.9 69.9	68.5 74.3	0.3 0.2	0.5 0.4
High-income countries 1994 2015/6/7	9.3 4.6	17 13	76.1 80.4	72.8 77.8	79.5 83.1	0.1 0.1	0.1 0.1
Low-income countries 1994 2015/6/7	101.9 48.6	908 479	51.3 62.9	49.9 61.1	53.4 64.8	1.4 0.6	3.7 1.3
Sub-Saharan Africa 1994 2015/6/7	104.2 51.5	944 547	49.9 60.4	48.1 58.7	51.7 62.1	1.7 0.9	4.0 2.0
South Africa 1994 2015/6/7	46.2 28.8	69 138	61.8 62.8	58.2 59.2	65.6 66.4	2.7 3.9	6.7 10.3

* The World Bank's World Development Indicators have data for the IMR and the proportion of the adult population living with HIV for up to 2017, but only up to 2016 for life expectancy and 2015 for the MMR.
(Source: World Bank 2010)

For most countries, improvements and progress in living conditions, medical services, nutrition, housing and sanitation lead to dramatic declines in child mortality rates. Mosley and Chen (1984) designed a model that describes the social and biological determinants of child mortality for poorer regions of the world. One of the key assumptions of the model is that child deaths are seldom the result of a single, isolated episode of illness, but rather the consequence of multiple episodes of illness and morbid conditions and their biosocial interaction.

According to Mosley and Chen's framework (1984), socioeconomic variables, including income and education, influence child survival through one or more of the five sets of proximate determinants:

1. *Maternal factors:* certain births present a high risk for infant mortality, such as births to very young women (those in their teenage years), births to older women (those at the end of their reproductive lifespan), births that are too closely spaced (ie birth intervals of less than two years) or a high number of births to one mother (more than six). Family planning and the use of contraceptive methods to prevent births that present a risk to the health of the mother and her child can curtail infant mortality rates.

2. *Environmental contamination:* polluted drinking water, for example, can cause diarrhoeal disease, and insect vectors (carriers) can spread malaria.

3. *Nutritional status:* factors such as a brief period of breastfeeding, followed by underfeeding and malnutrition, increase the risk of infectious diseases and conditions that affect child mortality. Longer periods of breastfeeding prevent further pregnancies and reduce mortality figures in this way.

4. *Accidents and injuries:* children may, for example, fall onto an open cooking fire, drink paraffin, eat poisonous plants or be the victims of violence.

5. *Personal illness control (including the use of medical services):* antenatal and postnatal care, immunisation against childhood illnesses (eg measles, whooping cough, tetanus, diphtheria) and the timely treatment of illnesses (eg diarrhoea) can prevent deaths.

These are socioeconomic, cultural and political factors that do not in themselves lead to mortality, but indirectly influence the proximate (direct) causes of mortality. Mosley and Chen (1984) name the following:

- *Ecological factors:* topography, soil fertility, rainfall and climate affect food production and water supply, and are also related to the occurrence of parasites and viruses that cause disease and deaths.

- *Individual factors:* the mother's level of education, occupation, social class and residential area are also related to her knowledge of and access to resources that promote health or, conversely, increase the risk of child mortality.

- *Household factors:* the quality of sanitation, drinking water and dwelling structure (formal, traditional or informal) and the physical environment of the home determine the child's exposure to infectious diseases and injury.

- *Institutional factors:* governments are responsible for providing certain social services to a population in order to limit the proximate determinants of child mortality. These include mother and child healthcare services, family planning services, education and health education. Governments are also responsible for putting the necessary legislation in place, together with the financial, human and other resources required to implement it.

- *Cultural factors:* values, traditions and practices relating to the prevention and treatment of disease can have a negative effect on health and lead to deaths. An example here is prejudice against immunisation or advice.

South Africa endeavoured to cover interventions for achieving SDG3 in its National Development Plan (NDP), especially in Chapter 10. Specifically, the goals are to reduce the MMR and IMR and to progressively improve TB prevention. In terms of the latter, South Africa has one of the worst TB burdens in the world, with reported cases of 600 per 100 000 of the population in the early 2000s increasing to 950 by 2012, with the most extensively drug-resistant (XDRTB) cases globally (Mayosi & Benatar 2014). The plan also intends reducing the prevalence of non-communicable chronic diseases (such as heart disease and diabetes), and the incidence of injury, homicide and violence. In addition, Chapter 10 of the NDP refers to the need to address disparities in health outcomes in the country by ensuring that there are primary healthcare staff and by equalising access to quality preventative health care. How do you think we are faring in this regard? Read Case study 5.1 again. Are you now better able to offer some informed answers to the questions posed at the end of the case study?

5.10.3 Migration

The third and final population process we consider in this chapter is migration. Keeping the population balancing equation in mind, we can argue that, whereas in terms of the world population, births add people and deaths subtract them, migration merely influences their global distribution.

The last decade has seen great interest in migrant movements across the globe, stirring fears about foreignisation of countries or other stereotypical negative responses to mass movements of people. With the current obsession about unwanted migration streams, it is easy to forget that mass migrations have occurred over the course of human history. For example, we can argue that people migrated from and to Africa for many millennia. Think of early explorations, the colonisation of Africa by settler migrants, the Transatlantic slave trade and the resultant African diaspora, or the Mfecane/Difaqane/Lifaqane. Africa has always been a continent on the move.

Migration refers to spatial movement of people from one geographic area to another with the intention of settling permanently in the new area. This movement has the potential to change the size, growth and composition of a population (both in the area migrated from and the area migrated to). However, defining migration is problematic as human movement across geopolitical borders can take on a myriad of forms. For this reason, migration is linked to the notion of permanency. The United Nations regards residence for a period of one year or longer as permanent for this purpose, but what about tourists, migrant labourers, seasonal cross-border farm workers, diplomats or students who are temporarily in a foreign country? What about nomadic tribes such as the Khoi and San hunters of the Namib Desert and Botswana? Can you see that in terms of the intentions of these categories of people to settle permanently, they are likely to be excluded from our definition of a migrant? The ideas of a nation-state and of a national border thus feature strongly in our conceptualisation of migration.

Definitions

There are many types of migrants and different forms of migration. These will be looked at in this section, which should give you a glimpse of the complexity of defining legal and irregular international migration. Keep in mind that these definitions are contested and constantly changing in terms of policy and legal directives.

Internal migration is a movement from one permanent place of residence to another within the borders of a country. Internal migrants are referred to as out-migrants when leaving their area of settlement and as in-migrants in terms of the destination to which they migrate.

International migration refers to people who migrate permanently to another country. Such a person is referred to as an emigrant in respect of his/her country of origin and as an immigrant in the country of his/her destination.

Legal immigrants have legal and political permission from the country of destination to settle there permanently. Legal migration is regarded as *voluntary migration* based on the migrant's own decisions to relocate. Other forms of migration that do not adhere to this definition of legal migration are often referred to as *irregular migration*, economic migrants or *displaced peoples*.

Illegal, clandestine or *undocumented immigrants* enter the country of destination (1) without valid documentation or with fraudulent documents; (2) as refugees or asylum seekers; or (3) with valid visas but remain in the country in contravention of their authority (eg by staying after the expiry of a visa or work permit, through sham marriages or as bogus students).

Fugitives are people who leave their country and cannot or do not wish to return there either because they have actually been persecuted or because they have good reason to fear that they will be persecuted as a result of their race, language, religion, political convictions or membership of a particular social group. When a fugitive arrives at the country of destination, such a person can apply for asylum – protection against persecution or arrest in or extradition to his/her country of origin.

Asylum seekers are people who have moved across an international border in search of protection under the *1951 Geneva Convention Relating to the Status of Refugees*, but whose claim for refugee status has not yet been determined (Martin 2010).

A *displaced person* is a refugee with no apparent home country.

According to the *1951 Geneva Convention Relating to the Status of Refugees* (Martin 2010), a refugee is a person who, because of a well-founded fear of being persecuted for reasons of race, religion, nationality, membership of a particular social group or political opinion, is outside the country of his/her nationality. Sub-Saharan Africa hosts more than a quarter of the world's refugees, many fleeing from the Central Africa Republic, Nigeria, South Sudan and Burundi.

Internally displaced persons (IDPs) are persons who have been forced to flee their homes, but who have not crossed an internationally recognised border. Displacements occur as a result of interethnic or interreligious conflicts, violence, land disputes or environmental disasters. There are large numbers of IDPs in Africa, especially in Nigeria, the Democratic Republic of Congo and Sudan.

Assisted migration refers to international migration propelled by assistance illegally offered to undocumented migrants and includes the categories referred to as smuggled migrants and trafficked persons. However, the distinction between smuggled migrants and trafficked persons remains a matter of debate. One example illustrating the contentious nature of assisted migration is the so-called 'mail-order bride' industry where matrimonial industries advertise the availability of women as potential wives for European or American men. Such industries arrange the necessary travel documentation and the women in question may or may not find themselves in exploitative situations (Van Liempt 2011).

Smuggled migrants are moved illegally across borders for profit and may include those who have been forcibly displaced as well as those who have left their homeland in search of better economic and social opportunities. The main difference between a trafficked and a smuggled person is that the former is a transaction about control over the person, whereas the latter is transaction for illegal entry into a country. This does not dispel the fact that smuggled migrants are often mistreated, robbed, raped, exploited or abandoned along the route by their smugglers (Campana 2016; Van Liempt 2011). The United Nations' (2000) *Protocol against the Smuggling of Migrants* says:

> *Smuggling of migrants shall mean the procurement, in order to obtain, directly or indirectly, a financial or other material benefit, of the illegal entry of a person into a State Party of which the person is not a national or a permanent resident.*

This definition precludes acts of migrant smuggling that are not directed by illicit or criminal commercial gains, such as when the International Organisation for Migration smuggled Syrian refugees to across the border into Jordan and Lebanon to escape the armed conflict in Syria (Aljehani 2015).

Trafficked people are recruited or procured by threat, force, intimidation, coercion, abduction, kidnapping, fraud, deception or debt bondage and exploited for commercial sex work, domestic servitude, child sex tourism, organ harvesting, agricultural labour, labour in the garment industry or other labour. This definition stems from the 2000 *Protocol to Prevent, Suppress and Punish Trafficking in Persons*, commonly referred to as the *Palermo Protocol* (Campana 2016). Human trafficking is a global problem. It

is estimated that 800 000 to 900 000 people are trafficked annually, but accurate statistics are hard to find. South Africa is regarded as a source of human trafficking as well as a transit and destination point for international trafficking in human beings. This phenomenon is fuelled by factors such as poverty, porous borders, inadequate border control, lack of legislation, gender-based violence, political unrest and a demand for trafficked persons. Some commentators lament the conflation of commercial sex work and human trafficking, highlighting the fact that some persons may be coerced into commercial sex work due to dire economic circumstances, yet not fit the strict definition of victims of trafficking because they agreed to the exploitative conditions out of their own volition (Swart 2011).

In addition, the precise migrant status of a person can change many times and relatively quickly, meaning that migration status can be seen as a process or strategy instead of an immutable end state. Linked to the problems of definitions and categorisation is the problem of accurate, up-to-date and verifiable data on migration streams. Statistics on irregular migration, for example, may be especially difficult to find and the popular media often exaggerate the highest estimates of illegal migration (Bloch & Chimienti 2011; Swart 2011). Irregular migration has become a feature of **globalisation** in which the demand for both highly skilled and low-skilled labour increases along with stricter immigration controls, leading to a clash between the economic and political forces that drive migration. In fact, it can be argued that it has become increasingly difficult for people to undertake legal migration and that it is limited to the privileged few (Bloch & Chimienti 2011).

In terms of international migration flows, emigration holds serious consequences for the country of origin (ie the country which has been migrated from), especially when large numbers of highly skilled people emigrate and the investment made in human capital creation is thus lost. Such a phenomenon is popularly referred to as a *brain drain* or *human capital flight*. A recent example of a brain drain is the mass exodus of skilled and educated people from Zimbabwe (especially healthcare professionals), negatively impacting on the education and healthcare sectors of that country. Skilled and educated migrants are attracted by the promise of higher wages and better living conditions, but many fall prey to downward economic and vocational mobility in their destination countries. They could, for example,

- suffer job insecurity (not be considered for permanent positions)
- be forced to take a job below their skill level (skill downgrading) or their years of experience

- not have their academic credentials recognised in the host country
- face decreased access to housing or social services
- earn lower wages (a large immigrant–native wage gap)
- be forced to work for longer hours and in bad working conditions
- or face hostility and violence from members of the host society. This trend is referred to as brain waste. Brain gain describes a situation where people return to further education in the hope of emigration (Pires 2015).

In terms of internal migration, you have already been introduced to the fact that the world is becoming increasingly urbanised. Part of the **aetiology** of this trend is the internal migration from rural to urban areas and the tendency for immigrants to settle in the urban and metropolitan centres of the countries to which they migrate.

Another important issue that spans both internal and international migration is that of labour migration. In this regard, the apartheid policies in South Africa pre-1994 were enforced by legislation that inhibited and controlled the urbanisation and free movement of Africans (both citizens and foreign born) and encouraged a system of *circular internal labour migration*. The pre-1994 labour migration in South Africa was a male-dominated phenomenon in which mostly men migrated to areas offering employment and remitted their incomes to family members residing in Bantustans or other prescribed areas of settlements inside South Africa and its neighbouring countries (Posel 2003).

Post-1994, internal migration in South Africa became less of a research focus, with much attention instead focused on the issue of undocumented migration into the country from neighbouring countries such as Zimbabwe and Mozambique. However, accurate estimates of the numbers of undocumented migrants are hard to come by, and range from four to eight million people. Along with negative stereotyping of undocumented migrants in the press, increasing unemployment, jobless economic growth (in which the economy shows growth but its level of employment stagnates or even decreases), deep structural socioeconomic inequalities, housing shortages, and a normalisation of the use of violence to advance sectional interests, foreign-born nationals have become the target of sporadic xenophobic attacks in South Africa since May 2008 (Dobson 2010; Everatt 2011; Posel 2003).

Trends indicate that internal labour migration has increased in South Africa since 1994 and so has the proportion of women who become migrant labourers. This

feminisation of labour migration in South Africa post-1994 is unrelated to labour market conditions. It is instead linked to household decisions to maximise their survival strategies in a harsh economic climate by sending as many members (irrespective of gender) to obtain gainful employment while still retaining a rural base and membership in rural households. The same feminisation trend has been reported for circular labour migration streams between South Africa (as a migrant-receiving destination) and other countries in sub-Saharan Africa (in particular Zimbabwe, Lesotho and Mozambique as migrant-sending countries) (Dobson 2010; Everatt 2011; Griffin 2011; Posel 2003).

5.11 Social change, population and identities

We tend to associate the word 'identity' with the traits of an individual. In sociology, we understand that larger groups, societies and nations can also be characterised as having specific identities. In this sense, the identity of a given population becomes a signifier that carries with it symbolic meaning in terms of politics, exclusion or inclusion, and status. Social groupings or aggregates can draw on their demographic characteristics to assert or contest identities. This has been especially pertinent in our discussion of migration above.

In a similar fashion, demographic measurement and representation can influence the politics of identity. A census can become part of the politics of social identity and representation. Censuses are used by governments for various planning activities, but deciding on census categories can be complex and these decisions are influenced by political ideologies. If as sociologists we treat the multiplicity, intersectionality and mutability of identities as technical categories by which to report aggregated measurements, we disregard a major dimension of population dynamics. By understanding that a population has spatial and identity connotations, we are able to investigate how particular collective identities have come to be the conventional aggregate units used in demographic data collection and analyses.

The deepening divide between richer and poorer countries may well mean that social identity politics will play an increasing role in demographic decision making in future years. As ecological, economic and political pressures encourage further ambitions for emigration from poorer regions of the world, migration and the status of refugees and asylum seekers will become increasingly important. By now you should be able to understand that population growth and change and the resultant pressure on resources have the capacity to exacerbate social problems already present in societies. An understanding of such demographic dynamics can help us better comprehend issues such as claims about nationalism, political conflict and backlash against immigrants.

The spatial identity of a population implies the centrality of a 'home', 'homeland' or 'nation' that conjures up notions of belonging, a sense of place, a sense of belonging, heritage and loyalties, a moral location, a symbolic anchor and a source of identity. Migration is linked to identity formation as it is a simultaneously selective and strategic process – one that reshapes social relations, is instrumental in ethnic minority formation and is an economic, social and political process.

5.12 Population and development

Throughout this chapter, we emphasised the centrality of population, demographic characteristics and trends in social concerns. Among such concerns are the eradication of poverty and the achievements of so-called sustainable development. It should be evident to you that population dynamics such as growth rates, age structures and trends in fertility, mortality and migration influence social and economic development.

Thomas Robert Malthus wrote *An Essay on the Principle of Population* in 1798 in which he argues that human populations tend to grow faster than the food supply they need to sustain them. His principle of population holds that human populations tend to increase geometrically, and therefore grow exponentially and can possibly double every 25 years if left unchecked. Malthus argues that food supply and resources, such as land for agricultural production, are finite. This means that at some stage, population growth will outstrip agricultural production, causing food prices to rise and incomes to fall. To balance these two unequal powers (population growth and food production), Malthus argues that two checks can be imposed, namely 'positive checks' and 'preventive checks'.

Positive checks, according to Malthus, were increases in the death rate of a population due to famine, disease, malnutrition, poverty and war. Such increases in mortality relieve the pressure put by people on food supplies. Preventive checks, according to Malthus, implied moral restraint through the postponement of marriage and refraining from premarital or extramarital sex (ie remaining celibate). Such behavioural checks on fertility lead to a decline in the fertility rate and thus to a new equilibrium between people and food supplies.

The historical and social context in which Malthus wrote his Essay is of importance, because he commented on the rapid increase in the British population after 1740 and especially after 1781 when early industrialisation and mercantile capitalism were well established. In the years during which Malthus penned his famous Essay, Britain experienced a five-year period of poor harvests and resultant food shortages. However, he did not foresee the Agricultural Revolution and the rapid improvement and expansion in transportation technology that were to follow, or the improvement in human longevity (at the time of writing his *Essay*, life expectancy at birth was less than 50 years) and much of his principle of population assumed that very small improvements in human life expectancy were possible.

The importance of Malthus's work to demography is in part the criticism and debate it sparked. Notable among these is the Marxist critique of Malthusianism which asserts that poverty is not a consequence of rapid population growth. The Marxist perspective on the relationship between population growth and resources is that overpopulation is the consequence of capitalism and that within a socialist system with an equitable distribution of resources, population growth is absorbed by the economy. An important idea in the Marxist interpretation of population and development is the idea of an industrial reserve army of workers created by an exploitative capitalist system – in other words an oversupply of labour that makes jobs redundant in certain sectors and fuels labour force flexibility, lower wages and chronic livelihood insecurity for the poor. Do you think that policies in liberal democracies and the clout of organised labour, social assistance offered by governments and better bargaining powers for workers have rendered these ideas out of date? Szreter (2018) asks us to consider the following matters that demand a reinterpretation of Marxist ideas:

- Neoliberal capital continues to extract surplus value from workers through the growth of short-term, zero-hour, piece-rate and freelance contract labour, or the so-called gig-economy (Standing 2011) or precariat.
- In many countries (LDCs and MDCs alike), the younger generation are less likely to own homes.
- The Fourth Industrial Revolution may see further job losses.

By the end of the 19th century, Malthusian views lost favour in the West as fast-growing populations were seen as beneficial to industrial and agricultural advances. The view was that a youthful, fast-growing population provided vitality, a stimulus for technological progress and the possibility of more producers (instead of merely more consumers as in Malthus's principle of population). However, by the 1970s, the West reconsidered the possibility of a Malthusian threat to earth's non-renewable resources and this gave rise to neo-Malthusianism.

There were several reformulations of Malthusian and Marxist perspectives on population, but the demographic transition theory in the mid-1940s was the first attempt at a unified demographic theory apparently capable of explaining global trends. This theory held that all demographic trends are responses to structural changes associated with the development of a mature industrial society. Demographic trends in 1945 to 1955, however, seriously questioned the adequacy of the theory. A baby boom occurred in industrialised countries, presenting a problem for the assumption that no significant fertility changes would occur after the birth rate reached low levels in response to 'modernisation'. Furthermore, the 1950s witnessed continued declines in mortality rates that were not dependent on general economic development. In the less-developed countries, growing numbers of people living in abject poverty made economic development, which was seen as the precursor of fertility decline, highly improbable.

The International Conference on Population and Development (ICPD) in Cairo in 1994 acknowledged the importance of the empowerment of women in socioeconomic development efforts. Since the 1970s up to the ICPD and immediately following it, works by feminist demographers gave central focus to gender and contextual issues in demographic dynamics. By considering the important role played by the socioeconomic context in influencing demographic behaviour, feminist demographers have brought the problems of social inequality and notably gender inequality into sharper focus. Such ideas formed the basis for the MDGs and SDGs. What do you think?

Summary

- Individual demographic acts (such as migrating, getting married or making decisions that influence one's health and chances of survival) on the aggregate produce macro-level trends in fertility, mortality, migration and nuptiality.
- These trends or population processes in turn give rise to a particular population composition.
- Sometimes a given compositional structure can give rise to societal changes.
- This idea of the flow between actions, aggregate results and further societal change fits into sociological understanding of agency and structure.
- The tools and insights gained from a sociological study of population will be increasingly important in grappling with emergent issues such as population ageing, migrant populations and environmental collapse.
- This chapter introduced you to concepts and sources of information to help you develop your sociological imagination to include an understanding of population as a key force in social change and the causes and mechanisms of that change.

ARE YOU ON TRACK?

1. What is the focus of the sociological study of population?
2. What are dynamic and static features of a population?
3. What are the causes of rapid population growth?
4. What is the importance of the age composition of a population?
5. What are the pros and cons of a population census?
6. What is vital registration information?
7. What influences the birth performance of a population?
8. Which proximate and distal factors influence child survival in disadvantaged societies?
9. Is the world facing a migration crisis?
10. Does population influence development or is this a purely ideological debate?

More sources to consult

Books

Betts A. 2013. *Survival Migration: Failed Governance and the Crisis of Displacement*. New York: Cornell University Press. A good overview of the push and pull factors in migration from fragile states.

Livi Bacci M. *A Concise History of World Population*. 5th ed. Oxford: Wiley-Blackwell. A trustworthy text on the history of world population with projections for 2050.

Lundquist JH, Anderton DL, Yaukey D. 2015. *Demography: The Study of Human Population*. 4th ed. Long Grove: Waveland Press. A cogent, understandable book covering the field.

Kok P, Gelderblom D, Oucho J, Van Zyl J (eds). 2006. *Migration in South and Southern Africa: Dynamics and determinants*. Pretoria: HSRC Press. An authoritative work on migration in Southern Africa.

Siegel JS, Swanson D, Shryock HS (eds). 2004. *The Methods and Materials of Demography*. Elsevier Academic Press. This is a seminal work covering the methods and methodology of population measurement and analysis.

Websites

Demography matters: https://sites.google.com/site/demographymatters/home

Gap-minder: http://www.gapminder.org

John Week's blogspot: http://weekspopulation.blogspot.com/

Statistics South Africa: http://www.statssa.gov.za/

The Population Council: http://www.popcouncil.org

The Population Division of the UN: http://www.un.org/en/development/desa/population/

The Union for African Population Studies (UAPS) is a scientific organisation, created in 1984. UAPS promotes the scientific study of population in Africa through research, training and technical assistance. Membership is not open to students, but rather to established population scientists: http://uaps-uepa.org/home-page/

The World Health Organization: http://www.who.int/en

Journals

Demography
International Journal of Aging & Human Development
International Migration
Population
Population and Development Review
Population Studies: A Journal of Demography
Southern African Journal of Demography

References

Aljehani A. 2015. 'The legal definition of the smuggling of migrants in light of the provisions of the Migrant Smuggling Protocol'. *The Journal of Criminal Law*, 79(2): 122–137.

Becker G. 1960. *An economic analysis of fertility*. [Online] Available at: http://www.nber.org/books/univ60-2. [Accessed 17 September 2013].

Bloch A, Chimienti M. 2011. *Irregular Migration in a Globalizing World*. Surrey: Ethnic and Racial Studies.

Bradshaw D, Pillay-Van Wyk V, Laubscher R, Nojilana D, Groenewald P, Nannan N, Metcalf C. 2010. *Cause of Death Statistics for South Africa: Challenges and Possibilities for Improvement*. Cape Town: Medical Research Council Burden of Disease Research Unit.

Campana P. 2016. 'The structure of human trafficking: Lifting the bonnet on a Nigerian transnational network'. *British Journal of Criminology*, 56: 68–86.

Dobson B. 2010. *Locating Xenophobia: Debate, Discourse, and Everyday Experience in Cape Town, South Africa*. London: Africa Today.

Draper P, Howell N. 2006. *Changes in Co-survivorship of Adult Children and Parents: Ju/'hoansi (!Kung) of Botswana in 1968 and 1988*. Tokyo: Senri Ethnological Studies.

Easterlin RA. 1966. 'On the relation of economic factors to recent and projected fertility changes'. *Demography* 3: 131–153.

Eaton JW, Rehle TM, Jooste S, Nkambule R, Kim AA, Mahy M, Hallett TB. 2014. 'Recent HIV prevalence trends among pregnant women and all women in sub-Saharan Africa: Implications for HIV estimates'. *AIDS*, 28(Suppl 4): S507-14.

Everatt D. 2011. *Xenophobia, State and Society in South Africa (2008–2010)*. Pretoria: Politikon.

Feeney G, Lutz W. 1990. *Future Demographic Trends in Europe and North America: What can we Assume Today? Distributional Analysis of Period Fertility*. Lutz W (ed). New York: Academic Press.

Frejka T, Calot G. 2001. *Cohort Childbearing Age Patterns in Low-fertility Countries in the Late 20th Century: Is the Postponement of Births an Inherent Element?* Rostock: Max Planck Institute for Demographic Research.

Griffin L. 2011. 'Unravelling rights: "Illegal" migrant domestic workers in South Africa'. *South African Review of Sociology*, 42(2): 83–101.

Hirschman C, Tolnay SE. 2005. 'Social demography' in *Handbook of Population*, Poston DL, Micklin M (eds).

New York: Kluwer Academic/Plenum Publishers, 419–449.

Hobbs F. 2004. *The Methods and Materials of Demography: Age and Sex Composition.* Siegel JS, Swanson DA, Shryock, HS (eds). 2nd ed. Amsterdam: Elsevier Academic Press.

International Conference on Population and Development (ICPD). 1994. Conference proceedings held in Cairo, Egypt. 5–13 September 1994. Coordinated by the United Nations.

Klasen S, Woolard I. 2009. 'Surviving unemployment without state support: Unemployment and household formation in South Africa'. *Journal of African Economies,* 18(1): 1–51.

Kohler H-P, Ortega JA. 2001. *Period Parity Progression Measures with Continued Fertility Postponement: A New Look at the Implications of Delayed Childbearing for Cohort Fertility.* Rostock: Max Planck Institute for Demographic Research.

Longman T. 2001. *Documenting Individual Identity: The Development of State Practices in the Modern World: Identity Cards, Ethnic Self-Perception, and Genocide in Rwanda.* Caplan J, Torpy J (eds). Princeton: Princeton University Press.

Mayosi BM, Benatar SR. 2014. 'Health and health care in South Africa – 20 years after Mandela'. *New England Journal of Medicine,* 371: 1344–1353.

Malthus TR. 1998. *An essay on the principle of population, 1798.* [Online] Available at: http://www.esp.org/books/malthus/population/malthus.pdf [Accessed 17 September 2013].

Martin SF. 2010. 'Gender and the evolving refugee regime'. *Refugee Survey Quarterly,* 29(2): 104–112.

Massey DS, Durand J, Malone NJ. 2005. *The New Immigration. Principles of Operation: Theories of International Migration.* Suarez-Orozco MM, Suarez-Orozco C, Qin DB (eds). New York: Routledge.

Medani S. 2016. *Why urban and rural classifications matter.* [Online] Available at: https://www.ee.co.za/article/urban-rural-classifications-matter.html [Accessed 28 January 2019].

Moodley J, Pattison R. 2018. 'Improvements in maternal mortality in South Africa'. *South African Medical Journal* 108(3a): s4–s8.

Mosley WH, Chen LC. 1984. 'An analytical framework for the study of child survival in developing countries'. *Population and Development Review,* 81(2): 140–145.

Mostert WP, Hofmeyr BE, Oosthuizen JS, Van Zyl JA. 1998. *Demography: Handbook for the South African Student.* Pretoria: HSRC.

OECD Stats. nd. [Online] Available at: https://stats.oecd.org/Index.aspx?DataSetCode=HISTPOP

Oosthuizen MJ. 2018. 'Bonus or mirage? South Africa's demographic dividend'. *The Journal of the Economics of Ageing,* 5(C): 14–22.

Our World in Data. nd. [Online] Available at: https://ourworldindata.org/ [Accessed 8 January 2019].

Pires AJG. 2015. 'Brain drain and brain waste.' *Journal of Economic Development,* 40(1): 1–34.

PopulatonPyramid.net. 2018. [Online] Available at: https://www.populationpyramid.net/south-africa/2018/ [Accessed 8 January 2019].

Population Reference Bureau. 2018. *2018 World Population Data Sheet.* Washington, DC: Population Reference Bureau.

Posel D. 2003. *Have migration patterns in post-apartheid South Africa changed?* Paper prepared for Conference on African Migration in Comparative Perspective. Johannesburg, South Africa.

Setel PW, Macfarlane SB, Szreter S, Mikkelsen L, Jha P, Stout S, AbouZahr C. 2007. *A Scandal of Invisibility: Making Everyone Count by Counting Everyone.* Cambridge, MA: Monitoring of Vital Events (MoVE) writing group. Lancet.

Standing G. 2011. *The Precariat. The New Dangerous Class.* London: Bloomsbury.

Statistics South Africa. 2001. *Census 2001: Concepts and Definitions.* Pretoria: StatsSA.

Statistics South Africa. 2003. *Census 2001: Investigation into Appropriate Definitions of Urban and Rural Areas for South Africa.* Pretoria: StatsSA.

Statistics South Africa. 2006a. *Migration and Urbanisation in South Africa.* Pretoria: StatsSA.

Statistics South Africa. 2006b. *Mortality and Causes of Death in South Africa, 2003 and 2004.* Findings from Death Notification. Pretoria: StatsSA.

Statistics South Africa. 2011. *Revised Census 2011 – Strategy Document.* Pretoria: StatsSA.

Statistics South Africa. 2018. *Mid-year Population Estimates.* Pretoria: StatsSA.

Swart DN. 2011. Problems surrounding the combating of women and child trafficking in southern and South Africa. *Child Abuse Research: A South African Journal,* 12(1): 26–37.

Szreter S. 2018. Marx on population: A bicentenary celebration. *Population and Development Review,* 44(4): 745–769.

Turok I & Borel-Saladin J. 2014. Is urbanisation in South Africa on a sustainable trajectory? *Development Southern Africa,* 31(5): 675–691.

Udjo E. 1993. *Fertility and nuptiality: Analytical aspects.* Unpublished lecture notes. Pretoria: University of Pretoria.

United Nations. 2000. [Online]. Available at: https://www. unodc.org/documents/middleeastandnorthafrica/ smuggling-migrants/SoM_Protocol_English.pdf [Accessed 20 January 2019].

United Nations Population Division. 2017. *The 2017 Revision of World Population Prospects.* New York: The United Nations.

Van der Ven R, Smits J. 2011. *NiCE Working Paper: The Demographic Window of Opportunity: Age Structure and Sub-national Economic Growth in Developing Countries.* Nijmegen: Nijmegen Center for Economics (NiCE). Institute for Management Research. Radboud University.

Van Liempt I. 2011. 'Different geographies and experiences of 'assisted' types of migration: A gendered critique on the distinction between trafficking and smuggling'. *Gender, Place & Culture,* 18(2): 179–193.

Weeks JR. 2015. *Population: An Introduction to Concepts and Issues.* 12th ed. Belmont: Thompson Wadsworth.

WHO, UNICEF, UNFPA and the World Bank. 2010. *Trends in Maternal Mortality in 1990–2008.* Geneva: WHO.

World Bank. nd. *World Bank open data.* [Online] Available at: https://data.worldbank.org/ [Accessed 3 March 2019].

World Health Organization. 2015. *Strategies toward Ending Preventable Maternal Mortality.* Geneva: WHO.

World Health Organization. 2018. *World Health Statistics 2018: Monitoring Health for the SDGs.* Geneva: WHO.

Part

2

The Individual and Society

Socialisation and identity

Khosi Kubeka

Much of our lived experience is shaped by the learning processes of our upbringing. We become *socialised* into the habits, traditions and ways of thinking of our particular family, school and university, community, work occupation and society. Some scholars also call this the process of enculturation. Socialisation is a powerful force shaping the identity of the individual. It can therefore seem that individuals are a result or product of the culture and society in which people grow up, but which also constrains us as individuals in powerful and important ways. If individuals are thus shaped by the processes of socialisation, is it then also possible that we can act with free will? This chapter demonstrates that the very possibility of freedom is the result of an intensive socialisation process. This socialisation process (or processes) determines and restricts freedom, but at the same time enables self-awareness for human agents to act in such a way that they can surpass and transcend the limitations imposed on individual identity.

Philosophers call *identity* an 'indexical'. This is a technical term which means that identity is a one-to-one relation. You can only be identical to yourself. Only 'I' can refer to myself as 'I'. Only you – personal pronoun singular – can refer to yourself as 'I'. In South Africa – as elsewhere – we all have discrete, separate and individual identity numbers. Legally speaking, this unique number defines us as separate and unique individuals. What constitutes *individual identity*, however, is a much more complicated issue. Philosophy continues to debate it. Psychology continues to explore it. Sociologists are, unusually, united in the view that the formation of identity is intimately related to the processes of socialisation.

This chapter explores this central issue which grapples with the perplexing question of what it is to be human. The two opening case studies starkly illustrate that individuals who are not properly socialised literally fail to become healthy and useful human beings through no fault of their own. Once you have read these two case studies, spend some time reflecting on the powerful, if controversial, sociological dictum that the individual is, in a very meaningful way, formed and shaped, 'created' even, by society – yet has the capacity to exercise individual freedom. This profound sociological insight remains the subject of much theorising, discussion and debate. To engage with it does require becoming familiar with the terms of this debate regarding the extent to which society exercises a powerful influence over the individual. The very early conceptual distinction made between socialisation and identity in this chapter must hence be taken seriously as we engage in the process of intellectual self-formation in tertiary education.

Sociologists generally lean to the one side of this singularly important debate. We argue that identity is fundamentally a *social* process. As you will soon see in this chapter, this is the 'nurture' side of the debate. The other side of the debate considers 'nature' as basic and fundamental to the individual identity of persons. In this chapter you will confront various theoretical perspectives, formulated by modern authors, who have sought to address this matter. Sociologists might agree on the central idea that the formation of individual identity can only be understood in relation to the processes of socialisation. This does not mean, however, that they either share a single perspective or agree on which theory provides the best explanation of how socialisation lies at the heart of how individual identity is formed.

This crucial chapter needs to be read carefully. The text is conceptually dense, especially the first part which tackles a range of theories addressing this thorny issue. Do ensure that you understand the meanings of the concepts discussed. Consult the Glossary at the beginning of the textbook if you are not sure of the meaning of a term or concept. You then need to pay special attention to how the various concepts in each theory are linked together in order to grasp the overall point and argument the theories are making. Once you have seriously engaged in this intellectual task – which will take some effort on your part – you will be in a position to compare and contrast the various theories and be able to express them in your own words. You will then find yourself enabled to choose and argue, on the basis of reference to the various theories and the evidence they present, which theory you think best explains the relationship between socialisation and identity.

The effort of grappling with the concepts and theories will be worth it and the slightly easier final third of the chapter will make greater sense. In the final part of the chapter the agents of socialisation are discussed. The examples taken from South African life will be familiar to you. You might find the sections on ethnic identity and non-racialism particularly illuminating, especially if you read these sections together with Chapter 11 on families and households, Chapter 9 on race, Chapter 7 on gender and Chapter 10 on class. If you do so you will find yourself dealing with the age-old sociological issue of the relationship between the individual and society. You will be doing so while firmly grounding this complex but fascinating issue and its debates in the context of our own society. Because we as sociologists – and other social scientists – are part of the world we study, we inevitably learn about ourselves as we study the social world around us. This chapter enables us to do just that.

Case study 6.1 Isolation

A little girl named Genie from the United States was kept in isolation by her father from the age of 20 months, only to be discovered at age 13. By the time a psychologist, Dr Susan Curtiss (1977), met Genie, her emotional and linguistic capabilities were severely impaired. She could not walk or speak and was unable to focus her eyes beyond a certain boundary. During her time in confinement, Genie spent most of her days naked and tied to a potty seat. At night she was placed in bed in a straightjacket. The house was often quiet with no radio or television in sight. Genie's exposure to abuse during her formative years had harmful effects on her development in later years. She spent the rest of her life institutionalised (Source: Curtiss 1977).

In KwaZulu-Natal, a five-year-old boy, called Saturday Mthiyane, was discovered by the inhabitants of Sundumbili. He had been living with and appeared to have been reared by monkeys near the Tugela River. When he was discovered, Saturday displayed strange, animal-like behaviour, climbing trees and rooftops, was aggressive and ate fruit and uncooked raw meat. He was also institutionalised and placed in a special school for the disabled where he was diagnosed as mentally retarded. He also has severe speech impediments which appear to be permanent. He now struggles to relate to others and repeated efforts to teach him social skills have failed (Source: *Mail&Guardian* 2012).

Key themes

- Definition of socialisation and identity
- Theories of socialisation and identity
- Agents of socialisation
- Re-socialisation
- Social identity
- Identity as construction
- Identity and globalisation
- Ethnic identity.

6.1 Introduction

The two tragic stories in Case study 6.1 point to the kind of damage that isolation and lack of socialisation can have on human beings. They demonstrate the significance of the nurturing we all yearn for and deserve from our significant others, especially our parents and/or guardians in shaping our sense of self and place in an ever-changing world. They also demonstrate how most of our human learning occurs through our interaction with others in our surroundings. In short, our very identities – or what sociologists refer to as **identity formation** – are shaped by this social contact. In fact, even in the animal kingdom researchers found that severe isolation and deprivation of 'social' contact in young monkeys led to long-term deep psychological and emotional distress later in life (Mason 1968). How are we then to understand the critical importance of the processes of socialisation? This chapter aims to introduce this central question in sociology and which will be structured in the following way. The terms socialisation and identity will be defined and a range of theories centred on these two key concepts will be introduced. Such is the central and foundational importance of these two central concepts in sociology, this review of key theories will take up half of the chapter. The chapter then moves on to discuss the agents of socialisation, those institutions in which the process is embedded, the family, school and peer groups. The world of work further serves as a powerful socialising agent on the individual. The formative power of the mass media today is so pervasive that it too has been recognised as a powerful socialising agent. In instances where individuals fail to be fully functioning members of society and find themselves in mental hospitals or prisons for instance, we can then talk about the process of *re-socialisation* which is formally instituted. The question of social identity is then discussed and finally, in order to stretch your **sociological imagination**, individual identity is discussed in the current context of globalisation before some conclusions are drawn.

6.2 The nature versus nurture debate

Scholars have long been engaged in debates about what it means to be human. In *On the Origin of Species* (Darwin 1859), the English naturalist Charles Darwin asserted that natural adaptation is at the core of human development. Darwin argued that humans and other species undergo a process of evolution in response to the environment that makes demands on them to adapt, develop and evolve or become extinct. The famous phrase 'survival of the fittest' was coined to refer to the competition for scarce resources among all species as they seek to successfully keep up with

the demands of survival. Those forms of life, including *homo sapiens*, with greater inherent adaptive capabilities are more likely to survive and pass on the survival genes to the next generations. Species lacking in such features, however, naturally cease to exist and are thus eliminated from the evolutionary record.

Darwin's claim sparked a massive response from the entire scientific and religious community. His work saw the beginning of a long, drawn-out debate that led to the development of a range of postulations and theories regarding the development of the human species. At the centre of what has come to be known as the *nature versus nurture debate* is an effort to elucidate how human beings have evolved over time. Two opposing observations are at the centre of the debate. There are those who view humans as animals with advanced capabilities that set us apart from other animals (nature). On the other hand, there are those who believe that we are essentially *social* beings (nurture).

From a sociological perspective, although nature plays a crucial role in human development, especially in the beginning of life, it is our interaction with our surroundings and our immediate caregivers that significantly influences our identity formation and lays the ground for who we become later in life. In other words, in posing questions about our own unique individual consciousness, the interactions and social relationships – which occur within very different environments – are what primarily shape the individual. In addition, to understand both individual and shared forms of behaviour within groups of people, such behaviour needs to be observed within the context of specific events, happenings and social processes. This means that there are always events (stimuli) that precede behaviour (response), which in turn give rise to consequences (reward, punishment, or neutral effect). So significant is the role of the environment in human development that early philosophers such as John Locke (1632–1704) thought that human beings were born as a 'blank slate' – or *tabula rasa* – in which he compared the mind to a blank sheet of paper. Locke believed that each experience a person encounters fills the page of the mind with ideas from past experiences that are unique from person to person. This is how human beings came to interpret their world differently according to this theory of human development. Human agents, over time, accomplished our interaction with our societal environment and other human beings who cross our path.

This thoroughly **behaviourist** view of how human intelligence developed was, however, to be challenged. Rather than being a blank slate, the mind itself should rather be viewed as an organ brimming with capacity to absorb perceptions and generate ideas as it interacts with its immediate natural and social environment as the socialisation of individuals unfolds.

It was the social psychologist George Herbert Mead (1934) of the Chicago school of sociology, who first argued that it is through *human interaction* that meaning and understanding is derived. Who we are, Mead carefully argued, is determined by 'the social'. Our first acquaintance with and knowledge of the world occurs within a social setting and our place in it is facilitated through the use of language which develops as human beings interact. Therefore, it is through human interaction that language and the transmission of meaning, derived from the very first learning experiences at our mother's breasts, that we become members of society. It is these experiences which are the first building blocks of identity formation and in which the new-born human infant plays an interactive role, Mead argued. As such, new-born humans – as well as other mammals especially – are introduced into some form of pre-existing social organisation. This led Mead to talk of the 'priority of the social' in the formation of individual identity. In brief, the behaviour of individuals and the very development of increasingly complex societies can only be understood through the many daily interactions between human agents that make up 'the social'. These interactions are, in turn, framed by the wide range of particular environments within which different forms of social organisation have developed.

Sociologists firmly hold that we learn ways of being and acting through our interaction with those present in our lives. This occurs through the process of **socialisation**, which is how we come to understand and internalise the norms, values and expectations of behaviour that we carry with us throughout our lives. These attributes inform the roles we occupy and the kind of relationships we form and maintain. It is hence through the processes of socialisation that a person's identity is constructed. **Identity** is the socialised part of the self that comes in a form of meanings that define who we are based on our position in society.

What this chapter now goes on to present is hence a series of sociological explanations of how socialisation, which occurs through our interaction with individuals and groups at familial, community and societal level, inform the development of our sense of identity. As the influential contemporary English sociologist Anthony Giddens (1991) has powerfully argued, socialisation is the process whereby we become members of society.

6.3 Theories of socialisation and identity

Sociological theories of socialisation and identity help us understand how our self-concept – the view that we have of ourselves – emanates from our social environment in various ways. One long-held view was developed by the influential American sociologist Talcott Parsons (1902–1979) who dominated much of sociological theorising for over a generation. He called his theoretical approach **structural functionalism**. Central to this approach was the view that society was made up of *institutions* in which individuals each played different roles. Individuals were guided by sets of norms of behaviour and which functioned interdependently, yet in an integrated manner. This ensured social order and stability in society. The *function* of socialisation was to entrench and perpetuate social order and stability and ensure its continuity. Here, through key societal institutions such as the family, school and community, among others, we learn important norms and values as well as *roles* that will enable us to integrate, conform and become well-adjusted members of society. Well socialised individuals would, in turn, contribute to societal stability and social cohesion.

Conflict theories and the **conflict perspective**, on the other hand, do not stress social order and the integrated functioning of society as a whole, but focus rather on the impact of *social change* and *social difference*. Conflict theorists take the different contexts in which socialisation takes place very seriously. Very different environments and different social situations into which individuals are socialised are subject to constant change and often results in competing claims for resources. This results in conflict between different groups of people in society. The process of socialisation takes place very differently in these different contexts. The different and often competing views, norms, values and sets of behaviours into which individuals are socialised reflect not only these differences, but also the unequal power relationships which develop within societies. In other words, socialisation reproduces differences and inequality. To put it crudely, the 'haves' and 'have-nots' are socialised differently. Powerful social groups control and determine the nature and structure of social institutions which regulate social life. The foundation of this power, for conflict theorists, generally lies in ownership and control over the economic resources of society and which is the source of political and social power.

You might have noticed how George Herbert Mead's explanation of identity formation and 'the priority of the social' for identify formation and within which socialisation takes place, underlies both the structural functionalist and conflict perspectives of society. Mead's views were central to a cluster of theoretical views which fall under the name of **symbolic interactionism** – also referred to as *social interactionism*. As must have been evident from what was said about Mead's views, symbolic interactionism holds that socialisation is a major, if not *the* major determinant of human nature. This is because socialisation involves learning shared meanings which lie at the heart of human interaction and which makes *social action* possible. From this perspective, human behaviour is determined not only by the objective facts of a situation, but also by how people define that situation – that is, by the meaning or meanings they attribute to it.

Note how both structural functionalist and conflict theorists highlight the importance of **social structure** in explaining identity formation and the central role of socialisation. Individuals reflect the wider social structure with membership of social categories based on a hierarchically structured and well-ordered and functioning society for the structural functionalists. For the conflict theorists, how socialisation takes place depends on membership of particular social groups or social classes. Despite these different views, at the core of the relationship between self and the environment are values and beliefs. Although socially patterned or socially structured, these values are actually deeply personal. Thus, since personal identity and its formation is built up over time as individuals navigate their social world to achieve certain goals, values are embedded in that process and assist in the development of self and indeed, self-formation. This has brought us back to the key refrain of the symbolic interactionists. Symbolic interactionist theorists such as Mead, Charles Horton Cooley (1864–1929) and Irving Goffman (1922–1982) help us understand more deeply how we are essentially products of social interaction, how we use other people's responses to help us shape our self-concepts, and how we present ourselves in everyday life.

6.3.1 Mead and the social self

In a very important book called *Mind, Self and Society* (Mead 1934), which was actually written by students attending his lectures, George Herbert Mead, following Darwin, sought to demonstrate how human beings, despite their biological animal status, developed into thinking beings with minds who possessed a sense of self, unlike other animals. Early humans survived and evolved as a special kind of self-conscious animal by learning to communicate through the development of language.

Non-verbal communication first occurred through the emergence and development of making signs to each other

and developing communicative gestures. Before language developed, a grunt or a growl was a vocal gesture – a symbol for wanting food or warning of danger. These signs and gestures became significant symbols of communication. Through such symbolic interactions, language gradually took shape. Central to this process was the realisation of what Mead called 'the other'. In learning to communicate through making signs and gestures, human beings came to recognise that they were each distinct from other human beings as they interacted in the early social group of the tribe or clan in order to gather food and survive. They learned – or perhaps it should be said that *we* learned – to assume the role of 'the other'. Others would respond to our gestures and vice versa. From this recognition – a revolutionary moment in the development of the human mind – a sense of self emerged. Central to Mead's careful philosophical reasoning as a social psychologist – but who referred to his own work as **social behaviourism** – was his powerful insight that 'mind' and 'self' do not exist independently of their social environment. For Mead then, society or 'the social' as he liked to say, was the very foundation for the emergence of individuality. For Mead, we become individuals by virtue of engaging in *social acts*. We use each other's actions, or what he called gestures, to guide our own actions and thus behave and interact with others in certain ways. During this process, both our actions and those of the people with whom we interact undergo a change. It is not just a case of *responding* to *stimuli*. We adjust to the stimuli and responses we present to each other through the gestures or communicative signs we observe or vocal gestures we hear.

Mead used a famous example of a dog-fight to illustrate what he called the 'conversation of gestures' which led to the formation of language. The behavioural 'act' of each dog becomes the stimulus to the other dog which elicits a response. There is then a communicative relationship established between these two dogs about to engage in a fight. In response to a growl (a threatening gesture) from the first dog, the other dog responds – either by fleeing or making a responding challenging growl. The very fact that the second dog is ready to either flee or attack the first dog becomes a further stimulus to the first dog to change its own position or attitude. The second dog has no sooner done this than the change of attitude in the first dog in turn causes the second dog to change its attitude. We have here a 'conversation of gestures' (Mead 1934: 42–43). In this example, Mead argues, the gesture of the first dog summons up an appropriate response from the second dog and which has a symbolic meaning attached to it. This determines how they then respond to each other in what is essentially a 'social' process of behaviour. When it comes to human beings, a similar 'conversation of gestures' is both a process of learning that includes the shaping and development of capacities of survival, and represents a mutual awareness of what is happening in our, mutually influencing, social interactions. It is within this process at the heart of 'the social', for Mead, that the *emergence of mind* takes place. The mind, therefore, emerges as we embrace and internalise the attitudes of others as they respond to our gestures and actions.

What is important here is that, for Mead, the mind and its biological functions are social phenomena. The development of the subjective experience of the individual (which we unreflectively take for granted), he argues, has its origin in and relates directly to the 'natural, socio-biological activities of the brain in order to render an acceptable account of mind possible at all' (Mead 1934: 133). This is because our individual experiences are only made possible by the workings of the brain, the development of which could only take place within the context of group interaction or, to use Mead's favourite locution, within the context of 'the social'.

The self is hence not something with which we are born. Following Mead, we acquire the notion or sense of 'the self' from our interactive relations with our social environment. In addition to language, Mead traces the emergence of 'the self' (or self) in two stages of childhood development. He refers to these two stages as 'play' and 'game'. During the 'play' stage children begin to view themselves as belonging to an organised community or social group to the extent that they assume the attitudes of others in their social environment.

The attitude of the other players, which the participant assumes organise into a sort of unit, and it is that organisation which controls the response of the individual (Mead 1934: 154).

During the 'game' stage, however, children learn how to take on the role of many others. It is this organised community or social group which Mead refers to as 'the generalised other' that gives an individual a sense of self. Here, individuals use the generalised attitudes of the other members in their social group to define their own behaviour. In other words, they come to perceive themselves from the viewpoint of the generalised other, thereby developing a sense of self and self-consciousness, the 'embryo of mind'.

In addition to these two stages of development Mead goes on further to distinguish between the 'I' and 'me' as components of the self. This can be quite tricky to grasp. Whereas the former – the 'I'– refers to the unpredictable and creative part of the self that instantaneously responds to others, the latter – 'me'– is that part of our selves which constitutes the attitudes of others that the individual assumes. The 'I' can only act in the present. 'I' is the part of the self which creates the part of the self which becomes the 'me' and which can only then fall under the reflective gaze. In other words, the 'I' is the creative, selfish and independent part of the self. The 'me' is the reflective, selfless part of the self. The 'me' comes to light as we evaluate how 'I' have done in the light of how *others* have responded to what 'I' did. After we have done something – acted as an independent individual out of the strength of our 'I', we then evaluate and say: 'How did I do?' I should be proud (or ashamed) of *myself'*. The 'me' is powerfully dependent on how we think and assess how others saw us and is hence powerfully dependent on the norms, values of our own social group or, in other words, how society itself is organised.

What is the significance of all of this? It is quite simply that human society, Mead argues, would not exist if it were not for minds and selves. At the same time, however, both minds and selves are the products of the very social processes that constitute the interaction between human beings and their environment. Mead hence argues that at the basis of all forms of society, regardless of complexity, whether primitive or industrialised, lies what he calls the 'socio-physical relations among individual members' (Mead 1934: 133). Mead goes on to argue that the family is the fundamental social unit or what we will later refer to as the first **agent of socialisation**. This is because it is in the family where these socio-physical relations are most pronounced by virtue of its ability to reproduce and maintain the human species. Note that even larger institutional units of society, such as governments, were originally ultimately extensions of the interactions between families.

Mead consequently viewed identity and identity formation as stemming from the solid web of social relationships that are organised and grouped differentially so that individuals are classified by race, class, gender and religion, among others. People tend to fall within different segments of this classification simultaneously. At any given time, therefore, human agents develop and comprise a multifaceted identity by virtue of different roles they play and which are deeply embedded in these social networks. Furthermore, given that the positions or social roles people occupy require certain expectations of behaviour, identity then become the internalisation of such role expectations.

6.3.2 Erving Goffman's 'presentation of the self in everyday life'

If identity can be meaningfully said to be closely related to social recognition and acceptance, then how we *present* ourselves in social settings is clearly an important aspect of identity. Goffman (1959) built on the work of the symbolic interactionists who preceded him and on Mead and Cooley especially. Goffman was interested in elucidating how we manage our personal identity in our everyday lives. In his 'dramaturgical' theory of self (a theory using the drama of the theatre), Goffman depicts the self as a multifaceted entity with its components forming an identity that is closely tied to the social structure. As in the drama of the theatre, in life there are actors, scripts, stages and props. Goffman presents six components of the dramaturgical analysis.

The first component is the performance wherein we stand in front of others, 'the audience,' and act out impressions that in turn confirm our identity. A continuous exchange of information and meaning making occurs as actors interact with their audience. The performance takes place in a setting represented by scenery, props and locations that vary in terms of the audience and which thus requires the actor to be flexible in the delivering of his/her performance. It is through appearance, that is, how the actor portrays him/herself, that the audience come to know the actor's social status. For instance, the way the actor is dressed and the props he/she uses serve to communicate race, gender, socioeconomic status, occupational status, age and personal commitments. The manner in which actors perform their role serves to make the audience aware of what to expect. Any inconsistencies between the manner and appearance can unsettle the audience. This occurs, for instance, when the actor's behaviour or performance goes against or violates socially defined and accepted norms that accompany their social status position. The 'stage', also known as the script, forms part of the performance and functions to provide an image or an impression the actor seeks to portray. Some social scripts become institutionalised – resulting in stereotypes and expectations. Here, given their roles, social actors are expected to behave in a particular way.

Finally, Goffman observes that the stage wherein the drama of life is performed is divided into three areas: front stage, backstage and off-stage. The 'front stage' is where the actor performs in accordance with the values and norms associated with his/her role and which is meaningful to the audience. The 'backstage' is where the actor can behave differently because there is no audience watching him/her. This is where the actor *prepares* for his/her performance. Actors get to both put on and remove the mask and become who they really are in the absence of the roles they perform in front of an audience. The 'off-stage' is where the individual actors meet the audience members who are not part of the performance team on the front stage.

To illustrate how we perform our roles on the stage of life, imagine Thembi, a university student who is pursuing a Bachelor of Social Sciences degree, majoring in sociology and political science. After a difficult transition in her first year, from high school to a university far away from home, Thembi has come to a place of comfort in her role as a university student. Every day she juggles different roles and performs according to the stage and audience. Thembi typically begins her day by attending classes from morning until lunchtime. When she is in class, she takes on the role of a student watching a teacher perform a teaching role, while she performs her student role by sitting, listening and taking notes. During lunchtime, Thembi switches roles and therefore her performance. She is the chairperson of a student society on campus promoting human rights. She facilitates events and runs workshops with students on campus, educating them about respect for human rights and diversity on campus. On Fridays, Thembi ends her day by switching to her role as a waitress at one of the restaurants off-campus frequented by students. Here she takes orders and serves a lot of different people at the same time. This is how she earns extra money. All these role identities involve preparation behind the scenes, preparing props and performing on stage in front of an appropriate audience. Thembi's multifaceted identity is thereby formed and developed as she acts out different roles on the public 'front stage' of life, each one having been carefully prepared privately 'backstage'.

The question now arises how we conceptually link the micro-symbolic interactionist account of Thembi's experience with a broader social structural level of analysis. How do the activities of the many Thembi's relate to the patterning forces of social structure?

6.3.3 Charles Cooley and 'the looking-glass self'

Only the most unreflective person has never asked themselves the question: 'Who am I?' We all seek to understand who we are, how we fit in, what is going to happen to us. Sociology and the views of one symbolic interactionist in particular provide some thought-provoking and insightful answers. Charles Cooley coined the phrase, *the looking-glass self* (*LGS*). A leading sociologist of his day and a close contemporary of Mead, Cooley (1902) similarly held that self-formation is informed in part by our perception of how others view us. In other words, through interpersonal interactions, we constantly engage in the process of living 'in the minds of others without knowing it' (Cooley 1902: 208). Our self-concept is largely shaped by the way in which we respond to how we think others view us and behave towards us. We interpret and internalise the attitudes of others and how they respond to us. We thus invoke within ourselves powerful emotions of either pride or shame depending on the nature of the reflection we are focusing on. Hence:

> We are ashamed to seem evasive in the presence of a straightforward man, cowardly in the presence of a brave one, gross in the eyes of a refined one and so on. We always imagine, and in imagining share, the judgments of the other mind (Cooley 1902: 184–185).

Sometimes we also actively manipulate other people's view of us to serve our needs and interests.

The tendency to evaluate ourselves in response to the judgements of others begins during our formative years as we interact with our parents or other significant figures. It then extends to the wider social world that we navigate as we make the transition into adulthood. Our self-concept or self-understanding evolves as we continue to engage with others and internalise their expectations and perceptions of us.

Cooley's surprising, yet reassuring, response to the question 'Who am I?' would be that the question is not a **mystical** or **metaphysical** one with no ready answer. We ultimately understand ourselves in the light of the way in which others see us. We evaluate and assess our behaviour and actions and indeed our very selves, largely in social terms. We might have strong ideas and differences to those around us. We might see ourselves as a rugged and independent individualist. Yet the extent to which we can realise our view of ourselves lies in the extent to which we successfully negotiate and manage to express these qualities – and by extension ourselves – in our social context. To a large extent who I am or who we are insofar as we try to fathom the nature of identity – and especially our own – could be said to be intimately tied to social recognition and acceptance – even if that takes time.

6.3.4 Peter Berger's and Thomas Luckmann's social constructivism
Given that the mind and the self emerge from interaction with the social environment, it is not surprising that two sociologists went on to argue that identity is 'constructed' by that environment. This view is emphasised in the **social constructivist** perspective of Berger and Luckmann (1966),

which stresses that society is a human product. As a collectivity of people with 'different spheres of reality' and 'multiple realities', we engage in meaning-making within a 'human environment' marked by complex sociocultural and psychological components. Such a context is sustained by the presence of order, direction and stability. The use of language plays a very critical role in the process of the creation of a shared sense of order and meaning. It enables us to see how our individual 'inter-subjective world' corresponds to that of others in our social environment.

Furthermore, for these theorists the social construction of society occurs in three stages, namely: externalisation, objectivation and internalisation. First, human beings express themselves through language, art and in what they produce. Berger and Luckmann call this 'externalisation'. These 'cultural products' are then organised in social institutions and are held together by common values and beliefs. When they come to fruition, the products created have become 'externalised' and stand outside of the human beings who produced them. This is when 'objectivation' takes place. Some thing or product has been created or produced. The products produced – the actual objects – take on a life of their own. Social life progresses. New objects are created. As individuals, we overlook or even forget that it is as a result of generally collective human endeavour which has been responsible for the creation of the social and cultural environment which we then seek to interpret and understand.

Precisely because our attempts at expressing ourselves in the process of externalisation – in creating or producing – results in *objects* or objectification, the objective world – the overall product of our collective efforts – is taken for granted as a normal part of life. We then, thirdly 'internalise' these 'objective facts' through the process of socialisation. This is how they become a part of a shared human consciousness wherein members belonging to the same cultural group come to share, understand and interpret reality in similar ways. This influential view in sociology has been further elaborated by giving greater weight to the role of self-formation in human agency in the social construction of reality.

6.3.5 Anthony Giddens's structuration theory
In recent years there has been a shift in thinking that tends to embrace the idea that the environment and individual capacities interact in significant ways to influence human behaviour. Here **structure** (the way social life is patterned and organised) and **agency** (the ability of the individual to make choices) are key determinants in and of human development. The debate in sociology between structure

and agency – in some ways often an alternative to the nature versus nurture debate – has often been seen as a case of either 'structure' or 'agency' being the key determinant in explaining human behaviour and social events. Giddens sought to integrate 'agency' and 'structure' and argues that human behaviour, while embedded within social structure and enabled by it, contributes to changing it. In what Giddens refers to as the concept of structuration, 'the constitution of agents and structures are not two independently given sets of phenomena' (Giddens 1984: 25). There is continual interplay between agency and structure. In this interplay, the organisation of social relationships is based on *rules* (guidelines of behaviour) and *resources* (access to tools and materials) that people have at their disposal as they engage in 'the production and reproduction of social action' (Giddens 1984: 19).

While human behaviour is shaped by the social environment, people in turn influence this environment through their actions. Thus, people are not merely passively influenced or restricted by either imitation or the powerful patterning influence of social structures, but instead use these as resources for independent human behaviour. In essence, the social structural patterning 'rules', 'resources' and 'social relationships' of social life are produced and reproduced through processes of social interaction by social actors who have a strong sense of agency. The relationship between structure and agency is *reciprocal* – each influences the other. This relationship is characterised by a repetition of a process wherein individuals reproduce the structure, but which is then in turn subject to a subtle process of social change. Giddens says we are actively and constantly engaged in constructing our identity and positions because we are reflexive agents or beings. **Reflexivity** here highlights our ability to actively reflect on the events, experiences and messages we observe and receive from our environments and make choices about decisions about how we want to interpret them. Giddens points out that such a process is even more pronounced in modern societies where self-identity becomes a reflexive project. He concluded, therefore, that identity is not a fixed set of traits or observable characteristics. Identity is our own reflexive understanding of our lives. In addition, identity is not static, but is instead imbued with continuity, which means that identity is 'a product of the person's reflexive beliefs about their own biography' (Giddens 1991: 53).

The notion that identity is in fact multifaceted emerges from the interplay between mind and self, and self and structure. If one takes Mead and Giddens together, this was further developed by contemporary sociologists such as Sheldon Stryker (1980) among others. Stryker pointed out that individuals are always acting in the context of a complex social structure out of which a multifaceted identity emerges. Stryker goes further to argue that there is a **salient identity** that emerges out of different circumstances and situations. One's salient identity tends to stand out as dominant and is frequently active across different contexts. It also determines how a person may behave in any situation. Furthermore, what makes an identity *salient* is a person's commitment to that identity. Commitment can be informed by the number of people within the social structure with whom one has ties as a result of that identity. Commitment may also be informed by the stronger and deeper ties that one has to others through that identity. A salient identity would be manifest, for example, in a stay-at-home mother who spends most of her time tending to the needs of her children and being with other mothers who are in the same position. Other examples are a traditional healer who spends most of the day engaged in healthcare and training a new generation of traditional healers or a student who spends years in a classroom at school taking courses, studying and interacting with teachers and peers. All of these role identities could be experienced by these people as salient identities across time and space for as long as these socially constructing circumstances dominate their lives. The most prominent of these 'socially constructing circumstances' are the institutional agents of socialisation.

6.4 Agents of socialisation

Up until now in this chapter we have spoken about socialisation and the process or processes of socialisation. The discussion went in two directions. One direction was to show the centrality of socialisation for explaining how individual or personal identity emerges and is shaped in the process. The other direction pointed to how socialisation relates to the broader analysis of society as a whole. This discussion, you might have noticed, continually moved from the individual to the structural and back again. The discussion tied the micro (small) *individual* and macro (large) *structural* foci into one single, increasingly integrated and complex whole. The question which now arises addresses those *social institutions* which drive, embody or serve as the *agents* of the processes of socialisation. The three most important of these agents of socialisation are: the family, schooling and the work environment. In addition, the role of the mass media has been seen as an increasingly important and hence fourth agent of socialisation. Before looking at each of these **agents of socialisation** in turn, it is useful to adopt a broad, **ecological** perspective.

One of the greatest contributions to the under-standing of how external social environments and contexts influence the operation of families as the primary agent of socialisation, and the implications of such on human development, is the ecological theory of Urie Bronfenbrenner (1986). In Bronfenbrenner's ecological theory, personal characteristics and the interaction between the institution of the family and the environment are significant for the development and social adjustment of young people, particularly children and adolescents. He identified the environmental systems that influence intra-familial processes. The first is the *microsystem*, which describes the set of roles and relationships within the immediate family environment. The second is the *mesosystem*, which describes how different types of microsystems, such as home and school environments, interact to exert mutual influence on children and adolescents. The influence of the third kind of environmental system, the *exosystem*, is more indirect and a function of the individual's (especially children and adolescents) exposure to peers, teachers and community members. Finally, individual development is also affected by the *macrosystem*, which are the dominant socio-political and cultural patterns of the larger society in which they live. From this theory's standpoint, all these systems are intertwined, with the individual placed both at the centre and at the receiving end. It is also useful in understanding our individual socialisation experiences within different social and broader environmental contexts.

6.4.1 The family

As the most significant agent of socialisation, the family context probably has the greatest impact on human development. The socialisation that takes place within the family is known as **primary socialisation** and it occurs as soon as children are born, with their sense of self yet to develop. The family is the primary site wherein children learn values, beliefs and norms of behaviour to prepare them for the outside world. The nature of the interpersonal relationships children forge with their parents or guardians is critical in this process. The family's central positioning as the first point of entry into the world makes it the only space wherein the strongest of emotional ties are forged, namely between the child and the parents or other significant family members. It is also where the imitation of adult significant others is most pronounced. Children are prone to copy parental behaviours they observe around the house, such as domestic chores and other activities.

As children become youth, they experience physical and emotional changes that signal their transition to adulthood.

Here, familial socialisation plays an even more critical role in enabling the youth to cope with these changes. In many societies youth undergo initiation ceremonies as they move from childhood to adulthood, often through formal religious ceremonies such as the Christian confirmation service and when Jewish young people become Bar Mitzvah (men) or Bat Mitzvah (women).

Figure 6.1 Xhosa circumcision initiate (*Umkhweta*) photo of *kwekudee*
(Source: Photograph courtesy of Kopano Ratele)

In South Africa, particularly among African ethnic groups (Nguni, BaSotho, BaVenda and Shangaan), such traditional rituals and ceremonies form part of the ancestral and traditional family life. They are practised in both rural and urban families and communities. While their appearance may differ from one ethnic group to the next, the basic principles are similar. Pre-adolescent boys and girls are, however, subjected to different processes. These rituals always signal the end of childhood and the beginning of adulthood (Nel 2012).

For the boys, the initiation process usually lasts from a few days to several months, after which they then enter the second phase of their initiation. Among Sotho, Venda, Ndebele and Xhosa communities for instance, initiation takes place in the mountain where boys set up camp, concealed from females or children who are not allowed to be present. They have to build shelters out of grass, wood and branches. They are then instructed on tribal laws and customs, are taught respect for their elders and how to hunt and fend for themselves. The initiation process usually ends with circumcision as a sign that they have entered manhood (Nel 2012).

Girls go through a communal form of initiation process. Among different groups we find ceremonies such as *vusha* and *domba* (Venda), reed dance (Swazi and Ndebele), and *bojale* (Pedi). Initiation among the Zulu and Xhosa groups is more individualistic and occurs at the beginning of puberty. Here girls begin lessons on matters relating to sexual behaviour, tribal etiquette, wifely duties, married life and agriculture (Nel 2012).

As we can see from these social practices, the ways in which children and youth are socialised within families are also influenced by the sociocultural environment within which they are located. Old established traditions, for instance, often dissolve in the shift from rural to urban environments. In our current global society, moreover, due to advances in technology people are able to forge intimate relationships with individuals more broadly than ever before and indeed, from other parts of the world. One of the challenges this presents for parents is that through such connections, their children may be exposed to values and beliefs that are contradictory to those they are trying to instil. This tension becomes especially pronounced when children make the transition to adolescence and young adulthood. In our contemporary information driven society, young people are more likely than before to challenge parental authority in their attempts to assert themselves and define their own identity.

6.4.2 The school
With increasing numbers of children entering nursery schools, primary socialisation can be said to continue beyond the family environment as children begin the first stage of schooling. A child's first day of school often marks a critical transition into another important socialising platform outside of the family context which also powerfully influences their development. This is the beginning of **secondary socialisation**. Unlike in the generally private and confined environmental space of the family, socialisation within the school is considerably more socially open and formal in nature. It is enforced through a set of standards and requirements children are expected to absorb. Through both formal schooling as well as the **hidden curriculum** – those unwritten yet powerful rules of interaction – schools prepare children for transition to adulthood and membership of society at large.

Beyond the confines of the family, at school children are subject to social interactions which result in the development of strong bonds which influence their behaviour and shape who they are to become as fully socialised adults. Obtaining affirmation, acceptance and approval from people, such as teachers and friends, potentially becomes more important for the development of the individual than during the course of primary socialisation. What the individual learns over 12 or more years of schooling is the meaning and significance of group conformity, belonging and co-operation. It is during this period that young people are faced with the challenge of developing the aptitudes and capacities to effectively adjust to changes in their interpersonal relationships with parents and other significant adult figures in their lives. If socialisation in the family has resulted in what sociologists call a **prescribed** (or *acquired*) **identity**, now the beginnings of an **achieved identity** take shape. For instance, even children and certainly young people begin to actively develop the capacity to deal with potential family tensions that may be triggered by their strong desire to assert their independence from their parents or guardians. They also have to maintain self-control in the face of peer pressure, while at the same time sustaining strong friendship ties and networks. In addition to these intra-personal and inter-personal changes, young people in contemporary societies also have to navigate institutional changes. These relate to changes in school settings during early adolescence with the transition from primary school to secondary school. For older adolescents the change involves moving from matric to tertiary educational settings, employment or starting a family (Spencer et al 1988).

6.4.3 The peer group
Secondary socialisation continues as peer group influence becomes more significant in the lives of young people. It is within this context of interaction that developing a sense of agency, identity and autonomy becomes critical. Young people tend to be drawn more to their peers at this stage, spending less and less time with their parents and family. The shared understanding, interests and age groups often makes young people feel more comfortable and understood. Peer groups provide young people with new and fresh and different perspectives about life. Therefore, adolescents are more likely to consult their friends on issues that are of value to them, such as appearance, lifestyle, fashion, social activities, intimate relationships and sexuality. Furthermore, beliefs and behaviours that receive disapproval from peers – playing the role here of the 'generalised other' to use a concept from Mead's theory – are less likely to be displayed again by an individual. Conversely, peer-group influence can also have negative consequences, particularly when the interaction with the peer group falls outside of the protective institutional and socially framing contexts of school or work in which much social contact originates. Deviant peers have

been counted among the strongest models that reinforce experimentation with risk-related behaviours among young people. We might call this *negative socialisation*.

6.4.4 The mass media

With the advancement in information technology, the global mass media is now recognised as a particularly powerful socialising agent. Information transmitted through media such as television, newspapers, magazines and more recently, online social networking sites, exerts a strong influence on people's beliefs and behaviours. To give one example, studies have long found that children who spend a significant amount of time watching television and playing video games with violent content are more likely to display aggressive behaviour. With its strong influence, beginning early on in life and continuing as people advance into adulthood, the media could be described as both a primary and secondary agent of socialisation. Children in contemporary societies, including South Africa, are exposed to educational television shows such as *Takalani Sesame* and other game shows aimed at instilling cultural values and norms of behaviour that prepare children for adjustment in society. Furthermore, online social networking sites such as Facebook and Twitter are used especially by young people to connect with other people across the globe and develop 'virtual' relationships. These networks are also used as spaces for the assertion of identity and are sites to state views and opinions on events and issues of significance to them.

6.4.5 Work and employment

If socialisation is broadly understood as the process whereby we learn to become members of society, it is generally assumed that this process has been completed by the time adulthood arrives. Yet with entry into the labour market occurring prior to adulthood, the experience of work should also be considered as an agent of socialisation. Even adults switching jobs have to re-learn new sets of skills and ways of behaviour. They must temporarily undergo a process very similar to the learning processes embedded in both primary and secondary socialisation.

The importance of the role played by the formal institutional agents of socialisation of the family, school and work and the informal, non-institutionalised socialising role played by the peer group, comes to the fore when they are absent. Take the example of unemployment. For a very large number of young people in South Africa today, especially those who come from socioeconomically disadvantaged family backgrounds and who are more likely to drop out

of school, the likelihood of unemployment and remaining stuck in the cycle of poverty, looms large. Those who are unemployed must somehow develop their own coping mechanisms and survival strategies. There is no guiding and formal institutional social structure which assists them. Such people find themselves beyond the nurturing protection and stability the institutional agents of socialisation provide. Even the sense of the passing of time changes for such individuals and every day is the same. The temporal rhythms and patterns of the institutional agents of socialisation no longer play their structuring role. The unemployed person is often out of kilter within his/her own family. Even reliance on the previous informal agent of socialisation of the peer group is often not possible as the peer group itself would have been central to the school or workplace with which the unemployed person no longer has contact. After long periods of unemployment getting and holding on to a new job can be a challenge. There is a sense in which people need to learn again how to live and work with others, to be re-socialised in an important sense. Re-socialisation can, however, be very purposively implemented and it is to this topic that we must now turn.

6.5 Re-socialisation

In his groundbreaking work *Asylums*, Goffman (1968) examined the ways in which people are subjected to a process of re-socialisation upon entering total institutions. Goffman defines the total institution as:

> *... a place of residence and work where a large number of like-situated individuals cut off from the wider society for an appreciable period of time together lead an enclosed formally administered round of life* (Goffman 1968: 11).

Using the **total institution** model, Goffman compares mental institutions to prisons, concentration camps, orphanages and the military within which people lose a sense of control and independence over their lives. The migrant labour compounds which dominated the South African mining industry have been viewed as total institutions. In order to gain an insider perspective of life in a total institution, Goffman relied on the subjective experiences of patients. He gathered their accounts by using an ethnographic, participant observation research method and conducted interviews while spending time at a mental hospital. He concluded that people confined in total institutions are often detached from the larger society. Their behaviour and movement is strictly monitored by authority figures who are appointed to enforce rules of conduct. The ultimate objective of total institutions such as mental hospitals, Goffman observed, is to dismantle an individual's old self and create a new one. In the process, the individual's sense of identity is broken down. The social roles they came to occupy and enact are stripped off through physically and socially abusive institutional practices and routines. The physical structure and the rules and regulations of these institutions also assure that inmates have little or no contact with the outside world. Visitations from family, friends and kin are restricted and strictly monitored. Goffman argued that often the usual response from inmates is that of conversion, wherein they adopt the official or staff view of them and act out the role of the perfect inmate. Goffman claims that among inmates in total institutions there is a strong feeling that time spent there is time wasted. The inmate learns that, if released, life will never again be what it was.

In his work on prison life in South Africa, Jonny Steinberg (2004) applied Goffman's theory to demonstrate how total institutions can transform people's sense of self and behaviour. After conducting research in one of South Africa's largest prisons, Steinberg concluded that the prison perpetuates a behavioural subculture. Steinberg identified four types of adaptation in a total institution. First, some prisoners tended to undergo what Goffman terms a *situational withdrawal*, which is when the inmate mentally detaches from the prison. Here, the inmate withdraws from everything except events immediately around his body. Second, inmates may respond by adopting prison life, preferring it to life outside. This kind of adaptation is known as 'colonisation'. Third, inmates may choose to act out the role of the perfect inmate. Fourth, some inmates may choose to oppose the legitimacy of the institution and rebel against authority in various ways, such as embarking on a hunger strike or instigating violence, and so on. These are some of the ways in which prison inmates cope with the dehumanising effect of total institutionalisation.

6.6 Social identity

Given that identities form and take shape within the context of our interaction with those with whom we share similar group membership, namely our families, communities and the general structuring patterns of organised social life, it is important to understand intergroup identity dynamics. The fact that we have multiple groups within hierarchically structured societies, intergroup issues such as stereotyping, discrimination and separation, have significant effects on intergroup relations within and among societies. The social

identity perspective provides insights into these dynamics and their impact on human development.

6.6.1 In-group and out-group

The *social identity* perspective emerged from Henri Tajfel's 1960s and 1970s research on intergroup relations (Tajfel & Turner 1985). This perspective sought to explain the social psychological nature of group membership – that is, the psychological processes of self-identification with or feelings of 'belongingness' to a particular group. Belonging to a group is a psychological process distinct from being a sole individual and which bestows social identity; a symbolic perception of self is shared among members of the same group and which determines intergroup and intra-group behaviour.

The social identity approach is based upon the assumption that 'society comprises social categories which stand in power and status relations to one another' (Tajfel & Turner 1985: 14). In other words, people are distinguished in terms of race, class, nationality, gender, religion and occupation, among others. Some categories enjoy greater power, status and prestige than others. The function of *categorisation* is to accentuate similarities among individuals belonging to a particular group or category, while stressing the differences between in-groups and out-groups.

Furthermore, people's self-concept consists of a complete set of self-descriptions and evaluations which are 'textured and structured into circumscribed and relatively distinct constellations called *self-identifications*' (Tajfel & Turner 1985: 24). A distinction is made between self-identifications that are either social identifications or personal identifications.

6.6.2 Categorisation

The fact that societies place people within categories (race, class, gender, occupation and religion) that often stand in relation to one another in terms of power, status and prestige, contribute to development and escalation of intergroup tension. This occurs especially when the dominant, materially powerful social group imposes its own value system and ideology (designed to benefit the powerful group) in seeking to legitimise and maintain the status quo. Socialised under these conditions, individuals tend to internalise their membership of these groups, which may lead to the development of either a positive social identity (for those who belong to the dominant group) or a negative social identity (for those belonging to the subordinate group).

6.6.3 Stereotyping

Stereotyping refers to people's tendency to oversimplify or severely limit our perception of other social groups. This results in generalisation about people and groups based on characteristics such as race, ethnicity, age, gender or sexual orientation. Stereotypes can either be positive or negative particularly when they are directed at members of the out-groups, for example when members of certain subordinate racial, ethnic or cultural groups are labelled as having low intellectual capacity. Such stereotypical generalisation about other groups is narrow because it ignores individual differences or the subjective aspects that make each individual human being unique. Where do stereotypes come from? One of the most important contributions to our understanding of the nature and impact of stereotypes as part of intra- and intergroup dynamics is explained by social identity theory. Tajfel and Turner, for instance, dispute the popular conception of stereotyping as a way in which people process information. Rather, they view stereotyping as a tool that members of the in-group use to justify their behaviour towards those of the out-group. Therefore, stereotyping is a critical component of the social identity process in that it implies perceiving members of a given category as possessing various common attributes, in other words, being seen as more similar to one another than they are to members of another category. Stereotypes serve a number of social functions that provide individuals with a social identity. At an individual level, stereotypes enhance our positive view of ourselves as part of a group that is distinct and valuable when compared to others. At a communal and societal level stereotypes function to organise groups in stratified status positions that determine access to resources and which regulates how groups relate to each other. This can result in subordinate out-groups being used as scapegoats for societal problems.

The xenophobic attacks that spread throughout South African townships in 2008 is an example of how vulnerable groups in society, in this case African foreign nationals, were targeted and blamed for contributing to persisting poverty. Clashes between disadvantaged and poor South Africans and foreign immigrants were reported around the world and condemned as criminal behaviour. Social factors contributed to the violence (Citizens Rights in Africa Initiative (CRAI) 2009). The post-apartheid government failed to bring about sufficient improvements in service delivery and economic conditions in marginalised communities in which little had changed in many poor households after democracy in 1994. Local South African residents perceived that foreign nationals competed unfairly with them for scarce jobs and income and who were accused by poor South Africans of 'stealing jobs'. Another source of tension was the competition for trading spaces in the informal sector. The depiction of foreign nationals by the press as 'illegal aliens', as well as references to 'alien terror' and 'war on aliens', who were deemed responsible for the perpetuation of crime in the country, received considerable coverage in the media and can be seen as having had a negative socialising effect on the South African collective psyche.

Box 6.1 Non-racialism in post-apartheid South Africa

Realising a non-racial society was at the core of the activities of the liberation movements that dominated South Africa during the apartheid era. This was because race, as a category, was used by the apartheid system to place individuals in groups hierarchically structured with unequal access to socioeconomic resources. The divisive nature of such a system also created segregated and unhealthy intergroup relations that were, and continue to be, characterised by racial stereotypes and distrust.

What is the meaning of non-racialism in post-apartheid South Africa?

In her analysis of data from focus group interviews with individuals from all racial categories, Kate Lefko-Everett (2012) explored how ordinary people understand the notion of non-racialism in the new South Africa. She found that for most South Africans, race continues to form a foundation for their sense of identity. She noted that most 'self-describe in terms of a number of different identities. While for many this includes national identity, it is often coupled with race, ethnicity, gender and language, and this was a common practice'.

Although most participants still defined their sense of identity in terms of their racial categories, they were more likely to embrace integration with other groups. This can be attributed to the fact that there is more intergroup interaction taking place in public spaces such as schools, recreational facilities and the workplace. People of all different racial groups tend to reject racism and embrace a South African identity.

However, racial group stereotyping still persists within private spaces. The participants in the study believed that non-racialism can only be achieved by the young generation who grow up in a more racially integrated society. However, given that social identity is learned through socialisation, the author wonders if children will be able to discard the stereotypes about individuals who belong to racial groups different from their own.

6.7 Identity and globalisation

Contemporary theories of identity stretch our sociological imagination by explaining how identity formation and enactment is shaped by globalisation. Anthony Giddens (1991) and Manuel Castells (2010) are among notable scholars who theoretically integrate identity into comprehensive analyses of our contemporary global society. In his analysis of *Modernity and Self-Identity*, Giddens argues that 'transformations in self-identity and globalisation are the two poles of the dialectic of the local and the global in conditions of high modernity' (1991: 32). In other words, the more globalisation rapidly dominates, the more local traditions lose their relevance and influence on people's lives. As a result, life is reconstructed 'in terms of the dialectical interplay of the local and the global, the more individuals are forced to negotiate lifestyle choices [from] among a diversity of options' (1991: 5). This is a reflexive process wherein self-identity, based on life experience, is structured and restructured in the midst of this dialectical relationship of the global and local contexts. Giddens observes that ideally, a stable self-identity is nurtured during childhood through our ongoing interactions with the people in our social environment, but which can be fractured in the context of the rapid changes which accompany globalisation.

As with Giddens, identity forms part of Castells' analysis of the global age. Castells argues that the 'conflicting trends of globalisation and identity' stand in contradiction to each other and shape and reshape people's lives in significant ways. On the one hand, the technological revolution that has given rise to 'the network society' has made the world even more complex. It is characterised by:

… the transformation of capitalism, and the demise of statism; and characterized by flexibility and instability of work, individualization of labour, network forms of organization, a 'culture of real virtuality' based on complex media systems, transformed material foundations of life, space and time, and the rise of new cosmopolitan ruling elites … (Castells 2010: 2).

At the same time, identity formation and expression also evolves in a complex, persistent and enduring way despite the powerful forces of globalisation in the form of a:

…. widespread surge of powerful expressions of collective identity. … [these are] multiple, highly diversified following the contours of each culture, and of historical sources of formation of each identity (Castells 2010: 2).

These multiple identities are increasingly acted out through the media and telecommunications systems and '… challenge globalization and cosmopolitanism on behalf of cultural singularity and people's control over their lives and environment' (Castells 2010: 2).

This persistent and enduring ability of an individual's self-identity, Castells stresses, makes it constant, transcending time and space. It continuously reinvents itself while maintaining its essential features, resulting in subsidiary identities and social roles that have significant meaning to individuals and the context in which they function. These identities and their associated meanings are created through the process of 'individuation'. While the governing social institutions, social roles and values may provide important foundations for identity construction, they only form part of an individual's identity, however, when and if individuals *choose* to internalise them. Identity is therefore seen as an active process of construction wherein the individuals determine their own sense of self and the meaning thereof. Castells is of the view that identities in modern societies are constructed through:

building materials from history, from geography, from biology, from productive and reproductive institutions, from collective memory and from personal fantasies, from power apparatuses and religious revelations. … Social groups process, reorganize these materials and their meaning, according to social determinations and cultural projects that are rooted in their social structure, and in their space/time framework (2010: 7).

This process of identity construction occurs within contexts marked by power relationships. He proposes three types of collective identities: legitimising identities, resistant identities and project identities. A legitimising identity is used by dominant groups in society to justify and reinforce their dominant status over ordinary citizens. In contrast, resistant identities are appropriated by marginalised groups in society who are hurt by their conditions and stigmatised, '… thus building trenches of resistance and survival on the basis of principles different from, or opposed to, those permeating the institutions of society' (2010: 8).

In South Africa's past one can clearly see the emergence, enactment and enforcement of both legitimising and resistant identities within both white and black racial groups. For instance, one may argue that the formation of apartheid as a legalised system of racial discrimination was influenced by the emergence of Afrikaner nationalism, an ideology that promoted Afrikaner supremacy and pride in response to British invasion and colonisation as well as the threat from the majority indigenous population, who were resisting subordination (Worden 1995). During this period, the Afrikaner nation had endured British colonial rule throughout most of the 19th century. They were sustained by maintaining their cultural identity through their language (Afrikaans) and religion (Dutch Reformed Church), in this way cultivating a sense of group nationalism. Winning political power thus put the Afrikaners in a position to steer the country in the direction which would serve their group and its values. The objective of the National Party was to take over the major institutions, that is, the economy and the political and educational systems. In order to achieve its goals, it had to design a system which would elevate whites over other racial groupings through economic and political deprivation (Zungu 1976).

During the apartheid era, the Black Consciousness ideology formed a central and critical part of the credo of most anti-apartheid political and **social movements**, whose mission was to fight against the subjugation of black people in the country. Black Consciousness is predicated on the belief that because black people are often confined to poor living conditions, they develop a state of alienation and rejection of self that tends to associate anything positive to whiteness. This 'self-negation' usually begins in childhood and persists throughout one's life. The only way to rid oneself of this sense of unworthiness is by refuting the notion that black is a deviation from the 'normal', which is white (Biko 1978). The objective of Black Consciousness is to raise racial awareness and critical consciousness among black people. Black Consciousness encouraged black people to refute the perception perpetuated by the apartheid government depicting black people as unworthy and inferior as a racial group. These tactics served as impetus for the mobilisation of the masses for political action in black communities across the country. In the post-apartheid era, beginning with the first democratic elections in 1994, however, Black Consciousness and radical political action gave way to a non-racial ethic and the accompanying sentiments of national unity, reconciliation and the encouraging of interracial group tolerance and contact.

The majority of black South African adolescent respondents in a study by Farred (2006) were born during this era of racial reconciliation, often referred to as 'the New South Africa' or the 'Rainbow Nation'. Farred (2006) describes the 'rainbow' as symbolising:

… the disjoining of the 'old' South Africa from the new; the rainbow of the present represents a "racially" complementary harmony as opposed to the Apartheid past where the disunion of the various peoples was the predominant racist logic (2006: 231).

In the spirit of post-apartheid nation building, the notion of, or efforts to build the 'rainbow nation', has been accentuated in the media and political platforms. The aim has been to encourage racial reconciliation and tolerance through the emphasis of patriotic sentiments among all racial groups. Studies have documented that, while people embrace 'South Africanness' as an umbrella identity, their racial, linguistic and religious identities and occupational categories take precedence. Therefore, intergroup behaviour, rather than interpersonal behaviours, is more predominant in our society (Burgess & Harris 1999). In their examination of self-categorisation tendencies among a select group of South African youth ('Birth to Twenty') from different racial backgrounds, Norris et al (2008) found that, when compared to their white counterparts who had a more individualistic sense of identity, African and 'coloured' youth were more likely to embrace their collective sense of identity as South Africans. They had more positive perceptions of the new South Africa.

A project identity is constructed when members of society draw on existing cultural materials to create new identities so as to reframe their status in society. Castells cites feminism as an example and highlights how women's movements:

move[d] out of the trenches of resistance of women's identity and women's rights, to challenge patriarchy, thus the patriarchal family, and thus the entire structure of production, reproduction, sexuality, and personality on which societies have been historically based (Castells 2010: 8).

While growing, this project identity is relatively small when compared to other ways in which social identities are constructed.

6.7.1 Ethnic identity

Notwithstanding our democratic transition in 1994, ethnic identity remains a powerful social identity and which refers to the extent to which we identify with our particular ethnic group. This identification provides us with a sense of belonging and strongly influences our thinking, perception, feelings and behaviour. Components of ethnic identity include an understanding of our own and other groups (ethnic awareness), the labels bestowed upon our group (ethnic identification), our feelings about our group (ethnic attitudes) and the patterns of behaviours associated with belonging to a particular group (ethnic behaviour) (Regmi 2003).

What makes ethnic groups distinct from one another are cultural attributes such as systems of belief, practices, religion, languages spoken and even physical appearance. These attributes are consolidated through a shared destiny, status, ideas, behaviours, feelings and the meanings we attach to these attributes of our particular ethnic group. Members of ethnic groups often make an 'us' and 'them' distinction to assert their uniqueness thus setting themselves apart from others.

Two main approaches to the understanding of ethnic identity have been documented, namely: primordialism and constructivism. The former views ethnicity identity as ascribed and fixed, while for the latter, ethnic identity is constructed, situational, subjective and instrumental. Edward Shils (1957) and Clifford Geertz (1973) are credited for advocating the primordialist view of ethnic identity. For these scholars, ethnic groups are the precursors or constitute the core foundation of nations. For Shils, for instance, modern societies are:

held together by an infinity of personal attachments, moral obligations in concrete contexts, professional and creative pride, individual ambition, primordial affinities and a civil sense which is low in many, high in some, and moderate in most persons (Shils 1957: 131).

Shils conceptualised family groups as primary groups and sought to show how these are linked to larger societal structures. He argued that through interpersonal interaction social groups are formed, which in turn expand to form ethnicities. The outcome is an amalgamation of ethnicities that form nations. Geertz concurred with this view and added that the primordial ties are based on what he calls 'givens' of 'immediate contiguity and kin connection mainly, but beyond them the "givenness" that stems from being born into a particular religious community, speaking a particular language … and following particular social

practices' (1973: 259). The six primordial ties are assumed blood ties (based on invisible but commonly known kinship or quasi-kinship relationships), race (those phonotypical physical features such as skin colour), language differences, region or geographical boundaries, religion, and cultural customs and rituals.

In contrast, constructivists challenge the depiction of ethnic identity as fixed and ascriptive. Rather, ethnic identity is viewed as fluid, flexible and subject to constant redefinition. The appropriation of an ethnic identity is a means to an end. In other words, ethnic groups use their collective identity as a tool to achieve certain privileges and accentuate their position within the social structuring of society. Solidarity within groups and competition among groups is at the basis of human interaction in societies. An emphasis is placed on how elites manipulate ethnic identities in an effort to rally support for materialistic interests. In such instances, ethnic identities are often evoked and used as offensive and/or defensive weapons to protect or realise such interests. As such ethnicity is politicised and manipulated by those in power 'to protect their well-being or existence or to gain political and economic advantage for their group as well as for themselves'. It should be clear how very different political implications flow from these two different sets of theoretical perspectives.

6.7.2 Hybrid identity

If the formation of identity was not already complicated enough, the notion of hybrid identities further complicates matters. Hybrid identities are considered to be one of the outcomes of cultural globalisation. By definition, cultural hybridity is '… the way in which forms become separated from existing practices and recombined with new forms in new practices' (Smith & Leavy 2008: 3). A hybrid identity stems from a reflexive relationship between the local and the global cultural practices. The local and the global unite to create new identities which are distinct within a specific context. This results in a form of hybridity that 'signifies the encounter, conflict and or blending of two ethnic or cultural categories' which results in a complex identity structure that reflects the uniqueness of individuals. Most of the research on the impact of globalisation on identity formation has had the youth as its focus. These studies sought to unpack the impact of broad global changes on the process of transition from childhood to young adulthood in nations around the world. The focus has been on the intersection between the context and individual behaviour resulting from changes in an individual's access to especially informational resources combined with their specific/personal attributes during the transition to adulthood.

The accelerating economic and cultural integration driven by technological changes is said to influence the process of transition in significant ways. At the same time, adolescents increasingly form multicultural identities because they grow up being aware of and knowing about diverse cultural beliefs and behaviours. As such, understanding identity formation in rapidly changing contexts has become exceedingly complex. A local example is instructive.

In her ethnographic study of how youth construct racial selves within a multiracial school context in South Africa, Dolby (2001: 63) argues that:

African [black] students are poised at a three-way juncture: an ever-changing traditional culture that exists for many, in the imagination; the urbanization of modernity; and the globalizing thrust of postmodernity.

She stresses the ways in which these students draw heavily upon Western, particularly African American 'icons and symbols of the global popular' to construct and express their racial identity. Her respondents seem to have discovered ways to engage in processes of creating what Massey (1998) calls a hybrid culture, which '... involves active importation, adoption, and adaptation' of various sources of influence as they construct and make sense of themselves. In other words, they have perfected the art of 'symbolic creativity' in which they combine their indigenous cultural practices and traditions with global popular culture as they aesthetically enact and re-enact their personal and communal identity. Blending contemporary styles of dress, for instance, with traditional African flavours to create a hybrid style is an example of creating a hybrid identity. Preserving one's indigenous accent when expressing oneself in a non-native language and doing so with a strong sense of pride, is another. Here we see the autonomous ways in which these young people frame and use cultural practices to construct their identities as they '... creatively combine elements of global capitalism, transnationalism, and local culture' (Bucholtz 2002).

Furthermore, Lene Jensen (2003) highlights three important issues relating to the formation of multicultural identities. First, Jensen argues that for contemporary youth, a multiculturally informed identity involves having both direct and indirect contact with a diverse set of people. Adolescents are exposed to first-hand contact with people from different cultures as a consequence of migrations and tourism within their own countries. They are also exposed to cultures other than their own traditional culture indirectly through media. As a result, they develop their 'local identity'

based on their indigenous tradition, as well as a 'global identity' based on their exposure to a global (often Western) culture conveyed through the media. In addition, cultural identity formation based on access to media exposure tends to be more *subjectivised* or *individualised* than cultural identity formation based on first-hand interactions. The agent-orientated creative use of the media facilitates more individual interpretations of identity than first-hand messages derived from within an immediate group context. Second, youth cultural identity formation may take diverse developmental paths depending on the particular cultures involved. This means that while notions of individual autonomy and family obligations are typically important aspects of people's cultural identities, these appear to develop in different ways and in varying orders across cultural traditions during adolescence. This makes cultural identity formation more complex as adolescents have been exposed to a considerable number of cultural styles and ways of being. This is because they have to form identities in the face of cultural traditions that may hold out different goals and different pathways to those goals.

Third, there are both gains and losses that occur when youth form a multicultural identity rather than an identity based primarily on one cultural tradition. Youth may face challenges associated with having to adjust psychologically as they engage in the process of forming a multicultural identity. Some youth experience a form of 'culture shedding' which involves leaving behind or unlearning aspects of their parents' culture. This may result in a sense of loss in some cases. In others, it may lead to a positive sense of leaving behind undesirable beliefs and practices. Other youth may experience a 'culture shock' brought on by difficulties in forming a coherent identity in the face of culturally distinct world views that are difficult to reconcile. Finally, **psychopathology** may be another response resulting in failure to adapt. Here youth may be prone to problematic and deviant social behaviour – the extent of substance abuse, prostitution, armed aggression and suicide which has occurred in a variety of traditional cultures and may, in part, have resulted from processes linked to globalisation and identity confusion and the sense of marginalisation in the face of diverse cultural values that are difficult to reconcile. Finally, the extent to which adolescents are able to adjust and form a multicultural identity is further informed by factors such as age, gender, level of education, degree of social support, inter-group attitudes and discrimination. Such is the complex, but fascinating, set of issues sociologists have dealt with in trying to understand how we form our identities in the context of our fast-paced globalised world.

Summary

- This chapter sought to outline theoretical frame-works that explain the processes of socialisation and identity formation as determinants of human development. The discussion has highlighted the significance of social context in shaping individual development and identity formation.

- Socialisation is the process wherein we learn to be our unique selves through our interaction with significant others in our environment and it is absolutely crucial in our navigation of life and in establishing our sense of being and role in an ever-changing world.

- Sociological theories of socialisation clearly articulate the role of our environment in shaping our sense of self and role in the world. This is facilitated by our interaction with significant people in our lives within societal structures that have evolved over time.

- Key theorists such as George Hebert Mead, Erving Goffman, Charles Cooley and Anthony Giddens, help us understand a) the connection between mind and self and how these interact within a social environment, b) the importance of how we are perceived by others around us as we present ourselves and play out our roles in shaping our sense of identity, c) how we interpret, process and internalise people's perceptions of us as we develop our sense of self, and d) the way in which this process of acting out roles and reflecting is influenced by the structural environment to which we are exposed. Our development of self and identity occurs within specific contexts and social institutions and through our interacting with significant people in our lives. These are known as agents of socialisation. They teach, guide and instil values that inform our sense of self and behaviour.

- The social identity perspective helps us understand how, through the process of socialisation, our identities take shape. Here our sense of who we are and our position in society becomes clearer as we navigate our social lives.

- Our individual sense of identity is also tied to our collective sense of identity. Here our sense of belonging within groups of people with whom we share similar characteristics becomes meaningful. It also influences our perceptions of others who belong to groups that are different from our own. While this is important in nurturing our sense of belonging, it can also negatively affect the way in which we interact with people who are different from us, thus leading to tensions based on perceived differences.

- Given the fact that we now live in a global society means that our socialisation is no longer confined within our immediate environment. Through the global social media, we are exposed to a wide variety of cultures, belief systems, lifestyles and values that have a strong influence in shaping our sense of identities. We develop multiple identities and hybrid identities wherein we enact both the local and global ways of living.

Are you on track?

1. What is socialisation and why does it matter in human development?
2. Discuss each of the agents of socialisation and their role in human development. Provide examples from your own or other people's experiences.
3. Compare and contrast the psychological and sociological explanations of identity formation.
4. What is the difference between ethnic identity and hybrid identity?

References

Berger PL, Luckmann T. 1966. *The Social Construction of Reality.* Garden City, NJ: Anchor Books.

Biko S. 1978. *I Write What I Like* (with personal memoir by Stubbs A). New York: Harper & Row.

Bronfenbrenner U. 1986. 'Ecology of the family as a context for human development: Research perspectives'. *Developmental Psychology*, 22(6): 723–742.

Bucholtz M. 2002. 'Youth and cultural practice'. *Annual Review of Anthropology*, 31: 525–552.

Burgess SM, Harris MJ. 1999. 'Social identity in an emerging consumer market: How you do the wash may say a lot about who you think you are' in *NA – Advances in Consumer Research*, 26: 170–175. Arnould EJ, Linda M, Scott LM (eds). Provo, UT: Association for Consumer Research.

Castells M. 1997. *The Power of Identity.* Oxford: Blackwell.

Castells M. 2010. *The Power of Identity: The Information Age: Economy, Society and Culture* (Vol II). Oxford: Blackwell.

Citizenship Rights in Africa Initiative (CRAI). 2009. 'Tolerating intolerance: Xenophobic violence in South Africa: A report. July 2009'. Kampala: CRAI.

Cooley CH. 1902. *Human Nature and the Social Order*. New York: Charles Scrivener's Sons.

Curtiss S. 1977. *Genie: A Psycholinguistic Study of a Modern-day 'Wild Child'*. Boston: Academic Press.

Darwin C. 1859. *On the Origin of Species by Means of Natural Selection, or the Preservation of Favoured Races in the Struggle for Life*. London: John Murray.

Dolby N. 2001. *Constructing Race: Youth, Identity, and Popular Culture in South Africa*. New York: SUNY Press.

Farred G. 2006. 'Shooting the white girl first: Race in post-apartheid South Africa' in *Globalization and Race: Transformations in the Cultural Production of Blackness*. Clarke KM, Thomas DA (eds). Durham: Duke University Press.

Geertz C. 1973. *The Interpretation of Cultures*. New York: Basic Books.

Giddens A. 1984. *The Constitution of Society: Outline of the Theory of Structuration*. Berkeley, CA: University of California Press.

Giddens A. 1991. *Modernity and Self-Identity*. Cambridge: Polity.

Goffman E. 1959. *The Presentation of Self in Everyday Life*. London: Penguin.

Goffman E. 1968. *Asylums*. Harmondsworth: Penguin.

Jensen L. 2003. 'Coming of age in a multicultural world: Globalization and adolescent cultural identity formation'. *Applied Developmental Science*, 7(3): 189–196.

Lefko-Everett K. 2002. 'Leaving it to the children: Non-racialism, identity, socialisation and generational change in South Africa'. *Politikon: South African Journal of Political Studies*, 39(1): 127–147.

Locke J. 1632–1704. *An Essay Concerning Human Understanding*. Oxford: Oxford University Press.

Mail&Guardian. nd. [Online] Available at: http://paul.chattaway.com/entertainment/stf/stf18.html [Accessed 29 November 2012].

Mason WA. 1968. 'Early social deprivation in the nonhuman primates: Implications for human behaviour' in *Environmental Influences*, 70–101. Glass DC (ed). New York: Rockefeller University and Russell Sage Foundation.

Massey D. 1998. 'The spatial construction of youth culture' in *Cool Places: Geographies of Youth Cultures*. Skelton T, Valentine G (eds). New York: Routledge.

Mead GH. 1934. *Mind, Self, and Society*. Chicago: University of Chicago Press.

Nel J. nd. [Online] Available at: http://myfundi.co.za/e/Initiation_cycles_of_traditional_South_African_cultures [Accessed 29 November 2012].

Norris SA, Roeser RW, Richter LM, Lewin N, Ginsburg C, Fleetwood S. 2008. 'South African-ness among adolescents: The emergence of a collective identity within the Birth to Twenty cohort study'. *Journal of Early Adolescence*, 28(1).

Regmi R. 2003. 'Ethnicity and identity'. *Occasional Paper in Sociology and Anthropology*, 8: 1–11. Kathmandu: Central Department of Sociology and Anthropology, Tribhuvan University.

Shils E. 1957. 'Primordial, personal, sacred and civil ties: Some particular observations on the relationships of sociological research and theory'. *The British Journal of Sociology*, 8: 130–145.

Smith KI, Leavy P. 2008. *Identities: Theoretical and Empirical Examinations (Studies in Critical Social Sciences)*. Chicago: Haymarket Books.

Spencer MB, Dobbs B, Swanson DP. 1988. 'African American adolescents: Adaptational processes and socioeconomic diversity in behavioural outcomes'. *Journal of Adolescence*, 11: 117–137.

Steinberg J. 2004. 'Nongoloza's Children: Western Cape Prison Gangs During and After Apartheid'. Braamfontein, South Africa: Centre for the Study of Violence and Reconciliation.

Stryker S. 1980. *Symbolic Interactionism: A Social Structural Version*. Menlo Park: Benjamin Cummings.

Tajfel H, Turner JC. 1985. 'The social identity theory of intergroup behaviour' in *Psychology of Intergroup Relations*. 2nd ed. 7–24. Worchel S, Austin, WG (eds). Chicago: Nelson-Hall.

Worden N. 1995. *The Making of Modern South Africa: Conquest, Segregation and Apartheid*. Oxford: Blackwell Publishers.

Zungu Y. 1976. 'The education for Africans in South Africa'. *The Journal of Negro Education*, 202–218.

Gender

Marlize Rabe

Powerful arguments have been presented that gender as a construct is one of the most important forces in the socialisation of individuals. Gender as a social construct has been described as personal and social, plural, relational, dynamic, an active product and inscribed in power relations.

Feminism – broadly speaking the view that men and women should have equal rights – has fundamentally challenged the theoretical basis of sociology and transformed its view and understanding of society. Few other theoretical perspectives or world views can make this claim. This does not mean that feminism is a single, unified perspective. The extent of its challenge to social analysis and social understanding is too far-reaching for this to be the case. Feminism, this chapter will go on to show, has been expressed in different ways by radical feminism, Marxist feminism, liberal feminism, black feminism, eco-feminism, conservative feminism and new feminism.

This chapter provides more than simply an introduction to gender and feminism. It concisely treats the critical theoretical standpoint feminism has articulated under patriarchy – the power some men exercise over both women and other men. This standpoint is based on the justifiable, historical and contemporary struggles by women for political, economic, health, educational and sexual rights. However, this analysis does not exclude the involvement of men in the struggle to establish more equitable relations between people in society. One of the variants of feminism you will learn about in this chapter makes this clear. This does not mean that feminism is united on this issue. It is not. What might surprise you is how masculinity studies can be said to have arisen out of or responded to feminism.

Serious study of this chapter will challenge your social understanding of gender. None of us is exempt from this learning process as we have all been subjected to specific social constructions of gender. The issues discussed in what follows, however, are not conceptually difficult to grasp. What is perhaps difficult, is to learn to meaningfully look at the world from different gendered perspectives. This is due to the powerful and deeply entrenched forces of our own gendered socialisation processes which have shaped the formation of the identities of most people. What is conceptually challenging is the scope of other issues implicated in the study of gender. In South Africa the way in which gender intersects with race and class is often prominent in shaping identities. It has long been recognised in South African gender and feminist studies, for instance, that black women in South Africa under apartheid were subject to the 'triple oppression' of gender, race and class. In brief, if there was ever an instance in the study of sociology – where a serious attempt should be made to extract and distance ourselves from the forces of socialisation in order to understand society and our own role within it anew, the study of gender is a case in point.

Gender inequality and the oppression of women continue to be serious issues in South African society. This is despite the hugely significant role and contribution women played in the struggle for democracy and without whom it might not have been achieved. That gender inequality is widespread is especially evidenced by the way those who experience it acutely have mobilised themselves into social movements to collectively express their rights to equal treatment in social life. The way in which many such activist groups have formed and continue to struggle for social recognition and the acceptance of difference from dominant and often oppressive social norms, are briefly outlined towards the end of this chapter.

Initiated and empowered by the standpoint of feminism and rightly opposed to oppressive forms of gender socialisation, South African society has, for instance, only in recent times seen the emergence of a focus on sexual minorities such as bisexual, intersex, transgender, transsexual and asexual individuals. The rights of whom, it is argued, are only recently given much attention, even in fairly new theoretical paradigms such as Lesbian and Gay Studies.

When you next see or read of (or take part in) Gay Pride marches, now part of the South African social landscape, you might consider the important conclusion to this chapter that there is a general lack of tolerance for diversity and difference regarding sexual orientation on the African continent, which includes South Africa.

Case study 7.1 Gender issues in South Africa

During the #FeesMustFall movement in 2015, the following was reported at Wits University by Pontsho Pilane in the *City Press*:

' ... Incoming students' representative council (SRC) president Nompendulo Mkhatshwa addressed the student crowd and asked that they sit so that there could be some kind of order. Some male protesters shouted: 'We won't be told by a woman!'

They refused to sit down, even though most people were pleading with them. I then asked two of them why they refused to sit and whether this had to do with the gender of the person instructing them. They said it didn't, but they continued to say that 'feminism must *voetsek*'.'

(Source: Pilane 2015)

Case study 7.2

At 8 a.m. on 16 June 1976 Tsietsi Mashinini interrupted the school assembly to lead the first group of students out of the gates and on the march that started the Soweto uprising. They were protesting the use of Afrikaans in schools. A reward was posted for his capture and one afternoon Security Police checked every student leaving the grounds. Mashinini, who was a prefect at the Morris Isaacson School, escaped detection by dressing up as a girl. After the march he never slept at home again and fled the country two months later (Segal & Holden 2008).

(Source: Courtesy of SAHA)

Case study 7.3

The ANC Women's League called on the department of transport and safety to act ... This was in response to the humiliation on Sunday of Nwabisa Ngcukana (25), when taxi drivers and hawkers at the rank tore off her clothes to cheers from a crowd who said she was being taught a lesson for wearing a miniskirt. Taxi drivers allegedly put their fingers in her private parts while others poured alcohol over her head and called her names.

(Source: SAPA 2008)

Key themes

- Gender
- Social construction
- Embodiment
- Socialisation and gender
- Power relations

- Patriarchy
- Feminism
- Masculinity studies
- LGBTI (Lesbian Gay Bisexual Transsexual Intersex) studies.

7.1 Introduction

During the #FeesMustFall protests massive numbers of students in South Africa highlighted, through demonstrations, how financial barriers prevent students from accessing higher education in the country. These protests were initially focused and appeared undivided. As the movement gained momentum, divisions between students became clear and gender was extensively commented upon in the mass and social media. The first case study is a short excerpt from an article titled 'Patriarchy must fall' in the *City Press* by Pontsho Pilane (2015) that cast some light on gender divisions. From Pilane's first-hand experiences, it is clear that female leaders were not always given the same respect as their male counterparts. Particular male supporters wanted to focus on the issue at hand and not let it be diverted to other issues such as gender. Yet these same male supporters exhibited clear forms of sexism. One can deduct from this that gender permeates our lives and that it is often difficult, if not impossible, to separate gender from human struggles.

In the case of Tsietsi Mashinini (Case study 7.2) his leadership qualities in the student resistance movement against specific apartheid legislature are highlighted. He escaped on more than one occasion by disguising himself as a girl; apparently the police officers did not consider this possibility when lining up suspects. Clothing is very much linked to gender as particular pieces of clothing are only associated with being either male or female. If we reflect on what these first two short overviews tell us about gender, then it highlights how gender identity intersects with other identities. The term **intersectionality** is often used and it focuses on how different social identities interact. In the case of Tsietsi Mashinini we can see how gender is constructed through the use of socially expected norms of how a person of a particular sex 'should' present themselves. Both the intersection of identities and the social construction of a gender identity will be further discussed in this chapter.

The third case study is an incident that took place in an urban area, Johannesburg, in the democratic South Africa in the 21st century. Ironically, this case was reported on in 2008, after the release of the Criminal Law (Sexual Offences and Related Matters) Amendment Act 32 of 2007. Although the behaviour of these men was unlawful and they could be theoretically charged for their behaviour according to this Act, it will be very difficult for a female victim to bring charges against a group of men who humiliated and hurt her in a public space in full view of spectators who did nothing to help her. In this example we see how certain men want to control the way in which a woman, and by implication all

women, presents herself in public spaces. This violence and humiliation against women is an ongoing, alarming trend in the 'new South Africa' which will be highlighted below from a feminist and a masculinist point of view.

Why should sociologists concern themselves with issues related to gender in South Africa? Can we not simply argue that women's rights are entrenched in the Constitution, among all other human rights, and that we should move on? Although some people may take such a stance, daily news reports (as Case study 7.3 shows) tell us a different story. In South Africa we are bombarded with newspaper articles on women falling prey to domestic violence and being raped by strangers as well as by men they know. Terms such as the feminisation of poverty and the traditional role of men are used in political speeches to justify certain public expenditure patterns. Specific interpretations of traditions are often claimed (sometimes referred to as the invention of tradition) by especially men to ensure that specific forms of patriarchal power stay intact. We read and hear about lesbian women and gay men being attacked simply because they are homosexual. Certain churches do not allow women to become priests or pastors while others do not allow homosexual people to fill such positions. If we look at the pictures on the back pages of newspapers they either contain men in action doing sports or inactive women in bathing costumes posing for the camera in order to be gazed at. The overwhelming majority of political leaders, rock band members, engineers, medical specialists, taxi drivers, garbage collectors and gardeners are men while the vast majority of teachers, nurses, models, figure skaters, cleaners and secretaries are women. Despite maternal deaths at childbirth, women in general live longer than men. Girls outperform boys in primary school but later on in life men receive much higher salaries compared to women with equal levels of education. We are baffled by certain gender differences and inequalities in popular books, sometimes satirical in nature, that sell like hotcakes. In short, we live in a gendered world where our gender sometimes restricts and sometimes enables our life chances. In trying to understand how individuals are shaping and being shaped by larger structures, forces and institutions, it is impossible to ignore how gender takes centre stage.

On the one hand, bodies have certain desires, functions, capabilities and limits that point to a gendered nature. Men cannot bear children, for example. On the other hand, children are taught from a young age to act in a specific way according to an assigned gender, for example 'girls should not act like that'. Both the biological aspects of gender and the social moulding (construction and re-construction) of gender are therefore of importance and both of these issues will be discussed in more detail in the next section.

7.2 Gendered bodies

In many early introductory courses to gender it became a standard practice to distinguish between **sex** and **gender**. The former is defined as referring to the biological features of being male or female and the latter to context-specific social definitions of maleness and femaleness. Critics regard such a distinction between the biological and social dimensions of gender as artificial because the one influences the other. For example, the fact that certain women bear children influences working conditions for pregnant employees. Although biological analyses of gender can be used negatively or in a pseudo-scientific manner such as: 'It is that time of the month for her, you know' and 'Boys will be boys'; biological aspects are not unimportant for the gender discourse. Hormonal fluctuations and genetic potential form an important part of who we are, but they are constructed within a specific context. **Biological determinism** is unacceptable to sociologists because the way in which we analyse and perceive biological characteristics is greatly influenced by social or cultural and ideological beliefs.

7.2.1 Binary claims of the gendered body: Boy or girl?

Before or directly after the birth of a baby many family members, friends and other interested people often ask whether the baby is a boy or a girl. There are many reasons why people want to know the sex of the baby such as a general interest in the baby's life, wanting to know whether they should start planning for bride wealth, expectations about assigning family names and so forth. This general interest in the sex of the baby already indicates the social expectations assigned to men and women in specific socio-historical milieus. The interest in the baby's sex may also signal gender stereotypes such as 'look at those dainty fingers, she will definitely be a "lady"' or 'the boy's big feet will definitely be able to kick soccer goals soon'.

The assumptions about men and women on a daily basis become even clearer when the answer to whether a newborn is a boy or a girl is: 'We don't know', often leaving the questioner stunned. It is estimated that one out of 1 500 people are **intersex** babies but there is disagreement about the exact criteria for being defined as an intersex person and accurate records are not being kept (Strachan & Van Buskirk 2011). By and large, external genitalia are used to determine the sex at birth, but in some cases the external genitalia may be atypical. In other cases the reproductive

anatomy of an individual may not match external genitalia and this may only be discovered later in life. People who are intersex were often assigned the gender that their genitalia resembled the closest and as technology developed, surgical procedures were also used to remove or modify specific bodily parts (Wiesner-Hanks 2011). Later on in life the gender identification by such a child may match or contradict the decisions made at birth about the sex of the child which may lead to emotional trauma for the intersex individual and other people involved.

The social pressure to divide people into males and females is also highlighted in sports where men and women usually compete in different categories. The assumption is that men are bigger, stronger and faster and therefore should not compete against women. The result is that a type of 'gender detection' is set in motion to identify any person who may compete as a woman but who may appear male in some way. In 2009, the South African athlete Caster Semenya was subjected to a range of invasive procedures to 'prove' that she is a woman and therefore eligible to take part in women's athletics at an international level. The fact that she was raised as a girl, has always competed as a female athlete and identified herself as female was not considered as enough evidence since she was said to 'have a certain look' and she regularly outperformed her competitors. The procedures that she had to undergo, not only consisted of an examination of genitalia and reproductive organs, but also of chromosomes and hormones even though both chromosomes and hormones may contain ambiguous and contradictory indications of maleness or femaleness.

What is clear from the above 'interventions' and 'examinations' is that there is an insistence within general society that one must be either male or female and nothing else. It is only with great difficulty that the activist group 'Intersex South Africa' became established and managed to add references to intersex people to South African legislation.

Where intersex people challenge the certainty with which many people assign the categories male or female (and nothing else), transgender or transsexual people challenge the assumed link between biological categories and gender identities. **Transsexual people** view themselves as living in a body that does not match their gender identity and choose (or desire) to live as a person of another gender. Complex surgery and hormonal treatments make it possible for people to actually change their sexual category to align it with their gender identity. Such medical interventions are a slow, expensive process and it is accompanied by intense psychological therapy. **Transgender** is an umbrella term that not only refers to transsexual people but a variety of people that includes certain cross dressers (people that voluntarily dress up in clothes associated with people of the other gender, either on occasion or regularly) and a variety of people who live and express themselves beyond approved restrictive male and female behavioural patterns (Norton & Herek 2012: 66).

Box 7.1 Gender identity

Figure 7.1 'celebrating The Freak' by Germaine de Larch (1 in a series of 5, 2013)

Germaine de Larche is a gender non-conforming transgender person, a writer, artist and documenter of life. They explain the image above entitled 'celebrating The Freak', in the following manner:

Luciano and Ivanka are gender non-conforming people living in the urban suburbs of Alexandra and Tembisa in Johannesburg. These suburbs were known as 'townships/locations' during apartheid, and are still mostly inhabited by people of colour from South Africa and the rest of Africa. Luciano and Ivanka identify as neither male nor female and as people with both feminine and masculine energies. They express their gender outside of the limitations of society's conflation of sex and gender; its narrow definition of sex as being only male or female, and gender being only man or woman. While their gender and the way they express it is a daily threat to their physical safety, they, in their own words, 'celebrate The Freak'; reclaiming the pejorative term for themselves as a form of empowerment and self-determination in a disempowering and oppressive culture, society, country and world.

* Do you think that embracing such a controversial title can be empowering?

De Larche goes on to explain that their portraits are about:

Collaboratively documenting selves, outsider voices from inside. I am not a photographer; these are not my subjects. I make images of me through relating to myself on my human journey. I make images of you with you, through relating to each other's journeys as human beings. Portraits from, of and dedicated to everyone on a journey who embraces and celebrates 'there is no one more YOUer than YOU'. My pronouns, as well as the pronouns of Luciano and Ivanka, are 'they', not 'he' or 'she'.

De Larche uses the portraits to show the life that they live, while telling the story that is theirs.

* Do their statements make you rethink gender identity?

7.2.2 Changing technology and the gendered body

Modern medical technology makes the re-assigning of a person's sex possible (although only people with access to such medical resources can make use of it). This same medical technology is also used to determine a clear sex category in the case of many intersex people. In the former case the wishes of the individual are catered for, but in the latter, the wishes of the individual are sometimes ignored or not yet known (as in the case of infants). The same medical technology can thus either aid or hinder the individual's embodiment of a chosen gender identity, thus illustrating the power of certain cultural developments on people as gendered beings. **Embodiment** theorists see people as social beings but stress the fact that humans are biological organisms. This latter aspect has implications for how we are perceived by others, what we can do or not do, what we have done and not done and so forth – in sum, the body tells a story.

The pervasive effect of cultural developments on gender experiences can be seen in the widespread availability of the oral contraceptive, the 'Pill', since the 1960s. Although different contraceptive methods have always been used with varying degrees of success, the availability of *effective* and 'easy-to-use' contraception changed women's life choices dramatically since it enabled them to plan childbirth far more accurately than ever before by delaying, spacing or even preventing the birth of children. This decision-making power regarding childbirth had dramatic consequences for women since bearing children had influenced their social position in all cultures, positively or negatively. In industrial and post-industrial societies, pregnancy and childbirth could end or dramatically alter a woman's career prospects since childbirth is seen as a disruption of employment. It has been argued that the introduction of the Pill was one of the major driving forces of the emancipation of women in the 20th century (see development of feminism in section 7.3).

Apart from the well-known example of contraception and its effect on women's life choices, other examples of cultural developments also had a huge impact on women's fertility patterns. The feeding practices of infants for example changed dramatically with the invention of the first artificial nipples, made possible by the manipulation of rubber. This invention allowed successful feeding of young infants without the presence of the actual breast of a woman, which implied more freedom of movement for women if this device was used. In even earlier times it was only once humans started planting crops and domesticating animals that they produced food, especially cereals, that was soft enough for young children to eat and digest and women could wean their children at a younger age. In most gathering and hunting societies, the food was (is) too hard for young children to eat and women had no choice but to breastfeed their children until the age of three or four years. However, breastfeeding children for such long periods contributed to fairly large intervals between the births of children (since breastfeeding suppresses ovulation) compared to more settled communities (Wiesner-Hanks 2011). It can thus be seen that changes in diets, inventions and technological developments have a direct impact on the body that may lead to shifts in the way people live as gendered beings in their society.

Other examples of technological inventions changing gender relations relate more to the role of men. Mary Wiesner-Hanks (2011), using a wide socio-historical lens, argues that in almost all known societies women generally performed a subordinate role with limited references to the dominant role of women, usually individual women, and not women as a social category. The subordinate role of women was sharpened in communities where land ownership became fundamental, since warfare often followed. During times of war, before the invention of sophisticated war technology, men played a central role as soldiers and therefore their status in such societies was elevated. Armies were even described as sites where **hypermasculinities** developed. Only once warfare became more dependent on strategy and sophisticated technology, as opposed to brute strength, did women enter warfare

in larger numbers. Similarly, in agricultural societies where ploughing developed, men tended to dominate this task due to perceived (and often actual) physical strength. Ploughing yielded more agricultural products and therefore heightened the importance of men's work in society.

Technology can thus influence the very distinctions between the male and female categories dramatically. Furthermore, technological developments also altered the way in which the roles of men and women were understood within different societies over centuries.

7.2.3 Challenging heteronormativity

Heteronormativity is an underlying assumption in society (including social institutions such as schools and churches) that all people are heterosexual and specific roles are assigned to men and women. In a publication entitled *Undoing gender*, Judith Butler (2004) argues that transgender and transsexual people, as well as the intersex movement, challenge the current set of norms that have been established regarding gender. Butler asserts that the experiences of bodies have to be 'reworked' in order to contest the normative ideals of bodies. For her this relates to what it means to be human and actualising a 'liveable life' for larger groups of people.

Butler goes further and argues that not only transgender, transsexual and intersex people challenge established norms but also lesbian, gay and bisexual people. The acronym LGBTI is commonly used today to refer to lesbian, gay, bisexual, transgender and intersex people. In the case of the former three the structure of the body is not the issue per se, but rather the sexual orientation or desire emanating from the body. Note that not all activists are satisfied with grouping these different categories of people under one umbrella term since the focus of each group is regarded as too distinct. Opening up debates regarding the validity of the normative nature of heterosexual relationships is not welcomed by all people as physical violence against and other forms of derogatory behaviour and discourses towards LGBTI people clearly illustrate.

Stevi Jackson (2006) argues that 'institutionalized, normative heterosexuality regulates those kept within its boundaries as well as marginalizing and sanctioning those outside them'. The author is thus arguing that heteronormativity not only excludes homosexual people but also regulates heterosexual people according to narrow criteria. The latter perpetuates specific forms of gender division and thus not only sexuality but also gender is regulated by a specific normative concept of heterosexuality.

In this section the interplay between body and cultural aspects was alluded to repeatedly. Although the examples related to the development of medical technology point to the ability of individuals making life choices in relation to gender, it has to be kept in mind that these choices are not available to everybody. For example, in many parts of the world women do not have access to effective birth control methods since they are not available or their use is forbidden. In such cases where technology is rejected, the social construction of gender in specific communities, rather that invention of technology, determines the life choices available to gendered beings. We will now turn to these social constructions of gender, keeping in mind that biological aspects of gender are important.

7.3 The social construction of gender

The social construction of gender refers to the way in which people interact on a daily basis with an established view of how men and women 'should behave'. Mostly, such gender expectations are on a subconscious level but it can be observed in how people dress and groom themselves, how they interact with each other and what they say in casual conversations.

In explaining a social constructionist approach, Margaret Wetherell (1996) argues that 'individual social identities' should be regarded as *projects* that are made and remade. Such a construction process is based upon 'collective understandings' of socially significant categories such as gender, race and class. These collective understandings flow from dialogue, experiences, observations and both local (eg immediate experiences and conversations) and global (eg through the mass media) sources are used to arrive at such collective understandings. This implies that one is not born with a social identity, but that it unfolds within an individual's life. Individuals try to make sense of identity by presenting it as a 'unified narrative' (a story that makes sense) of the diverse relationships and activities that form part of their lives. In trying to construct such a unified narrative, a continuous struggle with internal conflict and repression can be observed.

In other words behaviour, thoughts, emotions or experiences that do not make sense, are seen as 'out of character' or regarded as undesirable and then erased or downplayed in a life story. Certain individuals never achieve a unified narrative due to irreconcilable contradictions in their lives. In trying to construct a life story, there is an *active* element of construction, but since the individual lives within certain limitations, a *passive* element is also present. Furthermore, the multiple versions of one life story hint at the fragmented and contradictory nature of identities.

Figure 7.2 Lejeanne Marais, five-time South African women's figure-skating champion

Let us look at the social constructionist view of gender in a more systematic manner by paying attention to the following elements: gender is personal and social, plural, relational, dynamic and an active project that is linked to power.

7.3.1 Gender is personal and social

How do social constructions of gender come about? Families, as with all socialisation aspects, form the institution that 'gets there first with the most'. Parents, siblings, grandparents and so forth all provide us with information, role models and implicit expressions of what gender is or 'should' be. Friends, schools, the mass media and churches are further avenues to convey specific meanings associated with gender to individuals. Yet, individuals do not necessarily accept these social constructions. Wetherell (1996) explains such dual processes of identity formation by stating that identity is not only 'collective, historical and social' but also 'personal, private and individual'. If we apply this perspective to a gender identity, then gender is constructed on an individual level albeit with knowledge about present gender identities. 'Given identities' may be accepted, adjusted or rejected by an individual in order to make the identity fit with a personal life history.

Michael Kimmel (2009: 102) states the following about the relationship between the personal and the social aspects of gender:

A sociological perspective examines the ways in which gendered individuals interact with other gendered individuals in gendered institutions. As such, sociology examines the interplay of those two forces – identities and structures – through the prisms of socially created difference and domination.

7.3.2   Gender is plural
'Personally, when I read what social psychologists wrote about the "male sex role" I always wondered whom they were writing about. "Who me?" I thought.' (Kimmel 2009: 93). This observation by Kimmel reveals that generalisations of one form of masculinity exclude the variety of gender manifestations. Because different individuals vary so much in their expressions and embodiments of gender, the plural forms, namely *masculinities* and *femininities*, are preferred to indicate the variety of gender identities. For example, different male sex roles are envisaged when thinking about a professional rugby player and a florist.

Wetherell (1996) also points out that gender can be plural *within an individual* by stating that 'identity can be fractured, multiple and contradictory'. The same person can present different aspects of a gender identity in different milieus in relation to different people which indicate the fluidity of gender. If we use the same example, then a professional male rugby player becoming a florist shows different identities by the same person.

7.3.3   Gender is relational
Gender identities are constructed in relation to other people. Relational aspects can firstly refer to how women and men construct their identities in relation to each other. It has been argued that women have often only been understood in juxtaposition to men (being their mothers, wives, sisters and so forth) until the feminist project placed the experiences of women at the centre. Secondly, it is important to note that women also construct their gender identities in relation to other women, just as men construct their gender identities in relation to women and other men (Wetherell 1996).

7.3.4   Gender is dynamic
The dynamic aspect of gender refers to the shifting nature of gender across time and place. Again feminism exemplifies clearly how the understanding of women changed dramatically during the 20th century (see for example advertisement images), where amongst other things, the economic and political roles of women altered dramatically in especially Western societies. Feminist views therefore provide clear-cut examples of replacing specific constructions of gender with other constructions of gender (Wetherell 1996). Advertisements in the mid-20th century often portrayed women as being restricted to domestic roles. Advertisements today do not carry such blatant forms of sexism, but subtle examples of gender specific roles may still be present. Can you think of any examples in this regard?

7.3.5   Gender is an active project
The world we live in today emphasises the differences between men and women in various ways, for example, schoolgoing children are required to wear school uniforms according to their gender and a multitude of personal attire and grooming products (from shoes to moisturiser) are aimed at a specific gender. We are constantly reminded of our gender, but we are not passive recipients since we actively buy and wear the 'correct' school uniform and buy the appropriate products. From a social constructionist perspective gender is thus not something that one is born with, but it is an active project that is continuously under construction (Wetherell 1996).

7.3.6   Gender and power relations
Power relations are described by many as central to gender. One of the strong motivational forces for the feminist movement(s) was a general unequal power distribution between men and women. **Patriarchy**, for example, is an expression of power that can be observed in almost all societies. The church has often functioned as a secondary socialisation agent that has reiterated patriarchy. Today certain churches still play such a role, while other churches play an activist role to promote equality.

Having given this broad perspective on how a gender identity can be understood, the focus will now be on the largest and most enduring social movement of the 20th century that challenged gender relations in every sphere of life. This movement became known as feminism.

7.4   Feminism
The term **feminism** is widely used, defined and misunderstood. For example, one often hears that a woman would say: 'I am not a feminist, but ...', and then they make a statement that resonates with core feminist thinking. A certain stereotype of 'a feminist' (eg someone who does not like men and dresses and grooms herself in a specific manner) seems to have developed over the years and many

women do not want to be associated with such an image. Despite the reluctance of many women to be typecast as feminists, the core meaning of the term is largely accepted, at least publicly, in South Africa. A general definition of feminism is that men and women should have equal rights. Such rights are interpreted in their broadest sense to include important spheres of life such as political, economic, health, educational and sexual rights. Certain authors refer to **women's rights movements** as the main catalyst for reforming the political climate so that women are treated as equal self-determining individuals – gender is thus a dynamic construct that is actively reconstructed by feminists. Beyond women's rights, feminism developed as a critical theoretical standpoint that focuses on the experiences of women.

However, according to Amina Mama, not all women's movements are necessarily feminist in principle as women organisations are even (ab)used to mobilise for the ideologies of undemocratic regimes. In this regard she cites an example of Nigerian wives who sponsored women's programmes in order to secure support for 'corrupt dictatorships run by their husbands' (Salo 2001). Various other examples of the support women give to 'masculinist hegemonic domination', as described by Theresa Barnes, are listed by Desiree Lewis (2008). When defining specific women's movements as part of the larger feminist struggle, such movements should encompass the basic principle of equality since gender equality cannot transpire within a society where human rights of particular groups of people are under threat or undermined. We will return to this issue when discussing intersectionality, feminism and men's social movements in South Africa in the next section.

The development of feminism is often analysed by referring to the three waves of the women's movements. The first wave was observed towards the end of the 19th and beginning of the 20th centuries. The second wave gained momentum in the 1960s and dominated for almost three decades and the third wave emerged in the early 1990s. The first two waves are associated with European and North American developments, mostly led by white middle-class women, and it is only in the third wave that feminism is giving wider recognition in more countries and socioeconomic classes. Other outlines of feminism do not refer to the different waves but focus on the different strands of feminism, each with a particular history embedded within a specific world view (eg liberal, radical, black and Marxist feminism). Yet the observed waves of feminism draw our attention to certain historic events in the late 19th and 20th centuries that served as an impetus to broaden women's rights movements. The Industrial Revolution, World War II

and globalisation all played a role in the development of women's movements in general and feminist theory in particular.

The Industrial Revolution challenged existing gender relations profoundly since changed labour relations came into existence. According to Wiesner-Hanks (2011) the women's rights movements were one strand of social movement amongst many that wanted to counter the social problems associated with industrialism. This notion of a 'family wage' was developed which was paid to certain men in specific occupations. Women and children were paid a pittance compared to men, even though they may have worked the same number of hours. Eventually certain types of jobs were reserved for men and the economic production of women and children decreased.

Decades later, during World War II, women took over many jobs, especially in manufacturing, since large numbers of men were occupied in the war. With the end of the war, men wanted to return to their jobs and therefore the image of women as full-time homemakers was upheld in the public domain to encourage women to give up their jobs and the concomitant independence it brought. The result was that large numbers of women who became full-time housewives felt something amiss in their lives. Women, especially middle-class women in Western countries, were by and large excluded from economic production and economic consumption was under the control of husbands, for example a married woman could usually not buy a house (or make any large purchase) independently from her husband. In addition, effective contraception meant smaller families, children attended formal educational institutions for increasingly longer periods and more home appliances meant less heavy work in middle-class, and even working class households. Within such a socio-historical milieu feminist writings, such as those by Simone de Beauvoir, became widely read (in different languages). De Beauvoir (1949) argued that men were seen as the norm or the 'Subject'. Women, almost as an afterthought are described as the 'Other'. In this regard the theorist Anna Tripp (2000) highlights this general division between men and women within the family context by referring to an archaic English expression 'the world and his wife'. Similarly, Wiesner-Hanks (2011) states that in many societies women's life stages could be summed up in relation to their reproductive phase that is linked to their relationship with men: 'virgin, wife, widow'. Critical feminism and specific socio-historical conditions gave the Women's Movement momentum on an unprecedented scale – the second wave of feminism.

A singular 'sisterhood' never existed but black women, women from a working class background, women from developing countries, women from the East, women within particular religious traditions and a multitude of women from other socio-historical contexts made their voices increasingly heard. The 1995 Fourth Women's Conference in Beijing is a well-known example where not only activists and academics, but also policy-makers and women in key positions, came together and reached the conclusion that the specifics of a socio-historical milieu may divide women more than the term 'women' can unite them. The discussion on intersectionality in section 7.4.9 will illuminate these thoughts that are related to the third wave of feminism. A discussion on the South African scenario will also show the complexity of the challenges experienced by women.

The explanation is intended to provide a basic outline of different types of feminist thinking and it does not take the nuanced developments of the different strands into consideration. Each of these types of feminism has been criticised and counter-arguments have been developed which, over time, led to an increase or decrease in the popularity of specific strands. The radical, Marxist and liberal strands of feminism can be seen as three early strands of theoretical feminism.

7.4.1 Radical feminism

In radical feminism it is argued that men are the beneficiaries of gender exploitation and hence the blame for the inequalities between men and women should be placed on the shoulders of men. Childcare and housework are seen as unpaid work that women do for men and which simultaneously ensures that women are excluded from any positions of power in society. Clearly the family is a central institution of oppression within such an argument where men have power and women do not – the classical definition of patriarchy. In order to change this state of affairs, women have to take action and many radical feminists believe that this should happen without the help of men. It is even further argued by specific groups of radical feminists (a 'radical' form of radical feminism) that only lesbian women can be true feminists since only they can have meaningful domestic lives and intimate relationships independently of men. An even more extreme belief by a small group of radical feminists is that women are morally superior to men and matriarchy should replace patriarchy. In this view men are not only responsible for the exploitation of women but also other negative aspects such as war and the destruction of the environment. A more moderate radical feminist view is that men and women

are basically the same and that differences between them are largely the result of social construction (Haralambos & Holborn 2000).

7.4.2 Marxist feminism

According to Marxist feminists the root of women's exploitation is capitalism. They do not deny that men in general benefit from women's unpaid work, but capitalists are the primary beneficiaries of this work. In addition, women also bear and raise future generations of workers for the benefit of capitalists. It is postulated that the notion of private property and not owning the means of production are disadvantaging women. A distinction is drawn between women from the ruling class and the proletariat and, unlike radical feminists, it is believed that men and women from the working classes can work together to change society. It is believed that in a new socialist society with its emphasis on communal ownership, gender inequalities will disappear (Haralambos & Holborn 2000). The importance of gender in relation to class is thus underlined here, but with the aim to eradicate the differences by wiping out class and gender divisions within a new social order.

7.4.3 Liberal feminism

Liberal feminism probably appealed to the greatest number of people since its inception, as the core views are not considered as extreme as the previous two types of feminism. According to liberal feminists both men and women are disadvantaged when living in a society of gender inequalities since neither men nor women can live full, rich lives in such societies. Whereas women cannot develop their skills to step into positions of power, men cannot express their emotions adequately, which means that potentially intimate relationships (such as father–child relationships) are superficial or distant. Within this line of thinking a change in the culture and the thinking of individuals is required to reach greater gender equality. Changing the socialisation of children, developing and practising policies that give equal access to opportunities for men and women and removing sexist images in the media are examples of strategies that contribute to greater gender equality (Haralambos & Holborn 2000).

All three of the above expressions of feminism developed within a Western framework and understanding of gender inequalities. All three of them have developed and became more nuanced over time but above are their initial core assumptions. In reaction to these expressions of feminism, black feminism became a strong fourth voice within such societies.

7.4.4   Black feminism

Black feminism, in for example the UK and the USA, developed because many black women felt that the feminist movement did not address their experiences. For example, the family lives of middle-class white women were used as the norm, but many black women had entirely different family experiences – there was thus a 'racist bias'. Black women in the USA struggled side by side with black men for civil rights but in these organisations men dominated and women's specific concerns did not receive much attention – there was thus a 'masculinist bias' (Haralambos & Holborn 2000).

A basic premise of black feminism is that black women should draw from their own experiences. A classic example from the 19th century is often cited to illustrate this point. In the USA in 1852 it was argued by white males that women should not have equal rights to men because they are fragile and physically weak. The fragile portrayal of femininity was often used by men, but on this occasion it was challenged by an African-American activist with a passionate speech containing the famous expression 'Ain't I a Woman?' (Weldon 2008). She was referring to the experiences of slave women working as farm labourers who had to do hard physical labour. Through this speech she highlighted very different expressions of femininity that were condoned by white males.

7.4.5   African feminism

Black feminism should not be equated with African feminism since the former often developed in contexts where black women are a minority (in actual numbers and in terms of power). In the African context women are not a minority in numerical terms but may still have less power than men. Elaine Salo (2001) asserts that there are in essence two views on feminism in Africa. The one view, portrayed by Patricia Macfadden, is that gender hierarchies were embedded in African societies and that such power inequalities were intensified by colonialism. The other view, portrayed by Gwendolyn Mikell, is that gender inequality on the African continent is by and large the result of colonisation. In this view women were integrated in the societal structures of the pre-colonial times. In tandem with this latter view, Oyeronke Oyewumi argued in *The Invention of Women; Making an African Sense of Western Gender Discourses* (1997) that gender is not a central social category for the Yoruba (in western Nigeria) but rather seniority as it relates to chronological age. She argues that one person is always senior or junior to another person within the kin system. With increasing age one usually becomes more senior.

According to her analysis seniority is more important than wealth, rank or sex in the stratification of society. She argues that the Yoruba language does not indicate gender and social distinctions are not made according to anatomical differences. She concludes that power is not assigned according to gender as is the case in Western societies. Although she has been admired for challenging the entrenched gender construct, she has also been criticised from various quarters by pointing out that seniority on its own is not the determining source of power in all contexts in the Yoruba society. Seniority in relation to other constructs forms the basis of power. Further, the fact that gender is not indicated so explicitly in language does not mean that it does not play a role (Bakare-Yusuf 2002).

As pointed out by Amina Mama, the way in which African feminism is defined will largely determine which of the above two views in relations to colonialism are supported, but what is perhaps of greater importance is the experiences of African women today. Although many women are trapped in the basic task of surviving on the African continent, many African women aspire to the same feminist principles of political, economic and social equality that are aspired to everywhere (Salo 2001).

7.4.6   Eco-feminism

Eco-feminists equate women with nature. Eco-feminists argue that similar to the way women are under the domination of patriarchal rule, nature is dominated by culture. It is further postulated that these dominations by culture and men originate from a similar world view. A kind of logic of domination exists where it is believed that human beings are morally superior to things such as rocks and plants and therefore humans are morally justified to subordinate plants and rocks. Eco-feminists are protesting against a kind of thinking wherein the wellbeing of other beings is separated from one's own wellbeing, which then leads to a way of life in which one does not care for other beings. Among other things, eco-feminists want to underscore the feminine side of human beings and believe in living in harmony with nature. In this regard certain expressions of eco-feminism have been taken to task for not really being feminist since they want to assert expressions of femininity without critically reflecting on whether those expressions of femininity are damaging to women or not (Davion 1994).

Apart from eco-feminism, other newer forms of feminism are described as backlashes against the initial formulations of feminism. One such complicated form of feminism, the status of which many question, is conservative feminism.

7.4.7 Conservative feminism

Classic forms of conservative feminism insisted that women should be treated with respect. The traditional roles of wife and mother are underscored in this form of feminism and men are urged to fulfil their roles as caretakers of families. Such views resonate with many conservative religious groupings. According to Judith Stacey, new conservative feminism also has a 'profamily' stance where the general feminist view that the 'personal is political' is seen as too invasive and even threatening to family life. Second, conservative feminists regard gender differences as positive and characteristics that are traditionally associated with women, of which mothering is a prime example, are embraced. And thirdly, it is believed that there are more important political struggles than the struggles against male domination. Betty Friedan argued that women struggle so much to have careers and public achievements and in the process they cannot realise or admit their basic needs for intimacy, having children and a family. In short, the goals of feminism are seen as a stumbling block for women. It is believed that both men and women want families and will join in new egalitarian families with childcare needs being realised (Stacey 1983).

Although it may almost appear as if such articulations are not really feminist, conservative feminism is reacting against the **androgynous** expressions that certain early feminists believed we should be heading towards. Furthermore, families are the prime institutions for raising children and other models or experiments in raising children did not succeed on a wide scale. It is argued that egalitarian relationships struggle to succeed in the long term partly because there are not clearly demarcated spheres of life (Stacey 1983).

Another form of backlash feminism has been termed 'new feminism'.

7.4.8 New feminism

In many developed countries such as the UK, or even in developing countries such as South Africa, certain sectors of women (often white and middle class) may feel that feminism is not applicable to their lives. Feminism can be seen as consisting of 'politically correct language' that places restrictions on women's personal lives including what they should wear and think or how they should engage in sexual pleasure. One can argue that feminism may not resonate with such women by oversimplifying the relations between men and women (Haralambos & Holborn 2004). Ironically, the main reason why these women do not feel that feminism applies to them is exactly because they are reaping the benefits from the gains made by feminists in the past. Women associated with new feminism had access to good educational institutions, they are recognised as legally mature persons who can buy cars and houses which they may drive and live in alone if they choose to. They can take part in sport, marry who they like or marry nobody, travel alone and go to bars without 'male escorts'.

Has feminism thus achieved its goals for such women? It could be argued that despite the strides made towards gender equality, women are still not paid equally or given the same opportunities if they venture into acting or directing, engineering, the diplomatic service or competitive sport. In others words, men still dominate many powerful sectors of society. Moreover, if women decide to have children, they will probably experience that combining a career and motherhood is somehow more difficult for them than their male counterparts. For example, in academic sectors across the world, it is still found that men are promoted much earlier in life compared to women because of women's lack of (or lack of access to) professional networking skills, their nurturing nature, childcare responsibilities and so forth. These observations of career patterns resonate with the experiences of women in many economic sectors of society and it is mostly young women at junior levels of their careers who report that they are experiencing sexual discrimination. As they become older and more senior new forms of discrimination present themselves (Rabe & Rugunanan 2012).

Apart from 'new feminism', the term post-feminism also developed. Postfeminists reject a 'single metanarrative' to explain the plight of women. Where the three early feminist strands focused on the inequalities between men and women, postfeminists highlight the differences between women (Haralambos & Holborn 2004). Yet, this was not an entirely new development in feminism since Marxist feminism drew our attention to the simultaneous effect of class and gender from the outset. Black feminism highlighted the importance of both race and gender. In addition, a strand of feminism that has been dubbed 'queer feminism' that is clearly articulated in, among others, the work of Judith Butler (2004), focuses on gender and sexual orientation. Such diverse formulations that grew out of diverse experiences are formalised in the theoretical term intersectionality.

7.4.9 Intersectionality

The term intersectionality is attributed to Kimberlé Crenshaw. In 1989, Crenshaw used it to illuminate the different experiences of different women. As was described under black feminism earlier, the famous expression 'Ain't I a Woman?' (Weldon 2008) that highlighted the interplay between race and gender gave impetus to the fact that gender discrimination does not happen in isolation. Weldon argues though that one cannot simply use the discourse of the 'double oppression' of race and gender that black women experience (or the often cited 'triple oppression' used to describe black women's race, gender and class experiences during the apartheid years in South Africa), since it does not give justice to how race and gender can intersect. In other words there are no women without race and the racial category of any woman will influence her gender experiences. Being white and/or heterosexual thus also intersects with gender. The hierarchical nature of the constructs of race and gender and how they influence each other within a specific context is thus of importance. Social divisions that are thought to be 'enduring' such as class, race, sexual orientation and (dis)ability, intersect with gender in any individual's life. Similarly, men's race, class, sexual orientation and (dis)ability have a simultaneous influence on their experiences as men. Categories of social relations can thus not be understood in isolation (Weldon 2008). These expressions resonate strongly with the third wave of feminism.

This diversification of identity is commented on by Lennard Davis (2002) in terms of identity politics and social movements. According to Davis all identity struggles are characterised by 'the establishment of the identity against the societal definitions that were formed largely by oppression'. One of the central aims is to replace negative descriptions with positive ones so that an identity can be 'normalised'. In practice this would imply that basic rights have to be acknowledged to combat discrimination. In trying to achieve more political power, group solidarity is needed amongst the members. Only once this has been achieved, can a redefinition of the struggle emerge wherein the focus is diversity within the group and the subtleties and nuances of identity are acknowledged. Yet this acknowledgement of diversity in identities may entail conflict among various group members. The recognition of the diversities between women that is formalised in the term intersectionality, is thus expected when looking at the development of feminism as a social movement over several decades.

This tension between a unified gender struggle and acknowledging the different experiences of different women clearly manifests itself in the South African context.

7.4.10 South African feminism

South African feminism should of course be understood within the broader context of African feminism, but let us look more closely at the specific South African situation in relation to feminism.

Feminist research in South Africa

In South Africa the intersectionality of gender experiences seem to have been present from early on in feminist work. The main reason for this is probably that in South Africa women had such diverse experiences based on their racial categorisation. As mentioned, the so-called 'triple oppression of black women' (race, gender and class) has often been repeated as it was such a salient aspect of South African society. To be classified black meant that one was excluded from middle and upper socioeconomic classes and patriarchy in its various forms was experienced.

Jacklyn Cock's (1980) book, entitled *Maids and Madams*, provided a clear example of how the experiences of black women, working as domestic workers, differed from their white female employers. Although Cock's work preceded the theory on intersectionality, the way in which these different identities are connected and interwoven are clearly demonstrated. Shireen Ally (2010) furthered the understanding of domestic workers in the 'new South Africa' with new labour legislation by analysing the complicated overlap of the private and public spheres in the daily lives of domestic workers. Cock presented one of the few early works in South Africa where the hierarchical power relations between women are laid bare, again preceding the identified gender hierarchy amongst men as explained by Connell (see section 7.5.2).

Other influential works over the years focused on the specific experiences of black women as they relate to other significant identities. The seminal book *Women of Phokeng* by Belinda Bozzoli (1991) not only focuses on being a black woman of a particular class, but also on being born at a particular place and having experiences of urbanisation during a particular historical period. The fact that both Bozzoli and Cock are well versed in Marxist feminism explains their sharp grasp of the class and gender intersections in South Africa and the reality of the racial divisions could hardly be ignored (even though other sociologists underplayed it). Much later work by Elaine Salo (2002) on the women in Manenberg, Cape Town, and Kamilla Naidoo's and Kavita Misra's (2008) work on the women in the Winterveld area had a similar strong geographical and historical setting that enhanced the understanding of women with a particular racial and socioeconomic standing. In Naidoo's and Misra's work the added realities of living with HIV also form part of the experiences of women.

Activism and feminism in South Africa

A further characteristic of feminism in South Africa is the strong activist element. The 1956 march by women to the Union building in Pretoria to protest against the carrying of 'passes' and the current protests outside courts during prominent cases of rape and violence against women are examples of this. (A pass was an identity document that all black people in so-called 'white' areas had to carry to prove that they were there 'legitimately'. It was usually obtained if employed by a white person.)

Yet, if the protests by women during the apartheid years are studied more closely, it transpires that women protested against the pass laws by arguing that they could not fulfil their roles as mothers, wives and even domestic workers effectively under such conditions. Making claims to those roles that are associated with the domestic world of women proved successful since black women, unlike men, were not required to carry passes until much later. Such claims by women clearly resonate with conservative feminism but in a more dynamic manner, which is referred to as 'conservative militancy' (Britton & Fish 2009).

Black women in South Africa also shared the predicament of black women in the USA during the civil rights movement that gave rise to black feminism. The struggle against a racist regime often necessitated a united front (with men) against the state and by necessity women's rights took a back seat. The strong racial divides in South Africa also made any sisterhood across racial boundaries difficult but a few organisations, most notably, The Black Sash, tried to overcome such divides. Initially, the organisation had a white leadership to demonstrate that not all white people supported the apartheid policies of the time. In the 1960s this ideology shifted and women from different racial categories worked side by side in the organisation addressing issues such as human rights and providing legal assistance for families of political prisoners (Britton & Fish 2009).

During the early 1990s towards the end of the apartheid rule in South Africa, different women's organisations, civic movements, religious groups, informal groups and women in exile were brought together under an umbrella organisation called the Women's National Coalition (WNC). This was not an easy process. As Shireen Hassim (2003) remarked, women's protests tended to be sporadic and often centre on specific issues with the result that women's social movements were characterised by upsurges and declines. The tension between addressing racial and gender injustices continues in present-day South Africa.

Challenges facing feminism in South Africa

There are disturbing occurrences of women's groups supporting or turning a blind eye to authoritarian masculine rule in South Africa after the first 1994 democratic election in South Africa. Hassim (2003) used the term 'gender pact' to portray how the belief amongst gender activists exists that the state will ensure gender equality. Indeed, the young democracy of South Africa developed various quotas and reached milestones for employing relatively high percentages of women in seemingly powerful positions. This, however, does not ensure equality in itself, just as it was stated above that all women's movements are not feminist movements. All women's leadership does not entail feminist leadership (Lewis 2008).

A further challenge is the extreme violence and humiliating acts that are perpetrated against women who fall outside 'the patriarchal heterosexist family' for wearing short skirts, being lesbian or not being 'proper' in some way. These incidents are described as part of 'the regulatory ethos of masculinist post-colonial nation-building' (Lewis 2008). One of the responses to these attempts to control women's bodies, is the first so-called 'Slutwalk' that took place in September 2011 (widely advertised on social networks such as Facebook), by particularly younger women of all races. This march follows similar ones in places such as Toronto, Mexico City and Delhi. Dressing up in a provocative manner (as so-called 'sluts') the message of the march is that women may not be raped regardless of how they present themselves, in other words rape is not okay and 'no' to any type of sexual act means 'no' regardless of the circumstances. An attempt is thus made to reclaim public spaces for women. Criticising overt gender discrimination and laying bare hidden gender oppression have become characteristic of South African feminist thinking. The feminist mantra that the 'private is public' should still be taken seriously, otherwise, as Raewyn Connell (2011) remarked, we may be one of the few countries where public patriarchy is being eradicated but we are losing the battle against private patriarchy.

It could be argued that the strength of the feminist work produced in South Africa is its close links to the lived experiences and struggles of women in different sectors of society. This feminist strength in South Africa resonates with feminist traditions in other developing countries that are sometimes referred to as Third World feminism (Ackerly & Attanasi 2009). Despite this rich tradition of activist feminism, Amanda Gouws (2010) analyses how local feminist movements continue a struggle to be heard alongside a particular government discourse on women (grouping them with children and people living with disabilities) that she describes as 'State feminist inactivism'. Local feminist movements are also being excluded from international feminist debates due to financial barriers that prevent many women from partaking in decision-making forums.

Both political struggles and feminist typologies are helping us to understand the 'similarities, differences, and critical dialogues among feminisms' (Ackerly & Attanasi 2009).

7.5 Masculinity studies

From the long and complicated history of feminist studies it is clear that women reconstructed the way gender is understood forever, but what does this imply for men? From a liberal feminist point of view, both men and women should be involved in changing current gender relations. Tripp (2000: 11) argues that:

[i]n any individual context, femininity is only intelligible through its differences to masculinity and vice versa. If this is the case, then feminist redefinitions of what it means to be a woman will have a knock-on effect on understandings and experiences of what it means to be a man.

In addition, Connell argues that there are multiple reasons for the involvement of men in changing gender relations such as the fact that gender relations are embedded in the way people live their daily lives. Gender relations are dynamic and are continuously shifting and if women change the way they live their lives, it necessarily demands changes in the way men live since it entails new ways of engaging in economic arrangements and emotional and power relationships. Moves towards gender equality require the co-operation of men since it touches on every aspect of life (Connell 2003).

In the South African context, two leading masculinity studies researchers, Robert Morrell (2001) and Kopane Ratele (2008), both argued that the negative perceptions about men have to be addressed since they are not applicable to all men. The third opening case study to this chapter refers to the actions of men as perpetrators of violence, but we should guard against generalising such horrific cases of violence and disrespect against women to all men. In fact, various groupings of men also fall victim to violence perpetrated by other men.

However, not all feminists are prepared to work with men as there are deep suspicions that men are redefining feminism and women's issues as gender issues. In other words, gender is a term that can be hijacked by men to get it under their control. The tensions between masculinity studies and feminism will probably continue and perhaps it is a healthy state of affairs since it would guard against reversing the gains made by feminism.

But what are masculinity studies then? Have men not always been studied? Have they not always been the 'Subject' as Simone de Beauvoir and others proposed? The answers to these questions are yes and no. Men have been studied as if they were the 'given' or the 'norm', but they have not been studied in past times as gendered beings. For example, where women complained about always being seen in relation to men (daughter, wife, sister, etc), men's relations with women, from the perspective of men, did not receive much attention. These previous gaps in research changed dramatically in the last three decades or so and the literature on masculinity studies grew in leaps and bounds. Tripp (2000) states that masculinity is no longer regarded as singular and monolithic but also as complex, plural and a cultural product. The outline of the social constructionist approach to gender above should make it clear that all people are regarded as gendered beings.

7.5.1 Patriarchy revisited

One of the key themes associated with men from a feminist perspective relates to patriarchy and power. This term is complex but closer inspection helps us to understand the hierarchal order that not only exists between men and women but also between men.

Patriarchy may be understood as the power that men have over women, but a more precise definition would be the power that certain men have over women and men. Within the family context a father who controls the finances, owns the property and has the final decision-making power is the patriarch. Young men thus may become patriarchs if they reach a certain age, but this is not always a given. However, women are given over to husbands by fathers in patriarchal societies and thus stay under the rule and control of men.

Patriarchy is not limited to one form though. Sylvia Walby (1997), for example, distinguished between private patriarchy and public patriarchy. The former refers to patriarchy in the domestic sphere, usually referring to control by the father, while the latter refers to power in the public domain where legislation and embedded structures are denying women certain rights and discriminate against them on a collective level. Another example of different forms of patriarchy is 'dual patriarchy' that refers to the combined power of colonial administrators and husbands/

fathers over women in colonised countries (Wiesner-Hanks 2011). Bozzoli (1983) analysed such a manifestation of dual patriarchy by focusing on the formation of the state and patriarchy in the South African context. Bozzoli argues that *patriarchies*, instead of a singular simplified form of patriarchy, must be acknowledged. Similar to the establishment of a 'family wage' for certain male labourers in the formation of industrialisation in England, different reasoning was adopted with male labourers earning much higher wages than black labourers in the context of the mining sector. For example, in the case of white mineworkers it was believed to be beneficial that a man should settle with his wife and children in town near the mine, but black mineworkers should work without their family members in close proximity.

In the South African context then, black men and white men were placed in a hierarchical order during the colonising and apartheid periods, with black men always taking a secondary position. Even currently in South Africa, certain sectors of the white community may still regard white superiority as a given, a fact that is possibly fuelled by thousands of black male labourers working for 'white bosses' in, for example, the construction and maintenance industries.

However, in present-day South Africa *dominant* black masculinities come to the fore more regularly and openly and 'tradition' is often cited as a justification for chauvinistic and scandalous behaviour towards women. The taxi rank incident was justified by the men involved by pointing out that the woman wore a mini-skirt that is 'not traditional' (note that similar cases took place in Kenya and Swaziland). This invention of tradition by men to suit or support any action has been commented on extensively by anthropologists (Van der Vliet 2001; Spiegel & McAllister 2001). In addition, contested masculinities are 'performed' (or constructed) in the South African mass media on a daily basis in advertisements and speeches by certain male politicians. A particular notion of what it means to 'be a man' is regularly enacted while at the same time other forms of masculinity are being excluded. In this regard Theresa Barnes (2007) observed that many of the current high profile struggles within universities centre on black masculinities replacing white masculinities.

7.5.2 Male experiences

Focusing on these extreme cases ignores the majority of men who are neither perpetrators of violence nor present themselves as powerful individuals. Kimmel (2009) states that discussions on male power make men uncomfortable and defensive. He sums up the reaction by certain men in

the following way: 'What do you mean men have all the power? What are you talking about? I have no power at all. I'm completely powerless. My wife bosses me around, my children boss me around, my boss bosses me around. I have no power at all!' On an individual level, men do not necessarily feel powerful, in fact they may see themselves as victims of reverse discrimination. But Kimmel states that power is not the possession of individual men, rather it is 'woven into the fabric of our lives' and 'it is most invisible to those who are most empowered'. Kimmel argues that power is more prominently in the hands of certain groups of men as opposed to all men.

It is on this note that Connell's (1995) analysis of a hierarchy of power between men, with hegemonic masculinity at the top, is useful. According to Connell, *hegemonic masculinity* refers to a dominant expression of masculinity that could be regarded as the 'ideal type' within a particular society. In Western societies, such an expression of hegemonic masculinity would include employment, being heterosexual, married and a father and have at least moderate sporting abilities. Hegemonic masculinity is often held up as the ideal or standard that boys should aspire to. However, not many men embody all aspects of hegemonic masculinity yet they may be complicit in hegemonic masculinity. The remaining identified forms of masculinity include complicit masculinity as well as marginal and subordinated masculinities. *Complicit forms of masculinity* neither embody nor challenge hegemonic masculinity, but refer to a large number of men who benefit from being male in general. Men in this category are not blatantly authoritative, but they benefit from the dividend of patriarchy, albeit in a limited way. They make compromises with women but benefit from the general privileged position of men. *Marginal masculinities* are often interlinked with class and race in opposition to hegemonic masculinity. Neither race nor class are fixed identities either and these aspects differ in importance for men in different contexts. Connell refers to black sportsmen in the USA to explain marginal masculinities – although certain sports are dominated by black men (eg basketball) the high status given to black male athletes does not filter through to black men in general. A fourth identified masculinity refers to relations between men where dominance and *subordination* are noted. If the hegemonic masculinity for a particular society is heterosexual, homosexual men are viewed as exemplifying a subordinate position. Connell regards subordination as more than stigmatisation since it can, for example, entice homophobic attacks. A variety of men can be placed in such a subordinated position, depending on the situation, and it is often signified by name calling such as 'pushover' or 'wimp'.

Masculinity in crisis?

A question that has been asked repeatedly in masculinity studies is whether there is a 'crisis in masculinity'? Men's extreme demonstrations of violence, boys' general poor performance in school compared to girls, an increasing number of health problems among men, their lack of responsibility as fathers, increased suicide rates and their struggles with unemployment all seem to point to such a crisis of masculinity. The feminist project empowered women, but did it in the process emasculate men?

There are various answers to these questions in Western societies and on the African continent. In South Africa specifically it seems as if men struggle to define their place in the new democratic era of South African history. Some may embrace the changes brought about by the new Constitution and the possibilities it opens up for new forms of masculinity. For other men these changes undermine their sense of self as men especially since they are often portrayed as 'the enemy' and they feel lost or react violently to reclaim the power they have lost (Walker 2005).

Kopano Ratele (2008) focused on African masculinities and the perception that African men are reluctant to support feminist action. He argues that the term hegemonic masculinity describes the hierarchical power differentials that include the subordination of women (as a group) to men (as a group). This subordination of women is clearly visible in society when looking at acts of violence against women by men. Ratele relates male practices and experiences to social conditions and psychosocial realities. Within this understanding, men who are subordinate to other men, but part of the 'powerful gender group', require specific analysis. Ratele identified occupation and income as well as age as key factors to the understanding of African masculinities – more specifically, the intersection of gender, age and unemployment/poverty on the African continent. In Marlize Rabe's (2006) study on fatherhood amongst black mineworkers, the centrality of being a breadwinner, for working class men in particular, has been reiterated. However, if working class men are not working, men feel worthless and ashamed of their unemployed status. The high unemployment figures in South Africa and the vulnerability of specific economic sectors (such as construction and mining that are dominated by male workers) to economic cycles, imply that thousands of South African men are unemployed and unable to change their economic prospects. On an individual level then, many South African men are in a vulnerable position since they are, or may become, unemployed, and they have not found new avenues for constructing an acceptable self-image.

Men's social movements

What then about men on a collective level? Morrell (2005) reiterated that dramatic shifts towards gender equity in South Africa have been made in policies, but in reality, gender inequality is still rife. Morrell argued that within this climate of slow change towards gender equality, men's movements have been under pressure to support gender transformation. Men's movements can be defined as targeting men to address specific gender challenges (not to be confused with a movement that consists largely of men but with a different aim, eg firearm enthusiasts or certain sports clubs). Although men can contribute towards gender transformation on an individual basis, men can augment such individual initiatives and do far more on a collective basis. Although certain collective action by men has been successful in this regard, men's organisations are by and large not geared towards gender equality or not even supportive of feminism. A distinction has thus to be created between 'men's movements' that are seen as 'reactive, antifeminist and committed to the restoration of male power' and 'new men's movements' that are believed to be 'profeminist and committed to gender justice'.

In practice, most men's movements cannot be categorised in such a distinct manner. In an analysis of South Africa's men's movements, of which there are relatively few, Morrell (2005) uses Michael Messner's model and classifies three distinct types. The first type is defending male privilege where hegemonic masculinity is enshrined and the 'losses' of men are bemoaned. Such a movement will either limit the gains by women or highlight how men are disadvantaged. These movements seem to be short-lived in South Africa and without major followings. The second grouping that strives towards gender justice often addresses the high rates of rape and domestic violence against women in South Africa (see section 11.7 on domestic violence in Chapter 11). Movements with such a specific goal seem to be more successful than those that strive towards general gender equality. The third type deals with the 'crisis of masculinity'. Although this crisis has been in dispute ever since it was first mentioned, such organisations focus on the things they believe men should do. Many of these organisations in South Africa have a religious basis and issues relating to 'responsible fatherhood' often form a major theme.

Although the overt expressions of the latter movements' goals are aimed at sharing responsibilities with women, an underlying implication is the restoration of male authority.

Gay organisations do not seem to find a haven in any of the above categories and therefore they operate separately, often with a distinct racial character in the South Africa context.

7.5.3 Masculinity and homosexuality in South Africa

Queer feminism was referred to above and the experiences of lesbian women as activists or as victims of violence were mentioned. Similar to the study of feminism, the experiences of homosexual men played an enormously important role in the study of masculinities. Challenging hegemonic masculinity has been a contributing factor to the importance of studying homosexual men, but, again similar to feminism, the experiences of homosexual men are placed at the centre of this approach. HIV initially spread the fastest amongst homosexual men in Western societies (in South Africa the pandemic is as much a heterosexual as a homosexual phenomenon) and this also added to the attention given to homosexual men by researchers from various disciplines. Queer theory is a term coined by Teresa de Lauretis. It is a large discipline on its own. In addition to focusing on gay and lesbian experiences, it incorporates a focus on sexual minorities such as bisexuals, intersex, transgender, transsexual and asexual individuals, all of which were given scant or no attention in modern theoretical paradigms such as Lesbian and Gay Studies (Halperin 2003).

Glen Elder (2005) analysed the representations of homosexual men of South Africa by focusing on the tourism industry of Cape Town. The leisure industry has targeted gay men for the past few decades as they supposedly have more money to spend – the 'pink dollar'. However, in targeting gay men as tourists to Cape Town, Elder uncovered the subtle (or not so subtle) racial bias in this industry which marginalises black gay men:

Promotional materials also have pictures of twenty something, well-defined white men making clear that the 'expected' clientele, once again, is white, middle-class and male.

It is as if the existence of black homosexual men is almost silenced.

This 'invisibility' of black gay men points to another important issue relating to homosexual acts – the argument that homosexual acts are 'unnatural' and not African. In countries such as Zimbabwe homosexual acts are even criminalised, a practice that was common in many Western countries a few decades ago as well. Earlier evidence of homosexual acts between black men on the mines and in prisons (Moodie 1994; Niehaus 2002) was deprecated as imitations of heterosexual unions in the absence of wives. Men having sex with men (MSM) has become a common term to use, especially in HIV and AIDS research, to avoid the complexities of whether men identify themselves as homosexual or not. Although this was indeed the case for many men, Dunbar Moodie in his research clearly indicated that certain men continued living as homosexual men long after leaving the mines. Marc Epprecht's (2005) research in Lesotho is an example of the open, long standing existence of homosexuality within black communities. Although homosexual unions may be specific to a particular African context (Reid 2005), the existence is undeniable.

The lack of tolerance for diversity on the African continent, including South Africa, is in fact the problem. The feminist observation that the insistence on the normative pattern of the 'patriarchal heterosexist family' that is used to control women, may also be used by men who support a particular hegemonic model of masculinity and are trying to suppress other forms of masculinity.

The work of Sylvia Tamale (2013) in Uganda is of importance here. She argues that there are links between 'civil liberties and the protection of nonconforming sexualities' where African leaders (just as in other places in the world) invent a 'moral panic' (such as homophobia) to divert attention from serious socioeconomic and political crises facing societies.

Summary

- This chapter on gender theory aimed to sensitise you to the centrality of gender in everyday life.
- The way in which we experience our bodies as well as the things we believe about ourselves and the way in which we present ourselves all have a strong gender basis.
- Feminism in its broadest sense changed and continues to change the way in which we think about gender.
- Both the critical and the activist components of feminism are of importance in the South African society where large numbers of women are still treated as second-class citizens despite the 'celebrations' of a handful of women in powerful positions.

- Narrow versions of femininity are often presented in the public domain to undermine the increasing variety of feminine power that women display in their everyday living.
- Masculinity studies challenge the one-dimensional view of men as the aggressive patriarch.
- The different responses of men in reaction to changed gender power relations have to be underlined as mainly negative portrayals of men are seen in the mass media. The variety of masculine experiences and actions should be recognised and given prominence.

ARE YOU ON TRACK?

1. Explain the importance of 'the body' in understanding gender.
2. Describe the social construction of gender.
3. Provide an outline of the different strands of feminism.
4. Write short notes on women in South Africa in relation to feminism.
5. Do you agree that masculinity studies are of importance in gender studies? Give reasons for your answer.

More sources to consult

Britton H, Fish J, Meintjies S (eds). 2009. *Women's Activism in South Africa. Working across Divides.* Scottsville: University of KwaZulu-Natal Press.

Gasa N (ed). 2007. *Women in South African History.* Cape Town: HSRC.

Gevisser M, Cameron E (eds). 1995. *Defiant Desire: Gay and Lesbian Lives in South Africa.* New York: Routledge.

Mkhize N, Bennett J, Reddy V, Moletsane R. 2010. *The Country We Want to Live In: Hate Crimes and Homophobia in the Lives of Black Lesbian South Africans.* Cape Town: HSRC Press.

Morrell R (ed). 2001. *Changing Men in Southern Africa.* Pietermaritzburg: University of Natal Press.

Reid G, Walker L (eds). 2005. *Men Behaving Differently. South African Men since 1994.* Cape Town: Double Storey Books.

Ruiters G (ed). 2008. *Gender Activism: Perspectives on the South African Transition, Institutional Culture and Everyday Life.* Grahamstown: Rhodes University Institute of Social and Economic Research/Rosa Luxembourg Foundation.

References

Ackerly B, Attanasi K. 2009. 'Global feminisms: Theory and ethics for studying gendered injustice'. *New Political Science*, 31(4): 543–555.

Ally S. 2010. *From Servants to Workers. South African Domestic Workers and the Democratic State.* Scottsville: University of KwaZulu-Natal Press.

Bakare-Yusuf B. 2002. '"Yoruba's don't do gender": A critical review of Oyeronke Oyewumi's *The Invention of Women: Making an African Sense of Western Gender Discourses*'. *African Gender in the New Millennium.* Dakar: CODESRIA.

Barnes T. 2007. 'Politics of the mind and body: Gender and institutional culture in African universities'. *Feminist Africa*, 8: 8–25.

Bozzoli B. 1983. 'Marxism, feminism and South African studies'. *Journal of Southern African Studies*, 9(2): 139–171.

Bozzoli B. 1991. *Women of Phokeng.* Johannesburg: Ravan Press.

Britton H, Fish J. 2009. 'Engendering civil society in democratic South Africa' in *Women's Activism in South Africa.* Britton H, Fish J, Meintjies S (eds). Scottsville: University of KwaZulu-Natal Press, 1–42.

Butler J. 2004. *Undoing Gender.* New York: Routledge.

Cock J. 1980. *Maids and Madams: A Study in the Politics of Exploitation.* Johannesburg: Ravan.

Connell R. 1994. 'South African Sociological Association's Congress'. University of Pretoria, 2011.

Connell R. 1995. *Masculinities.* Cambridge: Polity Press.

Connell R. 2003. 'The role of men and boys in achieving gender equality'. United Nations, EGM/Men-Boys-GE/2003/BP.1.

Connell R. 2011. *Confronting Equality: Gender, Knowledge and Global Change.* Cambridge: Polity Press.

Davion V. 1994. 'Is ecofeminism feminist?' in *Ecological Feminism.* Warren K (ed). Abingdon: Routledge, 8–27.

Davis LJ. 2002. *Bending Over Backwards. Disability, Dismodernism and other Difficult Positions.* New York: New York University Press.

De Beauvoir S. 1949. *The Second Sex.* London: Picador.

Elder G. 2005. 'Somewhere, over the rainbow: Cape Town, South Africa, as a "gay destination"' in *African Masculinities.* Ouzgane L, Morrell R (eds). Scottsville: University of KwaZulu-Natal Press, 43–59.

Epprecht M. 2005. 'Male-male sexuality in Lesotho: Two conversations' in *Men Behaving Differently.* Reid G, Walker L (eds). Cape Town: Double Storey Books, 183–204.

Gouws A. 2010. 'Feminism in South Africa today: Have we lost the praxis?' *Agenda: Empowering Women for Gender Equity,* 24(83): 13–23.

Halperin DM. 2003. 'The normalization of queer theory'. *Journal of Homosexuality,* 45(2/3/4): 339–343.

Haralambos M, Holborn M. 2000. *Sociology. Themes and Perspectives,* 5th ed. London: Collins Education.

Haralambos M, Holborn M. 2004. *Sociology. Themes and Perspectives,* 6th ed. London: Collins Education.

Hassim S. 2003. 'The gender pact and democratic consolidation: Institutionalizing gender equality in the South African state'. *Feminist Studies* 29(3): 504–28.

Jackson S. 2006. 'Gender, sexuality and heterosexuality. The complexity (and limits) of heteronormativity'. *Feminist Theory* 7(1): 105–21.

Kimmel M. 2009. *The Gendered Society.* New York: Oxford University Press.

Lewis D. 2008. 'South Africa, African feminism and challenges of solidarity' in *Gender Activism: Perspectives on the South African Transition, Institutional Culture and Everyday Life.* Ruiters G (ed). Grahamstown: Rhodes University Institute of Social and Economic Research, 56–71.

Moodie D. 1994. *Going for Gold: Men Mines and Migration.* Johannesburg: Witwatersrand University Press.

Morrell R. 2001. 'The times of change. Men and masculinity in South Africa' in *Changing Men in Southern Africa.* Morrell R (ed). Pietermaritzburg: University of Natal Press, 3–37.

Morrell R. 2005. 'Men, movements, and gender transformation in South Africa' in *African Masculinities.* Ouzgane L, Morrell R (eds). Scottsville: University of KwaZulu-Natal Press, 271–288.

Naidoo K, Misra K. 2008. 'Poverty and intimacy: Reflections on sexual exchange, reproductive dynamics and AIDS in South Africa'. *South African Review of Sociology,* 39(1): 1–17.

Niehaus I. 2002. 'Renegotiating masculinity in the South African Lowveld: Narratives of male-male sex in labour compounds and in prisons'. *African Studies,* 61(6): 77–97.

Norton AT, Herek GM. 2012. 'Heterosexuals' attitudes towards transgender people: Findings from a national probability sample of US adults.' *Sex Roles,* 66.

Pilane P. 2015. 'Patriarchy must fall'. *City Press,* 25 October 2015.

Rabe M. 2006. 'Black mineworkers' conceptualisations of fatherhood: A sociological exploration in the South African goldmining industry'. Doctoral thesis, UNISA.

Rabe M, Rugunanan P. 2012. 'Exploring gender and race amongst female sociologists exiting academia in South Africa'. *Gender and Education,* 24(5): 553–566.

Ratele K. 2008. 'Analysing males in Africa: Certain useful elements in considering ruling masculinities'. *African and Asian Studies,* 7: 515–536.

Reid G. 2005. 'A man is a man completely and a wife is a wife completely: Gender classification and performance amongst "ladies" and "gents" in Ermelo, Mpumalanga' in *Men Behaving Differently.* Reid G, Walker L (eds). Cape Town: Double Storey Books, 205–229.

Salo E. 2001. 'Talking about feminism in Africa. Interview with Amina Mama'. *Agenda,* 50: 58–63.

Salo E. 2002. 'Condoms are for spares not the besties: Negotiating adolescent sexuality in post-apartheid Manenberg'. *Society in Transition,* 33(3): 403–419.

Sapa. 2008. 'Outrage over attack on miniskirt-wearing woman'. *Mail&Guardian.* [Online] Available at: http://mg.co.za/article/2008-02-19-outrage-over-attack-on-miniskirtwearing-woman [Accessed 8 September 2011].

Segal L, Holden P (eds). 2008. *Great Lives: Pivotal Moments.* Johannesburg: SAHA/*Sunday Times* Heritage Project: Jacana Press, 56.

Spiegel AD, McAllister PA (eds). 2001. *Tradition and Transition in Southern Africa*. New York: Harper & Row.

Stacey J. 1983. 'The new conservative feminism'. *Feminist Studies*, 9(3): 559–583.

Strachan DC, Van Buskirk J. 2011. 'Intersex resources in libraries' in *Serving LGBTIQ Library and Archives Users*. Greenblatt E (ed), 13–25.

Tamale S. 2013. 'Confronting the politics of nonconforming sexualities in Africa'. *African Studies Review*, 56: 31–45

Tripp A. 2000. 'Introduction' in *Gender: Readers in Cultural Criticism*. Tripp A (ed). Houndmills: Palgrave, 1–17.

Van der Vliet V. 2001. 'Traditional husbands, modern wives? Constructing marriages in a South African township' in *Tradition and Transition in Southern Africa*. Spiegel AD, McAllister PA (eds). New York: Harper & Row, 219–241.

Walby S. 1997. 'Theorising patriarchy' in *Sourcebook on Feminist Jurisprudence*. Barnett H (ed). London: Cavendish, 124–126.

Walker L. 2005. 'Negotiating the boundaries of masculinity in post-apartheid South Africa' in *Men Behaving Differently*. Reid G, Walker L (eds). Cape Town: Double Storey Books, 161–182.

Weldon SL. 2008. 'Intersectionality', in *Politics, Gender, and Concepts: Theory and Methodology*. Goerts G, Mazur AG (eds). Cambridge: Cambridge University Press, 193–218.

Wetherell M. 1996. 'Life histories/social histories' in *Identities, Groups and Social Issues*. Wetherell M (ed). London: SAGE, 299–342.

Wiesner-Hanks ME. 2011. *Gender in History. Global Perspectives*, 2nd ed. West Sussex: Wiley-Blackwell.

Sexualities and sexual orientations

Jacques Rothmann

No other academic discipline challenges our own socialised beliefs as does sociology. We realise how profoundly deep these beliefs are when we come across forms of social behaviour with which we were not previously familiar or even which we were taught are wrong. Confronting norms and mores that conflict with our own upbringing, and most especially often our religious faith, presents us with a test of how well we are able to adopt a sociological approach when viewing the world. This can be a significant challenge for it means reflecting on some of the earliest learning of our own primary socialisation, yet, needless to say, it is not only sociologists who are required to be sensitive to social difference. All South Africans are required to respect each other despite the very different ways in which we express our social being.

It is useful to rehearse the section on Equality in Chapter 2 of our Bill of Rights where sexual orientation is mentioned before embarking on this chapter. Taking paragraphs 3 and 4 together, section 9 of the Constitution is clear that neither the state, nor any person, may unfairly discriminate against anyone on the grounds of their 'race, gender, sex, pregnancy, marital status, ethnic or social origin, colour, sexual orientation, age, disability, religion, conscience, belief, culture, language or birth'. We will all differ with others on many issues related to these grounds. Our civic duty is not to unfairly discriminate against others. Our intellectual challenge is to understand diversity and difference, and the social contexts of those with whom we do not agree.

The two paragraphs above could serve as an introductory preface to a good number of chapters in this textbook. They preface this particular chapter for the simple reason that we need to squarely recognise that we live in a deeply homophobic society. While social attitudes have changed and continue to do so, there remains much gross intolerance of others who express and enact their sexual preferences differently from heterosexuals. For a start, it is useful to immediately point out that sexual orientations and behaviour, other than the heterosexual norms into which most people are socialised at this point in the social evolution of our own society, are as old as history itself. Some readers might even be surprised to learn in this chapter how pre-colonial African attitudes to sexual orientation were widely socially accepted and that the unfair discrimination our Constitution expressly forbids became institutionalised with the colonial encounter and the introduction of Christianity in southern Africa.

This chapter develops and expands key concepts introduced in the previous discussion around gender and introduces new ones. If you read carefully, you will see how the definition of some of these key concepts in the field of medical science were socially determined by the mores of late 19th century European society. This enables us to see how discriminatory social attitudes produced bad science. Instead, we now know how wonderfully fluid the expressions of human sexuality are and that, as we saw in Chapter 6 on socialisation and identity, we are in fact taught to act and behave in certain ways, whether along heteronormative or homonormative lines. You should, from the previous chapter, be familiar with one of these terms. By the end of this chapter you will be familiar with both of them and can add them to your conceptual repertoire and expanding sociological outlook.

Following a major methodological approach in this textbook of presenting a historically sensitive sociology, this chapter briefly covers how human sexuality was racially policed in South Africa. It also follows a major theoretical orientation of this textbook by analysing human sexualities and sexual orientations by expanding the number of conceptual lenses of the different approaches outlined in its first chapter. Like much of sociology, how key concepts in defining and understanding sexualities and sexual orientations are contested and debated are discussed. The chapter ends where this brief preface started, namely the importance of exercising our civic constitutional duty by recognising and respecting the right to equality of all people to express their sexuality freely.

Case study 8.1 Religious views on sexuality and sexualities

In 2012, the Lights of Nations Church leased a billboard in Pretoria East on which they appealed to South Africans to attend their services and in so doing, become free of a range of troubles and difficulties (see Figure 8.1). Included in the list was homosexuality, alongside such issues as divorce, pornography, depression, drugs and lies. Complaints were brought before the Advertising Standards Authority (ASA) for the inclusion of homosexuality, which implied that it was a 'sin' that could 'cured' through Christian salvation. Although the church removed the term from the billboard, its co-founder, Dr Deric Linley, argued that the intention had been to emphasise the everyday challenges that people face rather than to name homosexuality a 'sin'. He noted: 'Besides homosexuality, diets, rejection and depression are also listed. It was never [our] intention to discriminate against any group, but purely to offer a non-judgemental refuge for people.'

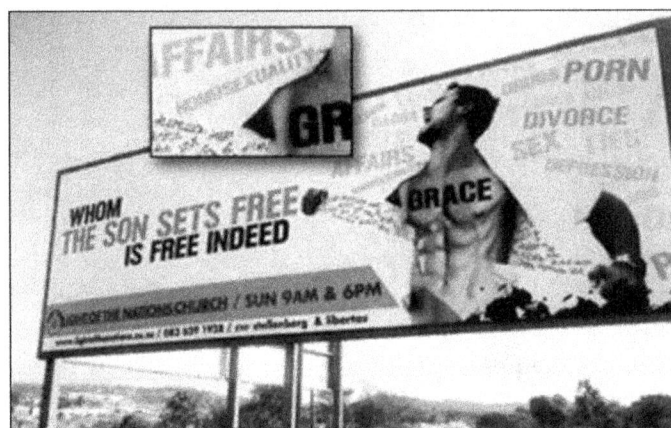

Figure 8.1 The Lights of Nation's billboard
(Source: Mamba Online)

In 2014, a Cape Town minister of *Calvary Hope Ministries*, Oscar Bougardt, reached an agreement with the South African Human Rights Commission to refrain from using any anti-gay statements, following remarks he posted on his Facebook page calling homosexuality a 'curse', a 'disgrace' and perversion 'from hell'. This notwithstanding, Bougardt actively continued to collaborate with another anti-gay evangelist, the American pastor Steven Anderson. Together they were working towards establishing South African religious congregations based on *Anderson's Faithful Word Baptist Church* model in Cape Town. In 2016, however, as a result of pressure from the gay and lesbian community, the South African Department of Home Affairs invoked clause 26 of the Home Affairs Act, banning Anderson from entering the country on grounds of demonstrated discrimination on the basis of sexual orientation.

Following this, Bougardt stated publicly that homosexual people posed a 'danger' to heterosexual people, particularly children. He further equated homosexuality with paedophilia: 'Why should we be tolerant of their criminal lifestyle? Ninety-nine percent of paedophiles stem from homosexuality … it is proven that 99% of the paedophiles have a homosexual background'. In response, GaySA Radio chairperson Hendrik Baird warned that such statements were 'inflammatory and could lead to further violence and discrimination against LGBTI people, something which you could and should be held liable for'.

In May 2018, Bougardt was sentenced to 30 days in prison, suspended for five years, for contempt of court. The presiding judge in Cape Town's Equality Court noted that Bougardt's comments encouraged 'hatred and were clearly discriminatory'. In blatant disregard of the judgement, Bougardt reaffirmed his anti-homosexual stance by telling the media that gay people are 'perverted' and advocated efforts to 'deal with them like they do in Nigeria'. He even blamed the Cape Town drought on 'wickedness and homosexuality and church leaders who fail to preach the Bible and sodomite abomination' (Petersen 2018; Serra 2018).

Case study 8.2   Bisexuality in South Africa

In contemplating his bisexuality in an article for the South African gay-orientated publication, *Gay Pages*, Werner Pieterse provides an insightful narrative about how he continuously attempts to navigate his sexual attraction to men *and* women while being married to his wife:

It has become a bit of an alphabet soup acronym, hasn't it? The LGBTQI+ umbrella term hoping to encompass all minority sexual and gender identities … At any rate, here I am! Smack bang in the middle of it: 'B' for bisexual. Sometimes feeling slightly affronted when others believe that the term is merely a convenient place to 'park' before you acknowledge that you're gay.

Explaining to people who are not bisexual how I experience my feelings, emotionally and physically, is tough and challenging. I often sense a level of confusion from listeners, more so if they've boxed themselves as either gay or straight … I am a guy, and as far back as I can remember, I have been attracted to both men and women, physically and emotionally … I want to emphasise that bisexuality is a very complex sexual orientation … because [it] comprises the whole spectrum between straight and gay (Pieterse 2018: 65).

After deciding to 'come out' to his wife, both had to establish an 'ethically non-monogamous' (or polyamorous) relationship, affording them the opportunity to engage in more than one intimate relationship with the consent of the other partner.

8.1 Introduction

This chapter's main focus centres on a concept commonly linked to and sometimes even conflated with **sex** and **gender: sexualities**. Sylvia Tamale (2011: 11) notes that gender and sexuality 'go hand in hand; both are creatures of culture and society, and both play a central role in maintaining power relations in our societies'. These power relations become apparent in how we expect people to behave based on their biological sex, captured in Raewyn Connell's (2005) reference to **hegemonic masculinity** and **emphasised femininity**. The latter refers to the 'traditional' roles associated with women, including an affinity to be nurturing, soft-spoken, sexually alluring and domestic. Hegemonic masculinity requires men to be competitive, dominant, muscular and aggressive. While gender and sexuality are closely related, each have different meanings and should therefore not be used interchangeably.

The case study that opened the chapter highlights how religious views and discourse inform the way in which many South Africans are taught to think about sexuality. These discourses often have a negative view of sexual identities and forms of behaviour that fall outside the parameters of heterosexuality (ie people who are attracted to the opposite sex). Homosexuals – commonly referred to as gay men and lesbian women – are emotionally and sexually attracted to people of the same sex. It will, however, become clear that such attraction is also characterised by differences.

Moreover, as the second case study showed, heterosexual and homosexual identities are not the only possible sexual identities. Bisexual people are attracted to both men and women, and they often face difficulties not only because they contradict the expectations of heterosexual attraction, but do not identify as either gay or lesbian. Bisexuality demonstrates the fluidity of human sexual attraction. Tamale (2011: 4) emphasises the plurality and diversity associated with human sexualities, as well as the localised and context-specific nature of sexual behaviour and attraction. There is thus not only one sexuality, but rather many *sexualities*. The range of influences on sexualities is broad, but they have all been fundamentally defined and shaped by society in various ways: from colonialism, globalisation and class, to religion, law and culture, and patriarchy, gender and age. One should, for example, not simply assume that your sexual identity as a South African heterosexual or gay man will be precisely the same as a man living in the US or Nigeria. Specific factors (including certain laws, religious views and family upbringing, among others) influence how you will be able to enact your sexuality in public and private or be prohibited from doing so. Several studies point to the daily discrimination gay and lesbian people face because of their sexual identity in South Africa and around the world. There are multiple reports of verbal and physical harassment, and imprisonment. Some countries, such as Iran and Sudan, even impose the death penalty on people who are openly gay or lesbian in public. Certain African traditional and religious leaders, politicians and ordinary people consider gay men and lesbians as 'un-African'. This implies that such sexual identities originated in the US and European countries and were 'imported' to Africa through colonialism, but is this really the case?

This chapter examines contemporary debates regarding the challenge individuals face as a consequence of their sexual identity. Such challenges generally arise from the **homophobic** (physical and/or verbal discrimination toward people who identify as gay or lesbian) prejudice against people who do not conform to the perceived 'acceptable' ways of being a man or being a woman.

8.2 Defining 'sexualities': Navigating the conceptual landscape of sexual identities

Sociologically speaking, **sexuality** involves much more than the biological sexual behaviour of human beings. Sexualities reflect the deeply embedded rules, regulations and patterned behaviour prescribed by particular cultural expectations and social institutions.

8.2.1 Medical definitions of sexuality

Some of the earliest examples of the rules and prescriptions around sexuality arose with the birth of **sexology** as a field of study in the West. Initially, Victorian doctors believed that it was harmful for women to display any interest in sex, since any form of sexual indulgence could result in damage to their reproductive organs or lead to hysteria.

Michel Foucault (1978) argues that with the rise in scientific research by medical professionals in general and psychiatry in particular, people were increasingly categorised based on their attraction to people of the same or opposite sex. This was done in order to better understand and deal with changes in sexual practices in society. By doing so, doctors were able to determine specific norms that differentiated 'acceptable' and 'unacceptable' sexual behaviour. In 1869, Karl Maria Kertbeny created the category of 'the homosexual'. Homosexuality was regarded as a form of deviant behaviour in opposition to the heterosexuality that was considered normal and thus acceptable. What followed was a prolonged period of intense medical and legal policing of sexual desire and behaviour.

In 1886, German psychiatrist Dr Richard von Krafft-Ebing argued that homosexuality should be regarded as a 'sexual perversion', describing it as an abnormal and unfortunate inborn trait. Other sexologists, including German physician Karl Westphal, identified so-called effeminate characteristics among men who were attracted to other men by the display of 'feminine' behaviour. His work supported fellow physician, Karl Heinrich Ulrich's reference to homosexuals, particularly homosexual men, as being overly effeminate. Homosexual activist and sexologist Magnus Hirschfeld refuted the association of homosexuality with mental illness and sexual perversion. Instead, he considered homosexuals a 'third sex' who displayed both masculine and feminine traits. These thoughts informed the work of British sexologist Havelock Ellis (1897; 1937), who attempted to provide a fair and scientific view of homosexuality. He argued that three contextual factors determined the sexual attraction to someone of the *same sex: seduction* by someone of the same sex, *disappointment* in romantic relationships with someone of the opposite sex, and *situational absences* of the opposite sex, such as the separation of boys and girls in boarding schools or men working in situations, such as mining, where they *mainly* or *only* interact with people of the same sex (Meem, Gibson & Alexander 2010).

Regardless of these mainly historical views, local thinker and writer Kopano Ratele emphasises the *political* nature associated with the act of naming or labelling people in terms of their sexuality. Ratele notes that by 'calling ourselves or being called homosexual or bisexual men or women ... women who love women, women who have sex with women [could be an] act of submission or resistance, supportive of the status quo or defy prevailing structures' (2011: 44). This means that, through labelling, we confirm or deny who we are and what we do as sexual beings. In doing this, we either *challenge* the status quo through activism or hide our sexual identity to avoid discrimination. By not conforming to a hegemonic form of masculinity or femininity associated with African manhood and womanhood, gay men and lesbian women respectively face not only marginalisation but violence. This occurs since they are thought to threaten 'the dominance of masculinity and masculine lesbian women challenge and try to assume male dominance and therefore these individuals need to be punished for not conforming to the "natural" social order' (Judge 2014: 69).

8.2.2 The Kinsey scale: Human sexuality as fluid and plural

Sexualities comprise two components: **sexual behaviour**, such as sexual intercourse, and **sexual orientation**, which is a person's emotional, psychological and physical attraction to another person. One of the first sociological studies related to human sexuality was that of a zoologist, Alfred Kinsey. Based on interviews with over 5 000 white men and women on their sexual histories, Kinsey (1948; 1953) provided a comprehensive analysis of sexual practices. Considered immoral by some members of the public, Kinsey's work is significant because it was an objective scientific study that avoided a moral view of human sexuality. Kinsey argued that homosexuality is based on a stimulus–response effect. Such an approach viewed homosexuality not as deviant, but rather as one of various forms of human sexuality. In support of this, he identified the social aspects – age, marital status, education, race, class and gender – that influenced the way in which people express their sexual identity (Rothmann 2014). His research was, however, subjected to criticism. In the first instance, his study could not be replicated, focusing as it did on men and women in the Midwest of the US, and secondly, the findings could thus not be generalised outside of that country (Herzog 2006).

Notwithstanding these criticisms, the strength of Kinsey's research lay in his identification of *sexual diversity*. He argued that one should avoid classifying people as only heterosexual or homosexual, since there exist a number of ways in which people choose to define and express their sexuality. All individuals, given the necessary physical stimulus, will experience sexual arousal towards another person, regardless of his/her sex or sexual orientation. **Bisexuality** is a case in point. Often defined in a very superficial way, some studies place bisexuality in the 'middle' of heterosexuality and homosexuality as a 'homogenous middle ground that bridges two **mono-sexual** (heterosexual and lesbian/gay) anchors' (Galupo, Ramirez & Pulice-Farrow 2017: 109). This creates the

simplistic impression of bisexuality as solely based on a continuum between what is considered 'same-sex' versus 'opposite-sex' attraction. Rather, there are a multiplicity of ways in which bisexuals choose to define their sexuality, based on their given context. Several typologies have been used to describe bisexuality, all of which emphasise Kinsey's earlier point of sexuality as diverse and fluid rather than static. These typologies include those persons who are sexually attracted to males and females; individuals who are not prevented from being sexually attracted to another person based on their sex; people sexually attracted to their own sex but who have, in the past, engaged in sexual intercourse with persons of the opposite sex; people in a stable and long-term monogamous sexual relationship with a person of the same or opposite sex, but display sexual attraction towards persons of either the opposite or same sex respectively; and persons who have sex only with other bisexuals (men or women) (Halperin 2009).

To substantiate his argument, Kinsey devised a seven-point scale or continuum upon which individuals could position themselves, depending on their degrees of heterosexual or homosexual attraction, in place of a polarised either/or approach. Known as the **Kinsey scale** and widely used by researchers to chart human sexual attraction, the seven points on the scale represent fluidity in terms of human sexual and erotic dispensations, as is evident from Figure 8.2.

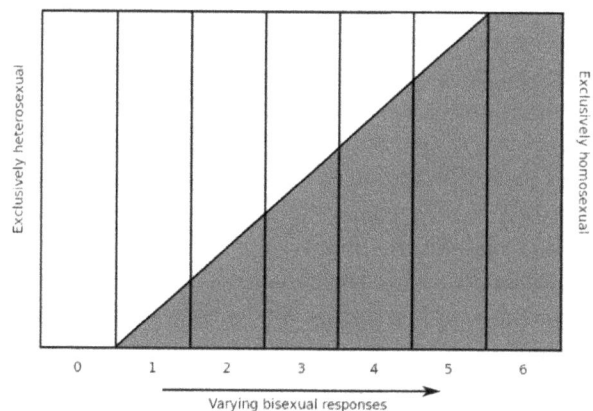

Figure 8.2 The Kinsey scale
(Source: Rothmann 2014)

The seven points on the scale include the following positions:

0: Exclusively heterosexual

1: Predominantly heterosexual with only incidental homosexuality

2: Predominantly heterosexual with more than incidental homosexuality

3: Equally heterosexual and homosexual (ie bisexual)

4: Predominantly homosexual with more than incidental heterosexuality

5: Predominantly homosexual with only incidental heterosexuality

6: Exclusively homosexual

The main findings from Kinsey's study:

- Of the male population, 37 per cent had engaged in some homosexual behaviour which culminated in orgasm.

- Five to 12 per cent placed themselves on either the 5 or 6 axes of Kinsey's scale.

- About 10 per cent of men between the ages of 16 and 55 identified as exclusively homosexual – hence the argument of 'one in 10' men as gay.

Kinsey's work primarily focused on behaviour and not identity (Rothmann 2014).

A recent explorative study with 172 North American adults emphasised the main point of Kinsey's research: the importance of recognising diversity, fluidity and plurality of sexual identities versus the rigidity of sexual identity categories (Galupo et al 2017). People described their sexual orientation in many ways, referring to themselves as bisexual, **queer**, **pansexual** and **polyamorous**, among others.

A *queer identity* suggests an acceptance of the 'openness, plurality, diversity and difference' of varied forms of sexual identities and intimate relationships (Haralambos & Holborn 2013: 123). *Pansexuality* is one such example, and refers to people who express sexual desire towards people regardless of their sex or gender. Another example related to pansexuality is the *polyamorous* or 'open' relationship. This is a desire for engaging in multiple intimate relationships with more than one partner with consent by all involved. Schippers (2016: 17) argues that polyamorous relationships allow for mutual equality, cooperation and freedom among partners, obviating the need for one 'cheating' on the other. Such relationships underline the necessity for trust, open communication and emotional connectivity. Furthermore, bisexuality and polyamorous sexualities thus 'unravel the notion of fixed gender and sexual identities' (Schippers 2016: 26) by questioning fixed identity categories.

Given their Western origin, many labels such as 'bisexual' or 'queer' may not necessarily have a specific linguistic equivalent in Africa. Those men and women who express attraction to both sexes may merely 'prefer to be loved in a sexual way by a woman or man or both at any point in time of their lives' (Ratele 2011: 44). Social scientists therefore need to acknowledge the *context specificity* of sexualities in South Africa and in other societies. In acknowledging and enacting their sexuality, people constantly have to consider what is culturally, legally and socially 'acceptable' and 'allowed' in their community, culture or country – in short, their social context. Will they, for example, face imprisonment or the death penalty for being openly gay or lesbian? Conversely, do they enjoy the same legal rights, such as the right to marry, adopt children or serve in the military, as those who identify as heterosexual? The importance of the social context in shaping expressions (or not) of sexual intimacy and desire point to a question which is at the heart of this chapter: why is it that one form of sexuality – heterosexuality – is dominant over other possible forms of human sexuality?

8.2.3 Pre-colonial sexual relationships

Context-specific views of sexual identities were particularly evident in pre-colonial Africa. There are numerous examples of how same-sex practices were culturally and socially accepted in various parts of Africa prior to the introduction of Western religious and medical influences. Olaoluwa (2018: 20) argues that it is through these influences that same-sex practices became vilified.

Same-sex relationships as 'un-African'?

The introduction of religious doctrines and medical science by Western countries during the era of colonialism in Africa served as the foundation for the idea that same-sex attraction is 'un-African'. McAllister (2013: 88) notes that:

> … *identifying with what is so visibly a Western image of gayness exposes … sexual minority communities to the most dangerous of the justifications for homophobia in Africa, the argument that sexual dissidence is a neo-colonial conspiracy to subvert 'African values'.*

Arguments against the Western influence on Africa have used the idea that same-sex attraction and behaviour are Western imports into Africa, which undermine African values and traditions. This is, however, *not* the case. Same-sex attraction is not a Western import. There is much evidence to suggest that same-sex attraction and practices existed long before the conquest of Africa by colonial rulers. What is, however, of importance is the medical and religious condemnation of same-sex attraction and practices, facilitated by the introduction of the category of 'the homosexual'. Some Christian missionaries showed little regard for issues regarded as important to indigenous African people, since their main objective was to replace existing traditional values with their own – thus displacing the acceptance of same-sex expression. Epprecht (2013) argues that these misconceptions and resulting violence associated with same-sex relationships as being 'un-African' persist for a number of reasons: Firstly, some political and religious leaders consider same-sex behaviour as 'taboo' in Sub-Saharan Africa. Secondly, the introduction of 'the homosexual' to Africa through colonial and post-colonial Christian evangelism, perpetuated and reinforced homophobic religious rhetoric on the topic. Brown (2012: 52) reiterates that a number of Western 'faith-based' non-governmental organisations (NGOs) invest a considerable amount of time and money into 'evangelising Africa' and intensify negative beliefs and practices on the continent. Although these accounts suggest that homosexuality is a 'foreign' practice introduced by early Portuguese colonisers in Western Africa, among others, later research of the 20th century has provided ample evidence of same-sex behaviour in traditional African tribal societies.

In addition to colonialism, continued adherence to the notion of African tradition today plays a significant role in undermining the expression of same-sex relations. A recent example where male same-sex behaviour was subject to intense scrutiny was with the release of the film *Inxeba* (*The Wound*) in 2018. The film, which depicts a sexual relationship between male Xhosa initiates, was met with varied and heated responses. The controversy revolved around two key issues: one, its depiction of same-sex relations between *African* men, and two, its depiction of these relations taking place during a sacred process and rite of passage for young men into manhood. The Film and Publication Board (FPB) initially awarded the film a 16SLN rating, indicating it contained sex, strong language and nudity. Following an appeal from the National House of Traditional Leaders and a suspension of the film's screening at several cinemas, the FPB's Appeal Tribunal awarded the film a rating of X18SNLVP, thereby classifying it as hard-core pornography (Khoza 2018). A legal battle ensued, and the film's producers were able to repeal this classification.

The film merely echoes the findings from a South African study on the experiences of gay Xhosa men during traditional male initiation or *ulwaloko*. The researchers found that some of their nine Xhosa participants, aged between 18 and 26, in the Eastern Cape wanted to remain closeted and conform to the traditional teachings of the Xhosa culture,

owing to the influence of African tradition. They attended these initiation ceremonies to prove their manhood and physical and emotional strength in the hope that they could potentially convert them from their homosexual orientation. Some, however, withdrew or resisted participating in the rituals, while others attempted to prove that they could be gay and successfully complete *ulwaloko*. The study highlights the range of possible responses in negotiating sexual identity amidst cultural challenges and threats (Ntozini & Ngqangweni 2016).

Numerous other examples of human rights infringements based on sexual and gender identity exist in Africa. One such example includes a police raid on gay pride events in Kampala, Uganda in August 2016. Although the Ugandan government initially sought to persecute sexual minorities through the enactment of the 2014 Anti-Homosexuality Act, it was later repealed. Section 145 of the Ugandan Penal Code, however, still allows for harsh penalties, including life imprisonment. This has resulted in many Ugandans fleeing the country for their own safety (Oluoch & Tabengwa 2017).

In spite of controversy and the challenges of freely expressing a sexual identity that does not conform to the accepted norm, there is some evidence for an increase in visibility of human rights and activist movements on the continent (International Lesbian, Gay, Bisexual and Intersex Association 2017). One example is the 2014 'Resolution on Protection against Violence and Other Human Rights Violations against Persons on the Basis of their Real or Imputed Sexual Orientation or Gender Identity' (Resolution 275), passed during the 55th Ordinary Session of the African Commission on Human and Peoples' Rights in Luanda, Angola. The resolution condemned 'the increasing incidences of violence and other human rights violations' directed at people on the basis of their sexual orientations.

Same-sex relations in southern Africa

While the existence of same-sex relationships in ancient Greece between older men and younger boys (called pederasty) is fairly well known, similar (and sometimes very different) same-sex relationships on the African continent are less so. In his discussion of African homosexuality, Dlamini (2006) emphasises the longstanding existence of same-sex practices in indigenous African cultures. A number of studies refute arguments that emphasise the novelty of same-sex behaviour in Africa, citing migrant labour mining hostels, male prisons and domesticated same-sex relationships as examples of how same-sex intercourse and relationships were, and in certain settings continue to be, socially acceptable.

Mining compounds

Same-sex relationships in South Africa have been evident in the mining industry. These relationships are called mine marriages and are based, in part, on the principles of the Grecian practice of pederasty. Partly as a consequence of the absence of women, experienced male miners tied themselves to more recent recruits, who became known as mine wives. Such relationships incorporated household practices that are traditionally associated with a husband and wife. Evidence strongly suggests that younger mine wives generally assumed a passive sexual role, similar to that which is associated in the main with a monogamous heterosexual husband and wife relationship. In addition, they performed domestic functions – cooking, cleaning, washing and ironing – in return for financial reward and protection from the older masculine male miners.

Despite both being male, these men in fact formed a heterosexual union in which their roles were either that of male (older male) or female (younger male). Upon leaving the mine compounds, some of the mine-wives would return home with their mine-husbands, and were accepted by the rural community, including the older husband's wives and elders (Dlamini 2006). Although socially and culturally accepted, these relationships did not supplant the importance of family ties and sexual reproduction within a patriarchal and heterosexually dominant African culture (Gevisser 1995). When the mine-wives grew older and took on the more active sexual and masculine role, these relationships would end, and they could now take on male wives of their own (Moodie 1994). Although these relationships, as noted, are characterised by a power relationship along gender lines, with a dominant masculine male role and a submissive effeminate one, findings from other studies do note the freedom such relationships provide men. Achmat (1993: 106) comments on how these mine marriages 'partially freed' men from cultural expectations which associated sexual intercourse with only procreation, and serve as an example of the social acceptance of same-sex relations in Africa.

Prisons

Niehaus's (2009) research among former male prisoners in the South African village of Impalahoek yielded interesting findings. His participants identified a number of features which characterised male-to-male sexual relationships in prisons. Inmates distinguished between *consensual sex* and *coercive sex* or *rape* or *go kata*, which translates as 'to push down'.

Consensual sex relationships were described by former inmates in terms of two roles: a *lebosa* or a *papa*, the more masculine male or father figure, and the *mfana wa misa* or *picanini*, the boy-wife or small boy. Other similar typologies include the distinction between 'men' or 'husbands' and 'women' or '*wyfies*' (literally 'little wife') or 'wives', with the latter performing the role of 'wife'. The *lebosa* or 'man'/'husband' usually proposes to his younger partner, providing the latter with extra food, money or cigarettes. He was also expected to provide protection to his boy-wife at all times and only he was allowed to engage in the old custom practised by young heterosexual couples wishing to avoid unwanted pregnancies, namely thigh or anal sex. In exchange, the 'wives' are responsible for taking care of the 'home space', namely the prison cell, and to be sexually available to the 'husband'. The *lebosa* could be polygynous – having more than one sexual partner at the same time – as long as he was able to provide for the material and physical needs of the younger submissive partner. What is evident from these 'marriages' is the pervasiveness of traditional gender stereotyping, where the gender and sex roles of inmates are conflated: dominant 'men' display hegemonic masculinity and the more submissive 'men' emphasise feminine features (Gear 2005: 94).

Gendered power relationships are also evident in the more coercive examples of same-sex relations in prisons. Here male inmates had very little or no choice of *whether they wanted to* engage in sexual intercourse or *with whom*. This form of sexual domination relates to the existence of prison hierarchies where gang members, almost exclusively dominant 'men', are ranked more highly than the submissive 'women' and are thus entitled to establish sexual relations with the more passive 'wyfie'. Such sexual violence 'changes' the submissive men into 'women', who are effectively subject to rape. The 'men', on the other hand, retain their masculinity and thereby protect themselves from rape (Gear 2005). Specific examples of these complex relations include those established by members of the 'the Numbers' (the 28s, 26s, 27s and Big 5s) gangs in South African prisons, who rape newcomers to initiate them into prison life. Although their codes of conduct may differ, these gangs organise 'wives' into having sex on a regular basis. In many instances prison wardens either ignore such behaviour or rape young prisoners themselves, paying them to ensure their silence. Niehaus (2009) shows how, unlike the men who engaged in male-to-male sex in mining hostels, many prisoners expressed fear of such sexual relations in prisons. They were particularly concerned about contracting diseases that would make them physically weak and unable to defend themselves when necessary. Although prison authorities and educationists have initiated HIV/AIDS information interventions and provided prisoners with condoms, many male prisoners still disregard the dangers of unprotected male-to-male sex.

Female same-sex relations

Prisons also provide the backdrop for relationships between women. Dirsuweit (1999) uses Butler's (1990) work on 'performing gender' to analyse the role allocations of female inmates in South African prisons. She notes that female inmates do not only emulate heterosexual gender and sex roles in ways similar to their male counterparts, but challenge the supposed stability of a natural gendered and sexual order. 'Butch' female prisoners assume the traditional heterosexual masculine gender role in order to enforce their dominance over feminine or 'femme' inmates in general and in sexual relations. By assuming the traditional submissive gender role, the more feminine partner in turn confirms her womanhood. Unlike the context of the male prison, such relationships are not necessarily coercive in nature. Studies have indicated that '[w]hile some [inmates] were extremely homophobic … others were lesbians themselves [some even in relationships with prisoners]' (Dirsuweit 1999: 77). Even while taking on these traditional heterosexual roles, it is also possible that these inmates 'parody the notion of gender as the natural and stable outcome of particular sex' (Gear 2005: 93). This means that, in the absence of men, women are able to display different types of masculinity as opposed to the one hegemonic form of male aggression and control. They thus engage in different ways of performing their female roles – whether it be more masculine or feminine.

In addition to these typologies, other examples of consensual female same-sex relationships have been recorded in Lesotho. Considered as same-sex sexual friendships among women, the 'mommy–baby' relationships, which originated in the 1950s, were also organised according to an age difference between younger and older women. They served both an emotional and sexual purpose, particularly for younger women prior to marriage. Owing to strong emotional connections established between partners, some relationships continued to exist after the younger woman's entry into a traditionally gendered heterosexual marriage. In some cases, the older partner remained in such a relationship well into her 30s to avoid marriage. Same-sex female marriages were found to be evident in over 30 other African contexts. Such arrangements would provide *female husbands*, obliged to pay bride wealth, and in return having the power to decide on and approve appropriate

heterosexual relations to secure progeny for the female same-sex couple (Wallace 2010). Other studies highlight the importance of acknowledging such diversity among women by citing Rich's (1980) reference to a 'lesbian continuum'.

These fine-grained studies confirm Kinsey's findings on the fluidity and diversity of human sexuality. The freedom to express and live one's preferred sexual orientation has subsequently found social acceptability in many societies. In others, the dominance of heteronormativity has become further entrenched. Where sexual freedoms have been extended, a new limitation has expressed itself in the form of **homonormativity**. In short, the freedom of choice in respect of sexual orientation has become socially acceptable in many contexts, *provided* it is expressed as and mirrors heterosexual relationships.

8.2.4 Two sides of the same sexual coin: heteronormativity and homonormativity

Social expectations and limitations arise regarding the free exercise of sexual orientation. **Heteronormativity**, most clearly, reproduces and maintains hegemonic beliefs, privileges, sanctions and rules in favour of heterosexuality. These gendered and dominant socialised traditions generally include prejudice against other forms of sexual orientation, such as homosexuality and bisexuality. Most societies are heteronormative, with the expectation that both romantic love (itself a relatively recent social construction) and sexual desire are to be expressed in a heterosexual framework. This expectation is linked to the assumption that one's biological sex (male or female) aligns with the matching gender identity (masculine or feminine). The term **cisgender** has recently been used to describe people whose biological sex matches their gender identity, which, it must be said, describes the vast majority of people. To this, however, a further important dimension must be added: in our heteronormative culture, a key aspect of the cisgender identity is the expectation of a heterosexual sexual identity. To be a man, therefore, means not only that one has male genitalia and fulfils the obligations of the masculine gender, but that one is also 'straight' (ie heterosexual). The same is true of women, except, of course, in terms of female biological characteristics and a feminine gender identity. These gender identities and a heterosexual orientation are what is considered to be 'normal' and even 'natural'. Underpinning this is an acceptance that there is a clear-cut distinction between heterosexuality on the one hand and homosexuality on the other.

Research has shown that this distinction creates the false impression that *only* heterosexuality is morally acceptable. Valocchi (2005: 753) argues that the uncritical acceptance of and conformity to heteronormative expectations has the effect of maintaining social inequalities that exert 'power over those who do not align normatively within the binary constructs' of masculinity and femininity.

This power is exercised through negative attitudes and prejudicial behaviour towards gay men *and* heterosexual men who do not exhibit masculine traits associated with a cisgender male. Specific examples include name calling (eg derogatory language such as *faggot* and the Afrikaans and isiXhosa versions *moffie* and *stabane* respectively) which posits such men as weak, unmanly and unacceptable. In a similar vein, pejorative terms like *dyke, butch* and *lesbo* are equally directed at both lesbian and heterosexual women who do not portray the requisite feminine characteristics.

In their study on homosexual migrants in Africa, Koko, Monro and Smith (2018) also provide a number of examples of prejudice people face because of their homosexuality. They note that in certain African countries, including Nigeria, Uganda and Zimbabwe, people may face criminal charges by simply expressing their gender and sexual identity. They cite research which shows that gay men in the Congo, Malawi and Uganda, among others, have been denied access to basic social services, been beaten or stoned by police, and received death threats for being gay. In response, they may attempt what Rich (1980) calls *compulsory heterosexuality*, in other words, act heterosexual in order to avoid prejudice, physical assault or imprisonment. This highlights the centrality of heterosexuality in society and the marginal position of gay and lesbian people.

While heteronormativity is now extensively recognised in the scholarly literature, **homonormativity** as a concept has fairly recently emerged to deepen our understanding of the socially constructed dimensions of human sexuality. The concept has two meanings. The first refers to those stereotypical 'traits' associated with being gay and lesbian. Simply put, there is an expectation that homosexual people act in a way that conforms to the stereotype that heterosexuals have of homosexuality. Some of the stereotypical attitudes, traits and behaviours include effeminate and flamboyant behaviour, a preoccupation with physical appearance and style of dress, a 'superior sense of fashion, design, and taste' (Ghaziani 2014: 127), and a sexually promiscuous lifestyle. Downs (2006) argues that these expectations are not exclusive to heterosexuals, and homosexuals themselves may have similar expectations. Many contemporary gay men wish to overcompensate for not being 'manly' enough with an excessive focus on exercise to attain a muscular body and living in the most beautiful homes or having the best jobs. As a result, people

may attach such stereotypes to all gay persons, reinforcing the idea that heterosexual and homosexual people are completely different. In some cases, these stereotypes then result in anti-gay and anti-lesbian groups to justify prejudice and discrimination towards homosexual people.

The second meaning of *homo*normativity actually *supports* the principles of *hetero*normativity. Provided their homosexuality is played out *by acting in a heterosexual way*, gay men and lesbian women are accepted and afforded the opportunity to succeed in a heteronormative society. In this way, heterosexuality is in fact further enforced. Ghaziani (2014) argues, for instance, that the representation of gay men in the media provides a good example of this. He cites the American sitcom *Modern Family* (2009), in which the two gay characters (Mitchell Pritchett and Cameron Tucker) *imitate* the behaviour of heterosexual couples. They are in a monogamous marriage, adopt a child, live in a suburban area and display gendered behaviour in terms of the division of household tasks (Mitchell as the main breadwinner and Cameron the *caretaker* of their daughter and home). These men thus perform similar roles to those of their heterosexual counterparts. By presenting the couple in this way, the idea that gay men can 'belong' in mainstream society if they emulate heterosexual behaviour is encouraged.

Writing from a South African perspective, Milani and Wolff (2015: 165) refer to homonormativity as 'the queer skin under the otherwise straight masks'. In their view, homonormativity supports the dominant assumptions and institutions (eg the traditional family and religious views) of society. It does this by differentiating socially acceptable and unacceptable homosexual behaviour. In this regard, the 'bad gay' is effeminate, perverse, predatory and politically persuasive. The 'good gay' is more 'straight acting', private and discreet (Greenland & Taulke-Johnson 2017). In short, these writers argue that gay and lesbian individuals who are 'good' do not challenge the centrality and dominance of heteronormativity in mainstream society.

Let us now consider some actual examples of *how* we are in fact 'taught' to act in a hetero**normative** or homo**normative** way.

8.3 Teaching people to be sexual: Reinforcing 'normativities'

Jackson and Scott (2010), writing from a feminist perspective, argue that people are 'taught' to act in a sexually 'correct' way in contemporary society. More specifically, people are provided with the *skills* they need in order to be sexual beings. Although human sexuality may be considered as inherently biological and natural, social scientists have indicated that men and women (regardless of their sexual orientation) are 'taught' to correctly internalise, enact and interpret principles associated with their sexual behaviour and identity. This process of 'sexual skilling' provides particular guidelines, principles and advice which in turn emphasise the importance of a healthy sexual existence and conforming (or aspiring to conform) to a particular 'blueprint' of heterosexual or homosexual culture. This is necessary for individuals' sexual health and integration into a society's sexual culture. Through the influence of the mainstream mass media, among others, individuals are skilled to have mastery over their sexual needs in terms of their physical, emotional and psychological behaviour. Examples include the use of magazines, sex manuals, advertising, 'how to do it' DVDs, pornography and other print or electronic media. Jackson and Scott (2010: 63) argue that '[b]eing "good at sex" is increasingly equated with other indices of "having style" like wearing the right clothes or having the right mobile technology – a qualification for and an indicator of our worldly success and social integration'.

In one of the earliest analyses of this process, Giddens (1992) argued that human sexuality has evolved from being a secretive and revered activity in heterosexual marriages to something more open and less hidden in contemporary society. Contemporary romance and sexuality, according to Giddens, are characterised by *confluent love* and *democratised relationships*. Confluent love has replaced the importance attached to finding a 'one-and-only' monogamous partner and saving one's virginity for marriage. Confluent love is a more 'active and contingent love, in which intimate relationships are characterised by personal understandings between two [or possibly more] people' (Chambers 2012: 35). He argues that this provides individuals with agency to negotiate equality in their intimate relationships, and affords them the chance to move from one relationship to another until they find emotional and sexual fulfilment, with one or more people if necessary. Men and women who challenge conventional and traditional ideals associated with heterosexual monogamy are more likely to engage in such relationships. Beck and Beck-Gernsheim (1995) share Giddens' view on the increased emphasis on *individualism* in contemporary society. They warn, however, that a preoccupation with 'our*selves* and our *personal* relationships within a rising tide of narcissism' (Chambers 2012: 39) may result in the fragmentation of more permanent intimate relationships. People are thus more prone to take care of their individual self-fulfilment as it relates to their sexual identity and behaviour instead

of focusing on the wellbeing of the other person involved in the relationship or marriage.

However, mastering the skills to be a good sexual citizen is not necessarily as easy as one might expect. We cannot escape the principles of heteronormativity or homonormativity, which subtly dictate the correct way in which we should behave sexually. Men and women are always held to a particular standard and assessed in how they perform sexually. The following section examines issues related to male and female sexuality in South Africa.

8.3.1 South African male sexualities in the *Gay Pages* and *Men's Health*

These two South African publications illustrate the process of sexual skilling. Both target particular niche markets: *Men's Health* has a mainly heterosexual male readership (with a monthly circulation of about 29 305 as of 2018) while *Gay Pages* caters for gay males. Figure 8.4 reproduces the South African cover pages of the autumn 2018 edition of *Gay Pages* and the 2012 'sex issue' of *Men's Health*. The cover lines on these front pages, which inform the reader of the content of the magazine's articles, are indicative of the kind of sexual skills that we learn through the mass media. They also help to reinforce the norms for constructing a heterosexual and gay masculine identity. While the media and these magazines in particular are not the only means of reinforcing the expectations of these identities, they provide a good example of how ordinary people are exposed to heteronormative and homonormative ideas about the ideal heterosexual and gay man.

The cover page of the *Gay Pages* magazine makes it clear that the articles are directed at a gay readership. This 2018 edition highlights the importance of male beauty ('Photos: hot boys about town') and confluent sexual relationships ('How to do friends with benefits'). An excerpt from an earlier edition of the magazine describes some photographs as 'extremely sexy and absolutely convincing. With aplomb and appeal, these ever so sweet guys show that they have plenty of raw ... sexual energy in them after all' (*Gay Pages* 2017). Research on gay men's proclivity for an athletic, lean and muscular physique as ideal and their attraction to men who display such physiques is well documented (Varangis et al 2012). This is closely associated with the importance ascribed to hegemonic masculinity through embodying both a muscular and powerful appearance and the avoidance of being viewed as effeminate. Studies indicate a definite link between a man's gender identity and his sexual orientation, since it may be considered shameful if one is unable to conform to the expectations of the masculine male. As such, gay men aspire to attain (and retain) the ideal image of 'gay masculinity' (Halkitis, Green & Wilton 2004). In assessing these magazines, we need to note that, on the one hand, their articles risk reinforcing stereotypical interests or behaviour associated with heterosexual and gay

men. On the other hand, the articles establish a sense of communal identification and sense of 'brotherhood' among gay and heterosexual men as a result of their shared values (Rothmann 2018).

Figure 8.3 Cover pages of the South African editions of *Gay Pages* and *Men's Health* magazines
(Sources: *Gay Pages* Autumn 2018; *Men's Health* July 2012)

Hall (2015: 998) argues that physical appearance has become very important for men (regardless of their sexual identity) in modern and individualised consumer societies. He notes that such 'modern pressures' require men to exercise regularly, eat healthily, dress well, drive the right car and engage in particular sexual activities to 'fit in' with their male counterparts. These themes are evident in the cover lines of the *Men's Health* magazine ('Build big arms! 4 weeks to muscles women love'). Similarly, the South African writer, Kopano Ratele (2011) emphasises the importance of the external physical attractiveness of men. Research has indicated that the 'ideal masculine body type is characterized by broad, muscular shoulders, and a thin waistline, appearing physically strong, powerful, and able to successfully compete' (Watson & Dispenza 2015: 146). In this regard, heterosexual men are increasingly expected to engage in body grooming practices that focus on external aesthetics (a feature traditionally associated with women) such as facials, waxing and the application of face and body lotions. The men who do are referred to as **metrosexuals**. Metrosexuality is a phrase coined in the 1990s by British journalist Mark Simpson, and specifically refers not to a

sexual orientation but especially to young heterosexual men who spend their income on products and services to improve their physical appearance. By identifying as metrosexual, heterosexual men are in fact given 'permission' to participate in the noted activities which are stereotypically associated with women or gay men.

Although each magazine is directed at a different readership, they display similarities in how they depict masculinity in general – an expectation of rugged attractiveness, an emphasis on physical stamina and strength, strategies for attracting a sexual partner, managing the demands of an intimate relationship, and so forth. As noted, research has shown that heterosexual men aspire to conform to heteronormative and hegemonic masculinity. Gay men may do this to overcompensate for not being heterosexual and believe that by acting in this more manly way, they may gain more acceptance and less prejudice in society. Regardless of their reasons, both groups emphasise Arxer's (2011: 416) view that there exists a 'plurality of hegemonic masculinities', meaning that heterosexual *and* gay men display hegemonic ideals in their appearance and actions.

8.3.2 Female sexuality in 'mommy pornography'

In addition to its presence in magazines, sexuality has become more mainstream in contemporary South African society and abroad. This encourages men and women to feel less shame in experimenting with their sexual agency, even though the possibilities for this may vary depending on how conservative their immediate social context is. One example of the mainstreaming of sexuality can be found in the erotic novel genre, most especially those directed towards women. Labelled as 'mommy porn', the name is derived from the appeal of erotic and sexual literature to middle-class women in the 30–50 age bracket, many of whom are wives and mothers. The impact of 'mommy porn' illustrates how sexually explicit media have become part of a more mainstream environment that is available to a wider audience. Consider the fact that these books are sold by franchises such as the CNA and Exclusive Books and online on Takealot, among others. This has been made possible by the repeal in the mid-1990s by the democratic government of the apartheid legislation that had banned all pornographic material (Loots 2001).

Writing from a South African perspective, Van Reenen (2014: 226) cites the unprecedented success of EL James' erotic fiction series *Fifty Shades of Grey*. The book's focus on the sexual relationship between a college graduate, Anastasia Steele, and a young business magnate, Christian Grey. They contain explicit erotic scenes featuring elements of sadomasochist sexual practices and role play. Although panned by literary critics, the series is one of the fastest selling of all time, with worldwide sales exceeding 70 million copies overseas, and is fourth in South Africa on the list of the most books sold with 166 149 copies as of 2018 (Andersen 2018). Its success was attributed to a number of reasons: the provocative nature of the story, the privacy provided to consumers who purchased the book online in e-book format, and the 'discreet and tasteful' cover pages of the novels, which did not resemble pornography. The success of the novels also encouraged sex shops in South Africa and overseas to produce and sell sex toys associated with the titles. This results in a 'conversion of erotic fiction into [the] erotic reality' of fans of the series who want to engage in similar sexual acts in their private lives (Martin 2013: 981). As with *Gay Pages* and *Men's Health*, mommy porn is only one example of introducing consumers to the centrality of sexual appearance and behaviour in contemporary society. This genre also extends to South African titles, including the series *A Girl Walks Into ...*, *Folly* and the Afrikaans publication of 54 erotic short stories called *Bloots* (2011). These novels created an environment where women were

not only defined by their availability for sex to men but as sexual agents who have an interest in sex (and their own sexuality) (Attwood 2011).

Karin Eloff, one editor for the *Bloots* publication, argues that mainstream South African audiences, including their Afrikaans-speaking niche market, are 'way more open-minded than before. Erotic literature is at a point where it has to move on and evolve to stay interesting. It is not enough anymore to describe sex. Some of my favourite stories in *Bloots* have a very unromantic backdrop, such as war ... there is eroticism to be found in those circumstances as well'. *Folly's* author, Jassy Mackenzie, and the three-woman writing team behind the erotic series *A Girl Walks Into* ... argue that writing their so-called mommy porn provides them with the opportunity to introduce men and women to the redeeming effects of sex.

There are varying interpretations of the effects of mommy porn. On the one hand, critics have commented that the male character is overly controlling and abusive towards the female protagonist in *Fifty Shades of Grey*, but others contend that this is overstated, as Ana had to give consent for Christian's preferred sexual practices (Barker 2013). Likewise, the characters in *Folly* and *A Girl Walks Into* .... take on the more sexually dominant role and have men 'just letting go for a while, to just have a strong woman taking control'. These books are significant because, as Moffett (in Sidley 2013: 53) argues, to 'explore their sexuality women need to be free to make choices. And without empowerment and knowledge, women can't have freedom and choice. In my 20s I was hugely influenced by books like *Our Bodies Ourselves*, which emerged from the pro-sex, pro-pleasure element of the women's movement. They encouraged women to explore what they wanted sexually, not what they thought men wanted'.

8.4 Sociological perspectives on sexuality: A South African view

Sexuality and sexualities are powerfully shaped by our specific social contexts. There are also strong links and overlaps between our sexual orientation and other aspects of our identity, including our social class, race and gender. Specifically, a person's race, class, gender and ethnic position, among other things, influence the ways in which one is able to access particular resources to construct and enact a sexual identity. This has been very evident in South Africa. What follows then is a brief overview of sexuality in the South African social landscape before engaging with different sociological perspectives on the matter.

8.4.1 Policing sexuality in South Africa: A brief history

Since the transition to democracy in South Africa, there has been a dramatic shift in attitudes to and the corresponding representations of sexuality in mainstream society. Posel (2011: 131–132) argues that South Africa's new Bill of Rights (included and enacted in the 1996 Constitution), allows individuals more rights and responsibilities related to their sexual identities. She notes that 'sexuality has been thrust into public prominence', as evidenced by the portrayal of explicit sex scenes on television and in films, sex talk on radio, the proliferation of sex shops and strip clubs, and the unbanning of the pornography industry as common daily features of post-apartheid South Africa. Sexuality, according to Posel, is 'boldly and openly on display', with women and men attempting to sexualise their appearance (in body image and dress code). This was not, however, always possible. The apartheid regime enforced 'draconian policing' strategies and prohibitions over sex and sexuality. In addition to the South African Publications Act of 1974, which outlawed the production, distribution and consumption of sexually explicit material, two other examples of policing sexuality under apartheid are worth noting here: the Prohibition of Mixed Marriages Act 55 of 1949 and legislation associated with homosexuality.

The Prohibition of Mixed Marriages Act 55 of 1949

This 1949 apartheid Act sought to criminalise marriages between Europeans and all those deemed non-European. The then Minister of the Interior, Dr TE Dönges, argued that the law was not racist, since it applied equally to both races and that both white and black persons expressed their opposition to such marriages. While largely accepted by the white population, most Indian, coloured and black African people regarded it as racist and inhumane. Additional legislation supported the objective of preventing marriages across racial lines. These included the Immorality Act 21 of 1950, which declared intimate sexual relations across the races illegal, the Population Registration Act 30 of 1950, which required that all people be classified in terms of a race grouping, and the Group Areas Act 41 of 1950, which formed the basis of racially segregated residential areas (Sherman & Steyn 2009).

Such laws determined *who* could perform *which* sexual acts with *whom* – with a particular focus on a person's race. Sex (whether consensual or violent) under apartheid was considered a private and domestic matter, and not open to public debate. Despite this, in protecting the supposed 'purity' of the white race, where perpetrators of

sexual violence happened to be male and black, and the victims white (and male or female), the 'public outrage was virulent' (Posel 2011). Given national and international condemnation, the South African government initiated steps to investigate the possibility of repealing these laws in 1983. A parliamentary select committee was appointed for this purpose and in 1985 the government withdrew its support for the laws. The then Minister of Home Affairs and National Education, FW de Klerk, noted that although 'sex across the colour line would create social problems … it was time to remove the issue from the political realm' (Sherman & Steyn 2009: 67). Although interracial marriages were decriminalised, these couples could not live together, based on the provisions of the Group Areas and Separate Amenities Acts. These laws, too, were later repealed in post-apartheid South Africa in line with the provisions of the Constitution, which recognises the basic human rights of all South Africans, regardless of race, gender and sexuality.

Legislation policing homosexuality in South Africa

In addition to these laws, in 1968 the National Party government sought to criminalise homosexuality under the amendments to the Immorality Act of 1957 (later renamed the Sexual Offences Act) in 1968. Drawing on the idea of homosexuality as an 'alien' import and an English and Jewish threat posed to young Afrikaner boys, the apartheid government justified its aim to criminalise homosexual acts by compulsory imprisonment of up to three years. This led a number of white, middle-class gay men (who formed the Law Reform Movement) to raise an amount of R40 000 to afford the services of a lawyer to prevent the enactment of such legislation. Owing to their efforts, the proposed legislation was not passed, but the homosexual community was made aware that they were to be discreet under the watchful eye of a conservative government (Gevisser 1995).

Only in 1982 did the first national gay organisation emerge in Johannesburg. The Gay Association of South Africa (GASA) was frequented by wealthy white middle-class gay men. Its mission statement emphasised the organisation's lack of political motive, eventually resulting in its demise. Its then National Secretary-General, Kevan Botha, stated that 'we cannot begin to enter any debate on political structures or ideologies, neither our own country's nor any others' (Croucher 2002: 318). For not supporting one of its few black members, Simon Nkoli, who was on trial for high treason in the anti-apartheid struggle, GASA was criticised both by some of its members and by the International Lesbian and Gay Alliance (ILGA). Later organisations therefore had to exhibit a more visible link to the social and political turmoil facing South Africans (along racial, gender and sexual lines). This resulted in the formation of the Gay and Lesbians of the Witwatersrand (GLOW), chaired by Nkoli with a majority black membership. Under his leadership, GLOW sought to address the struggles of gay individuals, attesting that homosexuality was a ubiquitous racial problem embedded within a larger political struggle. Nkoli noted that 'I'm fighting for the abolition of apartheid, and I fight for the right of freedom of sexual orientation. These are inextricably linked with each other. I cannot be free as a black man if I am not free as a gay man' (Cock 2003: 36). It was through the creation of the Organisation of Lesbian and Gay Activists (OLGA) in Cape Town, aligned with the United Democratic Front (UDF), an affiliate organisation to the African National Congress (ANC), that much change would result in the early 1990s (Croucher 2002).

In the years preceding the legalised prohibition of discrimination on the basis of sexual orientation in South Africa's Constitution, 42 organisations came together across South Africa to form the National Coalition for Gay and Lesbian Equality (NCGLE). This movement played an important role in the eventual Constitutional protection of sexual minorities. Its key objectives were to have an explicit reference to sexual orientation in the Equality Clause of the final Constitution, to campaign for the decriminalisation of homosexuality and to challenge homophobic discrimination. As part of sections 9(3) and (4) of the Constitution of the Republic of South Africa, Act 108 of 1996, the equality clause includes sexual orientation as one of several identity markers against which the 'state may not unfairly discriminate directly or indirectly against anyone'. In addition to this legal victory, other legal judgements resulted in abolishing the crime of sodomy in 1998, providing same-sex couples equal rights in terms of immigration regulations (1999), pension benefits (2002), recovering funeral expenses (2003), adoption (2002) and marriage (2006), either as a civil or marital union (Reddy 2010).

So how do the different strands of sociology engage debates on sexuality?

8.4.2 Sociological perspectives on sexuality

Sociology offers a number of different ways to look at sexuality in contemporary society. Some value its role in stabilising family relationships. Some encourage us to acknowledge the similarities between people regardless of their different sexual identities. Others, however, are more critical about how sexuality is used as a site to exploit certain groups. We may not necessarily agree with all or some of the following sociological perspectives, but we demonstrate a sensitivity towards the diversity of views on the topic.

The structural functionalist perspective: Assimilating into heteronormativity

Proponents of structural functionalism argue in favour of establishing and maintaining order and stability in society. They acknowledge that change and conflict take place, but believe that measures need to be introduced as quickly as possible to retain the status quo. In order to do this, members of civil society need to reach consensus about the importance of certain values and practices in society. When we relate this to sexuality, two points are of interest. First, these theorists identify the particular **roles** that people are assigned based on their gender and sexual identities. These roles ensure that people know precisely what is acceptable and unacceptable in society and to avoid unnecessary change and conflict. One of the earliest structural functionalists to write about this was Talcott Parsons. His work was of particular value in the US in the late 1940s and early 1950s. He distinguishes between two distinct roles performed by men and women in society. Men perform the instrumental role of breadwinner, father figure and patriarchal husband in their marriages. Women perform an expressive role, taking on a more empathetic, supportive, caretaking and nurturing performance in the domestic sphere. These roles recall the earlier references to Connell's distinction between hegemonic masculinity and emphasised femininity. Role division of this sort maintains the centrality of the institution of the family as primary source of socialisation and stratification of men and women along gender lines. Reid's (2013) South African study on gay male sexuality among black gay hairdressers in the town of Ermelo provides an example of how these men emulate heterosexual male and female roles. The men distinguished between the more masculine gay males, labelled as the *gents*, and their more effeminate and submissive male counterparts, the *ladies*. Findings from the study indicated that the ladies take on the traditional gendered roles of women and are thus vulnerable and submissive. In contrast, the gents are more masculine, and determine the nature of sexual relations, among other matters, in their relationships. Although a degree of negotiation is evident in how these men perform their roles, it should be clear that this relationship is characterised by a distinction between masculine and feminine roles.

A second important point related to structural functionalism is the importance it assigns to *assimilation*. This means that if we recognise the rights of, for example, gay and lesbian persons, the latter group is required to 'become one with' and emulate heterosexual behaviour in society to gain equal status. Heteronormativity is thus not critiqued or questioned. Such rights include the legal right to get married to one's same-sex partner, adopt children, be included in the military and inherit from a deceased partner after his/her death. Conforming to principles associated with heteronormativity is the best possible decision for gay and lesbian individuals, since it acknowledges same-sex rights within the existing sexual framework of heteronormativity. In her discussion of the principles of an assimilationist approach, Van den Berg (2016: 28) refers to the defence of same-sex marriage as a means to establish or even 'guarantee equal citizenship and societal worth for lesbians and gay men'. This 'normalises' homosexuality and provides gay and lesbian persons equality before the law. Critics of the assimilationist approach point out that such 'normalisation' poses a threat to a much-needed self-assertion by gay and lesbian individuals in South Africa and abroad. They argue that assimilation further marginalises, silences and denies sexual diversity within a heteronormative society (Van den Berg 2016).

Contemporary approaches have, however, become very sceptical about the applicability of Parsons' work insofar as more women are entering the labour market, serve in political leadership positions in the South African government and abroad, and also engage in sexual behaviour outside the institutions of family and marriage. Proponents of this approach have also been criticised for ignoring the impact of domestic violence, rape and sexual exploitation of children in the family.

Conflict perspectives: Feminist and liberationist discourses

The newfound freedoms in post-apartheid South Africa did not come without some trepidation. Fears abound regarding contracting sexually transmitted diseases (eg HIV/AIDS) and experiencing homophobia and sexual violence (eg domestic violence and 'corrective' rape) (Jackson & Scott 2010). As opposed to structural functionalism, conflict theorists present a more revolutionary critique of the social order in society. Its proponents favour change and a destabilisation of the existing status quo to limit inequality between dominant social groups on the one hand, and racial, gender and sexual minorities on the other.

South African feminist discourses

Writing from a feminist perspective, Lewis (2011: 206) argues that African men and women have been misrepresented in academic and public discourse. She notes that with regard to their sexuality, they are defined in terms of 'sexual excess … and deviance', thus preoccupied with sexual behaviour. Previous and current academic scholarship focuses on how the sexual expression of African men and women has been controlled and punished. Judge (2017) asserts that the apartheid government enforced colonial principles to control sexual expression. These principles viewed white men as powerful and in control, whereas black men and women were seen as subordinate and in need of management. Men too, have been subjected to Western and South African feminist critique.

This relates to the differentiation in the degrees of control men and women have to exert their sexuality in African culture. Men, for example, have been able to exercise control over women in patriarchal societies, and in so doing maintain their superior position over them. Women are, in certain contexts, seen as the sexual property of men. In so doing, expression of their sexuality is considered 'in service' of men in the domestic and public spheres (eg as wives, lovers, sexual partners or sex workers). A clear South African example is the practice of **transactional sex**. It is defined as a purely sexual relationship outside the confines of marriage, where men and women engage in sexual intercourse 'in exchange for, or in anticipation of, material possessions or favours' (such as money, clothing, transportation and school fees) (Ranganathan et al 2016:1). Those who participate in this exchange do not consider the relationship as a form of sex work. The reason for this is that there is no predetermined price negotiated before engaging in transactional sex, whereas sex work requires an upfront specification of payment. In traditional patriarchal terms, it is usually the older man (the 'blesser') who provides the younger woman (the 'blessee') with gifts. Women engage in such relationships for a number of reasons: to gain more social status, pressure from their families or peer groups, or because of material needs. Although this relationship may be characterised by a reciprocal negotiation between the two parties under certain circumstances, South African feminists remain critical of the woman's supposed agency. Research has commented on the risk of contracting HIV or other sexually transmitted diseases (STDs) (Ranganathan et al 2016). This is mainly attributed to the fact that men may exert their power over women by refusing condom use in practising safe sex. Constraints on the agency and power of South African teenage women emphasises the fact that these women are 'on the receiving end of patriarchal power and almost defenceless when it comes to negotiating heterosexual relations' (Jewkes & Morrell 2012: 1729). Having multiple sexual partners is not necessarily frowned upon for men, since it affords them respect and a higher social status among their peers. This may legitimise their exertion of intimate partner violence and rape of women (Morrell 2001).

In keeping with the view of women as the sexual property of men, McRobbie (2010) provides a pessimistic view of the increased sexual freedom of women. She argues that the increased consumption of sexual imagery by women in particular, as more sexually confident agents, actually inhibits individual choice and freedom. When women consume and participate in specific products and activities that mirror the narcissistic behaviour of their male counterparts and engage in behaviour traditionally associated with men, including drinking, swearing and casual sex, this results in a so-called 'double entanglement' for women. While engaging openly in sexual behaviour and expressing diverse identities, such sexual freedom fuels 'sexual permissiveness' on the part of women, making them more apathetic and depoliticised. This means that they do not question the stereotypical representation of themselves as sexual objects, which helps to maintain the dominance of heteronormativity and patriarchy (McRobbie 2010: 43). Levy (2005) echoes these sentiments when she argues that the increased emphasis on women's sexuality creates a so-called 'raunch culture', which refers to women's tendency to freely use their bodies in order to titillate men. Examples include the use of hard-core pornographic media and more soft-core examples where young girls are encouraged to expose their naked bodies to male and female spectators (Bradley 2013). Levy (2005: 33) comments cynically on women's position in this regard: 'Proving that you are hot, worthy of lust, and – necessarily – that you seek to provoke lust remains women's work'. This double entanglement of women exercising their sexual agency in such ways enforces the dominance of male behaviour and their own sexual subordination and exploitation.

South African liberationist discourses

Conflict theorists disagree with functionalists that the provision of legal equality to gay and lesbian persons, such as the right to marry and to adopt children, will advance freedom of choice regarding sexual orientation. Proponents of this approach argue instead that assimilation will only result in making gay and lesbian individuals more 'heterosexual', 'ordinary' and subordinate (Van den Berg 2016). Eribon (2004: 115), for example, disassociates himself from advocating for same-sex marriage. In his view, the institution of marriage itself is discriminatory because 'every time a justice of the peace [marries gay and lesbian persons],

he or she not only marries two people, he or she also re-enacts all the rules (and the laws) of marriage – thereby reproducing the social and juridical exclusion of gay people'. Originating from the liberationist movements in the US of the late 1960s, this liberationist strand of conflict theory is critical of the dominance of heterosexuality in the gay and lesbian community's fight for social and political freedom. They argue for the construction of a separate community and culture as affirmation *against* a heterosexual society that only accommodates them if they conform to heteronormative principles. Instead, the aim is a fundamental challenge to sexual, gender and other social inequalities (Jagose 1996).

Efforts to create such communal gay and lesbian settings include the Castro District in San Francisco and the Cape Town suburb of De Waterkant. These communities provide its constituents with political, social and economic resources in order to redress the dominance of heteronormativity. Such self-imposed segregation does, however, throw up a series of contradictions. On the one hand, it emphasises the autonomy of the gay and lesbian community, and on the other it renders the community as too separate and distinct from mainstream heterosexual society. In doing this, gay and lesbian identities may in fact be 'hardened', resulting in strengthened 'othering' of homosexuality and reinforcing the impression that gay and lesbian people are somehow completely different from heterosexuals. This links to the earlier discussion on **homonormativity**. Although the creation of a separate sexual context may be laudable, the boundaries between a heterosexual and gay geographical context have become more permeable in recent years (Rothmann 2018). Elder (2004), Rink (2013) and Tucker's (2009) critical reading of the South African city of Cape Town as a 'gay village' is significant here. In addition to providing a communal environment for white gay men in particular, they argue that De Waterkant helps to promote Cape Town as a 'gay destination'. This boosts monetary income (for a heterosexual society) through gay and heterosexual tourism, despite a largely homophobic African continent, with South Africa thus becoming the destination for gay and lesbian travellers. This makes the gay community even more politically apathetic and uncritical of heterosexist discrimination directed against them. Tucker (2009: 188) refers to substantiated reports on the exclusion of 'non-white queers' from particular gay male social contexts (eg bars and clubs), supposedly on the basis of their not being 'regulars' or 'members'. Elder (2004: 580) notes that this reinforces a 'myth of [gay] community', insofar as such spaces cater mainly for certain gay men (gay white men) to the exclusion of others.

Liberationists are, moreover, critical of the longevity of such communities. Recent studies have indicated that gay villages such as San Francisco's Castro District are disappearing for three likely reasons. First, we have seen the increasing assimilation of heterosexual families into those contexts mainly populated by gay and lesbian persons, who in turn moved into mainstream heterosexual neighbourhoods. Secondly, owing to shifts in social and political views on homosexuality (eg South Africa's progressive Constitution), mainstream society has also become a 'gay village' of sorts for all sexual citizens. Thirdly, generational changes also indicate that younger gay and lesbian individuals attach less importance to a physically separate space for homosexual people. This has been spurred on by the availability of online dating platforms and digital applications such as *Grindr*, a platform for gay men wishing to date, network or meet up for sexual intercourse. Gay and lesbian youth are able to interact with members of the wider gay and lesbian community without having to meet them in a club or bar (Ghaziani 2017).

Regardless of their different foci, South African feminists and liberationists are both concerned about the detrimental effect of **homophobia** in society.

Critiquing homophobia: A conflict and feminist view of corrective rape

One of the earliest definitions of **homophobia** described it as 'the dread of being in close quarters with homosexuals' (Weinberg 1972: 4). More recent accounts regard homophobia as a fear of homosexual people that informs the attitudes and behaviour towards such individuals. Homophobia relates directly to **heterosexism**, which refers to discrimination towards those who do not conform to heteronormativity. Two forms of homophobia are particularly evident in society: **institutional** and **internalised homophobia**. Institutional homophobia centres on the various forms of oppression and discrimination (verbal and physical) that homosexual persons may experience through their interaction with social institutions in mainstream society. This happens in the family, schools and universities, the workplace and in religious institutions (Butler 2007). Internalised homophobia refers to an internal and self-hatred of one's own homosexuality. It may create a degree of 'in-group-hostility', which results in feelings of dislike, contempt or even stigmatisation of other more visible homosexual persons (Halperin 2012: 430). As a result, these persons may engage in intense self-regulation. When people feel compelled to regulate themselves in this way, the result may be 'deeply rooted tensions within themselves, leading

to censored self-expression'. Let us consider corrective rape as an example of the impact of homophobia on lesbian women in South Africa.

Since lesbian women may be considered as a minority, due to their sexual identity, they have become susceptible to corrective rape (Nkabinde & Morgan 2006). This sexual offence refers to a heterosexual male raping a lesbian woman to 'cure' or 'correct' her lesbianism in order for her to be attracted to men, not women. A male participant from a South African study supported the rape of lesbian women. He noted that '[i]f there is someone who is trying to rape a lesbian, I can appreciate their thing. It's just to let them know that they must be straight … Once she gets raped, I think she'll know which way is nice' (Mieses 2009). Judge (2017) argues that with corrective rape, in practice and in the acceptance of it, black lesbian women are portrayed as being passive victims without any social or sexual agency. She cites three reasons for her view. One, prefacing the rape with the word 'corrective' typifies the rape of lesbians as a 'separate class of rape'. Secondly, the reference to 'corrective' or 'curative' introduces the possibility of reforming or correcting the sexual preferences of the lesbian woman towards becoming heterosexual. Finally, academic and mainstream (eg media) usage of the phrase posits lesbians as passive victims of male sexual violence, making them more vulnerable, powerless and 'rapable', affording them no or very little agency (Judge 2017: 69).

Notwithstanding its obviously negative impact, Judge (2017: 90) critiques a singular view of a purely homophobic African context. Buying into the 'un-African' view of homosexuality only perpetuates the false idea that African prejudice is fixed and not open to change. The source for homophobic rhetoric in Africa stems from the colonial imports of Western religious discourse which sought to vilify same-sex behaviour among men and women. Regardless of its source, Gqola (2018) echoes this argument in reflecting on the rape and murder of Eudy Simelane, activist and player for Banyana Banyana (the South African national women's soccer team) in 2008:

The manufacture of female fear is concerned with regulating women's … sexuality and behaviour. What has been dubbed 'curative' or 'corrective' rape is a manifestation of this desire to control, monitor and police all aspects of women's lives. Lesbian women are marked as inappropriately sexual and the motivation or justification for raping and/or killing them often surfaces the desire to render them heterosexual … [Lesbian women] are also to be rendered fearful of living their lives on their terms, in a collision of patriarchal and homophobic power that lies behind rapist men's senses of entitlement to women's bodies (Gqola 2018: 92).

Gqola emphasises the fact that male sexual predators use 'corrective rape' to reinforce patriarchal dominance by controlling, humiliating and 'changing' their female victim. This is similar to Smuts' (2011) findings from her research among black lesbian women living in Johannesburg. Smuts engages the linear movement associated with the construction of a gay and/or lesbian identity. Her study reaffirms how the incongruence between the South African Constitution and the actual treatment of lesbian women in society actually provides them with little leeway to construct their sexual orientation without fear. The women in her study would progress towards the next stage in their identity construction (eg from acknowledging that they were lesbian to identity acceptance) and then, after experiencing discrimination, revert to the initial stages of shame and fear for being lesbian. This, according to her, relates to the lack of access of these women to a 'matrix of power ... and the extent to which [they] can tap into this power, and gain agency' because of heteronormativity and homophobia (Smuts 2011: 38).

The symbolic interactionist perspective: the influence of reflexivity

Proponents of symbolic interactionism focus on how people construct their social selves in relation to other people through social interaction. Primarily informed by the work of George Herbert Mead, the main tenet of this theory centres on how we are able to constantly reflect on our surroundings and conversations with ourselves and others to construct meaning. The perspective thus emphasises the possibility to constantly construct, reconstruct or deconstruct our social (and sexual) selves based on the different meanings we attach to our experiences. Given the foregoing references to the possible decline in communal social and sexual identification, Plummer (2015: 66) claims that contemporary society foregrounds a greater degree of reflexivity on the part of individual persons. This, he argues, provides individuals the opportunity to negotiate their personal and *individualized sexualities*. Choices now extend to how we will live our personal lives, with whom we will live, the kinds of sex and love we pursue and, ultimately, what we will do with our lives'. Plummer (1998) advocates acknowledging the 'messiness' (in other words, the plurality and diversity) associated with the lived experiences of gay men and

lesbian women in order to distinguish between contrasting experiences within what functionalists and conflict theorists consider as a homogeneous group (meaning that all gay men are the same and all lesbian women display the same traits). Symbolic interactionism encourages us to appreciate the 'pluralization, individuation and multiplying choices ... for new kinds of sexualities' (Plummer 2003: 520).

Because of this, proponents of this view emphasise a more fractured, fluid and heterogeneous view of sexual identities. For example, Sedgwick (2008) argues that one needs to acknowledge the inherent diversity which characterises individual experiences, regardless of whether these persons share the same racial, ethnic, class or sexual orientation category. She identifies several examples of how people engage with meanings that they attach to their sexual lives. These include the importance people attach to having sexual intercourse, the role of their sexual identity as dominant feature in their lives or only one of several identity components, the frequency with which individuals engage in sex or the choice for or against the use of sex toys during intercourse. Other studies on the sexual proclivities of gay and lesbian individuals are also highlighted in the recommendations of Nardi (2002). He emphasises initial sources for sexual practices, the 'types' of attractions among gay men (based on bodily appearance), as well as the way in which different nationalities, racial groups, classes and age groups engage in sexual acts. In addition, diverse forms in the gay community also result from particular sub-categorisations that men may wish to ascribe to, particularly around whether these are more effeminate or masculine. Examples of these include the more masculine gay men or 'muscle marys', the cultured and effeminate gay male or 'opera queen' and the more feminine or 'butch' lesbian (Roseneil 2002).

The queer theoretical perspective: A poststructuralist discourse on sexuality

Queer theory originated from a post-structural approach that critiques fixed understandings of sexual identities along binary lines. Its proponents view sexual identity as a 'socially constructed fiction that prescribes and proscribes against certain feelings and actions' (Giffney 2009: 2). What we regard as acceptable or unacceptable is not merely a natural given, but it is something that was socially constructed to exercise power over certain people based on their gender and sexual identity. The dominance of heteronormativity over heterosexual *and* homosexual people is basically seen as the above mentioned 'fiction' that we have to constantly question. Queer theory represents 'whatever is at odds with the normal, the legitimate, the dominant' (Halperin 1995: 62). Queer theorists contest the stable meanings of identity categories and labels of, among others, gay and lesbian or heterosexual and homosexual. They do this to critique the dominance, stability and morality associated with heteronormativity. Writing from a South African perspective, Msibi (2018: 22) provides an interesting way of looking at queer theory. He notes that the theory 'views identity as a process and not a final destination'. It therefore 'questions the "normalized", "known", "assumed" and "taken for granted" ideas about identification'.

Queer theorists maintain that focusing solely on the binary logic (ie the distinction between one group and another) simply reinforces the idea that the group on the one side of the continuum is more dominant and significant (eg heterosexuality, men) than the one on the other side (eg homosexuality, women). This approach proposes that we rather acknowledge the *fluidity* and *multiplicity* of sexual expression *outside* a specific identity category (Butler 1990; Dillon 2014). In short, 'you are just *you*', regardless of your sex, gender or sexuality. You determine what the rules are in terms of your behaviour and appearance – *no one else!* Quite strange, isn't it? We have all been socialised to fit into specific 'boxes' or 'categories' to know *who we are, where we belong* and *what we should do.* Identities have become a very important component of all of our lives, but they have also, according to queer theory, prevented people from being their 'true selves'. This is because most of us try to conform to the expectations of 'accepted' gender and sexual identities in order to 'fit in', 'be accepted' or better understand ourselves. For example, questions like 'how should I act because I am gay?' or beliefs such as 'I should be sexually submissive to my husband simply because I am a woman' only reflect the power of society and societal expectations. These theorists thus share the appreciation symbolic interactionists have for sexual diversity, but they are critical of retaining an identity category.

Seidman (1996) argues that regardless of how different theoretical perspectives (eg assimilationists, liberationists and symbolic interactionists) approach sexual identities, they fail to adequately challenge or eradicate the dominance of heteronormativity. Conflict and liberationist theorists bring to light how the category of 'the homosexual' is used to discriminate against gay and lesbian persons. Structural functionalists and assimilationists celebrate the sameness of heterosexuals and homosexuals to gain equal rights. Both, however, adopt an approach that values an appreciation of specific categories: on the one hand, a unified homosexual category that challenges heterosexual principles (conflict and liberationist theorists), and on the other a homosexual category that shares the values of heterosexual society (assimilationist and functionalist theorists). In short, then, queer theory destabilises the noted binary logic (heterosexuality versus homosexuality) to alert us to how this division reproduces power for some, at the expense of others, which leads to social inequality based on sexual orientation (Dillon 2014).

You have now been introduced to a number of concepts, debates and theories on sexualities and sexual orientations. It is evident that discourses on sexuality and sexual orientation are a contested terrain, and that the sociological theoretical traditions approach the topic in different ways. Two specific points are worth highlighting:

1. The importance of appreciating and respecting the right of all people to express their sexuality freely. Irrespective of where your theoretical inclinations lie, note that each of the theories presented in this chapter provide invaluable insights into the constant interplay between a person's sexual agency and their surrounding community and country.

2. Noting that one can never assume that everyone enjoys equal rights when it comes to their sexual identity, every country has its own unique cultural traditions, laws and ideologies about what is acceptable or unacceptable. This should alert you to the fact that identity is always open and contested, and shaped by the social context in which it is located.

Summary

- This chapter on sexualities and sexual orientations aimed to introduce you to the central concepts, current debates and practical applicability of both constructs in people's everyday lives.
- You were sensitised to the fact that your sex, gender and sexual orientation are not the same thing and should not be conflated or confused – instead, they are interrelated.
- The way in which we enact our sexual identities is not just a natural given because we are socialised to internalise and exhibit particular behaviour based on our sexual orientation(s) in a certain context.
- South African society is characterised by a variety of lay and activist approaches, views and movements that seek to challenge or uphold certain forms of discrimination and exclusion based on a person's sexual identification and orientation.
- It is important to note the different theoretical approaches that are used by academics to understand a person's sexuality and sexual orientation.
- Sociological theories challenge the taken-for-granted importance and dominance of heteronormativity, homonormativity and patriarchy in South African society and abroad to emphasise the rich variety and plurality associated with sexuality and sexual orientations.

ARE YOU ON TRACK?

1. Shortly explain why sexuality and sexual orientation should be considered as social constructs.
2. Explain how a person's sex, gender and sexuality are interrelated.
3. Do you agree with arguments that view same-sex behaviour as 'un-African'? Give reasons for your answer.
4. Shortly explain how people are 'taught' to be heterosexual, gay and lesbian. Refer to specific South African examples as part of your answer.
5. Provide a discussion in which you distinguish between the different sociological perspectives on sexuality.

More sources to consult

Aldrich R (ed). 2010. *Gay Life and Culture: A World History.* London: Thames & Hudson.

Francis D. 2017. *Troubling the Teaching and Learning of Gender and Sexual Diversity in South African Education.* New York: Palgrave Macmillan.

Gevisser M, Cameron E (eds). 1995. *Defiant Desire: Gay and Lesbian Lives in South Africa.* New York: Routledge.

Nardi PM, Schneider BE (eds). *Social Perspectives in Lesbian and Gay Studies: A Reader.* New York: Routledge.

Richardson D, Seidman S (eds). *Handbook of Lesbian and Gay Studies.* London: SAGE.

Seidman S (ed). 1996. *Queer Theory/Sociology.* Cambridge: Blackwell Publishers.

Tamale S (ed). 2011. *African Sexualities: A Reader.* Cape Town: Pambazuka Press.

References

ABC Analysis. 2018. 'ABC Analysis Q1 2018: The biggest-circulating consumer mags in SA'. http://www.marklives.com/2018/05/abc-analysis-q1-2018-the-biggest-circulating-consumer-mags-in-sa/ [Accessed 19 January 2019].

Achmat Z. 1993. '"Apostles of civilised vice": "Immoral practices" and "unnatural vice" in South African prisons and compounds, 1890–1920'. *Social Dynamics*, 19(2): 92–110.

Andersen N. 2018. 'Top selling books in SA history: The President's Keepers takes the crown'. https://www.thesouthafrican.com/top-selling-book-in-sa-the-presidents-keepers/ [Accessed 19 January 2019].

Arxer SL. 2011. 'Masculine power: Reconceptualizing the relationship between homosociality and hegemonic masculinity'. *Humanity & Society*, 35: 390–422.

Attwood F. 2011. 'Sex and the citizens: Erotic play and the new leisure culture' in *The New Politics of Leisure and Pleasure*. Bramham P, Wagg S (eds). London: Palgrave Macmillan, 82–96.

Barker M. 2013. 'Consent is a grey area? A comparison of understandings of consent in Fifty Shades of Grey and on the BDSM blogosphere'. *Sexualities*, 16(8): 896–914.

Beck U, Beck-Gernsheim E. 1995. *The Normal Chaos of Love*. Cambridge: Polity Press.

Bradley H. 2013. *Gender*. 2nd ed. Cambridge: Polity Press.

Brown R. 2012. 'Corrective rape in South Africa: A continuing plight despite an international human rights response'. *Annual Survey of International & Comparative Law*, 18(1): 44–66.

Butler J. 1990. *Gender Trouble: Feminism and the Subversion of Identity*. New York: Psychology Press.

Butler AH. 2007. 'Navigating institutional homophobia'. *Journal of Gay & Lesbian Social Services*, 19(1): 71–88.

Calhoun C. 2008. 'In defence of same-sex marriage' in *The Philosophy of Sex: Contemporary Readings*. 5th ed. Soble A, Power N (eds). Lanham: Rowman & Littlefield, 197–215.

Chambers D. 2012. *A Sociology of Family Life: Change and Diversity in Intimate Relations*. Cambridge: Polity.

Cock J. 2003. 'Engendering gay and lesbian rights: The equality clause in the South African Constitution'. *Women's Studies International Forum*, 26(1): 35–45.

Croucher S. 2002. 'South Africa's democratization and the politics of gay liberation'. *Journal of Southern African Studies*, 28(2): 315–330.

Dillon M. 2014. *Introduction to Sociological Theory*. 2nd ed. West Sussex: Wiley Blackwell.

Dirsuweit T. 1999. 'Carceral spaces in South Africa: A case study of institutional power, sexuality and transgression in a women's prison'. *Geoforum*, 30: 71–83.

Dlamini B. 2006. 'Homosexuality in the African context'. *Agenda*, 20(67): 128–136.

Downs A. 2006. *The Velvet Rage: Overcoming the Pain of Growing up Gay in a Straight Man's World*. Cambridge: Da Capo Press.

Dowsett GW. 1996. *Practicing Desire: Homosexual Sex in the Era of AIDS*. Stanford: Stanford University Press.

Elder G. 2004. 'Love for sale: Marketing gay male p/leisure space in contemporary Cape Town, South Africa' in *A Companion to Feminist Geography*. Nelson L, Seager J (eds). London: Blackwell, 578–589.

Epprecht M. 2013. *Sexuality and Social Justice in Africa: Rethinking Homophobia and Forging Resistance*. London: Zed Books.

Eribon D. 2004. *Insult and the Making of the Gay Self*. (Translated by Michael Lucey). London: Duke University Press.

Foucault M. 1978. *The History of Sexuality*, Volume 1. New York: Vintage.

Galupo MP, Ramirez JL, Pulice-Farrow L. 2017. '"Regardless of their gender": Descriptions of sexual identity among bisexual, pansexual, and queer identified individuals'. *Journal of Bisexuality*, 17(1): 108–124.

Gansen HM. 2017. 'Reproducing (and disrupting) heteronormativity: Gendered sexual socialization in preschool classrooms.' *Sociology of Education*, 90(3): 255–272.

Gay Pages. Autumn 2018. https://gaypagessa.com/

Gear S. 2005. 'Rules of engagement: Structuring sex and damage in men's prisons and beyond' in *Men Behaving Differently: South African Men since 1994*. Reid G, Walker, L. Cape Town: Double Storey, 89–110.

Gevisser M. 1995. 'A different fight for freedom: A history of South African lesbian and gay organization from the 1950s to the 1990s' in *Defiant Desire: Gay and Lesbian Lives in South Africa*. Gevisser M, Cameron E (eds). New York: Routledge, 14–86.

Ghaziani A. 2014. *There Goes the Gayborhood?* New Jersey: Princeton University Press.

Ghaziani A. 2017. *Sex Cultures*. Cambridge: Polity.

Giddens A. 1992. *The Transformation of Intimacy: Sexuality, Love & Eroticism in Modern Societies*. Cambridge: Polity Press.

Giffney N. 2009. 'Introduction: The 'Q' word' in *The Ashgate Research Companion to Queer Theory*. Giffney N, O'Rourke M (eds). Surrey: Ashgate, 1–13.

Gqola PM. 2018. *Rape: A South African Nightmare*. Johannesburg: MF Books.

Greenland K, Taulke-Johnson R. 2017. 'Gay men's identity work and the social construction of discrimination'. *Psychology & Sexuality*, 8(1–2): 81–95.

Halkitis PN, Green KA, Wilton L. 2004. 'Masculinity, body image, and sexual behavior in HIV-seropositive gay men: A two-phase formative behavioral investigation using the internet'. *International Journal of Men's Health*, 3: 27–42.

Hall M. 2015. '"When there's no underbrush the tree looks taller": A discourse analysis of men's online groin shaving talk. *Sexualities*, 18(8): 997–1017.

Halperin DM. 1995. *Saint Foucault: Towards a gay hagiography*. New York: Oxford University Press.

Halperin DM. 2009. 'Thirteen ways of looking at a bisexual'. *Journal of Bisexuality*, 9(3–4): 451–455.

Halperin DM. 2012. *How to be Gay*. Cambridge, MA: The Belknap Press of Harvard University Press.

Haralambos M, Holborn M. 2013. *Sociology: Themes and Perspectives*. 8th ed. London: Harper Collins.

Herzog D. 2006. 'The reception of the Kinsey reports in Europe'. *Sexuality & Culture*, 10(1): 39–48.

Hupperts C. 2010. 'Homosexuality in Greece and Rome' in *Gay Life and Culture: A World History*. Aldrich R (ed). London: Thames & Hudson, 28–55.

Jackson S, Scott S. 2010. *Theorizing Sexuality*. New York: Open University Press.

Jagose A. 1996. *Queer Theory: An Introduction*. New York: New York University Press.

Jewkes R, Morrell R. 2012. 'Sexuality and the limits of agency among South African teenage women: Theorising femininities and their connections to HIV risk practices'. *Social Science & Medicine*, 74: 1729–1737.

Judge M. 2014. 'For better or worse? Same-sex marriage and the (re)making of hegemonic masculinities and femininities in South Africa'. *Agenda*, 28(2): 67–73.

Judge M. 2017. *Blackwashing Homophobia: Violence and the Politics of Sexuality, Gender and Race*. London: Routledge.

Keegan T. 2001. 'Gender, degeneration and sexual danger: Imagining race and class in South Africa.' *Journal of Southern African Studies*, 27(3): 459–477.

Khoza A. 2018. '*Inxeba* (The Wound): Court rules that film is not hardcore porn'. [Online] Available at: https://www.news24.com/SouthAfrica/News/inxeba-the-wound-court-rules-that-film-is-not-hardcore-porn-20180628 [Accessed 1 October 2018].

Koko G, Monro S, Smith K. 2018. 'Lesbian, gay, bisexual, transgender, queer (LGBTQ) forced migrants and asylum seekers: Multiple discriminations' in *Queer in Africa: LGBTQI Identities, Citizenship, and Activism*. Matebeni Z, Monro S, Reddy V. New York: Routledge, 158–177.

Levine MP. 1998. *Gay Macho: The Life and Death of the Homosexual Clone*. New York: New York University Press.

Levy A. 2005. *Female Chauvinist Pigs: Women and the Rise of Raunch Culture*. New York: Free Press.

Lewis D. 2011. 'Representing African sexualities' in *African Sexualities: A Reader*. Tamale S (ed). Cape Town: Pambazuka Press, 199–216.

Loots L. 2000. 'Looking for women's rights in the rainbow pornography, censorship, and the "new" South Africa' in *Feminism and Pornography*. Cornell D (ed). New York: New York University Press, 423–437.

Mamba Online. http://www.mambaonline.com/2012/07/12/health4men-condemns-gay-cure-billboard/

Martin A. 2013. '*Fifty Shades* of sex shop: Sexual fantasy for sale'. Sexualities, 16(8): 980–984.

McAllister J. 2013. '*Culture, Health & Sexuality:* An international journal for research, intervention and care.' *Culture, Health & Sexuality*, 15(S1): S88–S101.

McRobbie A. 2010. *The Aftermath of Feminism*. London: SAGE.

Meem DT, Gibson MA, Alexander JF. 2010. *Finding Out: An Introduction to LGBT Studies*. London: SAGE.

Men's Health. July 2012. https://www.mh.co.za

Mieses A. 2009. 'Gender inequality and corrective rape of women who have sex with women'. [Online] Available at: http://www.gmhc.org/files/editor/file/ti-1209.pdf [Accessed 20 September 2018].

Milani TM, Wolff B. 2015. 'Queer skin, straight masks: Same-sex weddings and the discursive construction of identities and effects on a South African website'. Critical Arts, 29(2): 165–182.

Moodie TD. 1994. *Going for Gold*. Johannesburg: Witwatersrand University Press.

Morrell R (ed). 2001. *Changing Men in Southern Africa*. Pietermaritzburg: University of Natal Press.

Msibi T. 2018. *Hidden Sexualities of South African Teachers: Black Male Educators and Same-sex Desire*. New York: Routledge.

Nardi PM. 2002. 'The mainstreaming of lesbian and gay studies?' in *Handbook of Lesbian and Gay Studies*. Richardson D, Seidman S (eds). London: SAGE, 44–54.

Niehaus I. 2009. 'Renegotiating masculinity in the Lowveld: Narratives of male–male sex in compounds, prisons and at home' in *The Prize and the Price: Shaping Sexualities in South Africa*. Steyn M, Van Zyl, M. Cape Town: HSRC Press, 85–111.

Nkabinde N, Morgan R. 2006. 'This has happened since ancient times … it's something that you are born with': Ancestral wives among same-sex sangomas in South Africa. *Agenda*, 20(67): 9–19.

Ntozini A, Ngqangweni H. 2016. 'Gay Xhosa men's experiences of *ulwaluko* (traditional male initiation)'. *Culture, Health & Sexuality*, 18(11): 1309–1318.

Olaoluwa S. 2018. 'The human and the non-human: African sexuality debate and symbolisms of transgression' in *Queer in Africa: LGBTQI Identities, Citizenship, and Activism*. Matebeni Z, Monro S, Reddy V. New York: Routledge, 20–40.

Oluoch A, Tabengwa M. 2017. 'LGBT visibility: A double-edged sword' in *State Sponsored Homophobia*. 12th ed. Carroll A, Mendos, LR (eds). [Online] Available at: http://ilga.org/downloads/2017/ILGA_State_

Sponsored_Homophobia_2017_WEB.pdf [Accessed 16 September 2018].

Petersen T. 2018. 'Cape Town pastor found guilty of contempt of court for anti-gay slurs'. [Online] Available at: https://www.news24.com/SouthAfrica/News/cape-town-pastor-found-guilty-of-contempt-of-court-for-anti-gay-slurs-20180518 [Accessed 1 October 2018].

Pieterse W. 2018. 'The Big B in LGBTIQI+'. *Gay Pages*, Autumn, 85: 64–65.

Plummer K. 1998. 'Afterword: The past, present, and futures of the sociology of same-sex relations' in *Social Perspectives in Lesbian and Gay Studies*. Nardi PM, Schneider BE (eds). New York: Routledge, 605–614.

Plummer K. 2003. 'Queers, bodies and postmodern sexualities: A note on revisiting the sexual in symbolic interactionism'. *Qualitative Sociology*, 26(4): 515–530.

Plummer K. 2015. *Cosmopolitan Sexualities*. Cambridge: Polity.

Posel D. 2011. '"Getting the nation talking about sex": Reflections on the politics of sexuality and nation-building in post-apartheid South Africa' in *African Sexualities: A Reader*. Tamale S (ed). Cape Town: Pambazuka Press, 130–144.

Ranganathan M, Heise L, Pettifor A, Silverwood RJ, Selin A, MacPhail C, Delaney-Moretlwe S, Kahn K, Gómez-Olivé FX, Hughes JP, Piwowar-Manning E, Laeyendecker O, Watts C. 2016. 'Transactional sex among young women in rural South Africa: Prevalence, mediators and association with HIV infection'. *Journal of the International AIDS Society*, 19: 1–13.

Ratele K. 2011. 'Male sexualities and masculinities' in *African Sexualities: A Reader*. Tamale S (ed). Cape Town: Pambazuka Press, 399–412.

Reddy V. 2010. 'Identity, law, justice. Thinking about sexual rights and citizenship in post-apartheid South Africa'. *Perspectives*, 4(10): 18–23.

Reddy V, Monro S, Matebani Z. 2018. 'Introduction' in *Queer in Africa: LGBTQI Identities, Citizenship, and Activism*. Matebeni Z, Monro S, Reddy V. New York: Routledge, 1–16.

Reid G. 2013. *How to be a Real Gay: Gay Identities in Small-town South Africa*. Scottsville: University of KwaZulu-Natal Press.

Rich A. 1980. 'Compulsory heterosexuality and lesbian experience'. *Signs*, 5(4): 631–660.

Rink BM. 2013. 'Que(e)rying Cape Town: Touring Africa's "gay capital" with the Pink Map', in *Tourism in the Global South: Heritages, Identities and Development*.

Sarmento J, Brito-Henriques E (eds). Lisbon: Centre for Geographical Studies, 65–90.

Roseneil S. 2002. 'The heterosexual/homosexual binary: Past, present and future' in *Handbook of Lesbian and Gay Studies*. Richardson D, Seidman S. (eds). London: SAGE, 27–43.

Rothmann J. 2014. '(De)constructing the heterosexual/homosexual binary: The identity construction of gay male academics and students in South African tertiary education'. PhD thesis. Potchefstroom: North West University.

Rothmann J. 2018. '"To gay or not to gay, that is the question": Permeable boundaries between public and private spaces of gay male academics and students in South Africa'. *Gender Questions*, 16: 1–24.

Santos AC. 2013. 'Are we there yet? Queer sexual encounters, legal recognition and homonormativity'. *Journal of Gender Studies*, 22(1): 54–64.

Schippers M. 2016. *Beyond Monogamy: Polyamory and the Future of Polyqueer Sexualities*. New York: New York University Press.

Sedgwick E. 2008. *Epistemology of the Closet*. Updated version. Berkeley: University of California Press.

Seidman S (ed). 1996. *Queer Theory/Sociology*. Cambridge: Blackwell Publishers.

Serra G. 2018. 'Bougardt could be sent to prison'. [Online] Available at: https://www.dailyvoice.co.za/news/bougardt-could-be-sent-to-prison-13672440 [Accessed 1 October 2018].

Sherman R, Steyn M. 2009. 'E-race-ing the line: South African interracial relationships yesterday and today' in *The Prize and the Price: Shaping Sexualities in South Africa*. Steyn M, Van Zyl M. Cape Town: HSRC Press, 55–81.

Sidley K. 2013. 'Meet four South African women who have taken over where *Fifty Shades* left off: Except this time, the women are in charge'. *Fair Lady*, 6(1): 50–53.

Smuts L. 2011. 'Coming out as a lesbian in Johannesburg, South Africa: Considering intersecting identities and social spaces'. *South African Review of Sociology*, 42(3): 23–40.

Tamale S. 2011. 'Researching and theorising sexualities in Africa' in *African Sexualities: A Reader*. Tamale S (ed). Cape Town: Pambazuka Press, 11–36.

Tatchell P. 2005. 'ANC dashes hopes for gay rights in SA' in *Sex & Politics in South Africa*. Hoad N, Martin K, Reid G (eds). Cape Town: Double Storey, 148–150.

Tucker A. 2009. *Queer Visibilities: Space, Identity and Interaction in Cape Town.* West-Sussex: Wiley-Blackwell.

Valocchi S. 2005. 'Not yet Queer Enough: The Lessons of Queer Theory for the Sociology of Gender and Sexuality'. *Sociologists for Women in Society*, 19(6): 750–770.

Van den Berg E. 2016. '"The closet": A dangerous heteronormative space'. *The South African Review of Sociology* 47(3): 25–44.

Van Reenen D. 2014. 'Is this really what women want? An analysis of *Fifty Shades of Grey* and modern feminist thought'. *South African Journal of Philosophy*, 33(2): 223–233.

Varangis E, Lanzieri B, Hildebrandt T, Feldman M. 2012. 'Gay male attraction toward muscular men: Does mating context matter?' *Body Image*, 9: 270–278.

Wallace L. 2010. 'Discovering homosexuality: Cross-cultural comparison and the history of sexuality' in *Gay Life and Culture: A World History.* Aldrich R (ed). London: Thames & Hudson, 249–269.

Watson LB, Dispenza F. 2015. 'The relationships among masculine appearance norm violations, childhood harassment for gender nonconformity, and body image concerns among sexual minority men'. *Journal of Gay & Lesbian Mental Health*, 19(2): 145–164.

Whitton G. 2001. 'Masculinities and *Men's Health*'. *Agenda*, 16(47): 99–104.

Youdell D. 2010. 'Queer outings: Uncomfortable stories about the subjects of post-structural school ethnography'. *International Journal of Qualitative Studies in Education*, 23(1): 87–100.

Race

Ran Greenstein

During the apartheid period, South Africa constructed one of the most thorough and complex systems of racial domination. This means that racial distinctions were legally entrenched and had profound social, cultural and political implications. Apartheid focused on the physical features of race, and the differences between members of racial groups, despite there being no specific basis for 'race'. What really mattered was that no normal social relationships could be formed and people were damaged by racial segregation and division. The legal foundations of apartheid are no longer with us, and yet the general legacy of racial differences continues to manifest itself in the public sphere in South Africa and beyond its borders. In order to understand the ongoing operation of race as a way of dividing people in society and shaping their political and cultural interests, this chapter discusses the race concept and its social expression within their historical contexts and in their diverse forms.

Because race has had such a long history shaping South African society, from early colonial conquest through apartheid to the present, we need to make an effort to focus on its ongoing impact. Under apartheid race was deeply entrenched in processes of socialisation and identity formation, but despite the fact that race became real for people in their living experiences, it was never a *natural* or biological phenomenon. The colour of our skin and the shape of our hair are real but irrelevant features of who we are. Race is rather a set of *material practices* and *cultural meanings*. It has a defined historical origin. It cannot be understood outside the experience of slavery and the *colonial encounter* and its expression in a range of political and economic processes. Race is, in addition, a *global* phenomenon that is not confined to any one society. These powerful social forces made race important. This is what is meant by the statement that race is socially constructed.

Since the advent of democracy in South Africa, the abolition of racial legislation and the enshrinement of equality in the Constitution, we are facing a serious challenge in creating a society that is not continually affected by its racially scarred past. This challenge requires of us to recognise the shifting meanings and impacts of race. At the same time, however, as this chapter discusses, we must avoid two pitfalls. We cannot assume that nothing has changed and that the old language of race can be used to make sense of our society today. And, we cannot assume that everything has changed and that race is consequently no longer relevant in understanding contemporary South African society.

The centrality of race in South African history and social theory makes this chapter essential reading for critical people, not just sociologists out of whose discipline this analysis of the concept of race and its practices flows. You need go no further than #BlackLivesMatter to realise the full extent of this claim.

Case study 9.1 Race and identity

In March 2011, Jimmy Manyi (then Director General of Labour, government spokesperson until 2012) said in a television interview:

> Coloured people in the Western Cape should spread in the rest of the country ... they must stop this over-concentration situation because they are in over-supply where they are [the Western Cape], so you must look into the country and see where you can meet the supply.

In response to this statement, Minister Trevor Manuel published an open letter, in which he accused Manyi of expressing racist sentiments by referring in the way that he did to 'the sons and daughters of those who waged the first anti-colonial battles against the Portuguese, the Dutch and the British when they set foot on our shores'. Coloured people, said Manuel, were also black and therefore entitled to claim equity in employment and to be regarded as a 'designated group' that had been discriminated against under apartheid and therefore deserves redress now. They are not different from other black people in the country in that respect.

Manuel was careful to note that although he himself was from the Western Cape, and was regarded as a 'coloured' person under apartheid, he was not speaking as a representative of that particular group but as a concerned activist, 'not as a coloured but as a non-racist determined to ensure that our great movement and our constitution are not diluted through the actions of racists like you'.

(Source: *Mail&Guardian* 2011)

Questions

1. Why was Manuel so critical of Manyi's approach?
   - Was it only because they differed on the correct way to refer to coloured people (as a separate group or as part of a broader black collective)?
   - Was it because they disagreed on how precisely to apply employment equity laws? Or was it, perhaps, because of a dispute over the links to be made between race, labour and social rights?
2. Why was the controversy brought out into the open a year after Manyi had made his statement, shortly before the 2011 municipal elections?
3. Are there more fundamental issues related to race, identity, economic position and political power that the exchange forces us to examine?

Key themes

- The concept of race and its multiple uses
- Historical perspective on the emergence of race: colonialism, slavery and empire
- The different dimensions of race: economic, political, cultural
- Critical race theory to South African history
- The significance of race.

9.1 Introduction

Ever since the beginning of European expansion into overseas territories, a process that has become known as **colonialism**, race has been a central element of social stratification. This has been true at the global level for the last five centuries, as well as in many local sites, of which South Africa is a notable example. Few other societies have been associated with the notion of race to the same extent as has South African society. But, we must recognise that the specific expressions of race, and its impact on society and politics, have changed over time. In examining race in our context we need to be aware of such changes, as well as appreciate the fact that we operate in a global context, which shapes the meanings we attach to the concept and the ways in which it affects us.

South Africa has been notorious for its use of the notion of race to justify social inequalities and political exclusion. Race as a social and political tool was thoroughly discredited with apartheid's demise and to this end, we can expect that it would no longer be used in the public sphere. But is that really the case?

This chapter will address issues of race with a focus on three dimensions: labour and the economy, power and politics, and identity and culture. It is important first to identify a theoretical framework within which we can examine the notion of race and its derivations (racial, racist, racism, and so on).

9.2 What is race?

American sociologist Howard Winant provides us with a good starting point for the theoretical discussion of race. He defines race as a concept 'that signifies and symbolizes socio-political conflicts and interests in reference to different types of human bodies'. He goes on to clarify that the concept of race 'appeals to biologically based human characteristics'. At the same time, the focus on particular human physical features (such as skin colour, hair, and so on), in order to indicate race, 'is always and necessarily a social and historical process' (Winant 2000). There is simply no biological basis for distinguishing human groups along the lines of race, he argues. The categories we normally use in order to identify different groups, and distinguish between them, are always imprecise and at times completely arbitrary. In other words, they have no basis in biology and science.

For this reason, it is important to note that sociological theories of race do not pay much attention to the physical features that are associated in the popular imagination with the concept of race. This is not because such features are not visible or are not real. The sociological approach does indeed recognise that some groups of people tend to have darker skin than others, or differently shaped and coloured hair, and they may tend to be taller and leaner, or shorter and heavier. But, it regards all these physical characteristics as irrelevant to people's qualities as individual human beings and as collective groups. These *physical* features of their bodies are not meaningful when considered on their own, in isolation from the meanings attached to them by *social*, *cultural* and *political* forces.

9.2.1 Racial meanings

The notion of meaning is central here. We use it in order to understand how people respond to the reality around them. Their responses are shaped by their perceptions of reality, which in turn are shaped by their prior experiences, cultural background, belief systems, habits of mind and social and political ideologies. All these factors play a role in making sense of social differences and dealing with them. Such differences become meaningful for us and form a basis for undertaking social action in line with the meanings they acquire.

Physical features associated with race (such as skin colour and hair) have been used in various historical circumstances to classify people, separate them into groups, judge their ability to perform various tasks, and provide them with differential access to social and political rights and economic resources. In other words race, in this sense, as a concept referring to a series of physical differences related to the body, is important. This is because it has had an impact on how people are treated, what they have been entitled to possess and what their life chances have been. In that way it has become meaningful.

It is precisely the use of *socially meaningless* features of the body, in order to make *meaningful social distinctions* that give race its unique status as a theoretical concept and as an important historical force. Other systems of classification usually rely on culture, origins, ethnicity, language, religion, and related factors, in order to distinguish between different groups. It is race alone that has linked some of these factors to physical features. This link is essential to the concept, and to the ways in which it has been used historically to create and perpetuate inequalities.

The use of the concept of race has varied between societies and over time. In some of them – South Africa, southern USA – it has been crucial to the entire evolution of the social and political system. In others, most European countries, it has had relatively little impact internally until recently, with the arrival of large numbers of people from formerly colonised countries. Historically, of course, race played a major role in shaping the process of European colonial expansion, even if its full impact was not noticeable on the home front. Despite these differences, all of these societies have been profoundly affected by the global rise of race from the 16th century onwards.

This focus on social and political dimensions is not meant to deny that people who live in different geographical conditions, physical and climatic environments who enjoy different diets and engage in different activities, tend to develop certain physical differences. These may have an impact on their ability to perform tasks involving the use of their bodies, for example excelling in various branches of sports that require different levels of endurance, having higher probability of experiencing certain genetically based diseases, or being more or less tolerant of harsh climatic conditions. The common wisdom of the social sciences is that all of these have nothing to do with mental and social processes and therefore do not affect individual and collective abilities and entitlements in all other fields, beyond the physical one.

9.2.2 Race as an emergent identity

A key implication of this approach, which focuses on the social significance of physical differences, is that it casts doubt on the objective existence of race. It regards race as an idea, a concept, a sign and a symbol. In other words, race is a way of making sense of social and political issues by interpreting them and linking them to real or imaginary physical appearances. The operation of the concept of race in this way does *not* mean that races – that is, distinct groups of people whose members are united by common features – really exist in nature. In some societies people of certain background were treated as if they were all members of the same group, and were seen by the legal system to be unified. South Africa under apartheid is the obvious example. These people were given or denied rights on that basis. In other societies this kind of treatment is more informal. But, whether formal or informal, racial groups exist only as the products of society, culture and the legal system, not as part of nature.

This point needs clarifying further. People of lighter and darker skin colours have always existed in different parts of the world. As a result of colonial expansion, enslavement and migration, they have become mixed to some extent in various locations. They are no longer confined to specific geographical areas. However, all those people who share such physical characteristics as skin colour had nothing to unify them historically beyond the fact that they may have looked similar to outside observers. They were divided on the basis of language, religion, culture, social structure, economic occupation, and so on. They were not part of a group with shared identity, a sense of common past and future destiny. It is only with the rise of colonialism that they were lumped together on the basis of their physical features, but even then they remained divided on all the other grounds listed above. In that sense, they have never become a global *group* (or race) with a unified position based on common interests. However, in specific times and places people may have formed a common racial identity over time, based on their shared legal and political position.

To pursue the example of apartheid South Africa, what is it that made whites a distinct group of people in this country? It was not their language or religion (they were divided on that basis between English, Afrikaans and other languages), it was not physical appearances (Jews from Eastern Europe look very different from Portuguese immigrants, or from white Afrikaners), it was not their culture (Afrikaans-speaking whites have much more in common culturally with Afrikaans-speaking coloured people than with some other groups of white immigrants), or any of the other features that normally unify people around a common identity. Rather, it was the fact that they were regarded by the legal and political system as members of the same group, entitled to the same rights and privileges. That was the primary factor that created some sense of identity among them.

Before the 20th century, the ancestors of people in Europe never regarded themselves as having anything in common. It was their specific historical experience in South Africa that allowed them to develop feelings of commonality defined in racial terms. Their ongoing historical experiences in post-apartheid South Africa may shatter that sense of identity, reinforce it or serve to merge their identity with that of other groups of people (for example those of Indian origins), even if they do not share physical features. We need to look at the role of such experiences in creating a group sense and identity among people of diverse origins, and also look at how changing circumstances usually lead to changing perceptions of identity.

We need to explore the extent to which our notions of what constitutes a racial group shift over time, which groups we include and exclude when we think of race classification and why we make links between racial features and mental abilities.

Case study 9.2 Nature, leisure and race in South Africa

Another story has raised additional questions related to race. It was in response to news about the South African National Parks' (SANParks) intention to build a five-star hotel in the Kruger National Park (KNP), with upmarket black clients, called 'black diamonds', having been identified as the key target audience for such a venture. An angry resident of Nelspruit (the main city close to the southern part of the Kruger Park), wrote a letter to a local newspaper, asking: 'Does one really expect the visiting 'Black Diamonds' entering the KNP in their high speed luxury cars to obey the 50 km per hour speed limit? … Are these people going to be happy to sit in the hotel after sunset and listen to the sounds of the African bush? Before long, there will be in-house entertainment; a night club and then a casino to keep the money moving.'

➡

SANParks responded by denouncing this as a racist attack, disguised as an attempt to protect nature. Government went ahead and approved the construction plan in August 2011.

QUESTIONS

1. What questions are raised by this incident?
2. How do notions of nature, leisure and race become connected in people's minds?
3. What images of the ways in which wealthy black people spend their money are exhibited in this case?
4. Are these images merely a reflection of reality, a bunch of offensive stereotypes, or a response by people to feelings of frustration and marginalisation?

9.3 History of the race concept

It is obvious that when whites in South Africa started regarding themselves as a racial group, they did not invent the concept of race from scratch. Rather, they relied on pre-existing notions that were widespread in the country itself, as well as in Europe and globally. But where did the notion of race originally come from?

9.3.1 Origins of race

Awareness of physical differences between groups of people from various geographical and climatic backgrounds may have been a feature of human consciousness from time immemorial. Likewise, a distinction between 'us' and 'them' or between 'self' and 'other' has been a part of the way all groups of people define their identity wherever they are, from the ancient Greeks to medieval Christians and the residents of the Arab and Islamic empires. However, the conversion of such general awareness into the systematic identification of physical features as crucial, and their consolidation into a rigid system of classification into distinct racial groups, is more recent in time. It can be traced to the rise of three historical processes which took place simultaneously over centuries and in close relation to one another.

These three processes were the rise of the European-centred colonial empires from the 16th century onwards, the emergence of the capitalist world system during the same period, and the consolidation of the modern scientific study of nature and society. Together, these processes created the foundation for a new way of looking at the world. This new mode of rationality and logic served to organise our thoughts and our observations of nature and shaped the ways in which we govern it. In combination these processes gave rise to what is known as modernity.

In its modern sense, the concept of race cannot be attributed to any particular individual, but rather is a product of studies and debates within various scholarly disciplines over many decades, which took place in the context of European overseas expansion. However, it is associated at times with the names of the great German philosophers Kant and Hegel. Their ideas are still of interest to us today due to their general influence on modern thought, but we must look at them in the context of their times, rather than try to evaluate them in view of our current ideas and norms. In other words, our purpose is to understand their contributions, not to blame them for some problematic practices that others have adopted independently of them.

9.3.2 Kant and Hegel on race

In the late 18th century, Immanuel Kant argued that all humans belonged to the same species and were all descended from the same line, and yet they could be classified into distinct racial groups. He defined race as a concept that indicated 'a radical peculiarity that announces a common descent' together with several 'persistently transmitted' qualities that appeared in the 'developing characters of successive generations'. Races were not different species, but 'deviate forms', meaning variants on the same basic human theme, which came about as 'a further development of purposive primary predispositions implanted in the line of descent'. While all human beings carried with them the same potential to develop, specific physical features emerged in response to encounters with the diverse geographical and climatic environments in which people found themselves as they dispersed and populated the planet (Bernasconi 2001; Kant 2001 [1788]).

It is important to recognise both aspects of Kant's approach: that all humans share the same line of descent, but also that in the process of dispersal throughout the world, racial differences became consolidated. Once that happened, they could not be overcome or reversed. This means that the division of the world's population on the basis of physical appearances is here to stay, though the relations between the groups that emerged as a result of that process may change over time. Whether physical features also lead to different levels of mental capacity, and as a result to different entitlements to recognition and resources, are questions that Kant did not discuss directly. In a sense, both the notion that all humans are equal despite diverse physical appearances, and the notion that they can be classified into distinct groups with their own abilities and rights, may follow logically from Kant's perspective.

Another famous philosopher of the period, GWF Hegel, writing in the early 19th century, argued that physical differences cannot tell us anything about what goes on inside people's minds. For that reason, we can recognise the existence of races, but cannot judge their ability to take equal part in society and its institutions on the basis of physical differences. At the same time, cultural and historical processes may mean that people who live in various parts of the world develop in their own ways: white, black and other people tend to face different challenges and therefore develop their own skills and capacities to cope with such challenges. These capacities are not biological in nature but a product of physical and social conditions. Hegel concluded that white people, living in temperate zones, showed greater ability to shape their environment, but this was not due to superior biology. People of other racial backgrounds could acquire similar abilities if exposed to the same conditions.

These general statements on race must be seen against another saying by Hegel, in his *Philosophy of History,* that the continent of Africa, 'is no historical part of the World; it has no movement or development to exhibit'. Africa is an expression of 'the Unhistorical, Undeveloped Spirit, still involved in the conditions of mere nature, and which had to be presented here only as on the threshold of the World's History' (in Taiwo 1998). This statement does not deal directly with questions of race but rather with history and culture. Yet, the negative attitudes towards Africa shown here have had obvious implications for the ways in which Europeans regarded black people. Even if Hegel personally did not hold the position that black people (most of whom originated in Africa) were mentally inferior, it is likely that most of his readers would have reached such conclusions from his work. In fact, such attitudes towards Africa and African people are still common today, and are one of the most serious problems created by the legacy of colonialism.

The approach adopted by people like Kant and Hegel and their followers may be better referred to as **Eurocentrism** than racism. It assumes that Europe enjoys mental and technological superiority in relation to most other cultures and civilisations, but does not regard that as the outcome of physical differences. It bases this view on an interpretation of social and cultural developments rather

than on biological theories. We must realise, though, that in the popular mind these factors frequently are closely related. This means that not only the intentions of writers are important, but also the likely impact of their words, and the many – sometimes contradictory – ways in which they could be interpreted by readers, activists and other thinkers and writers.

Kant and Hegel were merely the most famous in a line of European (and later also North American) philosophers and thinkers who dealt with this set of issues: the relations of Europe and its peoples to the rest of the world, and the consequences of that for questions of race. We cannot cover in this chapter in any detail the long list of people who made a contribution to debates over these matters. Karl Marx is one 19th century thinker who must be discussed directly because he studied the matter from a different perspective and left a lasting and distinct legacy.

9.3.3 Marx on race
Although Marx was a product of similar social and intellectual conditions to those of Kant and Hegel, who preceded him by a few decades, his theoretical approach was radically different. Known as the Materialist Conception of History, it examined social forms of organisation in the context of the social and economic developments of society as a whole. This was accompanied by a focus on the rise of capitalism as crucial to modern race relations. Marx is known for his study of capitalism – an economic system based on private property and the operation of market forces. Unlike classical economists though, Marx emphasised the role of violence and coercion, especially in capitalism's early stages, which he referred to as primitive accumulation – a process 'dripping from head to toe, from every pore, with blood and dirt', and the history of which is written 'in letters of blood and fire' (Marx 1867).

Exploitation of workers and their coercion into the labour market are central features of capitalism. Marx referred to that as 'wage slavery', which was distinguished from formal slavery in degree only. While slavery does not have any necessary relation to race, and it has existed in various forms since ancient times, it acquired a specific racial character under capitalism. Capitalism spread over the world and became global by using coercion to force diverse people and populations to work for it:

The discovery of gold and silver in America, the extirpation, enslavement, and entombment in mines of the indigenous population of the continent, the beginnings of the conquest and plunder of India, and the conversion of Africa into a preserve for the commercial hunting of black skins are all things that characterize the dawn of the era of capitalist production (Marx 1867a).

Marx failed to discuss race as a concept in its own right and did not dedicate space to it or to other questions of identity in his theoretical approach. He did leave a legacy to subsequent theorists of race, centred on looking at its role in the rise and growth of capitalism. In particular, three aspects have been central to such theory:

- The rise of race as a mode of identification and organisation of society was historically linked to European colonial expansion, the creation of overseas empires, and the emergence of a global capitalist economic system.
- The use of racial distinctions to facilitate the exploitation of vulnerable populations and the imposition of poor working conditions and low pay on them in order to increase profits.
- The ideological use of race in order to turn workers against each other and prevent them from forming a united front against their employers.

The role of race as an ideology was noted in a famous quote from a letter to two of his colleagues, in which he discussed how racial and ethnic prejudices were used to undermine workers' organisation:

Every industrial and commercial centre in England now possesses a working class divided into two hostile camps, English proletarians and Irish proletarians. The ordinary English worker hates the Irish worker as a competitor who lowers his standard of life. In relation to the Irish worker he regards himself as a member of the ruling nation and consequently he becomes a tool of the English aristocrats and capitalists against Ireland, thus strengthening their domination over himself. He cherishes religious, social, and national prejudices against the Irish worker. His attitude towards him is much the same as that of the "poor whites" to the Negroes in the former slave states of the U.S.A. The Irishman pays him back with interest in his own money. He sees in the English worker both the accomplice and the stupid tool of the English rulers in Ireland. This antagonism is artificially kept alive and intensified by the press, the pulpit, the comic papers, in short, by all the means at the disposal of the ruling classes. This antagonism is the secret of the impotence of the

English working class, despite its organisation. It is the secret by which the capitalist class maintains its power. And the latter is quite aware of this (Marx 1870).

This statement by Marx is based on the assumption that race and ethnicity may be genuine identities that reflect people's sense of common destiny with their 'own kind'. In other words, people feel that race is real, and this feeling is important for their sense of self-identity, even if it is ultimately based on unimportant physical differences. However, such feelings are dangerous when used to claim privileges at the expense of those who belong to the 'wrong' group and therefore are denied equal rights. Racism is a term normally used to refer to such attitudes of superiority and support for inequality. Not all identification in racial terms is racist, especially when those subjected to discrimination use racial identity as a source of self-empowerment (as in 'Say it loud – I'm black and I'm proud'). But, claims to an elevated status on the basis of different historical origins fall under this label. To prevent race from serving as a means for dividing workers and undermining their struggles, three additional aspects of race can be derived from the legacy of Marx's approach (though he rarely discussed them directly):

- Since race played a major role in facilitating the rise of capitalism and its ongoing growth, the struggle for racial equality is an essential component of the struggle against all forms of exploitation and oppression. Solidarity with and support for the rights of people oppressed on the basis of race, ethnicity or nationalism serves the interests of workers.
- Race has consequences for people's material conditions (their life chances, access to jobs, services, and so on). It also has ideological and cultural implications in that it affects images, stereotypes and perceptions of race, which are disseminated through the media and other means of mass communications.
- The politics of race – the ways in which race is conceptualised, understood and fought over, as well as serves to organise various groups – are thus central to our understanding of modern society.

9.3.4 The consciousness of race: Du Bois, Fanon and Biko

The European theorists discussed above examined race as part of their overall approach to society and history, rarely focusing on it directly. In contrast, many theorists from Africa and the African diaspora paid more attention to race as an independent factor in analysis and action, frequently drawing on their personal experiences.

In his 1903 book *The Souls of Black Folk*, African-American academic and public intellectual WEB Du Bois coined a prophetic phrase: 'The problem of the twentieth century is the problem of the color line – the relation of the darker to the lighter races of men in Asia and Africa, in America and the islands of the sea.'

Black people experienced a unique sensation, which Du Bois called double consciousness, a 'sense of always looking at one's self through the eyes of others,' of having to deal with prejudice and bigotry, being judged and having to measure 'one's soul by the tape of a world that looks on in amused contempt and pity'. The natural response to that might be despair, since black people are forced to stand 'helpless, dismayed, and well-nigh speechless; before that personal disrespect and mockery, the ridicule and systematic humiliation, the distortion of fact and wanton license of fancy, the cynical ignoring of the better and the boisterous welcoming of the worse, the all-pervading desire to inculcate disdain for everything black, from Toussaint [rebel leader in Haiti] to the devil.'

But, there is an alternative, 'the unifying ideal of Race; the ideal of fostering and developing the traits and talents of the Negro, not in opposition to or contempt for other races, but rather in large conformity to the greater ideals of the American Republic, in order that some day on American soil two world-races may give each to each those characteristics both so sadly lack.' What might the contribution of black people be, then? Du Bois focused on culture and spirituality: 'the wild sweet melodies of the Negro slave', American fairy tales and folklore derived from native American and African legacy, an 'oasis of simple faith and reverence in a dusty desert of dollars and smartness', providing a balance to the American materialist culture, 'light-hearted but determined Negro humility', and 'loving jovial good-humor' as well as 'the soul of the Sorrow Songs'.

At the time, such distinctions between races, seen as mutually exclusive groups, were common. But decades later, when Du Bois returned to the issue in his 1940 book *Dusk of Dawn: An Essay towards an Autobiography of a Race Concept*, he emphasised history more than culture:

> *the fact that since the fifteenth century these ancestors of mine and their other descendants have had a common history; have suffered a common disaster and have one long memory. The actual ties of heritage between the individuals of this group, vary with the ancestors that they have in common and many others … But the physical bond is least and the*

> *badge of color relatively unimportant save as a badge; the real essence of this kinship is its social heritage of slavery; the discrimination and insult; and this heritage binds together not simply the children of Africa, but extends through yellow Asia and into the South Seas. It is this unity that draws me to Africa.*

In making the case for Africa's contribution, Du Bois recognised European scientific knowledge and technology but asserted that 'African life with its isolation has deeper knowledge of human souls. The village life, the forest ways, the teeming markets, bring in intimate human knowledge that the West misses, sinking the individual in the social.' At the same time, he went beyond culture and highlighted, in a Marxist vein, 'the close connection between race and wealth. The fact that even in the minds of the most dogmatic supporters of race theories and believers in the inferiority of colored folk to white, there was a conscious or unconscious determination to increase their incomes by taking full advantage of this belief'. This means that race prejudice was caused by the quest for profit rather than by theories of race inferiority.

The psychological impact of segregation, making its victims, concerned only with their own issues, resentful but also loyal to their own group members, was a different dimension of race addressed by Du Bois. It was taken up later on by another prominent intellectual and activist from the African diaspora, Frantz Fanon, in his 1952 book *Black Skin, White Masks*. Standing out as a black man in Europe, having to deal with the burden of historical prejudice and racial stereotypes, Fanon felt he was made to be 'responsible at the same time for my body, for my race, for my ancestors. I subjected myself to an objective examination, I discovered my blackness, my ethnic characteristics; and I was battered down by tom-toms, cannibalism, intellectual deficiency, fetishism, racial defects, slave-ships, and above all else, above all: "Sho' good eatin" [making fun of black slang].'

Fanon attributed racial prejudice to projection of 'the most immoral impulses, the most shameful desires', which lie dormant within the unconscious of all people, onto others, in this case the black world. He called this process 'transference', which means taking what you find objectionable about yourself and transferring the burden to others by blaming them for your own fantasies. Some black people internalise these stereotypes, thereby mentally enslaving themselves. The way to deal with this is neither to adopt negative images of black culture nor to reject them uncritically, but to move beyond stereotypes and 'reach out for the universal'. This means avoiding getting bogged down in arguments over specific ethnic and racial histories by embracing humanity on all its achievements, wherever they come from.

Fanon said: 'Every time a man has contributed to the victory of the dignity of the spirit, every time a man has said no to an attempt to subjugate his fellows, I have felt solidarity with his act. In no way should I derive my basic purpose from the past of the peoples of colour. In no way should I dedicate myself to the revival of an unjustly unrecognized Negro civilization. I will not make myself the man of any past. I do not want to exalt the past at the expense of my present and of my future.' It is through political struggle for dignity, freedom and justice that people can regain their value, not through a search for the real or imaginary glorious past of their ancestors.

In his last and most famous work, *The Wretched of the Earth* of 1961, Fanon focused on colonialism rather than race, and advocated the use of insurgency and counter-violence in order to overcome the legacy of structural violence unleashed by colonial forces on indigenous people. This approach was inspired by the struggle waged by the Algerian national liberation movement, which Fanon joined, against French colonialism. Its goal was to re-shape the consciousness of indigenous people, who had been subjected to consistent attempts to undermine their culture, self-esteem and confidence in their ability to run their own affairs. A resolute struggle which included the use of force and military violence would allow subordinate people to regain control over their lives and become active participants in shaping a new society free of colonial oppression.

A decade later, a similar focus on consciousness was offered by South African activist, Steve Biko. Like Fanon before him, Biko noted the internalisation of racial stereotypes by black people who suffer from 'inferiority complex – a result of 300 years of deliberate oppression, denigration and derision'. The necessary response was 'a very strong grass-roots build-up of black consciousness such that blacks can learn to assert themselves and stake their rightful claim'. Since blacks were subjugated as a group in apartheid South Africa, he asked, 'what can be more logical than for us to respond as a group?' Not mincing words, Biko portrayed 'the black man' as 'a shell, a shadow of man, completely defeated, drowning in his own misery, a slave, an ox bearing the yoke of oppression with sheepish timidity'.

The first step in political action therefore is 'to make the black man come to himself; to pump back life into his empty shell; to infuse him with pride and dignity, to remind him of

his complicity in the crime of allowing himself to be misused and therefore letting evil reign supreme in the country of his birth ... This is the definition of "Black Consciousness".' Only people who defy white supremacy and refuse to 'willingly surrender their souls to the white man,' can be defined as black. Black Consciousness is 'the realisation by the black man of the need to rally together with his brothers around the cause of their oppression – the blackness of their skin – and to operate as a group in order to rid themselves of the shackles that bind them to perpetual servitude.'

Challenging a simplistic version of class analysis, Biko saw apartheid South Africa as:

a case of haves against have-nots where whites have been deliberately made haves and blacks have-nots. There is for instance no worker in the classical sense among whites in South Africa, for even the most down-trodden white worker still has a lot to lose if the system is changed. He is protected by several laws against competition at work from the majority. He has a vote and he uses it to return the Nationalist Government to power because he sees them as the only people who, through job reservation laws, are bent on looking after his interests against competition with the 'Natives'.

Race was 'the greatest single determinant for political action', but it was also linked to class, since blacks were 'the only real workers in South Africa'. There were no prospects of class alliance across the colour line, as 'the greatest anti-black feeling is to be found amongst the very poor whites whom the Class Theory calls upon to be with black workers in the struggle for emancipation.' Later on, the term 'racial capitalism' was used by Biko's supporters to refer to the apartheid system in which class exploitation and racial oppression were intertwined, necessitating a joint struggle against both.

The different perspectives outlined above point out that we need to understand race in a comprehensive manner, on all its different dimensions, with a focus on the three key aspects of:

- economics/class relations
- politics/state power and resistance, and
- ideology/identity/culture/consciousness.

In the following sections, each of these aspects will be discussed in turn.

Case study 9.3 Power, politics and race

In August 2011, in an article entitled 'Haffajee does that in the service of white masters', Eric Miyeni, writing for the *Sowetan* newspaper, attacked *City Press* editor Ferial Haffajee for singling out black politicians as suspects in corrupt practices. He said:

> Who the devil is she anyway if not a black snake in the grass, deployed by white capital to sow discord among blacks? In the 80s she'd probably have had a burning tyre around her neck.

(Source: *Sowetan* 2011)

QUESTIONS

1. What notions of power, politics and race are displayed in this attack?
2. How can we understand the complaint (frequently heard) that critical black journalists and analysts follow a 'white agenda'?
3. How do accusations of corruption – and denials of such accusations – serve as a political tool in a racially charged atmosphere?
4. What role do the media and other means of communication play in disseminating racial images and linking them to issues of violence and distribution of economic resources?

9.4 Race, class and economics

In many places around the globe the notion of race has been associated with the specific economic positions occupied by people of different backgrounds. For example, the institution of slavery was – and to some extent still is – central to the experience of people of African origins in North America, the Caribbean and Brazil. The experience of working on plantations and mines has been central to the experience of indigenous people in Mexico, the Andean countries of South America and southern Africa. Even after colonised countries achieved their independence from European rule, in the course of the 19th and 20th centuries, racial conditions forged during the colonial period continued to shape the economic structure of society. The abolition of slavery in the USA in the 1860s was not accompanied by granting social and political equality to black people, descendants of slaves, especially in the South. It took a century for the majority of black people in the southern States to be able to exercise the right to vote, and they still occupy there a low position in the social and economic order to this day.

In a similar manner, the abolition of apartheid in South Africa in the 1990s was an important step towards political equality in the country, but has not resulted in major changes to the racial structure of the economy. Economic inequalities are still very high in post-apartheid South Africa, possibly even higher than they were under apartheid, and they have a pronounced racial character. Despite the rise of a layer of wealthy black people in the state and business sectors, the majority of black people in South Africa remain poor, especially in townships and the rural areas, while the majority of white people remain relatively wealthy. Growing inequalities *within* the black population coexist with ongoing racial inequalities *between* different groups. The economic legacies of colonialism and apartheid continue to dominate society.

9.4.1 Colonialism and slavery

Why is it that these legacies continue to dominate? To answer the question, we have to understand how, in the early stages of the colonial era, powerful economic forces shaped the relationships between different groups of people in a way that affected their conditions for centuries to come. There were multiple motivations for European overseas expansion. The desire for fertile land, gold and lucrative trade routes played a role alongside the quest for empire building, exploration, knowledge and domination, and a sense of religious mission. There is little doubt though that the search for gold (and other riches, minerals and precious commodities such as spices) was paramount. Plunder of indigenous resources allowed European conquerors to get rich quickly. But, a more systematic long-term exploitation of the commercial opportunities that opened up with the takeover of new territories was a more difficult prospect.

European economic expansion across the globe required the creation and organisation of and control over vast numbers of able-bodied, docile and productive workers. It was these workers who mined the gold and silver that enriched Europe at the expense of the Americas, who worked in the sugarcane plantations of Brazil and the Caribbean islands, who toiled in the fields of the American South, harvesting tobacco and cotton, who produced the wheat and wines that sustained the colonial Cape economy, and who mined the Witwatersrand goldfields that gave rise to Johannesburg.

Different options were available: free European workers could have been recruited, but the cost of their labour was usually too high, especially when they had to be transported and settled in remote and hostile places and enticed with promises and rewards. Indentured labourers from Europe, who worked to pay off debts, usually were difficult to control as they sought to become independent. The obvious choice in the Americas was indigenous people (native Americans), who did labour in the colonial mines, but they frequently fell prey to contagious diseases to which they had developed no immunity, and died out in their millions. What European commercial and political interests eventually settled for was the system that came to dominate life in most of the colonies in the New World: the massive use of African slave labour. It is this historical development above all else that has shaped the notion and meanings of race in the modern world.

Why was Africa (sub-Saharan Africa to be precise) the main source for slaves at that time? There are a number of answers to this question. For one, it was ruled by relatively weak and fragmented political units, which allowed Europeans to gain access to its coast without facing much resistance. It was also internally divided and dominant local groups facilitated European efforts to capture and transport members of competing groups, and make a profit in the process. Its people – unlike west Asians and north Africans – had not had much contact with European religious, intellectual and economic forces, and therefore were easily stereotyped as heathen savages who were only good for manual labour. In other words, they were vulnerable to a greater degree than other potential sources of labour. It is this vulnerability, rather than racial prejudice that was primarily responsible for their predicament. There is no reason to believe that people living in similar social and political circumstances, albeit with different skin colour, would have been treated differently. Conversely, dark-skinned people living in different social and political circumstances (in India, for example) were not subjected to the same treatment from which Africans suffered. However, once the link between slavery and dark skin colour was made, it persisted for a long time.

This combination of factors served to brand Africans, and by extension all black people, primarily as suppliers of unskilled labour power, which was subjected to a variety of coercive measures. The association between black skin and a range of negative characteristics (lack of education and skill, physical strength combined with low mental ability and so on) can be traced back to the rise of racial slavery. Slavery of course was not new – it has been practised for

thousands of years in various societies and geographical locations – but it had not been systematically linked to skin colour, and therefore had had no specific racial character. Racial images conjured up by this initial historical link of the modern era were crucial in shaping cultural attitudes for centuries to come. The changing conditions of work and economic development continued to have a direct impact on the way people of different racial origins were viewed by others and on their self-perceptions as well.

9.4.2 Labour coercion: past legacies and present conditions

In addition to slavery itself, these material conditions consisted of:

- various forms of labour organisation (indenture, tenancy, migrancy, wage labour)
- places of work and residence (on commercial farms, small holdings, compounds, townships)
- political conditions (restrictions on movement and union membership)
- working conditions (long hours, low wages, tight control, lack of opportunities for promotion).

The great diversity of conditions affected all people in the labour market, not only those of African origins. All workers, including those in Europe and of European origins, were subject to restrictions on their social and geographical mobility, political organisation, and access to rights. In many places indigenous people under colonial rule were living under conditions similar to slavery even when they were nominally free. One needs to realise that not all Africans were treated in the same manner, whether in Africa itself or in the Americas. With all these qualifications in mind, it is important to recognise that, as a group, black people consistently tended to occupy the lowest positions in the global economy that came into being as a result of colonial expansion and conquest.

South Africa is useful as an example of the diverse circumstances under which people lived during the colonial period and beyond it (to some extent at least, all the way to the present). It combined different forms of labour subjugation. Indigenous people were tied to the land and forced to work on farms in exchange for being able to graze their cattle and sheep and grow crops on small plots. Those of them who lost their means of livelihood worked for white farmers in the fields or the residence to get access to shelter and food. Slaves were imported from Madagascar and East Africa to work on farms, and from Indonesia and other Indian Ocean territories to work mainly in urban areas as craftsmen. Various arrangements of tenancy existed in parts of the country, which required of families to contribute the labour of some of their members for some for the time, to enable other members to work on their own land. Share-cropping arrangements led to division of the crops between the workers and the landowner. Commercial companies held title to land and employed workers who were paid in money or in kind, and so on. Even when wage labour became the norm, it was usually accompanied by coercion: workers were forced to live in compounds and hostels; they were tightly monitored and denied basic freedoms of movement and association. Many of these older arrangements have declined over time but have not been eradicated completely.

In all the situations above, most of those performing the manual labour were black, while those who owned the land – outside the areas of communal settlement – were predominantly white. Landowners clearly benefited economically from the work of labourers, and were dependent on them, and therefore had an interest in maintaining these relations of inequality between them. Racial distinctions facilitated their ability to do so. This pattern of white employers/bosses and black employees/subordinates has been a crucial feature of South African society since its inception. We cannot understand the central role of race in South African history without focusing on the links between racial origins, social status and labour market position. In other words, we need to look at how racial classification and race-based political domination enhanced the welfare of some groups in society at the expense of other groups. In recent times coercion and violence play a smaller role, but it is still largely the case that black people provide labour services for white employers, in business, factories, farms, service industries, and homes. Not all employers are white, of course, and the rise of the black middle class has changed the demographic composition of the wealthier groups in the country, but the farm workers, manual labourers, and domestic workers remain almost exclusively black (these days growing numbers of such workers come from other African countries, such as Zimbabwe and Mozambique, but racially they are not distinct from their South African counterparts).

9.4.3 Avenues of further exploration

All this is not to say that race simply is a reflection of the operation of economic forces. Other dimensions of race, such as its relationship to political power, to identity and to culture must be considered as well, in order to provide a comprehensive picture of race in society. We can look at this issue in theoretical terms from different angles. The following questions are particularly interesting for further exploration (although we cannot pursue them in this chapter, they are useful in setting the agenda for additional study, reading and research):

- How have white people and social forces used existing racial differences to their economic advantage?
- How have racial images and stereotypes been created in order to justify granting material advantages to some groups and denying them to others?
- How have black people and social forces used racial identity to organise in the workplace and at communities to challenge exploitative practices?
- At a more fundamental level, how have economically exploitative relations given rise to, but also been shaped by, racial images?

Taken together, these questions guide us to look at race as a set of practices, which forge links between economic inequalities on the one hand, and social distinctions, power and cultural images on the other. The relations between the economic, political and cultural aspects of race are thus seen as being mutually reinforcing, all of which are crucial in shaping race. The precise weight of these factors in accounting for specific historical instances must be established concretely for each case.

In South African history, race was used as a mechanism for dispossessing indigenous people, taking away their land and the livestock resources which were essential for independent existence and forcing them into working in the service of white-dominated enterprises. Under apartheid, racial mechanisms became more formal and were applied more tightly than previously but along similar lines.

9.4.4 Race and class post-apartheid

In the post-apartheid period, race continues to play a role in the allocation of resources in a number of ways:

- Through the operation of existing economic forces tied to global trends, it replicates the racial structure of the labour market with no need for formal race distinctions.
- Through affirmative action and black empowerment policies it acts to redistribute jobs, contracts and funds to well-connected black people.
- Through informal networks of business and expertise, it allows well-connected white people to maintain positions of economic power and influence.
- Through ongoing residential and educational segregation, which keeps poor black people in a disadvantaged

position, it retains wealth, skill and status in suburban areas (where the majority of whites and a minority of privileged black people live).

In other words, while race ceased to operate as a formal mechanism of inequality it still operates informally to achieve similar broad effects, albeit with some important changes.

Race relations in South Africa are based on economic inequalities, which affect ownership of land, property and other assets, acquisition of skills, job opportunities, wages, and access to services and socioeconomic rights. It is not surprising therefore that overcoming such inequalities has been a central goal of the struggle for justice and freedom in the country. Significantly, in his famous statement from the dock at the 1964 Rivonia trial, before he spoke about the demand for equal political rights, Nelson Mandela declared:

Africans want to be paid a living wage. Africans want to perform work which they are capable of doing, and not work which the government declares them to be capable of. Africans want to be allowed to live where they obtain work, and not be endorsed out of an area because they were not born there. Africans want to be allowed to own land in places where they work, and not to be obliged to live in rented houses which they can never call their own. Africans want to be part of the general population, and not confined to living in their own ghettoes. African men want to have their wives and children to live with them where they work, and not be forced into an unnatural existence in men's hostels. African women want to be with their menfolk and not be left permanently widowed in the Reserves. Africans want to be allowed out after eleven o'clock at night and not to be confined to their rooms like little children. Africans want to be allowed to travel in their own country and to seek work where they want to and not where the labour bureau tells them to. Africans want a just share in the whole of South Africa; they want security and a stake in society (Mandela 1964).

It is clear that many of the grievances of black people in South Africa at the time had to do with concrete social and economic concerns linked to race classification. This continues to be the case today. The quest for political equality is seen, in large part, as a means to enable workers and other socially and economically deprived sections of the population to organise to meet their needs. The decades-long alliance between the African National Congress, the Communist Party, and the main trade unions (SACTU and, since 1985, COSATU) is a testimony to the connection between race and class, between material needs and political organisation, in South Africa. Similar connections can be found in other contexts as well, though perhaps they are not as strong elsewhere. The precise nature of such links is a key theme in the ongoing study of race.

Affirmative Action and Black Economic Empowerment (BEE) are seen as means to redress this situation. One of the big questions facing us today is the extent to which such policies serve indeed to meet that task. BEE policies have managed to transfer a small, but significant portion of ownership of economic sectors, such as mining and finance, into the hands of newly emerging black businesspeople. The benefits of such change have been restricted to a small elite and have not trickled down to the level of ordinary black people.

In the civil service in particular, affirmative action has resulted in an important shift in the demographic composition of state employees, at all levels of the administration. At the same time it has raised concerns about the quality of the service, given that many senior jobs have been allocated to people based on their political links to the ruling party, rather than skills and competence to do the job. How to combine the quest for racial redress with the maintenance (and improvement) of civil service standards remains a challenge.

9.5 Race, state and resistance
Alongside the economy, politics is another crucial arena on which race is shaped. In one sense, everything that affects the distribution and exercise of power in society is political. In another sense, politics is the specific field of power as exercised in public life, primarily by the state and by forces operating in relation to it. State policies, challenges to them, resistance to power and exercises of power in spheres independent of the state, are the focus of politics.

9.5.1 The rise of empire
As a concept and a central organising principle of social and political relations, race first emerged in the context of European overseas expansion and imperial rule. Both the subjugation of indigenous people in the Americas and the institution of racial slavery were aspects of the building of new transatlantic empires. These empires initially stretched from the western edge of Europe into the Caribbean, North and South America and then further into Asia and Africa. Empire thus became the dominant organisational form of world power for four centuries: from the rise of Spain and Portugal in the 16th century to their decline by the

beginning of the 19th century, when they were decisively overtaken by the British and French empires which survived until the middle of the 20th century. Smaller powers such as Holland, Italy and Germany also contributed to the spread of empire, though their mark on the world was less pronounced.

These New World overseas empires were different from the Old World land-based counterparts – the Russian, Austrian and Ottoman Empires – that dominated Europe, Central Asia, the Middle East and North Africa. Both types of empire included people of diverse racial, ethnic, and religious backgrounds. However, race did not become the central principle of political organisation in the old world, even though it was not completely unknown, while in the New World empires it did play a central role. Why was that the case?

The new mode of imperial rule applied under conditions of massive expansion of territory, which saw the rapid incorporation of a large number of people of different cultural and social origins into the new political frameworks created by colonialism. Regarding all these people ('the natives') as rights-bearing citizens or as entitled to legal and political protection would have undermined the foundations of political rule in the colonies, since people of European origins were a minority in most cases. We need to realise though that ordinary Europeans (not only the new colonised populations) did not enjoy equal rights at home during the era of colonial conquest (from the 16th to the 19th centuries), which took place long before notions of citizenship and democracy became prominent in political discourse. And yet, most Europeans did possess certain customary rights and were protected to some extent from absolute control by their royal rulers. In contrast, colonised populations did not benefit from such protection and were subject to power that was exercised with a relative lack of inhibition and restraint.

9.5.2 Slavery and emancipation

To appreciate the radically new nature of colonial conquest, we need to look at it against the background of imperial expansion overland, which had been part of European history for centuries, and was more gradual in nature. It involved the conquest and integration of people whose cultures and religions (orthodox Christianity, Islam) were more familiar to the core European powers and not so different from them in terms of their social organisation and access to technology. In contrast, overseas colonialism was based on a more fundamental distinction between those regarded as 'civilised' and those regarded as 'uncivilised' or 'savages'. The latter could more readily be enslaved and

subjected to the use of force to guarantee compliance and submission. That was especially important in cases where the conquering Europeans were a small minority of the overall population. In societies based on the massive exploitation of slave labour to cultivate tropical products, such as sugar cane, slaves outnumbered their masters by far, and had to be controlled by military force and superior technology as well as by political and cultural mechanisms – such as religion – that aimed to ensure their subservience.

That was the case in most Caribbean islands, Brazil and the American South. Granting slaves political rights was out of the question, as they could easily overwhelm the European settler dominant group and undermine the foundations of the economy. For centuries then, societies that emerged out of the colonial encounter displayed sharp political inequalities between citizens and subjects. This state of affairs gave rise in many instances to authoritarian states, controlled by elites that relied on the use of force rather than persuasion to sustain their rule. It is not a coincidence that military regimes brought to power by violent coups have been a feature of many parts of the post-colonial world.

The way to political equality was slave rebellions – as happened in Haiti – but more frequently the gradual removal of the specific political aspect of forced labour and its replacement by informal social mechanisms, which retained class distinctions without explicit race-based legislation. That was the case in the Cape Colony (essentially our current Western Cape province, which included parts of Eastern and Northern Cape as well), after the abolition of slavery in the 1830s. Repressive labour legislation replaced racial laws, without seriously affecting the nature of the social structure. In Brazil later in the 19th century, people of African origins were incorporated politically in a similar manner, as a group that is socially subordinated with no use of direct racial mechanisms. In the USA, slaves in the Southern states were emancipated with the victory of the North in the civil war of the 1860s, but remained subjected to discriminatory laws and practices for another century. It was only with the civil rights movement and other struggles of the 1950s–60s, which involved passive resistance and defiance campaigns, marches and attempts to mobilise black people (at times together with supportive white people), and was led by people such as Martin Luther King Jr and Malcolm X, that black people finally won full political equality in that country.

9.5.3 Conquest and incorporation

In other colonies, where slavery was less common and indigenous people retained some form of political organisation, attempts were made at times to incorporate local elites into the structure of power. This allowed a measure of political integration, though within the framework of overall imperial domination, as was the case in parts of central America, West Africa and India. It was a mode of rule based on the assumption that effective long-term control could be secured if indigenous structures were not thoroughly disrupted, but rather co-opted into the colonial state. Indirect rule through the mediation of chiefs and indigenous authorities, exercising 'customary law', became the norm in many British and French territories in Africa. After independence, the role of such authorities usually remained powerful and hampered attempts at democratisation (Mamdani 1996).

A similar approach was applied in parts of South Africa as well, beginning with the 'Shepstone System', which was used in colonial Natal in the mid-19th century and was extended later to other parts of the country. It was based on the employment of chiefs to play a major role in the daily life of people living on communal land. Although these 'traditional leaders' were autonomous, they exercised their rule and maintained order on behalf of the colonial state. Their areas of operation became known as the 'native reserves', and in the second half of the 20th century, under apartheid, were given an institutional role as the Homelands, also referred to as Bantustans.

The Homelands became the cornerstone of the apartheid government's plan to guarantee political stability by granting limited powers to traditional authorities, in exchange for their participation in enforcing the rule of the white-dominated state. African people were supposed to exercise their political rights in these ethnic homelands and abandon their claims to political representation in South Africa itself. Thus, even if they were the majority of the overall population in the country, including in the white-designated urban areas, their numerical dominance was neutralised politically by deflecting it to limited and marginalised geographical areas. Because those areas were poor, without proper infrastructure, and usually fragmented into numerous pieces of land interspersed with white farms and towns, they could not establish any real political or economic control, and did not serve as a foundation for African independence.

In adopting the Homeland policy in the 1960s, the South African government embarked on a concerted effort to abandon the language of race and replace it with the more respectable notion of ethnicity – which displaced the outdated and offensive term of tribalism – and national self-determination. It divided black people in the country into different ethnic groups, each with its own language, culture, history and a right to its own territory and political institutions, eventually leading to a series of independent states alongside 'white South Africa'. It did not succeed because, at the same time it talked about ethnicity and culture, it kept the notion of race alive. Only black people were regarded as ethnic in nature, while white people retained their political unity in the central state, regardless of their own internal ethnic differences. This duality, using race to put white people in charge and relegate black people to the margins, and using ethnicity to divide black people among themselves, was internally contradictory and could not be sustained for long. The history of race, used by the state to separate and subjugate black people, but also used by black people to mobilise themselves, meant that it continued to serve as a focus for the politics of struggle and resistance to apartheid. The complex relationship and tensions between these different types of identity (centred around notions of race, ethnicity and nationalism) is an important aspect of identity formation processes that needs to be studied further.

9.5.4 Settlers and indigenous people

In general, we need to realise that racial divisions between European settlers, Native Americans, slaves and indigenous Africans, never overlapped completely with political divisions and allocation of rights. Among Europeans in the Americas, a split opened up between those who came directly from Europe (including most colonial officials) and the creoles. These were white people whose historical origins were in Europe but who developed an identity of being of the New World, where they were born and to which they owed their loyalty. In some places in Latin America, these creoles rebelled against the Spanish authorities and recruited indigenous people and slaves with the promise of political equality. In the USA, settlers rebelled against the British Empire, and then became divided between the Northern and Southern states, adopting different positions regarding slavery. In Africa, European colonial authorities were more willing than white settlers were to move towards a measure of integration of indigenous people from the late 19th century onwards. There was never uniformity in the responses of all white people towards the prospect of equal political rights for blacks and other indigenous people.

The political responses of indigenous people, slaves, and other groups subordinated on a racial basis were not uniform either. In cases where political power was exercised by empires ruling from afar, the residents of colonies opted for complete independence. In some places they achieved independence through peaceful negotiations and organised transition (most countries in West Africa, for example), in others through a combination of negotiations and militant struggle (India for instance), and still others through armed uprising against stubborn colonial authorities or settler regimes (Zimbabwe, Namibia) or through a combination of various other methods.

Only in a few countries, favourable environmental conditions and good economic potential led to the immigration of large numbers of European settlers. When these combined with practices of slavery and territorial expansion, this state of affairs led to race becoming the central organising principle of political relations and social practices. Most notably, the USA, Brazil and South Africa, among others, have been shaped politically by race from their inception. Their varying historical legacies, though, brought about different ways of dealing with the issue of race and its resulting politics.

In addition to race, ethnicity (language and cultural heritage) was used to classify people into groups, frequently referred to as 'tribes' in the colonial context. While ethnic differences played an important role in divide-and-rule policies of control, they rarely acquired the central political and social significance of race. Sharp divisions and conflicts on racial grounds characterise many societies that emerged out of the colonial encounter, while ethnicity separated groups horizontally (positioning them alongside each other) without usually involving them in relations of economic exploitation or political domination. In apartheid South Africa, for example, ethnicity divided the indigenous population into groups with their 'own' territories and administrations, but all of them were equally marginalised in relation to the central state and the system of white supremacy.

9.5.5 Civil rights movements in the USA

Race has been a major bone of political contention in the USA throughout the 19th and 20th centuries. It continues to play an important role today. With the Civil Rights Act of 1965 and the extension of equal rights to black people in the South, formal political equality was established, culminating in 2008 with the election of the first black president in US history, Barack Obama. At the same time, race still serves to distinguish between different political agendas. Conservative politicians affiliated mostly with the Republican Party argue that race has been formally eliminated as a legal barrier to jobs and public offices, and therefore must not be used as a consideration in gaining access to any public position. Progressive politicians affiliated with sectors of the Democratic Party, as well as some civil society groups argue that the legacy of racial discrimination exists long after its formal abolition. Therefore, race-based affirmative action policies may be needed to redress historical injustices and imbalances in the allocation of funds, jobs, educational opportunities and representative positions in public institutions. Debates over free market policies and the need for state intervention to ensure social progress and equality thus have profound racial implications, even when they do not address race explicitly.

Organising for change in the USA has involved a combination of political, legal, and mass action strategies. The civil rights movement, formed under the leadership of Martin Luther King in the 1950s, emphasised protest action alongside legal strategies that used the Constitution to promote equality and to campaign for political and civil rights for all people. More militant forms of struggle also emerged in the same period, leading in some isolated instances to armed action against the state. In some instances, such militant sentiments associated with the names of Malcolm X and the Black Panther party, have fed calls for separatism and the creation of black-led parties and public institutions. That black people are a small minority of the overall population, with no real chance of becoming a central force in society, has made such calls a problematic political prospect. A strategy of forging alliances with other minorities and dissident groups may seem more promising.

The majority of black people have focused on electoral politics, and engaged in a massive shift in support away from the Republican Party (historically associated with Abraham Lincoln and the fight against slavery) into the Democratic Party (historically associated with segregation in the South). This shift coincided with the northward migration of poor black people, growing urbanisation and joining the ranks of the industrial working class in the North. That the Democrats with their New Deal and Great Society policies adopted reform-orientated social programmes, using the state apparatus to advance marginalised groups and working people, has helped them gain the support of newly urbanised and industrialised black people. At the same time, this transformed the Republicans into a force opposing progressive change. They became associated with the white backlash against racial equality, and by implication against other forms of social and cultural diversity. Even though many people have been disappointed with the ability of electoral politics to change society fundamentally, and are sceptical about the viability of the Democratic Party as a driver of such change, they are still largely aligned with that party as the major political vehicle representing their concerns.

9.5.6 Struggle for racial equality in South Africa

In South Africa, the struggle for racial equality has taken many forms, reflecting the diversity of historical conditions in the country. Two common responses in the earlier periods, which shaped subsequent political approaches, were a quest for independence from colonial rule and a quest for incorporation on an equal basis in the new society into which enslaved and conquered people were forced. While the initial response of most people was to attempt to regain their freedom and liberate themselves from foreign rule, with the passage of time many of them changed orientation and began to seek equality under the circumstances in which they found themselves. By the early 20th century, most racially oppressed people had abandoned the notion that pre-colonial conditions could be restored and accepted the boundaries of the Union of South Africa, established in 1910 and remaining effectively the same to this day, as the framework for solving the racial question.

Most black political movements in the 20th century called for civil and legal equality within the South African state and society. While differences existed with regard to the degree of desirable ethnic or cultural autonomy, the demand for 'one person, one vote' became the dominant theme in political mobilisation, from the post-1945 period to the demise of apartheid in 1994. Within this context, some political forces focused more on ethnic identity (the Inkatha Freedom Party, for example, with its Zulu ethnic-cultural focus), or black racial identity encompassing all those excluded from the system of white supremacy (the Black Consciousness Movement), or black African racial identity (the Pan-Africanist Congress). But, it was the African National Congress (ANC), with its call for racial equality as part of an overall national liberation of the country, which became the dominant voice in the anti-apartheid campaign. This position became known as non-racialism.

Non-racialism was never defined officially by the ANC, but it does *not* mean denying the role of race or ignoring the fact that many people identify themselves in racial terms. Rather, it usually is interpreted as a perspective that combines overall national liberation tasks (granting the vote to all citizens, incorporating all members of society on an equal basis, extending access to services to all, and so on), with recognition of the specific historical oppression of black people in this country. Because race played an important role in subjugating people, it must also play a role in redressing their situation after liberation has been achieved. This means, among other things, that affirmative action policies, which have an explicit racial component, are a legitimate means of redress. However, racial considerations in state policy are only temporary in nature, a measure meant to redress the historical imbalances produced by colonialism and apartheid. They should not become a permanent feature of South African society and politics.

The leading role of the ANC in the liberation struggle before 1994 allowed it to retain a key position after the demise of apartheid. This meant that non-racialism became the official state approach although its precise meaning is subject to dispute. Politically, non-racialism is as ambiguous as the notion of race itself. Does it mean ignoring race altogether or regarding it as crucial but only until racial equality is achieved? If it means the latter, what concrete indicators would tell us that our goal is within reach? And even if we regard race-based policies as merely a measure needed to redress historical inequalities, how can we prevent its continued use from reinforcing its impact and creating new inequalities? And, whenever we invoke race in a positive manner in order to address the legacies of apartheid, do we not grant the concept renewed power that is difficult to control? It is not the intention here to provide conclusive answers to these questions, merely to suggest that the political use of race has unintended consequences that cannot be anticipated in advance, and may subvert the intentions of policy makers.

9.5.7 Avenues of further exploration

We can summarise the section on the political aspects of race by outlining different theoretical tasks that follow from it. The following questions are particularly interesting for further exploration (although we cannot pursue them in this chapter, they are useful in setting the agenda for additional study, reading and research):

- How did white people and social forces use state power to enhance their social and economic domination and use their economic power to gain control over the state?
- How were racial images and stereotypes created in order to justify granting political rights to some groups and denying them to others?
- How have black people and social forces shaped racial identity (and linked it to ethnic and national identities) to organise politically in order to challenge their legal and social marginalisation and exclusion?
- How have politically unequal relations and positions given rise to, but also been shaped by, racial images?

All this means looking at race as a practice in which the quest for political power is linked to cultural images and legal differentiation: the relations between the economic, political and ideological aspects of race are thus seen as being mutually reinforcing. In South African history, race was used to entrench legal and civil inequalities, destroy pre-colonial states and reshape pre-colonial forms of organisation to facilitate white domination. Under apartheid, racial political exclusion became more formal and was applied more tightly than before, but along similar lines.

9.5.8 Race and power post-apartheid

In the post-apartheid period, race continues to play a role in the allocation of political power in a number of ways, though with significant differences from earlier periods:

- By aligning the South African state with global democratic norms, the racial structure of the state was radically changed. It is no longer dominated by white people, and its managers broadly reflect the demographic composition of the South African population.
- Through affirmative action and black empowerment policies, the state acts to re-allocate political positions and government contracts, and jobs in the state apparatus and civil service to black people, and thus serves as a major vehicle for social and economic upliftment of a section of the black population.
- It is an open question whether the changing demography of the state means a change in the nature and impact of its policies: critics argue that the post-apartheid state pursues the same broad policies as its apartheid predecessor, in that it continues to marginalise the majority of poor black people in the rural areas and urban townships. Others praise the changes in the rhetoric used by the state, and its benevolent intentions, but see these as insufficient in the absence of clear changes in budgetary allocations and capacity to implement new policies.
- This means that although race ceased to operate as a formal mechanism of political and legal inequality in 1994, it may still operate informally to achieve similar effects, albeit with some important changes. This may be the result of failure to transform the mode of operation of the state, which had been geared in the past to serve the needs of business and political elites. These elites have become racially mixed, and in the political arena specifically whites are a minority force with little formal influence. And yet, whites continue to hold substantial economic power and to benefit from the historical legacy of racial inequalities. The majority of impoverished black people may have no more ability today to make the state listen to them and address their needs than they did before 1994.

In what meaningful ways the state has changed its racial character is a key question for us to consider in coming years. From a theoretical perspective, this section has highlighted the need to pay attention not only to political rhetoric – what state officials say about their own actions and plans – but also the actual organisation of state institutions and the racial impact of their policies. This approach encourages us to look at race and politics as a multidimensional arena: progress on one front may clash with lack of progress – and even retreat – on another. For example, growing representation of black officials in state structures can go together with growing inequalities in society as a whole and growing impoverishment of the black rural masses. We need to look out for such potentially contradictory trends to appreciate the full picture.

9.6 Race, identity and culture

Understanding race requires looking at processes of identity formation, and examining how social relations and practices acquire and impart racial meanings through contestation over power. It is important, however, not to regard race as a narrow political construct. Although racial meanings emerge in a political process, they are not necessarily generated in or directly impact on the formal state and party-political arena. Rather, they are shaped on many terrains which include culture, geography, gender, scholarship and media. To make sense of them we need to study how different aspects of race come together in specific situations, each of which displays a different combination of forces. This focus on specificity does not mean that racial meanings are restricted to a particular space/time condition. Racial images and concepts have been disseminated through world-wide networks for centuries through scholarship, art, literature, political exchanges and debates, and so on, and have never been confined to any single country.

9.6.1 Media, culture and racial images

The terrains of media and culture are particularly interesting in this respect. They do not merely reflect existing popular notions and perceptions of race but also serve actively to construct these racial representations. This is done by advancing explicit and implicit notions of race-linked practices and traits, such as those of:

- tradition (involving medicine, initiation rites, witchcraft)
- physical and mental characteristics (energy, laziness, defiance, criminality, stubbornness, acquiescence, promiscuity, size of various bodily organs)
- cultural tastes (in dress, music, dance, storytelling, food)

- family patterns (polygamy, women's subordination)
- religious values (the role of ancestors, spiritual attitude to the world)
- politics (tribalism, faction fights, respect for authority) and various other social aptitudes.

It is not usually the case that any particular individuals or institutions set out consciously to portray certain groups in a derogatory light. Rather, inherited historical prejudices may combine with misconceptions about more scholarly findings, ignorance and popular understandings, and real differences in culture, to produce an image of 'us' and 'them' or of the unknown 'other'. All these acquire racial meanings through their association with what is globally defined as race in the world today, as well as in the specific conditions of South Africa.

This process of developing racial meanings does not apply only to black people, of course. Race defines white identity as well, not only in a negative and visible form of creating boundaries of separation that exclude black and other racially defined people, but also in an affirmative sense that links notions of technology, cultural standards, residential patterns, behavioural patterns, and generally the 'Western' or 'civilised' way of life, to social and institutional arrangements. The formation of white identity, which has affinities with, but is not identical to simple-minded racism, is crucial to the analysis of the rise and demise of racial discourses. It continues to have great significance in the transformation of white social, cultural and political organisation in the post-apartheid era.

Exploring the meanings of race and how they are debated and developed politically should be combined with an understanding of their cultural and institutional dimensions. The effectiveness of racial meanings – the extent to which they appeal to some people and make sense of their situation – depends on a context that makes some of them more credible than others.

A useful illustration of the operation of these forces was provided in 2012 by the case of The Spear, a painting by South African artist Brett Murray. In it, President Jacob Zuma was portrayed with his genitals exposed, standing in a position similar to that of a famous poster of Lenin, the Russian revolutionary leader. Different meanings, reflecting political, racial and cultural agendas, were displayed in the controversy that erupted as a result of the exhibition of the painting in a Johannesburg gallery, and its reproduction in the *City Press* newspaper.

Questions of power and political control, of media responsibility and free expression, of sexuality and pornographic images, of gender and race stereotypes, were all mixed up in the public debate. Was it right for the artist to express his feelings in that way, even if he used – intentionally or not – racial images of colonial origins (about black men and their uncontrolled sexuality)? Given the President's own use of cultural symbols with racial meanings (animal skins, a spear as a traditional weapon), was he not setting himself up as a legitimate target for criticism? Given his powerful political position, can he really be regarded as a victim of racial abuse by the media? Were protesters, marching against the gallery and organised by the ANC and SACP, expressing legitimate complaint against white cultural domination or rather using the 'race card' in applying bullying tactics against dissident minorities? Who was responsible for Zuma's image (combining gender and race aspects) as a typical African 'macho' man who needs multiple partners to satisfy his needs?

We cannot answer all these questions here, but need to draw attention to their importance in understanding how race, as a social and cultural force, shapes reality and is being shaped through the creation of meanings in the public sphere, their dissemination through different media, and their discussion in various political and civil forums (see further discussion of some of these issues in Dodd 2012).

9.6.2 Race and identity in South Africa

To understand how racial meanings operate under the unique South African conditions we need to examine the emergence of racial concepts and their evolution over time. This requires looking at the interaction between colonial, settler and indigenous voices in the making of racial identities (both of 'self' and 'others'). While the former two sets of voices have been heard frequently through official state reports, legislation, and media analysis, indigenous voices have not been studied as extensively. The reluctance to engage seriously with indigenous racial conceptualisations (such as the meanings and applicability of notions of blackness, African identity, in the country itself and across the continent) has been explained away in the past in light of the use made of racial classification by the apartheid regime. After the demise of apartheid this reason is no longer valid. Since race is not a direct instrument of oppression as it used to be, it is important to understand how it operates today and what are the consequences of its continued use by people in their daily lives, as well as by political forces and state institutions. Reluctance to do so, because it may be socially embarrassing, or awkward politically, or because it raises uncomfortable questions, is clearly unhelpful in addressing the issue.

Focusing on shifts in racial meanings and in usages of other identity terms is a useful way of accounting for changes in South African identity politics. Notions of nationhood, race and cultural identity have been competing for legitimacy and popular support. These are not mere manipulations or reflections of different social and political interests. Rather, contestation over racial meanings and shape of identities serves to define and consolidate these social interests.

For example, the post-1994 National Party, followed to a large extent by the Democratic Alliance in the last decade, put forward an implicit definition of nationhood based on social stability and civilised standards, giving rise to a new community with racial characteristics, mostly comprising whites, coloured and Indian people. This new identity is characterised more by whom it excludes – the mass of black African people – than by whom it includes: people concerned above all with a stable social order, regardless of their skin colour. This process of constructing meanings has not taken place in a social void. It has been linked to material concerns over housing, jobs and security. The crucial point, however, is that it would not have been possible without a clear shift in racial meanings – dismantling notions of blackness which lumped coloured people together with black Africans, and constructing new notions which may be defined in negative as well as positive terms: the current understanding of blackness may exclude those not perceived to be truly indigenous to the country, or the dominant form of coloured identity may exclude black Africans and be more open towards racial alliances with white people, and so on.

A different racial project has been offered by the ANC, which, true to the contradiction contained in its own name, sought to retain a focus on African identity while also claiming a leading role in South African nation building. Without neglecting, but also without highlighting, a specific sense of African identity, the ANC has managed to combine it with a sense of nationhood in which Africans are perceived as prominent members whose role has finally been given due recognition. The ANC thus projects both racial and non-racial images, in its attempt to appeal to different constituencies. The success of this project has been uneven. It enjoys massive support among black Africans, but has not been able to project a convincing non-racial image among other groups in the country. It probably served, though, to facilitate an attitude of reconciliation and acceptance of majority rule among non-Africans, which might not have been possible had a more undiluted African racial image prevailed.

The relative success of these racial projects can be seen against the failure of competing racial images. The Pan-Africanist Congress (PAC) and adherents of the Black Consciousness Movement have not developed wider definitions beyond race – African and Black respectively. They thus offer a one-dimensional image, which has not been appealing to many. We must keep in mind, though, that electoral success should not be simply equated with the power of racial images. African identity and Black Consciousness cannot be reduced to the parties claiming to speak on their behalf. The combination of racial and non-racial meanings in ANC policy and practice makes it possible to extract more racially explicit elements and use them to create a new identity building on the ongoing power of race as a concept signifying social, economic and cultural relations.

9.6.3 Avenues of further exploration

Based on this understanding, some avenues of further study open up. The following questions are particularly interesting for further exploration (although we cannot pursue them in this chapter, they are useful in setting the agenda for additional study, reading and research):

- How have cultural notions of civilisation, modernity, strict standards, stability and other positive values become associated with white and European identities, both as a form of internal self-regard and external evaluation?
- How have derogatory racial images and stereotypes become associated historically with blackness and African identity, and other non-European cultures?
- To what extent have such negative stereotypes been appropriated or internalised by members of the targeted groups, and how have such attitudes affected their self-esteem?
- How have black people and social forces used racial identity to organise culturally to defend their collective interests?
- How have race-based cultural notions affected people's positions in society, and shaped their practices of maintaining the social order or organising to transform it?

All of the above means looking at culture as a set of practices that shape social distinctions and affect access and claims to power and legitimacy.

In South African history, cultural differences and collective identities based on them (but also reinforcing them) served to entrench white settler control over indigenous people, but also allowed oppressed people to organise effectively to assert their identities and claim their rights.

9.6.4 Race and identity post-apartheid

In the post-apartheid period, race-based identities continue to play a role in shaping culture and social relations in a number of ways:

- Through a combination of local developments and global trends, they keep the notion of race alive, even when it no longer has legal validity in most areas.
- Through affirmative action and black empowerment policies race acts to enhance notions of blackness and Africanism, as personal, cultural and political identities.
- Through the impact of affirmative action, race acts to reinforce different notions of whiteness: as a powerful obstacle to change and also as a victimised and threatened identity.
- Through informal networks of knowledge, artistic production and expertise, it allows well-connected white people to maintain positions of power in the cultural field, as well as in the economic sphere, though usually without blocking the advancement of black people. Perceptions vary on this point and it is an interesting topic for further exploration, as is the extent to which black people manage to join these networks or form other cultural networks for their own use.
- In other words, race has ceased to operate as a formal mechanism of inequality, except for purposes of redress, but it still operates informally, albeit with some important changes, in the post-apartheid period.

It is this last point which is particularly central for us today. Globally, since the 1950s, and in South Africa since the 1990s, race has fallen into disrepute as a concept that serves to organise social relations. It is not considered respectable to invoke it openly as a justification for inequalities or denial of rights. At the same time, we must realise that it has never disappeared as a cultural code, providing meanings for economic and political relations, and shielding them from critical scrutiny. It is working in a less visible and open manner to re-shape society, both to maintain existing relations of power and privilege and to overturn them. It can be used to defend the social order as well as to undermine it. Perhaps it is this great flexibility of the concept, and its ability to work for different and even contradictory purposes, which keeps it alive long after it seemed to have lost its naked power.

In reflecting on these issues we must keep in mind a simple notion powerfully expressed by then Deputy President Thabo Mbeki back in 1998. Issues of race are shaped by material conditions that divided the country into two nations: 'One of these nations is white, relatively prosperous, regardless of gender or geographic dispersal. It has ready access to a developed economic, physical, educational, communication and other infrastructure ... The second and larger nation of South Africa is black and poor, with the worst affected being women in the rural areas, the black rural population in general and the disabled. This nation lives under conditions of a grossly underdeveloped economic, physical, educational, communication and other infrastructure.'

Mbeki added: 'This reality of two nations, underwritten by the perpetuation of the racial, gender and spatial disparities born of a very long period of colonial and apartheid white minority domination, constitutes the material base which reinforces the notion that, indeed, we are not one nation, but two nations.'

Two decades later, are these words still valid for South Africa? We refer to it as a Rainbow Nation, as indeed it is, but the different colours of the rainbow are not necessarily and always equal. Some shine brighter than others and some are obscured at certain times but not at others. We need to understand race in South Africa in all its different dimensions and nuances: equality under the law, persistent economic inequalities that reflect the historical conditions under apartheid, and a more mixed and internally diverse picture in the areas of politics, media and culture. At the same time, let us not forget that South Africa is also an 'ordinary country' shaped by the global dynamics of economy, society and state, like all other countries, regardless of its specific racial legacy. Both its unique and general features must play a role in the analysis.

By way of conclusion, and in order to illustrate some of the points raised here, it would be instructive to return to the examples mentioned in the beginning of the chapter. Let us examine them each in turn, offering some possible interpretations.

9.7 Illustrations of race

The exchange between Manuel and Manyi (Case study 9.1) is a good example of how race is linked to economic realities (and perceptions of reality), as well as to politics. It reflects lingering resentments that date back to the apartheid era, when coloured people in the Western Cape were given preference in housing, residence rights and employment opportunities, while black Africans, mostly from the Eastern

Cape, were treated like undesirable immigrants. The Western Cape was indeed declared a Coloured Labour Preference Area during that time. With the demise of apartheid, this legacy was converted into a call by some politicians for affirmative action specifically for Africans, excluding coloured people as not eligible. Manuel was responding not really as a representative of that group, but as a defender of the anti-apartheid tradition of struggle, especially in the 1980s, which put a great deal of emphasis on overcoming the racial boundaries that were created by the apartheid state in order to sow divisions and turn some blacks against others. The need to appeal to voters in the impending 2011 elections when 'the coloured vote', contested bitterly between the ANC and the DA, was going to decide who would win elections for provincial municipalities, was never far from the mind of senior political leaders. A long history of racial conflict within the ANC camp in the province contributed additional fuel to the exchange.

Beyond such political analysis, it is important to consider the racial images and negative stereotypes that play a role, though usually implicitly rather than openly: that coloured people are unnaturally concentrated in the Western Cape, that they are people without their own identity, being a product of forced sexual relations between whites and Africans (historically inaccurate and offensive notion captured by the misleading term 'mixed race'), that they are using that position to gain illegitimate advantages, that black African people are not getting their fair share as a result, that there is some kind of informal alliance between white and coloured people to subvert the African majority, that coloured people were not 'white enough' under apartheid and not 'black enough' in the post-apartheid period, and so on. It is only by considering all the dimensions of the issue – not only economic and political but also cultural – that we can account for this specific exchange.

The SANParks story (Case study 9.2) directs particular attention to the cultural aspect of race. Stereotypes (which are one-dimensional, usually derogatory images of racial characteristics or behaviours) are clearly at play here. Black people are seen as not capable of interest in the environment or wildlife, being loud and inconsiderate. Their sole concern is to show off their flashy possessions; white people alone appreciate the simple joys of the bush. One response to such images is to portray comments by white, usually older, people as being more concerned with nature than with people. This is a reflection of the old apartheid attitude that reserved areas such as the Kruger National Park for the use of white families and officials, and regarded them the only

ones who truly appreciate nature (even if many black people happen to live close to it).

Class issues may not be central to this matter but they do sneak in: the black people in question are the newly enriched 'diamonds' portrayed as having plenty of money but neither the manners nor the understanding of how to use it properly. A sense of resentment is evident here, a frequent element of the new white discourse of South Africa today. It is directed against black elites who are seen as undeserving, not having worked hard for their money but benefiting from access to power and riches because they are politically connected. Racial jealousy and fear are hereby projected onto an unsuspecting group of people, whose sole guilt may be the wish to gain access to nature and wildlife while experiencing luxurious accommodation (hardly an unusual combination in this country).

The intentions of those waging a campaign against a hotel in the Kruger Park may well be noble, but it is not surprising that they are seen as guardians of white privilege. This is not because they are racists, but because they seem unable to conceive of any other way of enjoying nature than their own traditional way: in their minds this has everything to do with respect for nature and nothing to do with race. Their critics, however, cannot separate such respect from the racial privilege that used to underpin it during the apartheid era. Racial meanings can be found not only in what some people say, but also in what other people hear.

The final example, raised in Case study 9.3, is related to the politics of identity, both in assertive and defensive forms. The view of society in terms of 'us' and 'them' results in a mode of group identification that allows no freedom from race. It is understandable perhaps, but also regrettable, that race should acquire such power that nothing can be said outside of its framework: journalists are not judged by the accuracy of their reporting, or the validity of their analysis (of corruption in this case), but by the extent to which they promote or hamper the interests of the group to which they are assigned. They are either loyal to the group's cause or are seen as traitors. There is not a semblance of independence from race in this approach: for black ideologues, accusations of corruption are an expression of a 'white agenda'; for white ideologues, corruption in politics and business practices is part of 'black culture'. A rational analysis, followed by praise or condemnation for individuals, black or white as the case may be, simply has no place in such a racially loaded atmosphere. The politics of 'my group, right or wrong', accompanied by a sense of permanent victimisation and search for vindication, takes over completely.

All the foregoing examples represent extreme responses by individuals to conditions of racial tension in a society that had long experienced the pain of forced segregation. They are caused by the difficulties of adjustment to the open society made possible by the demise of apartheid, a new space in which people of different backgrounds frequently live and work together, sometimes against their will. In one sense, these are positive responses despite the hostile clashes, because they show that desegregation is making progress. In another sense, to the extent that they reflect typical attitudes, they show that there is a long way to go before we can overcome the legacies of the apartheid era.

Summary

- Race is a set of *material practices* and *cultural meanings*. This means it is a way of organising society and operating within it (the material aspect), as well as a way of making sense of its history and current shape (the cultural aspect). All this is done by referring to the nature of the different groups within it, groups that are defined by their physical features.
- Race as a key theoretical concept emerged in the course of the *colonial encounter*, a long period during which forces based in Europe took over and re-shaped indigenous societies in Africa, Asia and the Americas.
- *Slavery*, a form of labour control involving physical subjugation of people, was central to the rise of race. It led to the forced relocation of millions of people from Africa into the New World (the Caribbean islands, North and South America), to work on plantations growing sugarcane, cotton and tobacco, in order to meet the demands of consumers and allow European industries to flood the world market with their products.
- From its inception race was global in scope: it was never confined to the boundaries of a single society. This remains the case today. *Race is a global phenomenon*, even if it manifests itself in somewhat different ways in specific times and places. We need to understand it as a worldwide force but should also not forget its specific nature.
- South Africa and the role that race has played in its history is unique, but it also bears similarities to other places.
- Colonisation and slavery, territorial expansion and conquest, white settlement and black resistance have all shaped race relations in South Africa. While these forces are no longer operating to entrench racial domination, their legacy continues to affect the society that has emerged from these processes.
- The most important analytical challenge facing us today is how to recognise the shifting meaning and impact of race, while avoiding two traps: (1) assuming that nothing has changed, and therefore we can use the old language of race as it was to make sense of our society today, or (2) assuming everything has changed and race is no longer relevant.
- We therefore need to appreciate both continuity and change as they manifest themselves in different dimensions of society (the economic, political, social, cultural fields) to acquire a comprehensive understanding of the ongoing significance of race, globally and in South Africa.

ARE YOU ON TRACK?

1. Is the distinction between physical differences (skin colour, hair) and their various social and political implications, which may change from time to time and place to place, clear?
2. Do you understand the role that forced labour and struggles over land and resources played in entrenching racial distinctions?
3. Are you aware of the processes through which racial meanings are created by different social actors and media?
4. Can you think of a way of using the understanding of race, as outlined in this chapter, in order to make sense of some South African political debates?
5. Looking at music, sports and other cultural activities, can you see how they express the global nature of racial identities?

More sources to consult

Back L, Solomos J (eds). 2009. *Theories of Race and Racism: A Reader.* Abington: Routledge.

Durrheim K, Mtose X, Brown L. 2011. *Race Trouble: Race, Identity and Inequality in Post-apartheid South Africa.* Pietermaritzburg: University of KwaZulu-Natal Press.

Essed P, Goldberg DT (eds). 2002. *Race Critical Theories: Text and Context.* Oxford: Blackwell.

Fredrickson G. 1988. *The Arrogance of Race: Historical Perspectives on Slavery, Racism, and Social Inequality.* Connecticut: Wesleyan University Press.

Gilroy, P. 2010. *Darker than Blue: The W.E.B Du Bois Lectures.* London: Harvard University Press.

Philomena E, David TG (eds). 2002. *Race Critical Theories: Text and Context.* Oxford: Blackwell

Rattansi A. 2007. *Racism: A Very Short Introduction.* Oxford: Oxford University Press.

Seekings J, Nattrass N. 2005. *Class, Race, and Inequality in South Africa.* New Haven: Yale University Press.

Winant H. 2001. *The World is a Ghetto: Race and Democracy since World War II.* New York: Basic Books.

References

Bernasconi R. 2001. 'Who invented the concept of race?' in *Race.* Bernasconi R (ed). Oxford: Blackwell, 11–36.

Biko S. 2007. *I Write What I Like.* Johannesburg: Picador Africa.

Dodd A. 2012. *Spear and Loathing: The Image that Undid Us.* Johannesburg: Mampoer Shorts.

Du Bois WEB. 1903. *The Souls of Black Folk.* New York: Penguin.

Fanon F. 1952. *Black Skin, White Masks.* New York: Grove Press.

Fanon F. 1961. *The Wretched of the Earth.* New York: Grove Press.

Kant I. 2001 [originally 1788]. 'On the use of teleological principles in philosophy' in *Race.* Bernasconi R (ed). Oxford: Blackwell, 37–56.

Mail&Guardian. 2011. [Online] Available at: http://mg.co.za/article/2011-07-01-kruger-row-becomes-racist-game [Accessed 25 October 2012].

Mamdani M. 1996. *Citizen and Subject: Contemporary Africa and the Legacy of Late Colonialism.* Princeton: Princeton University Press.

Mandela N. 1964. Statement from the Dock at the Rivonia Trial, 20 April 1964. [Online] Available at: http://www.anc.org.za/show.php?id=3430 [Accessed 16 July 2013].

Marx K. 1867a. 'The secret of primitive accumulation', Chapter 26 of *Capital*, Volume 1: [Online] Available at: http://www.marxists.org/archive/marx/works/1867-c1/ch26.htm [Accessed 18 October 2013].

Marx K. 1867b. 'Genesis of the industrial capitalist', Chapter 31 of *Capital*, Volume 1. [Online] Available at: http://www.marxists.org/archive/marx/works/1867-c1/ch31.htm [Accessed 18 October 2013].

Marx K. 1870. Letter to Meyer and Vogt in New York, 9th April, 1870. [Online] Available at: http://www.marxists.org/archive/marx/works/1870/letters/70_04_09.htm [Accessed 18 October 2013].

Miyeni E. 2011. 'Haffajee does it for white masters'. *The Sowetan,* 1 August.

Taiwo O. 1998. 'Exorcising Hegel's ghost: Africa's challenge to philosophy'. *African Studies Quarterly,* 1(4): 3–16.

Winant H. 2000. 'Race and race theory'. *Annual Review of Sociology,* (26): 169–185.

Class

Paul Stewart & Ran Greenstein

Sociology is the study of groups in society, just as psychology is the study of the individual. The concept of class refers to the way in which people in society are divided into social groups or layers, each of which share similar experiences, orientations and habits. Class has consequently assumed a hugely controversial role in sociology, and South African sociology is no exception. This was especially the case when class overshadowed race to explain apartheid. Much like the concepts of race and gender, the concept of class has been used as a prism through which fundamental lines of division in society have been drawn – or what sociologists refer to as social stratification. Emanating from Marx and the conflict perspective, class has been presented as a factor that not only stratifies society into social groups, but shapes almost every aspect of our lives. This line of division has, however, proved increasingly difficult to draw. The extent to which class is an organising factor in contemporary society is also not simple, especially as modern capitalist society has become increasingly stratified in terms of social classes. The result is that 'class' has, over time, been imbued with many meanings. Its central role as an explanatory concept has, however, diminished.

Once the theory of class of the classical thinkers Karl Marx and Max Weber has been introduced, this chapter will present key aspects of three post-classical theorists who use a class analysis to understand advanced 20th-century capitalist societies. These theorists, who were selected due to their impact on the work of scholars who have examined South African society, have something in common. One is an analytical philosopher, another an internationally leading sociologist while the third is a radical historian. They share an intellectual and ontological commitment to class as a concept which serves as a foundational conceptual tool when analysing society. Many social theorists think this commitment needs to be retained when we analyse and explain contemporary society. The conceptual picture looks a lot more complex when we recognise that the concept of class and class analysis cannot account for everything that happens in society.

This becomes clear when the chapter takes a look at how class analysis was used to understand apartheid society. In the 1970s a fierce intellectual debate surfaced. It became known as the 'race–class' debate and pitted Weberian-inspired writers, who used race to analyse South African society, against Marxist-inspired ones who used class to understand racial capitalism. Marxist analyses came to dominate. Yet the recent rediscovery of Weberian class analyses must still be integrated with and into class analyses, particularly if class is to remain a salient concept to capture the nature of a complex, previously racially divided society long dominated by capitalist economic development.

With that in mind, democratic South Africa then becomes the focus. The specific focus is a recent major collaborative sociological study conducted over a long period by academic scholars from the University of Johannesburg. This *Class in Soweto* study illustrates very well how class is used to analyse and understand the social configuration of South Africa's '*most populous and politically important township*'. The findings of this Marxist-orientated empirical study are surprising in terms of our common sense intuitions and view of the immediate world around us, yet they confirm the findings from the Weberian-orientated studies of 40 years ago.

The chapter ends by asking you to identify your own class position and to establish whether this is an important exercise in the sociological imagination. In this case it means you will need to apply the theoretical orientations in this chapter to your own life experience.

Case study 10.1 Class and race

I am black middle class. I matriculated from a prestigious girls' school in Pretoria, obtained a degree in economics and worked for a global consulting company. I live in the hipster capital of Johannesburg, am a wine, tea and coffee snob, and my favourite form of exercise is yoga. Naturally, I picked up a few white friends along the way. I really do love my white friends, but I often find myself struggling to be in an honest relationship with some of them.

A few weeks ago, I found myself in a passive–aggressive exchange with a dear (white) friend about gentrification. In my view, the model was capitalism's version of the 1913 Land Act, substituting economic power with political mandate and in the end black and coloured people were being displaced. In her view, I was racialising an economic issue, making it unnecessarily complex and besides 'as a middle-class person [I was] part of the problematic class and therefore complicit and guilty by association'.

Over time I have had to constantly remind myself that my white friends and I occupy the same spaces but live in different worlds. They do not understand why I am a proud product of numerous legislations meant to transform our society by raising the economic participation and living standards of those who had previously been excluded. To them this is an unfair advantage. To me, this is barely fair and not enough to dismantle centuries of methodical amassing of power to exercise over others.

Sometimes even black people can be guilty of misappropriating the experience of the poor and working class to further their own interests. Poverty is as systematic as racism, and requires that black middle-class people also pay attention to how their own actions deepen rather than alleviate it.

Still, although 'middle class' denotes an income and lifestyle identity, it does not fully define every experience, especially in ridiculously complex South Africa.

(Source: Ndlovu 2014)

QUESTION

Hold a discussion about Zama Ndlovu's experience and then repeat the exercise once you have worked through this chapter – ideally with the same university colleagues.

Key themes

- Defining class in the classical sociological tradition
- Outlining Marx's and Weber's theories of class and introducing key concepts related to class
- Going beyond classical class analysis and introducing integrated perspectives
- Reassessing and modifying class analysis

- Reviewing classical class analysis in South Africa under apartheid
- Noting non-reductionist analyses of class
- Empirically examining class in contemporary South African society.

10.1 Introduction

The concept of class has been used for a long time to divide society into distinct social groups. The word *classis* was first used in ancient Rome over 2 000 years ago to divide the population into tax groups (Dahrendorf 1959). The concept was introduced into English in the 16th century (Williams 1976). Society as a whole can be understood in terms of class analysis. The popular division of society into the 'haves' and the 'have-nots' can, for instance, be taken as a rough description to express this social scientific concept to which you were introduced in the first chapter of this textbook.

There you learned that social scientific concepts, carefully defined, pick out and identify some or other aspect of the social world. You also saw that theories are constructed by linking concepts coherently. You might have noticed how class was defined in different ways by Karl Marx and Max Weber. In other words, the *same* concept can be applied very differently and so pick out different aspects of social life to draw different lines of division between people or stratify them into different social groups.

In this chapter we are going to trace some of the ways in which the concept of class has been defined, understood and developed. Importantly, it will also show how the concept is embedded in different theoretical accounts of society. The power of this concept and how it enables competing perspectives and often fierce debates about the nature of the social world will come into view when its significance is located within the theoretical conceptions of Marx and Weber. The chapter will show how these perspectives have subsequently been developed by key theorists who influenced South African sociological studies. Class analysis – using class divisions to understand society – is applied to how sociologists, historians and economists tried to explain apartheid. The analysis of class – using class to distinguish and understand social groups – is then applied to explain South African society under democracy.

10.2 Defining class

All concepts are abstract, but this is especially true of the concept of class. It can also be widely applied. The concept is especially abstract as it does *not* include non-economic factors such as culture or race. It also fails to point to any actual economic conditions which a group of people share. One celebrated theorist put it quite plainly: 'Class is an obviously difficult word as class both conveys a range of meanings', and 'is particularly complex when it describes a social division' (Williams 1976: 51). Even when carefully defined, it is not immediately clear what the concept picks out or identifies when we examine society empirically. In order to understand concepts generally, such as class, we must follow the advice of Marx's great teacher, Georg Hegel. He said we must first 'grasp' and 'grip' a 'concept' and 'mentally … get hold of it and hold it still' (cited in Marx [1857] 1977: 28). Marx agreed this was a good place to start, but alerted us to the fact that concepts 'become fluid in the further course of development' (Marx [1857] 1977: 28–29). Concepts change and develop as we apply and test them in the light of empirical research. Concepts do so for the simple reason that we are trying to grasp and understand something which is continually changing and developing – society itself.

This textbook has already introduced two different definitions of the class concept. Marx defines class in relation to production, while Weber defines class in relation to the consumption of goods and services available on the market. Put another way, for Marx the background keyword for class is *exploitation*, while for Weber, it is *life chances*. More specifically, Marx defined class in terms of the ownership and non-ownership of economic resources (the 'means of production'), while Weber defined class in terms of the opportunities or life chances available to an

individual in a society dominated by the market. The concept of class is embedded in a distinct theoretical perspective, which asks its own set of questions (Wright 2005). In order to meaningfully discuss class we also need to discuss the concepts related to it in whatever conceptual framework or theory the concept is used.

10.3 Marx's theory of class

The concept of class is most strongly associated with the theories of Karl Marx. It is surprising then to realise that Marx never offered a clear, well-structured theory of class. To understand his approach, we must examine his historical writings and from these extract relevant definitions and discussions of the concept and its implications.

Early in his career as a thinker and activist, Marx developed what he called the **materialist conception of history**. As Chapter 14 on work will explain, this conception was based on the notion that history consists of human beings organising themselves in relation to nature, in order to meet their basic material needs. In so doing they enter social and political relations among themselves. Their role in production, and the system of division of labour and resources, shapes their consciousness about their position in society.

For Marx, it was essential to recognise that people did not operate in society as individuals only, but primarily as members of larger units that he termed classes. Classes developed historically as a result of conflicts over control and ownership of resources. In Marx's own society and time – Europe in the mid- to late 19th century – two classes had emerged as central. These were the **bourgeoisie** (the capitalist class) and the **proletariat** (the working class). The dynamic system of production in which these two classes operated was built on the constant growth of markets, territorial expansion, technological innovation, and ever-changing social relations. Marx called this **capitalism**.

Capitalism set in motion a period of unprecedented economic growth and guaranteed huge profits for the bourgeois class. It quickly became the dominant economic arrangement globally and continues to occupy that role. Marx argued, however, that capitalism has a critical weakness. For capitalism to succeed, a large number of workers need to be employed. Their labour is essential for the industrial production of goods to be sold in the marketplace. However, when workers get together in large-scale modern industrial enterprises, they inevitably begin to organise to defend and promote their own interests as a class. These interests are opposed to those of the capitalists. Whereas capitalists seek to increase their profits at the expense of workers' wages, the workers naturally seek the opposite – to reduce their exploitation and increase their share in the global economic pie. This, Marx argued, undermines capitalism as an economic, political and social system as a whole. As capitalism grows, so does the level and scale of organisation of its opponents. In that way it produces – in Marx's words – its own 'grave-diggers', the social forces that would destroy it eventually.

10.3.1 Class as the starting point

Class is not only central to Marxist theory, but it is also Marx's theoretical starting point (Bottomore 1983). According to Marx, there were no social classes in primitive communal societies where the institution of private property had yet to emerge. Classes only emerged as social relations became more complex with the division of labour and as the ancient communal mode of production gave way to feudalism and then capitalism. Class, for Marx, consequently refers to a historical phenomenon. Talking about capitalism, Marx writes in the *Poverty of Philosophy* (ch 2, sect 5): 'Economic conditions had in the first place transformed the mass of people into workers. The domination of capital created the common situation and common interests of this class' (cited in Bottomore 1983: 76). Yet Marx did not think even his own historical-philosophical theory could fully capture the complexity of class and the class structure of especially capitalist society. In order to properly apply the concept of class to society then, it should in each case be based on – again in Marx's words – the 'empirically given circumstances' (Bottomore 1983: 77).

Consistent with his own historical materialist approach, Marx's own view of class underwent development as he examined the society of his day. How Marx initially thought about class under early industrial capitalism, when the landowners of the previous feudal mode of production remained prominent, is often missed. It is to be found in the final, unfinished chapter of *Capital* Vol III, edited by his collaborator Friederich Engels. In this fragmentary note on class, Marx poses and then answers his own question:

What constitutes a class? – and the reply to this follows naturally from the reply to another question, namely: What makes wage-labourers, capitalists and landlords constitute the three great social classes? At first glance – the identity of revenues and sources of revenues. There are three great social groups whose members, the individuals forming them, live on wages, profit and ground-rent respectively on the realisation of their labour-power, their capital and their landed property (Marx [1894] 1977: 886).

In this definition class is defined in relation to income or revenue. As capitalist society matures and the influence of the landowners fades – the concept of class becomes more clearly defined in relation to production and the economy. As capitalism took root and capital replaced land as the primary source of wealth in society, the bourgeoisie (or capitalists) and proletariat (or working class) emerged as the two primary and *fundamental* social groups in capitalist society. Alongside these two great social classes – as no actual society involves *only* two classes – Marx further identified two subordinate groups, the petty-bourgeoisie (mainly small traders, teachers and professionals) and the *lumpen*-proletariat (the homeless, indigent, permanently unemployed and marginalised social groups). Marx's use of the concept changed and developed along with changing social and economic conditions. Similarly, the manner in which it has been applied has also changed and developed. The immediate question which arises is, how are classes formed?

10.3.2 Class formation

Marx famously wrote in the *Contribution to the Critique of Political Economy*:

In the social production of their life men enter into definite relations that are indispensable and independent of their will, relations of production which correspond to a definite stage of development of their material productive forces (Marx [1959] in Tucker 1978: 4).

Human beings must relate to one another in order to produce what society needs to survive. What starts out as a series of **social relations of production** between people soon turns into relationships between different social groups. For Marx, class identifies the antagonisms between social groups which arise in this historical process in successive modes of production. The beginning of social class formation is described in the Communist Manifesto as follows:

The proletariat goes through various stages of development. With its birth begins its struggle with the bourgeoisie. At first the contest is carried on by individual labourers, then by the workpeople of a factory, then by the operatives of one trade, in one locality, against the individual bourgeoisie who directly exploits them. They direct their attacks not against the bourgeois conditions of production, but against the instruments of production themselves; they destroy imported wares that compete with their labour, they smash to pieces machinery, they set factories ablaze, they seek to restore by force the vanished status of the workman of the Middle Ages (Marx [1848] in Tucker 1978: 480).

It is worthwhile reading the Communist Manifesto in full to see how this process unfolds and how the labourers are initially 'an incoherent mass scattered over the whole country', how the bourgeoisie 'is compelled to set the whole proletariat in motion', how 'the proletariat not only increases in number' but 'becomes concentrated in greater masses, its strength grows and it feels its strength more' (Tucker 1978: 480 ff). Read how machinery develops, workers' livelihoods become more precarious, how workers combine to form trade unions, how 'every class struggle is a political struggle' and how 'the bourgeoisie finds itself in constant battle' and how, for Marx: 'The proletarian movement is the self-conscious, independent movement of the immense majority, in the interests of the immense majority' (Tucker 1978: 480 ff).

There are many examples of the 'definite social relations' which emerge in the process of class formation in these passages, just as there continues to be definite social relations between the modern employer who pays a wage and the contemporary worker who earns one.

It is important to note that while the two primary classes are locked into antagonistic social relations in order to produce an economic surplus for society, they cannot survive without each other. Despite the antagonistic, yet co-operative social relation in production that the concept of class identifies, the immediate social consequence is poverty and inequality. Chapter 22 on poverty specifically addresses this. The point is that the concept implies the existence of different social classes.

10.3.3   Class as a relation

Society is a whole. This whole is stratified into different classes that stand in specific sets of social relations to one another. Class is hence not a thing, for Marx, but rather expresses *a relation*. This relation – as we will see in the next section – is, for Weber, expressly a *relation of domination*. For Marx, the relational nature of class is defined in terms of who owns (and does not own) the **means of production**. This refers to the land, raw materials, tools, equipment, machinery, factories and mines – needed when work is being performed. The social relations of production emerge when work is performed. These are intimately linked with how the economy and the productive forces in society develop and become organised in terms of the class of capitalists and the class of workers. The productive forces (or **forces of production**) in society do not only consist of the *means* of

production, but also include the *development* of machinery and technology, sources of energy and the education of the proletariat as well as science, particularly as it is applied to industry. Any such economic development requires social organisation. Class, for Marx, captures how, historically, the two major social classes are organised and stand opposed to one another, particularly under capitalism.

Understood as a relation and not as a thing, class must not be understood as a static concept and hence neither must social classes be understood as such. Social classes undergo continual change as:

at a certain stage of their development, the material productive forces of society come in conflict with the existing relations of production, or – what is but a legal expression for the same thing – with the property relations within which they have been at work hitherto and from forms of development of the productive forces these relations turn into their fetters. Then begins an epoch of social revolution (Marx [1859] in Tucker 1978: 4–5).

The formation of social classes is hence rooted in conflict. As the British sociologist Anthony Giddens put it: 'class of necessity involves a conflict relation' (1971: 37).

10.3.4   Class conflict and class struggle

The conflict between capitalists and workers is known as **class struggle**. To quote an even more famous statement from Marx, more fully cited in Chapter 22 on poverty: 'The history of all hitherto existing society is the history of class struggles'. This conflict relation is a perpetual and irreconcilable tension, whether overt or covert or whether hidden in production or when it bursts open in society such as when workers go on strike. It involves a clash between the direct producers (workers, peasants) and those who own and control crucial economic resources – the means of production in other words. This group of people can use their ownership and control to benefit from the labour of the direct producers. Marx refers to such benefits as **surplus value** – what capitalists get from the process on top of their investment. He regards it as being a form of **exploitation**: profit made at the expense of the workers' efforts. In each society there may be more than one class of producers and of owners, but usually one set of class relations is dominant.

Marx hoped to forever change the dominant social relations of production in capitalist society and the need for class struggle. He first expressed this idealistic hope as a young student and later wrote in ringing tones how:

[a]n oppressed class is the vital condition for every society founded on the antagonism of classes. The emancipation of the oppressed class thus implies necessarily the creation of a new society. The condition of the emancipation of the working class is the abolition of every class ... (Marx [1847] in Tucker 1978: 218–219).

For Marx, it is the class struggle which provides, in his words, the 'motor of history' – the dynamic structural tension that propels any class-divided society forward and lies at the heart of social change. This conflict relation between the two fundamental classes, however, extends well beyond the confines of the factory gate or the company office. It ripples out across society and impacts on virtually every aspect of people's lives. Hence, while the social relations of production are primarily economic in nature, they have social, political and ideological dimensions as well.

The multiple dimensions of social relationships between classes mean that the class struggle can acquire different forms. In the direct economic dimension, it is usually conducted through union organisation, labour negotiations, strikes and other forms of protest. In the social dimension it may be conducted through community-based organisation and civil society alliances. In the political dimension it may be conducted through the formation and operation of class-based political parties and their work on relevant legislation and policy. In the ideological dimension it may be conducted through struggles over the content of education, in the media and through campaigns by various forces meant to shape people's class consciousness. In short, in the process of class struggle, those who belong to a particular class will come, for Marx, to understand themselves in relation to those in a different class and understand themselves as a definable social group or class. So important is the notion of class struggle – when classes express their collective sense of agency when confronting each other – that the famous 'structuralist' Marxist, Nicos Poulantzas, came to adopt a radically subjectivist, agency-orientated reading of class. He went as far as to conclude that 'classes have existence only in the class struggle' (1982: 101) as they attempt to advance their class interests. This brings us to the issue of how a class understands itself.

10.3.5 Class consciousness

The notion of **class consciousness** – the understanding a particular group of people has of itself – was central to Marx even though he did not offer a dedicated discussion of the issue. He did, however, use the concept of class in both an objective and a subjective sense. Both of these senses are captured in the following quote from Marx ([1847] 1978: 168) that, once capital had created 'the common situation and common interests of this class ... Thus this mass is already a class in relation to capital, but not yet a class for itself. In the struggle ... this mass unites and forms itself into a class for itself. The interests which it defends become class interests'. Marx uses the concept of class 'in-itself' to refer to a specific group of people who belong to either the working or the capitalist class. This 'objectivist' sense in which Marx used the concept has had far-reaching implications and has led to a wide range of understandings of how society should be analysed in terms of class. Capitalist society must first be viewed then in terms of the dividing line offered by an 'objective' reading of class. Then we will examine the 'subjective' aspect of class and class consciousness.

Class understood as 'objective' – or 'in-itself'

To say that classes exist objectively means there is an empirically identifiable group of people who share a similar position in the system of production. Class could be empirically and hence *objectively* defined – one could, in other words, count who worked for a wage (working class) and who did not (capitalists or some of the professionals in the petty bourgeoisie or middle class). Marx argues that people who share the same objectively definable material conditions will most likely share the same **class interests**. This idea was to have an enormous impact on social analysis and was at the foundation of his approach to class. Such a class Marx called a class 'in-itself'. The actual identification of such groups (or classes) of people was much easier in Marx's day. But when society divided into a wide range of social groups, this development blurred Marx's social stratification into the two major and two subordinate classes. This was particularly true with the increased differences amongst the middle classes.

Stressing the 'objectivist' reading of class, however, often suffered the fate of boiling down or *reducing* everything to the single notion of class. When class is defined in economic terms to the virtual exclusion of any other key non-economic factors, such analyses become examples of economic class **reductionism**. This is especially true in the South African context. What this means is that class does not capture other ways, like race, in which people think of (or are aware of) themselves as a group. As we will later see, class expresses itself in other, 'subjective' ways. Groups of people may well *objectively* be working class or a class 'in-itself', but may understand themselves *subjectively* as a nation, as Africans, as 'the people' or as 'the poor'.

Class understood as 'subjective' – or 'for-itself'

When waged workers become aware of their situation and the commonality of their interests and begin to organise accordingly in order to pursue their goals, they are transformed into a class 'for-itself'. This means that such a social group becomes aware and conscious of its class belonging and acts to consolidate and advance itself.

Used in this way, the subjective aspect of class – a class which acts in its own interests – has enjoyed less prominence than in the objective sense. The subjective sense was, however, crucially important for Marx. For it was only when the working class became *aware* of and came to understand how their combined labour power was exploited under capitalism and understood themselves as a distinct class and acted on the basis of that self-understanding – that capitalism could be overthrown. Marx thought this would lead to a 'class-less' society – one free of oppressive social relations.

If the working class did not, however, come to this collective awareness and realisation that they constituted a class 'for-itself' or there was an absence of awareness of their common class interests, members of a class may suffer from what Marx called **false consciousness**. This is a distorted vision of reality, their place within it, and their real needs. The struggle between true and false consciousness is waged in the education system, public media, arts and culture, and other spheres of society.

Herein, however, lies the problem with the highly abstract concept of class. Because of the abstract nature of the concept, it does not specify its various dimensions and how it is experienced. Because the working class in South Africa was predominantly a black working class, *the experience of class* was racialised and assumed racialised forms of expression. Workers felt themselves oppressed collectively because they were being discriminated against in terms of race. It was not necessarily as a *class* that the *objectively* definable South African working class understood themselves. Rather, class consciousness was expressed in terms of being oppressed as Africans, as black, or as an oppressed nation of people. White workers in the Rand Revolt in 1922, on the other hand, understood themselves as a class, but understood this in starkly racialised and hence, contradictory terms. This was because they rejected their working-class comrades on the other side of the racial divide. The Rand Revolt is described further in Chapter 14 on work.

By way of contrast to not only the proletariat in South Africa but also the proletarian working class internationally, it is the bourgeoisie who seem to have understood themselves more clearly as a class 'for-itself' by virtue of their immense economic, political and social power in society. The basis for this sense of themselves as a class 'for-itself' is explained in the Communist Manifesto:

> *The bourgeoisie cannot exist without constantly revolutionising the instruments of production and thereby the relations of production, and with them the whole relations of society* (Marx [1848] in Tucker 1978: 476).

In playing what Marx deemed to be a historic role in the development of human progress, the bourgeoisie experienced themselves to be a powerful social class. Their own system compelled them to revolutionise production and hence their relations with the working class. As the bourgeois class felt they were leading and changing society, they became ever-increasingly conscious of the need to pursue their own interests as a class 'for-itself'.

Social action, then, is shaped by shared class interests, which are formed on the basis of social and economic location. In the immediate term such interests revolve around wages, working conditions and control in the workplace. A longer-term view may focus on economic policy matters: budgets, taxation, public services, industrial relations and so on. Ultimately, structural issues of class power and resources at the level of state and society as a whole may come to the fore. We can look at interests as ranging from the concerns of individual members of the class in their daily lives to broader concerns of the entire class about its overall position, all linked by a common class identity.

10.3.6 Class and material inequality

Behind the notion of class interests there is an understanding that class relations are driven, above all, by **material inequalities**. This aspect is dominant in popular meanings of class. Material inequalities normally refer to inequalities of income, assets (property, cars, appliances) and access to services (water, electricity, housing). For Marx all these were important components of inequality, but were of secondary significance. The basic inequality has rather – from a strictly Marxist perspective – to do with access to productive resources, between those who own them and those who do not, and the extraction of surplus value. Although some workers may receive high wages and can afford to buy consumer goods (including expensive ones), *structurally* they occupy an inferior position, having to work for employers who exploit them. Workers may improve their position and experience upward mobility as individuals, but as a class they remain subordinate to capitalists who subject them to wage slavery and extract profits (surplus value) from them.

The combination of material inequalities and different degrees of consciousness – born in class struggle – leads to political organisation and a struggle over power. Class may serve as a foundation for unions, social movements and political parties. But the relations between classes and their political representatives are not simple. As the economic power of the bourgeoisie developed and advanced with the growth and establishment of capitalism as the dominant economic system globally, so did their political power. Marx and Engels defined the role of the bourgeois capitalist class in relation to government – whose role was to administer the affairs of the state in the interests of *all* citizens – in the following way: 'The executive of the modern State is but a committee for managing the common affairs of the whole bourgeoisie' (Tucker 1978: 475). By this they meant that government policies in modern states serve the interests of the bourgeoisie as a class, though not necessarily those of each individual capitalist (because they are many and have divergent interests). In other words, economic power under capitalism could not be separated from political power which the bourgeoisie usurped in their own class interests – to the detriment of not only the working class but society as a whole.

10.3.7 Class and politics

Much has changed since this view – that the bourgeoisie exercises direct control over state political power – was expressed by Marx and Engels. In democratic regimes today, political parties – with different class and other interests – compete for popular votes and frequently claim to be acting in the service of certain classes to attract support. The degree to which they truly work for the classes in whose name they speak varies a great deal. Trade unions usually represent workers more directly against employers because they are based on membership within sectors and workplaces. Yet political parties and trade unions alike take part in a struggle for power and, to some extent at least, shape government policy in accordance with class interests. For more on this issue, read Chapter 16 on politics and governance.

Regarding the role of classes in capitalist society, the final point to be made here is that Marx envisaged that political forces representing the working class would gradually acquire power and use it to change the balance of class forces in favour of workers against capitalists. This would, he thought, eventually lead to more thorough political transformation, which would see the demise of the class-based capitalist state and the rise of a new regime representing the exploited masses, headed by the working class. This revolutionary process would mean that capitalism will be replaced by a more just, egalitarian and 'classless' society.

We have seen how Marx regarded class as a central concept, one that changes in order to reflect the changing class relations and fortunes of society; how it shapes all economic and social relations and how it will play a crucial role in the political transformation of society in the future. This discussion has, however, also noted criticisms of how the single concept of class and a class analysis of society is not straightforward. This examination of class will now turn to Max Weber, the thinker who had to work in the shadow of Marx.

10.4 Weber's theory of class

Class is used in sociology as a marker to distinguish between groups of people. Class is one way sociologists develop systems of social stratification. While Marx was preoccupied with a single aspect of stratification, namely class, Weber had a considerably more complex, multidimensional view of social stratification – the division of society into social groups. What underpins the phenomenon of social stratification is the notion of power, and this is more explicit in Weber than in Marx. Simply put, if one social group or class has access to the productive forces in society (as for Marx) or one social group enjoys better life chances on the market due to owning property (as for Weber), these social groups possess significantly more power than a social group or class that does not have access to material resources. While the notion of power is difficult to define or pinpoint, let us use the following working definition derived from Weber: power is the ability to make others do what you want them to do whether they like it or not. Parents have power over their children, teachers over their learners, employers over their employees. The state, via the law and law enforcement agencies (the police and the military), exercises power over all citizens. In brief, power can be personal or structural, positive or negative and it ebbs and flows. Power is a dynamic potential.

Weber claimed that in order to *understand* society, it was important to recognise how *power* underpinned the way in which society was socially stratified. This idea was introduced in a few paragraphs in Chapter 1, which might be worth revisiting at this point. Whether in the classical theorists Marx or Weber, or in the post-classical theorists, class is defined and embedded in different conceptual frameworks. In the case of Weber, the range of concepts within which class needs to be embedded is broader than in the case of Marx.

10.4.1 Rationalisation and class

If the complex conceptual framework and theories of Weber could be encapsulated in a single word or concept, the word might well be 'rationalisation'. Both individual social action and the social action of collectivities, for Weber, are increasingly required to conform to legal–rational forms of social action. The only way to organise an increasingly complex industrial society is to continually improve and amend the rules, procedures and laws by which the various bureaucratic systems and structures administer and regulate society. In fact, so important was the need for bureaucracy and increasing rationalisation in society that Weber even attributed the demise of slavery to the lack of *rationality* and *calculability* in the economy under slavery. In order to develop and thrive, society must become increasingly rational. As Weber studied industrial society, moreover, he noticed that it was becoming increasingly characterised by various processes of rationalisation. As industrial society became more complex, so the number of social groups proliferated and became more differentiated from one another. Bear this key insight of Weber in mind as his notion of class, as well as his two other key concepts of social stratification, are defined and applied to identifying social divisions in society.

10.4.2 Weber's definition of class

While Marx did not provide a formal definition of the concept of class, Weber pursued an opposite approach by providing a formal definition. In his influential *Economy and Society* (Part II Chapter 4) Weber wrote:

> The term 'class' refers to any group of people …
> [who have the same] typical chance for a supply of
> goods, external living conditions, and personal life
> experiences, insofar as this chance is determined by
> the amount and kind of power, or lack of such, to
> dispose of goods or skills for the sake of income in
> a given economic order… 'Class situation' is, in this
> sense, ultimately 'market situation' (cited in Gerth &
> Mills [1948] 1974: 181).

Life-chances are based on people's ability to compete in the market. This competition favours those who possess property or other assets. Those without property have to sell their labour in order to survive, and are thus at a disadvantage. What distinguishes those who have property from those who do not is, consequently, that the two groups have different *interests*. For example, it is in workers' interest to earn the highest possible wage,

while it is in employers' interest to get as much work out of workers as possible. More rational ways of working must continually be introduced in the interest of progress and profitability and generally to serve the interests of employers.

10.4.3 Class interests and social action

Above all, according to Weber, the factor behind class is *economic* interest. On this point Weber could not have been clearer: 'According to our terminology, the factor that creates "class" is unambiguously economic interest, and indeed, only those interests involved in the existence of the "market"' (Gerth & Mills [1948] 1974: 83). Hence, for Weber, classes are specifically related to interests linked to the market, which involve an exchange of property, skills and abilities, for income and other assets. With 'class' understood in this way, shared interests of such a 'class' of people may (or may not) serve as a basis for **communal action** – which Weber defines as 'action which is oriented to the feeling of the actors that they belong together' (Gerth & Mills [1948] 1974: 83). Such 'class' interests may serve (or not serve) as a basis for **societal action** – which Weber defines as action 'oriented to a rationally motivated adjustment of interests' (Gerth & Mills [1948] 1974: 83). Such action – whether communal or societal – may take a more or less organised form.

For Weber, how social action is organised is crucial to understanding the relation between class as rooted in the market economy and the extent to which society as a whole is becoming increasingly rationalised. For him, it is hence *not* inevitable that shared material or class interests necessarily result in class-based social action as Marx thought.

Organised social action – such as a workers' strike that can be interpreted as an expression of their 'class situation' – depends for its basis not *only* on their shared circumstances. Crucially such social action, for Weber, depends also on circumstances such as general cultural and political conditions and on 'the *transparency* of the connections between the causes and the consequences of the "**class situation**"' (Gerth & Mills [1948] 1974: 184) (our emphasis). In other words, communal and societal action – which both have their base in shared interests and which are both related to the market – will depend on the way people *interpret* the situation, and the extent to which it shapes their consciousness. This is a far more complicated explanation of how groups of people behave collectively. Unlike Marx supposed, there is no *direct* relation between social conditions and voluntary, but consciously organised, collective social action.

To put Weber's explanation of consciously organised collective social action another way, common economic interests do *not* automatically lead to class action, because as Weber puts it:

In our terminology 'classes' are not communities; they merely represent possible, and frequent, bases for communal action (Gerth & Mills [1948] 1974: 181).

For any social group to be a community – as opposed to a class sharing a similar set of life chances – they must feel they share common ways of life, meanings and doing things. Social groups do not just act due to sharing similar economic circumstances. Something else is needed to spur people to social action. If, for instance, inequalities are regarded as part of the natural order of things, or as a just reward for people's different abilities and efforts, no organised action is likely to follow. When the same inequalities are seen as a result of unfair distribution of resources, or as a result of economic structures and policies that provide some people with advantages while disadvantaging others, action based on people's association to pursue common goals may follow. An example of this is the service delivery protests in South Africa today.

In this approach, the relationship between class 'in-itself' and class 'for-itself', which was established by Marx, becomes more complicated. It is no longer simply a matter of class members learning to recognise their true interests and to act on them. Rather, there are different ways in which these interests may be defined and serve as a basis for action. We do not know in advance what they are, and there is no necessary end result to the process. Unlike Marx, Weber did not assume that outsiders, or insider-activists speaking in the name of the class, could determine how interests would be interpreted and what action should be taken. In this sense Weber's approach is more flexible and open to diverse outcomes.

We saw earlier that Marx adhered to the materialist conception of history, which regards production as the foundation for social, political and ideological arrangements. From that perspective, class is based primarily in the relations of production. These are the relations between groups with different positions in the process of agricultural and industrial production. They shape secondary aspects such as class consciousness, identity and political organisation. As briefly indicated in Chapter 1, Weber introduced two other concepts to explain these relationships which he did not think could be reduced to class.

10.4.4 Status and party

While Weber recognised the economic nature of class and class situations, he also acknowledged other forces. He called these **status** and **party** and they played a role in the process of translating class positions into communal identities and political action. Weber defined status in the following way:

In contrast to classes, status groups are normally communities ... often of an amorphous kind. In contrast to the purely economically determined 'class situation' we wish to designate as 'status situation' every typical component for the life fate of men that is determined by a specific, positive or negative, social estimation of honour (Gerth & Mills [1948] 1974: 186–187).

Groups of people – or 'status groups' – who find themselves in the same 'status situation' do not have a clear structure. They are based on 'social estimation of honour' (or prestige). This is a consideration of a *non-economic* factor. Status is related to the ways in which people identify themselves and are identified by others. The class situation and the status situation are not necessarily linked and may even be opposed to one another, with status *dividing* people of the same class or *uniting people across class lines*.

Although Weber gave a few examples of status groups, these were drawn mostly from contexts that have limited relevance for us. One type of status, however, stands out: that of ethnicity and race, which use real or imaginary common heritages as a foundation for identity. Race in particular (Weber uses the term 'caste') is not just about difference but also relations of domination, which serve as a basis for mobilisation – to entrench domination or to fight it.

Weber identified the difference between the class situation and market order on the one hand, and the status order on the other. Note how carefully he compares the difference between class and status:

With some over-simplification, one might say that 'classes' are stratified according to their relations to the production and acquisition of goods; whereas 'status groups' are stratified according to the principles of the consumption of goods as represented by special 'styles of life' (Gerth & Mills [1948] 1974: 193) (Weber's emphasis).

In other words, the class situation and market order are concerned with 'functional interests' only. Work must be performed efficiently and transactions must be conducted in a rational manner. Weber says: 'the market and its processes knows no personal distinctions' (Gerth & Mills [1948] 1974: 192). Status, identity and culture play no part here. The status order is defined in terms of the social estimation of 'honour' and of 'styles of life' peculiar to status groups. This status order or status situation *interferes* with the free operation of the market. During supposedly rational transactions on the market, a person of high social standing often receives preference over someone of low social status. Sometimes such interference can act to reduce economic inequalities and sometimes to reinforce them. The point is that we must study the impact of the status order in each case concretely and empirically, instead of simply assuming that it will always be in the same relationship to the class order. At a more general level – in Weber's 'complex multidimensional view' – the class situation and the status order remain strongly related:

> And today the class situation is by far the predominant factor, for of course the possibility of a style of life expected for members of a status group is usually conditioned economically (Gerth & Mills [1948] 1974: 190).

In other words, status is linked to the economic position of groups and what they can afford to buy and their consequent 'styles of life'.

It is within this nuanced relationship of class and status that Weber introduces another element to the discussion.

> Whereas the genuine place of 'classes' is within the economic order, the place of 'status groups' is within the social order, that is within the sphere of the distribution of 'honour'. From within these spheres, classes and status groups influence one another and they influence the legal order and are in turn influenced by it. But 'parties' live in a house of 'power' (Gerth & Mills [1948] 1974: 194).

The notion of parties that 'live in a house of power' allows Weber to introduce the element of **political action**. Such action is required to realise goals of an ideal or material nature, involving the group as a whole or some of its members. 'Party', for Weber, can refer to diverse social entities, such as a social club or the state. Parties represent interests derived from the class situation or status situation or some combination of the two. Their mode of operation is shaped by relations of power in society or what Weber refers to as the 'structure of domination'.

In essence, both Marx and Weber see a relationship between class, identity and power, but whereas Marx tends to see the latter two as derived from the former key concept of class, Weber regards them as three independent, but interrelated dimensions. When looking at the economic dimension itself, Marx focuses on relations of exploitation and conflict, while Weber's focus is more on opportunities derived from skill, will (or agency) and taking advantage of market positions.

10.5 Integrated perspectives

Is there a way of integrating the two approaches? Can Marx's focus on the centrality of class be retained, but combined with Weber's notions of status and party, in order to address issues of culture, power and identity? Let us look at some attempts to move beyond the classical theories in this vein.

10.5.1 Eric Olin Wright and *class*

The American analytical philosopher and social theorist Erik Olin Wright has written extensively on class (Wright 1978; 1985; 1997). The distinction he makes between class structure and class formation is a useful starting point to see how he goes beyond classical class analysis. **Class structure** 'defines a set of empty places or positions filled by individuals or families' (Wright 1985: 10). What is important about this way of understanding class structure for Wright is that it provides *limits* to the possible variations of not only class formation, but also to the forms that class struggle and class consciousness can assume (1985: 27).

This becomes clear when we see that **class formation** is defined as 'the formation of organised collectivities *within that class structure* on the basis of the interests shaped by that class structure' (Wright 1985: 10) (our emphasis). It is obvious from these definitions that class structure is the basic element in the analysis and that it *logically precedes* and is a *precondition* for the processes of class formation. To help clarify further, Wright distinguishes between these two concepts by suggesting that:

> If class structure is defined by social relations between classes, class formation is defined by social relations within classes, social relations and collectivities engaged in struggle (Wright 1985: 10) (our emphasis).

For Wright then, the material interests that are the foundation for class formation are based on relations of exploitation that are generated by the class structure. They can be defined with precision 'regardless of the subjective states of the actors' (Wright 1985: 108). In other words, structures exert a *decisive* influence and *determine the limits* within which processes of class formation, consciousness and struggle take place. Central to class analysis, from this perspective, is 'the role of class structures and class struggles in understanding the overall trajectory of historical development' (1985: 114). This role is guided in turn by 'the development of the forces of production' (1985: 131).

Wright recognises that non-class mechanisms operate in society, that class structure does not determine everything on its own, and that it is not always the most important factor in the explanation of social developments. But what emerges from his work is that class structure is the *primary* factor that sets limits on all other factors – among which are gender, power and identity. The latter do not constrain and act upon one another in a similar way to that of class, nor do they have an impact on the class structure. The relations between these concepts are *asymmetrical*. This simply means there is *no direct relation* between class structure and class formation.

Looking at class in this way directs our attention *towards* important issues (how class shapes power and identity), but also *away* from other important issues (how power and identity shape class). But because Wright maintains a conception of class in solely objective terms and focuses solely on objective class interests – despite the *limits* he acknowledges – such a view overlooks the *capacity of people* to define different sets of interests on the basis of similar circumstances. When class is viewed solely in objective terms, analysts are given the power to decide what their 'real' interests are and whether their class consciousness fits their position in society or constitutes 'false consciousness'. Wright assumes that interests follow directly from class structure. This removes from the analysis the processes of construction of classes and their interests through culture, identity and politics. This is what is interesting from a historical perspective. The *capacity of people* must then be brought back into the analysis to restore the agency of class actors to class analysis.

10.5.2 Michael Burawoy and *The Politics of Production*

In the introduction to his influential book, *The Politics of Production* (1985), Michael Burawoy makes it explicitly clear that workers should be brought back into class analysis. This develops the argument first made in *Manufacturing Consent* (Burawoy 1979). Burawoy studies the industrial working class. Going beyond Wright, he

argues against the notion of a class 'in-itself' that can be defined in objective terms – the size and composition of class in terms of its relation to ownership of economic resources. His focus is on how workers under capitalism and state socialism alike resist, as well as collaborate and, surprisingly, even *consent*, to their own exploitation in productive activity. This goes well beyond the classical analysis of the overall trajectory of capital and the *determining* role of class structure. As Burawoy explains: 'There is no "objective" notice of class prior to its appearance on the stage of history' (1985: 39). Rather, class is constituted by acting on the historical stage. Viewed in this way, 'class becomes the *effect* of a set of economic, political and ideological structures found in all spheres of social activity' (ibid.). Hence, class cannot be located in a specific economic realm only.

Moving from capitalism in the abstract to detailed empirical studies in the practical **politics of production**, Burawoy asserts that:

there are no longer any objective laws of development of the capitalist mode of production: different political apparatuses of production lead to different struggles and thus to diverse patterns of accumulation (Burawoy 1985: 255).

What Burawoy means by the 'political apparatuses of production' is the role of the state, especially in the organisation of work. In this he takes a step towards the recognition that classes and the interests that organise the life of workers are not determined solely by economic structures, but are also shaped by power (of the state) and culture (of workers). Production politics, in other words, brings the role and power of the state, as well as the agency and lived experience of workers, into the account of how classes are formed, act and struggle against one another.

Burawoy hence incorporates economic, political and ideological aspects into his understanding of class and production. His perspective does not, however, grant an independent role for non-class forces. He recognises that gender and race may play *a greater role* in society and politics than class, but he regards class nonetheless – in a manner similar to Wright – as the *basic* principle of organisation of contemporary societies. He does so for the following reasons:

First, class better explains the development and reproduction of contemporary societies. Second, racial and gender domination are shaped by the class in which they are embedded more than the forms of class domination are shaped by gender and race. Therefore, any attempts to eliminate non-class forms of domination must acknowledge the limits and character of change within capitalism and socialism, considered as class societies (Burawoy 1985: 9).

This statement, however, gives rise to two problems. The first is that the claim that class provides a better explanation for the development of contemporary societies is based on the definition in class-related terms. If we do *not* take the class analysis framework as our starting point, our understanding of what constitutes the structure of contemporary societies and what counts as development will change. From a race- or gender-centred perspective, the transition from one pattern of class relations to another, and from capitalism to socialism, are not *necessarily* the crucial developments that are in need of explanation.

The second problem is that, since gender and racial domination are admittedly more tenacious than class domination, it is *not* clear why they are to be seen as more importantly shaped by class than the other way around. This is particularly the case in a racially divided South Africa. We consequently need to develop an analysis that looks at *all* social identities, interests and structures *without* reducing them to any particular concept. We should rather identify connections between class, identity and power. But we should do so without assuming that they are always linked in the same way and with class always emerging as the dominant force.

10.5.3 EP Thompson and *The Making of the English Working Class*

A more flexible formulation of class analysis, which appeared before Wright and Burawoy wrote their works, is found in the work of British historian EP Thompson. In his book *The Making of the English Working Class* (1963), he regards class as:

a historical phenomenon, unifying a number of disparate and seemingly unconnected events, both in the raw material of experience and in consciousness. I emphasize that it is a historical phenomenon (Thompson 1963: 9).

Class for Thompson is not a 'structure' or a 'category', but 'something which in fact happens (and can be shown to have happened) in human relationships' (1963: 9). It happens when people perceive the identity of interests among themselves and against others as a result of common experiences. This

class experience, which is at the basis of consciousness and action, is 'largely determined by the productive relations into which men are born – or enter involuntarily' (Thompson 1963: 10). For Thompson 'class consciousness is the way in which these experiences are handled in cultural terms: embodied in traditions, value-systems, ideas and institutional forms' (ibid.). Understood in this way the concept of class suddenly becomes less abstract. We can relate the concept of class now to our own 'traditions, value-systems and ideas' instead of to the more 'objective' criterion of our relation to ownership of economic resources in society, which is often not straightforward.

The important point is that Thompson rejects the notion of objective material interests just waiting to be discovered by class actors. Class does not exist *outside* of a historical process, he says. Class is rather practically defined 'by men as they live their own history, and, in the end, this is its only definition' and so Thompson reminds us that 'class is a relationship, and not a thing' (1963: 11). Class consciousness, in other words, is not determined by the relations of production and does not follow any necessary direction towards a specific outcome. To understand how consciousness is developing over time, we need to observe patterns of relationships between people, institutions and ideas. Class is an identity that is produced historically in interaction between structure and agency, experience and consciousness: 'The working class made itself as much as it was made' (Thompson 1963: 213).

Thompson has, in his construal of class, powerfully recognised the agency of class actors. This means that people formulate their own interests, based on their specific history and social position, instead of following objective interests defined by others. In understanding class in this way, Thompson set the stage for theorists to recognise fully the role of culture and power in the formation of class and class consciousness. Subsequent theorists then started to look at class and community, languages of class, and class experience.

10.6 Class, people and community

Social scientist Craig Calhoun (1982) focuses his contribution on the need to recognise the diversity of positions occupied by workers, which makes it difficult to lump them all together under the same label of 'the working class' (in the singular). He argues that the majority of the working masses in the period considered in Thompson's work (Britain in the 19th century) identified themselves as 'the people' rather than as 'the working class'. They adhered to community-based populist ideologies, not class-specific movements, and succeeded in mobilising people precisely because they did not call on them to abandon their different identities in favour of a single category of 'working class'. This gave them a sense of being part of a larger group, as did the concept of 'the nation'. The concept of class did not have the same political mobilising capacity as that of 'the people'. Communal organisation, building on existing bonds, provided a more powerful basis for action.

Calhoun's arguments refer to a point in time and space remote from ours, but it may be applicable to other situations as well: people organise on a variety of issues, using different components of their identities, of which class is only one – and not necessarily the most important. Three components of collective association are particularly important: people, community and nation. The three are not mutually exclusive with regard to class or one another. They can be seen as partially overlapping and partially competing principles of identity and organisation.

All these concepts – people, community and nation – allow people to define themselves in terms that address a particular set of circumstances, without committing themselves to a potentially divisive identity. Class appears as a more contentious and, therefore, a more problematic basis for action. People, community and nation are inclusive concepts that have a unifying dynamic, creating a sense of being a majority of the population and occupying the moral high ground. Class identification, therefore, involves more of an uphill struggle than popular or communal and national identification.

Another critique of mainstream approaches to the question of class was provided by British historian Gareth Stedman Jones (1983). Stedman Jones questions the notions of experience, consciousness and interest. He directs our attention to the ways in which our political language (or **discourse**) serves to conceptualise and define our social interests. We must study the production of interests, identities, grievances and aspirations, as they are formulated within the terms of political discourse. This means that we cannot assume in advance that the particular language of class necessarily expresses people's experiences, even if we restrict ourselves to the spheres of work and production.

As a consequence, we must examine how class concepts become central (or not) to the way people represent themselves and their experiences at specific historical moments. In the words of historian Joan Scott, 'we should attend to the process by which one definition emerged as dominant, looking both for explicitly stated and implicitly structured political relationships' (1988: 88). Seen from

this perspective, class becomes a field that always contains multiple and contested meanings. The analysis of class should proceed by 'interrogating its meanings – not only its terminology and the content of its political programs, but the history of its symbolic organisation and linguistic representation' (Scott 1988: 90).

Putting *meaning* and *representation* at the centre leads Scott to question the notion of lived experience as a foundation for class consciousness. Experience, she argues, is constructed historically, and what passes as meaningful experiences for people and groups are themselves produced through the operation of culture and power. At times these experiences bring together people of different backgrounds on the basis of their shared class circumstances. At other times the same unifying aspect of experience also serves to exclude other aspects of human activity by not counting these aspects as being experiences with any significance for social organisation and politics. When class becomes an overriding identity, other components of identity – such as gender and race – are incorporated into it, and our focus on class results in diverting attention away from these. We also ignore other important spheres of life such as meaningful beliefs and traditions, for example. How some experiences become more prominent than others is hence a central question to bear in mind and which your further studies will hopefully explore.

10.7 The conceptual status of class

Where does the preceding discussion leave us? As Marx initially put it in his iconic general principle:

It is not consciousness of men that determines their being, but, on the contrary, their social being that determines their consciousness (Marx 1977 [1859] in Tucker 1978: 4).

Given the importance of the system of economic production for Marx and the 'predominant factor' of the class situation for Weber, class must be retained as a conceptual category when analysing society. Yet even taking the spheres of production and the market together, this does not *determine* the ways and forms that social consciousness, collective identity and political involvement can assume. There must be room for independent thought and opinion at the heart of individual and collective agency. Having said that, we must recognise that it is largely Weber's contribution which has compelled us to adopt this view. In short, no mono-causal explanation for the complexity of social reality is possible. While class is a powerful conceptual variable, it cannot account for the full array of human experience, whether individual or collective. Where Marx relied too heavily on class, Weber alerted us to a more complex and multidimensional analysis of social stratification and hence to a more nuanced analysis and understanding of society.

This is a debate in which we hope you will actively engage. Culture, identity and power are all forces that operate alongside class. These forces shape class perhaps as much as class shapes them. In other words, we need to look at the interrelationships between all these forces rather than derive their impact from the primary concept of class, as Marx tended to do.

10.7.1 Modifying class analysis

Recent attempts seeking to modify class analysis have built on Weber's initial insights to expand the field of investigation. There is more emphasis today on a broader range of concepts. Notions of lived experience, social meanings, political discourse and symbolic representation, for instance, help overcome the gap between class as objective (class 'in-itself') and class as subjective (class 'for-itself'). For Marx, it was just a matter of time and education before class forces (particularly the working class) would realise what their interests are and how to act on them. As you well know, Weber introduced status and party as additional concepts that make the transition from objective class existence to active class identity more complicated. Status and party may bring people of different classes together and may divide people of the same class. Hence, we need to consider their operation independently, without assuming that they necessarily align with class as a social force. Instead, they may subvert and undermine it, and vice versa.

Introducing discourse (the languages of class) and representation (how people present themselves as a group) into the class picture makes its different components even less clearly aligned. This means the position in the system of production may acquire different meanings for individuals, and then may serve as different bases for identity formation, and in turn become different bases for action. In other words, people who share similar social positions may juggle between different identities and modes of political action, and the straight line from objective class interests (class 'in-itself') to subjective political action (class 'for-itself') is not so clear and obvious any longer.

How all this works in practice must be the subject of a case-by-case study of concrete interactions over time. Recall the brief quote at the beginning of this chapter how Marx argued that the analysis of class should, in each case, be based on the 'empirically given circumstances' (Bottomore

1983: 77). In the South African context in particular, we need to examine how notions of class have interacted historically with notions of community, people and nation. In other words, how have class identity and organisation overlapped, but at times also contradicted the language and politics of community and popular and national mobilisation? This is not just a conceptual question. It also means looking at alliances between class-based unions and parties, community-based organisations and popular and nationalist movements. This is not a small intellectual and social scientific task. It is ongoing and one you are invited to join. This chapter has only been able to introduce the issue. Bearing all this in mind, our empirical focus must now, however, turn to our own society.

10.8 South African society and class analysis

Given the dominance of race in South African society – from colonial times, through segregation and apartheid and even into democracy – it is understandable that the concept of race was the starting point in understanding our racially divided society. Race as a central concept was, however, displaced by the concept of class in the social sciences in the 1970s. This sparked a major debate which became known as the 'race–class debate' (see Posel 1983). Yet we know from our discussion earlier, that any mono-causal explanation of race, class or any other single conceptual category is bound to have limitations. There are three important lessons to be learned from this, but which also can be more generally applied. The first is that understanding South African society in a scholarly manner leans on studies conducted in the past. The second is that it is instructive to see how conceptual and theoretical analyses develop and advance – and to note what they often overlook entirely. The third lesson is that there is still work to be done and that is where you come in.

The 'race–class debate' took place between thinkers following the liberal modernisation theory on the one hand and thinkers following in the Marxist tradition on the other. The former used race – or what Weber called *caste* – as their key concept. The latter used the concept of class. In hindsight, the debate turned out to be somewhat sterile as it resulted in the '"either-or" quality of this debate' (Posel 1983: 50). The issue turned on the importance and impact of race and racial policies in South Africa for the development of capitalism on the subcontinent of Africa. The Weberian-orientated scholars who focused on race, argued that racial policies were *dysfunctional* for the development of capitalism and progress in South African society. The Marxist-orientated scholars, also referred to as the revisionists, who focused on class, argued that racial policies were *functional to and necessary for* the development of capitalism based on mining.

10.8.1 Weberian class analysis of apartheid

Max Weber's important essay *Class, Status, Party* only became known to social scientists in South Africa in 1948 with the translation from German of Max Weber's work by Gerth and Mills ([1948] 1974). From the late 1940s through to the 1960s, Weber's ideas inspired a wave of pioneering studies on social stratification in South Africa (Seekings 2009). Yet these analyses, recently rediscovered by Jeremy Seekings, were overlooked as Marxism – and its conception of class – came to dominate the intellectual climate in South Africa in the 1970s. You can read about this in the final chapter of this textbook. Before this occurred, leaning on Weberian scholars in America, the central issue was the relationship between class and Weber's notion of *caste* – or race.

The first South African theorist to examine the class–caste relation was the Weberian-inspired thinker Leo Kuper. Like both Marx and Weber:

Kuper acknowledged that there was a proletariat in South Africa: black people did not own the means of production or had access to too little such productive property to subsist, and were, therefore, compelled to work for wages ….

But, Kuper argued, someone's class situation was less important *than their racial position in determining their life chances … White workers, despite their lack of property, benefited from and thus had an* interest *in maintaining the system of racial discrimination* (Seekings 2009: 870) (our emphasis).

Race prevented black workers from being free to sell their labour, acquire skills and education and:

… finally the lack of productive property is itself a consequence of race criteria which determine the distribution of available land in South Africa and rigorously control the right to acquire property (Kuper 1949: 152 cited in Seekings 2009: 870).

Citing Weber on both caste and class, Kuper argued that 'the proletarianisation of the Native is one of the forms in which race conflict is expressed' (1949: 153). What drew Kuper's attention, however, was not the working class or the capitalist class, but the small emerging African middle class.

The African middle class

In 1950 in South Africa the African middle class only constituted between 2 and 3 per cent of the total African population (Seekings 2009). It comprised mainly small traders, clerks in the mining industry and a very small handful of professionals. Status is key to understanding this class which 'was a class determined to differentiate itself from the African working class' (2009: 871) and, like the African-American middle class, was 'obsessed' with the 'struggle for status' (Frazier 1957: 236, cited in Seekings 2009: 871). A study by two later anthropologists, Monica Wilson and Archie Mafeje, confirmed the concern of the African middle class with social status:

They pride themselves on being respectably dressed and gentle and polite in their manner … English is used in many situations among themselves … Those with the highest status in Langa are those who have absorbed most of Western culture (Wilson & Mafeje 1963: 26 & 145, cited in Seekings 2009: 871).

Among the middle class who were engaged in small business in Langa outside Cape Town, not only was status a concern, it was also strongly suggested that 'class distinctions plainly exist in Langa' (Wilson & Mafeje 1963: 28, cited in Seekings 2009: 872). What is of particular interest, Seekings argues, is that despite the Weberian influence on Kuper, there is a 'lack of clarity about the relationship between (occupational) class and status (or prestige)' (Seekings 2009: 873). In the complex South African situation, it does seem, however, that while class distinction rested on a slender material basis of being primarily small business owners, it coincided with status. Significant, however, was Kuper's view that the racial policies of apartheid were responsible for pushing this class into radical and even revolutionary politics.

A later study on the African social 'elite' sought to distinguish class from status by drawing a line of division between this 'social elite' and an 'occupational elite' on the basis of social status (Brandel-Syrier 1971). This middle class was apparently contemptuous of 'African culture' and drew selectively on Western culture (Seekings 2009: 873). In grappling with how to apply Weberian concepts to a starkly racialised society and – as ever – comparing Marx and Weber, a further study by the sociologist Pierre van den Berghe concluded that:

[s]ocial classes in the Marxian sense of relationship to the means of production exist by definition, as they must in any capitalist country, but they are not

meaningful social realities. Clearly, pigmentation, rather than ownership of capital or labour, is the most significant criterion of status in South Africa (Van den Berghe 1965: 267 cited in Seekings 2009: 876).

You can see here in this Weberian-inspired study, how race and class were viewed as distinct and separate, much as they were in the liberal vs Marxian 'race–class debate'. As we have already concluded, this was not a satisfactory way of understanding South African society.

While Weberian analyses, which emphasised race in the South African context, were to disappear with the adoption of Marxism, Seekings concludes that one of the weaknesses of this approach was that the origins of the status order and the class structure was largely missing from these accounts. However, he also argues that:

The key strength of the Weberian approaches was that, notwithstanding a lack of clarity in key details, they suggested that status distinctions coexisted with differentiation by occupational class – a point that was frequently overlooked when class was reduced to its Marxist variant (Seekings 2009: 877).

As Seekings points out, Marxist analyses would shift from examining social life to studying the organisation of production – and that of the gold mining industry in particular.

10.8.2 Marxian class analysis of apartheid

The decisive shift from the Weberian emphasis on race to the Marxist focus on class can be traced to what became the most quoted academic article ever in the social sciences in South Africa. This article was entitled *Capitalism and Cheap Labour Power in South Africa: From Segregation to Apartheid* (Wolpe 1972). Its author, the sociologist and activist Harold Wolpe, wanted to explain why apartheid had been instituted. He argued that apartheid was not merely the intensification of the previous government policy of racial segregation. Wolpe controversially argued that the shift to apartheid was *not* centrally about the racial policies of the state, but occurred as a result of a changing relationship, at the wider level of political economy, between the 'capitalist and African pre-capitalist modes of production' (Wolpe 1972: 425). To successfully establish capitalist mining in South Africa, the collective labour power – the capacity to work – of the African mining proletariat had to be paid *below* its costs of social reproduction. The term reproduction refers to the costs of maintaining the working-class family. In order to establish itself, mining capital needed a supply of *cheap*

labour. The key and central point is this: when the migrant labourers have access to a means of subsistence outside the capitalist economy and they then enter wage relationships in the formal capitalist economy, they do not have to be paid the full cost of their reproduction. This is because they live, in part, off the pre-capitalist African agricultural economy between migrant labour contracts and especially when ill or old. Capital pays the worker *below* the cost of his/her reproduction. In other words, this saves the capitalist economy *part of the cost* of maintaining the working-class family.

Apartheid, in other words, was simply the specific political mechanism to maintain a cheap labour-power regime by rationalising the existing racially organised system of segregation and developing a complete system of domination and control. For Harold Wolpe, then, the shift from the political policy of racial segregation under British imperialism to the new local nationalist political policy of racial apartheid was *not* to be explained in terms of race and the rise of the National Party in 1948. This shift in policy was *not* a case of increased racial oppression due to a racist and totalitarian ideology. Apartheid did *not* differ in degree only from segregation by representing an intensification of racial domination. Apartheid was *not* simply an increase in white domination, *nor* was it merely the modernisation of segregation. Rather, apartheid was to be explained in terms of Marxist political economy and class analysis. In short, apartheid was necessary for the development of capitalism based on mining. This argument put Marxist class analysis firmly at the centre of sociological inquiry. The key methodological and conceptual point Wolpe made is that any political policy of the state – in this case the racial policies of apartheid – must *themselves* be explained in terms of a specific historical moment by accounting for its 'ideology, political practice and the mode of production' (Wolpe 1972: 427).

The issue is, for Wolpe, not about race per se. Rather, while the state is an instrument of racial domination, it is also 'an instrument of class rule in a specific form of capitalist society' (Wolpe 1972: 429). The state – whether colonial, segregationist or under apartheid – always served to develop capitalism, especially by acting through the law to facilitate its development. What apartheid made clear in South Africa was that the state does not just *appear* to intensify racial domination and segregation – continued from British rule – but that racist policy and ideology really are a means to reproduce capitalism.

By presenting this class-based analysis, Wolpe wanted to break through the mask of racial ideology which hides the capitalist nature of society. Racial ideology and practices, for Wolpe, mask the way in which capitalism as a mode of production, in his words, 'articulates' with the previously independent pre-capitalist African agricultural mode of production – as capitalism tends to do elsewhere. What this means is that there were not two separate and unrelated economies in South Africa – namely an African subsistence agricultural economy and a capitalist mining economy. Two economies implies independence and separation. For Wolpe, modes of production *articulate* with one another because capitalism 'enters into, lives off and transforms the rural African economy' (Wolpe 1972: 433).

The consequence of this – more obvious now even than when Wolpe wrote 40 years ago – is that capitalism not only transforms previous pre-industrial modes of production, but destroys them. Already having begun under the political policies and systems of colonialism and segregation, under apartheid the pre-capitalist mode of production was systematically destroyed through soil erosion, a decline of production and the impoverishment of the people resulting in starvation, malnutrition and a high death and debilitation rate. The majority of black South Africans ended up living *below* the level of subsistence in the predominantly rural reserves.

Not able to survive in the rural reserves led to increasing urbanisation and permanent proletarianisation. This went against the policy of apartheid. Industrialisation developed as the capitalist economy gradually expanded from the primary sector (maize and gold) to the secondary sector (manufacturing). The pure idea of apartheid as a system based on the complete division of society based on race, then had to accommodate a black urban working class, which resulted in the building of the townships with black people subject to a raft of racially discriminatory legislation, the Pass laws and the very limited right of residence in particular. This generated conflict not just over wages but all aspects of social life and brought the entire structure of a class-based capitalist, yet also racially divided society, into question.

Resistance and the emergence of a radical black, largely middle-class intelligentsia developed in the 1940s. The Mandela generation was responsible for the radicalisation of the African National Congress. Apartheid became economically untenable as there were simply not enough whites to provide the skills for the development of a capitalist economy. Spurred on by international pressure against South Africa's legalised racist policies, although not without enormous political struggle and individual sacrifice, the end of apartheid loomed and the prospect of democracy arose.

For Wolpe, apartheid was a response to the rural and urban challenge of the black working class and the changed conditions of migrant labour-power. He notes a range of aspects of apartheid and its difference to the previous policy of racial segregation and how apartheid perfected the mechanisms of control of the 'Non-white population' (Wolpe 1972: 446). In brief, apartheid removed the last political rights for black people through racial legislation. Anti-communist legislation was passed to prevent class from becoming a mobilising factor for black African nationalism. Black African and other 'non-white' geographical and job mobility was restricted. Powerful police, security and white civilian army reserves were established. Strikes by black workers were outlawed and trade unions of African workers – although never officially outlawed – were effectively repressed in order to keep wages down.

The central aspect of Wolpe's argument was that the African reserves, referred to as 'Bantustans' by the apartheid regime, which were the source of cheap labour power, began to break down under segregation. But under apartheid, state power over residence and movement of all black people was asserted by repressive means to continue to supply to capital a source of cheap black, still largely, migrant labour-power, 'but in a new form' (Wolpe 1972: 448).

Weberian class analysis, in terms of class–caste (or race) was entirely eclipsed by a slew of new 'revisionist' Marxist class analyses following Wolpe's hugely influential article. One of the problems with Wolpe's analysis, and which he himself recognised and corrected, was that he had ended up with a *reductionist* understanding of class as he had not taken the question of the national struggle and the *capacity of people* to fight against racial oppression into consideration. In such reductionist Marxist analyses (and Wolpe's was not the only one):

> ... 'the class for itself' is collapsed into 'the class in itself' – that is to say, no space is allowed for the contribution of non-economic conditions to the formation of class interests (Wolpe 1988: 15).

What Wolpe then did was to suggest that the relation between race and class had to be reconceptualised in order to develop a *non-reductionist* theory of class within Marxism. To do this, the specific conditions of the relationship between capitalism and white domination needed to receive attention. It would be mainly social historians who would move in this direction by conducting detailed empirical studies examining lived experience, consciousness, power and identity.

10.8.3 Non-reductionist perspectives on class

In order to break away from class viewed in purely economic and objective terms, an influential group of social historians took a step back from studying apartheid and began to study the formation of the African mining working class. The first major work was that of Charles van Onselen in his book *Chibaro* ([1976] 1980) – which means 'forced labour'. In his detailed historical study of African mine labour in Southern Rhodesia (now Zimbabwe) Van Onselen identified patterns of resistance among black miners. He argues that desertion from the mines and harsh conditions in the compounds are an index of worker consciousness.

Desertion as a rational and conscious attempt to avoid exploitation is perhaps most clearly evident in the response of workers to the death and disease that was rampant in the compounds (Van Onselen [1976] 1980: 239).

Following the perspective of other European social historians, such as EP Thompson, abstract concepts such as race and class then became embedded in the details of workers' experience of work and life on the mines.

What developed was a wide range of 'local histories', 'popular history' or writing 'history from below' that often made use of oral history – taking the actual accounts of ordinary black workers and people seriously. Given the importance of class rooted in capitalism, labour history became a focus (see Webster 1978). Township life, patterns of protest, culture and worker experience and action became the focus in the book entitled *Labour, Townships and Protest* (Bozzoli 1979). A wide array of social issues and history was treated in two volumes of *Working Papers in Southern African Studies* (see Bonner 1979; 1981). This scholarly work has continued apace. In brief, the major conceptual themes of class, race and gender have been closely investigated by examining how they interrelate to one another in specific social and historical contexts. Culture, lived experience and the self-understanding and consciousness of ordinary people are central to the formation of identity and to understanding the exercise and use of power in society.

The class structure of South African society has consequently proved to be considerably more complex than scholars anticipated. Understanding class under democracy would be no less difficult.

10.8.4 *Class in Soweto*

Class in Soweto is a major exercise in sociological research. It is an empirical study of class. The three guiding theoretical issues which inform it will be familiar to you:

- the strength of Marx's concept of class is the level of its abstraction (it can be widely applied)
- class is principally about production, but also about aspects of reproduction (although the gaps between classes are wider than in Marx's day)
- subjectivity is important.

With regards to subjectivity, the authors are concerned with three further matters. The first is a focus on agency, for agency is responsible for social change. Secondly, while the distinction between class 'in-itself' is recognised as something objective and class 'for-itself' is recognised as capturing the notion of subjectivity, the authors acknowledge the key point about class made in this chapter – that class includes other dimensions, but which they do not explore. They write:

In this formulation [of class in and for itself], subjectivity could include subjectivities according to race, gender and so on, but we focused narrowly on class subjectivities (Alexander et al 2013: 5–6).

Thirdly, they provide a rationale for their choice by suggesting that holding onto Marx's distinction between objective (class 'in-itself') and subjective (class 'for-itself') aspects of class:

discourages slippage into assumptions that capitalism inevitably leads to socialism, and instead opens up possibilities for researching the relationship between the two dimensions (Alexander et al 2013: 6).

The study then is based on an orthodox Marxist conception of class. Unlike previous Marxist studies, however, the book reviews the previously overlooked Weberian studies of class stratification noted in this chapter.

This important study, which is well worth hunting down, is an impressive examination of the analysis of class. In order to expand on the concept of class as rooted in production, the notion of *employment category* is formulated and represents the objective aspect of class.

No less than nine employment categories emerge from the empirical findings. While these employment categories are not classes, the authors argue that 'One can see them as defined in relationships to production, whether direct or indirect, and of relationships between the different categories' (Alexander et al 2013: 7). Class as a relation is hence strongly maintained, both empirically and conceptually. Noted in Table 11.1 are nine employment categories, the relation of each category to production, the number of respondents who participated in the quantitative survey and the estimated percentage of Sowetans in each category. The table provides a useful objective picture of class.

A key conclusion drawn from this data is that Soweto is a proletarian township. 'Soweto's proletariat is a differentiated unity' where proletarian is defined to mean:

that group of people who have access to only one main means of production – their own ability to work – and whose opportunities for exploiting this ability are, therefore, circumscribed by the availability of employment (Ceruti 2013: 97).

Yet what this data shows about the class structure of this proletarian township is rather startling given that: '… 69 per cent of adult Sowetans [are] either not in the labour force, unemployed or engaged in survivalist strategies' (Alexander et al 2013: 3). Given this broadly based tenuous relation to productive resources – including the ability to sell one's labour – what Sowetans very broadly share is:

a dependence on availing themselves for exploitation. When opportunities to do so are absent, their dependence is often manifested in deprivation (Ceruti 2013: 119).

Table 10.1 The structure of employment and unemployment in Soweto (all Sowetans aged 16 and over)

Employment categories	Relation to production	No of respondents (unweighted count)	Estimated percentage of Sowetans (weighted)
Capitalists	The owners of productive resources	3	0
Managers	Those who exercise some control and surveillance over workers	24	1
Regularly employed workers	Non-owning waged workers – including public service workers	582	24
Partial workers	Day labourers and short-term workers	251	11
Unemployed (our definition)	Marx's 'reserve army of labour'	535	24
Survivalist self-employed	Independent people, but who would prefer to be employed	225	10
Petty bourgeoisie	Self-employed and small business owners	129	6
Students	Neither employed nor available for employment	261	12
Pensioners and disabled	Those permanently outside the labour force	309	12
Total		2 319	100

(Source: Adapted from: *Class in Soweto* survey 2006 (Alexander et al 2013: 107)

Yet despite this sobering finding, in the 2006 *Class in Soweto survey* (Alexander et al 2013) on the aspect of subjectivity in the study and how people identify themselves, 90 per cent of Sowetans could classify themselves in class terms. Almost four tenths (38 per cent) used a single class label (working class, middle class, etc) with the strong finding that 'Most Sowetans had *multiple* class identities' (Alexander 2013: 3). A surprising 66 per cent of Sowetans described themselves

as middle class. As Mosa Phadi and Owen Manda note in the study, citing the 1977 work of the anthropologist Philip Mayer: 'Africans tended to use the term "middle class", not in the Western sense to refer to professional people or business people; but to refer to "medium people" or people in the middle – *"abantu abaphakathi"*. These people were "neither well off nor very poor or dissolute" (Mayer 1977: 67)' (Phadi & Manda 2013: 203). Students often described themselves in this way as middle class due to being supported by their families and hence felt they had been given opportunities (Phadi & Ceruti 2013: 157).

Another surprising finding is that while 41 per cent of Sowetans described themselves as working class (as one of the series of options of class labels respondents were given), only 3 per cent of Sowetans chose the *single* label of working class as their preferred class identity.

There is a wealth of such data and material in *Class in Soweto*. What very strongly emerges from this study, however, is that the objective conditions of class do not translate into the subjective definition of class. Hence the more difficult task of exploring the interrelationships between class, identity, power and culture – argued for in this chapter – powerfully asserts itself empirically.

A further point about this study can be made in the light of this chapter. In *Class in Soweto*, social class distinctions rested on the notion of *affordability* (Alexander et al 2013: 3) and the ability to consume and maintain a certain lifestyle. Affordability is clearly closely related to work and production.

Yet access to goods and whether they can be afforded or not and how affordability is regarded in Soweto surely impacts on social status? But perhaps this is a question for further empirical research on the complex nature of class and its relation to the range of concepts that have been used to illuminate it and the nature of South African society more generally.

What this chapter has done is to come back to its conceptual starting point where class was defined solely in relation to the economy. When applied empirically in a context that differs considerably from when Marx, Weber or most of the theorists wrote, the identification of 'employment categories' was formulated to illustrate how the abstract concept of class can be usefully applied to explain something about our contemporary society – the essentially class-based character of the sprawling and historically important place called Soweto. What must be clear is that this is but a starting point to understand ourselves, our own neighbourhood and the society in which we live. Many illuminating discoveries await the exercise of our sociological imagination.

Summary

- Class is an abstract concept, the strength of which makes it widely applicable. However, the difficulty is that it does not include non-economic factors, nor does it point to any actual economic conditions a class of people share.
- When using class to analyse and understand society, it is closely related to a range of other concepts in theories of class – particularly in the case of both Marx and Weber.
- Class can be used as a way to understand society as a whole. This would be an example of 'class analysis'. It can also be used to understand the nature of social groups themselves. This would be an example of 'the analysis of class'.
- Marx saw class as having both objective and subjective factors. This was illustrated in his distinction between a class 'in-itself' and a class 'for-itself'. For Marx the subjective aspect of class is directly related to the objective aspect, while for Weber there is no direct relation between the 'class situation', status groups and social action.
- For Weber, the additional concepts of status and party are required to elaborate what he referred to as the 'class situation'. The reason for this is that Weber did not think class, on its own, adequately captured the broad range of ways people saw and understood themselves and others.

- A range of post-classical theorists discussed in this chapter integrated aspects of the work of the classical theorists.
- When the concept of class is closely interrogated, a further range of concepts such as power, culture and identity come to the fore. The interrelationship between class and these concepts needs to be explored.
- In using class as a conceptual perspective to analyse society, this chapter argued that it is Weber's more complex multidimensional view that needs to be taken seriously.
- When using the concept of class, class must always be analysed in the empirical and historical contexts in which it occurs. Both Marx and Weber make this clear and we must not lose sight of this.
- The major empirical study of class referred to in this chapter, *Class in Soweto*, illustrated how the concept of class needs to be examined anew. It also shows that it is complex as it has both objective and subjective aspects. Questions about the salience of class therefore remain on the agenda of the social sciences.

ARE YOU ON TRACK?

1. Carefully define both Marx's and Weber's concept of class, as well as the two other important concepts Weber uses in his model of social stratification.
2. Explain Marx's distinction between class 'in-itself' and class 'for-itself'.
3. Why, according to Weber, are common economic interests in the 'class situation' not directly related to class identity and social action?
4. Explain the difference between 'class analysis' and 'the analysis of class'.
5. Explain how *one* post-classical theorist (Wright, Burawoy or Thompson) go beyond Marx in his conception of class.
6. Define class formation and explain how the South African black mining working class was formed. (Hint: start with

Karl Marx's account in the *Communist Manifesto* on the formation of the working class and go through the textbook for empirical and historical detail illustrating how this has occurred in South Africa.)

7. What is your class and status position in your community?
8. How would you go about identifying your own class and status position?
9. Do class and status overlap in your case? If so, describe and explain how they do to someone who is not familiar with your neighbourhood.
10. How did grappling with these questions – as an exercise in the sociological imagination – reveal something new about your society? Give reasons for your answer.

More sources to consult

Bendix R (ed). 1966. *Class, Status and Power.* 2nd ed. London: Routledge & Kegan Paul.

Bozzoli B. 1991. *Woman of Phokeng: Consciousness, Life Strategy and Migrancy in South Africa, 1900–1983* (with the assistance of Mmantho Nkotsoe). Johannesburg: Ravan Press.

Crompton R, Devine F, Savage M, Scott J (eds). *Renewing Class Analysis.* Oxford: Blackwell Publishers/The Sociological Review.

Giddens A, Held D (eds). 1982. *Classes, Power and Conflict: Classical and Contemporary Debates.* London: Macmillan.

Grusky DB (ed). 1994. *Social Stratification: Class, Race and Gender in Sociological Perspective.* Oxford: Westview Press.

Vidich AJ (ed). 1995. *The New Middle Class: Life-Styles, Status Claims and Political Orientations.* London: Macmillan.

Wolpe H. 1988. *Race, Class and the Apartheid State.* London: James Currey.

References

Alexander P, Ceruti C, Motseke K, Phadi M, Wale K. 2013. *Class in Soweto.* Scottsville: University of KwaZulu-Natal Press.

Alexander P. 2013. 'Affordability and action: Introduction and overview' in *Class in Soweto.* Alexander P, Ceruti C, Motseke K, Phadi M, Wale K (eds). Scottsville: University of KwaZulu-Natal Press.

Bonner PL (ed). 1979. *Working Papers in Southern African Studies.* African Studies Institute, Johannesburg: University of the Witwatersrand.

Bonner PL (ed). 1981. *Working Papers in Southern African Studies* Vol 2. Johannesburg: Ravan Press.

Bottomore T. 1983. *A Dictionary of Marxist Thought.* Oxford: Basil Blackwell.

Bozzoli B (ed). 1979. *Labour, Townships and Protest.* Johannesburg: Ravan Press.

Brandel-Syrier M. 1971. *Reeftown Elite: A Study of Social Mobility in a Modern African Community on the Reef.* London: Routledge & Kegan Paul.

Burawoy M. 1979. *Manufacturing Consent.* Chicago: University of Chicago Press.

Burawoy M. 1985. *The Politics of Production: Factory Regimes Under Capitalism and Socialism.* London: Verso.

Calhoun C. 1982. *The Question of the Class Struggle: Social Foundations of Popular Radicalism During the Industrial Revolution.* Chicago: University of Chicago Press.

Ceruti C. 2013. 'A proletarian township: Work, home and class' in *Class in Soweto.* Alexander P, Ceruti C, Motseke K, Phadi M, Wale K (eds). Scottsville: University of KwaZulu-Natal Press.

Dahrendorf R. 1959. *Class and Class Conflict in Industrial Society.* London: Routledge & Kegan Paul.

Frazier F. 1957. *The Black Bourgeoisie: The Rise of a New Middle Class.* New York: The Free Press.

Gerth HH, Mills CW (trans and eds). 1974 [1948]. *From Max Weber: Essays in Sociology.* Boston: Routledge & Kegan Paul.

Giddens A. 1971. *Capitalism and Modern Social Theory: An Analysis of the Writings of Marx, Durkheim and Max Weber.* Cambridge: Cambridge University Press.

Kuper L. 1949. 'The South African Native: Caste, proletariat or race?' *Social Forces*, 28(2).

Marx K. 1978 [1847]. *The Poverty of Philosophy.* Peking: Foreign Language Press.

Marx K. 1977 [1857]. *Grundrisse: Foundations of the Critique of Political Economy (Rough Draft).* (Trans and Foreword by Nicolaus M.) Harmondsworth: Penguin Books (in association with *New Left Review*).

Marx K. 1977 [1859]. *A Contribution to the Critique of Political Economy.* Moscow: Progress.

Marx K. 1977 [1894]. *Capital: A Critique of Political Economy (Vol III).* London: Lawrence & Wishart.

Ndlovu Z. 2014. 'Some of my very best friends are white …'. *Mail&Guardian*, 30 September. [Online] Available at: http://mg.co.za/article/2014-09-30-some-of-my-very-best-friends-are-white [Accessed 13 November 2014].

Nicolaus M. 1977. 'Foreword'. Marx K. *Grundrisse: Foundations of the Critique of Political Economy (Rough Draft).* (Trans and foreword by Nicolaus M.) Harmondsworth: Penguin Books (in association with *New Left Review*).

Nyquist T. 1983. *African Middle Class Elite.* Grahamstown: Rhodes University Institute for Social and Economic Research.

Phadi M, Ceruti C. 2013. 'Models, labels and affordability' in *Class in Soweto.* Alexander P, Ceruti C, Motseke K, Phadi M, Wale K (eds). Scottsville: University of KwaZulu-Natal Press.

Phadi M, Manda O. 2013. 'The language of class: Confusion, complexity and difficult words' in *Class in Soweto.* Alexander P, Ceruti C, Motseke K, Phadi M, Wale K (eds). Scottsville: University of KwaZulu-Natal Press.

Posel D. 1983. 'Rethinking the "race–class debate" in South African historiography'. *Social Dynamics*, 9(1): 50–66.

Poulantzas N. 1982. 'On social classes' in *Classes, Power and Conflict: Classical and Contemporary Debates.* Giddens A, Held D (eds). London: Macmillan.

Scott JW. 1988. *Gender and the Politics of History.* New York: Columbia University Press.

Seekings J. 2009. 'The rise and fall of the Weberian analysis of class in South Africa between 1949 and the early 1970s'. *Journal of Southern African Studies*, 35(4): December.

Stedman Jones G. 1983. *Languages of Class: Studies in English Working Class History, 1832–1982.* Cambridge: Cambridge University Press.

Thompson EP. 1963. *The Making of the English Working Class.* Harmondsworth: Penguin.

Tucker RC. 1978. *The Marx–Engels Reader.* 2nd ed. New York: WW Norton & Co.

Van den Berghe P. 1964. *Caneville: The Social Structure of a South African Town.* Middletown, CT: Wesleyan University Press.

Van Onselen C. 1980 [1976]. *Chibaro: African Mine Labour in Southern Rhodesia: 1900–1933.* Johannesburg: Ravan Press.

Webster E (ed). 1978. *Essays in Southern African Labour History.* Johannesburg: Ravan Press.

Williams R. 1976. *Keywords: A Vocabulary of Culture and Society.* New York: Oxford.

Wilson M, Mafeje A. 1963. *Langa: A Study of Social Groups in an African Township.* Cape Town: Oxford University Press.

Wolpe H. 1972. 'Capitalism and cheap labour power in South Africa: From segregation to apartheid'. *Economy and Society*, 1(4): 425–456.

Wolpe H. 1986. 'Class concepts, class struggle and racism' in *Theories of Race and Ethnic Relations.* Rex J, Mason D (eds). Cambridge: Cambridge University Press.

Wolpe H. 1988. *Race, Class and the Apartheid State.* London: James Currey.

Wright EO. 1978. *Class, Crisis and the State.* London: Verso.

Wright EO. 1985. *Classes.* London: Verso.

Wright EO. 1997. *Class Counts: Comparative Studies in Class Analysis.* Cambridge: Cambridge University Press.

Wright EO. 2002. 'The shadow of exploitation in Weber's analysis of class'. *American Sociological Review*, 67: 832–853, December.

Wright EO. 2005. *Approaches to Class Analysis.* Cambridge: Cambridge University Press.

Part

3

The Institutions
in Society

Families and households

Marlize Rabe

The family is the oldest and most enduring of all social institutions. It has consequently assumed a multiplicity of forms and instituted the bedrock of society long before it was even thought of as an institution. Yet the concepts family and household are both difficult to define and you will be challenged with various expressions of these concepts in this chapter. The family is the primary source of that most powerful process, socialisation. Identity formation cannot therefore be understood without surveying the family's impact. For the majority of people, whether it is the family or the household, this primordial institution is the original source of the experience of social cohesion. It is hence no wonder that the family and households are often regarded as at the core of both society and the study of it. In brief, the family is often believed to be central to the health of social life. What this chapter will alarmingly show, however, is that a significant number of South Africans have not enjoyed the benefits of family life in a stable household. Despite the longevity of the family as an institution, families are often at risk and alarmists regularly warn us that it is under threat.

Owing to the fact, already noted in this textbook, that sociologists are part of the society they study, the family as a concept is not readily subject to analysis because, for the most part, we are so intimately related to it. The emotional bonds to the family and the household in which we grew up remain with us throughout our lives regardless of whether the lived experience of socialisation was positive or negative. Being adaptable, despite enormous external pressures exerting themselves upon it, the family remains a reference point for most people. Do read the opening case study in this chapter carefully since it exemplifies the profound impact the passing of a beloved family member has on the individual.

This chapter will challenge you to grasp the social implications of the fact that so many children have not had the nurture, comfort and benefits of the critical process of socialisation the family can offer. The realities of dysfunctional families should be acknowledged and dealt with without trying to romanticise family life or clinging to only certain positive notions of it. In fact, idealised views of family can easily inspire narrow ideological notions of what families should be, and it will be shown how such narrow views can even undermine dealing with the realities families have to face.

This chapter invites you to examine the individuals within the life course of families by focusing on childhood, parenting and being a grandparent. The various stages within an individual's life which may include living with or away from a partner are also briefly introduced to provide you with insight into the dynamic nature of family life.

As ever in sociology, the view of the family expressed here can be critically examined from a range of theoretical perspectives – the bases with which you are already familiar. Whatever theoretical perspective(s) you are developing or favouring as you progress in your sociological studies, they have to be critically analysed here in relation to families and households. Likewise the usefulness of concepts such as social class and race in framing the current state of families and households in our society should be critically evaluated.

Families and households are experiencing stresses and strains as they have for centuries. Our society is no different. It is, however, an explicit aim of this chapter to alert students and scholars of society that understanding the causes and reasons for abuse and violence within the family is an important starting point in preventing their occurrence. In this case, as often in sociology well practised, an objective assessment of the facts evokes a moral response. When it comes to the factual study of families and households, social science and moral conscience, it seems clear, are intricately intertwined.

Case study 11.1 A grandmother

Read the case study below and answer the question that follows.

By mid-morning medical staff confirm that Grandma is no more. She was 97 … She remains to this day, the most resilient, the most constant, most consistent and most reliable presence in my life. With no real memory of my own mother, Grandma was the only tangible evidence that I did really have a mother once upon a very short time. But Grandma was more. Grandma was mother. Upon the death of my mother, she took over the motherhood function so seamlessly, it took me a long time to realise she was not my mother … Grandma was an ordinary, rural, illiterate South African woman. I have no hope that a monument will ever be erected in her honour. She will never receive a National Order. She was not perfect either. She sniffed copious amounts of snuff and took traditional beer as well as the odd non-traditional beer from time to time. Playing with matchsticks one day in my toddler years, I burnt an entire winter's harvest of rondavel roof thatch that she had harvested and collected by hand over many months. She was livid. On that occasion, she said things to and about me that are simply unprintable. Yet it all ended with her lovingly embracing me even as she watched the blazing fire consuming months of her hard work in an instant. We were both crying … The old woman who brought me up with her bare hands and a heart pulsating with love was my greatest teacher. I have encountered few people as forgiving. Again and again, at various stages of my life, she has snatched me from the jaws of hell. For me she was and will always be a great South African woman.

(Source: Maluleke 2011)

QUESTION

List differences and similarities between this story and the family in which you were raised.

Key themes

- Complexities in defining households and families
- Overview of families in South Africa
- How different theories of the family provide different outlooks on families

- The importance of families for individuals from birth to death (intergenerational relationships)
- Patterns of joining and dissolving unions (marriage, cohabitation and divorce)
- Family violence in South Africa.

11.1   Introduction

The overwhelming majority of people grow up in families. In fact many people live with or close to their family members their entire lives. Based on this familiarity with families, introducing the 'sociology of families' seems unnecessary. We all know what family life is about and the fact that there are different types of families also comes as no surprise. Why then a chapter on families? Although some people believe that it is a waste of time to study something as mundane and well known as families, it is often more difficult to look at such a familiar phenomenon in a systematic manner. Either broad generalisations about families (based on no systematic information) or very specific knowledge about a few families are used in everyday conversations to make assumptions about families. Similarly, the mass media present information on families in a haphazard fashion

which may result in distorted knowledge about families. You can look at the gross overestimation of divorce rates as a case in point (see the discussion on divorce in section 11.2).

If we were to collect the different personal responses to Case study 11.1 above, we would find a myriad of experiences being described. In this chapter on families, you are firstly invited to look at this diversity of families but also to move beyond only general observations of families and understand the reasons for this diversity. Specific theories will be explained to help you identify underlying assumptions, entrenched values and links between broad socioeconomic dynamics and families. Intergenerational relations in families will be addressed by highlighting childhood, parenthood and grandparenthood. Attention will then be paid to the different ways in which people constitute relationships such as marriages and cohabitation followed by pertinent notes on divorce (one of the most prominent ways in which marriages end). Finally, information on the different types of domestic violence will be provided. The different theories of domestic violence will be considered and the current views and practices which deal with domestic violence in South Africa looked at.

11.2 To be or not to be … a family

It is difficult to define families in general. In order to avoid the 'fuzziness' of a term such as family, certain researchers prefer to use the term **household**. A household is commonly defined as a group of people living in a dwelling. It usually includes the sharing of meals and other resources. Household members pool their resources, which implies that certain decisions have to be made about how the income of the household will be used to provide for the needs of each of its members. Economists and statistical surveys focusing on households often explore the income and expenditure patterns of households in great detail. It is important to note that household members may be family members, but they may also not be related to one another in any way. Households can therefore be subdivided in two main forms, namely **family households**, for example a husband, wife, dependent children and a grandparent living together, and **non-family households**, for example university students sharing a residence. Of course households do not always fall neatly into these two types as a family household may also have a household member that is not related to them. Also, in the case of students sharing a house, two of them may be brothers. One other type of household is a **single-person household**, which refers to a person living alone.

A further complication with the definition of households is that family members not sharing the household may contribute to the income or the expenditure of the household. For example, parents with dependent children may not live with their children, but they may still support them financially by sending them money on a regular basis. Such a pattern of financial resources flowing between households is particularly important in the South African context due to our long history of widespread migrancy. Breadwinners of households often do not live with their families. Consider live-in domestic workers or mineworkers living in hostels on mine premises. During the apartheid years in South Africa this pattern of migrancy was particularly common since black people were legally prohibited from living with their families in so-called white areas. In this regard, Spiegel, Watson and Wilkinson (1996) coined the term **stretched households**, which refers to the joint financial commitment to a particular household even though the individual family

members are not able to eat together and sleep in the same dwelling on a regular basis. In such stretched households the financial aspect becomes the ultimate criterion for defining the household. Although all such legal prohibitions on where South African citizens may live have been abolished, there are still practical and preferential reasons that divide families geographically. Examples of family members living in more than one household could be a husband and wife who cannot find employment in the same city, a couple who prefer to live separately from one another or parents placing their children with family members who live near a good school.

Now that we have some perspective on the definition and complexity of households, what then is a family? More importantly, do we really have to define families? Certain family researchers prefer not to define families and only work with the definitions provided by research participants themselves. Although this is a workable strategy for some research projects, a common understanding of families is still sought by some such as policy-makers, financial institutions and maintenance courts. In each of the latter cases, benefits have to be extended to specific family members and clear definitions are needed to inform decisions on who should benefit and who not. Furthermore, dependent family members such as young children, the frail elderly and mentally handicapped individuals need specific care. Responsibility for them is assigned to family members even though the responsibility may be (or should be) shared by the state. If a competent family member who is willing to share in the care of such dependent individuals cannot be found, it usually becomes the responsibility of the state. Important aspects can be deduced from this – family members have enduring intimate relationships that include certain *responsibilities* (such as care) and *rights* (such as financial entitlement) towards one another.

At the core of all definitions of the family is the parent–child bond and/or the bond between those adult members of the family who can be described as a couple and usually have sexual relations with one another (often believed to be of an exclusive nature). Usually it is only in cases where these primary bonds are non-existent (due to death or abandonment) that relationships with other kin become important. Much clearer definitions of families have been formulated by distinguishing between the different forms of family, which will briefly be defined in the next section.

A **nuclear family** refers to two adult members living with their dependent biological or adopted children in one household. Originally this term referred exclusively to heterosexual couples, but homosexual couples with adopted children also fit this description. Another major family form is the **extended family** where at least three generations of a family live together in one household (multiple 'vertical' levels) or in polygamous marriages where more than two marriage partners share a household (multiple 'horizontal' levels). You may notice that there is an overlap between households and families in these two definitions (as is the case with the other definitions of families) and other terms were developed to describe the relationships between households with strong family ties such as the **modified extended family**. In this latter type of family the family members live in different households, but they exchange services and goods on a regular basis. An example is where grandparents who are living near their adult children might assist them by babysitting their grandchildren and in return they might get help from their adult children with general repairs to the house.

Figure 11.1 Extended family
(Source: Photograph courtesy of the extended Pheiffer family)

There are many variations of the modified extended family in South African society, including **assisted families**. These include live-in domestic workers, nurses or nannies responsible for childcare or frail care. Clearly only more wealthy families will be able to include such help while poorer families may make use of **survival kinship networks**. In these networks the parents send their dependent children to other family members, for example to relatives on farms for better food or to relatives in town for schooling. Another family form termed **surrogate families** refers to unrelated individuals providing support for one another, such as runaways forming gangs.

A **single-parent family** refers to a single parent who lives with dependent children in a household. Although the single parent may be either male or female, women are the heads of such families in most cases. Single-parent families may also have different resources nearby, such as a divorced woman whose ex-husband helps in taking care of the children and makes a substantial financial contribution to the upkeep of the children, or parents who live nearby and help practically and financially to raise the children (see the concept of the stretched household mentioned earlier). However, a single-parent family may also imply that a mother (or father) has no other help and raises the children alone. Another related term that is increasingly common in the South African context is a **child-headed household**. In these households the parents have either passed away (often due to AIDS-related illnesses) or are unable to look after their children. As there are no other adults that can assume full-time responsibility for the household, older siblings will then take control of the household with varying support from other kin or community members.

The last major family type that we will define here is a **reconstituted** or **joint family**. Such a family is formed when divorced, widowed or never married parents marry or cohabitate. The newly formed couple may also have children together and this gives rise to a situation where there are 'my children, your children and our children'. Complicated extended family patterns may also be involved here with various sets of grandparents, uncles, aunts and cousins who may all have different ideas on things such as how much to spend on gifts for children and how children should be raised (children born from polygamous marriages – discussed under section 11.6.1 – may also experience such complicated family relations).

It is possible that over the lifespan of an individual various types of families are lived in: You may be born within a nuclear family, your parents then get a divorce and you live in a single-parent family. After a while you move with your mother to live with your grandparents,

which means living in an extended family. Your mother then remarries a widower with children and you live in a reconstituted family. As you become a young adult you move out of the house to live on your own in a single-person household. Although some people may live in extended or nuclear families their entire lives, changes in the types of families we live in over a life cycle is very likely for the majority of people living in present-day society.

11.3 An overview of family life

The variety of family forms is almost overwhelming yet certain family patterns are more common than others. In this section we will focus on such common patterns by taking a bird's eye view of the South African scenario and looking at certain historical trends that gave rise to the current family patterns as can be observed in Table 11.1.

Table 11.1 Percentage distribution of children aged 0–4 years by year and living arrangements with biological parents, 2002–2012

	2002	2003	2004	2005	2006	2007	2008	2009	2010	2011	2012
Unspecified	0.1	0.0	0.0	0.2	0.3	0.2	0.2	0.6	0.6	0.6	0.4
Lives with neither parent	16.9	18.7	17.6	17.1	20.8	19.4	19.9	22.3	18.8	18.4	18.7
Lives with biological mother only	41.8	41.3	43.0	43.6	40.4	42.7	41.6	39.9	43.2	44.3	42.5
Lives with biological father only	1.7	1.4	1.5	1.8	1.5	1.6	1.3	2.7	2.1	2.2	2.0
Lives with both biological parents	39.5	38.6	37.9	37.4	37.0	36.2	37.2	34.5	35.4	34.4	36.4

In Table 11.1 (StatsSA 2013a: 26) an overview of family households of young children in South Africa over an 11-year period is provided. It can be seen that less than 40 per cent of South African children younger than four years live with both their biological parents. Further, when adding the percentage of young children who live only with their biological mothers and those who live with neither biological parent, it transpires that over 60 per cent of young children do not live with their biological fathers. These same trends continue for older children. If this phenomenon is analysed according to racial category, it is found that 69.3 per cent of black African, 45.1 per cent of coloured, 15.5 per cent of Indian/Asian and 21.5 per

cent of white children under the age of 18 years do not live with their biological fathers (StatsSA 2013b: 9). These percentages require explanation. Why do you think so few children in South Africa live with their biological fathers? Before discussing these results in more detail, we should also consider another interesting aspect of South African household arrangements, namely the living together patterns of adults.

In Figure 11.2 (in StatsSA 2013b: 7 compiled from the 2011 census) it is shown that people who are married or 'live with a partner' are likely to share a household.

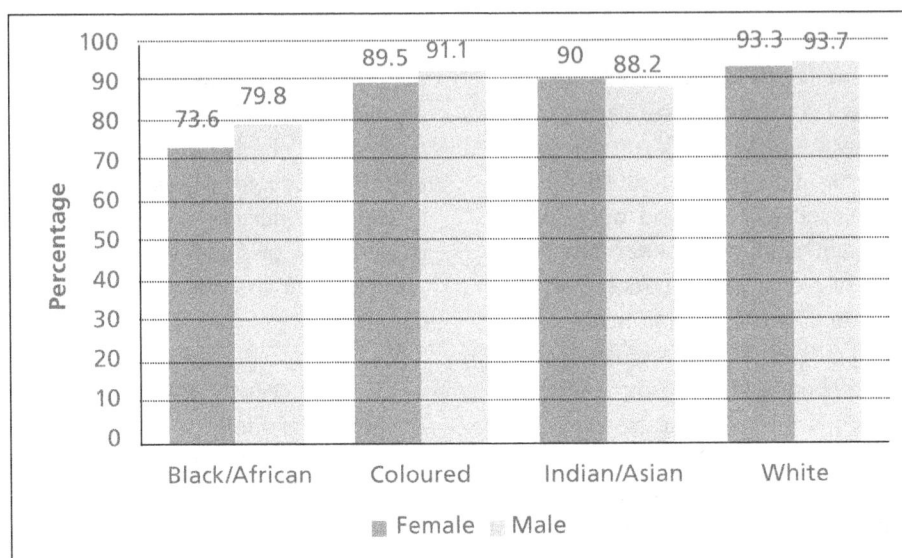

Figure 11.2 Percentage of people married or living as husband and wife whose partner is a member of the same household, by sex and population group, 2011

This would imply that children living with their biological mothers, have a good chance to live with stepfathers or 'social fathers'. In order to make sense of these statistics, let us consider the histories of South African families in a little more detail.

11.3.1 Selected historical trends amongst families

We will cast light on the above family trends if we employ a historical lens to show how different patterns emerged and replaced others over time, even though all of these patterns are still discernible today.

Coltrane and Collins (2001: 66–69) describe five general types of societies (dominating in certain historical periods and in different geographical locations) and the families commonly found within each of them.

The first type is *hunting-and-gathering societies* which are characterised by small groups of people moving around in search of food and water. Such nomadic groups are particularly associated with the Stone Age even though they are still found today in certain parts of the world, including Africa. In southern Africa the San, or Bushmen, exemplified this hunting-and-gathering lifestyle until relatively recently. In such societies families are often simple units consisting of parents and their offspring. It is suggested that since ownership of property is not common in these societies, women are also not regarded as being 'owned' in the way they may be viewed in strict patriarchal societies.

The second type is *'primitive' horticultural societies* where agricultural activities emerge and a division of labour between men and women is observed. For example, men may clear land for planting crops while the women may take responsibility for the planting and harvesting of certain crops. Marriages in such societies nestle within large kinship networks that determine complex marriage rules. Matrilineal or patrilineal descent (meaning heritage through the maternal or paternal line respectively) as well as matrifocal or patrifocal residence (living with the mother's or the father's family respectively) help to regulate the society. Herding or fishing societies may still be structured along these lines today.

In the third type of society, *advanced horticultural societies,* larger populations (from 10 000 to 1 million people) live together and stratification becomes prominent. Stratification is linked to the owning of land and other resources (such as cattle) and the social positioning of families. Such societies are characterised by complex family structures. An example of such a society is the Incas empire in Peru prior to its contact with the Spanish people.

In the fourth type, *agrarian societies,* the state may emerge. The establishment of the state is made possible by the diversification of tasks in a society. Such diversification is dependent on the cultivation of a surplus of food. This implies that farmers have to be able to produce enough food for a large number of people who are freed from farming activities and therefore able to focus on different tasks. In agrarian societies the production of such a surplus of food was made possible by ploughing techniques that used *animal power* as opposed to the exclusive use of human labour. If a central state developed in such agrarian societies, the importance of the complex kin structures eroded. Specific families, for example the military aristocracy, became important and such powerful families employed various other categories of people that were not related to them, such as servants and/or slaves, in their households. The class structure thus replaced the kin structure as the most prominent stratification system. An historic civilisation, such as the Roman Empire, is an example of such a society.

Lastly, *industrial society* emerges where *non-animal sources of power* are used with the invention of technology relying on steam power and electricity. In industrial societies the bulk of production moved from taking place within the family system to factories. In industrial societies, the family system is characterised by simplified structures where monogamy and nuclear families are commonly found.

The above simplified account of societies and family structures helps to illuminate the historical dynamics of families in southern Africa since different societal and family patterns could be found at the same time in one place. When Europeans arrived in the Cape in the middle of the 17th century, they brought with them notions of the importance of the state and owning property. To them, class structure was largely determined by a person's family of origin. At the same time the San (Bushmen) had no such views of ownership. Complex stratification systems (whether based on kinship or not) were also foreign to the San. Concurrently with these diverse views of not owning property (Bushmen) and wanting to enforce views of a foreign state (European countries), various African groupings of people lived in different stages of horticultural and agrarian societies where kinship structures were of huge importance at the southern point of Africa (South Africa today). Such diversity in the same geographical area led to intergroup relationships that ranged from trading to violent clashes over access to land and livestock. In the process, indigenous African people and imported slaves (eg from Malaysia) ended up working for families of European descent. Working full-time for other families often transformed their own family lives, but relatively small sections of African families were affected by this.

The discovery of mineral riches towards the end of the 19th century in South Africa and the sudden demand for large numbers of labourers profoundly disrupted family lives of Africans in the ensuing decades, often with the help of the state and industry (capital). The migrant labour system that became synonymous with the mining industry in South

Africa was one of the most prominent examples of this. The majority of Africans were not keen to leave their families to go and work on the mines (or in white households, on farms or in other industries) but by imposing various forms of taxes and withdrawing access to land, able-bodied men (and later women) were forced into the cash economy by working for wages. This practice took people away from their established kinship structures and new family patterns emerged. The process continued, even though it went through different cycles, throughout the greater part of the 20th century to the increasing detriment of African families (Rabe 2006).

While colonialism, and later apartheid, dramatically affected the lives of families in southern Africa, the development of sociological theory as applied to families was formulated in different parts of the world. The first prominent sociological theories of the family focused in particular on the relationship between growing industrial capitalism and families.

11.4 Family theories

In the previous section it was postulated that industrial societies are associated with simple family forms where production is segregated from family life. As the industrialisation process intensifies, urbanisation follows since workers are needed in a central place. Nuclear families thus accompany the workers and the so-called fit between the nuclear family and the industrial society was often highlighted by family theorists. The sociologist Talcott Parsons (1902–1979) in the United States of America (USA) was especially prominent in developing the theoretical foundations for how the nuclear family was understood in terms of structure and function. These ideas of Parsons are outlined in the next section after which the critical perspectives on family life are highlighted. Most notable are the criticisms of the conflict approach of which the groundwork was laid in the work of Friedrich Engels (1820–1895), a friend and colleague of Karl Marx, and the criticisms by feminist theorists. Although the views developed by feminism are paramount for an understanding of family theory, only a short overview will be provided here and it is recommended that this section be read in conjunction with Chapter 7 on gender.

Both the conflict and structural functionalist theories developed by analysing large structural elements of society (macro theories), but elements of these theories also operate at the interpersonal or micro-level of societies. Another general sociological theory that has been applied to the family is the social exchange theory, which will be the fourth theory focused on here. Lastly, the life course approach which developed in specific relation to family life will be highlighted.

11.4.1 Structural functionalism

The anthropologist George Murdock (1897–1985) analysed data on family and kinship from 250 societies. The author admits that he only had extensive data on 85 of these societies and that the data from the remaining societies were of varying quality. Despite these misgivings, Murdock confidently proclaims that 'the nuclear family is a universal human social grouping' (Murdock 1949: 2). Murdock's definition of a nuclear family presupposes that at least two adults of the opposite sex live together, have a socially sanctioned sexual relationship and have at least one child through birth or adoption. Cohabitation of family members, heterosexuality as a norm and children are all characteristics of Murdock's version of a family. Murdock (1949: 10) also ascribes four functions to the family. These are sexual regulation, economic tasks, reproduction and education. Murdock explains a 'polygamous family' as nuclear families that are joined through plural marriages and extended families are explained as nuclear families strung together through extended parent–child relationships.

The sociologist Talcott Parsons, in collaboration with Robert Bales, expanded on these premises of family life as explained by Murdock, but focused his attention on families living in the USA in the mid-20th century. Structurally, Parsons and Bales (1955: 10–12) regard the nuclear family as isolated due to the separate dwelling that it occupies and its economic independence that is made possible by the earnings of the father. Parsons and Bales (1955: 16–17) state that in a 'highly differentiated society' the family has lost certain functions (such as economic production and comprehensive education of children) and the two primary functions assigned to families in such societies are the 'primary socialisation of children' and 'the stabilisation of the adult personalities'. The diversification of tasks was believed to be best divided according to gender. Thus the mother/wife took care of the expressive aspects such as emotional support to all family members and the father/husband of the instrumental tasks by earning an income through employment (Parsons & Bales 1955: 46).

It is clear that Parsons is assuming that all families have one male breadwinner. He does concede in his discussion that not all families have male breadwinners, yet he considers such cases as deviant and as such 'scarcely needs mentioning' (Parsons & Bales 1955: 12). Although the data

Parsons was working with were very different from the data available on families today (in the USA, globally and in South Africa), it is clear that Parsons worked with a rigid gendered view of the family.

Structural functionalism in its original form and subsequent developments add to our understanding of the family. Unfortunately, the application of some of the central views of the nuclear family became ideological and even detrimental to the wellbeing of families in certain cases as we shall see below when highlighting family life in the Zambian Copperbelt during colonial times.

Parsons' theory was influential in the USA and beyond during the 1950s, but it was increasingly criticised for focusing on white, middle-class families. For example, in many so-called working class families in the USA, women had little choice but to work. Further afield evidence suggested that a much greater variety and complexity of family forms existed in pre-industrial Europe and England (Cooper 1999). Furthermore, distinct trends were identified in different European countries. In South Africa fierce debates developed between prominent family scholars on whether (or to what extent) the nuclear family existed amongst all racial groupings (Ziehl 2002). The absence of proper censuses amongst all racial groups (the first census inclusive of all racial groupings took place in 1996 in South Africa) meant that such disputes could not easily be resolved in a satisfactory manner.

Over the years the nuclear family advanced from being a commonly observable phenomenon in certain sectors of specific societies to an 'ideal family' for some. A deplorable example can be seen when, during colonial times, the mineworkers of the Copperbelt in Zambia were encouraged to settle with their families near the mines. Such families were regarded as 'stabilised families' or 'modern families' (note that this is the exact opposite approach to the migrancy pattern of mineworkers in South Africa) and the observed nuclear family model that Parsons identified (husband as provider and wife as homemaker in the 1950s in the USA) was encouraged. The absurdity between such an 'ideal' nuclear family and the reality experienced by Zambians is shown below:

The image of Copperbelt women as housewives was already a bit hard to swallow. With the economic crisis, women were less likely to be staying home and looking after the housekeeping than to be trading in used goods, making smuggling trips to Zaire or Malawi, or juggling lovers who might be persuaded to help out with the bills. Many women were, indeed, struggling to keep afloat at all; some were losing children to disease and malnutrition. The juxtaposition of such realities with an unselfconsciously stereotypical image of smiling 1950s happy homemaker seemed little short of ludicrous. But there the women were, sitting in classrooms, being taught how to bake angel food cake or to sew a tea cosy (Ferguson 1999: 167).

Note that not only the nuclear structure but also foreign middle-class roles were enforced on these families. Prior to colonisation, Zambia was characterised by matrilineal descent and Vaughan describes how this derailed the nuclear family housing schemes in Zambia:

Colonial experts looked on in dismay as their neat lines of nuclear family housing took on the more familiar appearance of an African village settlement with new huts erected next to brick houses and the 'colonial village' fragmented into what was essentially a set of lineage settlements (Vaughan 1998: 173).

Ferguson has demonstrated how traditional family patterns were typecast as 'pathological' and nuclear families as being 'normal', but eventually the reality (matrilineal families with many unfulfilled economic needs) and the ideology (nuclear families with assigned roles to men and women) clashed. Clearly, when studying family life, ideology and reality should not be confused. The nuclear family is thus only one of different family forms that may be the most common in specific contexts.

Another prominent theory of the family is the systems theory that developed within the discipline of biology and then spread to the social sciences. This theory has remarkable similarities with the structural functionalism of Parsons' grand theory in which families form part of a subsystem of broader society. Similar to Parsons' theory, systems theory is criticised for not being able to explain radical change (although it must be noted that later formulations of structural functionalism and systems theory addressed the criticism of not dealing adequately with change in society in a comprehensive manner).

The next theory has no such problem with explaining change; in fact, bringing change about as well as the reasons for doing so are central to the conflict theory.

11.4.2 Conflict theory

The conflict theory of the family has its roots in the writings of Karl Marx and Friedrich Engels. At the heart of Marxian theory is control of material production in society where two positions are possible – people who own the means of production and others who sell their labour to those who own the means of production. A scarcity of resources would result in conflict over such resources with the aim of gaining power over the limited resources. With the development of the conflict theory, both conflict between and within groups is focused on. The 'European family', as an example of conflict within a group, is regarded by Engels as a microcosm of society where the first opposition between two parties or classes appeared in the form of the division of labour according to sex. The oppression experienced by women in the marriage is described as the historical, original, class oppression (White & Klein 2008). It should be noted that Marx and Engels developed their observations and views at a time when many Western European countries were experiencing the effect of the Industrial Revolution where poverty was rife among the working classes.

Similar to structural functionalist views of the family, the conflict approach to families also became blurred with ideological aspirations. Unlike a structural functionalist approach that saw the nuclear family as an ideal fit for capitalist societies, the conflict approach was furthered in communist countries (eg China and Russia in the mid-20th century) where the family was at times regarded as an obstacle to the advancement of a classless society. The unpaid labour of women within the domestic sphere was believed to make life bearable for the male worker and therefore less likely to take up the revolutionary ideas in fighting for a classless society. In this regard wives were even famously described as nothing more than prostitutes exchanging domestic labour and sexual services for a stable family income. Abolishing the family itself or the power of parents over women were both experimented with in specific communist countries. Such examples of ideology were manifest in the 1920s in Russia where there was a move to abolish families. In one of the most deliberate attempts to manipulate people into abandoning primary relationships formed within families, the fertility rate dropped dramatically, juvenile delinquency increased and many children and young women found themselves destitute. The Russian state made a U-turn in their policies in the 1930s where the importance of the family and marriage was dramatically reinstated to counter these unforeseen results of their initial policies (Timasheff 1960). There is thus also a link between families and larger ideological projects in the conflict approach.

Apart from such a macro analysis, the conflict approach also operates at the micro level of interpersonal conflict in families. Georg Simmel (1858–1918) gave a different slant to conflict theory by regarding the family not as a microcosm of society, but as units that are comprised of special, small group interpersonal relationships such as dyads and triads. Mother–father–child-triads (relationships consisting of three people namely the mother, the father and the child) and sibling-dyads (relationships consisting of two brothers or two sisters or a brother and sister) are examples of specific groupings that are formed within families. Power dynamics, alliances and ties to one another are formed within the family just as in other small groups. Conflict in such relationships is a type of catalyst for emotional growth and it may result in 'love, partnerships, hate, and solidarity' (White & Klein 2008: 198–192).

Similar to the conflict theory, feminist theories also argued that families have to change for the benefit of the family members and society at large.

11.4.3 Feminist theories

Feminist theories are discussed in more detail in Chapter 7 on gender. Yet they are briefly discussed here because feminist thinking has had a huge impact on the way families have been understood. Feminist theories have a critical approach to families since the family is identified as a major site for the oppression of women and a central aim of feminist theory is to change such oppression. When reading about feminist theories, keep in mind that feminism is an interdisciplinary approach that also has various links with activist groups. Furthermore, feminism contributes to our understanding of the overlap between the private/family/domestic sphere and the public sphere, which will also become clear when discussing domestic violence (see section 11.7).

Feminism is usually described as consisting of three waves. The first wave of feminism took effect in the beginning of the 20th century and is associated with the general rights of women such as voting and owning land. The second wave of feminism became prominent in the 1960s partly in reaction to a singular view of the nuclear family where the man is the breadwinner and the wife the homemaker (a view much supported by structural functionalism as described above). Women's rights to employment and equal pay for the same work were further issues that the second wave of feminism advanced. The third wave of feminism emerged during the 1990s and the main theme is to acknowledge the diversity of women globally within varied local contexts. The previous waves of feminism were often experienced as the project of white middle-class women in Western societies,

which excluded the experiences of many women. There is no unified 'sisterhood' but rather a variety of experiences linked to the local context where identities other than a gender identity intersect with being a woman. This latter point is of particular importance for South Africa since the majority of women in this country suffered from combined racial, gender and class oppression. These combined forms of oppression, or 'triple jeopardy', were especially apparent in the lives of live-in black domestic workers (see Chapter 7 on gender for further details). However, for the purposes of family theory, the second wave of feminism is of particular importance.

Early feminists of the second wave described a prescribed role for women restricting them to the domain of family life. The nuclear family was believed to be the ideal place for women where they could raise children and be 'happy homemakers' (as described within a structural functionalist approach). However, the nuclear family is associated with patriarchy where the husband had legal, sexual, physical and economic power over his wife. Private individual patriarchy within the family was backed up by larger societal institutions such as legal and financial organisations. The next section on domestic violence illuminates the most extreme examples of how patriarchal power can undermine the rights of women. Furthermore, since middle-class women were discouraged from seriously pursuing a career, many women found the isolation imposed on them by the structural constraints of the nuclear family unbearable. It was described above how economic production mostly took place within families in non-industrial societies. In industrialised societies in the mid-20th century middle-class women had no specific economic purpose and effective family planning methods meant that women had fewer children than in previous generations. In addition, the education of children was taken over by schools and a growing number of household appliances meant that women had less labour-intensive household chores. In South Africa, which was characterised by large economic inequalities, cheap household labour was readily available, which meant that middle-class (especially white) women had fewer household duties. Together these factors created an environment that was conducive for dramatically changed gender relations within families and beyond.

Different strands of feminist theory developed and each viewed patriarchal power and the family differently. Certain strands of feminist theory viewed the relationship between the state and the family as problematic. Marxist feminism, for example, viewed the nuclear family as serving a capitalist state where the class position of the family determined the role of women. Overthrowing the state and replacing it with a classless society would therefore address the plight of women as well. In contrast, radical feminism moved for the overthrow of patriarchy on all levels, identifying men (and not the state or the economic system) as the root cause of women's oppression. The different strands of feminism are discussed in more detail in Chapter 7 on gender, but it is important to note that all feminist theories (except certain expressions of conservative feminism) identified the specific family relations of the mid-20th century as a major stumbling block for the advancement of women.

The previously mentioned three theories are linked to one another. Conflict theorists and feminist theorists both criticised the basic assumptions of the original structural functionalist theory on families with its said strong link to capitalism and specific gender roles within a nuclear family. The following two theories developed largely independently from these discussions and therefore different focal points of families are identified.

11.4.4 Rational choice and social exchange theory

Rational choice and social exchange theory, as applied to families, provides explanations for decisions of an individual and interpersonal nature – the micro level of human interaction. The rational choice and social exchange theory makes a number of assumptions about human nature. Firstly, it assumed that the larger social phenomena are constructed through the *actions of individuals*. The family is therefore regarded as a collection of individuals or actors. Secondly, it is believed that in order to understand human interaction, the *motivation of the actor* should be understood. Thirdly, this implies that humans are *rational*. To be rational within this tradition means that individuals weigh up costs and rewards. Rewards are anything the actor (or the acting individual) believes is beneficial to his/her interests while costs are regarded as detrimental to the actor's interests. Lastly, it is believed that actors are *motivated by self-interest*. Even in cases where it may appear that individuals are acting altruistically, closer inspection will reveal that self-interest is still at the heart of the action (White & Klein 2008).

The above theory may seem rather simplistic but the idea of *profit* makes the theory more complicated. White and Klein (2008: 71) define profit 'as the ratio of rewards

to costs for any decision'. Actors will therefore take the different ratios of rewards and costs attached to actions into consideration when making a decision. The action carrying the greatest profit will be chosen by the actor. This general theory is then applied to families especially when important decisions have to be made regarding marriage, divorce or the care of dependent family members. For example, if a woman is dissatisfied with her husband's behaviour and she considers divorcing him, she may decide to weigh the advantages and disadvantages of being married and being divorced against each other. If she decides that there are more disadvantages to being divorced than married, she considers that there is 'profit' in being married (according to this theory) and decides against a divorce.

The next theory is again concerned with understanding individual actions within larger socio-historic milieus.

11.4.5 Life course approach

One of the strengths of the life course approach is that it links individual and family narratives with larger societal changes. The life course perspective focuses on change or transitions and development over the lifespan. The unique circumstances of an individual's life are linked to the broader socio-historical context to form a clear picture of the agency of individuals within such a specific context. The life course perspective is concerned with transitions while taking individual differences and generalisations into consideration. Within families one person's life course influences and is influenced by another person's (White & Klein 2008). The timing of a transition which the individual or the family undergoes (such as the birth of a baby or the death of a family member) in relation to historical events (such as the outbreak of a war or the discovery of gold), and the cumulative impact of earlier transitions on current transitions, are central to this theory. The multiple identities of the individual, such as employee or spouse, are all taken into consideration when discussing individual transitions (Elder 1978). The changing nature of the social context and the agency of the individual are thus focused upon simultaneously.

The above five theories approach the study of families in very different ways and the aim of a specific research project will influence the type of theoretical approach used by a researcher.

Structural functionalism	Conflict theory	Feminist theories	Rational choice and social exchange theory	Life course approach
• Talcott Parsons • Focuses on specific functions of the family • Concerns with fit between family structure and society	• Friedrich Engels • Family is seen as a microcosm of larger class divisions • Family is regarded as an obstacle to a classless society	• Different historical waves of feminism • Different strands of feminism • The patriarchal family restricts women's life opportunities	• Focuses on micro level of family • People are regarded as rational and motivated by self-interest • Within family relationships rewards and costs are calculated	• Links individuals and family narratives with societal changes • Focuses on transitions and development over the lifespan

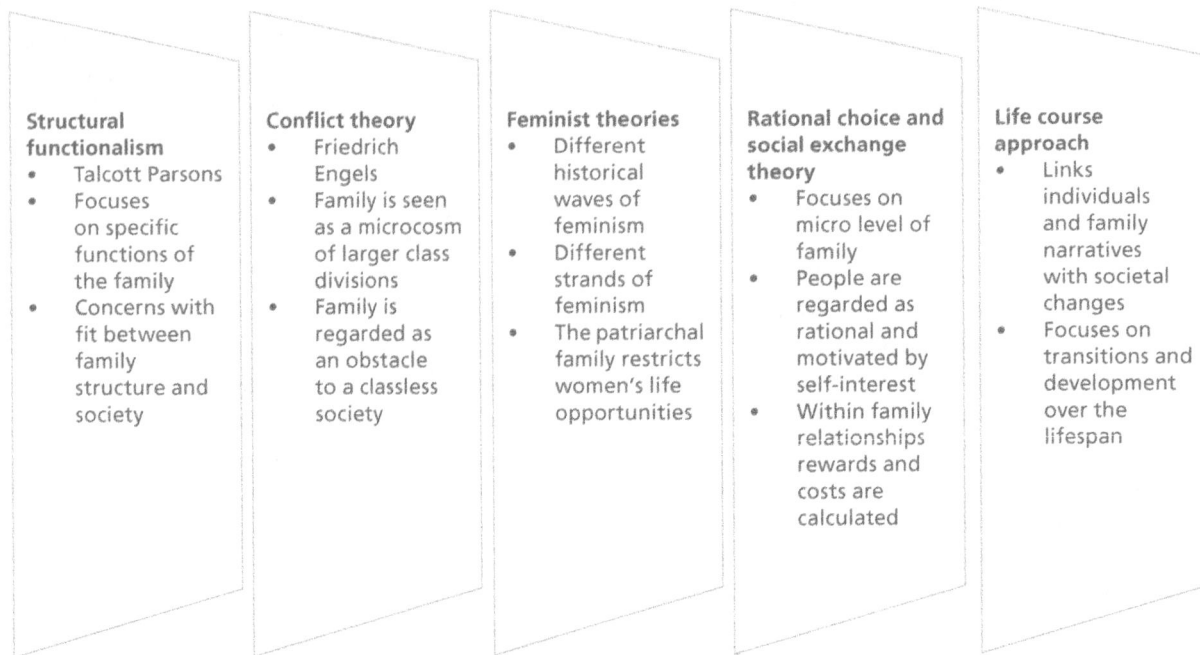

Figure 11.3 Comparison of initial formulations of theories as applied to families

11.5 Intergenerational relations

The relationships between different generations is the focus of this next section. For children, families are usually the primary socialisation agents and caretakers and therefore relations with parents, siblings, grandparents and other family members are hugely important. Becoming a parent or grandparent are two additional, clearly identifiable stages in families which constitute new intergenerational relations. Each of these will be given attention.

11.5.1 Childhood and youth

According to the 2001 South African census, 32 per cent of the population was under the age of 15 (StatsSA 2003: 30), but this figure dropped in 2011 to 29.6 per cent of the population (StatsSA 2012: 28) demonstrating the continuous decline in the South African fertility rate. A World Development Report on the youth (World Bank 2006) stated that in 2006 1.5 billion people were in the age category of 12 to 24 and of these, 1.3 billion people were in developing countries. It is the largest number of people in this age category ever and it will probably never be repeated since populations are ageing and fertility rates are declining worldwide (although there are a few developing countries with different population trends). Such a staggering number of young people, in particular in developing countries,

requires a well-grounded understanding of this life stage to try and achieve a quality of life for this generation and for the future.

Seeing childhood as a distinct age category and children as having specific needs that are not exactly the same as those of adults is a fairly recent phenomenon. Until recently (and in some contexts even today) children were considered similar to adults and expected to work and contribute to the family's upkeep in the same way as adults (Coltrane & Collins 2001). Contributing to the view that children have different needs to adults is the increased complexity of contemporary societies. Ever more skilled and educated workers are needed and hence children have to spend progressively longer periods in formal educational environments. In 2011 more than 95 per cent of children aged seven to 14 attended school in South Africa (StatsSA 2012: 47) and 73 per cent of people between the ages of five and 24 attended an educational institution (StatsSA 2012: 46). Spending a lot of time with peers in schools and other educational institutions facilitated the development of youth cultures with distinct tastes in things such as music, clothes and leisure time activities.

In economic terms children can be regarded as an 'asset' in a rural, non-mechanical agricultural environment, but a 'liability' in an urbanised industrialised setting where they are expected to attend school. Caldwell (in Weeks 2005: 95) explains this view in the wealth flow perspective: in pre-industrial societies, wealth flows from children to parents by children supporting parents in old age and taking part in family labour throughout life. However, in a society where income is linked more with formal educational levels, the cost of having children far outweighs the possible financial rewards they may provide (compare with rational choice and social exchange theory discussed in section 11.3.4).

How do these large percentages of children/youth (and their specific needs) tie in with families? The family is often described as a primary socialising agent of children where the parents play a particularly important role by instilling valued qualities in relation to the social context in which families live. However, children can also be seen as socialising agents of their parents as adults become parents, grandparents, uncles and aunts with the birth of children. Specific examples of children socialising their parents include the use of technological equipment (in many families children know more about the use of social network sites, such as Facebook, Twitter and Instagram, than their parents). Many children learn languages that are different to that of the family (children often learn new languages quicker than adults do) and many illiterate parents depend on literate children to help them with various forms of written material. Parent–child relationships can thus be described as complex processes with reciprocal influencing (Peterson & Hann 1999: 327–328; 341).

11.5.2 Parenting

Thousands of South African children grow up without the benefit of living with their biological fathers on a daily basis and much less than half of South African children live with both their biological parents (as can clearly be seen in Table 11.1). As a young scholar interested in sociology you may ask yourself, firstly, why this is the case and, secondly, whether we should be concerned about this picture of parenting.

The first question is easier to answer since a vast amount of anthropological and historical literature is available to illuminate the reasons for these family household patterns. The long history of apartheid where employed men were not allowed to settle with their families at or near their workplace certainly still contributes to family arrangements in the 21st century. The huge differences between the different racial categories also support such a view. A pattern of **oscillating migrancy** (moving between one's workplace and home on a circular basis) became entrenched in the lives of many people as can clearly be seen with certain employment sectors such as mining and domestic work (although both

sectors are slowly changing with more employees living at home). The fluidity of households became a dominant theme in understanding the family lives of especially poor black people towards the end of apartheid and beyond. Often children are moved from household to household to ensure that they have access to adult supervision (grandparents, uncles, aunts) and that they are close enough to schools. Furthermore, there is not a close link between fertility and marriage (or even cohabitation) in South Africa (as will be discussed in section 11.6 in more detail) which in practice, often implies that children grow up with their mothers or maternal grandparents.

The second question of whether we should be concerned about this pattern of children living away from their parents, is more complicated. There are definitely activist groups that are trying to convince especially biological fathers that they should take up their parenting role within households, but this is not a realistic option for many families. Below we will look at the different ways in which parenting can materialise and it will be clear that biological parenthood can be distinguished from other parenting roles. Not living with biological children does not mean that parents are not involved in their children's lives. Parents who are not able to live with their children on a daily basis may still be active parents who undertake various parenting tasks.

Let us now consider different views on motherhood and fatherhood keeping in mind that in various contexts the following still holds true: '[w]hile women's lives have been characterised primarily in terms of motherhood, men's lives have been characterised largely without reference to fatherhood' (Bruce et al 1995: 49).

Motherhood

As we have seen in section 11.4.3 when discussing feminist theories, gender relations have been dramatically reshaped in the past sixty years. Yet researchers find a continued role division according to gender in which women are primarily responsible for childcare (Ramphele 1993; White 1999) to such an extent that women are socialised into believing that 'having children is a primary source of self-identity' (Newman 1999: 268). The term 'intense mothering' (Hay in Ranson 2004: 88) captures the notion that children need the constant attention of their mothers and often mothers set extremely high expectations for themselves in this regard.

An active attempt to place motherhood on a pedestal can be seen in the 1950s, after the World War II (which ended in 1945). After women took on the role of 'workers' during this war, returning soldiers had to reclaim their roles as breadwinners and women were encouraged to take mothering seriously by regarding it as a full-time occupation (especially in the USA and Western European countries) leaving the available jobs to men. Women's roles as caretakers within nuclear families were emphasised (note that this was also the time in which the structural functionalist theory became prominent). In South Africa, during the apartheid years, similar processes could be seen among Afrikaners where 'volksmoeders' (mothers of the nation) were encouraged to build a 'nation'. Among a different section of South Africa, but in similar vein, the famous uprising against pass laws in 1956 by mainly black women was at times cast as being inspired by their roles as mothers and being primary caretakers of children.

Motherhood is often narrowly defined as biological motherhood since women are not only expected to have children, but also to raise those children. A view that biological mothers are 'real' mothers easily flows from this latter premise as illuminated by Downe (2004: 165–178) when reflecting on her status as a stepmother. Since she had not undergone the rites of biological motherhood, she often experienced that her motherhood status was not regarded as real. She struggled to get time off from work while other women with less urgent child responsibilities were easily granted time off. Although policies may accept wider categories of motherhood, experiences of mothers who are not biological mothers (including grandmothers) point to far less support from employers and other community members.

Next, the distinctions between different forms of fatherhood will be analysed.

Fatherhood

The roles of fathers towards their children have been subdivided into economic, social and biological fatherhood. **Biological fatherhood** refers to the procreation of children. Although this does not seem like a complex aspect of fatherhood, multiple sexual partners may obscure, and *in-vitro fertilisation* (IVF) cases where donor sperm is used, may complicate the identity of a biological father. **Economic fatherhood** refers to the financial upkeep of children where more than one man can be involved in providing financial contributions to children. This aspect of fatherhood is often referred to as the breadwinner role, which is easily equated with being a responsible father. In industrial capitalist societies the breadwinner role is mostly linked to waged labour. High levels of unemployment imply that financial support by fathers is not always feasible, yet fathers themselves, mothers and children easily regard fathers as irresponsible or even 'worthless' if they are not

able to meet the material needs of children sufficiently. **Social fatherhood** implies multiple roles which may entail living with a child or taking care of a child in some way – including teaching, playing with and nurturing them. As it is in the case of economic fatherhood, social fatherhood can be undertaken by more than one man in relation to a specific child (Morrell 2006; Rabe 2006).

The above three roles of fatherhood summarise the relationships between men as parents and children, but how does fatherhood manifest itself in South African society? Rabe (2006) identified three expressions of fatherhood that are dominant in different communities in different time periods in South Africa. These three manifestations of fatherhood are patriarchy, the breadwinner and 'new' fatherhood. Patriarchy, within the family context, refers to the power men exert over women and children by taking decisions on their behalf that largely determine the way they live. However, Bozzoli (1983) had already indicated three decades ago how patriarchy denotes a dynamic relationship that can adapt to changing circumstances. Patriarchy can therefore imply that a man can control almost every aspect of his wife's and children's lives by owning all property and other assets of the family, dominating other family members (even to the point of domestic violence, see Section 4.6) and controlling the family's interaction with external institutions (eg school, legal services and social networks). In other versions of patriarchy a man may consult his wife and children and have a more compassionate bond with them, but the decision-making power still rests in his hands.

Being a **breadwinner** can overlap with patriarchy or new fatherhood, but the importance of this role is central to evaluating the worth of fathers in various South African communities. If financial support is the only link men have with their children, the father–child relationship is at huge risk in cases of unemployment. The migrant worker often has no choice but to take on only the breadwinner role but even in cases of resident fathers (men living with their children on a daily basis), some fathers provide little direct care towards or have little interaction with their children.

The so-called **new fatherhood** refers to a man who takes on the various social roles towards children referred to above. Such a father may be able to meet the material needs of children but, more importantly, he has an emotional and caring relationship with a child. It is referred to as *new* since it is believed that men generally did not fulfil such roles towards their children in the past. It is argued that within industrial capitalism the absence of emotional and caring ties between fathers and their children became more apparent (Smit 2005). This argument is strengthened if it is taken into account that industrial capitalism also implies that the educational role of the father diminishes (in agrarian or horticultural societies trades and skills are often directly transferred from fathers to children). However, there are also clear cases where fathers deny their fathering responsibilities and refuse to take up the demands of fathering.

From this, it seems as if men have more options in terms of parenting compared to women but the lack of a constantly involved father figure may be contributing to such accepted multiple father identities. The absence of material wellbeing for many South African children may also contribute to emphasising the breadwinner role associated with responsible fatherhood. A general negative perception of fatherhood exists in South Africa and the extreme levels of domestic violence by men certainly contribute to this. Abandonment of children by fathers is equally detrimental to the view of fathers. Yet, not all fathers are uncaring towards children and specific portrayals of 'positive fatherhood' are launched from time to time to boost the general image of fathers in South Africa (eg Fatherhood Project HSRC). Instead of trying to vilify or idolise fatherhood, it seems that more realistic portrayals of fatherhood are needed where the joys, obstacles, responsibilities and mundane aspects of being a father are addressed.

11.5.3 Grandparenthood

Since large numbers of people live increasingly longer, the population of elderly people (or older persons, which is the preferred term in United Nations documents), is growing fast (Kalache, Barreto & Keller 2005: 30). Despite the AIDS pandemic and reduced life expectancy at birth in Africa, the actual number of the elderly continues to grow rapidly since the majority of African countries are growing in size due to a current or recent high birth rate. According to a WHO report, the number of older adults (older than 60 years) in sub-Saharan Africa will increase from 46 million in 2015 to 157 million by 2050 (WHO 2015: 43). According to the South African Census of 2001, persons aged 65 and older comprised 4.9 per cent of the total population – approximately 2.2 million people from a total of 45 million (StatsSA 2005: 156). In ten years' time the number of people older than 65 grew to 2.7 million, or 5.3 per cent of the total South African population, according to the 2011 census, with a staggering 1.3 million people in the age category of 60 to 64 years (StatsSA 2012: 28).

The growing number of elderly people gives rise to a general 'verticalisation' of family relations where the number of families comprising three generations or more is increasing

(Hodgson 1995: 155). The family structures of developing countries in relation to age categories is often characterised by age-condensed families. Such families have small age differences between the generations due to early fertility patterns. In contrast, the pattern in developed countries is characterised by age-gapped families. Age-gapped families refer to families where there are big age differences between generations as a result of late fertility (Lowenstein & Katz 2010: 190). South Africa is characterised by women who give birth to their first child at an early age (StatsSA 2013b: 25) although age-gapped families may be found among more wealthy families where specifically women spend long periods in formal educational institutions and pursue careers that require long working hours. However, the general pattern of age-condensed families implies that people become grandparents at an early age in South Africa.

Grandparenthood can take many forms that range from a 'fun-relationship' to that of being the permanent caretakers (in effect parents) of grandchildren. The latter is a very common pattern in South Africa when parents have to work away from their children, when parents may have passed away or when parents abandon their children. In cases where parents are alive, they usually control the amount of time grandchildren spend with grandparents. Other factors that influence this relationship between grandparents and grandchildren include the physical distance between them, the age and gender of both the grandchildren and grandparents. Young and healthy grandparents (who are not full-time caretakers of children) are more likely to have a 'fun' relationship with their grandchildren, especially among the middle- and upper-class families (Roberto & Stroes 1995: 141–142).

These three main generational positions in families are largely dependent on the way in which couples are joined whilst they can be hugely influenced by the splitting up of couples.

11.6 Patterns of joining and dissolving families and households

A demographer, John Weeks (2005: 402), stated that the dominant pattern of households being created by marriage and dissolved by death, with children between these two events, has been transformed. This described dominant pattern has been replaced with a variety of household and family forms due to dramatic changes that are often referred to as a family and household transition. It has already been noted in section 11.2 of this chapter that South African society has always contained complex patterns of households and families, and the patterns of joining and dissolving families are no less so. The current variety of these patterns is indicated, among other things, by the fact that South Africa legally acknowledges customary marriages (Customary Marriage Act 1998) and same-sex couples (Civil Unions Act 2006). Unlike the 'dominant pattern' Weeks refers to, a variety of trends could be seen in South African society for more than a century that can be attributed to phenomena such as migration. Yet, 'newer trends' that gave rise to the family and household transition are also affecting South African families and households. These trends include the general increased longevity of people, which implies that marriages also became longer since partners are less likely to die before old age, the general emancipation of women over the last few decades (see also Chapter 7 on gender) and the growing secularisation or at least ideological changes regarding marriage itself (see also Chapter 13 on religion). Such factors contributed to the diversity of living conditions as can easily be noticed in certain statistical trends such as the number of children born out of wedlock and the divorce rate.

11.6.1 Cohabitation and marriage

The use of certain terms helps us to understand the intimate and sexual relationships between people (as was the case when defining families). The term **monogamy** refers to one man being married to one woman. Homosexual couples may also refer to their unions as monogamous, but that would only be accurate if they were legally married. Being monogamous therefore implies a marriage and it should not be confused with the term **fidelity**, which refers to being committed to a sexually exclusive union. **Polygamy** refers to a sanctioned marriage between one person and several partners of the opposite sex at the same time. This term should not be confused with bigamy, which refers to a person being illegally married to more than one person and the persons involved are unaware that their partner is married to another person. Polygamy can be subdivided into polygyny and polyandry. **Polygyny** refers to one man being married to several wives at the same time and **polyandry** refers to one woman being married to several husbands at the same time. Polygyny is associated with customary African marriages in southern Africa while polyandry is not. It is important to note that in societies that allow polygamy, monogamy is still the norm.

Serial monogamy refers to being married several times, but with one partner at a time. Apart from the death of a partner, serial monogamy is only possible in the case of divorce since one has to legally separate from one's partner before being married again in the case of monogamous relationships.

Studying the marital patterns of South Africa reveals that South Africans tend to marry very late (StatsSA 2005: 77; StatsSA 2016: 3). For at least the past decade the median age at first marriage for men was in their early thirties (fluctuating between 32 and 34 years) and for women three to four years earlier (fluctuating between 28 and 30 years). The validity of the figures has been questioned (Budlender et al 2004), but if other sources of data, such as census data and the South African Demographic and Health surveys, are examined, the same pattern is observed (although the median age may be slightly lower). Namibia and Botswana (Garenne 2004) share this atypical African pattern of late marriage with South Africa. The influence of migration patterns is once again considered as a possible reason for this phenomenon.

You may wonder why this high age at first marriage should be of interest to sociologists. In North American and West European countries a general rising trend of age at first marriage has been observed for the past few decades. This pattern is the result of a variety of general societal changes, such as the increasingly longer education periods young people are engaged in, women who are more career orientated and not wanting an early marriage to interfere with their career aspirations and the greater permissiveness of non-marital sex that separated the close link between marriage and sex. Such factors that indicate the ability of especially women to choose between different life options certainly play a role in South Africa since older women tend to have married at a younger age than younger ones, but it cannot explain the trend entirely. Kalule-Sabiti et al (2007: 95–99) state that the link between **nuptiality** (marriage rate) and fertility (bearing children) is particularly weak in South Africa. In other words, although South African women (especially from the black and coloured racial categories) have children at relatively young ages, they marry later in life if they marry at all. Late age at first marriage is thus not necessarily an indication of women's emancipation as is the case in many other countries.

Single-parent households are common in South Africa and this is partly due to marriage at a late age of especially black South Africans and partly due to the high number of divorces among especially white South Africans (see discussion in section 11.5.2 on divorce in this regard).

When discussing marriage and cohabitation, heterosexual couples are usually the focus of the discussion. This tendency has been labelled **heteronormativity**, meaning that heterosexual couples are the norm and hence the families of homosexual couples are ignored or even denied. When looking at the number of registered civil unions, it is reported by StatsSA (2016: 31) that 1 144 such unions were registered in 2014 compared to 888 in 2010. There is thus an increase of people choosing to legally register homosexual unions or marriages. A growing interest in the family dynamics of same-gendered couples is also noticeable in South Africa, and often challenging the way we think about nurturing, mothering and fathering (Lubbe 2007). In certain sectors of the South African society, such as heterogeneous urban environments, same-sex couples are more likely to live with their children in a supportive environment.

11.6.2 Dissolution of relationships

Apart from death, relationships come to an end when people separate. The only way in which the dissolution of relationships are regularly measured, is by calculating divorce rates. We simply do not have reliable South African figures to determine the number of people who break up after cohabiting or separate informally without obtaining a divorce (although regular censuses may start to shed some light on these patterns in future). Even when calculating the divorce rate, certain problems arise. Divorce rates are regularly mentioned in popular media discussions (eg talk shows and articles in 'women's magazines'). Steinmetz, Clavan and Stein (1990: 481–482) discuss three ways of calculating the divorce rate. The first method, often used in the mass media, involves comparing the number of divorces with the number of marriages in a given year. The divorce rate is thus calculated in relation to the number of new marriages in a given year. This method is not advisable since various population factors may influence this calculation such as the number of marriages for the particular year (eg a downward trend in the marriage rate will result in the divorce rate appearing higher) and even changed divorce legislation. A second method is to report the number of divorces per 1 000 members of the population, known as the crude divorce rate. This calculation presents an unrealistically low rate since children, widows/widowers and never-married people are also included (in the youthful population of South Africa such a method will present a particularly skew picture). A third method is to calculate the number of divorces per 1 000 married couples. The latter method provides a more accurate reflection of the divorce rate since only the population at risk (the married) regardless of the length of the marriage is included.

Generally divorce rates are much higher today than in previous generations (hence the statement by Weeks earlier in this section). One of the main reasons for the higher incidence of divorce is that 'no-fault divorce' legislation became the norm in many countries. This simply means that

people can get a divorce if they wish to and, unlike previous times, they do not have to prove that either party is to blame for the breakdown of the marriage. The increasing longevity of people is regarded as a driving force for this changed divorce legislation. Many marriages dissolved because one partner died, but with higher life expectancy, marriages became longer. Longer marriages mean that unhappy marriages are more likely to dissolve in divorce rather than death (Weeks 2005: 419–420).

In South Africa there are wide disparities in the divorce rates according to race: The white population has a divorce rate of 11.6, the Indian or Asian population 6.7, the coloured population 6.3 and the black African population a rate of 2 per 1 000 married couples. The overall divorce rate is 5.3 per 1 000 married couples (StatsSA 2006). (Subsequent reports on the official marriages and divorces in South Africa by StatsSA do not give the divorce rate per 1 000 couples, only the crude divorce rate.) In 2014 it was reported that 55.4 per cent (13 676 couples) of divorces registered in 2014 were by couples who had children under the age of 18 (StatsSA 2016: 42). The emotional, financial and practical implications of divorces are substantial and clearly large numbers of children are affected by this. Of course other forms of dissolution, such as abandonment, separation and living with a new partner, also exist, but it is even more difficult to form a reliable and valid statistical picture of these patterns in the South African society.

11.7 Domestic violence

South Africa is often described as one of the most violent countries in the world and the staggeringly high numbers (see discussion in the next section) of domestic violence against children and women contributes to this view of the country. The Domestic Violence Act (1998) is the most important legislation for protecting people from various forms of violence by family members or partners. In addition, the Older Persons Act (2006) and the Children's Act (2005, amended 2007 and 2008) provide further specific legislation for the rights of the aged and the young. Although important legislation to protect people is in place in South Africa, these Acts and Bills are not always enforced, partly due to the reluctance to interfere with 'private affairs'. Activists have campaigned to transform domestic violence from a private matter to a public concern (Harne & Radford 2008: 1), yet there is reluctance to intervene in the private family sphere (Kurst-Swanger & Petcosky 2003: 27). This results in domestic violence often carrying on for years without any intervention from outside the family.

11.7.1   Types of family violence

Domestic violence can be categorised as physical violence; sexual violence; coercion and control; and economic control and material deprivation.

Physical violence may involve the perpetrator using body strength alone (eg kicking or punching) or it may include the use of weapons and objects (eg guns and knives). The availability of certain objects, such as widespread gun ownership, as is the case in South Africa, or having an argument in the kitchen where many sharp objects are at hand, easily leads to more serious physical harm being inflicted on the victim of domestic violence.

Sexual violence includes rape and any other sexual act in which a person is forced or pressured to take part. Sexual violence is often accompanied by physical violence and verbal abuse or threats. Marital rape may not always be regarded as a valid form of rape in all communities since women may be 'expected' to fulfil their partner's sexual desires at all times. Clearly, such reasoning may contribute to widespread sexual violence against women. However, in South Africa marital rape is recognised as an act of domestic violence although it is difficult to prove and therefore to convict a partner of such an offence.

Coercion and control involve a range of acts such as screening a person's phone calls, preventing them from visiting friends or family on their own or making them believe that everything (including the violence) is their fault. This type of violence is the most difficult to prove. Coercion and control should not be confused with the socialisation of children where certain rules are laid down and punishment is given when rules are disobeyed, for example when a child is prevented from attending a party because they hit their siblings. Although specific manifestations of coercion and control are used in the socialisation of children, extreme forms are regarded as abuse, such as when children are never allowed to visit friends. Any form of coercion and control between adults is most likely a form of abuse.

Economic control and material deprivation are not related to poverty but to the unequal distribution of resources in the family. It can again include a wide range of actions from the absolute control of all financial resources by one partner to actually depriving someone of food or other necessities. This type of violence is often accompanied by the threat of physical violence (Harne & Radford 2008: 3–7).

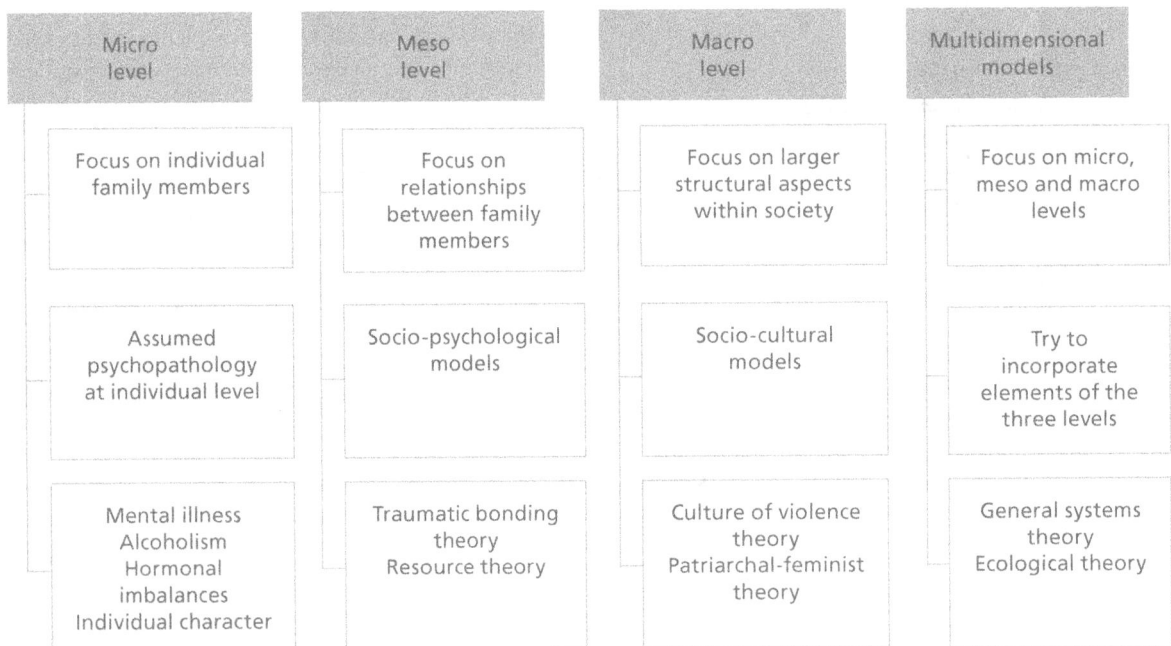

Micro level	Meso level	Macro level	Multidimensional models
Focus on individual family members	Focus on relationships between family members	Focus on larger structural aspects within society	Focus on micro, meso and macro levels
Assumed psychopathology at individual level	Socio-psychological models	Socio-cultural models	Try to incorporate elements of the three levels
Mental illness Alcoholism Hormonal imbalances Individual character	Traumatic bonding theory Resource theory	Culture of violence theory Patriarchal-feminist theory	General systems theory Ecological theory

Figure 11.4 Different theoretical approaches to domestic violence

11.7.2   Theoretical views

A multitude of theories aim to explain domestic violence. To make sense of all these theories, Kurst-Swanger and Petcosky (2003: 34–35) divide the different theories into three levels of theoretical models. Firstly, on the micro level, the individual family members are under scrutiny. At this level the focus is on the assumed psychopathology amongst individual family members, which may include mental illness, alcoholism, hormonal imbalances or specific characteristics of the victim. Secondly, at the meso level, socio-psychological models focus on the relationships between family members. Examples on this level include the traumatic bonding theory that highlights the unique relationship between the victim and the abuser and the resource theory that explains family violence in terms of the person with access to most of the social, personal and economic resources in the family. Thirdly, at the macro level socio-cultural models analyse larger structural aspects. One of the most prominent theories on this level, that is applicable to South African society, is the culture of violence theory. In terms of this theory, family violence can be attributed to the general norms and values within a particular society that condone violence. A further explanation for family violence at the macro level emphasises structural inequalities within a society that is based on aspects such as race and socio-economic status. The patriarchal-feminist theory, which attributes gender family violence to general male domination in society, will also be categorised under the macro level. Also take note of the general systems theory and the ecological theory that are considered multidimensional models. Multidimensional models try to incorporate all the above-mentioned variables (psychological, socio-psychological and socio-cultural) in explaining family violence.

11.7.3 Perpetrators and victims

In the majority of cases of family violence, the perpetrators are the more powerful members of the family and the victims the less powerful members. Physical strength often plays an important role in the different forms of family violence since family violence often carries the threat of physical violence even if it does not involve physical violence in every instance. Children, frail elderly people and women are therefore particularly vulnerable, and they are also the most likely to be in need of medical care on a regular basis in extreme cases of physical and sexual violence. Domestic violence as gender violence, child abuse and abuse of the elderly will each be discussed in more detail.

Gender violence as a form of domestic violence
The term gender violence refers to the worldwide pattern in which women are the most likely victims of domestic violence due to the unequal power relations that exist between men and women (Harne & Radford 2008: 17). Theories at the micro and meso level help to explain why

specific people are victims or perpetrators of domestic violence, but the culture of violence theory and the patriarchal-feminist theory on the macro level, postulate that the general high level of violence against particularly women enhances the risk of domestic abuse in a society. The South African figures for intimate partner violence (IPV) that result in death, the most extreme form of domestic violence which is most likely the final act in years of abuse, support such a view. The availability of guns, mainly owned by men, is a risk factor in domestic violence as guns are used to control, hurt or kill partners. The latter is referred to as intimate femicide, which is murder by an intimate partner. Based on large representative South African studies (including national homicide studies), Abrahams, Jewkes and Mathews (2010) report that 2.7 per 100 000 women are killed through gunshot by an intimate partner in South Africa, which is almost double the rate of all gunshot killings of women in the USA. Interestingly, almost a fifth of men who kill their wives in South Africa with a firearm, commit suicide within a week after shooting a partner. A similar high number of women reported being threatened or attacked with guns. Based on another national study of mortuaries, Abrahams et al (2009) report that 8.8 per 100 000 women (14 years and older) died as a direct result of IPV (not only caused by gunshot). This rate is two and a half times higher than any other reported study of IPV in any other country. In such cases where South African women died from IPV, almost a third had reported IPV with the police at least once before.

Internationally women are far more likely to be victims of domestic abuse than men and if being a woman is coupled with another minority status (eg not having full citizen status, such as 'guest workers' or refugees, or being forced into prostitution by family members), it makes abused women even less likely to be able to seek help. The experiences of women with disabilities sheds some light on the added difficulties women with minority status encounter when faced with domestic violence. There are two patterns in this regard. Firstly, women with disabilities are particularly vulnerable to domestic violence and they have to face additional barriers in accessing services and protection from domestic violence. Perpetrators of domestic violence may also create more barriers for women with disabilities by hiding or removing certain aids (eg wheelchairs or special communication systems designed for deaf people) or reinforce stereotypes of certain conditions (eg mental illnesses) when women do seek help. Secondly, women may also become disabled or experience permanent impairment due to injuries from domestic violence. Disabilities therefore heighten women's vulnerability to domestic violence and in some cases it is the result of domestic violence (Harne & Radford 2008: 14–15).

The most effective programmes to reduce IPV are enhancing gender equity by targeting boys and men, changing institutional cultures, policies and laws (addressing domestic violence on the macro level). Further interventions include a reduction in alcohol abuse, restricting access to guns and better mental health services (thus addressing domestic violence at the micro and meso levels) (Abrahams et al 2009: 553).

Men are also victims of domestic violence but it is believed to be far less widespread compared to domestic violence against women. If we look at the number of women who die from IVP (the most severe outcome of IVP) and suffer detrimental physical, emotional and financial consequences due to IVP, the belief that men are more likely to be perpetrators than victims of domestic violence is justified. However, the much lower incidence of domestic violence against men does not make the violence less serious for the men concerned.

Domestic violence against men is sometimes complicated to understand and should not be confused with women who defend themselves against abusers or retaliate after years of abuse. Rautenbach (2006) found in a qualitative study on violence against men that victims may experience verbal, psychological and physical violence on a daily or weekly basis. Although such violence may be embedded in broader familial conflict, it is not the result of women retaliating to domestic violence against them. Men sometimes have to face ridicule against them when they report domestic violence. Men as victims of violence have not received much attention, they are not receiving much support from helping professions and it is likely that their needs are very different from those of women (Kurst-Swanger & Petcosky 2003).

Gendered violence may not only occur between men and women but also between women and between men in lesbian and gay men's relationships respectively. Although there are claims that domestic violence is as common in homosexual relationships as it is in heterosexual relationships, there is not enough conclusive evidence to support this. In the case of lesbian relationships in particular, researchers tend to use wider and more inclusive definitions of what constitutes domestic violence compared to definitions used when looking at domestic violence amongst heterosexual relationships (Harne & Radford 2008: 16–17).

Child abuse

The four main forms of child abuse are neglect (eg inadequate care or abandonment), physical (eg injuries or corporal punishment), sexual (eg rape or sexual exploitation) and emotional (eg kidnapping) abuse. Identified immediate risk factors associated with child abuse include factors such as alcohol and drug abuse, teenage pregnancies and inadequate accommodation or overcrowding. These factors fit in with theories at the micro and meso levels of explaining the incidence of domestic abuse. At the macro level contextual factors such as poverty and a lack of daycare facilities contribute to the prevalence of child abuse (Makoae et al 2009). Yet, it should be kept in mind that even though some situational factors contribute to a greater likelihood of children being maltreated, child abuse takes place within families from all socioeconomic groupings.

Child neglect can be divided into deliberate neglect and situational neglect. The former refers to wilfully ignoring the needs of the child while having the means to fulfil those needs, such as not providing balanced meals to children on a regular basis. Situational neglect results from not being able to meet the child's basic needs. Not feeding a child regularly due to family poverty is an example of the latter. Not all forms of neglect are physical; for example, not ensuring that a child receives education can be described as educational neglect and withholding medical treatment as medical neglect (Makoae et al 2009: 6–7).

Where child neglect refers to the failure of doing something, **child abuse** is the active maltreatment of children physically, sexually or emotionally. Physical abuse refers to non-accidental injury of children. Sexual abuse involves not only any sexual contact with a child but also non-contact sexual abuse, such as exposing them to pornographic material or voyeurism (Makoae et al 2009: 8).

The extent of child abuse in South Africa is difficult to determine as it is underreported. Screening young adults and school children on their experiences of child abuse often exposes much higher incidences of child abuse than what is ever reported (Andersson & Ho-Foster 2008). Promoting the wellbeing of children through putting policies in place is important, but resources are needed for such policies to make a difference in the lives of children. There is a general re-orientation in South African policies and approaches towards child abuse by focusing on prevention of such abuse and trying to identify children at risk. Such an approach aims to minimise the extreme act of removing children from families, known as tertiary intervention, when they are maltreated and no other options are available (Makoae et al 2009).

Abuse of the elderly

Defining what constitutes elder abuse is difficult as varied definitions exist where some focus on abuse by close relatives or people in whom trust is placed while others focus on human rights in general. The latter definition complicates estimating elder abuse in South Africa with its long history of the violation of human rights of black people in general for decades. When aged research participants are asked to report forms of abuse, general infrastructural deficiencies are mentioned. All poor communities suffer under these deficiencies and not only the elderly. Where the needs of the white elderly started to be addressed towards the end of the 20th century, systemic abuse (arising from the system) towards the elderly is still ingrained in South African society – for example struggling to access social grants and being treated poorly in residential care facilities for the aged (Ferreira & Lindgren 2008). Owing to the lack of empirical data on elder abuse in South Africa, '… "elder abuse" has become a veritable catch-all term for any social, economic or political injustice or inequality that older persons perceive is discriminatory of themselves' (Ferreira & Lindgren 2008: 103). The structural inequalities of South African society that are categorised under the macro level theoretical explanations of domestic violence described above, are thus contributing heavily to the experiences of abuse by the elderly.

An NGO that has campaigned for the rights of the elderly, *Action on Elder Abuse South Africa*, has installed a national toll-free telephonic service in South Africa named the Halt Elder Abuse Line (HEAL). The aim of HEAL is to try and prevent elder abuse, provide general information, intervene in cases of elder abuse, link victims with sources of assistance in the case of abuse and do follow-up work on reported cases of abuse if possible. Physical abuse is the most likely to be reported, followed by financial abuse. In research among the aged, older people also identified marginalisation and disrespect in addition to violence and exploitation as part of discriminatory practices against them (Ferreira & Lindgren 2008: 99–104; Marais et al 2006: 188).

South African society thus has the challenge to address domestic violence by eradicating structural violence, replacing the general climate of violence with tolerance, making more quality care facilities available to children and re-educating men in particular in finding acceptable ways to express themselves in relationships.

Summary

- The aim of this chapter was to introduce and sensitise you to the complexities inherent in studying families. Despite the difficulties encountered within families, it remains one of the most enduring institutions of all times. In times of need, celebration, birth or death, family members are often the first people that we turn to in order to share our problems, joys, grief or responsibilities.

- Although there is often an alarmist view that describes 'the family as if it is in crisis', families are able to adapt to the demands of the time by changing in structure and losing or gaining functions along the way, as was noticeable when describing the different family and household forms as well as the different patterns of joining and dissolving relationships of couples.

- In order to understand families we have to look closely at what happens within families. At the same time we have to form a broad picture of the trends of family life in specific societies.

- General theoretical views and specific statistical information of stages in the lives of family members were given. Our hope is that you were able to simultaneously gain a more in-depth and wider view of families than the one you have of your own family or those of the few people you know well.

- In the last section of this chapter domestic violence within families was looked at. An overview of the types of theoretical views on the causes of domestic violence was provided, with the focus on the dynamics of specific forms of violence. The aim is to use such information to curb the alarming trends of domestic violence in this country. The available policies to protect different vulnerable members of families should be strengthened by supporting families in more proactive ways before domestic violence escalates into an uncontrollable and damaging force within specific families.

More sources to consult

Amoateng AY, Heaton, TB (eds). 2007. *Families and Households in Post-apartheid South Africa: Socio-demographic Perspectives*. Cape Town: HSRC.

Lubbe-De Beer C, Marnell J (eds). 2013. *Home Affairs: Rethinking Lesbian, Gay, Bisexual and Transgender Families in Contemporary South Africa*. Johannesburg: Fanele and GALA.

Makiwane M, Nduna M, Khalema NE (eds). 2016. *Children in South African Families: Lives and Times*. Newcastle upon Tyne: Cambridge Scholars Publishing.

References

Abrahams N, Jewkes R, Martin LJ, Mathews S, Vetten L, Lombard C. 2009. 'Mortality of women from intimate partner violence in South Africa: A national epidemiological study'. *Violence and Victims,* 24(4): 546–556.

Abrahams N, Jewkes R, Mathews S. 2010. 'Guns and gender-based violence in South Africa'. *South African Medical Journal,* 100(9).

Andersson N, Ho-Foster A. 2008. '13,915 reasons for equity in sexual offences legislation: A national school-based survey in South Africa'. *International Journal for Equity in Health,* 7(20). [Online] Available at: http://www.equityhealthj.com/content/7/1/20 [Accessed 20 June 2011].

Bozzoli B. 1983. 'Marxism, feminism and South African studies'. *Journal of Southern African Studies,* 9(2): 139–171.

Bruce J, Lloyd CB, Leonard A, Engle PL, Duffy N. 1995. *Families in Focus. New Perspectives on Mothers, Fathers, and Children*. New York: The Population Council.

Budlender D, Chobokoane N, Simelane S. 2004. 'Marriage patterns in South Africa: Methodological and substantive issues'. *Southern African Journal of Demography,* 9(1): 1–26.

Coltrane S, Collins R. 2001. *Sociology of Marriage and the Family*. 5th ed. Belmont: Wadsworth.

Cooper SM. 1999. 'Historical analysis of the family' in *Handbook of Marriage and the Family*. 2nd ed. Sussman MB, Steinmetz SK, Peterson GW (eds). New York: Plenum Press, 13–37.

Downe PJ. 2004. 'Stepping on maternal ground' in *Mother Matters. Motherhood as Discourse and Practice*. O'Reilly A (ed). Toronto: Association for Research on Mothering, 165–178.

Elder GH. 1978. 'Family history and the life course' in *Transitions, the Family and the Life Course in Historical Perspective*. Hareven TK (ed). New York: Academic Press, 17–64.

Ferguson J. 1999. *Expectations of Modernity: Myths and Meanings of Urban Life on the Zambian Copperbelt*. Berkeley: University of California Press.

Ferreira M, Lindgren P. 2008. 'Elder abuse and neglect in South Africa: A case of marginalization, disrespect, exploitation and violence'. *Journal of Elder Abuse and Neglect,* 6 20(2): 91–107.

Garenne M. 2004. 'Age at marriage and modernisation in sub-Saharan Africa'. *Southern African Journal of Demography,* 9(2): 59–79.

Harne L, Radford J. 2008. *Tackling Domestic Violence. Theories, Policies and Practice*. Berkshire: Open University Press.

Hodgson LG. 1995. 'Adult grandchildren and their grandparents: The enduring bond' in *The Ties of Later Life*. Hendricks J (ed). New York: Baywood Publishing Company, 155–170.

Kalache A, Barreto SM, Keller I. 2005. 'Global ageing: The demographic revolution in all cultures and societies' in *The Cambridge Handbook of Age and Ageing*. Johnson M (ed). Cambridge: Cambridge University Press.

Kalule-Sabiti I, Palamuleni M, Makiwane M, Amoateng AY. 2007. 'Family formation and dissolution patterns' in *Families and Households in Post-apartheid South Africa: Socio-demographic Perspectives*. Amoateng AY, Heaton TB (eds). Cape Town: HSRC.

Kurst-Swanger K, Petcosky JL. 2003. *Violence in the Home. Multidisciplinary Perspectives*. Oxford: Oxford University Press.

Lewis S, Rapoport R, Gambles R. 2003. 'Reflections on the integration of paid work and the rest of life'. *Journal of Managerial Psychology,* 18(8): 824–841.

Lowenstein A, Katz R. 2010. 'Family and age in a global perspective' in *The SAGE Handbook of Social Gerontology*. Dannefer D, Phillipsen C (eds). Los Angeles: SAGE, 190–201.

Lubbe C. 2007. 'Mother, fathers, or parents: Same-gendered families in South Africa'. *South African Journal of Psychology*, 37(2): 260–283.

Makoae M, Warria A, Bower C, Ward C, Loffell J, Dawes A. 2009. *South Africa Country Report on the Situation on Prevention of Child Maltreatment Study*. Cape Town: HSRC.

Maluleke T. 2011. 'A great South African woman'. *Mail&Guardian* [Online] Available at: http://www.thoughtleader.co.za/tinyikosammaluleke/2011/05/25/a-great-south-african-woman-2/ [Accessed 20 June 2011].

Marais S, Conrad G, Kritzinger A. 2006. 'Risk factors for elder abuse and neglect: Brief descriptions of different scenarios in South Africa'. *International Journal of Older People Nursing*, 1: 186–189.

Morrell R. 2006. 'Fathers, fatherhood and masculinity in South Africa' in *Baba. Men and Fatherhood in South Africa*. Richter L, Morrell R (eds). Pretoria: HSRC, 13–25.

Murdock GP. 1949. *Social Structure*. New York: Macmillan.

Newman DM. 1999. *Sociology of Families*. Thousand Oaks: Pine Forge Press.

Parsons T, Bales RF. 1955. *Family. Socialization and Interaction Process*. New York: The Free Press.

Peterson GW, Hann D. 1999. 'Socializing children and parents in families' in *Handbook of Marriage and the Family*. Sussman MB, Steinmetz SK, Peterson GW (eds). New York: Plenum Press, 327–370.

Rabe ME. 2006. *Black Mineworkers' Conceptualisations of Fatherhood: A Sociological Exploration in the South African Goldmining Industry*. Pretoria: University of South Africa.

Ramphele M. 1993. *A Bed Called Home: Life in the Migrant Labour Hostels of Cape Town*. Cape Town: David Phillip.

Ranson G. 2004. 'Paid work, family work and the discourse of the full-time mother' in *Mother Matters. Motherhood as Discourse and Practice*. O'Reilly A (ed). Toronto: Association for Research on Mothering, 87–97.

Rautenbach EA. 2006. *'n Kwalitatiewe Ondersoek na Huweliksgeweld teenoor Wit Suid-Afrikaanse Mans*. Stellenbosch: University of Stellenbosch.

Roberto KA, Stroes J. 1995. 'Grandchildren and grandparents: Roles, influences and relationships' in *The Ties of Later Life*. Hendricks J (ed). New York: Baywood Publishing, 141–153.

Smit R. 2005. 'Involved fathering: Expanding conceptualisation of men's paternal caring'. Paper presented at the Department of Sociology, University of Johannesburg.

South Africa. 1998a. Customary Marriage Act 120 of 1998. Pretoria: Government Printer.

South Africa. 1998b. Domestic Violence Act 116 of 1998. Pretoria: Government Printer.

South Africa. 2005. Children's Act 38 of 2005. Pretoria: Government Printer.

South Africa 2006a. Civil Unions Act 17 of 2006. Pretoria: Government Printer.

South Africa. 2006b. Older Persons Act 13 of 2006. Pretoria: Government Printer.

Spiegel AD, Watson V, Wilkinson P. 1996. 'Domestic diversity and fluidity among African households in Greater Cape Town'. *Social Dynamics*, 22(1): 7–30.

Statistics South Africa. 2003. *Census in brief*. Report no. 03-02-03 (2001). Pretoria: StatsSA.

Statistics South Africa. 2005. *Census 2001. Stages in the life cycle of South Africans*. Report no. 03-02-46 (2001). Pretoria: StatsSA.

Statistics South Africa. 2006. *Marriages and divorces 2004*. Statistical release P0307. Pretoria: StatsSA.

Statistics South Africa 2012. *Census 2011. Census in brief*. Report no 03-01-41. Pretoria: StatsSA.

Statistics South Africa. 2013a. *South Africa's young children: their family and home environment, 2012*. Report no 03-10-07. Pretoria: StatsSA.

Statistics South Africa. 2013b. *Gender statistics in South Africa, 2011*. Pretoria: StatsSA.

Statistics South Africa. 2016. *Marriages and divorces 2014*. Statistical release P0307. Pretoria: StatsSA.

Steinmetz SK, Clavan S, Stein KF. 1990. *Marriage and Family Realities. Historical and Contemporary Perspectives*. New York: Harper & Row.

Teachman JD, Polonko KA, Scanzoni J. 1999. 'Demography and families' in *Handbook of Marriage and the Family*. 2nd ed. Sussman MB, Steinmetz SK, Peterson GW (eds). New York: Plenum Press, 39–76.

Timasheff NS. 1960. 'The attempt to abolish the family in Russia' in *A Modern Introduction into the Family*. Bell NW, Vogel EF (eds). New York: The Free Press (originally published in 1946).

Vaughan M. 1998. 'Exploitation and neglect: Rural producers and the state in Malawi and Zambia' in *History of Central Africa. The Contemporary Years Since 1960*. Birmingham D, Martin PM (eds). London: Longman, 167–201.

Weeks JR. 2005. *Population. An Introduction to Concepts and Issues.* 9th ed. Belmont: Wadsworth.

White C. 1999. 'Gender identities and culture: Some observations from fieldwork in Soweto' in *Identity? Theory, Politics, History.* Bekker S, Prinsloo R (eds). Pretoria: HSRC, 95–111.

White JM, Klein DM. 2008. *Family Theories.* 3rd ed. Los Angeles: SAGE Publications.

World Bank. 2006. *Development and the Next Generation.* Washington: The World Bank.

World Health Organization (WHO). 2015. *World Report on Ageing and Health.* Geneva: WHO.

Ziehl S. 2002. 'Black South Africans do live in nuclear family households – A response to Russell'. *Society in Transition,* 33(1): 26–49.

Education

Pragna Rugunanan & Shandré Hoffmann-Habib

The origin (or etymology) of the term 'education' comes from the Latin verb *educare* which means to train or mould. After procreation, teaching the young in the family household is the most fundamental activity in which human beings engage. Without education of some form, individuals are not socialised, families cannot cohere, work cannot be performed, and society cannot develop. Ever since the introduction of mass schooling in 19th century Europe, however, education has become formally institutionalised, and plays a central role in modern societies. Needless to say, without having successfully been through primary and secondary education, you would not possess the skills to study this book. This chapter enables you to stand back and examine this process you have undertaken over the past 12 or more years of your life. It also examines the tertiary educational system in South Africa, both before and after democracy. This chapter on the sociology of education is another opportunity to exercise and develop your own sociological imagination.

After having defined the sociology of education and the role education plays in society, the chapter begins by reviewing how the three classical perspectives in sociology understand and analyse education as a key institution in modern society. This part of the chapter should leave you with a growing sense of how these perspectives lie at the basis of sociological understanding and analysis – which will deepen as you progress through the study of this book. The chapter then turns to the historical narrative of education in South Africa. This review of the background to studying education as an institution reveals the importance of the social context in the study of any social phenomenon, thereby showing how sociology needs to be sensitive to history.

There are at least three reasons why this historical background is particularly important in this instance of studying education from a sociological perspective. The first is the important role of Christian missionary education that provided black Africans with their first experience of Western culture and education. The impact of missionary education and the acculturation of Western culture that accompanied it under colonialism are, of course, open to much debate. Its impact, however, cannot be denied. The second reason relates to how black South Africans, across all social classes, were denied a decent education under apartheid which, among other things, closed down the mission schools. The serious consequences of this part of the story of education in South Africa can hardly be denied. The impact of over 40 years of the massification of black education, but which was of an inferior quality, continues to make its influence felt. The third reason for the importance of the historical narrative is to highlight and celebrate the significant contributory role played by secondary school students in the liberation of our country, signalled by the student uprisings of June 1976. The fact that it was high-school students whose collective social action in June 1976 challenged the 'high' period of apartheid is a remarkable chapter in the history of our country. It speaks volumes about the broader role education can play in society. In 2015 and 2016 it was the turn of university students at historically advantaged universities (see Case study 12.1) to shake South African society by demanding new ways of thinking about it and calling for free education. This chapter discusses the significance of these watershed events.

If you want to gain insight into the tertiary educational process you are undergoing right now, the critical discussion of the restructuring of education post-apartheid, taken right into the present day, is essential reading. Apply each of the three sociological perspectives to this part of the chapter as an exercise in developing a sophisticated and nuanced sociological imagination of your educational experience. You will be able to apply your now rapidly developing sociologically informed mind to the social institutions of the state, society, schooling and the family in this regard. This is an exercise you can do for yourself or together with your colleagues. Perhaps your lecturers will set this as a task in developing your own sociological perspectives. Ultimately, however, at tertiary level only you can educate yourself. Carefully applying your mind to this exercise in the sociology of education will go a long way towards understanding your country and being able to position yourself within it as an active citizen, for without education and the meaningful contribution of those who have the privilege of enjoying a university education, empowered and able to authoritatively discuss this critical social issue, the prospects for a better life for all could be bleak. If that sounds like a lecture, it is not intended as such. It is rather a call to take our precious education seriously. It is sorely needed. There is much evidence in this textbook which could be cited to support this claim. Just do it!

Case study 12.1

In a recent study of alternative voices in the national student movement, one Master's student, Marcia Vilakazi, asked why it was that student protests were only centred in public discourse when formerly white institutions took part. One participant in the study asked: 'Are we not important enough in the government's eyes to be heard on our own without support from Wits, Stellenbosch and UCT?' University of Limpopo students interviewed lamented that when they had raised issues about rape and shootings on campus there had been no response. 'There were countless protests, countless shut-downs and efforts, but these were not given the same space as the #FeesMustFall movement'.

(Source: MISTRAy 2017)

Case study 12.2

The South African Democratic Teachers Union (SADTU) said the situation was disappointing and that its members were being forced to operate without crucial tools. This comes after the department conceded that dozens of schools in the province had yet to receive stationery and additional textbooks. According to SADTU, Grade 10 and 11 pupils were the worst affected. 'We are extremely worried that the same situation we were subjected to in 2012 is about to repeat itself,' said SADTU provincial secretary Matome Raphasha. In 2012, the province was embroiled in controversy when a court order declared that the non-delivery of textbooks to thousands of pupils was a failure by the Provincial and National Departments of Education. The court found that it was paramount to a 'violation of the rights to a basic education [and] equal dignity'. The decision was taken on appeal and last year the Supreme Court of Appeal upheld the High Court's findings.

(Source: News24 2017)

Case study 12.3

A South African man from Kliptown in Soweto is one of 10 finalists for the 2012 CNN Hero of the Year award ... Madondo was nominated for his work with the Kliptown Youth Programme (KYP). Madondo is a founder of the organisation and its chairperson. The main focus of the initiative is its tutoring programme, which runs four days a week. It provides tutoring for grade two to seven pupils and uses professional teachers to help grade eight to 12 children with subjects such as maths and science. Madondo is Soweto's ordinary hero who has made it his life mission to change his community. Growing up in Kliptown, in a one-room shack that he shared with seven other siblings, he knows the challenges of young people in this area. His family did not have enough money to keep him and all his siblings in school, but he was determined not to drop out.

He washed cars to earn enough money to pay his school fees and went on to become the first member of his family to graduate from high school. With his schooling behind him, he wanted to become an accountant, but his family did not have the means to send him to university. Looking back on his childhood, Madondo realised that education is the most powerful tool to empower people, and this led him to co-find the KYP. 'We feel education is the only key out of these challenging conditions that people live in,' he says. Kliptown is one of the oldest residential areas of Soweto and is home to about 45 000 people. Here people live in informal housing, some don't have access to services such as electricity and there is a high rate of unemployment. Many children from this community drop out of school because they don't have school uniforms and textbooks.

(Source: CNN 2012)

Key themes

- Formal education and informal education
- The role of education as a transmission of culture in society
- Hidden curriculum
- Bantu Education system
- Restructuring of education in post-apartheid South Africa
- Role of family in education

- The role of higher educational institutions in society
- Education and the labour market.
- Student protest for curriculum transformation #RhodesMustFall and #FeesMustFall
- Education in the Fourth Industrial Revolution
- The function of education in society.

12.1 Introduction

Education is a formal social institution that plays a decisive role in society by transmitting society's values and morals, shaping its views, upholding traditions, regulating our behaviour and bringing about change. The aim of this chapter is to show how one institution can contribute to the benefit of the entire society. The value of education is such that the right to education is a fundamental human right enshrined in the initiatives of the United Nations Declaration of Human Rights (United Nations 1948) and the Millennium Development Goals (United Nations 2000).

The three introductory case studies provide different viewpoints about schooling and education. In the first one the recent student protests since 2015 at higher education institutions (HEIs) reflect the prevailing and growing inequality in South Africa. The second one reflects how the state, under a system of democracy, is perpetuating inequality in the schools in Limpopo and disadvantaging its learners. The third one reflects how an ordinary citizen of South Africa, despite his deprived circumstances, runs an organisation that provides meals for children, helps with their school fees and provides after-school tutoring and assistance to about 400 children.

The case studies highlight that, although education is an integral component of society, our education system is part of a transforming society marked by vast inequalities and poverty. Learning begins the moment we are born

and continues throughout our lives. The act of learning is found in every society and transmitted both formally and informally. The process of learning can be taught in classrooms or in the fields, verbally, visually and orally. The institutionalisation of education is a central feature of modern societies. Not all children receive a formal education in a formal setting. Without formal education, many children can be disadvantaged for the rest of their lives. This is simply because education opens up opportunities for personal growth, social mobility and the capacity to be useful members of society. In the words of Nelson Mandela 'education is the most powerful weapon which you can use to change the world'.

12.2 Definition of sociology of education

The sociology of education is defined as the systematic study of the social institutions and the interrelationship between these institutions from a sociological viewpoint. Education can be viewed from a broad (or macro) perspective. Such a perspective focuses on how institutions such as economics, politics and religion influence and mould the education system. Education prepares young people for participation in society and is a powerful agent of socialisation. At the micro level, sociologists want to understand how basic factors such as having a meal, school uniforms, school fees, and access to public or private schooling can affect individuals and their interaction at schools.

The sociology of education is characterised by two dominant streams of thought: those who view education as imparting science and those who argue that education serves broader social functions. To fully understand this distinction, we examine how early theorists came to understand the role of education in society.

12.3 Theoretical frameworks of education

When looking at education from a sociological point of view, the traditional three distinct theoretical perspectives or frameworks are identified. These are the positivist or functionalist, the conflict and the interactionist perspectives. As you know from Chapter 1 in this textbook, the writings of early theorists such as Durkheim, Marx and Weber serve to lay the foundation for sociologists of education who used these theoretical underpinnings to understand the roles of education and schools in society. You will, throughout, need to think about which aspects of these theories articulate your own experience of higher education in South Africa today in the light of Africanisation or, better perhaps, Africanism and decolonial theory. Indeed, what are the central theoretical questions that need to be posed in the sociology of education in South Africa today?

12.3.1 Positivist or functionalist theory

From this theoretical perspective, strands of functionalism can be found in structural-functionalism and consensus or equilibrium theory. Durkheim, one of the early scholars to examine education from a sociological perspective, reflected on how education equipped children for their positions in later life (Hallinan 2000: 2). The functionalist approach has always used the popular analogy of the human body to understand society. The human body consists of numerous organs with specific functions all working together to create a harmonious whole. If one part breaks down, this has an effect on the entire system. Similarly, education makes up one part of the system in society; it is linked and contributes to the larger functioning of society as a whole. The economy, family, political and religious systems are interconnected and interdependent. The way each of these institutions work is towards maintaining social order. Education was particularly important for Durkheim in the maintenance of social order.

Durkheim's foremost contributions to sociology of education reside in his works entitled *Moral Education, The Evolution of Educational Thought* and *Education and Sociology* (Ballantine 1989). He placed significant weight on the position of values in society and the function of schools in transferring those values to the students. Further, his work

focused on analysing the relationship between schools and other public institutions, the interplay between education and social change and 'between schools and the function of a social system' (Hallinan 2000: 2). Critical to Durkheim's sociology is the 'notion of [the] primacy of *society* over the individual' (Meighan 1981: 232). Durkheim holds that a moral order is created by members of society to guide our actions. As one of his commentators argues, '[s]ociety commands us because it is exterior and superior to us, the moral distance between it and us makes it an authority before which our wills defer' (Meighan 1981: 232). Durkheim insisted that it was not possible to divorce the educational system from society. Education and society replicate each other. Durkheim emphasised the view that 'any change in society reflected a change in education and vice versa' (Ballantine 1989: 8). The highly influential American sociologist, Talcott Parsons, supported this view of Durkheim. Parsons (1959) understood schools as a social system. He examined how schools transmitted values and promoted social order and stability in society (Hallinan 2000: 2).

Functionalists consider the educational system as working or functioning to transmit the traditions, rules, values and skills from one generation to another (DeMarrais & LeCompte 1995). Structural functionalists argue that education maintains the 'accepted' culture (DeMarrais & LeCompte 1995). This view of 'accepted culture', however, infers that there is a consensus on what this 'accepted' culture is. Collective values or consensus is important in order to keep the system in balance. Sever (2012: 652) contends that knowledge must work toward 'solidarity and integration rather than pluralism and differentiation'. In Sever's view of Durkheim's understanding of education, teachers are seen as 'agents of legitimate knowledge transmission' while occupying themselves with teaching 'only for societal goods' (Sever 2012: 652). In line with this thinking, schools are also used to prepare students for work roles in adult life and to allocate and train a future workforce. This is the open or *manifest* intention of education. The *latent* or hidden function, however, is to train a future workforce by teaching skills and inculcating values and the attitudes of punctuality, cooperation and conformity, encourage socially appropriate behaviour and the acceptance of authority. Schools further function to sort or grade learners in terms of academic ability by measuring their performance in assessments. The same principles apply to all students, irrespective of ascribed factors of sex, race, family background or class. In this way, schools create a meritocracy whereby status is realised on merit alone. A *meritocracy* is a system based on an individual's ability and achievement. This creates a social hierarchy based on ability, and students or learners are distributed along this hierarchy in terms of academic achievement.

Given South Africa's legacy of apartheid and the **Bantu Education system**, the conflict perspective's critique of functionalism is highly critical of Durkheim's stance. Both conflict theorists and interactionists argue that Durkheim's theory did not address 'the function and allocation of adult roles; the gap between societal expectation of schools and actual school performance' (Ballantine 1989: 8). The functionalists' emphasis on value consensus, integration and stability all work to keep society in balance. Societies today are multicultural with highly diverse communities and schools that reflect this diversity. The concept of a shared culture in schools must be replaced in recognition of a multicultural one. While consensus and balance are required for the system to work, the functionalist perspective tends to ignore the diversity of interests, thoughts, ideologies and opposing interest groups in society. Society is not a homogeneous entity. Instead, it is highly heterogeneous with many subgroups, each with their own interests that they wish to advance.

12.3.2 Conflict theory

While functionalists view education as contributing positively to social order in society, conflict theorists adopt a different stance. The conflict approach points out the tensions in society resulting from both individuals and social groups competing for resources (Ballantine 1989). Two main groups are identified: the dominant and subordinate groups with differential access to power in society. Some authors loosely refer to these groups as 'haves' and 'have-nots'. The dominant group or 'haves' command power and privilege, and have access to resources and goods. The 'have-nots' lack power in society and this power dynamic between the two groups results in tensions and conflict between them (Ballantine 1989). Conflict theorists are concerned with the type of education given to children of the working classes, and the manner in which they receive it operates to serve ruling-class interests. The conflict theorists share the view with the functionalists that education prepares learners for their future roles in the family, the economy and society in general. It transmits the values of society to learners and serves to produce productive citizens. Marx (1977) had a different perspective, arguing instead that the education system perpetuated the dominance of one class over another. Two Marxist theorists, Bowles and Gintis (1976), contend that schools are used by the dominant class to retain power and control in society. Schools support the status quo (the social order as it is) and preserve inequality in society, especially under capitalism.

Education is known for exhibiting both *manifest* (obvious, stated) and *latent* (concealed, covert) functions of society. The manifest function is recognised and intended to provide skills and prepare learners for their future roles in society. The latent function is unrecognised and unintended, and is sometimes referred to as the **hidden curriculum** which prepares students to accept what is given and not to be critical or question things. The hidden curriculum is referred to as all the things that are learnt at schools that are *not* explicit, blatant or obviously taught as part of the curriculum. Teachers teach a set curriculum with a specific object in mind, yet at the same time unconsciously transmit a hidden meaning or subtext. For example, the emphasis on a Eurocentric curriculum tends to negate and undermine the knowledge context of authors from the global South. On the other hand, critiques of Euro-Northern American-centric perspectives often lean on thinkers from these environments who were critical of their own societies – some of whom supported struggles emanating from the global South.

The education system in America, squarely in the global North, according to Bowles and Gintis, is moulded by the capitalist economy to reproduce its particular needs. Education is thus shaped by economic needs, and reproduces citizens to serve the capitalist economy. Education hence perpetuates class inequalities in society. Bowles and Gintis (1976) show how schools train learners for their future occupational positions based on their social class position. While the manifest function is to train students for a useful productive life based on merit, working-class children are encouraged to be subservient, take orders and be obedient. Children of professional and more affluent parents are treated differently and encouraged to pursue leadership roles in society. For conflict theorists, this is the *manifest function* of education. In contrast, to repeat, the *latent functions* are the unintended and hidden outcomes of the objectives of educational institutions. The manifest function of the Bantu Education system in South Africa was to produce a docile, unskilled and obedient workforce. In contrast to the functionalists, Bowles and Gintis did not believe that education in capitalist societies was meritocratic. Instead, class background served as the important determining factor. The education of the black African working class under apartheid in South Africa is a clear example of this, but with racial oppression as key, yet underplayed in the main by Marxist theorists and scholars.

Conflict theorists also take issue with the concept of **credentialism**, which is the idea that some people are better than others based on their educational credentials. Credentialism is a status marker and denotes knowledge or expertise in an area. While the functionalists insist that credentialism rewards people for their achievements, conflict theorists argue that it perpetuates and further creates social divisions in society and rewards people unequally on basis of their class position. Conflict theorists argue that schools merely propagate social inequality in society. Although **race** was a major determining factor in South Africa, basic inequalities generally centred on social **class** in conflict theories. Education in South Africa instead was a centrally institutionalised part of a *racist, capitalist system* and major change was (and is) needed to bring about its transformation if this theoretical perspective is correct.

Although Weber's writings did not explicitly relate to education – with notable exceptions such as 'The typological position of Confucian education' (Weber, Gerth & Wright Mills 1991) – his work on bureaucracies, organisations and status provided a macro overview of how schools are organised. These writings also provided an interpretive perspective on how these situations came about and how we define them (Ballantine 1989). Weber's structure of an ideal type organisation, with its characteristics of the division of labour, administrative hierarchy, rules and regulations, formal relationships and rational behaviour, did thus enable him to provide a framework for the formal organisations of schools (Ballantine 1989: 2). Weber also considered the issue of 'status cultures' and how schools perpetuated this relationship among groups both inside and outside of schools. Power was an important component and together with conflicting interests and groups in society, could sway and put pressure on the education system in the interests of the dominant group. Weber argued that teachers and academics should keep their values under control in a classroom. The teacher or academic should only teach 'facts'. Weber was consciously arguing against Marx's position that facts and values were closely interwoven (Ritzer 1992). Weber also disagreed with Marx's analysis of stratification in terms of economic factors only. For Weber, the concept of stratification was multidimensional, and society was stratified in terms of economics, status and power (Ritzer 1992). His work, along with that of Georg Simmel (see Ritzer 1992), lay the basis for interactionist perspectives on education.

12.3.3 Symbolic interactionism

Symbolic interactionists put a lot of emphasis on how meanings are constructed. The focus of interactionist theory concentrates on the interactions of individuals and the behaviour of small groups. The macro theories of functionalism and conflict theory focused on large-scale broader institutional patterns of interaction. Those individuals sharing a culture have much in common in terms of their immediate experiences and norms and values, but differences are also recognised because of the individual's experiences of class and broader social experiences (Ballantine 1989). In our context, the experiences around race, of course, are crucial here. Educational perspectives using the interactionist approach concentrate on interactions between teacher, student, parental and peer-group relationships. Tracking and labelling theory are found within the interactionist perspective. Tracking or streaming is a sorting mechanism used to assign students to particular programmes or educational streams on the basis of evaluations. While some educators believe that this approach is beneficial to students as their specific needs can be catered for, the approach has also been criticised for creating and reinforcing inequality in society. Tracking can also lead to 'labelling' when educators distinguish between children as either 'gifted', 'bright,' 'dumb' or 'slow'. Labelling has been shown to lead to a self-fulfilling prophecy where students either aspire to the teacher's high expectation or perform poorly due to the low expectation of the teacher. The interactionist perspective is criticised for failing to acknowledge the agency of individuals in the education process. The emphasis on an exclusively micro-perspective by the interactionist perspective, however, fails to acknowledge how macro-level factors, such as the control of access to resources, can affect a school and its learners.

In the section that follows, a brief historical background of education in South Africa is given to provide an understanding of how the apartheid state used education to create and perpetuate an unequal society in South Africa. The move to democracy in 1994 required a transformation of the education system and a reconfiguration of the institutions of learning.

12.4 Historical background of education in South Africa

In 1945, a National Party politician, Mr JN le Roux, said: 'We should not give the natives any academic education. If we do, who is going to do the manual labour in the community?' This view resonated with the even earlier perspectives of British colonialists on the provision of education to the indigenous population in the 1800s. Formal schools did not exist in pre-colonial African societies. Instead, learning took place via observation, storytelling and the transmission of oral history. Children learnt alongside their elders by observing and copying tasks, and taking instruction, and past traditions were passed on through the medium of songs, stories and poetry (Christie 1985). Before the arrival of white settlers from Europe in 1652, the land was inhabited by different ethnic groups. The Khoi hunters and San herders were based around the Cape, the Xhosa-speaking people occupied the Eastern Cape, while the Nguni speakers lived in what is currently known as KwaZulu-Natal. Sotho speakers lived further inland. All these groups were subsistence farmers who lived off the land. Once Europeans from different countries arrived to settle in the Cape as farmers and traders, they dispossessed the indigenous groups of their land. Some farmers, known as the *trekboers*, set up farms far in the interior and were not very concerned about the government in Cape Town (Christie 1985). These first settlers operated under the umbrella of the Dutch East India Company (DEIC). Little attention was given to education, which was left mostly in the hands of the churches. The only schooling available for the Boers was limited to a few church-run schools, and 'two slave schools' were available for Africans (Johnson 1982: 215).

The first organised attempt at providing a formalised system of education was established by the British in 1806. They asserted their hegemony by using education as a tool to enforce the language and culture of the British. Here we begin to see the establishment of a dominant culture being put into place. The enforcement of English as the official language, with schools being organised in the British tradition with teachers from Britain, illustrates the dominance of one group over another. In 1812, a system of free schooling was implemented with English as the medium of instruction. The British imposed a deliberate plan of Anglicisation towards the Afrikaners, resulting in the near extinction of Dutch as a medium of instruction (Johnson 1982: 215). Afrikaner culture and language were systematically excluded from the formal educational system. From a conflict perspective, we can see how the British used education as a form of social control.

In 1839, a department of education was set up that funded local schools. The establishment of schools, at first sporadic, began mushrooming, with no control over the quality of education. Private schools, a few state schools, some state-aided schools and mission schools emerged (Christie 1985: 34). Access to schooling along social lines was already taking place. Wealthier families sent their children to private schools. While primary schools were free, secondary schools restricted access to those parents who could afford to pay school fees. After 1893, the government ensured that

the mission schools received funding to provide education for poorer white communities. Class cleavages were also becoming apparent between schools in towns and those in rural areas (Christie 1985). The schools were initially racially mixed, providing learning to whites, Africans and those of mixed race. It reflected the liberal thinking of the time. Functionalists would argue that this was an attempt to establish social order and achieve value consensus in society. By firmly placing English as the medium of instruction, it also served to establish the dominance of European culture. The conflict perspective would regard this as the domination of one group over another.

According to historians, schools functioned to provide basic reading, writing and arithmetic. This was the open, stated aim of the schools at that time, while at the same time enforcing 'discipline, obedience and the value of work' (Christie 1985: 36). Together with the overt manifest function of mission education, part of the agenda was also to instil a Western, more 'civilised' life for Africans and to impress upon them the value of hard work and a Christian way of life. The British government assisted the mission schools with funding and contributed to teachers' salaries. This had the dual function of having some sort of control over the mission schools, which in turn brought Africans under their power. The social control function of schools is evident here. This is not to say that all Africans attended schools or even attended regularly, but the British governors were also anxious about providing education to Africans as they were seen a pool of cheap, unskilled labour (Johnson 1982). The latent function or aim of education was to create a subservient, docile and racialised labouring class.

The bitter conflict between the British and the Afrikaners resulted in the South African War of 1899–1902. As victors, the British continued with their enforcement of Anglicisation in education. Recognising the 'socialising power of schools', the Afrikaner community insisted in being taught in their mother tongue (Johnson 1982: 216). The Afrikaner community was larger than the British, and this strength in numbers allowed them to successfully resist the British plan for assimilation. The protection and safeguarding of their language and culture led to the rise in Afrikaner nationalism. While the competing interests of these two groups of Europeans underplayed the racialised character of colonial society, poor white communities, mostly Afrikaners, were educationally disadvantaged in the process. A ripple effect was the increase in conflict between poor whites and Africans, who often competed for the same jobs. This led to strong Afrikaner opposition to the provision of education for Africans (Johnson 1982). A growing demand for the segregation of education, by Afrikaners in particular, led to a separate set of public schools for whites so their children did not have to attend the same mission schools as Africans. The interests of the British and the Afrikaners reflect the conflict theorists' views of domination of one group by another, but in the case of South Africa, this was a clear case of the predominance of racial domination. Access to resources was controlled by dominant groups, and education was used as a tool to subjugate a black labour force who were denied both political and social rights. Christie and Gordon (1990: 402) report that schooling for Africans was neither free nor compulsory; it was 'largely in the hands of missionaries; … poorly funded, sparsely provided and of varying quality'. In aligning itself with the pressures from the Afrikaner community, the British withdrew their support for African education and promoted segregated education. This meant that Africans needed to finance their own education. The significance of this tacit complicity between the British and Afrikaners against the Africans show how race defined lines of hierarchy and stratification and how they used the educational system to reinforce these differences in society as well.

This brief introduction to the establishment of an education system in South Africa demonstrates how education was used to cultivate social and racial cleavages in the 1800s. It also shows how the control of education, whether by the state or the church, was contested during the 19th century. In the latter part of the 20th century, a number of significant dates impacted on the direction of education in South Africa. In 1948, the victory of the National Party resulted in the implementation of apartheid, which legally entrenched and further institutionalised racial segregation under British colonial rule. While education for whites was freely available and compulsory, for the majority of black South Africans, education was marked by the lack of funds, and insufficient schools and teachers, with only a very small proportion of black children attending school. The Eiselen Commission was appointed in 1949 to review African education. Part of its recommendations was the passing of the Bantu Education Act in 1953, providing the mandate that all black South African schools be registered with the state. The term 'Bantu' in the policy of Bantu Education was a derogatory one and disrespectful to black people (Nel & Binns 1999). This referred to an inferior system of education when compared to that of whites. The enforcement of the Bantu Education Act resulted in a significant growth in the number of black children attending school. This Act, however, effectively closed down all church missionary schools that had provided reasonable education to many

black children, many of whom were to go on to assume the country's political leadership over 40 years later. The control of education was securely located in the Department of Bantu Education. The 1953 Act effectively removed the financing of education for Africans from state funding to the direct taxation paid by Africans themselves. Given the poor wages and dire conditions of the vast majority of black South Africans, significantly less money was spent on black children in comparison to white children.

During the period 1954 to 1955, black teachers and students protested against Bantu Education. Segregating education even further in line with apartheid policy, the Coloured Person's Education Act was passed in 1963 regulating the education of people of mixed race. Schooling was made compulsory under the Department of Coloured Affairs. Similarly, the 1965 Indian Education Act was passed with education for Indian children also made compulsory and with control of Indian education falling under the Department of Indian Affairs (Christie 1985: 55). In 1967 the National Education Act was promulgated enforcing the principles of Christian National Education. A summarised view of Christian National Education is provided in Van Niekerk (1999: 18):

> Christian National Education was embodied within the white education system and enforced in all former white schools, especially in Afrikaner schools. The official value system was that schools should have a broad Christian and national (meaning Afrikaner nationalist) character. The non-official value system was that of inculcating ethnocentrism and attitudes of both superiority and obedience … towards the state. The aim was obvious – namely to legitimise an own separate education system and maintain white supremacy and privileged social and economic positions.

After the establishment of Bantu Education, the numbers of African children attending schools increased, but the dropout rate was equally high. The education system represented 12 years of formal schooling with a matriculation certificate being written in the last year. The apartheid educational system firmly established patterns of segregation, discrimination and inequity across the different race groups and served to entrench social cleavages across South African society. From 1948 to 1993, the system of education was used to reflect the ideology of those in power and to cement their racialised control over society. Schools for Afrikaans and English children were free, and incorporated books and stationery. It was also compulsory from age seven until 16 or 'passing the school leaving certificate' (Johnson 1982: 219). On the other hand, education for Africans was not free or compulsory, and the medium of instruction was in an African language. The choice of subjects differed greatly between the white and African students, thus providing access for the Afrikaans and English children to better job prospects while confining African students to menial jobs. White students had a superior quality of education, while education for African students was of a poor quality, with under-resourced schools, overcrowded classrooms and poorly trained teachers (Johnson 1982). The conflict perspective of dominant and subservient class positions can be clearly seen, while the function of training workers for their roles in society is also apparent. The control of access to resources further served to strengthen the dominant class's superiority over the poorer classes. The institutionalisation of this stratification, which legitimately empowers one group over another, reinforces the conflict view of dominant and subordinate groups in society.

However, in the 1970s the need for a better-educated and skilled black workforce compelled business to put pressure on the apartheid government to build new schools in Soweto. This was in contradiction to the government's stance that students should attend school in their relevant homeland. Under pressure, 40 new schools were constructed in Soweto. This saw a significant surge in students attending high school, with the numbers increasing from 12 656 in 1972 to 34 656 in 1976 (see http://www.sahistory.org.za/topic/bantu-education-policy).

With an increase in the development of urban schools and the rise in numbers of young black South African students continuing their education, schools in predominantly black areas became the organs of protest and politicisation of the youth. One of the organisations in the forefront of this struggle was the South African Student Organisation (SASO), formed in 1969. A defining moment in history, on 16 June 1976, the Soweto uprising ruptured a nation and brought home the glaring disparities of the education system. The seams of the apartheid system were coming apart. In quoting the words of professor of sociology and central architect of apartheid, Dr Henrick Verwoerd, the 1976 Soweto Students Representative Council's stance on Bantu Education was unequivocal: 'We shall reject the whole system of Bantu Education whose aim is to reduce us, mentally and physically, into hewers of wood and drawers of water' (see http://africanhistory.about.com/od/apartheid/qt/ApartheidQts1.htm).

Figure 12.1 Hector Pieterson photo epitomising the 1976 Soweto uprising

When the high-school students, protesting against Afrikaans as a medium of instruction and for a better education, took to the streets, police responded with live bullets and teargas. The unleashing of anger by the youth, in one of the most brutal riots against the apartheid state and the equally aggressive reaction by the South African police, ushered in a new era of action against the state. Over 660 black South Africans were killed in the uprising, and both black schools and universities were burned down, and buildings destroyed as a result of the revolts (Hare & Savage 1979). The shocking pictures made international headlines and pressure on the South African government to amend its policies intensified. It all came a little too late. June 16 is now observed as a South African national holiday. Youth Day honours the countless young people who gave up their lives in the struggle against apartheid and Bantu Education.

With the 1976 uprising putting the spotlight firmly on Bantu Education, the 1980s saw an intensification of the struggle for liberation. Very little formal schooling took place in black schools. The motto was 'liberation first, education later'. These students became known as the 'struggle generation' or the 'lost generation'. Student boycotts and protests, together with brutal acts of violence by the South African police against students, became commonplace. During the period 1988 to 1994, about 6 000 young people under the age of 25 lost their lives and a number of schools were burnt down in the KwaZulu-Natal area (Jacobs 1999: 117).

Owing to the politicisation of black schools in the 1980s, the schools were characterised by a 'boycott culture'. This inherited legacy continued in the early 1990s with the absence by both teachers and students at schools, political standoffs by both groups, lack of resources and inequalities in school resources (Nel & Binns 1999). Schools in townships and working-class areas had overcrowded classrooms and low matriculation pass rates between 1994 and 2006 (Chisholm 2012). These schools were also fenced off for protection and shown to have high learner absenteeism rates. Coupled with this, the long-lasting effects of Bantu Education were 'underdevelopment, a poor self-image among learners, economic depression, unemployment, crime and a highly unskilled and poorly educated workforce' (http://www.sahistory.org.za/topic/bantu-education-policy). The findings support Johnson's (1982: 214) argument that education was 'manipulated for stratification purposes' and served as an 'instrument of social engineering'. The discussion above is a clear example of how education can be used as a form of social control and stratification as argued by conflict perspective sociologists.

The higher education sector did not remain unscathed by the apartheid government. As all areas of learning were racially grouped, universities were also created in the 1960s along the lines of being 'racially/ethnically separate and unequal' (Hugo 1998: 11). The geographical location of universities reflected the uneven geographies of the apartheid state. The English-medium universities of Cape Town, Witwatersrand, Natal and Rhodes opposed the formation of these racially designated universities. The universities of Cape Town and Witwatersrand were regarded as 'open universities' and permitted students of colour to register on the basis of academic merit (Hare & Savage 1979). However, after 1959, the government passed the Extension of University Education Act, which restricted black students from attending the 'open universities' except under special conditions. The Act instituted separate universities for blacks at the University of the North (1960), the University of Zululand (1960), the University of Western Cape (1960), the University of Durban-Westville (1960), the Medical University of South Africa (1976) and a multi-campus institution called Vista University (1982). The independent 'homeland' states created by the apartheid government founded the University of Transkei (1977), the University of Bophuthatswana (1980) and the University of Venda (1982) respectively (Hugo 1998) and incorporated the University of Fort Hare (1916).

The apartheid-led South African government also openly supported and comprehensively funded some institutions over others, creating further divisions among universities. This reinforced the privilege of a select group of white South African institutions over others. The conflict perspective's view of one privileged group having access to better resources over another is clearly evident. The universities of Cape Town, Witwatersrand, Stellenbosch, Rhodes, Natal and Pretoria and technikons such as Port Elizabeth, Witwatersrand and Pretoria became known as historically advantaged institutions (HAIs). In contrast, 17 institutions, comprising universities and technikons restricted to the enrolment to blacks (African, coloured and Indian) students, became known as the historically disadvantaged institutions (HDIs). These institutions were underfunded and under-resourced in comparison to the HAIs. Further, the obvious 'unequal funding regimes' for the HAIs and the HDIs produced different results for the two sectors (Barnes 2006).

Although the HDIs were academic institutions, the freedom of academics was severely curtailed under apartheid. Many of the students attending these institutions came from underprivileged backgrounds and fell into arrears. Compounding this situation were limited educational facilities, administrative incapacities, reduced academic offerings, few sporting and cultural facilities and opportunities, and high teaching loads of undergraduate courses. Junior and inexperienced academics, insulated from established academics, were often appointed at HDIs and looked down upon from the established HAIs (Barnes 2006). The academic institutions thus also became sites of contestation. They came to represent a microcosm of apartheid society. Students gave voice to their anger by protesting against their perceived inequality at the HDIs, but these forms of protest represented a larger call for the inequality in society as a whole. The HDIs thus experienced high levels of unrest and boycotts against the bureaucratic administration, and served as sites of violence and brutal police action.

12.5 Restructuring of education – post-apartheid South Africa

The transition to a new democratic South Africa necessarily implied a complete overhaul of the country's major educational institutions and schooling system. This was required to take place within a framework of transformation to address the three main issues of access, equity and redress. How can a new sociology of education begin to address these changes, and from which theoretical standpoints – functionalist, interpretivist, conflict or decolonial – will best describe, analyse and chart a way forward for this new framework? The reality of 1994 was that a large percentage of South Africa's workforce was unskilled – one of the manifest functions of the Bantu Education system. McKay (2007) argues that a high number of adults were functionally illiterate. Literacy levels were so poor that many were unemployable. There was a severe shortage of professional, technical and skilled expertise in the country. Even after the year 2000, skills were still in short supply (Kraak 2007). Medical, engineering, nursing and teaching graduates were being lured by lucrative work offers in foreign countries, leaving a growing and severe skills shortage in the country, which further compounded the skills shortage problem.

The new government recognised that the previous educational system was dysfunctional and that it failed to address the needs of a new democratic South Africa. At the same time, the restructuring of education must be contextualised within the contradictory pressures South Africa was facing. On the one hand, it needed to reconstruct every sector of society, and on the other it needed to meet the demands of the global economy and produce skilled knowledge workers to do so. In line with the transformation of the broader education system, a new curriculum was being engineered with a variety of stakeholders, under the auspices of the National Training Board, during 1991–1997. The stakeholders included COSATU, several government institutions such as Transnet, Eskom, the technikons, the National Education Department and industrial training boards attempted to create a curriculum that would effectively prepare learners for beyond the classroom and make them productive citizens (Jacobs 1999: 118).

As early as the 1970s, black trade unions had taken up aspects of this attempt by demanding a living wage from employers. This demand was refused on the basis that workers were unskilled and therefore could not ask for a living wage. Training was, however, viewed as an important step towards improving workers' skills. Training is a form of learning that can take place at the workplace to improve the skills, knowledge and competencies of workers to improve their work performance. Part of the vision of the new collaborative institutional arrangements, the National Training Board was to integrate education and training and to view learning as a continuous and lifelong process (Erasmus & Van Dyk 2003). To facilitate this, in 1995, the ministers of labour and education established a statutory body, the South African Qualifications Authority (SAQA), to oversee the development and implementation of the National Qualifications Framework (NQF). All education and training bodies in South Africa must affiliate themselves to the principles and guidelines of the NQF, which records levels of learning achievement and ensures that the skills and knowledge that have been learned are recognised throughout the country. The objectives of the NQF as outlined in the NQF Act 67 of 2008 below and illustrated graphically in Figure 12.1 (NQF Act 2008) are:

- to create a single integrated national framework for learning achievements

- to facilitate access to, and mobility and progression within, education, training and career paths
- to enhance the quality of education and training
- to accelerate the redress of past unfair discrimination in education, training and employment opportunities.

The link between schooling, tertiary education and training cannot be overemphasised. The new government sought to ensure that learning should take place at every level in society and was a way to upgrade the skills of workers in a post-apartheid South Africa. To enable this possibility, a core principle of the NQF was to ensure a new way of thinking about education, a paradigm shift that viewed education as a process of lifelong learning. A further aim was to remove not only the traditional barriers between how education and training was viewed but to remove the barriers between 'different knowledges, disciplines or subjects' (Ensor 2004: 340). Ensor hoped that this would erode the deeper barrier based on race and class as well. We begin to see how education under the new framework is very different to how it was perceived in the past, both from a functionalist and conflict perspective. As we will see, however, the challenge from a decolonial perspective was still to arise.

A further important objective of the NQF states that it is 'designed to contribute to the full personal development of each learner and the social and economic development of the nation at large' (NQF Act 2008). In line with this objective, the aim of the NQF was to bridge the chasm between formal academic education and vocational training (Ensor 2004: 340). Learning here also encompasses different types of learning: part-time, full-time, adult basic education and in-company training (Erasmus & Van Dyk 2003). This essentially linked the worlds of training and education. From the vantage of the government, this important step recognised that learning and education were intimately connected to the development of the person as a whole and to prepare graduates for the workplace and society in general. This sounds like a functionalist view of education. How would a conflict or interactionist theorist argue differently? What does decolonial theory have to say in this regard?

In line with these changes, South Africa elected to introduce a system of outcomes-based education (OBE) in schools. The system was phased in by 1998 and was officially known as 'Curriculum 2005'. The principles of OBE are listed below (Erasmus & Van Dyk 2003: 4):
- It is learner centred, and takes the learners' needs into consideration.
- Takes the learners' differences into account.

- Encourages parents and learners to participate democratically in their experience of education.
- Focuses on responsibility.
- Allows learners to achieve their full potential.

The decision to implement OBE was a political one taken by the new government with the aim of removing racial inequalities inherited from apartheid education. Countries that have successfully implemented the OBE system are Canada, Australia, New Zealand and the US. In many of these countries, a period of 10 years was taken to implement such a system. But the government wished to introduce the new system in just four years. Questions about the haste at which the government sought to implement such a policy, given the state of the schooling system post-1994, abounded. The prerequisites of a successful implementation of an OBE system are well-trained teachers and well-resourced classrooms. The ushering in of OBE in schools in 1997 was founded on the view that teachers would develop their own curricula and supplement their teaching and learning resources from a wide array of references and sources (Chisholm 2012). This belied the assumption that teachers in the majority of schools had access to the available resources. The opposite was in fact true.

In 2002, the minister of education requested a review of the OBE system or Curriculum 2005. The review committee found that implementation of the system was compounded by factors such as:
- a skewed curriculum structure and design
- lack of alignment between curriculum and assessment policy
- inadequate orientation, training and development of teachers
- lack of learning materials and variation of the quality of them
- policy overload and limited transfer of learning in classrooms
- shortages of personnel and resources to implement and support Curriculum 2005, and inadequate recognition of curriculum as the core business of education departments (Chisholm 2012).

The Committee also found that the system needed 'sufficient resourcing, manageable time-frames for implementation and consistent monitoring and review'. Teachers in the majority of the poverty-stricken areas had neither the resources nor adequate training on how to use the varied resources available in the classrooms (Chisholm 2012). Furthermore, the teachers themselves had been trained

in a 'rigid, authoritarian education system' (Nel & Binns 1999: 121). This move from an authoritarian functionalist-orientated model to a participatory democratic approach involved a variety of stakeholders, and required a paradigm shift or new way of thinking.

Box 12.1

What theoretical viewpoint do you think best interprets the decision to implement OBE? Do you think the functionalist approach describes this approach as it was supported by the capitalists as being positive for the economy and for the social development of society? Or do you think a combination of the functionalist and symbolic interactionist can be applied here, as the OBE approach is focused on the interaction of the learner and the teacher, and the learner with other learners? What would have been different had a decolonial perspective been applied in this instance?

In short, as a result of the review, in 2010 the Department of Basic Education decided to introduce the Curriculum Assessment Policy Statements (CAPS) to strengthen the current National Curriculum Statement (NCS). This reformulated policy is a comprehensive document to provide for what teachers need to teach and assess on a grade-by-grade and subject-by-subject basis. One of the aims of the new revamped policy was to reduce the administrative load on teachers and to provide for more consistency across teaching. The new curriculum intends to provide a 'week-by-week planning for teachers to follow, provide clear guidance in terms of pacing and progression and in terms of assessment requirements' (see http://www.oxford.co.za/page/about-us/newsroom/489550-CAPS-What-you-need-to-know).

The discussion above briefly illustrates the far-reaching efforts of transforming the education system post-1994. It explains the path the current South African government uses to frame its educational policies. The education system was overhauled in line with the democratic government's views on transformation and principles of access, equity and redress. New structures such SAQA and the NQF were institutionalised to steer change in the education sector. At a school level, these changes manifested in the form of Curriculum 2005 and OBE. Curriculum 2005 was the framework through which this change was managed, and OBE was an approach looking at what is being learned and how is learning taking place (De Waal 2004). The CAPS system, implemented in 2012, was used to strengthen the current national curriculum and to reduce the administrative load on teachers.

The higher education sector found itself in a state of immense flux as it welcomed the ending of the isolation of apartheid. At the same time, pressing concerns for change in the higher education sector impacted on the sector, both at home and globally. The massification of higher education put additional demands on an already pressured higher education system. Universities were compelled to be accountable for their products and services to the public. Students were becoming selective consumers of knowledge, and chose courses that would gain them entry into the marketplace. For black students, the emergence from decades of apartheid education and the hope for a new democratic, free and equal society created enormous expectations, particularly among those immersed in the struggle for free access to universities and hope for a better future. This expectation has yet to be realised. The HDIs continue to be under-resourced and experience problems alluded to earlier in the chapter. The economy could not afford, in the era of neoliberal globalisation, to inject more money into already overburdened system. From a conflict perspective, previously advantaged institutions were still being privileged over the historically disadvantaged ones. Even under a democratic dispensation, privilege over access to resources exist and certain groups were given preference over others, reinforcing the conflict perspective of exclusion and inclusion, 'the haves' and the 'have-nots'.

In 1994, the higher education system consisted of 36 separate institutions in South Africa. Historically, South Africa's HEIs reflected the racial makeup of the country, resulting in 'black' and 'white' institutions. In 2004, a major overhaul in HEIs took place, resulting in the mergers of some institutions, some remaining untouched and others closed down. From 36 institutions, only 23 publicly funded universities remained. Transformation on all levels was urgently required. The universities reflected the problems in society: there was a disproportionate level of access and opportunities for staff and students across race, gender, class and even geographical locality. Disparities in the ratio of black and female staff compared to whites and males remained worrying. The racial profile of university councils, staff and students needed radical transformation. In line with the discriminatory practices of the universities, there was also a shortage of skilled graduates in science, engineering, technology and commerce, as well as black and

female graduates in these fields (Strydom & Fourie 1999). Suitably qualified black academics across all disciplines were in short supply, and many institutions implemented affirmative action programmes to redress the imbalances. Compounding the problem was the 'academic brain drain', where black academics were enticed by lucrative government positions promising higher status and substantially better salary packages. Universities could not compete with these salary packages and lost highly skilled black academics to the government and private sector. Lucrative salaries were not the only factors. University environs were slow to embrace change. Together with the bureaucratisation of academia, large teaching loads and pressure to publish prompted black academics into the government or private sector (Hugo 1998). As a result, the sector was characterised by low staff morale, uncertainty and large-scale resignations (Maree 2010).

This section of the chapter highlighted the transformation and challenges facing the higher education sector in South Africa post-1994. The next section elaborates on the current scenario in South Africa and the education sector in particular to understand the impact of the transformative educational policies that the government has put in place.

12.6 The current scenario: Challenges facing the education system

Current research and literature on education in South Africa indicates that the state's education goals have not yet been achieved. The majority of the population continues to reside in poverty, and unemployment remains a pressing concern. The interconnection between the state, broader socioeconomic issues and society's impact on the individual and the family within the context of education cannot be overemphasised. From the discussion in the previous section, do the functionalist, conflict and symbolic interactionist perspectives begin to provide for an understanding of the transformative agenda of education in a democratic South Africa? Do we need a new theoretical approach to understand how educational institutions must serve society in a transformative context? Can decolonial theory serve this purpose?

This section will contextualise the many challenges facing education within a framework of the state, society, schooling and the family. The relationship between these institutions and education is graphically illustrated in Figure 12.1 and will be discussed further in the following four sections of this chapter.

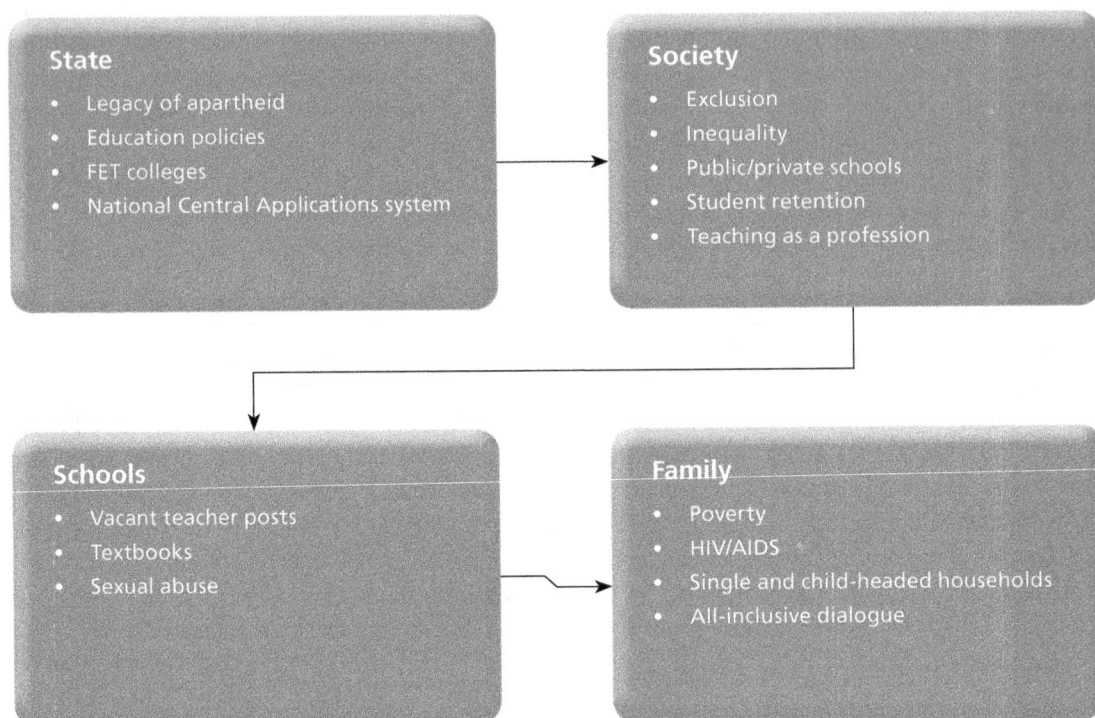

Figure 12.2 Framework for education
(Source: Adapted from Maree 2010)

12.7 State

After 25 years of democracy, the problems with all levels of schooling and higher education in South Africa remain dire. The government has successfully reconstituted the education system into a single unified national system. Statutory bodies such as SAQA and the NQF are in place to monitor and oversee quality assurance in education, skills development, adult education and early childhood development. The state embraces education from the perspective of early childhood development to adult basic education through to skills development at the workplace, and ensures quality assurance bodies are in place to monitor and evaluate these processes. This reflects a functionalist perspective to ensure that the different parts of the education system cohere and create consensus in society. The government has also been proactive and implemented pro-poor education policies such as the fee-free schools, nutrition and transport programmes (Motala 2017). An interactionist perspective shows that factors such as the lack of school fees, basic food and transport services clearly have a negative effect on the development of learners.

Deeper tensions in society remain. Poverty, rising unemployment and increasing levels of inequality tarnish South Africa's image of a successful democracy. The wealth distribution in South Africa remains largely in favour of

white South Africans. This inequality is evident in the public schooling sector as well. The country has 26 000 public schools (Schools4SA 2019). Some of these schools are in a decrepit state with basic facilities such as sanitation, running water and safe buildings still sorely lacking. Equal Education, a non-governmental organisation (NGO), highlighted the state of public schools by pointing out that 20 000 public schools have no libraries, 76 per cent have no water supply, 4 500 still use pit toilets and 913 have no toilets at all (Nal'ibali 2019; SABC News Online 2019).

Besides infrastructural concerns, studies show that South African learners are far behind their contemporaries in language literacy, language skills and reading (Wanner 2019). The Department of Basic Education decision to lower the requirements to achieve a National Senior Certificate (matric) pass has been widely criticised and debated. To pass matric, a learner needs to pass three subjects with a minimum of 40 per cent and three subjects with a minimum of 30 per cent, one of which must be a home language with a minimum of 40 per cent. In 2018, matriculants passed the National Senior Certificate exam, achieving a pass rate of 78.2 per cent. However, only 33.6 per cent of these students qualified for admission into Bachelor studies. With the current pass barrier of 30 per cent, it was recorded that 58 per cent of matriculants passed mathematics in

2018. However, if the pass rate were set at 40 per cent, this number would decrease to 37.1 per cent. The systematic lowering of matriculant pass rates has serious consequences for tertiary education. Lowering of standards at secondary level creates a first-year cohort of students who are academically unprepared for tertiary education. This is one contributor to the alarmingly high dropout rate among first-year university students. According to Viljoen (2019), 50 per cent of university students in South Africa drop out in their first year.

The lowering of standards has been criticised by widely respected educationists, and raises concerns about the quality of learners entering higher education and their ability to cope at tertiary level. In turn, some universities have instituted their own entrance level assessments to filter students. This has had an impact on the quality of graduates produced by HEIs and the length of time taken to complete a qualification. In higher education, about 50 per cent of registered students drop out of their studies during or at the end of their first year of study and only 15 per cent complete their studies in the minimum time required. In 2014, the Centre of Higher Education launched a multi-institutional research and development project to assess the implementation of extended curriculum programmes. The programme aims to alleviate the 'articulation gap' – the jump between schooling and higher education that remains a problem in South Africa (Prince & Yeld 2012). The move to a four-year degree would go a long way towards assisting students manage the gap and transition from school children to young adults at HEIs. Extensive preparation in terms of career guidance and counselling also needs to be provided to assist with this transition. The 2014 project found that the programmes have played a significant role in the retention and success of underprepared black students and are therefore promising for the redress of the South African tertiary curriculum (CHED 2016).

Just after the 2012 matric results were released, school leavers and their parents remained unconvinced that further education and training (FET) colleges could compete alongside a university qualification – to which it is viewed as a poor second cousin. In 2012, the Higher Education and Training (HET) minister Blade Nzimande mobilised resources to attract learners to the 50 public FET colleges. Despite Nzimande's media campaigning, negative stereotypes of FET persisted. For the post-1994 generation and especially first-generation entrants to university, graduating at a university is seen as matter of immense honour and prestige, especially for students from previously disadvantaged backgrounds. There is a social expectation that university degrees are more

highly valued and will allow for greater mobility in society. The value of achievement as espoused by the functionalist is evident here. The view from students and parents alike is that a FET education is a 'lowering of one's standard' and will disadvantage these students against university qualified graduates. The view by parents is that government is 'trying to provide a dumping site, while pretending to help our children access higher education' (Nkosi 2013: 6).

In 2019, the FET debate erupted once again in the mass media with the introduction of the General Education Certificate (GEC) which will allow pupils to leave school after the completion of Grade 9. The GEC is currently in development through a pilot study expected to conclude in July 2020. The fundamental argument for the proposed GEC is that it will 'equip learners with the values, knowledge and skills that will enable them meaningful participation in society and establish a firm foundation for skills development that will prepare students for the workplace' (Hans 2019: 2). Moreover, it is argued that it will be able to fill the annual gap of 10 000 artisans in the South African labour market (Hans 2019). However, the GEC has received criticism for its potential to devalue education, thereby decreasing the skills of the future South African labour market.

Alongside the valuing of a university education are contending notions of space and access to universities. In this regard, the Council on Higher Education (CHE) was seeking to implement the first phase of a national central applications system by 2013. The Department of Higher Education and Training (DHET) publicised the Central Applications System (CAS) in 2012 as a mechanism to deal with the complications arising out of the large volumes of late applications. In April 2019, the DHET legislated the CAS Bill, which will provide for a one-stop application where students can apply at multiple institutions on one form and with one application fee. While the central applications system will be phased in, it will not resolve the problems of lack of space in tertiary institutions. For example, in 2017 the University of Johannesburg received more than 135 000 applications but only had space for 10 500 first-time students while the University of Witwatersrand handled 69 000 applications and can only allocate 6 200 undergraduate positions (Seeth 2017). This raises important questions about our higher education system and the provision of access to these institutions. Who controls access to them and how can one institution receive 135 000 applications and only have space for 10 500 students? The central admissions system will also eliminate the problem of late applications taking place at the beginning of each year where long queues of hopeful applicants line the admissions doors of many tertiary institutions. On a deeper level, the sheer numbers of these applications indicate a hunger for education and the expectations of what a tertiary qualification can do, not only for individuals but also their family and community. Maree (2010: 87) refers to the trap that learners and communities find themselves in – that is, 'inequality, unemployment and poverty' – which appears to be more prevalent now than in 1994. Education is seen as key to overcoming these traps and as an opportunity of uplifting oneself out of poverty. There is thus this huge demand for a tertiary level education, together with the view that a degree offers more prestige and will make the graduate more employable.

Theoretically speaking, the evidence challenges the functionalist view of education as a meritocratic system; clearly, opportunity is not available for everybody with all competing on equal terms. Bowles and Gintis refer to this as the 'myth of meritocracy'. The point is that that inequality remains pervasive in South Africa and is reflected in access to and the experience of higher education, as the three case studies in the beginning of the chapter only too clearly show.

12.8 Society

South Africa is still a society marked by deep cleavages of disparities in income. Research by the Social Policy Research Group at Stellenbosch show that 'the persistence of these patterns of income distribution ...overlap between race, language, culture, education level and neighbourhood' (Van der Berg et al 2011). The research further emphasises how the quality of teaching and schooling in poor communities further embeds 'exclusion and marginalisation' in society (Van der Berg et al 2011). Various authors indicate that resources in township schools are still lacking compared to those in formerly white schools (Nel & Binns 1999; Vally & Dalamba 1999; Motala 2006; Robinson 2019). Early in the 1990s, many black parents took to either moving to former 'white' areas or transporting their children over long distances to better resourced and wealthier schools in these suburbs (Nel & Binns 1999; Nzimande 2009). They were convinced that the quality of education and resources were superior in former 'white' or 'Indian' areas. Research by Fataar (2009: 3) shows that 60 per cent of learners preferred to attend schools away from their area of residence, and Fataar (2009) and Jansen (2012) support the view that township schools have continued to produce insignificant results. The inequalities in the disadvantaged communities continue to persist and appear embedded in the schools as well, to which the focus now turns.

The public schools are structured in terms of 'quintiles'. The lowest or poorest 20 per cent of the schools are in quintile one and the richest in quintile five (Ogbonnaya 2019). The poor and under-resourced schools are in quintiles one to three and can be found in the rural areas and townships. These schools remain under-resourced and as a result perform much more poorly. Research by Van der Berg et al (2011) shows that by the age of eight, children in the top 20 per cent of the population (top quintile) far outperform those in the lower four quintiles. Thus, from an early age, obvious disparities are apparent in the performance between children from poorer communities and those from well-off homes. The results of the education system then seem to reinforce the social classes in society and reflect the conflict view that education serves as a tool for reproducing the class structure in society. The schooling environments in these poorer communities exhibit poor discipline, weak management and poor administrations, coupled with a lack of suitably qualified and experienced teachers (Van der Berg et al 2011). Overcrowding remains a concern in schools located in quintiles one to three, and the lack of mathematics and physical science teachers in these schools is also worrying (Nkosi 2013; Ogbonnaya 2019). While the Department of Education has emphasised that school infrastructure and development is a priority, there are still 300 mud schools in the Eastern Cape (Nkosi 2013). The legacy of the apartheid system still remains imprinted on society. While the equality of opportunity under democracy is available, social class inequalities still persist, and this acts as a barrier to growth for all.

The private or independent schools, as defined by the South African Schools Act (DoE 1996), comprise about three per cent of the entire schooling population (Ryan 2019). Some analysts were critical of the expansion of private schools, arguing that the state resources would be better directed at those schools in abject poverty. Private schools were seen as hurdles to nation building and regarded as elitist (Motala & Dieltiens 2008). Functionalists see education as providing for upward mobility, but for the conflict theorists this mobility is restricted because of the lack of access to resources and the privileging of certain groups in society.

The Independent Schools Association (Isasa) has made it a precondition that if schools wish to remain members of the organisation, then they should be committed to diversity and hire more black teachers. It was recognised that a growing black middle class was a key determining factor in the growth of private schools (Govender 2012: 6). It seemed that race was still being equated with quality and that 'whiteness' was synonymous with excellence, according to the head of Isasa, Dr Jane Hofmeyr (Govender 2012). Divergent views are offered for this statement.

The association argues that both black and white parents originally argued against the employment of black teachers, and black parents in particular still held the belief that 'white teachers provided a better quality of education' (Govender 2012: 6). Private schools also found it difficult to recruit and then retain black academic staff. However, black teachers employed by private schools end up teaching African languages or subjects such as Life Orientation or Technology rather than those in which they specialise. Race here has been equated with 'whiteness' and excellence. Black parents are themselves perpetuating discrimination by arguing that black teachers are not suitably skilled. The issue then is not one of race but rather of class. Thus, the deep-seated views of racial prejudice have not yet been overcome by 25 years of democracy, but instead rears its head in new ways, such as both racial and class bigotry.

What adds to redressing past inequalities is the lack of a sufficient pool of black graduates who choose teaching as a career. Initiatives are being taken to address these challenges, and internships at some private schools have been implemented to groom young people to become teachers. However, teaching as a profession is not highly regarded in society, not least because salary scales are low in comparison to the important function of teaching and education. Greater effort clearly needs to be made by the state in uplifting the profession and value of teaching, and the remuneration associated with it.

12.9 Schools

Problems in the schooling sector have already been alluded to in previous sections. There are many pressing issues that require urgent attention. In 2013, 21 000 vacant teacher posts remained unfilled (Nkosi 2012). While this number has significantly decreased to 2 041 unfulfilled posts in 2018, schools in rural and township areas and urban areas are disproportionately affected (Magubane 2018). The consequence is that poorer schools are compelled to limit their range of subject offerings as they are unable to afford the teachers and have to deal with larger class sizes, all of which impacts of the quality of delivery (Nkosi 2012). The South African Democratic Teachers' Union (SADTU) criticised the funding model used by the Department of Education to determine posts as it focused on numbers of pupils as opposed to the 'subject needs of specific schools' (Nkosi 2012). Township schools and rural-based schools do not have enough teachers. Unlike urban schools, they are unable to employ additional teachers with funds from their school governing funds. Moreover, the DHET reported that 5 139

teachers in South Africa are un- or underqualified, with the vast majority located in rural KwaZulu-Natal (Savides 2017). The problems in the teaching sector remain grave. How do we begin to address them? The problems stated above do not only pertain to the education department but reflect the structural inequalities still prevailing in society.

Since democracy, one of the more controversial highlights of the 2017 school calendar was the non-delivery of textbooks in the Limpopo province as provided in Case study 12.2. The textbook crisis not only highlights some of the problems in the provision of education, but in fact reveals deeper tensions in the country as a whole regarding lack of service delivery, problems of mismanagement of funds, corruption and fraud. The problem needs to be taken a step further and analysed in terms of access and perpetuating inequality in society. From the conflict view, access to resources is still being controlled by a dominant group. While the provision of textbooks to schools appears to have improved, questions remain as to how a new sociology of education can begin to argue for a change in access to resources and provide workable responses to a range of similar issues that continue to confront education in South African today.

Deeper concerns in the schooling system, for instance, relate to the increasing rate of sexual abuse at schools. A 2001 Human Rights Watch report on sexual violence and sexual harassment of female pupils in South African schools states that the high rate of teenage pregnancy results from 'sexual harassment or rape by male pupils or teachers' (John 2012b). At a conference held in 2012 attended by civil society organisations, education and child's rights NGOs, the conference detailed alarming figures and information relating to issues such as 'pupil-against-pupil sexual violence, the selling of sexual videos, the development of 'taxi-queen' pupils who offer sex in lieu of taxi rides, incidents of violent rape cases, to other cases involving the exchanging of sex for marks' (John 2012b: 13). These stories are indicative of deeper problems in our social fabric manifesting in the abuse of children. The current spate of gender-based violence against women in particular reflects the deep-rooted violence pervasive in our society. How do we begin to explain this from a sociological point of view? From a functionalist perspective, is it a breakdown of norms and values of society or, from a conflict perspective, does it reflect a lack of social power from certain groups in society? Is the prevailing social inequality in society contributing to this problem? To repeat, how does a new sociology of education begin to address these issues in South Africa?

12.10 Family

Education in South Africa is now compulsory for all children of school-going age. The Department of Education, however, remains concerned that a large number of such children are not attending schools. Some of the factors that have been identified are poverty, HIV and AIDS, unemployment and household responsibilities (Patel 2006). Other pertinent issues affecting learners are overcrowded homes, and the increasing number of single-parent families and child-headed households that prevails in South Africa. Parents from poor socioeconomic backgrounds are also under pressure to bear the 'indirect costs of schooling in terms of transport, school fees, and uniforms' (Motala 2007).

Education as an institution thus cannot be divorced from rest of society – learners, parents, teachers and educators are all intimately linked. Witten (2012: 39) talks of an 'inclusive education dialogue' where all stakeholders, not only important role players such as academics, education officials and policymakers, are involved, but at a micro level, parents, teachers, community organisations and NGOs need to come together to talk about how to support each other's initiatives and contribute to the holistic development of the learner. Witten (2012) illustrates how this 'inclusive education dialogue' is taking place in the Eastern Cape, a province known for its poverty and systemic education crisis. In the area, basic needs such as the provision of basic nutritious food, school uniforms and fees are lacking in households, and this affects the cognitive and developmental functioning of school pupils. These are the social problems that learners face at home and are brought to school as well, adding to the already heavy load of teachers. However, if a collective effort is made to address the issues, then the problem does not only lie on the shoulders of the Department of Basic Education.

What emerges from all of this is that the role of education in a new democratic South Africa is closely intertwined with the development of the nation-state. To what extent can the functionalist view of education promote a sense of national identity and social solidarity? Or in a society divided by such deep poverty and inequality, can we still talk of social cohesion? This chapter has already shown that student protests in South Africa are a common practice to contest the education system in ways that will make it more transformative and accessible for all students. South African universities saw major student protests in 2015 and 2016, with the #RhodesMustFall and #FeesMustFall movements gaining international attention, and these continue unabated especially in institutions of

higher learning previously designated as disadvantaged institutions or historically black universities.

12.11 Student protest for curriculum transformation: #RhodesMustFall and #FeesMustFall

The call for decolonisation of the South African curriculum was popularised by the University of Cape Town student movement #RhodesMustFall, which resulted in the removal of the statue of Cecil John Rhodes on 9 April 2015. The movement, however, entailed more than the removal of the symbolic significance of the Rhodes statue. #RhodesMustFall was deeply rooted in the broader discontent for higher education to transform since 1994 and the preservation of structural practices that exclude many black Africans.

Historically, South African tertiary education institutions were formed to enlighten the African mind through Eurocentric curricula rooted in capitalism, patriarchy and racism. Today, Eurocentrism ingrained in the curriculum excludes many African students and staff who feel underrepresented in and marginalised by their institutions. To make the curriculum more inclusive, calls for decolonisation were conceptualised as the meaningful inclusion of African theories and language, increasing the number of black students and staff across campuses nationally, incorporating marginalised LGBTQI, female and disabled student bodies, removal of colonial symbolism and addressing racist campus culture in formerly white universities (MISTRAy 2017).

At the centre of attention for the decolonisation movements were historically advantaged, formerly white institutions of tertiary learning. The #RhodesMustFall, Luister Stellenbosch (which calls to decolonise the language of the curriculum at Stellenbosch) and #TransformWits movements were commonly reported by the media. Similar struggles taking place at historically black universities have not generally assumed the degree of national media attention despite deep fissures of race and class divisions characterising them. While formerly white institutions are gradually expanding to include black students and academic staff, exceedingly few or no white students enrol in formerly black institutions, which continue to be marginalised by their locality, insufficient resources and limited course selections. Moreover, many black learners enrolled at formerly black institutions feel further marginalised by their Eurocentric curricula.

Smith (1999) offers processes through which the curriculum can be decolonised: deconstruction and recon-struction; self-determination and social justice; ethics; language; and the internalisation of indigenous experiences, history and critique. Deconstruction refers to breaking down the curriculum unsuited to learners who are receiving it and reconstructing it to be more suitable. In South Africa, this means deconstructing the Eurocentric curriculum and restructuring it to be centred on African theories and history. To establish equity and social justice, it is important that students are equipped with theories in their entirety rather than only receiving part of the information as this will create well-informed members of society. Social justice refers to the emancipation of Africans from the negative and inferior narrative commonplace in Eurocentric literature.

Eurocentric knowledge was legislatively entrenched in the Bantu Education system designed to oppress along the lines of both race and class. Today, legislation could potentially play a positive role. Research is needed in this complex domain if tertiary institutions are not only to address past inequity but also ensure course offerings relevant to their local context.

One major issue is that of language. The standard South African curriculum is one which maintains English and Afrikaans as dominant languages of learning and instruction. South Africa has 11 official languages. Arguably, the inclusion of indigenous African languages into the curriculum will advance decolonisation. The University of KwaZulu-Natal was, for instance, the first institution to make an indigenous African language (isiZulu) compulsory for students. At the University of Zululand, at least one PhD has been submitted in isiZulu.

Figure 12.3 #FeesMustFall reminiscent of the 1976 Soweto Uprising protests

(Source: Photograph courtesy of Christian I de Witt)

Capitalising on the momentum of #RhodesMustFall, the #FeesMustFall protests gained momentum on 14 October 2015 with student demonstrations taking place at the University of the Witwatersrand following the announcement of a proposed fee increase of 10.5 per cent. In the groundswell that followed, the #FeesMustFall

movement was rapidly adopted on a national scale, reflecting the depth and breadth of dissatisfaction among university students, which was in turn a reflection of the scale of inequality and poverty that underpinned the movement. In addition to decolonisation, students demanded free education and the erasure of historical student debt. The 2015 protests only came to a halt when government, not without controversy, declared a zero per cent fee increase for the following academic year. However, in 2016, the movements gained momentum as the reality of South African tertiary education saw a continuation of financial exclusion of students. In December 2017, former president Jacob Zuma declared fee-free education for students from lower- and working-class backgrounds.

While #FeesMustFall was recognised internationally for bringing attention to the funding crisis in tertiary education in South Africa, students' protests over the cost of tertiary education are not recent. Students from historically black universities have engaged in fee protests since the inception of democracy (Langa 2016). Decolonising the curriculum leads us to debating how, among the slew of issues this generation of students has raised, crucial questions arise around how universities prepare students for the new world of work in the much-vaunted Fourth Industrial Revolution.

12.12 The Fourth Industrial Revolution in South Africa

We are living in an era characterised by extraordinary technological advancements known as the Fourth Industrial Revolution (4IR). More than ever before, we are connected globally in a technological community, which enables us to be more efficient in every facet of our lives. The Fourth Industrial Revolution is driven by the integration and development of sophisticated technologies creating nanotechnology, artificial intelligence, robotics, genetics and 3D printing, all of which promise, according to their originating proponent, to revolutionise the future of work – and which thus implicates education (Schwab 2016). It is important to understand the implications of the Fourth Industrial Revolution for education. Higher education in this era (HE 4.0) has the potential to positively transform society (Xing & Marwala 2017).

In the foreseeable future, it has been strongly propounded, no industry will operate without the use of digital and robotised technologies. This, it is foreseen, will change the nature of work by creating new jobs not in existence today. What is needed, it is argued, is a workforce with new skills capable of keeping up with this advancing society (World Economic Forum 2018). Education needs to be at the forefront of the reskilling of students, preparing them to be adaptable and flexible in workplaces. While we are expected to work with technology in workplaces of the future, it is essential to remember that we still work with and beside one another (World Economic Forum 2018). For this reason, human skills are important. Courses that consider the needs of the labour market need to be developed. It is necessary to consider skills required by the current economy as well as soft skills that will be relevant in the foreseeable future. To distinguish themselves from machines, human agents need to be able to do what machines cannot (Xing & Marwala 2017). For this reason, all students need to be equipped with skills such as critical thinking, the ability to manage complex social contexts and environments, particularly around human diversity, the capacity for emotional intelligence, judgement, negotiation, cognitive flexibility, and the production and management of knowledge. Such skills, it is argued, will be invaluable (Xing & Marwala 2017). Whether the envisaged technological advances become generalised and unevenly distributed across and within societies or left behind and permanently marginalised, shifts are already occurring toward interdisciplinary academia with the hard sciences converging with the soft ones. An interdisciplinary approach would appear to be the most appropriate way of ensuring that tertiary educational institutions equip their students with not only the skills to engage in and with newly, but seemingly rapidly emerging technologies, but are also enabled to manage the political and ethical consequences for the societies in which they operate (Khathu 2019).

The advancement of technology in South Africa needs to be deracialised and revolutionised in a way that will provide students with quality, accessible education (Khathu 2019). The reskilling of workers to develop and maintain marketable skills needs to be done in an efficient manner that allows for both practical and rewarding independent lifelong learning if leisure is to become a more significant aspect of daily life. The question remains, however, whether rampant unemployment and marginalisation are not more likely scenarios.

To embrace lifelong learning, the traditional learning method of university curriculum dominated by attending lectures needs to shift significantly to embracing methods of teaching that are learner centric and innovative. The use of technology in teaching has created several ways to make education more economical. As technology can link people in an online global community, educational courses will now be accessible remotely. This is made possible by massive online open courses (MOOCs) that allow students to receive educational instruction through online platforms (Xing 2015). The resulting implications are twofold. More students will have access to the course as there is no limitation on physical space. These courses will be more affordable than those we know today as input costs will be lower. Blended learning converges face-to-face learning with e-learning, which allows students to attain a conceptual understanding of their curriculum as they can apply theory to real-world scenarios. Competency-based education (CBE) allows students to expand their current knowledge base by equipping them with the critical skills that they lack. Timeframes to CBE learning are flexible, and students pass through levels of learning when they can demonstrate a mastery of skills.

Summary

- The disjuncture in the social contract between government and society on the delivery of basic services on something as fundamental as education and basic services such as water and electricity are indicative of wider fissures in society.
- The rapidly modernising and global world has a direct effect on patterns of education and South Africa has not remained unmarked from the effects of globalisation and neoliberal state policies.
- The massification of higher education, pressure to publish, growing student numbers, bureaucratisation of schools and academia, increasing administration overload, the demand for tertiary education coupled with the lack of space and access are all indicators of a system under pressure.

- Huge income and poverty gaps reinforcing the privilege and domination of a few over the majority of the country's citizens makes this situation worse.
- Education is intimately linked to employability, which in turn reflects on the country's economic wellbeing. This means the better educated your workers are, the more productive your workforce is, which increases living standards for the country and makes the economy more competitive. Investment in education is thus a win–win situation for the country as a whole.
- NGOs, community organisations, business organisations and individuals far and wide in the country have pledged their support and in their own little way have begun to make a difference in educating others.

➠

- The powerful #FeesMustFall and #RhodesMustFall student movements illuminated the deeply rooted inequalities in education that were discussed throughout this chapter. These movements provide promising strides toward a more inclusive curriculum in terms of access to universities for students from marginalising backgrounds and prioritising the teaching and producing of knowledge from African perspectives.
- In the epoch of the Fourth Industrial Revolution, universities need to provide students with skills that

can enable them to compete in the job market: critical thinking, the ability to manage complex social contexts and environments, particularly around human diversity, the capacity for emotional intelligence, judgement, negotiation, cognitive flexibility, and the production and management of knowledge.

- Technology is changing the way we traditionally view education: lifelong learning is emphasised and made possible through forms of blended and online learning.

ARE YOU ON TRACK?

1. Provide a definition for the sociology of education.
2. Explain the functions of education.
3. Identify the manifest and latent functions of education in your schooling career.
4. Compare the different theories of education as outlined in the chapter.
5. How have ordinary citizens in South Africa helped communities with teaching and learning resources at schools?

6. How have student movements such as #FeesMustFall and #RhodesMustFall contributed to the reform of the South African tertiary education system? Give examples.
7. How should education in the epoch of the Fourth Industrial Revolution prepare students for a market economy that does not yet exist?
8. How can the lifelong learning of skills required for a fast-paced workforce be made accessible to minimise marginalisation?

References

Ballantine JH. 1989. *The Sociology of Education: A Systematic Analysis*. New Jersey: Prentice Hall Inc.

Barnes T. 2006. 'Changing discourses and meanings of redress in higher education, 1994–2001'. *Journal of Asian and African Studies*, 41(1/2): 149–170.

Bin Ali-Al-Thani A, Botman R. 2012. 'Chaos could start a wave of learning'. *Mail&Guardian*, 16 November.

Bowles S, Gintis H. 1976. *Schooling in Capitalist America*. New York: Basic Books.

Braskamp L, Wergin J. 1998. 'Forming new social partnerships' in *The Responsive University: Restructuring for Higher Performance*. Tierney W (ed). Baltimore: Johns Hopkins University.

Centre for Higher Education Development (CHED). 2016. *New Generation Extended Curriculum: Report*. [Online] Available at: http://www.ched.uct.ac.za/news/new-generation-extended-curriculum [Accessed 20 October 2019].

Chisholm L. 2012. *Corruption in education: the textbook saga*. Delivered at a symposium hosted by the Public Affairs Research Institute (PARI) and innovations for successful societies, Princeton University.

Christie P. 1985. *The Right to Learn: The Struggle for Education in South Africa*. Johannesburg: Ravan Press.

Christie P, Gordon A. 1990. 'Politics, poverty and education in rural South Africa'. *British Journal of Sociology of Education*, 13(4): 399–418.

CNN. 2012. *This Year's Heroes*. [Online] Available at: https://edition.cnn.com/SPECIALS/cnn.heroes/2012.heroes/thulani.madondo.html [Accessed 17 January 2019].

Cummings W. 1998. 'The service university movement in the US: Searching for momentum'. *Higher Education*, 35(1): 1–8.

DeMarrais KB, LeCompte M. 1995. *The Way Schools Work. A Sociological Analysis of Education*. USA: Longman Publishers.

Department of Education. 1996. National Education Policy Act 27 of 1996. [Online] Available at: https://www.education.gov.za/LinkClick.aspx?fileticket=I73mPb_ja4c%3D&tabid=419&portalid=0&mid=4023 [Accessed 17 January 2020].

DeMarrais KB, LeCompte M. 1995. *The Way Schools Work. A Sociological Analysis of Education*. USA: Longman Publishers.

De Waal T. 2004. 'Curriculum 2005: Challenges facing teachers in historically disadvantaged schools in the Western Cape'. MA of Public Administration, University of the Western Cape.

De Witt C. 2015. '#FeesMustFall protests: photographer Imraan Christian documents South Africa's "born free" generation uprising'. [Online] Available at: https://i-d.vice.com/en_au/article/feesmustfall-protestsphotographer [Accessed 6 March 2019].

Ensor P. 2004. 'Contesting discourses in higher education curriculum restructuring in South Africa'. *Higher Education*, 48(3): 339–359.

Erasmus BJ, Van Dyk PS. 2003. *Training Management in South Africa*. Cape Town: Oxford University Press Southern Africa.

Fataar A. 2009. 'Schooling subjectivities across the post-apartheid city'. *Africa Education Review*, 6(1): 1–18.

Govender P. 2012. Call to hire more black teachers. *Sunday Times*, 28 October 2012.

Hallinan MT. 2000. *Handbook of the Sociology of Education*. New York: Kluwer Academic/Plenum Publishers.

Hans B. 2019. *GETC covers Grades R to 9 but not a 'real qualification'*. [Online] Available at: https://www.parent24.com/Learn/High-school/Grade-9-the-new-matric-20090904 [Accessed 20 October 2019].

Hare P, Savage M. 1979. 'Sociology of South Africa'. *Annual Review of Sociology*, 5: 329–350.

Hobsbawm EJ. 1992. *Nations and Nationalism since 1780. Program, Myth, Reality.* Cambridge: Cambridge University Press.

Hugo P. 1998. 'Transformation: The Changing Context of Academia in Post-Apartheid South Africa'. *African Affairs*, 97(386): 5–27.

Jacobs M. 1999. 'Curriculum' in *Contemporary Education: Global Issues and Trends*. Sandton: Heinemann Higher and Further Education (Pty) Ltd.

John V. 2012a. 'Improved assessment results impossible, say academics'. *Mail&Guardian*, 7 December.

John V. 2012b. 'Sexual abuse at schools "a pandemic"'. *Mail&Guardian*, 16 November.

John V. 2012c. 'Treasury confirms budget reallocations for education'. *Mail&Guardian*, 12 November. [Online] Available at: http://mg.co.za/article/2012-11-01-treasury-confirms-budget-reallocations-for-education

John V. 2013. 'Angie's new school norms blasted'. *Mail&Guardian*, 17 January.

Johnson WR. 1982. 'Education: Keystone of apartheid'. *Anthropology & Education Quarterly*, 13(3): 214–237.

Khathu R. 2019. *4IR and the SA Education System*. [Online] Available at: https://www.bizcommunity.com/Article/196/371/193213.html [Accessed 14 October 2019].

Kraak A. 2007. *Human Resources Development Preview*. Cape Town: HSRC Press.

Langa M. 2016. 'Researching the #FeesMustFall movement' in *#Hashtag. An analysis of the #FeesMustFallMovement in South African Universities*. Langa M. South Africa: Centre for the Study of Violence and Reconciliation.

Lemmer E. 1999. 'Higher education policy and practice' in *Contemporary Education: Global Issues and Trends*. Lemmer E (ed). Sandton: Heinemann Higher and Further Education (Pty) Ltd.

Meighan R. 1981. *A Sociology of Educating*. London: Holt, Rinehart & Winston Ltd.

Mola T. 2012. 'Why parents need some teaching too'. *Mail&Guardian*, 30 November.

National Qualifications Framework. 2008. National Qualifications Framework Act 67 of 2008. [Online] Available at: http://www.dhet.gov.za/SiteAssets/About%20us%20new/2National%20Qualifications%20Framework%20Act%20No.%2067%20of%202008.pdf [Accessed 17 January 2020].

Patel F. 2006. 'Opening the doors of learning: changing schools in South Africa'. *Quarterly Review of Education and Training in South Africa*, 13(2): 386–401.

Presence C. 2012. 'Rector calls on government to declare crisis in education'. [Online] Available at: http://mg.co.za/article/2012-10-03-rector-calls-on-govt-to-declare-crisis-in-education [Accessed 20 December 2012].

Maree K. 2010. 'Critical appraisal of the system of education and prospects of meeting the manpower and developmental needs of South Africa'. http://hdl.handle.net/2263/16042 [Accessed 18 October 2019].

Magubane T. 2018. 'Education suffers as two thousand posts remain vacant due to lack of funds'. [Online] Available at: https://www.iol.co.za/mercury/education-suffers-as-two-thousand-posts-remain-vacant-due-to-lack-of-funds-14837019 [Accessed 14 October 2019].

McKay V. 2007. 'Adult basic education and training in South Africa' in *Review of Adult Learning and Literacy: Vol 7: Connecting Research, Policy, and Practice*. Comings JP, Garner B, Smith CA (eds). National Center for the Study of Adult Learning and Literacy Series: Routledge.

MISTRAy. 2017. 'Decolonisation for South Africa's historically black institutions'. [Online] Available at: http://www.mistra.org.za/Media/.../Decolonisation%20Article_MISTRAy_20170615.pdf [Accessed 4 March 2019].

Motala S. 2006. 'Education, resourcing in post-apartheid South Africa: the impact of finance equity in public schooling'. *Perspectives in Education*, 24(2): 79–93.

Motala S. 2007. 'Remembering June 16 – 30 years later'. *The Star*, 16 June.

Motala S. 2017. 'Introduction – Part III. Achieving 'free education' for the poor – a realisable goal in 2018?' *Journal of Education*, 68(1): 14–19.

Motala S, Dieltiens V. 2008. 'Caught in ideological crossfire: Private schooling in South Africa'. *Southern African Review of Education*, 14(3): 122–136.

Nal'ibali. 2019. 'School libraries matter'. [Online] Available at: https://nalibali.org/news-blog/blog/school-libraries-matter [Accessed 20 October 2019].

Nel E, Binns T. 1999. 'Changing the geography of apartheid education in South Africa'. *Geography*, 84(2): 119–128.

News24. 2017. 'No textbooks or stationery for Limpopo schools'. [Online] Available at: https://www.all4women.co.za/971548/news/south-african-news/no-textbooks-stationery-limpopo-schools [Accessed 13 October 2019].

Nkosi B. 2012. 'No money means poorer education'. [Online] Available at: http://mg.co.za/article/2012-10-25-no-money-means-poorer-education/ [Accessed October 2012].

Nkosi B. 2013. 'Matriculants want universities – not FETS'. *Mail&Guardian*, 14 January.

Nzimande BS. 2006. 'Parental "choice": The liberty principle in education finance'. *Perspectives in Education*, 24(2): 143–156.

Nzimande BS. 2009. 'It's a "Catch 22 situation": The challenge of race in post-apartheid South African desegregated schools'. *International Critical Childhood Policy Studies*, 2(1): 123–139.

Ogbonnaya U. 2019. 'Quintile ranking of schools in South Africa and learners' achievement probability'. *Statistics Education Research Journal*, 18(1): 106–119.

Papier J. 2012. 'Making public colleges effective'. *Mail&Guardian*, 7 December.

Parsons. T. 1959. *The School Class as a Social System: Some of its Functions in American Society*. Boston: Harvard Educational Review.

Prince R, Yeld N. 2012. 'A bridge too far for school leavers'. *Mail&Guardian*. 12 October.

Review Committee on Curriculum 2005. 'A South African curriculum for the 21st century'. [Online] Available at: http://citeseerx.ist.psu.edu/viewdoc/download?doi=10.1.1.361.5200&rep=rep1&type=pdf [Accessed 18 October 2019].

Ritzer G. 1992. *Classical Sociological Theory*. USA: McGraw-Hill, Inc.

Robinson N. 'Are elite former white schools the best?' [Online] Available at: https://mg.co.za/article/2019-02-22-00-are-elite-former-white-schools-the-best [Accessed 20 October 2019].

Ryan C. 2019. 'Private schools are thriving in SA'. [Online] Available at: https://citizen.co.za/business/2167297/private-schools-are-thriving-in-sa/ [Accessed 20 October 2019].

SABC News Online. 2019. 'Public schools in SA still surrounded by poor infrastructure'. [Online] Available at: http://www.sabcnews.com/sabcnews/public-schools-in-sa-still-surrounded-by-poor-infrastructure-survey/ [Accessed 20 October 2019].

Sanderson SK. 1991. *Macrosociology: An Introduction to Human Societies*. New York: HarperCollins Publishers Inc.

Savides M. 2017. 'South African schools have 5 139 teachers who are unqualified or under-qualified'. [Online] Available at: https://www.timeslive.co.za/news/south-africa/2017-06-06-south-african-schools-have-5139-teachers-who-are-unqualified-or-under-qualified/ [Accessed 14 October 2019].

Schools4SA. 2019. 'South African comprehensive school directory'. [Online] Available at: https://www.schools4sa.co.za/ [Accessed 20 October 2019].

Schwab K. 2016. *The Fourth Industrial Revolution*. New York: Crown Business.

Seeth A. 2017. *Limited space: Universities face thousands of first year queries*. [Online] Available at: https://city-press.news24.com/News/limited-space-universities-face-thousands-of-first-year-queries-20170111 [Accessed 14 October 2019].

Smillie S. 2013. 'Slipping through the cracks'. *The Star*. 3 January.

Sever M. 2012. 'A critical look at the theories of sociology of education'. *International Journal of Human Sciences*, 9(1): 651–671.

Smith L. 1999. *Decolonising Methodologies: Research and Indigenous Peoples*. London: Zed Books.

Strydom AH, Fourie M. 1999. 'Higher education research in South Africa: achievements, conditions and new challenges'. *Higher Education*, 38(2): 155–167.

United Nations. 1948. *Declaration of Human Rights*. [Online] Available at: https://www.un.org/en/universal-declaration-human-rights/ [Accessed 17 January 2020].

United Nations 2000. *Millennium Development Goals*. [Online] Available at: https://www.who.int/topics/

millennium_development_goals/about/en/ [Accessed 17 January 2020].

Vally S, Dalamba Y. 1999. *Racism, 'racial integration' and desegregation in South African public secondary schools.* Education Policy Unit. Johannesburg, South Africa: University of Witwatersrand.

Van der Berg S, Burger C, Burger R, De Vos M, Du Rand G, Gustafsson M, Moses E, Shepard D, Spaull N, Taylor A, Van Broekhuizen H, Von Fintel D. 2011. *Low Quality Education as a Poverty Trap.* Social Policy Research Group, Stellenbosch University.

Van Niekerk P. 1999. 'Values and ideologies' in *Contemporary Education: Global Issues and Trends.* Lemmer E (ed). Sandton: Heinemann Higher and Further Education (Pty) Ltd.

Veriava F. 2012. 'Righting the wrongs of school costs'. *Mail&Guardian*, 6 November.

Viljoen J. 2019. 'South Africa's first year dropout rate is not unique'. [Online] Available at: https://krugersdorpnews. co.za/362800/xmas-back-2-school-south-africas-first-year-drop-out-rate-is-not-unique/ [Accessed 20 October 2019].

Wanner Z. 2019. 'Illiteracy is part of the ticking time bomb'. [Online] Available at: https://mg.co.za/article/2019-05-10-00-illiteracy-is-part-of-a-ticking-time-bomb [Accessed 20 October 2019].

Weber M, Gerth H, Wright Mills C. 1991. *From Max Weber: Essays in Sociology.* London: Routledge.

Witten A. 2012. 'Learning does not occur in a vacuum'. *Mail&Guardian*, 16 November.

World Economic Forum. 2018. *The Future of Jobs Report.* Doha: World Economic Forum.

Xing B. 2015. 'Massive online open course assisted mechatronics learning a hybrid approach' in *Furthering Higher Education Possibilities through Massive Open Online Courses.* Mesquita A, Peres P (eds). Hershey, USA: IGI Global.

Xing B, Marwala T. 2017. 'Implications of the Fourth Industrial Age on higher education'. *The Thinker*, April.

Zibi S. 'Education: Celebrating failure says it all'. [Online] Available at: http://mg.co.za/article/2013-01-11-education-celebrating-failure-says-it-all [Accessed 12 November 2012].

Chapter 13

Religion

Johan Zaaiman

Religion is a feature of all societies, whether past or present. The word 'religion' comes from the Latin *religio*, meaning fear of the supernatural. One Latin dictionary suggests that the term may stem from *religio* meaning 'to bind together'. Since time immemorial, religion was the chief source of social cohesion and constituted the 'glue' that holds society together. Even today in a society such as ours, in which the vast majority lays claim to being a member of some or other faith community, religion continues to serve the purpose of binding communities together. It is hence no accident that both Durkheim and Weber paid studious attention to religion in their scholarly work.

But religion can also have a negative impact on society. Religious conflict and wars have raged through the ages and influence global politics today. Marx thought that religion was 'the opium of the people' as it deflected the working class from their daily struggles to liberate themselves from the shackles of exploitation. Religion, as a topic of sociological inquiry, is therefore clearly of significance.

It is not easy, at the best of times, to stand back from cherished beliefs and study and analyse them sociologically. This is especially true of religious beliefs, but this is what this chapter does in presenting a sociological perspective on religion. Do, however, take immediate note that, as the introduction makes abundantly clear, sociology does not pronounce on the validity of religious beliefs – whether they are right or wrong, true or false. The first few paragraphs of this chapter make this point very clearly. Religion is presented and studied here as a social phenomenon in all its rich diversity and complexity.

There are a diverse number of religions in South Africa. Religion and the performance of religious rituals were prominent features of the earliest communities in southern Africa and to which were added many more, as this chapter describes. The variety and diverse ways in which society can be bound together by religion are responsible for the difficulties in defining religion, but with which this chapter grapples. The word 'grapples' is intentionally used here as the roots of religious experience run deep in the collective psyche of humanity. For despite the promise of science to provide certainty in the human mind and in social affairs, as this chapter will show, the need for certainty continues to make its presence felt as the preliminary nature of science did not live up to its early promise. There has been renewed interest in moral guidance, and religion continues to be a socially binding cultural resource as two contemporary social theorists, discussed in this chapter, argue. Alongside its traditional function in contemporary society, however, religion has lost much of its traditional power and so this chapter also deals with topics such as the relation between religion and inequality, and its role in gender relationships, and discusses in some detail what is known as the secularisation debate. The relatively recent upsurge in religious fundamentalism and the relation between religion and social change are topics which are also broached.

These topics in the sociology of religion provide the background to looking, as always, at how the three main sociological perspectives treat the social phenomenon of religion. There is much room for serious thought here in discussing this profound subject. There is also, as usual, more than one conclusion that can be drawn from studying religion sociologically. Does religion have greater functional or dysfunctional social effects? Does religion distort social reality? Was religion the motivating force for the emergence of capitalism in the West or was it a result of early capitalism? How can or does religion as a system of meaning contribute to progressive social change in our society? These are all weighty questions with no easy answers, but which demand the serious application of the scholarly mind and sociological investigation.

Whether you are of a religious disposition, agnostic or atheist, or fascinated by but do not know much about Zen Buddhism, the Hare Krishna movement or Sufism, this chapter can do no other than excite your interest in the study of a social phenomenon that cannot be ignored. The sheer depth and power of religious beliefs, the profound nature of religious socialisation, the impact on social behaviour of religion and the importance of faith communities in South African society are all almost certainly paid insufficient attention in sociology today. Perhaps it is because these are difficult issues, but in grappling with them the insights sociology reveals enables it to present itself as a discipline of unparalleled fascination. Taken seriously, the diligent student cannot fail to be enthralled by studying the social phenomenon of religion introduced in this chapter.

Case study 13.1 Skin taken off the religious practice

In South Africa, a traditional custom, informed by religious motives, has a detrimental impact on its society and the environment. The Nazareth Baptist Church, also known as the Shembe, is a mixture of Christianity and Zulu culture. In this religion, leopards are seen as a symbol of pride, beauty and wealth. Leopard skins are therefore viewed as essential for church elders, who wear them around their necks during traditional ceremonies. The Shembe is one of the largest traditional religious groups in South Africa (approximately five million members). As the church grows, it could push Africa's leopards, already listed as 'near threatened', towards extinction.

According to the Convention on International Trade in Endangered Species (CITES), the sale or possession of leopard parts is illegal in South Africa. Those who do wear a leopard skin as traditional gear need permits issued by the state. At Shembe church gatherings, however, skins are traded openly and there are no laws enforced. Increasingly poachers are killing leopards to profit from this huge demand.

Tristan Dickerson is a conservationist at the Phinda Game Reserve in KwaZulu-Natal. He attempted to solve the conflict between traditional values and contemporary environmental responsibility by using modern technology. He got the idea to manufacture fake leopard skins (made from nyala skin), and travelled as far as Beijing in China to produce the most acceptable fake leopard fur.

In Ekuphakameni, where the church was founded, Tristan visited a church gathering and showed his fur samples to a senior preacher. The conservationist understood that he had to target the older generation and the leaders to accept his proposal. The preacher responded: 'It's beautiful, but it's not the real thing. It's like a blanket. After some time, it will wear out.'

The senior preacher was not aware that the trade in leopard parts was illegal. He conceded that the continuing demand for church attire may lead to the extinction of leopards. He agreed that it would be a shame that the following generations would not have the privilege of experiencing these proud animals, but as an elder of the religion he could not wear a fake costume. However, as church membership continued to grow and the price of leopard skin escalated, he could see a possibility among the membership: 'It will help the congregation and protect the leopard from extinction.' Although there is a growing awareness among the younger generation of the need to conserve our natural resources, this cultural custom is entrenched in the religion. It was thus back to the drawing board for manufacturers of fake leopard skin attire.
(Source: Mabuse & Ko 2012)

QUESTIONS

1. How does religion impact on society and the surrounding environment?
2. Which shift in focus occurred in modern-day society from traditional values to those of a society with interdependent systems?
3. How do your religious practices differ from those of the previous generations (eg your parents or guardians and grandparents)? Talk to them about this if you do not know. Copy Table 13.1 from this chapter and complete it to indicate the shift in the different aspects:

Table 13.1 Changes in the religious practices of people across generations

Religious practices	Similarity and difference to your parents' practices	Similarity and difference to your grandparents' practices
Worshipping practices		
Reading of sacred texts		
Dress practices for worshipping		
Religious dietary practices		
Celebration of sacred days		

Key themes

- The development of the diverse religions in South African society
- The tension lines between traditional African belief systems and other religions that were introduced to the country
- The sociological approach to the study of religion and how these views build on a definition of religion's unique contribution to society
- Religion's role in modern-day society and the three basic viewpoints
- The relationship between religion and inequality, and the basic social themes

- The two points of entry for the secular debate and secular theory and their impact on religious theory and practices in society
- The emergence of religious fundamentalism as a countermove to defend traditional beliefs, and how religion can indeed bring about social change
- The three classical sociological perspectives on religion and how they still influence the approach to religion today
- The organisation of religion and the three basic types, the elements, as well as relevant criteria to measure **religiosity**.

13.1 Introduction

This chapter introduces you to a sociological perspective on religion. Owing to sociology's interest in social phenomena, it evaluates religion from a social perspective. It therefore focuses on the social aspects of religion and attempts to interpret the nature and role of religion from the perspective of its place in society. This therefore implies a specific perspective on religion. Sociology studies religion as an embedded aspect of societal functioning. This means that sociology does not evaluate the validity of a religion or aspects thereof. Its aim is rather to interpret the role of religion in a society.

In this chapter you will first be introduced to the historical development of the diverse religious systems in South Africa. The focus will then shift to a study of religion as a social phenomenon. The reader will understand the challenges of seeing religion as part of larger social interrelations. Instead of attempting to define religion as an isolated entity – either

as a function of society or as a sacred substance within it – the sociological view relates religion to other social factors, such as social class or socioeconomic position in society. In this way, specific sociological questions can be asked:
- What is the relationship between religious theory and practice, and internal contradictions (eg inequality) in society?
- How does religion affect social change?
- How are religious institutions organised within society?

When studying religion in terms of its interrelatedness to modern-day society, it can also be analysed and assessed against the theoretical frameworks of modernity and postmodernity, and measured against the threat of secularism. From a sociological perspective of religion, readers get acquainted with the three classical theorists and their different angles on religion's contribution to society: as social function, conflict dynamism and unique system of meaning. Through case studies, this focus on religion as a social phenomenon is contextualised in the South African social environment with its diverse religious systems, which reflects the rich and complex pluralism of diverse religious societies in modern-day society.

13.2 The development of South Africa's diverse religions

13.2.1 Indigenous beliefs

The first indigenous people of South Africa, the San, had a deep awareness of the **supernatural** realm consisting of a god or gods and evil spirits. They named their high god *!Kaggen*. The San portrayed their awareness of the supernatural communally through their powerful ritual dance. In a San camp, some members acted as medicine men and mediated between the groups and the gods. Of the early indigenous people, the Khoi emerged as a later grouping. They also entertained a variety of beliefs. To a lesser extent than among the San, the medicine man also played the role of **mediator** between the Khoi people and the supernatural forces. The Khoi recognised and revered three supernatural beings: the *Tsui Guab* (a good being), *Guanab* (an evil being) and *Heitsi Eibab*, an **ancestral** figure influencing the fortunes of individuals.

The indigenous African people of South Africa believed in a continued existence after death. They therefore had an awareness of family ancestral spirits with whom interaction is possible. This was an important feature in their religious **rituals**. They were also aware of other supernatural beings and of a supreme being, whom they named *Modimo* or *Nkulunkulu*.

13.2.2 Religions introduced through immigration

Immigration, whether voluntary or forced, helped to introduce the world religions to South African society. These religions included Christianity, Islam and Judaism, as well as Hinduism and Buddhism from the East.

European settlers brought the Christian religion to Africa. During the colonial period in South Africa, each colonial power established its religious preference as the official faith. A characteristic feature of this period was the intolerance shown by the Dutch, French (Huguenot) and later the British settlers towards Catholic settlers. Catholic priests were forbidden to live or minister in the Cape colony. The Catholic Order of Jesuits was allowed to visit the Cape in 1685, but they were not permitted to perform Mass. This was mainly due to the religious wars that raged in Europe between the Protestants and Catholics.

Eventually freedom of religion was extended to all citizens in South African society. This was entrenched in the various constitutions of South Africa: first in the constitution of the Union of South Africa in 1910, then in the amended constitution of the Republic of South Africa in 1961 during the apartheid system, and finally in the constitution of the new democratic government after 1994. However, in the earlier constitutions this freedom in practice meant **tolerance** rather than equality.

The Dutch permitted only the Reformed Church to operate in the Cape Colony. Despite the prohibition of other faiths, the Islamic faith was introduced to the Cape with the arrival of a number of Malay slaves not long after the Dutch had established their settlement there. Sheik Yusuf, who was banished from Malaysia in 1758, formally founded the Islamic faith in South Africa together with other followers. This was done even though the public practice of Islam was prohibited by the Dutch. It was only in 1804 that freedom of religious expression was recognised by the Dutch colonial power. In 1789 the former Indonesian, 'Abd Allah ibn Qadi 'Abd al-Salam, who had been imprisoned on Robben Island, managed to establish the first Islamic mosque in Cape Town.

Another world religion, Hinduism, was brought to South Africa in the mid-1800s. In the 1850s the sugar-planters in the British colony of Natal (currently known as KwaZulu-Natal) began to experience labour shortages, and in 1859 persuaded the authorities to import labourers from India. With the immigration of 150 000 Indian people between 1860 and 1911 to work as labourers, Hinduism was introduced to the country. Approximately 60 per cent of these workers were from the lower caste – mainly Tamil and Telegu speakers from southern India. Others formed part of the higher caste, and were mainly Hindi and Gujarati speakers from the north of India. These divisions of class, language and place of origin resulted in diverse forms of Hinduism in South Africa. The first Hindu temple was erected in Durban in 1869.

13.2.3 Missionary activities

The first known attempts at Christian **missionary** work in southern Africa were carried out by the Jesuits of the Roman Catholic Church in the vicinity of Zimbabwe (as it is now) in 1560. After the Cape was occupied by the United East India Company, the Dutch Reformed Church became its official church. This church initiated some missionary work in 1737 but it was only in the 1800s that this started to flourish in South Africa. Initially the British colonial rulers, who took over the Cape in 1806, acted antagonistically towards Roman Catholics, Lutherans, Methodists and Muslims.

Roman Catholics were only allowed to enter the Cape colony in 1820. The first resident Catholic bishop, Raymond Griffith, arrived in 1838 and the first Anglican bishop in 1848. This religious intolerance by the British administration also affected other Christian denominations. The first Methodist minister who arrived in 1806 was not allowed to preach. Eventually the British opened up the field for other denominations to do missionary work. This resulted in British, German, French, Scandinavian, Finnish, Swiss and American missionary societies establishing missionary centres in South Africa. After slavery was abolished in the Cape in 1834, these missionary societies ministered actively to the liberated slaves and helped enhance their livelihood.

From early on, Christian and Muslim religious leaders were intolerant towards traditional African beliefs and culture, which they saw as 'uncivilised'. This caused a split between Western religion and African beliefs. Beliefs in ancestors supported traditional political and economic systems and maintained age-old customs. In this sense, traditional African religions could be employed to mobilise resistance against **colonialism**.

13.2.4 Binary tension

Political and economic conditions in 19th century southern Africa required the image of a superordinate god whose authority would extend beyond the homestead and the **chiefdom**. Such an extended god concept was provided by the Christian and Muslim missionaries. The problem was that the missionaries equated Christianity with European cultures. Africans had to adopt both the religion and the culture. This state of affairs divided African societies along Christian and traditional lines. Bishop Stanley Makgoba described how his village was literally divided by a donga (a cleft in the land caused by erosion). This physical divide ran between converts to Christianity and people with more traditional beliefs.

These tension lines between the two forms of beliefs can be illustrated further by the tragic events that took place in 1856 to 1857. There had been a long and bitter conflict between the amaXhosa and the colonial powers in the Eastern Cape. The amaXhosa's beliefs were also being challenged by the missionary teachings, European technology and the outbreak of lung disease among their cattle. A negative reaction was brewing among the amaXhosa. It is alleged that in 1856 the ancestors addressed Nongqawuse, a niece of Mhlakaza, who was a councillor to Paramount Chief Sarhili. She received the message that the ancestors would rise from the dead on 18 February 1857 and a whirlwind would sweep all white people and

the non-traditional amaXhosa into the sea, but for this to happen, all cattle had to be slaughtered and no lands were to be cultivated. The people then had to dig new granaries and erect strong cattle-folds to house the plenitude which they would then receive from the ancestors. Historians estimate that about 300 000 head of cattle were killed between April 1856 and May 1857. On the predicted day, however, nothing happened. The amaXhosa was then faced with a severe crisis. It is believed that about 30 000 died of hunger, 30 000 had to migrate and only approximately 30 000 people remained. The result of this tragedy was that both Chief Sarhili and Sir George Grey, the then governor of the Cape, were accused of engineering the crisis through Nongqawuse. Nongqawuse was arrested by the British authorities and imprisoned on Robben Island. After her release, she lived on a farm in the Alexandria district of the Eastern Cape and died in 1898. This incident demonstrates the tension that the introduction of new religions had on worshippers in South Africa.

13.2.5 Dynamic relationship

However, the binary tension of Christian faith and traditional beliefs did not remain static. Numerous African people adopted the Christian religion but **indigenised** it (translated it to fit their indigenous beliefs). The result was the establishment of a variety of so-called **independent churches** that combined traditional and Christian beliefs. The independent churches that originated at the beginning of the 20th century can be seen as an assertion of Africanist identity. The Ethiopian churches were established as a response to white-dominated **mainline** Christian denominations. The Zionist churches reinterpreted Christian teachings within an African context. They offered care and fellowship which the mainline congregations could not match. Throughout the 20th century, the **charismatic** movement grew in South African and later on established loose alliances among themselves, such as the International Fellowship of Christian Churches (IFCC). The affinity between the charismatic movement and the churches with an African identity is that both emphasise direct contact with the supernatural.

During South Africa's colonial period, Christianity enjoyed a privileged position over other religions, although it did not act as an official religion. Under British rule, the bond between the state and the Christian religion was severed, but under the Nationalist government it was reinstated. The government claimed that it stood for and would defend Christian values and integrated this in a system of Christian-Nationalism. This sanctification of the Nationalist government's ideology introduced a civil religion in South Africa. Civil religion can be viewed as a quasi-religious faith in which beliefs, values, rituals, texts, symbols, sites and heroes are accentuated to ensure cultural and social integration. Bellah (1967) argued that America also had a civil religion. This entailed a religious orientation that supported the American societal dispensation at that time. Such a religious orientation masked petty interests and harmful passions that were rife in American society.

In the apartheid state, religion played a similar role and was used to justify apartheid. It was assumed that God took a special interest in South Africa and that the country had a special, elevated destiny. South Africa was seen as a new Israel and the Afrikaners as the new chosen people, therefore certain forms of Afrikaner culture were elevated to an almost sacred status. Such forms of culture include the commemoration of the Day of the Covenant (16 December) and the Voortrekker Monument. This type of civil religion was also used to rally white South African citizens against ideological opponents, such as 'godless communism'. In that sense, religion was employed to justify military involvements in states such as Angola, Mozambique, Zambia and Zimbabwe from the mid-1970s to the mid-1980s.

This form of civil religion continually played a part in motivating the colonial powers to introduce their civilisation and the Christian **gospel** to the African continent. Presently, there is in general a stronger division between state and religion in African countries. The 1996 Constitution of South Africa defines the country as a secular society in which religion is neither suppressed nor supported.

13.2.6   Current situation

Religion is still a major influence in South Africa. Christianity, in many forms, is the dominant religion with currently approximately 80 per cent of the population professing to be Christian. Other significant religions are traditional African beliefs, Islam and Hinduism. However, the estimate is that people not adhering to any religion is currently about 10 per cent of the South African population. In Christianity there is no dominating denomination. Mainline churches (eg Anglican, Catholic, Dutch Reformed, Lutheran, Methodist and United Reformed) have considerable followers, but at present there is a growth in Pentecostal/Charismatic and African-initiated churches (churches attempting to escape white control and accommodate Christian beliefs within an African world view). Main groupings in the African initiated churches are Ethiopian, Messianic, Israelites and Zionist churches. The Zion Christian Church (or ZCC) is the largest African-initiated church with a following of about four million

members. It gathers yearly during Easter at the church's headquarters at Zion City, Moria in Limpopo province, attracting over one million pilgrims. Experimentation with new or alternative religious movements also currently occurs. Religion is also creatively used in media. The Gospel Music industry is an example thereof and for the film *Black Panther* different Wakandan religious cults and related deities were conceptualised and integrated in the film.

13.3   The sociological study of religion

Studying religion is a challenging undertaking for the sociological imagination. The reason is that a wide diversity of beliefs and rituals is to be found in various human cultures. Within this, sociologists must show sensitivity towards the convictions of believers. Social scientists must respect their ideals that are built on eternal and mundane goals. This diversity of religious beliefs and modes of conduct must therefore be recognised and respected, but the nature of religion as a general social phenomenon must also be probed.

13.3.1   A sociological approach

Sociologists do not study religion as believers of a particular faith. They do not view religious beliefs as being true or false. Émile Durkheim viewed all religions as true in their own fashion. Sociologists therefore have a very specific approach to religion. This approach holds a number of important implications for the sociological study of religion, as outlined below.

- Sociologists view religion as a social phenomenon. They study expressions of a religious faith as a socially constructed entity. Sociologists are therefore not concerned about whether beliefs are true or false. The personal beliefs of social analysts are therefore not relevant when they study religions through a sociological lens.
- Sociologists do not focus on the personal, spiritual or psychological factors that may motivate religion. They are more interested in the type of social forces that may have caused the formation of a religion. For people, religious beliefs can be a deeply personal experience that includes a sense of connection with forces transcending their everyday life. However, sociologists focus on the factors in the social order that contribute to the formation of religions, rather than examine the individual's psychological response to these deeper experiences.

- Sociologists view religion as an important element within the functioning of society and as a phenomenon that can be studied. Many sociologists point out the important role that religion plays in society. Religion creates social solidarity by providing a common set of norms and values. Religious beliefs, rituals and bonds are therefore viewed as important guidelines that inform people how to behave towards one another, and by doing so, create a 'moral community'.
- Sociologists are interested in the wide variety of social forms that religion presents. Religion presents many forms and changes over time in terms of beliefs and practices. It is important for sociologists to study this religious diversity, seeing that religion is such an important institution in society.
- Sociologists view religion as an institution which is an integral part of society and also a source that provides deep-seated norms and values. Because religions are among the most important institutions in society, sociologists are particularly concerned with the social organisation of the social phenomenon of religion.

Although religion is such an integral part of societies, the original nature of religion within societies is unknown. Archaeology discovered early evidence of religious practices at burial sites, such as the dead being buried with gifts and food for use in a next world. Remains of altars used by early peoples indicate religious practices. This evidence was found at archaeological sites where human societies existed previously. This indicates that religious beliefs were present in every known human society. However, the variety of religions seemed to be endless. This provides challenges in defining religion.

13.3.2 Defining religion

A definition assists the researcher in explaining a field of study. The difficulty in defining religion in sociology is how to outline satisfactorily what religion entails in society, and to include the wide variety of religious beliefs and practices. Such a definition should also demarcate the phenomena to be excluded – those which are not normally thought of as religion. There are two main approaches that could be followed in defining religion sociologically. On the one hand there is the functional approach and on the other the approach that focuses on substance.

Functional system

One way to define religion is by describing the function it fulfils for society and individuals. For instance, Yinger defined religion as follows:

A system of beliefs and practice by means of which a group of people struggles with the ultimate problems of human life (Yinger 1970: 7).

This definition defines religion in terms of the function it performs where it supplies an answer to the ultimate problems in society. In this sense, religion is viewed as part of culture; it consists of beliefs, norms, values and ideas that create a common identity among a group of people within a society. This identity is upheld by certain behavioural patterns. Such behaviour entails ritualised practices in which believers take part and which identify them as members of a religious community. These beliefs, symbols and rituals help humans to experience life as ultimately meaningful and contribute to the sense that the universe has a purpose. All of these features unite the adherents of a religious experience.

The function religion provides to society is to explain comprehensively and compellingly those otherworldly aspects that overshadow everyday life and to bind people together. For instance, according to African traditional beliefs, respected ancestors are bound to the family and so create a broader community and identity. Religious beliefs guide people to transcend material reality. Religion answers existential questions such as: 'Why am I here?' It also provides answers to deeper questions with which people often struggle – why they exist, the meaning of birth and death, anxiety about the future, ageing, illness, suffering, tragedy, injustice or uncertainty about life.

Religion therefore also helps to define **rites of passage**, such as births, weddings and death in a community. Initiation of the youth in some African communities is an example of religion's input in the sphere of cultural practices. Religion also gives these practices absolute moral significance and provides definite standards. In that sense, religion is a yardstick for judging people's ideals and actions. Other cultural aspects cannot provide this dimension.

A difficulty with such a definition of religion in sociology is that the 'ultimate problems' in societies are to a large extent determined by culture and environmental conditions, therefore they vary strongly between different countries. Another difficulty encountered by a functional definition is its large scope. Such a definition can even include ideologies, such as communism, that also aim to present society with ultimate answers to its critical problems, although communism explicitly rejects religious beliefs. Lastly, the definition is undermined by the vagueness of 'ultimate problems', which would be open to a wide range of interpretations. The issue here is that some ultimate life problems can also be dealt with by medication. The definition based on religion's societal function is therefore too inclusive. The functional definition is, however, widely employed by sociologists because it is a useful tool to describe religion. At the same time the weaknesses of such a definition must be taken into account.

Sacred substance

Another way to define religion in sociology is to focus on its substance or content. Religion would then be defined as *that which is sacred in society* against the profane aspects in society. The **sacred** in society are those aspects that are holy, supernatural and extraordinary, and which create a sense of respect, veneration and awe among believers. These sacred features can, for instance, be objects, places, ceremonies or states of consciousness that are protected by specific rituals and rites. These prescribe how people should behave in the presence of that which is sacred or supernatural, and can include songs, chants, prayers, offerings, purifications, commemorations and sacrifices. Over and against the sacred is the **profane**. The profane refers to the worldly or **secular** aspects of life – those that stand apart from the sacred. Usually contact between the sacred and the profane is viewed as dangerous, subversive and something to be be avoided.

Other definitions based on substance focus on the existence of supernatural beings or **culturally postulated** superhuman beings (in other words, the existence of such superordinate beings is assumed as evident within certain cultures). The problem with such definitions is that certain belief systems which are also commonly regarded as religions (eg Buddhism) do not hold a belief in supernatural beings. Such a definition of religion could therefore be too exclusive, and to counter this, a more precise description is necessary.

Typically, where religion is defined by content it refers to the following:

A system of beliefs and practices by which a group of people interprets and responds to what they feel is sacred and, usually, supernatural as well (Johnstone 1997: 13).

This kind of system has an organisational structure in which members are socialised. Adherents to religions are therefore organised around beliefs, practices and symbols. This gives religion an institutional character in society. It is also in the context of defining religion as a response to what is sacred that **civil religion** can be defined as a set of beliefs, rituals and symbols that sacralises (makes sacred) the values of society. Civil religion presents the *nation* as the ultimate system of meaning, therefore the nation's values and national events assume a sacred quality.

A way out of this difficulty in defining religion is to focus rather on the questions that sociologists would like to answer about the phenomenon of religion in societies. Relevant questions are as follows:

- How are religious belief and religious practice related to other social factors, such as social class, race, age, gender and level of education?
- How are religious institutions organised?
- How does religion influence social change?

The following sections present an overview of some of the sociological thought expressed on religion. The questions posed above will be addressed in the course of this discussion.

Case study 13.2   Nation building depicting civil religion

After the National Thanksgiving Service held on 8 May 1994, the rainbow symbol gained widespread popularity in the new democratic South African society even to the level of a civil religion.

Thousands of people from very different religious and political backgrounds gathered in solemn confession, mutual forgiveness and common reconciliation. In front of the crowd with the television cameras of the world trained on him, Archbishop Tutu announced: 'We are the rainbow people of God. We are free – all of us, black and white together!' This was the birth of a new syncretistic civil religion to which all South Africans could subscribe (Møller, Dickow & Harris 1998: 252).

Newly elected President Nelson Mandela again referred to this symbol of the rainbow when he was inaugurated as president of South Africa on 10 May 1994. Since then, South Africans are known all over the world as the 'rainbow people'. It also became commercialised:

The rainbow symbol has been exploited for commercial purposes as well as political ends. It features in the title of business and community enterprises and adorns products boasting South African origin from clothing to coffee cups to band-aids (Møller et al 1998: 246).

Bellah, who 'revealed' the American civil religion, defines civil religion as 'a genuine apprehension of universal and transcendent religious reality as seen or, one could almost say, as revealed through the experience of the … people' (Bellah 1967: 12).

In 1996, a study on national pride and happiness was undertaken as part of the Quality of Life Trends Study by Møller et al. According to them:

… the study showed that the unifying civil religion of the 'rainbow people' is more than a superb feat of social engineering; it has captured the public imagination. It has promoted national unity and harmony, inspires happiness as well as pride, and commands a wide following among diverse groups in South African society. Moreover, supporters of the rainbow symbol of peace are also optimistic about the future (Møller et al 1998: 276–277).

Figure 13.1 National celebration – depicting civil religion?

QUESTIONS

1. How did the religious symbol of the rainbow – representing a covenant between God and a chosen people – become a political symbol?
2. Taking into account Bellah's definition of civil religion above, which features of a civil religion can you point out in this 'rainbow people' symbol of nation building?
3. How was the unifying movement of the rainbow people more than ingenious social engineering built around a myth? Give a reason for your answer. (Hint: keep in mind the link between national identity and social wellbeing.)

13.4 Religion and society

Religion can be found in every society. The general fact that it exists in society can be related to its relevance to the basic aspects of the human condition. Religion presents humans with the following: a sense of significance, meaning, support, consolation and help in transitional stages, **a transcendence** of everyday reality, identity and purpose. Other practices, views and institutions can undeniably also provide humans with meaning in their lives. Examples of these are the family, friends, neighbourhood ties, occupation and nation. However, religion presents people with a unique **transcendental** orientation that plays a continuous and unique role in human lives. This holds true for stable societies. However, in times of social upheaval or during natural disasters new religious movements frequently develop, or people fall back on established religious institutions. There exists therefore a close relationship between society and religion. The next subsections discuss aspects of this relationship.

13.4.1   Religion in current society

Different views exist on how current society can be described, which leads to diverse views on how religion's role in society can be explained. This subsection will examine the views of three sociologists: Anthony Giddens, Zygmunt Bauman and David Lyon. Each of them poses a specific understanding of what is important in present-day society and how religion fits into it.

A need for certainty

It is the view of Anthony Giddens (1990) that modern society moved into a new phase of high modernity (ie it developed its modernity to the point that it radicalised certain features of it). One such feature is increased reflexivity (thoughts and actions 'bend back' towards themselves). Any society is continually monitoring itself with the aim of improving its functioning. The result is that people within that society are increasingly willing to change their practices, beliefs and institutions in the light of new experiences and knowledge. Although these new developments seem to offer certainty through scientific knowledge, people are unsettled by the uncertainty of the constant change confronting them.

A second feature of radicalised modernity is the fundamental changes in people's organisation of time and space. Modern communication technology and the globalisation of social life resulted in social relationships being played out between people who are separated in time and space. People develop globally close relationships with others in the absence of face-to-face interaction. Locality is not as important or necessary for relationships as it was in the past.

A third feature of modernity that flows from its radicalisation is the experience of **disembeddedness**. In other words, people have the feeling that their lives are not determined by what happens in their immediate locality, but rather by distant events. People can therefore not depend on those in their immediate locality for the functioning of their lives. Their fate is to a large extent determined by expert systems that are out of their reach and by events that occur outside their locality.

Giddens argues that this form of high modernity provides the conditions for the resurgence of religion. A revival of religious or spiritual concerns seems to be fairly widespread in modern societies. The one condition that leads to a resurgence of religion is people's radical doubt about any certainties. This deep-seated doubt exists in radicalised modernity. This is accompanied by the situation in high modernity where **existential** questions are separated from everyday life. The increasing doubt among people stems from the fact that modern knowledge is not final, but preliminary. Knowledge claims are presented as the truth but are in principle continually open to revision. As a result, nothing can be seen as permanent. People thus develop an interest in religion due to their need for certainty.

This links closely to Giddens' second condition for the revival of religion: the fact that existential questions are not addressed in high modernity. People are separated from experiences and situations that link their lives to issues of morality and finitude. They are isolated from thoughts about death or from intrinsic ethical motivations for their actions. Therefore, in high modernity, people function in a moral vacuum, which can be filled by religion, spirituality, self-actualisation programmes or commitment to a cause that gives a sense of fulfilment. In this sense, Giddens also views religious **fundamentalism** as a reaction to uncertainty in life. Fundamentalism presents an alternative world view in which no compromise is tolerated. Against the openness of high modernity, this view presents a closed system to people by simplifying reality – as if it is based on certain knowledge. Giddens identified the conditions that may presently support a religious or spiritual awakening. The general critique against his viewpoint is that it overemphasises function; he views religion solely from the *function* it fulfils in society. Other viewpoints on religion are also possible, as will be indicated later.

Renewed interest in moral guidance

Zymunt Bauman (1997) follows a very similar argument to Giddens' one. In Bauman's view society is not in a state of modernity or high modernity as Giddens argued, but rather in a state of postmodernity. Bauman distinguishes modernity from postmodernity in the sense that in modernity universal truths were sought, whereas in postmodernity posited truths are **deconstructed**. People do not have the same blind respect for authority as they did in the past – they do not accept any situation in which external authorities can impose rules on them. Such an absence of rational rules guiding people's lives can lead to an emphasis on personal ethics and morality. There are only two sources for establishing true moral beliefs:

1. People can make use of experts to justify their moral choices.
2. People can follow the masses in their choices and thereby follow the trends.

Religious leaders are viewed as experts in morality and therefore people will seek guidance from them. The lack of moral guidance produced by postmodern society renews people's interest in moral agencies and ethical debate.

The critique against Bauman's argument is that he identifies the need for expertise and moral guidance within the context of the postmodern era, but he points out that in this era people actually resist expertise and guidance from authorities. Therefore, although Bauman's argument about the renewed interest in moral guidance seems to make sense, the anomaly indicated in this paragraph undermines his argument to some extent.

Revalued as cultural resource

According to David Lyon (2000), postmodernity introduces two social changes in particular. First, technology makes it possible for information to be globally available, which undermines the inflexibility of belief systems. Secondly, this contributed to the consumer approach that also impacted on people's search for insight into their existence. People want to be able to choose their own **narrative** or story for their lives. They want to be free to choose their own options in religion. This does not mean that religion is at present losing ground – it has merely changed from being a social institution to being used as a cultural resource and as such remains important in people's lives. In this sense, religion is not confined to worshipping within church buildings anymore, but rather expressed in contemporary culture. Religion has thus been loosened from tradition (detraditionalised) and from set rules (**deregulated**).

Furthermore, with regard to religion in current society, some sociologists of religion argue that people are attracted to theologically conservative churches because of the clear and consistent practice and steadfast doctrine they advocate. However, where mainline churches have attempted to accommodate the modern secular world, this seems to have lessened these churches' appeal. A number of people also change their religious membership during their lifetimes. The main reasons for this change may be young people's desire to leave mainline churches, to adopt the same religion of their spouse, or to worship with people of similar socioeconomic status.

It is clear that Giddens, Bauman and Lyon view religion as important in present-day society. However, it is also their opinion that the function, role and place of religion in society has changed. In the next subsection, the place and role of religion within society is viewed from a different angle. An important aspect of contemporary society is the awareness of inequality, so it is important to view religion in the light of forms of inequality.

13.4.2 Religion and inequality

This subsection focuses on the relationship between religion and inequality. Studies have already indicated a relationship between religion and **marginality**. This is the first theme of this section. Secondly, the subsection examines the issue of women and religion.

Marginalised groupings

Max Weber (1922) argued that from **marginalised** groups in society religious groupings will emerge that have no ties with established churches. If groups are of the view that they are sidelined in society with regard to prestige and/or economic rewards, they may seek explanations for their situation. **Sects** are religious organisations that stress emotionalism and individual mystical experiences (the use of the term 'sects' in sociology will be clarified later in this chapter). Such religious organisations can present members of marginalised groups with reasons for the inequity they have to suffer, and provide them with a promise of a better life in the afterlife or in a future new world.

Sects can also provide spiritual relief from the experience of **relative deprivation**, which is a feeling of being economically deprived in comparison to other groups. This experience can also exist in the middle classes. People enjoy material wealth but may feel that they lack a sense of community, which sects provide.

Wilson (1982) is of the view that sects arise in times of disorder. When traditional meaning is undermined and social relationships lack coherence and consistency, sects come to the fore presenting a sense of security and order. This is an indication of how the disruption of traditional norms undermined conventional institutionalised religions. This disruption encouraged people to consider alternatives that are not as traditional. People became more tolerant of diversity and religious **pluralism** – multiple religions in one society. The result was that the popularity of cults increased. It is important to remember that social studies have a distinct view on cults that differs from the traditional one. From a sociological view, cults are seen as religious groups lacking organisation and receiving their inspiration from outside the predominant religious culture. They require fewer sacrifices and commitments than churches and sects.

Inequality in gender relationships

Another kind of inequality that stands out in many religious organisations relates to the relationship between men and women. Men can use religion to dominate and oppress women, but at the same time women are compensated for their second-class status. Radical feminist theory argues that religion is a product of patriarchy – a society under male domination where the father figure has a prominent place. Women are given a false belief of compensation in the afterlife and in that way are kept subjugated. However, some scholars argue that in many cases religion actually protects women from the excesses of patriarchy and from abuse. In contrast to those who emphasise the active role that religion continues to fulfil in society, an intense debate is also raging in sociology on whether religion is indeed continuing to play any significant role in society. This matter is discussed in the next subsection.

13.4.3   Secularisation debate

Do people take part in religion to a lesser extent today than previously in history? Secularisation refers to a process in which a society becomes less religious. This tendency can be viewed in different ways.

- First, it can be done by measuring the extent to which people are members of a church and attend services. The decline of membership and participation can then be viewed as an indicator of secularisation.
- Second, it can be viewed as the extent to which the prestige and social influence of religious organisations decline in society. In earlier societies, religious organisations had considerable influence, but do not demand the same respect in society as they did in the past.
- Third, secularisation can refer to a diminishing effect that religious beliefs and values have on people's lives. People orientate their lives less according to what they believe about the supernatural.

Favouring secularisation

Auguste Comte believed that human history passes through three consecutive stages:

1. The first is the **theological** state where *religious beliefs* would be important.
2. The second is the **metaphysical** stage where *philosophy* is dominant.

3. In the final **positivist** stage *science* will be the leading principle.

Another sociologist from earlier times, Émile Durkheim (1912), also argued in favour of the secularisation process. His view was that in an industrial society the division of labour is highly specialised. In such a society religion will lose its significance as a force that integrates society.

Max Weber (1930) also anticipated the decline of religion. His view was that increasing **rationality** will undermine religious influence. Karl Marx believed that religion legitimised the inequality in class societies. He therefore did not expect religion to decline under industrial capitalism that entrenched inequality between the workers and the owners of capital. However, according to him, when capitalism is replaced by classless communism, then religion will cease to have any social purpose.

Wilson (1982) defined secularisation as the process whereby religious institutions, as well as religious thought and practice, lose social significance. Contemporary sociologists supported the views of the founders of sociology by indicating that modern society is incompatible with a context in which the central role of religion is retained. Several factors undermine the significance of religion. Among these is the increasing specialisation of labour, the ascendancy of science and rationality, as well as the decline of traditional values in society.

People's belief in a personal god or some sort of spirit or life force is decreasing. People are becoming increasingly sceptical about religious beliefs. The social fragmentation of society led to a plurality of religious and cultural groups, which caused individuals to view their beliefs as a matter of personal preference. Religious commitment has become a matter of choice and is not a necessary part of being a member of society, as is the case in religious societies in which there is only one faith and one church. This condition is helped along by the fact that people in modern-day society do not have a sense of building a community. The reason is that people's lives are dominated by impersonal bureaucracies, therefore it is difficult for them to relate to the closely knit communities provided by religious organisations. People explore in a wider sense the cultural services and the cultural diversity that are open to them. The result is that they hold their beliefs with less certainty.

Social scientists view the process of secularisation as well advanced and irreversible. The belief in supernatural powers as a cultural trait is viewed as doomed because scientific knowledge is becoming increasingly **diffuse** and is deemed adequate to provide answers to life's problems.

The notion developed that science would ultimately answer questions that had previously been in the realm of religion. This is due to the rapid growth in technological solutions to the daily problems of living and the scientific understanding of them. The result is that religion's influence on thought and behaviour is gradually reduced or removed. Societal elements become separated from spiritual or religious influences or connections.

This decline in religion's influence led to a situation where religion only retained its influence within the family environment. Religion is seen to be largely irrelevant in the circles of government, the marketplace and education. Nationalism and political and secular ideologies became the cohesive forces in societies. Religion became a matter of personal conviction rather than an expression of a social reality. Religious norms and values do not function on a societal level. The concepts of sin and salvation, or heaven and hell, have lost much of their importance in modern-day society. Moral rules that are enforced by religious and supernatural sanctions have become less strict. The realm of the supernatural is viewed as not important for the modern world anymore.

Rationality involves action to achieve a goal that is thought out. Capitalism places a primary emphasis on maximising profit. In the light of such a goal-orientated emphasis, religious beliefs tend to fade into the background. Society is then **desacralised**. This means that supernatural forces are no longer seen to control it. People's actions are not directed by religious beliefs but by secular goals. The world is characterised by disenchantment. Magic and mystery are not leading powers in society anymore. According to Wilson (1982), a rational world view is the true adversary of religion. Motives and meaning that determine action are in this case taken as rational. Rational procedure and the testing of arguments are the basis for meaning in modern-day society. Truth is assessed by what can be measured objectively and **quantified**. Religion is viewed only as an option that comes into reckoning when scientific alternatives have all been exhausted.

Secularisation, on the one hand, refers to the declining power of religion. On the other hand, it also points to the effect that ideas of the modern world have on religious policies and doctrinal views, for instance those on the role of women and gays. Traditional religious institutions increasingly have to accommodate outlooks from the modern world view. In a global society, religion does not present an overarching set of beliefs and values, but takes on a relatively marginal, limited and privatised role. In this sense, religion can only deal with personal questions, such as the meaning of life for an individual

Critique of secularisation

Currently among sociologists there is a strong critique of the idea of secularisation. It is their opinion that a decline of religion in its institutional state does not necessarily indicate a decrease in religious commitment and belief. It is not essential for people who hold religious beliefs to belong to a religious institution. In today's world, people can express their religious beliefs in different ways. Polls indicate that many more individuals hold religious beliefs than those who belong to religious organisations. Religion still shows a surprising vitality. Conservative and fundamental religious groups, in particular, have growing numbers of followers. In these organisations good and evil are clearly distinguished, and individual effort is emphasised and sometimes rewarded. In many cases such groupings use the mass media and social networks effectively to spread their message. This conservative reaction attempts to defend beliefs and structures against secularisation, which can be viewed as a counter-secularisation response. This stems from uncertainty and anxiety about the danger of secularisation undermining their religious position. They maintain only a practical and instrumental relationship with the secular world and resist moral relativisation. This position is found among groupings that resist secularisation within Christianity, Judaism and Islam. They build a strong counterculture in order to maintain a steadfast religious identity among future generations by means of a committed and continuous religious socialisation.

Talcott Parsons (1949) argues that society has evolved through a process of **structural differentiation**. During this process, parts of the social system have become more specialised, which resulted in the parts performing fewer functions without lessening their importance. Religious beliefs can therefore still provide significance and meaning to an individual's life. Such specialisation does, however, limit the church's involvement in non-religious matters. This enables the capitalist logic of efficiency, calculability and profit to play a more dominant role, while the roles of religious faith and that of morality diminish. Furthermore, religion can play an important role in defending cultures or by lending support during cultural transitions. In such cases, religion helps people cope with change or in times when their culture is threatened. Religion also supports the world view of its followers' culture and gives members reason to defend it.

Gilles Keppel (1994) argues that Islam, Judaism and Christianity have experienced a resurgence in the modern world. These religious revivals are reactions against modernity and represent a process of resacralisation: restoring religious meaning or the quality of the sacred to society. Stark (Stark & Bainbridge 1985) views the religious dimension as more dynamic than it is depicted in typical secularisation theories. He suggests that secularisation thrusts religion into new directions. Some religious organisations become orientated more towards the world, while others evolve to fill the vacuum produced by secularisation. Through innovation there emerged new kinds of religions and forms of religious organisation. Many organisations shift their emphasis away from the supernatural, but they still satisfy people's religious needs. Thereby religion still retains a form of otherworldliness by presenting people with an escape route from the demands of the modern world. In modern-day society, different patterns of religious practices develop continually in all parts of the world.

The problem with the secularisation theory is that it is not clear what the extent of spiritual fervour or scepticism was among tribal societies in the past. The nature of religious practices and beliefs was not studied throughout the centuries before the social sciences were established, but since the development of the social sciences, the ways in which religion is to be measured remain a contested terrain. Measurement depends on what definition of religion is being employed, an aspect on which scientists differ significantly.

The existence of a secularisation process in society is therefore not evident in a straightforward manner. The identification of such a process invariably depends on how religion is defined. Against those highlighting a secularisation process, others do still view religion as a critical force in the social world. It seems that religion will still appeal to people for a long time because it provides people with meaning and answers to complex questions about life that cannot be explored when limited to a rational perspective. Huntington (1997) is of the opinion that religion will become more important in global terms. People tend to identify themselves in terms of civilisations that are made up of history, language, culture, tradition and religion. In the light of this identification, clashes between civilisations will increase because they exist geographically close to each other. In such an environment, the divide in relations between 'us' and 'them' will enlarge and breed continual conflict, a huge part of which will be related to religious divisions., Globally, therefore, religion will become more rather than less important. In this conflict the identity of Western Christian civilisation will be increasingly challenged.

Sociologists further argue that global politics, science and the economy do not offer an identity to individuals or to social groups. People do not have a single or general sense of who they are in modern-day society. Within this lacuna, religion can be used to provide an overarching identity. Religion can be abused to assert one group's superiority over another group, or it can be employed to mobilise marginalised groups to seek influence or power within a global world. Religion can also be used to bring together people of different beliefs and faiths. Globalisation limits the influence of religion but does not lead to the end of all religion.

Rationality caused the modern world to become fragmented to such an extent that many people find it difficult to draw a satisfying identity from their public life. Work became a means to an end and does not offer people lasting satisfaction and fulfilment. People do not sense a **calling** to their work and may not identify strongly with their co-workers. In such cases religious movements can restore a sense of fulfilment in people's lives. In order to construct an idea of secularisation, an ideal religious society has to be envisaged against which the idea of secularisation can be measured. Such an ideal religious society is to a large extent the product of a particular researcher's judgement. This should caution readers about how they interpret conclusions drawn in the secularisation debate.

In modern-day society the religious field changes continually. Alternative religions develop, Christian and Muslim political parties are established, and the Africanisation of Western religions takes place in Africa. Outside of the mainstream institutions, charismatic and Pentecostal groups and religious movements function with vitality. These trends could slow secularisation or reverse it. The future of the relationship between religion and society is thus not clear.

13.4.4 Religious fundamentalism

Religious fundamentalism is a term that came into common use only in the last two or three decades. Modernisation undermined traditional elements of society, thus religious **fundamentalism** developed as a countermove to defend these traditional beliefs. Religious fundamentalists interpret basic scriptures or texts literally. They view such texts as sacred and therefore believe in their timelessness and authority. Fundamentalists believe that their own interpretation and doctrines are correct, and no other interpretations are possible or permissible.

Religious fundamentalism is a learned disposition and is dependent on the insight of privileged interpreters who thereby have considerable power in religious and non-religious matters. All aspects of life are interpreted in terms of faith-based answers, therefor this social grouping views their doctrines as fully applicable to family, political, social and economic life. To them history is not merely a sequence of events, but rather a cosmic struggle between good and evil. The good is outlined in certain principles and the evil is identified as that which digresses from those principles. Such a divisive imagery does not take into account that human life is complex. Truth is viewed as unchanging and knowable. According to this view, truth does not vary over time and place. This way of dealing with reality can fuel hate and conflict, and thereby produce martyrs and deadly foes. Religious fanaticism can thus stem from fundamentalism. If such religious fanaticism is embodied in the state, then leaders can use military power, government structures and propaganda to wield total power, which can lead to crimes against humanity. Religious fundamentalists tend to be highly patriarchal. The power of men and the subordination of women are notions that are emphasised in fundamentalism. Gender equality is viewed as a symptom of a declining moral order that needs to be reversed.

All fundamentalist movements believe that secular values aim to wipe out their religions completely. Such movements therefore develop in reaction to a perceived threat or crisis, whether it is real or imagined. Fundamentalism is found among Christians, Jews and other religious groupings, but it is Islamic fundamentalism that currently plays an important role in world politics and is shaping world history. The Islamic faith involves the whole of human life and a clear distinction is made between what is sacred and what is secular. For Muslims their religious prescriptions cover all aspects of their life. In this faith, Western values are viewed as a threat to what Muslims view as sacred. The radical faction in Islamic fundamentalism views their religious traditions as under threat from a degenerate Western society and they often take extreme measures to protect their religion. Other religions are not tolerated, and Western culture is vilified.

This religious fundamentalism is a response to experiences of failures of legitimacy and authority in modern Muslim states. It views Islam as a way of life that is relevant to the whole of society, therefore the subversive, secular and materialistic Western view of life cannot be tolerated. Islamic law must be introduced, and Islamic values must be reflected in the use of science and technology. Islamic fundamentalists range from those who would want to promote an Islamic state within current political arrangements to the fanatics who want to establish political change in a violent way.

The motivation for the establishment of an Islamic state is not driven solely by religion. It is a complex matter which includes the revival of traditional ways of life combined with modern lifestyles. The rise of fundamentalism can be attributed to people's experience that their belief system is challenged. People feel they cannot tolerate the challenge and have to reaffirm their belief. They often use political means to further their cause.

13.4.5 Religion and social change

The practice of religion can change over time. For instance, currently the practice of much religious activity is highly **commercialised**. A large industry has developed through selling religious music and 'spiritual' publications. Theorists debate the changing role that religion plays in society. Most functionalists, Marxists and feminists generally dismiss the possibility that religion is able to transform society. They view religion as a **conservative** force. In their view it is society that rather changes religion and not vice versa. In this context fundamentalism is presented as an example of religion playing a counter-revolutionary role. However, religion can indeed play an important role in liberation movements. This is what happened in South Africa during the time of the anti-apartheid movements. Some churches in this instance functioned in a similar way to civil rights movements and raised the consciousness of people to understand their state of oppression in order to engage in acts of resistance.

The potential of a religion to affect society depends on the overlap between the religion and the culture of the society, as well as the social location of religion in such a society. The more influence religion exerts in a society, the more it can impact on it. If an influential religious belief system promotes change, then the society will be directed by this focus.

13.5 Sociological perspectives on religion

The three classical sociological theorists – Durkheim, Marx and Weber – still strongly influence sociological approaches to religion. All three of these theorists expected the significance of religion to decrease in modern times. Each of them believed religion was fundamentally an **illusion**. This means that they viewed it as a false image or representation of what is real. This view stems from the period in which they lived where rational thought was valued more highly than religious beliefs.

13.5.1 Structural/functionalist perspective: Religion and social stability – product of society

Worshipping society itself

Émile Durkheim (1858–1917) studied religion, particularly in small-scale, traditional societies. He published his work *The Elementary Forms of the Religious Life* in 1912. This provides us with one of the most influential interpretations of religion from a functionalist perspective.

Durkheim studied the **totemism** of Australian Aboriginal clans as the most basic form of religion. A totem is an object, plant or animal that is revered by a clan as a symbol, and therefore viewed as sacred, in contrast to what is seen as profane. A totem is used for rituals and is treated with respect. In the case of the Australian Aborigines, the totems differ among the clans. The clans select a totem for themselves, which is usually an animal or natural object. Examples of totems are kangaroos, trees, rivers, rock formations and other animals or natural phenomena.

A clan is like an extended family. The members share duties and obligations, and practise **exogamy** – members are not allowed to marry within the clan. Within these clans the totem is represented by drawings in stone or wood, which are considered as equally sacred as the figure they represent. The totem distinguishes the clan from all the other clans and as such is the most sacred object used in the Aboriginal clan ritual.

Durkheim concluded that each totem is a symbol of the group itself, representing its cohesion and values. The respect shown towards the totem is in fact respect for the values of the group and for the group as such. The ceremonies and rituals related to the totem are essentially meant to bind the members of the group together and to express the group's unique identity. The collective ceremonies create, reinforce and express group solidarity and unity.

In Durkheim's view, this applies to small traditional societies, as well as to modern societies. He therefore views religion as a cultural universal that can be found in all societies because it meets basic human needs and serves important societal functions. Religion establishes a collective consciousness that gives people a sense of belonging and guides them to let go of individual self-interest. In religion, members of society communicate, express and understand the moral bonds which unite them. Within the religious rituals, full of reverence and drama, the integration of that particular society is strengthened. In this sense, religion can be seen as a worshipping of society. The actual object of religious worship is the society and the members who depend on it.

Critics of Durkheim do not support his view that religion is in general the worship of society as such. This observation may be applicable to small, non-literate communities where culture and religion largely overlap, but it is less applicable to modern, industrial societies. Modern-day society is diversified, with different cultures, religions, institutions and social groups. This pluralism stands in direct contrast to Durkheim's theory of religion's role to ensure unity and solidarity. It is also pointed out in the critiques that Durkheim studied only a small number of Aboriginal groups and these groups were somewhat atypical of other Aboriginal tribes. It may therefore be misleading to make generalisations based on the Aboriginal groups Durkheim studied and, on this basis, to try and work out universals for religion.

Coping mechanism for stress

Malinowski (1884–1942) used data he obtained from studying small-scale, non-literate societies to interpret religion. He did his fieldwork mainly in the Trobriand Islands off the coast of New Guinea. As with Durkheim, Malinowski (1948) was of the opinion that religions reinforced social norms and values, and promoted social solidarity. However, he did not view religion as the worshipping of society itself. For him it is rather concerned with situations of emotional stress that threaten social solidarity within the society.

Malinowski noted that religious rituals are associated with life crises and events that cannot be controlled or predicted. Life stages such as birth, puberty, marriage and death all are enclosed in religious rituals. Life crises tend to disrupt social life or produce tension and anxiety. Rituals tend to reduce the anxiety, provide confidence and strengthen group unity. Malinowski was critiqued for exaggerating the role of religious rituals in this matter. Other studies indicated that many rituals merely maintained the prestige of the custom and were not related to strengthening solidarity and addressing fear and uncertainty.

Providing answers to ultimate issues

Talcott Parsons (1902–1979) argued that beliefs, values and systems of meaning directed human action in the social system. These guidelines were provided by the cultural system of which religion formed a part. The function of religion was to provide guidelines for human action within this system. Human life can be disrupted by unforeseen circumstances and is therefore characterised by uncertainty due to uncontrollable factors. To cope with such possible crisis situations, people need religion. Religion provides answers to those issues that cannot be understood. Religion presents meaning in view of events and problems that threaten to shatter people's meaning of life. An example of this is *suffering*, for which religion can provide answers to a person's piercing questions. From a religious perspective, suffering can be presented as a test of faith, a punishment for sins or as temporary hardship that will be rewarded in the afterlife.

A problem with the functionalist perspective of the theorists above is that they tend to emphasise the positive contributions of religion and neglect the **dysfunctional** aspects. According to this perspective, the focus is on functional aspects such as solidarity, integration and harmony. However, the many ways in which religion can be disruptive and divisive are not placed under scrutiny. For instance, in the religions of the ancient Greek and Roman Empire, the gods did terrible mischief to one another and to human beings. The social order had to stand on its own moral and ethical laws. The gods (from the supernatural realm) were portrayed as uninterested in the mundane doings of human beings.

The idea that the supernatural is deeply involved in the lives of human beings is to be found in the major world faiths, such as Christianity, Judaism, Islam and Hinduism. Not all religions acknowledge the existence of a god or gods. Taoism, Confucianism and ancestor worshipping have a belief in an overarching mystical force that governs life. The effect of religion on individual morality depends on the images people have of the supernatural. Only when the supernatural is viewed as *morally concerned* will the religious rites and rituals help impose human morality. Morality depends, therefore, primarily on the people's view of how important the supernatural is for moral behaviour.

Religion: Functional or dysfunctional effect?

The functional perspective's main contribution is that it sensitises people to the functions that religion can fulfil in society. However, religion can also have a dysfunctional effect on society. Below is a list of some functions, followed by a list of possible dysfunctions.

The important functions that religion can play in societies are the following:

- Religion can promote social cohesion and a sense of belonging. It can thereby emphasise the importance of shared symbols and practices. Religion can bind members of a society together through rituals and rites. It assists people to experience on a subconscious level the power society exerts over the individual.
- Religion strengthens society's norms and values. It controls human behaviour and provides a foundation for social organisation. If personal wishes conflict with society's requirements, religion offers rewards to those who subordinate their desires to society's interests. In that way religion controls deviant behaviour and sanctions conformity. If people deviate from the religious norms, they may expose themselves to supernatural punishment or bad fortune. These sanctions extend to unseen deviance as well. In this way religion is a major influence on an individual's conscience. In religion there are also ways of forgiveness so that transgressors can be received back into the religious community. This ensures social control and reduces tension.
- Religion presents meaning to human life. It places the lives of people in a universal context. This is especially true of poor and oppressed people who are presented with deliverance from their hardships and inequality by a message of social salvation. Religion presents the destitute and downtrodden with a high moral status, which compensates for their low socioeconomic status. Religion can also influence the higher classes to be more conscious of inequality. They are called to acts of kindness, charity, mercy and sharing with those who are less fortunate.
- Religion gives family life special meaning. Marriage rituals are important in most religions. Religious norms on marriage include the following: it prescribes the way in which sexual activity should take place, it discourages divorce, equalises couples' norms and limits mistreatment of spouses. According to the oral traditions, familial relationships are also present among the divinities of different religions, for instance the father–son (filial) relationship between God and Jesus. In ancestral veneration, the aim is to appease the deceased male family members so that they will continue to care for the clan. In some instances, these ancestors can also be female family members. Mother figures are also worshipped, as seen in the case of the Hindu goddesses, and also with the veneration of Mary, the mother of Jesus according to tradition. The family has a special place in religious rituals and worship, and is closely associated with it. Religion can therefore determine the normative functioning of families' lives – a functioning that is in most cases transmitted to new generations.
- Religion can play an important role to **legitimise** the authority of government. In this sense, religion stabilises societies and persuades people to accept government laws. Such legitimisation is very prominent in Islamic countries. The South African Constitution has a secular grounding, and religion is therefore not directly

supportive of the government. However, religious groupings can align themselves with the government and thereby support government initiatives. Traditional chiefs in rural areas can also uphold traditional rites and rituals. In their area they can legitimise their authority by means of appealing to religious views.

In general, the functionalist perspective does not point out the dysfunctional effect that religion can have on societies. However, it is clear that religion can contribute to a society being more dysfunctional. Below are some examples:

- Religion can encourage the subordination of women to men. A submissive position for women is prescribed in some religious groupings. This usually implies that women are excluded from certain religious activities. Among the Nguni who practise **exogamy** (marrying outside of the group), the women remain strangers in the homestead and can more easily be accused of witchcraft. In groups that practise **endogamy** (marrying within the group) like the Venda and Sotho, the wife is normally not accused of witchcraft by her husband. However, women can also play an important role in religion as seen among the Venda and Swazi. Women sometimes fulfil the role of **prophets** in some African independent churches and also act as diviners (*isangoma*) among the Zulu.
- Religion can make it difficult to resolve political conflicts. Political struggles are occasionally about valued resources such as land and water. When the opposing parties identify with different religions, the political dispute becomes difficult to resolve. The struggle is then elevated to a higher level of conflicting values and beliefs. This is the case with the dispute between the Palestinians and Israelis in the Middle East.
- Religion can prevent change. When the religious establishment supports the prevailing culture, norms and values, it presents the status quo with a revered character. In such instances it becomes difficult to motivate the population to work for change of the existing conditions. The support of some religious groupings for the apartheid system made it more difficult for these groupings to consider the possibility of changing the system.

The next angle on religion – the conflict perspective – focuses on religion and its role in resisting change. Where the functionalist perspective views religion's primary function in

society to be a stabilising influence, the conflict perspective underscores the problematic effect that this function can have on society.

13.5.2 Conflict perspective: Religion and change

Karl Marx (1818–1883) did not study religion directly. He derived his ideas from Ludwig Feuerbach (1804–1872), who viewed religion as ideas that humans form during their cultural development. They then project these ideas and needs as personalised religious forces and gods. Through this projection people alienate themselves from their own cultural creations. Karl Marx accepted this notion of alienation as being central to religious practice. Marx argued in a famous phrase that religion is 'the sigh of the oppressed creature, the heart of the heartless world, and the soul of soulless conditions. It is the opiate of the masses'. By this he meant that religion promises happiness in an afterlife and thereby causes people to accept the existing conditions of life. Religion helps to alleviate the pain of their living conditions. Marx views religion in this sense as an illusion that makes the world bearable for people who place their hope in supernatural intervention. This also makes suffering a virtue.

It is clear that, according to this view, religion actually distorts reality. People are led to accept blindly the existing conditions of life because religion justifies such acceptance. This preserves the social order, as well as the social inequality inherent in it. In this way religion is a force that encourages resistance to change and gives capitalists the opportunity to mislead the workers whom they are exploiting. Religion then becomes a tool for class oppression and a mechanism for social control. Religion thus coaxes the oppressed to accept their socioeconomic constraints and simultaneously creates a false consciousness by explaining and justifying these social conditions. The purpose is to blind members of the subjected class to their own interests and to persuade them to support the capitalist system, even to their detriment. In this way they do not realise their oppression and help the ruling classes to maintain their capitalist power.

In contrast, in a classless society, religion would not be necessary, because people would not have the need to escape reality. In such a society the means of production will be communally owned, therefore no social conditions will exist to produce religion. All of the illusions and distortions within the social reality will disappear, according to Marx. Some evidence from our time confirms religion's role in resisting change. Typically, the conservative Protestants in the US, the so-called New Christian Right, support the right-wing political candidates in the Republican Party. From this political platform they attack the more liberal candidates in the Democratic Party, who champion socioeconomic transformation.

The critique of Marx's theory of religion is directed towards his view that religion cannot contribute towards change or towards a revolution in society. Religion can indeed play a significant part in helping to bring about change and the total transformation of society. Examples are the religious wars, terrorism and genocide that contributed to some of the many violent and tragic episodes in world history. Many national revolutions were fuelled by religious beliefs. Examples of these are the Protestant Reformation of the 16th century and the current Islamic militancy that foments radical social upheavals. The Protestant Reformation united diverse groupings of people who were dissatisfied with the existing social system. It drew support from the city and country, as well as the lower and upper classes. Within the Reformation all of these groupings could be united to become a strong force in reshaping society.

Another example where religion contributed to a national revolution was the fall of the Iranian monarchy in 1979. This revolution was driven by Shiism, a fundamentalist branch of Islam. The leader of the Shiite clergy, the Ayatollah Khomeini, engineered the revolution from exile, became the new leader of the country and transformed it into an Islamic republic. This fusion of religion and the revolutionary movement successfully ensured the overthrow of the Shah of Iran. The religion of Shiism provided the revolutionaries with communication, supporters, structures and ideas to fulfil their mission.

13.5.3 Interpretive perspective: Religion as a system of meaning

The interpretive perspective views religion as a socially constructed belief system. Max Weber (1864–1920) studied different religious systems: Hinduism, Buddhism, Taoism, ancient Judaism and Christianity. In studying these religions, he concentrated on the relationship between religion and social change. Weber describes how religions have often produced social transformation. He explained in particular how Protestantism, and especially Calvinism, contributed to the capitalist outlook of the modern Western world. Max Weber pointed this out in his book *The Protestant Ethic and the Spirit of Capitalism* (1930). Weber argues as follows: whereas development in manufacturing and commerce as well as urbanisation did take place in traditional India and China, it did not fully develop because the religions in those societies inhibited the process.

In contrast, Christianity contributed to the radical social change in the Western world. Weber regarded Christianity as a religion built on salvation. That means that humans are **sinners** who can only be rescued by God's **grace**. The psychological tension created by either being lost or saved did not exist in the Eastern religions and this impeded change. The origins of the belief system within Christianity that led to capitalism were identified in Protestantism by Weber. He posed the question why capitalist leaders were overwhelmingly Protestants. He claimed that this tendency stemmed from the religious teachings of the Protestants. The Calvinist branch of the Protestant tradition in particular contributed to an ethic that supported the orientations required by capitalism.

Weber pointed out that the founder of Calvinism, John Calvin (1509–1564), emphasised a doctrine of **predestination**. This is a belief that God decided in the beginning who would be saved and who would perish. Because people cannot know for sure whether they are saved, they look for earthly signs of their salvation. This psychological problem of Protestants led them to search eagerly for clues of 'being elected'. High income due to hard work was believed to be a clue of believers being elected by God. The Protestants' work ethic was not an attempt to 'get to heaven', but to convince themselves that they were 'chosen for heaven'. Protestants therefore toiled hard but did not indulge in the fruits of their labour. They maintained the belief that the present world is temporary and that it is more important to focus on heaven as the final goal of life. This meant that they practised **asceticism**. They abstained from the pleasures and luxuries of this world and developed an austere lifestyle. They did not collect luxuries or enjoy possessions. Key features of the Protestant ethic were hard work and self-denial. The adherents criticised laziness, time wasting, sexual pleasures and unnecessary sleep. Recreation was only permitted to improve health to be fit for the individual's calling (calling refers to the work that God expects of one to accomplish on earth). Anything that may distract people from their calling was condemned. This methodical and single-minded pursuit of a calling led to an ethic that produced a stockpiling of wealth. Owing to this ethic, Protestants invested their wealth in their businesses and did not spend it on themselves. In combination with the development of steam power and mechanisation at that time, this led to an astronomical increase in production, which ensured surplus income to develop the businesses further. The result was, according to Weber, the development of capitalism. This production system eventually developed its own norms and became a socioeconomic force in itself.

From the Marxist viewpoint, Weber was criticised for granting Calvinism such a prominent position in the development of capitalism. The Marxists indicated that Calvinism developed in cities where commerce and early industrialisation already existed. They view Calvinism rather as a result of early capitalism than the cause of this economic system. It is clear from an interpretative perspective that religion is described as a *system of meaning* that is developed to interpret the position of humans in relation to the supernatural. This presents religion as a dynamic process of interpretation and in that way it can indeed contribute to change in society.

13.6 Organisation of religion

The language of economics can be used by sociologists to describe the way religion is organised in society (Stark 2007: 395). This is called economy of religion. In the same way that the economy has markets and firms, there is a demand for religion (market) with religious organisations (firms) fulfilling the demand. In accordance with economic language, religion in society can also be characterised by a free-market system or by monopolies. There can be an active interplay between different religious groups, or the 'market' can be dominated by one or only a few religious organisations. Religious pluralism stands in opposition to religious monopoly. A religious monopoly is only possible with strong support from the state that enforces an adherence to one religion. In such an economic interpretation of religion in society, it is said that the greater the number of competing religious groups, the greater will be the proportion of the population who will be active in religion. A variety of religious groups that cater for 'niche markets' can satisfy a greater scope of religious needs and tastes in society. On the other hand, if only one religious institution exists, this will not satisfy everyone's religious needs, and participation levels will therefore be lower. For a religious organisation to be competing successfully in the economy of religion, its beliefs and rituals have to be appealing to the religious 'consumers'. Such a religion should compete successfully with other religious groups, and must therefore have efficient 'sales representatives' who spread the word and display good marketing skills.

The dynamics of this theory hold for societies with a variety of religious organisations, which gives people the opportunity to make a free choice. In societies where religious pluralism is not as prevalent with fewer deeply committed believers, there may be less religious mobility. It is likely that people will rather practise their childhood religion without considering alternatives. Such a society will therefore have a rigid economy of religion. The motive for using economic terms in a religious context is to give a general description of how religious organisations function in society. More generally, sociologists attempted to distinguish different types of religious organisations, their elements and the members who participate in them.

13.6.1 Types of religious organisations

In sociology, religions can be classified in different ways, one of which is in terms of the object of worship. For instance, the major religious groups in the West – Christianity, Islam and Judaism – are characterised by worshipping only one god. This type of religion is described as **monotheist**. In contrast to this there are **polytheist** religions where more than one god is worshipped. Hinduism could be seen as a polytheist religion; however, the different 'gods' that are worshipped are also seen as manifestations from the 'One Spirit'. Other religions such as Confucianism, Buddhism, Shintoism and Taoism can be seen as expressions of **transcendental idealism**. Adherents of these religions do not worship a god, but rather focus on a set of moral, philosophical and ethical principles of an ideal life. Other forms of religion that can be highlighted are:

- ancestor worship – the reverence granted to deceased relatives
- animism – the belief that spirits inhabit the material world and operate actively in this world
- totemism – the veneration of an object from nature.

For an extended period in sociology, the typology used mostly to study religions focused on the types of *religious organisations* that can be found. Sociologists used different ways to categorise the types of religious organisations. However, it is indeed a question whether, with the increasing pluralisation of religious organisations, they can all be categorised in a meaningful way. For a while, some theorists in sociology categorised religious organisations according to four types: church, denomination, sect and cult.

Church as a religious organisation

The organisation of church depicts a large, bureaucratically organised religious organisation that accommodates all the members of the society concerned. This organisation is fully integrated and institutionalised into the dominant culture of the surrounding society. The following features can be highlighted:

- Churches are organisations with a strong intellectual and teaching tradition.

- The organisation has a clerical and administrative hierarchy, and it is founded on elaborate dogma that is expressed through detailed rituals.
- It draws its membership from all classes of society, but especially from the middle and upper classes.
- The members can participate fully in social life and need not reject the present world in favour of an afterlife ('heaven').
- The church generally represents the country's official religion and has a close relationship with the government.
- It does not tolerate challenges and therefore guards its monopoly on religious truth.

The current upsurge in religious pluralism put pressure on these types of monopolies. This caused such religious structures (churches) to act strongly in a protective mode and to maintain their primary and religious-based controlling position. Membership commences with birth and is not voluntary. An example of this is Islam in Iran presently.

Denomination as religious organisation

The second type of religious organisation is called a **denomination**. This is similar to a church and displays the same hierarchical organisational structure together with formally trained leadership. A denomination differs from a church in the following fashion:

- It does not appeal to the whole of society.
- It approves of the separation between church and state.
- It does not claim monopoly on religious truth.
- It cooperates with other religious organisations towards a greater cause.
- Denominations do not define the values of the society but rather accommodate them.
- Members largely share the values of the host society.
- Members are mostly drawn from the middle and working classes.
- New members are mainly the children of present members with more flexible commitment.

Examples within South Africa are the Catholic Church in South Africa, the Anglican Church of Southern Africa, the Methodist Church of Southern Africa, and the Dutch Reformed Church.

Sects as religious organisation

The third type of religious organisation, **sects**, refers to religious groups that are not part of mainstream organisations. They are actually the opposite of churches.

Elements that are important in this kind of organisation are emotionalism, purity of faith, mystical experiences and less structure. Features that can be highlighted are the following:

- Sects are generally small organisations that reject aspects of the established religion.
- They call for a return to **purity** – unblemished moral conduct.
- They believe God is present and active in members' lives.
- The members form a close-knit community in which they experience solidarity and a stand in opposition to the world.
- In view of the previous point, the membership of sects usually includes those persons who are disconnected from their positions in life and who oppose the direction of the state and society.
- Sects actively recruit members and only admit truly committed converts.
- Children do not automatically become part of the sect but join it willingly as adults and accept its prescribed lifestyle.
- In many instances, sects are formed by members who have severed ties with existing religious organisations.
- Sectarian leaders usually lack formal training but exercise personal charisma.
- Members are actively involved in the organisation, and the structure has very little hierarchy.

The difficulty in defining sects is that as the membership increases, the structure can become more hierarchical and starts to display the characteristics of a denomination. As the children of the original members of a sect grow up and become members themselves, they may not be able to sustain the fervour of the initial generation. When the sect begins to take on the form of a denomination, members become dissatisfied and break away to form a new sect. Sects can also come under pressure when the charismatic leader dies, or members can improve their socioeconomic status in society and the marginality of a sect loses its attraction to them. However, sociologists differ on the point whether all kind of sects will tend to develop into denominations. There is a view that this will depend on the nature of the sect.

Cults as religious organisation

The final type of religious organisation is **cults**. Sociology assigns a specific meaning to this concept, which differs from the popular usage that views a cult as a small and unconventional religious grouping that provokes social disapproval. In contrast, sociology uses this term to describe a group without a fixed religious doctrine. The following features can be pointed out:

- The beliefs that members of a cult hold are vague, and members tolerate individualistic beliefs.
- The cult has a charismatic leader and a loose organisational structure.
- Whereas sects call people to return to a pure belief system, cults devise new belief systems with accompanying symbols and rituals.
- The cult's belief system may be based on a new insight or revelation from a prophet.
- The goal is to present the adherents of this religious formation with a spiritual experience.
- The cult can offer services directly to their clients or make use of mass media, social networks and conferences.

Three kinds of cults can be distinguished:

- Countercultural cults are offshoots of especially Asian religious traditions. Examples are Zen Buddhism, the Hare Krishna movement and Sufism. They have a charismatic leadership and emphasise direct personal religious experience.
- Personal-growth cults have a Western origin and are more quasi-religious in nature. They want to put their followers in touch with the ultimate meaning of life. Scientology, Transcendental Meditation and the New Age Movement are examples of such cults. Members are not fully involved in these cults, but rather follow them to solve specific problems in their lives.
- Neo-Christian cults include groups such as the Children of God and Jews for Jesus that emphasise direct religious experiences.

Sociologists agree that sects and cults are the result of people's reaction to swift social change or their attempt to relieve feelings of deprivation. The deprivation can be social and can stem from lack of prestige and status, or economic because of the struggle to make ends meet. Such deprivation can also be psychological where somebody feels rejected from mainstream society or alienated from the values of the society. The view exists that sects develop especially in an environment of economic and social transition and deprivation, and that cults thrive on psychological deprivation. If circumstances change and the deprivation disappears, the related sects or cults tend to dissolve or turn into different organisations.

Wallis (1984) differentiates between new religious movements that reject, accommodate or affirm the world.

- World-rejecting new religious movements carry a definite conception of God. The movements are critical of the outside world and expect their members to break with conventional life; some even encourage a communal lifestyle. Contact with the outside world is not allowed. These movements actively seek societal change and expect God to intervene in bringing this about.
- World-accommodating new religious movements are, in contrast, new formations (secessions) that broke away from existing religious organisations. Their aim is to re-establish morally pure conduct in religion.
- World-affirming new religious movements offer members success in terms of the dominant values of society. Personal achievement is emphasised and is seen as a solution to personal problems. They use courses and training to unlock the spiritual powers within individuals. These movements have weak control over their members. World-affirming new religious movements can be based on Western psychotherapy or on oriental spiritual views.

The examples above indicate how sociologists tried to compose typologies of people's religious activities. However, sociologists at present agree that such typologies are only vague descriptions of all religious activities. The diversity of religious activities makes meaningful typologies very difficult, therefore sociologists tend nowadays not to identify types of religions. Nevertheless, to distinguish religions in view of their characteristics will remain an important research endeavour in sociology.

13.6.2 Elements of religion

In religion a distinction is made between the profane – elements of everyday life – and the sacred – that which evokes awe and respect. The separation of the profane and the sacred is typical of any religious orientation. The basic religious orientation is to worship that which is viewed as sacred. What is the source of viewing something as sacred in religion? This can be ascribed to supernatural beings or to authoritative declarations. People experience the sacred when they are in the presence of something that exposes them to a power larger than themselves. This power surpasses their ordinary life experiences, therefore the sacred becomes desirable and attracts people. However, the dimension of the sacred can also raise feelings of dread.

Box 13.1 Things that are sacred

In religions the spectrum of objects that are viewed as sacred is very broad. 'Sacred' can refer to people with rare abilities (eg a prophet), material objects (eg a cross, totem), locations (eg a cave, spring), unusual occurrences (eg a flood, lunar eclipse) or particular times (eg sunrise, Easter). In religious conduct, a ritual is an established formal pattern of behaviour that is associated with the sacred. Rituals are practised to show reverence to the sacred and clearly set it apart from the profane. In religions the rituals are also practised to ensure the goodwill and blessings of supernatural beings towards the worshippers. Ritual also brings the believers in a group together and the repetition of rituals creates feelings of solidarity, integration, security and identity. The close association of the rituals to the dimension of the sacred can cause worshippers to view rituals as also sacred.

The system of religious beliefs in elementary religions links the rituals to those aspects which are viewed as sacred. This belief system explains the purpose and meaning of rituals. In more complex religions the systems of religious beliefs go beyond such a linkage and include moral **propositions**, which are considered to be truths that ought to be the foundation of the particular society. In this way the believers of those truths may expect the moral propositions to inform the different aspects of that society: family life, gender relationships, the economy, politics and education. Societies with diverse religions therefore rather opt for constitutions that do not favour a single religion in order to create less chance of religious conflict.

13.6.3 Religious organisations and their members

Religious organisations can have systems of religious beliefs, rituals and sacred objects. Such organisations are only significant to the extent that their members adhere to them. It is therefore important to consider members' religious participation and their religiosity.

Religious participation

Religious participation must be distinguished from religious preference and membership. In general, far fewer people participate in religious rituals than those who indicate that they are affiliated with the religion. Attempts have been made to attribute the variation in church attendance to the fact that people belong to different socioeconomic classes. For instance, it was argued that upper classes need fewer benefits from religion and will therefore participate less in religious activities. Similarly, it was noted that there may be less involvement from the lowest classes due to economic factors. It could be that they are unable to afford clothes for church attendance or are not able to support the church financially. However, it seems that the factor of class does not adequately explain the different patterns of religious participation. Attempts have therefore been made to examine other factors that lead to a variation in religious participation.

One such a factor is *gender*. A difference in religious participation that has been noted is that women seem to be more likely than men to practise religion and hold religious beliefs. Different arguments have been set forward to explain this tendency. One reason may be that boys and girls are socialised differently. It may also be argued, as in theories on crime and **delinquency**, that men demonstrate more risky behaviour and less self-control than women. Religious belief may be regarded as encouraging a lifestyle with fewer risks, making it therefore less attractive to men (Stark 2007: 394).

Religiosity

In their study of religion, sociologists are eager to measure religiosity. In attempting this, they encounter major problems. In the first place it is difficult to get consensus on the indicators of religiosity because it means different things to different people. Membership of a religious organisation is therefore not an accurate indicator of religiosity. Many deeply religious people prefer to practise their religion in private rather than publicly. Furthermore, members of religious organisations differ widely in their knowledge of religious doctrine, their participation in religious activities and their level of commitment to the religion, thus membership as such is an unreliable indicator for religiosity. In cases where sociologists set out to measure religiosity they differentiate between its various dimensions. An example of such an attempt is the five dimensions proposed by Glock and Stark (1965).

1. The first is the *ideological* dimension that relates to the believer's commitment to the religious beliefs.
2. The second is the *intellectual* dimension that refers to how knowledgeable the believers are of their religion.
3. The third is the *ritualistic* dimension that refers to the level of participation by the believers in the rituals of the religious organisation.

4. The fourth is the *experiential* dimension that refers to the degree of emotional attachment the believer has to the supernatural.

5. The fifth is the *consequential* dimension that reflects how the believer's behaviour is determined by religious participation in and commitment to the organisation.

Therefore, it is no simple task to measure religiosity. The practice of religion presents various dimensions to consider.

Summary

This chapter described religion from a sociological perspective. The following aspects of religion were dealt with:

- How the diverse religions were introduced and then developed within the South African society
- The tension lines between the traditional African belief systems and the other 'imported' religions
- The sociological approach to the modern study of religion based on two different definitions of religion as social function or sacred substance
- Religion's role in modern-day society – the three basic viewpoints, as well as how religion is linked to inequality within society
- The secular theory and its understanding of religious activity
- Religion as an instrument for social change and the emergence of religious fundamentalism
- The three classical sociological perspectives and their influence on today's approach to religion
- The organisation of religion: the four basic types of organisations, the elements of religion, as well as means to measure religiosity.

ARE YOU ON TRACK?

1. What does it mean for a sociologist to study a society with diverse religions?
2. How did the historical tension lines between indigenous and 'imported' faith systems develop in South Africa?
3. Modern-day society and its complex issues could provide the conditions for the resurgence of religion. Do you agree with this statement? Motivate your answer.
4. What is the twofold effect that secularity could have on religion?
5. Outline the three classical sociological perspectives on religion – how do these viewpoints influence the approach to religion today?
6. Compare the four types of religious organisation (church, denomination, sect and cult) in terms of their membership and structure.

More sources to consult

Bellah RN. 1967. 'Civil religion in America'. *Daedalus*, 96: 1–21.

De Gruchy JW, De Gruchy S. 2005. *The Church Struggle in South Africa*. Minneapolis: Fortress Press.

Prozesky M, De Gruchy J. 1995. *Living Faiths in South Africa*. London: C Hurst & Co.

Thomas D. 2002. *Christ Divided: Liberalism, Ecumenism and Race in South Africa*. Pretoria: University of South Africa.

References

Bauman Z. 1997. *Postmodernity and its Discontents*. Cambridge: Polity Press.

Bellah RN. 1967. 'Civil religion in America'. *Daedalus*, 96: 12.

Durkheim E. 1912 (2001 printing). *The Elementary Forms of the Religious Life*. Oxford: Oxford University Press.

Giddens A. 1990. *The Consequences of Modernity*. Cambridge: Polity Press.

Glock CY, Stark R. 1965. *Religion and Society in Tension*. Chicago, IL: Rand McNally.

Huntington SP. 1997. *The Clash of Civilisations and the Remaking of World Order*. New York: Touchstone.

Johnstone R. 1997. *Religion in Society: A Sociology of Religion*. 5th ed. Upper Saddle River, NJ: Prentice Hall.

Keppel G. 1994. *The Revenge of God: The Resurgence of Islam, Christianity and Judaism in the Modern World*. Cambridge: Polity Press.

Lyon D. 2000. *Jesus in Disneyland: Religion in Postmodern Times*. Cambridge: Polity Press.

Mabuse N, Ko V. 2012. 'Wild leopards threatened by religious tradition in Africa'. *Eco-Solutions, CNN*, 17 September. [Online] Available at: http://edition.cnn.com/2012/09/16/world/africa/leopards-shembe-south-africa/index. html [Accessed 11 December 2012].

Malinowski B. 1948 (1982 printing). *Magic, Science and Religion and Other Essays*. Atlanta, GA: Doubleday.

Møller V, Dickow H, Harris M. 1998. 'South Africa's "Rainbow People", national pride and happiness'. *Social Indicators Research*, 47(3): 245–280. [Online] Available at: http://www.jstor.org/stable/27522393 [Accessed 11 December 2012].

Parsons T. 1949. *The Structure of Social Action*. Glencoe, IL: Free Press.

Stark R. 2007. *Sociology*. 10th ed. Belmont, CA: Thomson Wadsworth.

Stark R, Bainbridge WS. 1985. *The Future of Religion: Secularization, Revival and Cult Formation*. Berkeley: University of California Press.

Wallis R. 1984. *The Elementary Forms of the New Religious Life*. London: Routledge and Kegan Paul.

Weber M. 1922 [(1979 printing Roth G, Wittich C (eds)]. *Economy and Society: An Outline of Interpretive Sociology*. London: University of California Press.

Weber M. 1930 (1990 printing). *The Protestant Ethic and the Spirit of Capitalism*. London: Unwin Hyman.

Wilson BR. 1982. *Religion in Sociological Perspective*. Oxford: Oxford University Press.

Yinger JM. 1970. *The Scientific Study of Religion*. New York: Macmillan.

Work

Paul Stewart

Work is a universal human activity. Through the purposive activity of work, the humanly constructed world and society are created. This is qualitatively different from the way in which other animals construct their own habitations by instinct. For, as Marx incomparably put it, the difference between the best bee and the worst architect is that the architect first erects the structure to be built in his/her imagination. Work is at once both a cognitive and physical activity. The purposive physical activity of work has hunger and the need to survive as its motivating driving force and out of this activity, ideas of how to ensure survival are born. The purpose of work is hence to make or produce something useful and needed to satisfy human wants and needs. In the earliest of communal societies, production would have been intimately bound up with religious rites, rituals and festivals. But in all social contexts, past and present, it is work that creates society and ensures its survival.

This chapter will first offer a definition of work and then make the explicit argument that work is at the centre of human consciousness, the formation of individual identity and the creation of communities and social classes. The analysis thus presented is explicitly a materialist one. Understanding ourselves and the social world must start from the mundane everyday things we have to do in order to survive and flourish. As human beings overcome nature and work with tools according to a purpose, the human species shapes itself in the process.

As work is very largely collective – including intellectual work such as preparing this textbook – specific forms of social relations between people develop. In the beginning of human development, under different conditions and over time and with the application of different aptitudes, the more successful would have gained power and ensured that others worked for them. Much work was soon to be reduced to labour – hard toil done under the pain of subservience and compulsion. This kind of work is not the choosing of the slave, the peasant or the worker. Under these conditions, free purposive work transformed into labour becomes a tool of domination and exploitation.

The nature and organisation of work shapes all societies. This can be seen when the four great transformations in the world of work fall under the sociological gaze. Where this chapter departs from all other accounts in the sociology of work is to go back to the way in which mining took root in Africa some 60–70 000 years ago, before looking at how the mining of diamonds and gold on an industrial scale fundamentally changed the shape of African societies.

In short, the argument and evidence presented in this chapter shows how work shapes society. Space here does not permit showing how the *absence* of work and employment has similar effects. Instead, what follows traces the increasingly rational way in which the collective work of its members is organised as the division of labour rapidly became more complex. With China rapidly establishing itself as the factory of the modern global economy, elsewhere much work is related not as much to production as to provision of services. If you are a waiter or shop a assistant, you must smile at customers and hence present what sociologists call emotional labour. As two leading sociological theorists of work powerfully show, our consent is *manufactured* and the human heart is now *managed* in the contemporary world of work. The global economy now exerts its influence over South African society and its prospects. Much work has become precarious. It must be clear that not having work, not being employed and unemployment in our modern age are a critical social concern of our times.

Case study 14.1 Learning to lead in the Fourth Industrial Revolution

Professor Alwyn Louw, President of Monash South Africa, said the following in an article in the *Mail&Guardian*:

Ultimately, the security and resilience of tomorrow's employees does not lie in their ability to do a job. It is inextricably linked to their ability to adapt and their capacity to harness the constant flow of new knowledge to create the tomorrow they desire – for themselves, and their fellow man.

(Source: *Mail&Guardian* 2017)

QUESTIONS

1. What is the role of work in society?
2. What are knowledge workers, and can everyone be one?
3. What is the Fourth Industrial Revolution?

Key themes

- Introducing the concepts of work, labour and production
- Work as a universal human activity
- Defining the concept of work
- The evolution of work and corresponding forms of society
- Transformations in the world of work
- Tracing the sociology of work in Africa

- Pre-industrial mining and the first great transformation in production
- The rise of scientific management
- Fordism
- Post-Fordism
- The future of work.

14.1 Introduction

Work is a universal human activity, and has always played the central role in economic and hence perhaps even social life. The activity of work has taken many forms and continues to evolve. New kinds of work emerge while others disappear. Work shapes not only the individual's social position and status within society, but the character of society itself. Simply put, the result of the collective work of all active members of society creates society itself. It is through this collective activity that society makes and remakes itself. It has done so under the most extraordinary variety of conditions throughout the course of human history. The individual members of society are likewise created and formed – in the self-same moment – by the society they create. This is the central conceptual insight arising out of the perspective in the sociology of work presented in this chapter. In brief, the very identity of individuals who make up society is powerfully fashioned by the work they do. How work is at the very centre of individual identity formation and the creation of communities and social classes is hence a key theme in what follows.

To elaborate on this central insight, people's perceptions, their social interactions and general behaviour are powerfully influenced by their occupation or profession or, crucially, whether they are even employed at all. To give a simple example, the experience, perceptions and social position of a plumber and a public relations officer of a multi national company are very different. Obviously, the chief executive officer of a major company and workers on the factory floor do very different kinds of work. They consequently see the world and act within it from very different perspectives. In general, the work of the company executive is abstract and conceptual. It is largely **mental labour**. The work of the factory floor worker is concrete and practical. It is largely **manual labour**.

Labour is, however, to be distinguished from work. To labour implies not just to work hard, but to toil and do heavy, often painful, back-breaking work under duress or compulsion and which is not under the worker's control. Much work, such as that of slaves, is this kind of labour and this often continues to be the case. The term 'labour' has, probably not incidentally, also come to be used to refer to the social group of workers as a whole. This strongly suggests that much of their work is inordinately hard and performed under circumstances not of their own choosing. When one studies the nature of work, how and why much of it has become labour and the ways it has undergone significant transformations, this chapter will suggest, it is noteworthy how significantly work defines the character of the human agents who perform it and the societies they create.

In following on from these preliminary observations in the sociology of work, what this chapter will further show is that we cannot understand society without understanding the nature of work: what it is, why it is necessary, how it is performed and how it changes. In brief, what the chapter even further wants to show is how work remains at the heart of the social and economic life of every society across time and space.

This chapter will present the case that one form of society gives way to another due to the transformations occurring in the world of work. These transformations have been remarkable. Agricultural society dominated by the horse and the farrier (a person who puts shoes on horses) is very different from industrial society dominated by the motorcar and the mechanic. How different again is industrial society from that of the post-industrial automated machine-making robotised **production** systems driven by communication technologies? Will technologies still to be invented dispense with work altogether? Is this at the heart of the Fourth Industrial Revolution? For new forms of work, such as the call centre operator and the cell phone salesperson, are rapidly being taken over by talking machines and online advertising.

To tackle such questions, this chapter begins by defining some key concepts in the sociology of work. The chapter will use the concept of work to delve into the earliest beginnings of human experience. Clearly, for instance, agricultural work dominated society for the greatest part of human history as it still does in Africa and elsewhere in developing societies today. When Africa is the focus, however, what seldom attracts attention is how mining, over a 1 000 years ago, was an integral part of agricultural society and was responsible for a major transformation in the world of work, fundamentally changing African society. When **industrialisation** later exploded onto the stage of human history and initiated the beginnings of a global society, this marked the single most important change in human evolution and social experience. This astonishing historical moment will absorb our attention in this chapter, not only because it is responsible for initiating the modern era in which we currently live, but also because of the way in which it changed the way we think about the world around us as well as ourselves.

The chapter then turns to discussing these developments. It specifically notes the four major transformations of work which take place with the advent of industrial capitalism. The rediscovery of precious metals and the beginning of modern mining in South Africa, how **scientific management** was implemented in the goldmines and how Western forms of work organisation were implemented in mines and then factories in South Africa, becomes the focus. In discussing these themes in the sociological study of work, the broader story of the world of work and its intimate relationship to society at large is introduced.

The chapter ends by posing an important question as to the future of work. This and similar questions are noted as of critical importance in trying to understand both South African society and the global world around us. In short, such is the centrality of work that one prominent theorist has asked the question whether work is not in fact *the* key sociological category (Offe 1985).

14.2 Work as a universal activity

It is doubtful whether society will ever attain the dream of science fiction, namely **artificial intelligence** – a state where fully automated robotised machines run a world in which people are idle and superfluous. Or is it? For the foreseeable future, the workplace will remain a central feature of society despite its ever-changing nature. Thousands of years ago the ancient Greeks thought work was a necessary evil. Founded on **slavery**, Greek citizens constituted a social class who never did any actual physical work. Around the same period, in the Judeo-Christian-Islamic tradition, work was seen as a curse. In our modern globalised world, dominated by capitalism, it is a curse if you are unemployed and do *not* have work. What, we may ask, is this thing called work? How has it changed, how is it changing and what is the future of work?

14.3 Work as a purposeful activity

Work can be defined as the purposeful activity or effort of using tools and materials to make or create something useful. The primary tools of work were always the human hand and brain. Current technologies such as the cell phone, tablet and laptop can be viewed as extensions of the human hand and brain. If work was previously viewed as a necessary evil or curse, the 19th century thinker Karl Marx, once referred to as the 'philosopher of work', shared the view of his contemporaries, who saw work in a much more positive light. Marx correctly saw it as a universal condition of human existence. Work, he thought, is the first and necessary historical act in which human beings engage. Work is, moreover, fundamentally collective. It is, he suggested, the very fountain of the development of human consciousness. If this is true, the study of work must surely be the very starting point of social understanding.

These are big claims. They are made for the following simple but profound reason. Human beings need to engage in the activity of work or what can be called material production to satisfy their basic physical needs of food, shelter and clothing before they do anything else. Logically speaking, the instinct of survival precedes the formulation of ideas. Only once basic physical needs have been satisfied can ideas fruitfully emerge, often first expressed as art painted or etched onto rock. Surely it was only through the struggle for survival that traditional and practical rules of life then gradually developed, later to be inscribed in modes of education, law and politics? These activities have in turn resulted in different occupations and kinds of work. In the context of engaging in some activity, that of work especially, ideas develop. In short, work is an activity devoted to the practical end of producing something as a service or good to be consumed. It does not matter whether work is predominantly manual or mental, or practical or intellectual. Work is the centrally crucial activity in which human beings have had to engage in creating and sustaining society from its very first beginnings.

14.3.1 Work as constitutive of individual identity

It is hard not to agree with Karl Marx that it is through work that we become fully human or 'realise our species being', as he put it. Through actively engaging with the world around us, we gain mastery over nature and over ourselves. Are we not all pleased when a job of work is done well? It could have been a simple household chore, a school project or a task performed in a part-time job. In fact, through actively engaging in the world through the activity of work, we interact with others in society and in the process transform the identity we acquired at birth. This is the identity ascribed to us by factors such as our race, sex and socioeconomic position and over which we had no control. We can change this **ascribed identity** into an identity we have achieved for ourselves. For better or worse, we are continually required to develop ourselves and thereby gain social recognition. We then become more confident of our role in the world. Much of such an **achieved identity** has to do with our performance in our working environment which, for those engaged in some form of work, generally absorbs a significant proportion of time across the span of a lifetime. If this is true, then the seriousness of being unemployed and *not* having work or something meaningful to do to sustain life becomes self-evident. As we will also see, however, much work has become repetitive and monotonous with soul-destroying consequences.

14.3.2 The origin of work

Work originated alongside the most primitive forms of social organisation in the domestic household. The home was for a long time the basic social unit of the economy. The immediate environment of the family or kinship group, despite significant differences in the ways it has been organised in the course of development of the human species, would have provided the first experiences of social contact and social co-operation. The very first sets of social relations would have formed as the household needed to hunt and gather, and thereby survive as a social group. Through such basic forms of collective behaviour and action, social life began to take shape and assumed a variety of different forms. More complex forms of organisation, such as settled agriculture and larger hunting and gathering parties, production for barter and, as we shall see, the activity of mining began to appear.

The survival of any form of society more complex than nomadic hunting and gathering requires that more must be produced than is immediately consumed. Every social group of human beings must create a surplus. In a rural economy the seed needed for planting for the next season is, for instance, often jealously guarded by the women to prevent the men from consuming it.

If work then was originally necessary for survival, today one needs **money** to make a livelihood and survive. In a modern economy, even those who are not formally employed need to find some way of acquiring money. In our modern globalised economy especially, work generally means access to money. When people are put to work and paid, whether this is a **salary** or a **wage**, work becomes paid or wage labour. When that is the kind of work we do, we expect something in return. We can hence expand our definition of what work is by saying that work is the purposive productive activity or *effort* applied at a specific *time* and particular *space* for a *reward*. The reward might not be in the form of money. As soon as we adopt this definition of work, a wide range of different forms and different kinds of work come into view.

Work must be understood more broadly than the activity associated with formal employment earning a wage or a salary. Much work, for instance, continues to occur in the home or is what sociologists call domestic or reproductive work, yet this is often not paid work. There might only be the reward of satisfaction or a 'thank you'. An increasing amount of work further occurs in the informal sector where there is generally no wage paid, but where manufactured articles might be resold, such as in 'spaza' shops or on a street corner. There are an increasing number of people who provide services, such as cleaners, nurses, teachers and those in law enforcement – the police and military. But before we look at how the activity of work eventually evolved into these different occupations, there is one curious thing we must note about work.

14.3.3 Work as a function of social circumstances

Work is central to the development and fortunes of society, yet one and the same activity can be either work or play. Take the example of baking a cake. If you are enjoying baking a cake for your party, it is a kind of play or recreation. If you are a chef cooking or a domestic employee baking a cake, then that is work. The same activity (baking or cooking) is either work or play depending on its *social circumstances*. We need, in other words, to look at the sets of social relations within which the activity is located before we can define that activity as work. Is the activity being paid for? Is there an owner and a worker, a self-employed worker/ owner or is there no financial transaction taking place? If the same activity can be either work or play, can we imagine a society in which work becomes play? Was work in the dim and distant past more playful than it is today? Or was work always the product of the sweat from one's brow?

14.4 The evolution of work

Since the dawn of human history, work has assumed many forms, but has always been closely related to different types of economy. These types of economy can themselves only be understood once those very forms of work are examined. The history of work can be divided into three types. By dividing societies into this three-fold conceptual typology, this does not mean that the previous types of society and forms of work disappear entirely. There are still parts of the world in many developing societies where work is still performed much in the same way as it was centuries ago. Across southern Africa in far-flung rural areas you can still witness the tilling of the land with a rudimentary hoe often wedged onto a sturdy shaft of wood. This work is generally done by women. The point is that analytical distinctions – such as between different *types* of society – are not meant to necessarily follow chronologically or can ever fully characterise the extraordinary variety of forms of social existence.

14.4.1 Nomadic, pastoral and agricultural societies

Before the advent of science and modern industrial technology, all societies were either nomadic or pastoral, and based on agriculture. These were pre-industrial societies. In such societies work was embedded in the extended family, clan,

tribe or immediate community. The social group of clan or tribe was primary with little differentiation between individuals. Everyone knew one another and relationships were close. Seniority, generally of the men, was the hallmark of decision making. The way in which work was divided, the **division of labour**, was based on gender. Generally, men hunted or looked after the cattle and were responsible for cultural rituals while women worked the fields. Such forms of society were fairly homogeneous. Everyone did much the same kind of work. The surplus produced in such economies was shared. The contemporary legal notion that land could be **private property** was foreign. Work took place in the context of webs of traditional obligations and duties. The collective collaboration which work demanded signalled strong bonds of social **solidarity** or what Émile Durkheim called **mechanical solidarity**. In southern Africa, the ancient San communities were nomadic. The Khoi-Khoi were cattle breeders and clashed over grazing lands with the early Afrikaner farmers in the Cape who were often partly nomadic and partly, like the Khoi-Khoi, cattle farmers. Economic wealth in such settled agricultural societies would have been measured in terms of the number of cattle the social group or community possessed. In rural communities in South Africa and elsewhere, this is still the case.

Since time immemorial then, apart from nomadic groups of people, society was based primarily on agriculture. The driving force of this type of society was human labour, aided by the domestication of animals. Camels and horses were used for transport, and draught animals such as oxen would draw ploughs in the fields. All manner of crafts and industrious forms of activity evolved. Populations increased in size and society became more complex and heterogeneous. Some people ended up working for others. Some, like slaves, would have had to devote all their time to the masters who owned them. Even freemen and their families – such as agricultural peasants – would have had to give a significant proportion of their **labour time** to work for their traditional chiefs, as would serfs for their lords in European traditions. At every step of the way, as societies became more complex, various forms of social organisation developed which mirrored the forms of work and production with which those societies were engaged. With the density of the world's population increasing, ever greater congregations of people formed themselves into villages and towns. Ancient civilisations built great cities. Civilisations rose and fell. The shift from agricultural to industrial society would mark the single most critical change in human history. The division of labour exploded and specialisation of work and its labours, occupations and professions and their many tasks became the way of life. Every person came to require the contribution of a great many others to satisfy their needs. Society would now hold together, as Durkheim explained, through complex forms of **organic solidarity**.

14.4.2 Industrial society

The invention of electricity and steam engines in Scotland and the emergence of industrial society followed the **Industrial Revolution** in the mid-19th century in England and spread to the rest of the world. These developments transformed virtually every aspect of human experience and social life. No longer was brute human energy and animal power the driving force of work. The power of steam and electrically driven machines completely transformed work (see Berg 1979). Industrial societies developed. Urban populations grew. People now thought of themselves as more advanced and even superior to other societies that were not urbanised and industrialised.

With the advent of industrialisation, the amount, performance and intensity of work which could be performed was thoroughly revolutionised. Machines came to dominate work. Men, women and children became slaves to ever bigger and more efficient machines that now produced great masses of commodities and products. This new form of work overwhelmed the old familial and communal sets of social relations which had nurtured and sustained it as an activity. The invention of machines brought with it an astonishing array of different kinds of jobs and an explosion in an increasingly complex division of labour. Where previously there may have been miners digging at the earth with crude implements, now they would employ sophisticated machinery at great depths underground. An entire social class of artisanal and technical trades emerged. These artisans worked increasingly powerful industrial lathes designed by engineers. The widespread use of the internal combustion engine, still found in effectively every motor vehicle today, despite the looming of electrically powered driverless cars, transformed society entirely.

Beyond the productive heart of industrial society in the factory, these changes were foundational ones. Every member of society, across all social classes, now became a consumer. The availability of goods and services, previously the exclusive preserve of the wealthy aristocratic elite, now became potentially available to everybody. With the production of whole new ranges of commodities, markets increased rapidly, became hugely sophisticated and continue to extend their global reach. Work and society, now freed from deeply entrenched age-old traditions and

obligations and ways of doing things, became increasingly embedded in an economy dominated by the market. In these new marketplaces the emerging middle classes were free to buy and sell, and invest their money. Stripped from communal land, the newly formed urban industrial **working class** would sell the only commodity they had at their disposal, namely their **labour power** or, in other words, their capacity to work.

Accompanying this process of industrialisation, an entire range of planning, conceptual and organisational forms of work emerged to regulate, control and administer the new capitalist **mode of production** which characterised industrial society. With the family and traditional obligations around which work cohered overwhelmed, written and contractual obligations become dominant in defining human and social relationships. New organisations came into being. The old **guilds** of the skilled craftsmen who worked by hand were replaced with the **trade unions** of the semi-skilled industrial workers who tended the new machines. Small family firms were rapidly swallowed up by emerging national and then multinational companies and corporations. The legal contracts these new institutions required became increasingly complex as specific production processes developed and required ever-increasing amounts of money and capital. More sophisticated and complex financial institutions emerged with the expansion of the legal system. New branches of law evolved to regulate the ownership of the economic resources in society. The **means of production** rapidly became considerably more complex. Wealth would now be measured in terms of the money and capital circulating in a society. The institution of private property would take the place of shared and communal ownership. Ever-expanding and advancing industrial technologies enabled the manufacturing of the everyday goods and commodities which continue to form the foundation of all modern urban lifestyles – from electric light bulbs to skyscraper elevators, and movie houses to jet-powered passenger aircraft.

With the advent of modern industrial society, great advances came with great costs. Ordinary men and women were forced to relinquish the control they had over their own work. The greatly enhanced social surplus was no longer commonly owned, but was increasingly privately appropriated by the formation of a powerful new social class which drove this revolution in society and became intertwined with it – the hugely progressive entrepreneurial, capital-owning class or bourgeoisie. Under industrial capitalism, economic growth and profit were to become the guiding principles dominating society. Work increasingly came to dominate social life. The time allocated to work regular and standardised hours, measured by the clock, would now powerfully shape society.

14.4.3 Post-industrial society

In an ever rapidly changing and fast-paced world where daily life can seem to pass in a blur, the emergence of the third type of society is perhaps less socially visible, until one pauses to reflect how much has changed in one or two short generations. Sociologists suggest that society entered the post-industrial age with the dropping of the atomic bomb on the cities of Hiroshima and Nagasaki in 1945, which ended World War II. It signalled the explosive birth of the global village in which we now live. At the level of daily experience, the 'wireless' radio, long-playing records, reel-to-reel tape recorders and landline telephones were shortly to be replaced by cellular telephony and our current rapidly expanding ever increasingly remote-based communication technologies. In short, now the technologies of the post-industrial age powerfully shape our lives. When separated from our cell phones, for instance, we are suddenly isolated and can even feel lost. Such is the power of the productive forces in society, born out of the socio-technical conditions of contemporary, largely automated production systems.

Nuclear power now drives many advanced capitalist societies. While coal mining remains the mainstay of the generation of electricity in South Africa, and the nuclear future remains uncertain, our age is an electronic and informational one. In advanced capitalist societies, the importance of industrial manufactures has shrunk as automated computerised electronic technologies and robotisation produce new goods and commodities at an ever-accelerating rate. A wide variety of service industries has overtaken manufacturing in the technologically advanced societies of Europe and North America, and South Africa stands on the cusp of the same development with the increase of the so-called knowledge economy.

In what are called 'emerging economies' such as South Africa, brands such as 'Made in China' and 'Made in Malaysia' signal the industrial workshops of the world as powerfully as 'Made in England', 'Made in Hong Kong' or 'Made in Japan' ever did. All manner of technologies, both industrial and post-industrial, are in evidence in these societies. The advance and development of a global information technology, where virtually anything can be Googled, has accelerated in an ever more closely interconnected world economy. Businesses which were the most widely known brand names in the industrial

era, such as Coca-Cola and Ford, while still around, have been replaced by Amazon and Microsoft. Everything now seems to be subject to the power of the market – available for sale and purchase. Sociologists call this phenomenon and process **commodification.** Alongside this process that was previously communal and social has become commercialised.

With these changes a seismic shift in the world of work has occurred. Full-time jobs in the formal sector of the economy are no longer the norm. What was once the regular structuring capacity of working hours, shaping the form social life assumes, is for many now a thing of the past. Work is increasingly part-time, piecework, casual, outsourced, contracted out or conducted at home. These are generally precarious forms of employment and the struggle of many people is now to find some **decent work** or any work at all. Work has become increasingly temporary and precarious. Where manufacturing and industry dominated industrial society, social classes divided fairly neatly into a working class and socially identifiable ruling bourgeoisie. Now the financial and banking sectors and an increasingly faceless global super-rich, **transnational elite,** a growing *precariat* – those who only ever find temporary work – and those who have been marginalised and permanently unemployed and unemployable increasingly characterise post-industrial society.

Box 14.1 Work

How has work and society changed from the time when your grandparents were your age?

Ask them – or one of their peers:

- to describe what work they did
- to tell you how long they spent working
- how they listened to music – or did they have to make their own?

14.5 Transformations in the world of work

We need to take a closer look at the nature of these transformations. The key sociological question posed here is whether the shape and form of work really does give us the society in which we live.

The sociology of work generally begins with the transformations of work in industrial society which has assumed a capitalist form of society. We are, however, going to go back further and delve into the rich past and blur a distinction often imposed on Africa and other developing societies. The distinction is often made between an unwritten pre-history of 'primitive' societies and the recorded history of more technologically and industrially advanced or so-called 'civilised' societies. It is to the former and the case of the deep history of the southern African continent this chapter now turns.

14.5.1 Stone Age mining of iron oxides and Iron Age farmers in southern Africa

Virtually all South African studies in the sociology of work begin with mining and the discovery of diamonds in 1868 in Kimberley and gold in 1886 on the Witwatersrand. African societies had, however, been mining and processing ore-bearing rock thousands of years before. It is clear from archaeological evidence that the mining of oxides for use as a pigment and the work of mechanical processing was undertaken around 70 000 years ago towards the end of the Middle Stone Age. The existence of finds of both ground and polished ochre attests to significant pigment production which was processed by **shamanic labour**. The shaman was the medicine-man, healer or *inyanga* in these early societies. The production of pigment was of central importance to these early communities. Pigment was used as a medium of cultural expression, both artistically and for body paint to signal the growing complexity of social position, status and identity.

In the Later Stone Age, archaeologists suggest that ochre and pigment were not used purely for symbolic purposes, but played a more complex social role. Weberian-orientated sociologists would nod in agreement with the conclusions of two contemporary archaeologists, Shadreck Chirikure and Simon Hall (2008), who suggest that:

> *the processing of pigment and the tools of its application are inseparably linked to the deeply religious structures these images communicated. Pigment itself has an essence that was integral to meaning.*

The systematic decorations made of ochre and the use of mined oxides represents evidence of abstract and symbolic thought and are crucial in debates around cognitive development and the display of modern forms of human behaviour. The decorative work of these early human beings, in other words, tells us that African societies were considerably more advanced than Euro-North American epistemic frameworks held.

14.5.2 The first great transformation of production

The first major transformation in the production of pigments and ochre was from the mechanical crushing of pigment-bearing mineral ores by stone to a complex, heat-driven chemical transformation of the smelting of these oxides. This significant technological advance in production occurred early in the Early Iron Age, the period up to the year 1000. At this point, by means of a complex pyrotechnology (using fire), clay was transformed into ceramics, and iron ore into metal. Although the history is contested, it appears this technology was introduced into southern Africa by trade with communities from the north as part of a complex package of new food producing economies to which the settled Bantu-speaking agriculturalists were central.

This discovery was interpreted by means of cultural idioms. The chemical transformation of mineral ores into metals was associated with birth, and the furnaces themselves were decorated with symbols representing the female gender. The placement of these furnaces was located *away* from the household, much in the same way the human birthing process was separated from the sight of the community. Work and production hence were intimately connected with the form of social organisation these societies assumed. The point is that the very process of metal smelting production was both shaped by the archetypal gendered division of labour and provided the structuring architectural landscape of the household economy.

Even more importantly, during the Middle Iron Age (from around 1000 to 1300) and the Late Iron Age (1300 up to the 19th century) the mining of a range of metals went hand in hand with agriculture. African pre-industrial societies were not then, as is often simplistically understood, merely agricultural societies. The mining and production of metals for decorative purposes, and also for the production of tools such as hoes for agriculture and axes for times of war, were integral to larger social systems. The African states, such as Great Zimbabwe state and Mapungubwe (1220–1290) in present-day Mpumalanga, are examples of significant sophisticated pre-industrial civilisations.

The point of work in society is to create a social surplus, and with the production of an economic surplus comes trade. Social interaction between people immediately becomes more complex. Trade in metals in Africa was extensive during the whole of the Iron Age (1000 to the 19th century) with the mining of gold, for example, occurring in placer (alluvial) deposits as well as underground deposits. Alluvial goldmining was conducted seasonally after the rains had brought down auriferous (gold-bearing) sands to the riverbanks, which would be winnowed and separated from the silt until all that was left was gold dust. Weighed down by weights, African miners would dive into rivers and collect auriferous sand in bowls which would be carefully washed off to leave the gold dust behind. It is clear that the organisation of this kind of work was vastly different to that of agricultural work even if we know very little what forms of organisation this work assumed.

Early African mining was not, however, simply confined to sifting alluvial deposits of gold. Underground mining involved using iron gads, stone hammers and the setting of fires to break the ore-bearing rock. A copper mine near Phalaborwa, dated to the year AD 800, was found, but destroyed by modern mining. This ancient African mine excavated copper carbonates (malachite and azurite) from a complex of adits, shafts and chambers. This kind of mining required considerably more complex forms of social organisation than did mining alluvial deposits washed down streams and rivers.

The range of metals mined and processed during pre-colonial times was remarkably extensive. Literally thousands of tons of iron, gold, copper and tin ore were mined. In counties neighbouring South Africa, such as Zimbabwe and eastern Botswana, over 500 copper and 4 000 pre-colonial goldmines have been identified as well as evidence of copper mines in Musina and Phalaborwa over 1 000 years ago. Production debris from AD 500 has been found at Broederstroom just north of Johannesburg in Gauteng province. Tswana copper miners worked large amounts of copper and produced surplus copper and iron for regional trade at Zeerust and at Marothodi in the Pilanesberg. Sotho and Tswana tin miners produced an estimated 2 000 tons of tin ore or casserite at Rooiberg, in both opencast and underground mines from the 15th century. The discovery of the iconic gold rhino, together with gold beads, bangles and wound helices signalling gold as a status metal, first appeared at Mapungubwe going back to the Middle Iron Age (1000–1300).

Not only was production sophisticated, but trade was extensive. During the Middle Iron Age, copper beads were found in Natal where there are no copper mineral deposits. Gold was traded with the Indian Ocean Swahili Arab states, creating wealth for elites early in the second millennium from around 1100 to 1300. Later, around the year 1500, Tswana copper had found its way through trade to the Eastern Cape. These historical facts, uncovered by the science of archaeology, challenge Western-orientated sociological conceptions of the nature of southern African society. And the story does not end here.

Iron, for instance, was particularly important. Iron tools were not only central to the viability of agricultural societies and to warfare and hunting, but also enabled these societies to develop in scale and complexity of organisation. Trade evened out the availability of these metals where sources of mineralogical deposits were poor or did not exist, such as in the Free State and the Northern Cape. Iron Age sites are scattered all over southern Africa. As Chirikure and Hall (2008) tell us:

[m]etal was active in all spheres of political, social and economic life and the practical and utilitarian cannot be separated from social structure and meaning.

These findings powerfully challenge Western-orientated sociological conceptual categories and theorisations. They suggest a radical rethinking of the concepts sociologists in Africa often uncritically inherit from contexts in which they were first formulated. In this instance, the concepts of work, production and economy clearly need to be conceptualised in a much closer relation to the meanings that African sociologists attach to social and political life.

14.5.3 Slavery and indentured labour

The pre-industrial rhythm of agriculture and mining that structured African societies for over 2 000 years came to an abrupt end when Portuguese explorers first rounded the Cape of Good Hope, and later with the establishment of the Dutch settlement at the Cape. The colonists brought with them a wide range of skills and paraphernalia of European society – resources previously unknown to the continent. But crucially, these Europeans had a need for labour, particularly unskilled labour. The Dutch brought with them the institution of slavery, the majority of the slaves being imported in small numbers over a long period of time from Asia. The institution of slavery provided for every conceivable kind of work required to build the Cape colony. Slaves worked as herdsmen and household servants, and did the bulk of the physical work in the growing though scattered settlement for the first 150 years of the colonial period. The arrival of the Dutch settlers was intimately linked to the expansion of the economies of Europe. Progress and development were slow, which stood in marked contrast to the settlement of Europeans in North America. The simple reason for the relatively stagnant development of the Cape under Dutch rule was due to the role of the Dutch East India Company (DEIC/VOC), which required a refreshment station at the Cape midway between Europe and India.

No great surplus needed to be produced at the Cape as it was only the requirements of a refreshment station of the VOC which needed to be met. The only market was the VOC itself, which was largely a law unto itself and was keen to keep its costs down. This frustrated the small but slowly growing group of Dutch free burghers who began to farm independently beyond the reaches of the Cape Town fortified castle which was the VOC's headquarters. These Dutch farmers, it was envisaged, would supply all the basic food supplies Cape Town needed. In what is a complex history, these free burghers associated closely with the Malay slaves, some of whom attained manumission (freedom) from their slave status and constituted the basis of the early Afrikaner communities out of which the language of Afrikaans developed in distinction to the 'High Dutch' spoken in the urban Cape.

These farmers, partly nomadic and partly settled, quickly learned they too had need of additional labour to till their lands. They instituted their own form of slavery, a form of bonded or indentured labour acquired by warlike raiding parties that captured the children of the Khoi-Khoi. The farmers 'booked them into' their own household economies and so these children were hence called *inboekselings*. When the *inboekselings* became adults, having shared close and intimate though patriarchal relationships with the early Afrikaner farming families, they were set free and became known as *oorlams* – literally meaning the 'left over' slaves. They often continued to live and work as part of the Afrikaner household economy (see Delius & Trapido 1994).

These farmers increasingly established themselves beyond the reach of the VOC. They soon found themselves in stiff competition from a society much like themselves, the independent pastoralist Xhosa peoples of the Eastern Cape. A series of wars were fought with the Xhosa communities across the Eastern frontier over grazing lands, with each group thieving and raiding each other's cattle. Both pastoralist groups, however, faced the poisoned arrows of the San who raided the easy target of the cattle of both the established Xhosa and the emergent Afrikaner farmers.

The Afrikaner settlers' agricultural mode of life was to be sorely threatened. Only a few decades after 1806, when the British annexed the Cape, the prospect of the abolition of slavery and the consequent freeing of their agricultural labour interfered with the generations-old relationship of master and servant, and thus with the very foundation of their still somewhat fragile agricultural economy. The economic foundation of the early Afrikaner communities, slavery in other words, was being threatened. This was a

major reason for these farmers leaving the Cape to settle in what became known as the Boer republics of the Orange Free State and Transvaal.

This series of struggles and wars all went to the heart of a pre-industrial, agricultural mode of production and the centrality of both land and labour which underpinned it. The nature of agricultural work for a great many Africans of different communities changed in the process. People were no longer free to work the land which was shared by their communities at large and was conducted under the authority of traditional rights and obligations. Work for the indigenous peoples of South Africa was conducted under the pain of bondage or low wages. This was to continue until the single most significant transformation of work was to occur with the *rediscovery* of precious metals in Kimberley and what was to become known as Egoli or Gauteng – the mining tent-town of Johannesburg.

14.5.4 Modern mining and industrial manufacturing

The Industrial Revolution in England was marked by the rise of a new institution devoted specifically to make work more efficient. Whereas work had previously been conducted within the 'cottage industries' under the control of the family, the establishment of factories brought workers together under a single roof. The very word 'factory' comes from the Latin word 'facere' and means 'to make'. This new environment, well documented as a cruel institution in which a regime of inhuman discipline developed, undermined the traditional handicraft technologies. Agricultural peasants were deprived of their land through Acts of parliament and had only their labour to sell. In the first factories this early **proletariat** was subject to tight control and close supervision, and worked extraordinarily long hours to ensure greater productive efficiencies and the maximisation of profit. What skills remained were rapidly to be eroded as machinery was increasingly introduced.

In South Africa we cannot talk about the rise of the factory, which only developed later to support the mining industry (see Callinicos 1994b), but rather the revolution of both production and society brought about by modern mining. Peasant farmers from across southern Africa initially flocked to the Kimberley diamond fields to work. Shangaans from the coastal plains of the Gaza empire, for instance, arrived alongside men from Basotholand, and men from the eastern Transvaal tramped down the Xingwedsi and Pafuri rivers to Pretoria, while others followed the Olifants and Sabi rivers to converge in Kimberley to be employed in the diamond mines (Harries 1994). When the new phenomenon of cash wages, paid in exchange for work, was cut, Pedi and Sotho workers left. Such behaviour is associated with a modern industrial proletariat. Other African workers quickly took their place, a common occurrence under industrial capitalism and evidence that South African society had entered a new stage of development.

The experience of what it meant to work in southern Africa was dramatically transformed. The historian Patrick Harries (1994) tells how agricultural and crude mining implements were replaced not only by the pick and shovel, the bucket and the wheelbarrow, but men also learned to work with windlasses, washing machinery, carts and wagons. The introduction of the rotary washing machine, driven by horse or steam power, accelerated the rhythm and pace of work, while hundreds of steam engines were imported from Britain to pump water from the ever increasingly famous and fabulously rich Big Hole at Kimberley. Work went on by day and night, and changed long-held conceptions of both time and work. Time now no longer simply 'passed' – but had to be 'spent' (Thompson 1967). With time itself turned into a commodity, the industrial clock replaced the rhythm of the natural seasons. This revolution in time continues to discipline the whole of society today.

Central to the Mining Revolution in South Africa, Harries (1994: 50) tells how 'Mine labour required an unrelenting discipline and regularity' with a new definition of work being imposed by 'the fist, the boot and the whip'. Under these circumstances work became labour. In the workplace, working conditions were dismal, as were the living conditions around the mines. The food was poor and wages were low. The very idea of working for a cash wage, for instance, was the result of a constant process of negotiation and contestation. Despite all this, workers at Kimberley were not only able to press for higher wages, but also managed to struggle for and settle on a pace of labour closer to the rhythm of work with which they were familiar back home by getting the working day reduced from 13 to nine hours. To attract workers, the European diamond diggers had to provide workers with 100 lbs of maize meal a month (Harries 1994: 53). Some workers were provided with *boer* tobacco, cotton blankets and large iron cooking pots. These commodities, new to southern Africa, would transform rural households and local economies far away from the mines.

With the establishment of industrial production there is generally a shift from the predominance of natural resources (land) as central to production to the mastery of production technology and capital to support it. This development

originally occurred in the context of science and Newton's mechanical theories and world view, and was transported into Africa and elsewhere. Capital harnesses science, productivity is dramatically increased and new technologies are born. Mechanisation is introduced. In the instance of the immigrant skilled artisanal European workers, this resulted in the deskilling of their traditional craft trades. As tasks became simpler and semi-skilled, initially unskilled African workers, themselves facing a new form of industrial work, replaced the craftsmen. To generalise sociologically, the organisation of the factory and mine not only characterises modern production systems, but also imposes its hierarchical form of organisation across society. To put it more specifically, in southern Africa a new African proletariat was born out of diamonds in Kimberley and the goldfields on the Witwatersrand (see Callinicos 1980).

The rise of scientific management
The new temporal and generally rigid discipline of the factory and mine provided the foundation for a further impetus to greater efficiencies and productive output. In 1911, an American engineer by the name of Frederick Winslow Taylor published *The Principles of Scientific Management*, which was responsible for the development of what became known as Taylorism or scientific management. In a famous series of experiments at Bethlehem Steel in the United States, Taylor focused on the time it took to perform each aspect of a job in a production process. He wanted to cut the time to its minimum and establish scientifically the time units each part of a job should take. The attempt was to make people act in as predictable and machine-like manner as possible in a hierarchic structure with managers at the top. The managers' job was one of *conception*: how and in what time frames jobs should be done. Workers were simply required to attend to the *execution* of the job at hand. A key objective was to prevent them from being idle while at work and ensure they worked at their maximum physical capacity. Like many of his contemporaries, Taylor thought workers were loafers and lazy. This view was to be overlaid by racial stereotypes on the South African mines where black workers were, in addition, considered to be slow and passively resisted the new advanced scientific consciousness of industrial society. Science proved, however, to have a blind side.

The role of science was to gain significantly greater control over the production process. Developed at the turn of the 20th century, the broader social context for scientific management was a strong belief in rationality (as Weber pointed out) and the limitless opportunities of technology.

The momentum for these views was accompanied by the strong belief that Europeans were bringing Christian 'civilisation' to the so-called 'dark continent' of Africa which decolonial theorists have examined at length. Scientific progress was, however, not to be halted. The immediate result of applying science to the organisation of work and production, justified by a religious ideology, were that workers become appendages to the speed and pace of the industrial machine. The intensity of work was greatly increased, thinking (*conception*) and doing (*execution*) were seen as separate realms of activity with no need for workers to have overall knowledge of the production process or a broad set of skills. Craft work was consequently broken further down into its most simple and distinct parts.

The consequences of scientific management soon became clear. Power was now concentrated in the manager-engineer, the productivity of labour was dramatically increased, while the value of labour-power – the capacity to work – was cheapened in the process. Worldwide, the social effect of the changes to factory work was the emergence of a new, more homogeneous social class of unskilled and semi-skilled workers. On the South African gold mines, the institutional effect was similar to what happened elsewhere, except that race became a central aspect (see Allen 1994). Elsewhere industrial trade unions emerged for semi-skilled workers to protect them from unskilled workers. These industrial trade unions replaced the older craft guilds of skilled workers established by pre-industrial European traditions and effectively protected European workers from the mines employing African workers at lower rates of pay. This trade union was, at times, to be courted by the mine owners and political authorities alike. What happened at work on the mines, in other words, impacted on the politics in society as a whole. Despite later being able to establish a 'colour bar' preventing black workers from doing skilled work, organised white labour was unable to prevent disenfranchised and compounded (see Callinicos 1994a) yet capable African mineworkers from taking over much of the work performed by unskilled whites, including Afrikaner workers, at lower rates of pay (see Johnstone 1994).

To control this new mass labour force, American engineers, well versed in scientific management, had proved that African mineworkers could drill more than the one hole per shift by hand as they were required to do. African mineworkers however, refused to drill more than one hole as they knew that would become the norm for a day's work. The implication is clear. These early African mineworkers may have been formally uneducated, but had quickly picked up a modern industrial consciousness despite having been only recently **proletarianised** as technically unskilled migrant workers.

Drilling by hand with a hammer and chisel was, however, to be replaced by machines and resulted in a range of social consequences. By 1899 mechanisation at the rockface resulted in a dramatic change to the composition of the labour force. African workers, previously engaged solely in hand-drilling, unskilled lashing work underground and responsible for all physical labour, were employed to assist with operating the new machines, supervised by the now de-skilled white miner. This represented a degradation of work, as explained by Harry Braverman (1974).

14.5.5 The rise of Fordism

Every sociology textbook will tell how Henry Ford instituted the **assembly line** production system in his factory. This proved so successful and became so widely generalised in production systems worldwide that this great transformation of work in capitalist societies has become known as **Fordism**.

Whereas previously workers would move around at work, under Fordism workers were stationary and the job was brought to them on a continually moving conveyor belt assembly line system. Fordism integrated workers and machines into the **labour process** and specified the position and work tasks of every individual worker. The concept 'labour process' refers to the combination of workers and machinery organised in production in order to produce a useful commodity. The study of the capitalist labour process transformed the sociological study of work in South Africa (see Webster 1999).

Nowhere is the centrality of the labour process seen more clearly as when the assembly line labour process is studied and revealed to signal the virtually complete loss of a worker's control over his/her work. While work itself became hugely degraded, the power of this form of the organisation of work resulted in both positive and negative social effects.

Under Fordist assembly line production processes, the worker became subject to the rule of the speed of 'the line'. Standardised product design was now possible. Every manufactured item – motorcars in the case of Ford's factories – was the same. This came along with extensive use of new machine technologies and the parallel social development of higher wages to stimulate consumption. Fordism is in fact usefully conceptualised as *mass production* plus *mass consumption*. Ford instituted not only a revolution in production, but also in society. For the first time even ordinary workers could afford to buy a car, which literally mobilised and completely transformed American society.

In brief, not only were the lives of ordinary Americans transformed by this development, but Fordism also had a significant impact on government planning, politics, the legal system and a change in culture. Fordism initiated unprecedented economic growth and social development in North American and shortly all European industrial societies. Even more, Fordism created a homogeneous class of semi-skilled assembly line production workers whose job was regimented and monotonous in a system where one worker could technically stop the entire plant and cause huge disruption.

The system called Fordism transformed human capacity and consciousness positively and negatively. It did so positively by providing significantly enhanced access to consumer goods and an increase in standards of living. The negative impact of Fordism was that the hugely increased rate of repetitive work it demanded resulted in fatigue, stress, high levels of absenteeism, high labour turnover and a general sense of alienation among the workforce. The social effect of this production system was contradictory. Fordism degraded work for the homogenised worker, but also empowered workers collectively as the shared experience of monotonous work resulted in the rise of militant trade unionism which spread worldwide.

Fordism consequently had a deep impact on American life and globally. American technology and its productive power was decisive in World War II from 1939 to 1945 and a shattered Europe was rebuilt quickly using this scientific model in production. In line with the question we are examining – as to the centrality of work and its commanding influence on society – the case of Fordism is a classic example. The question confronting us now, however, is how Fordism played itself out in South Africa and how have scholars in the sociology of work understood this phenomenon. For one, why did African workers working in the assembly plants of Uitenhage and Port Elizabeth and in Pretoria *not* also drive cars like their American counterparts? The short answer is that in South Africa under apartheid, labour was 'cast in a racial mould', a book by that title being prescribed reading for any student of the sociology of work in South Africa (see Webster 1985).

The assembly line brings together and integrates a large number of workers with similar levels of skills who share the same monotonous working regime, both in terms of experience and working hours. The immediate social consequence of this homogenising workplace resulted, as it did elsewhere, in an upsurge of militant trade unionism in South Africa. We can but note here that

the car plants in the Eastern Cape and Pretoria, instances of assembly line production, were to become an important basis for the re-emergence of the modern mass-based industrial trade unions for black workers which emerged after the Durban strikes in the early 1970s. By 1979 the apartheid state would accept the recommendations of the Wiehahn Commission to recognise the right of all workers to associate freely and join trade unions.

The most prominent of these unions were formed under the umbrella of the Federation of South African Trade Unions (FOSATU) which combined in 1982 with trade unions in the African National Congress tradition to form what remains, despite a split in 2017, with the formation of the South African Federation of Trade Unions (SAFTU), the largest trade union federation in the country the Congress of Trade Unions of South Africa (COSATU) (see Baskin 1991).

14.5.6 The emergence of post-Fordism

It should be clear that the Fordist assembly line was not only a rigidly organised workplace, but that its products were similarly standardised. This resulted not only in the alienation of workers and resistance, but was also unable to satisfy the needs of the market and customer choice. All vehicles were similar initially, even their colour. When Henry Ford's factories began to produce motorcars, they were only painted black.

This was to change as producers gradually came to see they had to accommodate increasingly specific customer requirements. Producers began to vary their products, often serving niche (specialised) markets and ensuring ever greater degrees of product variety. In order to do this, workers had to learn how to perform a wider range of tasks and learn different skills. This has been termed **multitasking** (performing a series of different tasks) and **multiskilling** (learning and exercising more than one skill). Initially this impetus came from Japanese producers who reorganised assembly line work to be less alienating, more flexible and able to cater for a more diverse market and its needs. This orientation – often referred to as Quality Circles or Green Circles – was also accompanied by the emergence of personnel management and industrial relations departments within firms as it became increasingly recognised that the worker was a human being with human needs. This is not to say that the assembly line has disappeared or lost much of its rigidity. It continues to be a boring, repetitive and monotonous form of work and is found in virtually all large manufacturing enterprises that have not been fully automated. There were attempts to break up the assembly line where smaller groups of workers would assemble an entire vehicle. Where the auto manufacturer Volvo famously reorganised production at their Kalmar plant in Sweden, the initiative did not last long for one simple reason: it gave workers too much control over production, which threatened managers' authority and control over the process.

Such initiatives nevertheless signalled the beginning of the contemporary period in the transformation of work known as Post-Fordism. While the ability of producers to move in the direction of making work more meaningful and satisfy a wider range of consumer requirements, there were limits to the extent of the changes which were constrained by the very structure of production itself. Post-Fordism, however, became characterised by workplace flexibility at a number of levels. This would ensure a different kind of control over work in the interests of especially large multinational corporations. Workplace flexibility has almost certainly not served the interests of those who work for weekly wages. In order to meet the demands of an increasingly discriminating consumer market – the people who buy products, in other words – companies became more flexible in the way they both hired and used labour.

There are four forms of workplace flexibility. The first of these is **functional flexibility**. This involves ensuring workers exercise a range of skills or perform a range of tasks, referred to above as multitasking and multiskilling. This went hand in hand with job rotation – workers being moved around to do different kinds of jobs – and experimenting with forms of teamwork. Interestingly, where this was attempted in the South African goldmines, workers were found to drift back to the jobs they had got used to, so where a worker who used to be a winch driver was also required to do timbering work or pipe laying, winch drivers would often gravitate back to their old jobs (see Phakathi 2002).

Temporal flexibility is the second form of workplace flexibility. It suited large companies to introduce different kinds of shift systems and when orders for their products did not come in, to put workers on part-time work or, where possible, to perform work at home (like the 'cottage industries' of old) or offer temporary working arrangements instead. For worker employees this introduced considerably greater uncertainty than before, with few advantages except for women who did not want to work full time in order to continue with childcare activities at home. It seems only a minority of workers like shift systems and irregular working time arrangements, such as working four days on and then four days off – a shift configuration on some South African collieries.

Wage flexibility was the third form of workplace flexibility. Various forms of performance-based pay, incentive schemes and productivity bonuses were introduced to encourage greater commitment to work and make working time more intensive.

A fourth form of flexibility has been called **numerical flexibility**. Instituting this kind of work regime means companies can be flexible in the numbers of workers they employ. Workers are employed on short-term contracts or simply retrenched if sales of the companies' products decline. Combined with temporal flexibility, seasonal labour, casual or subcontracted forms of employment would be offered instead of full-time employment. Such workers are notoriously hard to organise into trade unions to protect their interests and so have begun to organise themselves (Lenka 2017). In South Africa and elsewhere, subcontracted and other part-time workers generally do not qualify for medical insurance, or pension benefits, and the time they spend at work is often not recorded. Such workers are also well known for often not being properly registered for statutory Unemployment Insurance Fund (UIF) benefits, for instance. This deprives them of claiming the modest yet important state-instituted benefits when they are not employed. Workers organised and protected by trade unions have also been known to complain that they feel less secure at work when subcontracted workers are employed and work alongside them at lower rates of pay and often for longer hours. Subcontracted work then threatens trade union organisation built over long years in winning benefits and improved pay and better working conditions from employers.

Employer business organisations, on the other hand – as well as political parties who support them – often accuse trade unions of not being interested in poorer workers and of depriving them of entrance into the formal labour market. Initiated by the International Labour Organisation (ILO), this has raised huge contemporary questions over the last 20 years about what has been called decent work. The movement from the factory to the office has often been thought of as providing better opportunities for decent work.

The rise of service work

Post-Fordism is best characterised by a fundamental shift that has taken place in the very structure of the global economy and which applies to South Africa as well as many similar **emerging economies.** This shift has seen the decline in the importance of and the number of workers being employed in manufacturing and the rise of what has become known as **service work**. Since the Industrial Revolution and the rise of the factory – or in the South African case the emergence of mining – a large number, if not the majority, of workers were employed in the manufacturing sectors of the economy. In South Africa, the numbers of mining and manufacturing jobs have dropped dramatically over the past generation and continue to do so.

Economists often refer to the service sector as part of the tertiary sector of the economy. As its name suggests, this sector is not concerned with production of products and commodities, but provides a wide range of services instead. Those employed in the hospitality and entertainment sectors; the banking sector; the educational sector; the law enforcement agencies such as the police, prisons and military; and the health sector comprising clinics, hospitals and laboratories all provide a specific service in an increasingly complex post-industrial or Post-Fordist society. In South Africa, the broad services sector now employs nearly three-quarters of all formally employed workers, having replaced manufacturing and industry as the largest economic sector. What adds to the complexity is that some of these sectors are part of the formal capitalist economy while others are part of the public sector and paid for by the taxes of citizens. Where trade unions, for instance, used to confront profit-making businesses as their employers to make their demands, public sector trade unions, currently representing the largest number of workers in COSATU, are now confronting the government as their employer and whose wages come out of the public purse.

To make the overall point of this chapter again, then, the dominant form of work and its organisation in a society powerfully shapes much of what happens elsewhere in that society and changes many of the relationships within it. Hence, when COSATU embarks on strike action in the interests of its members, it now no longer often confronts big business or capital to claim a greater share of its profits, but confronts the ANC government with which it stands in a tripartite political alliance alongside the South African Communist Party (SACP). This introduces a considerably more complex set of interactional dynamics between different social groups in contemporary South African society, as simply opening any newspaper today will reveal.

It is not only relationships *between* different social groups with different and competing interests which emerge under Post-Fordism. The very nature of the relationship between individuals changes as well. Under the previous three forms of the organisation of work, the primary relationship in the workplace and reflected in the social

classes in society, is that between employer and employee, or capitalist and worker. A third agent enters the relationship under Post-Fordism and that is the consumer or customer. The employer/employee relationship is replaced, in other words, by an employer/employee/customer relationship for services are now increasingly directed towards the individual consumer.

Work has become more people orientated and involves what theorists have called emotional labour. Shop assistants, public officials and flight stewards are required to be friendly. They must sell their smiles and create a welcoming attitude in us – their consumer customers. Nobody likes a grumpy waiter when ordering a cup of coffee when out at a café with friends. One theorist, whose work has been influential, has suggested this places a demand on the service sector worker and has been called the 'management of human feelings' or what has become known as 'emotional labour' (see Hochschild 1986). If you work as a waiter in a part-time job to get yourself through university, you have to go to work with a smile even though you may not feel like doing so. We as customers and consumers expect such behaviour from those offering services. The market of consumers – us as citizens – increasingly expects this when we are face to face with someone doing their job of serving us.

Box 14.2 People at work

Next time you have coffee with friends, closely observe the service worker who is serving you and ask yourself:
- Is their smile natural?
- How are they interacting with their fellow workers?
- Can you gauge their response when they get a tip or if they do not get one?
- Is what they are doing work or labour?

Control and supervision of the body

This new three-fold relationship (employer/employee/customer) in the world of work has implications for those who perform this kind of work. Some theorists have explained these implications in terms of the exploitation of the body (see MacDonald & Sirianni 1996). Employee workers must often stand all day while at work and must present a disciplined, smiling and sympathetic attitude to their customers. They need to be aware of and are required to manipulate the feelings of their customers so they will come again. Service sector employees must use their bodies and personal talents to market the services they represent.

This has a further implication for control within the workplace. The locus of control is now no longer a supervisor exercising external, coercive control, but has become internal. Employees are not coerced or forced to work, but rather must willingly consent to work and conduct themselves at work as the new consumer-based and globally orientated economy requires. So powerful is the socially structuring character of the modern workplace that theorists have persuasively argued that consent itself is in fact *manufactured* (Burawoy 1979) and the human heart is now *managed* (Hochschild 1986).

14.5.7 Work in South Africa today

The great transformations in the world of work do not mean that older forms do not continue. In fact, instances of all of these forms of work can be found in South African today. If the nature and organisation of work indeed shapes society, as the beginning of this chapter suggested, this signals the variety, diversity and uneven development which characterises our society.

In South Africa today in rural areas, whether serviced with running water and electricity or not, women work in pre-industrial ways – with a hoe using ancient indigenous knowledges (Garutsa & Nekhwevha 2016). Men can be seen herding cattle as in pre-colonial times. In urban and industrial areas, the ideas of scientific management in the world of work have long taken root as managers remain concerned with efficiency and how long it takes to get a job of work completed, dispatched and invoiced. Fordist assembly line forms of work have become generalised in manufacturing across industrial sectors. Under Post-Fordism, work and workplaces everywhere increasingly require flexibility with precarious forms of work and the struggle for decent work having become a dominating feature in our context.

Sociologists in South Africa have examined and widely explored the *idea* of work, the *nature* of work and the *experience* of work. The expending of emotional labour is often evident in workers' experience, whether politely working the telephone lines in call centres (Omar 2005), smiling and waving at petrol stations (Du Toit 2012), managing access control to companies and institutions such as schools, despite rude school children (Sefalala & Webster 2013) or equally rude university students (Du Toit 2015). In the police services, workers are required to provide a 'polite, efficient, purposeful service to people seeking information of laying complaints' (Faull 2013: 29) as professionalism

becomes a focus. While for many workers, such as in the hospitality and tourism industry and in agriculture, work is seasonal. In municipal services and even in manufacturing in large industrial centres, work has often become equally precarious. This applies to both non-South African (Smit & Rugunanan 2014) and local workers (Barchiesi 2011).

Meanwhile, the increasing use of electronic devices and the internet to provide, allocate, perform and control work on digital platforms has seen the rise of work done from home. Whether we use digital apps for play or work, we live in an increasingly digital society shaped by a digital or **gig-based economy**. One prominent example is when commuters download an app to call an Uber taxi driver, whose name is sent beforehand by SMS, to safely collect commuters from home, saving them having to queue for a minibus taxi. So popular has Uber become across the world that sociologists of work have called this the Uberisation of work under what has become known as **platform capitalism** (Webster 2020). Platform capitalism represents a major shift in how companies operate. Major companies, such as Google, Apple, Facebook, Siemens and Uber, transform themselves into platforms that provide the hardware and software on which other companies can operate. These companies attract large numbers of people who are treated as independent contractors with self-employed status.

There are three key features of digital work – or the Uberisation of work. Firstly, the app is the now the common point of production – where worker and customer encounter one another. Secondly, customers' feedback now enables ranking and rating of the service provided, as well as the self-employed contractor, in effect an individual worker, who must expend emotional labour to achieve favourable ratings. Thirdly, a new form control is now exercised remotely by managers who are invisible and inaccessible. In short, while working remotely offers increased flexibility, this is a heavily constrained freedom in the working and personal lives of workers (see Webster 2020). This is the contemporary transformation in the world of work.

To summarise the transformations of work discussed in this chapter, under industrial capitalism the working class was firstly subject to the control of time under Scientific Management and then the pace of the assembly line under Fordism. With the emergence of Post-Fordism and the rise of the tertiary sector and service work, the 'precariat' became subject to the uncertainties of informalisation and precarious forms of work, with nearly half of all workers in South Africa falling into this category (Bezuidenhout et al 2017). Now, with work increasingly performed and controlled at a spatial or physical distance, we see that with remote work, the worker with self-employed status or **cybertariat** has come of age (Huws 2014).

The acceleration of remote work with Covid-19

The Covid-19 pandemic and the lockdown of many societies significantly accelerated the trend towards remote work, including that of academic work. It quickly became apparent that the urgent turn to remote work – such as Emergency Remote Teaching (ERT) in schools and universities – exposed a division between those who were connected and could work remotely from home and those who were not connected or whose jobs required their physical presence at the workplace. In between these two groups of workers, only essential service workers continued to work under the abnormal conditions of the pandemic.

With the rise of platform capitalism, the digital economy and the much discussed Fourth Industrial Revolution has been widely promoted globally. Proponents of the new technologies of robotisation, digitisation and artificial intelligence use the term 'creative destruction' to explain how, while old jobs have been and will be lost due to these technological transformations in the world of work, new jobs will arise. A local report, *South Africa in the Digital Age*, for instance, sees new income opportunities in areas such as the provision of services that can be traded globally, digital platforms that can absorb labour and how these developments can serve as a technology hub in which new opportunities, products and markets for goods and services can emerge (Webster 2020).

Platform capitalism, however, focuses wealth and power increasingly in the hands of a few global corporations with a small highly technically skilled and well-paid workforce and a large group of expendable peripheral self-employed workers who may receive their work orders and instructions remotely, but who do not work from home. Delivery transport workers and Uber drivers are the most prominent examples of these peripheral workers in platform capitalism. The promise is that many young people can now work flexibly as independent self-employed contractors and hence manage their own work–life balance. Their belief that they are self-employed or in 'partnership' with the company often dissolves when they discover they have no pension, health and other benefits or stable contracts as they are considered 'self-employed'. In other words, the mass of jobs in the digital economy tend to be inferior to full-time employment and are precarious with low pay and poor working conditions.

14.6 *The End of Work?* Recent perspectives on work and labour

In 1995 Jeremy Rifkin published a book entitled *The End of Work: The Decline of the Global Labor Force and the Dawn of the Post-Market Era*. It was not so much China that was becoming the workshop of the world that explained how jobs were disappearing elsewhere. Instead, work was going to the robots. In an interview with the German magazine *Der Spiegel*, Rifkin summarised much of this chapter in the following way:

Everybody used to be on the farm, then it automated with machinery and they went to the factories. Then in the 1970s and 1980s the factories were automating, so we went to the service industries.

Well, the intelligent technologies are penetrating just as quickly now into the service industry as they are in the factories – be it banking, financing, wholesale or retail trade … where are the telephone operators or librarians or bank tellers, the middle managers, the secretaries? The traditional jobs are all going … its happening in the professional and conceptual categories, too, like architecture, law and accounting where you need the best and brightest talent.

You are never going to see mass workers in software companies, nanotech companies and biotech companies. They don't exist. The new workforce is a specialised professional one.

Rifkin's book sharpened the view that in the digital age of a globalised society dominated by the market, the study of work, the workplace, labour relations and trade unions and consequently the working class, belonged to the past. The evidence seemed to bear this out. In the context of globalisation, with much work informal, irregular, temporary and hence precariously unstable, trade unions struggled to organise workers dispersed across these sectors. The result was a decline in trade union membership worldwide. The study of work and its transformations and how trade unions had emerged to respond to these changes and had become important institutional players in modern society, for instance, was increasingly seen as of mere dry academic interest. In a few countries, such as in Latin America, however, a new form of people's mobilisation – social movement unionism – emerged outside the gates of factories, mines and workplaces as trade unions joined up with social movements or fought alongside struggles for national liberation, such as in South Africa. This renewed studies of work and labour. One recent approach is noted here to end this chapter.

14.6.1 The labour process and political economy

Unsurprisingly, industrial sociology and the sociology of work traditionally had the workplaces of factory, mine, farm, office and school as their dedicated focus. At the heart of sociological description and analysis was the *labour process* which, in addition to the definition provided in this chapter, can be seen as the socio-technical processes in production within workplaces. Labour process theory, emanating from the critical tradition stemming from Marx, concerned itself with understanding how the nature of work and production in the economy shaped society as this chapter has tried to show. Workers' struggles at the point of production, enmeshed with technological innovations and managerial strategies, shaped trade unions and industrial and labour relations. Labour process theory consequently had to address the politics of production and the role of the state which intervened in regulating what happened inside workplaces (Burawoy 1985).

In short, workplace studies have focused on *control* by managers via supervision and the organisation of work, *resistance* by workers to managerial control, workers' *consent* in collaborating in their exploitation by treating work as a 'game' as Burawoy showed (1979) or as part of a 'moral economy' as Moodie (1994) has shown on the South African mines. Overall, *accommodation* between workers and their trade unions and managers and employers has taken place.

The vast literature on the sociology of work, however, was distanced from important aspects of its Marxist roots (see Thompson 1989) which led to the emergence of critical management studies. The study of work went in two directions. On the one hand control by managers in the factory and the reorganisation of work became an intensified focus in order to deal with the old themes of conflict and resistance by workers. Even the introduction of self-directed teamwork, for instance, that promised greater initiative, co-operation and collaboration while at work by way of introducing multiskilling and multitasking, came widely to be seen as yet a new form of control over workers.

On the other hand, the study of work extended outwards. It has been argued that the interests of labour process theory need to be in conversation with a disciplinary trend which has had broader comparisons between different political economies as their subject matter. Comparative political economy developed within political science and industrial relations. If the study of work started from how relations in the labour process ripple out and shape society, comparative political economy argues that national institutional contexts regulate and powerfully shape what happens at work. We saw how the Wiehahn Commission in 1979, for instance, enabled the beginning of the transformation of racialised social relations of work by recognising trade unions for black workers in South Africa.

To conclude, work in the past gave us a certain kind of society. The question is now the future of work in an increasingly digital economy and knowledge-based society. Both globally and locally, the world of work is shrinking. The result has been the informalisation of work, by way of an exceedingly diverse range of activities serving as generally poorly paid work. Over 60 per cent of workers globally are in the informal economy, predominantly in developing countries such as ours (ILO 2018). This stands in contrast to formal sector work dominated by an ever-smaller skilled professional elite and an increasing number of workers engaged in precarious forms of work, even though the majority of workers have the official status of being self-employed. These two worlds of work, formal and informal, are linked.

In South Africa instances of all the transformations of work can be observed. In the formal economy there are the ascendant globally dominant high-tech companies continually transforming the world of work and their small, highly skilled workforce and a larger number of 'self-employed' workers. The formal economy includes manufacturing and service work, whether in the private or public sectors. In the informal sector, an exceptionally wide variety of activities serves as work which is generally low paid with poor working conditions and few, if any, benefits. Then there is work performed, whether linked to either sector or not, such as subsistence farming. Here women in particular can be found still working as in pre-industrial times with access to a modest plot of land and still tilling with an Iron Age hoe in her hand and a cell phone in her pocket and who has weathered all the transformations in the world of work.

Summary

- This chapter argued that the activity of work is central to the structure and shape society assumes and the formation of individual identity and subjectivity.
- Four major transformations in the nature of work in industrial societies developing along capitalist lines were identified and discussed.
- Work includes and integrates us into society as citizens, but which brings to the fore the social significance of joblessness and unemployment.
- Looking at South African society today in the context of Post-Fordist or post-industrial globalisation, work is increasingly experienced as flexible and precarious. Work, understood as wage labour, is increasingly dominated not by a regular, secure routine, but by outsourcing, piece work, contract and temporary work.
- This raises significant sociological questions about South African society, but which are also applicable elsewhere in emerging economies especially. How are those excluded from work to be included as fully fledged citizens capable of exercising their human rights and adopting their place within society as a whole?

ARE YOU ON TRACK?

1. Define the concept of work and explain why it is different to the concept of labour.
2. Why is 'work' seen by Claus Offe to be the central concept in sociology?
3. What are the four major transformations of work in capitalist society?
4. How is the human body exploited in post-industrial society?

More sources to consult

Burawoy M. 1979. *Manufacturing Consent: Changes in the Labor Process under Monopoly Capitalism.* Chicago: University of Chicago Press.

Callinicos L. 1980. *A People's History of South Africa, Volume 1: Gold and Workers.* Johannesburg: Ravan Press.

Moodie TD (with Ndatshe V). 1994. *Going for Gold: Men, Mines and Migration.* Berkeley: University of California Press.

Webster E, Alfred L, Bethlehem L, Joffe A, Selikow T (eds). 1994. *Work and Industrialisation in South Africa.* Johannesburg: Ravan Press.

References

Allen VL. 1994. 'The genesis of racism on the mines' in *Work and Industrialisation in South Africa.* Webster E, Alfred L, Bethlehem L, Joffe A, Selikow T (eds). Johannesburg: Ravan Press.

Barchiesi F. 2011. *Precarious Liberation: Workers, the State and Contested Social Citizenship in Post-apartheid South Africa,* New York and Scottsville: State University of New York Press and University of KwaZulu-Natal Press.

Baskin J. 1991. *Striking Back: A History of COSATU.* Johannesburg: Ravan Press.

Berg M. 1979. *Technology and Toil in Nineteenth Century Britain.* London: CSE Books, Humanities Press.

Bezuidenhout A, Fakier K. 2006 'Maria's burden: Contract cleaning and the crisis of social reproduction in post-apartheid South Africa'. *Antipode,* 38(3): 462–485.

Bhana D, Nkani N. 2016. '"What can I do, the child is already here?"' Caregivers, gender, poverty and the contradiction of care in supporting teenage mothers at school', *South African Review of Sociology,* 47:(2): 13–18.

Braverman H. 1974. *Labour and Monopoly Capitalism: The Degradation of Work in the Twentieth Century.* New York: Monthly Review Press.

Burawoy M. 1979. *Manufacturing Consent: Changes in the Labor Process under Monopoly Capitalism.* Chicago: University of Chicago Press.

Burawoy M. 1985. *The Politics of Production: Factory Regimes under Capitalism and Socialism.* London: Verso.

Callinicos L. 1980. *A People's History of South Africa, Volume 1: Gold and Workers.* Johannesburg: Ravan Press.

Callinicos L. 1994a. 'The compound system' in *Work and Industrialisation in South Africa.* Webster E, Alfred L, Bethlehem L, Joffe A, Selikow T (eds). Johannesburg: Ravan Press.

Callinicos L. 1994b. 'New factories, new workers' in *Work and Industrialisation in South Africa*. Webster E, Alfred L, Bethlehem L, Joffe A, Selikow T (eds). Johannesburg: Ravan Press.

Chirikure S. 2010. *Indigenous Mining and Metallurgy in Africa*. Cape Town: Cambridge University Press.

Chirikure S, Hall S. 2008. 'The archaeology of indigenous mining and metallurgy in South Africa: A brief overview'. (Unpublished paper.) Johannesburg: The Platinum Centre.

Delius P, Trapido S. 1994. '*Inboekselings* and *oorlams*: The creation and transformation of a servile class' in *Work and Industrialisation in South Africa*. Webster E, Alfred L, Bethlehem L, Joffe A, Selikow T (eds). Johannesburg: Ravan Press.

Du Toit D. 2012. 'Beyond the smile and wave of petrol attendants: A case study on male petrol attendants' use of emotional labour'. *South African Review of Sociology*, 43(3): 129–145.

Du Toit D. 2015. 'Working as a security guard on Potchefstroom Campus: issues challenges and coping strategies'. *South African Review of Sociology*, 46(4): 97–114.

Faull A. 2013 'Towards a "New professionalism" for the South African Police Service'. *South African Review of Sociology* 44(2): 18–35.

Garutsa TC, Nekhwevha FH. 2016. 'Labour-burdened women utilising their marginalised indigenous knowledge in food production processes: The case of Khambashe rural households, Eastern Cape, South Africa'. *South African Review of Sociology* 47(4) :106–120.

Gilbert L. 'Re-engineering the workforce to meet service needs: Exploring 'task-shifting' in South Africa in the context of HIV/AIDS and antiretroviral therapy'. *South African Review of Sociology* 44(2): 54–75.

Harries P. 1994. *Work, Culture and Identity: Migrant Labourers in Mozambique and South Africa, c 1860–1910*. Johannesburg: University of the Witwatersrand Press.

Hauptmeier M, Vidal M. 2014. *Comparative Political Economy of Work*. Houndmills, Basingstoke: Palgrave Macmillan.

Hochschild A. 1986. *The Managed Heart: The Commercialisation of Human Feeling*. Berkeley: University of California Press.

Huws U. 2014. *Labor in the Global Digital Economy: The Cybertariat Comes of Age*. New York: Monthly Review Press.

Johnstone FA. 1994. 'Class conflict and colour bars in the South African gold mining industry' in *Work and Industrialisation in South Africa*. Webster E, Alfred L, Bethlehem L, Joffe A, Selikow T (eds). Johannesburg: Ravan Press.

Lenka. 2017. 'Precarious workers, the Casual Workers' Advice Office and the 2014 Labour Relations Act Amendments'. MA thesis, University of the Witwatersrand.

MacDonald CL, Sirianni C. 1996. *Working in the Service Society*. Philadelphia: Temple University Press.

Mail&Guardian. 2013. 'Numsa: We don't want DA policies in the NDP'. [Online] Available at: http://mg.co.za/article/2013-03-19-numsa-reiterates-ndp-rejection [Accessed 16 August 2013].

Marx K. 1976. *Capital: A Critique of Political Economy* (Vol 1). London: Penguin Books.

Moodie TD (with Ndatshe V). 1994. *Going for Gold: Men, Mines and Migration*. Berkeley: University of California Press.

Offe C. 1985. 'Work: The key sociological category?' in *Disorganised Capitalism: Contemporary Transformation of Work and Politics*. Offe C (ed). Cambridge: Polity Press.

Omar R. 2005. 'New work order or more of the same?: Call centres in South Africa'. *Beyond the Apartheid Workplace: Studies in Transition*. Webster E, Von Holdt, K (eds.). Scottsville. University of KwaZulu-Natal Press.

Phakathi S. 2002. 'Self-directed work teams in a post-apartheid goldmine: Perspectives from the rock face'. *Journal of Workplace Learning,* 14(7).

Rifkin J. 1995. *The end of work: The decline of the global labor force and the dawn of the post-market era*, New York: G.P. Putnam's Sons.

Sefalala T, Webster E. 2013. 'Working as a security guard: The limits of professionalisation in a low status occupation', *South African Review of Sociology*, 44(2): 76–97.

Smit R, Rugunanan P. 2014. 'From precarious lives to precarious work: The dilemma facing refugees in Gauteng, South Africa'. *South African Review of Sociology*, 45(2): 4–26.

Standing G. 1999. *Global Labour Flexibility: Seeking Distributive Justice*. Basingstoke: Macmillan.

Taylor FW. 1911. *The Principles of Scientific Management*. London: Harper & Row.

Thompson EP. 1963. *The Making of the English Working Class*. London: Penguin Books.

Thompson EP. 1967. 'Time, work-discipline and industrial capitalism'. *Past and Present,* 38: 56–97.

Thompson P. 1989. *The Nature of Work: An Introduction to Debates in the Labour Process*. 2nd ed. London: Macmillan.

Webster E. 1985. *Cast in a Racial Mould: Labour Process and Trade Unionism in the Foundries.* Johannesburg: Ravan Press.

Webster E. 1999. 'Race, labour process and transition: The sociology of work in South Africa'. *Society in Transition,* 30(1): 28–41.

Webster E. 2020. 'The Uberisation of work: The challenge of regulating platform capitalism'. *International Review of Applied Economics*, 34(4).

Webster E, Alfred L, Bethlehem L, Joffe A, Selikow T (eds). 1994. *Work and Industrialisation in South Africa.* Johannesburg: Ravan Press.

The South African economy

Paul Stewart

The word 'economy' means the management of the home. The modern economy includes everyone who works to produce, distribute and consume the resources of the society in which these activities are embedded. This includes the *goods* or commodities we buy or sell or the services we want and need and for which we are generally required to pay. Individuals, workers, small traders, businesses, corporations, banks and governments are all economic actors in the national economy of specific countries as well as in the global economy. The informal sector, where economic activities are neither taxed nor monitored by government, is an increasingly important part of economies in the global South. How all these agents and activities are organised and the health of any country's economy in the current era of globalisation are of critical importance to the welfare of its citizens.

The chapter first lays the foundations for examining the economy from a sociological perspective. It starts by describing how economists divide the economy into three sectors: the primary (agriculture and mining), secondary (manufacturing) and tertiary (the provision of services) sectors. It then notes that the economy can be planned or unplanned, but that all economies have elements of both in the ways they are organised. It then argues that you cannot meaningfully talk about the economy without talking about the state and politics – the dedicated focus of which is the chapter to follow. All states control or regulate their national economies in some way, yet some economists strongly believe that the economy and markets must be free from any state intervention. To confront this issue head-on, the chapter then dives straight into the longstanding ideological debate about the economy, which, to put it bluntly, involves the question of whether and to what extent it should be regulated or unregulated. This debate continues worldwide and has not been resolved. Decisions have nevertheless to be made about economic policy and which programmes of action are most appropriate for economic growth and prosperity. Such decisions are of particular concern to especially developing and emerging market economies such as South Africa.

This chapter has the South African economy since 1994 as its focus. While political freedom and the implementation of democracy understandably took centre stage with the ending of apartheid, the central issue of how our economy was reintegrated into the global economy was sidelined. The question was, and remains, how best to do this? In order to present the different sides of the debate in this ongoing ideological and political struggle, the chapter divides the debaters into the 'defenders' and the 'critics' of capitalism, and shows how governments have the unenviable task of 'managing' the capitalist economy.

The specific set of challenges our economy faces today are briefly outlined. The tough choices over economic policy the new ANC government faced after April 1994 are then discussed in some detail. The issues are thorny ones. The loss of massive amounts of capital through illegal capital flight, the departure of major South African-based companies to London, the promotion of black capitalism and the policy of Black Economic Empowerment (BEE), and the serious problem of unemployment, especially among South African youth, are some of the issues discussed. What did the new democratic government decide about these issues? What are the RDP (the Redistribution and Development Programme) and GEAR (the Growth, Employment and Redistribution) programme? How does the ANC's guiding policy of the National Democratic Revolution impact on economic policy decisions made? How was the globally dominant economic policy imposed on South Africa managed after 1994? What impact has the reintegration of our economy had on work and employment? Should the state rethink the question of intervening in the economy? These are some of questions this chapter confronts. There are no easy answers, not in this textbook or anywhere else. Every society across the globe confronts similar questions in one way or another.

One of the great strengths of sociology is its ability to understand what happens in society by way of analysis and critique. It often does less well at providing practical alternatives to the social problems it identifies, for which a final section – entitled: 'Economic possibilities and alternatives?' – serves as a potential remedy. A range of practical measures regarding economic policy, virtually all of which are controversial, are proposed. Should every South African could be forced, by the state, to save some of their earnings? Is that even possible in a constitutional democracy? As you will see, there is much scope for the study, analysis and active engagement of social scientists when the economy is the topic of debate in South Africa today.

Case study 15.1   The South African economy and society

South Africa has a highly developed economy and advanced economic infrastructure. South Africa is one of the world's largest producers and exporters of gold, platinum, and other natural resources. It also has well-developed financial, legal, communications, energy, and transport sectors as well as the continent's largest stock exchange. Low commodity prices have weakened economic growth. Rates of formal-sector unemployment and crime are high.

South Africa was able to retain its investment-grade credit rating because of significant policy improvements after President Cyril Ramaphosa took office in February 2018. The new government has restored macroeconomic stability but still faces rising public debt, inefficient state-owned enterprises, and spending pressures that have reduced the country's global competitiveness. The judicial system is increasingly vulnerable to political interference, and scandals and political infighting have severely undermined government integrity and weakened the rule of law.

(Source: Index of Economic Freedom 2019)

QUESTIONS

1. What options do South African economic policy makers have to improve the assessment above?
2. Which economic policy would best serve industrial and economic development and address formal-sector unemployment, crime and poverty?
3. Why has economic policy remained essentially the same under presidents Mandela, Motlanthe, Zuma and Ramaphosa?

Key themes

- The economy in the era of globalisation
- The division of the economy into its different sectors
- The role of the state, economic policy, and planned and market economies
- The reintegration of the South African economy into the global economy
- Two competing views regarding the direction of economic policy

- Core features of the South African economy
- Economic policy interventions since 1994
- The National Democratic Revolution and black capitalism
- Debates regarding neoliberal economic policy
- Rethinking state intervention in the economy.

15.1 Introduction

The economy is central to any society. In order to survive, all societies must produce more than they immediately consume and retain the surplus production for future use. Even a simple agricultural subsistence society must keep some seeds for planting after winter. In any society, everyone must be able to gain access to the resources produced and services provided to satisfy a broad range of needs. The basic needs are food, shelter and clothing, to which should be added energy, clean water, garbage management and sewage treatment. The economy is hence made up of those activities, informal networks and institutions where the resources and services necessary to sustain social life are produced, distributed and consumed. The nature, form and quantities of the resources and services required by different societies at different times to satisfy these needs are as varied as human experience itself.

Instead of describing and analysing the economy in the abstract, this chapter will explain what happened in the South African economy since democracy in 1994. It will examine, for instance, how the South African economy was reintegrated into the global economy after decades of isolation under apartheid. The focus is thus our own economy in the context of the modern era of globalisation which started from around the 1970s.

The key features of modern globalisation are a reduction in transport and communications costs; reduced barriers to trade, often referred to as **trade liberalisation**; access to increased information technology; and the massively increased speed of information flow. These features of the **global economy** and society have resulted in our fast-paced and closely interconnected world. What happens in the global economy and the powerful forces it unleashes have an immense effect on the fortunes of every society. This is because what happens in a country's economy is closely related to what happens in the global economy.

The post-apartheid South African economy covers the lifetime of most of this book's readers. The sociological challenge is, as always, to ask how our own individual lives are influenced by the structure of South African society and in this case, by the state of the economy. As a functionalist thinker might ask, what is your role in how the economy works in South Africa today? Or as Weber might ask, how are you as an individual inserted into the economy and how does your position within the economy frame your personal 'life chances'? Or as Marx might ask, what is the extent of your access to resources and services, given your social class position? Whatever approach you prefer, how do we think of this thing called 'the economy'? How are South Africans

going to fare given that the World Bank predicts a very low (0.9 %) growth rate for the South African economy in 2020? (Buthelezi 2020). A growth rate of 4 to 6 per cent is the ideal range of growth under contemporary conditions of globalisation.

The chapter starts out by showing how **neoclassical economics** divides the economy into sectors, notes the important role the state plays in the economy and how all economies lie on a continuum of being either centrally planned or left completely free to regulate themselves. No economy functions in isolation from politics. The impact of apartheid politics, for instance, left the new democratic government with a 'failed' and ultimately bankrupt economy (Moll 1991). Global and other local circumstances and conditions framed the choices the new African National Congress (ANC) government faced in attempting to redress the past and reintegrate South Africa back into the world economy. While the details and economic choices made after 1994 are complex (Gelb 2010), the main features of the South African economy are then outlined and its challenges are highlighted. The economic policies, the debates and contestations around economic policy are introduced. The interventions of the new democratic state, and the results of these interventions, assume a central role in the chapter. The way in which the state promoted black capitalism, the fortunes of BEE and why whites still remain dominant in a centralised and skewed economy will be discussed. The role of those who did not benefit from these developments will be seen to be powerful yet limited.

In treating these issues and by analysing the policy choices made under difficult economic circumstances since 1994, this chapter aims to explain how the economy powerfully frames what happens in society.

15.2 The sectors of the economy

Modern mainstream **neoclassical economics** divides the economy into the primary, secondary and tertiary sectors. The **primary sector** produces raw materials and is made up of agriculture and animal husbandry, forestry and mining. Without the farms, forests and mines and the people who work there, no further development of an economy can take place, hence its importance as the primary sector of the economy.

The **secondary sector** is largely concerned with manufacturing and construction. This sector takes the raw materials produced in the primary sector – food from agriculture, animals reared for consumption, wood from forestry and precious minerals from mining – and transforms them into useful products to sustain life and build society's infrastructure. The secondary sector is generally the most productive one of an industrialised capitalist economy, but this is not the case in the South African economy, as you will see.

The **tertiary sector** provides the wide range of services supporting all economic activities in the primary and secondary sectors. The tertiary sector therefore provides services such as security, health, education and information, hospitality and entertainment and, of course, an ever increasingly complex set of financial products and services. In any economy more developed than a simple subsistence or **household economy**, banks and financial institutions provide loans to producers and consumers alike. The financial sector – the banks, other financial service providers, the big insurance companies and the JSE – can be thought of as the nerve centre of the economy. In **post-industrial societies**, this tertiary sector, dominated by the technologically driven global information and knowledge economy, assumes the central focus of developed modern economies, including South Africa.

Finally, one very significant, often ignored part of the economy must be highlighted, and that is domestic work, the greater part of which is unpaid. The unpaid work of women in the home (and a miniscule number of men) is often overlooked, and without it the economy would not function. Millions of unpaid domestic workers (or generally very poorly paid ones) contribute to sustaining the workforce – whether manual labourers or white-collar professionals (Dalla Costa & James 1972).

Wherever people produce the resources, goods and commodities, as well as provide the wide range of services, information and knowledge a modern economy requires, these sites and the people who work there are all part of the economy. All economies assume a particular shape and size. Each one is characterised by different levels of technological development, forms of organisation and complex sets of networks. The extent of the formal institutionalisation of the economy, consequently, exercises a profound impact on and is integrally enmeshed in the society in which it is deeply embedded.

15.3 The role of the state

In any economy more sophisticated than a simple household-based or pre-industrial, nomadic or agrarian economy, some form of social organisation has emerged as government or the state. By formulating **regulations** and law, the modern state ideally serves the interests of society as a whole. A key role of the state has been to levy taxes on all income derived from economic activity, again ideally in the collective interest of society as a whole. Without the collection of **tax**, no state and certainly no modern state can exist. States have consequently always had a complex and intimate relationship with the economy. In capitalist societies especially, governments and the state have generally sought to organise economic activity around which the art, science and practice of politics centrally turns.

15.3.1 Planned economies and market economies

In many variations and to different degrees the economy can be planned or unplanned. In a **planned economy**, the state plays the central role to control the production and distribution of resources and services. The economy can also be unplanned; the state does not interfere in economic transactions, and leaves buyers and sellers to do as they please. Unplanned economies are referred to as **market economies**. What is produced and how the distribution of resources and services takes place is the result of the many individual decisions taken in the marketplace.

Markets were first very simple and were, of course, preceded by bartering. This is where two individuals, or producer groups from simple household economies, exchanged the things or products they had made. The quantities in which things were bartered were based on their value – usually measured by the time they had spent labouring over their respective products. The role of labour was seen the source of economic value and wealth, with **labour time** as its measure. This was the foundation of the **classical economics** of Adam Smith (1723–1790) and David Ricardo (1772–1823) and their chief critic, Karl Marx (1818–1883). The focus in economics shifted, however, from production to the market. It was not *production* (the time spent making a product), but rather the *market* (the amount a purchaser was prepared to pay for a product) that became central to economics. The idea is that the most rational way to organise society is through the '**invisible hand**' of the many millions of daily transactions on the market. This thinking dominates economics in our current globalised marketised economy today – often referred to as **neoliberalism**. The problem is that when society is organised on this principle, social inequality is further entrenched. Often the vast majority of people in society, including economically productive workers, are not able to access the resources and services they need to live a decent life. As a result, after socialist-inspired revolutions of oppressed and exploited workers and peasants, attempts have been made to plan economies on rational grounds instead of leaving the economy to the chaos of the unplanned market. How to achieve this, and how and to what extent the state should regulate economic affairs, remains an unresolved economic and political issue to this day.

Where planned economies have been attempted, markets and trading in resources and the provision of services have, however, always emerged, no matter how centralised and planned an economy might be. Obviously, not everything can be planned. By the same token, there is much planning in so-called unplanned or market economies. Clearly, not all decisions taken in the market are completely free, hence neither the few planned economies that have ever existed, nor the unplanned but sophisticated modern market economies, have ever appeared in a pure form. The South African economy is no exception. It displays features of both forms of economic organisation and can be called a **mixed economy** – as are most economies across the globe today. This is despite the fact that the idea of the rationality of the 'invisible hand' of the market dominates global economic thinking. Despite this stress on the central role of the market, substantial centralisation and concentration of purchasing power occur in market economies and often powerfully override how independent individuals behave in the market. Large businesses, corporations, conglomerates and monopolies, for instance, dominate advertising and the current global market. Yet the web of politics surrounding market activities in turn profoundly influences both access to and the control over the almost infinite number of products and services available on local and world markets. The question arises as to how individual governments and states deal with the overall and ever-changing impact of these transactions that find expression as externally imposed global economic and political forces.

15.3.2 Ideological struggle and the economy

For the purposes of this introductory text, the background to the two main perspectives of how to organise modern societies needs to be outlined and put into historical context. Let us only go back to 1989 and the fall of the Berlin Wall, which not only divided Germany into East and West Germany, but also represented the two different ways in which society can be organised – through **centralised planning** (former East Germany) or via the dictates of an open **market economy** (former West Germany). You may be familiar with the expression of the 'Cold War' – the undeclared post-World War II ideological struggle between the Soviet Union and the US. The Cold War was fought over the competing ideas of communism and capitalism (ie ideas about how society should best be organised). The US fought for the idea that everyone should be free to invest their

money or sell their labour wherever they liked and that the market would rationally distribute the product of society's collective labour. This is the key argument for capitalism and is based on the liberal ideal of the freedom of the individual. The Soviet Union fought for the idea that the organisation of society and the economy should be planned in order to ensure that everyone benefited equally from what society produced that capitalism had failed to achieve. This is the key idea of socialism which, following Marx's ideas, leads to communism and is based on the ideal of cooperation and sharing among independent human agents. As always in sociology, as in social life, however, there are complexities. There is a very strong argument, made especially by socialists, that the Soviet Union was not socialist at all, but was really a form of state capitalism. But that just is more evidence that one cannot talk about the economy without talking about the state, whatever form either assumes.

Needless to say, both socialism and capitalism (respectively preferring a 'planned' and a 'market' economy) are what Max Weber would call 'ideal types'. **Anarchists** who reject the very need of a state would reject both of the forms of organisation that these opposing views often assume in practice – capitalism or socialism in the guise of state capitalism. Much heat has been generated over these two competing ideas. Some think this ideological debate died when the Cold War ended and the Soviet Union and its planned economy collapsed. Yet aspects of this debate are still very much alive in South Africa today. In fact, these two opposing ideological views underlie any discussion on how or to what extent the state should intervene in economic affairs in the interest of its citizens. These two ideological perspectives each have practical implications that need to be noted when looking at the South Africa economy in the current era of globalisation.

15.3.3 To regulate or 'free' the capitalist market economy?

The capitalist system dominates the global economy. For neoclassical economists, the four factors of production are land, labour, capital and entrepreneurship – the factor of entrepreneurship only having been recently added to the first three. Capital takes the form of money and **credit**, and is the repository of wealth and gives its owner a stream of income. The capital invested in a *spaza* shop is modest, yet in a gold or platinum mine the capital investment would be massive. The accounting of monies in a spaza shop would be simple – adding the difference between the purchase and resale price of everything sold. The accounting of a multinational corporation – from intricately structured credit arrangements with banks to changing currency values across time zones – is complex. Both must make a profit. Profit drives the modern capitalist system, which mainstream neoclassical economics refers to as the free market or **free enterprise** system.

All governments in capitalist societies claim that their interest is either to regulate or free the capitalist market economy to work in the best interests of society as a whole. Whether and how the economy should be planned and regulated, or left to its own devices and not regulated at all, lies at the basis of competing views about the economy. These two ideological perspectives frame the analysis of the economic trajectory of any contemporary society. The South African case is, again, no exception. This simply means that the economy cannot be adequately treated from a sociological point of view without reference to the role of the state and politics.

The key question motivating this chapter and which arises, when both the local South African economy and the current modern capitalist global economy are under consideration, is then this: Can or should the state *regulate* the economy or leave the decisions of buyers and sellers to determine the shape of the economy and society? In short, what is the best way for the economy to serve the interests of society as a whole?

15.4   The economy and politics

When the South African economy is viewed in its social and political context, the relation between the economy and politics is a two-way street. Political developments have the capacity to structure the economy in much the same way as the economy shapes society. What happened politically and historically, colonisation for instance, had a profound structural impact on their economies and society. A *structural* factor is one which has a powerful defining influence on other social factors. For instance, no South African university student needs to be reminded of how the racially exclusive policy of apartheid denied not only the vote, but also skills and equal education to the majority of South Africans. This political ideology completely excluded black entrepreneurs from leadership roles in the formal economy. After only a single generation of 30 years, however, it was evident that apartheid was dysfunctional to the development of the South African economy. There were simply not enough whites to fill all the positions in the economy. Lacking skilled and educated personnel in virtually all occupations and professions, the attempt to sustain a racially based political system failed. Faced with international political opposition and the isolation of the apartheid state by way of **economic**

sanctions, the apartheid economy was shortly to become hugely indebted and was the foundation for its eventual demise. This was the economic legacy the new popularly elected democratic government of the ANC had to face when assuming political power.

15.4.1   Reintegrating the South African economy

The first challenge the new ANC government faced in 1994 was to reintegrate the previously isolated apartheid economy into the internationally globalised one. The best way to do this was highly contested. Was the new government to finally implement the policies based on the Freedom Charter it had espoused as a **liberation movement** and which had long been strongly influenced by socialist policies, most notably **nationalisation**? In socialist economic thinking, labour is not merely 'a factor of production', a *thing*, but is instead the source of all economic wealth. Nationalisation (ownership of all economic wealth by the nation) has traditionally been a key element of socialist thinking and is an economic policy which seeks to transfer the private ownership of capitalist sectors of the economy to the state. Nationalisation of the economy was certainly entertained by the ANC before it assumed political power – in its rhetoric at least. Was the new ANC government to follow its liberation politics or was it to show to the world that the new black majority-based democratic government would follow the dominant economic policies espoused especially by international financial institutions such as the World Bank and the International Monetary Fund? These institutions were central in defining the economic policy widely known as the **Washington consensus**. Such an economic policy for developing countries was characterised by strict control over the money supply, minimal 'political interference' or intervention by government in the economy, low taxes for businesses especially and maximum freedom for privately owned companies. The rationale of this view is that following such an economic policy encourages investment and results in job creation. In brief, national economic (state) policy should not attempt to regulate the economy, nor should the government 'interfere' in the economy and advocate spending as a way to respond to downturns in the economy. Both of these principles had been the hallmarks of governments until World War II when, following the British economist John Maynard Keynes (1883–1946), it was realised that certain 'safety nets' had to be introduced by the state to protect disadvantaged groups such as workers and the poor.

This view has since been challenged by big business. In the Washington consensus, **neoliberal** view, the economy and the market should be entirely 'free'. There should be no barriers to trade. Taxes for businesses should be low. Taxes to pay for education and health should be removed – such institutions should be **privatised**. This means schools, universities, clinics and hospitals should be economically self-supporting, which in turn means they should make a profit, even if it is a small one. Where there are barriers to trade, such as tariffs to pay when goods cross a national border, these should be dropped. Economists refer to the removal of such barriers as *trade liberalisation*. In this view, the state should certainly *not* take over or nationalise privately owned businesses and companies.

There is still much disagreement among thinkers, social analysts, economists and scholars in the social sciences, as well as between politicians and the capitalist business community on these two basic orientations regarding economic policy. These disagreements were, as usual, intimately related to the competing interests of different social groups. Each proposed different policy initiatives and measures to be adopted emerging from conflicting theoretical perspectives about both the nature of society and the direction economic policymaking should take. The debate after 1994 was a rigorous one. Economic policy was to take the path of capitalism (see Carmody 2002: 255).

15.4.2 The 'defenders' vs the 'critics' of capitalism

The main contenders of the two views on economic policy could be called the 'defenders' and the 'critics' of capitalism. These two opposing and highly contested sets of views continue to find their expression in South African politics today. The 'defenders' are represented by mainstream neoclassical economics which argues that the market economy, based on the freedom of the individual and the institution of private property, should be independent of any government interference. Broadly speaking, this is the liberal view and analysis of society, but the form it currently takes is often referred to as neoliberalism. Thinkers from the positivist and even the interpretive approaches in sociology largely support such an analysis of society.

The 'critics', on the other hand, argue that the capitalist economy cannot be and is not in practice separable from the

political sphere. Governments must make economic policy choices, but are constrained by the capitalist economy, yet they need to protect vulnerable citizens whose interests are not served by the inequalities generated in a capitalist society. Capitalism is a form of society in which an increasingly small number of people dominate and marshal the bulk of the resources and economic wealth. The rationale for this view is that capitalist production is inherently exploitative, and the uncertainties and chaos of the market do not in fact ensure that everyone benefits from this way of organising society. Broadly speaking, this is the radical view and analysis of society. The conflict or Marxist approach supports such an analysis of society.

In the current era of globalisation, the state can be viewed as 'managers' of capitalism at the national level. The South African state has been shown to be trying to 'manage' or 'negotiate' globalisation (Carmody 2002: 258). The state 'manages' capitalism not only by creating conditions for global capital to invest, but also by using the threat of the impact of the global market to discipline both capital and labour locally. In the South African state, both 'defenders' and 'critics' of capitalism are to be found as it seeks to 'manage' capitalism. Both ideological stances can be found within the tripartite alliance of the ANC, the Congress of South African Trade Unions (COSATU) and the South African Communist Party (SACP).

Once the decision was made to follow a capitalist path of development, the key question arose as to how the new democratic government should play its role as 'manager' of capitalism. How should the failed and bankrupt apartheid economy be restructured in the era of globalisation? There were, and still are, different responses to this question. The extent to which and how the government is involved in the economy is really at the centre of the debate.

Before examining how this matter was tackled, we first need to understand something about the nature and structure of the South African economy itself. We need to ask what kind of economy the ANC inherited and what its key features were.

Case study 15.2

Are you a 'defender' or 'critic' of capitalism?
- List the arguments and evidence for both of these competing views, choose which side of the debate you are on and give reasons for your choice. (Hint: Do the exercise and then go and find a classmate who made the opposite choice. Conduct your debate in a rational and reasoned manner and try to stick to the evidence for your argument).
- Are you able to argue on both sides of the debate?

15.5 The South African economy in context

The South African economy and society is a mix of features of developed societies and those now referred to as 'developing'. In societies displaying entangled combinations of 'developed' and 'developing' societies, such as in South Africa, some multi- or transnational corporations have improved the quality of their product *beyond* that of European or North American standards. Parts of the economy and society are very well developed. Some South African producers are able to compete with the global best, yet many **peri-urban areas** are not yet serviced with running water and electricity, and remote, economically deprived rural areas especially lack basic services.

Despite stark differences in the South African economy, it was the largest economy in Africa, eclipsed only recently by Nigeria. Economies in Africa, however, remain small in global terms. In 2009, Africa's total **gross domestic product (GDP)** represented only 2.3 per cent of the world's economy (Carmody 2002: 256). In 2017 this had risen to between 2.6 and 2.7 percent. South Africa's proportion of global economic activity in 2018 was 0.59 per cent of global GDP (https://tradingeconomics.com/south-africa/gdp). Our small economy had, moreover, been slowing down for decades: from 4.1 per cent growth in 1979, to 3.2 per cent in 1980 and to 2.5 per cent in 1990 just prior to democracy. From this point onwards, during the transition from apartheid to democracy, from 1990 to 2000 the South African economy grew consistently for 10 years, but only at an average of 2.9 per cent (Gelb 2010). This was nowhere near a growth rate of 4 or 5 per cent, which was, however, achieved between 2004 and 2007. Growth has, however, subsequently slowed down again. In 2018, for instance, the growth rate was 1.1 per cent, and slowed further to 0.9 per cent in 2019 (https://trading economics.com/south-africa/gdp). This, as noted, has again been predicted for 2020.

We need, however, to look at the structure of the South African economy before returning to the issue of the rate of **economic growth** to get a sense of the meaning of such figures often cited by economists and politicians.

15.5.1 The Minerals Energy Complex (MEC)

Historically, the South African economy was dominated by the *primary sector*. The pre-industrial economy was dominated by agriculture and the production of maize. Since the discovery of diamonds in Kimberley in 1868 and gold on the Witwatersrand in 1886, the industrial economy was dominated by mining, which depended heavily on the exploitation of black workers who worked for low wages

over long hours and who served increasingly long migrant labour contracts for over a century. This labour was the basis of the South African economy, which was the world's biggest producer of gold and underpinned the paper currencies of the world's largest economies – America and Europe. These were the richest gold deposits ever discovered, but were also the deepest goldmines in the world. To mine gold successfully required a massive concentration of capital, and the industry's demand for energy from coal-fired power stations was enormous. Mining quickly became controlled by a few major mining producer groups, to which the rest of the economy and its development were subordinated. This concentration of economic wealth powerfully influenced state economic policy as mining was its major tax base.

While the secondary sector, dominated by manufacturing, has surpassed mining in terms of its contribution to GDP, South Africa remains rich in mineral reserves and, according to the American banking giant Citigroup, is still the richest nation in the world by 'commodity wealth', with reserves estimated to be worth $2.5 trillion (Ashman, Fine & Newman 2010: 179–180). This works out to an amount of R35 trillion if the exchange rate is taken to be R14 to $1. The sheer scale of this wealth can be appreciated when compared to the GDP of South Africa, which in 2018 was $366.3 billion or nearly R4.7 trillion! (Note: A billion is a 1 000 million – 1 000 000 000; a trillion is a million million – 1 000 000 000 000.)

The South African economy remains dominated by what has been called the Minerals Energy Complex (MEC). Mining does not only contribute to the economic weight of the economy, but also to its direction (Ashman et al 2010: 180). Mines require massive amounts of energy, and are powered by electricity. Mining hence determines that electrical energy be produced, which in turn requires the mining of coal to fuel power stations. Energy is thus included with minerals in the idea of the MEC. It is then not surprising – especially since South Africa produces 75 per cent of the whole of Africa's electricity – that at the time of democracy the South African economy was 'uniquely dependent on electricity and is uniquely electricity intensive' (Fine & Rustomjee 1996: 8). Note that black South Africans were, until a generation ago, generally not included in the electricity power grid and even then, services of electricity were both of low quality and expensive for ordinary households despite the cheap electricity provided to the mines. Since the 1980s, however, the electricity grid in southern Africa has been extended to low-income and rural areas on such a dramatic scale and at a pace which, one writer says, is unprecedented in modern history (McDonald 2008). At a period when the economy was growing, however, former president Thabo Mbeki admitted that government did not heed the warnings of Eskom regarding problems with the power supply to the national grid, which has led to cutting electricity to businesses and homes alike for specified periods (known as 'loadshedding'). This has had a serious impact on the South African economy – and its people – since 2007.

15.5.2 A weak secondary sector

Despite the power of the South African economy, the secondary sector of manufacturing is relatively weak. Manufacturing has been centrally dependent on mining, which has resulted in a weak industrial or secondary sector. The structure of the South African economy is consequently not balanced, but skewed. In 1994, for instance, 83 per cent of the JSE was owned by only four mining conglomerates (Carmody 2002: 255–275). A conglomerate is made up of one or more corporations under which separate and often different businesses fall, but where there is some form of centralised reporting. The sheer economic power of the four mining conglomerates represented a structural weakness in the economy. This came about as a result of a compromise between two powerful competing groups in the economy – English mining interests and the powerful Afrikaner political establishment of which the farmers, in the primary sector of agriculture, were very important electoral constituents under apartheid. The South African economy was, of course, also shaped by racial oppression and social control, particularly over the lives of black workers. With people's resistance supressed, Afrikaner farmers were given a stake in mining. This can be seen as the forerunner to the current policy of BEE. A portion of the lucrative goldmines was transferred to Afrikaner business interests in the 1960s at favourable rates of **interest**. This maintained the dominance of the primary sector of the economy over the secondary one and further entrenched the control over a disenfranchised black working class and the majority of the population. In brief, the main activity of the economy was centred on the export of raw materials, mainly precious metals and minerals. At its height, the goldmining industry alone employed between 700 000 and 760 000 workers. Mining overall still formally employs around 456 000 workers and the economy remains largely a supplier of raw materials to the global economy. An estimated 30 000 illegal *zama zama* miners (an isiZulu word meaning those who take their chance) are, however, currently changing the face of the mining industry.

Mining dominated the secondary industrial sector where a wide range of economic manufacturing and construction activity generally takes place. The South African economy hence did not adequately diversify, but instead developed in a stunted and limited manner. The importance of the industrial sector is that it requires a wide range of unskilled, semi-skilled and skilled labour, and thereby provides substantial employment in any balanced economy. This did not happen in the South African economy. Light **manufacturing industries**, for instance, which are labour intensive, did not develop extensively and this further entrenched high levels of **unemployment** in the local economy. To compound matters, employment fell in the two critical primary sectors of agriculture and goldmining shortly after 1994 and negatively affected the secondary sector (Ashman et al 2010).

15.5.3 Financialisation and de-industrialisation and the minerals–energy–finance complex

Following trends of economic liberalisation, both globally and in Africa since the 1970s, rapid expansion, extension and disproportionate growth of the financial sector has taken place in the South African economy (Carmody 2002: 270). Economists refer to this process as **financialisation**. This process has been so powerful, it has been argued, that we should now refer to it as the *mineral–energy–finance complex* (Ashman 2015). Financialisation reduces levels of real **investment**, gives priority to **shareholders**, extends **commercialisation** and deepens its influence over economic and social policy. One of the reasons for financialisation is that companies can earn greater profits by investing in the financial market than by manufacturing products. Companies hence choose to rather invest in the financial market and the short-term flow of funds from one country to another in order to make a profit on the interest rate differential rather than engage in the hard work of building industrial plants and factories, which creates employment. This kind of investment – **financial speculation** on the stock exchange in particular – is referred to as 'hot' money, which increased globally from $15 billion in 1973 to $1 000 billion *daily* in 2006. Speculation in the foreign exchange markets was reported in 2019 to have ballooned to $5 trillion a day globally! (https://www.investopedia.com). The banks and other financial institutions, however, obviously benefit massively from these enormous flows of funds. Such financial speculation not only fails to contribute to employment, but also contributes to de-industrialisation, which occurs when manufacturing and the secondary sector does not grow but contracts. In the process, where there is a lack of employment, households have become increasingly involved with financial institutions and moneylenders, and become more indebted. The same applies to governments who run a deficit, which results from overspending. Government budget deficits are generally measured as a percentage of GDP, South Africa's being high at 55 per cent at the end of 2019. This in turn means people (or businesses and governments) are less able to save, which in turn means there is less money in the economy for productive, labour-creating investment.

In South Africa, massive state involvement and expenditure in 'mega' projects such as at Saldanha Bay and Coega have somewhat prevented the degree of de-industrialisation as has occurred elsewhere in Africa. While the South African economy grew after 1994 and experienced economic growth for a full 10 years from 1998 until the global 2008 financial crisis – precipitated by bankers seeking super-profits – this was essentially what is called **jobless economic growth**. There is more money in the economy, but this money does not translate into employment. Under these conditions, poverty persists for very many South Africans. This is despite the fact that the ratio of the income of (the average) white to (the average) African income has shifted from 15:1 in 1970 to 8:1 in 2011 to 5:1 in 2019 (SAIRR 2019).

While the racialised income gap has narrowed, with more money in the economy, or what economists call **liquidity**, banks have more money to lend and so extend credit to the private sector and middle-class households in particular. This saw household debt – the ratio of household debt to disposable income (or what you owe as a percentage of what money you have once all necessities are paid) – increase from just over 50 per cent to over 75 per cent between 2002 and 2009 (Mohamed 2010: 42); rise to 86 and 84 per cent in the crisis years of 2008 and 2009, and settle at 72 per cent in 2017 and 2018 (https://tradingeconomics.com/south-africa/households-debt-to-income). Just as a new black middle class was emerging, this social group became significantly more indebted to the banks as indebtedness has risen (Neves 2018).

These key features – the massive concentration of capital dominated by the primary sector and the MEC and de-industrialisation (or at minimum stalled industrialisation) – characterised the South African economy in 1994. In this structural context, financialisation and low economic 'jobless growth' came to mark the South African economy and entrench already high unemployment despite some gains regarding social inequality in the economy.

15.5.4 Unemployment and the informal economy

The single most critical feature of South African society and central to the economy is unemployment. Unemployment has always been a major problem for capitalist societies, but is particularly acute in South Africa. Note the definitions of unemployment and how it is measured change in Chapter 22 on poverty. Compare, for instance, the one million loss of jobs in the economy in 2009 – when the GDP growth rate fell from nearly 6 per cent to nearly – 2 per cent – to those of the most recent National Population Census of 2011. This was discussed in Chapter 5 on population.

Box 15.1 Unemployment and social inequality

Find an accurate source for these general indicators of social inequality:

- Between 20 and 26 per cent of workers are officially unemployed in South Africa.
- Some sources cite 50 to 55 per cent of South Africa's youth as unemployed.
- South Africa and Brazil are the most unequal societies in the world, registering very high on the **Gini Coefficient** scale, which measures social inequality. (On the Gini scale, 0 represents perfect equality and 1 represents maximum inequality. What are the scores for these two countries?)

The unemployment crisis in South Africa, which is high by world standards, has resulted in a massive shift to informal work or what social analysts refer to as **informalisation**. Without formal work, people perform informal work by opening a *spaza* shop, for instance, or by trying to make a small profit selling cigarettes and sweets on the street. In this growing **informal economy** – small by standards of other emerging economies such as India – people earn much less than they would if they were employed.

The key challenges facing our economy and society are addressing unemployment and the extent of social inequality. Despite this, the power of the South African economy is such that it has been suggested that South Africa is to Africa what the US is to the world: a powerful economic player defining the lives and fortunes of societies beyond its borders. We can only make sense of this anomaly by bearing in mind the global scenario and the skewed structure of the economy, and by examining what economic policy choices have been made over the past 25 years.

15.6 Economic policy interventions since 1994

There has been a series of major economic policy interventions since 1994, the RDP, GEAR and the National Development Plan (NDP), launched in 2012, being the most significant developments. The detail of other important policies, such as the Accelerated and Shared Growth Initiative for South Africa (ASGISA) and the Industrial Policy Action Plan, now in its 10th iteration (2018/9–2020/1), will not be discussed in this chapter, neither will the National Growth Path (NGP), released in December 2010, which failed to bring unemployment down to 15 per cent by 2020.

15.6.1 The Reconstruction and Development Programme (RDP)

The first priority of the post-apartheid government was to redress the past social and economic imbalances resulting from apartheid and its failed economy and polity. The first major economic policy instituted was the RDP, which saw **social inequality** as the main obstacle to economic growth. With high unemployment levels and the poor unable to generate income, there is very little spending. The domestic **demand** for goods and services hence remains weak as there is little financial capacity to pay for them. Small business entrepreneurship is further hampered as the majority of South Africans do not possess the required business skills or have the resources to pay for learning new skills.

The RDP consequently focused on **domestic production** in order to build capacity among the majority of South Africans. The drive was to create economic equality. Emphasis was placed on land reform, cooperatives and micro-enterprises. The new democratic state engaged in a massive expansion of infrastructure, housing, education and welfare which could provide jobs. The institution of the Expanded Public Works Programme (EPWP), a top-down state initiative, is a good example of how this economic policy strategy is usually attempted. All these initiatives were designed to build local capacity – especially the development of skills designed to empower individuals to win through to economic independence. Regarding the example of cooperatives, there is evidence, for instance, that worker cooperatives in particular, based on 'principles of democratic ownership, one-member-one-vote, collective decision making and an ethic of cooperation and solidarity', are capable of doing just this (Satgar & Williams 2011: 202). Worker cooperatives in South Africa today, however, are only a tiny element in the South African economy.

The economic policy strategy of the RDP relied very heavily on the state to integrate social and economic strategy, to build job-creating industries and to drive programmes to alleviate poverty and restructure formal production. This is no small feat. It presupposes massive capacity – planning and skill and the dedication of public-sector officials in particular. The necessary skills were largely missing due to the legacy of apartheid. This policy was short-lived and abandoned in 1996, not least due to the criticisms of the 'defenders' of capitalism whose preferred strategy of organising society won out, as will be seen. The legacy of the RDP is most popularly remembered in that it left us with RDP houses. Between 1994 and 2008/9, the South African government achieved the building of 2.6 million RDP houses, yet this was insufficient to supply houses for all (Gelb 2010). The RDP was replaced by a mainstream economic policy, GEAR.

15.6.2 The shift to GEAR

It has been suggested that South Africa emerged as a new economic and political factor in Africa in the mid-1990s. The then president, Thabo Mbeki, envisioned a new African Renaissance, a new 'flowering' of economic and consequently social life. The overall strategy adopted was to engage in widespread trade liberalisation by dropping **tariff barriers** which were designed to protect local businesses and whole sectors of the economy. Export-driven trade and the development of a transnational elite social group were encouraged. The idea of export-driven trade is to encourage local economic development in order to bring **foreign exchange** into a country to improve that country's standards of living. Mbeki sought to do this by aiming at a more competitive economy to attract foreign direct investment (FDI). He aimed at integrating South Africa's economic growth and development with that of Africa via a broad policy initiative known as the New Partnership for African Development (NEPAD), but such a policy required the active intervention of the well-resourced, yet still primarily white-owned private sector. This policy aligns with the 'defenders' of capitalism, especially those of the neoliberal mainstream economic view of how globalisation should be tackled by societies with developing or emerging economies. An economy following this policy, the 'defenders' of neoliberal economic policy argue, would attract investment, employment would increase and wealth would 'trickle' down to everyone in society. As elsewhere where this kind of policy has been implemented, it did not achieve the majority of its objectives.

Ironically, the adoption of a neoliberal policy in the era of globalisation requires the centralisation of state power.

Thabo Mbeki sought to do this. This meant shifting political power from the liberation movement of the ANC to a centralised executive government which had already been strongly centralised in the last years of apartheid.

The outcome of Thabo Mbeki's choice of economic policy initiative did, however, result in 10 years of sustained economic growth, running as high as 5 per cent from 2004 to 2007 (Mohamed 2010: 39). The spending of late apartheid was brought under control (Gelb 2010), but the 'critics' questioned whether this was the right kind of economic growth as it was largely jobless. While GEAR led to some investment and marginally increased employment, this was generally not in productive sectors and the policy ended up reinforcing existing structural imbalances inherited from the past. Social grants, paid for by taxation, *did* improve the standards of living of some of the very poorest South Africans. The delivery of social services for many South Africans, however, remained weak or was even non-existent. In brief, this strategy did not result in improving the living standards of a sufficient number of ordinary South Africans quickly enough and brought about two waves of community protest around the lack of social delivery and municipal services in 2004 and 2007, which have continued virtually unabated since then.

While there was an increase in **GNP** over these years, this signalled an increase in financial capital. In brief, the banks and financial institutions benefited from this economic growth. As we will see, generally white-owned large and medium-sized businesses were also beneficiaries. While GEAR was designed to attract FDI, well-placed South African companies invested abroad instead, thereby contributing to an *outflow* of capital. In short, 'a better life for all' was deferred and this lay at the basis of Jacob Zuma's appeal to many ANC members that resulted in the recall by the ANC of Thabo Mbeki as the president of South Africa after the ruling party's crucial meeting in Polokwane in 2009. It is doubtful this would have happened had Thabo Mbeki's economic policy been successful in significantly meeting, or being seen to be meeting, the basic needs of South African society as a whole. Given the best of circumstances, let alone under the conditions of what happened in the local economy after 1994 as analysed thus far, this was, under conditions of capitalist globalisation, perhaps an unrealistic proposition for any emerging economy. In this instance, however, the economic situation powerfully shaped what took place at the political level.

Deregulation and privatisation

As part of GEAR, there were further attempts made to address issues facing the post-apartheid economy: unemployment, the slow rate of economic growth, the continuation of stark social inequality and the racially skewed ownership structure of the economy.

The question arises as to whether economic growth can occur without addressing massive inequality in income and wealth. Thabo Mbeki's ANC administration further attempted to encourage competition in the economy by opening it up to global forces via deregulation and privatisation. **Deregulation** is the process of relaxing the guiding rules and procedures protecting a national economy from its competitors across the globe. **Privatisation** is the opposite of nationalisation and entails transferring state- or partially state-owned enterprises to private business. The rationale for deregulation is to impose fewer controls on business and hence make it easier for international investors to invest in a country and hence contribute to employment creation. The aim of privatisation is to release the state from the costs of running state-owned enterprises and hence potentially reduce taxes on businesses and citizens. Lower taxes on businesses would encourage them to invest in South Africa, and lower taxes on citizens means there is more money to spend. This in turn stimulates demand for goods and services, which opens more opportunities for businesses to develop. The aim was also to make these now privatised, previously state-owned enterprises more efficient. The argument is that when a business enterprise is driven by the profit motive it will cut costs and find ways to be more productive. When this policy is followed, this means that countries must compete against each other for investment by global capital. The country with the lowest costs and in which the lowest labour costs feature prominently is the most likely to attract investment ('critics' often refer to this as 'the race to the bottom'). Countries with the lowest wages and taxes attract foreign investment.

Ending subsidies and tightening monetary policy

To further enhance the efficiency of the economy, GEAR included two other policies. The first was to end state subsidies in production – those granted to especially white-dominated agriculture under apartheid. State support of this component of the primary sector finally interrupted support of the political constituency of the white farmers, which historically went back all the way to Paul Kruger (1825–1904), president of the old Transvaal. White farmers today still decry the end of these long-established subsidies as well as the increases to the minimum wage granted to farm labour in March 2013, which followed farmworkers' strikes and social unrest. Ending subsidies also aimed at forcing farming businesses to become more efficient by cutting costs and working more productively. This result, however, it has been argued, 'has made South Africa one of the most vulnerable agricultural economies in the world' (Atkinson 2010: 378).

The second major element in the cluster of GEAR policies was to follow austere or tight **monetary policies**. The rationale for stricter monetary policy (ie not to print too much money) was to guard against **inflation** and hence protect the value of the local national currency – the rand. For if the state prints and puts money into circulation more rapidly than the production of goods and services available for purchase, inflation occurs and the value of money decreases. Further, when a local currency loses its value, imports become more expensive, which hurts the local economy.

When all these policies geared towards efficiency were implemented, it was understood that some businesses would go bankrupt. While this would be painful for many businesses, it was argued, it would be temporary and good for the economy as whole. Such a view is a cornerstone of the 'defenders' of capitalism and those who argue for a free, unregulated market or neoliberal economic policy such as the Mbeki administration largely implemented. As we will see, due to trade union power and going against neoliberal-inspired economic policy, the **labour market** was *not* deregulated. Also going against neoliberalism, due to having to address the imbalances of the past, the state spent money on **social welfare**. How and to what extent economic policy was implemented was highly contested within the ruling party. There was no general agreement about how this economic policy fitted in with the ANC's guiding policy of the National Democratic Revolution.

15.6.3 The National Democratic Revolution

If the implementation of GEAR was self-imposed in order to respond to external global economic forces, an even more important political policy orientation was internal to the politics of the new democratic government. Still dominating is the politics of liberation as expressed in the idea of the National Democratic Revolution (NDR) in particular. The politics of the NDR comprises the view that a developing country must embrace capitalism and build socialism gradually by promoting an indigenous capitalist class. It is envisaged that this capitalist middle class will be 'patriotic' and hence assist with national development in the interests of the nation as a whole. It should not be underestimated

how the NDR constrained the government, and arguably still does so, from intervening with a single voice unified around economic policy.

The theory of the NDR dominant in the ruling ANC serves a range of functions. It legitimises the historic role of the ANC as it requires the assumption of political power of the state as a condition of transforming the economy. It consequently validates the need – against the view of strict 'defenders' of capitalism – for an **interventionist state** to transform society, preferably by introducing a 'mixed' economy. The NDR clearly justifies the existence of a black bourgeoisie and hence endorses the need in the South African context to cooperate with white capitalism (Southall 2004).

There is little question that the South African economy *had* to be de-racialised. As one sociologist indicated, the ANC provided the 'absolutely necessary condition' of legitimising the state and capitalist business, both of which had for decades been under attack by the liberation movement and the ANC in particular (Southall 2010: 13). While necessary, the question arises whether black capitalists could *afford* to be 'patriotic' and contribute to social and economic development in the face of established white business and under tough market conditions in the era of marketised globalisation.

Promoting black capitalism

In the context of engaging in widescale restructuring in order to become more globally competitive, partially or fully state-owned **parastatal institutions** shed **non-core assets** to respond to a neoliberal economic policy agenda. A range of assets **unbundled** from both **private** and **public enterprises** was taken over by BEE companies. In the public sector, the controlling boards of directors were taken over by a new elite and served as the springboards for black capitalism. This resulted in an intense political struggle for tenders and the emergence of the phenomenon of **tenderpreneurship** – a newly coined term for businesses built on winning large government tenders resulting from political connections.

The origins of promoting black capitalism under the rubric of BEE can be traced to the initiatives of big business (Lindsay 2011), but fitted well with one interpretation of the NDR. Adopted by the new democratic post-apartheid state, the report of the Black Economic Empowerment Commission (BEEC) was designed to redress the imbalances of the past and facilitate black-owned businesses and entrepreneurship. The commission recommended a wide series of state-driven programmes to set targets, regulations and obligations to realise the aims of BEE. After a widely publicised 'initial flurry of politically driven' big business deals between 1994 and 1997, black ownership on the JSE stood at around 10 per cent (Jacobs 2002, cited in Southall 2004: 318). The financial value of BEE deals as a percentage of mergers between companies increased from 5 per cent in 1996 to 31 per cent in 2002. The number of top and senior black managers in the private sector increased from 18.5 per cent in 2000 to 32.5 per cent in 2008 (Southall 2010: 11). The 2019 Commission of Employment Equity Report, however, noted that in the private sector black African managers still only constituted 15.1 per cent of top management positions while occupying 76 per cent of these positions in government (DoL 2019).

While small, the emergence of a new black middle class heralded an important and significant moment in social class formation in South African society. But how were previously disadvantaged South Africans promoted as capitalists when they had no *capital*? This was achieved mainly via the complex financial instruments of Special Purpose Vehicles (SPVs) and 'N' Shares. The designated few gained control of parts of unbundled companies undergoing restructuring by being granted significant proportions of shares on the understanding that these would be paid for by profits in the future. Such deals, however, were exceptionally sensitive to share price fluctuations and in some cases did not initially result in 'real' ownership as the 'owners' of the shares did not have voting rights until the shares had been paid for.

The new black middle class

Important members of the new black middle class are public sector leaders and managers who have assumed leadership positions in the state. They are well paid, and their positions in government have often served as a springboard to shift to the private sector. A more socially visible set of members of the new black middle class are those senior managers and spokespersons in the private sector. Notable among this group are a small number of entrepreneurs who astonishingly managed to build businesses *during* apartheid, some of whom were able to flourish under the more open trading conditions and access to resources of democracy while others, it has been argued, did not (Randall 1996). These are largely individual entrepreneurs who have been joined by the new and generally more powerful BEE-based business class, some of whom established significant footholds in the financial sector through, in some instances, establishing businesses out of trade union investment and pension funds. A range of professionals in the media, academic realm and other occupations can also be included in this new social class. The state has attempted to broaden this social group into even more significant economic players, but this has been limited. To what extent a new generation of genuinely independent black entrepreneurs is emerging and expanding the size and composition of this new middle class is a topic that sociologists need to examine more carefully.

The limitations of black capitalism

As a result of the mixed fortunes of black capitalism since 1994 and due to BEE only having assisted a highly socially visible elite, the policy drew much criticism from within the ruling ANC and beyond. For instance, initially only about 200 BEE entrepreneurs benefited from buying assets of companies that had unbundled. In mining, financial services and a few other sectors, this remained a small elite with the structure of BEE largely precluding either genuine entrepreneurship or ownership.

Tensions manifested themselves in the ANC/COSATU/ SACP alliance over the strategy, and BEE came to be seen as accessing economic power via political connections. The dangers and evidence of **crony capitalism** and corruption became evident. One sociologist has gone so far as to argue that the intentions of this economic policy turned into its opposite: this was not a 'patriotic' but a 'parasitic' social class and holds the potential of social class conflict in the future (Southall 2004: 327). As a result of these criticisms, BEE was broadened out and reformulated with the passing of the Broad Based Economic Empowerment Act 53 of 2003 (South Africa 2003). By 2008, the value of deals showed an average increase of 18.5 per cent. Under such schemes, shares in companies were given to generally relatively small fractions of workers and employees, and have also often proved not to have worked well. Workers, for instance, have been known to treat these shares as emergency funds and sell them when there are problems at home, such as funeral expenses for example.

Despite the broadening of BEE, there have been limited inroads by black Africans into private capital. Ironically, Afrikaner capital benefited by regionalising businesses into sub-Saharan Africa and capitalising on their economic power established under apartheid, and because their money was less exposed to the global market. The upshot is that the structure of the South African economy has remained largely in the hands of economic players who are white. This has not only proved to be a disappointment to the new political elite, but raised the question as to whether the NDR is adequate in serving as a guide for economic policy. This does not mean, however, that the emergence of a new black middle class has not been an important development in social class formation in the new South Africa. The question as to whether this new middle class can serve as a buffer between a well-resourced minority and a poorly resourced majority in a society marked by a vast gulf of social inequality and the lack of social cohesion remains a significant one.

15.6.4 Opposition to economic policy

The danger of the GEAR policy strategy for economic development was experienced and interpreted as legitimising the existing and already highly unequal power relations in South African society. The policy had the effect of mirroring the relations of global domination and subordination between developed and developing countries and within countries, especially one such as South Africa, between rich and poor people.

It was the political power of the majority that responded to calls for regime change within the ruling party of the ANC. Thabo Mbeki's 1996 'class project'– a focus on the elite, the shift to GEAR and the centralisation of power within the state administration – had not benefited the majority. It has been argued that the change of one ANC administration to another – from Mbeki to Zuma – meant that political power shifted back to the ANC headquarters, Luthuli House; in other words from the state back to the political party. This is perhaps a controversial view. Whatever the case, the broader sociological point regarding the profound impact of the economy on society is that democratic *political power* in turn impacts on the policy decisions framing the economic situation. So what actually happened in the South African economy after 1994?

15.7 The effects of a neoliberal economic policy

Despite playing by the rules of the global economy, the introduction of GEAR did not result in the tide of the economy turning. Foreign direct investment (FDI) did not stream into the country as the 'defenders' suggested it would. The World Bank's view that trade liberalisation – deregulating trading rules such as dropping tariffs (taxes) when goods enter a country – would 'facilitate the development of indigenous-owned small and medium-sized enterprises in "labour intensive", light manufacturing industries', for instance, clearly did not happen (Carmody 2002: 259). This requires close examination. What were the reasons for the poor performance of GEAR?

One social analyst explains why this policy did not have its intended effect. Carmody (2002) examined the role and logic of the two key institutional players in economic restructuring: the state and capital (big business). The state attempted to 'manage' globalisation at first by imposing restructuring on itself. This represents an 'inside out' policy – the attempt, in other words, to take the initiative and be *independent* by aligning the South African economy with global economic trends. This is essentially a 'defenders' of capitalism policy. To be more streamlined and competitive and to avoid falling rates of profit due to a strengthened US dollar, companies unbundled, which simply means shedding non-core assets. These are assets companies had accumulated, but which were not directly related to their main economic activity. BEE companies bought up these assets on credit, with the effect that white-owned companies transferred risk to black capital. The big corporate companies meanwhile won *political mileage* in the process and used money from the sale of non-core assets to invest overseas. The state followed suit in selling off assets of state-owned enterprises, both to make them more focused and to advance the policy of BEE.

The striving for a measure of independence in the face of the global economy, however, shifted to an 'outside in' policy; in other words, one of *dependence*. The economy was instead subject to external global forces which proved too powerful to resist. Carmody explains why conglomerates moved to London and why the state allowed them to do so. This was seen as part of South Africa's reintegration into the global economy. It enabled the big conglomerates access to cheaper capital which would 'unlock' shareholder value as many of these companies' assets had been undervalued in an economy previously isolated from the global economy. The argument was that this move would facilitate global expansion and make them more globally competitive; in other words, 'facilitate increased investment in the South African economy' (Carmody 2002: 263). Very significant, well-known business groups such as Anglo-American, Old Mutual, SA Breweries and Dimension Data moved their headquarters abroad. When Anglo American moved their head office to London, for instance, the value of their shares immediately increased by 37 per cent (Carmody 2002: 264). This move signalled that the South African economy had in fact quite rapidly become embedded in the global economy, but in fact it *limited* the possibilities of these companies to engage in national development as many companies **rebundled** through new mergers in order to compete more effectively on the global market. A stunning example is how the old established South African insurance group, Old Mutual, 'in partnership with Nokia, IBM and Dimension Data, became the first unit trust company in the world to offer online trading via cell phones, in 2000' (Carmody

2002: 266). Such developments do not significantly facilitate investment in the local economy, which, as we have seen, faced its own structural challenges.

The economist Neva Seidman Magetla (2004) has noted the structural situation characterising the South African economy. There has been low growth of around 2.2 per cent since 1994, which is currently even lower as noted above. Figures range from 1.5 to 3.2 per cent. On top of this, population growth also ran at around 2 per cent. What this means, quite simply, is that there was not and has not been sufficient economic growth to catch up and redress the huge racialised social imbalances after apartheid, while *at the same time* meeting employment needs and preventing the deepening of poverty – explicitly acknowledged by President Cyril Ramaphosa in his 2020 New Year's message to South Africa's citizens.

Given this situation, the three main *economic* issues the government has faced since 1994, Magetla (2004) argues, are:

- the relationship between *economic growth* and *redistribution* of resources across society – ie between 'rich' and 'poor'
- the 'relevance of structural factors on underdevelopment'
- the role of the market and the state.

We have seen how the state attempted to respond to this situation via trade liberalisation and privatisation, yet continued to spend money on social grants to meet the basic needs of the poorest of South Africans. Magetla (2004) argues, however, that this economic policy orientation separates *economic policy* and *anti-poverty measures*. In other words, the money coming to the state (via taxes) was spent on social welfare in the form of social grants such as pensions, child grants and disability grants, as well as on education. In fact, around 17 million out of 57 million South Africans rely on these kinds of grants as their sole source of income. This has lifted many of the very poorest of South Africans out of the worst deprivations of poverty. The problem was that the beneficiaries of these grants would not be directly involved in the economy and be actively engaged in productive work. People were not meaningfully involved in the 'growth strategy' of the ANC government, but were and remain dependent on government grants. As a leading economic thinker in the ANC put it, '[t]he unemployed should not be treated as recipients of welfare, but as potential producers' (Turok 2008: 101). The awarding of grants has had social consequences and had a profound impact on communities. Many poor black families, young people especially, are dependent on their grandparents'

pensions. There is competition, often within families, as to who gets the grants and there has even been debate whether single young women intentionally fall pregnant in order to secure a child grant.

Such are some of the social consequences of economic policy. This is an ongoing debate, not just in South Africa, but worldwide and especially in emerging economies. The change in the ANC administration from presidents Mandela to Mbeki to Zuma to Motlanthe to Ramaphosa, however, did not result in any clearer resolution emerging regarding economic policy. The chief reason is quite clear. A country cannot alienate international financial investors. One important consideration for any investor is that if taxes (which the state depends on) are too high or if wages are relatively high (as a result of strong trade unions), international investors would rather invest where the costs of doing business are lower. The result is that changing the current economic policy strategy, even though it did not provide jobs in the formal sector, has been deferred. But the social consequences of GEAR were not the sole factor in deciding what money and resources were available in the economy. Other important factors were also at play.

15.7.1 Capital flight

It is insufficiently recognised how the South African economy experienced a massive outflow of capital after 1994. This took place in two main ways. First, to show that South Africa was a good place to invest, we saw how the government permitted major companies to shift their headquarters from the JSE to London where they could be closer to the international markets. At the same time there was much financial speculation, and trading in stocks and bonds, and especially in currencies, on the stock exchange. Such speculative ways of making money, as we noted above, do not result in real investment and jobs.

Second, the problem of *illegal* capital flight exploded out of control. Under apartheid, between 1980 and 1993, illegal capital flight ran at around 5.4 per cent of GDP. Under democracy, from 1994 until 2000, this increased to 9.2 per cent. Between 2001 and 2007, this figure increased to an average of 12 per cent, peaking at an extraordinary level of almost a quarter or 23 per cent of GDP in 2007. Take this statistic seriously – almost a quarter of GDP was lost to illegal capital flight. The responsibility for illegal capital flight across South Africa's borders lies squarely at the feet of primarily large conglomerates and those in mining in particular (Ashman et al 2011). The usual mechanism used to take money illegally over the borders is mis-invoicing – generally by over-invoicing, ie inflating the prices of goods.

This is white-collar company fraud on a massive scale. This loss of money 'contributes to low levels of domestic investment, so perpetuating unemployment, inequality and domestic development' (Ashman et al 2011: 9).

The developments noted above all impact on employment and unemployment, and have crucial racial and social dimensions. Just before the most recent crisis in the world economy, caused by the American bankers (Stiglitz 2009) in the third financial quarter of 2008, we noted how one million jobs were lost, resulting in employment falling by 6 per cent in 2009. This translated into a loss of 9 per cent of jobs for Africans, while other racial groups were not quite as hard hit at 4 per cent (Magetla 2004: 67–68). While the government had aimed of halving poverty in South Africa by 2014, even if this could have been achieved, it would still mean that 35 per cent of South Africans would continue to live below the then poverty line of R2 500 per month.

15.7.2 The role of the trade unions

Trade unions are a feature of all capitalist economies. In fact, South Africa is one of the very few countries on the globe where union density (the percentage of employed workers who belong to trade unions) increasing in the contemporary period. While trade unions in South Africa significantly improved wages and working conditions for many workers, both before and since the advent of democracy, there has been the threat of eroding the gains that were made. The key role of trade unions has traditionally been an economic one, namely to improve the wages and working conditions of their members. In South African labour history, however, trade unions have often played a political role. The exclusively white Mine Workers Union (MWU) played this role throughout its history, supporting racial exclusion, whether under segregation from 1924, when the MWU was recognised by the Chamber of Mines or under apartheid, from 1948 through to 1994, until 2002 when its name was changed to Solidarity. Most importantly, the MWU managed to secure all important jobs in mining for their white male members in 1924. From that date, black workers were not even formally recognised as employees, and their trade unions were severely harassed throughout their turbulent history until 1979 when a government commission, known as the Wiehahn Commission, recommended that trade unions for black workers be recognised by the apartheid state. As all political organisations for the majority of South Africans were banned, the trade unions increasingly took on a political role in the quest for national liberation. In brief, the trade union movement and especially the National Union of Mineworkers (NUM) provided a major support base and played a central role in ending apartheid, not least as the trade union movement was able to push through important legislation protecting workers. When the ANC came to power, it could not ignore its most powerful ally – **organised labour** in the shape of COSATU.

The strength of organised labour, however, was of concern to the mainstream 'defenders' of capitalism. The neoliberal-inspired economic policy did not work, these 'defenders' argued, as organised labour constituted a privileged group in society and maintained high wages for workers. The 'defenders' argued that high wages were a disincentive for international investors to invest in the South African economy. High wages prevent job creation by small businesses, the 'defenders' argue. This argument can be found in most newspapers, articulated especially by the official opposition in parliament, the Democratic Alliance.

The 'critics' of capitalism respond to this argument by saying that employers manage to avoid legislation protecting workers in a number of ways, especially in a period dominated by what Chapter 14 on work explains are Post-Fordist forms of organisation of production such as **outsourcing**, subcontracted labour, part-time work and piece work. If workers earn too much, they simply face **retrenchment**. This is supported by legislation. An employer simply needs to argue that the retrenchment of employees is required for 'operational' reasons or, in other words, if the company has to restructure itself and become more 'flexible' in order to continue making profits. The 'critics' powerfully argue that companies and businesses simply revert to forms of 'flexible' labour such as casualisation and the outsourcing of jobs if wages are thought to be too high. This is a precarious form of employment in which employees generally enjoy no benefits such as medical aid or pension funds, have no security of tenure, are paid lower wages and work often illegally long and longer hours than organised workers and whose conditions of work are invariably poor. The conditions of such work are not 'regulated' and so these temporary workers are hence cheaper to employ. One sociologist, however, has argued that all wage labour is 'precarious' and that this is the permanent condition of workers under capitalism (Barchiesi 2012).

In brief, the transition to democracy, the 'critics' have argued, has not improved the situation of workers as they hoped. In a summation of working conditions since the end of apartheid in the primary sector, focusing directly on mining, agriculture and forestry, two analysts evoke a statement by Marx and that 'workers are now weighed down by the dull compulsion of economic forces' (Pons-Vignon & Anseeuw 2009: 895).

15.7.3 Other debates concerning neoliberal economic policy

A further reason the 'defenders' cite why their policies – and GEAR in particular – have not succeeded is that South African workers generally have low levels of skill. At a broader economic level, they further admit that unfair international trade rules apply, that Africa as a whole is considered 'risky' for investors and that this is yet another reason for low levels of investment by international corporations (Magetla 2004: 269). One of these risks is that the costs of HIV/AIDS are high which adds from 3.5 to 6 per cent to the wage bill.

To make matters more complicated, where the mainstream GEAR-type neoliberal economic policies were introduced in the export sectors, such as automotive manufacturing, such initiatives were too small to provide employment except for a few highly skilled workers. Employment fell even in sectors where an export strategy, designed to make local businesses more competitive, was implemented (Magetla 2004). In short, the new capital investment in manufacturing only required a small number of highly skilled workers, which meant cutting back on both unskilled and semi-skilled labour, deepening the gap between a large, low-skilled labour force and these highly skilled workers. There was, in other words, a direct relation between economic policy and the world of work, which had further social consequences and needs highlighting.

15.7.4 Work and employment

How did a neoliberal economic strategy for economic growth for an emerging economy such as South Africa impact on the world of work and unemployment? Broadening out the example noted above will make this clear. With the focus on exports, large manufacturing corporations were encouraged to invest in South Africa of which the auto manufacturer BMW is a case in point. As BMW has to compete internationally, its organisation of production in South Africa had to be as advanced as BMW and other competing auto manufacturing companies elsewhere in the world. This meant introducing automated assembly lines where robotisation, a major feature of the so-called Fourth Industrial Revolution, replaces workers performing semi-skilled manual work. In 2006, for example, BMW produced 24 000 motor vehicles for export using this advanced technology. This resulted in a few very highly skilled jobs. The upshot of this was that only a relatively small number of both companies and workers were able to benefit from economic integration with global markets.

In addition, while there was a measure of FDI in the automotive industry, local components manufacturers faced more competition. Hence, once again, big capital benefited, not medium-sized locally based business. Something similar happened to the 'white goods' industry, ie manufacturers of fridges, stoves and household appliances.

Local manufacturers faced competition from the international conglomerate LG whose prominent TV advertisements were widely seen. Such big international conglomerates further crowded out small, medium and micro enterprises (SMMEs), which were unable to grow under these conditions. Labour-intensive industries suffered, with female workers, as usual, being among the most affected, in the clothing industry for example.

15.7.5 Regionalisation

Meanwhile, regionally within sub-Saharan Africa, there was an opportunity for the expansion of already established South African businesses. In fact, after 1994, South African companies expanded very rapidly into the southern African region in a process called **regionalisation**. Well-known companies such as Shoprite Checkers and SA Breweries, for instance, were able to expand into undeveloped markets where there was a need for consumer articles, commodities and other goods. Local established businesses grew. Local Afrikaner business share on the JSE, for instance, rapidly grew from 24 to 36 per cent between 1994 and 1999 (Carmody 2002: 265). Overall, it has largely been business as usual for the main corporations, despite complaints of having to comply with additional regulatory legislation with which business has to comply, yet which is much more of an administrative burden for smaller businesses. Mainly white-owned companies and individuals who had benefited from apartheid legislation benefited again after democracy.

15.7.6 Decreasing employment

In the post-apartheid period, in addition to the factors already mentioned, many mines were coming to the end of their productive life. Hundreds of thousands of jobs were shed. While platinum overtook goldmining in terms of the number of workers it employed, only relatively few were able to make the shift from gold to platinum. In February 2012, starting in the platinum industry, workers went out on a strike wave across the South African mining sector demanding higher wages at a time when the demand for platinum weakened on the global market. The construction industry did not fare any better. Stagnation took place in construction with the state, traditionally a major player in this sector, cutting back on expenditure for major infrastructural projects, except for the World Cup stadiums leading up to 2010 which partly offset the stagnation in this sector. Even in the flourishing financial sector, uncompetitive branches of banks were closed, mainly in small towns and in rural areas. Elsewhere in the economy, in the name of efficiency, small businesses were taken over by larger ones. Many farmers did not manage to survive under the new conditions and others mechanised their operations, leading to a further influx of unemployed workers and their families to the peri-urban informal settlements around the main cities.

Box 15.2 Managing capitalism in an emerging economy such as South Africa

- If you were the Minister of Finance in South Africa after 1994, how would you have managed the emerging South African economy?
- What economic policy choices would you have made?
- Do you think South Africa was – and remains – inevitably captured by global economic forces or that different choices could have been made?
- Look up and explain why the Minister of Finance, Tito Mboweni, issued a strong warning about 'structural reform inertia' regarding the economy in January 2020.

Give reasons for your answers in each case.

15.8 Rethinking state intervention in the economy

Even before many of the developments noted in this chapter so far, in 2004 – a decade after the advent of democracy – it had become apparent that the strict application of mainstream neoclassical, neoliberal economic policy of GEAR had not delivered on its promises of temporary economic pain which was to result in economic recovery. The state consequently attempted to intervene in the economy and formulated the idea of a 'developmental state'. This was but a moment in the full story of the evolution of ANC economic policy since the Freedom Charter in 1955 (see a full account in Turok 2008).

Government spending began to rise, with the World Cup, the Gautrain and the Gauteng Highway Project being good examples. Note, however, that this spending took place in the main urban centres, with rural areas, as usual, being ignored when investment and economic development take place. This point aside, the 'critics' of capitalism, however, asked whether this was the right kind of spending. The new emphasis on job creation was not clear, and neither was

the new stress on state planning, with the National Planning Commission established under Trevor Manuel appearing to reinforce many aspects of GEAR. Greater support advanced for economic cooperatives aiming to provide employment, has, for instance, shown little progress. Critically, these initiatives do not appear to have been formulated sufficiently broadly to constitute a new integrated social and economic strategy.

One initiative which did and has continued to have a major impact has been mentioned – the awarding of **social grants** to the poorest of South Africans. In 2010 there were 13.9 million such grants relating to pensions, child grants and disability grants. This rose to 17 million out of a population of 57 million by 2017 and is predicted to rise to 18.1 million beneficiaries by 2020–2021 (Mtantato 2018). There is little doubt that these widely extensive grants, though small, have significantly assisted the poorest of the population who, in many cases, depend solely on them as their only source of income. They have not been sufficient, however, to significantly alter the heavily unequal structure of the economy as a whole. The further consequence of social grants which delinks recipients from work and economic development has been noted. This perpetuates the existing structures of social class.

15.9 The question of land

At the same time another big cost to the state, which did not make much headway, must receive some attention in this introduction to the South African economy. The new ANC government has focused on *ownership* of land, yet has not done well in ensuring access to land in the primary sector of the economy, for black farmers.

One social analyst has made a very strong claim in this regard, namely that 'black farmers have been set up for failure by a government bureaucracy which is out of its depth when it comes to a vast programme of social engineering' (Atkinson 2010: 364). The evidence appears to bear out this strong claim. Since the 1913 Land Act, which relegated 87 per cent of South Africa's population to 13 per cent of the land, over a decade after 1994 land ownership by black Africans was still only around 16 per cent and came again under review. While this whole issue is highly contentious politically, initiatives that began with the principle of the 'willing buyer/willing seller' – transferring ownership of land from private farmers to the state, which would then redistribute land – proved too expensive for the state. The demand for 'expropriation without compensation' of land is an unfolding story with constitutional amendments likely.

Box 15.3 Community service to develop skills and the economy

Community service should be instituted by having every school leaver perform a year at work after school and before college or university.

QUESTIONS

1. Do you agree or disagree with this statement?
2. What are your reasons for doing so?
3. Who would pay for such a scheme?

15.10 Economic possibilities and alternatives?

The picture presented here is complex and somewhat bleak. Economic transformation may well be more difficult to achieve than the political triumph over apartheid (Carmody 2002). One example indicates this in a stark manner. Very high unemployment levels and increased income inequality, resulting in increasing crime rates, have had one especially noteworthy social consequence. Middle-class, predominantly white communities have attempted to protect and isolate themselves behind what have become known as 'neo-apartheid' gated communities. In Johannesburg's wealthy northern suburbs, one such 'gated community' is served by domestic workers from a nearby unserviced informal settlement. Is this simply apartheid of old under democracy or a new form of economic apartheid?

To finally conclude this chapter, what follows are a number of interventions the state could potentially initiate. Is it not reasonable that the state *should* intervene in the economy, seeing that the economic policy path that has dominated the democratic era has not resulted in its desired outcomes? The 'defenders', of course, suggest that the state has not gone far enough in *freeing* the economy from its intervention. Here we come to the nub of the ideological debate between the 'defenders' and 'critics' of capitalism.

There is evidence that effective state intervention in the economy is possible. For a start, a greater degree of autonomy from global capital should be a central aim. The state could reassert exchange controls over capital, otherwise inequality will not be addressed. Could citizens be forced to save some money as has happened in Chile

or would there be a constitutional outcry? Stress should be put on developing resources internal to the economy. For instance, surely a sustained and well-advertised mobilisation around cooperatives, community-based corporations and small businesses would provide a way forward for many jobless South Africans. This would, however, require greater engagement between the state and society, inter-government department cooperation and the strengthening of existing state institutions. The remarkable experience of one community and the introduction of a Community Work Programme (CWP) and a community-building Organisation Workshop (OW) strongly suggests that positive initiatives have shown success (see Langa & Von Holdt 2011).

In Africa the state has been the only resource previous liberation movements have at their disposal, hence the time has come when serious reconsideration of state intervention in the economy and society is back on the agenda. To this end the Expanded Public Works Programme should be intensified, the Sector Education and Training programme should be more strongly mobilised and local markets should be more forcefully encouraged. Incentives offered to business to explore labour-intensive strategies need more attention; and BEE should be entreated to build businesses from the ground up instead of buying into existing white business or relying on state tenders. Regarding this point, former president Jacob Zuma is on record as appealing for more black industrialists.

Further, capital controls could be reconsidered as China is doing today to keep its currency (referred to as the *yuan* and the *renminbi*) artificially high to guard against inflation. NEDLAC, the business, labour and government forum, should be strengthened. In short, potentially workable alternatives are not in short supply and greater use of available resources in the economy should no longer be ignored.

All these initiatives would build infrastructure and human capacity, and recombine work and the economy. Whether such initiatives are practically and politically possible in the current era of globalisation is another question. Will the dominant economic policy model remain supreme? Will possible alternatives for economic policymaking and implementation emerge more strongly? Regarding the economy, there is clearly much scope for study, analysis and active involvement for social scientists in general, and economists and sociologists in particular.

Summary

- The role of the economy in a global society cannot be understood sociologically without understanding how it relates to politics and the state.
- In the context of globalisation, the new democratic government had limited economic policy choices after 1994, the most important being the RDP and GEAR.
- Attempts to address the economic inequities of the apartheid past were, however, severely constrained.
- The shift from the RDP to the neoliberal economic policy of GEAR resulted in cutting expenditure on social services, and support for micro and small business and skills development were lacking.
- The attempt to diversify the economy away from the MEC did, in addition, not bear much fruit.
- Further constraints such as the depreciation of the rand in 1996, the Asian crisis in 1997 and the World Economic crisis in October 2008 represented structural global economic forces with which the South African economy, like all national economies, had to contend.
- Even further, increasing informalisation of the economy cut at the tax base, and capital flight exacerbated the general economic situation.
- In this context, black capitalism benefited only a few South Africans with the economy remaining largely in the hands of large white-led business corporations.
- Where some jobs were created in the informal sector, mainly by African immigrants, this had the social effect of contributing to xenophobia as many South Africans without such skills and expertise again felt disadvantaged.
- The debate about an appropriate development strategy for South Africa in the context of globalisation hence continues.
- Given the limited success of neoliberal economic policy to meet expectations of many South Africans, this chapter suggested it might be time to rethink state intervention in the economy and made a range of suggestions in this regard.

ARE YOU ON TRACK?

1. What is the economy and how is it divided into sectors?
2. What are the two main views and arguments regarding economic policy in South Africa today?
3. What are the main features of the South African economy and what are the social effects of the economy in our society?
4. What is black capitalism and how successfully was it introduced in South Africa?
5. Social science is capable of sharp social and economic critique. Should it also offer some alternative or potential way forward?

More sources to consult

Carmody P. 2002. 'Between globalisation and (post) apartheid: The political economy of restructuring in South Africa'. *Journal of Southern Africa Studies*, June, 28: 255–275.

Mohamed S. 2010. 'The state of the South African economy' in *New South African Review 1: Development or Decline?* Daniel J, Naidoo P, Pillay D, Southall R (eds). Johannesburg: Wits University Press.

Southall R. 2010. 'South Africa 2010: From short-term success to long-term decline?' in *New South African Review 1, 2010: Development or Decline?* Daniel J, Naidoo P, Pillay D, Southall R (eds). Johannesburg: Wits University Press.

Stiglitz J. 2009. *Freefall: Free Markets and the Sinking of the Global Economy.* London: Penguin Books.

Turok B. 2008. 'From the Freedom Charter to Polokwane: The evolution of ANC economic policy'. Cape Town. *New Agenda: South African Journal of Social and Economic Policy*, CTP Books.

References

Ashman S, Fine B, Newman S. 2010. 'The crisis in South Africa: Neo-liberalism, financialisation and uneven and combined development', in *The Crisis this Time: Socialist Register 2011.* Panitch L, Albo G, Chibber V (eds). Halifax: The Merlin Press, London, Monthly Review Press, New York, Fernwood Publishing.

Ashman S, Fine, B, Newman S. 2011. 'Amnesty International? The nature, scale and impact of capital flight from South Africa'. *Journal of Southern African Studies*, March, 37(1): 7–25.

Atkinson D. 2010. 'Breaking down barriers: Policy gaps and new options in South African land reform', in *New South African Review 1: Development or Decline?* Daniel J, Naidoo P, Pillay D, Southall R (eds). Johannesburg: Wits University Press.

Barchiesi F. 2012. 'Precarious liberation: A rejoinder'. *South African Review of Sociology*, 43(1): 98–105.

Buthelezi L. 2020. 'World Bank growth forecast shock could finally tank Moody's rating for SA – analysts'. Fin24. 9 Jan. https:///www.fin24.com/News/world-bank-growth-forecast-shock-could-finally-tank-moodys-rating-for-sa-analysts-20200109?isapp=true

Carmody P. 2002. 'Between globalisation and (post) apartheid: The political economy of restructuring in South Africa'. *Journal of Southern Africa Studies*, June. 28: 255–275.

Dalla Costa M, James S.1972. *The power of women and the subversion of the community*. Bristol, England: Falling Wall Press Ltd.

Department of Labour (DoL). 2019. *Fact sheet: CEE Annual Report*. [Online] Available at: https://www.gov.za.sites/default/files/19%20CEE%REPORT%20SUMMARY%20FACT%20SHEET%2021.06.2019.pdf

Fine B, Rustomjee Z. 1996. *The Political Economy of South Africa: From Minerals–energy Complex to Industrialisation*. Boulder, CO: Westview Press.

Gelb S. 2010. 'Macroeconomic development: From crisis to crisis', in *Development Dilemmas in Post-Apartheid South Africa*. Freund B, Wits H (eds). Durban: University of KwaZulu-Natal Press.

Index of Economic Freedom. 2019. https//www.heritage.org/index/country/southafrica

Jacobs S. 2002. 'About turn: The ANC and economic empowerment'. [Online] Available at: http://www.nu.ac.za/ indicator/Vol.19No.1/19.1htm [Accessed 5 November 2013].

Kariuki S. 2010. 'The Comprehensive Rural Development Programme (CRDP): A beacon of growth for rural South Africa?' in *New South African Review 1: Development or Decline?* Daniel J, Naidoo P, Pillay D, Southall R (eds). Johannesburg: Wits University Press.

Langa M, Von Holdt K. 2011. 'Bokfontein amazes the nations: Community Work Programme (CWP) heals a traumatized community', in *New South African Review 2: New Paths, Old Compromises?* Daniel J, Naidoo P, Pillay D, Southall R (eds). Johannesburg: Wits University Press.

Lindsay D. 2011. 'BEE reform: The case for an institutional perspective', in *New South African Review 2: New Paths, Old Compromises?* Daniel J, Naidoo P, Pillay D, Southall R (eds). Johannesburg. Wits University Press.

Magetla NS. 2004. 'The post-apartheid economy'. *Review of African Political Economy*, 100: 263–281.

McDonald D. 2008. *Electric Capitalism: Recolonising Africa on the Power Grid*. Pretoria: HSRC Press.

Mohamed S. 2010. 'The state of the South African economy', in *New South African Review 2: New Paths, Old Compromises?* Daniel J, Naidoo P, Pillay D, Southall R (eds). Johannesburg: Wits University Press.

Mtantato S 2018. 'SA's "welfare state" is in trouble'. *Mail&Guardian*, 28 September.

Moll T. 1991. 'Did the apartheid economy "fail"?' *Journal of Southern African Studies*, 17(2): June.

Nattrass N. 1996. 'Economic restructuring in South Africa and gambling on investment: Competing economic strategies in South Africa'. Transformation: *Critical Perspectives on Southern Africa*, 31: 25–42.

Neves D. 2018. 'The financialisation of the poor and the reproduction of inequality', in *New South African Review 6: The Crisis of Inequality*. Khadiagala GM, Mosoetsa S, Pillay D, Southall R (eds). Johannesburg: Wits University Press.

Pons-Vignon N, Anseeuw W. 2009. 'Great expectations: Working conditions in South Africa since the end of apartheid'. *Journal of Southern African Studies*, 35(4): 883–899.

Randall DJ. 1996. 'Prospects for development of a black business class in South Africa'. *Journal of Modern African Studies*, 34(4): 661–686.

Satgar V, Williams M. 2011. 'The worker cooperative alternative in South Africa', in *New South African Review 2: New Paths, Old Compromises?* Daniel J, Naidoo P, Pillay D, Southall R (eds). Johannesburg: Wits University Press.

Schmidt M, Van der Walt L. 2009. *Black Flame: The Revolutionary Class Politics of Anarchism and Syndicalism, Counter-power Volume 1*. West Virginia: AK Press; Edinburgh: Oakland.

South Africa. 2003. Broad Based Black Economic Empower Act 53 of 2003. Pretoria: Government Printer.

South African Institute of Race Relations (SAIRR). 2019. *FreeFacts* 1, No 11/2019/November. 19: 2.

Southall R. 2004. 'The ANC & black capitalism in South Africa'. *Review of African Political Economy*, 100: 313–328.

Southall R. 2010. 'South Africa 2010: From short-term success to long-term decline?' in *New South African Review 1: 2010: Development or Decline?* Daniel J, Naidoo P, Pillay D, Southall R (eds). Johannesburg: Wits University Press.

Stiglitz J. 2009. *Freefall: Free Markets and the Sinking of the Global Economy.* London: Penguin Books.

Trevor Chandler & Associates. 2010. *JSE Report on Ownership Competition.* Cape Town.

Turok B. 2008. 'From the Freedom Charter to Polokwane: The evolution of ANC economic policy'. *New Agenda.*

South African Journal of Social and Economic Policy, CTP Books.

Von Holdt K, Alexander P. 2012. 'Collective violence, community protest and xenophobia'. *South African Review of Sociology,* 43(2): 104–111.

Webster E, Adler G.1999. 'Towards a class compromise in South Africa's "double transition": Bargained liberalisation and the consolidation of democracy'. *Politics and Society,* 27(3): 347–385.

Politics and governance

Kirk Helliker

Politics is about power. Governance is about ruling. Institutionalised as administrators of the state, the formally constituted ruling powers regulate society: register its citizens, pass its laws, ensure national security, establish and maintain law and order and possess the monopoly over exercising legitimate force. The empirical focus is contemporary South African society.

This chapter starts by making a few key conceptual points. The chapter is then divided into three main parts. They can profitably be read as three interconnected essays. Being a sound exercise in sociological thinking, the first part is a historically sensitive account of segregation and apartheid. It is important to know that the authoritarian character of the state and the formalisation of racial segregation, following centuries of racial conquest and slavery, is the explicit reason why the ANC was established in 1912. Every student of South African society should know that the 1913 Land Act relegated 87 per cent of its people to 13 per cent of the land. In a few pages, this part of the chapter takes the reader through the nature of white politics and intra-white conflict and black oppression and black opposition to segregation leading to apartheid in 1948. It looks at intensified racial domination in the 1950s and 1960s, black consciousness and the Soweto Revolt in the 1970s, the partial nature of political reform under apartheid and the emergence of COSATU and the UDF in the 1980s and how the ANC inherited the apartheid state-form when it came to power in 1994.

The second part treats post-apartheid South Africa. It starts by locating the political tasks and challenges of our new democracy in the context of the restructuring of the global social system. Not surprisingly, the political choices open to the ANC government were constrained by the need for a strong economy and so echoes of the discussion in the previous chapter bounce into this one. Precisely due to the structural economic constraints imposed on the ANC's policies and programmes, racially based inequality and injustice could not be tackled as strongly as was hoped and envisaged throughout the years of the liberation struggle. Despite this, the ANC has continued to achieve resounding electoral successes. This is discussed alongside that of the ANC/SACP/COSATU tripartite alliance, how the ANC has had to deal with powerful internal lobby groups seeking to safeguard their own interests, the relation between leading state officials and dominant class and social groups, the needs of economically weak social groups and the emergence of new social movements.

The third and final part of the chapter broadens the discussion and addresses theoretical perspectives on the state and society. You have an open invitation. Of the three key theories presented, which is the most adequate in explaining the dynamics of the empirically based account just presented in the first two parts of the chapter? Does the pluralist view that the state is an honest broker which mediates between opposing groups in society explain politics and governance in South Africa today? Are the theories clustered under the concept of elitism, whether radical or conservative, a useful conceptual lens to analyse local political and governmental issues? Or are the instrumentalist and structuralist analyses located in a Marxist problematic better able to explain the often noisy sphere of contemporary politics and government?

Few people manage to avoid getting drawn into heated discussions about politics. This is surely because the issues are far too important to be ignored. Take this chapter seriously and you will learn how to be the informed voice of scholarly reason when it comes to hot political discussions. When tempers flare, you might have to be the one to bring the discussion back within the bounds of rational discussion. This conceptually dense chapter will have provided serious food for thought. Good luck!

Case study 16.1 Service delivery protests in South Africa

Over the past decade, there have been thousands of service delivery protests taking place in urban South Africa by poor black people, in which people publicly complain and demonstrate about the failure of the government to provide basic services such as proper housing, sanitation and water. These protests can be read about almost weekly in South African newspapers or seen on television news. In trying to make sense of these protests, Peter Alexander (2010: 26) argues:

> It appears that what we are attempting to grapple with is locally organised protests that place demands on people who hold or benefit from political power (which includes, but is not limited to, local politicians). These have emanated from poorer neighbourhoods (shack settlements and townships rather than suburbs). Perhaps this is best captured by defining the phenomenon as one of local political protests or local protests for short. The form of these actions relates to the kind of people involved and the issues they have raised. They have included mass meetings, drafting of memoranda, petitions, toyi-toying, processions, stayaways, election boycotts, blockading of roads, construction of barricades, burning of tyres, looting, destruction of buildings, chasing unpopular individuals out of townships, confrontations with the police, and forced resignations of elected officials.

South Africa has a long history of racial domination which officially ended in 1994 with the election in free and fair national elections of the African National Congress (ANC) under the leadership of Nelson Mandela. During the 1970s and 1980s there was massive resistance to the existing apartheid government by black organisations, including trade unions, the Black Consciousness Movement and the United Democratic Front. At that time, the ANC was banned in South Africa and had its offices outside the country. But it increasingly requested that black organisations in South Africa make the country 'ungovernable', that is, to totally disrupt economic and political activities in the country through – for instance – work stayaways, school boycotts and consumer boycotts. To a significant extent, the apartheid state reacted with brute repression and violence to black protest, as shown by the army and police action against the Soweto (and other) students in 1976 during school boycotts.

Nearly 20 years after the end of apartheid in 1994, South Africa has a progressive constitution which outlaws racism and holds regular democratic elections in which all races can participate. But the vast majority of black residents in both urban and rural areas live under conditions of extreme poverty and social inequality along racial lines remains prevalent. Because of this, demonstrations such as service delivery protests take place on a regular basis. In their demonstrations, people are using some of the same tactics that were used in the struggle against apartheid – including violent attacks against local government councillors and officials. Like the apartheid government before it, the ANC government has often responded with force against these protests. Further, the ANC has argued at times that the protesters are trying to undermine social and political stability – in fact, that they are trying to make the country 'ungovernable'. Again, like the apartheid government did, it is calling for peace and stability throughout South Africa.

Questions

1. Why has the South African government since 1994 not brought about any meaningful change to the lives of ordinary black people in terms of socioeconomic conditions of life and access to resources?
2. Is it an unwillingness to do so, or an inability?
3. Why does the post-apartheid government at times respond to the demands and protests of ordinary people in the same way that the apartheid government did?

These (and other similar) questions are critically important in trying to understand and explain contemporary South African society and its future. This chapter will assist you in trying to answer these questions sociologically.

Key themes

- Key conceptual points about state and society
- The state in segregation/apartheid South African society
- The state in post-apartheid South African society
- Theoretical perspectives on state and society.

16.1 Introduction

Why would two very different states in South Africa – an undemocratic racist apartheid state and a democratic non-racial post-apartheid state – both adopt similar approaches to social protests and focus on the need for political stability? More broadly, why do states do what they do, and how does state action relate to social groups that exist in modern, including South African, society? These are the type of questions that sociologists ask about state and society and this chapter seeks to assist students in answering them.

The overall aim of this chapter is to introduce you to the sociological study of state and society. This is an important field of study because it relates to two key sociological concerns, namely, social order and social change. An examination of the state is regularly seen as critical to addressing these concerns because of the central role played by the state in serving the changing needs of society. While the main emphasis in the chapter is on South African state and society, you are also introduced to broader sociological debates about state and society.

The chapter has four main themes:

- **Key conceptual points.** This theme details four main points that assist us in making conceptual sense of state and society issues. These points are relevant to any society, including South African society.
- **Segregation/apartheid South Africa.** The main empirical focus of this chapter is contemporary South African society, but this second theme examines the South African government historically before 1994. This is critical, because sociology seeks to understand contemporary social phenomena by looking deep into history.
- **Post-apartheid South Africa.** This involves a specific focus on post-apartheid state and society. This is a crucial theme in the chapter, and will help us in deepening our understanding of the opening case study.
- **Theoretical perspectives on state and society.** This theme broadens the debate by identifying and discussing key theoretical perspectives found in the existing sociological literature on state and society globally.

16.2 Key conceptual points

In order to discuss governments, including the post-apartheid South African government, it is critical to raise some conceptual points. Five points in particular are important.

The first point relates to **power**. The term 'power' is widely used within sociology and in a variety of different ways. A basic definition though is as follows: 'By power is meant the ability of individuals or groups to make their own concerns or interests count, even where others resist. Power sometimes involves the direct use of force, but is almost always accompanied by the development of ideas (ideologies) which *justify* the actions of the powerful' (Giddens 1989: 52, his emphasis). Power exists in all institutions in society (including the family, religion, education, the economy and politics) but also in deeply personal everyday relationships. Overall, the powerful in society therefore are able to ensure that their own interests are met.

When it comes to the political sphere, there are significant debates about which group is the most powerful. As we will see in this chapter, Marxists argue that the dominant group is the capitalist class and the government serves first and foremost the interests of this class. Radical elite theorists argue, however, that the government is controlled by a small power elite. Nevertheless, the quotation from Giddens has relevance to this sphere, and it connects to the important work of Antonio Gramsci (Haralambos & Holborn 2008: 539–540). Gramsci uses the term hegemony for the most powerful political group, or the group which dominates others politically. This power is expressed in different ways and Gramsci speaks about coercion (direct use of force) and consent (ideas or ideologies).

Often, the most powerful seek to justify their powerful position (and control of government) by way of ideas. People internalise these ideas through socialisation and, because of this, they do not challenge (or resist) the position of the powerful. For instance, if we are all socialised into believing that the best and only economic system possible is capitalism, we accept the ideology of the capitalist class and we will not struggle against it. This involves the powerful ruling on the basis of consent, as we see the position of the powerful as legitimate. This is regularly the most successful way to dominate. If we do not consent to the rule of the powerful, then they will use coercion or repression (through, for example, draconian laws and police action) to ensure that we do not revolt against the position of the powerful. This is rule by coercion. In any particular society, there is often a fluctuating combination of rulership by consent and coercion.

The second point concerns the distinction between government and state. The **state** and the **government** are not the same thing. The former term, the state, is in fact more all-encompassing. Often, a distinction is rightly made between the legislature, the executive and the judiciary. The legislature refers to the parliamentary and political party systems. The parliament is an elected body – it is comprised of members of parliament, as elected representatives, who pass legislation that affect citizens. The judiciary refers to the legal and court systems, from magistrate courts to the supreme and constitutional courts. The executive refers to all the government ministries, departments and apparatuses which implement legislation, for instance the Ministry of Basic Education in South Africa.

The term 'government' normally refers to the sphere of the legislature, so that the political party that has most members in parliament is said to form the government – or is the 'sitting government' such as the ANC in South Africa. The term *state* includes the legislature or government, judiciary and executive, and hence is a broader term. This is an important distinction because while a government may change, that is a new government is voted in, the state may continue functioning as in the past, without changing or changing only slightly. In other words, the state executive – including often vast state bureaucracies of ministries and departments – often has a certain degree of autonomy from government influence. The election of the ANC involved a change in government, but did it involve a significant change in the state? Also, a critical question often arises: where does power in the state reside? Is it in government or outside government in the executive? If it resides in the latter, then a change in government may not bring about any significant changes.

The third conceptual point relates to the notion of **state form**. Capitalism exists currently as a worldwide system. This is a system that privileges maximising economic growth and profit for companies, often at the expense of satisfying basic human needs. But different types (or forms) of states exist presently under capitalism, or existed in the recent past. The differences between states are regularly determined by the nature of the relationships between the legislature, executive and judiciary, and by where power resides. Three forms of states can be noted. There are 'military states' or military dictatorships in which the military, as part of the executive, is all-powerful and the government, if it exists at all, simply rubber-stamps what the military demands. These states were quite common in South America during the 1970s and 1980s, most famously in Chile from 1973 until 1990. There are also 'authoritarian states', including states in which large sections of the national population are formally excluded from the parliamentary system and are not recognised as citizens with the right to vote. South Africa under apartheid is a good example of this – this had a racially exclusive authoritarian state with an all-white parliament that oppressed the black population. Another

form of state is the 'liberal democratic state' in which all civic and political liberties are available to everyone such that all members of the nation are considered as full and equal citizens. These liberties include voting in free and fair elections, freedom of speech and the right to mobilise and organise, for instance, in trade unions. The post-apartheid state illustrates this state-form. This form of state is the most democratic form, but questions still emerge about the relevance and significance of the legislative arm of the state. It seems that the executive, which is unelected and often shielded from the demands of citizens, has over the past few decades become increasingly powerful even within liberal democratic states.

The fourth point is that states and governments are to be understood in relation to the twin concepts of 'domination' and 'struggle'. States often serve the interests of a particular dominant group in society, such as the white group in apartheid South Africa. Hence, they seemingly become instruments for social domination. Many sociologists argue that liberal democratic states also serve dominant interests in society, for example the dominant social class; countries with liberal democratic states are said to be democratic in name only, but in reality are undemocratic despite regular elections. Because of domination and the division of society into dominant and dominated groups, there are invariably social struggles taking place through which dominated groups seek to challenge the dominant groups and to democratise or to further democratise the state. These dominated groups organise and seek to make the state more responsive to their needs or to the needs of citizens in general. States therefore are the focus of social struggles to either defend the existing social order or to change it. These ongoing social struggles mean that 'politics' is not reducible to voting in elections or to electoral politics. There are constant struggles waged by dominated groups between elections. And many of these struggles are unrelated to the political party system, that is, they are not linked to the agendas or programmes of particular political parties. These struggles though, insofar as they seek to challenge the existing social order, involve 'politics' – they have an unambiguous political content.

The fifth point is that states in the modern world are linked to nations and form part of an international system of **nation-states**. The modern state, involving the legislative, the executive and the judiciary, arose alongside the emergence and consolidation of territorially delimited nations. Each state has its own spatial territory and is responsible for (and is supposed to be responsive to) the people that live within that territory, ie the citizens, and others who are non-citizens but live within the defined territory. States therefore are linked to national groups, including citizens and others, called nations, which have their own specific history. The term 'nation-state' is used to define these entities. Each nation-state, for example South Africa, is part of a global system of nation-states but there is vast inequality between nation-states. Some nation-states notably the USA are very powerful and they are able to impose their will on weaker nation-states.

16.3 Segregation and apartheid in South Africa

This section examines the South African state prior to 1994, during both the pre-apartheid segregation period up to 1948 and the apartheid period from 1948. South Africa as a distinct nation-state was formed in 1910 and hence segregation as a form of state-sanctioned racial domination formally began then, but this was preceded by centuries of British and Dutch colonialism based on racial conquest, slavery and segregation. The ANC was formed in January 1912 as a direct response to the formalisation of racial segregation as embodied in the South African state.

South Africa is normally defined as a former settler colony or society in the sense that there was – literally – a large settler presence in the country which was originally driven by the agricultural and then mining sectors of the economy. This is similar to the case of Zimbabwe and Namibia, but different to other countries in the region including Zambia and Malawi. In settler societies, this significant settler presence led to the massive dispossession of land once wholly possessed by indigenous populations – mainly Bantu-speaking people – and to the setting up of Native Reserves in different regions of the country. In the case of South Africa, this was formalised by the passing of the 1913 Native Land Act in which 13 per cent of South Africa became designated as black South Africa and 87 per cent was declared as white South Africa, which was a combination of white commercial farming areas and state-held lands. This dispossession eventually undermined the small-scale agriculture system engaged in by indigenous populations. Simultaneously, the movement by black people from the Reserves to urban centres became subject to restrictions by way of the pass law system. Black men in particular, through the burgeoning migrant labour system, gained employment in the expanding South African economy on white-owned commercial farms or in the mining and manufacturing sectors of the urban economy all located in white South Africa.

The South African state, through a range of policies and programmes pursued during the segregation period, engaged in activities that bolstered the fortunes of the different sections of the white population. For instance, the low-wage structure of the capitalist economy benefited the captains of the manufacturing industry; the migrant labour and Native Reserve systems maximised profits for the mining industry; the job colour-bar protected the interests of the more vulnerable groupings of the white population and guaranteed them sheltered employment; and massive state subsidies to white farmers and infrastructural development that serviced their farms permitted the growth and consolidation of the white agricultural sector. This consistent and sustained support by the state for the white population during segregation reflected the fact that the state served the general interests of the white population. The state under segregation was a racially exclusive state with a whites-only electorate.

It was clearly an authoritarian state as well, in that the state's relationship to the black population was built on subjugation and oppression. The state administered and controlled the black population through a separate sometimes unwieldy institutional apparatus known as the Native Affairs Department which had no black representation or input of any significance. This state administrative arrangement was found throughout the colonies ruled by Great Britain, even in non-settler societies. In addition, the segregation state in South Africa was more than willing to engage in outright violent repression in undercutting black oppositional activity to racial domination. The white population and its politics had all the hallmarks of a liberal democratic state – regular elections, freedom of speech, freedom to organise and so forth. Within this restricted democratic realm, different sectors of the white population, represented by different political parties, engaged in conflicting politics that led to changes in government at election time. The formation of the Pact Government in 1924 is a clear example of this. This whites-only politics, to emphasise, led to governmental changes, but essentially the state in its racially exclusive authoritarian form continued. Whites were citizens in the full sense of the term; blacks were and remained as non-citizens or, as sometimes called, *subjects*.

Intra-white conflict, as expressed in political party activity, was particularly intense during the 1940s in the years leading up to the change of government and institutionalisation of apartheid in 1948. This conflict took place at a time of heightened black opposition to segregation, including the famous 1946 mineworkers' strike and numerous community-based mobilisations by the ANC.

For over two decades after 1948, the main sociological literature on South Africa identified with the 'Liberal School' argued, almost without qualification, that 1948 marked a watershed in South African history. The year 1948 was seen as exemplifying the victory of Afrikanerdom or of irrational conservative Afrikaner racism over the rational requirements of – notably – the modernising urban market economy. In large part, this modern economy was associated by the Liberal School with supposedly enlightened English-speaking white interests; however, a significant portion of English speakers voted for and eventually sided with the National Party. Nevertheless, apartheid was seen more as a break with segregation than as a continuation. In other words, a change in government was said to have had effectively altered the state-form. Literature that emerged in the 1970s, sometimes called the 'Radical School', downplayed the extent of the change initiated by the apartheid government. For instance, it argued that the intensification of the pass law and migrant labour systems under apartheid – which restricted the permanent residence of blacks in urban centres – served the specific labour needs of white-owned mining companies and commercial farms without jeopardising the urban labour requirements of white manufacturing businesses.

There was little disagreement though about the intensification of racial domination during the 1950s and 1960s under successive National Party governments, including the establishment of the complex ethnic-based Bantustan system with Bantustan governments. Black opposition, notably by the ANC and including the pass law campaigns, was particularly pronounced during the 1950s and the repressive might of the state was deployed, most vividly in the 1960 Sharpeville Massacre during a protest organised by the Pan-Africanist Congress. White owners of urban-based manufacturing companies at times expressed a concern about the intensification of racial discrimination, arguing, for instance, for a relaxation of the pass law system to enable the formation of a more permanent urban-based black workforce, with workers and their families living together. But the South African economy experienced major growth, including during what became known as the economic boom decade of the 1960s. In this context, the Liberal School argument about the irrationality of apartheid seemed amiss as it did not tally apparently with the empirical evidence. The Radical School argued that apartheid was, in large part, functional to the South African capitalist economy. While the Liberal School tended to emphasise 'race' – with apartheid serving white interests, but particularly those of white Afrikaners – the Radical

School stressed 'class' in claiming that apartheid served, not white interests per se, but the interests of white economic leaders – or white capital – in particular manufacturing, mining and agricultural sectors. Both schools stressed the state's involvement in social domination – the former spoke about an ethnic–racial state and the latter a racial–class state.

During the 1970s and 1980s a limited process of political and social reform was undertaken by the apartheid state, and this process involved specific measures of de-racialisation. At times this simply entailed relaxing petty apartheid, such as segregated toilets and beaches. However, a number of more substantial actions were taken in the light of two important commissions, namely the Wiehahn and Riekert commissions, established in 1977 by the state: their recommendations led to the official recognition and registration of a number of black trade unions and to the granting of securer rights of residence to urban blacks living in white South Africa. The state itself was also reformed through the formation of the tricameral parliament in 1984, which allowed for subservient Indian and coloured representation in national government structures, with whites retaining overall control of central government. At the same time, Grand Apartheid or separate development was enacted more vigorously with the granting of 'independence' to the Bantustans of Venda, Transkei, Ciskei and Bophuthatswana from 1976 to 1981. Black Africans were still treated as non-citizens in white South Africa and were expected to pursue their political aspirations through their respective ethnic Bantustan governments.

These initiatives by the state were taking place during a time of great political upheaval in South Africa, after a political lull in the 1960s. The early 1970s witnessed the activities of the Black Consciousness Movement led by Steve Biko and the emergence of strong black trade unionism in Durban, Johannesburg and Cape Town. School students also became active in the struggles against apartheid – this became dramatically evident during the Soweto Revolt which began in June 1976. A range of political tactics were used, including rent boycotts, school boycotts, consumer boycotts and work stayaways. National organisations emerged in both workplaces and communities – particularly important were the Congress of South African Trade Unions (COSATU) which was formed in 1985 and the United Democratic Front (UDF) formed in 1983. The level and depth of black opposition was so extensive that the National Party government declared a nation-wide state of emergency in 1987.

The reformist moves by the state were in part a response to the heightened political struggles of the black population and were designed to dampen these struggles and thus limit social disorder – that is, reform was meant to give the black population less reason and justification to mobilise against apartheid. The state though was ready and willing to repress, through its army and police units, any black oppositional activities that were seen as trying not simply to reform or alter apartheid but to end apartheid altogether. In other words, the state engaged in a process of controlled reform. Racial domination was also seen as being increasingly dysfunctional to the changing needs of the South African economy. For instance, the economic development path in the 1970s and 1980s required large numbers of skilled workers and there was one key potential source of these workers which was not being tapped due to apartheid: the black population. A whole range of racist restrictions, including the entire racially based Bantu Education system, inhibited the growth of a skilled black labour force. Thus, there was an economic rationale for reforming apartheid, besides the political rationale of maintaining social stability.

Throughout the 1980s the pressures for ending apartheid became so immense that the ruling National Party and the African National Congress, then banned and operating from exile, entered into negotiations to end apartheid and to plot the transition from apartheid South Africa to post-apartheid South Africa. The early 1990s became known as the transition years and they led to the first nation-wide election for all South Africans in 1994 and to the overwhelming victory of the ANC. The ANC has formed the government since then. The ANC government effectively inherited the apartheid state or the apartheid state-form. This inheritance had important implications for the ANC in trying to build a post-apartheid society.

16.4 Post-apartheid South Africa

The ANC set out immediately to transform South African society and to bring about a non-racial society. After decades of entrenched racial domination under both segregation and apartheid, this would be a gigantic project by any standard. This section does not seek to provide a chronological overview of the post-apartheid period. Rather, it seeks to identify some of the key factors that shape the ANC's policies and programmes. Many of these factors inhibit the ANC government in successfully tackling racially based inequalities and injustices. The chapter therefore gives insights into the workings of a liberal democratic state.

Post-apartheid South Africa is undoubtedly a liberal democracy and has held free and fair elections on a regular basis since 1994 – at both national and local levels. All the civil and political liberties typically associated with a liberal democracy are to be found in South Africa. The country is also known for having one of the most progressive constitutions globally. For example, the state's obligation to provide basic socioeconomic rights to all citizens, for instance access to decent housing, clean water and proper sanitation, is enshrined in the constitution, although this is qualified by the notion of legitimate limitations on state capacity to deliver these basic services. However, the fundamental reality is that a significant proportion of the black population – despite now having the right to vote and exercising that right – remain unemployed, live in poor-quality housing and struggle to feed their families. Poverty is in fact pervasive. In addition, the spatial character of apartheid society continues. In urban centres, the majority of blacks are still confined to overcrowded townships and, in rural South Africa, the division between Bantustans and white commercial farming areas is in evidence. The transition to post-apartheid South Africa, therefore, has led to the realisation of political and civil rights but not to the realisation of socioeconomic rights. This has meant dashed expectations for the vast majority of the black population.

There are a number of reasons for this, including both global and local factors. In identifying and discussing these factors, we will get a sense of some of the key pressures and processes within which any nation-state functions in the modern world of capitalism. After reading about these factors, think about them with respect to the material covered in Case study 16.2 later in this section.

The main *global* factor relates to the restructuring of the world social system. The dissolution and collapse of the Soviet Union in 1991 led to the disintegration of the communist system that centred on the Soviet Union. The Cold War and dual-power system between the United States of America and the Soviet Union ended; and one power, namely the United States, emerged on the global stage. Simultaneously, the capitalist system was experiencing a crisis of profitability internationally and this led to the emergence of neo-liberal capitalism. Neo-liberalism refers to a political-economic system which stresses 'small states'; more specifically, states are not supposed to intervene strongly in the capitalist economy. Prior to neo-liberalism, **Keynesianism** as a political-economic system existed. Keynesianism arose in the USA and Europe in the 1950s – it stressed 'big states' that strongly intervened in the economy in order to regulate the economy. This was done in a manner intended to protect the specific interests of poorer sections of the population. In this regard, sometimes Keynesianism is described as entailing a 'welfare state' – for instance, workers who became unemployed were entitled to unemployment benefits and if they remained unemployed for extended periods they would receive welfare benefits. Trade unionism and employment contracts, which guaranteed long-term and stable employment for workers, and national minimum wages for all workers, were also emphasised. The equivalent type of state in independent Africa during this time was the developmental state – this state sought to bring about socioeconomic development to broad swathes of the African population, although normally unsuccessfully.

Emerging in the 1970s, neoliberalism, as noted above, stresses 'small states'. Insofar as they strongly intervene in society, states are expected to focus on maximising the profitability of the productive sectors of the economy such as manufacturing and mining; and to limit the amount of state investment in unproductive sectors such as health and education. Further, many services previously provided by the state, including water, should, where possible, be provided on a commercial basis by private businesses. In addition, rather than the state enforcing uniform regulations to protect all workers, business leaders should be given the flexibility to devise, in partnership with workers, their own regulations for their own particular sector of the economy. Because of this, neoliberalism is often associated with the dwindling of state protection and rights of workers. The USA and Europe, through the World Bank and International Monetary Fund, tried to impose neoliberal arrangements on states throughout Africa through structural adjustment programmes starting in the 1980s. These programmes were designed to adjust economies towards neoliberalism. Hence, they made any further international bank loans, and development aid or co-operation, conditional on the imposition of neoliberal reforms in African countries. For instance, Zimbabwe, which received independence in 1980, implemented a structural adjustment programme in the early 1990s. Amongst other initiatives focusing on tackling racial inequalities, the Zimbabwean state from 1980 pursued a large-scale programme to broaden access to health and education for blacks; under structural adjustment, this was considered unproductive government expenditure and hence was cut back considerably.

This is the global context within which apartheid South Africa ended in 1994. There was now only one global power and therefore countries like South Africa could not – as a strategy to receive maximum benefits for themselves – play off two world powers against each other. As well, there was one uniform global economic system based on neoliberalism that countries like South Africa had to slot themselves into if they wanted to be globally integrated and receive socioeconomic development packages from international agencies. South Africa, because of international sanctions against the apartheid regime, had in many ways been

excluded from any perceived benefits from the insertion of its national economy into the global economy. In this regard, there was a reasonable rationale on the part of any post-apartheid government to seriously consider integrating the South African economy more fully into the international system – despite any recognised drawbacks of neoliberalism. The ANC government has pursued this line of thought, but has tried to 'manage' its global re-insertion in a way that does not fully undercut its attempt at historical redress of racial inequality.

Besides global factors, there are a range of *local* factors that have inhibited the capacity of the ANC government to bring about significant socioeconomic change. The first factor is *structural*, referred to as a 'structural constraint', and relates to the primary function of any modern state in capitalist society. It is in the interests of all states to maintain social cohesion and minimise social instability; otherwise, states undercut the foundation of their very existence. The crucial dimension of any capitalist society is the economy. A productive and profitable economy provides a strong basis for the state's existence (for instance, in order to function, the state relies on taxation emanating from profitable companies). The ANC government, in 1994, could have initiated far-reaching socioeconomic change, if it so wished – possibly even change with a moderate socialist emphasis. It is certainly highly unlikely that the international community would have denounced such an initiative given the tremendous racial injustice of the past few centuries that needed to be vigorously addressed.

Despite this, the ANC government was faced with the problem that confronts all states: namely, the need for a strong economy. Any attempt at redistributing wealth and rectifying the injustices of the apartheid past could not be accomplished in a manner that undermined the profitability of the economy. Because of this, radical changes to the economy would not be appropriate. The ANC government initially introduced the Reconstruction and Development Programme (RDP) as a socioeconomic programme that laid a strong emphasis on socioeconomic redistribution, including most famously the provision of housing in urban centres (known as RDP housing) to address the slum/squatter problem. A few years later, the Growth, Employment and Redistribution (GEAR) programme was introduced – this primarily stressed economic growth seemingly based on more neoliberal principles. Considerable debate exists within both academic and policy circles about the relationship between the RDP and GEAR. The ANC always claimed that GEAR, with its stress on growth, would allow for the implementation of the redistributive goals of the RDP; critics argue that GEAR in fact undermines the RDP. On balance, it appears that the RDP sought to bring about 'growth through redistribution'; but without any guarantee that growth would in fact emerge, whereas GEAR involved 'redistribution through growth' in which growth would be the primary focus, which may or may not result in redistribution – which in fact has not taken place in any significant manner. The ANC has sought to redistribute wealth through the social grant system (old age pensions, child support grants), but its primary goal has always been economic growth and it has claimed, for example, that strong growth would lead to more employment opportunities for unemployed blacks. The key point is that, in a sense, the ANC government was forced to emphasise economic growth – capitalist society requires a strong economy and this regularly translates into social stability, something on which sitting governments thrive.

There are also *agency* explanations for the actions of the ANC-led state. In national elections since 1994, the ANC has constantly received over 60 per cent of the national vote. On this basis, it would seem reasonable to assume that the ANC would enact legislation and pursue programmes that served the particular interests of its voting constituency – mainly poor blacks – and redistribute wealth on a massive scale. Structural constraints, as noted above, prevent this. But there is another factor that is also important, and this relates to what takes place between elections. Between national elections, economically powerful groups lobby state ministries and departments and key politicians to ensure that their interests are safeguarded.

A key case in point is AgriSA, which represents white commercial farmers. AgriSA is a powerful organisation that has the economic resources to continuously advocate for policies that protect the interests of white commercial farmers. It has regularly met with top officials from national ministries responsible for land and agriculture in South Africa, and has stressed that land reform must be market driven and that compulsory acquisition of farms, like what happened in Zimbabwe from 2000, must not take place in South Africa. In doing so, it has claimed that agricultural productivity depends upon the on-going existence of large farms and that subdividing commercial farms into plots to be farmed by small-scale black farmers will undermine the agrarian economy. To a large extent, the relevant land and agriculture departments have bought into this 'big farm' argument, such that land reform in South Africa has taken place at a snail's pace since 1994. Land redistribution, involving the purchase of white commercial farms for resettlement by a number of black families, is for

instance well below even conservative government targets. Agricultural labourers, who work on commercial farms, are not well organised in South Africa. COSATU for instance (the national trade union federation) does not organise amongst farm workers because of the practical difficulties in organising workers who are dispersed widely throughout the countryside. The only farm workers organised are those working on large estates or plantations such as tea and sugar and those in agri-processing enterprises such as citrus.

In addition, as part of its redistributive and growth strategies, the ANC has pursued a Black Economic Empowerment (BEE) programme which is designed to integrate black people more fully into the South African economy. It is now called Broad-Based BEE. Though the programme was intended to benefit a significant number of mainly poor black people, for example through skills enhancement and employment equity, in many cases it has had the opposite effect in enriching a small elite occupying key ownership and management positions in the private sector. There has also been serious criticism of improper relations between ANC officials and leading black businesspeople to the mutual benefit of both parties, leading for example to undue influence being placed on government by black business. The government tendering process, in which government publicly requests companies or individuals to submit applications for government contracts, has also been condemned for its partiality – the notion of 'tenderpreneurs' has arisen to describe those black-owned companies successfully obtaining tenders despite supposed lack of capacity and competency. This had led to widespread claims about corruption. However, dubious links between political and economic leaders is common, if not endemic, to capitalist societies, including liberal democratic ones.

The ANC government's particular propensity and the propensity of leading state officials to engage in significant and ongoing relations with dominant classes and groups in South African society is in part a reflection of state, government and party structures in post-apartheid South Africa. First of all, liberal democratic South Africa is marked by representative, indirect democracy rather than by deeper, more direct, participatory forms of democracy as evidenced in Kerala, India. This tends to shield ANC political leaders from the pressures of ordinary citizens and makes them more susceptible to other influences. Secondly, the electoral process is marked by proportional representation. Proportional representation means that the number of seats in national parliament for each political party is determined by the percentage of votes each receives. The ANC, which receives about 65 per cent of the national vote, therefore receives 65 per cent of the seats, which are constituency based. The ANC uses a party list to assign members to a particular seat or constituency and, quite often, the selected member does not live in the constituency's territory. Again, this means that the ANC-led government may become insensitive to the demands of community members and prone to the influence of economic elites. Thirdly, there is sufficient evidence to suggest that there is a process of centralisation and centrism within both ANC party structures and state ministries, which was particularly evident during the presidency of Thabo Mbeki from 1999 to 2008. This provides fruitful conditions for wheeling and dealing behind closed doors, so to speak. These three issues do not necessarily inhibit powerful pressure groups such as mining companies from accessing government and state, but they do minimise citizenry ownership of state policies and programmes.

Despite this argument, and the fact that economically weak groups do not have the same scale of resources wielded by economically powerful groups in lobbying the state, there is no doubt that the ANC government is sensitive to the needs of economically weak groups – particularly considering that these groups represent the main constituency of the party. This explains, for example, the number of pro-poor policies put in place by the government since 1994. An excellent example is the massive social grants system, notably the old age pension and child support grant that the ANC has developed since democracy and that targets poor families in both urban and rural areas. The receipt of a grant is the only source of income for vast numbers of households and is often the difference between living on the edge of poverty and living deep in poverty. Yet the grant system has been criticised by certain opposition political parties, such as the liberal Democratic Alliance party, for being an unproductive investment (ie for investing in a manner that does not directly contribute to economic growth) and for supposedly breeding dependency amongst the poor. Despite these criticisms, the ANC has every intention of maintaining the social grant system and even expanding it.

The ANC is in fact formally in an alliance – a tripartite alliance – with the trade union federation COSATU and the South African Communist Party. The ANC is certainly the dominant member of the alliance, but it needs to cater for the interests of members of COSATU if it wishes to keep the alliance together. At times, COSATU has publicly declared deep concerns about the ANC government's economic and social policies, including its failure to ensure decent work standards nationally and to resist the casualisation of the workforce. COSATU argues that these

policies are in large part slanted in favour of business and against worker interests. There is mounting evidence that COSATU's voice is not being heard sufficiently within the alliance. COSATU remains faithful to the alliance, but retains the right to take to the streets in protest against regressive government policies.

Trade unions were critical in the struggle against apartheid and, in decades past, the union movement globally was very powerful. But other types of movements – called social movements – have always existed both internationally and in South Africa. In the fight against apartheid, civic movements based in communities, notably urban black townships, and student movements played particularly significant roles. These and other kinds of movements were organised nationally in the 1980s under the banner of the United Democratic Front (UDF). When the ANC came into power, the UDF was disbanded and the community organisations were de-mobilised. It is sometimes argued that the ANC did this intentionally, so that there would not be an important power base within the black population that would be outside of the grip of the party; in this way, it is claimed, the ANC could be in power with a docile citizenry that would not meaningfully challenge the authority of the ANC-led government and state.

Nevertheless, there is significant mobilisation and organisation in urban-based communities. Indeed, under post-apartheid conditions, the more visible and confrontational movements have not been worker-based movements or unions but community-based movements. This political activity is often designed to place pressure on the ANC state to enact policies that benefit these communities, because electoral politics does not seem to improve the lives of poor urban dwellers. On the one hand, there are shack dwellers' movements – the most famous is *Abahlali baseMjondolo* which began in Durban in early 2005 and now has branches in Cape Town. *Abahlali* members live in informal settlements or shacks which are outside official townships. These movements tend to refrain from engaging in party politics. They claim that no political party in the country currently represents the interests of shack dwellers and they argue that the ANC is not a progressive party. At times they have protested against local ANC councillors who fail to ensure that even minimum services such as water are delivered to informal settlements by municipal government.

On the other hand, there are 'service delivery' protests. Thousands of these protests have taken place across the breadth of South Africa, as urban residents express their frustration over the lack and poor quality of municipal services, such as housing and sanitation. The extent to which these protests arise from permanent organisational structures rather than more fluid ad hoc structures varies between protests. These protests, which take place in public places such as streets, often entail confrontations with the police and a number of protesters have been killed or seriously injured during such collective actions. Besides services, protesters also complain about unresponsive municipal government and corrupt councillors – although, the protesters are mainly ANC supporters. In this regard, the protests may be misnamed as 'service delivery' protests as they regularly focus on a lack of political accountability; hence, an important dimension to them is the deepening of democratic processes at local state level.

The state tends to be less accommodating to the shack dweller movements because the latter threatens the hegemony of the ANC in urban townships and provides a power base outside the sphere of its influence. *Abahlali baseMjondolo* has hence experienced the wrath of the repressive might of the state. The most notable incident took place on the night of 26 September 2009, with apparent

ANC complicity, at the Kennedy Road informal settlement in Durban, leaving two community members dead. The ANC disputes the legitimacy of service delivery protests, and argues that the protests are destabilising and fall outside the formal electoral channels. But it still feels obliged to respond positively in some fashion to these protests, seeing the protesters, not as citizens exercising their civil rights, but as poor people with some legitimate claim to state resources, albeit severely limited resources.

So far this chapter has focused specifically on the South African state, during both segregation/apartheid and post-apartheid periods. It identified the segregation/apartheid states as racial states that continuously sought to serve the overall interests of the white population. In examining the post-apartheid state, we specifically sought to identify the many factors that affect that state's capacity to bring about significant socioeconomic change – given the massive poverty and inequality that continues to haunt South African society despite nearly two decades of liberal democracy.

Case study 16.2 Inequality in post-apartheid South Africa

Apartheid formally ended in 1994. At the time there was considerable talk about the dawning of a 'new' South Africa which was envisaged by Archbishop Desmond Tutu as a 'rainbow nation'. The newly elected government led by the ANC insisted that the racial injustices of the past would be addressed in a forceful manner and that this would accomplish two things: first of all, it would end the intense conflict between racial groups that had marked apartheid South Africa therefore leading to peaceful co-existence between groups and, secondly, it would overcome the conditions of poverty within which the vast majority of black people had lived before 1994 thereby lessening the social and economic inequalities that were pervasive under apartheid. But nearly 20 years after the end of apartheid, glaring socioeconomic inequalities and entrenched racial identities continue to characterise South African society, and they are fuelling social polarisation and conflicts in the country. South Africa in the 21st century seems anything but a rainbow nation. Indeed, for a large proportion of the black population, who continue to live in abject poverty confined to urban townships and rural former Bantustans, post-apartheid South Africa may not seem vastly different from apartheid South Africa. Because of ongoing inequalities along primarily racial lines, current South Africa may best be described as late apartheid and not as post-apartheid. The important point is that the prevailing situation of racially based inequality and poverty exists despite the fact that a former liberation movement and now progressive political party (the ANC) has controlled the South African government since 1994, and has pursued racial levelling and material redistribution on a nationwide basis.

Questions

1. Why has the ANC government not been able to bring about significant socioeconomic change?
2. Which factors are more important – global or local?
3. Identify what you consider to be the three most important factors responsible for this.

16.5 Theoretical perspectives on state and society

The chapter now broadens the discussion about the state by moving beyond South Africa. It considers some of the existing sociological literature on the state. This literature has, in large part, arisen in the United States and Europe over the past century. There has been a proliferation of sociological writings on the state in recent decades, but this section focuses on three important theories only. These theories are not exhaustive of sociological thinking about the state, but outlining the theories offers you as students a good introduction to the diversity of sociological thinking. In fact the three theories are quite closely linked to key traditions in the sociological discipline. These theories are pluralism, radical elitism and Marxism. Pluralism is associated with Émile Durkheim and the functionalist school, radical elitism is linked to Max Weber and critical Weberianism and, needless to say, Marxism draws on the work of Karl Marx.

In discussing these theories, the focus is on the liberal democratic form of the state in capitalist society. How these theories relate to the earlier discussion about South African state and society and specifically the post-apartheid state is highlighted where relevant. As students of society, we do not want to impose these or any other theories on South African society, as if they provide ready-made theoretical solutions for making sense of South African history and society. Nevertheless, they do raise important points that assist in understanding – sociologically – the complexities that have always characterised politics in South Africa. Often these theories are seen in direct competition with each other and as mutually exclusive in the conclusions they make about the liberal democratic state. It is worth exploring though how the theories may in specific ways add value to or complement each other.

All three theories would accept in some way the significance of the claim by Max Weber that the state in capitalist society has 'a monopoly of the legitimate use of force'; although we will see that the theories have a different take on this. Weber's claim means that the state is a centralised form of coercion (standing in a way 'above' society) that effectively commands and demands consent: it is the centre of power in society to which all citizens owe obedience, but this obedience involves active acceptance, based on consent. This may seem odd and even contradictory, that is, the existence of a coercive institution in society that has the consent of citizens, but this is the very basis of the state's existence in capitalist society.

In trying to distinguish clearly between the three theories, the notion of **autonomy** will be highlighted. The term 'autonomy' is used here to refer to the relationship between the state and social groups in society, in particular dominant groups. Radical elitists argue that the state has no autonomy or is the instrument of the power elite. Pluralists claim that the state has complete autonomy, meaning that it is not serving the interests of one particular group; and Marxists broadly say that the state has **relative autonomy**, in relation to the capitalist class. The differences between these three understandings of autonomy and their significance, will become clearer as we now go on to discuss the first of the three theories, namely **pluralism**. The longest of the three discussions is on pluralism, because the other two discussions, on radical elitism and Marxism, in certain ways entail a critique of pluralism.

16.5.1 Pluralism

Pluralism claims that liberal democratic capitalist society is marked by a substantive or actual democracy, in which a diffusion of power prevails, buttressed and safeguarded by a number of important mechanisms and institutions. Democracy therefore is not simply guaranteed constitutionally, or exists in a formal sense, but exists in practice. This may seem like an uncontroversial claim, but we will see that both radical elitists and Marxists claim that democracy in these capitalist societies is a mere illusion.

Liberal democratic capitalist society is differentiated on many bases (by means of social stratification or horizontal divisions in society) including in terms of social class, gender, race, occupation, region, religion and age. In making decisions in the form of policies, pluralists argue that government cannot possibly please all groups in society at all times, including all social classes. Indeed, social class is often seen as the major fault line in capitalist societies. In making any particular political decision, for example enacting a piece of legislation, the state cannot meet the interests and preferences of all members of society. Simultaneously, however, pluralists believe that the exercise of power by the state ultimately benefits everyone in society on a largely equal basis. No particular group, including no particular social class, in capitalist society consistently wins out in terms of policy decisions made by the state.

Pluralists portray the state as an honest broker which mediates between social groups and takes account of all the competing demands of the different groups. In doing so, it ensures that all groups (such as social classes) influence government policy but no one group consistently gets its way. In large part, this is because political, social and economic resources are widely distributed in society amongst different groups; and these groups are all able in some way to effectively make known to the state their policy preferences. In this way, no group can be said to monopolise or control state power to its exclusive advantage. Hence, one can speak of multiple centres of power within capitalist society, where power is situational and non-cumulative, that is, power in one area of life does not give power elsewhere. This goes against the Marxist argument, which claims that the economic power of employers, or capitalists in Marxist terms, translate into political power almost by necessity. Different groups have varying degrees of influence at different times and over different issues. There is open political competition between social groups, and the overall result is a win-win situation for all.

Therefore, the elected representatives of citizens in liberal capitalist democracies, which are sometimes called the political stratum, are said to serve the interests of the people, or the national interest, the public interest or the general interest. Political decision makers are accountable to the citizenry because they are dependent fundamentally on regular elections for their own political survival and they almost by necessity pursue policies, or at least seek to do so, that are popular with the electorate. Formally recognised modes of representation are hence built into elections in capitalist democracy, but so is redress if things go wrong – if a particular politician or political party proves unpopular, they can simply be voted out of power in the subsequent elections. In this sense, politicians may choose between competing policy alternatives based on what is popular, even if this means going against the policy prescriptions contained in the manifesto of their respective political party. Politicians seek the national interest, such that the political stratum does not pursue its own selfish political interests or the particularistic interests of a dominant economic class or power elite, as argued by Marxists and radical elitists respectively.

In arguing their position, pluralists highlight the existence of two main mechanisms that act as bulwarks for inhibiting the concentration of power in capitalist society and for enhancing the diffusion of power: these are political parties and pressure groups.

Political parties are a mechanism for linking individuals and groups with the formal structures of state through government. Parties represent and aggregate or bring together a wide range of social group interests (under one roof so to speak) and on this basis they bring policy preferences and platforms into the democratic process, thereby shaping public policy in the interests of citizens. The political party system commits and unites conflicting groups

to the principle of an orderly and open competition for power in elections and therefore to the principle of majority rule in and through parliament, with the sitting government controlling parliament. Thus, conflict occurs within agreed-upon democratic channels and mechanisms. Pluralists also say that parties educate the public on political issues between and during election campaigns.

A number of criticisms of the pluralist argument about parties have been put forward. First of all, the degree of alternative choices offered by competing parties is more illusory than real, as fundamental differences between major parties in any liberal democratic capitalist society are rare. A good example is the Labour Party and Conservative Party in Great Britain; for example, the Labour Party under Prime Minister Tony Blair adopted socioeconomic policies that seemed to be consistent with the views of the Conservative Party. In the case of South Africa, because of the strong neoliberal thrust in post-apartheid state policy, it is sometimes suggested that differences in economic policies between the ruling ANC party and the opposition Democratic Party (DA) are not substantial. A second criticism is that party leaders (irrespective of the party – even socialist-inclined parties) in the main have upper class backgrounds and, because of this, their decisions often reflect the interests of the dominant class. Thirdly, contemporary political parties have a very inactive membership with only minimal participatory involvement in party structures; this makes parties unresponsive to mass membership such that party members have few if any policy-making teeth. Finally, parties in their education and campaign work are selective in what they raise publicly as issues for open debate – they define and influence what can become a public issue in a very selective manner and shape the climate in which it is discussed. As a result, certain economic programmes that might be of distinct advantage to workers, such as workers' control of factories, are never raised in the public sphere by political parties. In the end, the overall criticism is that the political party system has certain in-built biases vis-à-vis the diverse groups, including social classes, in capitalist society. Parties do not facilitate democracy but undercut it, which means that the party system does not serve the common good or national interest.

Pressure groups are based on interest groups. There are a vast range of interest groups that are organised in terms of social identity such as class, gender and ethnicity or policy issues such as abortion or crime. Members share a common interest and insofar as these groups seek to influence government they are referred to as pressure groups. To give an example in relation to social classes: workers are an interest group and their pressure group is a trade union, and employers are an interest group and their pressure group is an employers' organisation, for example the Minerals Council. Pressure groups do not seek to gain or win state power like political parties do, and they do not always claim to represent a large cross-section of the population like political parties do. A trade union for example only represents its members, which may be restricted to employees within a particular sector of the economy such as the automobile industry. These groups can exert pressure by giving funds to political parties, by appealing to public opinion on, for example, crime through campaigns, by giving government specialised knowledge for decision-making purposes, by civil disobedience, and even by bribery. They put pressure on the political stratum, including top officials within state ministries and departments, to make particular decisions on specific issues that serve their perceived or subjective interests. In the case of pressure groups, political decision-making involves weighing the different arguments articulated by pressure groups on a particular matter, for example pro- and anti-abortion groups' arguments, and trying where possible to accommodate the different demands. This has been labelled the politics of adjustment.

Pressure groups are seen as important by pluralists because voting for political parties in elections takes place only intermittently and the ongoing work of pressure groups animates democratic processes. Also, a specific political party gains power with a broad agenda, called a platform or manifesto, but pressure groups still need to ensure that specific parts of the agenda are pursued. As well, pressure groups provide an opportunity for those who voted for the losing party to influence government decisions. Lastly, new issues emerge in between elections, for example a corruption scandal in government, and pressure groups enable the public to make the diversity of their positions known on these issues.

As with political parties, criticisms have been put forward pertaining to pluralist claims about pressure groups. For example, it cannot be assumed that all interest groups have the capacity to form meaningful pressure groups, such as domestic workers and farm workers in the case of South Africa and, even if all interest groups can do so, they are unlikely to have the same degree of influence based on the resources available to them. Indeed, even within the working classes, employed workers have more resources than do unemployed workers – the latter are normally not organised and not represented by trade unions. In addition, it cannot be assumed that all groups have the same ease or privilege of access to decision-makers in state and government. For

instance, decision-makers feel more comfortable in the presence of business leaders than workers, if only because decisionmakers and business leaders are likely to have similar socioeconomic backgrounds.

Not all interest groups have the same position of importance in capitalist society in the minds of members of the political stratum. Associated with this is the fact that some groups can more easily claim that their specific interests are consistent with the public or national interest, which the state seeks to defend and promote. All states depend on a strong economy and hence business leaders often claim that a strong economy (meaning high profits for business) translates into a strong state which has sufficient revenue for education, health and other social services. Workers' specific interests, namely higher wages, is regularly seen as detrimental to a prosperous economy leading, for example, to runaway inflation detrimental to consumers. A final criticism about pressure groups is that all groups are supposed to play by 'the rules of the game' such as by lobbying, assembling petitions and rallying public opinion. Some groups are unable to have their voices heard through these normal channels, which in the case of South Africa has led to thousands of service delivery protests in recent years. Not playing by the rules though makes these groups appear illegitimate and even unpatriotic and criminal.

In general, pluralists identify and examine power in terms of observable or actual political decisions (ie political decisions on issues that are raised in the public sphere). This has been labelled as the first face of power. The two other faces of power will be discussed later in relation to the other two theories – these three faces have been made famous by Stephen Lukes (2005). This first face involves: a public issue which is openly debated such as abortion; a range of policy preferences which are articulated by different pressure groups such as pro- and anti-abortion groups and their lobbying of the state around this issue; and, eventually, a public decision made by government on the particular public issue. Hence, power is said to be openly and therefore democratically displayed and implemented. In analysing power in this way, pluralists come to the conclusion that no particular group in society dominates by having their preferences consistently translated into government policy. In other words, democracy actually exists in liberal democratic capitalist societies.

The relevance of pluralist theory to South Africa is problematic in relation to the segregation and apartheid periods, during which time liberal democracy did not exist formally let alone substantively. Insofar as there were signs of democracy during these periods, this flourished purely within the politics of the white population. Democracy existed for whites only. Pluralist theory, as a legitimate perspective within sociology, has only taken on relevance to South Africa in the context of the end of apartheid and the emergence of a non-racial, liberal democracy society.

16.5.2 Radical elitism

Elitism sits in stark contrast to pluralist theory. It denies that liberal democratic capitalist society is democratic; rather it is fundamentally undemocratic. It argues that the state serves the interests of a small and exclusive elite group, and thus the state maintains or reproduces relations of domination between the elite and the non-elite (the masses) within capitalist society. The state has no autonomy vis-à-vis the elite group in capitalist society. Elitism can be divided into two different theories: **conservative elitism** exemplified by Vilfredo Pareto and Gaetano Mosca and radical elitism exemplified by Charles Wright Mills and George William Domhoff. Conservative elitism condones the existence of an elitist power structure whereas radical elitism condemns the elitist power structure. Conservative elitists claim that the existence of elites is inevitable, as centralised authority based on expertise is efficient and indispensable given the inexperience and incapacity of the general populace in handling the affairs of the state.

In this chapter, we focus exclusively on radical elitism and the work of C Wright Mills because of its clear and explicit criticism of pluralism. Wright Mills speaks about the power elite. There is a version of pluralism that is sensitive to the criticisms made by radical elitists – this version argues that the political stratum is a pluralist elite that may at times act in its own interests and not in the national interest, and that the political stratum sometimes stands aloof from the democratic processes taking place in broader society. But, in the end, it comes to the typical pluralist conclusion about the existence of a vibrant liberal democracy.

Mills studied the US national power structure in the immediate post-World War II period, that is, during the 1950s, but its relevance to South Africa should also be considered (see Case study 16.3). He argues that during the post-war period the United States is well beyond the era of romantic pluralism. He speaks about the decline of politics as understood by the pluralists, that is, the decline of any vestige of substantive democracy. He goes on to show that the kind of politics that pluralists focus on is now located merely at the middle level of power in the United States.

Mills says that an elite power structure consisting of the power elite has always existed in the modern history of the US, and this includes the political, economic and military elite

combined into one overall elite group that dominates politics and political decision-making processes. The elite consists of those individuals who occupy the top positions in the state, the economy and the military organisations; considering that the military forms part of the state, when Mills speaks about the state elite he is referring to individuals in other parts of the state. These three elite subgroups come together and form the united and cohesive power elite. But over the years there has been a marked shift in the balance of power within the power elite.

In this regard, Mills argues that because of World War II and the significance of the military to war's victory, the military has become increasingly powerful within the elite group. He thus speaks about the warlords gaining decisive political ascendancy, about a coincidence of interest between military and corporate needs, and about how important political and economic decisions are now being made 'in terms of military definitions of reality'. Mills speaks about American capitalism being a military capitalism or a military-industrial complex. Some recent commentators have noted American intervention in the Islamic world, notably Iraq and Afghanistan, in the light of the 9/11 terrorist attacks on American soil as further consolidating the importance of the military elite, at least in relation to foreign policy.

Mills provides two main reasons for why the three groups of sub-elites come together to form a cohesive power elite. First of all, he refers to the common social background and personal lifestyles of the different elites: they intermingle socially on a regular basis and develop a common belief system on this basis. Secondly, he mentions the common organisational interests or structural coincidence of the interests of the three sectors that the elites command; in other words, their specific interests complement each other. For example, the economy receives a boost when America goes to war, such that one hears talk about a 'war economy'. This simply means that the armaments industry, which forms an important part of the American economy, needs to continuously supply the military with armaments during wartime and hence business booms for this industry under such conditions.

The complementary interests do not imply though that the elite are always a homogeneous entity. There are at times conflicts and individual ambitions that get in the way of complete unity; but in terms of making important decisions they invariably adopt a common policy position. Any autonomy that does exist between the sub-elites is in the end subsumed under the internal discipline and the community of interests that bind the power elite together. Hence, the three elites connect because of 'common beliefs, social congeniality, and coinciding interests'. From Mills' discussion (Wright Mills 1959), it is clear that he would not only reject pluralism but also Marxists' overall claim (discussed below) that the economic elite or capitalist class controls the state. He labels Marxism as economic determinism; more specifically he argues that Marxists understand capitalist societies purely in terms of the economy, such that political power is reduced to or derives from economic power.

Further, the power elite is characterised by considerable internal interchange and mobility; for example, retired army generals may wear civilian clothes and occupy a position in a non-military state department, or corporate executives may leave the private sector and take up a key position in state ministries involved in economic affairs. Those individuals who interchange positions in this way are said to be the inner core of the power elite and are able to transcend the particularity of interests in any of the three institutional set-ups, and thereby unite the power elite. In other words, they recognise most clearly what is in the best interests of the power elite as a whole, because of their personal experiences of working in more than one part of the power elite. The inner core comprises the individuals who are most active in organising the upper echelons of the power elite into an organised structure of power and sustaining it.

The power elite are an 'invisible' elite. Its members in a sense operate behind closed doors, and outside of the public eye and public scrutiny. There is thus increased official secrecy behind which great decisions are made. In this regard, radical elite theory takes us beyond the observable decisions that pluralists focus on, and it delves into a second face of power, or a second way in which power is exercised. This second face of power is the private face of power in which dominant groups or the power elite may prevent or exclude issues from becoming public and open to democratic debate. Thus some issues do not reach the stage of decisionmaking and only *safe* issues become public issues. The most important national decisions, the ones that have important implications for instance for national security, are made behind closed doors. Thus power is sometimes

about managing situations or influencing the definition of matters for public debate, with the interests of non-power elite groups becoming marginalised in this way. Pluralism is thus based on the unsound notion that visible issue-based conflicts reveal the power structures of capitalist society. This gives merely the illusion of democracy, according to radical elitists.

The power elite group is not accountable for its actions, either directly to the public or to anybody that represents the public interest. But the notion of the power elite, according to Mills, is not based on a conspiratorial theory. Therefore, he is not arguing that the elite are involved in some secret plot to dominate capitalist society. Indeed, he argues that the elite are not consciously organised as such and nor would its members consider themselves as an elite or as acting in the interests of the elite or of themselves. The elite would likely claim that they are genuinely acting in the 'national interest'. Yet, despite the self-conceptions of the elite members and their intentions, the overall effect of their actions marks them – for Mills – as the power elite.

Mills claims that the pluralist notion of power entailing a 'balancing society' is not applicable to the upper reaches of politics in contemporary America. For instance, there has been the relegation of the professional politicians to the middle levels of power. State power rests not with professional politicians but with the political directorate or higher echelons of the state administration or executive. There is hence a weakened formal democratic system, as only democracy in name or formal democracy exists. The middle level of power consists of government, the legislature and the political party system. The conventional lobbying activities of pressure groups, as focused on by pluralists, are normally conducted at the middle level of power. At this level, issues fundamental to national stability are not made. Mills also argues that contemporary citizens are in large part passive and not actively engaged in any significant manner in party politics and pressure groups – they are largely demobilised and thus he refers to them simply as the 'masses'.

Case study 16.3 Radical elitists in South African society

Radical elitists are in the in-between position between pluralists and Marxists – they disagree with Pluralists about the existence of democracy under capitalism but they do not reduce political power to capitalist economic power. Because of their middle position in this regard, it is worth using radical elitist theory to illustrate the deployment of state theory in making sense of contemporary South African society. ➡

There is no doubt that South African society is marked by vast inequalities which benefit the most economically powerful, including the owners of manufacturing corporations, mining conglomerates and large commercial farm estates. But the post-apartheid state's activities cannot be explained solely in terms of the needs of economic elites. On a diverse range of issues, economic leaders are highly critical of the ANC-led government – for instance, economic leaders argue that the labour markets are overly regulated by the state through labour legislation protecting workers and that the massive grant system amounts to unproductive investment to the disadvantage of economic growth. In other words, there are disagreements and conflicts between economic and political leaders such that economic power does not automatically translate into political power.

At the same time, there is an overall unity of interest between political and economic leaders in South Africa. The ANC government, though in alliance with COSATU, does not want the South African economy changed dramatically; for example, it refuses to listen to trade union calls for the nationalisation of the mining industry as it is felt that this will undercut the productivity and profitability of the gold mines. In this, it is strongly supported by the mining industry owners. There are also close personal connections between economic leaders and political leaders. This is clearly demonstrated by the existence and workings of the Presidential Commercial Agriculture Working Group. This group contains state departments and commercial agricultural organisations without any agricultural worker presence of significance. It was established by former president Thabo Mbeki in 2001, and meets intermittently with the state president. One of its first tasks was to develop the Strategic Plan for Agriculture. The participation of farm worker representatives has come only after the fundamental basis for agricultural and land reform has been designed in the interests of agribusiness and commercial agriculture. There is also movement between the economic and political leadership spheres. Tokyo Sekwale (past Minister of Human Settlements), for instance, had massive business interests but he has moved into politics and there were rumours that he may one day be state president. The closeness between the political and economic elite means that many policy decisions are made without public knowledge and are simply imposed on the general citizenry; the controversial arms deal is a case in point. This 'behind closed doors' policy-making exists despite quite vigorous democratic processes that seemingly exist, including multiparty parliamentary portfolio committees which scrutinise the work of state ministries and departments.

The use of radical elitist theory provides important insights in examining post-apartheid society and it clearly raises critical questions about the status of democracy in South Africa. The other two perspectives could likewise be used to generate insights into present-day South Africa.

16.5.3 Marxism

Like radical elitism, **Marxism** sees power concentrated in the hands of a minority. Political power, though, does not rest with those who occupy key positions in the state, because economic resources are the key source of power. Economic control means political control. The dominant class in capitalist society, that is the capitalist class or bourgeoisie, owns the means of production (the factories, equipment and so on) and the working class does not. The members of the working class sell their labour, or what Marx calls labour power or capacity to labour, to the capitalist class in order to earn wages and make a living. This economic domination is based on exploitation, and translates into political domination. The Marxist theory claims that the state in capitalist society is a *capitalist state*.

All citizens appear to be equal in power, for instance, through universal suffrage or the right to vote, and by way of mobilising and organising without hindrance, and thus the state and government appear to reflect the wishes of citizens or the national interest. This is mere appearance and reality in capitalist societies is far different. In this sense, for Marxists, pluralist theory is simply the ideology of capitalism dressed up in theoretical clothing that seeks to justify the continuation of a social system based on exploitation. According to Marxism, it does not matter which political party forms the government, as all parties end up supporting the maintenance of the capitalist system. Within Marxism, there are two broad approaches: **instrumentalism** as exemplified by Ralph Miliband (1983) and **structuralism** as found in the works of Nicos Poulantzas. These two approaches are not necessarily in opposition to each other but, in fact, may complement each other.

Instrumentalism means that the state is a direct instrument of the capitalist class, and that the capitalists directly intervene in ensuring that the state functions in the interests of capitalism. Miliband's theory has many similarities to radical elitism in terms of the evidence given to support his argument. He does not speak though of a power elite in which political and economic elites rule together because, for Miliband, economic elites have control over political elites. He says that the state elites who run central state institutions, such as military officers and cabinet ministers, are closely aligned to the capitalist class. He gives empirical evidence showing that a significant minority of political elites have a bourgeois or upper-class background or that they develop a bourgeois or pro-capitalist outlook on capitalist society. The overall claim is that the state acts at the behest of the capitalist class.

Compared to instrumentalism, structuralism does not stress the actions of individuals, for instance the activities of capitalists in putting pressure on the state, in making the state a capitalist state. Rather, it focuses on the importance of social structures and how social structures constrain and limit the actions of the state and government. The state in capitalist society exists in order to stabilise the capitalist system and it does not really matter whether there is capitalist pressure on the state to act in a way which benefits the dominant economic class. *The state exists to ensure that the capitalist economy functions profitably and smoothly and to ensure that social and political stability provides a solid foundation for economic growth and development.* State leaders by necessity recognise that a strong state and thus the very continuation of the state requires a strong economy. Insofar as the state pursues a vibrant economy, it serves the interests of the class, namely the capitalist class, that dominates the economy. The state works on behalf of the capitalist class but not at its behest, that is, not on its orders.

Theorists who stress structuralism often speak about the *relative autonomy* of the state in capitalist society. The ruling class or bourgeoisie does not directly govern (ie it is not the governing class). The governing 'class' are the political elites who control government and the state. But the interests of the ruling class are met through the actions of the state. In this sense, the state is relatively autonomous from the bourgeoisie; in serving the interests of the bourgeoisie, the state has a certain freedom and independence from the bourgeoisie. In fact, the state needs this autonomy in order to maintain the capitalist system. The capitalist class is itself internally divided, and often different sections of the capitalist class, including manufacturers and mining companies, place different demands on the state. The state

is not linked to any particular section of the capitalist class on an ongoing basis, and hence it has the freedom to act on behalf of the entire capitalist class. The relative autonomy allows the state to move beyond or rise above the sectional interests within the capitalist class in order to represent the class as a whole.

Plus, relative autonomy gives the state the freedom to respond to demands of the working classes, demands which the bourgeoisie might oppose. For instance, trade unions might put extreme pressure on a particular state to increase significantly the national minimum wage for all workers. The owners of the means of production might oppose this pressure, claiming that any such increase would jeopardise or compromise economic profitability. The state, though, may recognise that the scale and scope of mobilisation by trade unions around the issue of minimum wages might lead to substantial social instability. Hence, the state may decide to increase the national minimum wage. The state, therefore, seeks to ensure that the demands of the working classes are contained within the parameters of capitalism. According to Marxists, the existence of relative autonomy also promotes the myth that the state represents society as a whole.

One of the problems that Marxists have tried to explain is the disjuncture between capitalist exploitation of workers on the one hand, and the existence of a working class that generally does not seek to overthrow the capitalist system. In other words, Marxists claim that workers are exploited and that it is in their interests to end capitalism, but workers do not see it this way. They are normally quite satisfied simply to have their wages increased within the confines of capitalism. In this respect, Marxists speak about ideology and legitimation. This is linked to Stephen Lukes' third face of power. An ideology or world view that is supportive of the capitalist system is prevalent within capitalism and citizens are socialised into this ideology. As a result, capitalism as an economic-political system is legitimised. This, for Marxists, is a form of power – in this case, power entails shaping or influencing the world view and belief system of members of the working classes. This is not done necessarily intentionally by the capitalist class or the state, but nevertheless the predominance of a pro-capitalist ideology becomes an important source of social cohesion for liberal democratic capitalist societies.

16.6 Applying theory to the phenomenon of state capture

A central issue about politics in contemporary South Africa, and which is hotly debated publicly, is 'state capture'. In fact, state capture was investigated by the Zondo Commission, which was launched by state president Cyril Ramaphosa in August 2018. The commission investigated corrupt dealings between certain business interests (notably the infamous Gupta brothers), state-owned enterprises (such as Eskom) and leading figures in the ruling African National Congress (ANC) (including the former president of the ANC, Jacob Zuma, when he was state president). There is also significant concern that businesses linked to top ANC leaders are benefiting from tenders (or state contracts) granted to businesses for providing services to the state.

What, however, is 'state capture'? How do we make sense of this in relation to theories of the state? We can consider this question in relation to Radical Elitism and Marxism. Besides the judiciary, the state – as discussed earlier in this chapter – refers to the executive (ministries and departments) and the government (the parliament ruled by the ANC, which thus forms the government). As used in South Africa, 'state capture' normally refers to the capture of the government and executive by businesses. More specifically, it means that, in corrupt and illegal ways, certain businesses (like those of the Guptas) work closely with leading figures in the executive and government to ensure that their own business interests are met, while the executive and government leaders benefit financially from this collaboration as well. In other words, political and economic elites benefit mutually, but only those economic and political elites involved in these illegal and corrupt transactions.

What would Radical Elitism say about this? For Radical Elitism, even if all collaboration is legal and without corruption, political and economic elites constantly benefit from collaboration at the expense of non-elites. In other words, all economic elites benefit and not just some as under 'state capture'. This relationship of mutual benefit, therefore, is the normal state of affairs and not the exception (ie when 'state capture' exists). If this collaboration exists always, with both political and economic elites benefiting, then it is unlikely that Radical Elitism would use the term 'state capture'.

From a classic Marxist perspective, does 'state capture' (as understood in South Africa) fail to recognise a more fundamental form of 'state capture'? As indicated earlier, Marxism argues that the state acts invariably and always in the interests of the capitalist class (economic elites) or

of capitalism. In this, more fundamental, sense, the state in capitalist (including South African) society is a capitalist state. This would be the case even if the Zondo Commission on 'state capture' did not exist in South Africa. Again, it is the normal state of affairs.

Considering all this, as students of sociology we need to recognise that 'state capture' does not fully account for the relationship between state and business.

16.7 Thinking about the South African state and the Covid-19 pandemic

A number of scholars argue that, even in normal times, liberal constitutional democracies (including in Europe and North America) are not as democratic as they first might seem. These liberal constitutional societies are said to be sleepy democracies because of the immense power of the state executive that imposes its will on ordinary citizens. So what about abnormal times, like during the Covid-19 pandemic?

In his famous book called *Seeing like a State*, James Scott (1998) argues persuasively that the modern state acts in a top-down manner by re-ordering nature and society in particular ways. Through centralised plans, and without consulting citizens, the state rearranges nature and society so that it can understand and therefore control them. We see this in the difference between, for example, a natural and a state-managed forest, with a state-managed forest planned and managed through a grid pattern. Cities are planned in a similar manner. Interestingly, Scott also argues that the state justifies its re-ordering of nature and society on the basis of scientific knowledge. As we will see, this is used by states to justify their responses to the Covid-19 pandemic, including in South Africa.

In abnormal times, when states are experiencing a deep crisis (eg a political or economic crisis), Bob Jessop (2016) argues that they are even more inclined to forego democratic processes. In other words, during such times the state executive may even become stronger as it goes about planning and implementing programmes that all citizens must follow. It is also possible that the state executive might enact such programmes in response to a public health crisis, as in the case of the Covid-19 pandemic.

South Africa is a liberal democratic constitutional society in which citizens have a range of important civil and political rights and liberties, including freedom of movement. In times of war and internal strife, liberal democratic states may impose a state of emergency that restricts political and civil liberties in order to facilitate social stability. As a response to the Covid-19 pandemic, which has been described as a war against an invisible enemy, the South African state imposed a state of disaster in March 2020. Though this is one measure short of a state of emergency, the effects of a state of disaster can have similar consequences for ordinary citizens.

Box 16.1

Think back to the beginning of the year 2020. Imagine leaving your place of residence one morning to visit a friend and a police officer outside orders you back into your residence. Or think about how you were compelled to wear a face mask whenever you went out in public. These two incidences would be unimaginable if you thought of your life at the start of 2020.

In the midst of the Covid-19 pandemic, these incidences became the norm. What happened?

- Did these changes arise simply because of the existence of a pandemic?
- Or did something else also happen?
- Why did some countries not go into lockdown and yet seemed to manage the pandemic more successfully than some of those that did so, even early?

If we think of these questions deeply, we begin to realise how different our societies are and how states can reshape our lives in very dramatic ways.

In South Africa and elsewhere, states closed their international borders and implemented lockdown and stay-at-home orders, including closing universities and schools. In South Africa, the army and police patrolled the streets to enforce the lockdown, arresting people for violating the lockdown, even for simply walking down the street. While the World Health Organization (WHO) applauded these efforts of the South African state, globally the lockdowns have had devastating economic costs, leading to significant declines in economic growth, rising unemployment and deepening levels of poverty. Across the world, governments tasked with administering the affairs of states have

stressed their role as having to balance saving lives with ensuring economic survival. In trying to assess the various degrees of success, you will have noted how both medical epidemiological and social scientific surveys became virtually the only news of the day, both locally and globally. Politicians justified the Covid-19 responses, including lockdowns, on the basis of scientific knowledge about the pandemic. That is why we often saw scientific experts and not politicians being interviewed on television.

But by whom and how were these decisions made, and is the reason why as simple as it has been made out to be – namely saving lives under the conditions of the Covid-19 disease pandemic? Do some benefit more than others from these decisions? If so, how and why? From the perspective of this chapter, what theory of the state helps us best to answer these questions? There are no simple answers.

In the case of South Africa, a National Coronavirus Command Centre was formed, consisting mainly of state ministers. These political elites in the state executive made all the major decisions with only minimal consultation with the legislature. This goes contrary to the pluralist understanding of the state, in which the state incorporates the views of different interest groups (as represented, for example, in parliament) before making important decisions. Further, the economic effects of the Covid-19 pandemic closures have been detrimental to everyone, even large corporations. This goes contrary to Marxist views of the state. Radical elitism may provide the best explanation, because it highlights, even in normal times, the power of the state executive. But because it stresses that economic and political elite act in unison, it might have difficulty explaining why the state executive closed down businesses during the lockdown, and affected negatively the profits of large corporations.

One thing is sure: around the world, the Covid-19 pandemic has shown the tremendous power that exists, potentially, in the hands of the state executive and its willingness to use this power when it deems fit. What about the post-Covid-19 future? Has the Covid-19 pandemic further consolidated the power of state executives? And what does this mean for the future of democratic principles and processes in the liberal constitutional order in South Africa? How should we make sense of all this?

Summary

- Key conceptual points have been made with reference to the sociological literature on state and society, including highlighting the distinction between government and state.
- This distinction between government and state is important in identifying where power lies within the state and how the state is subject to pressures emanating from within society.
- The main empirical focus of the chapter has been contemporary South African society.

- South African history (before 1994) was also examined to highlight the changes and continuities between apartheid and post-apartheid society in relation to the state and politics. Explaining these changes and continuities is an important sociological endeavour.
- Examining the continuities and changes in South Africa, and trying to make sense of post-apartheid state and society, requires sensitivity to the range of sociological theories of the state. For this reason, the chapter outlined and discussed pluralism, radical elitism and Marxism.

ARE YOU ON TRACK?

1. Relate your experiences in your personal life to your understanding of the South African state obtained from this chapter. How do you feel about encounters with state officials? Do you find the experiences pleasant or alienating? And what do they tell you about the state more broadly? Further, when you read in the newspaper or hear on the television or radio news about the different policies and programmes pursued by the South African state, do you feel a sense of ownership of these policies and programmes?

2. Write down a list of all the main changes and continuities between apartheid South Africa and post-apartheid South Africa which you can identify. Which ones of these can you

attribute to the actions or inactions of the state? On what basis do you claim that the state is in some way involved in the continuity or change? Has the state since 1994 been more involved in contributing to change or contributing to continuity in South African society?

3. Examine a particular state policy or programme that you are aware of in present-day South Africa, such as the social grant system. Whose interests is this policy or programme serving and on what basis do you make this claim? Because one policy or programme is serving the interests of one group, can you then conclude that the state is controlled by that group? If yes, why? If no, why not?

References

Alexander P. 2010. 'Rebellion of the poor: South Africa's service delivery protests – a preliminary analysis'. *Review of African Political Economy*, 37(123).

Dahl R. 1961. *Who Governs?* New Haven, CT: Yale University Press.

Domhoff G. 1967. *Who Rules America?* New Jersey: Prentice Hall.

Giddens A. 2006. *Sociology.* 5th ed. Cambridge: Polity Press.

Haralambos M, Holborn M. 2008. *Sociology: Themes and Perspectives.* 7th ed. London: Collins.

Jessop B. 2016. *The State: Past, Present, Future.* Polity Press: Cambridge.

Lukes S. 2005. *Power: A Radical View.* 2nd ed. New York: Palgrave.

Miliband R. 1983. *The State in Capitalist Society.* London: Quartet Books.

Pierson C. 1996. *The Modern State.* London: Routledge.

Popenoe D. 1993. *Sociology.* 9th ed. New Jersey: Prentice Hall.

Saunders C. 1988. *The Making of the South African Past.* Cape Town: David Philip.

Scott J. 1998. *Seeing like a State: How Certain Schemes to Improve the Human Condition Have Failed.* Yale University Press

Seekings J, Nattrass J. 2005. *Class, Race, and Inequality in South Africa.* New Haven: Yale University Press.

Wolpe H. 1988. *Race, Class and the Apartheid State.* London: James Curry.

Wright Mills C. 1959. *The Power Elite.* London: Oxford University Press.

Organisations, bureaucracy and social movements

Prishani Naidoo

In contemporary times, organisations are a prominent social phenomenon. If organisations are defined, as they are in this chapter, as collective formations of people in society, then very few individuals manage to escape their influence. Organisations can also be understood as formal social structures with clearly defined goals, rules and principles that direct the activities of the individuals who compose them.

This chapter highlights the decisive role organisations play in contemporary society. This appeared when society became more ordered and stable half a century ago, but the chapter also describes the current shift to greater flux and flexibility that has occurred over the past 50 years resulting in social movements. Few would disagree that our present social reality is characterised by dynamic fluidity and accelerated social change. This shift also reflects the fact that people express themselves more freely than in the past. The authority of institutional social structures is no longer considered sacrosanct. In many terrains and areas of social life, in the quest for a fairer share of what modern society has to offer, people combine as communities and interest groups to make their voices heard.

By means of a wide variety of collective formations, people have come together and, in a sense, broken through the rigid way in which institutions previously dominated, regulated and restricted human behaviour. Without going too far, it is almost as if humanity worldwide has come alive in a new way in the past generation or so. Even the term 'organisation' does not quite capture many of these collective social responses. It should then not come as a surprise that sociologists and other social analysts have had to sharpen their conceptual tools and now widely use the term social movements to describe the groundswell of an awakened society in the late 20th and early 21st centuries.

The pre-eminent sociologist of organisations was, of course, Max Weber. His study of bureaucracy remains foundational when coming to grips with understanding the shape, form and motivation behind contemporary organised combinations or collectivities of people engaged in social action. It is argued in Chapter 1 on sociological theory that concepts and theories can tell us much about the state of society at the time they were formulated. As the shifts in conceptualising how people come together in formal ways, whether as organisations or social movements, Weber's analysis of bureaucracy reasserts itself and is discussed early on in this chapter. A number of theories grappling with the independent collective social actions in evidence across the globe today are discussed. These theories and theorists include one of Weber's contemporaries, a number of later 20th century sociologists, both Marxist and non-Marxist writers and a number of contemporary critiques of Weber's classic texts.

Sociology has the unenviable task of grasping phenomena in motion, hence the quest for ever more accurate conceptual formulations. This requires constant sensitivity to the social context to which sociological concepts apply and sociological theories seek to explain. What comes across very clearly in this chapter is how the key concepts of organisation, social movements and change need to be applied to a globalised world. To capture the remarkable way in which ordinary inhabitants of this planet seem to collectively be making their presence felt and voices heard, sociological concepts are hard-pressed to keep up. The reader will find references to 'old' and 'new' conceptual categories, terms such as 'new social movements' and 'new forms of organising' which describe how the social movements they identify have coalesced in the anti-globalisation social movement or, again in the quest for conceptual accuracy, the alter-globalisation movement. These are hugely significant developments on the world stage. The social composition of people involved in what has become a global collective social formation, perhaps best exemplified in the World Social Forum, is what is perhaps most interesting from a sociological point of view. Across the globe, in a multiplicity of forms and ways, ordinary people of extraordinary diversity are straining to find, it could be said, the voice of humanity itself. This relatively new-found global social 'awakening' is an amazing story and is what this chapter is all about – the unprecedented contemporary expression of global collective social action.

The concepts sociologists have formulated to describe and explain this global social phenomenon, which has taken shape in the relatively recent past, are not difficult to grasp. They are instead very fresh and young, somewhat like our still youthful democracy and the new social movements in South Africa that emerged after 1994, which are briefly noted as the chapter ends. If you want to follow the next instalment of this fast-paced sociological introduction to organisations, movements and social change, go out and buy a good newspaper or check the internet to see what is happening on the social movement terrain internationally, a brief discussion of which brings the story as up to date as a scholarly textbook could possibly be.

Case study 17.1 The Treatment Action Campaign

Founded on 10 December 1998 in Cape Town, South Africa, the Treatment Action Campaign (TAC) advocates for increased access to treatment, care and support services for people living with HIV, and campaigns to reduce new HIV infections. With more than 16 000 members, 267 branches and 72 full-time staff members, the TAC has become the leading civil society force behind comprehensive healthcare services for people living with HIV and AIDS in South Africa. Since 1998, the TAC has held government accountable for healthcare service delivery; campaigned against official AIDS denialism; challenged the world's leading pharmaceutical companies to make treatment more affordable; and cultivated community leadership on HIV and AIDS. Our efforts have resulted in many life-saving interventions, including the implementation of countrywide mother-to-child transmission prevention and antiretroviral treatment programmes. For their efforts TAC has received worldwide acclaim and numerous international accolades, including a nomination for a Nobel Peace Prize in 2004. On 30 August 2006 the *New York Times* named TAC 'the world's most effective AIDS group'.

(Source: *Ndifuna Ukwazi* (Dare to Know) – Treatment Action Campaign)

Key themes

- Sociological definitions of and theoretical approaches to the study of organisation/s over the history of the discipline
- The relationship between the development and practice of particular organisational forms and notions of capitalist efficiency and productivity
- The relationship between forms of resistance and the cultivation of particular forms of organising and organisations
- Bureaucracy as a form of organisation (primarily through the work of Max Weber)

- Bureaucracy as a form of control that works in the interests of the capitalist system of production (also through Weber's work)
- The debates that have arisen in relation to the concept of bureaucracy and its further use in theories about organising
- Social movements and contentious politics
- Theories of organisation, organising and social movements.
- Researching organisations and movements.

17.1 Introduction

From meeting the very basic needs required by all people for daily survival, to challenging the dominant political order in society, the coordination of processes and individuals for the sake of meeting and serving common goals and interests (in the form of **organisation**) is necessary. Since the emergence of sociology, sociologists have sought to identify, define and understand the different kinds of collective formations, organisations and institutions, and the role of such groups in the shaping of such a society.

The sociological study of organisations has included both a focus on those institutions serving as the foundations of a developing capitalist society (eg the factory and the state bureaucracy) as well as on the emergence of organised forms of collective resistance to aspects of capitalist development (eg in the form of social movements and trade unions).

This chapter provides an introduction to some of the theories, experiences and debates that have shaped sociological approaches to the question of organisation (as process) and organisations (as structures). It offers some working definitions and historical perspective with which to make sense of more contemporary experiences of organisation/s.

The chapter begins by defining organisations and **social movements**, and identifying the key differences between them. You will find that applying these definitions to an actual example of a social collective immediately becomes rather complex, especially when one does so in the context of social change. In order to address this challenge, this chapter will go on to outline and define key theoretical approaches to the study of organisations and movements in sociology.

17.2 Organisations and social movements

There are a large number and kinds of collective formations of people in society. They appear in an immense variety and forms. The concepts of organisation and movements – or social movements – do, however, broadly pick out and isolate most ways in which people come together to meet and address their common concerns. Some of these collective formations are becoming institutionalised as part of society while others might only exist as long as the need for them continues.

17.2.1 What are organisations?

An *organisation* is a social unit (or set of social relations) directed towards meeting a particular goal in society. The goal usually determined by its members (or by society on behalf of them). Members belong to it because they share a common set of characteristics, beliefs, values, interests and/or practices. Organisations are formal structures with clearly defined rules and principles that determine the engagement of members and the operations of the collective. They are different from social units like the family in that they tend to be more specialised and focused in meeting very clearly defined goals, and from other collectives like social movements.

17.2.2 What are social movements?

Social movements are less formally structured than organisations and are often the precursors of more formal ones. One form of organisation (eg bureaucratic) might provoke the emergence of a movement against the effects of its form of organisation; over time, this movement, if sustained, might become a more formal organisation. Often, groups come together informally around common problems and/or interests in less clearly defined movements. They are frequently without a clear leader, constitution, manifesto of demands or programme of action, and they only begin to take a clearer organisational form as they grow. They then find ways of sustaining themselves and become successful in meeting their goals. A clear example here would be many trade unions, which emerge in the first instance as informally organised labour movements that only develop into formal trade unions over time.

The term 'social movement' is used by most sociologists to refer to any conscious, collective, organised attempt to effect (or prevent) widespread social change outside the sphere of accepted institutions. However, some theorists (Piven & Cloward 1977) point out that such mainstream definitions of social movements fail to acknowledge the political nature of certain collective acts in society. For example, large-scale truancy from school or rising numbers of rent defaulters are not usually considered to be part of the field of analysis that is named social movement studies. Piven and Cloward (1977) write:

> [T]he effect of equating movements with movement organisations – and thus requiring that protests have a leader, a constitution, a legislative programme, or at least a banner before they are recognised as such – is to divert attention from many forms of political unrest and to consign them by definition to the more shadowy realms of social problems and deviant behavior (Piven & Cloward 1977: 5).

Based on their studies of mass protest movements in the US in the 1930s and 1960s, Piven and Cloward (1977) also argue that social movements tend to develop into formal organisations over time, emerging only at the height of their individual success. While collective acts of protest might begin in informally organised ways without proper structures and processes, over time social movements develop into formal organisations or **social movement organisations** (Zald & Garner 1966).

Writing in the 1960s in the context of the US, Zald and Garner (1966) coined the term 'social movement organisation'. They argue that social movements consist of a number of different organisations. These operate independently of each other, but come together at different times in joint movement activities. They state that social movements do not share all of the formal characteristics that the organisations comprising them might hold. For them, social movements are often the product of various organisations and organising attempts. So, for example, various trade unions, which often begin as social movement organisations before becoming more formally institutionalised, come together with individual resource people and activists, and other resource organisations in the even broader labour movement. While each **trade union** and organisation within the movement conforms to different sets of accepted rules and regulations, the broader movement they collectively comprise is more fluid and less structured.

17.2.3 Differences between social movements and organisations

There are various differences and similarities that exist between social movements and organisations, as discussed in the previous sections. However, it will be of importance for us to draw the attention of the reader to some major differences that exist in both organisational and social movement study. Following, MacAdam and Scott (2005: 8–11) social movement studies or theorising are informed by organisational studies framework, concepts and arguments.

Table 17.1 Differences between social movements and organisations

Organisations	Social movements
Structure	Process
Established organisations	Emergent organisations
Organisational field	Movement centric
Institutionalised authority	Transgressive contention
Localised regimes	Societal regimes

Box 17.1 How does a social movement organisation differ from other formal organisations?

Look at Case study 17.1 opening this chapter and decide whether the TAC is a formal organisation or a social movement.

(Hint: Zald and Garner (1996: 329–330) argue that a social movement organisation has 'goals aimed at changing the society and its members; they wish to restructure society or individuals, not to provide it or them with a regular service (as is typical of bureaucracies)').

17.3 Why study organisations?

Organisation (as a process) is what makes societies work in the ways they do, and studying it is therefore key to making sense of the character of social relations and the place of power in a particular society, as well as its dominant modes of thought. The emergence of formal organisations, with members identifying as part of bigger singular entities with commonly defined goals and rules, speaks to the various configurations of power that especially characterise colonial and industrial capitalist societies. While there were some formal organisations prior to industrialisation, it was only with the increasingly specialised division of labour accompanying industrialisation that formal organisations began to proliferate. These organisations were to define much of the character of social, political and economic life.

17.3.1 The emergence of organisations

The earliest forms of human society were characterised by a very simple division of labour that saw all adults involved in subsistence activities, with no time freed up for the development of specialised social units dedicated to tasks other than the collection of food. Sociologists point to the emergence of agriculture as the point at which a specialised division of labour and the development of independent, formal organisations began. With the growth of agriculture, a smaller proportion of the population was required to be able to meet the subsistence needs of a community, and so more people could specialise in tasks that were not directly related to subsistence. As the division of labour becomes more and more specialised, it needs coordination and management, resulting in the production of sets of rules and hierarchies of authority. An organisation is said to be formed when these factors are combined in the pursuit of a specific goal. The increase in the number of formal organisations in society is closely related to the increasingly specialised division of labour in an industrialising society.

Modern industrial societies differ from pre-industrial societies with regard to the number, size and scope of their organisations. It is also the case that social change is driven in modern societies by social movements and social movement organisations. Key to understanding how change is effected in the world, then, is the study of organisation and organisations.

17.4 Theories of organisation

Although one encounters the theme of organisation/s in the work of other 'founders' of sociology, such as Comte (1798–1857), St Simon (1760–1825), Durkheim (1858–1917) and Marx (1818–1883), it is the work of Max Weber (1864–1920) that has been most influential in the crafting of 'a sociology of organisations'. In particular, Weber's work on **bureaucracy** has provided material for much discussion and debate over many years, continuing into the present. It is for this reason that much of the discussion that follows focuses on the question of bureaucracy as an organisational form by examining the work of Weber, as well as of students and critics of his writings.

While Weber's analysis spoke largely of the experience of the state bureaucracy and economic enterprises, his ideas about organisation were applied by others (like Robert Michels 1876–1936) to the study of social movement organisations (such as trade unions and political parties). There have also always been attempts at organising that have refuted aspects of Weber's and Michel's analyses and the emergence of other theories to try to understand forms of organisation that do not conform to the bureaucratic model. After a close look at bureaucracy, this section moves on to look at other forms of organising and theorising organisation/s, drawing from Marxist writings, resource mobilisation theory and experiences of 'new social movements'.

17.4.1 Max Weber and the concept of bureaucracy

Modernity, rational action and bureaucracy
Writing about and trying to understand modernity and industrial society, Weber highlights that a particular organisational form comes to dominate with the ascendance of rational thought and action in the world. He names this organisational form *bureaucracy* and defines it as 'a hierarchical organisation designed rationally to co-ordinate

the work of many individuals in the pursuit of large-scale administrative tasks and organisational goals' (Weber 1978).

Before we go on to study this model of organisation in more depth, it is important to situate Weber's work on bureaucracy in the context of his more general theory of social action. To recap what was introduced in Chapter 1, for Weber all human action is directed by meanings. He identifies three kinds of action that are the result of different meanings given by people to the circumstances confronting them:

1. **Affective action:** resulting from the emotional state of an individual in a given context such as physical violence as a result of a loss of temper
2. **Traditional action:** the result of a habit or custom such as clapping at the end of a speech, often done without thought or awareness
3. **Rational action:** the result of clearly defined goals of which the actor has a keen awareness, and systematic planning towards attaining set goals such as the organisation of a workforce, workplace, production and distribution of goods with the goal of making a profit.

In Weber's words, rational action is 'the methodical attainment of a definitely given and practical end by means of an increasingly precise calculation of means' (Weber 1958: 293).

For any kind of action to take place among a large group of people, Weber argues that a section of the group will have to direct and control the actions of others, necessitating some form of legitimacy for those in positions of control over others.

17.4.2 Legitimacy and forms of authority

Legitimacy, Weber explains, derives from the three types of social action outlined above. Behind affective action lies a particular motive for obedience to authority based on emotion. Behind traditional action is a motive based on *custom*, while with rational action, *reason* provides the motive for why a group of people would choose to obey a select few within the group. Weber argues that these forms of legitimate control are *charismatic authority*, *traditional authority* and *rational-legal authority*, with each producing a different organisational form or structure.

Weber developed models or 'ideal types' for each type of authority, which should each be viewed as a system of control. An ideal type, you may recall, represents a 'pure' form of a set of relations, which is not expected to be found in real life. Weber's **ideal type** rather represents a situation towards which reality approximates or tends. In other words, a real situation might express some of the characteristics outlined by Weber in an ideal type, but not all of them.

Charismatic authority

In a system where charismatic authority determines the nature of control, leaders appeal directly to the emotions of their followers, drawing on strong feelings of devotion, dedication and loyalty to persuade and control them. Followers obey because of their devotion to a leadership perceived to be exceptional and outstanding. Examples from history of charismatic leaders include Jesus, Mohammed, Napoleon, Hitler and, of course, Nelson Mandela. Charismatic authority produces organisations that are poorly defined and structured, with no laws or rules governing them and no fixed hierarchy of officials. There is also usually no properly organised financial support for the organisation, and it seldom exists longer than the life of its leader. After the death of the leader, the organisation must take on the routines of a system in which traditional or rational-legal authority is central in order to survive.

Traditional authority

A shared belief in the correctness of certain customs and traditions provides the basis for traditional legitimacy and authority. Traditional status (usually inherited) is what commands obedience, and positions of power are maintained over long periods of time through customary practices that entrench loyalty and submission. A clear example of such authority is the European feudal system in which lineage and inheritance determined the superior positions of royalty and nobility, and custom and status worked together to hold in place the rigidly defined divisions and inequalities among different groups in society. Such traditional authority is evident in many rural areas in South Africa today.

Rational-legal authority

In a system characterised by rational-legal authority, the general acceptance of a set of impersonal rules is what produces the obedience of those in positions of authority. Legal frameworks grant authority to certain individuals in society, and set limits to this authority. Directed towards the attainment of specifically defined goals, these rules might be said to be rational (after Weber's definition quoted above). The particular form of organisation that rational-legal authority produces, Weber argues, is that of bureaucracy.

With modernity and the ascendance of rational thought and action, Weber argues, bureaucracy became the dominant form of organisation, its structure providing 'technological superiority' over any other forms of organisation, a superiority that suited the developing industrial capitalist society. In particular, he felt that the bureaucratic model was essential for the effective functioning of the state and economic enterprises.

We will now look more closely at the bureaucratic model of organisation (or ideal type) towards which, Weber argued, organisations in modernity tended.

17.4.3 Weber's ideal type of bureaucracy

Weber identified a number of characteristics of an ideal type bureaucracy and these are summarised here:

1. Tasks required for the proper functioning of the organisation are defined as clearly separate areas of responsibility and each administrative official is designated one of these in which he/she specialises. For example, a hospital has different divisions – management, human resources, admissions, casualty, various medical wards, catering, maintenance, laundry, etc. Within each of these divisions, each official specialises in a particular area of responsibility.

2. The structure of the organisation is hierarchical. As every official is made accountable to the person immediately superior to him/her, for every person below him/her a chain of command and responsibility is established.

3. The functioning of the bureaucracy is governed by 'a consistent system of abstract rules' and 'the application of these rules to particular cases'.

4. These rules lay down rigid procedures for the carrying out of each task, clearly marking out the limits of the authority that the different officials hold and working from the basis that obedience to them comes from a belief that the rules are correct. With the rules enforcing strict discipline and control, little room is left for creativity, personal initiative or discretion.

5. The actions of the officials are rational, not affective, as they do not allow personal consideration and feelings to come in the way of their being governed by the rules.

6. Bureaucratic administration is characterised by the exercise of control based on knowledge (making it rational). For this reason, officials are appointed on the basis of what their technical knowledge and expertise can contribute towards the attainment of the goals of the organisation. Once an official is appointed, he/she is a full-time paid employee and his/her occupation constitutes a professional career. An official is promoted based on a number of factors, including time spent in a position and achievements in the job.

7. With bureaucratic administration, there is a strict separation between private and organisational life, and in particular private and organisational income. The official does not own any part of the organisation or any of its assets, nor does he/she use the organisation for personal gain.

Weber argues that this ideal type of bureaucracy is most closely approximated in industrial capitalist society, in which it has become the dominant form of organisation (Weber 1978: 956–1005).

Disadvantages of bureaucracy

Although Weber believed that bureaucracy was essential to the functioning of industrial societies, he also acknowledged some of its disadvantages.

Distinguishing between *substantive rationality* (understood as suggesting concern with 'the values and desired end of an action') and *formal rationality* (as being concerned with 'calculable techniques and procedures'), Weber (1978: 85) admits that bureaucracies themselves produce tendencies to undermine substantive rationality by focusing on technical rules and processes without much concern for the broader aims of organisations (formal rationality). However, he argues that there is a force that disciplines bureaucracies in capitalist societies in the form of the market. When an economic enterprise becomes inefficient, its profits start to decrease, with bankruptcy being experienced in some cases, forcing institutional restructuring (or 'rationalisation') through the elimination of operational units that no longer function in the interests of organisational efficiency.

Weber also spoke about bureaucracy as a potential 'iron cage' limiting human freedom. As a strict and rigid set of rules works to limit individual freedom, uniform and repetitive tasks forbid initiative, creativity and spontaneity. This produces 'specialists without spirit' who seldom see the relationship between their individual work and the rest of the organisation. In relation to the control of state bureaucracies, Weber highlighted that in times of crisis a bureaucratic leadership would be useless if left in control of the administration as bureaucrats are trained to follow orders and routines, not to make on-the-spot decisions in response to crises.

It was also in relation to the state bureaucracy that Weber showed particular concern that high-level bureaucrats could be bought over by the interests of rich capitalists to reshape their official practices to better meet the needs of capital. Weber believed that it was only through strong parliamentary control of the state bureaucracy that

such potential problems could be prevented. Such control should take the form of professional politicians holding high-level positions in the different state departments, for example by providing strong leadership and improving the accountability of organisations.

However, history provides us with many examples where politicians in such positions in the state bureaucracy abuse their power in enacting their leadership roles and ability to decide what is shared in the public realm to serve their personal interests. Weber also points out that in many cases professional politicians do not have sufficient technical knowledge to fulfil their responsibilities without the assistance of the bureaucrats who control access to such knowledge. Politicians therefore become dependent on the bureaucrats and their advice about decisions they need to make, often being directed by them. Very often, then, bureaucrats are able to exercise much control over their political 'bosses'.

Noting its limitations, Weber offers, as his only solution to some of the challenges raised by bureaucracy, the cultivation of a strong parliamentary government in control of state bureaucracy. For him, the answer lay in making state bureaucrats directly accountable to parliament for their actions by requiring them to report to a parliamentary committee on a regular basis. While bureaucracy was, for Weber, necessary for the greater development of industrial capitalist society, it also represented the potential for adverse consequences for human freedom.

17.4.4 Some critiques of Weber

'Dysfunctional consequences of bureaucracy' – Robert Merton (1910–2003)

Writing at the end of the 1950s, Robert Merton argues that certain characteristics of bureaucratic functioning might have **unintended consequences** for the organisation that do not work in its interests, often preventing its attainment of its set goals. He called these 'dysfunctional consequences'. Like Weber, he points to the problem of bureaucrats being unprepared for crisis situations (that the rules of the organisation do not address) and unwilling to go beyond the rules in such situations for fear of jeopardising their individual interests in making progress upwards through the organisational hierarchy (by demonstrating acceptance and adherence to the rules). He goes on to argue that such strict upholding of the rules can also lead to the bureaucrat making the rules an end in itself (rather than a means to an end of the organisation overall). In this way, the official regulations can become a hindrance to the meeting of the goals of the organisation.

Merton also highlights that Weber's emphasis on the need for bureaucrats to be impersonal may result in conflict between officials and the public in particular contexts. For example, sick patients might expect sympathetic interactions from hospital staff dealing with their admissions, yet come up against the opposite in their engagements with the administrative clerks who are occupying their positions in the bureaucracy of the hospital. In this manner, the goals of the hospital (to provide a comforting and healing service for the sick) are compromised as patients end up frustrated and upset with their treatment on their very admission to hospital.

Informal structure – Blau (1918–2002)

A critique that has often been raised of Weber's work on bureaucracy is that he focuses too heavily on the formal rules, processes and hierarchies of organisations with very little attention to the informal relations and unwritten laws that emerge within them (that often work in the interests of the meeting of the overall organisational goals). With his critics asserting that 'the unofficial' has often become part of the overall functioning of an organisation, the argument has been made that any discussion of the character and functioning of organisations must include an analysis of unofficial groups, practices and unwritten common laws, etc.

Blau's (1963) work on different kinds of administrative jobs is exemplary in showing the need for attention to be paid to informal networks of exchange at both the level of the sharing of ideas and at the level of practice. In his study of a group of law-enforcement agents in a Washington DC federal bureau, he observes that accepted rules were informally flouted in the interests of increasing the efficiency of the group. In this particular case, where agents were investigating whether standards of employment had been broken, the rules prohibited discussion of cases among colleagues (in order to protect the confidentiality of the records of companies), and stated explicitly that if any problems or challenges arose they should be taken to the supervisor. With individual agents fearing that they would not be looked at positively by seniors responsible for their promotion (based on an assessment of their work), Blau shows how they came together to share and discuss information, actively seeking the advice of their colleagues in direct contravention of the official rules. While the formal rules and regulations were not upheld, Blau argues, an

unofficial practice emerged that improved the efficiency of the agents and the bureau.

Through other studies, Blau (1974) illustrates further the importance of the informal in analyses of organisations. He argues that in all organisations, groups of workers form their own norms of engagement around their work that become a central part of the structure of the organisation. While management might succeed in increasing efficiency by monitoring the adherence to rules, it is impossible to be able to predict all potential problems in a particular organisation. These informal, unanticipated norms that emerge can either work for or against the interests of improving the efficiency of the organisation.

Degrees of bureaucratisation – Gouldner (1920–1980), Burns (1913–2001) and Stalker

The research of Gouldner (1954), and Burns and Stalker (1961) highlights problems with Weber's assertions that all modern organisations tend towards bureaucracy; that the advance of bureaucracy is inevitable; that all organisations necessarily direct themselves towards the meeting of clearly defined organisational goals; and that there are set forms into which organisations develop in the interests of meeting set goals.

In Gouldner's work on a gypsum plant in the US, he highlighted differences in social context that related to what he called 'degrees of bureaucratisation' in organisations. With the plant consisting of two distinct parts – a gypsum mine and a factory using gypsum to make wallboards – Gouldner observed a clear difference in the levels of bureaucratisation in each part. He established that the organisation was more fully developed and bureaucratic above ground than it was below ground and in the mine. He concluded from his close study of the structures and processes at play in both parts that a predefined set of rules was not suited to the unpredictable conditions that defined work in the mine while factory production demanded the kind of fixed and predetermined sets of rules that bureaucratic organisations provided. Strong informal networks of solidarity and support also emerged in the mine as a result of the dangers that workers were confronted with underground. Gouldner's study also shows how such networks sometimes facilitate and permit collective resistance to bureaucratisation through the experience of miners actively preventing a new manager from introducing stricter measures to enforce the formal rules and to eradicate any informal ways of operating.

Basing their arguments on a study of 20 English and Scottish firms (largely in the electronics industry), Burns and Stalker (1961) offer support for Gouldner's claim that the bureaucratic form of organisation lends itself best to situations in which routine and predictability are defining characteristics. They argue that the technical and commercial context in which most of the electronics firms emerge is highly unpredictable and continuously changing, suggesting that the bureaucratic model may not be the dominant form of organisation in the future. In an attempt to understand the nature of the organisations they were studying, Burns and Stalker (1961) developed two ideal types of organisation – 'mechanistic' and 'organic' – the former conforming largely to Weber's bureaucratic model. Organic organisations differ in that it did not have clearly defined areas of responsibility or a complex division of labour with an accompanying fixed hierarchy. This allowed for tasks to be shaped collectively through discussion and the taking on of problems as they arose rather than through the following of predetermined rules. The firms that they studied fell between these two poles.

In addition to showing that organisations differ in structure based on their specific tasks, responsibilities and context, Burns and Stalker's (1961) research showed that when organisations were faced with unstable and therefore unpredictable conditions, not all of them turned to organic forms of organisation, and many clung to their old mechanistic ways. They explain this as relating to the behaviour of individual members and the emergence of sectoral interests within an organisation.

First, organic systems demand greater commitment to the organisation from individuals, who no longer have a specific area of specialisation, but have to participate in the broader, general discussions and processes towards making the organisation work. Several senior managers refused to give up on mechanistic systems as they provided them with a security of knowledge that participation in the development of new approaches did not.

Secondly, Burns and Stalker (1961) point out that the goals of the organisations studied were often replaced by the interests of groups that emerged within them to compete for resources, organic systems being prevented from being established due to internal political battles. In this way, they show that how organisations develop and the forms they take do not follow any predetermined path, but are also subject to the internal political dynamics of an organisation and to individual aspirations as well as group interests and goals.

Robert Michels – 'The iron law of oligarchy'

While Weber's analysis of organisations focuses largely on the state and economic enterprises, his model of bureaucracy was also recognised (and studied) by other theorists in organisations seeking fundamental change in society and its dominant institutions. One such theorist was Robert Michels, an Italian sociologist (and a student of Weber), whose work of 1911 focused on European socialist parties and trade unions, in particular the German Socialist Party. While these organisations claimed to be democratically organised and to directly represent the interests of their members, Michels (1962) shows that in practice they did not come anywhere close to the perfect picture they painted. Running through his analysis of these organisations is the inability for any democratic practice to exist in society without any form of organisation. However, he contends that with organisation comes the inevitable emergence of a form of rule that works against the spirit of democracy.

While Michels (1962: 61) observes that 'democracy is inconceivable without organisation', he also points out that it is indeed organisation that eventually leads to the death of democratic practices within an organisation. What does he mean by this? Michels asks us to consider the nature of social interaction in large complex societies, in which, he argues, the formation of organisations is the only way for the majority of individuals to effectively express their desires and campaign in their interests. However, direct participation by large numbers of people in the decision making and everyday functioning of an organisation is impossible in practice (or would take impossible amounts of time and other resources to accomplish, making it inefficient and generally undesirable). For this reason, representative forms of democracy are introduced through which individual members delegate their responsibilities to elected or appointed representatives. However, according to Michels, even this system fails to ensure democratic participation.

He argues that once a representative system of 'democratic engagement' is set up in trade unions and political parties, fulltime officials and professional politicians are appointed to ensure that the goals of the organisation are met. As the necessity to fulfil administrative tasks grows, a bureaucracy invariably emerges. With the efficiency and effectiveness of the organisation requiring a specialised division of labour, a **hierarchy** emerges through which control from above is maintained, and room for democratic consultation and engagement narrows. As the administrative functions of the organisation increase with overall organisational growth, it becomes increasingly difficult for all members to understand all aspects of these functions, and those without specialist training and knowledge fall behind. In this manner, ordinary or 'rank and file' members tend to leave decisions to their leaders, and organisations start to be run by executive committees rather than the general membership. Hence the very structure established to facilitate individual expression and action within a collective results in the exclusion of people from decision making within that structure. Michels claims that organisations inevitably produce **oligarchy** – that is, rule by a small elite. In sociology, this is known as the 'iron law of oligarchy', and that all modern organisations inevitably produce bureaucracy, which results in the rule over an organisation by a small elite within it (Michels 1962: 50–51).

Michels does not see any possibility for representation of 'rank and file' members in a bureaucratic system of organisation. He argues that once a leadership is in place, it becomes preoccupied with maintaining its own power. Using the German Socialist Party as an example, Michels shows how the maintenance of the status and privileges that come with positions of leadership begins to take priority over the goals of the organisation, and preservation of the organisation becomes the *goal* rather than a *means* to the attainment of a more broadly defined set of goals. Conservatism also sets in as leaders become fearful of threatening their individual positions within an organisation by straying from the rules and the expected paths. In the Socialist Party, Michels argues, the commitment to the overthrow of the capitalist state retreated as leaders of the party became part of the national ruling elite through taking up positions in the existing political structure in the country (Michels 1962: 333–341).

Michels also shows how leaders cultivate and use certain skills that they develop as part of the positions they hold in the bureaucracy of organisations to maintain their positions of power. For example, they are able to control meetings, communication to the rank and file (through organisational media), the appointment of officials, and so on. At the same time, he believed that groups of people have the psychological need to be led, often resulting in the worship of leaders who are fashioned into cult figures. Often, as a result of such experiences of power, leaders begin to believe in their own greatness and make the organisation into a vehicle for the attainment of their own interests. Michels argues that they are often unable to distinguish between their own interests and the maintenance of the organisation (Michels 1962: 389–391).

17.4.5 Alternative approaches to organisation/s and bureaucracy

Weber's ideal type of bureaucracy has been used widely by other theorists. His ideal type has been applied to the study of social movement organisations, primarily through the work of Michels on trade unions and political parties. This has meant that much of the literature on social movements and their organising practices and organisations (usually seeking to effect change in society) has borrowed heavily from and/or tried to refute claims made in the Weberian tradition. In addition, as the nature of work has changed with the development of capitalist society, theories have emerged to understand new arrangements of social relations and aspects of production within workplaces. These arrangements often do not conform in their entirety to the bureaucratic model. While theories on social movements have tended to be produced in the sociology of collective action and change, those on formal organisations have been produced from within industrial sociology in an attempt to understand the continued functioning of capitalist society. Below is just an introduction to some of the thinking (through and against Weber) about different organisational forms in relation to the study of social movement organisations. We will not, however, have time in this chapter to look at the various ways in which organising practices within the capitalist firm and state administration have changed. These are areas for study further in your sociology degree.

Marxist thought and practice

On bureaucracy
Marxists argue that in a capitalist society, bureaucracy (primarily in the form of the state administration) exists to fulfil the interests of the ruling class or bourgeoisie – that is, those who own the forces of production. In a communist world, where ownership is collectivised and in which there are no classes, democratic institutions would ideally take the place of hierarchical structures designed to control. The tasks and responsibilities required for the proper functioning of society would be shared equally among all people and rotated such that no group would bear any particular burden.

As Marx and Engels put it:

When, in the course of development, class distinctions have disappeared, and all production has been concentrated in the hands of a vast association of the whole nation, the public power will lose its political character. Political power, properly so called, is merely the organised power of one class for oppressing another. If the proletariat during its contest with the bourgeoisie is compelled, by the force of circumstances, to organise itself as a class, if, by means of a revolution, it makes itself the ruling class, and, as such, sweeps away by force the old conditions of production, then it will, along with these conditions, have swept away the conditions for the existence of class antagonisms and of classes generally, and will thereby have abolished its own supremacy as a class. In place of the old bourgeois society, with its classes and class antagonisms, we shall have an association, in which the free development of each is the condition for the free development of all (Marx et al 1992).

(Excerpt from *The Communist Manifesto*, written by Karl Marx and Friedrich Engels in 1848.)

Marx and Engels looked to the participatory, collectivised forms of organising that characterised the Paris Commune, the system of administration established at municipal level by Parisian citizens involved in the rebellion against their own centralised hierarchy of command in 1871 in their imagining of the system to be produced in a communist society.

There has, however, been no easy path imagined (or practised) by Marxists from a society in which a bureaucratic state ensures its functioning to an ideal communist society. While Marx argued that a 'dictatorship of the proletariat' would be necessary in the transition from capitalist to communist society, he did not offer many concrete suggestions for what this might look like or how it might be constituted. This has meant that there has been much debate among Marxist thinkers about what form such a 'dictatorship of the proletariat' should take. Existing experiences of revolutions in which the organised working class has played a central role have also produced varied forms of administration, many of which have reproduced the bureaucratic model in some way.

In the case of the Soviet Union, for example, Lenin believed that the revolution of 1917 would usher in an era of state administration in which democratisation would be effected through the appointment of state administrators. These administrators could be recalled at any point. Their wages would be set at the level of any ordinary worker, and administrative tasks would be simplified to allow anyone with basic numeracy and literacy skills to perform them. This would allow almost every member of society the potential to be a part of the state administration. While Lenin believed in the possibility and necessity for mass participation in a system of state administration based on 'control and supervision by all', the experience of the USSR after 1917 (in particular under the reign of Stalin) does not demonstrate the disappearance of the state bureaucracy, but in fact its expansion over time. It is difficult to find cases in history

that illustrate the possibility for sustainable and large-scale non-bureaucratic, democratic forms of state administration.

On working-class movements and organisations for change
While Marx himself spent little time on the question of organisation, those who came after him have contributed to its theorisation along Marxist lines and continue to do so today. For Marx and Engels, the emergence of organised forms of working-class struggle were understood as a result of the structural conditions of capitalist society, with historical forces determining when the **contradictions** between the working class and the bourgeoisie were developed enough to produce the conditions conducive to revolution. A working-class revolution would produce the conditions for the establishment of new social relations that would not resemble the unequal and exploitative hierarchies that sustain capitalist society.

But Marx himself did not offer much in the way of defining what prevented revolutions from happening in particular contexts in spite of conditions being ripe for struggle or how it was that revolutions are actually made (ie the resources that go into the making of a revolution). Apart from a cursory discussion of 'false consciousness' as the reason behind the failure of revolutions to materialise in certain contexts, Marx spends little time thinking through the nuts and bolts of organised collective action. Since Marx there have been too many different theories that have been developed to discuss them properly in their entirety here. Instead, we will look very briefly at some of the main points of debate and disagreement that have characterised (and continue to mark) engagements between Marxists since Marx. These have related to questions of political consciousness, organisational forms and mechanisms of power.

In the years prior to the 1917 Russian Revolution, Lenin proposed the need for a **vanguard political party** to lead the workers' revolution. Noting that a majority of workers did not see their exploitation as a class and the need to struggle against it as a collective, Lenin argued that they possessed a 'narrow trade union consciousness' and needed to be guided towards a more collective, political consciousness or a 'working-class consciousness'. This guidance should, he believed, be provided by a small party of individuals possessing working-class consciousness who would also steer the working-class revolution in the form of a vanguard political party, a hierarchical form of organisation. There have been various adaptations of Lenin's theory of the vanguard by Marxist theorists since him, as well as debates with those who have disagreed with his approach. Within Marxist thought and practice, there are continuing differences in approach and often major debates between differing groups, not least in our own society.

Contemporary South African politics reflects the diversity of thinking in relation to the need for a political vanguard. For example, the South African Communist Party (SACP) views itself as a **vanguard** of communists working to lead those organised in the mass formations of the African National Congress (ANC) and the Congress of South African Trade Unions (COSATU). These three formations are in a political alliance with each other.

Vanguard political groups also exist within social movements to the left of the alliance. For example, the Socialist Group (SG) and Keep Left are two small political formations in Johannesburg that belonged to the Anti-Privatisation Forum (APF) in the period 2000–2012, operating to direct the work of the APF as organised vanguards of like-minded Trotskyist activists.

Some Marxists (eg those belonging to the Italian tradition of **autonomist Marxism**) disagree with the need for political vanguards, and argue strongly against the creation of hierarchies with regard to how consciousness and decision making are thought about and treated. They speak about the possibilities for 'self-valorisation' – that is, for members of the working class broadly (both inside and outside the factory) to govern themselves (without the need for leaders to speak on their behalf or to make decisions for them). Such thinkers call for more democratic practices to be shaped to facilitate the participation of the majority in the production of their collective and individual lives. In practice, *autonomist approaches* encourage forms of political organising that are horizontal, anti-bureaucratic and non-vanguardist.

Many **anarchists** also reject the need for vanguards, arguing that they are reproduced through authoritarian practices and entrench inequality through hierarchy. There have been various experiments by anarchists since the 19th century with horizontal forms of organising. Perhaps the most famous experience is that of the Industrial Workers of the World (IWW), more popularly known as 'the Wobblies'. The IWW was founded in Chicago in 1905 as one of the first industrial unions in the US and is known for its championing of 'rank and file leadership'. Administrative and leadership tasks and roles were rotated on a regular basis and there was no creation of a permanent leadership or bureaucracy. Ordinary workers took up different tasks, and collective responsibility for the life of the union was prioritised.

Today the IWW continues to organise workers across both industrial and non-industrial workplaces.

* Social Movements and Social Transformation
* Organisations, Power and Contentious Politics
* Globalism Activism, Networking Hope and Radical Change
* Collective Resistance and Uprisings in Africa and South Africa
* Contestations, Insurgency and Activism in Post-apartheid South Africa
* Evaluating South African Social Movements
* Researching Organisations and Social Movements
* Sociological Theorisation on Social Movements and Collective Organising

Box 17.2 Strike action

At a point in the massive strike wave across mining in South Africa 2012, involving between 80 000 and 100 000 mineworkers, these workers formed their own strike committees and rejected any trade union involvement.

QUESTIONS

1. Do the perspectives in this chapter account for this phenomenon?
2. If so, which of these theoretical perspectives best explain workers' actions?
3. Can you provide reasons for your answer?

What is clear is that non-bureaucratic, independent worker action has long been a feature of working-class struggles. As the experiences of working-class struggles and organising showed that particular configurations of structural conditions did not always produce the same kinds of responses from individuals and groups, questions began to be asked by Marxists about **agency** and **ideology**. In particular, the Italian Marxist, Antonio Gramsci, encouraged an approach that considered the place of culture in the making of consensus in society, and hence in collective action and social change. Gramsci (1971) argued that in a capitalist society, the dominant ideas are those of the ruling class. These ideas come to be held by all members of society (including the working class) as 'common sense' through the ways in which institutions, like the media, schools, universities and religious formations, function to produce this common sense. He used the word **hegemony** to refer to the ideas, values, beliefs and knowledge that come to be accepted as the norm (or as common sense) by the majority in society through a process of consensus building within and between classes and organisations. Working-class organisations should strive to build *counter-hegemony* – that is, consensus around acting against the ideas, beliefs, values and knowledge that dominate in defining and constructing the society we live in.

Gramsci (1971) made a distinction between two kinds of struggle:
1. *War of Manoeuvre* = physical attack on the coercive and administrative power of the state (in *political society*)
2. *War of Position* = a more gradual process of building consensus and coalitions to challenge ruling class hegemony (across civil society).

Since Gramsci, there have been others who have highlighted the need to explore the place of culture and other social aspects of structural processes and formations. For example, the work of the radical English historian, EP Thompson (1965), which emphasises the social nature of class, has been influential in producing a school of social historians whose work is dedicated to showing the centrality of cultural (and social) questions to the understanding of class relations and working-class struggles. In South Africa, a group of researchers working in the History Workshop at the University of the Witwatersrand in Johannesburg also took up the ideas of Thompson in their studies of different groups in South Africa's cities and countryside.

Non-Marxist approaches to social movements and organisations

As the experience of social movements and organisations grew in Europe and the US, greater theorisation began to happen about organised forms of collective action. While there are a number of different approaches for us to consider, we will sample just a few that have come to be recognised as schools within the study of social movements and collective action. Social movements continue the debates with Weber and Michels. They can be seen to emerge in the context of specific experiences of collective action and attempts to make sense of the specific character of shifts or changes in experience.

Collective behaviour and grievances theories

Until the 1960s, sociologists tended to think about social movements as existing outside the societal institutions accepted as normal, grouped under the sign 'collective

behaviour'. This could include anything from a rumour to a big party, a riot, a movement or a revolution.

For this group of theorists, individuals facing common problems come together to ensure that their common grievances are addressed, producing initially 'spontaneous' forms of collective action that might be sustained for longer periods of time necessitating more structured and formal organisation. The word 'spontaneous' is in scare quotes because not all sociologists agree with the analysis that any mass form of protest can happen without any organisation (even if on an informal level) as the word suggests should be the case.

Gustave Le Bon's and George Rude's work on the French Revolution are examples of such theorising that take two completely opposite views on riots and crowds as forms of collective action. For Le Bon (1896), riots must be viewed as the actions of 'mobs' or 'crowds' – that is, forms of collective behaviour in which the individual, by virtue of being part of a crowd, loses certain inhibitions and forms of rational engagement that he/she would otherwise have, and acts 'irrationally' together with others. For Rude (1959), however, it was important to understand the actions of the crowd as the result of rational individuals driven to act in certain ways together by their common circumstances.

Following Rude, Kornhauser (1959) highlights that some dysfunctional aspect of society can usually be apprehended behind each social group, movement or organisation that drives individuals to find ways to address it (and inevitably brings them together with others in the formation of a collective). Social movements and organisations emerge and exist, then, to correct some aspect of the overall social system that is not working in the interests of individuals across a part of the system.

Box 17.3 Service delivery protests

Social delivery protests have characterised South African society under democracy.

QUESTIONS
1. Are such collective social actions rational?
2. How do different theories explain social delivery protests?

Resource mobilisation theories

In the 1960s, scholars (many based in the US) began to focus more on the 'hows' of organisation and less on the 'whys'. The existence of common grievances was often not enough on its own to provoke collective action. Scholars wanted to understand what else was needed for movements and organisations to emerge, in particular in contexts where narrow self-interest often guided individual decisions and choices. The work of Olsen (1965) spurred others, like Zald, Garner and McCarthy (Zald & Garner 1966; McCarthy & Zald 1973; 1977), to think and write about what allowed organisations to emerge in spite of individual interest often determining how members of a collective worked. They turned to the resources available to people in enabling the creation and sustaining of particular forms of organisations.

In particular, McCarthy and Zald (1973; 1977) identified the industrial period of capitalist development as best suited to the mobilisation of resources for collective action in the form of professionalised social movement organisations which was defined above. They tried to understand the ways in which particular collective formations sustain themselves and operationalise their plans by focusing on their various mobilisations of different kinds of resources. This group of theorists map out various processes and steps in the building of an organisation and identify different ways in which resources, both internal and external to a collective, can be mobilised successfully.

While Zald and McCarthy played an important role in focusing research on the sphere of the actual functioning and internal makeup of an organisation or movement, they came under criticism for their neglect of the political sphere in which movements and organisations came to be formed. In the 1970s, Charles Tilly led the critique by highlighting a problem in their analysis of African-American social movements as being enabled to become more formal and professionalised social movement organisations (and therefore more successful) as a result of their being granted donor funding from elite groups. Tilly (1978) argues that a distinction has to be made between 'insiders' (like well-resourced lobby and advocacy groups) who are able to use their particular positions and knowledge of the system as members of entitled interest groups in society to intervene in the system on behalf of their own or others' interests, and 'challengers' (like the poor, black US groups) who are only able to exert pressure on the system through their collective acting against it in what Tilly calls 'contentious collective action' or 'contentious politics' (Tilly 1978).

McAdam (1982), Tarrow (1998) and others joined Tilly in fashioning a new theory of resource mobilisation called 'political opportunity' or 'political process' theory. This revised approach emphasised that it was the mobilisation of resources from within a group that sustained movements and organisations mobilised in critique of and in opposition to the accepted political institutions. It also highlighted

that collective action, social movements and organisations emerge in response to 'political opportunities and constraints' – that is, shifts in the political order that change the ways in which individuals can come together to try to effect change in their lives. Tarrow writes:

> By political opportunity structure, I refer to consistent – but not necessarily formal, permanent, or national – signals to social or political actors which either encourage or discourage them to use their internal resources to form social movements. My concept of political opportunity emphasises not only formal structures like state institutions, but the conflict and alliance structures which provide resources and oppose constraints external to the group (Tarrow 1998: 19–20).

We can try to understand this concept of political opportunity structure in relation to the South African experience before and after apartheid. Under apartheid the black majority were constrained in various ways to act collectively and politically. The political opportunity structure was such that it prevented black people from participation in the formal political system, and outlawed any form of collective political mobilisation. This resulted in particular forms of organising and imagination of politics among black South Africans. The political constraints against them forced black people into underground, clandestine, illegal, armed forms of protest and made transparent, participatory forms of democratic engagement among activists difficult. Since the 1990s, however, the political opportunity structure changed to facilitate the formal participation of black people in politics through electoral and other representative forms of democracy. This produced the conditions for greater party political mobilisation, as well as for organising in civil society formations and community structures. New kinds of movements and organising experiences emerged as a result of the ability for different and new kinds of mobilisations of resources among individuals.

Theories emphasising culture in relation to organising
Towards the end of the 1970s, theorists began to emphasise another aspect to organising that had not received much attention in work produced prior to this period – culture. When trying to analyse choices made by individuals in relation to their participation in movements and organisations, as well as the ways in which collectives choose to approach their role and actions in society, more attention was given to the influence of certain cultural aspects on the behaviour of

individuals in relation to organising and movements and the effects of this on collective action and organising.

Much like Gramsci and EP Thompson, theorists of social movements and collective action in the 1970s began to argue for greater attention to be paid to the meanings given by individuals within collectives to their actions. The reasons behind individuals choosing to engage in collective action and particular forms of political engagement were seen to relate to particular cultural aspects of their being in society. Religious differences, for instance, might explain the choice of a particular group affected by a problem to revolt and another similarly affected group not to do so.

Others theorists emphasised the importance of studying the ways in which collectives choose to 'frame' their issues and demands (ie how they choose to win sympathy and support for their cause from a broader audience) and how groups cohere and choose to identify publicly (ie around what identities and attributes groups of people choose to publicly define themselves). As experiences of collective action, social movements and organising grew to include those of people organising deliberately along lines of identity and cultural difference in the 1970s and 1980s, theories that emphasised culture grew in popularity during this period.

In trying to study organisations today, it is probably best to draw from each of the sets of theories above to best understand both the internal and external influences on movements and organisations, and the interrelatedness of political, economic and social questions in their exploration and analysis.

17.4.6 'Old' and 'new' forms of organisations

Thus far we have understood how the bureaucratic form has tended to characterise those organisations that are dominant in industrial, modern capitalist societies – nation-states, capitalist firms and companies, political parties and trade unions. We have also looked at some of the debates that emerged at the height of the period of industrial capitalism (eg in relation to bureaucracy and oligarchy) and political approaches (eg towards the state).

We will now look at another set of experiences and theories about social movement organisations (and social movements) that began at the end of the 1960s, many of which continued to speak to the ideas and experiences that came before (and that have been discussed above). In particular, the perceived failure of certain socialist and nationalist struggles (characterised by particular forms of organising common to both) to address the problems produced by capitalist and colonial administrations was

to ignite a renewed questioning of the different *forms* of organising and collective action.

'Old' and 'new' as conceptual categories

The distinction between 'old' and 'new' forms of organising appears first (and mostly) in studies of those movements and organisations seeking to effect change in the world. Wallerstein (2003) invented the term 'anti-systemic movements' to refer to collectives fighting for socialism (socialist movements), and those demanding the right to govern themselves as nation-states (nationalist movements). The primary examples that he gives of socialist movements are trade unions and socialist parties (which we have defined above as social movement organisations). Nationalist movements either fought to bring together different political units into a single national system (eg in Italy) or to break ties with or secede from oppressive political systems (eg in the colonies). He uses the word 'anti-systemic' because these are movements that demand a complete change in the system that governs society – that is, the capitalist system (Wallerstein 2003).

While nationalist and socialist movements are often seen in history to be pitted against each other, Wallerstein argues that they shared some common characteristics in the period 1850–1970. This makes them recognisable as a category of movements, particularly after the emergence of a new set of organising experiences (different in character) in the 1970s. These common characteristics include the following:

- Socialist and nationalist movements were bureaucratic in their organisational form.
- Socialist and nationalist movements adopted what is known as the 'two-stage theory' of revolution (ie to fight for control of the existing state apparatus and then to use it to transform society).
- Both these sets of movements struggled with the implementation of two-stage theory in practice, and had to face disagreement among members about this approach.

However, by the 1960s already, these movements and organisations that had come to dominate in the context of industrial capitalist society were being criticised for their failure to deliver systemic transformation in the interests of the majority. Critics spoke directly to the failure of bureaucratic forms of organising and two-stage theory in their analyses of the problems they were facing.

Wallerstein writes:

Once 'stage one' was completed, and they had come to power, their followers expected them to fulfil the promise of stage two: transforming the world. What they discovered, if they did not know it before, was that state power was more limited than they had thought. Each state was constrained by being part of an interstate system, in which no nation's sovereignty was absolute. The longer they stayed in office, the more they seemed to postpone the realisation of their promises; the cadres of a militant mobilising movement became the functionaries of a party in power. Their social positions were transformed and so, inevitably, were their individual psychologies...

Analysis of the world situation in the 1960s reveals these two kinds of movements [nationalist and socialist] looking more alike than ever. In most countries they had completed 'stage one' of the two-step strategy, having come to power practically everywhere. Communist parties ruled over a third of the world, from the Elbe to the Yalu; national liberation movements were in office in Asia and Africa, populist movements in Latin America and social democratic movements, or their cousins, in most of the pan-European world, at least on an alternating basis. They had not, however, transformed the world (Wallerstein 2003: 63).

From the end of the 1960s, we begin to see increasing criticism of these formations, and experimentation with different forms of organising and approaches to effecting social change. As groups began to experiment with less hierarchical models of organising and to question the centrality of the state to effecting change (as well as the two-stage approach in some cases), those organisations and movements conforming to the bureaucratic model described above came to be known as 'old'. 'New' came to refer to the growing number of formations that structured and co-ordinated their activities and relations differently from 'the old'. It is important to note that 'new' and 'old' refer to particular forms of organising and do not signify the particular moments in history (or time) at which formations emerge. This means that we can find both old and new forms of organising in society today. For example, the Congress of South African Trade Unions (COSATU) is an old social movement organisation by the definition provided by Wallerstein above. COSATU is bureaucratic in its structure, it is governed by the belief that control of the state is central to the transformation of society in the interests of the

working class, and it upholds a notion of two-stage theory. At the same time, we find formations like the TAC, which is characterised by some new forms of organising, as we will see below.

Many theorists highlight the year 1968 as holding particular significance for the questioning of the continued relevance of old forms of organising (bureaucratic; state-facing) and the birth of forms of experimentation with new forms of organising (non-hierarchical or less hierarchical; non state-facing or anti-state). In 1968, mass political protests resounded across the world. Most famous are the student and worker uprisings in France that produced mass stayaways for a period of three weeks, bringing the entire country to a standstill in May that year, as well as demonstrations in the US against the war against Vietnam. In these gatherings, activists fought against what they saw as the failures of bureaucratic forms of power in the form of the political party and trade union and the nation-state. They called for new forms of politics and organising that would actively seek to build less hierarchical and more democratic forms of engagement between and among large groups of people and to prevent unequal power relations from determining the character of social relations.

'New' forms of organising

Theorists (like Wallerstein) identify significant changes in the character of collectives or organised groups from the 1960s onwards. In particular, they categorise groups focusing on 'women's issues', gay rights, environmental activism, and the Black Power movement in the US as 'new social movements'. In our context, #RhodesMustFall and #FeesMustFall and, more broadly, #BlackLivesMatter fall into this category of 'new social movements, highlighting the following similarities among them (that mark them as different from the 'old social movements'):

- Unlike Wallerstein's anti-systemic movements, which target the entire social system for change, new social movements tend to focus on a single issue through which societal transformation is approached (eg women's oppression, racial inequality or environmental degradation).
- New social movements consciously experiment with forms of organising that attempt not to produce hierarchies and unequal power relations.
- New social movements tend to critique the role of the state in effecting transformation, seeking alternatives to social change that prioritise the role of actors other than the state.

- New social movements are often critical of any approach that speaks of a two-stage approach to addressing the particular problem they are fighting.

More recently, the terms 'new social movement' and 'new forms of organising' have emerged once again in relation to descriptions and discussions of movements and organisations making up the alter-globalisation (or anti-globalisation) movement.

Towards the end of the 1990s, an increasing number of movements and organisations began to emerge to fight against various effects of neoliberal policies across the world. Their presence was felt at both a local and global level, with local protests and forms of organising speaking at once to both local and global audiences, and global convergences beginning to characterise the growing movement. These separate experiences began to be spoken of as one through the label **anti-globalisation movement**, as their similarities began to be recognised, particularly in the mainstream media. The coming together of different but similar experiences of resistance in this global movement has also been referred to as 'a movement of movements'. This term signifies both a singularity of experience and purpose in relation to a commonly identified enemy (neoliberalism and its conductors) and difference with regard to imaginings of and approaches to the struggle against it and alternatives to it.

As more and more groups began to protest against the various effects of neoliberal policies all over the world, the mainstream media and commentators began to refer to them collectively as the anti-globalisation movement. While this term was initially embraced by the growing movement, over time activists from within began to question this label. They argued that although the movement was against corporate forms of globalisation (or neoliberal globalisation), there were also strong calls for and imaginings of a different kind of globalisation. There were certain aspects of globalisation, after all, that the movement had benefited from such as the internet and the ability to organise across national borders. They therefore called for the name 'alter-globalisation movement' to be used when referring to the collection of formations organising against neoliberal policies and their effects instead, signifying 'another' kind of globalisation different from that produced by neoliberalism.

Once again, in the struggles of these groups, organised formations conforming to old forms of organising came under criticism, with the bureaucratic, stagist approaches to transformation that prioritise the place of the nation-state being opposed by those wanting to experiment with less hierarchical and more creative forms of organising. In several cases, alternative forms of organising emerged, with varying levels of success for activists depending also on the ways in which they conceived of change.

Some of the experiences within the alter-globalisation movement that have come to be seen as constituting alternative forms of organising and politics include the Zapatistas in Mexico (self-organised indigenous communities); social movements and organisations of self-organised unemployed people in Argentina; movements and organisations of landless people in Brazil and Argentina; affinity groups in the US and Canada bringing friends together in targeted demonstrations against corporate capital and collective and communal living arrangements; and social centres in Italy.

Activists in the alter-globalisation movement have come to be known for their experimentation with forms of internal organising that try not to reproduce inequalities and hierarchies among activists. Forms of protest action have come to be known as **direct action** against corporate capital and the state. Forms of organising that facilitate **transnational communication** and coordination among activists and collectives have been developed, as well as forms of politics that think beyond, against and outside of the state and political parties.

Another important characteristic of many of the collectives making up the alter-globalisation movement relates to their conception of how an alternative to neoliberalism (and capitalism) should be fought for and what it would look like. These forms of mobilisation stand in stark contrast to the single vision that characterised the 'old' alternatives imagined and fought for by Wallerstein's anti-systemic movements. Many of the formations making up the alter-globalisation movement conceived of alternatives as being imagined, fought for and shaped in the process of struggle together with others involved in the struggle (ie without being predetermined or known before embarking on struggle). A popular slogan from the Zapatistas illustrates this thinking: 'Walking we ask questions'. This means that any alternative must be made in the process and experience of struggle (walking), a process characterised by uncertainty (we ask questions, not knowing the answers). This uncertainty is confronted collectively. This was a very different imagination of politics and organising from that of socialist parties and trade unions, whose members' participation in politics was characterised by the certainty of the correctness of the two-stage approach and what it would result in and produce. Within the alter-globalisation movement, then, were two very different imaginations of politics that sat side by side.

This can be seen clearly in the experience of the World Social Forum (WSF), a space of global convergence for the movement that began in 2001 in the city of Porto Alegre, Brazil. This forum stood in direct opposition to the meeting of the world's political and economic leaders in the World Economic Forum (WEF) in Davos, Switzerland. Since 2001, people involved in struggles against various effects of neoliberal policies have organised in both the 'old' and 'new' ways. A range of different forms of mobilisation and organisation can be identified – from direct action networks and neighbourhood collectives to political parties and trade unions, as well as non-governmental organisations (NGOs) and international donor organisations. These organisations have come together annually to declare their unity in opposition to neoliberalism and to share and discuss experiences and strategies as well as to develop joint and global campaigns and approaches to struggle. While the diversity and difference that characterise the WSF were initially celebrated by most, over time this became the subject of major conflict within the WSF between activists seen to be part of 'the old left' and those coming from new social movements and organisations. In particular, lines were divided around the conception of how an alternative to neo-liberalism (and capitalism) should be imagined and fought for. While activists from socialist parties and critics like Wallerstein began to argue for the WSF to develop a single manifesto spelling out a single conception of an alternative, others from experiences of new forms of organising rejected any moves towards the development of such a manifesto.

New social movements in South Africa

In South Africa, the term 'new social movement' has been used in relation to a set of struggles that emerged after 1994, beginning in 1998 with the formation of the TAC. As the ANC government began to implement various policy changes after 1996, differently affected groups of people (in particular the poor) began to come together and organise in their interests. For example, in fighting against the failure (and refusal in certain instances) of the state to deliver proper healthcare for people living with HIV/AIDS, people came together in various forms of protests to demand that this issue be taken seriously, resulting in the formation of TAC. TAC brought together seasoned activists from different parts of the liberation movement

and civil society with ordinary people living with HIV/AIDS in different forms of protest, including direct action, legal cases, marches and pickets. As the state enforced the duty of all citizens to pay for basic services (like water and electricity), other movements (like the Concerned Citizens Forum (CCF) in Durban and the Anti-Privatisation Forum (APF) in Johannesburg) were formed as residents who could not afford to pay for services had their water and electricity cut off. Like the TAC, the CCF and APF were formed by activists from within different organisations that made up the liberation movement as well as ordinary residents who were affected by the cut-offs. This can be said of most of the post-apartheid movements and organisations that have emerged. Analysts have argued, therefore, that while these movements certainly reflect an experimentation with new forms of organising, they were also strongly shaped and influenced by the individual and collective experience and knowledge of organising gained in old movements and organisations. Often, activists within these movements and organisations fought among themselves about whether to employ old forms of organising (such as formal, hierarchical decision-making structures) or to experiment with new forms (such as less formal coordinating structures that did not allow for hierarchies to emerge).

New social movements internationally

New forms of organising have also been present in the most recent cycle of protests that have been experienced in the form of the **Arab Spring** and the Occupy movement. In fact, some of the major lines of cleavage within the emergent movements have related to the need for formal, hierarchical organising structures versus more horizontal and less formal networks of communication and coordination; and the place of the state and forms of democracy in the new orders being shaped to fill the political vacuums left by recent deposition of leaders.

The term 'Arab Spring' refers to a series of mass uprisings that began in December 2010 in Tunisia, followed by Egypt, Libya, Syria and other countries across the Arab world, in which people demanded an end to authoritarian forms of rule and corrupt leadership.

The Occupy movement has come to consist of several groups around the world speaking out and acting against what they identify as undemocratic and unjust in contemporary economic and political practices and processes, beginning in December 2011 with a group of activists calling their demonstration in Zucotti Park, New York City, 'Occupy Wall Street'. As similar protests sprung up across the world, a common narrative began to emerge linking the different expressions of resistance from Egypt to the US under the banner of 'Occupy'.

Box 17.4 Organisations

QUESTIONS

1. Make a list of all the organisations you have come into contact with and/or have been a part of in your life.
2. In relation to each of them, ask whether you would have been able to accomplish whatever they assisted you to do without them.
3. Then identify the characteristics they share. Is there anything that distinguishes them from each other?
4. Finally, reflect on whether there was anything about them that frustrated you.

Your list might have included hospital, religious group, school, youth group, factory, company/business, political party, volunteer group/association, community group, NGO, university, sports club, trade union or any collective of people united in their interests and/or actions towards a common end.

In this chapter we looked at some of the differences between organisations and other collectives (like social movements), as well as at the differences between organisations. You will have seen how the range of theoretical perspectives and theories discussed has advanced the common sense understanding of what an organisation is – a formalised set of relations among a group of people in which there are certain shared interests and common aspirations supported by accepted rules and principles governing it.

Summary

- By now you should have a sense of what organisations are and how they are different from social movements.
- You should also understand the use of the term 'social movement organisations', and the relationship between social movements and organisations.
- You should be able to draw from a range of theories (developed in different contexts and in relation to various experiences) to analyse forms of organising and organisations over the development of capitalist society – from early industrial capitalist society to the contemporary – and have a sense of some of the debates that have emerged in relation to forms of organising and strategies for social change.

ARE YOU ON TRACK?

1. Return to the list of structures you put down as organisations in Box 17.4.
2. You should now be able to tell whether each one is an organisation or a social movement, or a social movement organisation.
3. You should also be able to explore the nature of each in terms of the various theories you have encountered in this chapter.
4. If you can also answer the following few questions, you are on track:
   a. Why do social movements occur?
   b. What are some of the theories that have emerged to explain how social movements develop over time?
   c. What is the relationship and difference between social movements and social movement organisations?
   d. What is 'bureaucracy' and why is it so important in the study of movements and organisations?
   e. What is 'the iron law of oligarchy'? How does it relate to Weber's ideas about bureaucracy?
   f. What does the distinction between 'new' and 'old' refer to when used in relation to social movements?

References

Blau PM. 1963. *The Dynamics of Bureaucracy*. Chicago, IL: University of Chicago Press.

Blau PM. 1974. *On the Nature of Organisations*. New York: John Wiley & Sons.

Burns T, Stalker GM. 1961. *The Management of Innovation*. London: Tavistock.

Gouldner A. 1954. *Patterns of Industrial Bureaucracy*. Glencoe: The Free Press.

Gramsci A. 1971. *Selections from the Prison Notebooks*. Hoare & Smith (eds and transl). New York: International Publishers.

Kornhauser W. 1959. *The Politics of Mass Society*. Glencoe: The Free Press.

Le Bon G. 1896. *The Crowd. A Study of the Popular Mind*. New York: The Macmillan Company.

Marx K, Engels F, Moore S, McLellan, D. 1992. *The Communist Manifesto*. Oxford: Oxford University Press.

McAdam D. 1982. *Political Process and the Development of Black Insurgency 1930–1970*. Chicago, IL: University of Chicago Press.

McCarthy J, Zald M. 1973. *The Trend of Social Movements in America: Professionalisation and Resource Mobilisation*. New Jersey: General Learning Press.

McCarthy J, Zald M. 1977. 'Resource mobilization and social movements: A partial theory'. *American Journal of Sociology*, 82: 1212–1241.

Merton RK. 1968. *Social Theory and Social Structure*. New York: The Free Press.

Michels R. 1962a. *Political Parties: A Sociological Study of the Oligarchical Tendencies of Modern Democracy*. Ohio: Crowell-Collier.

Michels R. 1962b. *Political Parties*. (transl Eden PC). New York: The Free Press.

Ndifuna Ukwazi (Dare to Know) – Treatment Action Campaign. [Online] Available at: http://nu.org.za/what-we-do/organisations-supported/treatment-action-campaign/ [Accessed 26 August 2013].

Olsen M. 1965.*The Logic of Collective Action: Public Goods and the Theory of Groups*. Cambridge, MA: Harvard University Press.

Piven FF, Cloward RA. 1977. *Poor People's Movements: Why They Succeed, How They Fail*. New York: Pantheon Books.

Rude G. 1959.*The Crowd in the French Revolution*. Oxford: Clarendon Press.

Tarrow S. 1998. *Power in Movement: Social Movements and Contentious Politics*. Cambridge: Cambridge University Press.

Thompson EP. 1965. *The Making of the English Working Class*. London: Victor Gollancz Ltd.

Tilly C. 1978. *From Mobilisation to Revolution*. New York: Random House.

Wallerstein I. 2003. 'New revolts against the system'. *New Agenda*, Fourth Quarter: 62–65.

Weber M. 1958. *The Protestant Ethic and the Spirit of Capitalism*. New York: Scribner's.

Weber M. 1978. *Economy and Society Volume II*. Roth & Wittich (eds). Berkeley: University of California Press.

Zald MN, Garner RA. 1966. 'Social movement organizations: Growth, decay and change'. *Social Forces*, 44: 327–341.

Media and technology

Chapter **18**

Grey Magaiza & Phephani Gumbi

The first mass media of newspapers, radio, television and cinema revolutionised society. Ever since, the permanent revolution in technology and communication accelerates daily. Fuelled by the increasing desire and need for information, it is not about to end. The full implications of the contemporary electronic and digitised age are still poorly understood. Our current capacity for communication, from individual self-expression, via the creation of virtual selves and mass social mobilisations, via SMS, WhatsApp, Facebook and Twitter, have made their own social and political revolutions. Their impact has been felt across the globe. Google and Facebook own their own advertising markets based on the personal information you, me and millions of others across the planet provide these Big Tech electronic giants. We are now their products. We are maximised for profit every time we share information about ourselves and reveal our interests online.

One implication is the need for a qualitative paradigm shift in what the classical sociological concept of social cohesion means, but which has yet to take shape. However social science is construed in the future, it must surely point back to the remarkable age in which we now live.

The very first sentence of this chapter succinctly lists the ways in which communication is currently commonly transmitted. The second sentence points to the diversity of global forms of communication. The third sentence neatly defines the media. You would do well to go through this chapter carefully in this way. It communicates much, as opposed to many fast forms of communication, because you can take it slowly and thoughtfully at your own pace. Like all of the chapters in this written and bound textual form of communicative media, there is a lot in this chapter. But it moves fast. No synopsis could do it justice. The information on the background to the media has all occurred in the past 20 years and hardly qualifies as 'history'. Only fairly recently have the mass and social media, for instance, been recognised as powerful agents of socialisation. By now you are all too familiar with the family, schooling and work as its main agents. Here and now socialisation is much more immediate. Exercising the sociological imagination – or a range of emerging decolonial imaginations – now becomes urgent if we want to find even a small measure of objective distance from the object of our sociological study – if that is still at all possible as we are part of the 'hyper-object' of surveillance capitalism. A 'hyper-object' envelopes and surrounds us but which is so close and so large we cannot see it in its entirety. The internet is a prime example, others being global warming, evolution and nuclear radiation.

In this chapter the application of the three classical perspectives suddenly has a different kind of conceptual quality and dense form of expression. The language has changed. It is very modern and contemporary as it struggles to conceptualise these new times in which we live. It is in and of the world of immediate contemporary experience. The names of the contemporary theories are ultra-modern and even postmodern: the 'hypodermic syringe' model, the 'inoculation' model, the 'two-step flow' and the cultural effects theory. Now you really do have to start thinking. Sociology is now a wave threatening to engulf you. You dare not stop reading fast just to keep up. You will just have to read it again more slowly. You will be asked to go and look up a whole range of new concepts used globally in the modern electronic mass media. And then you will need to speed up again and change your focus to the local – because how on earth does one understand the young, slay queens who live in the public glare through various social media platforms?

How do we understand this local, youthful sub-cultural social phenomenon which is global but has taken on a South African flavour? Alternatively, is American pop culture and the obsession with their celebrities going to smother Africanisation and the call for Africanism? These are some of the questions this chapter raises. The chapter hopefully propels you into the fastest moving area of study in which you can possibly engage.

Case study 18.1 Social media and you

'Have you been tweeted, blogged, YouTubed, Snapchatted, Instagrammed, Kindled, interacted, texted, sexted, crowdsourced and socially networked to the edge of your sanity?'

The writer of these opening words to his book, *Digitized Lives*, is really concerned about what the new media is doing 'to our brains, to our sex lives, to our parent-child interactions, to our politics, to our education system, to our identities as individuals and as community members (Reed 2019: xi).

From a University of Winchester and First Direct study, which identified different types of social media behaviour, can you identity yourself from the list below?

The Ultras

For many habitual social media users, the networks are their primary communications link to family and friends, so the enforced changes did, in some cases, make them feel isolated. Some felt the feelings of isolation from the first few days, while for others those feelings were triggered later in the experiment by missing out on information, or a conversation, that had taken place on their networks.

The Deniers

Deniers are those who maintain social media doesn't control their lives. They reckon they can easily live without it. The reality, however, is very different. Whenever they can't access their favourite network for an extended period, they become anxious and feel cut off from the rest of the world.

The Dippers

Although many signed up to Facebook or Twitter, not all are regular users. Dippers access their pages infrequently, often going days – or even weeks – without tweeting or posting an update.

The Virgins

Every day, new people are signing up to social networks. These virgins are taking their first tentative steps in social media. They can often struggle initially to get to grips with the workings of Facebook and Twitter, and until they build up their own networks of friends and followers, they may question why they've joined. The first couple of months will determine whether they go on to become ultras!

The Lurkers

Hiding in the shadows of cyberspace, they watch what others are saying on social networks but rarely (if ever) participate themselves. They will complain publicly about the 'mundane drivel' that is posted, and privately they worry they don't have anything interesting to say, but they keep an eye on others' conversations.

The Peacocks

A Peacock can be easily recognised on Facebook, Twitter and Instagram because they see social networks as an opportunity to show everyone just how popular they are. They judge their social standing on how many followers or fans they have, and the aim of each post or tweet is to secure as many 'likes' or re-tweets as possible.

(Source: *The Telegraph*, 11 April 2013)

1. Do you see yourself in any of these social media user characterisations?
2. Who has been left out of this list which is already 7 years old?
3. What forms of social media do you use?
4. Are there others that you are not using?
5. What do you use social media for?
6. Do you think social media has relevance in today's society?

Case study 18.2   The most viral video of all time?

KONY2012 The impact of new media on society

Early in 2012 a YouTube video called KONY2012 was uploaded by an organisation called Invisible Children in an attempt to raise global awareness about the so-called 'conflict-ridden' Uganda. It received unprecedented attention across the internet, thought by some to have been the most viral video of all time. Through the video the organisation hoped to spark international action by appealing to people across the globe, specifically those in resource rich Western countries. The intention was to help capture Joseph Kony the Leader of a group called the Lord's Resistance Army (LRA). The LRA is one of many groups said to be responsible for various atrocities in Uganda including the abduction of children to make them into child soldiers or sex slaves. In the 30 minute video, which was watched 50 million times in four days and received 2.5 million 'likes' on Facebook and six million tweets on Twitter, the group's leader urges Americans and the rest of the world to join forces and bring Joseph Kony to Justice by the end of 2012.

The video and the campaign, however, received much criticism, mostly from people in Uganda. The video is criticised for:
- an oversimplification of issues, especially in a region that has experienced fighting and conflict for over 20 years
- the charity's appeal for further US intervention in securing the arrest of Joseph Kony
- being 'naïve' in believing that raising awareness alone can solve complex problems
- suggesting that there is an expiry date for solving a political situation.

As of 2018 it appears little or nothing is known of Joseph Kony.

1. What do you think the role of the media is in a social crisis of this kind?
2. Do you think creating unprecedented media attention around an issue will galvanise society into action?
3. Do you have other examples of issues where the mass media was used to mobilise for action on an issue?

Key themes

- Sociological frameworks used to analyse mass and social media and technology in society using sociological perspectives
- The role of mass and social media in facilitating new ways of thinking about social, cultural and political arrangements and identities in South Africa today
- How the media and technology affect different individuals, groups and institutions in society

- Social media, social networks, cyber communities and surveillance in contemporary society
- Theoretical perspectives on media and society
- Social networks and communication culture in contemporary South African society

18.1   Introduction

'Whatever we know about our society, or indeed about the world in which we live, we know through the mass media', claims an intellectual giant of the 20th century, the systems theorist Miklas Luhmann (2000: 1). What, we might ask, does this mass media of newspapers, magazines, radio, television, film/movies, billboards, emails and the internet have in common? In short, they are all different ways in which information and news can be communicated to *large numbers of people who are dispersed globally* at the *same time*. Mass media can hence be defined as:

> … *[t]he institutions and techniques by which powerful, specialised social groups disseminate standardised commodities (in the form of symbolic content) to large heterogenous and geographically dispersed audiences.* (DMMA 2009)

The mass media is one of the most influential, visible social institutions of our time with an exceptionally powerful worldwide distribution and impact on the information-driven future of our globalised world. As long as a quarter of a century ago the prominent sociologist, Anthony Giddens (1990) persuasively argued that globalisation, even before the current state of our electronic media highway, represented the 'compression of time and space'. The immediacy of the media, which drills itself into our lives even if we try and ignore it, has resulted in the simultaneous spread of news and information to exceptionally large numbers of people over great distances. A consequence of globalisation and its accompanying technological innovations is that information is readily available globally in real time. Over 850 million people internationally watched the 2010 Soccer World Cup in South Africa. As Anthony Giddens' argued, the universalisation and liberalisation of time and space, has 'stretched' relationships between the local and the global and 'local happenings' are now 'shaped by events occurring many miles away and vice versa' (1990:63-65). With digital technology underlying globalisation, widespread changes such as the informalisation of the economy (Castells 2005) and the **virtual reality** of corporations beyond the reach of regulators (Sassen 2006) which accompany a new capitalism (Boltanski & Chiapello 2005) has taken place (see Kirkpatrick 2014).

The ability of the mass media to communicate the same message to many people over vast distances has far reaching implications. The mass media is a powerful agent of social change and reproduces its **cultural hegemony** in the way it spreads ideas and influences people.

In exploring the relationship between media and society, pertinent questions must include whether the media and technology are moulders or reflectors of social structures, and whether media are agents of social change and in what way, or reinforcers of the status quo (Glasser 1997; Rosengren 1981).

This chapter will explore different ways of understanding and experiencing this relation between the media and society.

18.2   The 'new' mass media

The internet is 30 years old in 2021, with access to information at the press of a button, yet only a century ago, information used to be a luxurious commodity. Limited communication and information, coupled with sluggish technological advancements, especially in transport, made the transmission of information very slow. Society had few newspapers and magazines which contained local and regional news, advertisements and some entertainment. Such media was only available in print form. However, as technological advancements occurred in print and with the invention of the telephone and television, media platforms combined with increased literacy levels in society. The reach of the *mass media* widened. The classic work of Daniel Bell (2004) argued that the growth from a pre-industrial society to a post-industrial one was due to the slow but successful transition focused on the importance of knowledge and information. In just over half a century, from modern computing in the 1960s and 1970s to the transformation of these technologies in the 1990s (Kirkpatrick 2014) coinciding with 'informational capitalism', these developments accelerated considerably. What Bell (2004) was emphasising, however, is what has been taken for granted all along: information is power. One consequence of this is that competition propelled information to become a powerful entity and a central globally available social resource (Bell 2004: 88).

In South Africa, the 20 daily newspapers and 27 major weekly newspapers has remained fairly stable over the past 25 years. The 440 consumer magazines are down from a highpoint of 690 in 2008, as are business-to-business publications which are also down from 775 in 2008 to 480 in 2018. Interestingly, community newspapers and magazines have grown from 475 in 2008 to 490 in 2018 as have the number of radio stations – from 135 in 2008 to 260 in 2018. This suggests a focus on local, community and regional networks along lines of language, class, ethnicity and race, representing a shift away from the dominance of centralised news media of the past. Yet, perhaps unsurprisingly, however, the number of television (linear channel) stations has shown the greatest growth – from 85 in 2008 to 300 in 2018 – with over 90 per cent of South Africans who participated in the poll to determine these figures saying they had watched television the day before the poll (SA Media Facts report for March 2018, OMD Media Direction). Currently low economic growth, however, is impacting negatively on this growth.

The same poll further estimated there are 31.3 million registered IP addresses of all types in South Africa today. As of January 2019, regarding internet connectivity, there are now 5.11 billion unique mobile internet users worldwide, up a 100 million since the year before, with 51 per cent of South Africans now connected, but which points to the 'digital divide' stratified across class and racial lines (VPUU 2019). This ever-widening divide, namely the gap in access to ICT and internet usage, it has been argued, has become 'one of the most crucial challenges of the 21st century' (Nxasana 2001, cited in Lesame 2005). For what it means to be a member of a digital society and what new notions, such as 'digital citizenship' mean, are by no means simple issues, though they are some of the burning ones of our time (see Lindgren 2017).

It is now a century ago that the media moved from a predominantly print medium to different media such as radio, later followed by television, which significantly also provided entertainment with its motion pictures. While figures change daily, the popular television programme, *Uzalo*, for instance, was watched by nearly 10 million South Africans, followed by the other popular television programmes *Generations: The Legacy*, *Skeem Saam*, *Scandal* and *Muvhango*.

What is clear is how the mass media plays a prominent role in South African society, providing us with news, information about various topics, education and entertainment. The mass media has become a vehicle for nation-building and democratic communication. While radio and television, which are more widely accessible than the internet – though *electronically connected* South Africans spend more time on the internet – these two media outlets have been ascribed multiple and often contradictory roles in the process of democratic transition and consolidation in South Africa. After the advent of democracy these media were important stages for symbolic representations of the 'rainbow' concept of 'One Nation, Many Cultures' (Barnett 1999), a notion which appears to have subsequently waned over the last decade.

In recent years social scientists have been questioning the effect of television and more recently the internet on its audiences, given the fact that it is so easily accessible

to people, particularly children. There are more questions than answers – and hence a huge area for sociological investigation. How does mass media consumption influence people's behaviour? Can mass media consumers and audiences be assumed to be *victims* – by simply taking on the messages the established media throw their way? While some approaches to media seem to implicitly assume this to be the case, another strong tradition of research into audiences has answered this question with a very strong: 'No!' Later in the chapter we will discuss various perspectives on the media and its effects on and relation to audiences. Before we tackle these theoretical issues or look at the media and technology in the 21st century, however, a brief overview of what preceded these developments is required.

18.3 The mass media and its colonial legacy

African society was, as is well known, artificially carved up by the European colonial powers in Berlin from the 1880s 'the scramble for Africa' – of which Thomas Packenham's history by that name is the definitive account (1991). Ethnic and linguistic groups became divided by artificial boundaries with little logic or shared history apart from that of the new colonial masters. With radio broadcasting first established in South Africa in 1920, by the end of the decade the BBC had set up the Empire Service across its colonies and by the end of the 1930s African personnel using indigenous languages were broadcasting religious services and music and entertainment took root. Similarly established in Francophone Africa, initially the express aim of radio broadcasting was to counter resistance by educated African elites to colonial rule, but which was to turn to preparing the way for independence in the 1950s, including using indigenous languages to communicate colonial perspectives, norms and values. With new political and economic orders established after the end of the decade, with political decolonisation mirroring the fractured African societies inherited from colonialism, modern Western-oriented elites would inherit post-colonial governments and come to control generally centralised government-operated mass media. Countries with a British colonial legacy, for instance, would have taken over broadcasting agencies modelled on the British Broadcasting Corporation (BBC) (Bourgault 1995). Liberation leaders, such as Jomo Kenyatta in Kenya, Kwame Nkrumah in Ghana, Nnamdi Azikiwe in Nigeria and Hastings Banda in Malawi, were quick to recognise the power of radio (Bourgault 1995). By the late 1960s, however, Louise Bourgault goes on to show, with widespread disappointment in post-liberation regimes, various means were found 'to curb media access' and which continued through to the 1990s in the 'vast majority' of African countries, at least in sub-Saharan Africa (1995: 75).

With changes sweeping the continent in the 1990s in the wake of the collapse of the Soviet Union, there is a general liberalisation of the airwaves. Private radio stations begin to appear, the African press and independent print journalism flourishes along with electoral freedoms while television in Sub-Saharan Africa becomes the means whereby political agendas are promoted, yet all of which – radio, the press and television – tend 'to be an elite and an urban phenomenon' (Bourgault 1995: 103). 'Rural Radio', in both Anglo and Francophone Africa, struggled to take root (Ilboudo 2000). In South Africa there have been major changes in the media since apartheid (Wasserman 2018). With rapid political and economic developments over the decade of the 1990s, 'continuity and change have characterised media and communication' with the media opening up to 'diverse and pluralistic interests' in the context of democratisation of our society (Moyo & Chuma 2010: 1) unlike under apartheid. In its dying days tough questions were asked about the future of media freedom under democracy (Mazwai et al 1991). In short, however, key to the 'project of modernity' (Giddens 1990) and how liberation movements only had the state – and its centralised media at their disposal to build new **post-colonial** (or **neo-colonial** regimes), industrialisation and modernisation, along with the mass media in Africa, has given way, it is clear, to the **information society** in an era of global interdependence (Bourgault 1995) and the **knowledge economy**.

18.4 The mass media in 21st century society

Digital technologies have extended the speed and reach of the mass media to global dimensions. Theorists now talk about 'online' and 'offline' communities and networks as 'we have the internet. We have smartphones. We have apps, social network services, blogs, and media sharing platforms' (Lindgren 2017:3). The internet has clearly been the most influential determinant affecting social interaction in our daily lives. Manuel Castells noted that the new 'Internet Society' is:

> ... a social structure built on networks. But not any kinds of networks, since social networks have been an important dimension of social life since the origins of humankind. The networks that characterize contemporary social organization are information networks powered by microelectronics-based

information technology ... The emerging pattern is one of self-directed networking ... it does not substitute for face-to-face sociability or for social participation. It adds to it.

Modern mass media has had a diverse impact on social interaction. There has been an uneven penetration of the global media into local cultures, as clearly shown by how, for instance, the 'different worlds' inhabited by African and white students, with Indian and coloured students positioned in between, 'powerfully structure preferences for global and local media' (Strelitz 2005: 103). In the same breath, developments are so rapid that it is 'axiomatic' that any update on 'the media will be out of date as soon as it is printed'! (Bourgault 1995). Within South Africa, the discourse on rights, especially those enshrined in the constitution, has been communicated through the media filtering to the general citizen, whether internet connected or not. For those with resources and connected on the empowered side of the digital divide, the increased use of chat rooms, for instance, has meant that distance and time are not key determinants of communication as the development of virtual communities has altered conventional face-to-face social interaction. The same can be said of smart phones which only partly bridge the digital divide, as teaching and learning during the Covid-19 lockdown showed all too clearly. The impact of these technologies is highly likely to increase in the future as, ever rapidly expanding, they alter our ability to communicate with one another locally, nationally and around the globe. Modern mass media are not only used for communicating information. The news and even entertainment raise complex, interconnected, global issues such as the many social and environmental problems of contemporary societies. It is becoming increasingly difficult to know whether social change is becoming more rapid or whether we simply have much readier access to news and events than ever before. Moreover, computers and the internet have revolutionised contemporary education with applications, for instance, such as WebCT and BlackBoard. The use of e-mail, online chat rooms and the creation of virtual communities have permanently altered our abilities to communicate and interact with others in our everyday lives.

The development of new mass media, such as the internet, has not, however, entirely replaced the need and uses of either print media or radio, although it has markedly shifted and in cases reduced print media in particular. Yet there are exceptions, such as noted above relating to community print media and local or regional radio linking networks of like-minded people across geographies.

In short, sociologists have tried to understand and analyse this phenomenon of the modern mass media.

Sociologists have an interest in the mass media for a number of reasons. These include how the mass media cultivates personal values, its role in cultural processes and the effects of the mass media on general behavioural patterns in society. To begin this brief discussion of how to think about the mass media, we will begin with a few simple questions:

Who owns the media in South Africa and globally? Do you think there is a link between media ownership and media content? Can South African society be described as a *mediated* society? How free is the media in South Africa? Do you wish you could sometimes speak, dress and behave like a celebrity? Do you think there is a **culture of consumption** in South Africa? If so, what drives this consumptive culture?

Such are the kinds of questions we need to pose to understand and explain the role of the media and its influence on society. In certain instances, contemporary sociological perspectives will be highlighted, but at the same time links with classical sociological theories will be illustrated.

18.5 Media ownership in South Africa

South Africa has a large mass media sector and is one of Africa's major media centres. The large daily newspapers are owned by a small clutch of media firms, which our theories seem to suggest must lead to pro-corporate bias. The major media owners are Media24, Independent News and Media, Avusa and the Caxton and CTP Group. In addition, the SABC, the public broadcaster, is funded by the government and this has implications for what freedom of speech and what it means to be a public broadcaster.

Press and other media freedoms have a chequered history in South Africa. While some sectors of the South African media openly criticised the apartheid system and the National Party government, they were hampered by various degrees of government censorship during the apartheid years. This was because of the strict licensing regime before democracy and the need to follow the party line or risk serious censure. For example, renowned journalist Donald Woods fled to exile in the United Kingdom after helping to expose the truth behind the philosopher and activist of Black Consciousness, Steve Biko.

The year 1994 ushered in a new democratic dispensation, which enacted a new constitution and a Bill of Rights. This guarantees that every citizen has the right to freedom of expression. This freedom includes freedom of the press and media; the freedom to receive or impart information or ideas; freedom of artistic creativity; academic freedom and freedom of scientific research.

These freedoms are generally respected in practice and our press is considered relatively free. Laws concerning the media and political control over its content are generally considered to be moderate and there is little evidence of repressive measures against journalists. There have, however, been criticisms of certain aspects of the freedom of the press in South Africa (Pillay 2011; Duncan 2011; Skinner 2011). Is the mass media as manipulative and controlling and thus hegemonic as the analyses just presented might suggest?

18.6 Theories of the media and theories of society

Attentive readers of this chapter may have noted and asked themselves the question why its title is 'Media and Technology' while up until now the term 'mass media' has been used. This has to do with the close relation between the media and society. The 'new media' in the late 19th and early 20th centuries – the popular press, radio, television and the cinema and recording industry – for the first time, enabled communication with the general citizenry – or 'the masses'. This new media, powered by technologies which enabled them, changed society. In a relatively short period of time large numbers of people could be reached and had access to the news and entertainment as never before. The assumption was that the new media addressed an undifferentiated mass of people. They would be served by the new media technologies and the mass media. The educated political and economic elite would, however, come to use the mass media to communicate their ideas, norms, morals and values to the masses. In other words, behind the idea of the *mass media* lay a *theory of mass society*, namely one which was divided into the elite and the masses. This influential theory of society – argued as late as the 1960s to have been the most influential theory of society in the Western world (see Bell 1960, cited by Bennett 1982) – has determined the way we have looked at the media, its role and even how we ask questions about the media – or mass media, the term which, despite criticisms of mass society and its cognate terms, 'mass culture' and 'the culture industry', has continued to remain in use (see Adorno 2001).

The big question which arose in scholarly debate in the North Americas and Europe was from what perspective the media, or mass media, was to be viewed. The answer on both sides of the debate related to the *theory of society* underpinning two very different perspectives. Firstly, inspired by Marxist materialism, critics of urbanisation and industrialisation and the emergence of the mass media, pointed to how the media, via ideological control of the masses, *served elite interests*. Then, inspired by pluralist liberal political philosophies, American 'mainstream' approaches, held that general consensus underpinned society and that the mass media simply *reflected* the competing interests in society. For the conflict theorists, the mass media are powerful instruments aiding the maintenance of minority social class interests. For the political liberals, the mass media are important instruments functional for maintaining pre-existing shared norms and values in society (Hall 1982).

It is within these two starkly contrasting views of both society and the media that all subsequent theorising has taken place. Needless to say, the very character of the mass media is intimately related to the technologies which underlie it.

18.6.1 Functionalist theory

Functionalist perspectives continue to provide the basis for the 'mainstream' understanding of the mass media, despite their decline in the 1960s along with the challenge to functionalist thinking. Functionalist theorists assert that each aspect of society is interdependent and contributes to the consensual functioning of society as a whole. Emile Durkheim, Robert Merton and Talcott Parsons are the most prominent sociologists to whose work this approach can be traced. Functionalist perspectives regarding the media focus on the *purposes* or *functions* of the media in society. Despite the remarkable advance in communications and forms of media with which we are all too familiar, the very early functionalist approach of Laswell (1948) retains its useful *descriptive role* by identifying four basic functions of communication via the mass media in society, but which have been somewhat adapted here. These functions are:

- Surveying the environment for news and information – the *surveillance* function
- Monitoring social responses – the *interpretation* or *editorial* function
- Entertainment – the *diversion* function
- Transmission of culture – the *socialisation* function

Before looking at how Laslow described these four functions, we need to briefly update the technological and accompanying terminological shifts in the first function he identified seventy years ago, namely that of *surveillance*.

Surveillance and the surveillance function

It has been claimed that 'The Internet is the *greatest surveillance device ever invented* (Reed 2019) (emphasis in original). New concepts have been coined to describe this device of our new **digital culture**. Internet service providers and search engines such as Google and Yahoo and social media sites such as Twitter, Instagram and most controversially, Facebook, have employed what has become known as **dataveillance**, namely data as surveillance (see Reed 2019: 78).

As suggested in the opening case study to this chapter, you have probably received unsolicited information on your smartphone, tablet or laptop advertisements or information specifically tailored to your own interests of news on topics which you have searched or sites you have visited. Your data has been kept under *dataveillance*. **Data mining** of your personal preferences and official information, posts you thought had been limited by your own 'privacy' settings and communications with your virtual friends *can and have been used* by a range of different institutional agencies. Theorists and media studies researchers have shown that data mining can fall into a number of categories.

- Interpersonal surveillance – 'spying' on each other
- Institutional surveillance – universities and employers 'watch over us'
- Market surveillance – businesses spy on customers, especially regarding personal preferences expressed online
- Government surveillance – authorities can spy extensively on our activities and even what we might discuss we are going to do (Trotter 2012, cited in Reed 2019: 79)

In addition to these forms of surveillance, the phenomenon of 'redlining', to exclude certain groups has now been broadened and the term 'updated' to **weblining** or '**data profiling**'. Such forms of surveillance are seen as major invasions of privacy which has developed to the extent, it has been reported, that Facebook was 'even working on apps that utilise the cameras on your smartphones and laptops to gain information on you by *reading your facial expressions*'! (Silver 2017, cited in Reed 2019: 85) (emphasis added).

Beyond how technology users are being monitored via the use of our electronic devices, in today's society, media disseminators such as journalists, TV stations, bloggers and newspapers have a presence all over the world. These individuals guarantee a flow of information and news to the public about events occurring within and outside the country. The news is distributed to everyone who has access to the mass media, thus, somewhat more positively, stimulating a form of egalitarianism. This is what the surveillance function of the media does and is hence a description of it. Note how this functionalist theoretically oriented formulation has recognised that the effects of the mass media are not evenly distributed.

We can break the surveillance function into two key forms: the *warning surveillance* and the *instrumental surveillance* (Aggarwal & Gupta 2001). The warning surveillance includes those moments when the media informs us about threats. This may include the threat of disease, changes in weather patterns and wars. When the Covid-19 was spreading globally, for instance, the media in South Africa warned the public by distributing information about the symptoms and communicated information regarding simple preventative measures. This kind of warning surveillance function helped manage the potential pandemic locally.

The instrumental surveillance function transmits information that is useful and helpful for everyday living. Such useful information includes information on stock prices, latest fashion, and new products among others. Such information would serve different interest groups in society, thereby playing its socially integrative regulatory role. We will see how conflict theorists consider this to be ideological. Aggarwal and Gupta (2001), however, argue that not all examples of surveillance occur in traditional news media or represent the role of the elites as conflict theorists would argue. Instead, even local soap operas might perform an instrumental function by portraying new fashions and hairstyles, ways of behaviour as well as glamorising celebrity status. There are also added functions associated with the surveillance role of the media. These include enhancing social control on society by placing deviant behaviour in the public arena. In South Africa 'corrective rapes' against lesbian women have been drawn to the public's attention as a consequence of media reports. The media attention on any form of sexual violence has created some, though by no means sufficient, awareness against sexual violence which people have been encouraged to report. While these are all positive functions, surveillance through mass communication has proven to result in dysfunctional aspects for society. Invasion of the privacy of the individual has, for instance, proven to be of significant concern.

Further, living in an era of **post-truth** and **fake news**, poorly and purposively incorrect or false information is harmful for society. The current drive by the World Health Organisation to encourage male circumcision as an HIV preventative measure, for example, has not yielded expected results in some African countries. This is because some circumcised males stopped using condoms and other preventative measures thinking that circumcision was enough to protect them against the HI virus.

Whether positive or negative, this all amounts to the process of the *normalisation of surveillance* and the invasion of privacy, a trend the media watcher, TV Reed, thinks is probably unstoppable as the data about us as individuals, the key commodified product of the Big Tech companies, simply continues to increase (see Bennett et al 2014).

The interpretation or editorial function

The interpretation function is closely related to the surveillance function. Mass media communication clearly has undesirable and unintended social consequences. This is recognised by the Big Tech and other mass media companies. It is hence important for the media to evaluate and interpret events in order to respond to readers, viewers and listeners. When the price of petrol goes up in South Africa, for example, it is important for those in control or managing the mass media to analyse the significance of this for a variety of stakeholders: the petrol industry, the transport industry, commuters, vehicle owners, businesses and ultimately the economy as a whole. An interpretation function serves to collate all the viewpoints around the different interests and meanings attached to and the significance of a petrol price hike. This will give the consumer of media, you and me, access to viewpoints other than we would get through our interpersonal contacts – at least those of us living under democratic regimes. Many analytical articles, radio and TV documentaries and panel discussions on an event or issue also perform this function. This enables an individual in society to evaluate an issue and arrive at a (relatively) informed decision – where there is at least some real or even a nominal tradition of media freedom.

The interpretation function is not, however, immune from criticism. Sometimes, depending on the issue, people may not be served with a sufficiently in-depth or accurate picture of events being reported. Is or can the full cost of corruption by high level government officials be exposed to public view? How can the interpretation function be performed without risk of breaking other laws such as confidentiality? What happens when the laws regulating the media change as a result of a successful exposé of highly placed individuals or government misrule? An added critical issue regarding the interpretation or editorial function of the mass media is that people can become passive by relying too heavily or uncritically on the media analysis and consequently do not (or cannot) develop their own independent critical faculties.

Box 18.1 So you thought you were a *digital native* and not a *digital immigrant*?

How many of these terms can you define? Check them out!

- Affinity portals
- Augmented reality
- Bots
- Brain computer interfaces
- Cyberbullying
- Cyberfeminisms
- Cyberghettos
- Cyberstalking
- Cyberterrorism
- Cybertypes
- Cyborgs
- Default identity

- Default subject position
- Digital civil disobedience
- Digital humanities
- Electronic civil disobedience
- Ethnic portals
- Fake news
- Green computing
- Locative media
- Massive open online courses (MOOCs)
- Massively multiplayer online role-playing game (MMORPG)

- Mesh media networks
- Microserfs
- Militainment
- Netroots activism
- Post-truth
- Prosuming
- Robot apocalypse
- Slacktivism
- Slow technology movement
- Technological imagery
- Wikidentities

(See Reed *Digitized Lives* 2019)

The entertainment function

Most of us are probably passive consumers of entertainment precisely because we want to relax and perhaps switch off our active, overly busy and critical minds and simply be entertained. Reaching for the remote and putting on the TV set to watch a game of sport is less wearisome than playing it in the field. Highly personalised entertainment, like console and computer games, has become so endemic that the result for many individuals has been a withdrawal from the public sphere into *private life*. We create alternative, 'safe' and impersonal and distant associations with others – if we can afford it! The entertainment function of the media cannot be separated from this significant social change occurring in contemporary society. As people get more leisure time, they tend to fill up the spare time with entertainment. Furthermore, as developments in technology facilitate easy access to technologically inspired entertainment innovations, a whole new market and culture has developed. This has made entertainment a sought-after commodity. In traditional societies, entertainment could not be separated from the primary socialisation of children. This function was fulfilled by interpersonal communication including storytelling, folk songs and folk dances (Aggarwal & Gupta 2001). In today's society however, the mass media has made entertainment available to large numbers of people at low cost. This form of entertainment is in many respects impersonal, but also connects people. Within the music industry, for example, artists have become global icons capable of influencing attitudes and behaviours of millions of people at any single moment. You may want to ask whether the mass production of entertainment has improved the quality of its content! Aggarwal and Gupta (2001) argue that while entertainment appeals to a mass audience, the media content accompanying it often appeals to the lowest common denominator of taste.

The socialisation function

The media transmits values which socialise individuals into socially acceptable ways and forms of behaviour. This transmission of values, the socialisation function theorists argue, results in the emergence of common values and therefore creates common bonds between people. On the other hand, the kinds of values and cultural information portrayed are selected by media organisations to reflect the values and behaviours that encourage the status quo (Dominick nd). In fact, the values that are being transmitted through the media may not be neutral values. Over two decades ago, the often well-thumbed copies of a well-known South African Sociology textbook, Popenoe, Cunningham and Boult (1998), noted how film and television industry story lines promoted law and order in our society. This continues today as any glance at contemporary films and crime dramas will attest. Have you ever noticed how the 'bad guy' is always caught? The media must portray the law as superior and therefore serve the function of maintaining social order. Do you ever wonder why there is no 'getting away with murder' in the movies? Having the media as **agents of socialisation** often results in individuals seeking role-models from television and movies. As noted above, socialisation via the media can be both functional and dysfunctional for society and will affect different social groups in different ways.

The functionalist perspective is indeed one of the oldest theoretical traditions in sociology. Functionalists consider the media as contributing to societal stability by creating a common consensus. This common consensus, achieved through the various media programmes, functionalists argue, is essential for order in society. It creates a kind of predictability. Functionalists explain the media in terms of its cohesive functions within an interconnected, socio-cultural system. One of the big criticisms against classical forms of functionalism, as you know, is its failure to account for social conflict.

18.6.2 Conflict theory
No reminders are needed that conflict theorists, whether Marxists or not, emphasise power and struggle between social classes over resources as key determinants of social change. While you now know well that functionalists focus on order and consensus as the basis for social stability, conflict theorists assert that order stems from domination of a social class or elite in the social system. Domination, also a Weberian formulation as you also by now well know, occurs when one class exercises control over the means of cultural and moral production – the production of ideas, beliefs, values and norms which constitute the **dominant ideology**. The classic formulation was that of Marx and Engels:

The ideas of the ruling class are in every epoch the ruling ideas: i.e. the class which is the ruling material force is, at the same time, its ruling intellectual force.

So how does this relate to the media? Media are part of a cultural industry that functions to mask the exploitative and oppressive character of capitalist society. The role of media is to distract and pacify people by feeding those standardised images and messages which stifle capacity for independent and critical thought. The conflict theorists, therefore, view the media as a tool of domination used to control others in society by reproducing the *dominant ideology* that maintains the status quo. Conflict theorists thus stress that the media communicates symbols consistent with the interests of the dominant classes. In fact, the media is seen as an extension of the **repressive apparatus** that leaves the audience with limited access to alternative meaning systems that would enable them to reject the

definitions offered by the media in favour of consistently oppositional definitions. While the above statements lay the basic principles for a conflict analysis of the media, there are, however, three critical approaches that underlie an analysis of the media as informed by the conflict perspective: *the manipulative, control of the media* and *hegemonic models.*

The manipulative model
The manipulative model argues that the mass media corporate owners, some directed by high-profile, powerful individuals, purposefully manipulate mass media content to determine how the audience will receive it. There are various techniques used to manipulate media content, including the use of logical fallacies and propaganda techniques. The manipulative model perceives the audience to be passive recipients of information. During the holocaust in Nazi Germany, Hitler used both techniques to great effect in his quest to exterminate the Jews. Many whites in South Africa say they did now know of the excesses of the apartheid state, dominated, as it was, by a centrally controlled, restricted and censored mass media. Are they justified in this belief?

Other manipulative tactics include ensuring journalists follow official editorial policy. This usually means that stories are structured to suit editorial policy. This can be further linked to the employment policies for media practitioners who are required to practise considerable self-censorship to maintain the status quo favouring capitalists and the ruling class who own media establishments – even if the individual journalists do not agree with the dominant ideology. In pre-1994 South Africa, needless to say, government censorship ensured that the media 'towed the line' in terms of the apartheid government's policies (DMMA 2009). More broadly and as noted, movies and other forms of popular culture encourage consumers of media products to side with the forces of law and order or a particular 'line' – usually that of government and the establishment. According to this stance, the mass media, therefore, functions to produce a generalised cross-class popular *false consciousness*. Media products become monolithic transmitters of ruling class values, which ignores any diversity of values within the media or the possibility of oppositional readings by media audiences. While much has changed under democracy in South Africa, the mass media continues to exercise powerful effects on its audiences to generate attitudes which are both uncritical and supportive of the capitalist status quo.

Control of the media model

This model is related to the manipulative model. Media proprietors use the media to entrench their own views throughout society. In South Africa, according to the Digital Media and Marketing Association (DMMA) report of 2009, media ownership is regulated by Independent Communications Authority of South Africa (ICASA) licencing regulations. These require applications for broadcasting licences to indicate ownership and control at both shareholding and management levels. For example, the primary shareholder for the South African Broadcasting Corporation (SABC) is the government, while eTV and DStv have more private shareholding arrangements. If a news agency is government owned, it is usually expected to report in the **public interest**.

The concept of public interest is highly controversial because it has multiple meanings. With regard to the media, in most instances the public interest usually means protecting the interests of the elite and powerful. This also ties in with the notion of media freedom – another contested concept! While the media may not have an extended responsibility to the audience, the same cannot be said of shareholders and other media owners. The mass media, entangled with significant corporate financial interests, always has particular interests to pursue and these are predominantly commercial. For the primary purpose of the existence of any business is to survive – and the media survive chiefly through advertising revenues and other sponsored programmes.

Box 18.2

QUESTIONS

1. Have you noticed any differences in the news presented by the SABC and eTV?
   If so, why do you think this is the case?
2. Do you think 'the media' in South Africa is free?
   Is the reporting objective?
3. Who owns the media in South Africa?
   ANC cadres complain they do not have its own newspaper
4. Draw a mind map of the issues implicated in this statement!

The hegemonic model

The term **hegemony** was used by the Italian Marxist Antonio Gramsci to describe how the dominance of a ruling class is maintained over civil society by the continual re-establishment of its cultural legitimacy through various forms of ideological persuasion. Applied to our context here, the concept entails that bourgeois hegemony of the media does not need to deliberately manipulate audiences. The reason for this is that the persuasive power and exercise of hegemonic control, via intellectual, moral and ideological means, represents not only political and economic control, but also the ability of the dominant class to project its own way of seeing the world. Even at the most superficial, yet immediate level, have you ever noticed just how similar many media practitioners are? They usually have a college education, professional media qualification and a middle-class outlook on life. The news is usually interpreted according to the world view of the front-line person presenting it. Such news presentations are encoded in the language, camera shots and how interviews are conducted. This common background of journalists means that a similar message is transmitted – no matter what the medium and despite the apparent variety of institutions in the press and publishing media. The continuous consumption of media products results in society accepting the situation as 'common sense' and 'natural'. Common sense, suggests Geoffrey Nowell-Smith, is 'the way a subordinate class lives its subordination' (cited in Alvarado & Boyd-Barrett 1992: 51). Gramsci noted that 'common sense is not something rigid and immobile, but is continually transforming itself' (Gramsci, cited in Hall 1982: 73). As John Fiske (1992: 291) puts it:

> Consent must be constantly won and rewon, for people's material social experience constantly reminds them of the disadvantages of subordination and thus poses a threat to the dominant class ... Hegemony ... posits a constant contradiction between ideology and the social experience of the subordinate that makes this interface into an inevitable site of ideological struggle.

A focus on the mass media in terms of an ideological site of struggle is pervasive in the analysis of those influenced by this approach. So, what does this all mean in light of what we are discussing now? In simple terms, the hegemonic theory of the media stresses that the media does not deliberately manipulate audiences but strives to perpetuate the existing social class arrangements by persuasively presenting and interpreting the views of the ruling class. As you will see in some of the practical examples, the ruling class tends to have strong views when it comes to race, gender and class which are broadcast through the media. Theories based on the concept of hegemonic, however, gives agency to the audiences. This theoretical perspective does not regard audiences, ourselves in other words, as passive, but as receivers endowed with the capacity to interpret messages in various ways.

18.7 Feminist theories of the media

You probably need to quickly rehearse the varieties of feminist thought in this textbook. Not to be too simplistic, feminist thought generally considers a gender divide whereby men oppress women and weaker men, but which especially disadvantages women. Strong on the agency of the individual, considerable work has been done on how women's structurally socialised oppression often contributes, even by women themselves, to the common negative stereotypes of the position of women in society. Although feminist theorists agree on the need to improve the position of women in society, there is much disagreement on how to proceed to tackle gender oppression. This has resulted in many variants of feminist theory which provide for critically rethinking analyses of the intersection of media and society. This section of the chapter will, however, only focus on a general discussion of feminist strands and their position regarding the media.

Elizabeth Meehan (1983), in an analysis of representations of women in popular culture, argued that the way women are presented in films and movies is likely to be an extension of women's caring, nurturing roles or focus on their appearance and sexual attractiveness. Women are often stereotypically portrayed as playing passive, submissive and dependent roles. The concept of sexual objectification and, in particular, the objectification of women, is of fundamental importance to feminist theory. Feminists rightly regard sexual objectification as objectionable and which plays an important role in gender inequality. Such gender representation is, again correctly, seen to be a natural carryover from the institution of patriarchy. The roles of women as cleaners, care givers and even sexual objects are, under **patriarchy**, deemed to be natural and representative of social reality. The media is thus hypothesised to fulfil the structural needs of a patriarchal and capitalist society by reinforcing gender differences and inequalities (Van Zoonen 1994). Many studies of gender representations are grounded on the assumption that the mass media contributes to systems of representation that contribute to ideological processes and social constructions. Patriarchal ideology distorts reality and supports male dominance. Mass media in all its forms, whether television, radio, the internet and the press, are not solely a source of information. Mass media also plays an important role in shaping our attitudes, beliefs and behaviours towards the social issues, society and our

self-perception (Henslin 2008). The various forms of mass media socialise us and inform public opinion in gendered ways. In short, our social perceptions and stereotypes about not only gender, but race, culture, class and disability have been influenced by how key institutions are portrayed in the media. This comes through to us via gendered portrayals of the institutions of the family, education, religion, the economy and government on television, magazines and internet (Hickey 2005).

18.8 Pluralist perspectives on the media

The defining characteristic of pluralist theories is the assumption of their overarching democratic credentials. It has been argued, for instance, that democracy and freedom of speech are the necessary means to protecting political pluralism – the expression of many views and interests in society. (Keane 1992, cited in Karppinen 2013). Political pluralism begins from the view that political power in society is divided among a wide variety of political parties and pressure groups representing different interests. While disagreements may emerge from time to time, pluralists say that these are resolved through existing political institutions without need for radical structural political transformation in a socialist or authoritarian mould.

South Africa is widely touted to boast a most progressive constitution that allows redress for aggrieved individuals and communities. In the context of the media, pluralist perspectives imply that the media consists of multiple role players with different interests. Unlike the conflict theorists discussed earlier, who assume that the ruling class shapes and controls media content to reproduce subordinate-dominant relationships, pluralists do not hold believe in the existence of a dominant ruling class. Pluralist theories stress the existence of many competing groups with different interests. In South Africa today, there are many media outlets including newspapers, radio and TV stations which all broadcast different news and provide different angles on the same story. Pluralists stress that the media content is not driven by some ideological interests of the ruling class, but by practical issues like circulation, viewership and profit. In fact, according to the pluralists, the media have considerable independence to broadcast and therefore make important contributions to the maintenance of democracy. In South Africa, the existence of multiple media houses is guaranteed under the constitution, but with certain checks and limits on how the media operates. An example is the media ombudsman and the Broadcasting Authority of South Africa who has a constitutionally mandated function to oversee media activities.

Pluralist thinking, moreover, assumes the state to be a neutral enabler taking decisions in the national interest. It is essential to note, however, that during those instances in South Africa, when the state has tried to impose controls and regulations on the media, there has been resistance from society. One example is when the state tried in 2011 to introduce the Protection of State Information Bill – known as the 'Secrecy Bill' by its opponents – in Parliament. The state was forced to retreat as media organisations, pressure groups and political parties, which would otherwise normally express different and conflicting sets of interests, cohered and their resistance coalesced around opposition to the Bill and out of which the 'Right to Know' campaign was established (Wasserman 2018). The Bill remains in draft form. Pluralist thinking would argue that this example points to the validity of its basic premise about society and by extension the media, namely that society is constituted of and represents different interests in all its multiplicities and which gives rise to individual choice.

This view has, of course been the target of conflict theorists who argue that the praise of multiplicity and choice in society simply masks class interests. Long aware of this rejoinder to their position, sophisticated pluralist thinkers have recognised that media pluralism needs to take into account power relations in society and acknowledge that social inequality and power differentials exist not only in society, but also in how the media operates and communicates (Karppinen 2013). As indicated towards the beginning of this chapter, liberal media pluralism and conflict theories regarding the media continue to frame how we understand both society and the media.

Box 18.3

QUESTIONS

1. When it comes to mass media, do you think the state in South Africa is neutral?
2. How would you describe and analyse the relationship between the state and media in South Africa?
3. Can you argue from three different perspectives whether the media should be regulated and controlled or should it be free of state control?

4. What might Africanising and/or decolonising the mass media in South Africa mean?

Note: More adequate answers to these questions than is possible in a brief lecture room debate would require an in-depth analysis of the role players in the South African media and elsewhere.

18.9 Symbolic interactionist theories

Modern classic symbolic interactionists, such as George Mead, Herbert Blumer and Erving Goffman laid the basis for communication studies. The interest of sociology in the effects of the media and 'public opinion research', however, fell away as the United States government during the Cold War heavily funded 'propaganda' studies and took over an area of research and work established by these sociologists (Weisbord 2014).

Contemporary interactionist theories have subsequently taken up a range of communication related issues and concerns: agency and social interaction; audience studies; media representations and digital technologies, the self and society and the like. Interactionists continue to focus on social interaction but also now address broader issues as framing social contexts in understanding the powerful symbolic status in how the mass media both presents and projects itself and its content. Symbolic interactionists stress that human beings use symbols to construct all forms of social reality; churches, teams, schools and civilisation in general. Altheide (2003) states that the mass media has become a significant part of our lives because it reflects both the form and content of our cultural categories and experiences. Locally, it was through the media that the notion of a 'rainbow nation' was disseminated and became a worldwide description of our country. It is also through the media that new fashions and ideas are acquired. Some symbols communicated via the media become common place.

In 2019 Siya Kolisi became a symbol and representation of the deracialisation of rugby, Nelson Mandela's vision of a peaceful society, new possibilities of South Africans 'working together' and renewed hope in progress towards becoming a more equal, humane society. The kinds of event for which Siya Kolisi became the brand, winning the 2019 Rugby World Cup, clearly resulted in changing the quality of interactions between strangers often across social divides. While hard to pin down and difficult to quantify, sociologists studying the mass media and its impact and role would be to study and analyse what such symbolic representations as the name Siya Kolisi means, how it becomes known, how widespread it is, among which social groups it holds significance and how long the social effects endure and how people make meaning and interact with others around such representations. For interactionists, it is of importance how people attach meanings to such symbols, how behaviour and interactions with others are affected and hence how people act according to their subjective interpretation of those symbols. Such ways of thinking have increasingly become part of the way in which sociologists grasp and analyse society. It is hard to understand our own responses to what we see or hear or read and the meanings we attach to news of events without the resources that interactionist perspectives provide. When those are shared with others, often relayed through the power of the media and its analysis, broader structural features of society appear on our conceptual horizon. For all of us are, after all, part of the audience of the media and it is to our collective response to the media that the media, in turn, must respond. For the media need to keep us as media consumers – as well as the raw human material to mine for the biographical detail of our lives!

18.10 The media and its (mass) audience

There are a range of conceptual and theoretical resources available to understand and explain the relationship between the media and our collective social selves as its audiences. James Curran (2002), for a start, argues that while the media are important agencies of influence, they exert this influence in a complex and **contingent** manner. In other words, while it is obvious that the media affects and influences people, the manner through which this occurs is unclear. To use a relatively recent term popularised by the media, audiences can 'push back' against the media and affect social change such as when there is a 'media outcry' in response to some event or other.

In the quest for an adequate response to this problem, this chapter concludes by noting a selection of theories that seek to explain how and in what ways the media effects human behaviour. The four theoretical explanations of the relation between the media and their different audiences are the *hypodermic syringe model*, the *inoculation model*, the *two-step flow theory* and the *culturation theory*.

18.10.1 The 'hypodermic needle' or 'hypodermic-syringe' or 'magic bullet' theory

A hypodermic syringe contains injects drugs into a body. In this model, or theory, the media is seen as a syringe that transmits or injects messages *directly* into the collective body of mass society or its *audience*. The theory emerged in the 1930s and 1940s after the direct impact of the mass media of the glamour of Hollywood and the horror of Nazism were observed – two glaringly different contexts. This theory was supposedly disproven by the two-step theory, discussed below, in the 1950s but has reasserted itself in the contemporary context of Big Data and Big Tech.

The idea behind this model or theory was rooted in the behaviourist belief that the media stimulates human behaviour by eliciting various *responses* to their content. A violent film for example can elicit negative feelings. A heroic film can elicit positive feelings. This theory, following a behaviourist methodology and epistemology, presupposes a *cause and effect* relationship between the *media* and their *audience*. The underlying assumption is that media content has an immediate influence on human behaviour. It assumes a passive, as opposed to an active, *audience*.

Today's society is in many respects a mass society, where individuals are increasingly socially isolated and the media exceptionally powerful as the very first sentence of this chapter, citing the major thinker Miklas Luhmann, suggests – everything we know we know through the media! Taken together with the atomised social isolation of swathes of modern society implies that individuals become receptive to all media content as the media is the only source of information. The media therefore feeds information to a starved population that develops behavioural tendencies in accordance with the media content.

Box 18.4

QUESTIONS

1. Did media saturation about HIV and AIDS result in individuals' changing their sexual behaviour?
2. How might you answer this question empirically?
3. Assume it *can* be empirically shown that sexual behaviour changed as a direct result of the mass media. How would you explain this shift in human sexual behaviour?

18.10.2 The inoculation model

The inoculation model is also known as the cumulation theory. It suggests that extended exposure to repeated media messages makes audiences immune to them. This is a process called *desensitisation*. This simply means that audiences tend no longer to be shocked by scenes or news of especially violence as they are exposed to it time and again. The more violence you watch on television, the more violence you will need to be satisfied. In fact, the inoculation model assumes that mass media is like a narcotic drug. As society becomes addicted, the dose of certain imagery needs to be increased. This may mean more real pornography or more real violence. Do you remember your initial reaction to the following:

- Scenes of starving refugees fleeing war in Darfur, Sudan
- Statistics showing a woman is sexually assaulted in South Africa every minute
- Photograph of a Mozambican immigrant being burnt alive during the 2008 xenophobic attacks
- Scenes of the police shooting mineworkers at Marikana now widely referred to as the Marikana Massacre – a term widely used in the alternative media.

Answers to these questions would most likely reveal your level of sensitivity to mass media imagery. What do your answers say about the nature and types of mass media content in South Africa?

18.10.3 The two-step flow theory

The two theories above assume a direct, one-step effect – or direct one-way relation – between the impact of the media on their audiences. The two-step flow theory, resulting from a study conducted by Elihu Katz and Paul Lazarsfeld in 1955 was for long thought to have refuted the one-step theory. This two-step flow theory suggested messages flowed from the media to opinion formers. Opinion formers are individuals who directly receive a message and have the social influence to convey it to others. In many respects, opinion formers are our significant others – such as parents, teachers, spouses and siblings, among others. These significant others play the role of opinion leaders within our immediate social circles. These opinion leaders filter and disseminate messages, thus creating a two-step communication flow from the news source to the opinion leader to the individual in society. The study conducted by Katz and Lazarsfeld had voting patterns as its focus. How, you might ask, do you decide for which political party to vote and how are people's voting habits established? The

study showed it was not the media, but rather those close opinion makers in family, school or community, who played a crucial role in individual decision making.

Box 18.5

Most people can recall important moments in certain conversations which changed the way we think. Such moments might have been about history, the economy, politics or religion or about love and intimate relationships.

QUESTIONS

How have your own viewpoints regarding other, less dramatic, moments developed?

18.10.4 Cultural effects theory

First formulated by Stuart Hall, the cultural effects theory assumes that certain ideological representations have long-term effects on beliefs and values. The mass media presents ideal images which capture our imaginations. Celebrities or other attractive powerful individuals are presented or able to present or brand themselves as possessing membership of a certain social class, or status, or wealth or elite group to which many people in society aspire. This feeds into the consumptive tendencies of capitalism. Although we have discussed the hegemonic theories of the media and society, we can still apply them to this section on cultural effects as well. From this neo-Marxist perspective, the media police and control society through the promotion of ruling class ideas. This theory argues that the media are deeply ingrained in the class structures of the society in which they operate. In fact, the media is a tool to reproduce and reflect ruling class interests via the exercise of hegemony which encourages, over time, ways of thinking about society and therefore human behaviour.

The media do this by exercising a hegemonic role which entails guiding and advising audiences. Do you think the media in South Africa performs a hegemonic role of advising and guiding the South African population? Your answer to this question will need you to reflect and link this theory to the other theories we have discussed as well.

In Case study 18.3 we will look at one more practical example of a dramatic instance that attracts media attention and the social effects this has in society.

Case study 18.3 The *Izikhothane*

The *Izikhothane* were groups of young people who lived in the Katlehong township in the East Rand of Johannesburg. *Izikhothane* is township slang for 'the one with the most expensive clothes'. The *Izikhothane* were comprised of groups such as the 'Born-Agains' and the 'Overspenders'. They regularly challenged each other and competed for the title of best dressed or as they call it in the township: the group with the most 'swagger'. For these *Izikhothane*, clothes make or break an outing. They made sure that they look the part. The price tags of these clothes were a very important aspect. If one is to get any recognition from other groups, the pricier the clothes, the better. Only expensive brands of clothing were bought and worn by the *Izikhothane* groups. Gold teeth and flashy accessories completed the look of these young people. The aim is to be the most expensively dressed at any outing so as to please the crowds and their peers and to get the most attention when they are out on the township streets. They had also to be seen drinking the most expensive alcoholic beverages, driving expensive cars and doing the most creative stunts at social outings. Displays of abundance in the form of money, clothes and style determine the winner. The young people from these groups only desired the best, even though they came from working-class backgrounds. What drove this new youth-culture in some of the townships of South Africa? Has it mutated into other forms on Social Media like the so-called slay queens and slay kings? From the knowledge you have just learned about the media and their influence on the audience, which theory can better explain the behaviour of the *Izikhothane* in your view?

Summary

- The technologies driving mass media revolutionised society by introducing new forms of communication of ever-increasing scope and impact. Globally encompassing technological companies, it has been argued, now are central to what has been called surveillance capitalism with the internet being a 'hyper-object' which is close but so large we cannot see it in its entirety.
- Mass media has become an integral part of the contemporary lived experience of human beings.
- The pervasive ability of the mass media contributes to both social order and social change and continues to powerfully shape social structure and forms of human communication and interaction.
- The mass media is intimately interconnected with our contemporary information society and burgeoning knowledge economy, with surveillance and intrusions into the privacy of individuals emerging as a growing concern.
- It remains an open question whether, how and to what extent the mass media shifts and changes between serving the interests of ruling elites and reflecting competing interests in society to which it must respond.
- Classic sociological perspectives introduced in this chapter have been foundational to a variety of theories which have attempted to explain the relation and interaction between mass media and mass society.

- Functionalist perspectives argue that communication via the mass media functions in the interests of social order.
- Functionalist perspectives have identified various functions of the media; the surveillance function, the interpretation or editorial function the entertainment function and the socialisation function. While these functionalist perspectives were formulated in the 20th century, they were discussed in the light of the modern electronic media and the internet.
- Conflict perspectives argue that the mass media is central to masking the exploitative nature of capitalism and serves class interests by reproducing the dominant ideology of elite groups.
- Conflict perspectives have identified various forms of social domination in and by the media in the manipulative model, the control of the media model and the hegemonic model.
- Feminist theories cut across and challenge classical perspectives of the media and range broadly with the focus in this chapter being how patriarchy underpins much of what the mass media communicates. Feminist perspectives importantly point to how perceptions and stereotypes regarding not only gender, but race, culture, class and disability are portrayed in the media.

➠

- Pluralist perspectives, based on the centrality of democracy and the freedom of speech, see the media as reflecting how society is constituted by different groups and competing interests which find expression in a variety of views by multiple role players in the media.

The relationship between the mass media and its audience is a key area of concern for media studies. Old questions and old theories relating to human agency and social control are again raised as and show their relevance in our contemporary electronic age. The 'hypodermic needle' theory, thought to have been superseded, has reasserted itself with the growth of the Big Tech and Big Data companies. The inoculation model and the two-step flow theory and the classic cultural effects theories are viewed in the light of our local context.

Gorman and McLean (2009: 289) point to the direction analysis should take in an effort to answer the question regarding the role of the media in society:

Media ... have continued to be shaped by tensions, competition, and contradictions: between democratic expansion and oligopoly, between public service and commerce, between information and entertainment, between information and manipulation, between the national and the global.

In many ways this is what we have attempted to do here. The perspectives theories and examples sought to offer, not only a general sociological exploration of the media but also to develop your own thinking regarding the media industry.

ARE YOU ON TRACK?

1. In your view, do the media have a constraining or enabling effect on society?
2. What has been the influence of technological revolutions on the media?
3. Does media ownership influence the media content?
4. Do you think the social media will 'undo' established media forms like newspapers and radios?
5. Do sociological theories of the media capture fully and reflect social reality?

More sources to consult

Cannadine D (ed). 2004. *History and the Media*. Basingstoke: Palgrave Macmillan.

Curran J, Gurevitch M (ed). 2005. *Mass Media and Society*. 3rd ed. London: Arnold.

Held D, McGrew A (ed). 2000. *The Global Transformation Reader: An introduction to the Globalisation Debate*. Cambridge: Polity Press.

Papathanassopoulos S (ed). 2011. *Media Perspectives for the 21st Century*. New York: Routledge.

Seib P (ed). 2005. *Media and Conflict in the Twenty-first Century*. New York: Palgrave Macmillan.

References

Adorno T. 2001. *The Culture Industry*. London: Routledge.

Aggarwal VB, Gupta VS. 2001. *Handbook of Journalism and Mass communication*. Delhi: Concept Publishing Company.

Altheide DL. 2003. 'Notes Towards A Politics of Fear'. *Journal for Crime, Conflict and the Media*, 1(1): 37–54.

Alvarado M, Boyd-Barrett O. 1992. *Media Education: An introduction*. London: British Film Institute.

Barnett C. 1999. 'The limits of media democratisation in South Africa: politics, privatisation, and regulation'. *Media, Culture and Society*, 21(1): 649–671.

Bell D. 2004. 'Post-Industrial Society' in *The Information Society Reader*. New York, NY: Routledge, 86–102.

Bennett T. 1982. 'Theories of the media, theories of society' *Culture, Society and the Media*. Gurevitch M, Bennett T, Curran J, Wollacott J (eds). London: Methuen, 30–55.

Bennett CJ, Haggerty KD, Lyon D, Steeves V. 2014. *Transparent Lives*. Athabasca: Athabasca University Press.

Boltanski L, Chiapello E. 2005. *The New Spirit of Capitalism*. London: Verso.

Bourgault LM. 1995. *Mass Media in Sub-Saharan Africa*. Bloomington and Indianapolis: Indiana University Press.

Castells M. 2005. *The Network Society: From Knowledge to Policy*. Washington, DC: Johns Hopkins Center for Transatlantic Relations.

Curran J. 2002. *Media and Power*. London: Routledge.

Digital Media and Marketing Association (DMMA). 2009. [Online] Available at: http://www.dmma.co.za/?s=media+ownership [Accessed 7 October 2013].

Dominick JR. nd. *The Dynamics of Mass Communication.* London: McGraw Hill.

Duncan J. 2011. 'The print media transformation dilemma'. *New South African Review 2: New Paths, Old Compromises.* Daniel J, Naidoo P, Pillay D Southall R (eds). Johannesburg: Wits University Press.

Fiske, J. 1992. 'British Cultural Studies and Television', in *Channels of Discourse.* Allen RC (ed). Chapel Hill: University of North Carolina Press.

Giddens A. 1990. *The Consequences of Modernity.* Stanford: Stanford University Press.

Glasser CK. 1997. 'Patriarchy, mediated desire, and Chinese magazine fiction'. *Journal of Communication,* 47(1): 85–108.

Gorman L, McLean D. 2009. *Media and Society into the 21st Century: A Historical Introduction.* West Sussex: Wiley-Blackwell.

Gramsci A. 1971. *Selections from the Prison Notebooks.* London: Lawrence & Wishart.

Hall S. 1982. 'The rediscovery of "ideology": Return of the repressed in media studies'. *Culture, Society and the Media.* Gurevitch M, Bennett T, Curran J, Wollacott J (eds). London: Methuen, 56–90.

Henslin JM. 2008. *Essentials of Sociology: A Down-to-Earth Approach.* 8th ed. USA: Pearson.

Hickey S. 2005. 'The politics of staying poor: Exploring the political space for poverty reduction in Uganda'. *World Development,* 33(6).

Ilboudo J-P. 2000. 'Prospects for rural radio in Africa'. *African Broadcast Cultures: Radio in Transition.* Fardon R, Furniss G (eds). Oxford: James Currey; Harare: Baobab; Cape Town: David Philip, Pages 42–71.

Karppinen K. 2013. *Rethinking Media Pluralism.* New York: Fordham University Press.

Katz E, Lazarsfeld P. 1955. *Personal Influence.* New York: The Free Press.

Kirkpatrick G. 2014. 'Digital media technology and the spirit of the new capitalism: What future for "aesthetic critique"?' in *Media Sociology: A Reappraisal.* Weisbord S (ed) Cambridge: Polity Press.

Lasswell H. 1948. *The Structure and Function of Communication in Society.* The Communication of Ideas. New York: Institute for Religious and Social Studies.

Lesame NC. 2005. (ed). *New Media: Technology and policy in developing countries.* Hatfield, Pretoria: Van Schaik.

Lindgren S. 2017. *Digital Media and Society.* Los Angeles/London/New Delhi/Singapore/Washington, DC/Melbourne: Sage.

Luhmann N. 2000. *The Reality of the Mass Media.* Cambridge: Polity Press.

Luo Y, Hao X. 2007. 'Media Portrayal of Women and Social Change'. *Feminist Media Studies,* 7(3):281–298.

Mazwai T, Konigkramer A, Molusi C, Nyatsumba K, Lindberg D, Abrahams L, Mathiance N, Thloloe J, Kane-Berman J. 1991. *Mau-Mauing the Media: New Censorship for the New South Africa.* Johannesburg: South African Institute of Race Relations.

Meehan D. 1983. *Ladies of the Evening: Women Characters of Prime Time Television.* New Jersey: Scarecrow Press.

Moyo D, Chuma W. 2010. (eds). 'Policing the media in Southern Africa in the global era: An introduction'. *Media Policy in a Changing South Africa: Critical reflections on media reforms in the global age.* Pretoria: UNISA Press.

Nxasana S. 2001. 'Building a bridge across the digital divide: Focus on the ITU Telecom Africa 2001'. *Sunday Times Business Times,* 4 November: 23.

OMD Media Direction. 2009. 'South African Media Facts 2009'. [Online] Available at: http://www.omd.co.za/media_facts/samediafacts2009.pdf [Accessed 19 September 2013].

Packenham T. 1991. *The Scramble for Africa.* London: Abacus.

Pillay D. 2011. 'Media transformation and the right to know'. *New South African Review 2: New Paths, Old Compromises.* Daniel J, Naidoo P, Pillay D Southall R (eds). Johannesburg: Wits University Press.

Popenoe D, Boult B, Cunningham P. 1998. *Sociology.* 1st ed (South Africa). Cape Town: Prentice Hall.

Reed TV. 2019. *Digitized Lives: Culture, Power and Social Change in the Internet Era.* 2nd ed. New York and London: Routledge.

Rosengren KE. 1981. 'Mass media and social change: some current approaches', in *Mass Media and Social Change.* Katz E, Szecsko T (eds). Beverly Hills, CA: SAGE, 247–264.

Sassen S. 2006. *Territory, Authority, Rights: From Medieval to Global Assemblages.* Princeton: Princeton University Press.

Schefermann M. 2013. '"You can help" campaign'. [Online] Available at: BizCommunity.com [Accessed 7 October 2013].

Silver C. 2017. 'Patients reveal how facebook wants to capture your emotions, facial expressions and mood'. *Forbes.* 8 June. www.forbes.com/sites/curtissilver/2017/06/08/how-facebook-wants-to-capture-your-emotions-facial-expressions-and-mood/#9302cee606014c.

Skinner K. 2011. The South African Broadcasting Corporation: The creation and loss of a citizenship vision and the possibilities of building a new one'. *New South African Review 2: New Paths, Old Compromises*. Daniel J, Naidoo P, Pillay D, Southall R (eds). Johannesburg: Wits University Press.

South African Audience Research Foundation (SAARF). *AMPS*. [Online] Available at: http://saarf.co.za/AMPS/amps-evolution.asp [Accessed 19 September 2013].

Sparkes M. 2013. 'What type of social media user are you?' *The Telegraph*, 11 April.

Strelitz L. 2005. *Mixed Reaction: South African Youth and their Experience of Global Media*. Pretoria: UNISA Press.

Trotter D. 2012. *Social Media as Surveillance*. London: Routledge.

Van Zoonen L. 1994. *Feminist Media Studies*. London: Sage.

VPUU. 2019. 'Bridging the digital divide'. Newsletter, *Violence Prevention through Urban Upgrading* newsletter, 20 May. http:// vpuu.org.za/ict4d/digital-divide-South-Africa/ [Accessed 5 November 2019]

Wasserman H. 2018. *Media, Geopolitics and Power: A View from the Global South*. Cape Town: UCT Press.

Weisbord S (ed). *Media Sociology: A Reappraisal*. Cambridge: Polity Press.

Health, disease and care

Engela Pretorius

Without sustained health and freedom from disease, no individual or society can flourish. This only truly strikes home when we are seriously ill or injured and need care. What is less obvious is that whatever the reason for being sick, it more often than not fits into a social pattern or is a function of social circumstances. The occurrence of rare diseases aside, health, disease and the extent and quality of care received is largely socially determined. The very first paragraph of this slightly longer chapter cites extensive scientific research which makes this most basic point in the sociology of health and disease – the affluent are less prone to disease than the less affluent. The chapter is longer than most chapters in this book for one simple reason. The wide-ranging effects and impacts of health and disease make it the largest of the sub disciplines in sociology. These effects and impacts concern us all and because this sub-discipline closely tracks the developments in medical science – often with a critical stance – it is increasingly being viewed as complementary to bioscience.

The chapter starts by contrasting biomedicine with the sociological perspective on health and disease and traces how this important sub-discipline developed. The biomedical and social models of health and disease are then contrasted and not without a fascinating reference to the history of thought you encountered in the introduction to this textbook. The criticisms the social model makes of the biomedical model must not be read as detracting from the modern marvels of medical science. It is precisely due to the valid criticisms the sociology of health and disease has made that its role as complementary to and convergent with medical scientific practice has increasingly been recognised.

It is perhaps the serious nature of the subject which points to another convergence, this time within sociology itself. You may have gained the impression that, for example, when it comes to examining politics, a positivist or structural functionalist approach focusing on social order *competes* with the conflict approach which emphasises social change. When it comes to the sociology of health and disease, there is no tension in understanding the sick role as defined in structural functionalist terms or by the conflict perspective – both contend that social inequality also extends to healthcare. It is hence appropriate that it is only after discussing the three main approaches in sociology that the chapter turns to defining health, disease and illness – these not being as obvious as they may at first appear. Make sure you understand the difference between the concepts of medicalisation and iatrogenesis! In brief, as you will see, health is not merely the absence of disease, but includes a sense of wellbeing. When looked at from at least one African perspective, you might be surprised to learn that even disease is understood as a gift, signalling a calling to the vocation of healer.

Having laid this basis, the chapter then turns to how healthcare was gradually institutionalised and much improved over the course of centuries. It then describes the development of the primary healthcare movement and how this took root in South Africa, especially from the 1940s. This is followed by a fuller discussion of the role of African traditional healthcare and the emergence, in the 1980s, of complementary and alternative forms of medical practice. While African traditional healthcare has not been accepted and hence not integrated or institutionalised within the biomedical tradition (although the North-West University Mafikeng Campus has specifically addressed this issue), there has been a significant degree of legitimation and acceptance of complementary and alternative medicine by biomedicine.

Case study 19.1 Stephen Hawking

One of the world's most famous scientists, Professor Stephen Hawking, died on 14 March 2018 at the age of 76. This British theoretical physicist is regarded as one of the most brilliant since Einstein. In 1962, when he had just turned 21, he was diagnosed with ALS, a form of degenerative motor neurone disease. Generally, people who suffer from this condition do not live beyond five years after being diagnosed. Hawking, however, defied established medical opinion by managing to live 55 years beyond the two years he was given. He was almost entirely paralysed and spent the greater part of his life confined to a wheelchair. He was only capable of communicating by means of a speech-generating device and was dependent on a number of nurses and assistants. Yet, while Hawking was physically constrained by his disabled body, his intellectual feats are a clear demonstration that his mind was unconstrained and 'undamaged' (Penrose 2014; The Stephen Hawking official website 2013).

When people looked at Stephen Hawking, most considered him to be a very sick person or severely disabled. This is the case because we all know what constitutes disease and what health is – or do we really? One thing is certain – health is not the opposite of disease – just as 'body' or 'lung' does not have an opposite. In this chapter you will be introduced to the phenomena of health and disease, to the complexities involved in defining these concepts and to the ways in which society has come to deal with them.

Key themes

In this chapter, the following themes are addressed:

- The sociological perspective on health and disease
- Models of health and disease
- The major theoretical approaches to health and disease

- The concepts *health*, *disease* and *illness*
- Healthcare contexts: hospitals, primary healthcare, African traditional healthcare and complementary and alternative medicine.

19.1 Introduction

Life on earth is characterised by various kinds of inequality – be it in respect of material possessions, income or education. These socio-economic inequalities have a direct impact on the health of individuals and thus on that of populations. Whether one lives in a developed country or a developing one, the picture is the same: those who are more affluent live longer and are less prone to disease than the less affluent. These differences cannot be explained in terms of individual differences alone. An ever-increasing body of literature is pointing to the role of the social environment regarding health. In view of this, the World Health Organization in 1998 commissioned the following report: *Social determinants of health – the solid facts* (Wilkinson & Marmot 2003). The evidence on which this publication was based came from thousands of research reports. From this massive source of research data, a number of significant universal principles regarding the health of populations were determined. One principle is that creating a just and caring society requires an understanding of the interaction between material advantage and its social significance. Thus, while it is apparent that socio-economic inequality affects health and causes disease, the social meaning of being poor,

unemployed, socially excluded or otherwise stigmatised, also matters. It has therefore come to be acknowledged that to be able to understand and deal with health and disease, biomedical knowledge needs to be supplemented by knowledge generated by disciplines such as sociology, psychology and economics. Within the discipline of sociology, the speciality dealing with health, disease and care only developed a clear identity from around the 1950s.

19.2 The sociological perspective on health and disease

Sociologists – because they are students of society – do not have the same kind of interest in the phenomena of health and disease that medical professionals do. For one, sociologists do not believe that value-free, scientific knowledge about health and disease is possible. According to this view, rather than being an objective science, medical knowledge is both produced in a particular societal context and reflects the structural features of that society. Phenomena considered by biomedicine to be 'natural' are considered social phenomena from a sociological perspective. Therefore, questions such as why a member of the working class is more prone to sickness and consequently dies earlier than one from a more affluent class and why women are more frequently diagnosed ill than men require a sociological explanation rather than a biological one.

A sociological perspective on health emphasises that one is unable to understand health and illness unless one has a clear understanding of the social order. In this view, knowledge of health and disease is created in a social, political and cultural environment. The sociological perspective therefore aims to complement the biomedical model of disease by examining the social functions of medical knowledge. Based on their research, sociologists are able to demonstrate that knowledge about and therefore treatment of disease result from the interactions of socio-economic class, professional interests, power, religion, gender and ethnicity. As such, health and disease are considered social constructs, 'products' of social organisation rather than of nature, biology or even individual lifestyle choices. Moreover, everything we know about health and disease or of the professions that deal with them or how we respond to and experience being healthy or ill are moulded by the society in which we live and our place in that society. It is therefore possible to say that it is not enough to urge individuals to change their lifestyles or to spend more and more money on healthcare technology so as to prevent disease. What is required is to take into consideration the prevailing societal influences, not as inconvenient or irritating add-ons that need to be done away with as quickly as possible because they stand in the way of 'real' medicine, but as major determinants of disease.

Three distinct characteristics of this perspective can be summarised as follows: (White 2002)

- The focus is on social patterns rather than on individual behaviours. Therefore, while sociologists would not deny that individual personalities play a role in intimate partner violence, they would probably find it more useful to explore whether social forces can explain why wife abuse is more common than husband abuse or why abused wives remain with abusive husbands. The issue with which sociologists deal – and are able to deal – is not why an individual is ill, but rather the characteristics of the group to which the individual belongs that put the person at risk of being ill. The most significant such groups into which we are born and that either facilitate or impede our life chances – and consequently our chances of becoming ill – are socio-economic class, gender and ethnicity/race.
- Sociologists are not interested in appropriating the medical professionals' job or even prescribing to them as to how to do their job. Because of their research,

sociologists are, however, able to provide information on many aspects of disease causation other than biological variables – on patterns and trends pertaining to various diseases, on the practice of medicine and on people's perceptions and experiences of and also their responses to being ill.

- From a sociological perspective the way in which certain conditions are labelled and treated boils down to a form of social control. What is defined as a disease and how it is to be treated is often a product of social assumptions of what constitutes appropriate behaviour rather than of biological necessity. White (2002) cites the example of Professor Herbert Green, a gynaecologist at the National Women's Hospital in Auckland, New Zealand. In what became known as the 'unfortunate experiment', he chose to withhold treatment from women diagnosed with cancer in situ of the cervix. He considered women's role as child bearers, thus their fertility, more important than their health and did not perform **hysterectomies** – then considered the conventional treatment for this type of cancer. The women did indeed remain fertile, but many died. His non-treatment was as much a product of his view of women as it was of clinical medicine.

19.2.1 The development of the sociology of health and disease

The development of this speciality within sociology was influenced by the relationship between sociology and medicine. Three distinct phases in this development process can be identified. The speciality first developed a distinct identity during the 1950s. The second phase spanned the 1960s and part of the 1970s, while the third phase developed from the 1970s onwards.

Sociology in medicine

In the first phase – depicted as the sociology in medicine – sociology was considered to be subordinate to medicine. Medicine was regarded as the embodiment of what constituted 'science'. Sociologists were only too aware of the prestige of biomedical science and were eager to bathe in its reflected glory. In their research, sociologists working in this field therefore tackled issues problematic to the medical profession. One such topic was patient compliance/non-compliance. It was important for doctors to be informed as to why patients would not follow their instructions and to be able to change such behaviour once they understood it.

Sociology of medicine

During this second phase of the development of this speciality, sociologists designed their research to answer questions of interest to sociologists in general. Whereas sociologists would, during the first phase, view something like patients' non-compliance to be a problem of the patients concerned, they now came to view the issue of compliance through the patients' eyes. They would then come to realise that patients sometimes ignored medical advice because of ignorance or because they did not understand the doctor's orders or that financial constraints sometimes prevented them from adhering to medical advice (Weitz 2010; White 2002).

Sociology versus biomedicine

The third phase of the development of this branch of sociology, which spans the last three decades, is characterised by a critical perspective on the organisation and practice of medicine. Sociologists have come to challenge medical worldviews and to point out how doctors' power and authority enable them to frame society's ideas about health, disease and healthcare. During the 1970s, sociologists first came to recognise that the healthcare institution had been expanding into aspects of people's lives previously defined as 'non-medical'. The result was that patients consulted doctors for conditions previously considered to be 'normal' – such as baldness, unattractive facial features, fatigue, jet lag, shyness, the inability to focus on tasks, childlessness, pregnancy and childbirth and growing old. They termed this multi-faceted phenomenon the 'medicalisation of society'. It entails a reclassification of certain social phenomena – formerly regarded as either morally deviant (sin) or as socially deviant (crime) – as disease. Examples include various dependencies (alcohol and drugs), homosexual love and obesity. Another aspect of **medicalisation** is that it transforms a problem at the level of social structure – such as stressful work demands, unsafe working conditions and poverty – into an individual problem under medical control.

As the number of problems and behaviours labelled as disease increases, so do the ethical issues surrounding them. One such ethical issue relates to patient safety. Because pharmaceutical and biotechnological companies spend considerable amounts of time and money in developing and marketing their products, they aim to sell them to as many customers as possible. A case in point is the prescription rate of medications for children with attention deficit hyperactivity disorder (ADHD), which is two to four times higher in the US than in other countries. This may be the result of aggressive marketing by companies to ensure profit

taking. While such drugs have been approved, the ethical question that arises is whether it is safe to use drugs or devices we do not really need.

When we look at society and defining disease, it becomes apparent that there is also a reverse pattern, called **demedicalisation**. Thus, some behavioural aspects previously medicalised and identified as medical conditions are no longer regarded as such, for example homosexuality. Before the 1970s, same-sex relationships were considered to be a mental illness. However, in time and because of campaigning against such labelling, it has been demedicalised. Today, the medical community neither regards homosexuality as a medical condition nor considers it to be medically treatable (Steele & Price 2008). The move towards recognising patient rights can also be considered a step towards demedicalisation. In a post-modern era, the present-day 'consumers' of healthcare are a far cry from being docile lay persons. With increased concerns over risk and a decline of trust in expert authority, they play an active role in either bringing about or resisting medicalisation.

19.3 Models of health and disease

From the previous section, two quite different models of health and disease present themselves, namely the **biomedical model** and the **social model of health and disease**.

19.3.1 The biomedical model of health and disease

This model is widely used in Western healthcare. It emerged from the idea that science can be applied to the solution of human problems – an idea developed during the 19th century from **Enlightenment** views. Biomedicine as we know it today developed because of a number of important influences and spectacular breakthroughs, namely the Cartesian revolution, the development of the clinical method, the institutionalisation of healthcare and the doctrine of specific aetiology.

The Cartesian revolution: Mind/body dualism

During the Middle Ages, the development of medicine was severely constrained by the influence of the medieval church, the dominant institution at the time. During that time, the church had placed a religious embargo on the study of human anatomy because of the belief that body and soul were inseparable. It was thought that if the human body were not preserved intact, the soul would be unable to ascend to heaven. In these circumstances, human dissection was virtually impossible and without knowledge of anatomy, medical science could not really progress.

In the 17th century, science was able to break loose from the constraints of tradition, which made it possible for the best minds of the age to become involved in scientific inquiry. One of them, the French mathematician and philosopher René Descartes, also made anatomical dissections. He paved the way for the development of a medical science by emphasising **mind/body dualism**, arguing that the mind was, in principle, able to survive the death of the body. This way of thinking about the mind and body removed the obstacles to developments in medicine, and laid the foundations of medical science as it is practised today.

The clinical method

Towards the end of the 18th century, a major change occurred in the organisation and provision of healthcare in Europe, mainly because of the efforts of Herman Boerhaave (1668–1738). He was a Dutch doctor to whom the idea of a 'bedside manner'[1] is attributed. He revived the Hippocratic tradition of teaching students at the patients' bedsides as a regular part of the university course for medical students at Leyden in the Netherlands. To combine practice with theory, Boerhaave founded a hospital in which he gave clinical instruction to his pupils, thus introducing the clinical method into medical education.

Institutionalisation of healthcare

Before the 19th century, healthcare in the West was mostly delivered within the home by household members and non-professionals. During the early 1800s, there was a move away from the home to institutions – called hospitals – to deliver healthcare.

At first hospitals were only capable of providing what some would call 'primitive' treatment (see also section 7.1). The conditions were dreadful because of poor ventilation and overcrowding and sanitary standards were virtually non-existent. All of this gave rise to the perception that the hospitals of the time were places where only the lower classes went to die, and it took several decades to change this negative image. One of the factors that assisted in changing the negative image was the development of the germ theory, which affected the standards of hygiene and led to the realisation that infective patients constituted a risk to people suffering from other conditions. Patients were consequently isolated, which made hospitals much safer. Because of developments such as these, a new image of hospitals evolved as institutions where patients of all social classes could expect to find the highest-quality medical care and could reasonably expect to be cured of their disorders.

The doctrine of specific aetiology (germ theory)

Throughout history, infections have posed the biggest challenge to human health. The orthodox medical view of disease causation was that it was the result of *miasmata* or 'bad air' arising from dirt and lack of hygiene. In 1882, Robert Koch isolated and grew the tubercle bacillus in the laboratory. In this way, he was able to demonstrate that a specific micro-organism caused tuberculosis – the most virulent disease of the day. Scientists thus came to realise that infection was the result of the action of invisible micro-organisms – the invasion of one living organism by another. The research of Louis Pasteur in France and that of Robert Koch in Germany in the 19th century thus led to the development of the germ theory (Alais 1995; Berche 2012; Weiss & Lonnquist 1997).

Long before scientists became aware of the existence of micro-organisms, mortality from infective causes had, however, already been declining and continued to do so. This was due to the rising living standards and public health measures that had come about because of sanitary reforms. While the sanitary reformers did not understand precisely how infection occurred, they were quite aware of the role played by poverty, overcrowding and pollution in infection. Even today, in the 21st century, infectious diseases such as cholera and tuberculosis coincide with the fault lines created by poverty and inequality.

The germ theory had important consequences. First, it triggered a hunt for pathogens: within 20 years, the bacteria responsible for most infectious diseases – such as leprosy, tuberculosis, diphtheria, cholera and bubonic plague – were discovered. This was followed by new methods to combat infectious diseases, such as hygiene, pasteurisation and vaccines to prevent the spread of epidemics. Its relevance was extended to public health through the concept of the epidemiological triad. So as to control of disease outbreaks effectively, it was emphasised that attention be paid to all three corners of a triangle: the host (the person who has been infected), the vector (the carrier of an infectious pathogen into another living organism) and the environment (Berche 2012; Chotiner 2020; Da Cunha, Fonseca & Calado 2019).

Because of the consolidation of the germ theory in the 19th century, the fight against infectious disease advanced dramatically to the extent that it seemed that man's battle

---

[1] *Bedside manner* refers to a doctor's way of talking to and dealing with patients.

against such diseases had been all but won. Nothing could be further from the truth. Well into the 21st century, we are now faced with the most devastating of infectious diseases, which has resulted in a global lockdown of unparalleled magnitude. The outbreak of Covid-19 at the end of 2019 necessitates a more in-depth look at infectious diseases throughout history.

Infectious diseases

Infectious diseases generally remained the leading cause of death up to the 19th and 20th centuries. Only then did effective medical treatment become available because of major pharmacological breakthroughs, such as Louis Pasteur's development of vaccines and Alexander Fleming's discovery of penicillin (Da Cunha et al 2019; Denworth 2020). In 1928, Fleming discovered this extremely potent antibiotic substance, which is said to have changed the course of history by having saved and continuing to save millions of people around the world. It was instrumental in conquering some of humankind's most ancient scourges such as scarlet fever, gonorrhoea, pneumonia, meningitis, diphtheria, gangrene and tuberculosis (Tan & Tatsumura 2015). After the commercialisation of antibiotics by the mid-1900s, the mortality of infectious diseases in a country like England was minimised to under 1 per cent, and antibiotics came to be regarded as a 'medical miracle' (Da Cunha et al 2019).

The period between 1940 and 1960 – when most of the antibiotic classes in use today were identified – is referred to as the antibiotic golden age. In the late 1960s, this gave rise to a pervasive, dangerously complacent attitude among international public health authorities. A common belief was that, given the rate at which antibiotics had been discovered, infectious diseases would soon be a controlled public health issue because most pathogenic organisms – such as the parasite that causes malaria – would be eliminated by the end of the 20th century. In view of this conception, two prominent US universities closed their infectious disease departments during that time, sure that the problem they studied had been solved (Da Cunha et al 2019). According to Spinney (2019: 326), 'the starkest reminder that the battle is not won, however, is that only one infectious disease has been eradicated globally: smallpox'. She points out that cases of measles and mumps are on the rise again in Europe and in the United States, that new infectious diseases are emerging at an unprecedented rate and that 'the threat of the next pandemic keeps philanthropist Bill Gates awake at night' (Spinney 2019: 324). Therefore, despite a 36 per cent increase in human use of antibiotics from 2000 to 2010, today approximately 20 per cent of deaths worldwide

are still related to infectious diseases. This situation is exacerbated by the expected rise in deaths from antibiotic-resistant infections by 2050 (Da Cunha et al 2019). Once considered a resolved health issue, infectious diseases have resurfaced as a topic requiring urgent action. What is more, we seem to be repeating many of the mistakes that triggered or exacerbated epidemics or pandemics in the past. It was Louis Pasteur who said 'it is the microbes who will have the last word'.

- **Terms to describe the occurrence of infections**

Various terms are used to describe infections, namely *endemic*, *outbreak*, *epidemic* and *pandemic* (Grennan 2019). An *endemic condition* is present at a fairly stable, predictable rate among a group of people, who might be all the inhabitants of a town or county, or larger areas like countries or continents. Malaria in Africa is an example. An *outbreak* is limited to a relatively small area and refers to a sudden increase in the number of people with a condition. Examples include cholera after the 2010 Haiti earthquake. An *epidemic* is an outbreak that spreads over a larger geographical area. Examples include the Zika virus, which started in Brazil in 2014 and spread to most of Latin America and the Caribbean. An epidemic that spreads globally is a *pandemic*. Pandemics are, for the most part, disease outbreaks that become widespread as a result of the spread of human-to-human infection (Grennan 2019; Qiu, Rutherford, Mao & Chu 2016/17).

These definitions may seem straightforward, but applying them in evolving real-world situations is complicated. An example could provide clarity: HIV/AIDS started in the Democratic Republic of Congo in 1920. During the 1980s, there were signs of a growing epidemic, which lasted for decades. By the late 20th century, it took on the form of a pandemic because of its widespread occurrence. Two decades into the 21st century, one can now reasonably state that HIV/AIDS has become endemic in some parts of the world (Avert 2019; Grennan 2019).

- **Pandemics in human history**

Viruses constantly mutate. The extremely novel ones trigger pandemics because the human immune system is not capable of recognising them quickly enough as being dangerous invaders. They force the body to create a new line of defence, which involves new antibodies and other immune system components. In the short term, many people become ill, while social factors such as crowding and the unavailability of medicine serve to increase the numbers. Many people die because of such novel viruses, but ultimately antibodies are developed by the immune system to resist the invader. In this way, the antibodies linger in enough of the affected population to provide longer-term immunity and limit person-to-person viral transmission. This process, referred to as **herd immunity** (to be discussed later), can, however, take several years and before it happens, havoc reigns (Denworth 2020).

Humanity has gone through several large epidemics and pandemics throughout the ages. In the 20th century, there were three influenza pandemics. The most famous example was the H1N1 influenza outbreak of 1918–1919 – also known as the Spanish flu. It became known around the world as thus because Spain was hit hard by the disease and was not subject to the wartime news blackouts that affected other European countries (History.com editors 2020). Doctors and public health officials had far fewer weapons than they do today. Over two years and three waves, the pandemic infected more than one-third of the world's population (500 million) and was thought to have killed more than 50 million people. It ended only as those who recovered acquired natural or herd immunity. Only 90 years later, in 2008, it was announced that researchers had discovered what had made the 1918 flu so deadly – this was a group of three genes that enabled the virus to weaken a victim's bronchial tubes and lungs, and thus clear the way for bacterial pneumonia (Denworth 2020; History.com editors 2020).

The H1N1 strain became endemic as a less severe infectious disease and circulated for another 40 years as a seasonal virus. It took a second pandemic, the so-called Asian flu (H2N2), which caused about two million deaths during 1957–1958, to destroy most of the 1918 strain. In essence, one flu virus replaced another one, leaving scientists baffled. Human efforts to do the same have failed. The third influenza pandemic of the 20th century was the so-called Hong Kong flu during 1968–1969, which caused one million deaths (Denworth 2020; Qiu et al 2016/17).

In 2009, yet another novel H1N1 influenza virus – known as swine flu – caused a pandemic. It sounded immediate alarm bells because of its similarity to the 1918 killer. Fortunately, the pathogenicity of the virus was not very high and only six months after the virus appeared, scientists were able to develop a vaccine for it. As a result, the virus much more rapidly went the way of the 1918 virus, becoming a widely circulating seasonal flu, from which many people are now protected either by flu vaccinations or by antibodies from a previous infection (Denworth 2020).

In 2003, before the occurrence of swine flu, a severe acute respiratory syndrome (SARS) epidemic occurred. This was not caused by an influenza virus but by a coronavirus, namely SARS-CoV. There are seven known human coronaviruses, four of which circulate widely, causing up to a third of common colds. The coronavirus that caused the SARS outbreak was far more virulent. Thanks to aggressive epidemiological tactics such as isolating the sick, quarantining their contacts and implementing social controls, dangerous outbreaks were limited to a few locations such as Hong Kong and Toronto (Denworth 2020). These outbreaks could be contained because people who were infected quickly fell ill with serious symptoms such as fever and troubled breathing. Most importantly, they transmitted the virus after getting quite ill, not before. This means that patients with SARS only really became contagious once their symptoms appeared. Moreover, if they could be identified within that week and put into isolation with effective infection control, the disease was contained and unable to spread. The result was that, globally, only 8 098 SARS cases and 774 deaths occurred. The world has not seen a case since 2004 (Denworth 2020).

However, global health experts have been warning for years that another pandemic that matches the speed and severity of the 1918 influenza epidemic was a matter not of *if* but of *when* (Gates 2020). In October 2019, Spinney (2019) wrote that 'a future flu pandemic is currently ranked among the leading threats to global security'. These words would prove to be prophetic.

- **Pandemics in South Africa**

Since societies are unique, each one experiences a crisis such as a pandemic differently. As many countries worldwide, South Africa has a history of pandemics. Renowned South African historian, Howard Phillips, describes five epidemics and pandemics that have hit the country since the 17th century, namely smallpox, bubonic plague, the Spanish flu, polio and HIV/AIDS (Koorts 2020).

Pandemics are characterised by certain similarities. One such a characteristic is the spread of the disease by means of human mobility. In 1713, infected sailors of the Dutch East India Company brought smallpox to the Cape. While a quarter of the Dutch Colonists and 35 per cent of the Company's slaves died, entire clans of the Khoikhoi population were wiped out. Anecdotal reports from the Khoikhoi themselves stated that about 90 per cent of the original Khoikhoi population of the south-western Cape had succumbed to the epidemic (Koorts 2020; Phillips 2013; South African History Online 2020). Recent estimates, however, vary between a 36.3 and a 53.7 per cent decline in population numbers (La Croix 2018).

After World War I, the returning troops brought with them an extremely dangerous virus, namely that of the Spanish flu. It was brought inland from the coastal harbours along the most prominent transport routes. In South Africa, the first cases were reported in Cape Town, soon followed by Durban and Johannesburg. Although the official figures indicated 139 471 deaths, it is estimated that between 250 000 and 350 000 people died (Du Plessis & De Bruyn 2020).

During pandemics, there is often the search for scapegoats or, as Phillips (Pick 2012) describes it, the 'politics' of epidemics or pandemics. In this country, there is ample evidence that 'the "victim blaming" took on racial, religious, geographical and xenophobic tones with slave, Khoi, Muslim, migrant, the German Kaiser, the British, blacks, whites, Christians, and others, cast as villains responsible for the outbreaks'.

Invariably, the poor suffer most when health measures are enforced. In South Africa, the poor have always comprised more blacks than whites, which adds a racial dimension to epidemics and pandemics. At the outbreak of the Anglo Boer War in 1899, Britain shipped thousands of horses and tons of grain to South Africa. The grain harboured infected rats, which led to the outbreak of smallpox in harbour cities. Soon, fingers were pointed at poor blacks and Indians living in 'unhealthy' circumstances. This offered authorities the excuse to remove these people from inner cities, destroy their homes and isolate them in quarantine camps. Within a few years, these camps were transformed into municipal locations. This modus operandi was repeated during the Spanish flu when 1923 saw further steps towards apartheid when these measures became laws. Later on, the apartheid government would merely build on this. The establishment of Ndabeni, Langa, Klipspruit (later Pimville) and Soweto, among others, were some 'macropolitical' consequences of epidemics (Koorts 2020; Pick 2012; Spinney 2019).

Positive spin-off of epidemics and pandemics in South Africa have, however, been the establishment of a ministry of health, the emergence of health-orientated NGOs and the production of vaccines (Pick 2012).

• **Covid-19**

On 31 December 2019, a pneumonia of unknown cause was detected in Wuhan and was first reported to the WHO Country Office in China. On 31 December 2019, the WHO declared the outbreak a Public Health Emergency of International Concern. On 7 January 2020, a novel coronavirus was identified from the throat swab sample of a patient. The International Committee on Taxonomy of Viruses (ICTV) named this pathogen severe acute respiratory syndrome coronavirus 2 (SARS-CoV-2) and on 11 February announced a name for the new coronavirus disease, namely Covid-19. Within the first 50 days, it killed more than 1 800 people and infected over 70 000. It rapidly spread across continents and on 11 March 2020, the WHO declared it a global pandemic. The rapid spread of and the high mortality rate caused by Covid-19 soon forced an unprecedented worldwide lockdown – one that humans had never experienced on such a scale (Harapan et al 2020; Lupia et al 2020; Moore, Lipsitch, Barry & Osterholm 2020; Shereen, Khan, Kazmi, Bashir & Siddique 2020; WHO 2020).

○ *Characteristics of Covid-19*
The characteristics of the Covid-19 disease render it particularly deadly. SARS-CoV-2 is a novel viral pathogen to which the global population has little to no pre-existing immunity. This results in worldwide susceptibility. It is transmitted quite efficiently in that the average infected person spreads the disease to two or three others, creating an exponential increase rate – infecting millions of people and moving rapidly around the globe (Johns Hopkins University 2020). It also has a longer incubation period than flu. Whereas the average incubation period for influenza is two days (range: 1–4 days), the average incubation period for Covid-19 is five days (range: 2–14 days). Its carriers may, moreover, infect others even when they are **asymptomatic**. This fact, together with the longer incubation period, allows the virus to move silently in different populations before being detected, making it harder to contain.

○ *Combating Covid-19*
The fact that Covid-19 is such a deadly disease immediately raises questions about ways to combat it. The first and safest public health strategy is to prevent the onset of the coronavirus at all costs. This involves extraordinary restrictions on free movement and assembly – commonly referred to as **lockdown** – and also aggressive testing with a view to interrupting its transmission entirely. In the case of Covid-19, this has proved to be impossible given its global spread. What this action can, however, do is to buy time by 'flattening the curve' so that hospitals and care facilities are not flooded with cases all at once (Basu 2020; Regalado 2020).

A second strategy would necessitate a significant percentage of the population acquiring immunity, a state to which epidemiologists refer as *herd immunity* (Johns Hopkins University 2020). As with any other infection, there are two ways to achieve herd immunity, the best way to do so rapidly being by means of vaccination. A vaccine delivers a small amount of a virus into the body and the immune system learns how to fight it off without falling ill. In this way, diseases like smallpox were eradicated (Regalado 2020). To date (July 2020), a vaccine for Covid-19 has, however, not been developed. While scientists are working feverishly to develop an effective vaccine, experts agree that it will take a year or longer from the outset of the pandemic for a highly effective vaccine to be developed, tested, mass produced and administered (Basu 2020; Johns Hopkins University 2020; Regalado 2020).

The other way to acquire herd immunity is to let the virus keep on spreading. Eventually many people will be infected and – if they survive – become immune. In this way, an outbreak peters out because it becomes harder for the pathogen to find susceptible hosts (Regalado 2020). To understand this concept, one should know how individuals acquire immunity. A person can become immune (or resistant) after being exposed to a disease-causing agent, such as the coronavirus. In response to intruder organisms, the body produces antibodies specific to the virus. Once it has resisted the disease, it retains a 'memory' of the virus for future protection, which means that the person has become immune to that specific virus and is naturally 'protected' (Basu 2020; Sanchez 2020). If a large number of people – 'the herd' – become immune to a virus to such an extent that people who are not immune are also protected (indirect protection) because of the high population immunity, herd immunity has been acquired. For example, if 80 per cent of a population is immune to a virus, four out of every five people who encounter someone with the disease will not become ill and thus not spread the disease any further, essentially because it runs out of hosts to infect. In this way, the spread of infectious diseases can be controlled.

Depending on how contagious an infection is, typically 50 to 90 per cent of a population must be immune to achieve herd immunity. Based on early estimates of how transmissible the coronavirus is, at least 60 to 70 per cent of a population will probably need to be immune to achieve herd immunity (Basu 2020; Brock & Prescott 2020; Johns Hopkins University 2020; Regalado 2020; Sanchez 2020). The point at which herd immunity is reached is mathematically related to the propensity of the virus to spread, expressed as its reproduction number or R_0 (pronounced 'R naught'). The basic reproduction number (R_0), is an epidemiological metric used to describe the contagiousness or transmissibility of infectious agents (Delamater, Street, Leslie, Yang & Jacobsen 2019). It has a higher R_0 than flu, which means that more people will need to be infected and become immune before the pandemic can end. Scientists estimate that the R_0 for the

coronavirus is between 2 and 2.5, which means that each infected person passes it to about two other people without any measures to contain the contagion (Regalado 2020). However, if the coronavirus spreads more easily than the experts think, more people will need to be infected before herd immunity is reached. For example, an R_0 of 3.66 per cent of the population has to be immune before the effect is reached, according to the simplest model. According to Regalado (2020), whether the figure is 50, 60 or 80 per cent worldwide, billions could be infected and millions could be killed. The enormity of the problem emerges when one is confronted with figures such as the following. One expert analysis found that creating herd immunity in the UK would require more than 47 million people to be infected. With a 2.3 per cent fatality rate and a 19 per cent rate of severe disease, this could result in more than a million people dying and a further eight million needing critical care (Basu 2020). Such predictions based on models need, however, to be treated with caution.

Experts therefore warn against striving for herd immunity without a controlled vaccine in place. Sweden has taken such a risk by opting for a relaxed approach, which aims to minimise the impact on the economy and to slow the spread of the virus by means of herd immunity. According to Brock and Prescott (2020), the country has failed to contain outbreaks around their elderly population, resulting in more than 80 per cent of their deaths occurring in nursing homes.

It is poor consolation that the more slowly the pandemic unfolds, the greater the chance for new treatments or vaccines to be discovered. Regardless of the specifics, achieving herd immunity by means of the repeated process of infection of one person, recovery and immunity will take a long time – many months or even years (Sanchez 2020). Delamater et al (2019) estimate that the current outbreak will likely last up to between 18 and 24 months for 60 to 70 per cent of the population to become immune. These authors also predict that, depending on control measures and other factors, cases may come in waves of different heights – as was the case with the Spanish flu. The data so far suggest that the virus has a case fatality risk of around 1 per cent compared with the 2 per cent of the 1918 influenza pandemic (Gates 2020).

Apart from the biology of the virus, as ever, the social determinants of health will also be drivers of the outcomes of the pandemic. Social determinants such as levels of income and education, access to healthcare, not being essential workers, not being able to self-isolate and not being able to work from home are sure to influence the outcomes of the Covid-19 pandemic (Brock & Prescott 2020).

• The effects of pandemics

It is safe to say that each pandemic has harmed human life and economic development. In 2019, Frank Snowden, a historian at Yale University in the USA, wrote *Epidemics and Society: From the Black Death to the Present.* His global history – which spans more than a millennium of outbreaks and covers diseases like the bubonic plague, smallpox, malaria, the respiratory illness, SARS and Ebola – explains the longer-term social, political and cultural consequences of such vast outbreaks of infectious diseases on society (Spinney 2019). According to Spinney (2019), 'Snowden's broader thesis is that infectious diseases have shaped social evolution no less powerfully than have wars, revolutions and economic crises'.

The first and most obvious impact of pandemics are the health consequences.

○ *Health effects*

Pandemics invariably affect millions of people by causing widespread serious illness and thousands of deaths. In the 14th century, for example, the 'Black Death' plague killed half of the population of Europe (Qiu et al 2016/17). As already mentioned, the Spanish flu infected more than one-third of the world's population (500 million) and killed more than 50 million people. By August 2020, the Coronavirus had infected more than 21 million people worldwide – more than four times as many as three months earlier:

Table 19.1 Covid-19 situation – globally: 6 May 2020 and 16 August 2020 (WHO 2020a; WHO 2020b)

Area	Confirmed number of cases		Total number of deaths	
	6 May	16 August	6 May	16 August
Globally	3 588 773	21 294 845	247 503	761 779
Africa	33 973	945 165	1 202	18 476
Americas	1 507 148	11 420 860	81 070	414 326
Eastern Mediterranean	221 230	1 723 673	8 290	45 704
Europe	1 593 828	3 754 649	147 780	214 092
South East Asia	76 998	3 040 168	2 821	59 875
Western Pacific	154 884	409 589	6 327	9 293

At the beginning of May, the Americas and Europe were clearly the leaders in terms of the number of confirmed cases. South East Asia (including, among others, India, Bangladesh, Indonesia and Nepal) surpassed the May numbers of the Americas and Europe in August – although with much lower death rates. China, where the pandemic had had its origins, forms part of the Western Pacific with countries such as the Philippines, Singapore and Japan. According to the WHO (2020a; 2020b), China reported only a slight increase in both the number of cases and the number of deaths between May to August 2020: the number of cases increased from 84 406 to 89 761, while the number of deaths only increased by 67 (from 4 643 to 4 710).

In Europe, the countries occupying the top four positions remained the same between May and August 2020, merely changing their order:

Table 19.2 Covid-19 situation – Europe: 6 May 2020 and 16 August 2020 (WHO 2020a; WHO 2020b)

Country	Ranking in Europe		Confirmed cases		Number of deaths	
	6 May	16 August	6 May	16 August	6 May	16 August
Spain	1	2	219 329	342 813	25 613	28 617
Italy	2	4	213 013	253 438	29 315	35 392
United Kingdom	3	3	194 994	316 371	29 427	41 358
Russian Federation	4	1	165 929	922 853	1 537	15 685

In May, the United States of America had 1 171 185 confirmed cases (WHO 2020a), but reached the milestone of five million by 16 August 2020. At the same time, the number of deaths increased from 62 698 (WHO 2020a) to more than 167 201, which made the USA the world leader in this pandemic (Pineda 2020).

With a total number of about 34 000 cases and a mere 1 202 deaths in May 2020, Africa had by far the lowest numbers globally (see Table 19.1). This was to change dramatically by 16 August 2020, with confirmed cases totalling 945 165 and

deaths rising to nearly 18 476. It also became obvious that South Africa stood out in terms of numbers and occupied the top position. By 16 August 2020, South Africa had the highest number of cases in Africa (583 653, with 11 677 deaths), followed by Nigeria with 48 770 cases and only 974 deaths (WHO 2020a; 2020b). South Africa comprised about half of the overall cases in Africa (africanews 2020; eNCA 2020). In contrast, South Africa's closest neighbours had far lower numbers of both confirmed cases and deaths:

Table 19.3 Covid-19 situation – South Africa and neighbouring countries: 6 May 2020 and 16 August 2020 (WHO 2020a; WHO 2020b)

Country	Ranking in Europe		Confirmed cases		Number of deaths	
	6 May	16 August	6 May	16 August	6 May	16 August
Botswana	40	36	23	1 214	1	3
Eswatini	30	22	119	3 745	1	69
Lesotho	–	41	–	903	–	25
Mozambique	34	24	80	2 791	0	19
Namibia	43	20	16	3 907	0	35
South Africa	1	1	7 439	583 653	148	11 677
Zimbabwe	39	16	34	5 176	4	130

Not only did South Africa rank first in Africa, but, by August 2020, the country became a global hot spot, ranking fifth in the world after the USA, Brazil, India and Russia – this amid ever-increasing Covid-19 confirmed cases. This is an alarming statistic, given that South Africa has the smallest population of this group of countries (africanews 2020; eNCA 2020).

The rapid increase in the global numbers of Covid-19 and the absence of a cure serve to underscore the urgent need for prevention. It is therefore promising that, globally, the biotechnology industry is working at a frenetic pace to develop therapeutic and vaccine measures to combat the disease. At the time of writing (July 2020), globally, 626 unique Covid-19 therapeutic and vaccine candidates were being developed, 223 of which were being tested in clinical trials (Bio 2020).

On 23 June 2020, the first clinical trial in South Africa and on the continent for a Covid-19 vaccine was announced, led by Shabir Madhi, Professor of Vaccinology at Wits University and Director of the South Africa Medical Research Council (SAMRC) Vaccines and Infectious Diseases Analytics Research Unit (VIDA). Wits University is collaborating with the University of Oxford and the Oxford Jenner Institute

on the South African trial. The vaccine is already being evaluated in a large clinical trial in the UK where more than 4 000 participants have already been enrolled. A similar and related studies are about to start in Brazil, while an even larger study of the same vaccine with up to 30 000 participants is planned in the USA (africanews 2020; SAMRC 2020). Yet, all indications are that this pandemic will not be conquered in the immediate future.

Apart from the debilitating and often fatal consequences for those directly affected, pandemics have a range of negative economic, social and political consequences.

While the number of new cases and disease fatalities are slowing down in some parts of the world, indications are that it will only reach its current peak in the global South during September or October 2020 (Moore et al 2020).

Apart from the debilitating and often fatal consequences for those directly affected, pandemics have a range of negative economic, social and political consequences.

○ *Economic effects*
Pandemics wreak havoc with the economies of the world – to the point of causing them to become unstable. Pandemics could become a long-term burden and have both direct and

indirect costs. The direct costs of dealing with the disease outbreak can be very high. In 2016, the Global Health Risk Framework for the Future (GHRF) Commission estimated that the global economic loss from potential pandemics could be more than $60 billion per year. The current pandemic is bound to exceed this figure by billions. The direct health-related costs include, among others, testing for the virus, organising and rearranging healthcare facilities, providing the necessary protective equipment to healthcare workers and providing quarantine facilities. Indirect costs include everything that contributes to a decline in gross domestic product (GDP) and can be equally devastating. Significant numbers of industries across the spectrum – from tourism, agriculture, construction and mining to retail and wholesale – suffer enormous losses, as does informal trade. Large numbers of companies do not survive the lockdown periods, causing millions to lose their livelihoods. This in turn results in substantially decreased tax income for governments, who, at the same time, have to provide increased assistance to those already receiving grants or to the growing numbers of other dependants. Recovery from the Covid-19 pandemic for global economies is bound to take years.

○ *Social effects*

Pandemics have a destructive effect on societal structures. In fact, the social impacts of pandemics are no less severe than the economic ones. In South Africa, the victims of the Spanish flu were mostly between 18 and 40 years of age, which left a generation of impoverished, traumatised orphans. This pattern repeated itself during the HIV/AIDS pandemic. Family structures, already debilitated by the migrant labour system, were further compromised. It is common knowledge that in a society characterised by disrupted families, social problems are rife. Because of HIV/AIDS, millions of orphans now have to be raised by their grandparents – precisely those who are most vulnerable to Covid-19 (Koorts 2020).

In the case of a pandemic with true potential for high morbidity (the rate of disease in a population) and mortality (death rate), severe measures need to be implemented. In a globalised, media-connected world, national borders are no barriers to real or perceived threats – especially in the case of a virus, therefore travel has to be severely restricted, while schools, businesses, markets and sport activities have to be closed. One such measure, namely school closure and reopening, raises a range of ethical and social issues, particularly since families from underprivileged backgrounds are likely to be disproportionately affected by the intervention (Qiu et al 2016/17).

○ *Security effects*

In its 2016 book, *The Neglected Dimension of Global Security – A Framework to Counter Infectious Disease Crises*, the GHRF Commission states that '[a] range of factors, including increasing population, economic globalization, environmental degradation, and ever-increasing human interaction across the globe, are changing the dynamics of infectious diseases. As a consequence, we should anticipate a growing frequency of infectious disease threats to global security'.

Few other risks pose such a threat to human lives and few other events can damage economic activity as do pandemics. As already mentioned, the GHRF Commission's estimated global economic loss from potential pandemics could exceed $60 billion per year. Yet, compared with the resources spent on national security or avoiding financial crises, nations devote only a fraction of their resources to the prevention of and preparation for pandemics. The latter measures are far more effective – and ultimately far less expensive – than reacting to them when they occur (GHRF Commission 2016). The GHRF Commission's 2016 estimate of the likely occurrence of at least one pandemic and a 20 per cent chance of seeing four or more over the next 100 years has become a reality with the outbreak of Covid-19. The global devastation caused by this pandemic attests to the fact that pandemics – far from merely being matters of health – are essential aspects of both national and global security.

It stands to reason that an effective and efficient emergency response is required as protection against the pandemic spread of infectious diseases and to reduce avoidable mortality and morbidity. This is conceptualised as *health security* (Qiu et al 2016/17; Yates, Dhillon & Rannan-Eliya 2015). There is no simple definition of health security. It can mean, variously, human security, the prevention and control of infectious diseases, and the complexity of global health security (Horton & Das 2015). In a report published in 2003, the UN's Commission on Human Security advances a more constructive interpretation of health security, namely that it means both protecting *and* empowering people (Chen & Takemi 2015). According to this report, health security – as human security – is people centred. It is important to be people centred because 'irrespective of the threat, what matters is people – not borders, not international relations, not even money and economics' (Chen & Takemi 2015: 1887). However, apart from the health risks that threaten human survival and wellbeing, people face multidimensional security threats, such as extreme poverty and deprivation. As mentioned earlier, the disconcerting fact is that these multidimensional security threats are interactive. Thus, while the economic and political effects of an outbreak of an infectious disease can be catastrophic, other insecurities such as conflict and poverty can intensify a society's vulnerability. Faced with multiple threats, governments' responses to pandemics should go beyond merely containing an infectious agent. The economic and social effects of pandemics should likewise be addressed (Chen & Takemi 2015).

This very fact seems to create an obsession among some governments and/or its ministers to regulate every aspect of people's lives during the pandemic. It draws the attention away from the two critical problems, namely the virus disease and its devastating consequences. Not only is the coronavirus a novel one, but globally countries have been caught unawares as to how precisely to deal with it. This has driven changes in behaviour and public policy, and has often led governments to implement non-scientifically based actions, which exacerbate the negative economic impacts, such as travel bans, quarantines and blockades on the import and export of food, wine and other items.

Horton and Das (2015) warn that to invoke arguments of global health security might encourage violent responses and give governments – especially authoritarian-minded ones – permission to use health crises as justification for sometimes extreme curbs on liberty or citizens' political, economic and social rights. This was evidenced during the outbreak of the Ebola virus between 2014 and 2016 when photographs appeared in the news media of police brutality against the public for breaching curfews.

Unfortunately, this phenomenon again initially surfaced in a couple of countries, South Africa being one, during the Covid-19 pandemic. While the WHO applauded South Africa's efforts to curb the spread of the disease (Brandt 2020), the UN stated that it had received numerous complaints about murder, rape, the use of firearms and corruption in the country during the lockdown period. In general, the UN has spoken out on what is regarded to be 'a toxic lockdown culture in some countries', which includes the use of excessive and sometimes deadly force by security forces to enforce lockdowns and curfews (Farge 2020). According to Hartley and Mills (2020), during the first three weeks of the lockdown, more than 100 charges were laid against the South African police for instances of abuse.

Many of the steps taken by governments to limit social interaction are indeed necessary and legitimate. However, in times of turmoil, apprehension and uncertainty amid a deadly pandemic, there needs to be a balance between measures required to contain the spread of a virus and respect for democratic rights, and between individual liberties and the needs of the economy and public health. An extreme health crisis of pandemic proportions therefore requires, on the one hand, what Robins (2020) calls a 'listening government' and, on the other, citizens who are prepared to make sacrifices.

- **Some concluding remarks on infectious diseases**

Infectious diseases have threatened health security since the beginning of civilisation. As exploration, trade and warfare spread, so did disease. Infectious disease pandemics represent one of the most potent threats to humankind, both in terms of potential lives lost and in terms of potential economic disruption. Our current globalising world provides new contexts for infectious pandemics, namely larger human populations, unprecedented volumes of transnational movement and rapid travel. This world is also characterised by increasing global inequalities in respect of both economics and health. In many countries, the healthcare infrastructure is deficient, and comorbidities such as other infections (eg HIV, TB, malaria), malnutrition and chronic respiratory disease are common. The impact of Covid-19 and any future pandemics could be even more severe in such areas (Moore et al 2020).

The characteristics of biomedicine

Biomedicine is characterised by the following:

- It adopts a technological imperative. This means that physicians are trained to want to provide the best possible medical care; invariably, to them this means the latest and the most advanced technological care. Sometimes, the merits of technological interventions are overplayed.

- It is reductionist in that it reduces disease to chemistry and physics. Biochemical or biophysical abnormality becomes the criterion for diagnosing the disease and treating it. Because the explanations of disease thus focus on biological changes, social and psychological factors are often neglected.

- It is an objective science, based on empirical observation and induction. Medicine thus claims to offer the only valid response to the understanding of disease and illness.

These characteristics translate into medical practice that has the following features:

- The nature and causes of health and disease: Health is regarded as the absence of biological abnormality. All diseases have specific causes or origin – that is, a specific aetiology (or origin) such as a virus, parasite or bacterium. Disease is viewed as an alien intruder that needs to be expelled.

- The patient: Because of the mind/body dualism and the mechanical metaphor, the focus of the treatment is on the patient's body.
- The nature of the intervention: The focus is on cure, the aim being to manipulate the physical symptoms so as to make them disappear. The most appropriate place for treatment is considered to be a medical environment, such as the consulting room or the hospital.

An evaluation of biomedicine

Factors such as the escalating costs of healthcare and the increasing prominence of alternative and complementary therapies have given rise to criticism of biomedicine. At the same time, however, one cannot discount the successes of this kind of therapy.

Successes of biomedicine

The 19th and 20th centuries saw major pharmacological breakthroughs, such as Louis Pasteur's development of vaccines and Alexander Fleming's discovery of penicillin. Biomedicine has been able to eradicate many infectious and parasitic diseases, and to lower the infant mortality rate. Successes have also been achieved in respect of certain chronic diseases, such as diabetes mellitus and skin cancer. The development of new and safer surgical techniques resulted in bypass heart surgery and organ transplants. In 1967, South Africa's Christiaan Barnard performed the first heart transplant in the world. Because of all of these medical improvements, healing occurred, and many lives were saved.

Criticism of biomedicine

During the past four to five decades, the institution of medicine and the biomedical model have increasingly been challenged by criticism from both popular and academic sources.

- Efficacy is exaggerated

Most of the decline in the mortality rate achieved in the West from the late 19th century to the middle of the 20th century was the result of sociocultural factors. It thus comes as no surprise that both from within its own ranks and from disciplines such as sociology, it has been argued that medicine's efficacy has been overplayed. McKeown, a professor of social medicine, was especially responsible for demonstrating that the decline of mortality in Western societies to a greater extent resulted from social phenomena – such as nutrition, hygiene and patterns of reproduction – than from medical interventions such as vaccinations or treatments. Ivan Illich, an Austrian philosopher and social critic, went even further by declaring biomedicine to be

a major threat to health. The central theme of his book, *Medical Nemesis – The Expropriation of Health*, is that of iatrogenic disease – disease caused by medicine itself. Examples would be complications from plastic surgery or removing the wrong kidney. The death of pop star Michael Jackson is a classic example of **iatrogenesis**. His doctor, Conrad Murray, was held responsible for his death by having provided him with excessive drugs and he was imprisoned for involuntary manslaughter.

- Professional medical dominance

In numerous Western societies, but principally in the US, no group has gained such dominance as the medical profession. The medical profession is accorded exceptional status vis-à-vis other health professionals, based firstly on claims of the superior efficacy of medical methods over other healing arts and, secondly, on its lengthy period of education and training. The members of the profession – and by extension the institution of medicine – therefore play a dominant role in defining health and in the organisation of healthcare. This dominance was not evident from the outset but over the course of 150 years, medicine has developed into an institution of social control. Medical power can be seen to be functional in many ways. Both patients and allied health workers appreciate doctors' confident expertise. However, while the power of the medical profession is said to be used solely in the interests of health and in attempting to help humanity, it can also be said that on the strength of this power, doctors exert influence on patients, on co-practitioners and on the public in matters that fall not only within but also beyond their jurisdiction – the latter referring to the phenomenon of **medicalisation**.

Professional medical dominance, and by implication biomedicine's presumed superiority in relation to other forms of healing, is continually being challenged. While biomedicine has questioned the basis of **complementary and alternative medicines** (CAMs), arguing that they are 'unscientific' and therefore incorrect, another view – which suggests that all knowledge is conditional – would imply that CAM remedies are of equal validity. It would appear that there is a decline in faith in biomedicine with more and more people opting to seek help from and are successfully being treated by CAM practitioners. In Section 6.4, we look at this healthcare option.

- Disregard for the social context of health and disease

Owing to its indifference regarding the social and material causes of disease – mainly because of the germ theory – the biomedical model fails to account for the social inequalities in health. Another consequence of this neglect of the social context is that the focus is on the isolated individual as the site of disease and the appropriate object of treatment. This places the burden of health predominantly on the individual rather than on the social system and its health sector.

- Patient's body is isolated from the person

By focusing its treatment merely on the patient's body, biomedicine disregards the link between physical and mental well-being. Even the medical specialisation of psychiatry – concerned with the diagnosis and treatment of disorders with mainly mental or behavioural symptoms – predominantly seeks organic causes for the conditions it treats. Related to this problem is the biomedical view that patients are passive rather than actively thinking persons. While they have no medical training, patients do have their own valid interpretations and accounts of their experiences of health and illness – as we have gathered from Weber's interpretivist perspective (see section 4.3). Also, people's perceptions and experiences of health and illness are not merely reactions to physical bodily changes but are influenced by sociocultural factors. For treatment and care to be effective, these subjective perceptions and experiences must be acknowledged. In an attempt to address this problem, more attention is now being given to communication skills and to the behavioural and social sciences in the curriculum of healthcare providers.

- Medical control of women's health

Perhaps the most powerful criticism of biomedicine has come from feminists such as Ann Oakley. In her book, *The Captured Womb: A History of the Medical Care of Pregnant Women* (1984), she argues that women's lives have been subject to far greater control and regulation by the medical profession than those of men. An example is that of pregnancy and childbirth. In the 19th century, the institution of medicine took the control of childbirth out of the hands of women and managed to ensure – despite the lack of any sound evidence of benefit – that by the 1970s virtually all babies were born in hospital. In the process, what is primarily a woman's experience was removed from the domestic domain to the public one of the hospital, in which a male-dominated branch of medicine – obstetrics – had control. Moreover, pregnancy and childbirth came to be treated as 'disease' and therefore subjected to an entire array of technological interventions. Thus, something previously viewed as a 'natural' event attended by women was medicalised. For one strand of feminism, namely Foucauldian feminism, at issue is how women are able to challenge their medicalisation, especially given the pervasiveness of medical

knowledge, even in so-called self-help movements. Feminist Foucauldians argue that large parts of the women's health movement have been incorporated into a patriarchal net of self-surveillance.

Women, especially from the women's health movement, have, during the past few decades, effectively exposed and challenged the way in which medicine came to control their bodies. Medical discourse has contributed to the construction of women's bodies as fragile, passive vessels that routinely require medical monitoring and interventions. Because women often experienced that doctors dismissed their own interpretations of their bodily experiences as subjective and irrelevant, they have produced an entirely new health literature for women and have developed forms of medical care based on alternative philosophies to those supported by the dominant institutions of medicine.

- Scientific method only way to obtain truth about disease

Biomedicine assumes that it is able to identify the truth about disease by means of its scientific method. According to sociologists, disease categories are not merely accurate descriptions of anatomical malfunctioning, but are socially created – that is, they develop because of arguments that also have a social content. Thus medical belief systems, like any others, are dependent on the society that produces them. However, the apparent 'truth' of medicine means that values may be transformed into apparent facts. For example, the belief that women were unsuited to education in the 19th century was supported by so-called medical evidence. Moreover, the fact that concepts of and explanations for disease have and continue to change over time, attests to their being social constructs. One example is the early medical explanation for the condition of hysteria, namely that it is the result of the womb of a hysterical woman moving around in her body.

19.3.2 The social model

Because of the criticism levelled at biomedicine and also some major societal changes, medicine is increasingly called upon to return to the health problems of the *whole* person. While biomedicine has advanced over the past century, a range of other disciplines – such as sociology, psychology, epidemiology and economics – has explored the role of factors other than physiological ones that influence health and these factors have provided a different yet complementary way of understanding and addressing health and disease. Apart from considering the physiological aspects of illness, biomedical practitioners must, to a greater extent, develop insight into other aspects regarding the people they treat. Thus, the characteristic behaviour of their patients – the *psychological* aspects of the condition – and the context in which their patients live – the *social* aspects of illness conditions – must also be considered. Singular causes of disease are no longer the main focus. Contemporary physicians are often required to deal with health disorders that are described as 'problems in living'. As the name indicates, these are dysfunctions that involve many causes, not all of which are biological in nature. Research has indicated that how we respond to social, psychological and cultural influences affects not only whether we become sick, but also the form, duration and intensity of symptoms and disabilities. This more holistic way of looking at health has resulted in several models. One such model is the biopsychosocial model, proposed more than three decades ago by the American psychiatrist Dr George Engel.

By employing the biopsychosocial model, one will be able to understand how suffering and disease are affected by multiple levels of organisation – from the societal to the molecular. In determining the health status of people, the emphasis is on the role of people's behaviour, what work they do, and how and where they live. People are no longer regarded as passive victims of disease, but can themselves participate in their own recovery and in maintaining and promoting their health. Because of the impact of societal and environmental changes, social solutions are sought to the problems of health and disease. Whereas the biomedical model keeps health in the biological context, the biopsychosocial model puts it in the social context, thus offering a broader perspective. The emphases of sociological perspectives on health and disease are thus on aspects of healthcare such as prevention of illness, rehabilitation and the social management of illness, rather than on biological and medical aspects of healthcare.

A social model questions the ability of biomedicine to explain all important health issues. By highlighting the role of social factors – such as class, gender, ethnicity and inequality – and processes in influencing and patterning health and illness, whole realms of experience that do not readily lend themselves to purely biomedical explanations have been identified.

The social model of disability

A useful way to illustrate how the social model differs from the biomedical model is to compare the biomedical approach of disability with that of the social model. According to the biomedical model, disability is the result of an accidental trauma or bodily abnormality that cannot be corrected by medicine. In this approach, disability is equated with

disease or impairment. Rehabilitation focuses on 'curing' people with disabilities or helping them to act 'normally'. However, if this is not feasible, the route to be taken is that of removing such people from society and institutionalising them so that they can receive specialist care.

According to the social model, disability is firmly located within the social environment. This model therefore focuses on the barriers that the social environment may present to people with disabilities to participate in society. People with disabilities are not so much prevented by their own bodies' inabilities from participating in economic and social activities as by society's discriminatory attitudes and oppressive ideas.

The social model has had considerable influence on society regarding people with disabilities. It has been used for politicising the rights of people with disabilities and has resulted in many countries passing legislation in respect of matters such as access to buildings. South African equity legislation has also set a target of 2 per cent participation of people with disabilities for the public service sector. In 2011–2012, people with disabilities comprised only 0.8 per cent of the total workforce reported. (Department of Labour 2012).

One should however be mindful of the fact that the social model does not apply to the entire range of conditions defined as 'disability'. In the main, it only explains the situation of people with stable sensory and/or mobility impairments and of those who do not experience pain (Bradby 2009).

Convergence between the biomedical model and the social model

The matter of whether biomedical practice is limited to the biomedical model is still being debated and seems to vary among its practitioners. So, for instance, practitioners in public health, paediatrics and family practice are especially likely to question some of the assumptions of the biomedical model. There is, however, ample evidence that, in general, biomedical practitioners' assumptions about the nature of health and disease have been broadened to include insights garnered from other disciplines. In fact, doctors often use a number of interpretations and practices from beyond the parameters of clinical science. A case in point is that of the independent humanitarian organisation, Doctors Without Borders/Médecins Sans Frontières (MSF), which epitomises a broad-based, sociological understanding of disease and healthcare. Not only do the organisation's healthcare workers treat disease, but it also speaks out against the social causes of disease, death and disability, such as the attitude towards women that underlie the use of rape as a military tactic and the role of international economics in the short and brutal lives of street children (Weitz 2010).

19.4 Theoretical approaches to health and disease

By now you must be well aware of the fact that theories are the key tools for sociological investigation. In Chapter 1, we were told that sociology is perspectival, meaning that it comprises many theories and many perspectives – each providing a very different way of understanding social phenomena. Also, when it comes to studying health and disease in society, the theories and perspectives with which you are now familiar provide different accounts of the social causes of disease and of the role of the medical institution.

19.4.1 Structural functionalism

It was Talcott Parsons (1951) who applied the structural-functionalist perspective to the study of health and illness by highlighting the social dimensions of these phenomena. He developed the concept of the **sick role** to analyse sickness as a social role. In order for society to operate properly, sickness has to be managed in such a way that the majority of society's members are able to perform their normal social roles and obligations. Too much disease would be dysfunctional and disruptive to society as a whole – for example, the economic system would not be serviced and there would be an unsustainable demand on healthcare services. Society therefore regards disease as a form of deviance, which has to be regulated by the medical profession. In this way, the medical profession represents the interests of society as a whole by acting to curb the deviant tendencies of individuals who otherwise might try to escape their social roles.

According to Parsons, disease threatens social stability in that people – either consciously or unconsciously – use ill health to evade their social responsibilities. What intrigued Parsons was how society allows illness, yet succeeds in minimising its impact. To him, there had to be a 'formula' for allowing a certain amount of 'legitimate' sickness. This led him to develop the concept of the **sick role**.

The sick role is a temporary role and refers to social expectations regarding how society, on the one hand, should deal with sick people and how, on the other, sick people should behave. The sick role is based on the assumption that, generally, the sick person does not deliberately choose to become ill. Society accordingly allows people who accept the sick role to gain two rights (benefits) but also imposes two explicit behavioural requirements (two obligations):

- The sick person has the right to be excused – temporarily – from social responsibilities. Society however requires a physician's validation of the problem to maintain some

control and to prevent people from lingering in the sick role.
- The sick person is not held responsible for the illness and society accepts that the sick person must be taken care of by others, such as healthcare professionals.
- The sick person is obliged not to get so accustomed to the sick role or enjoy the lifting of responsibilities that he/she loses the motivation to get well.
- The sick person is expected to seek medical advice and to co-operate with healthcare experts.

Parsons has been criticised for the fact that the concept of the sick role does not allow for variation in the experience of ill health due to factors such as age, gender, social class, race and culture. This is the case because Parsons assumed that the urge to recover from ill health and return to optimum role functioning to be universal. In some cases, the sick role does not apply, such as when people are not able to take advantage of their rights when sick. Women who have to care for their children often find it difficult to adopt the sick role. Certain diseases are stigmatised (for example AIDS and alcoholism), which means that the victim is blamed for contracting the condition. In this case, the right to be held unaccountable for contracting the disease is denied.

Parsons was also criticised for not differentiating between different medical conditions and their social and cultural implications. For one, the sick role cannot be applied to chronic diseases. Remember that from the second half of the 20th century, **life expectancy** increased, with more and more people now living into their 70s, 80s and beyond. Older people are more prone to suffer from chronic or relapsing diseases and are often unable to meet all the obligations of the sick role, particularly the one stipulating that it is a temporary role that has to be vacated as soon as possible. Society therefore has to modify these social obligations so that they are less rigid. One solution is that the sick person may have to take on another role, that of 'disabled'.

Parsons has also been criticised for assuming that the process of normalisation – of vacating the sick role and returning to normal social functioning – is consensual. Often, patients engage in prolonged illness behaviour despite the professional declaring him or her to be healthy because it is 'comfortable' role to occupy – other people take over some of the person's responsibilities and such a person is pampered.

In all fairness, one has to say that Parsons did not believe that his model of the sick role could be found in every case of ill health or that medical practitioners and their patients performed consistently in their respective roles. What he presented was an ideal type – a model that could be used with a view to understanding a particular phenomenon (in this case sickness).

Despite the fact that Parsons conceptualised the sick role in the middle of the last century and that his frame of reference was the US, he remains relevant today. His notion of the sick role remains important partly because it was the first truly sociological theory of disease. His research moreover proved to be important because it stimulated later research on interactions between ill people and others (Morrall 2001; Weitz 2010; White 2002).

19.4.2 Conflict theory

According to the conflict theory, inequality and injustice are the sources of conflict that permeate society. Because resources and power are distributed unequally in society, some members of society and also some institutions have more material goods, power, influence and prestige than others. Individuals and groups in society therefore have to compete for limited resources, such as money, leisure and sexual partners. Social inequalities, however, also extend to health and healthcare.

Inequalities in health

Before the industrialisation of society, which developed about 200 years ago, mortality was mostly the result of infectious diseases, such as cholera, dysentery and the plague. These infectious diseases did not discriminate between the members of impoverished classes and those of more affluent classes in that such diseases thrived among both classes. Because of certain social developments in the West from the late 19th century to the middle of the 20th century, death rates declined dramatically. Economic development caused improvements in people's diets as agricultural techniques developed and transportation of produce became faster and more efficient; people also started taking nutritional supplements, for example vitamin C for scurvy – all resulting in people becoming more resistant to infections. Some biomedical advances also contributed to the decline in infectious diseases. In 1928, Alexander Fleming discovered an extremely potent antibiotic substance. Penicillin is said to have changed the course of history by having saved and continuing to save millions of people around the world. It was instrumental in conquering

some of humankind's most ancient scourges, including **syphilis**, **gangrene** and **tuberculosis**. The result of all of these changes and developments was a general increase in longevity. However, this progress has not extended to all parts of the world and nearly a century later, inequalities in respect of health and access to healthcare among different societies and also within the same society persist.

By now, you must be familiar with Marx's stratification of society into two major social classes, depicted as the 'haves' and the 'have-nots'. While some sociologists have – because of strong evidence for the class basis of inequality – sought to retain the usefulness of class for the sociology of health and disease, others consider class to be largely redundant and outmoded under the impact of postmodern analyses that claim to focus on complexity, difference and identity. Be that as it may, by classifying South Africans according to 'race', the apartheid system actually divided the society into the two-class system proposed by Marx – those who were accorded specific rights and those who were denied them. Because the apartheid policies caused immense hardship for blacks in this country, it stands to reason that it had an equally harmful effect on the health of the majority of South Africans.

In essence, the relationship between social class and health refers to health inequalities. Therefore, whether one belongs to the so-called haves or to the have-nots, it is bound to influence one's chances of experiencing disease and premature death. Being born into deprivation and moreover continuing to live in deprivation increase one's chances of disease and early death. Although the associations between poverty and health have been recognised for over 150 years, these inequalities in health still persist – and in some cases are widening – in the context of rapid economic and social change. On the one hand, there are significant discrepancies in the health statuses of developed and developing countries. Two factors in particular tell us much about the health and living conditions of populations. The first of these is life expectancy, which is the average number of years that a group of people can expect to live. The other factor is the child or under-five mortality rate – the number of deaths among children under five years old for every 1 000 live births – but especially the infant mortality rate – the number of deaths among infants less than one year old for every 1 000 live births.

Table 19.2 reflects a comparison of some developing and some developing countries in respect of their life expectancies to illustrate the discrepancies among them.

Table 19.4 Life expectancy: International comparisons, 1990, 2011 and 2020

Country	1990	2011	2020
Australia	77	82	82
Kenya	57	61	59
Spain	77	82	81
South Africa	62	53	61
United Kingdom	76	81	80
Zimbabwe	61	51	60
Germany	75	81	80
Nigeria	46	52	55

(Sources: United Nations Department of Economic and Social Affairs 2019; World Bank 2013)

From Table 19.2 it is evident that in the case of all of the more developed countries, life expectancy has increased in the three-decade period between 1990 and 2020. Among the less-developed countries listed here, Nigeria shows a steady increase (nine years) in life expectancy over the 30-year period, while Kenya displays an increase of four years between 1990 and 2011, followed by a slight decrease of two years by 2020. South Africa and Zimbabwe display similar trends, namely a drop of nine and 10 years respectively between 1990 and 2011, followed by increases to the 1990 levels. In respect of these two countries, the HIV/AIDS pandemic was, in the main, to blame for these decreases. Since 2000, HIV prevalence rates have appeared to be stabilising – partly due to the rollout of antiretroviral medicines during the last decades of the 20th century. This has led to a recovery in life expectancy, as seen in the cases of South Africa and Nigeria. These levels are, however, still about 20 years less than those in more developed countries (Pretorius, Matebesi & Ackermann 2013; World Bank 2013; Worldometer 2020).

The other indicator of the health of populations is under-five mortality. Globally, considerable progress has been made in under-five mortality rates (U5MRs). In 1990, more than 50 countries had U5MRs above 100 deaths per 1 000 live births compared with only six countries in 2018. Between 1990 and 2018, the U5MR was reduced by 59 per cent from 93 to 39 deaths per 1 000 live births. The total number of under-five deaths thus dropped from 34 000 per day in 1990 to 15 000 per day in 2018, yet children continue to face widespread regional disparities in respect of their chances of survival. Sub-Saharan Africa remains the region with the highest U5MR in the world, with one in 13 children dying before the age of five. This is 16 times higher than the average ratio of one in 199 in high-income countries (UN Inter-agency Group for Child Mortality Estimation 2019).

In Table 19.3, the U5MR demonstrates the differences between more-developed and less-developed countries.

Table 19.5 Under-five mortality: International comparisons, 1990 and 2018

Country	1990	2018	Annual reduction rate
More-developed regions	13	5	3.3%
Less-developed regions	103	42	3.2%
Australia	9	4	3.3%
Botswana	241	73	4.3%
Spain	9	3	3.9%
South Africa	59	34	2.0%
United Kingdom	9	4	2.8%
Zimbabwe	80	46	2.0%
Germany	9	4	3.0%
Nigeria	211	120	2.0%

(Source: UN Inter-agency Group for Child Mortality Estimation 2019)

From Table 19.3 it is apparent that all of the more developed countries depicted here (in shaded rows) have made great strides in reducing their already low U5MRs. Overall, more developed regions managed a reduction rate of 3.3 per cent within three decades, while less-developed regions only managed 2.4 per cent.

Not only are there differences between countries in respect of health status, variations also occur within countries – once again attributable to social inequalities. The significant variation among South African provinces in respect of under-five mortality rates correlates with the poverty levels within the respective provinces.

Table 19.6 Under-five mortality by province, 2011 and poverty measures by province, 2015

Provinces	Under-five mortality rate[?]	Poverty levels
Eastern Cape	52.7	72.9%
Limpopo	36.7	72.4%
KwaZulu-Natal	60.8	68.1%
North West	59.6	64.3%
Mpumalanga	52.4	59.3%
Northern Cape	48.3	59.0%
Free State	68.3	54.9%
Western Cape	24.2	37.2%
Gauteng	29.8	33.3%

(Sources: StatsSA 2016; 2017; 2019)

Table 19.4 indicates the significant variation among provinces, with the Western Cape having recorded the lowest under-five mortality rate (24.2) and the Free State the highest (68.3). The two provinces with the lowest poverty levels – Gauteng and Western Cape – also have the lowest U5MRs. Except for Limpopo, there is a direct correlation between poverty level and the U5MRs of the provinces.

In 2015, the World Health Organization published a report, *Health in 2015: From MDGs to SDGs*, which described new global development goals. The Sustainable Development Goals (SDGs) were broader and more ambitious than the Millennium Development Goals (MDGs) and were to come into effect on 1 January 2016. Almost all of the SDGs are directly related to health or will contribute to health indirectly. One goal (SDG3) specifically sets out to '[e]nsure healthy lives and promote well-being for all at all ages' (WHO 2016). In line with the SDG3 targets, South Africa is committed to an under-five mortality rate of < 25 per 1 000 live births by 2030. While U5MRs in South Africa have fallen substantially, especially in the past decade, the author does not share the optimism displayed by Bamford, McKerrow, Barron and Aung when they state that the SDG target is achievable. Except perhaps for the Western Cape – which has already reached the goal – and Gauteng, the author does not consider the target of fewer than 25 per 1 000 live births by 2030 to be achievable (WHO 2015).

Marxist approaches

Researchers in the Marxist tradition have produced one of the most powerful sociological accounts of the social patterning of the production of disease. According to them, the medical institution – when in a capitalist society – is said to reflect the characteristics of capitalism: it is profit oriented, it blames the victim and it reproduces the class structure and the accompanying inequalities. In this view, medicine serves a key function in capitalist societies in that victims of disease are blamed for their own conditions, while diseases are actually caused by capitalists' pursuit of profit. Medical professionals act as agents of social control, especially in respect of the working class. One way of doing this is by controlling access to the sick role, for instance by issuing (or not) medical certificates. This is done to secure a workforce for the ruling capitalist class.

A contemporary sociologist working in the Marxist tradition is Vicente Navarro, editor of the influential *International Journal of Health Services*. According to him, both the causes of inequalities in health between different social classes and the reasons for the continuation of this situation are attributable to the alliance of interests between the ruling classes and the medical profession. Both these parties share a willingness to perpetuate the belief that the principal causes of ill health are personal and physical rather than social. Not only does this strengthen the position of the medical profession in explaining ill health to the lay population but it also promotes a dependency on medicine to cure disease. In his view, the medical profession occupies a position of ideological dominance, which is based on the claim that the most notable improvements in the health of populations are the result of medical advances and medical technology. Admitting that patterns of disease and illness are largely determined by economic and social factors would deprive the medical profession of its professional dominance. The alliance between the ruling classes and the medical profession therefore serves the interests of both, on the one hand by maintaining the professional dominance of the latter and, on the other, by sustaining a reasonably healthy working population for the ruling classes.

Navarro maintains that morbidity and mortality, especially in the poor parts of the world in which the majority of the human race lives, are not the result of a scarcity of resources, of industrialisation or the population explosion. Rather, morbidity and mortality occur because of a pattern of control over the resources of those countries in which the majority of the population have no control over access to resources: 'It is not *inequalities* that kill, but *those who benefit from the inequalities* that kill' (Navarro 2009: 440).

When thinking about those who benefit, the pharmaceutical and medical technology multi-national companies invariably come to mind. The apparently inexhaustible demand for healthcare, together with the medicalisation of areas not previously considered to be medical (such as infertility, short stature and sexual performance) mean that the opportunities for the accumulation of profit are considerable. Consequently, the profit motive in such multi-national pharmaceutical companies makes the eradication of national and global health inequalities unlikely in the foreseeable future (Bradby 2009).

Michel Foucault

The French philosopher Foucault (1926–1984) was a social theorist who concerned himself with the development of the category of disease, which he regarded to be the product of the professionalisation of medicine. In his view, the medical profession acts on behalf of the administrative state, firstly by defining categories of people, such as the sick, the insane, the criminal and the deviant. The state then – via the surveillance of its citizens – polices 'normal' behaviour and enforces compliance with the 'normal'. Foucault compares modern society with Max Weber's idea of the iron cage.

Foucault's understanding of and argument about power challenges that of Marxists. Whereas the latter regard power

to be centralised in the hands of the capitalist class, Foucault points out that power is diffuse throughout society and not only located in any one group. The power over life, so-called *biopower*, emerged with the development of the modern state and its need to guarantee the health of its population. In *The Birth of the Clinic* (1973), Foucault contends that the development of modern positivistic medicine was instrumental in this process of gaining scientific control over humans. According to him, the history of medicine is at the same time the history of the **depersonalisation** of humans and their subjugation by the institution of medicine. He identifies three distinct periods in the history of medicine:

- The period from the Middle Ages to the 18th century was that of *bedside medicine*. Doctors had a holistic orientation to the patient and care comprised the whole person. Disease was conceptualised as a lack of balance in the human being and involved both physical and spiritual factors. In accordance with the spirit of this period, the doctor would ask the patient the following question: 'What is the matter with you?'

- The second period, which covers the 19th century, was as the era of *hospital medicine*. By this time, doctors had commenced the road to professionalisation and patients became dependent on them. Disease was considered a problem of the pathology of a specific organ, detached from the entire existence of the individual. Thus, the medical practitioner was only interested in specific information that pertained to the patient's physical condition and would ask the patient, 'Where does it hurt?'

- The period from the mid-20th century – in which both patient and doctor are displaced by scientific tests – is depicted as *laboratory medicine*. Disease becomes a biochemical process, dealt with by scientists and laboratory technicians. The patient as person is entirely superseded by statistical tests of biological normality. Doctors, too, become subservient to the biochemical process in that they no longer want to elicit information only from the patient, so they tell the patient: 'Let's wait and see what the tests say'. According to Foucault, the increasing 'scientisation' of life is inevitably followed by a disenchantment: we learn more and more about the workings of the body as an artefact of the laboratory, and less and less about health and happiness.

Interestingly, there are a number of parallels between the work of Michel Foucault and Talcott Parsons. They share the view that medicine is not only concerned with healing, but that it acts as an institution of social control in that medical professionals play a key role in inducing individuals to comply with social roles. However, while Foucault views modern societies as systems of organised surveillance, individuals conduct the surveillance on themselves because they have internalised the professional models of what is deemed appropriate behaviour. Both Parsons and Foucault argue that, in modern society, disease is constructed as deviant behaviour. In Parsons's case, this can be the motivated deviance to enter the sick role and thus avoid social obligations. For Foucault, this happens when a sick person is identified as being sick by the 'helping professions' of modern society (White 2002).

19.4.3 Symbolic interactionism

Contrary to the assumption of structural functionalists that we are socialised to act according to the rules and expectations of that society – which 'made us all "dupes" of the social system' (White 2002: 56) – symbolic interactionism views humans as acting, rather than as being acted upon. The interactionist theorist thus sees humans as active and creative participants who construct their social world, not as passive and conforming objects of socialisation.

This perspective has a long intellectual history, beginning with the German sociologist and economist, Max Weber (1864–1920). In Chapter 1, you were introduced to Weber's concept of *Verstehen* – deep empathic understanding. Weber's sociology has made notable contributions to social policy in respect of health and disease. For example, whereas most disease-prevention programmes in Western countries and those advocated by the World Health Organization (WHO) at first adopted quite a prescriptive, almost authoritarian approach of telling people how to live less-diseased lives (for example stop smoking; stop binge drinking; stop eating fatty, sugary and salty foods; and stop being lazy), the approach of such programmes has been modified – now being more in line with Weber's *Verstehen* approach. While the aim is still to steer people towards changing their potential self-destructive lifestyles, it has now become an acceptable part of health-promotion policies to try and *understand* why certain social groups persist in unhealthy actions, and to try to *accommodate* the meanings people attach to their actions (Morrall 2001: 30).

Another prominent social theorist in this tradition is Erving Goffman (1922–1982). He used this theoretical framework to analyse mental hospitals and the experiences of their inmates. He described mental hospitals as *total institutions* – institutions where a large number of individuals lead highly regimented lives separated from the outside world. In these institutions and the circumstances that prevail there, mortification of the self occurs. This refers to a process in which a person's self-image is damaged and is replaced by a personality adapted to institutional life. Goffman identified the following aspects of institutional life that cultivated such mortification.

- *Master status*: Because the inmates are isolated from work and family – which usually give one a sense of self – they only have one available role, namely that of patient. The role of patient becomes their master status and all behaviour is interpreted through the lens of illness.
- *Depersonalisation*: Because each staff member has to manage many patients, the best way to do this is to limit and even disregard individual desires, needs and personalities. Patients therefore may not choose what to wear, when to sleep and when to wake up, when to eat and what to eat.

Since the second half of the 20th century, several studies subsequently supported Goffman's idea of the negative consequences of institutionalising people experiencing mental problems. This has resulted in a process of deinstitutionalisation and the development of alternatives to hospitalisation – among them halfway houses (Weitz 2010).

19.5 Defining health, disease and illness

Defining the conditions *health* and *disease* is not as obvious as one might believe. In everyday language, we use the concepts *disease* and *illness* as synonyms. However, sociologists draw a distinction between these two concepts. Accordingly, disease refers to the presence of physical signs, whereas *illness* or *illness behaviour* refers to the subjective experience when one is subjected to certain physical signs. The implication of this distinction is that disease can occur without illness, and illness can occur without disease being present. One can thus be seriously diseased without being ill – for example if a person is unaware of a malignant tumour growing internally but regularly runs a marathon. Conversely, one can be ill without being diseased – for example with severe depression in response to a loss.

19.5.1 Defining health

In its Constitution of 1948, the World Health Organization (WHO) defines health in terms of physical, psychological and social criteria (http://www.who.int/hhr/en/). This is one of the earliest attempts at a holistic view of health. Over time, many disciplines involved in health have come to acknowledge and accept this view.

People not professionally involved in health issues also have perceptions of health. Such lay beliefs or more popular perceptions of health are not – as is often believed by biomedical practitioners – merely superstitions. Rather, they are people's attempts to make sense of their lives and to deal with the complexities of health issues. Whereas the biomedical concept of health takes as its starting point the anatomical parts and the physiological systems of the body, many lay beliefs about health have their origin in the wholeness of human beings. What seems to matter to people is the wholeness or integrity of the person. It is thus believed that health remains if one maintains inner strength and the ability to cope.

Sustained research since the 1970s has indicated that concepts of health vary in many respects. This has resulted in a growing recognition of the influential role of culture, class, gender, ethnicity and age in respect of the subjective experience of health and healthcare. For example, it has been found that younger men tend to think of health as physical fitness, while younger women emphasise energy and coping. In middle age, the emphasis moves towards notions of mental and physical well-being, while older people stress the ability to do things, contentment and happiness. As a result of research findings such as these, it has also been recognised that lay perceptions need to be taken into account when organising healthcare provision (Bradby 2009).

A wide range and variety of ideas about health have been described in literature. We will take a look at four of these.

Health as the absence of disease

This way of thinking is generally associated with the medical profession and has been described as 'an impoverished understanding of good health' (Bradby 2009). People are considered healthy as long as they show no signs of physical abnormality – regardless of how they feel about themselves.

The main criticism regarding this way of defining health is that the notion of abnormality (or pathology) implies that there are certain universal 'norms' or 'standards' of what constitutes health and of how the body *should* function when it is healthy. However, because there are wide-ranging variations in human anatomy and physiology, one may well ask whether such standards actually exist. Careful consideration of this idea makes it clear that there are quite a few shortcomings. For instance, when somebody has a benign tumour that does not seem to be a problem at that moment, is this person healthy or sick? Somebody may be HIV positive but not show any symptoms of AIDS – is this person healthy or sick? Someone who has suffered brain damage at birth may have reduced mental capabilities but above-average physical capabilities. Is this being healthy or ill?

Health as an ideal state

The definition of health used by the World Health Organization mentioned earlier states that 'health is a state of complete physical, mental, and social well-being and not merely the absence of disease or infirmity' (http://www.who.int/hhr/en/). It is not only about whether a person is ill or injured, but it has a social dimension, namely that a *sense of well-being* is also an important aspect of being healthy.

This definition has been criticised for being too idealistic – in other words, it specifies a state of being that is unattainable. It also presents an absolute view of health, which means that a person is unhealthy unless he or she has attained *complete* physical, mental and social well-being. The value of this definition is however that it encourages people to think of health more holistically, as something that relates to a wide range of human capacities and qualities.

Health as a commodity

The idea of health as a product suggests that health is something that can be *bought* (by a subscription to a medical aid scheme or to a gymnasium), *sold* (by health food stores and health centres), *given* (by surgery and drugs) and *lost* (following accident and disease). This is part of the current movement to enhance and control personal health called healthism (Bruhn 1991). This involves, inter alia, taking all kinds of supplements (eg tonics, vitamins and minerals), despite the fact that some physicians remain sceptical of the real efficacy of such preparations.

This point of view has been criticised for suggesting that health is, in a sense, a technical matter – removed from the individual. It is something that experts perform in respect of the individual – be it a doctor who administers medicines or performs surgery or a personal trainer. The idea of health as a commodity also discounts the constraints of structural inequalities. In other words, at odds here are first-world consumerism and third-world resource scarcity: people struggling to make ends meet are in no position to 'buy' health (Aggleton 1990; Bradby 2009).

Health as a human right

This perspective challenges the idea that health is a privilege that can be bought, and modifies it as an obligation that must be met. Several international declarations have included statements about health as a human right, such as the Universal Declaration of Human Rights, adopted by the

UN in 1948, the Constitution of the WHO and the Dublin Declaration on HIV/AIDS. 'Health as a human right' has also been written in our Constitution, bringing us in line with global developments of the past 50 years.

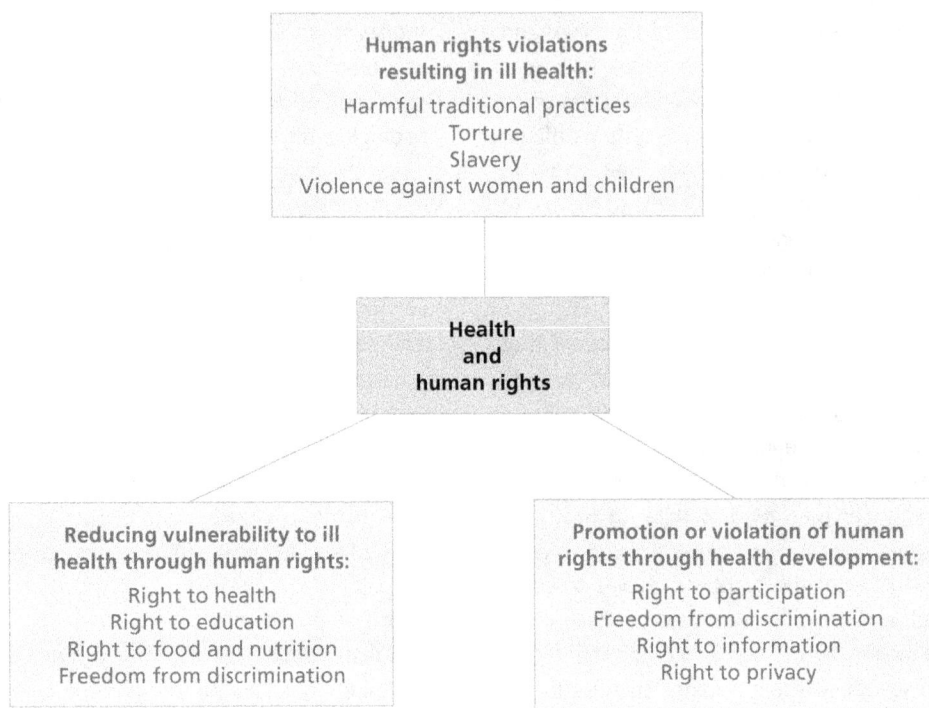

Figure 19.1 Examples of the links between health and human rights
(Source: WHO 2002)

19.5.2 Defining disease

In a Western context, **disease** refers to:

- a biomedical term
- pathological changes of the biological organism diagnosed by signs and symptoms
- an objective entity that can be defined by a licensed person (a doctor), by means of instruments (thermometer) and that can be monitored medically (prescribing medicines).

If disease were an objective and precisely measurable entity, it would always and everywhere be the same. However, there is evidence indicating that the concept *disease* is not fixed, but *varies over time*. One example is that of homosexuality. Once it was defined as a disease, specifically a mental illness, but it is now more socially accepted as a lifestyle choice. Alcoholism used to be viewed as immoral, therefore a sin, but it is now often typified as a disease. These changes are largely attributable to the fact that diseases are social constructs – thus when society changes, so medical perception and thus disease definition can change over time.

The definition of disease also *varies according to the particular social context*. In other words, what is considered to be disease in one society would not be considered such in another. Mental illness, for example, is very much rooted in culture in that what is considered abnormal behaviour varies between cultures. An extreme example would be the labelling of political dissidents as mentally ill, as happened in the former Soviet Union where such people were committed to in mental institutions.

In the same way, beliefs about *what causes disease* vary. In some societies, it is believed that disease is caused by supernatural forces – angry gods or ancestral spirits that inflict suffering on those who have broken moral codes or the forces called up by witches and sorcerers. On other occasions, supernatural intervention is regarded as a general imbalance between a community and its environment. While disease may, at times, be seen as punishment for wrongdoing, at other times it is considered an honour or a gift. The Nguni term *thwasa* describes a 'disease' sent by the ancestors to call a person to the vocation of traditional healer. Whereas most Western anthropologists define the condition in pathological and psychological terms – namely as behavioural disturbances or symptoms of mental illness – the amaXhosa regard it as an inborn gift. These symptoms are viewed as normal processes to force a person to accept the *ubizo* or calling (Mlisa 2009).

An illustration of how beliefs about the causes of disease vary is provided by Helman (1994). He describes how the modern-day AIDS pandemic has given rise to a number of ideas about its causes expressed by way of images or metaphors:

- AIDS as a plague – an invisible, spreading, destructive force that brings with it chaos, disorder and the breakdown of ordered society
- AIDS as an invisible contagion – an unseen influence transmitted by virtually *any* contact with an infected person, at *any* place, at *any* time
- AIDS as moral punishment – victims of the disease are divided into two groups: those who are 'guilty' (those who have multiple sex partners; homosexuals; prostitutes) and those who are 'innocent' (those who contracted the disease by means of a blood transfusion; partners of those who have multiple sex partners)
- AIDS as invader – this involves prejudice against foreigners or tourists as being 'alien AIDS carriers'
- AIDS as a war – a war waged on conventional society by 'immoral' lifestyles, promiscuity, foreign influences and stigmatised minorities (gays, drug abusers)
- AIDS as a primitive or pre-social force or entity – characterised by unrestrained and unconventional sexuality

These metaphors reflect how people – in the face of no cure being available – attempt to make sense of the disease and its devastating effects. Sontag has indicated how conditions with an unknown cause and seemingly ineffective treatment attract extraordinary levels of either fearfulness or disgust. This was the case with tuberculosis in the 19th century, but it has been replaced by cancer and AIDS as the mysterious, fearsome and objectionable diseases of the 20th century (Morrall 2001).

19.5.3 Defining illness
Illness refers to how people experience their symptoms, what meanings they ascribe to them, and how they act upon them. It must be clear from this that different people will define symptoms differently and will respond differently to them.

According to the biomedical model, illness behaviour is a direct response to physical pathology: the individual contracts a disease or sustains an injury that causes him or her to respond and behave in a certain way. For example, a broken leg will necessarily cause pain, impaired ability to walk and some form of clinical intervention in order to heal successfully.

From a sociological point of view, the study of illness is about behaviour in its social context rather than in relation to a physiological or pathological condition. When individuals become diseased, they (and others) try to make sense of their symptoms and choose what to do about their experience of illness. Illness cannot be established objectively by physical signs and is therefore not amenable to investigation by the methods of biomedicine because its study depends on the analysis of experienced suffering through individual self-reports and behaviour. Also, patients are mainly concerned with their illness (ie their pain, suffering and distress), while doctors are more concerned with their disease (Jennings 1986; Wainwright 2008).

One might think that the nature and severity of a disease would be the main determinants of an individual's response, and in the case of very severe diseases this is indeed often true. We do, however, know that many people fail to see a physician or go very late in the disease process despite the presence of serious symptoms, while many others see physicians regularly for trivial or minor complaints. Again, it would seem that apart from the physiological conditions, illness behaviour is also influenced by social and cultural factors. This is the case because people not only gain both their experience and their knowledge in this respect from sources such as their doctors and the media, but also from their broader culture.

The process of interpreting one's symptoms is not exclusively conditioned by individual traits, but is the product of shared cultural beliefs and expectations exchanged within the individual's social network or the lay referral system.

19.6 Places and sources of care
It is a widely held belief that all healthcare occurs in the hospital setting and is delivered by doctors and nurses. In this section it will become apparent that there are indeed many contexts in which healthcare is provided by diverse healthcare providers.

19.6.1 The institutionalisation of healthcare
For centuries, healthcare was mostly provided at home by family members and other laypersons. Only in medieval

times, institutions called hospitals developed across Europe and were linked to monasteries and abbeys to offer food and shelter – literally, hospitality. They were run on charity principles, and offered food and shelter to those not part of mainstream society – the poor, the aged, orphans, and people with physical and mental disabilities – regardless of whether they were sick or healthy. Because of the variety of patients that they could accommodate, hospitals provided doctors with a context in which they could do research and 'experiment'. By the end of the 16th century, hospitals were mere boarding houses where poor patients received free treatment in exchange for acting as 'guinea pigs' for medical students (Hart-Davis 2007).

By the 18th century, medical treatment was recognised as the primary function of the hospital. However, the level of the treatment can only be described as primitive, while they provided appalling living conditions: they were poorly ventilated and overcrowded; often more than one patient was placed in a single bed regardless of their disorders, and the treatment was usually carried out publicly in the ward itself. Surgery (mostly amputations and childbirth), the purging of fevers with various potions, bloodletting, and the removal of the dead all occurred in the same general area where patients ate and slept. The physicians and surgeons also did not practise even the most rudimentary standards of hygiene, moving from bed to bed and treating a great variety of diseases, including those that were infectious, without washing their hands or changing their clothes. They also performed surgery without masks, and the entire room was often filled with observers wearing ordinary clothes (Hart-Davis 2007).

Only in the 19th century, was the negative image of the hospital changed and they became centres for treatment, open to all who were able to pay. One of the factors that assisted in this process was the development of the doctrine of specific aetiology (germ theory). The standards of hygiene that resulted from practising the principles of the germ theory made hospitals much safer. The germ theory also led to the establishment of laboratories – a specialised medical environment where tests could be performed in hygienic conditions. Facilities such as operating theatres – so called because students were able to view surgery – and equipment, such as the first X-ray machine – were centralised in hospitals so that they could be available to most physicians. In addition, the process of diagnosis came to rely less on the verbal reports of patients and more on technological machine and drug-aided tests for symptoms. Especially since the end of the 19th century, a new image of hospitals evolved as institutions in which patients of all social classes could expect to find the highest-quality medical care and could reasonably expect to be cured of their disorders.

19.6.2 The primary healthcare movement

During the 1970s, international health policy took a new direction, its aim being to have countries move away from expensive, hospital-based, urban, curative, high-technology interventions. The aim of the primary healthcare approach, which encompassed a holistic view of health, was to bring services to people in rural areas. The philosophy on which primary healthcare was based was not so much about cheap services, but rather on a desire to move from a top-down approach in healthcare delivery to promoting grassroots community participation and development, thus giving ordinary people more of a role in their own health healthcare (Wainwright 2008).

In 1975, the World Health Organization (WHO) formally adopted the primary healthcare approach. In 1978, the Declaration of Alma-Ata was issued – the first international declaration underlining the importance of primary healthcare. Among the important basic values or principles of primary healthcare identified in the Declaration are those of social justice, equity and community participation and solidarity (WHO 1978).

Primary healthcare in South Africa

In the 1940s, long before Alma-Ata, primary healthcare (PHC) principles were being practised in South Africa in a small unit situated in rural KwaZulu-Natal called the Pholela Health Centre. The unit was initiated by Dr Eustace Cluver, the South African Secretary of Health, and Dr Harry Gear, the Deputy Chief Health Officer, as a means of establishing more appropriate healthcare services in the mostly ignored Bantustans. This was quite a progressive endeavour in that the healthcare providers integrated curative care and preventive health services in a comprehensive community-based package. They incorporated health education and health promotion as essential ingredients of their healthcare delivery. In addition, their focus was on the health of families and the community rather than on that of the individual alone. It also emphasised community empowerment and participation in healthcare delivery. This was done, among other things, by recruiting and training community members as healthcare assistants (Kautzky & Tollman 2008).

In 1944, the Gluckman Report envisaged a national health service – based on the Pholela model – funded by taxation and available to all the people of the country.

Gluckman's Commission envisaged the establishment of a comprehensive health service. At the centre of this health service would be health centres that would serve as the primary unit in the delivery of integrated healthcare. With a view to supporting the development of the planned health centres, the Institute for Family and Community Health (IFCH) was established in Durban in 1946, which was later attached to the Natal University Medical School as a teaching unit. Apart from financial backing from the then Department of Health, the IFCH was also generously supported by the Rockefeller Foundation. This support contributed, among others, to the establishment of 44 affiliated health centres throughout South Africa by 1949.

The proposed programme was, however, fiercely opposed and given a mortal blow when the Nationalist Party came into power in 1948. The new priority of the medical profession was to establish a private health sector base and they therefore offered no support for the proposals made in the Gluckman Report. By 1960, nothing was left of the community-oriented primary care movement, and its most ardent proponents and practitioners had emigrated. Each of the 44 health centres that had been established were abruptly closed or converted to provincial outpatient clinics (Kautzky & Tollman 2008).

During apartheid, there were two significant developments that would eventually culminate in 'a uniquely South African form of PHC explicitly born of the struggle against apartheid' (Kautzky & Tollman 2008: 22). The first was the direct result of the 1976 Soweto uprising. Because of the unsafe conditions, many healthcare workers could not enter the township, while more than half of the doctors at the (Chris Hani) Baragwanath Hospital and its affiliated referral clinics in Soweto either resigned or requested transfers. The local primary care clinics had to close down, resulting in heavy overloads at the hospital. To address the crisis, the chief superintendent of the hospital, Dr Koos Beukes, initiated a clinical skills training course for nurses, which culminated in a new type of healthcare worker, namely the primary healthcare nurse. The PHC nurse was able to assess and diagnose patients, prescribe treatment and dispense medication – responsibilities previously limited to general practitioners. This development had both a positive and a negative spin-off. On the positive side, the South African Nursing Council in time recognised this course as a postgraduate diploma, which allowed thousands of 'nurse clinicians' to be trained. At the same time, this development reinforced the idea that primary healthcare was nurse based, perpetuating the idea that doctors in the

public sector should work in hospitals and nurses should provide clinic-based care.

The second development during the 1980s was that of organisations that aimed to promote a national PHC strategy for South Africa. One such organisation, the National Progressive Primary Health Care Network (NPPHCN) strove for the implementation of a progressive PHC system in the country. It was to be based on four key principles: commitment to socioeconomic development; community accountability; concerned health worker practice; and comprehensive care (Kautzky & Tollman 2008).

Despite the progressive initiatives pertaining to PHC over the course of six decades, and despite the political will to implement socially accountable and responsive healthcare, effectively implementing PHC has proved to be a significant social challenge – as has been the case globally. There are numerous reasons for this state of affairs, the most important being health worker shortages and the HIV and AIDS pandemic (Kautzky & Tollman 2008; WHO 2008).

It is impossible to implement and provision district-based health services in South Africa without sufficient, trained healthcare personnel. On the one hand, staff shortages are the result of the unequal distribution of human resources between the private and the public sectors. During apartheid, most healthcare professionals worked in the private sector, which served only 20 per cent of the population. In 1998, 53 per cent of general practitioners, 57 per cent of professional nurses and 76 per cent of all specialists worked in the private sector. This situation has deteriorated in that 63 per cent of general practitioners now work in this sector. An estimated 62 per cent of the national health expenditure goes towards the private sector, and it now caters for about seven million people – which leaves 38 per cent of the national health budget for 35 million people. On the other hand, healthcare professional shortages are partly the result of the emigration of trained staff. In 2011, the Department of Health estimated that health professionals leave the country at a rate of 25 per cent per year (Van Rensburg et al 2012: 417).

The HIV and AIDS pandemic has also had devastating effects on the country's ability to transform its healthcare system. Not only the disease as such, but also the way in which the government has handled the crisis has posed significant and substantial barriers to the implementation of locally appropriate services. The proposed new National Health Insurance has all the potential to enable the creation of an efficient, equitable and sustainable health system.
One of the important characteristics of the primary healthcare movement is its holistic approach to health,

which includes an endeavour to respect communities. It therefore follows naturally that the PHC movement has also taken an interest in traditional healing systems.

19.6.3 African traditional healthcare

Before Europeans settled in Africa, the indigenous healthcare system was politically influential in both the public and the private spheres. Later, under missionary influence, and also because of repressive colonial ideologies, African medical practices were condemned as 'heathen', 'primitive', 'barbaric' and 'uncivilised', and ultimately outlawed (Fako 1992; Ulin 1980). Although such measures were justifiable in the case of those traditional healers who committed ritual murders and used human substances as medicinal ingredients, there were also those who practised traditional healing in a benevolent way. Traditional healing was also not able to escape increasing Westernisation, which brought about new values, preferences and behavioural patterns. While these developments eventually led to an erosion of traditional African cosmology and culture, the indigenous healthcare system managed to survive as a fairly well-established healthcare system. Whereas in the past, traditional healing was the only source of care for millions of people in times of illness, today it is still a refuge for large portions of the black population, not only because of limited other choices, but also because they deem it acceptable and functional.

Several developments, both locally and internationally, have resulted in the dawning of a new dispensation for traditional healthcare systems in South Africa, Africa and globally. Internationally, the WHO has played a pivotal role in promoting collaboration with traditional healthcare systems.

African views on disease causation

The original African notion of disease causation encompasses various factors: disease is ascribed to natural factors, but also supernatural ones (white and black magic), to ancestral spirits, to a violation of taboos, to transgressing kinship rules or failing to observe religious obligations. There are thus two distinct aetiological categories – the natural and the supernatural. Foster (1976) characterises these as *naturalistic* and *personalistic*; however, the existence of two categories does not imply that reality is experienced or classified in a dualistic fashion.

Naturalistic explanations

Africans accept that there are natural causes of disease, and even if these are not known, this has not been an overt concern. There is an acceptance that disease can be caused by infection, even though the infective agent is a mystery. There is considerable knowledge regarding which leaves, roots and berries possess beneficial healing properties and which are poisonous or even lethal. The deciding factor whether or not an illness episode has natural causes is the progress of the disease and not so much the symptoms. Therefore, natural diseases do not last unusually long, do not recur regularly and, apparently, do not form part of a series of misfortunes (Kriel 1999).

The nature of the treatment is in accordance with the cause. Natural causes require a specialist in symptomatic treatment, and although this specialist can be a traditional healer, it is generally accepted that medical doctors trained in Western medicine understand and know how to treat diseases caused in this way.

Personalistic explanations

As soon as a disease appears to be unusual, knowledge about the cause – especially whether it is natural or not – becomes imperative so as to decide on the nature of the treatment. In the case of disease and misfortune, Westerners seek an explanation in terms of concepts such as germ theory and fungal infection. The question as to why a particular person suffers disease or misfortune cannot be answered by science. In Western thought, the concept of chance is applied but the traditional African worldview makes little provision for accident or chance (Hammond-Tooke 1981). In this view, disease or misfortune is ascribed to the active, purposeful intervention of an agent, which can be human (a witch or sorcerer), non-human (a spirit or ancestor) or supernatural (a deity or other very powerful being). Foster (1976) terms this mode of explanation 'personalistic'.

Personalistic aetiologies comprise multiple levels of causality: (1) an *immediate* cause – *what* was done to the person and *what* was used; (2) an *efficient* cause – *who* did it or *what* it did to the person; and (3) an *ultimate* cause – *why* it happened to *this specific person at this point in time*.

In the case of personalistic explanations, healers with supernatural and/or magical skills are required because patients and their families are not principally concerned about the immediate cause of the disease, but rather about the *who* and the *why*. Patients opting for a personalistic aetiology will not accept that tuberculosis is caused by the tuberculosis bacillus – even if they were to see it under the microscope or were to acknowledge its existence. It would still not explain why the bacillus is active now, or why it is in their lungs and not someone else's.

Culture-related syndromes

Diseases that require personalistic explanations are known among the amaZulu as *ukufa kwabantu* (diseases of African people). They are understood only by Africans and can therefore only be treated by African traditional healers. Five such culture-related syndromes have been identified (Pretorius 2012):

- *Spirit possession* manifests in two forms, the first being ancestral spirit possession (*thwasa*). This Nguni term describes a 'disease' sent by the ancestors to call a person to the vocation of traditional healer. A second kind of spirit possession, *mafonfonyane*, is principally ascribed to sorcery and is brought about by harmful medicines controlled by the spirits of the deceased.
- *Sorcery* is usually held responsible for *poisoning*. Specific conditions associated with sorcery are, for example, *sejeso*: a sorcerer places something in a person's body to harm him or her. *Nehelelo* is caused by placing something in a place frequently visited by a person. If the person touches it, he or she falls ill.
- *Pollution* is a mystical force that reduces a person's resistance to illness and causes misfortune and repulsiveness, and as a result, people take a dislike to that person.
- *Ancestral displeasure* causes the ancestors to withdraw their protection. Their dissatisfaction is activated by conflict in the family or by failure to observe ritual sacrifices. This leads to a condition called *moloa badimo* (shade burns).
- *Disregard of cultural norms* is also associated with ill health. It involves ignoring social taboos and the non-observance of ritual sacrifices during key life events.

Traditional treatment

In accordance with Africans' holistic cosmological views, traditional treatment is holistic because of its comprehensive approach. Traditional treatment aims not only at curing the disease, but also at healing the patient. As illness is seen as being the result of a disturbance or imbalance at the psychological, physical, material, interpersonal or spiritual levels, all of these are taken into account when diagnosing and prescribing treatment. Some of the wide variety of procedures and methods are the following: blood cleansing, charms, incisions, drumming, sacrifice or prayer to ancestors and piercing ('African acupuncture') (Felhaber & Mayeng 1997; Mkwanazi 1987; Wessels 1985).

Types of traditional healers

Traditional healers do not all perform the same functions, nor do they fall into the same category. Just like practitioners of biomedicine, traditional healers can be divided into various fields of specialisation. The Traditional Health Practitioners Act 22 of 2007 identifies four types of such healers, namely diviners, herbalists, traditional birth attendants and traditional surgeons (RSA 2008).

A type of healer category of more recent origin is the prophet or faith healer, who divines and heals within the framework of the African Independent Churches (AIC). Although this kind of spiritual healer is not included in the aforementioned Act, and is a debatable issue, it is included here for discussion, because fundamentally and initially these healers are practitioners of traditional healing.

Diviners

Diviners isiZulu: *sangoma*; isiXhosa: *amagqira*; Sesotho/Setswana: *ngaka (ya ditoala)*) concentrate on the diagnosis of mysteries. They analyse the causes of specific events and interpret the messages of the ancestral spirits. Their function is mainly that of divination, but they often also provide the medicaments for the specific case they diagnosed. There are three methods of divination. Sometimes the diagnosis is made by *bone throwing* – by casting and studying a divination set (*litaola*). The second method is by means of *psychic/clairvoyance* or *telepathic ability*, while divination can also occur through *dreams and visions*.

African diviners experience a very definite calling by an ancestral spirit. Such a person presents the symptoms of a mysterious disease – *ukuthwasa*. Initiates may have symptoms of mental anguish, experience emotional turmoil, develop physical pains, suffer depression, become moody, nervous, restless and fearful, experience palpitations and insomnia, and have vivid dreams or even audible communication from the ancestral spirits. This 'sickness' does not respond to conventional treatment, and a traditional healer is usually consulted to diagnose whether the condition has a physical cause or whether it is a calling to the vocation of traditional healer. In the event of the latter diagnosis, the person is entrusted to the care of a traditional healer and training as a diviner commences. This is a long, complicated and secret process (Mlisa 2009).

Herbalists

Herbalists (isiZulu: *inyanga*; isiXhosa: *amaxhwele*; Sesotho: *ngaka e chitja/ya ditlamatlama*) do not, typically, possess occult powers but have acquired an extensive knowledge of magical technique (Hammond-Tooke 1974: 342). Herbalists are aware of the importance of ancestral favour, but they do not have the same close alliance with the ancestral spirits as do diviners. To them, the remedy itself is central to their treatment. They are expected to diagnose and prescribe medication for ordinary ailments and diseases, to prevent and alleviate misfortune and disaster, to provide protection against sorcery and misfortune, and to promote good fortune and happiness.

Herbalists acquire their skills by serving an apprenticeship with an eminent herbal practitioner. When they feel that they have learned enough, they leave their mentors and establish their own practices. In some cases remedies are, as it were, 'inherited', and secret remedies are passed down from father to son or from an uncle to a favourite nephew or niece.

Traditional pharmacopoeia is largely herbal (herbs, bark and roots), but a few are of animal origin. The herbalist's remedies often have strong symbolic significance. The general principle is that whatever characteristics plants, birds and animals may possess, they may be transmitted to humans. The Tswana traditional healer, for example, uses animal skins that symbolise coolness – such as that of a water iguana or of crocodile, to 'cool down' a patient (Reyneke 1971).

Faith healers/prophets

Faith healers or prophets (Nguni: *umthandazi*; Sesotho: *moprofeta/mosebeletsi/morapelli*) actually indicate a syncretism, a reinterpretation of orthodox Christianity to be reconcilable with traditional culture. Strictly speaking, prophets are not traditional healers, yet they have the following in common with the typical traditional healer: a shared theory of disease and health; a similar means of divination – even if God or the Holy Spirit, rather than the ancestral spirits, aids them; and the treatment of various diseases, including the so-called culture-related syndromes (Sundkler 1961). Such traditional healers are affiliated with the African Independent Churches (AIC) – also called African Indigenous Churches or African Initiated Churches, and they dispense their services within this framework.

Legitimisation and professionalisation of traditional healthcare in South Africa

Although, from both a legal and a Christian point of view, traditional healthcare in this country had 'no right of existence' for most of the previous two centuries, it has managed to survive into the 21st century. The new societal dispensation in South Africa brought with it an affirmation of African identity, which paved the way for, among other things, a re-evaluation of the indigenous healing system. The Constitution provides the framework for accommodating the traditional healthcare system. People's right to consult

healers of their choice is considered a basic human right and is thus enshrined in the Bill of Rights s15(1) and s31(1) (RSA 1996). Similarly, traditional healers have the right both to choose and practise their trade, occupation or profession freely, but they are, however, subject to legal regulation.

Immediately after the elections of 1994, government adopted a course of constructive engagement with a view to officially recognising this healthcare system. More than a decade would pass before enabling legislation was promulgated in 2008. The Traditional Health Practitioners Act 22 of 2007 was signed by the president on 7 January 2008, but only sections 7, 10, 11(3), 12–15, 47, 48 and 50 were made operational in April 2008. These deal mainly with establishing an Interim Traditional Health Practitioners' Council and the power of the Minister of Health to issue regulations in terms of the Act. More than three years after the Act had been promulgated, the Minister of Health set in motion the selection process for constituting the Council by publishing a Government Notice relating to the appointment of such members (Rautenbach 2011).

The future of traditional healthcare in South Africa

The importance of traditional healthcare is evident from a number of factors. The first and obvious reason is the number of traditional healers. Pretorius's estimate of between 150 000 and 200 000 has been confirmed by Gqaleni et al (2007) – their research indicating the more precise number of 185 477. The African traditional healthcare system also constitutes an important economic factor in that its annual contribution amounts to 5.6 per cent of the national health budget (R2.9 billion). In addition, approximately 133 000 people (mostly rural women) are employed in the trade in medicinal plants (Rautenbach 2011).

While it is a heartening fact that the required legislation in respect of traditional healthcare is finally in place, complete institutionalisation has not yet been attained. Regulatory measures regarding reimbursement by medical aid schemes are still in its infancy and only certain sections of the Traditional Healers Act are in effect (Gqaleni et al 2007). Illiteracy among traditional healers and incorporating a healthcare system with metaphysical qualities into a bureaucratic system are bound to produce some challenges (Moagi 2009). Also, in the Green Paper on National Health Insurance in South Africa (2011) no mention is made of the possible role of traditional healthcare (DoH 2011).

19.6.4 Complementary and alternative medicine

Up to the end of the 1980s, the term 'alternative medicine' was used for describing approaches to healthcare outside the sphere of conventional medicine. In time and as this type of healthcare became more acceptable – especially among physicians – the term 'complementary and alternative medicine' (CAM) became more widespread.

A characteristic of CAM is that it is based on the holistic philosophy of healthcare. Practitioners of holistic healthcare differ from biomedical practitioners in that they concentrate on the concept of *health* rather than merely on disease. For this kind of healthcare, the main goals are therefore the prevention of disease and the promotion of health, rather than the treatment of disease. Also, the focus is on the patient as the subject rather than the object of the treatment.

Diversity of therapeutic and diagnostic methods
CAM modes of healing comprise a range of therapeutic methods, various diagnostic methods and several healing systems. An example of a *therapeutic method* is reflexology, which entails the use of hands to apply pressure to specific points of the foot. The foot is regarded as a microcosm of the entire body, thus certain parts of the body relate to certain sensitive areas on the foot, called reflex points. For example, the toes correspond to the head and neck, and the ball of the foot to the chest and lungs. Stimulation of a particular part of the foot will have a response in a distant organ (Vincent & Furnham 1997).

A widely used *diagnostic method* is iridology – the study of the iris of the eye. Various marks, signs and discolouration in the iris reveal certain strengths and weaknesses. Iridology cannot detect a specific disease but can detect over- or under-activity in specific areas of the body, for example, an under-active pancreas might indicate a diabetic condition (Vincent & Furnham 1997).

Both in South Africa and globally, chiropractic is the most widely accepted and most 'mainstream' of the CAM *healing systems*. This is clearly illustrated by the fact that it is the modality most commonly covered by medical aid schemes. The primary goals of chiropractic therapy are relief of musculoskeletal pain and restoration of mobility.

Other well-known CAM healing systems are homoeopathy, naturopathy, Chinese traditional medicine and acupuncture. By way of illustration, the focus will only be on homoeopathy.

Homoeopathy aims at restoring the self-healing potential of the organism. This is accomplished by using the lowest possible dose that would provoke a reaction in the organism. The use of vaccines to stimulate the production of natural antibodies is a parallel approach. This aspect of homoeopathy has caused most controversy because

homoeopathic remedies are frequently, though not always, diluted to the point where it seems inconceivable that a single molecule of the original substance could remain. Various explanations are given for the action of these remedies, one being that a dissolved substance leaves an imprint in water after high dilution. Others consider homoeopathic remedies to operate at a subtle level not open to scientific investigation. Homoeopathy is also based on the principle of *like cures like*. According to this principle, a disease may be cured by means that cause similar symptoms in healthy persons. For example, if a given drug induces symptoms such as a headache in healthy individuals, this very drug can be employed in patients who suffer from headaches. The use of vaccines to stimulate the production of natural antibodies is a parallel approach (Aakster 1986; Allied Health Professions Council of South Africa 2011; Vincent & Furnham 1997).

Integrating biomedicine and CAM
Not only are physicians accepting CAM, but there seems to be an overwhelming thrust towards integrating CAM into the mainstream. This was borne out by a review by Astin et al (1998) of 19 international surveys. They concluded that large numbers of conventional physicians were either referring patients to or practising some of the prominent and well-known forms of CAM. The following are some examples of such surveys:

- In Britain, Perkin et al (1994) found that 70 per cent of hospital doctors and 93 per cent of general practitioners had suggested referral to a CAM practitioner at least once. They also found that 12 per cent of hospital doctors and 20 per cent of general practitioners were practising some form of CAM, mostly acupuncture.
- In the Netherlands, Visser and Peters (1990) established that in their sample of 360 almost all of the doctors reported referring to CAM practitioners.
- An Australian study (Pirotta et al 2000) found that more than 80 per cent of the surveyed GPs had referred patients to practitioners of acupuncture, hypnosis and meditation.

Also indicative of this new marriage between conventional medicine and CAM is the fact that in the US, 60 per cent of medical schools teach courses on CAM practices.

Present status of CAM in South Africa
At present, 11 CAM modalities are registered according to the Chiropractors, Homoeopaths and Allied Health Service Professions Second Amendment Act 50 of 2000. The Act established a professional council – the Allied Health

Professions Council of South Africa – to regulate a wide range of CAM practitioners, each with a professional board:

- Professional Board for Ayurveda, Chinese medicine and acupuncture, and Unani-Tibb
- Professional Board for therapeutic aromatherapy, therapeutic massage therapy and therapeutic reflexology
- Professional Board for chiropractic and osteopathy
- Professional Board for homoeopathy, naturopathy and phytotherapy

Under subsection 13 of Act 50 of 2000, all practitioners – including biomedical practitioners who also practise CAM – are required to register separately under each therapy. Thus, a medical doctor practising acupuncture must have dual registration, first with the Health Professions Council as a medical doctor and also with the Allied Health Professions Council as a Chinese medicine practitioner (Allied Health Professions Council of South Africa 2011).

The National Health Reference Price List (NHRPL) published annually serves to provide medical aid schemes with a reference/guideline for reimbursement for treatment conducted by registered CAM practitioners.

The future of CAM

CAM in South Africa has progressed from being considered 'deviant' to being legitimised. It would, however, seem that what is still required is that the public be educated about which practices are allowed by a specific kind of registration. While CAM practitioners may display registration certificates, such certificates do not stipulate the exact nature of their mandate. A CAM practitioner (Jonker 2011) maintains that it often transpires that CAM practitioners transgress in this regard. Some use some of the machines – used by homoeopaths and/or doctors – to diagnose and prescribe, despite lacking the requisite theoretical training, which in the case of homoeopaths amounts to seven years. The various professional boards are only able to regulate their members to the extent that they are made aware of offences, and in this regard the public has an invaluable role to play.

Summary

This chapter set out to demonstrate that the true nature of health and disease cannot be comprehended without taking into account the social aspects involved. The social model in which the sociological perspective on these phenomena culminates was contrasted with the biomedical model, but convergence between the two models was also indicated. Next, the three main theoretical approaches to health and disease each provided a different lens for viewing these phenomena and as such highlighted different aspects. An analysis of the concepts health and disease was augmented by including the subjective experience of these phenomena, termed illness or illness behaviour. Finally, the places and sources of care available when health fails were discussed.

ARE YOU ON TRACK?

1. Why is a sociological perspective on health, disease and healthcare important?
2. Which qualities would you expect someone to display if he or she were to be considered:
   - Physically healthy
   - Socially healthy
   - Mentally healthy?
3. South Africa has a high maternal mortality rate (the death of women during pregnancy or childbirth or within 42 days after delivery) when compared with some of our neighbouring countries and when compared internationally. Try to think of possible reasons for this.
4. What do you think has been the impact of the Covid-19 pandemic on the South African society?
5. When we say that health is a basic human right, what does it mean in practice? What societal measures need to be taken to ensure that every citizen is afforded this right?
6. Why are the children of poorer parents more prone to disease than those of richer parents?
7. Do you think that we are witnessing the demise of the medical profession's dominance of healthcare provision because of the recognition of the wide array of healthcare options? If this is the case, is it a negative development? What would this development indicate?
8. What should the relationship between biomedicine and traditional healing be? What, in your opinion, is the future of traditional healthcare in South Africa?

References

Aakster CW. 1986. 'Concepts in alternative medicine'. *Social Science & Medicine*, 22(2): 265–273.

Aggelton P. *Health*. London: Routledge.

Alais C (ed). 1995. *Sociology of Health and Illness*. Johannesburg: Lexicon.

Allied Health Professions Council of South Africa. 2011. http://www.ahpcsa.co.za [Accessed 8 May 2012].

Astin JA, Marie A, Pelletier KR, Hansen E, Haskell WL. 1998. 'A review of the incorporation of complementary and alternative medicine by mainstream physicians'. *Archives of Internal Medicine*, 158(21): 2303–2310.

Avert. 2019. *Origin of HIV and AIDS*. https://www.avert.org/professionals/history-hiv-aids/origin [Accessed 28 April 2020].

Bamford LJ, McKerrow NH, Barron P, Aung Y. 2018. 'Child mortality in South Africa: Fewer deaths, but better data are needed'. *South African Medical Journal*, 108(3 Suppl 1): S25–S32. doi:10.7196/SAMJ.2018.v108i3.12779 [Accessed 15 April 2020].

Barry A-M, Yuill C. 2008. *Understanding the Sociology of Health – An Introduction*. 2nd ed. Los Angeles: SAGE.

Basu A. 2020. 'The "herd immunity" route to fighting coronavirus is unethical and potentially dangerous'. *The Conversation*, 17 March. https://theconversation.com/the-herd-immunity-route-to-fighting-coronavirus-is-unethical-and-potentially-dangerous-133765 [Accessed 12 May 2020].

Berche P. 2012. 'Louis Pasteur, from crystals of life to vaccination'. *Clinical Microbiology and Infection*, 18(5): 1–6. https://www.clinicalmicrobiologyandinfection.com/article/S1198-743X(14)61355-0/fulltext [Accessed 5 May 2020].

Brandt K. 2020. *WHO praises South Africa's efforts to curb spread of Covid-19*. https://ewn.co.za/2020/04/23/who-praises-south-africa-s-efforts-to-curb-covid-19 [Accessed 5 May 2020].

Bradby H. 2009. *Medical Sociology: An Introduction*. Los Angeles: SAGE.

Brock E. Prescott V. 2020. 'The merits, risks and politics of Sweden's herd immunity strategy'. *GPB Radio News* 8 May. https://www.gpbnews.org/post/merits-risks-and-politics-swedens-herd-immunity-strategy [Accessed 12 May 2020].

Bruhn JG. 1991. 'Ethics in clinical sociology' in *Handbook of Clinical Sociology*. Bruhn JG, Rebach HM (eds). New York: Plenum Press: 99–115.

Chen L, Takemi K. 2015. 'Ebola: Lessons in human security'. *The Lancet* 385: 1887–1888. https://www.thelancet.com/action/showPdf?pii=S0140-6736%2815%2960909-6 [Accessed 3 May 2020].

Chotiner I. 2020. 'How pandemics change history'. *The New Yorker*, 3 March. https://www.newyorker.com/news/q-and-a/how-pandemics-change-history [Accessed 7 April 2020].

Da Cunha BR, Fonseca LP, Calado CRC. 2019. 'Antibiotic discovery: Where have we come from, where do we go?' *Antibiotics (Basel)*, 8(2): 45. Published online 24 April. doi:10.3390/antibiotics8020045 [Accessed 23 April 2020].

Delamater PL, Street EJ, Leslie TF, Yang YT, Jacobsen KH. 2019. 'Complexity of the basic reproduction number (R0)'. *Emerging Infectious Diseases* 25(1): 1–4. doi:10.3201/eid2501.171901. https://www.ncbi.nlm.nih.gov/pmc/articles/PMC 6302597/ [Accessed 3 May 2020].

Denworth L. 2020. 'How the COVID-19 pandemic could end'. *Scientific American*. https://www.scientificamerican.com/article/how-the-covid-19-pandemic-could-end/ [Accessed 28 April 2020].

Department of Health (DoH). 2011. *Green Paper on National Health Insurance in South Africa*. Pretoria: DoH.

Department of Health (DoH). 2020. *Covid-19 statistics in South Africa*. https://sacoronavirus.co.za [Accessed 7 May 2020].

Department of Labour. 2012. *Commission for Employment Equity Annual Report, 2011–2012*. https://www.labour.gov.za/downloads/documents/annual-reports/employment-equity/2011-2012/12th%20CEE%20Report.2012.pdf [Accessed 29 March 2013].

Du Plessis E, De Bruyn D. 2020. 'Groot griep onvergelykbaar'. *Bloemnuus*, 30 April, 5.

Engel GL. 1977. 'The need for a new medical model: A challenge for biomedicine'. *Science*, 196: 129–36.

Ernst E. 'Prevalence of use of complementary/alternative medicine: A systematic overview'. 2000. *Bulletin of the World Health Organization*, 78(2): 252–257.

Fako TT. 1992. *Survival and persistence of African ethnomedical systems*. Conference on Ethnomedicine and Health in the SADC Region, Maseru, Lesotho.

Farge E. 2020. *UN raises alarm about police brutality in lockdowns*. https://www.reuters.com/article/us-health-coronavirus-un-rights-idUSKCN2291X9 [Accessed 5 May 2020].

Felhaber T, Mayeng I. 1997. *South African Traditional Healers' Primary Health Care Handbook*. Cape Town: Kagiso Publishers.

Foster GM. 1976. 'Disease etiologies in non-Western medical systems'. *American Anthropologist*, 78(4): 773–782.

Gates B. 2020. 'Responding to Covid-19 – a once-in-a-century pandemic?' *The New England Journal of Medicine*, 28 February. doi:10.1056/NEJMp2003762/ https://www.nejm.org/doi/full/10.1056/NEJMp2003762 [Accessed 6 April 2020].

Global Health Risk Framework for the Future (GHRF) Commission. 2016. *The neglected dimension of global security. A framework to counter infectious disease crises*. http://nam.

edu/GHRFreport. doi:10.17226/21891 [Accessed 4 May 2020].

Gqaleni N, Moodley I, Kruger H, Ntuli A, McLeod H. 2007. 'Traditional and complementary medicine' in *South African Health Review 2007*. Harrison S, Bhana R, Ntuli A (eds). Durban: Health Systems Trust: 175–188.

Grennan D. 2019. 'What is a pandemic?' *Journal of the American Medical Association* 321(9): 910. https://jamanetwork.com/ [Accessed 7 April 2020].

Hammond-Tooke WD. 1974. *The Bantu-speaking Peoples of Southern Africa*. London: Routledge & Kegan Paul.

Hammond-Tooke WD. 1981. *Patrolling the Herms: Social Structure, Cosmology and Pollution Concepts in Southern Africa*. Johannesburg: Witwatersrand University Press.

Harapan H, Itoh N, Yufika A, Winardi W, Keam S, Te H et al. 2020. 'Coronavirus disease 2019 (COVID-19): A literature review'. *Journal of Infection and Public Health* (in press) doi:https://doi.org/10.1016/j.jiph.2020.03.019 [Accessed 9 April 2020].

Hart-Davis A. 2007. *History from the Dawn of Civilization to the Present Day*. London: Dorling Kindersley.

Hartley R, Mills G. 2020. 'An iron curtain is falling on our freedom'. https://www.dailymaverick.co.za/article/2020-04-30-an-iron-curtain-is-falling-on-our-freedom/ [Accessed 2 May 2020].

Helman CG. 1994. *Culture, Health and Illness: An Introduction for Health Professionals*. 3rd ed. Oxford, UK: Butterworth-Heinemann.

Heymann DL. 2015. 'Global health security: The wider lessons from the West African Ebola virus disease epidemic'. *The Lancet* 385:1884–1887. https://www.thelancet.com/action/showPdf?pii=S0140-6736%2815%2960909-6 [Accessed 3 May 2020].

History.com editors. 2020. *Spanish flu*. https://www.history.com/topics/world-war-i/1918-flu-pandemic [Accessed 22 April 2020].

Horton R, Das P. 2015. 'Global health security now'. *The Lancet* 385:1805–1806. https://www.thelancet.com/action/showPdf?pii=S0140-6736%2815%2960909-6 [Accessed 3 May 2020].

HSRC (Human Sciences Research Council). 2004. *Fact Sheet: Poverty in South Africa*. 26 July 2004. http://www.sarpn.org/documents/d0000990/ [Accessed 16 May 2013].

Illich I. 1976. *Medical Nemesis: The Expropriation of Health*. Harmondsworth, Middlesex: Penguin.

Jennings D. 1986. 'The confusion between disease and illness in clinical medicine'. *Canadian Medical Association Journal* 135: 865–869.

Jonker MH. 2011. Personal communication. 22 August.

Johns Hopkins University. 2020. 'Covid-19 and the long road to herd immunity'. *The Hub Staff Report*. 30 April. https://hub.jhu.edu/2020/04/30/herd-immunity-covid-19-coronavirus/ [Accessed 12 May 2020].

Kautzky K, Tollman SM. 2008. 'A perspective on primary health care in South Africa' in *South African Health Review 2008*. Barron P, Roma-Reardon J (eds). Durban: Health Systems Trust. http://www.hst.org.za/ publications/south-african-health-review-2008 [Accessed 16 May 2012].

Koorts L. 2020. 'Covid-19 hou 'n spieël voor ons samelewing'. *Beeld*. 25 April: 10.

Kriel JD. 1999. 'Liggaam en bloed in die siekte-etiologie van die Noord-Sotho' (Body and blood in the disease aetiology of the Northern Sotho). *South African Journal for Ethnology*, 22(4): 133–143.

La Croix S. 2018. 'The Khoikhoi population. A review of evidence and two new estimates'. *African Economic History Working Paper Series No 39/2018*. https://www.aehnetwork.org/wp-content/uploads/2018/03/AEHN-WP-39.pdf [Accessed 2 May 2020].

Lupia T, Scabini S, Pinna SM, Di Perri G, De Rosa FG, Corcione S. 2020. '2019 novel coronavirus (2019-nCoV) outbreak: A new challenge'. *Journal of Global Antimicrobial Resistance*. http://dx.doi.org/10.1016/j.jgar.2020.02.021 [Accessed 9 April 2020].

McKerrow N, Mulaudzi M. 2013. *Child mortality in South Africa: Using existing data*. http://www.healthlink.org.za/uploads/files/sahr10_5.pdf [Accessed 10 May 2013].

Mkwanazi I. 1987. 'Witchcraft and modern surgery'. *Congress of Theatre Study Group*, 24–25 July, Bloemfontein.

Mlisa LN. 2009. Ukuthwasa *initiation of* amagqirha: *Identity construction and the training of Xhosa women as traditional healers*. PhD thesis. University of the Free State, Bloemfontein.

Moagi L. 2009. 'Transformation of the South African health care system with regard to African traditional healers: The social effects of inclusion and regulation'. *International NGO Journal* 4(4): 116–126. http://www.academicjournals.org/INGOJ [Accessed 11 September 2011).

Moore KA, Lipsitch M, Barry JM, Osterholm MT. 2020. *Part 1: The future of the COVID-19 pandemic: lessons learned from pandemic influenza*. Center for Infectious Disease Research and Policy (CIDRAP), University of Minnesota. https://www.cidrap.umn.edu/sites/default/files/public/downloads/cidrap-covid19-viewpoint-part1_0.pdf [Accessed 2 May 2020].

Morrall P. 2001. *Sociology and Health. An Introduction*. 2nd ed. London: Routledge.

Naidoo K. 2013. 'Rape in South Africa – a call to action'. *South African Medical Journal*, 103(4): 210. http://www.samj.org.

za/index.php/samj/article/view/6802/4945 [Accessed 4 May 2020].

Navarro V. 2009. 'What we mean by social determinants of health'. *International Journal of Health Services*, 39(3): 423–441. doi:10.2190/HS.39.3.a http://baywood.com [Accessed 4 March 2013].

Penrose R. 2014. '"Mind over matter": Stephen Hawking obituary'. *The Guardian*, 14 March. https://www.theguardian.com/science/2018/mar/14/stephen-hawking-obituary [Accessed 18 April 2020].

Perkin MR, Pearcy RM, Fraser JS. 1994. 'A comparison of the attitudes shown by general practitioners, hospital doctors and medical students towards alternative medicine'. *Journal of the Royal Society of Medicine*, 87: 523–525.

Phillips H. 2013. 'The plague that came from the sea'. *Cape Times*, 12 February. https://www.pressreader.com/south-africa/cape-times/20130212/281865820865080 [Accessed 2 May 2020].

Pick W. 2012. 'Book review. Plague, pox and pandemics: A Jacana pocket history of epidemics in South Africa by Howard Phillips'. *South African Medical Journal*, 102(10): 783. amj.org.za/index.php/samj/article/view/6239/4526?fbclid=IwAR0Mbv2C5gfBnlsFdBtFxTdvgZjDgCPeyDakKt8qgDTmX9Zb2w91Z_iwSVI [Accessed 2 May 2020].

Pirotta MV, Cohen MM, Kotsirolis V, Farish SJ. 2000. 'Complementary therapies: Have they become accepted in general practice?' *Medical Journal of Australia*, 172: 105–109.

Pretorius E. 2012. 'Complementary and alternative medicine and traditional health care in South Africa' in *Health and Health Care in South Africa*, Van Rensburg HCJ (ed). Pretoria: Van Schaik, 593–652.

Pretorius E, Matebesi Z, Ackermann, L. 2013. *Juta's Sociology for Healthcare Professionals*. Cape Town: Juta.

Qiu W, Rutherford S, Mao A, Chu C. 2016/17. 'The pandemic and its impacts'. *Health, Culture and Society*, 9/10: 3–11. doi:10.5195/hcs.2017.221 | http://hcs.pitt.edu [Accessed 7 April 2020].

Rautenbach C. 2011. 'Institutionalisation of African traditional medicine in South Africa: Healing powers of the law?' *Journal for Contemporary Roman-Dutch Law*, 74: 28–46. http:ssrn.com/abstract=1780325 [Accessed 26 September 2011].

Regalado A. 2020. 'What is herd immunity and can it stop the coronavirus?' *MIT Technology Review*, 17 March. https://www.technologyreview.com/2020/03/17/905244/what-is-herd-immunity-and-can-it-stop-the coronavirus/ [Accessed 12 May 2020].

Reyneke JL. 1971. 'Towery by die Tswana met besondere verwysing na die Kgatla-Bagakgafela' (*Magic among the Tswana with specific reference to the Kgatla-Bagakgafela*). DPhil thesis, University of Pretoria, Pretoria.

Robins S. 2020. *Is the lockdown authoritarian creep or 'proportionate response'?* https://www.dailymaverick.co.za/article/2020-05-04-is-the-lockdown-authoritarian-creep-or-proportionate-response/ [Accessed 5 May 2020].

RSA (Republic of South Africa). 1996. Constitution of the Republic of South Africa Act 108 of 1996. Pretoria. Government Printer.

RSA (Republic of South Africa). 2000. Chiropractors, Homoeopaths and Allied Health Service Professions Second Amendment Act 50 of 2000. Pretoria. Government Printer.

RSA (Republic of South Africa). 2008. Traditional Health Practitioners Act 22 of 2007 (*Government Gazette* no 30660). 10.01.2008. Pretoria: Government Printer.

Sanchez E. 2020. *COVID-19 science: Understanding the basics of 'herd immunity'*. https://www.heart.org/en/news/2020/03/25/covid-19-science-understanding-the-basics-of-herd-immunity [Accessed 12 May 2020].

Shereen MA, Khan S, Kazmi A, Bashir N, Siddique R. 2020. 'COVID-19 infection: Origin, transmission, and characteristics of human coronaviruses'. *Journal of Advanced Research*, 24: 91–98. https://doi.org/10.1016/j.jare.2020.03.005 [Accessed 9 April 2020].

Snyman M. 2012. 'Steeds stralend'. *Rooi Rose*. 15 November. http://www.rooirose.co.za/article.aspx?id=31494&h=Steeds-stralend [Accessed 25 July 2013].

South African History Online. 2020. *Smallpox epidemic strikes the Cape*. https://www.sahistory.org.za/dated-event/smallpox-epidemic-strikes-cape [Accessed 25 April 2020].

Spinney L. 2019. 'How pandemics shape social evolution'. *Nature*. 574: 324–326. doi: 10.1038/d41586-019-03048-8 (accessed 10 April 2020).

StatsSA (Statistics South Africa). 2010. *Statistical release P0302 – Mid-year population estimates*, 2010. http://www.statssa.gov.za/publications/P0302/P03022010.pdf [Accessed 15 March 2013].

StatsSA (Statistics South Africa). 2013. *Millennium Development Goals – Goal 4: Reduce child mortality*. http://www.statssa.gov.za/nss/Goal_Reports/GOAL%204-REDUCE%20CHILD%20MORTALITY.pdf [Accessed 20 March 2013].

StatsSA (Statistics South Africa). 2016. *Community Survey 2016*. http://www.statssa.gov.za/?page_id=6283 [Accessed 10 April 2020].

StatsSA (Statistics South Africa). 2017. *Poverty trends in South Africa – an examination of absolute poverty between 2006 and 2015*. https://www.statssa.gov.za/publications/

Report-03-10-06/Report-03-10-062015.pdf [Accessed 12 April 2020].

StatsSA (Statistics South Africa). 2019. *National poverty lines.* http://www.statssa.gov.za/publications/P03101/P031012019.pdf [Accessed 10 April 2020].

Steele SF, Price J. 2008. *Applied Sociology: Terms, Topics, Tools, and Tasks.* 2nd ed. Belmont, CA: Thomson.

Sundkler BGM. 1961. 'The concept of Christianity in the African Independent Churches'. *African Studies*, 20(4): 203–213.

Tan SY, Tatsumura Y. 2015. 'Alexander Fleming (1881–1955): Discoverer of penicillin'. *Singapore Medical Journal* 56(7). https://www.ncbi.nlm.nih.gov/pmc/articles/PMC4520913/ [Accessed 24 April 2020].

The Stephen Hawking official website. 2013. http://www.hawking.org.uk/the-computer.html [Accessed 20 March 2013].

Ulin PR. 1980. 'Traditional healers and primary health care in Africa' in *Traditional health care delivery in contemporary Africa*, Ulin PR, Segall MH (eds). New York: Maxwell School of Citizenship and Public Affairs: 1–11.

UNICEF (United Nations Children's Fund), WHO (World Health Organization), World Bank & UN Population Division. 2012. *Levels & Trends in Child Mortality Report 2012.* http://www.who.int/maternal_child_adolescent/documents/levels_trends_child_mortality_2012.pdf [Accessed 24 May 2012].

United Nations Department of Economic and Social Affairs. 2019. *World Population Prospects 2019.* https://population.un.org/wpp/Publications/Files/WPP2019_DataBooklet.pdf [Accessed 15 April 2020].

UN Inter-agency Group for Child Mortality Estimation. 2019. *Children: Reducing mortality.* who.int/news-room/fact-sheets/detail/children-reducing-mortality [Accessed 14 April 2020].

Van Rensburg HCJ, Heunis JC, Steyn F. 2012. 'Human resources for health and the health professions in South Africa' in *Health and Health Care in South Africa.* Van Rensburg HCJ (ed). Pretoria: Van Schaik: 361–431.

Vincent C, Furnham A. 1997. *Complementary Medicine: A Research Perspective.* Chichester, NY: Wiley.

Visser G, Peters L. 1990. 'Alternative medicine and general practitioners in the Netherlands: Towards acceptance and integration'. *Family Practice*, 7: 227–232.

Wainwright D (ed). 2008. *A Sociology of Health.* Los Angeles: SAGE.

Weiss GL, Lonnquist LE. 1997. *The Sociology of Health, Healing and Illness.* Upper Saddle River, NJ: Prentice Hall.

Weitz R. 2010. *The Sociology of Health, Illness, and Health Care. A Critical Approach.* 5th ed. Boston: Wadsworth.

Wessels WH. 1985. 'Understanding culture-specific syndromes in South Africa: The Western dilemma'. *Modern Medicine of South Africa*, 10(9): 51–63.

White K. 2002. *An Introduction to the Sociology of Health and Illness.* London: SAGE.

Wilkinson R, Marmot M (eds). 2003. *Social Determinants of Health. The Solid Facts.* 2nd ed. Denmark: World Health Organization.

World Bank. 2013. *Life expectancy at birth, total (years).* http://data.worldbank.org/indicator/SP.DYN.LE00.IN [Accessed 24 May 2013].

WHO 2020a. Coronavirus disease (COVID-19) Situation Report – 107, 6 May 2020. https://www.who.int/docs/default-source/coronaviruse/situation-reports/20200506covid-19-sitrep-107.pdf?sfvrsn=159c3dc_2 (accessed 16 May 2020).

WHO 2020b. Coronavirus disease (COVID-19) Situation Report – 209, 16 August 2020. https://www. https://www.who.int/docs/default-source/coronaviruse/situation-reports/20200816-covid-19-sitrep-209.pdf?sfvrsn=5dde1ca2_2 (accessed 18 August 2020).

WHO (World Health Organization). 1948. *Constitution.* http://www.who.int/hhr/en/ [Accessed 12 August 2011].

WHO (World Health Organization). 1978. *Declaration of Alma-Ata.* Adopted at the International Conference on Primary Health Care, Alma-Ata, USSR; 6–12 September 1978. http://www.searo.who.int/LinkFiles/Health_Systems_declaration_almaata.pdf [Accessed 28 Mar 2011].

WHO (World Health Organization). 2002. *25 Questions and answers on health and human rights.* Geneva: Health and Human Rights Publication Series, Issue no 1, July.

WHO (World Health Organization). 2008. *The World Health Report 2008 – primary health care (now more than ever).* http://www.who.int/whr/2008/en/index.html [Accessed 16 May 2012].

WHO (World Health Organization). 2015. *From MDGs to SDGs, WHO launches new report.* https://www.who.int/en/news-room/detail/08-12-2015-from-mdgs-to-sdgs-who-launches-new-report [Accessed 17 April 2020].

WHO (World Health Organization). 2016. *Sustainable development goals.* https://www.who.int/sdg/targets/en/ [Accessed 15 April 2020].

WHO (World Health Organization). 2020. *Rolling updates on coronavirus disease.* https://www.who.int/emergencies/diseases/novel-coronavirus-2019/events-as-they-.happen [Accessed 1 May 2020].

Worldometer. 2020. *Life expectancy of the world population.* https://www.worldometers.info/demographics/life-expectancy/#countries-ranked-by-life-expectancy [Accessed 14 April 2020].

Yates R, Dhillon RS, Rannan-Eliya RP. 2015. 'Universal health coverage and global health security'. *Lancet*, 385: 1897–1898. https://www.thelancet.com/action/showPdf?pii=S0140-6736%2815%2960909-6 [Accessed 3 May 2020].

Sport and society

Kiran Odhav & Paul Stewart

All sports fans will know the experience of spontaneously finding themselves on their feet drowned in a sea of sound as their side scores the winning points to end a tense game. Not even Émile Durkheim's concept of *collective effervescence*, that feeling of social solidarity born of collective social rituals or his concept of *social currents*, that spur-of-the-moment power which fuels mob action, captures being caught up in the shared roar of celebration of the home side winning that critical game of the season.

Modern formal sport has become part of the fabric of our global society. Not even those disinterested in it can ignore its impact. Akin to religion for many, youngsters now play games on tablets or television screens and mimic their favourite sports celebrities who set fashions and often serve as beloved role models. Sport is a modern mass phenomenon attracting the attention of millions of people around the globe glued to their television screens or joining hundreds or thousands of other like-minded fans for big games and matches in community big-screen watching.

This chapter can only introduce a few of the themes in the sociology of sport. Even important ones such as the extent of its socialising power, sport's contribution to consumerism and relation to the media, violence at sports games or sport in the digital age are not discussed in this chapter. What does receive attention is how to analyse the social phenomenon of sport from different theoretical perspectives which all recognise how sport reflects the society in which it takes place. The origin of games and sport, how sport is defined, the characteristics of modern formal sport and how power and performance are central to the dominant form sport assumes in our contemporary world are among issues and themes discussed. The chapter moves from quick sketches of sporting personalities or sports stars, both past and present, each one revealing much about, not only South African society, but some of the major issues of our time. Yet sport is also a global phenomenon and subject to the forces which shape our world and to which this chapter makes constant reference.

Invariably, as sport played a key role in the transition from a racially divided society to democracy, a brief account of the historical trajectory of soccer illustrates how this course of events unfolds. The anti-apartheid movement and the sports boycott of South Africa which contributed to democracy is noted to show how politics and sport were inseparable for the majority of South Africans.

Despite democracy, however, significant challenges remain to ensure that access to sports facilities and resources are equally accessible across social classes. This has not happened and while celebrating the fun of games and sport, indigenous and formal, and how physical sporting activities emerged out of leisure, as usual, the sociology of sport does not shy away from asking why not all people are able to share in the pleasure of participation sport has to offer.

Case study 20.1   Running for hope

Jeanette Gcinimkhondo: Mahikeng campus, North West University

Figure 20.1 Jeanette runs at UJ racetrack centre

Figure 20.2 Children at Maiteko Early Learning Centre (MELC)

Jeanette Gcinimkhondo is from Tlapeng Village (Koster, North West Province in South Africa). She studied Sociology at Mahikeng campus, North West University. She registered for Honours in Development Studies (2019), although she sought to do sports management. She set two records for NWU (2012): 100m (13 sec) and 200m (±24 sec). She has since switched her efforts to long distance running, has won several certificates and trophies, and was awarded gold and silver medals in 2012 and 2013. Jeanette has dedicated time when she is not training to working with young athletes. She has established the Maiteko Early Learning Centre (MELC) and trains young athletes. She hopes to win the South African cross-country race and aims to raise strong athletes from her village. Jeanette receives no support from the private sector. Yet in the rural part of the North West province she has already made a significant contribution to the development of youngsters in her community through the medium of sport.

Figure 20.3 Young Tlapeng athletes in action

(Source of pictures: Ms Gcinimkhondo)

QUESTIONS

1. Can sociology explain Jeanette Gcinimkhondo's individual drive and leadership role in her community?
2. How does sociology relate sport, early education and socialisation?
3. On the basis of Jeanette Gcinimkhondo's endeavours, can you explain why sport is not merely a physical activity?

Key themes

- The relevance of studying sport and society
- Defining sports activity from various sociological viewpoints
- Modern sport and its characteristics

- South African sport and its challenges
- Introducing the history of soccer in South Africa
- Commodification and globalisation in sport
- Alternative forms of sport: leisure and indigenous games

Case study 20.2   Sport and sex

Caster Semenya and the International Olympic Committee (IOC) binary sex policy

Caster Semenya won gold in the 800 m athletics event in the Olympics in Berlin in 2009 and two silver medals in 2011 and 2012. She did, however, have to undergo medical tests to assess, on 'scientific' grounds, whether she was a woman. Semenya is not the first 'woman to face such scrutiny. Serena Williams and Martina Navratilova (tennis) and Brittney Griner (basketball) were also humiliated in similar fashion. The IOC has moved its position in a number of ways: from making women walk naked in front of male judges, to chromosome testing – until it was abandoned after eight women passed the test, to abandoning such tests altogether – until the Semenya 'case'. The IOC tested Semenya's testosterone levels (under the guise that they were doing drug tests) and found them to be too high for a female.

Figure 20.4 Caster Semenya

Experts see this form of 'medical' analysis as problematic. The question raised is whether a female athlete with high testosterone levels falls outside the definition of what it is to be a woman. It raises of the issue whether there is any upper or lower limit of testosterone in humans. Professor Kidd from Canada, who participated in the 1964 Olympics, believes that both gender testing and gender segregation need to be abandoned.

(Source: Adapted from Ellison 2012)

QUESTIONS

1. Why do you think there is genetic testing in modern formal sport?
2. Is the sexual division of sport justified or is it biased against women?
3. Is the enforced lowering of testosterone levels fair to female athletes?
4. Do such practices violate athletes' rights as people?

20.1   Introduction

This chapter introduces sports studies in the sociological tradition. The issues it addresses range from why people engage in sport, to how social scientists investigate sport and sporting activities, to how sport, as a major social phenomenon with global reach, played a significant role in social change in South Africa. The activities and lives of sports fans, players and organisations all come into focus to address these and a range of related issues.

The chapter begins with a definition of modern sport, but shows how games and sport emerged out of leisure. It illustrates how particular forms of the organisation of sport occur in specific historical circumstances. It shows how sport, in displaying particular cultural and political features and characteristics, reflects society.

Modern formal sport, on the one hand, involves competition and cooperation, both being central to contemporary identity formation and self-understanding.

On the other hand, sport assumes and represents significant media-linked institutional interests and **transnational corporate finance** at a global level. Encompassing a wide range of activities, sport includes displays of skill and drama, as well as often reflecting structural and societal conflict.

Familiar sociological perspectives will be applied to sport in this chapter. Functionalist, conflict and interactionist perspectives, it will be seen, emphasise quite different aspects of sport, sporting activities and the very different contexts within which they take place.

Sport in South African society, as elsewhere, has become increasingly central in contemporary social life. Whether as active sports people, whether professional or not, or as spectators at sporting events, or watching on television screens at home, or getting together in new forms of community 'big screen' watching, sociological perspectives expressed in terms of class, race or ethnicity clearly show how sport represents so much more than physical activity and exertion. Needless to say, even a brief glance at our local history of sport reveals the role it played in the anti-apartheid struggle with the international sports boycott of South Africa during **apartheid** having widespread repercussions (see Merrett 2009; Alegi 2004; Booth 2003; 1997). For anti-apartheid activists, the call was 'no normal sport in an abnormal society'. For apartheid politicians it meant attempting ever more difficult defences of a racially divided society. Long before apartheid, however, drawing from analyses of the making of the English working class (Thompson 1967) and an African working class (Atkins 1993), 'struggles over leisure time and the meaning and use of free time were crucial avenues for contesting, negotiating and shaping capitalist and colonial attempts to impose strict controls over workers' lives (Alegi 2010: 2).

While intimately centred on the body, sport has often had and continues to have major social and political implications and consequences. Who does not have an opinion on whether there should be racial quotas in national sporting teams? It might even be said that there are few topics sociology can study which so closely tie the individual and society together. Under democracy, we all know, sport has thrown up a range of tense issues surrounding **affirmative action** and the lack of '**transformation**' in sport (see Desai 2010; McKinley 2010). Precisely what 'transformation' means is contested and disputed. For some, 'transformation' refers solely to racial transformation. For others it means a deeper restructuring of institutions and social relations in society. The lack of structural transformation, access to sporting and related recreational activities, poor or little infrastructure, few or no resources and the absence of competent coaching remain a significant challenge for the majority of South Africans.

Despite all this, a range of formal sporting activities, and soccer in particular, which will come under special focus in this chapter, has developed and thrown up an array of talent over the years ever since the very first soccer match in the Cape on 23 August 1862. As we will also see, traditional and indigenous games and sports informally enacted go back long before the **colonial encounter**.

In November 2019, much of South Africa celebrated the global spectacle of Siyamthanda Kolisi, or simply 'Siya' – as the captain of the South African rugby team is more popularly known – lifting the Webb Ellis World Cup Rugby trophy. At least one journalist, although in a more sober tone now than in 1995 when Nelson Mandela donned the famous green and gold rugby jersey, is extolling the 'magic ability' of sport to bring South Africans together

'for a fleeting moment and rejoice in unity' (Basson 2019). That was indeed, only few would deny, the sheer drama of such moments and the collective feelings of belonging and solidarity in what Durkheim referred to as **collective effervescence**.

Box 20.1 Being a black Springbok

'What people do not know is what it took me to become the 708th Springbok or what the game is really like at the neglected core, where black African rugby players reside' (Mjikeliso 2017).

QUESTIONS

1. What are the sociological reasons for rugby and soccer being racially divided in South Africa?
2. What would have to change that no national sportsperson would ever again have to repeat Thando Manana's words?

Debate these questions.

Modern sport is a mass phenomenon, has immense financial implications and has major societal effects. Sport can be viewed from the perspective of well-rehearsed sociological themes such as equality, racism, secularism, celebrity status, role models and leisure – let alone issues of national pride and vanity projects – such as massive sports stadiums – which are raised as countries compete globally to host major sporting tournaments and events.

The chapter consequently notes the role of sport in relation to pertinent aspects of **globalisation** and how sport has become implicated in processes of **commodification** and **de-territorialisation** – top sportsmen and women are globally mobile as sport goes well beyond national boundaries. The final section of the chapter points to a series of what are argued to be alternative forms of sport that emerge out of play and leisure and include indigenous games with emerging public profiles in South Africa. For long before modern formal sport, in precolonial times:

... stick fighting, hunting, competitive dancing, foot races and cattle racing developed physical strength, honed bodily movements, facilitated competition and creativity, and called upon collective understandings needed for combat, game hunting and herding and raiding cattle (Alegi 2004: 8).

It would be in the context of such 'indigenous movement cultures', it has been argued regarding elsewhere in Africa, that British colonialism could plant the seeds of its sports (Bale & Sang 1996, cited in Alegi 2010: 14). Yet, as sport and controversy so often accompany one another, it would take a young South African athlete born of these local athletic soils a century later, Caster Semenya, to again raise, as we saw in an opening case study to this chapter, a particularly complex set of issues with international repercussions.

20.2 What is sport and why do we engage in it?

Sport or sports point to interest and engagement in physical activity and exertion and mastery over the body, whether as play and recreation or as work and financial reward. This includes cognitive aspects of strategy and tactics, notably when sport is competitive, but which, in turn, cannot occur without cooperation. Whether sport is informal or formal, it is invariably a social activity. In fact, sociologists try to show how the form and kinds of sport in a society reflect the society in which they are exercised and take place.

Every form of human society, from primordial times through to the era of slavery and contemporary modern society, appear to have engaged in particular kinds of play, games and sports. Whether swinging on jungle vines or diving off cliffs or playing with balls made from local natural materials or taking part in wrestling or fighting games or displaying some of other skill, humans have done so for a range of reasons and purposes. With sporting activities formalised by the Greeks around 3 000 years ago, sport has subsequently been a central aspect of human history. The Romans produced gladiatorial sport where slaves often had to fight to the death. Such contests were major public spectacles. Archaeological ruins still stand as testimony to these central events of the ancient world and are visited by millions of tourists. Agrarian traditions of physical prowess in precolonial southern Africa were equally major public spectacles 'serving leisure and socialisation's objectives' (Alegi 2004: 9)

20.3 Defining modern sport

As is often the case in sociology, problems arise when defining modern sport (Snyder 1974). Snyder asserts that sport embodies a range of sources of conflict inherent in society. He argues that the contours of conflict in the sports world stand out in stark relief when seen in the light of the manipulation of power in society. He thus sees the sports field as a natural laboratory in which to study group dynamics and conflict. In line with this, *sport can be seen as*

structured conflict embodied in organised physical activity, involving high competition set in long-established sporting traditions bound by the rules of the game.

For Coakley (2001), sport is more than just about games. Korr and Close would agree. They entitled their book *More than just a Game: Soccer v Apartheid* (2008). It is the story of the Makana Football Association established by political prisoners on Robben Island. The forms games and sports assume, as this instance shows, relate directly to and are expressions of specific sociocultural contexts. Human agency looms large in this instance of Robben Island. This is not always the case. Whatever the social conditions, however, specific stories and images are required to make sense of and explain and enable human beings to evaluate their connections to the world. Sports are such cultural practices and social constructions to which humans give form and meaning. Sociology provides concepts, theories and means of research to understand sporting behaviour and its meanings and social significance.

Box 20.2 So what is sport?

QUESTIONS

1. Why are only some activities referred to as sport?
2. Why is sport organised the way it is?
3. Why do different societies or social groups give different meanings to sport?
4. Who benefits from the organisation of sport in society?

Coakley's detailed and authoritative texts (2001) provide a substantive definition of sport as 'institutionalised competitive activities, with relative rigorous physical or complex skills.' In their later Southern African edition, Coakley and Burnett provide a more fundamental definition: *Sports are institutionalised competitive activities that involve physical challenges in which participants are motivated by internal and external rewards* (2009:4). Going further than a single definition, Coakley and Burnett suggest scholars instead pose pointed, critical questions to better understand how participants and spectators understand sports. This represents a significant methodological shift. Knowledge is not the sole preserve of educated elites. Rather, adopting this approach potentially results in scholarship reflecting the essence of what sport is when based on what participants and the public consider it to be. In short, to paraphrase Coakley and Burnett, participants are motivated by personal enjoyment, and external rewards and balance play with spectacle and drama to display skill within institutionalised formal rules, restrictions and regulatory enforcement (2009). Organisational and technical developments lead to the rationalisation of strategies and technologies to win and enhance participants' experience of sport and to which we might add, those of the spectators as well. Learning the skills of the game becomes formalised, the incremental complexity of activities advances and the stakes in competition grow, for which expert guidance is sought (see Coakley 2001).

The opening case studies to this chapter clearly embody aspects of this compressed description and analysis of what sport is and involves. Meanings are attached to sporting activities: the motivational aspects of participants, balancing play and skill and cooperation and competition, and enhancing participants' sporting experiences, all of which are of increasing complexity. Closely observed, this would become evident even in the young athletes receiving some form of expert guidance, coaching and training from Jeanette. If they are fortunate, they may later be exposed to more formal trainers, coaches or even experts in athletics or possibly a different sport entirely, an interest and competence in which they might trace back to their early introduction to sports discipline and proficiency. In the case of Caster Semenya, a similar such trajectory remains on display on the global stage. How are we to grasp such a biographical trajectory sociologically? (see Ingham 2004).

One useful way of understanding the reasons why humans have always engaged in some form of play or sport is to contrast undertaking sport for *pleasure and participation*, the organisation of which is generally *informal*, with sport undertaken to advance *power and performance* (Coakley 2001). The organisation of this latter form of sport is *formal* and is the current dominant form in our society. Bearing in mind these two very different forms sport assumes, we can begin looking at the phenomenon of sport more closely. We begin with contemporary, modern formal sport.

20.4 Characteristics of modern formal sport

At least four basic aspects of modern formal sport can be identified.

Firstly, modern sport comprises *organised activity* of various kinds, generally involving the internal structure of a team, distinct roles – coaches, athletes, referees, spectators and audiences, whether present or virtual and the following of formalised and generally evolving, often contested, sets of rules. Competition is invariably central to formal organised

sport whether undertaken as an individual or part of a team, but so is cooperation. Formal, professional organised sport, needless to say, is a global money-spinning industry with individual athletes earning astronomical amounts of money, with those at the very top earning even more through their endorsement of sporting products and other commodities and commercially available services.

Central to modern sport, secondly, is that it is based on *competition* and *contests* of power, strength and skill between individuals or teams. Competition entails not only mastery over body, self and others, but the quest for excellence and supremacy. Cooperation between athletes in team-based sports is generally subordinated to competition while remaining central to it. Further, serious sportsmen and -women seek not just recognition of their efforts in winning and the awarding of prizes and trophies, but also the glory of championship and sense and experience of ultimate, socially recognised achievement. Achievement at the highest level, particularly nationally and internationally, represents the attainment of lifelong recognition and social status. Both competitive behaviour and status achievement are underlying socially defined conditions of formal sporting activities. Without a will to win and a will to attain power and social recognition, there is no formal sport.

Modern formal sport has, thirdly, become *institutionalised and professionalised*. As these processes have taken place, via the regular organisation of competitions, from village to global level, different sporting activities have increasingly become rationalised and hierarchically centralised globally. Particular individual professionalised sporting activities have increasingly become monopolised and controlled, regulated and organised on a global level as major institutions. Although not all sports have evolved into monopolies, the Federation of International Football Associations (FIFA) is a prominent example of how one such institution has the monopoly on world soccer and its rules, as well as the selection of the countries to host World Cup games. FIFA, for instance, has established itself as a monopoly so powerful it virtually enforces World Cup host countries to serve it as tax free zones from which it gains huge wealth, thereby exercising a unique form of global domination.

Sport has, finally, become *formalised in academies* with its own relatively recently emerging discipline of Sports Science or Exercise Science, which studies the healthy physical body while engaged in exercise which is examined from the cellular level through to whole body perspectives. Sports Science consequently involves biokinetics, human anatomy and physiology generally offered in faculties of medicine or education. Qualifications are generally in the natural sciences, but which also feature the study of cultural, historical and political aspects and contexts crucial to a comprehensive understanding of sport as physical, tactical, strategic and intellectual activity.

Figure 20.5 Empire building
(Source: http://www.zapiro.com/cartoon/118045-100128mg#.U4C2F7-D5O0)

20.4.1 The current dominant form of sport

The current dominant form sport takes in our society is formal and has *power and performance* as central to its activities (Coakley 2001). In this sense sport reflects the broader social structuring of society. One theorist usefully suggests that any definition of sports will 'reflect the structure and organisation of relationships and social life in a particular society at a particular point in time' (Sokot 2009: 12). The focus here is the current dominant form that formal modern sport assumes. The chapter will later examine the origin of sport in leisure, and looks at contemporary games and sports engaged in for the purposes of *pleasure and participation*, some of which are moving in the direction of our current dominant sports form.

The following table is a summary outline of the characteristics of modern formal sport in which *power and performance* are dominant:

Table 20.1 Summary outline of the characteristics of modern formal sport in which power and performance are dominant

Characteristic	Description
Secularism	Power and performance sports entertain and create 'diversion.' Activity is not linked to religious beliefs, rituals or mysticism
Equality	Power and performance sports are ideally not based on birthright or social background. Participants in theory face the same competitive conditions irrespective of social circumstances
Specialisation	Specialists dominate in power and performance sports, with dedication to a single event or position in an event. Skills and responsibilities define positions served by equipment fitting the demands of particular activities
Rationalisation	Complex rules specify how athletes are required to pursue goals that regulate equipment, play techniques and the conditions of participation. Strategies involve increasingly rational training methods, affecting experience and the evaluation of participants

Characteristic	Description
Bureaucratisation	Complex organisations control the current dominant power and performance form of sports locally and internationally. Officials oversee and organise events, sanction players, enforce rules and certify records
Quantification	Participation in formal modern sport is subject to measurements and statistics: recording times, standardising distances, scoring individuals and monitoring events in communities, provinces, states and continents
Records	Formal sport stresses the setting and breaking of records. Performances across events are compared. Records are published. World records are thereby measured, officially ratified and publicly recognised

(Source: Adapted from Coakley 2001)

What is immediately apparent is that as soon as we put the dominant form that sport and sports take in modern society, we return to looking at a range of social phenomena and practices with which we are familiar. These social phenomena are readily identifiable characteristics of society as a whole and to which we need to apply our theoretical resources.

20.5 Theoretical approaches to modern sports

20.5.1 A functionalist perspective

Of the various perspectives in sports studies, three general and basic sociological approaches to the study of sports and society are outlined by Coakley (2001). *Functionalism* relates to a macro-perspective that is status quo oriented. It seeks to expand opportunities for sports participants and to oppose rule breakers – in short, cheaters and drug users. This perspective propounds a depoliticised view of sport, but has as its focus the function of sport and its role in social control in society. Functionalists see social order striving towards balance and stress consensus and shared values, which, this perspective argues, holds all the interrelated parts together for the overall operation of any system. The main concerns of this view are how sport fits into social life and how it contributes to personal development and social stability and efficiency. This approach thus concludes that sport is a valuable institution that benefits individuals and society at large and is a source of inspiration for individuals at a personal level. This perspective hence seeks to develop sports programmes to promote traditional values, build positive character and contribute to order and stability in society. Functionalists can be criticised for overstating the positive consequences of sport and ignoring power relations in how it can serve the needs of some people over others. Functionalist analyses generally do not fully acknowledge that sport is a social construction implicating race, class and gender stratification differences in society.

20.5.2 A conflict approach

Conflict-based approaches see social order as based on economic interests with social class shaping social structure and human relationships. This view focuses on how economic power is distributed and how the dynamics of class relations unfold. It identifies the privileged, exploited and socially excluded in such class relations. Typical questions asked by conflict theorists would be: how does sport maintain the interests of the administrators or how it contributes to maintaining the dominant ideas of competition instead of collaboration and cooperation or, indeed, how it *manufactures* social cohesion and *mirrors* social inequality while *masking* exploitation? Conflict theorists might inquire how the immense amounts of money paid to celebrity sportspeople distort the values of comradeship and ideals of fairness long associated with sportsmanship.

A strong version of this approach could go as far as to conclude that sport is a form of physical activity distorted by the immense amounts of money in professional support leading to its **commodification**, thereby replicating the logic and serving the interests of capital. Sport could further be seen as an opiate for those with no economic power and which distracts them from their own social problems by offering or imposing a collective focus and outlet and dominant topic of conversation. This view might want to assert the importance of raising awareness to eliminate the profit motive in sport and to rediscover lost notions of participation as a source of expression, creative experience and physical wellbeing. The problem with this view is that it generally overstates economic forces and the dominance of elites in society as if people in other social strata do not possess free human agency. This perspective can assume that those with economic power always shape sport to meet their own interests. It can tend to ignore the fact that sport can be, or is for many, across divides of social stratification, a site of creativity, the expression of individual agency and even of liberating experiences.

20.5.3 An interactionist theory of sport

The third view, *interactionism*, sees social order created from the bottom up, through intentional social interaction, of people's unique worlds. The stress is on democratic and alternative participation to create meaning and organisation in sports worlds. It looks at how meanings, identities and culture are created through social interactions between people and how people define their own lived realities and the world around them. Proponents thus ask: how do people get involved in sports, how do they become defined as athletes, and how do they derive meaning from participation and make transitions out of sports into the rest of their lives? It concludes that sports are forms of culture created through social interaction, with participation grounded in the decisions made by people in relation to their identities and relationships. It seeks to allow individuals the space for the creation of meaning and to shape sports to fit their definition of reality. Some versions of interactionism aim to make sport more democratic and less hierarchical. The focus of sound interpretivist accounts is both the culture and organisation of sport and how individual athletes attach meaning to their sporting activities. Despite its valuable contributions, this approach has its own limitations: it often fails to explain how meaning, identity and interaction are related to social structures and material conditions in society. Such approaches often also ignore issues of power relations and social inequality in society (Coakley 2001).

Box 20.3 Theorising sport

Split your class or tutorial into three debating or discussion groups.

Each group should take turns in representing a theorist from one of the three key sociological perspectives and answer questions from the other two perspectives.

The aim is to adopt or 'put yourself in the shoes' of a particular theory or perspective and to try to apply its concepts and explanations of sports phenomena, activities and institutions.

QUESTIONS

1. Are you sufficiently intellectually flexible to argue *for* and *against* all three perspectives?
2. Can you offer *novel* explanations?

20.6 Developing the three main perspectival sociological accounts

The above account of sport briefly presented the three dominant traditional sociological theoretical approaches or perspectives to analyse sport in society. The functionalist perspective, or more accurately the structural-functionalist perspective, dominated analyses from the late 1930s until the 1960s in North America and influenced much of sociology. Contemporary modern formal sport serves a variety of functions in society, economic functions having become especially significant, such as in the variety of often considerably powerful sports-based industries that emerge from particular sporting activities. These global corporate businesses, such as Nike and Adidas, can be understood as serving a conservative function to distract people from other needs that are necessary for their existence. The logic is that if one is satisfied through physical activity, one may not want to seek satisfaction in other aspects of one's life. This is, of course, not always the case. Take Nelson Mandela for instance: 'After a strenuous workout I felt both mentally and physically lighter. It was a way of losing myself in something that was not the struggle. After an evening's workout I would wake up the next morning feeling strong and refreshed, ready to take up the fight again' (Mandela 1994: 180, cited in Alegi 2004: 7)

The influence of structural functionalism waned significantly after the 1960s (Loy & Booth 2004). Along with Talcott Parsons, Robert Merton was a key thinker in this tradition, but began in the early 1970s to refer to himself as a 'structural analyst' (Loy & Booth 2004). The stress became, not how social phenomena, such as modern formal sport, were functional to the working of society by maintaining established norms and consensus, but rather how structural circumstances, such as socio-economic or racial disadvantage, shaped or governed choices members of such groups made.

Conflict perspectives reflect on the unequal distribution of power and resources in society. This view permits an appreciation of the foundational structural conflict between social groups based on social class, race, ethnicity and gender. The social institution of sport is powerfully shaped by these factors. The achievements of Siya Kolisi and the World Cup winning rugby team aside, rugby could never, for instance, replace soccer as the national sport in South Africa until everyone has equal access to grass playing fields. While South African rugby has gradually become more racially integrated, to be become a Springbok remains out of reach for members of the black African working class, not only as there are few grassed rugby pitches to play on, but also as the time, money and **cultural capital** are not readily accessible to poorly paid wage workers in industry or service sector workers working irregular hours. To a significant degree, as conflict analysts would argue, sport is indeed dependent on the development of the productive forces of bourgeois society (Brohm 1989, cited in Rowe 2004).

From the interactionist perspective, sport is important because it brings people together. From such interactions, sports institutions can emerge that may sustain themselves for generations. In some countries, sport takes on the characteristics of devotion to a religion. This could be said of sports such as cricket in India or soccer in Spain and England. Alegi's account of soccer, politics and society in South Africa, 'Laduma!', opens with the claim that South Africa has been described as 'the most sports-mad country in the world' (2004:1). The consequences of this are that many avid sports fans often craft their lifestyles around factors relating to sports matches or events. More particularly even, the work of the interactionist Irving Goffman has been to link his close interactional analysis to critical analyses. A single point worth mentioning is how Goffman's work on **impression management** has applied to the sociology of sport. Any leading sportsperson must *manage their performance* to the expectations of their peers, their managers and the public. They need to be '"cool" for their fans, demeaned for the management and dramatic for the fans' (Ingham 1975: 369, cited in Birrell & Donnelly 2004). This is no small task and can result in the alienated labour of the professional sportsperson.

Whatever theoretical perspective one adopts and regarding which much work has been done in combining these perspectives (see Giulianotti 2004), it is instructive to any study of sport to view its development in its historical context. The particular case of South Africa can be used to illustrate why the history of sport is of particular sociological interest.

20.7 Scanning the local sports literature

The case of South African soccer will be treated in this chapter as a case study of sport in South Africa. Many of its themes are suggestive of other national sports, both current and in the past. Do scan the fascinating local literature such as Desai (2016), Latakgomo (2010), Calland et al (2010), Merrett (2009), Korr and Close (2008), Alegi (2004) and Booth (1998) or broader accounts, such as Giulianotti and Robertson, on globalisation and football (2009). In South Africa the sports literature is broadening to address the silences inherited from our racialised past. South African

Rugby, the sports' coordinating body, in 2012, initiated, for example, the enormous task of documenting black rugby in South Africa.

Desai's story of cricket (2016), described as a 'brutal and brilliant analysis of transformation in cricket since the late apartheid years', could similarly serve as a focus alongside his earlier account of cricket in KwaZulu-Natal, cleverly entitled 'Blacks in Whites' (Desai et al 2002; see also Vahed et al 2010). To these two accounts could be added two keen foci on the politics of cricket in South Africa (see Odendaal 1977 and Gemmel 2004). Then there is also, of course, the seminal classic on cricket which 'explained' the game in terms of its deep social and cultural dimensions, *Beyond a Boundary* by CLR James written in 1963 (Stottart 2010).

The history of the last 90 years of black golf in southern Africa, incidentally, only appeared in 2019 (Cohen 2019). In fact, precisely because apartheid sport mirrored apartheid society, namely white ignorance and black marginalisation, there is much work to be done in the sociology of sport locally.

There are other sporting histories waiting to be written as segregated sport in South Africa, of course, long predated apartheid, with rugby, for instance, having been segregated since 1896. Under both segregation and apartheid, while sport beyond white sports was used as a form of social control, it received little official recognition by the government.

20.8 Sport under apartheid: The case of South African soccer

Soccer has a rich history in South Africa which well illustrates how sport mirrors society. The current definitive text is that of Alegi (2004). In terms of its numbers, soccer is clearly the country's majority sport. First played by colonial soldiers and administrators, black African soccer, prior to World War II, was informally organised (Couzens 1983) until the formation of the Durban and District Native Football Association (DDNFA) in 1916 which Natal exported to Johannesburg, with the Witwatersrand District Native Football Association (WDNFA) formed in 1917. Mine compound managers hoped the Association would 'curb militancy, increase discipline and production and improve health' among mine workers (Alegi 2004:39). The Chamber of Mines-owned newspaper, *Umteteli wa Bantu* – Voice of the People – considered there to be a 'definite moral enlargement in the *observance of the rules* of football, cricket, hockey and other healthy outdoor games' (Alexander 2013) (our emphasis). Soccer rapidly took root among clerks on the mines. In the decade of the 1930s, in which the Africanisation of its inherited institutions of British football was occurring, soccer had shown the 'remarkable ability' to have drawn in the poorest and most exploited sections of a newly industrialising South African society (Alegi 2004: 21). In 1932, significantly, the term 'native' was dropped from the name of soccer clubs and 'African' used, following the example of the African National Congress in 1923, signalling the ever-closer relationship between rising African nationalism in the 1920s and 1930s and the sport of soccer (see Alegi 2004: 31ff).

Black African and so-called 'coloured' players came together under the umbrella of the South African Soccer Federation (SASF), popularly known simply as *The Federation* in 1951, which organised regular competitions and professional football. The Federation was a highly centralised, relatively stable body, though not averse to accepting some white assistance for African recreation. Under the SASF high-quality football was played across the country in various local areas. There were also some friendly matches between teams from the Federation and the African league (NPSL). Players and administrators also moved between these leagues. Prominent names in this regard were Suli Bhamjee, Johannes 'Big Boy' Kholoane and Baldwin 'Groovin' Molope. Teams, however, mainly came from coloured and Indian townships, communities marginally better resourced than their black African compatriots.

Similarly, other black African sports organisations managed to survive despite the onslaught of apartheid. White officialdom, like the mine owners of earlier years, sought to instil 'proper behaviour' amongst Africans and saw it as an outlet for a non-political release of energy which was crucial for white minority rule to survive.

The world governing body FIFA admitted the whites-only SAFA to its ranks in 1952 only later to expel it as a result of the anti-apartheid sports boycott. International recognition for full representation of South African soccer was, however, to be a complex institutional struggle. The popular writer, Joe Latakgomo, tells the story (2010). FIFA rejected The Federation's affiliation for even non-voting status by claiming it did not represent football nationally, despite it being able to boast 46 000 players (see Latakgomo 2010: 77ff).

Over the following decades, as the institutional struggle for international recognition continued, the basis of the sport was laid with soccer growing to represent thousands of players in inter-district competitions representing streets, yards or sections in townships. The South African Soccer League (SASL), established by professionals and businessmen in 1961, sought to professionalise soccer to which The Federation, from which it broke away, was opposed. The SASL played an important role in promoting non-racial sport and the decision of FIFA to exclude the whites-only league in 1961. The NPSL, established to counter the SASL, which did not last long, consisted mainly of black African teams. What became clear to black African athletes and fans was that 'sport and politics were inseparable' (Alegi 2004: 117).

Under such racialised organisational conditions, South African soccer was not in a position to unite across the racial divide, despite the lead taken by the anti-apartheid South African Council on Sport (SACOS) on this matter.

Locally, however, there were individual sporting achievements despite the segregated sports regimes in South Africa.

Case study 20.3 Patrick Ace Ntsoelengoe: A multitalented soccer superstar

Figure 20.6 Ace in action

(Source: http://www.sowetanlive.co.za/sp ort/2013/05/16/we-look-back-at-amakhosi-titles#leaf)

Vignette: Youth dreams of sports stardom

Many young players dream about being soccer stars as they progress through their school or sports team. FIFA has officially warned that only very few will achieve this (see Coakley 2009:106). Little do young players realise that only unique athletes achieve 'stardom.' Many great players do not make it to the glittering world that such young players dream about. The idealism of youth makes sportspersons dream of reaching such a status and there are many factors that feed this form of idealism. Some, like Ace Ntsoelengoe, made it to the top of his game with pure raw talent and was idolised by many. At the early age of 17 he began to play for Kaizer XI where he spent his entire career (1970s to mid-1980s). He also played off-season in the USA and Canada, lasting 11 seasons in the North American Soccer league. He also played tennis, as well as the guitar and the organ. He was affectionately known as 'Ace'. Nicknaming players is a common phenomenon in South Africa, reflecting how fans claim such players as their own.

Ace played six seasons for the Denver Dynamos (later known as the Minnesota Kicks, 1976). When the Dynamos were about to fold, he was key in bringing them back to become one of the top teams. He also appeared in the Minnesota, Toronto and the Soccer Bowl series (1976–86). His talent was that despite being a mid-fielder, he attacked and scored more goals than strikers. Some saw him as the country's greatest footballer: Oscar Martinez (Argentina) saw him as the perfect player; and others like Clive Barker (ex-South Africa coach) and Eddie Lewis (Kaizer Chiefs coach), compare him to Zinedine Zidane (France), Christiano Ronaldo (Real Madrid) or Lionel Messi (Argentina). While sports stardom has its benefits and Ace used all the opportunities he got despite the limitations of apartheid, others were not so fortunate. Even after 1994, many footballers, particularly black sportsmen, did not always manage to go far after their short soccer careers, which generally last to the age of around 30.

QUESTIONS

1. How was Ace different from his peers in his soccer career? Is this a clear case of the power of individual human agency?
2. What are the opportunities and the risks of celebrity sports star status?
3. Is South Africa honing its sports talent? Are there structural or wider societal reasons why few black sportspersons manage to sustain their success as sports stars?

20.9 Resistance to sports domination under apartheid

While Ace Ntsoelengoe was one of the few with an international sporting status, SACOS took the political struggle to the international arena and clearly articulated the demands of the mass of disenfranchised communities with their call of 'no normal sport in an abnormal society' (Booth 2003). The call reflects how sport and society in South African were interlinked and intertwined.

Full-scale professionalism appeared in the 1970s when television was introduced and the modern era was born with the help of the midwife of the media and advertising. So strongly had soccer been established that it has even been claimed that the popularity of soccer 'defeated' apartheid society (McKinley 2010: 83). Gwede Mantashe, both a footballer and a National Union of Mineworkers organiser in the 1980s, was expected by some, for instance, to discourage the obsession with soccer on the collieries! (Alexander 2020: 164). On the playing fields, remarkable talent was being produced with gradually increasing numbers of players able to ply their trade internationally as professionals

before 1994. Off the field, sports administration became a key, if often a hotly disputed and contested area as a better-educated middle-class exercised political, economic and administrative control over the sport in a range of bodies, not without much controversy over the years, particularly regarding financial arrangements. After much institutional tussling a resurrected SAFA was formed as a racially united national association in 1991.

The fortunes of the national team in the early post-apartheid democratic era looked bright. Bafana Bafana won the Africa Cup of Nations in 1996 and qualified for the World Cup final rounds in 1998 and 2002. It was the hosting of the World Cup in 2010 which again put soccer securely in the national spotlight and gave coverage to the intensity with which soccer is received by players and spectators alike. Bafana Bafana has subsequently, however, performed poorly, with the administration of the sport having been described as being in an 'upside-down state' and has not led to the degree of genuine transformation in the sport as many hoped (see McKinley 2010).

20.10 Inequality in South African sport

Sport in South Africa since the earliest days was replete with class and race inequality, and an unequal provision of resources, infrastructure and access to the various codes of sport. Under apartheid a raft of discriminatory racial legislation made it illegal for the various legally defined 'races' to play any organised sport together. Apartheid, following established traditions of half a century of segregation, as we saw in the case of rugby, entrenched the separation of black and white sport across the national sports codes. One consequence was that sports audiences and supporters were likewise either physically divided in the stadiums or were socially divided in terms of support for their teams.

South Africa's insistence on white racial sport representing national entities became 'symptomatic of a white pathology about the body': white male bodies bonding in the context of forced white army conscription to defend white South Africa. In Bloemfontein, for instance,

'unpatriotic' crowd behaviour banned all black spectators (Nixon 1992). Yet a survey of white South Africans ranked the lack of international sport as one of the three most damaging consequences of apartheid.

20.11 International resistance to apartheid sport

With sport serving as a mirror of a racially divided society it would be the white 'national' sport under apartheid which would face the fiercest resistance from the international community regarding South Africa's racial policies. Rugby was emblematic of its white male Afrikaner credo. With the international community aiming for a total sports boycott of the country at the time, within South Africa the battle lines were drawn largely along race between those who supported the status quo – keeping politics out of sport – and those who opposed apartheid sport – 'no normal sport in an abnormal society'.

In a similar vein, the political protests orchestrated by Dennis Brutus, Peter Hain and Young Liberals (UK) in 1969 saw the South African rugby team retreat behind barbed wire and the British police. Two decades later, protesters tried to ensure the cancellation of the Springboks' cricket tour to England. Nixon (1992) reports that these actions became benchmark events in the international campaign to have apartheid's 'national team' barred from world competition. The power of such sports boycotts lay in its use of spectacle, as Nixon argues, and by accessing sports fans' passionate commitment – usually indifferent to international politics.

Figure 20.7 Police clash with anti-apartheid demonstrators
(Source (both): Nixon 1992)

Figure 20.8 Flour bags thrown at 1969 rugby match (All Blacks vs SA)

20.12 The sports boycott extends anti-racism internationally

The sports boycott became the most prominent and extended anti-racist campaign in the history of world sport. Not since the Berlin Olympics in 1936 and the appearance of the winning African American athlete, Jesse Owen, had race been of such international prominence. The boycott gained international status at the United Nations (UN) and the Organisation of African Unity (OAU). Owing to the predominantly white sports teams from South Africa, questions were raised about their representation. Questions were also raised about much contested issues such as nationhood, political representation, racial policies and racial discrimination. Elsewhere, the Maori cause in New Zealand, for example, gave fresh impetus to organised resistance to South African tours.

It was a surreal moment for many when, in the religious home of racialised right wing politics represented by rugby, the British Lions beat the Springboks in 1969 on South African soil. A commentator spoke of a double humiliation: losing on the field to the British Lions and being humiliated off the field by anti-apartheid protesters:

> To us in SA, rugby is a really our god with a small letter, and to be defeated like that – the mishaps, the players who were injured – it was abnormal. God spoke to us (Nixon 1992).

Resistance reached a peak, yet the conditions for black sports remained bleak. Conditions for sport were described as

> weather ravaged, over-extended, under-equipped, under-funded, and understaffed facilities in the black townships meant that sporting events promised not a flight from politics but an immersion in it (Nixon 1992).

The proponents of the sports boycott advocated the repeal of all apartheid laws. These included, among others, the Population Registration Act (which classified people in terms of race), the Group Areas Act (which controlled people's movements), the Reservation of Separate Amenities Act (which separated and provided unequal amenities for different races) and the Bantu Education Act (which provided unequal education for Africans). Internationally, the South African Non-racial Olympic Committee (SANROC) became more radical than its predecessors. It did not treat the racial composition of national teams as the index of deracialisation, but focused on the myriad of apartheid laws. These included

laws in education, health, housing, voting, residential and land rights, as well as access to amenities. All such laws that prevented black people from competing on equal terms represented fair game for SANROC. SANROC went into exile and South Africa was banned from the Olympics in 1964, with support from the African contingent (1966). After the Basil D'Oliveira affair, precipitated by a then so-called 'coloured' player who was not allowed to play for South Africa, a debacle which also embarrassed Britain and led to the expulsion by over 20 local sports bodies, more bannings occurred in South Africa (see Gemmell 2004: 1476ff). One such person was Morgan Naidoo of SACOS. Despite the apartheid regime's trying to continue with its rebel sports tours, the apartheid sports machine never quite managed to separate sport as it had done before. South African business began to support non-racial sport. South African Breweries (SAB) gave $2 million for such ventures. While whites constituted 15 per cent of the population, they owned 73 per cent of all athletic tracks, 82 per cent of all rugby fields, and 83 per cent of public schools. The regime spent between nine and 23 times more per capita on white than on black sports. This led to disastrous effects:

> [which carried]...apartheid into a sphere [where] ... boycotters tilted the balance of the game towards lawlessness and violence ... on and off the field. [Instead of] ... a carefully monitored, socially sanctioned outlet for unruly impulses, sporting contests became emblems of violence... bursting uncontrollably from the space-and-time frame of the game. This led the head or Rugby SA, Danie Craven, to state ... 'We can't go abroad without causing chaos. It's not pleasant to feel as if we're suffering from a disease' (Nixon 1992: 82).

After the ANC lifted the sports ban in 1991, it went on to promise to set up sports development programmes in the townships. The ANC, according to Nixon (1992), felt that it was taking the lead and commanding the pace and conditions of SA's admission into international sport. The pressing need, it was felt, was to democratise institutions. Between pressing international matters and those concerned with local issues, the former seems to have won out in an effort to act as a catalyst of change. The new effort did direct the flow of corporate funds to townships, and shift the 90 per cent that flowed to white communities. It was, in fact, a tussle between the last president under apartheid, Willem De Klerk and the ANC, as both attempted to gain the most mileage out of sport which had become a political weapon.

Yet the ANC's threat to re-impose the sports boycott did not materialise, even after the Boipatong massacre in 1992. The anti-apartheid inspired international boycott had already been dropped and negotiations towards a democratic South African well already underway.

Box 20.5 Sport, resistance and politics

QUESTIONS

1. Why did resistance to apartheid sport grow internationally?
2. What was the relation between sport and politics under apartheid?
3. What are the arguments for and against ending the sports boycott before the end of apartheid?

20.13 Sport in South Africa after 1994: A lack of transformation

In the new democratic political dispensation after 1994, the previously advantaged white constituencies gained the upper hand over the liberationists in sports structures. Liberation in the sports arena became more diffuse. Despite the advent of democracy, there was no systematic or decisive response to the financial needs of township schools: coaching, infrastructure and resources. This disabled building of strengths which had been developed under the adverse conditions of apartheid. Ashwin Desai thus asserts the following about what happened in cricket:

20% insiders enforced policy boundaries to an impoverished majority, arising from rampant commercialism in cricket that resulted in such a policy (Desai et al 2002).

After South Africa was readmitted to international cricket in 1991, to 'the strains of class and race', it has been argued, a 'contradictory transformation' took place in South African sport. 'Black gains were being forced onto unwilling whites.' Junior black sportsmen and women emerged, but were mainly from traditionally white schools and so continued to represent an elite. With an 'intact capitalist class structure', it has been further argued, this signalled a continuity between the old apartheid system and the new non-racial democracy. This is despite black cricket having been independent from white cricket over a century before when racialised imperial and capitalist interests supported segregated cricket. The hegemony of white cricket was attained by an 'evacuation of black cricket and absorption of

non-racial players and administration' (at provincial levels), with cricket development impacting mainly on areas that already had cricket. After rampant commercialisation, as in the post-1994 GEAR policy (see McKinley 2010), new race categorisations emerged, unrolling the meaning of 'black' in black consciousness due to historical and cultural conditions. Cricket entered a globalisation phase 'detaching it from its economic base', severing it from national expression and making it a 'subscription of capital'. Thus, the re-introduction of the amateur–professional division to save on costs and financial scandals in the sport reflected a dire governance and fiduciary crisis in national cricket administration (Desai et al 2002). Sports did not change much for most of the country's disadvantaged people. What follows is some explanation of the underlying issues relating to sport not transforming in more meaningful and structural ways.

20.14 Forms of affirmative action perpetuating social inequality

Despite all the strides and progress made by South African sport after political liberation in 1994, it remains in a state of mixture of progress and regression. Desai (in Habib 2008) cites the following as a sign of such a mixture: laws affirming race rather than class result in affirmative action and racial quotas, yet they leave black African and poor people further disadvantaged. This is exacerbated by the lack of change in sports laws to prescribe transformation. Sports transformationists may cite the 'logic of development', Desai argues, but they limit themselves to particular sports codes, franchised teams or how quotas compromise national teams by interfering with the branding and marketing of profit-driven events to the detriment of the sport. Government support for sport has been disabled due to its neoliberal macro-economic developmental path, McKinley has argued (2010).

The overall effect, Desai contends, is that the wider societal effects of the various policies and practices in sporting teams are waylaid. We then have affirmative action policies which become a vexed question with coaches accused of racism no matter how they choose their teams. Black African players are required to display disproportionately higher levels of proficiency to find social acceptance in selection. The question of how much or how far affirmative action is to be implemented or advanced is raised so as not to unfairly discriminate against white players who qualify for selection. The result is, as Desai argues, affirmative action broadly promotes race over class. The black middle class gains an advantage over working-class and poorer communities. Furthermore, the black middle class, Desai contends, is a key constituency of the ruling party (African National Congress): this is why this class rallies against an entitlement and dependency culture among the poor. With a lack of investment at all levels in advancing broader sporting development goals, the focus remains the top of the social pyramid and the perpetuation of elitism in sport is continued.

20.15 Infrastructure, resources and facilities in townships

In order for the development of a more broad-based and inclusive form of the organisation of sport, what is needed, for Desai, is that additional state support at all levels of resource allocation should be dedicated to the development of especially black African players irrespective of social class. Poor transformation in sport is, in short, due a lack of major investment in poor communities. The neoliberal Growth and Redistribution (GEAR) policies, characterised by focusing on economic growth without redistribution, entrenches social inequality. The result is a lack of linkages between sport and citizenship. This leads to a continuity of the status quo in sports arenas. This specifically affects the development of potential sportspersons in townships and in rural areas. The transformation of sport nationally is thus seriously compromised. Elite sports places remain confined to the privileged and transformation is 'contrived, uneven and contested'. Not just race, but targeting social class is therefore required for meaningful transformation in sport for Desai. This is not simply a matter of racial quotas or counting the number of black members of sports teams. Instead, genuine investment in poorer communities' sports infrastructure, coaching, talent identification and the like, need to be prioritised. This means policy has to shift the exercise of power for real change rather than 'disguising middle and upper-class interests as racial contestation'.

Mchunu and Le Roux (2010) concur in their finding that one main reason black school learners do not take part in sport in greater numbers, thereby developing a stronger social base for sport, relates to a lack of organised recreational facilities and the lack of upgrading of sports fields. A general lack of financial resources is the key reason for the lack of participation in formal sporting activities in many communities across South Africa. Clearly, this applies even more acutely to low-income families than it does for those from average-income ones. In short, access to sports and facilities remains grossly unequal in democratic South Africa across lines of race and social class.

Given this broad scenario makes the case of Jeanette Gcinimkhondo even more remarkable, for this represents an intervention at the individual level. While fortunate to have come from a sporting family and hence conditions in her socialisation which were conducive to achievement in sport, this does not explain her commitment to tackle the systemic lack of necessary equipment, resources or technical training or support that continues to characterise many schools, particularly in rural and disadvantaged communities (Desai et al, in Habib 2008). The case study is again noted here as it leads to discussing two further aspects of meaningful transformation of sport in our society.

20.15.1 Access and initiative

As noted earlier in this chapter, sport is not confined to being understood as solely a physical aspect of human behaviour. Sport, as both practised and enjoyed and as institution and source of wealth, is intimately implicated in the social construction of society. Despite the economic conditions of rural areas in South Africa, a social network was established by Jeanette, which is one among others also initiated by other like-minded individuals. The athletes train as a group, but will join other networks as they progress in life. Jeanette's running is also not an isolated individual event: it has precursors as her parents were sportspersons. While this individual may have a physiological disposition towards sporting prowess, her own inspirational efforts are grounded not only in her self-motivation as some psychologists may want to point out, but needs to be contextualised in her social being emanating from her family relations. Her early training at school, and in valiantly involving others in her efforts to achieve both academically and sports-wise, are crucial in her case. Such efforts are part of an ordinary person's sporting initiatives, for any of us can train youngsters, but in her case she has achieved awards in her running and seeks to pass this on even if she is not yet nationally or internationally famous. She is inspirational to those youngsters but is also providing some kind of access for them to achieve. Access to sport is an important issue, but it also needs other conditions that allow for growth and development.

Box 20.6 Sport and resources

Imagine yourself in a school with exactly the opposite of what you had for sports facilities in your school. Write down what you think. Ask others for their comments on what you wrote. Try this with a few people in your class and see if you can comment on what they have written (and vice versa). What have you learnt from this exercise?

The critical importance of an intervention, such as that of a Jeanette Gcinimkhondo, is that the first significant external and institutional community a child enters is the school. In this key institution of secondary socialisation, there remains a massive amount of socially charged energy, the 'raw' human material with which educationalists work. It is a crucial space for intervention. While there is much left to be desired for the resuscitation of the public-school system in South Africa, the challenge of sport development and infrastructure provision remains a massive (even hidden) challenge. This is ironic given the current global reach and impact of sport and to which topic this chapter now turns.

20.16 The globalisation of sport

The key processes of globalisation can be seen as primarily in terms of their economic or cultural aspects. The former view sees the worldwide spread of economic goods and services as crucial, while the latter view emphasises the cultural spread of ideas and lifestyles. Globalisation involves both processes, from the spread of ideas and cultural configurations to the multiplication of economic activities in the world from one country to others. One result is the development of economically globally active multinational or transnational corporations which constitute the global sports industry.

The reach of this global industry is extensive and is one with which we are all familiar, ranging from media displays of sport through to sports paraphernalia, to loans and transfers of players, and to the sale of teams, among a host of related industries. Modern formal sport is, however, at root, a Western product. As we have seen, its form mirrors and is powerfully shaped by the society in which it is embedded. The processes of globalisation, on which it built its extended landscapes after its 18th century bureaucratisation and specification, were interrupted after World War II, but taken up again in the new wave of globalisation in the 1970s. This process has subsequently been so successful that there are more member nations in the Olympics than in the United Nations! (Bale 1994).

Sports globalisation can, first, be characterised as a process rather than an outcome. There is internationalisation through cross-border trade of players, ideas, competitions and media ownerships. This has followed relaxing government regulation of business globally (Houlihan 2003). Sport has followed the internationalisation of the media and culture with competitions and mobility, for instance, subject to the European Union's ruling in 1995 regulating the transferability of players and specifying the number of national players allowed in a team.

Second, there is an increasing universalisation of culture, synthesised out of existing cultures. This produces homogeneous cultural experiences. The current global television sports diets are a case in point. Major European soccer games attract the widest audiences. Big games in tennis are dominated by Western countries.

Third, there is an American-dominated Westernisation that accompanies the international spread of modernity, capitalism and rational bureaucracy, industrialism and representative democracy. Sport has rational bureaucratic structures, written rules, leagues, achievement records, scientifically based talent identification and development efforts, a growing specialisation – on and off the field – and greater commercialisation.

Fourth, **deterritorialisation** alters spatial organisation of social relations, perceptions of space, location and distance. A good example of this phenomenon is how live television overtakes the actual live game and how global teams go beyond their own nation states as players are bought and sold in the international market of sports globalisation (Houlihan 2003).

20.16.1 The commodification of formal sport

Commodification is the process in which an increasing number of products and services are bought and sold on the market which were not previously for sale. The case of sport is instructive. Previously engaged in for pleasure and participation at an amateur level, sport, sporting activities, associated products and top players have become subject to this process. This commodification of sport in South Africa has, however, been uneven. The most popular and dominant sports are commodified in relation to market demand, while others lag behind, are marginal or are side-lined. The three main local forms of sport are cricket, soccer and rugby. All three are can be characterised as following the current dominant sports form and are highly commodified in various ways, of which the following are some examples.

First, while sports coaches stress the crucial relationship of the player to the ball, to the field or to other players, the market intrudes. The skills of players come up for sale, are advertised by a club and huge sums of money are transacted. In the case of exceptional sportsmen, these players become a willing commodity in the player market subject only to the last contract signed with their clubs.

Second, this system of commodification is sanctioned by rules and laws. There are, for instance, window periods for when to transfer players. There are rules of inclusion and exclusion regarding national and non-national players. There are rules of entry which relate to the number of games, foreign players, ranking between countries and ways of assessing the qualifications of players before they can apply for permits to play in countries other than their own.

Third, there are different forms of capital organisation of teams, clubs and leagues. There are also various forms of financial and administrative bureaucracies involved in sports. These all further testify to the commodity form of sport. It has been developing over a period of half a century in South Africa, with different forms developing in the different sporting codes. In rugby it is the franchise system that predominates. Rugby teams emerge out of a franchise, which is a financial organisation such as any other franchise. Such franchises make up professional rugby locally and are linked to universities and schools to buy players into contracts. It goes without saying that young players in this or other sports would strive to appear for their respective national teams.

20.16.2   The franchise system

The South African rugby franchise has a popular base. Supporters follow rugby, teams and players. Players consider selection into the system as an achievement. The media further popularises the sport on television. Franchise owners and clubs are run as business ventures and for successful players being part of the franchise system represents a livelihood. Rugby consequently is no longer merely about playing a good game, but is intimately interconnected with capital exchange and the control of markets in the different spheres related to the areas of activity which fall under its increasingly wide scope of commodification. These include media and advertising, sports paraphernalia, franchises, patents, betting agencies and the 'sports star' who achieves records and who is supported by large corporates. Sports men and women become one of a host of modern products in long economic and cultural value chains linking individuals, groups, companies or multinational corporations. This is not, however, the only form sport assumes, despite its being the current dominant one.

Box 20.7 The business of sport

Globalisation, commodification and sporting franchises have the market as a common factor. Explain the relation between sport and society taking your preferred modern formal sport as an example.

20.17   Alternative sports forms and indigenous games

Various forms of alternative sports, sporting cultures, traditions and sports paradigms attract less attention than the dominant sports and sporting forms which this chapter has been discussing. Many operate at local or regional levels, with some popular games and more informal sporting activities played out beneath the radar of media glare. South Africa society provides a number of examples where such games or sports constitute alternative sporting traditions to the dominant sports in the country. A number have emerged to sit alongside, while others remain marginal to them. These games or sports are based on principles different to the dominant forms and are based, not on power and performance, but instead manifest the original character of games and sport engaged in for pleasure and participation. These activities relate to play, games, leisure and recreation. How, we might ask, do we then also define the practice of indigenous games in South Africa? The chapter now turns to looking at play and leisure and has indigenous games as a focus. What will not be covered here, but is important for noting, is the growing area of recreation studies, an emerging and potentially increasingly important field of study which is offered at some universities in South Africa.

20.17.1   Play, leisure and indigenous games.

While modern sport may be highly competitive, some of its roots lie in the sublime notion of play. Krauss (1998) defines play as a 'self-motivated intrinsically purposive human activity, or behavioural style, generally pleasurable with elements of competition, creative exploration, humour and lack of structure, but it can have rules of prescribed actions'.

Play, as engaged in by children, is one of the earliest human experiences. Play cannot be separated from and is closely linked to education (Shiller & Rosseau in Krauss 1998). Play is also linked to active self-determination and social determination and is at the origin, it has been suggested, of the development of self-sacrificial attitudes and practices resulting in broader social welfare (see Krauss 1988). Play, however, has two sides: it can be characterised as fun, pleasure, enjoyment and preoccupation, but can also, as everyone knows, remarkably rapidly transform into a lack of harmony, which it presupposes, and result in discord, conflict and even violent physical behaviour.

Early Western theories of play were oriented to the individual to stimulate self-expression, rejuvenation or the enhancement of skill of the individual and have even been seen as socialising rehearsals via passing on customs and racial attitudes (see Spencer, Lazarus & Hall in Krauss 1998). Play can also be categorised into typologies, of 'agon' (competitive) and equality of participants and artificial forms of winning. Play has further been related to having no control over the outcome ('alea') and the creation of imaginary universes, illusion, simulated drama ('mimicry') and even to the generation of dizziness or vertigo, as in religious dance or trance states in many forms, of ancient origin, of traditional worship.

Such early categorisations of play show much that is neglected, especially in industrial civilisation. The second, typology serves to differentiate the various functions of play. An important tendency throughout history is the communal function of play through ritual, dance or music that serves as a healing rite or celebration of historic events. They serve to reinforce group ties and to transmit traditional beliefs and values across generations. Such accounts reiterate our earlier connections of sport to wider societal functions.

Huizinga (in Krauss 1998) has outlined the deeply ingrained nature of play in our everyday life: play as life pervading, as free of physical impositions, moral duty or physiological needs. Play has, moreover, been seen as set apart from ordinary life, taking place in special or 'safe' locations freed from 'rule demanding absolute order'. Yet at other times play is also marked by uncertainty and tension. It is this view of play which can be seen as standing in contrast to the formal rule-based organisation of modern sport, for example, when the Cameroonian national football club was (twice) involved in a controversy about their kit in international games: wearing a one-piece kit at the 2006 Confederation Nations Cup and sleeveless T-shirts at the Africa Nations (2002) that saw FIFA seeking to punish them. India were also disqualified from the soccer World Cup (1950) when they played barefoot!

The most salient of sport characteristics are contestation and representation of one or another broader aim, such as pleasure or power. In this view, play (and perhaps this also applies to sport in our modern era) has come to be seen as 'civilising' – with even law, it has been argued, emerging from play as a pure contest between competing individuals or groups conducted without concern for morality. On the path of social evolution, it is a short step from play to engaging in trials of strength, verbal contests or contests of chance to determine one's fate or testing one's resistance to torture (like children playing at holding their breath):

[M]yth and ritual ... [originate from] instinctive forces of civilised life: law and order, commerce ... profit, *craft ... art, wisdom ... science ... are rooted in the primeval soil of play* (Huizinga in Krauss 1998).

Huizinga's archetypal view of play sounds less fantastical when we can point to modern contexts of play, such as in politics, war or business, as forms of game or 'play'. There is also the historical pattern: play declines as technology advances. Psychologists relate play to psychological, emotional and intellectual development (Frank, Bruner & Piaget in Krauss 1998). For some, like Freud, play is about allowing mastery, while for Erikson it tests fate, order and causality and is for self-healing.

The activity of play may challenge players on the one hand or facilitate the powerful sense of relief, freedom, the unique 'sense of flow' (as in biking) or the well-known experience of the loss of time, peak level experiences (as in the 'second breath' of long-distance runners) or even altered states of consciousness. Krauss (1998) asserts that play studies are underexplored in the social sciences, with psychological theories overemphasising or limited to stressing individual behaviour only. This limits the communal aspects of play, its societal functions and the range of related phenomena just described. Play, however construed, must surely be seen as closely linked to leisure.

20.17.2   Notions of leisure

As noted in the chapter on work, the *same* activity can be play or work. The weekend golfer and the professional golfer are engaged in the same activity, but one is playing while the other is working. The original purpose of the activity, pleasure and participation, is leisure. The notion of leisure is hence closely related to that of sport. When we leave the arena of power and performance and return to the origin of sport, it is to leisure we return. This is, however, not a passive, but active form of leisure. Leisure may or may not involve competition, but not the competition of formal modern sport in which financial considerations play an inordinately central role.

Leisure is associated with being permitted, allowed or simply having free time. All of these relate to the absence of compulsion. In ancient Greece, leisure was a privilege of the aristocrats. The Greeks tied education and leisure in their meanings, to the notion of scholar or school – the Lyceum – as a place for discussion. The Greeks understood leisure in a more external institutional sense and not merely as an internal and mental sense as we think of it today. Krauss (1998) outlines six definitions of leisure as shown in Table 20.2.

Table 20.2 Definitions of leisure: use, limitation, contrast or similarity

1. The Greeks defined it for its own sake, in order to be rejuvenated and return to work	Defines a good life and culture, and includes art, music, community work and contemplation
2. Leisure, and its use and possession, is used as a symbol by the ruling classes for self-identification and social recognition	Limitation: leisure notions diffuse into other classes and the wealthy get involved publicly, hence leisure is not defined solely by the ruling classes
3. Leisure as 'free or discretionary time'	Problem: how do we separate leisure from work and can leisure have extrinsic purposes?
4. Leisure as amusement, to gain knowledge, skills or volunteer work	Leisure can be passive
5. Leisure as freedom for creativity and self-fulfilment	It contrasts to the more compulsive, highly competitive modern sports games
6. Leisure as spiritual involvement or expression	Work and play are complementary (eg in the Christian ethos) and relate to serenity or harmony (eg in Hinduism, Buddhism, Taoism)

(Source: Krauss 1998)

These diverse meanings of leisure need not confuse us. They simply show how different groups and societies define and use leisure time differently. There are two other aspects of leisure that relate to work, as cited by Krauss (1998): **compensatory theory** posits boring or strenuous work offset by leisure, or 'spill-over leisure' as an extension of work, where alienation of work or enjoyment spills over into life. Such tendencies have vast potential in two directions: being open to manipulation or compulsion, or to be the free expression in one's free time, which is not unproblematic as it assumes a strict separation of work and leisure.

It is well known that South Africa is a highly stratified society with one of the highest income gap levels and social inequality in the world. There are consequently vast differences in the kinds of leisure activity occurring in the various economic strata of society, concomitant with the level of resources, infrastructure, mobility and access (or lack of it) to leisure amenities in each stratum of society. These areas are rich but undeveloped areas of research, which could be followed up with Thorstein Veblen's ([1899] 1994) notions of **conspicuous consumption** of the upper classes or the kinds of township fashion among poor youth. But it is to some of the alternatives to the dominant forms of sport in South Africa that this chapter must turn.

20.18 Indigenous games as an emerging institution in South African sport

South African society can be proud of itself to have responded to the call by the government for an African Renaissance and to have created the Indigenous Games in

2003. The Indigenous Games emerged and developed into an institutional structure both locally and internationally. In 2015 the first World Indigenous Games were held in Brazil. South Africa in the same year celebrated the 10th National Indigenous Games.

These Games clearly provide a radical contrast with modern formal sport epitomised by the Olympic games which do not recognise indigenous sports. At the South African National Indigenous games, participants can enter for a range of nine alternative games and sports. These include indigenous games of *morabaraba*, *dibeke*, *kho kho*, *diteko*, *juksei* or *intonga* among a host of such traditional games. While not widely recognised, South Africans, under the auspices of the state, are preserving such games as part of its heritage.

There is a variety of such games that have been developed to continue at a competitive level as can be seen in Figure 20.10 showing the participation of enthusiastic youth. Such games create continuity between our traditional past and our present modern society. The Games also cater for youth activities and their health and wellbeing in the light of the impact of unemployment, township conditions and poverty. These Games also gave opportunities for some to represent South Africa abroad. Stick fighting is one such game which opens up such possibilities.

Durban youth represented South Africa in Lithuania at the Indigenous Games where there is usually a spectacle of games unique to the culture of different countries. It is held every four years by the Association for International Sport for All World Sport for All Games. South Africa showcased its games of *ingqathu* (rope skipping), *induku* (stick fighting), *amagenda* (stones) and *umlabalaba* (a board game). A recent Games South African delegation was made up of youth from KwaZulu-Natal, Mpumalanga, North West and Limpopo. Such games do not only ensure mental and physical development, but also involve skill acquisition and celebrate the spirit and traditions of locals. The South African Indigenous Games takes place in a different province each year, with KwaZulu-Natal at the top between 2010 and 2012 and again in 2016. The 2012 team captain who comes from Chesterville, Ntethelelo Gumede(20), participated in *ingqathu*, and saw it as a great experience for himself and his teammates to train and shine on the world stage and to learn about other cultures through sport (Mbanjwa 2012).

There are three categorisations of indigenous games: those needing physical skills (*kho-kho*, *do eke* and *kgati*), or physical skill and strategy (stick fighting and jukskei), or only requiring strategy (*Morabaraba*, *Ncuva*, *Moruba* or *Diketo*). Look up these games!

Figure 20.9 Stick fighting

(Source: Stick fighting tournament http://theafricanrenaissancecatalog.wordpress.com/2012/06/05/indigenous-games/)

Case study 20.3 Exercise on games

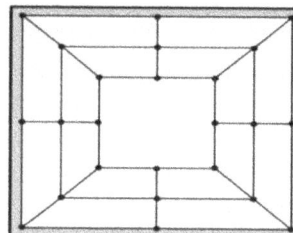

Figure 20.10 Indigenous games

The traditional South African game of *morabaraba*. The design used for morabaraba

Aim: Players must remove opposing players' 12 tokens.

Equipment: Two players. Each has 12 similar colour tokens or stones (*izinkomo*: cows).

Instructions: The game can take minutes or hours. Place tokens, one at a time, alternately, on a point of intersection. The aim is to form a line of tokens, three in a row. Opposing players try to block the other player from getting three in row. When a player gets three tokens in a row, they win that row, and must remove one of the other player's tokens from the board. Players can move their tokens to new intersections and keep trying to win each other's tokens. The game ends when all the opponent's tokens are removed.

(Source: http://theafricanrenaissancecatalog.wordpress.com/2012/06/05/indigenous-games/)

To download the game: http://www.morabaraba.org/computer

For local indigenous games rules see: http://www.srsa.gov.za/MediaLib/Home/DocumentLibrary/Indigenous%20Games%20Rule%20Book%20-%20Aug%202007.pdf

---

QUESTIONS

1. *Morabaraba* is similar to another board game that has cookies. Name that game.
2. What patterns do you notice in the game? What is unique in contrast to modern sport?
3. From what type of society do the above games emerge? Why are tokens seen as cows?

20.19 Conclusion

Sport is a multifaceted phenomenon. Definitionally it ranges from the prowess of the individual sportsperson to either formal or informal organisational and institutional arrangements through to global agencies. Sports superstars and celebrities are born or 'made'. Sport is a major focus in the media. Multinational organisations and corporate become household brand names. The public loves a spectacle.

Yet sport and its sociological analysis also concerns the particular and unique – individuals and social movements who do not always conform to the ideas and practices of powerful institutions, whether governmental or business, local or global. Sport remains connected to politics and power in a variety of ways, South Africa having proved to be a particularly stark instance. Currently, the dominant sports form mirrors the performance and power ethic moulding much of society. Social inequalities continue in sport in the country in our democratic era despite considerable advances made when the past is viewed. When the future is viewed, it seems sufficiently safe to say sport is likely to become an increasingly important aspect of the lives of South Africans but that there is a long way to go before resources and opportunities are equalised for all.

Summary

- Games and sport emerged out of leisure which is differentiated from play and sport with various definitions of modern sport discussed. Play is shown via one theorist to be the creative and origin of sport.
- Modern formal sport involves cooperation and competition, manifests particular cultural and political features and characteristics, and reflects the society in which it takes place.
- Sports can be defined as institutionalised competitive activities that involve physical challenges in which participants are motivated by internal and external rewards.
- The key characteristics of sport are that it comprises organised activity, is characterised by competition and contests, is institutionalised and professionalised and that Sports Science has become formalised in academies.
- The current dominant sports form is based on performance and power while games and informally organised sport goes back to its roots in leisure where pleasure and participation are the key forms games and sport assume.
- Sport can be analysed using functionalist, conflict and interpretivist approaches, all of which manifest limitations but which provide the theoretical and analytical resources to grasp the relation between sport and society and the different roles sport plays in the social construction of reality.
- Sport in South Africa reflects a divided society with sport and politics becoming bound together in the context of significant social inequality in access to opportunities and resources.
- Something of the extent of the scope of the literature on the various kinds of sports is introduced in the chapter.
- The chapter briefly outlined the most popular sport in South Africa, namely soccer.
- The role of sport in resistance to apartheid, the sports boycott of South Africa in the anti-apartheid movement which contributed to democracy in South Africa was presented.
- Social inequality of access and the issue of individual initiative, the lack of transformation in sport and broader issues of the commodification of sport and the corporate business model dominating much of local sport came under the spotlight.
- Games and indigenous sport in South Africa have been formally supported by the state and celebrated annually over the past decade and are noted in the chapter with a challenge to further investigate these traditional games.

More sources to consult

Coakley J, Burnett C. 2009. *Sports in Society: Issues and Controversies – Southern African Edition.* Hatfield, Pretoria: Van Schaik.

Coakley J. 2015. *Sports in Society: Issues and Controversies.* 11th ed. New York: McGraw Hill International.

Craig P. 2016. *Sport Sociology.* 3rd ed. London: SAGE Publications Ltd.

References

Alegi P. 2004. *Laduma! Soccer, Politics and Society in South Africa.* Scottsville: University of KwaZulu-Natal Press.

Alexander P. 2013. 'Recreation and resistance: Black worker culture, Witbank Collieries, 1900–1950. 'Digging for Treasure' Conference, Essen, Germany, 27 November.

Alexander P. 2020. 'Culture and classed identity on shaping unionisation' in *Making Sense of Mining History: Themes and Agendas.* Berger S, Alexander P (eds). London and New York: Routledge.

Atkins K. 1993. *The moon is dead! Give us our money: The Cultural Origins of an African Work Ethic, Natal, South Africa, 1843–1900.* Portsmouth, NH: Heinemann.

Bale J. 1994. *Landscapes of Modern Sports.* Leicester, UK: University Press.

Bale J, Sang J. 1996. *Kenyan Running: Movement Culture, Geography and Global Change.* London: Frank Cass.

Birrell S, Donnelly P. 2004. 'Reclaiming Goffman: Erving Goffman's influence on the sociology of sport' in *Sport and Modern Social Theorists.* Giulianotti R (ed). Houndmills, Basingstoke: Palgrave Macmillan.

Booth D. 2003. 'Hitting Apartheid for a Six, The Politics of South African Sports Boycott,' *Journal of Contemporary History*, July 1, 38: 477–493.

Booth D. 1997. 'The South African Council on Sport and the political antinomies of the sports boycott', *journal of Southern African Studies*, 23(1): 51–55.

Brohm J-M. 1989. *Sport: A Prisoner of Measured Time.* Pluto: London.

Calland R, Naidoo L, Whaley A. 2010. *The Vuvuzela Revolution: Anatomy of South Africa's World Cup.* Auckland Park: Jacana Media.

Coakley J. 2001. *Sport in Society: Issues and Controversies.* USA: McGraw-Hill.

Coakley J, Burnett C. 2014. *Sports in Society: Issues and Controversies – Southern African Edition.* Hatfield, Pretoria: Van Schaik.

Cohen B. 2019. *Blazing the Trail: Celebrating 90 years of Black Golf in Southern Africa.* Barry Cohen Publishing.

Coplan D. 1985. *In Township Tonight! South Africa's Black City Music and Theatre.* New York: Longman.

Couzens B. 1983. 'An introduction to the history of football in South Africa' in *Town and Countryside in the Transvaal.* Bozzoli B (ed). Johannesburg: Ravan Press.

Department of Sport and Recreation South Africa, Republic of South Africa. *The Indigenous Games Rule Book.* Mkhonto TK (ed). https://www.google.com/url?sa=t&rct=j&q=&esrc=s&source=web&cd=11&cad=rja&uact=8&ved=2ahUKEw

Desai A, Apalachee V, Vahed G, Reddy K. 2002. *Blacks in Whites: A Century of Cricket Struggles in KwaZulu-Natal*, South Africa: University of Natal Press.

Desai A (ed). 2010. *The Race to Transform: Sport in Post-apartheid South Africa.* Cape Town: HSRC Press.

Desai A. 2016. *Reverse Sweep: A Story of South African Cricket Since Apartheid.* Auckland Park: Fanele, an imprint of Jacana.

Desai A, Vahed G. 2010. 'Beyond the nation? Colour and class in South African cricket' in *The Race to Transform: Sport in Post-apartheid South Africa.* Desai A (ed). Cape Town: HSRC Press.

Ellison J. 'Caster Semenya and the IOCs Olympics Gender Bender'. http://www.thedailybeast.com/articles/2012/

07/26/caster-semenya-and-the-ioc-s-olympics-gender-bender.html [Accessed 20 October 2019].

Friedman G. 2001. *Madiba's Boys: The Stories of Lucas Radebe and Mark Fish*. Claremont: New Africa Books.

Gemmell J. 2004. *The Politics of South African Cricket*. London and New York: Routledge.

Giulianotti R, Robertson R. 2009. *Globalisation and Football*. London: SAGE Publications Ltd.

Ingham AG. 12004. 'The sportification process: A biographical analysis framed by the work of Marx, Weber, Durkheim and Freud' in. *Sport and Modern Social Theorists*. Giulianotti R (ed). Houndmills, Basingstoke: Palgrave Macmillan.

Habib A, Bentley K. 2008. *Racial redress, national identity and citizenship in South Africa*, HSRC: Cape Town, South Africa.

Houlihan B. 2003. 'Sports and Globalization' in Sport and Society, (Ch 19). Houlihan B, ibid.

Jarvie G (ed.). 1991. *Sport, Racism and Ethnicity*. Falmer Press: UK.

Korr C, Close M. 2008. *More than just a Game: Soccer v Apartheid*. London: Collins.

Krauss. 1998. *Recreation and Leisure in Modern Society*. Educational Publishers: USA.

Latekgomo J. 2010. *Mzanzi Magic: Struggle, Betrayal and Glory – The Story of South African Soccer*. Cape Town: Tafelberg.

Loy J, Booth D. 2004. 'Consciousness, craft, commitment: The sociological imagination of C. Wright Mills' in *Sport and Modern Social Theorists*. Giulianotti R (ed). Houndmills, Basingstoke: Palgrave Macmillan.

Magubane B. 1963. *Sport and politics in an urban African community: A case study of African voluntary organisations*. MSocSci thesis, University of Natal.

Mbanjwa N. 2012. http://theafricanrenaissance catalog. wordpress.com/2012/06/05/indigenous-games/)

McKinley D. 2010. '"Transformation" from above: The upside-down state of contemporary South African soccer' in *The Race to Transform: Sport in Post-apartheid South Africa*. Desai A. (ed). Cape Town: HSRC Press.

Mchunu S, Le Roux K. 2010. 'Non-participation in sport by black learners with special reference to gender, Grades, family income and home environment'. *South African Journal for Research in Sport, Physical Education and Recreation*, 32(1): 85–98.

Merrett C. 2009. *Sport, space and segregation: Politics and society in Pietermaritzburg*. Scottsville: University of KwaZulu-Natal Press.

Mjikeliso S. 2017. *Being a Black Springbok: The Thando Manana Story*. Northlands, Johannesburg: Macmillan.

Nixon R. 1992. 'Apartheid on the run: The South African sports boycott'. *Transition*, 58: 66–88.

Odendaal A. 1977. *Cricket in Isolation: The Politics of Race and Cricket in South Africa*. Cape Town. Odendaal.

Rowe D. 2004 'Antonio Gramsci: Sport, hegemony and the national-popular' in *Sport and Modern Social Theorists*. Giulianotti R (ed). Houndmills, Basingstoke: Palgrave Macmillan.

Snyder EE, Spreitzer E. 1974. 'State of the field: Sociology of sport: An overview'. *The Sociological Quarterly*, 15 (4): 467–487.

Sokot A. 2009. *Sociology of Sport: Conceptual and Topical Issues*. Doi:10.2478/v10141-009-0027-8

Stoddart B. 2004. 'Sport, colonialism and struggle: CLR James and cricket' in *Sport and Modern Social Theorists*. Giulianotti R (ed). Houndmills, Basingstoke: Palgrave Macmillan.

Vahed G, Padayachee V, Desai A. 2010. 'Between black and white: A case study of the KwaZulu-Natal Cricket Union' in *The Race to Transform: Sport in Post-apartheid South Africa*. Desai A (ed). Cape Town: HSRC Press.

Veblen T. [1899]1994. *The Theory of the Leisure Class*. New York: Penguin Books.

Wilson M, Mafeje A. 1963. *Langa: A Study of Social Groups in an African Township*. Cape Town: Oxford University Press.

Part

4

The Challenges
for Society

Social inequality

Christopher Thomas

When members of society do not have equal opportunities or access to resources, the result is social inequality. The uneven allocation and distribution of resources in society occurs along the lines of how society is organised hierarchically into different layers or strata. While many different forms of social stratification exist in different societies and which lead to different forms and degrees of social inequality, the most common and divisive types of social inequality are those based on race, gender and class. Opportunities, such as access to education and jobs, and resources, such as financial capital, land and property ownership, are organised along these lines of hierarchical stratification. Social inequality is consequently a major topic in sociology.

Social inequality is also a global societal challenge as it increases exponentially across many parts of the world. The extent of social inequality, most especially the extent of the economic stratification of society into elites (the rich) and commoners (the poor) has in fact played a central role in the last 5 000 years in the collapse of advanced, sophisticated and complex civilisations such as ours. This is the finding of a major study conducted in 2014 by natural and social scientists, led by the mathematician Safa Motesharrei and partly sponsored by the United States National Aeronautical Space Agency (NASA). It is well known that South Africa has consistently ranked as one of the most unequal societies in the world when measured by the Gini coefficient and that the topic clearly requires serious study. A 2010 study, using a modified Gini coefficient, found, however, that while still very high, the redistribution initiatives of government had achieved considerably more success than was immediately evident (Bosch et al 2010).

This chapter sets out how sociologists have traditionally understood social inequality, and how, what can be termed the hierarchies of power of race, class and gender account, for social inequality in South Africa in the aftermath of the colonial encounter predicated on slavery. Two of the classical accounts of social inequality are then discussed, followed by the way in which functionalist analyses argue that social inequality is inevitable in all societies. The work of a modern thinker, which suggests that schooling and the development of human capital are critical for overcoming social inequality, is then broached before taking a closer look at the extent and changing character of social inequality in South African society. It is with an exercise as to how social inequality has been pointedly addressed through legislation in democratic South Africa, however, that this chapter starts. Just before doing so, however, it is highly recommended that for this chapter and the next, students refer back to Chapter 9 on race, Chapter 10 on class, and most especially Chapter 7 on gender, the content of which is not explicitly discussed here.

Case study 21.1 Addressing the apartheid legacy of social inequality

Post-apartheid transformation is affected by the policy guidelines and legislation introduced by the ruling party, the African National Congress (ANC). The following are extracts from its statement on Black Economic Empowerment (BEE) and the Employment Equity Act of 1998. These persist in shaping the understanding of how to transcend the legacy of black poverty and social inequality rooted in a long history of white domination and privilege under colonialism, segregation and apartheid. Read the policy issues discussed in the following extracts and then answer the questions that follow.

Black Economic Empowerment

With regards to specific instruments to de-racialise the economy, the ANC's 1992 Policy Guidelines stated that:

Management of both the public and private sectors will have to be de-racialised so that they rapidly and progressively come to reflect the skills of the entire population. Equity ownership will have to be extended so that people from all sectors of the population have a stake in the economy and power to influence economic decisions.

In relation to ownership, the Reconstruction and Development Programme (RDP) stated:

The domination of business activities by white business and the exclusion of black people and women from the mainstream of economic activity are causes for great concern for the reconstruction and development process. A central objective of the RDP is to de-racialise business ownership and control completely through focused policies of Black Economic Empowerment.

Employment Equity Act 55 of 1998

… as a result of apartheid and other discriminatory laws and practices, there are disparities in employment, occupation and income within the national labour market, … [t]he purpose of the Act is to achieve equity in the workplace by –

(a) promoting equal opportunity and fair treatment in employment through the elimination of unfair discrimination; and

(b) implementing affirmative action measures to redress the disadvantages in employment experienced by designated groups, in order to ensure their equitable representation in all occupational categories and levels of the workforce (RSA 1998).

QUESTIONS

1. Why is there employment equity legislation in post-apartheid South Africa?
2. Why is there a need for Black Economic Empowerment?

Key themes

- Social stratification
- Social mobility
- Social inequality, race and class
- The conflict, interpretivist, functionalist and human capital approaches to social inequality
- Addressing social inequality in South Africa today.

21.1 Introduction

Social inequality is inextricably linked to the notion of poverty. But social inequality is not the same as poverty. The following example should clarify this important distinction at the outset. Imagine you are an employee of a company where you earn a monthly salary and can afford a small entry-level motor vehicle and a simple three-bedroom house. Your line manager and directors, however, own luxury cars and live in double-storey mansions with swimming pools. This is an indication of social inequality. When you encounter a beggar when stopping at a traffic light in your car, this is a situation of both social inequality and poverty. Possessing a car and enjoying food, shelter and clothing means that you are not poor like the beggar, despite the uneven allocation of resources between you and your managers. You may feel relatively deprived in relation to your managers, but your position in the social stratification hierarchy of social inequality is closer to them than you are to the beggar. While the chapter to follow discusses your sense of **relative deprivation** in contrast to the **absolute poverty** of the beggar, this chapter unravels sociological approaches to the phenomenon of social inequality in society.

Most of us will have come to understand the post-apartheid transition as meaning a transition to a society that simultaneously promises equal opportunities for all and **meritocratic** advancement. Exercising the sociological imagination, however, uncovers a social reality filled with obstacles to these promises in our context of marked degrees of social inequality. A range of theories and perspectives have offered explanations for its origins and reproduction and have formulated various approaches to reducing inequalities of all kinds in society. These attempts have, in addition, examined the possibilities of **social mobility**, in other words, moving out of the ranks of one group and into that of another in different social stratification systems. The study of social inequality is consequently entwined with studies of social stratification.

Sociologists have tackled the phenomenon of social inequality in a number of ways. Haralambos, Holborn and Heald (2004) claim the key issue regarding social inequality is 'the existence of *socially created* inequalities'. For these sociologists, whereas American sociology was dominated by a social stratification orientation, which conveys a geological imagery of the earth's surface made up of a series of layers called strata, it is rather about different forms of *humanly created social inequality* – where social groups are discerned in hierarchical strata or ranks determined by wealth or social esteem – that needs to be the focus. Peter Saunders (1990: 1–2) had previously suggested that

social stratification envelops both how inequalities originate, are maintained and change over time, as well as impact other aspects of social life. Erik Allardt (1968: 14) had some years before, however, usefully distinguished between two different *types* of theories of stratification. Allardt's distinction brings us to the key difference between competing approaches regarding social inequality. This will be a theme of this chapter and with which you will be familiar.

The first approach relates to the integration type of theories of Émile Durkheim and Talcott Parsons. These theorists see social order being maintained because of a sufficient level of consensus about society's values and that social stratification is an outcome of the **functional specialisation** which is necessary in any society. Simply put, society becomes socially stratified due to the *different kinds of work* required for the ordered regulation and organisation of the emergence of increasingly complex societies.

The second approach relates to the conflict type of theories of Karl Marx and the interpretivist perspectives of Max Weber. Despite their differences of which you are aware, both see the social order being maintained through different means of force and constraint. From this perspective social stratification is a consequence of the struggle for power. Two sociology textbook writers, Margaret Andersen and Howard Francis Taylor (2001: 180), get to the heart of social inequality by asking the following two questions:

- What features of society cause different groups to have different opportunities?
- Why is there an unequal allocation of society's resources?

Anderson's and Taylor's point is that to insightfully answer such questions about social inequality one would have to explain the *origins* of social inequality in the *structure of society*. In a society such as post-apartheid South Africa that promises equal opportunities for all, the unequal stations that people occupy in society are not due to the failings of individuals, but are instead due to the very structure of society itself, in this case a society subject to the colonial encounter, slavery, segregation and apartheid, and latterly a global marketised economy.

While our focus has thus far been the *origin* of and relation of social inequality to social stratification, and hence the social *creation* of inequalities, an important further point needs to be made. Many people regard differences between people in terms of status, education and wealth as arising out of *natural* inequalities, such as intelligence quotient (IQ) measures. A careful study of social inequality, however, reveals that many differences, even such differences in intelligence, can be more adequately understood as a *consequence* of social creation processes which impact on people's chances and possibilities or the lack of possibilities of social mobility in different stratification systems (Saunders 1990: 72–73). It is clear that a malnourished child will probably never develop their full physical or mental potential. But neither might a socially disadvantaged child develop their full potential when compared to one born higher up on the scale of social stratification. Even what we might think of as *natural*, differences associated with inequalities can be the result of systems of social stratification and of which there are a number of types.

21.2 Types of social stratification systems

21.2.1 The traditional typology of social stratification

Sociologists have historically identified four main stratification systems as they sought to understand social inequality from the perspective of the development of how social stratification embraced entire societies as a whole: **slavery**, **caste**, **estate** and **class**. Under the classic rubric of *caste*, *race* and *ethnicity* have often been included. While drawn from a Western, primarily European perspective, important aspects of this traditional typology nevertheless apply to African societies, including South Africa.

Slavery

As the chapter on race in this textbook so clearly showed, we cannot understand social inequality without an appreciation of the **colonial encounter** and the *institution of slavery*. Slavery was a stratification system and form of social inequality found in the agriculturally based economies of ancient societies. In the slavery practised since the modern era of European expansion from the 15th century and colonisation of territories on other continents up to the 1860s in America, the statuses of master and slave were largely ascribed by race as a determining factor. Dutch colonists who settled in South Africa after 1652 permitted the practice of slavery after 1658 and imported slaves from Dahomey, Angola, Madagascar, Indonesia and South-East Asia. When the British colonised South Africa and declared the emancipation of slaves in its colonies in 1833, it led to the emancipation of slaves throughout the British Empire and which numbered 36 278 in the Cape colony (Davenport & Saunders 2000: 25–27, 46–49).

Despite the abolition of slavery, however, a series of Ordinances were passed at the Cape. Ordinance No 1 of

1835, for instance, while it 'was supposed to prepare the slaves for freedom', 'changed little more than their name' (Simons & Simons 1969: 18). In fact, of this Ordinance, it has been claimed, that it was 'harsher by far' than a proclamation which regulated the conditions of slaves in 1818 before slavery was abolished (Simons & Simons 1969: 19). Worse, Simons and Simons suggest, was that 'the Masters and Servants Act of 1856, 'designed to enforce discipline on ex-slaves, peasants, pastoralists and a rural proletariat' was 'a law far more ruthless than its predecessors in the range of offences and the severity of the penalties prescribed for servants'. This Act was, moreover, 'a grim reminder of the country's slave-owning past and a sharp instrument for racial discrimination' (Simons & Simons 1969: 23). It is a salutary fact that this Act was only repealed in 1974, in the lifetime, in other words, of many of the parents and certainly the grandparents of those reading this textbook. In short, the extent of social inequality in contemporary South Africa cannot be adequately understood without an appreciation of the social stratification system of slavery.

The caste system

The caste system is most famously associated with more than 2 000 years of enforcement of the Hindu religion's belief in a hierarchy of ascribed social statuses in India. It entails the specialisation of different tasks in a social **division of labour** tied to each status and greater wealth marking higher status groups, and a range of practices to ensure segregation and avoidance of bodily contact between different castes. Generally, social mobility in a caste system is understood to be near impossible: one is born into a particular status in a hierarchy and remains there for life. However, Srinivas (1952: 271) contends mobility in castes in the middle of the hierarchy is possible by adopting certain practices associated with a higher caste. In South Africa caste distinctions were practised, although in a reconstructed form, among indentured Indian labourers and immigrants who settled in the country after 1860 (Chetty 2012; Ebr-Vally 2001). Features of the caste system are evident in the way in which, again, race especially, as well as ethnicity, have served to divide people into different social hierarchies and levels of social stratification which stamps its imprint on the form and character of social inequality.

Feudalism and the estate system

Much like the ancient systems of slavery and caste which continue to shape the present, the estate system was practised for about 1 000 years in the agricultural economy of Europe's feudal society before the emergence of industrial capitalism. Religion was used to legitimise different statuses and obligations between monarchs, landowning aristocrats and priests on the one hand and serfs on the other who produced crops on portions of lands the aristocrats supplied in exchange for military protection. Some mobility was possible, for instance, through marriage between persons of different estates. Undoubtedly, in the latter stratification systems women filled the most subordinate status, however, this chapter deliberately underemphasises an issue which is treated in the chapter on the sociology of gender.

What is of significance, however, is that it has been argued by some historians and social theorists that feudalism is not an exclusively Western social system of stratification (Spicer 2011). Even a critic of this view, Sharon Spicer, tells us Jack Goody (1969) concedes that 'there are similarities' between European and African societies when viewed through the conceptual lens of the feudal system of social stratification. Spicer goes on to note that Ethiopia only abolished **serfdom** in 1942, Eswatini (formerly Swaziland) continues to have a ruling monarch and that in South Africa 'certain socioeconomic conditions close to feudalism do exist', evidenced by the fact that agricultural **peasants** 'living in impoverished rural areas and using **subsistence farming** methods to survive, quite often do not own the land they live and work on' (2001: 55).

Class

While class is the dominant social inequality and stratification system in industrial capitalist societies, it is, as are the three forms of social stratification just discussed, deeply entwined and entangled with race. Unlike the systems of slavery, estate under feudalism and caste, class in contemporary society is, however, a comparatively fluid system which allows and even encourages in some instances social mobility *within* the social stratification system. Preliminarily, we can assert that the principal approaches to understanding social inequality in industrialised societies are the perspectives of Karl Marx and Max Weber. Influenced by Weber, even the structural functionalism of Talcott Parsons who, unlike Marx and Weber, thinks that social inequality is inevitable and is indeed *functional* for society, does not entirely ignore social class as we will see, which may come as a surprise for some readers. Each of these theorists spawned further scholarship which is intellectually indebted to their insights.

More recent theories, such as that of Pierre Bourdieu, for instance, are arguably indebted to both Marx and Weber. These mainstream approaches inform research about social inequality in South Africa.

Section 21.3 of the chapter summarises the gist of the four approaches, and expands upon the influence they have

had on later scholars. The chapter ends by asking what has happened regarding social inequality in South African since 1994. It presents three simple but clear graphs which speak for themselves as to the extent of social inequality and the racialised and gendered character of social inequality in South Africa today.

21.2.2 Overview of social inequality under apartheid

South Africa's political transition in 1994 heralded the arrival of an era where all citizens could formally enjoy participation in democratic processes. Democracy invigorated hope for a transition away from the social inequality generated by centuries of colonial dispossession and more recently, by four decades of apartheid rule. Haralambos, Holborn and Heald's (2004: 1) introduction to the theme of social inequality commences with a provocative claim: 'People have long dreamed of an egalitarian society, a society in which all members are equal.' They continue with the sober assertion that 'the egalitarian society remains a dream' and stress that forms of inequality pervade all societies. The central indicators of this are, first, inequalities in power or the capacity of individuals or groups to dominate others. The second is inequalities in prestige – that is, the social esteem people are recognised to have. The third is inequalities in wealth, that is, ownership of material possessions such as land, buildings, money, or machinery.

Our Constitution adopted after the political transition is sugar-coated with explicit and implicit egalitarian promises. Such promises include, for instance, equal protection before the law, equal enjoyment of citizenship rights, equal rights to dignity for all, and equal protection of citizens' rights to property. Our optimism about the political transition must be guarded – critical sociological insights illuminate limitations to the extent to which equality in general and social inequality in particular can be achieved in our society.

We need to understand a bit more of the context of where the optimism in our much-proclaimed Constitution comes from, that is, what was said about inequality and stratification before 1994. Three prominent sociological insights captured how divergent views were about inequality and stratification issues. Sam Mhlongo (1981) contended that apartheid policies were generally pernicious to all black people and consequently there was little class differentiation among the black population in the 1970s. Sam Nolutshungu (1982) gave considerable attention to the education system and its unlikely potential to create a co-opted black middle class. Harold Wolpe (1988) raised concerns about how poorly both academics and anti-apartheid political activists understood the changing dynamics of the interrelationship between race and class in South Africa.

The discovery of diamonds in Kimberley (1868) and gold on the Rand (1886) set South Africa on an industrial 'take off' that radically transformed the class structure of a largely agricultural economy to one with significant mining, commercial farming, and urban industrial manufacturing industries. Along with these economic developments came the attendant class structure of an industrial capitalist economy influenced by a history of European colonial settlement and domination. The growth of an economy dependent on black African labour came up against white settlers imbued with ideas of racial supremacy and influenced the policies of white governments. This is equally true of racial segregation in 1910 with the formation of the Union of South Africa and the virtually complete separation of races under apartheid from 1948 for which Afrikaner organisations, such as even the Dutch Reformed Church, called for and justified theologically. Apartheid policies upheld a racial order of white domination and black subordination and which intersected with class relations of a capitalist order dependent on cheap black labour.

Sam Mhlongo (1981) used official data sources compiled during the 1960s and 1970s to construct an analysis and description of a list of classes or a class structure and how these intersected with race in rural and urban areas:

- Rural landowners (not mentioned is how the Natives Land Act of 1913 and amendments secured ownership of 87 per cent of the land surface for white people)
- Farmworkers made up of 'African rural farm-workers'
- Foreign farm-owning companies that paid average weekly rates ranging between R3.17 and R8.69 to their African workers
- 'White rural workers' employed as technicians, mechanics, engineers, managers and overseers and who were paid higher than rural black workers
- The ratio of white to African wages in the mining industry was 20.6:1
- 'Indian and coloured rural workers'
- A 'rural black petty bourgeoisie' involved in trades like general dealers, butchers, bakers, cafés and restaurants, millers, grocers and fruiterers
- 'Like its counterpart in the urban areas, the rural black petty bourgeoisie aspires to the station of the bourgeoisie, which in South Africa is exclusively white'
- A 'white urban working class' that enjoyed a favoured and protected position in society and bourgeois democratic rights, like voting rights, recognition of their trade unions, and a job colour bar system enforced

through job reservation legislation. For instance, the Industrial Conciliation Act passed in 1924 and its amendments reserved high-wage, skilled jobs for white workers. When the job colour bar was relaxed and permitted black workers into jobs reserved for whites, they were not paid equally, sometimes as little as one sixth of white workers' wages

- Social classes in the urban areas – a bourgeoisie with two main factions, the rural land-owning class and the industrial bourgeoisie, who were divided on how much protectionism to extend to white workers.

Regarding the category 'bourgeoisie and petty bourgeoisie', Mhlongo (1981: 144) concluded: 'South Africa has no black bourgeoisie, only a petty bourgeoisie. Even the propertied classes among the Asian community in Durban could not be called as such because various legislative measures prevent them from full participation in the process of accumulation and expansion. Among the Africans, and the Coloureds also, a search for a bourgeoisie yields no positive results.' The urban African petty bourgeoisie were comprised of doctors, lawyers, teachers and nurses. None of the latter earned the same wages as whites. The urban industrial proletariat were mainly Africans. Mhlongo notes coloured and Indian workers organised in recognised unions. Furthermore, wage gaps worsened the race divisions created among the working class in all economic sectors.

Coloured and African businesses operated under very similar conditions. By way of contrast, an Indian trading class enjoyed some measure of success and in relation to the total Indian population were fairly numerous. Most Indians were descendants of indentured labourers and slaves brought to work in sugar plantations in 1860. Many of these descendants became an Indian proletariat in rural and urban areas. Nonetheless, the Indian trading class produced an educated professional group of doctors, lawyers, teachers and intellectuals. The imposition of the Group Areas Act ruined many Indian traders and restricted their ability to move higher into the ranks of a bourgeoisie although they owned factories and other enterprises that were restricted to employing mainly Indian labour (Mhlongo 1981: 145–146).

In Nolutshungu's (1982: 116) analysis of the circumstances of an African middle class he argued: 'Blacks who own or control means of production are few and are not represented in any of the major industries of the country. This is particularly true of Africans, who should, presumably, constitute the largest and most crucial component of a black middle class. It is more to salary earners than to entrepreneurs that the term "black middle class" is commonly applied, although it also includes small traders and businessmen.' Curtailed access to education opportunities stunted the growth of a black middle class. Nolutshungu drew on data about (the limited) educational provision for black people, particularly regarding university education or enrolments, and their attainment in the fields most relevant to bourgeois roles. This accounted for their poor representation in the middle class and why they would be slow to improve their situation.

As the industrial take-off unfolded, the position of the white working class was complicated by their racial proclivities and comparatively closer relation to state power and influence on policymaking compared to their black counterparts (Davies 1973). Skilled white labourers from England streamed in to the goldmines following gold discoveries in 1886. Following the South African War of 1899–1902 many Afrikaners were pushed out of rural livelihoods and sought employment in the mines while many were left unemployed. Enjoying the right to vote, they engaged in struggles to protect themselves from cheaper black African labour taking jobs they coveted for themselves. Over a number of decades this was done through a 'civilised' labour policy which protected white workers.

21.3 Mainstream perspectives on class inequality in industrialised societies

This presentation of the perspectives is organised chronologically in terms of the lifetime of the central or founding theorists, namely, Marx (1818–1883), Weber (1864–1920), Parsons (1902–1979) and Bourdieu (1930–2002). However, despite ebbs in the popularity of the perspectives they spawned in the academic arena, sometimes the research of their acolytes enjoyed simultaneous equally vibrant research, scholarly defence and esteem in the latter half of the 20th century.

21.3.1 The Marxist perspective

The classical contributions of Karl Marx and his lifelong friend Friedrich Engels reveal social inequality as a socially created phenomenon. The central concept used to signify inequality is class. They regard early human societies, or primitive communism, as ideally egalitarian since there is almost no institution of private property, nor the production of an economic surplus over and above that which is needed for the next season. Hunter and gatherer types of society have no classes. Class societies only emerged when humans developed technology or tools and organised the production of society's needs, that is, a more complex

social division of labour emerged in the material base (or 'economic base'), to produce a surplus above that needed for the subsistence of society. This began when humans became settled in agricultural societies that accepted the institution of private ownership, that is, private ownership of the land they cultivated, the tools used and the crop they harvested. Acceptance of the institution of private property allowed class societies to become more complex as humans made more advanced tools or machinery. Classes exist in a relationship where one dominant group exploits the labour of a subordinate class. It is a conflictual and antagonistic relationship. The subordinate class struggles to reclaim the fruits of its labour, but dominant classes are able to oppress subordinate classes since the main ideas about private property and institutions such as the state, which controls the police and army, enforce both laws protecting private property and regulations about contracts and relations between producers and owners. These are just some of the elements constituting society's 'superstructure' of ideas, laws and institutions protecting the interests of the dominant class.

In the earlier epochs of history, we find almost everywhere a complicated arrangement of society into various orders, a manifold gradation of social rank. In ancient Rome we have patricians, knights, plebeians, slaves; in the Middle Ages, feudal lords, vassals, guild masters, journeymen, apprentices, serfs; in almost all of these classes, again, there are subordinate gradations.

The modern bourgeois society that has sprouted from the ruins of feudal society has not done away with class antagonisms. It has but established new classes, new conditions of oppression, and *new* forms of struggle in place of the old ones.

Our epoch, the epoch of the bourgeoisie, possesses, however, this distinct feature: it has simplified class antagonisms. Society as a whole is more and more splitting up into two great hostile camps, into two great classes directly facing each other – bourgeoisie (the super-wealthy) and proletariat (precarious workers).

The foregoing outline prepares us for the Marxist perspective on class inequality in industrial capitalist society. Europe's feudal societies gave way to capitalist societies where the urban **bourgeoisie** made up the dominant class and the **proletariat** formed a subject class. The bourgeoisie emerged from small businesspeople, traders and factory owners in towns and cities. For Scase (1992: 5–6), the essence of a Marxist approach to class has little concern with discerning hierarchies or ranking occupations in industrial capitalist society into class categories or strata of occupations into status and income hierarchies. This type of emphasis on stratification was a popular trend in American sociology and is discussed in the structural functionalist theories of Talcott Parsons, Kingsley Davis and Wilbert Moore. Rather, it is understanding that classes are to be located in an analysis of economic production and the processes where commodities are produced, consumed and expropriated. It is about studying inherently exploitative and antagonistic relations in a social production process involving classes who produce an economic surplus and non-producing classes who own the tools, machinery, factories, mines, farms or means of production and control the labour process that puts these various forces to work.

Marx shows how wealth became concentrated in the hands of the landlords, merchants and urban capitalists who were dependent on the labour of the working class or proletariat. That proletariat emerged in the early stages of capitalism after peasants were pushed off feudal farms where they worked to maintain themselves and their families, and, not owning any means of production, were forced to survive by entering into wage labour relations with capitalists. The labour process performed in this capitalist context entails use of the workers' labour power in exchange for a wage (Fischer 1970: 94–124). Longer hours spent in factories, the constant drive to incorporate advanced machinery, and innovations in the **labour process** facilitate a process where capitalists increase workers' productivity and make profits above their investment in an enterprise once goods produced in their enterprises are sold on markets. This is the extraction of **surplus value**. The total value of wages at any time (as well as any other production costs) is below the economic surplus produced. That surplus can be reinvested in the enterprise and its improvement in order to cope with competition from other capitalists or be used to maintain a high quality of lifestyle for the capitalist. Even if wages are regarded as high, the working class is always regarded as living in relative misery since they are producing profits for the capitalist.

Marx predicted that as modern industry grows, so too would the size of the proletarian masses increase. The **peasantry** faces incorporation into the ranks of the waged labour class, but many continue to maintain some degree of control over land and hence avoid wage labour relations. Between the capitalists and the proletariat, a conservative 'middle class' or the **petty bourgeoisie** exists – small traders, shopkeepers and professionals. The members of this sub-class of the bourgeoisie always fear that they may lose their businesses, their economic resources and independent lives, and be incorporated into

the ranks of the proletariat. At the lowest rungs of capitalist society is the **lumpen-proletariat**, Marx's sub-class of the proletariat.

Many theorists have developed Marx's analysis of 19th century capitalism. It has been extended to analyse class inequality since the advent of **monopoly capitalism** by the end of the 19th century, the growing economic power of **transnational corporations** after World War II and the intensification of capitalism's linking of different parts of the globe by the dawn of the 20th century. To take two examples, the ideas of Greek Marxist theorist and sociology teacher Nicos Poulantzas and American sociologist Erik Olin Wright will be noted here.

Poulantzas (1982) asserts the classical Marxist position in that classes, he argues, are part of a wider *ensemble* or structure of social relations and only exist in class struggle. That is, classes are defined principally in economic terms, which locate their place in the production process or in the division of labour. Importantly though, Poulantzas elaborates the *political* and *ideological* criteria that are central to the determination of social classes. In this *ensemble of social relations*, it is possible to determine the 'place' of a particular class. But Poulantzas goes further than Marx by offering a theory and method of class analysis which accounts for there being no clear-cut confrontation between the bourgeoisie and proletariat. Instead, he argues, at specific historical moments, called 'conjunctures', there are complex class alliances of several fractions (parts) of classes and their chosen tactics called 'class positions'. To give an example, Thabo Mbeki referred to the ANC as a 'broad church' – or a cross-class alliance as politically expressed in the ANC–SACP–COSATU Alliance, but which would break up into its separate class constituencies as might be seen in the continued strains within this political cross-class Alliance.

Most Marxist explanations of class are about economic issues, such as identifying relations of economic ownership, that is, control of the means of production and exercising economic power that goes with ownership and the possession of such power, which is the capacity to get the means of production to work. Poulantzas goes further and seeks to explain that in the capitalist production process, which is about getting workers to make commodities and to exploit their production of a surplus, workers producing this surplus earn wages *below the value* of what they have collectively produced. However, not all wage earners are workers who produce surplus value due to the fact that they are involved in the wider process of the circulation of commodities and the realisation of surplus value. The incorporation of science and new technology has made the labour process more complex since it introduced the role of skilled engineers and technicians. Marxists have grappled with how to conceptualise the place of these higher paid strata of workers, such as supervisors and foremen, in the collective process of the production of *surplus value*. Poulantzas regards as *productive labour* those workers who have been exploited in the course of their producing surplus labour. Marxists shift between terms such as 'strata', 'fractions' and 'labour aristocracy' to refer to the phenomenon of higher paid workers. Poulantzas accepts the validity of these categories, but asserts that they still belong to one class, namely, the working class. His notion of 'fractions' of classes is also widely used to assert that the capitalist class has sectors with diverging interests at particular conjunctures. An example of 'fractions' within the capitalist class would be the competition between the agricultural and mining sectors for cheap black labour in South Africa.

Poulantzas expands on how the capitalist mode of production and its particular set of social relations should be understood as *coexisting* with other modes of production such as the indigenous African agricultural mode of production. The unique and particular set of social relations to which such coexisting modes of production give rise, together make up a concrete society or 'social formation'. So, no social formation has only two clearly distinct classes as might be assumed from Marx's use of the term class. Nevertheless, the social classes of the dominant mode of production are the major classes of that social formation. Poulantzas described an advanced capitalist society in the early 1970s.

Thus, in contemporary France, for example, the two fundamental classes are the bourgeoisie and the proletariat. But we also find there the traditional petty bourgeoisie (craftsmen, small traders), dependent on the form of simple commodity production, the 'new' petty bourgeoisie composed of non-productive wage earners, dependent on the monopoly form of capitalism and several social classes in the countryside, where vestiges of feudalism are still to be found in an untransformed state (eg forms of share-cropping) (Poulantzas 1982: 106).

This fact of a multiplicity of classes with their own interests is important in theorising about alliances between the working class and other classes. There often is the complex reality of such classes appearing as a popular mass of people with a common interest at particular conjunctures. While not discussed by Poulantzas, this account of social classes helps explain the cross-class alliance of predominantly black peoples' struggles mobilised around the Freedom Charter to abolish apartheid.

Poulantzas pays particular attention to an analysis of the petty bourgeoisie. This focus demonstrates that an understanding of social classes must take into account, not just the economic location of social classes, but must also look at the role of political and ideological criteria in the reproduction of social classes. Poulantzas saw the shrinking of the 'traditional petty bourgeoisie' – small-scale producers, small traders, artisans and family businesses (who do not extract surplus value from productive workers). However, the size of a 'new petty bourgeoisie' *grew* under monopoly capitalism. This class of wage earners does not produce surplus value and are merely exploited by the process of selling their labour power: he has in mind here the skilled engineers and artisans mentioned above (as well as people in government or the civil service – including teachers, lecturers, doctors and other professionals). Although the latter categories are different from the place of the traditional petty bourgeoisie in the production process, they have common unifying characteristics, or a similar political and ideological orientation, which serve to reproduce social classes of capitalist society. They fear working class revolution, live by a work ethic that social advancement is possible in capitalist society, aspire to a bourgeois social status, and believe that the state is neutral and not an instrument of a dominant class. To apply these ideas to our society, the *white petty bourgeoisie* can be described as having held such attitudes and views under apartheid and currently, as can also the emerging *black petty bourgeoisie* since democracy.

Eric Olin Wright (1982) feels that there is an alternative way to that of Poulantzas about understanding the ambiguous position of certain wage earners in the social division of labour. Wright famously used and prefers to call these **contradictory class locations**. Wright accepts that all class relations are antagonistic and contradictory. Some class positions in the class structure are, however, *doubly* contradictory. To make sense of this we need to understand that class relations have transformed in the advanced capitalist societies and produced three clusters of positions in the **social division of labour** with contradictory class relations. First, there are managers and supervisors occupying a *contradictory* relation between the bourgeoisie and proletariat. Second, some categories of semi-autonomous employees, who have considerable control over their labour process, are in a *contradictory* location between the bourgeoisie and proletariat. Third, there are small employers who occupy a *contradictory* location between the bourgeoisie and petty bourgeoisie.

These *contradictory class locations* originate from three structural changes that accompanied the development of capitalism. The *first* stems from the Taylorist deskilling process which took away artisans' and skilled workers' control of the labour process once capitalists redesigned the labour process, breaking it up into smaller tasks, and set workers to a pace determined by machines which increased their productivity. The *second* stems from the growing significance of management's role in the social division of labour, and the separation of ownership and control in determining class relations. The 19th century capitalist was characterised by legal and economic ownership of the enterprise, but these have become differentiated with the growth in the scale of enterprises, as well as the concentration and centralisation of capital. It became difficult for individual entrepreneurs to be involved in both ownership and the day-to-day management of production activities. This pressurised capitalists to recruit professional managers to cope with competition and to have managers of different sectors of an enterprise. Separation of formal legal ownership and real economic ownership enabled the growth of stock ownership of large enterprises. Class relations, however, have not changed because the institution of private property persists. The *third* stems from the development of complex hierarchies within corporations: the relations of possession in corporations have grown more complex as both the control of the means of production and the control of labour became more complex with the creation of further layers of supervisors. Then, there are also the complex relations of differentiating economic ownership: boards of directors, executives and managers have different functions and powers in what investments are made and what is produced.

An abstract model of capitalist society would depict two fundamentally antagonistic classes, workers and capitalists. However, complex hierarchies have arisen and people are found in contradictory locations between and within the fundamental class antagonisms. Compared to a 19th century factory situation, with foremen and supervisors being close to the working class, the situation has changed. While foremen and supervisors may have little real control over the physical means of production, they have acquired some control over **labour power** – usually because they convey orders from further up a hierarchy. Another instance of contradictory class locations is that of top or senior managers. They have limited economic ownership in enterprises compared to the bourgeoisie, yet both categories

conduct themselves in a similar way in the relations of production. Technical changes in the labour process allow middle level managers to have some measure of control over the labour process and over subordinates. One crucial issue about those located within this contradictory class position is with which side they would align in class struggle? To pose this question in our context, with whom would (or do) black and white managers align themselves when black workers in South Africa go on strike? Ultimately, any answer derived from whatever theoretical perspective would need to be informed by **empirical** research.

21.3.2 The Weberian perspective

Weber's view on social stratification is derived from his interest in how **power** is exercised and how domination is organised in human societies. Recall that Weber's understanding of social stratification is inextricably linked to his **methodological individualism** brand of sociology, that is, establishing the *meaning* behind the social action of individuals placed within larger social categories. Weber distinguishes between a legal order, an economic order, a social order and a status order, and shows their interrelationship in producing and sustaining social stratification. Recall also that Weber (1978: 926) defines power as the ability of individuals or a group to realise their will over others regardless of the latter's resistance. The exercise of power is not used only for economic enrichment. Sometimes its exercise may be used to realise social honour. A businessperson's wealth or economic power does not guarantee that he or she enjoys **social honour**. Sometimes the legal order enhances people's ability to hold power or social honour, but it cannot always be guaranteed to do so. The way in which social honour is distributed in a community Weber calls the 'social order'. The social order is influenced by the economic order or the mode of distribution and consumption of goods and services. But the social order can also have its own ways of reacting on the economic order. Classes, status groups and (political) parties are phenomena characterised by the fact that the distribution of power occurs within a community. Weber's concept of class is about a determination of collectives in the *economic* order. Status groups relate to the distribution of social honour in the social order. Weber's notion of party is about power in the legal order. Let us here briefly elaborate Weber's concepts of class, status and party introduced in the opening chapter of this textbook.

Weber on class

Weber's concept of class concerns people's position in the market situation or in economic relations. Sometimes people engage in social action and recognise themselves as of the same class when they do so. They recognise their common situation based on similarities in what goods they possess and their opportunities for an income. The basic distinction between people into classes in the market and with different life chances to set up businesses and accumulate further wealth or to survive by selling their labour, is their possession of property or the lack of property. Further distinctions can be made even amongst those who own property, that is, ownership of different types of property makes it possible to discern different classes – building owners, bankers, mine-owners, and so on. Differentiations can be made too among those who lack property but offer services. Having specified the possibility of several classes, Weber turns his attention to the **social action** that springs from these classes that are expected to act in their own interests.

Weber on status

Weber's concept of **status** groups refers to situations where people have either positive or negative estimations of the honour of others. Sometimes recognition of this status is because of the property or class situation of people, but property and class are not always the basis of status. Sometimes people with and without property are recognised as part of the same status group. People of a similar status group are recognised as having a similar style of life, or expected to have a similar lifestyle. The growth of a dramatic gulf between poor and rich black people in South Africa is manifested in some of the measurement approaches we referred to earlier as well as in different lifestyles. Look at how golf gained the reputation for being a lifestyle of white businessmen and provided occasions to network about business opportunities, and how that legacy pressured many black businessmen to adopt the lifestyle so they too may network with the right crowd. Golf is a costly pastime – equipment such as golf clubs and membership fees of a club as well as one day's fees for playing on the course are very expensive. Two black multimillionaire businessmen, Peter Vundla, a Johannesburg advertising company executive, and Jabu Mabuza, a Durban casino executive, state golf as their pastime (African Millionaire 2010). An advertisement by a golf estate north-west of Pretoria/Tshwane for the rich to buy exclusive residences on a gated golf course estate acknowledges that the apartheid history of privileged white access to sport facilities and denial of such to black communities is being followed by a new trend:

… it is not only the 'whites' who enjoy the game of golf and so already we are seeing a trend of 'black' businessmen taking to the links [golf courses] as part of the long-standing culture of modern business, where relationships are formed away from the boardroom (The Bay Golf Estate).

Sometimes a social group or closed circle of friends and acquaintances is a form of **social closure** in terms of marrying within the status group. Sometimes the stratification of status groups is based on people's place of residence. Now that apartheid laws prohibiting mixed race residential areas have been repealed, do black people living in historically white suburbs or newly created integrated suburbs assume a higher status than black people still resident in the old segregated apartheid-era townships? People sometimes may distinguish themselves as belonging to particular status groups by the clothing fashions they adopt, or by the family lineage they claim, and these later get recognition as status groups.

Weber asserts that status groups evolve into the characteristics of closed castes. In a caste stratification system, a person remains in the same social position for their whole life. An extreme situation sometimes develops where the consequences of the closure of status groups amounts to closure on an ethnic basis, and they may also be further distinguished as an ethnic community that performs a particular type of handicraft or art. Recognition of people as belonging to specific status groups allows them to claim certain privileges. For instance, what clothing items may be worn, foods consumed or trades performed can be restricted to members of specific status groups. Technological advances and economic transformations are two forces that can undermine status groups and make class situation a more prominent issue.

Weber on party

Weber sees a complex reciprocity where classes and status groups influence one another as well as the legal order, and these are also influenced by the legal order. Parties are the various forms of association that people adopt in order to acquire social power or influence the political order. Some of these associations are outside of the state and some are within the state. Such associations or political parties have clear goals and plans about how to achieve their various aims in different contexts. Parties are only possible when they are associations with a staff or membership who work for their ideals. They achieve their goals through violence, lobbying, bribery, persuasive speeches, creating rumours, or obstructing parliamentary committees. Perhaps an insightful illustration of how such well-organised influence on the state has successfully occurred in South Africa has been in the rise of a rich black elite who formed business associations and sometimes were facilitated by a background as 'former freedom fighters, communists and trade union leaders who have close links to the new political elite, having stood alongside them in the struggle against apartheid' (Simpkins 2004). The ANC government's formal promotion of a Black Economic Empowerment (BEE) policy and legislation has made multimillionaires of former trade unionist President Cyril Ramaphosa, former underground military activist Tokyo Sexwale, former political prisoner Mzi Khumalo (who moved into a gated golf estate), among many others.

British sociologist Frank Parkin – a pointed critic of the limitations of Marx's notion of class – made a notable attempt to take Weber's approach to class formation further by elaborating his concept of *social closure* as 'the process by which social collectivities seek to maximise rewards by restricting access to resources and opportunities to a limited circle of eligibles' (Giddens & Held 1982: 175). Parkin (1982), a contemporary of Poulantzas and Wright, was highly critical of the abstract formalism of their approach to class and explicitly opts for using Weber's notion of 'social closure' instead of their Marxist inspired, conflict-based formulations. For Weber, social closure is a means of explaining class formation and how social inequality is generated through excluding 'outsiders' and monopolising resources to which others have been denied access. Generally, these outsiders are discernible by attributes such as race, language, social origin, or religion. The two main mechanisms of achieving this are control over property and control over academic or professional qualifications and credentials. Both mechanisms involve legal arrangements which restrict access to rewards and privileges. Restrictions on property ownership constrain access to the means of production, while *credentialism* constrains entry into higher level positions in the division of labour. The effect of this exclusion is that one group secures for itself a privileged position while it simultaneously subordinates and creates a group, class or stratum that is legally defined as inferior.

This view of social closure occurs in two ways. *First*, social closure is effected mostly by *strategies of exclusion*, such as in the caste system mentioned earlier and through the stratification of racial and ethnic communities. What is also observed is that those who have been thus excluded also exclude others within their own ranks and thereby *increase* the number of social strata. *Second*, exclusion also results from *strategies of usurpation*. At one end of this continuum the usurpation causes *marginal redistribution* and at the other end there is *total expropriation*. In the first instance, the golf club president might claim the private dining room for himself and his closed group of friends only. More seriously, the social closure around race *usurped* all social and political rights, thereby *completely excluding* black people from participation in social life under apartheid – and which continues in subtle guises *despite* democracy.

The notion of social closure consequently offers a creative way of understanding the evolution of a **racial order** and social inequality in South Africa following its industrial take-off. On the one hand it offers insights into how a dominant class secured ownership of land and capital through the Natives Land Act No 27 of 1913. On the other hand, the social closure approach may be used to focus on the role of white workers' trade unions in securing a monopoly of positions and protection of privileges in the division of labour. The industrial take-off *attracted* English-speaking skilled-work immigrants and *expelled* independent small Afrikaans-speaking white agriculturalists from farms, thereby subjecting them to **proletarianisation**. Poor Afrikaners converged on mines and urban factories where they found themselves in competition with black workers whom employers chose because they were paid significantly lower wages. A climactic moment of this conflict is the 1922 white workers' rebellion and their utterly contradictory racialised class rallying cry under the slogan: 'Workers of the world unite, and fight for a white South Africa!' (Davenport & Saunders 2000: 292–297). Stanley Greenberg (1980: 223–327) and Eddie Webster (1985) provide rich empirical data and insightful analyses about how the activities of white artisan unions across the segregation and apartheid eras sought to *prohibit* lower-paid African workers access to the types of skilled jobs they controlled. The industrial relations framework further *denied* official recognition to trade unions of black workers and even *failed* to define African workers as employees or grant African trade unions bargaining rights white workers had fought for on a racialised basis.

21.3.3 The structural functionalist perspective

In the structural functionalist perspective 'social stratification is a social necessity' (Tischler 1996: 234). The perspective is indebted to Talcott Parsons' (1977) views regarding the **functional prerequisites** that must be satisfied in any **social system**. Parsons's ideas about the evolution of human society from simple to complex forms, is similar to evolutionary development in biological organisms. He discerns six **evolutionary universals** or 'structural complexes' that need to undergo adaptations in order for the social system to survive. However, only the first two are pertinent to the present discussion. Firstly, the *development of social stratification* permits the differentiation of societal functions and facilitates the change from primitive societies to modern societies. This stratification is about human society being characterised by people being found in different locations in a hierarchy of *lower*, *in-between* and *higher* social statuses (or 'upper', 'ruling' classes and the 'masses'). Stratification systems are *functional* and *necessary* for society to develop as they allow *advantages* to be gained when society's members *specialise* in performing different tasks or assume different roles in society's political, religious, education, defence, healthcare and production activities. Primitive societies are not stratified and in the evolutionary transition to modern society, stratification systems can evolve from simple two-class to complex four-class systems.

The second evolutionary universal, an independent *cultural legitimation* system, is closely tied to the stratification system and the move away from primitive society. Stratification and differentiation are important forces of social change, as well as sources of *social tensions* and *disruption*. Nonetheless, a legitimation system based on common values makes people identify and bond as a collective, and consequently legitimates society's prestige and authority arrangements. It accentuates the advantages of this order over the apparent burdens and inequalities some may feel. In effect, it generates *social solidarity* and *loyalty* to the system. Legitimation systems evolve from outdated types rooted in a religious belief system's justification for social arrangements to types where kings claim to be directly appointed by a god, to modern rational-legal cultural systems of justifying authority in modern industrial societies. For Parsons, American society's values emphasise individual achievement, efficiency and economic productivity. These values consequently provide legitimacy to the hierarchical social stratification system. For instance, the ambitious businessperson or executives at the top of corporations are considered to be fully deserving and consequently appropriately rewarded for their skills well above the salaries and wages paid to other members in a chain of interdependent occupations or tasks performed in a modern corporation.

American sociologists Kingsley Davis and Wilbert Moore (1945) expanded on this approach. In short, they argue that there is a 'universal necessity' of social stratification to maintain social order which supports 'the proposition that no society is "classless" or unstratified'. They saw social

stratification as a mechanism for the allocation of roles – or what is sometimes called positions or statuses – that must be fulfilled in order for the social system to survive:

> ... *the main* functional necessity explaining the universal presence of stratification is *precisely* the requirement *faced by* any *society of placing and motivating individuals in the social structure. As a functioning mechanism, a society must somehow distribute its members in social positions and induce them to perform the duties of these positions. ... A competitive system gives greater importance to the motivation to achieve positions, where a non-competitive system gives perhaps greater importance to the motivation to perform the duties of the position; but in any system both types of motivation are required* (Davis & Moore 1945: 242–243) (author's emphasis).

Society needs doctors, teachers, lawyers, bakers, truck-drivers, mechanics, musicians, radio and television announcers, farmworkers, authors, book printers, tree cutters, roadworkers, prison guards, mineworkers, mine supervisors, petrol pump attendants, car assembly workers, car assembly plant managers and supervisors, and so on. People are seen to have *natural* inequalities in their abilities and talents, and thereby fill different *roles* in society. The social stratification system gives different rewards and privileges to different roles, thereby getting the best suited people allocated to different roles because people are motivated to work for rewards. The high rewards 'built into' certain roles are an incentive for people to strive to obtain those roles.

People's qualification for certain roles, Parsons' structuralist functionalist theory further suggests, comes about through *inherent* capacity and training. Yet functional differentiation clearly does not always occur as a result of capacity. While many individuals have the mental capacity to learn and practise modern medicine, a medical education is burdensome and expensive. Furthermore, while positions that require great technical skill receive high rewards in order to attract the talented and those motivated to endure the training, such opportunities are not available to everyone. Such opportunities are not available to everyone precisely as a person's position in the system of social stratification *prevents* them from doing so, not because they *lack* the capacity to do so. A key criticism here is that the allocation of roles is not based on merit and capacity given that not all people in society have equal access to resources. Put differently, it is not the capacity or lack of capacity that determines where the individual is located in the social stratification system, but rather the means to do so, in other words social inequality itself. Parsons' structural functionalism ignores the formative structuring capacity of the social stratification system, which is explained as necessary and access to which is determined by individual capacity and merit. But this is clearly not the case as our own context only too readily reveals.

Understanding how social stratification unfolded in South Africa must take into cognisance a history of *racial domination* and *systematic privilege* which obstructed equal competition for roles and occupations in the division of labour. Racial segregation and apartheid policies in South Africa, which had as a consequence the unequal distribution of power, wealth and privileges on race lines, had its origins in the following:

- A political mythology of white peoples' ideas of race supremacy (Thompson 1985: 27–30)
- White peoples' claim to an 'empty land' (Marks 1980)
- The Afrikaner people's mobilisation to secure social, cultural, economic and political goals (Giliomee 1995)
- State-appointed commissions which advised the state on controlling the increasing numbers of blacks in urban areas (Ashforth 1990)
- The policies of white governments for the separation of races which Afrikaner organisations such as the Dutch Reformed Church called for (Dubow 1992: 212)
- The reality of white control of a modern economy dependent on African labour (Beinart & Dubow 1995).

In South Africa, white control of the state and the shaping of the education policy and institutions made its distinctive contribution to the sources of social inequality. The apartheid philosophy of Bantu Education deemed black people to be mentally inferior and conceptualised an education policy that was designed for the roles as manual labourers black people were to play in the economy (Davenport & Saunders 2000: 388–394, 674). This is contrary to Kingsley's and Davis' almost neutral view of how people pursue education in order to claim particular roles in a society's stratification system. Davis' and Moore's views on education as a means of social mobility are inappropriate in capturing the reality of the consequences of the overall education dispensation under apartheid.

What became characteristic of the overall education system was the unequal state spending on education per capita for different race categories, which partly explains the race inequality in the stratification system. More was spent on the education of white youth compared to any other race groups. The disproportionate spending on school education had further consequences with regard to preparation for tertiary education under apartheid. The race profile of tertiary education attainment shows that white enrolments for and completion of tertiary education qualifications outstripped the total for all the black groups put together (SAIRR 1977: 321; SAIRR 1977: 367).

Table 21.1 Professional, technical and related workers, by race, 1970

Occupational group	White	Coloured	Asian	African
Engineers	14 950	50	10	80
Technicians	19 240	240	250	560
Doctors, dentists	9 180	530	110	120
Nurses	26 260	960	5 640	27 800
Medical auxiliaries	8 510	190	220	720
Architects and quantity surveyors	3 530	20	10	–
Physical scientists	3 130	20	–	60
Teachers	56 000	6 340	16 350	43 960
Jurists	5 950	40	20	40
Surveyors	2 750	–	10	100
Working proprietors (commerce and trade)	22 980	8 110	1 420	9 720

(Source: Nolutshungu 1982: 117)

The 'colour bar' in the economy or the formal legislation which allocated occupations in the economy worsened the inequities of the education system, and is another important explanatory factor of social inequality in South Africa. Legislation passed between the 1920s and the 1960s specified 'the differential treatment of workers of various race groups in terms of these acts' (Scheepers 1974: 67). Apartheid served to buttress 'barriers, legal or conventional, to non-White advancement into semi-skilled or skilled jobs' (Scheepers 1974: 92). The information in Table 21.1 aptly illustrates concern about how the legacy of a stratification system informed by race is central to the shape social stratification and social inequality assumed under apartheid and continues under democracy.

21.3.4 Pierre Bourdieu's perspective

A brief look at Pierre Bourdieu's perspective on attributes which distinguish people from one another and contribute to social inequality will conclude our theoretical discussion. In Bourdieu's attempt to explain social inequality he sought to move beyond the focus on economic capital and resources which lie at the basis of both Marx and Weber. Indeed, he sought to go beyond both of these classic theorists by way of emphasising the importance of *cultural influences* arguably underemphasised or even ignored by Marx. Bourdieu certainly leaned on and further sought to more closely specify Weber's conceptions of status and class.

Bourdieu argues that we cannot understand the structure and functioning of the social world by focusing solely on the economic understanding of capital. Rather, we need to recognise the importance of other forms of capital, that is, what he termed *cultural*, *social* and *symbolic* forms of capital. Individuals or groups use these other forms of capital in order to gain an advantage and which also play a role in the structuring and lived experience of social inequality. These different forms of 'capital' function in different fields or sites of competitive social interaction. While economic capital is easily converted into money and can assume the form of property over which private rights can be exercised, the other forms of capital Bourdieu conceptualises are not quite so easily defined.

Bourdieu's notion of cultural capital

This form of capital relates to the social stature people acquire due to their educational background and the environment of their family upbringing which invests in them characteristics of different levels of cultural sophistication. The latter is no

doubt an advantage, for instance, in a competitive market for marriage partners. In addition, have you picked up how students try to assert their superior status depending on the education institutions from which they obtained their qualifications? **Cultural capital** cannot be transmitted in the form of a gift or as exchange for something else.

Bourdieu's notion of social capital

Social capital is a concept used and defined by several social scientists. In Bourdieu's conceptualisation it has to do with being part of social networks where one is recognised as part of a collective with a good reputation and that is taken as sufficient for credit and other advantages they seek. Mosoetsa (2011) talks about social capital among the poor in two communities in KwaZulu-Natal. Mosoetsa's view is, however, not entirely similar to Bourdieu's. She stresses the reciprocal relations among people to assist each other within social and kinship networks.

Bourdieu's notion of symbolic capital

This form of capital, symbolic capital, can be seen as an extension of Weber's notion of status. It can be further seen as located at the intersection of Weber's conceptions of class and status. It relates to status and prestige and other forms of social honour that set certain people apart, generally due also to more advantageous access such people have to opportunities to access and accumulate resources. By virtue of possessing or being imbued with such attributes, such people are elevated above the social standing of others. Symbolic capital is, moreover, identified with and is also subject to the cultural and historical frame within which it finds expression. The popular rubric attributed to someone who has what we South Africans call 'struggle credentials' – having been actively involved in the struggle against apartheid, especially in the military wings of the liberation movements – can be said to be imbued with symbolic capital. Political leaders who, in addition, have assumed positions of power, whether political or economic, possess even greater symbolic capital.

Bourdieu's different forms of capital can, without doing too grave an injustice to his concepts, be brought together under the notion of human capital. Not all sociologists will agree to describing human attributes and capacities in terms of capital. Nevertheless, the point regarding access to the different forms of **human capital** – cultural, social and symbolic – is that the possession or lack of human capital and position the individual occupies in the social stratification system will be both powerfully shaped by and influence access to, or the failure to access, opportunities and resources and hence locate the individual in the hierarchy of social inequality. In contemporary South African society, marked by a gendered, racialised and class-based system of social stratification, access to or the failure to access opportunities and resources, despite the possession of human capital, will more regularly than not ultimately depend on the complex confluence and intersection of a range of attributes defined, among others, by race, social class, gender, status and party.

21.4 Social inequality in South Africa today

What has happened regarding social inequality since 1994? Marxist, neo-Marxist, Weberian, neo-Weberian, structural functionalist, and Bourdieusian approaches continue to influence how social scientists see inequality unfolding in post-apartheid South Africa. Natrass and Seekings (2001: 476) synthesise some aspects of the latter approaches and construct a class and inequality structure comprising seven classes distinguished on the basis of professions and household incomes, overlapped with race, and the proportion of South Africa's total income that each class earns. Some more recent data in Table 21.2 provides useful information about how employment equity policies since the political transition have contributed to a changed

race profile in the hierarchy of occupations. This does not, however, broaden the picture in terms of the total share of **national income** each occupation category earns.

Poulantzas' and Wright's structuralist theories of class location and exploitation offer one way of understanding the role of the new black elite that has emerged largely through BEE. Until the 1960s, there was little **upward social mobility** and **class differentiation** in black African communities. In the past generation, however, a fairly highly differentiated class structure has emerged in this increasingly heterogeneous social group representing the majority of South Africans. In Terreblanche's view (2002), in all three black groups (African, coloured, Indian) a small elite has emerged, causing a shift from a racially skewed distribution of income to a class-based one. The white elite is argued to have co-opted the emergent black elite in a partnership that protects white wealth and privilege and has been accommodated by the former elites' adoption of the current globalised neoliberal economic policies, which have worsened the situation of the poor. The implication of this class-based elitism is that the political transition facilitated the emergence and co-option of a black elite into a lifestyle, a world view and policy preferences which separates them from those of the black underclass.

Table 21.2 Employment equity – employment by occupation, race and sex, 2015

	African % m/f	Coloured % m/f	Indian/ % Asian m/f	White % m/f	Foreign nationals % m/f	Totals % m/f
Top management	9.9 / 4.5	3.1 / 1.6	6.4 / 2.2	56.2 / 12.6	3.0 / 0.5	78.6 / 21.4
Senior management	13.7 / 7.4	4.6 / 2.8	6.8 / 3.4	40.1 / 18.1	2.4 / 0.7	67.6 / 32.4
Professionally qualified and experienced specialists, and mid-management	19.7 / 21.5	4.9 / 4.5	4.8 / 3.7	22.4 / 15.6	2.0 / 0.8	53.8 / 46.1
Skilled technical and academically qualified workers, junior management, supervisors, foremen, and superintendents	32.5 / 26.3	6.0 / 5.6	3.1 / 2.8	11.8 / 10.2	1.3 / 0.4	54.7 / 45.3
Semi-skilled and discretionary decision making	45.5 / 30.5	5.9 / 6.3	1.5 / 1.5	2.7 / 3.8	2.0 / 0.2	57.6 / 42.3
Unskilled and defined decision making	51.0 / 32.3	5.8 / 5.4	0.5 / 0.3	0.8 / 0.4	2.9 / 0.6	61.0 / 39.0

(Source: SAIRR 2017: 263)

The ANC is often seen as very closely aligned with an emergent black capitalist class and which has indeed 'been very deliberately engineered by the ANC' (Southall 2016: 65). The ANC committed itself to a BEE policy aimed at acquiring black ownership and control of productive property through the privatisation of state assets or companies and the selling of shares in historically white companies to black investors at discounted rates. BEE has economically empowered a narrow base of historically disadvantaged individuals. The party defends this as a redistributionist strategy where its BEE strategy would create a black capitalist class able to challenge white dominance of the economy. However, concern is raised that, while there has been improvement in the material circumstances of a broadly defined category called the 'black middle class', the poverty and inequality of a large section of the black poorer classes, with the exception of the 'poorest of the poor' who have benefited from social grants, has worsened. There is concern about the policies which favour the development of a black economic elite with a determination and official sanction to fast track their accumulation of wealth that undoubtedly places their economic policy preferences, their lifestyles and interests far above and removed from those of the black majority (Adam, Van Zyl Slabbert & Moodley 1998: 201). BEE creates a business elite who operate by principles or policies similar to any other capitalist (*Business Day* 2004):

Empowerment isn't creating any jobs and it isn't changing the way businesses run. Patrice Motsepe may be Harmony chairman, but that doesn't mean Harmony won't cut jobs when the cost to price ratio turns against it.

Defenders of the rise of a wealthy black elite warn that it is racist to object to the reality of black business people becoming millionaires. However, the strategy has had limited success, culminating only in the economic empowerment of a small black elite. It has not drastically altered the race profile of the wealthy and too often there is suspicion that the beneficiaries of the most lucrative empowerment deals are always those with connections to the ANC, consequently vindicating the 'elite pacting' argument that it is 'a device for white dominated corporations to build bridges with the ANC elite. Whatever wealth a relatively small segment of the black population has accumulated, it pales into insignificance given that whites, who make up 10 per cent of the population, continue to own and manage the vast bulk of the country's productive wealth and major companies. For some years after the 1994 political transition concern prevailed that black people still only controlled less than 4 per cent of shares in the JSE and that around nine out of ten senior management positions are held by white people (Carroll 2004). Since then a black elite (made up of African, coloured and Indian people) is steadily rising into the ranks of directorships in companies listed on the JSE (see Table 21.3).

Table 21.3 JSE black directorships, 2006–2016

JSE black directorships	2006	2011	2016	Change 2006–2016
Total number of black directors	485	1 035	1 043	115.1%
Black male directors	371	714	658	77.4%
Black female directors	114	321	385	237.7%

(Source: SAIRR 2017: 350)

Besides the BEE measures which have permitted considerable upward social mobility of a small black business elite we also need to look at the effects of legislation to transform the race hierarchy in the workplace and facilitate African, coloured and Indian upward mobility through affirmative action measures, namely the Employment Equity Act (RSA 1998). Data in Tables 21.2, 21.3 and 21.4 suggest what contribution affirmative action may be making to social mobility.

Table 21.4 Racial composition of top occupational categories, 2001

	Legislators, senior professionals, and managers	Professionals	Technicians and associated professionals	All three categories
African	25%	35%	52%	41%
Coloured	7%	8%	11%	9%
Indian	7%	7%	4%	5%
White	60%	50%	33%	44%

(Source: Seekings 2005: 312)

Summary

- Social inequality arises out of the social stratification system characterising that society. The social stratification system is humanly constructed and hence so is social inequality.
- This chapter introduced the traditional four main types of social stratification systems namely: slavery, caste (including race and ethnicity), estate and class.
- The depiction of the four social stratification systems showed their applicability to the South African context despite their origin in presenting the roots of social inequality in a society far removed from ours.
- A brief historical account of social inequality in the apartheid era with race as its central motif showed how in South Africa class was co-terminus with institutionalised and legislated racial discrimination.

- Overviews were given of four mainstream perspectives on class inequality in industrialised societies. These perspectives were those of Marx (1818–1883), Weber (1864–1920), Parsons (1902–1979) and Bourdieu (1930–2002).
- The chapter briefly concluded with noting some of the changes and continuities relating to social inequality in South Africa today. Improvements in social inequality were noted regarding access to senior positions in the state and the private sector were shown to have been accomplished in some areas.
- Social inequality remains a pressing issue in South African society today and regarding which increasing social scientific research can be anticipated.

ARE YOU ON TRACK?

1. What insights do Marxist, Weberian and functionalist perspectives offer you into how social inequality emerged during South Africa's industrial take-off?

2. What insights do Marxist, Weberian and functionalist and Bourdieusian perspectives offer you into new trends in social inequality following the policies adopted by government after 1994?

More sources to consult

Pillay U, Hagg G, Nyamnjoh F, Jansen J (eds). 2013. *State of the Nation. South Africa 2012–2013. Addressing Poverty and Inequality.* Pretoria: Human Sciences Research Council. A collection of recent essays on state policies, programmes and challenges to overcome unemployment, poverty and social inequality with special focus on industrial development strategies, housing delivery and urbanisation trends.

Seekings J, Natrass N. 2006. *Class, Race and Inequality in South Africa.* Pietermaritzburg: University of KwaZulu-Natal Press. Provides statistically detailed information on inequality across the apartheid and post-apartheid trends.

Seekings J, Natrass N. 2016. *Poverty, Politics & Policy in South Africa. Why Has Poverty Persisted After Apartheid?* Johannesburg: Jacana. Analyses aspects of neoliberal welfare state policy in post-1994 South Africa, persistent poverty and different perspectives on poverty and the effects of various welfare state measures to combat poverty.

References

Adam H, Van Zyl Slabbert F, Moodley K. 1998. *Comrades in Business: Post-liberation Politics in South Africa.* Cape Town: Tafelberg.

AFP. 2012. 'Mines unrest cuts S. Africa growth forecast to 2.5%'. [Online] Available at: http://au.news.yahoo.com/world/a/-/world/15227799/mine-unrest-cuts-s-africa-growth-forecast-to-2-5/ [Accessed 31 October 2012].

African Millionaire. 2009. [Online] Available at: http://theafricanmillionaire.blogspot.com/2009/12/jabu-mabuza-millionaire.html [Accessed 27 June 2011].

African Millionaire. 2010. [Online] Available at: http://theafricanmillionaire.blogspot.com/2010/11/peter-vundla-founder-of-herdbuoys-south/html [Accessed 27 June 2011].

African National Congress. 1992. 'Ready to govern: ANC policy guidelines for a democratic South Africa'. [Online] Available at: http://www.anc.org.za/show.php?id=227 [Accessed 28 December 2017].

Agüero J, Carter MR, May J. 2007. 'Poverty and inequality in the first decade of South Africa's democracy: What can be learned from panel data from KwaZulu-Natal?' *Journal of African Economies*, 16(5): 782–812.

Allardt E. 1968. 'Theories about social stratification' in *Social Stratification*. Jackson JA (ed). Cambridge: Cambridge University Press, 14–24.

ANC. 1994. *The Reconstruction and Development Programme. A Policy Framework.* Johannesburg: Umanyano.

Anderson ML, Taylor HF. 2001. *Sociology: The Essentials.* Connecticut: Wadsworth, Cengage Learning.

Ashforth A. 1990. *The Politics of Official Discourse in Twentieth-century South Africa.* Oxford: Clarendon Press.

Beinart W, Dubow S (eds). 1995. *Segregation and Apartheid in Twentieth-century South Africa.* London: Routledge.

Bourdieu P. 1986. *The forms of capital.* [Online] Available at: http://www.marxists.org/reference/subject/philosophy/works/fr/bourdieu-forms-capital.h... [Accessed 27 July 2017].

Carroll AB. 2004. 'Managing ethically with global stakeholders: A present and future challenge'. *Academy of Management Executive*, 18(2): 114–120.

Chetty K. 2012. 'Caste and religions of Natal immigrants'. [Online] Available at: http://scns.ukzn.ac.za/doc/SHIP/caste.html [Accessed 20 April 2012].

Davenport TRH, Saunders C. 2000. *South Africa: A Modern History.* 5th ed. New York; London: Macmillan.

Davies R. 1973. 'The white working class in South Africa'. *New Left Review*, 82 November–December: 40–59.

Davis K, Moore WE. 1945. 'Some principles of stratification'. *American Sociological Review*, 10(2): 242–249, April.

Dubow S. 1992. 'The elaboration of segregationist ideology' in *Segregation and Apartheid in Twentieth-century South Africa*. Beinart W, Dubow S (eds). London: Routledge.

Ebr-Vally R. 2001. *Kala Pani: Caste and Colour in South Africa.* Cape Town: Kwela.

Engels F. 1884. *The Origins of the Family, Private Property and the State.* Hottingen, Zurich: Penguin.

Fischer E. 1970. *Marx in His Own Words.* Harmondsworth: Penguin Books.

Fukuda-Parr S, Shiva Kumar AK (eds). 2005. *Readings in Human Development: Concepts, Measures and Policies for a Development Paradigm.* New York: Oxford University Press.

Giddens A, Held D (eds). 1982. *Classes, Power, and Conflict. Classical and Contemporary Debates.* Los Angeles: University of California Press.

Giliomee H. 1995. 'The growth of Afrikaner identity' in *Segregation and Apartheid in Twentieth-century South Africa*. Beinart W, Dubow S (eds). London: Routledge.

Goody J. 1969. 'Economy and feudalism in Africa'. *The Economic History Review*, 22: 393–405.

Greenberg S. 1980. *Race and State in Capitalist Development: Comparative Perspectives.* New Haven: Yale University Press.

Haralambos M, Holborn M, Heald R. 2004. *Sociology. Themes and Perspectives.* 6th ed. London: Collins.

Marks S. 1980. 'South Africa: The myth of the empty land'. *History Today*, 30(1): 7–12.

Marx K. 1979. *Capital: A Critique of Political Economy* (Vol 1). Harmondsworth: Penguin.

Marx K, Engels F. 1978. 'The Manifesto of the Communist Party' in *The Marx–Engels Reader*. Tucker RC (ed). New York: Norton.

Mhlongo S. 1981. 'An analysis of the classes in South Africa' in *Political Economy of Africa. Selected Readings*. Cohen DL, Daniel J (eds). London: Longman.

Mosoetsa S. 2011. *Eating From One Pot*. Johannesburg: Wits University Press.

Nattrass N, Seekings J. 2001. 'Democracy and distribution in highly unequal economies: The case of South Africa'. *Journal of Modern African Studies*, 39(3): 470–498.

Nolutshungu SC. 1982. *Changing South Africa. Political Considerations*. Manchester: Manchester University Press.

Parkin F. 1982. 'Social closure and class formation' in *Classes, Power, and Conflict. Classical and Contemporary Debates*. Giddens A, Held D (eds). Los Angeles: University of California Press.

Parsons T. 1977. *The Evolution of Societies*. Englewood Cliffs, NJ: Prentice Hall.

Poulantzas N. 1982. 'On social classes' in *Classes, Power and Conflict. Classical and Contemporary Debates*. Giddens A, Held D (eds). Los Angeles: University of California Press.

Republic of South Africa (RSA). 1913. Natives Land Act 27 of 1913. Pretoria: Government Printer.

Republic of South Africa (RSA). 1998. Employment Equity Act 55 of 1998. Pretoria: Government Printer.

Saunders P. 1990. *Social Class and Stratification*. London: Routledge.

Scase R. 1992. *Class*. Buckingham: Open University.

Scheepers JJ. 1974. 'Industrial legislation and non-white development' in *Labour Perspectives on South Africa*. Thomas WH (ed). Cape Town: David Philip, 67–77.

Seekings J. 2005. *Race, Class, and Inequality in South Africa*. New Haven: Yale University Press.

Seekings J, Nattrass N. 2006. *Class, Race and Inequality in South Africa*. Pietermaritzburg: University of KwaZulu-Natal Press.

Simkins C. 2004. 'What happened to the distribution of income in South Africa between 1995 and 2001?' [Online] Available at: http://www.sarpn.org/documents/d0001062/index.php [Accessed 5 October 2013].

Simpkins E. 2004. 'A new oligarchy rises in South Africa'. *Telegraph*. [Online] Available at: http://www.telegraph.co.uk/finance/2875635/A-new-oliarchy-rises-in-South-Africa [Accessed 27 June 2011].

Simons HJ, Simons RE. 1969. *Class and Colour in South Africa 1850–1950*. Harmondsworth: Penguin.

South African Institute of Race Relations .... 1997.....[[to be provided]]]]...............

South African Institute of Race Relations (SAIRR). 2017. *South Africa Survey 2017*. Johannesburg: SAIRR.

Southall R. 2016. *The New Black Middle Class in South Africa*. Johannesburg: Jacana.

Spicer S. 2011. 'Stratification systems and social inequality' in *Sociology: Supplement of Southern Africa*. Draper M, Galvin T, Graaf J, Hagemeier L, Lesetedi G, Malilal S, Mashaka K, Spicer S. Cape Town: Pearson.

Srinivas MN. 1952. 'The caste system in India' in *Social Inequality. Selected Readings*. Beteille A (ed). Harmondsworth: Penguin Books.

Terreblanche S. 2002. *A History of Inequality in South Africa, 1652–2002*. Pietermaritzburg: University of Natal Press.

The Bay Golf Estate. [Online] Available at: http://www.thebaygolf.co.za/EcoLivingMore.html [Accessed 27 June 2013].

The Sydney Morning Herald. 2009 '"Human calamity" warning amid crisis'. [Online] Available at: http://www.smh.com.au/business/human-calamity-warning-amid-crisis-20090427-akpr.html [Accessed 3 January 2018].

Thompson L. 1985. *The Political Mythology of Apartheid*. New Haven: Yale University Press.

Tischler HL. 1996. *Introduction to Sociology*. 5th ed. Fort Worth, TX: Harcourt Brace.

Weber M. 1978. *Economy and Society. An Outline of Interpretive Sociology*. Los Angeles: University of California Press.

Webster E. 1985. *Cast in a Racial Mould: Labour Process and Trade Unionism in the Foundries*. Johannesburg: Ravan Press.

Wolpe H. 1988. *Race, Class and the Apartheid State*. London: James Currey.

Wright EO. 1982. 'Class boundaries and contradictory class locations' in *Classes, Power and Conflict. Classical and Contemporary Debates*. Giddens A, Held D (eds). Los Angeles: University of California Press.

Poverty

Christopher Thomas

Poverty is a major societal problem. It is a tough topic to study. Poverty immediately raises the moral judgement that it is wrong and should be eradicated. This moral stance results in ethical concerns of what to do about it.

Poverty has rightly been construed in this chapter as *the* social question in applying the sociological imagination. This chapter consequently needs the careful application of a studious mind, but if you work through it diligently, the analysis and argument will become clear.

Conceptualising and defining poverty and impoverishment receives significant attention. This is because the way in which poverty is conceived leads, for instance, to different poverty reduction or poverty eradication strategies and conclusions about increases or decreases in poverty. This very way of thinking, however, it must immediately be said – that poverty needs to be reduced if not eliminated – is what the leading progressive economist, Samir Amin, calls 'a discourse of charity style of 19th-century thinking' which does not seek to understand the economic and social mechanisms which generate poverty. Amin's answer as to the fundamental cause of poverty in agriculture – which affects three billion farmers (nearly half of the seven billion people in the world) – is clear: modern capitalist agriculture and the maximisation of the return on capital in a market-led economy.

Despite Amin's unambiguous answer as to the cause of poverty, not everyone who investigates poverty, whether the ruling party, government departments or researchers, agrees about definitions, measurements or is in agreement about what constitutes a reduction in poverty. In defining poverty more closely, instead of using the three sociological approaches with which you are familiar, this chapter suggests the mainstream approaches to poverty are based on the question whether poverty is best understood and analysed from an objectivist, a subjectivist or a combination of these two approaches. The first, objectivist approach, assumes the self-evident fact of poverty as it exists as an external social reality. This approach is especially concerned with measuring poverty, with different measures having been established in trying to get to grips with identifying what poverty is. The measure of the poverty datum line remains an influential approach, popularised by the monetary value which signals falling below this line – one dollar a day. The second, subjectivist approach, seeks to examine the phenomenon from the subjective experiences of those who suffer poverty. Within this approach, the capability approach, the social exclusion and participatory approaches are discussed. The first approach, the capability approach, is the brainchild of Amaryta Sen. In following Sen's guide, these approaches all attempt to move beyond the objective monetary approach, not to replace it, but rather to gauge people's subjective experiences of poverty on which to base more effective policy interventions to alleviate, reduce or even eradicate poverty. In short, people suffering in and from poverty must be central in any understanding of poverty. Theoretically speaking, we here then return to the beginning of this textbook. *The* sociological imagination needs to be superseded by *many* decolonial imaginations – in this instance facilitating the articulations of those in poverty.

Consequently, the way in which people negotiate poverty in their lives and how poverty issues have been raised and treated in South Africa since 1994 becomes the focus of this chapter. Not having established consensus on poverty in South Africa, we remain a long way off from not only a 'discourse of charity' –

the quest for poverty alleviation, reduction and its eradication – but more seriously, how to transform our thinking about poverty and ensure those who suffer poverty can speak and act. When it comes to poverty then, sociology is not only sobering, but of critical concern in addressing the social question of our times.

Case study 22.1 Interpreting current poverty in South Africa

Poverty is currently increasing in South Africa. This is confirmed by the recent report of Statistics SA (StatsSA) on poverty trends which stated that in South Africa 55.5 per cent of the population was poor in 2015. Read in view of this the following extract and then answer the questions that follow.

Poverty trends

With regard to current poverty trends in South Africa, the StatsSA 2017 report on poverty trends in South Africa stated the following:

Despite the general decline in poverty between 2006 and 2011, poverty levels in South Africa rose in 2015. When applying the upper-bound poverty line (UBPL) (R992 per person per month (pppm) in 2015 prices), we see that more than one out of every two South Africans was poor in 2015, with the poverty headcount increasing to 55,5 per cent from a series low of 53.2 per cent in 2011. This translates into over 30,4 million South Africans living in poverty in 2015. While the recent increase in the headcount is unfortunate, we are still better off compared to the country's poverty situation from a decade earlier when it was estimated that two out of every three people (66,6 per cent or roughly 31,6 million people) were living below the UBPL in 2006.

QUESTIONS

1. When is a person poor and when not? When is a household poor and when not?
2. What level of poverty is reasonable for a country to tolerate?
3. How do you interpret the poverty situation in South Africa?

Key themes

- The phenomenon of poverty and inequality
- The relationship and differences between poverty and inequality
- Key sociological approaches to understanding poverty
- Poverty and inequality issues in South Africa

- The social question
- Measuring poverty
- Poverty lines
- Human development.

22.1   Introduction

On 10 May 1994 former political prisoner Nelson Rolihlahla Mandela was inaugurated as president of South Africa. The event signalled the end of apartheid policies that denied the overwhelming majority of the country's people the political franchise, powerfully contributing to the miserable existence of poverty and social inequality. Nelson Mandela's inaugural speech was an optimistic vision of the new democratic government's effort to transcend poverty and discrimination, and usher in a new era of prosperity, where all are 'freed to fulfil themselves' and have 'work, bread, water and salt' (Mandela 1994). Seventeen years later, the fourth post-apartheid president, Jacob Zuma (2011) acknowledged that, although the economy had grown, poverty persisted: this was against a background of a body of pessimistic research-based conclusions that claimed South Africa had become the most unequal society in the world and that poverty levels had worsened.

Under capitalism in South Africa apartheid poverty was racialised, seriously exacerbating the degree, extent and nature of poverty. Whites were generally better off than their black counterparts with concentrated pockets of not inconsiderable wealth among a small number of whites. Poverty was highly concentrated among a large proportion of the black African segment of the population. Capitalist social relations coexisted with apartheid policies creating a racialised system of social stratification compounding the problems of poverty and social inequality. The anti-apartheid struggle for the equal enjoyment of citizenship rights regardless of race culminated in a negotiated political transition to a constitutional democracy that promised civil, political and socioeconomic rights. This transition, it has now become clear, needed to be more cognisant of its shortcomings in the way British economist Thomas Humphrey Marshall argued how complicated the pursuit of equality really is. Marshall saw that the principle of citizenship promises formal equal status to all citizens. This is in tension with the social class inequalities rooted in capitalist market relations and the institution of private property. South African economist and poverty researcher Francis Wilson (2000) expressed wariness about the prospects of the political transition. Wilson has been proven entirely correct when he argued that achieving economic justice would become a leading political issue after the transition as the persistence of 'poverty based on huge and growing inequalities' would undermine respect for a praiseworthy constitution. The constitution itself has become an ideological resource in defining poverty in South Africa and a beacon for the new government to defend its achievements in reducing poverty (Magasela 2006).

How should we make sense of these concerns as sociologists? Debate has raged around the definitions, conceptualisations and measurements of poverty. The debate around how many people's circumstances have improved or worsened in post-apartheid South Africa is equally alive. The debate about poverty and widening social inequality within and between different racial groups has fuelled the construction of ominous scenarios depicting a fractured society and future social conflict. Case study 22.2 and the questions that follow are about some of the everyday issues facing post-apartheid poverty, inequality and social mobility.

This chapter on poverty and how to think about and measure poverty needs to be read in conjunction with Chapter 21 on social inequality to understand their connection to each other and build on the differences between poverty and social inequality. This will help you understand these phenomena through sociological theories, provide you with the necessary sociological skills to generate and analyse pertinent data, and consequently help you better understand how circumstances have changed, worsened or remained unchanged since the political transition. To grasp the present under capitalist democracy, this chapter starts by looking at how poverty and social inequality were woven together under apartheid racial capitalism.

22.2   Poverty as 'the social question'

Sociology emerged in an industrial society context characterised by extremes of poverty and inequality. The question of 'what do we do about the poor in society?' became known as 'the social question'. Frenchman Auguste Comte saw sociology's potential as a positivist science in the sense that it claims to be a systematic science about the nature and causes of problems in human affairs. He also saw how it could help us restore order, address poverty and improve human welfare. Sociology has often informed policies adopted to address social issues demanding urgent attention. It can claim to have contributed to social reforms and often aimed at structural social change. Much of early sociology has a 'meliorist' orientation – sociologists should produce knowledge about human society in order to shape policies and improve the conditions of the poor. Classical sociological theorists approached poverty and inequality in industrial capitalism differently. Émile Durkheim and Talcott Parsons saw poverty as a social problem, but thought that, overall, social inequality in society was inevitable and indeed functionally necessary for the existence of society, a view that has come under sustained attack since the 1960s. Karl Marx analysed how capitalism creates poverty and inequality for a subordinate class in a simultaneous process of enriching a wealthy ruling class. As you know, Marx argued for a transition to socialist society to overcome capitalist exploitation and hence, it follows, poverty itself. As you also know, Max Weber expanded on Marx's views regarding the economic basis of class and social inequality by adding the significance of status and power as dimensions of **social stratification**.

The immediate relevance of recalling these key theoretical signposts is that post-apartheid macro-economic policy, its relation to poverty trends and the framework of official measures to reduce poverty share a similar positivist orientation with Comte's view of sociology. Notions about measures to fight poverty, namely 'poverty relief', 'poverty alleviation', 'poverty reduction', and 'poverty eradication', as well as the concerted international campaign of the United Nations' Millennium Development Goals (2000–2015) and its successor, the Sustainable Development Goals (2016–2030), to reduce poverty, have a positivist tone about them too. This should make us stop and think and perhaps take up the suggestion at the beginning of this book to return to its first chapter on sociological theory – especially in the light of Samir Amin's criticism of 'nineteenth-century style thinking'.

Making sense of the prospects of tackling poverty in post-apartheid South Africa must have the type of 'sociological imagination' – and indeed the encouragement of decolonial imaginations – that understands and explains the interplay and mutual influences of circumstances in the lives of individuals and events and processes in a broader society – as well as the history of a larger changing world. The prospects of the new government to tackle successfully a legacy of poverty and inequality must take into account the new government's ascent against the backdrop of the global spread of a neo-conservative economic trend since the early 1980s. Conservative Party leader and British Prime Minister in the 1980s, Margaret Thatcher, led the way in the rise of the dominance of this line of thinking about shifting state involvement in the provision of services to the private sector. Whether called the 'Washington Consensus', or 'neoliberal globalisation', 'marketisation' or simply 'neo-liberalism', these variants of our current globally dominant macro-economic view and practice all prescribe to similar economic policy agendas about restructuring capitalist social and economic relations and dismantling welfare state measures. This is done through fiscal discipline as a means of reducing national budget deficits; re-ordering public expenditure priorities such as cutting subsidies of welfare programmes; trade liberalisation which opens economies to international competition; privatisation of the delivery of social services; and the protection of property rights as a measure to stimulate investment and entrepreneurship.

Case study 22.2 South Africa: Inequality not so black and white

Read the issues discussed in the following case study and then answer the questions that follow.

The growing gulf between the haves and have-nots in the black population has given South Africa the dubious distinction of becoming one of the world's most unequal societies, according to a recent report by the Organisation for Economic Co-operation and Development (OECD), an inter-government body.

'From a policy point of view, it is important to flag the fact that intra-African [black] inequality and poverty trends increasingly dominate aggregate inequality and poverty in South Africa,' noted the report, 'Trends in South African Income Distribution and Poverty since the Fall of Apartheid'.

'While between-race [black, white, coloured or mixed-race, and Indian] inequality remains high and is falling only slowly, it is the increase in [black] intra-race inequality which is preventing the aggregate [inequality] measures from declining,' the authors commented.

The demise of apartheid in 1994 left a skewed racial economic hierarchy that placed whites firmly at the top, followed by Indians, coloureds, and then blacks. Since then the African National Congress (ANC) government has made Black Economic Empowerment (BEE) a policy centrepiece, but by the party's own admission it has failed to improve the lot of the vast majority of black South Africans.

'We also have to admit that the "broad-based" part of BEE has seemed elusive. In the main, the story of black economic empowerment in the last 15 years has been a story dominated by a few individuals benefiting a lot,' Deputy President Kgalema Motlanthe said on 4 February 2010 at the first meeting of the BEE Advisory Council.

The country's ethnic composition has seen the black population expand from 70 per cent to 80 per cent between 1970 and 2001, compared to the shrinking proportion of whites – 17 per cent to 9 per cent – over the same period.

'Clearly such demographic change gives increasing importance to the intra-African distribution in driving the aggregate distribution,' the OECD report said. ⟶

Usual suspects

BEE has faced sustained criticism over the perception that it is benefiting a few, with the emergence of a disparaged class known as the 'usual suspects', like mining magnate Patrice Motsepe – whose wealth is estimated at about R14.2 billion (US$2 billion) – and ANC housing minister and struggle hero, Tokyo Sexwale, who is also a mining magnate.

Steven Hawes, manager of research and advocacy at Empowerdex, a company specialising in all aspects of BEE, told IRIN that the empowerment policy was not 'a vehicle for oligarchs' although its initial stages might have appeared that way. 'It's premature to say BEE as a policy has not worked. It needs time to spread its wings.'

He said the introduction of Broad Based Black Economic Empowerment (BBBEE) in 2007 was designed to benefit greater numbers of previously disadvantaged people.

The OECD acknowledged that the post-apartheid government could be seen as pro-poor, as it had expanded access to housing, water, electricity and sanitation. In 1993, for example, 51.9 per cent of South Africans had access to electricity for lighting, but by 2004 this had increased to 80.2 per cent.

'It should be noted that while the between-race component of inequality has fallen, it remains remarkably high by international norms, and its decline has slowed since the mid-1990s,' the report said.

'Moreover, the bottom deciles of the income distribution and the poverty profile are still dominated by Africans [blacks], and racial income shares are far from proportionate with population shares.'

Although the country's 'levels of poverty and inequality continue to bear a persistent racial undertone', poverty levels have been assuaged by social assistance grants rather than the labour market, despite the survey period – 1993 to 2008 – mirroring the longest period of growth the country has witnessed,' the report commented.

'Individuals with very low levels of education and with no workers in the household have the highest poverty incidence, but they have not become poorer over time … rather, those with no children have become poorer.'

Two-thirds of the income of the poorest 20 per cent was derived from social assistance grants, mainly child grants, but 'orphans are less likely to be receiving the Child Support Grant than children with both parents.

Social grants

South Africa's level of HIV/AIDS has undoubtedly contributed to its estimated four million orphans. 'Most significantly, there appear to be many eligible children in need who are not receiving the grant. The most common reason for not applying when eligible for the grant is found to be a lack of correct documentation,' the researchers noted.

More than a decade of uninterrupted growth ended with the global slowdown in 2008, but it had allowed for the rapid expansion of grants, and speculation that there might be some form of unemployment benefit.

'It is questionable whether a permanent income support for the unemployed would lead to the desired outcomes. Many of the unemployed are young school leavers, and while they clearly need some sort of social safety net or temporary social insurance, the longer-term goal of policy should be directed at helping this group enter the labour market and remain in work in the long term,' the report recommended.

Greater access to education has also not proved a boon to poverty alleviation. 'The fact that better-educated young people remain poor suggests that the labour market has not been playing a successful role in alleviating poverty, and that the education system is not delivering the skills needed in the labour market,' the OECD said.

'Thus, it is concluded that it is not the labour market but rather social assistance grants which have driven the relative improvement in poverty levels over time.'

(Source: IRIN 2010)

QUESTIONS

1. Can all black South Africans enjoy considerable social mobility as Tokyo Sexwale did?
2. What do you think the incomes and social statuses of the people who work in the businesses in which Sexwale has ownership and directorship interests may be like?
3. The businesses likely employ both black and white South Africans: what do you think their locations are likely to be in an analysis of the companies' hierarchies?
4. How do you understand the connections being made between political party association and social mobility?
5. What is the chief means whereby the circumstances of the poor have slightly improved?

22.3 Conceptualising, defining and measuring poverty

Systematic and comprehensive research of poverty dynamics in South Africa began in the early 20th century. The first major study, the Carnegie Commission on the Poor White Problem in South Africa between 1929–1932 (Davenport & Saunders 2000: 624–665), dealt with the circumstances of white people who lost access to land and subsistence farming, due to war, drought, pestilence-related death of their livestock, and the transition to commercial capitalism in the agricultural sector. Afrikaner whites, in particular, were unprepared for the competitive, low-wage conditions of the take-off of the mining and urban industrial economy. Following an electoral victory in 1948, the National Party government enforced sharper racial segregation policies in order to overturn white poverty. Apartheid policies, however, intensified the impoverishing processes among black South Africans and research on poverty shifted from the 'poor white problem' to unveiling and measuring the extent of poverty among black South Africans. The South African Institute of Race Relations annually reported on black poverty trends using some of the standard poverty measurement approaches. In the early 1970s the churches released a publication (Randall 1972) about black poverty. Worsening black poverty prompted The Second Carnegie Inquiry into Poverty and Development in Southern Africa (Wilson & Mamphela 1989) in the 1980s. That study drew from the approaches described further on in this chapter, namely the Poverty Datum Line, the Minimum Living Level, the Supplementary Living Level, the Household Subsistence Level, and the Household Effective Level. It recognised the link between poverty and inequality and referred to the **Gini coefficient** measures for South Africa. It also drew from **human development approaches** that go beyond **money metric approaches**. Researchers did not use a single definition or measure, instead they got people to talk and participate in the process of defining poverty. Researchers drew correlations between income, 'race' and 'colour-castes'. In 2012 social scientists were invited to discuss the need for a new Carnegie Commission inquiry into poverty in the post-1994 era in South Africa. A growing 'underclass' of poor and unemployed, worsening inequality and expectations of economic changes that transcend welfare handouts is seen to be nudging South Africa closer to the crossroads of intensifying violence and class conflict that threaten the security of post-apartheid democracy (see Mbeki & Mbeki 2016).

Poverty was structurally rooted in and a consequence of apartheid policies (Wilson & Mamphela 1989). Through the measures of a series of Urban Areas Acts black urbanisation was constrained. Black people in urban areas were constantly arrested and fined for contravening pass laws. There were limits on housing built for blacks in urban areas. This constrained black households from accumulating capital. Black people had to reside in geographically segregated areas and endured high transport costs because they had to travel to work in distant white areas. The forced removals of blacks out of 'white areas' to ethnic homelands and the enforcement of separate residential and business zones in urban areas by the Group Areas Act (1950) caused considerable loss of assets. The Bantu Education policy enforced from 1953 diminished the quality of black education and severely constrained the acquisition of skills among the black workforce; it also ensured that whites secured the higher income jobs in the economy.

Having inherited the poverty legacy created by apartheid, **poverty reduction**, as opposed to **poverty eradication**, which involves an overall structural change in social relations, is invariably a central policy issue in post-apartheid South Africa. The ANC published the Reconstruction and Development Programme (RDP) on the eve of the 1994 elections, which gives significant attention to a policy framework to undo poverty. President Mandela declared a 'war on poverty' in 1996. The ANC government conducted its first major study of poverty, *Key indicators of poverty in South Africa* (2007), with the Office of the RDP and the World Bank contributing to its authorship. In 1998, civil society organisations held a 'Speak out on poverty' campaign (Budlender 1999). Government also commissioned researchers for its *Poverty and Inequality Report* (May 1998) to investigate its extent and to analyse the effectiveness of the state's poverty reduction measures. Mandela's successor, President Thabo Mbeki, also reiterated the challenge of reducing poverty.

More than 20 years after the demise of apartheid, poverty patterns in South Africa remain similar to that of the apartheid era. When using the notion of 'households living in extreme poverty' we see that in 2014 approximately 21.7 per cent of African, 6.6 per cent of coloured, 1.4 per cent of Indian and 2.9 per cent of white households are regarded as extremely poor (SAIRR 2017: 454). Nonetheless, we need to use further concepts and measurement techniques to unravel the complexity of this situation.

We all have some notion of what poverty is. The ruling party, government departments, and social researchers in South Africa are not, however, always in agreement about definitions, measurements and achievements in poverty reduction. Poverty reduction measures may fall under one of two approaches or a mixture of the two. *Structural approaches* target the societal obstacles that force people into poverty, while in *agency-based approaches* the state assists individuals to empower themselves to move out of current poverty (NALEDI 2007: 18). Evaluating the achievements of poverty reduction strategies will always be held up against the chosen prevailing definitions, conceptualisations, and measurements of poverty.

The phenomenon of poverty and impoverishment is intrinsic to all analyses of the emergence and nature of capitalist social relations and market institutions in the classical sociological theory of the 19th century. It also is embedded in the theories developed in the course of the 20th century and contemporary sociological theory since the late 20th century, which has popularised the notion of the globalisation of ideas, culture, institutions and connections between different parts of the globe. Theorists acknowledged that capitalism and markets impoverish or produce poverty, but have offered different answers about whether the institutions of capitalism be improved or replaced by the institutions of a new type of social order.

Social historian Karl Polanyi conducted research in the mid-20th century on the institutions of the market economy. Polyani argued that the operations of these institutions contradicted some of the dominant ideas of freedom, as well as diminished the lives of the people who did not own productive capital (Harvey 2005: 36–37). Regardless of such warnings, since the 1970s an obsession with the logic and promise of markets to achieve economic growth and reduce poverty has influenced societies worldwide. While enforcing this trend in the 1980s, Margaret Thatcher infamously declared: 'There is no alternative!' (Harvey 2005: 40). Even more infamously, talking to *Women's Own* magazine on 31 October 1987, Thatcher asserted that: 'There is no such thing as society.' The basis for this claim is that 'society' is merely a collection of individuals. This view lies behind aspects of the British and American models of neoliberalism adopted worldwide. Neoliberal economic policies oppose one of the main poverty reduction strategies that advocates of the reform of capitalist institutions upheld through the 20th century, namely, that the role of the state should be increased through public and social spending – core features of a social democratic or welfare state. The economic growth policy-making measures associated with neoliberalism and the Washington Consensus have had the same impoverishing consequences anticipated in classical 19th century sociological theory. The swing to neoliberal economic policies has produced increases in

productive output and tremendous increases in wealth for some. Economic growth is certainly necessary for poverty reduction, but it does not translate into poverty reduction or a trickling down of wealth from its unequal concentration among a few at the top to a distribution among the masses at the bottom. In essence, economic growth simply does not reduce the number of people living in poverty.

It is widely acknowledged that unemployment, poverty and inequality have increased in developed, developing and underdeveloped countries. Poverty levels are highest in African, Asian, Latin American and Caribbean countries. European countries see their international development assistance as important because of its connection to combating a number of additional issues associated with poverty, namely, disease, illegal migration, environmental degradation, political instability, armed conflict, terrorism and crime (OECD 2001: 15). In September 2000, against the backdrop of the global dominance or hegemonic thinking about adopting neoliberal economic policies and acknowledgement of increased poverty globally, 189 member states of the United Nations (UN) identified eight global challenges to development and adopted the **Millennium Development Goals** (MDG) in New York City (UNDP 2001). The MDG policy was signed by 147 Heads of State who committed their governments to reaching the objectives. The MDG included the first objective of halving poverty by 2015. The MDG spoke in terms of reducing the number of people living below US$1.25 a day. (This was around R8.00 in mid-2012. As of October 2015, this was raised to US$1.90 – R26.85 at October 2017 exchange rates.) Each MDG signatory country was to adopt its own appropriate conceptualisation, definition and poverty measurement techniques – and report on their progress. The MDGs were followed by the Sustainable Development Goals (2016–2030), which continues the commitment to eradicate poverty. The current global economic recession since 2008 has worsened the economic situation in poorer countries as well as the numbers of people driven to extreme poverty. Nearly a decade ago this was held as threatening the possible successes of the UN's 2000 poverty eradication goals (Smith 2009). The final MDG report acknowledged that about 825 million continue to live in extreme poverty and 800 million people suffer from hunger. It concluded that 'the world is still far from reaching the MDG of eradicating extreme poverty and hunger' (United Nations 2015: 23). Although governments have proclaimed successes for their poverty reduction policies and programmes, they are held in doubt due to a plethora of definitions, conceptualisations and measurements of poverty. Because there are different ways of understanding the phenomenon, it also means that there are different choices of policies and actions to deal with it and claims of successes. Poverty reduction strategies require research that identifies the main causes of poverty, policies and plans of action to address its causes. Indicators must be useful to monitor or evaluate the successes and failures of plans of action. Identifying the poor, targeting poverty reduction measures and monitoring the outcomes are, to repeat, *complicated by the variety of conceptualisations, definitions and measurements.*

Since the 1960s there has been a growth in competing definitions, indicators, poverty reduction strategies and

toolkits. Poverty is a contested political concept and preferences for particular definitions and measurements reflect ideological and political choices. This partly explains sociologists' different conclusions about poverty trends in any particular country. One reason why the debate about poverty rages in South Africa is because there is no official definition of poverty and different researchers use different datasets. This chapter provides an overview of different definitions, conceptualisations, measurements of poverty, and integrates discussion of the structural origins and history of poverty in South Africa as well as trends since the 1994 political transition.

Case study 22.3 Surviving on US$1.90 (ZAR26.85) a day on the margins of the formal economy

Get a glimpse of a day in the life of an innovative recycler
by Kristian Meijer

Work for Eric Mkhinda (37) starts at 04:30 sharp, and after his morning chores he sets off on his trolley. He cannot afford to change clothes too often and this morning his clothes smell of his fire the previous night. Mkhinda is a street recycler, colloquially known as a 'trolley pusher'. He, like others, sift through dustbins for recyclable items. They then process and pack these items before selling them to recycling companies.

Mkhinda lives in a small squatter camp beneath the Gautrain bridge between Von Willich Avenue and Rabie Street. The camp is littered with cardboard and plastic bottles, ready to be sorted, packed and sold. He has a set route for each day where the municipality is collecting trash from dustbins. He made his trolley himself. A sort of 'frankentrolley' constructed from a flat piece of plastic and the handle of a broken shopping trolley. It has big, sturdy wheels.

'Nobody else has a trolley like this. If anybody steals it I will recognise it,' he said with a cheeky grin.

He is a veteran recycler, active in Centurion for more than 13 years.

'Everybody in Lyttelton, even the police, know me. I do not cause trouble,' he said.

Rekord joined Mkhinda on his Tuesday morning route, to see what he does, and how he was treated. We left at 04:05, setting off towards Glover Avenue. Mkhinda targets residential complexes where dustbins are packed closely together. At Emerald Park complex the dustbins have not been put out yet, so Mkhinda rolled a cigarette and waited.

'I know the guys who search dustbins in this street.'

When the bins arrived, he started his search.

'I never know what I will get. Sometimes I get a lot, or nothing.'

He aims for cardboard, paper and plastic bottles.

'I get R2.50 a kilogram for PET plastic.'

He sifted through 19 dustbins and salvaged several kilograms of cardboard, around 40 plastic bottles, two shirts, a pair of pants, two bags of cooked meat, two loaves of bread, three potatoes, two bottles of soda and a toy car. He can sell any of those items, the car for R2, and shirts and pants for R5. He packed everything in a big bag, and set off for the camp.

Rachel Isaacs looks after the camp while Mkhinda and others collect items. She helps sort the items. When everything is ready, she calls PWV recycling to collect the items. PWV could not be reached for comment at the time of going to print.

'I make around R800 a month. It is not much, but enough to survive,' said Isaacs.

The camp is a headache for residents, as it is next to a residential complex. Isaacs and Mkhinda were residents of the recently demolished camp in Von Willich Avenue that was torn down to make way for an office park.

(Source: Meijer 2016)

22.3.1 Mainstream approaches to conceptualising, defining and measuring poverty

The summaries below present the foundations of approaches researchers continue to debate. The conceptualisation dimension of the sociology of poverty provides a framework for the development of definitions and measurements (Lister 2004: 3–4). Conceptualisations of poverty attempt to give some meaning to the phenomenon such as in the notion of 'lack of basic needs'. Definitions, however, seek to be very precise about discerning between the 'poor' and 'non-poor'. Measurements are about operationalising definitions in ways that allow us to identify exactly who is poor, to count these people and to measure the intensity of their poverty.

Our focus is on definitions, concepts and empirical measurements that are the obvious building blocks of sociological theories and theories of poverty. This introduction to the topic does not deal with the range of theories of the social processes and structures behind poverty. One such approach examines the 'subculture of poverty'. This approach sees poverty as a self-perpetuating culture among the poor. Neither are the structural functionalist and Marxist theories (Townsend 1979: 61–92), discussed in Chapter 12, reiterated here.

Debate has steered the sociology of poverty to focus on the following issues:

- Gender power in the social structure and the consequent **feminisation of poverty**
- Whether it is appropriate to apply approaches used in developed countries to conditions in underdeveloped countries
- Questions about whether to focus on individuals or collectives (such as families or households)
- Whether it is appropriate to use the same definitions and measurements for both urban and rural conditions
- Whether poverty is a hopeless chronic condition or a transitory phenomenon (from which people can be rescued due to seasonal, new work opportunities emerging or as a consequence of successful poverty reduction measures)

- Whether poverty should be seen as an absolute, objective measurable phenomenon or a relative phenomenon.

The approaches can be grouped as *objectivist* and *subjectivist*. An objectivist approach has external reality 'out there' as its focus. Sociologists, economists and others can merely agree on a definition and proceed to measure poverty. Subjectivist approaches seek the participation of various stakeholders as well as, very importantly, the poor themselves in defining their circumstances. Some approaches attempt to reconcile the objectivist and subjectivist approaches.

Monetary approaches to understanding poverty

Two Englishmen are influential in the emergence of this objectivist approach, namely, Charles Booth's study of poverty in London in the late 19th century and Benjamin Seebohm Rowntree's study of poverty in York in the early 20th century. Booth explained his pioneering approach thus:

The divisions indicated here by 'poor' and 'very poor' are necessarily arbitrary. By the word 'poor' I mean to describe those who have a sufficiently regular though bare income, such as 18s [shillings] to 21s per week for a moderate family, and by 'very poor' those who from any cause fall much below this standard. The 'poor' are those whose means may be sufficient, but are barely sufficient, for decent independent life; the 'very poor' are those whose means are insufficient for this according to the usual standard of life in this country. My 'poor' may be described as living under a struggle to obtain the necessaries of life and make both ends meet; while the 'very poor' live in a chronic state of want (Booth 1889 in Ledger & Lockhurst 2004: 39).

Objectivist approaches regard poverty as a shortfall in income or consumption from a determined poverty line. One assumption behind this approach is that the subsistence needs of all individuals for food, clothing and shelter are the same; their situations, and their consumption needs and satisfaction thereof are taken as the same. Sociologists calculate the total market value of a specific basket of the minimum of essential items in a particular context. That basket of minimum items varies among different researchers using this approach, but generally the items include the monetary requirements for a nutritionally adequate diet, money for clothes and rent. Sometimes the basket includes items such as transport costs, education costs, and health services. Data is gathered on people's expenditure or incomes. This notion of income is somewhat broad in that it includes wages as well as subsidies and grants from state social security programmes. People with an income below the value of that basket of items are regarded to be living in poverty. They experience a shortfall in obtaining the minimum resources. They are below a threshold point, the poverty line. The 'one-dollar-a-day' approach (US$1.90 in 2015 – still applicable in November 2017) behind the Millennium Development Goals bears the imprint of an absolute monetary approach. The World Bank too includes this income or consumption approach in its reports on global poverty trends; it uses the following definition of poverty:

The inability to attain a minimum standard of living measured in terms of basic consumption needs or income required to satisfy them (World Bank cited in NALEDI 2007: 9).

If we were to rely on the one-dollar-a-day approach to observe poverty trends in South Africa, we see in Table 22.1 that it shows first an increase, then a declining absolute number and proportion of persons in these circumstances. The two-dollars-a-day measurement 'gives a better indication of the people living in poverty in an emerging economy such as in South Africa' (SAIRR 2012: 321). It would suggest that if you rely solely on this measurement technique you are likely to run into criticisms of your argument about poverty trends, hence our discussion of other measurements supports different perspectives on poverty trends. Furthermore, while this measurement technique provides some insight into poverty trends, we also would like to know what factors or policy-related measures may explain the positive changes. Transfers in the forms of grants and remittances to black households have increased tremendously: in the years 2009 and 2015 the respective increases in the number of African and coloured households that received grants were as follows: African households: 5 182 000 to 6 511 000; coloured households: 475 000 to 628 000. Contrarily, there was a decrease in grants to Indian households: 112 000 to 105 000 (see SAIRR 2017: 423).

Table 22.1 Number and proportion of people in South Africa living on less than US$2 per day

Year	Number	Proportion
1996	6 809 986	16.2%
2000	8 072 420	18.9%
2005	6 024 650	12.7%
2009	3 100 947	6.3%
2010	2 189 204	4.4%
2011	1 361 421	2.7%

(Source: SAIRR 2012: 321)

Criticisms have been levelled against the monetary approach. Its focus on food is seen as problematic because people have differing food tastes, individuals of different bodily proportions have different calorie intake requirements, and there is the issue of specifying what percentage of household income should be spent on food. Criticisms about the focus on individuals and families and assumptions about their subsistence needs saw the expansion of the approach and incorporation of the 'basic

needs' of larger units of local communities for safe drinking water, sanitation, public transport, health, education and cultural facilities. Furthermore, while the objective, monetary or absolute measurements continue to influence poverty research, concern about the poor's circumstances in relation to the rest of society and the sense of their exclusion has complemented the monetary approach. The idea of **relative deprivation** began to influence the definition and conceptualisation of poverty. The rationale here was that sociologists began to see the interdependence between a strictly numerical scientific (positivist) concept of poverty and the *social structure needs* to incorporate also a 'comprehensive and rigorous *social* formulation of the meaning of poverty' (Townsend 1993a: 33). The idea is to capture the changing relationship of deprivation and income taking into consideration the changed conditions in different moments in time and across communities in different places. Peter Townsend's (1979: 31) definition of this relative approach links objectivist approaches with social conventions about defining poverty:

Individuals, families and groups in the population can be said to be in poverty when they lack the resources to obtain the types of diet, participate in the activities and have the living conditions and the amenities which are customary, or at least widely encouraged or approved, in the societies to which they belong. Their

resources are so seriously below those commanded by the average family that they are, in effect, excluded from the ordinary living patterns, customs, and activities.

Using an objective monetary approach such as an official Poverty Datum Line in South Africa goes back as far as the 1940s (Frye 2005: 8) and continues up to the present. Discussion of poverty trends in the annual reports of the South African Institute of Race Relations (SAIRR) relies on monetary measures. Table 22.2 is an example of this; it discerns 16 income levels in rand, however, it does not give a breakdown of race group for each income category or the number of households in each income category in each province, consequently, it does not provide insight into countrywide differences in income and poverty.

Table 22.2 Number of households by income category in ZAR, 2015 (figures have been rounded)

Income levels in rand	Number of households
0–6 000	102 715
6 000–12 000	461 252
12 000–18 000	677 809
18 000–30 000	1 401 141
30 000–42 000	1 774 555
42 000–54 000	1 610 237
54 000–72 000	1 630 452
72 000–96 000	1 451 944
96 000–132 000	1 376 156
132 000–192 000	1 311 848
192 000–360 000	1 603 584
360 000–600 000	1 001 588
600 000–1 200 000	669 324
1 200 000–2 400 000	209 231
2 400 000+	44 203
Total	15 331 038

(Source: SAIRR 2017: 426)

Another way of representing this information is to divide the different income levels into equal 'deciles', or ten levels

from the highest to lowest incomes (sometimes levels of five 'quintiles' are used), and to count the number of households by race group found in the different deciles. Those found to be below the minimum income may be the households below a particular decile, say, the fourth decile, which could be set at about R1 000 per month, down to the first decile, which is an even lower monthly household income. If you examine Table 22.3 it means that, in 1996, 89 per cent of the poor in the fourth decile were African households, then coloured households made up another 6 per cent, then Indian households made up another 1 per cent, and

white households made up the remaining 4 per cent of households (totalling 100 per cent of the households at this income level or decile). An overall impression is difficult. Except for decile 10 where it is clear that white households are in the majority in this higher income level, however, from the upper income levels of 7 upward there are noticeably different amounts of representation of the different race groups compared to level 1.

Table 22.3 Racial composition of income deciles, 1996

Decile	African	Coloured	Indian	White
1	90%	4%	1%	1%
2	93%	3%	1%	3%
3	91%	5%	1%	3%
4	89%	6%	1%	4%
5	86%	8%	1%	5%
6	81%	10%	2%	7%
7	72%	12%	4%	12%
8	60%	14%	5%	21%
9	39%	12%	7%	42%
10	22%	7%	5%	65%

(Source: SAIRR 2001: 375)

The poverty line data can be aggregated to depict another poverty related phenomenon, that of inequality. Clearly, countervailing forces produced increasing inequality when using either the Lorenz Curve or Gini coefficient as indicators of trends. The Lorenz Curve, depicted in Figure 22.1 (NALEDI 2007: 36–37), is a method of representing inequality in a society on a graph and comparing it with other countries. The y-axis of the graph represents income and the x-axis represents population. This gives us an idea of how much a proportion of a society's income is controlled by a particular proportion of the population. In a society with perfect equality the line would be straight (actually it is at an angle of 45 degrees): the bottom 10 per cent of the population get 10 per cent of the income. Likewise, the bottom 25 per cent receive 25 per cent of the income. Once there is an unequal distribution of income, the line begins to curve. All societies, in fact, have a curved line, however, the more curved the line is, the greater the inequality.

The South African Institute of Race Relations uses the Gini coefficient to report on inequality trends in South Africa and uses the following operational definition:

The Gini coefficient is used to measure equality and inequality within countries or groups of people. It assigns a value between zero (perfect equality) and one (perfect inequality), where one household earns all the income.

For a considerable time, Brazil, a country regarded as being in the same middle-income group as South Africa, was noted for having the worst Gini coefficient. However, income inequality has worsened in South Africa and it is now the most unequal society in this group. The Gini coefficient increased from 0.596 in 1995 to 0.635 in 2001 (UNDP 2003: 43). The figures in Table 22.4 show a slowly worsening trend from 1996 to 2009 within the African and coloured groups but, after a brief spell of worsening within the Indian group, some slight improvement within the Indian and white groups.

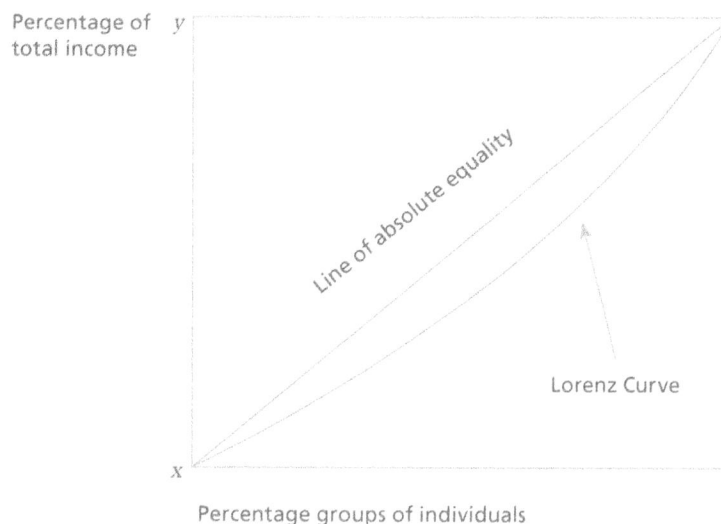

Figure 22.1 The Lorenz Curve

Table 22.4 Inequality within race groups

	African	**Coloured**	**Indian**	**White**	**Total**
1975	0.47	0.51	0.45	0.36	0.68
1996	0.53	0.51	0.51	0.48	0.61
2000	0.59	0.57	0.55	0.49	0.66
2005	0.58	0.56	0.52	0.48	0.65
2010	0.57	0.53	0.48	0.44	0.64
2015	0.57	0.53	0.47	0.43	0.63

(Source: SAIRR 2004/05: 191; 2000/01: 374; 2010: 251; 2017: 428)

The capability approach to poverty

The capability approach tries to move away from the emphasis of the monetary approach and gives attention to the 'quality of life'. Indian-born Cambridge University economist, Amartya Sen contributed to the evolution of the 'human development paradigm', which has sought to restore interest in the concerns of classical contributions to the development of economics as a discipline, that is, enhancing the quality of human lives, and not just measuring the production of commodities. Sen sought a multidimensional approach to poverty that integrates the insights of the different approaches to poverty; it is an attempt to integrate notions of economic development and social development. These ideas have influenced the United Nations Human Development Report emerging from 1990 and the notion of Human Poverty and a **Human Development Index (HDI)** in poverty research. Sen's influence permeates the human development report on

South Africa (UNDP 2003) and its conclusions about poverty dynamics. Public officials liberally sprinkle their speeches with references to this foremost contemporary theorist of poverty as an indication of the inspiration of his ideas on their poverty eradication policies.

The human development approach addresses income deprivation and other deprivations that reinforce poverty. Lack of education is characteristic of the poor and also means deprivation of other determinants of wellbeing, namely, employment, healthcare, clean water and sanitation. Poverty is seen as the deprivation of human development: 'the denial of basic choices and opportunities to lead a long, healthy, creative and free life' (Fukuda-Parr & Kumar 2005). The HDI is a composite of three variables measured in different units, namely:

- the life expectancy at birth index, which is measured in years

- the educational attainment index with regard to both adult literacy and the combined gross enrolment ratio at primary, secondary and tertiary levels, which is measured in percentages
- the gross domestic product per capita index, which is measured in dollars (Jahan 2005: 154).

The maximum value of the HDI is 1 and its minimum value is 0. Values that steadily approach 0 lead to conclusions that the quality of life is worsening. When the HDI improves, or moves closer to 1, it opens doors for other opportunities, improves the realisation of human rights, improves participation in society, reduces discrimination, and improves security.

The South African Institute of Race Relations uses the HDI in its annual reports on trends in human welfare, stating the following definition and purpose of the HDI:

The Human Development Index (HDI) is an index that combines normalised measures of life expectancy, educational attainment, and gross domestic product

(GDP) per capita for countries worldwide. It is used as a standard means of measuring human development, as well as to determine whether a country is developed, developing, or underdeveloped (SAIRR 2001: 71).

Looking at the HDI from the apartheid period and using 1975 as a base point where it was registered at 0.65, there was some improvement by the time of the political transition of 1994 when it was around 0.74, but it has steadily worsened after 1996 and was calculated at around 0.675 in 2005 (SAIRR 2009: 71). The United Nations (UNDP 2003: 44) reports on how this index declined after the ANC government's macro-economic policy, Growth, Employment and Redistribution (GEAR), veered towards neoliberal globalisation trends in 1996.

In Table 22.5 we see South Africa's ranking with the respective rankings of a selection of other countries when using the HDI for comparison.

Table 22.5 HDI of various countries, 2015

Ranking in the world, 2014	Country	HDI, 2015	Category of Human Development country
1	Norway	0.949	High HD countries
3	Australia	0.939	
11	United States	0.920	
91	China	0.738	Medium HD countries
111	Egypt	0.691	
119	South Africa	0.666	
151	Nigeria	0.527	Low HD countries
139	Zambia	0.579	
182	Mozambique	0.418	

(Source: United Nations 2016: 200)

Using composite figures for the components of the HDI in South Africa hardly helps illuminate the *differences* across the racial groups, arguably the chief goal of post-apartheid equality policies. The composite figure for life expectancy in 2015 was 57.7 years. For expected educational attainment it was 13.0 years of schooling.

Given that life expectancy and education attainment trends are two key factors in the determination of the HDI, it is worth isolating and examining their trends and projections over a number of years. In Table 22.6 the life expectancy variable for all race groups clearly shows a declining trend.

This may be due to the low figure for the African majority, which would explain the low composite figure of 57.7 years. A report on matric pass rates clearly tells that trends in education attainment are one factor that negatively affects the HDI for black Africans:

African pupils had the lowest pass rates for the matric exams in 2009, at 55%. White pupils had the highest pass rate, at nearly 99%. Pass rates for coloured and Indian pupils were at 76% and 92% respectively. (SAIRR 2010: 363)

The influence of the educational attainment variable on the calculation of the HDI is, however, quite complex. When comparing the different racial groups – on the number of persons aged 20 and older who have completed matric – we see significant changes for the two years of 2012 and 2015 (SAIRR 2017: 473). In 2012, 23.2 per cent of Africans completed matric. This moved up to 30.6 per cent in 2015. For people of mixed race, it moved from 23.6 to 32.5 per cent. For Indians it moved up from 48.0 to 51.3 per cent. Whites experienced a decline of 29.1 per cent when the figures moved downward from 72.9 to 51.7 per cent.

Table 22.6 Projected life expectancy

	2002	**2009**	**2012**
African	50.4	47.3	47.2
Coloured	62.2	60.8	59.7
Indian	66.7	66.3	65.8
White	71.6	71.5	71.0

(Source: SAIRR 2010: 48)

The social exclusion approach to poverty

The social exclusion approach emerged in Europe's rich industrialised countries with well-developed welfare state practices (Laderchi et al 2003). This approach has since also been used to research **deprivation** and consequent impoverishing processes in developing countries. The recognition and realisation of social and economic rights form the basis of the welfare state practices of the countries where the approach emerged. The gist of the definition of social exclusion is that it has the complete, or partial, exclusion of people from full participation in the society in which they live as its focus. The excluded are distinguishable collectives, that is, racial or ethnic groups, the aged or handicapped, rather than excluded individuals. Research using this approach is usually adapted to the conditions prevailing in particular countries. For instance, research in industrial countries focuses on indicators such as unemployment, access to housing, minimal income and democratic rights. Empirical research in developing countries using this approach, by way of contrast, has focused on *exclusion* from health services, education, housing, water supply, sanitation, pensions and land.

As you know, the political transition in 1994 introduced a widely acclaimed constitution (RSA 1996) with a Bill of Rights which recognises the right to certain social and economic rights. The key basic rights are housing (section 26), healthcare, food, water and social security (section 27) and education. (section 29). This approach may, arguably, be useful to account for considerable degrees of social exclusion processes, deprivation practices and impoverishment. Vusi Gumede (2006), an advisor to former President Mbeki,

regards monetary approaches to measuring poverty as a misleading representation of post-apartheid poverty trends. Gumede's reason is that monetary approaches do not take into consideration government spending on the **social wage**. The social wage, massively prominent in China incidentally, includes services actually delivered which enhance the quality of life of the poor. The entrenchment of socioeconomic rights in the constitution, of course, was that their exercise would have material expected redistributive effects. Researchers use the following operational definition of the social wage – so crucially important for the poor:

The social wage refers to benefits received by an individual that are supplied by the state in the form of such things as electricity, water, sanitation services, solid waste disposal, housing, education and healthcare (SAIRR 2009: 534).

In presenting the third and final approach to measuring poverty, in Table 22.7, we see calculations of state expenditures on different components of the social wage as gross values of these expenditures as well as average values per household.

The participatory approach to understanding poverty

Both the monetary and capability definitions and measurements of poverty have been regarded as externally imposed from above by researchers and their clients. The proponents of the **participatory approach**, such as Robert Chambers, argue that the views of the poor about what being poor means and what the *magnitude of poverty* is, must be taken into consideration. Both the World Bank and International Monetary Fund (IMF) have included this approach alongside others they use. The approach originated in development strategies that argued the poor are able to understand and analyse their own reality – and must be involved in the production of knowledge about their lives and reflect their strategies to deal with the lived experience of their conditions. Despite the ideal of the poor participating in this process, it usually turns out that

outsiders do the collection and interpretation of the data. Despite laudable commitments, the poor generally play a minor role in even these well-intentioned and deliberately chosen development strategies. In addition, there have been concerns that some segments of a community are excluded by others and are afraid of expressing their views. Another problem is that people have limited information and are conditioned to think of themselves in a particular way.

Table 22.7 Gross value of the social wage for 2004 (calculated in ZAR millions)

Component	Top 40% of households	Poorest 60% of households	Poorest 40% of households	All households
	Rm	Rm	Rm	Rm
Electricity	131	2 774	2 001	2 904
Water	72	1 816	1 312	1 888
Sanitation	34	514	350	548
Solid waste	66	934	638	1 000
Housing	1 179	2 357	1 572	3 536
Education	16 055	31 541	23 064	47 595
Healthcare	9 202	21 565	14 869	30 767
Total: Social wage	26 739	61 500	43 806	88 239
Social grants	4 179	18 901	14 365	23 081
Total	30 918	80 402	58 171	111 320

(Source: SAIRR 2009: 534)

Noble, Ratcliffe and Wright (2004) make the case for this kind of participatory approach to conceptualise, define and measure poverty in South Africa. They accept that objectivist, monetary approaches remain vital. These researchers also seek, however, to transcend the apartheid legacy of a divided society:

[I]t is crucial that a definition of poverty is found which reflects the common aspirations of all citizens ... A consensual definition would provide a truer reflection of what most South Africans think of as an acceptable standard (Noble et al 2004: 13).

Noble et al see a diminished role for professional, objectivist approaches:

Furthermore, a broadly consensual and socially informed definition of poverty would have the stamp

of democratic legitimacy in a way that 'expert' definitions, no matter how theoretically acute, do not. In a newly democratic country a bottom-up poverty measure, reflecting the views of most South Africans, could prove important in influencing the direction of poverty (Noble et al 2004: 14).

Frye (2005: 7) adds that such a participatory and relative definition of poverty would probably be the best way of gauging people's subjective experiences and would help guide the development of policies that address social inclusion.

The operationalisation of the consensual, participatory approach – and its definition and measurement of poverty – occurs in two stages. Firstly, a list of 'socially perceived necessities' needs to be drafted. Secondly, measures of the items of the list need to be created.

It should be noted, that in order to implement these two stages, for this human agent-sensitive approach to meet its aims, this strongly implies closing the often yawning social gap between researchers and the poor.

Poverty in everyday life

The foregoing gives considerable attention to the tools you would use as a sociologist to settle on the appropriate data to measure poverty, develop new knowledge about poverty in society and likely follow up through active engagement with state agencies and other civil society formations. Needless to say, the expressed intention of committed researchers is to influence or shape policy in the direct interests of the poor.

Poverty is a lived experience. The poor are in social interaction with others and create meaning in their social world. Poverty is a social condition of which the poor have some understanding of the larger social structural factors behind their impoverishment. The poor possess considerable sensibilities when comparing their circumstances with others in their society. Somehow, as a social group and individually, the poor cope with their lived experience of being poor. Too many of those who suffer poverty, however, clearly neither cope nor survive when compared with other social classes.

Often studies of the poor draw on the concept of **relative deprivation**. This term refers to individuals or social groups who feel or express their subjective sensibilities about being unfairly disadvantaged when they compare themselves to others. Relative deprivation occurs when those who share similar circumstances with others in their own society, or when they compare themselves to the overall standard of living in their society, experience a sense of disadvantage (Giddens & Sutton 2017: 1012). The sense of relative deprivation is independent of whatever research strategy might be followed. For within any system of social stratification, as in everyday life, people compare their fortunes to those of others. The concept of relative deprivation, however, remains a productive concept for studies that attempt to explain the discontent behind either the acquiescence or radical politics of the poor. As an exercise in evaluating the utility of this concept, consider watching television news reports about protests in low-income communities. Look out for statements made by protesters explaining their circumstances. Note when and how often such statements are made comparing their plight to other communities as reasons for their actions.

When it comes to reflecting on poverty in everyday life, the emphasis on quantitative approaches to understanding poverty discussed above must be seen as giving a one-sided and unbalanced view about poverty. Quantitative methods which measure and count, however important for social science, cannot capture but instead they minimise the importance of socio-cultural difference and the qualitative dimensions and lived experience of the life of the poor.

Qualitative-based approaches describe and explain the experience of being poor and how poor people understand their own poverty and the meanings they attach to poverty. Through interviews especially, qualitative approaches bring to the fore feelings of powerlessness, stigmatisation and discrimination, as well as the sense of belonging, co-operation and solidarity among the poor. The call for holistic approaches (see Poverty Analysis Discussion Group 2012) when doing research on poverty aims to represent more adequately the everyday lives and experience of being poor. Such holistic approaches acknowledge the fact that poverty is an economic and political phenomenon. Such approaches deal with power relations in society, which play a role in how opportunities and benefits are distributed. Such approaches also focus on the connections in the complex relationship between poverty and social inequality in society.

A brief case study

While the post-1994 government has moved away from the racial policies of the apartheid regime which contributed to black poverty, aspects of its neoliberal policies have contributed to the continuation of the wealth of whites and the enrichment of some black people. Current policy also contributes to unemployment, impoverishment, misery and a despairing sense of wellbeing among the poor.

In a study of two communities in KwaZulu-Natal Sarah Mosoetsa (2011) captures the voices of the poor, their understanding of the changing employment opportunities in relation to the new government's policies, their disappointment with aspects of the state's social services and their feelings of the lack of concern about their circumstances on the part of a new black elite. Objectively, given the continued high concentration of wealth among whites post-apartheid, the target of this poor community is misplaced – but that is a discussion for another day regarding methodology in sociological research.

This matter aside, Sarah Mosoetsa (2011) provides detailed insights into how impoverished households are mutually supporting, interdependent, depend on 'social capital' and are open to sharing with others in similar circumstances. The poor in this community and more generally are 'eating from one pot' (Mosoetsa 2011: 26). Furthermore, Mosoetsa tells about coping with changed gender roles – where the industrial economy socialised men into the role of breadwinner, buttressed by patriarchal culture. However, widespread male unemployment and households' shifting dependence on incomes brought in by women, Mosoetsa goes on to show, are behind a rise in gender violence. This is a study worth tracking down. It reveals something of the human face of poverty.

Post-apartheid poverty trends

What has happened since 1994? A reliable answer to this vexing question is pertinent to an evaluation of government's poverty reduction programmes. Some claim that poverty has worsened. Some claim that it has worsened drastically, others that it has worsened moderately. Still others believe that it has remained constant among certain categories of the poor. There are those who believe that income inequality has worsened and that there are different trends within and between the different race groups. Then, there are views that policy must simultaneously deal with poverty and inequality (see Chita-Mabugu et al 2016: 183). What adds to this being a vexing question is the fact that the post-apartheid state has adopted a range of policies and institutions characteristic of welfare states to provide safety nets and redistribute wealth. These include 'social wage' measures entailing state provision of basic services such as water, sanitation and electricity (Chita-Mabugu et al 2016: 182). Social protection measures entail social grants, state provision of primary healthcare and education. State spending on the spectrum of grants for child support, foster care, old age and pensions and disability has increased in billions of rand since 1994 and the number of recipients has increased by the millions – 31 per cent of the total national population are beneficiaries of some type of grant (Seekings & Nattrass 2016: 142–147; SAIRR 2017: 659). In addition, revenues for the Unemployment Insurance Fund (UIF) have risen from R13.9 billion in 2010/2011 to R28 billion in 2014/2015 (SAIRR 2017: 687). This UIF revenue is made up of monthly contributions by employers and employed workers. When workers who have contributed to the UIF become unemployed, they are entitled to draw from these revenues for a certain period of time to alleviate the immediate effects of being without an income. Further state-led initiatives such as the extended public works programme – to create work opportunities for unskilled workers – and land reform – to put productive assets at the disposal of the poor – have also been implemented with varying degrees of success.

As you have seen above, the choices of different definitions, conceptualisations and measurements undoubtedly contribute to generating a diversity of conclusions. Another reason for the diversity of conclusions is that researchers depend on different data sources. They use the October Household Surveys (OHS), the Labour Force Surveys (LFS), the General Household Survey (GHS), Income and Expenditure Surveys (IES), the All Media and Products Survey (AMPS) and the KwaZulu-Natal Income Data Survey (KIDS). Then there are the StatsSA national censuses, as well as the data researchers gather when conducting their own studies. Equally informative data sources are generated by the Development Bank of South Africa, the Bureau of Market Research, the SA Reserve Bank, the South African Advertising Research Foundation and the South African Institute for Futures Research. Not all of these institutions, however, will either provide access to researchers or disclose their data sources.

While apartheid policies left a tremendous legacy of poverty, South Africa's approaches to move away from the poverty and inequality have, however, not escaped the global trend to neoliberal economic policymaking. After 1994 the new government's RDP explicitly recognised a legacy of the mass of people living in poverty and spoke of redistribution (Everatt 2003: 81–83). Notwithstanding, the subsequent implementation, in 1996, of the Growth, Employment and Redistribution (GEAR) policy explicitly veered towards a neoliberal macro-economic framework to deal with economic growth and redistribution goals. This shift is widely acknowledged (Bond 2000; Marais 2001; Terreblanche 2002) to have generated higher unemployment rates and other inequality and impoverishing consequences similar to other countries where neoliberal economic policies were adopted. The adoption of the Accelerated and Shared Growth Initiative for South Africa (AsgiSA) in February 2006 promised to halve poverty and unemployment by 2014. That goal was not realised given a declining trend in gross domestic product, for instance, 3.3 per cent in 2011, 2.3 per cent in 2013, 1.3 per cent in 2015, and with forecasts of 0.4 per cent for 2016 (SAIRR 2017: 83–85). Unemployment steadily increased. The official definition put unemployment in 2016 at 26.6 per cent (5 634 000 people) while the expanded definition put it at 40.9 per cent (8 880 000 people) (SAIRR 2017: 84). Is it, however, reasonable to expect a massive successful transition away from the legacy of apartheid only two decades after the political transition? There has arguably been ample time to reflect on the trajectory and outcomes of the chosen set of policies. The current overall approach to addressing poverty takes place within a framework of realising constitutionally guaranteed social and economic rights (food, water, shelter, housing, healthcare, education, a job, social security), using 'legislative measures' and 'available resources'. Yet there is to date no official definition of poverty despite almost all government departments claiming their policies and programmes aim at reducing poverty (Frye 2005: 14). The debates about poverty measurement make it clear that different measurements have different poverty reduction policy recommendations. Everatt (2003: 82) contends that this

situation where 'poverty is endlessly elaborated but rarely (if ever) defined by government as a whole' can hold problems – poor definition means misguided policies and poor service delivery. While 'the poor' are regularly referred to as a category, if poverty is not consensually defined, it is difficult to argue what the trends are in terms of success or failure in reducing poverty.

Case study 22.4 Debating post-apartheid poverty trends

Read the article 'Government spending has reduced inequality sharply. The Gini coefficient ordinarily does not capture the impact of the social wage' by Joel Netshitenzhe, then answer the question that follows.

In a perceptive article on the wealth gap in our country, THISDAY (November 2) cited research on social inequality by the presidency contained in Towards a Ten Year Review. Alas, as often happens with headlines, the claim is made that this research asserts that the poor are 40 per cent richer than in 1994.

This simplifies complex research beyond recognition and distortions set in. What does the review say and what methodology is used to assess the effects of government policies on the poor?

The main assertion is that there has been a massive shift in government expenditure patterns since 1994 in favour of especially the poorest. Poverty is said to involve three critical dimensions: income, human capital (services and opportunity) and assets.

The point in identifying these dimensions is that a narrow focus on income can ignore critical redistributive aspects of a government budget, normally referred to as the 'social wage'.

This redistribution manifests itself especially in social spending on such services as education, social grants, housing, water and sanitation.

To quote two examples: since 1994, the government has increased spending on social grants from a racially skewed R10 billion to more than R34 billion equitably distributed this year. It has transferred assets worth about R50 billion to the poor through housing subsidies, transfer of title deeds and land reform.

It is this dimension that the Gini coefficient, as ordinarily used, tends to miss. The Gini coefficient measures how far the distribution of income or consumption expenditure deviates from a perfectly equal distribution.

A low Gini of zero means absolute equality among all citizens, its highest magnitude of 1 means massive inequality. This Gini coefficient, as ordinarily used, relies primarily on income and ignores the social wage.

An important contribution to this debate has been made by Servaas van der Berg, a professor at Stellenbosch University, in research that is increasingly being adopted by international institutions. He recalculated the Gini coefficient taking government expenditure into account.

This is ground-breaking research because in unequal and market-driven economies such as ours a critical question should be whether and how the government is playing its role as an agent of redistribution.

Starting off with the ordinary Gini, Van der Berg's calculations show that in 1997, taking into account only income before taxes and social transfers from the government, South Africa had a Gini coefficient of 0.68, reflecting extensive inequality. After taking into account taxes and social transfers, that is, after accounting for the social wage, the Gini coefficient is 0.44. So inequality is reduced by about 33 per cent through the social wage.

In 1993 the apartheid government's social expenditure was essentially neutral and had no effect on reducing inequality.

The researchers for Towards a Ten Year Review updated the information using Van der Berg's methodology and the 2000 Income and Expenditure Survey. This produced a pre-tax Gini of 0.57 and a post-transfer Gini of 0.35, a reduction of inequality of 41 per cent.

Van der Berg's methodology is important in at least two respects. It helps give quantitative expression to the three dimensions of poverty: income, services and assets. And it puts the spotlight on governments: are they doing enough as instruments of redistribution of wealth?

When all is said and done, income inequality cannot be discounted as just another dimension of poverty. Affected mainly by employment, it also raises the issue of the dignity of a job and if workers are receiving a living wage.

Further, a social wage, such as provision of electricity to those without a job, means that families use electricity only for lighting because they cannot afford stoves or heaters or, if they have them, they cannot afford the electricity bills.

So, in suggesting a trajectory for the second decade of freedom, Towards a Ten Year Review asserts the importance of a massive public-works programme, skills development, microcredit and land reform as well as decisions of the Growth and Development Summit, all critical for job creation and self-employment.

Government programmes over the past nine years have substantially reduced inequality among South Africans.

Though this may not have made the poor 40 per cent of our nation any richer, it has certainly made a significant improvement to their quality of life.

(Source: Netshitenzhe 2003)

QUESTION

What are your own perceptions about post-apartheid poverty trends and your views about how to measure these?

Summary

- This chapter began by describing the necessity of 'sociological imagination' to understand poverty in post-apartheid South Africa through understanding and explaining the interplay and mutual influences of circumstances in the lives of individuals and events and processes in a broader society as well as the history of a larger changing world.
- The chapter then described the definitions, concepts and empirical measurements that are building blocks of sociological theories of poverty but also describe the lack of agreement in view of the complexity of the poverty phenomenon. There exist different mainstream approaches to poverty.

- The first – objectivist – approach assumes the self-evident fact of poverty as it exists as an external social reality.
- The second – subjectivist – approach, seeks to examine the phenomenon from the subjective experiences of those who suffer poverty. Within this approach, the capability, the social exclusion and participatory approaches were discussed.
- The chapter closed by emphasising the importance of also understanding poverty as a lived experience that must be holistically analysed. In view of this the challenges and complexities in addressing poverty in a post-apartheid South Africa was then presented.

ARE YOU ON TRACK?

1. What insights do objectivist approaches offer in terms of understanding poverty trends in post-1994 South Africa?
2. What insights do subjectivist approaches offer in terms of understanding poverty trends in post-1994 South Africa?
3. How would you go about ensuring that the voices of the poor are included in a study based on the capability or participative approaches to studying poverty?
4. What is the difference between absolute poverty and relative deprivation?
5. What is a social wage?

More sources to consult

Pillay U, Hagg G, Nyamnjoh F, Jansen J (eds). 2013. *State of the Nation. South Africa 2012–2013. Addressing Poverty and Inequality.* Pretoria: Human Sciences Research Council. A collection of recent essays on state policies, programmes and challenges to overcome unemployment, poverty and social inequality with special focus on industrial development strategies, housing delivery and urbanisation trends.

Seekings J, Natrass N. 2006. *Class, Race and Inequality in South Africa.* Pietermaritzburg: University of KwaZulu-Natal Press. Provides statistically detailed information on inequality trends across the apartheid and post-apartheid trends.

Seekings J, Natrass N. 2016. *Poverty, Politics & Policy in South Africa. Why Has Poverty Persisted After Apartheid?* Johannesburg: Jacana. Analyses aspects of both neoliberal welfare state policy in post-1994 South Africa, persistent poverty and different perspectives on poverty and the effects of various welfare state measures to combat poverty.

References

Bond P. 2000. *Elite Transition: From Apartheid to Neoliberalism in South Africa.* Pietermaritzburg: University of Natal Press.

Booth C. 2004. 'Life and labour of the people of London' in *The Fin de Siècle: A Reader in Cultural History c 1880–1900.* Ledger S, Lockhurst R (eds). Oxford: Oxford University Press.

Budlender D. 1999. 'Patterns of poverty in South Africa'. *Development Southern Africa*, 16(2): 197–219.

Chita-Mabugu M, Mupela E, Ngwenya P, Zikhali P. 2016. 'Inequality, poverty and the state: The case of South Africa 2006–2011' in Plaatjies D, Chita-Mabugu M, Hongoro C, Meyiwa T, Nkondo M, Nyamnjoh F (eds). *State of the nation. South Africa: Who is in Charge? Mandates, Accountability and Contestations in the South African State.* Pretoria: HSRC Press.

Davenport TRH, Saunders C. 2000. *South Africa: A Modern History.* 5th ed. New York; London: Macmillan.

Everatt D. 2003. 'The politics of poverty'. *Development Update*, 4(3): 75–100.

Frye I. 2005. *Constructing and Adopting an Official Poverty Line for South Africa: Some Issues for Consideration.* Cape Town: NALEDI.

Fukuda-Parr S, Shiva Kumar AK (eds). 2005. *Readings in Human Development: Concepts, Measures and Policies for a Development Paradigm.* New York: Oxford University Press.

Giddens A, Sutton P. 2017. *Sociology.* 8th ed. Cambridge: Polity Press.

Gumede V. 2006. 'Research missed poverty line'. *The Star*, 18 April.

Harvey D. 2005. *A Brief History of Neoliberalism.* Oxford: Oxford University Press.

IRIN. 2010. 'South Africa: Inequality not so black and white. 8 February'. [Online] Available at: http://irinnews.org/Report.aspx?ReportId=88038 [Accessed 20 August 2011].

Jahan S. 2005. 'Evolution of the Human Development Index' in *Readings in Human Development: Concepts, Measures and Policies for a Development Paradigm.* Fukuda-Parr S, Shiva Kumar AK (eds). New York: Oxford University Press.

Laderchi CR, Saith R, Stewart F. 2003. 'Does it matter that we don't agree on the definition of poverty? A comparison of four approaches'. *QEH Working Paper Series.* Oxford: University of Oxford. [Online] Available at: http://www.qeh.ox.ac.uk/RePEc/qehwps/qehwps107.pdf [Accessed 26 July 2011].

Ledger S, Lockhurst R. 2004. *The Fin de Siècle: A Reader in Cultural History c 1880–1900.* Oxford: Oxford University Press.

Lister R. 2004. *Poverty.* London: Polity Press.

Magasela W. 2006. 'Towards a Constitution-based definition of poverty in post-apartheid South Africa' in *State of the Nation; South Africa 2005–2006.* Buhlungu S, Daniel J, Southall R, Lutchman J (eds). Cape Town: HSRC Press, 46–66.

Mandela N. 1994. Statement of the President of the African National Congress, Nelson Mandela, at his inauguration as President of the democratic Republic of South Africa. Union Buildings, Pretoria, 10 May 1994. [Online] Available at: http://www.africa.upenn.edu/Articles_Gen/Inaugural_Speech/17984.html [Accessed 28 June 2011].

Marais H. 2001. *South Africa. Limits to Change. The Political Economy of Transition.* London: Zed Books.

May J. 1998. 'Poverty and inequality in South Africa'. Report prepared for the Office of the Executive Deputy President and the Inter-Ministerial Committee of Poverty and Inequality. Durban: Praxis Publishing.

Mbeki M, Mbeki N. 2016. *A Manifesto for Social Change. How to Save South Africa.* Johannesburg: Picador Africa.

Meijer K. 2016. 'Get a glimpse of a day in the life of an innovative recycler'. *Centurion Rekord*, 22 April, 5.

Mosoetsa S. 2011. *Eating from One Pot. The Dynamics of Survival in Poor South African Households.* Johannesburg: Wits University Press.

NALEDI. 2007. *Fighting Poverty in South Africa. A Reader for Civil Society.* Johannesburg: National Labour and Economic Development Institute.

Netshitenzhe J. 2003. 'Government spending has reduced spending sharply. The Gini coefficient ordinarily does not capture the impact of the social wage'. *THISDAY*, 10 November, 11.

Nicolson G. 2015. 'South Africa: Where 12 million live in extreme poverty'. *Daily Maverick*, 3 February.

Noble M, Ratcliffe A, Wright G. 2004. *Conceptualizing, Defining and Measuring Poverty in South Africa: An Argument for a Consensual Approach.* Oxford: Centre for the Analysis of South African Social Policy, Oxford University.

Organisation for European Cooperation and Development (OECD). 2001. *The DAC Guidelines. Poverty Reduction.* Paris: OECD Publications.

Pretoria News. 2014. 'Big fall in SA poverty – Lehohla'. 4 April, 2.

Poverty Analysis Discussion Group. 2012. *Understanding Poverty and Wellbeing. A Note with Implications for Research and Policy.*

Randall P (ed). 1972. 'Power, privilege and poverty'. Report of the Economics Commission of the Study Project on Christianity in Apartheid Society, Johannesburg.

Republic of South Africa (RSA). 1996. The Constitution of the Republic of South Africa Act 108 of 1996. Pretoria: Government Printer.

Seekings J, Natrass N. 2016. *Poverty, Politics & Policy in South Africa. Why has Poverty Persisted after Apartheid?* Johannesburg: Jacana.

South African Institute of Race Relations (SAIRR). 2001. *South Africa Survey 2000/2001.* Johannesburg: SAIRR.

South African Institute of Race Relations (SAIRR). 2005. *South Africa Survey 2004/2005.* Johannesburg: SAIRR.

South African Institute of Race Relations (SAIRR). 2009. *South Africa Survey 2008/2009.* Johannesburg: SAIRR.

South African Institute of Race Relations (SAIRR). 2010. *South Africa Survey 2009/2010.* Johannesburg: SAIRR.

South African Institute of Race Relations (SAIRR). 2012. *South Africa Survey 2011/2012.* Johannesburg: SAIRR.

South African Institute of Race Relations (SAIRR). 2017. *South Africa Survey 2017.* Johannesburg: SAIRR.

Southall R. 2016. *The New Black Middle Class in South Africa.* Johannesburg: Jacana.

Statistics SA (StatsSA). 2011. *Quarterly Labour Force Survey.* Quarter 3, 1 November. Pretoria: StatsSA.

Statistics SA (StatsSA). 2017. *Poverty Trends in South Africa.* Report No 03 10 06. Pretoria: StatsSA.

Studies in Poverty and Inequality Institute. 2007. 'The Measurement of Poverty in South Africa Project: Key Issues'. [Online] Available at: http://www.sarpn.org.za/documents/d0002801/index.php [Accessed 14 October 2013].

Terreblanche S. 2002. *A History of Inequality in South Africa, 1652–2002.* Pietermaritzburg: University of Natal Press.

The Sydney Morning Herald. 2009. '"Human calamity" warning amid crisis'. [Online] Available at: http://www.smn.com.au/business/human-calamity-warning-amid-crisis-20090427-akpr.html [Accessed 3 January 2018].

Townsend P. 1979. *Poverty in the United Kingdom. A Survey of Household Resources and Standards of Living.* London: Allen Lane.

Townsend P. 1993a. 'Conceptualising poverty' in *The International Analysis of Poverty.* Townsend P. New York: Harvester Wheatsheaf.

Townsend P. 1993b. 'A theory of poverty' in *The International Analysis of Poverty.* Townsend P. New York: Harvester Wheatsheaf.

United Nations. 2015. *The Millennium Development Goals Report 2015.* New York: United Nations.

United Nations Development Programme. 2001. *Millennium Development Goals.* [Online] Available at: http://www.undp.org/mdg/basics.shtml [Accessed 2 April 2009].

United Nations Development Programme. 2003. *South Africa Human Development Report 2003. The Challenge of Sustainable Development in South Africa: Unlocking People's Creativity.* Oxford: Oxford University Press.

United Nations Development Programme. 2016. *Human Development Report 2016. Human Development for Everyone.* New York: United Nations.

Van der Berg S, Louw M, Yu D. 2008. 'Post-transition poverty trends based on an alternative data source'. *South African Journal of Economics*, 76(1): 58–76.

Wilson F. 2000. 'Addressing poverty and inequality' in *After the TRC. Reflections on Truth and Reconciliation in South Africa.* James W, Van Deventer L (eds). Cape Town: David Philip.

Wilson F, Mamphela R. 1989. *Uprooting Poverty. The South African Challenge.* Report of the Second Carnegie Inquiry into poverty and development in Southern Africa. New York: WW Norton.

Crime and deviance

Tapiwa Chagonda & Muhammed Suleman

Crime is anti-social behaviour which has serious social effects. Sociology understands acts of crime as a form of social deviance which violates norms and cultural standards generally accepted within a significant section of the community within which the crimes take place. Crime results from a variety of factors, not all of which can be explained within even the vast scope of sociology. The specialised study of crime, called criminology, is consequently multifaceted, complex, goes well beyond sociology and involves a range of disciplines. Questions as to who commits crime, why they do so, criminal capacity, statistics on crime, the different kinds of crime committed and the factors contributing to crime have resulted in a plethora of theories. These theories have emerged from not only sociology, but also out of the disciplines of biology, psychology and economics. The legal definition of crime is simple: a crime is a crime because the law defines it as such. Getting to the root of crime and deviance is, however, considerably more difficult.

The introduction to this chapter confirms the complexity attending the study of crime and deviance. At the risk of over-simplification, research shows that the majority of socially visible crimes are disproportionally committed by unmarried, young, urban-based males, a small proportion of whom are repeat offenders. Violent criminal offences increase in relation to the number of crimes a person commits. Nearly half of crimes committed in South Africa are violent and aggressive. A third of crimes are of a less socially visible economic nature. It is the capacity for aggression and violence and its deeply seated roots, where the problem of defining, explaining and understanding crime generally starts. As the case study at the beginning of this chapter clearly shows, brutalisation of the young is often the first step in the social recipe for the escalation of the development of criminal capacity in the biography of an individual. Central to understanding this process is the moral development, or lack thereof, in the socialisation of children. Yet how are we to understand the role of the lack of normative and moral standards in society when it comes to white collar fraud, theft and corruption? This crime is called white collar crime as it is usually committed within office environments and for personal gain.

In order to introduce the key aspects of a difficult topic to study, the first part of the chapter grapples with the definitions of crime and deviance. It then discusses the consequences associated with crime and deviance, social stigma for instance. The second part of the chapter interrogates the various sociological theories of crime and deviance. The major theoretical perspectives covered here are the functionalist, sub-cultural, conflict and interactionist paradigms. The contention is that post-apartheid South Africa has become an exclusive society. Our society is riddled with high levels of poverty, increasing levels of inequality between the rich and the poor and high levels of unemployment in a country still very largely divided by *spatial* apartheid. This social context explains much for the significant degree and extent of criminal activity in South Africa. That we continue to live in a society characterised by spatial apartheid means, of course, that crime affects different social and racial groups to different degrees. The nature and extent of crime – as well as forms of deviance – will express itself differently whether one lives in a suburban gated community, an inner-city high-rise complex, on a farm, in a rural community or in a township. In short, however, the poor experience crime to a far greater extent than other social groups.

The penultimate section in the chapter contends that social control that might curtail criminal and deviant activities can be enforced through conformity and obedience. This section argues, however, that in some instances, obedience to authority or conformity towards certain norms can be harmful, especially if the orders from the authority figures are questionable or unethical. The same applies to certain norms that might be considered wrong or inappropriate in the context in which they are applied.

If the chapter has had criminal activity among the youth as its focus, sight must not be lost of what one might call, perhaps controversially, the 'real criminals' – middle and upper middle class 'white collar' criminals engaged in fraud and corruption involving considerable amounts of money. Such criminal activity is often hard to detect, inevitably involves protracted legal procedures and is often unseen, yet robs society of badly needed resources, usually of a financial nature.

Finally, the chapter closes by reflecting on South Africa's high crime rate and notes that violent crimes are a huge problem which requires urgent and serious attention from the state and broader society.

Case study 23.1 Pre-sentence assessment of a young offender

The following case study is about a young adolescent, Joseph Hlongwane, who was recently charged for aggravated assault. The information was taken from a criminal capacity assessment report compiled by a forensic social worker at the local Magistrate's Court in Bloemfontein.

During the pre-sentencing interview, Joseph Hlongwane told the forensic social worker that he had a very difficult childhood. His biological father used physical force to discipline, intimidate, control and hurt both Joseph and his mother. This ranged from psychological intimidation to physical attacks to force obedience and respect. For the five-year-old Joseph, this situation was both frightening and humiliating and he quickly learned that submission brought relief. When asked to describe his most prominent feelings during this time, Joseph said: 'I am worthless, I hate them!' The violence only stopped when Ann Hlongwane divorced Joseph's dad and they moved elsewhere. When Joseph Hlongwane was 10, he transferred to a local junior school. He quickly got a reputation for being a 'bad kid' and many of his schoolmates remembered him for hitting a schoolteacher during an argument when Joseph refused to do as he was told. Due to this incident, Joseph was the subject of a school disciplinary hearing. He was suspended from school for three months after which he returned to school. He began to carry a knife to school which he used to victimise other children and extort money and goods. He used the money to buy drugs and alcohol. Meanwhile his grades were going down. He started skipping school to hang out with a group of older anti-social boys from his neighbourhood. Under the pressure of his friends, Joseph started to break into cars to steal radios and other items. He quickly graduated to vehicle theft. Although he was never caught, everybody knew he was involved in illegal activities. He became known as a 'gangster' by others in his neighbourhood. Joseph enjoyed the feeling and sense of power that came from being associated with a gang of thugs. He was also becoming increasingly aggressive towards his mother, Ann, and stepfather, Sam Radebe. This led to various arguments and family conflict. Sam felt that it was a mistake to ever have Joseph at home. Ann, on the other hand, kept on pleading on Joseph's behalf saying that it was puberty, a phase he would eventually get over. One night, Joseph came home under the influence of alcohol. Sam had had enough and threw Joseph out of the house and told him never to come home again. Joseph took out his knife and threatened to stab Sam. The two got into a physical struggle. In the ensuing scuffle Joseph stabbed his stepfather in the shoulder. The police were called by a neighbour and Joseph was taken into custody. A case was opened and the 14-year-old Joseph was charged with aggravated assault.

Key themes

- Defining crime and deviance
- Theoretical perspectives of crime and deviance
- Crime, poverty and social exclusion
- Mechanisms of enforcing social control
- Explanations for the high crime rate in South Africa.

23.1 Introduction

The above case of a troubled young adolescent illustrates the complexity of deviance and crime. What do we know about offenders? From the case study we note importantly that the crimes committed were by a young male. This is generally the case regarding socially visible crimes. In the words of Heidensohn 'gender is the single most important variable in criminality' (1988: 91). The fact that females make up only 4 per cent of prison population's worldwide, show that males are convicted more often than females, and more often than not for serious offences. Secondly, crime is a youthful activity, or as Smith & Rutter attest, 'an important fact about crime is that it is committed mainly by teenagers and young adults' (Smith & Rutter 1995: 395). The case study reflects the tendency of 15- to 25-year-olds committing more crime than any other comparable age group. This curve, which for individuals typically peaks in the late teen years, highlights the tendency for crime to be committed during the offender's younger years and to decline as age advances (Blumstein 1995: 3).

In the literature, data represented in this way represents the **criminal trajectories** of offenders. Criminal trajectory research makes a distinction between Life Course Persistent (LCP) offenders and Adolescence Limited (AL) offenders. AL offenders will engage in criminal behaviour for the duration of adolescence and will then cease such activities. The criminal behaviour of LCP offenders is, according to Moffitt (cited in Blokland et al 2005), rooted in early childhood factors: neurological difficulties and failing parent–child relationships set a small number of individuals on a life path of anti-social behaviour (Muntingh & Gould 2010). Violent offenders tend to be versatile rather than specialised and

thus commit a wide range of offences. They also exhibit other problems such as heavy drinking, drug use, have unstable employment records and are often sexually promiscuous. For violent offenders, the likelihood of committing a violent offence increases steadily with the total number of offences already committed. In other words, over time more of their total number of offences will be violent offences, suggesting that intervention at an early stage (when it becomes clear that a pattern is developing) may break the pattern of the criminal trajectory. Moving beyond these crucial variables of gender and age, we find more complex factors associated with the likelihood of committing crime. For example, differential association theory posits that delinquency, like much other behaviour, is learned in interaction with others in the process of communication patterns found in intimate groups. Young people who are strongly attached to their parents or their school, coupled with high educational and career aspirations, are less likely to become criminal offenders. Young people who do poorly at school, or have friends who are criminals, are more likely to resort to crime. Furthermore, crime is disproportionately committed by unmarried people, by people living in large cities and those living in areas of high residential mobility. One other aspect consistent with research to add is that while of the male population who are convicted, a much smaller proportion is convicted *repeatedly*. In other words, a small minority is responsible for high rates of repeat offending. For the sake of comparison, Table 23.1 gives a detailed breakdown of the major crime categories, the number of un-sentenced offenders, the number of sentenced offenders and totals per crime category for South Africa in 2011.

Table 23.1 Categories of crimes committed

Crime categories	Un-sentenced	Sentenced	Total
Aggressive	22 914	61 974	84 888
Economic	15 025	25 591	40 616
Sexual	6 578	18 084	24 662
Narcotics	1 437	2 698	4 135
Other	1 950	4 953	6 903
Total	47 904	113 300	161 204

(Source: Basic Statistical Report 2011)

From this table sourced from the Management Information System of the South African Department of Correctional

Services (Table 23.1), it can be seen that there were 161 204 offenders were incarcerated in the South African Department of Correctional Services. Statistically this table can be read as follows regarding the different categories of crime in 2011:

- 45.1 per cent were crimes of a violent or aggressive nature
- 33.1 per cent were crimes of an economic nature
- 8.3 per cent were crimes of a sexual nature
- 2.6 per cent were crimes involving narcotics.

Looking at these statistics, it is evident that by far the largest category and percentage (45.1 per cent) of crimes committed in South Africa were of a violent and aggressive nature. The second highest category or percentage (33.1 per cent) of crimes was of an economic nature. Crimes of an aggressive nature, in general refers to a wide variety of acts that involve attack, hostility, abuse and violence. According to the Diagnostic and Statistical Manual of Mental Disorders (American Psychiatric Association 1994), acts of aggression are typically motivated by any of the following:

- Fear or frustration in the aggressor
- A desire to produce fear or flight in others
- A tendency of aggressors to assert their own ideas, needs or interests at the cost of others.

When studying the crime categories of offenders who entered the **criminal justice system** and eventually ended up in prison in 2011, it is evident that most offenders had been incarcerated during this time for violent, aggressive or economic crimes.

Regarding economic crimes, in 2014, a report found that 69 per cent of organisations had been victims. The most prominent forms of economic crime were asset misappropriation, procurement fraud, bribery and corruption, and cyber fraud. While the last category of economic crime, cyber fraud, was on a par with international trends, all other categories were higher in South Africa (Global Economic Crime Survey 2016). Such 'white collar' or office-related crime we might refer to as largely *socially occluded* (hidden or invisible) crime. This chapter, however, has what we might call *socially evident* (socially felt or visible) crime as its main focus.

23.2 Defining deviance and crime

Deviance refers to behaviour that violates norms of a particular society. It refers to behaviour that goes against what is expected of people *in a particular society* (Schaefer 2013: 174). Someone wearing a swimming costume to a wedding is considered deviant. In such a situation, one would expect someone to wear a formal suit or dress. At the same time, one should remember that norms are not always universal. This means that different societies adhere to different norms. In South Africa, for example, a man who comes from a Zulu ethnic background, can have multiple wives. In 2010, President Zuma was criticised by the British media for having multiple wives, as bigamy (being married to two wives) and polygamy (having more than two wives) are illegal in the United Kingdom (Diffin 2010). In addition to not being universal, norms in one society can also change over time. This means that norms are not stagnant as they are always evolving within societies and do so differently. The apartheid government introduced the Prohibition of Mixed Marriages Act 1949, which prevented a white person from marrying anyone who was defined as non-white. Yet in 1985, that law was changed and interracial marriages became legal (SA History 2016).

In addition to norms not being universal, who decides what is right and wrong should also be questioned. It is often those who are in power and possess high status in society who decide what is right and wrong in a particular society. The normative attitudes of social elites generally become institutionalised. In the United States, for example, for many years, cigarette smoking was considered normal, despite clear medical evidence showing that smoking harms the health of individuals. Smoking was considered acceptable because of the power wielded by those who manufactured tobacco (Schaefer 2013). In South Africa, incidentally, the Tobacco Products Control Act 83 of 1993 (as amended) and subsequent Notices laid down rules and regulations regarding smoking in workplaces, public buildings, restaurants and even in your own car if transporting a child under the age of 12. If you break any of these regulations you are engaging in a criminal activity. You are not just being deviant, even if you are not caught, charged and prosecuted due to some of these laws being difficult to enforce.

If crime is easily defined in the legal system, deviance is less readily defined. Sometimes being deviant and even criminal, are necessary. Take Nelson Mandela, Steve Biko, Winnie Mandela, Oliver Tambo, Robert Sobukwe, Ahmed Kathrada and many other people who were part of the liberation movement. These political stalwarts and others did not agree with the norms and values of apartheid South Africa. They were considered deviant by the apartheid regime. They also broke many laws on purpose. Yet apartheid norms and legislation deviated from widely accepted international norms and laws. Sometimes conforming to particular norms in a certain context is considered harmful. For example, in some sections of South African society – as found elsewhere in Africa and Asia according to a study conducted in 2000 by the United Nations Population Fund (UNPFA) – it is considered acceptable for a husband to beat up his wife. Consequently, even if the wife is badly injured, people will often not question the norm. In this instance, *those questioning the rights of husbands* will be considered deviant (Rasool & Hochfeld 2005).

While the deviant and illegal behaviour of those involved in the liberation struggle in South Africa clearly served our society positively, in the majority of cases, deviance is viewed negatively. Often, those who deviate from accepted norms are stigmatised. After a former South Africa national cricket team captain, Hansie Cronje, was found guilty of and admitted to match fixing, he was always referred to as 'the disgraced' former Proteas cricket captain (Chapman 2012). Put simply, deviant behaviour has social effects for the individuals concerned.

While crime and deviance are often confused, there is a distinction to be made between the two phenomena. As already noted, crime refers to actions that break the laws of a country. If found guilty, a criminal offender will be punished by the criminal justice system of that country. Note that what may be a crime in one country is not necessarily a crime in the legal system of other countries. How is crime though different to deviance within a society? A person bunking school or talking in class is deviant, although pretty minor depending on the age of the learner. The learner is not, however, breaking any laws. Infringing on a school rule such as this is generally not a crime. Therefore, deviance is a much broader concept than crime. Deviance includes crime. In other words, sociologists recognise that all criminal acts are deviant and yet not all deviant acts are criminal. (Delinquency generally refers to acts of deviance and anti-social behaviour committed by adolescents.) Societies often use statistics in how they define or understand deviance. This is a misconception. If, for instance, someone has bathed three times a day, they are not harming anyone and yet they might be deemed to be deviant in the eyes of other people (Goode 1994). The most important aspect sociologists need to consider is that it is *society that decides* what is deviant and what is not (Haralambos & Holborn 2000).

The following sections will focus on some of the key theoretical frameworks that are helpful in understanding how crime and deviance occur in society.

23.3 Functionalist perspectives on deviance

Functionalist theorists focus on shared norms and values in society. They argue that a widely shared and generally accepted normative framework is a prerequisite for any society to maintain a sense of stability. If everyone in society agrees on which norms and values they should aspire towards, then social order is maintained. Bearing this in mind, one would think functionalists would view deviance negatively and yet this is not the case.

23.3.1 Deviance as functional for society

Functionalists argue that deviance is a necessary part of society, which contributes to the wellbeing of any society. Durkheim (1938) argued that crime is 'inevitable'. People come from different social backgrounds and are exposed to different circumstances. Hence, deviance is bound to happen, as not everyone will conform to norms in the same manner. To illustrate this contention, Durkheim imagined a 'society of saints'. Individuals in such as society would be considered perfect. Yet even in such an imaginary society, one would find deviance occurring as the standards set would be so high that the smallest mistake would be considered deviant. For example, if someone shares a different opinion they would be considered deviant. In addition to viewing deviance as consequently being inevitable, functionalists also consider deviance to be part of how society works and develops as norms and values change.

History teaches us that society cannot remain the same. Often those who made great scientific discoveries, especially in 17th and 18th century Europe, were considered deviant as they broke with the dominant theological and normative views of the world. Similarly, for society to progress, social norms also need to change and are indeed part of the process of change. Society needs to have different voices. While collective sentiments are important to maintain order, too great an adherence to collective sentiments prevents people from coming up with new ideas or opposing oppressive restrictions, neither of which benefits society. Therefore, a certain amount of deviance is required. The collective sentiments of society need to make room for this, even though political leaders, both of high moral and ethical standing, in this instance, Nelson Mandela and Martin Luther King Junior had to fight for their ideas which deviated from the accepted norms in their societies. On such grounds, Émile Durkheim and functionalists who have followed him have argued that deviance paves the way for a new morality and guiding sets of norms.

While arguing that deviance is necessary, functionalists have further argued that degrees and levels of deviance should not get out of control. As you know from your study of Durkheim, the absence of norms or anomie or a sense of normlessness results in the breakdown of social cohesion in society. The level of deviance should, therefore, be kept at a moderate level. The mechanism to ensure this is punishment so that collective sentiments are not completely disregarded (Graaff, Van Aswegen, Thomson 2002).

An American sociologist, Albert Cohen (1966), developed Durkheim's ideas. Cohen cited further social functions of deviance. He argued that deviance can act as a safety valve for society. People can express dissatisfaction with society without fundamentally disrupting the social order. The many protest marches, social service delivery protests especially, in South Africa could be taken as an example of collective actions which deviate from the normal daily order, but which signal that there is something wrong is society and act as a warning device (Haralambos & Holborn 2000). If people are stealing or children are engaging in unacceptable levels of truancy, it means something is wrong in a particular society. In these cases the source of the deviance can be addressed in order to solve the problem. When something goes wrong, people share their concerns and this strengthens the social solidarity of that community (Graaff et al 2002). Our current decolonial theoretical moment in South Africa since the #RhodesMustFall and #FeesMustFall campaigns of university students in 2015 and 2016, which stressed the need for the *disruption* of colonial norms and practices – which was a call for a 'new normal' social transformation – can be seen in this light.

Previous studies on deviance had focused on the individual. Individuals engaging in deviance were viewed as suffering from some form of psychological illness. Functionalists adopted a contrasting approach by focusing their analyses of deviance on society, instead of the individual. Robert Merton (1968), for instance, built on the works of Durkheim by developing a modified functionalist theoretical paradigm. Merton did not agree that deviance was a consequence of individual mental instability. His focus was *value consensus* and *normative* values in society. In other words, following Durkheim, his starting point was societal and normative, or *society as normative*. Merton advanced previous functionalist structuralist analyses as he argued that in any society, while members might largely share the same values and goals, they do not have the same opportunities to achieve these goals. Therefore, materially disadvantaged groups deviate from accepted norms in order to achieve their goals. When a dominant set of ideas or norms such as following the 'American dream' of success and wealth as in the society Merton studied, yet which not everyone is able to achieve due to the lack of resources, then people will often use any means necessary to achieve these goals. This can lead to scenarios in which norms are no longer followed. The overall result is a state of uncertainty due to the onset of normlessness or **anomie**.

When this occurs, deviant responses are most likely to occur according to Robert Merton's theory of structural strain (1968). Structural strain occurs where the *means* to which people have access – such as a job – are insufficient to meet the goals they wish to achieve – such as material success. The five forms of response Merton identified below, though interpreted somewhat differently to the way in which he applied his typology to American society, it is suggested, will differ very largely in social groups depending on their access to their means in relation to their goals.

Conformity

Over the long term, despite being punctuated by disruptions, economic distress, social upheavals and wars, human society is generally characterised by different degrees of order. Were it not so, human society would not have been able to produce its basic needs for survival. The need to conform is a strong one. Conformity entails people using socially prescribed means to achieve their aims and goals. Most people, across social groups, adhere to social conventions, the norms inculcated through successful socialisation and commonly accepted behaviours born of the strength of peer pressure, learning, habit and tradition. In short, most people conform to accepted standards, practices and the ways things are done in their immediate social context. For example, most readers of this textbook would hold to the belief that hard work (a means) will be rewarded and pays off in the long run as hard work achieves set goals. Predominantly socioeconomically middle class or aspiring to this social class in a context where education promises upward social mobility, most readers will hope to graduate from university, become self-employed or get a job, get married, buy a car and pay a bond on a house as the rest of an educated middle class has long done. Statistically speaking, you will probably try to live a useful, ordered and very largely a disciplined life, have children and hopefully grandchildren who will finally bury and remember you. Similarly, people who are poor or working-class poor, but who work hard are hopeful that if they persist in conforming to the ethic of hard work, life will improve.

Innovation

Merton suggested 'innovators' are those who adhere to the goals of society, such as success and the attainment of wealth especially, but do not have the means to achieve these socially accepted goals. They consequently reject the means, such as the belief in hard work which is rewarded, to achieve those goals. Such 'innovators' need to find ways of achieving social goals despite their lack of means or resources. This response is one most likely to come from people who form part of the working or poorer classes, because they lack the available means to achieve success goals. The jobs they occupy do not pay them enough money and so is an insufficient resource (means) to achieve what they may want or realise their goals. People who fall into this category are likely to feel more pressure to deviate from accepted norms. Hence, they are more likely than other social groups to resort to crime, such as pilfering from their employer, housebreaking and entry, petty or vehicle theft, or drug trafficking. Where such forms of deviant behaviour become accepted within segments of a population, this reinforces the rejection of norms such as that theft is wrong (Graaff et al 2003). Among the working poor this can also be seen as a *survivalist* strategy where people feel they have no choice but to break norms, which they may even continue to believe.

Ritualists

Those who accept the *means* to achieving socially accepted *goals*, but which prove insufficient do not relinquish their beliefs that hard work is rewarded for instance, but instead lower their expectations of what they can achieve. These individuals are people who are often socioeconomically middle class. They have steady jobs, yet these jobs do not pay them enough. Hence, they cannot achieve the goals they set out to achieve. At the same time, they have strongly internalised the norms of society. Consequently, they abandon their goals, or become more modest in the goals they try to achieve and stick to and appreciate the means they have. But by abandoning accepted social goals, they are still deviant as they have deviated from what is widely considered worthy of achieving. Many young middle-class married couples, for instance, not only locally but globally, discover that the price of owning their own house is beyond their means. They continue the daily ritual of keeping down their jobs, but relinquish the dream of becoming homeowners.

Retreatism

Statistically, this is the smallest social group that displays deviant forms of behaviour. Retreatists, in Merton's five-fold typology, are those who have fallen into the indigent or underclass in society. They have become homeless, are perhaps chronically addicted to alcohol or drugs so are unable to hold down the job they had and hence become beggars or vagabonds. Having been unable to succeed, they have ended up rejecting their previously internalised

normative standards regarding both the means and beliefs of society and its goals. Unable to achieve their goals, they retreat and drop out of society, socially isolating themselves in the process. Their failure to have achieved what they wanted to or to make a success of their lives may have been due to a wide variety of reasons, both individual and structural, or be a combination of factors. Such people are deviant because they reject *the means* to achieve the socially accepted goals in which they once might have believed. They consequently go on also to reject *the goals* which seems to be of no use to them anymore (Haralambos & Holborn 2000; Graaff et al 2003).

Rebellion

Those who resist and rebel against both the means and the goals of society can be members of classes across social groups. This is not Merton's view, but seems more applicable in our context. Often these are individuals who are members of a rising socioeconomic class who do not agree with the present state of society. Or they might be from militant working-class communities. Or they may be from criminal segments of society who feel they stand above and are independent of generally accepted norms and values. Empirical investigation would be required to test this view. The point is that such groups reject *the means* to achieve success goals. Unlike those who retreat, they endeavour to revolutionise society – or their own social and economic positions – by creating *new* goals and means (Graaff et al 2003).

Criticisms and defences of Merton's theory of structural strain

Some sociologists, noted in Haralambos' and Holborn's classic Sociology textbook (2000), have disagreed with Merton's views and they have raised the following issues:

Merton is accused by Steve Taylor (1971) of not considering the power dynamics at play in society. Taylor agrees that Merton does not consider that it is the political and economic elites in society, located in the apex of government and business hierarchies, who powerfully influence the shaping of values and norms of a particular society. Via the exercise of economic and political power, elites facilitate institutional mechanisms which make rules and regulations. This ensures the continuation and success of their social group. The norms and values are met and disseminated at the expense of other social classes. The 'rules of the game' which favour the interests of the elites are consequently not fair as they ensure only a certain category of people can win. This becomes internalised within society and are seemingly natural as captured in the expression 'life is not fair'.

Merton's theory has also been criticised for being too narrow in the sense that he assumes people who suffer from anomie will commit crimes. There are perhaps poor or working class people who suffer from anomie yet they do not commit any crimes or act in a deviant way. He also does not consider politically motivated crimes – such as challenging the state under apartheid – because the focus of his theory is on material rewards. Merton is also accused of *exaggerating* the crimes committed by the working class and *underestimating* the occurrence of white-collar crime in society. Furthermore, along with other structuralist functionalist theorists, Merton has been criticised for assuming that everyone in the United States, which was the society he studied, shares the same values. We saw in Chapter 1 on sociological theory that black scholarship pointed this out many decades ago.

Robert Reiner (1984) has come to the defence of Merton. Reiner argues that Merton did not ignore white-collar crime. He indicated that people become so driven by material success that they are not satisfied with what they have. Hence, they will use any means necessary to increase their wealth, including deviance and crime. While acknowledging that not everyone aspires to the same values in American society, these success values are shared to an extent that they account for working class crime. The criticism regarding political crimes, Reiner further suggests, can be addressed using the rebellious response to anomie.

23.4 Sub-cultural theories on deviance

Like functionalists, sub-cultural theorists explain deviance from a societal perspective. According to sub-cultural theorists such as Albert Cohen (1955) and Walter Miller, people who belong to disadvantaged socioeconomic groups, such as working class people, hold norms and values which have traditionally, over many years, qualitatively *differed* from the mainstream norms and values of a particular society. Hence, such social groups come to constitute a sub-culture within society. For example, certain social groups may admire, bestow status on and even reward criminal activity. This occurs, for instance, in the Western Cape where many young people, as well as others, admire gangsters whose criminal activity is intimately bound up with the local economy. Such criminal activity, in all likelihood, will, however, be disapproved of by mainstream society – especially when it becomes excessively violent. Individuals

belonging to these groups will seem very similar to members of the broader society, yet their behaviour, which is a result of adhering to distinctive norms and values of a particular group, differentiates them as deviant members of that society.

The following sections discuss different strands of sub-cultural theories.

23.4.1 A delinquent sub-culture

Albert Cohen (1955) modified the work of the functionalist, Robert Merton. Like Merton, he argued that deviance was a result of a discrepancy between goals and means. He argued that deviance was a response of a particular collective or social group, as opposed to Merton who had consensus around values as broadly shared across society, as a key focus. While the youth in society might aspire to achieving similar goals – popularity, celebrity status and financial success for instance – due to belonging to different social groups in society, it becomes difficult for them to achieve these goals. For example, young people from a working-class background and poorer schools and who often do not have jobs that allow them to achieve materialist goals are more likely to become delinquent. As a result of the lack of good schooling or access to jobs, they suffer from status frustration. In order to deal with this status frustration, they form groups with a sub-culture that includes norms and values which are different from society. They create goals and norms that allow them to achieve social recognition, status and even glory, so as to increase their self-esteem. Yet these norms and values fall outside those of society more broadly and are not in agreement with generally accepted societal norms and values. What broader society rejects, they accept. Truancy and disturbing the peace or membership of a gang are seen as legitimate means towards goals. Hence, they develop a delinquent sub-culture. Adhering to these norms and values, seen as delinquent from the mainstream normative value framework, brings joy to these individuals and increases their prestige among peers. This joy and prestige absolves them of the status frustration they experienced. What we notice here is that Cohen does not only focus on deviance committed to achieve material goals. We see sub-cultures formed that place high value on deviance such a disturbing the peace and rioting, which in general disrupts respectable middle-class life.

Cohen was criticised by theorists such as Steven Box (1981; 2000) who argued that his theory is only applicable to a small category of people in society. Instead of individuals or social groups suffering from status frustration, Box felt that those who come from a lower-class background behaved in a delinquent way because they did not agree with the norms and values, not of those held generally by society at large, but specifically of those who come from the upper strata of society.

23.4.2 Different types of sub-cultures

Richard Cloward and Lloyd Ohlin (1961), in advancing and differing from Albert Cohen's views, and working within Merton's theory of structural strain argued that individuals belonging to the ranks of the working class face more stress to deviate due to limited opportunities – especially that there are insufficient jobs (means). As a result of being blocked due to the lack of opportunities, an illegitimate opportunity structure emerges beyond the legitimate one where jobs are available. This can happen to working class youth, boys especially, who do succeed at school and do not become delinquent at school, but afterwards due to the lack of jobs which pushes them towards deviance and crime. These two theorists defined three types of sub-cultures.

When there is a strong illegitimate opportunity structure, individuals will find themselves adhering to a *criminal sub-culture*. They learn via mentors how to succeed in this environment, for example how to steal or deal in drugs. If they are successful, they are 'promoted' to higher positions. Individuals subscribing to this sub-culture engage in deviance, which will result in them gaining financial rewards for example, property theft, money laundering and white-collar crime (Haralambos & Holborn 2000).

In areas where there is overpopulation, and where the community lacks cohesion, one finds *conflict sub-cultures* to be most prominent. In these areas, there is a chronic lack of an illegitimate opportunity structure, again, access to jobs being of crucial importance. This results in individuals being frustrated. They deal with this frustration by using the illegitimate structures which are available, such as joining gangs and engaging in forms of gang violence.

Finally, there is the *retreatist sub-culture*. Individuals who form part of this sub-culture are those who have failed in succeeding in *both* the legitimate and illegitimate opportunity structures. Hence, they socially exclude themselves from society. They isolate themselves because they view themselves as failures. They often engage in deviant activities related to substance abuse.

While the work of Cloward and Ohlin has been lauded for modifying the work of Merton and Cohen whose analyses on deviant sub-cultures are intricate, they are in turn criticised for assuming that everyone in American society wants to achieve materialistic goals. Their classic work, now over 70 years old, however, needs to be revisited in the light of massive unemployment in our society where

the legitimate opportunity structure, access to jobs in particular, is increasingly limited especially for the youth. The existence of criminal and conflict sub-cultures is not simply trying to achieve goals of material success or status, but sheer economic survival.

23.4.3 Working class sub-culture

The previous sections pointed out that lack of materialistic success led to the development of deviant sub-cultures. Yet, there are sociologists who argue that deviant sub-cultures are developed not because of a lack of materialistic goals but because these cultures are *inherently* deviant. As noted, Walter Miller (1962) argued that a working-class sub-culture consists of norms and values, which are not in harmony with that of other classes in society. Existing for generations, working class sub-cultures contain norms and values, which encourage individuals to break the law. Working class culture, Miller argued, places special emphasis on toughness, smartness and excitement. Toughness places importance on being physically strong and not showing signs of being soft. This can lead to individuals engaging in physical assault and violence towards another person. Smartness refers to showing how intelligent you are, compared to others. This often leads to people becoming thieves, hustlers or conmen. Excitement involves sexual escapades and partying all night long. Manifestations of these characteristics can result in property damage and endangering the lives of people. Walter Miller argued that working class people engaged in this type of behaviour because they were bored of the blue-collar (low-skilled work) they took part in. Delinquency was a result of individuals being socialised into such sub-cultures, which historically normalised deviant behaviour.

Miller's work has, however, come under question. He has been criticised for painting a false and misleading picture of working-class individuals, 'living in a bubble', where they have no interaction with people from other classes. To apply his or any other theory in the South African context would need empirical research to be undertaken to test the validity of these theories.

23.4.4 The underclass sub-culture

Globally and in South Africa the formally employed working class has been shrinking. A new group of individuals comprising of unemployed people constituting an 'underclass' has been on the increase. People belonging to the underclass, live a qualitatively different life compared to others in mainstream society. The policies of social services towards the underclass have, controversially, been seen as encouraging deviance. There is no incentive for recipients of grants to seek employment, it is held. Factors such as unemployment, dispirited job seekers, rising social inequality and the emergence of illegitimate opportunity structures are instead reasons which need to be more carefully investigated in our context for the development of an underclass. The decreasing need for unskilled labour due to marketisation and in increasingly vulnerable 'precariat' (see Standing 2011) – those who only have part-time or casual jobs – has especially led to people becoming members of the underclass.

In South Africa, one of the leading sociologists who has examined the work of the underclass is Jeremy Seekings, for whom the underclass '...comprises households whose members have little prospect of finding employment or, we might add, establishing other livelihood strategies that yield more than meagre earnings' (2014: 139).

Theories on the underclass sub-culture have come under criticism. Murray in particular has been severely criticised. Countries such as Sweden which have a strong welfare service have not seen an upsurge in crime. Moreover, single parenthood in London did not lead to an increase in crime. Often individuals have been singled out as scapegoats for the lack of proper state governance in society These two societies are well resourced, but the argument holds even for less well-resourced societies such as our society. In South Africa, where young women were singled out for falling pregnant in order to get a child grant, this 'teenage pregnancy myth' has been exploded by the Statistician-General (Lehohla 2017). Teenage pregnancy has instead been understood as the result of a considerably more complex set of social factors than simply blaming the victim (Panday et al 2009).

23.5 The conflict perspective on crime and deviance

The conflict theory on crime and deviance draws its ideas from Karl Marx's writings on class conflict in society. Marx argued that under the capitalist economic system, there was bound to be conflict between the bourgeoisie (capitalists) and the proletariat (the working class) because of the exploitative nature of capitalism. The conflict perspective argues that laws are crafted by those in power (the capitalist class) to protect their rights and interests (Siegel 2000). Thus, they define crime and deviance to suit their needs. Larry Siegel, for instance, argues that law-making is often an attempt by the powerful to coerce others into their morality, and this explains why criminal law does not represent a consistent application of societal values, but rather competing values and interests. Laws are, thus, not an expression of value consensus but a reflection of ruling class ideology.

You will recall that from a conflict standpoint, the state ultimately represents ruling class interests. The capitalist state defends and protects private property, which is at the heart of capitalism and rarely directly passes laws that threaten capitalists' profits overall and instead spend large amounts of money to attract investment. The state offers tax concessions, cheap loans and grants to foreign companies that invest in their countries, in addition to building expensive infrastructure to help these companies operate successfully.

While crime is widespread in all social strata, conflict theorists argue that most of the serious anti-social and predatory acts committed in industrial countries are corporate crimes (Siegel 2000). Corporate crime, which is largely invisible, is seen as doing more harm than street crime and yet street crime is seen as more serious, partly as it is more socially visible. Corporate crimes cost more money and more lives than street crime according to conflict theorists. Moreover, when white-collar fraud and crime is prosecuted, it is small businesses that are more likely to be taken to court as opposed to big corporates. For Marxists, under capitalism, there is differential justice and this is where suspects are treated differently based on their racial, ethnic, or social-class background.

Furthermore, crime is viewed as a natural outgrowth of capitalist society which generates crime for the following reasons:

- The capitalist mode emphasises the maximisation of profits and the accumulation of wealth.
- Economic self-interest rather than public duty motivates behaviour.
- Emphasis on private property means personal gain rather than collective wellbeing is encouraged.
- Competition is encouraged under capitalism, which means that individual achievements are prioritised at the expense of the interests of social groups.
- Competition breeds aggression, hostility, and particularly for the losers, frustration.

Despite the merits which the conflict perspective holds in explaining how crime is viewed and operates in a capitalist system, as with all theories, it is also open to criticism. For instance, feminists argue that Marxism ignores patriarchy and racism and places undue emphasis on class inequality in its explanation of crime in society. Marxists assume that communism would eradicate crime but this did not happen in attempts at establishing communist states such as in the former Soviet Union, Cuba and China. The contention that capitalism will always breed high corporate crime rates is also debateable, given the low levels of such kinds of crime in capitalist countries such as Switzerland. Marxists have countered these criticisms, however, by pointing out that 'actually existing socialist societies' fall short of the ideals of communism and that wealthy, advanced capitalist societies continue to depend on the exploitation of developing societies for their standards of living, including low rates of crime.

23.5.1 Corporate crime in South Africa
While the conflict perspective has also been criticised for having concentrated too much on corporate crime at the expense of other forms of crime, its extent in South Africa currently suggests this may not be the case in our context. The problem of illegal capital flight in South Africa has been a serious problem over the last three decades and longer. The usual mechanism for this form of corporate crime to take money illegally out of the country is mis-invoicing – generally by over-invoicing, that is by inflating the prices of goods. Under apartheid, between 1980 and 1983, illegal capital flight ran at around 5.4 per cent of gross domestic product (GDP). Under democracy, from 1994 until 2000, this increased to 9.2 per cent. Between 2001 and 2007 this figure increased to an average of 12 per cent. The responsibility for illegal capital flight across South Africa's borders lies squarely at the feet of primarily large corporations and those in mining in particular (Ashman, Fine & Newman 2011). This form of corporate crime is white-collar company fraud on a massive scale. This loss of money 'contributes to low levels of domestic investment, so perpetuating unemployment, inequality and domestic development' (Ashman, Fine & Newman 2011: 9).

23.6 The interactionist perspective
Thus far, the work discussed has focused on deviance occurring because of social forces preventing individuals from achieving materialistic goals. The interactionist perspective places emphasis on how individuals create meanings of what it means to be deviant. These meanings are taken into the interaction process. Therefore, individuals who are working class are more likely to be labelled as deviant. Meanings that people create are, however, not cast in stone. During social interaction individuals may come to modify how they understand the world around them, most especially when coming to appreciate the lack of life opportunities of those they previously considered to be deviant. The most prominent social interactionist theories are the *cultural transmission* theory, the *social disorganisation* theory and the *labelling theory*.

23.6.1 Cultural transmission theory
The cultural transmission theory was first coined by Edwin Sutherland (1883–1950). Sutherland argued that people engage in deviance because they learn deviant behaviour in the same way they learn how to conform to the norms of a particular society. They do not only learn how to perform an act, but they also learn the rationalisations and motives behind engaging in specific forms of behaviour and social actions. Interaction with groups such as our family and friends exposes us to different ways of behaving. Sutherland referred to the notion of **differential association** to explain his point. Whether we become deviant or not will importantly be powerfully influenced by those with whom we interact. If the groups we engage with encourage deviance, we are more likely to engage in deviance. For example, a talented football player who manifests the hallmark of becoming a superstar may fail to achieve their potential if found frequently interacting with groups who engage in crime and other forms of deviance. The opposite might well be the case if the social environment is one which encourages conformity (Shaefer 2013).

This theory has been criticised as it does not explain impulsive behaviour leading to deviant acts or behaviour, nor does it consider the background of an individual which in turn may or may not have enabled the control of impulsive desires. The theory cannot explain why some people from a poverty-stricken background might steal while others do not. The importance of Sutherland's early theory, however, is that it points to the power of social context and social interaction within particular contexts and environments as key to influencing participation in forms of crime and deviance.

23.6.2 Social disorganisation theory
This branch of interactionist theory was developed by Phillip Zimbardo (2007). Zimbardo conducted an experiment where he abandoned a car in two different neighbourhoods. In one neighbourhood the car was left alone for two weeks, except that one person closed the bonnet. In the other neighbourhood the car was completely stripped. Social disorganisation theorists such as Zimbardo attribute this stark difference to a lack of social cohesion. Where the community had broken down there would be lack of jobs and healthy social structures such as proper schools and stable families. In this context a car would be stripped. This often occurs when urbanisation occurs at an intense pace. As a result, people might resort to deviant behaviour. In a well-resourced community an abandoned car would be largely ignored. Individual deviant behaviour is consequently

explained squarely in terms of social disorganisation in those parts of society in which it is most likely to occur.

23.6.3   Labelling theory

As crime is a crime if the law stipulates it as such, so some sociologists think there is no such thing as a deviant act unless people witnessing it consider it to be deviant. For example, a husband or wife wearing no clothes in front of each other, will consider this normal behaviour. Yet if a stranger walks in, then the behaviour might be considered deviant. Thus, it is important to consider the context, the audience witnessing the act and the person committing the act. When such acts are witnessed the resulting deviant identity is what people will remember them for. The following stages occur in a person becoming a deviant:

1. A person is labelled deviant by society. He or she is ostracised. They experience social exclusion. Their family and friends do not want to have anything to do with them.

2. The social exclusion or rejection they experience is likely to lead to the labelled individual engaging in further acts of deviance, often as this translates into no longer being employable such as if one has a criminal record.

3. Such people are then more likely to interact with those who are similar to them. This will lead to them engaging in deviant behaviour because the only people who are accepting of them are those who engage in similar forms of deviance.

4. A deviant sub-culture, complete with its own norms and values, is formed.

This theory like all other sociological theories has come under criticism for suggesting that a specific social audience decides whether an act is deviant or not. In certain cases, an audience will determine whether something is wrong or right, for example, someone killing another person in self-defence. Yet, premediated murder does not require an audience. The norms of most societies will deem such an act as both deviant and criminal. Secondly, this theory does not explain why deviance occurs in the first place. We find individuals engaging in different types of deviant acts and of different degrees of seriousness in terms of their impact on society, from petty theft to premeditated murder. These differences require explanation.

This theory is criticised for being too deterministic. It takes away the power of individuals to make decisions. It does not mean that once a person is labelled as deviant, they will necessarily continue on a deviant path. Just as that individual chose to act in a deviant way, they can also choose

to stop acting in a deviant manner, whether the form of deviance constitutes a crime as defined in their society or not.

The final criticism of this theory stems from its failure to consider power dynamics in society. It fails to explain why some actions are deviant and others not. Why is it that young brawlers in a township are considered deviant, yet a brawl in Sandton might be considered as youngsters letting off steam? Why is it that smoking marijuana is deviant, yet smoking cigarettes is considered normal? This is largely because it is the people who wield power in society who determine and decide what is deviance and what is not. The labelling theory consequently fails to recognise these power dynamics in society (Haralambos & Holborn 2000).

Interactionists have responded to this criticism. They acknowledge that deviance can be labelled as deviance without an audience being present. They call this *societal* deviance. Hence, *society*, interactionists are saying, *knows* murder is wrong. People do not need to witness it. At the same time, one needs to consider the audience's reaction. If an individual shoots someone who is trying to harm him or her, that might be regarded as self-defence depending on the circumstances, usually established in a court of law, even though 'the court of public opinion' might disagree with the verdict. Therefore, the reaction of the audience, and what one might call the societal view, is critical (Haralambos & Holborn 2000; Shaefer 2013).

Defenders of the labelling theory further do not agree that the theory is deterministic. Deviant individuals can decide to stop being deviant. Labelling theorists also reject the final criticism regarding power. This is an interesting position as they argue that it was the interactionists who created an awareness of the power dynamics in society. It was they who broached questions on who decides what is deviance and what is not within the field of deviance and crime. Here is an instance where the study of society and its findings have an impact on how society considers subsequent events and happenings within it.

23.7   Crime, poverty and social exclusion

In South Africa one can discern links between aspects such as poverty and social exclusion and crime. The rising levels of inequality between the rich and the poor and the growing levels of unemployment are clearly contributing to high levels of *socially visible* criminal activity that are witnessed in South Africa. These challenges largely have their roots in the legacy of apartheid which continues to manifest its influence in our society. This section of the chapter will present a straightforward definition of poverty discussed in greater depth in a previous chapter, social exclusion and it will end off with noting one theorist's discussion of inclusive and exclusive societies. The section concludes with the assertion that the idea of an exclusive society is helpful in understanding and explaining some of the crimes committed in post-apartheid South Africa.

23.7.1   Poverty

Simply put, poverty can be seen as lacking material resources. On this basis there are two types of poverty, generally referred to as **absolute** and *relative poverty*. When individuals are said to be in absolute poverty, it means they do not have the resources to maintain human life. Under such a scenario people do not have access to basic human needs such as nutrition, water, shelter and health. On the other hand, relative poverty refers to a situation where people lack the resources to participate in the community activities expected by the standards of a particular society at a particular time, for instance, inadequate educational opportunities, unpleasant working conditions and powerlessness.

If one looks at absolute poverty within the South African context, which can also be defined as those individuals living below the poverty line, one notices the dramatic impact of the global financial crisis of 2008/2009 on the livelihoods of South Africa's poorest people (StatsSA 2014). It is argued by Statistics South Africa (2014) that the number of people living below the food line increased to 15.8 million in 2009 from 12.6 million in 2006. Statistics South Africa (2014) also makes the contention that about 20 per cent of South Africa's population lived in absolute poverty between 2010 and 2013. Poverty in South Africa is also gendered and racialised (Chagonda 2016). Statistics South Africa (2014) found that women in South Africa are more impoverished than their men. In 2011, poverty levels of women stood at 47.1 per cent of the total female population and that of men stood at 43.8 per cent of the total male population in the country (StatsSA 2014). There are significant differences in poverty levels between the different racial groups in South Africa. In terms of poverty share, more than 9 out of 10 (94.2 per cent) poor people in South Africa in 2011 were black Africans. The high levels of poverty among this majority group in South Africa partly explains why some of these poverty-stricken people engage in criminal activities in order to survive.

23.7.2   Social exclusion

Social exclusion refers to the dynamic process of being shut out, fully or partially, from the social, economic, political and cultural systems which determine the social integration of a person in society. Social exclusion thus entails lack of access to resources, inadequate social participation, lack of social

integration and a lack of power. Individuals who are socially excluded from any of the above might also resort to criminal activities in a bid for them to feel included in society.

23.7.3   Inclusive and exclusive societies

Jock Young (1999) argues that between the 1950s and the 1970s in the global North societies could be understood as inclusive societies. Some of the key features of an inclusive society included the following:

- Secure employment
- Stability in the economy
- Welfare state provided citizenship rights for all members of society
- Women were increasingly included in the formal economy
- Family life was relatively stable
- Core values of population centred around work and family life
- There was a strong sense of community
- Most people were included within the social structure
- Values about right and wrong were absolute and not open to negotiation but society was tolerant of minor misdemeanours.

From the 1980s onwards, however, Young argues that an evolution took place as the period of 'late modernity' replaced the era of modernity. An *exclusive society* generally emerged which has caused individuals to turn to crime in order to survive in this era. An inclusive society gave way to an exclusive society as mass production of standardised products increasingly gave way to more specialist production of a wider range of products. Technology increasingly replaced human labour and the labour market has increasingly demanding less, but more highly skilled individuals (Young 1999). The exclusive society has also witnessed greater economic insecurity and increased levels of structural unemployment. Young (1999) argues that structural unemployment occurs when a labour market is unable to provide jobs for all job seekers as there is a mismatch between the skills of the unemployed and the more advanced skills needed for available jobs. Generally, for Young, an exclusive society leads to disgruntlement among those who are excluded and this results in higher levels of crime.

23.8   Social control

Social control can be defined as the techniques and strategies for preventing deviant human behaviour in any society. Social control occurs at all levels in society, whether in the family, peer groups, the university setting, organisations and within government. Social control within the family, as you know, normally takes place under the process of socialisation and sanctions can be imposed as a form of reinforcing social control. These sanctions can be penalties for deviating against certain norms and values or they might be rewards for abiding by societal expectations.

23.8.1 Conformity and obedience

Social control can be enforced through conformity and obedience. Conformity entails abiding by rules set by our peers who have no special right to direct our behaviour and obedience means compliance with higher authorities in a hierarchical structure. Under certain circumstances, both conformity and obedience can have negative consequences on people's behaviour. A highly controversial experiment was conducted at Yale University in the United States corroborates this point. The primary aim of what became known as the 'Milgram experiment' was to see how individuals in positions of power or authority could use their leverage to persuade other people to accept their understanding of deviance and to then influence these people to administer punishment. This experiment tested whether people would obey instructions to administer increasingly painful electric shocks to a subject. Ordinary people were selected and the results were themselves extraordinarily shocking. Social scientists were dismayed by results that came out of the experiment. They had predicted that virtually all subjects would refuse to shock innocent victims except only a pathological fringe of about 2 per cent which would continue administering shocks up to the maximum level. On the contrary, an astonishing 67 per cent of the participants administered shocks at the maximum level. Possible explanations of the shocking results of the Milgram experiment are that people are accustomed to submitting to impersonal authority figures whose status is indicated by a title. People also normally shift responsibility for behaviour to the authority figure by convincing themselves that they are doing their duty by obeying orders. Further studies have shown an even greater willingness to inflict shock if participants feel the victim deserves the punishment. A follow-up study on the Milgram experiment further showed that participants were less likely to impose shocks if they were moved physically closer to the victims. The Milgram experiment helps to explain some of the most horrific atrocities that have occurred in human history such as the harsh treatment of black people by the racist apartheid regime in South Africa, the Holocaust of World War II, or tortures at Abu Ghraib prison in Iraq and at Guantanamo Bay in the wake of the United States' and its allies' war against terror in Afghanistan and Iraq.

23.8.2 Control through laws and socialisation

Norms considered important to society are normally formalised into laws regarding people's behaviour and this is governmental social control. Some laws are directed at all members of society, for instance, prohibition against murder while others primarily affect particular categories of people for example fishing and hunting regulations. It should be noted that laws are not a static body of rules handed down from generation to generation. They reflect continually changing standards of what is deemed to be right and wrong, how to determine violations and the sanctions that are supposed to be imposed. Socialisation and the internalisation of norms are the primary source of conformity and obedience. Norms are seen as valid and desirable and we are committed to observing them. As individuals, we are normally socialised to want to belong and to fear being viewed as different or deviant.

23.8.3 Informal and formal forms of control

Informal social control is the casual use of mechanisms to encourage conformity and obedience such as smiles, laughter, frowns, raised eyebrows, ridicule or ostracism. Many cultures view spanking or slapping children as a proper and necessary means of informal social control. However, spanking children is increasingly being viewed in a negative light. It is inappropriate as it teaches children to solve problems through violence and can escalate into more serious forms of abuse. With respect to formal social control, this is carried out by authorised agents, such as police officers, judges, school administrators, employers, military officers etc.

23.8.4 Technology as a form of social control

Technology is increasingly being used to control people's behaviours through surveillance. The work of Michel Foucault (1979) on **governmentality** is of great utility in assisting us to understand the increasing use of technology to monitor people and in the process, control their actions. In his book *Discipline and Punish*, Foucault (1979) makes reference to a panopticon. A panopticon is a structure that allows someone in a position of power to observe individuals or a group of people. Foucault argues that the mere fact that people are always convinced they are being monitored by officials through panopticons, such as prison towers or cameras, acts as a form of social control. Being aware of being continually observed constrains people and forces them to behave in a way which conforms to certain social norms. In this present day of advanced technologies, people are increasingly being monitored by cameras, cell phones can be tapped, and internet use can be monitored by the authorities. Thus, technological advances have improved mechanisms of surveillance and in the process, the enforcement of social control.

23.9 Crime in South Africa

Crime is one of the biggest challenges facing South Africa today and as has been discussed earlier, the country is becoming more of an *exclusive society*. The country has moved away from the unique exclusivity of apartheid towards the more familiar forms of exclusion practised in late modern market societies. The period of transition has been long and many previously disadvantaged groups under apartheid remain disadvantaged. There is also a culture of violence in some communities and the triple threat of poverty, inequality and unemployment remains stark. The phenomenon of gangsterism and the rise of 'protest masculinity' in some communities, notably among the youth, as job opportunities decline, continue to be elusive. Poverty and unemployment also contribute towards the increase in marginalised and troubled masculinities as some men resort to criminal activities and violence because they feel insecure and challenged by successful women.

Crime has also been exacerbated by the history of a culture of violence. The experience of **institutional violence** during apartheid weakened parental control. The strategy of ungovernability by the oppressed majority bred a culture of violent lawlessness and distrust of authority. As a consequence, some of the murderous intolerance that is witnessed in the country is the result of the effects of apartheid, coupled with years of political violence and continued exposure to violence in the home and in especially poor neighbourhoods.

Violent crime is a major problem in South Africa as Figure 23.1 and Figure 23.2 show. Even though robbery with assault and common assault accounted for the most reported violent crimes in 2016, murder is a serious problem in the country as the graph in Figure 15.2 shows. The graph highlights the murder rate per 100 000 population in all of South Africa's provinces between 2013 and 2014. South Africa's murder rate during this period was 32.2 people murdered per 100 000 individuals. The international average during the same period was 6.2 people murdered per 100 000 population.

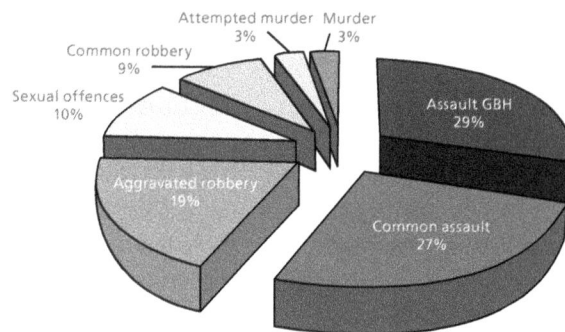

Figure 23.1 Breakdown of South Africa's violent crime categories as at end of 2016
(Source: Institute for Security Studies)

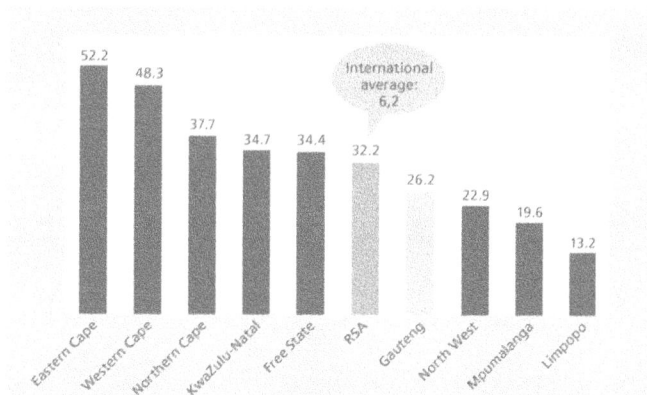

Figure 23.2 South Africa's murder rate at provincial level in 2013/2014
(Source: Institute for Security Studies)

Summary

- Deviance is the violation of societal norms, while crime entails breaking the laws of a country. All criminal acts are a form of deviance; however, not all forms of deviance are a crime.
- For the functionalists such as Durkheim, deviance is functional and inevitable in society. If changes are to occur in society, then some deviance has to occur. According to the functionalists, even though small doses of deviance are required in society, acts of deviance should not get out of control, otherwise that society will become dysfunctional.
- Sub-cultural theories of deviance argue that deviance normally occurs in groups when disgruntled or frustrated sections of society come together to constitute a deviant group that creates its own norms and values that are at odds with the norms and values of mainstream society. Once this happens, such a group can be said to have created its own sub-culture anchored in acts of deviance.
- The conflict theory on crime and deviance draws its ideas from Karl Marx's writings on class conflict in society. Marx argued that under the capitalist economic system, there was bound to be conflict between the capitalists and the working class because of the exploitative nature of capitalism. Under such a scenario, the conflict perspective makes the contention that laws are crafted by those in power (the capitalist class) to protect their rights and interests. This theory also argues that the most serious crimes that occur in society are of a corporate nature and are committed by the capitalists, and yet the law mostly focuses of 'less serious' street crimes that are committed by working class people.
- The interactionist perspective on crime and deviance argues that in order for us to understand deviance and crime in society, we need to look at the small-scale interaction that takes place between individuals, since it is individuals who decide and determine whether a particular act is a form of deviance or a crime or not.
- South Africa is becoming more of an exclusive society as it faces the major challenges of poverty, unemployment and rising levels of inequality. As a consequence of the exclusive nature of post-apartheid South African society, crime has been on the increase.
- Social control can be enforced through the process of socialisation or the promulgation of laws by the state. In contemporary societies, technology is proving to be a very useful tool in controlling people's behaviour and possibly even reducing acts of deviance and crime, as people can be monitored with devices such as cameras on the streets, buildings and other public spaces. However, the use of technology as a tool of surveillance has not eradicated criminal activities in society.
- Violent crimes are a major problem in post-apartheid South Africa. There is also the problem of gangsterism and the rise of 'protest masculinity' in some communities, notably among the youth, as job opportunities continue to be elusive. Poverty and unemployment also contributes towards the increase in marginalised and troubled masculinities as some men resort to criminal activities and violence because they feel insecure and challenged by successful women.
- Crime in the country has also been exacerbated by the history of a culture of violence. The experience of institutional violence during apartheid weakened parental control. The strategy of ungovernability by the oppressed majority bred a culture of violent lawlessness and distrust to authority.

ARE YOU ON TRACK?

1. Critically discuss the conflict perspective on deviance.
2. Critically discuss Merton's theory of anomie. Is his discussion relevant to the South African context?
3. Provide an explanation for South Africa's high crime rate.

References

American Psychiatric Association. 1994. *Diagnostic and Statistical Manual of Mental Disorders: DSM-IV.* 4th ed. Washington, DC: American Psychiatric Association.

Ashman S, Fine B, Newman S. 2011. 'Amnesty International? The nature, scale and impact of capital flight from South Africa'. *Journal of Southern African Studies*, 37(1): 7–25.

Bessadien RS, Hochfeld T. 2005. 'Across the Public/Private boundary: contextualising domestic violence in South Africa'. *Agenda*, 1(66): 4–15.

Blokland AAJ, Nagin D, Nieuwbeerta P. 2005. 'Life span offending trajectories of a Dutch conviction cohort'. *Criminology*, 43(4): 919–954 in *Towards an Understanding of Repeat Violent Offending.* Muntingh L, Gould C (eds). Institute for Security Studies, Paper 231, July 2012. [Online] Available at: http://www.issafrica.org/pgcontent.php? UID=31050 [Accessed 18 July 2012].

Blumstein A. 1995. 'Youth violence, guns, and the illicit-drug industry'. *Journal of Criminal Law and Criminology*, 86(1): 10–36.

Box S. 1981. *Deviance, Reality and Society.* London: Holt, Rinehart & Winston.

Chagonda T. 2016. 'Social stratification' in *Sociology: A South African Perspective.* Seedat-Khan M, Jansen Z, Smith R (eds). Singapore: Seng Lee Press.

Chapman M. 2012. 'Strong emotions about disgraced South Africa captain Hansie Cronje even 10 years after his death'. [Online] Available at: www.telegraph.co.uk [Accessed 12 July 2017].

Cloward RA, Ohlin L. 1961. *Delinquency and Opportunity.* London: Routledge.

Cohen AK. 1955. *Delinquent Boys.* Glencore: Free Press.

Department of Correctional Services. 2011. *Basic Statistics Report,* February 2011. Pretoria: Government of South Africa.

Diffin E. 2010. 'How do Zulus explain polygamy?' [Online] Available at: http://news.bbc.co.uk/2/hi/uk_news/magazine/8549429.stm [Accessed 24 August 2016].

Durkheim E. 1938. *The Rules of the Sociological Method.* New York: The Free Press.

Foucault M. 1979. *Discipline and Punish: The Birth of the Prison.* New York: Vintage.

Goode E. 1994. *Deviant Behaviour.* 4th ed. New Jersey: Prentice Hall.

Graaff J, Van Aswegen F, Thomson D. 2002. *Crime and Deviance.* Oxford: Oxford University Press.

Haralambos M, Holborn M. 2000. *Sociology: Themes and Perspectives.* 5th ed. London: Harper Collins.

Heidensohn F. 1988. *Women and Crime.* New York: New York University Press.

Lehohla P. 2017. 'South African Demographic and Health Survey (SADH 2016). Statistics South Africa (StatsSA). [Online] Available at: https://www.iol.co.za/news/south-africa/teenage [Accessed 9 November 2017].

Merton R. 1968. *Social Theory and Social Structure.* Ontario: Collier-Macmillan.

Miller W. 1962. 'Lower class culture as a generating milieu of gang delinquency' in *The Sociology of Crime and Delinquency.* Savitz W, Johnston N (eds). New York: John Wiley & Son Inc.

Muntingh L, Gould C. 2010. 'Towards an understanding of repeat violent offending.' Pretoria: Institute for Security Studies. 'We remember Steve Biko.' [Online] Available at: www. https://www.nelsonmandela.org/news/entry/we-remember-steve-bantu-biko [Accessed 24 May 2017].

Newham G. 2015. 'Crime in South Africa'. Paper presented at the UJ Sociology, Anthropology and Development Studies seminar series on 18 February 2015.

Pandy S, Makiwane M, Ranchod C, Lesoalo T. 2009. 'Teenage pregnancy in South Africa – with a specific focus on school-going learners'. Child, Youth and Social Development. Human Resources Research Council. Pretoria: Department of Basic Education.

PriceWaterhouseCoopers. 2016. *Global Economic Crime Survey 2016 – 5th South African Edition.* Johannesburg: PWC.

Reinar R. 1984. 'Crime, law and deviance' in *Durkheim and Modern Sociology.* Fenton S (ed). Cambridge: Cambridge University Press.

SA History.org. 2016. 'The Prohibition of Mixed Marriages Act commences'. [Online] Available at: http://www.sahistory.org.za/dated-event/prohibition-mixed-marriages-act-commences [Accessed 24 May 2017].

Schaefer RT. 2011. *Sociology in Modules.* New York: McGraw-Hill.

Seekings J. 2014. 'Taking disadvantage seriously: The underclass in post-apartheid South Africa'. *Africa* 84(1): 135–41.

Siegel LJ. 2000. *Criminology.* Belmont: Wadsworth.

Smith DJ. 1995. 'Youth crime and conduct disorders' in *Psychological Disorders in Young People: Time Trends and their Correlates.* Rutter M, Smith DJ (eds). Chichester: Wiley.

Standing G. 2011. *The Precariat: The New Dangerous Class.* London: Bloomsbury Academic.

Statistics South Africa. 2014. *Poverty Trends in South Africa: An Examination of Absolute Poverty Between 2006 and 2011.* Pretoria: Statistics South Africa.

Statistics South Africa. 2016. *Labour Survey Report.* Pretoria: Statistics South Africa.

Taylor L. 1981. *Deviance and Society.* London: Michael Joseph.

UNPFA. 2012. *Marrying too Young: End Child Marriage.* New York: UNPFA.

Young J. 1999. *The Exclusive Society: Social Exclusion, Crime and Difference in Late Modernity.* London: SAGE.

Zimbardo P. 2007. *The Lucifer Effect: Understanding How Good People Turn Evil.* New York: Random House.

Urbanisation

Cornie Groenewald

Urbanisation has become a permanent feature of modern society. Over half of the world's population is urbanised, and nearly two-thirds of South Africans live in urban areas. Over the past 25 years, the process of urbanisation has been rapid and is expected to accelerate in the future worldwide. Urbanisation qualitatively changes the shape of society by socially structuring the life experiences and opportunities of people. In this way it permits greater variety and more complex social relationships, thereby transforming the range and possibilities of human behaviour. An urban environment changes the forms of social cohesion in society and results in a range of social challenges such as crime and deviance, as we have just seen in the previous chapter. In addition, as this chapter will show, urbanisation often introduces the prospect of squalor, increased health risks, overpopulation, loss of privacy, loneliness, isolation and a loss of identity. But the urban environment is also concentrated, fast-paced, economically active, modern and exciting, and breeds a new kind of human being – the sophisticated, intellect-driven and ambitious urbanite. Few who enter this world return to the social slumbers and physical rigours of rural life. Not all who come to the city, however, realise their dreams of a better life and manage to conquer its immense power.

The urban environment is not a homogeneous social arrangement as the basic concepts used in studies of urbanisation clearly reveal. The spatial geography of the South African urban environment, while instantiating many of the concepts applying to towns and cities elsewhere – township, suburb, central business district, peri-urban area – retains its unique ecological patterns inherited from the past. Divided by the racialised patterns of colonial development and apartheid town and city planners, the urban cityscape of the built environment remains defined by the 'twin city' or the 'apartheid city'. This racialised spatial and demographic pattern, while evident more widely than the city itself, is also breaking down with new urban, commercial and industrial development occurring in what were once far-flung rural areas defined by apartheid geographers.

This chapter tracks urbanisation in South Africa. The main metropolitan areas, economic magnets of migration, have uniformly grown more rapidly than the provinces within which they are located. This means a movement of people into the urban areas within all of the provinces. Gauteng is now officially South Africa's first megalopolis – a seemingly urban sprawl, but officially called a conurbation, which is normally defined as an urban area with a population of over 10 million people. This pattern mirrors what has been happening in the rest of Africa and globally, as this chapter will show. Developing countries now have more people living in major cities than the developed world – and this is to quickly accelerate in the next few decades to come.

The factors driving this process in South Africa are discussed in terms of the competing forces of concentration and deconcentration. How urbanisation is contrasted with proletarianisation is discussed. Arguments about how to deal with uncontained urban sprawl and the development of peri-urban areas – which often contain the worst aspects of uncontrolled urbanisation – are noted. The consequences of urbanisation, in terms of its economic implications and the physical and social problems urbanisation presents, are treated in some detail. This chapter hence imbues the term 'developing society' with new significance and meaning. It notes how the way government sought to ensure the provision of urban amenities and facilities was outstripped by the rapid tempo of urbanisation and the rising expectations of a better life which accompanied it. These large-scale movements of people are crucial to understanding and explaining the corresponding increase in social service delivery protests that have occurred since 2004 and which are documented here.

This data is then set against an analysis of the rural–urban divide and refers to one of the famous debates in South African social science which attempted to explain these macro-sociological phenomena in terms of Francis Wilson's 'push-pull' model and Harold Wolpe's cheap labour thesis. The classical writers – Karl Polanyi, Ferdinand Tönnies, Louis Wirth and Georg Simmel – and their even more famous theories (which every sociology student should know) are all too briefly treated. As no account of urbanisation would be complete without noting the impact of migrant labour, the chapter ends by noting its importance in shaping the patterns of migration of millions of workers over the decades, and raises the relevance of Polanyi's analysis and research questions waiting to be posed. Here is yet another example of desperately needed sociological research awaiting, in this instance, its dedicated team of researchers.

Case study 24.1   The promise of urbanisation

Adegoke Taylor, a skinny, solemn 32-year-old itinerant trader with anxious eyes, shares an eight-by-ten-foot room with three other young men, on an alley in Isale Eko several hundred feet from the Third Mainland Bridge. In 1999, Taylor came to Lagos from Ile-Oluji, a Yoruba town a hundred and thirty miles to the northeast. He had a degree in mining from a polytechnic school and the goal of establishing a professional career. Upon arriving in the city, he went to a club that played juju – pop music infused with Yoruba rhythms – and stayed out until two in the morning. 'This experience alone makes me believe I have a new life living now,' he said, in English, the lingua franca of Lagos. 'All the time, you see crowds everywhere. I was motivated by that. In the village, you're not free at all, and whatever you're going to do today you'll do tomorrow.' Taylor soon found that none of the few mining positions being advertised in Lagos newspapers were open to him. 'If you are not connected, it's not easy, because there are many more applications than jobs,' he said. 'The moment you don't have a recognized person saying, 'This is my boy, give him a job', it's very hard. In this country, if you don't belong to the elite' – he pronounced it 'e-light' – 'you will find things very, very hard.' Taylor fell into a series of odd jobs: changing money, peddling stationery and hair plaits, and moving heavy loads in a warehouse for a daily wage of four hundred naira –about three dollars. Occasionally, he worked for West African traders who came to the markets near the port and needed middlemen to locate goods. At first, he stayed with the sister of a childhood friend in Mushin, then found cheap lodging there in a shared room for seven dollars a month, until the building was burned down during the ethnic riots. Taylor lost everything. He decided to move to Lagos Island, where he pays a higher rent, 20 dollars a month. Taylor had tried to leave Africa but was turned down for a visa by the American and British embassies. At times, he longed for the calm of his hometown, but there was never any question of returning to Ile-Oluji, with its early nights and monotonous days and the prospect of a lifetime of manual labour. His future was in Lagos … 'There's no escape, except to make it,' Taylor said.

(Sources: Anderson Literary Management, Inc 2006: 64; UNFPA 2007)

Key themes

- Demographic concepts relating to a good understanding of urbanisation
- The historical pattern of urbanisation in South Africa highlighting the process before and after 1986
- Urbanisation patterns in the world and its subregions, including Africa
- Reasons for establishing urban places and how their functions change over time

- The phenomenon of peri-urban areas and to assess their value of urban centres with specific reference to African urban centres
- The many implications of urbanisation with reference to the developed and the less-developed regions or countries of the world
- Differences in the quality of life of extremely poor South Africans with respect to urban and rural environments

⟶

- The sociological significance of urbanisation from a transformational perspective
- The phenomenon of urban–rural linkages, especially in African and South African contexts

- How urban dwellers from rural areas develop an urban identity that enables them to survive the challenges of the city.

24.1 Introduction

More than 60 per cent of all South Africans are currently living in urban areas. This is higher than the urbanisation level of the world population that in 2007, for the first time in human history, exceeded 50 per cent. The process of urbanisation has proved to be inevitable, driven by industrial forces that are irreversible on the one hand and by rural poverty on the other. Urban centres have the promise of a new future and new opportunities such as employment, education and a better quality of life. Urban centres also come with squalor, health and crime risks, overpopulation and loss of privacy, loneliness, isolation and a loss of identity.

In this chapter, we trace the transition from rural society to urban centres and the implications for our social and economic life. We consider economically developed countries as well as less-developed ones and the big challenge regarding poverty alleviation. We question the drivers of urbanisation and we determine how people affected make sense of urbanisation. While urbanisation holds a promise of improved lives for the poor, there are also challenges for people engaged in the process and for those with the responsibility to guide and manage urban life.

When this chapter uses terminology such as 'less' or 'least developed' and 'more developed', it simply follows the international practice of the United Nations to distinguish economic differences among countries and regions in the world. The same holds for the use of population categories, such as black, white, coloured, Indian/Asian and African, to indicate South African distinctions of the past when reference was made to the people of the country. We certainly do not support or justify in any sense racial or class connotations implied by these terms.

24.2 Basic urbanisation concepts

Urbanisation is the increasing proportion of a human population living in settlements such as cities, towns, **townships** and **suburbs**. These settlements are also known as **urban centres**. This is in contrast to rural areas that comprise villages, tribal areas, informal settlements and commercial farms. The proportion of the population living in urban centres is also expressed as a percentage, which is

then known as the **level of urbanisation** for the country or region. **Urban growth** refers to the growth in the urban population, which is the population already living in urban centres. Urban growth can be expressed in absolute numbers or as a growth rate, which is also a percentage but calculated over a period of time, such as one year or a five-year period. According to the United Nations, the level of urbanisation for South Africa in the year 2007 was 60 per cent, meaning 60 out of every 100 persons in the total population in the year 2007 were located in urban areas. The urban growth rate, as an average per year over the period 2005 to 2010, is calculated as 1.0 per cent which means the urban population is growing at one per cent on average per year (UNFPA 2007).

The criteria used to determine whether an area is urban are not clear-cut. In some instances, a certain number of people, known as the threshold size of population (eg 500 people), is the defining criterion. In other cases, a form of local government is required. Sometimes essential 'urban' services and facilities are required, such as a centre for law and order (a police station, for instance) or a communication centre (such as a post office), a shop, a school, a church, and so on. The cultural context also determines how urban centres are defined.

A city is a relatively large and permanent settlement. It has complex systems for sanitation, utilities, land usage, housing and transportation. Physical and business developments are concentrated in the same geographical area and draw large numbers of people. These enterprises benefit from the large numbers, which act as an economy of scale, meaning that services and products can be offered to the public at a cheaper unit price. A big city or metropolis includes various residential areas called suburbs within its area of jurisdiction, and often developments beyond its borders called exurbs (living areas outside the city boundaries but associated with the city) or **peri-urban areas** (similar to **exurbs**, but usually not as well developed as an urban environment). Large numbers of workers commute daily from these areas to urban centres of employment, a fact that creates the need for transportation systems such as railways, roads, buses and taxis. Once a city expands far enough to reach another city, the connecting cities form a **conurbation** or **megalopolis**. Administratively, we distinguish a city from a town or a smaller centre such as a village or a hamlet in terms of population size and type of local authority. Sociologically, we observe different ways of life and types of relationships among the residents of the various centres.

In a **city** or a large town, suburbs are different from the **central business area or district** (CBD), sometimes known as 'downtown' or the 'inner city'. The latter term carries the meaning of a **ghetto**, where people are often poor and where there is more crime. Owing to a process of urban renewal, known as **gentrification**, the character of a ghetto may be reversed to become an attractive area for inner city living, both for residential and business purposes. In some cities, for instance Paris (France), the inner city is the name given to the area where people with high incomes reside.

In South Africa, another distinction is used, namely township. Originally, the word referred to a segregated town, but under **apartheid** it came to mean a residential development that confined black people (black Africans, coloureds and Asians) to that area. A well-known township, Soweto, now a city in its own right, was established as a number of residential areas grouped together on the south-western borders of the city of Johannesburg. Soweto is an acronym for SOuth-WEstern TOwnships. Apartheid gave rise to a unique ecological pattern in the development of South African cities and towns. Tony Lamont labelled these 'twin towns', which refers to black and white towns existing in pairs next to each other (Swart & Lamont 1984: 101–105). According to the political and administrative policy of apartheid, which is traceable to colonial times in Africa, separate residential areas were earmarked for the different 'population groups' as defined by apartheid law. Under this law, blacks were seen as descendent from African nations, Asians included people from Indian descent, whites as descendent from European nations, and 'others' (called coloureds) were people of mixed descent. According to the Group Areas Act 41 of 1950 (superseded by Act 36 of 1966) under apartheid, indeed four different areas could be defined adjacent to each other to provide for these groups. In principle, the idea was that each group would have its own town with separate amenities for urban living, including a business district. In practice, this was not feasible or even possible, and different residential and social areas developed for each group while they were sharing the single industrial and business facilities of the white city or town. Urban living standards differed tremendously among the four groups, with a concentration of poor living conditions among the

black groups and far more wealthy living standards among the white groups. This fundamentally unjust system proved to be unsustainable. Mark Swilling coined it 'apartheid city', arguing that it had to give way through a process of urban transition to become a 'just city' that was to serve as a platform for developing the deracialisation of society, the reconstitution of the political system, and access to industrial work and urban space (Swilling, Humphries & Shubane 1991: viii–xx). After more than two decades since the scrapping of apartheid laws, many cities and towns still feature the remnants of apartheid. It has become one of the outstanding challenges of current urban South Africa to wipe out the historical legacy of the unequal 'twin city' and unjust apartheid status of urban centres in favour of unified cities for all in which full citizenship, earning potential, and social access and inclusion will be possible.

A kind of 'economic apartheid' based not on racial lines but class divisions stubbornly featured in South Africa's big cities and is expected to be a permanent feature of a capitalist-based urban system. A prominent example is downtown Johannesburg, characterised by overcrowded and dilapidated inner-city buildings versus Sandton with its modern, high-rise, well-maintained affluent architecture for business and residential purposes.

Three factors describe changes in the level of urbanisation and in urban growth (or decline). The first and immediate indication of most urbanisation is the net movement of people from rural to urban areas. This is part of human migration, which is a fundamental demographic process. Studies in human migration have shown that for every migration stream in one direction (eg from rural to urban areas) there is a countermovement (from urban to rural areas). Urbanisation occurs and increases when there is more migration from rural to urban areas than vice versa. The second factor in urbanisation is the natural increase of the existing urban population – that is, the net balance between the urban population's births and deaths. A third factor relates to the definition of an urban area, the geographic boundaries allocated to such an area and changes in these boundaries. Should the boundaries of a city or town expand, this will obviously include more people that as a result qualify as urban dwellers – purely because of the administrative change in the boundaries of the urban centre. Peri-urban areas are often targeted to be included in the city boundaries. Another example of the administrative factor in South Africa is the de-establishment of the Metsweding District Municipality and its two local municipalities of Kungwini and Nokeng tsa Taemane and the incorporation of the area into the metropolitan areas of

Tshwane and Ekurhuleni, both in Gauteng. The responsibility of the determination of municipal boundaries lies with the Municipal Demarcation Board, an independent authority protected by the Local Government: Municipal Demarcation Act 1998 and judgments by the Constitutional Court (http://www.demarcation.org.za).

It should be noted that the recognition of these three factors as demographic and administrative forces affecting urbanisation in South Africa contributes to the realisation that urbanisation has become a permanent feature of modern society and that political and administrative policies and arrangements to the contrary would only put a damper on society's developmental potential (Cilliers & Groenewald 1982: 37–39). In apartheid South Africa, the government's belief was that urbanisation was spurred mainly by the first (migration) factor and that influx control measures were necessary to keep rural black 'masses' from settling in existing white-controlled towns and cities. It was only after the recognition that urbanisation is characterised by all the mentioned factors and that influx control was therefore not a sustainable policy that these measures were scrapped. This happened as late as 1986 with the enactment of the Abolition of Influx Control Act 68 of 1986.

24.3 Urbanisation in South Africa

When looking at the urbanisation process in South Africa, we need to distinguish between urbanisation before and after 1986. Under apartheid rule, black South Africans found it extremely difficult to move and settle down permanently in urban areas of South Africa due to various legal and administrative instruments that operated as a bundle of influx control measures. One of the major legal instruments was the Natives (Urban Areas) Consolidation Act 25 of 1945 of which section 10(1) stated the conditions for black South Africans under which they would qualify for permanent residence. It was only men who could qualify for permanent residential rights under the most stringent conditions, such as finding a work opportunity and keeping it, preferably in the same place over a prolonged time (eg 10 years continuously at the same place or 15 years at various places). Difficult as it was for men to find a permanent job, it was virtually impossible under this system for the wives and other family members of the migrant workers to find a permanent abode in cities. One of the implications was that cities did not develop a social infrastructure to provide for the community needs of black urban dwellers. Another pillar of apartheid control was the Black Labour Act 67 of 1964 that controlled the employment of black workers in so-called prescribed areas – that is, towns and cities. Various protests,

many violent, led to reforms and eventually to scrapping the influx control measures in 1986. The freedom of movement and settlement for all citizens, men and women, of South Africa was finally and formally acknowledged in 1986. The new political dispensation that started eight years later has freed South Africans from all restrictive legislation based on race and sex, and opened up cities for all. After 1986, there was a period of 'corrections' to the rather skewed demographic pattern of urban dwellers, and with new family members being added to those already in the cities, urbanisation increased. According to estimates for 2015, South Africa was 65 per cent urbanised (UN, ECA & UNFPA 2016: 30).

The post-1994 reforms that took place in South Africa transformed the local government profile of the country. Today, no piece of land is not under the administration and jurisdiction of a municipality. A municipality is the area of jurisdiction of the third sphere of government, after national and provincial. It refers to local, district and metropolitan areas. There are four types of municipalities encompassing the whole country, including rural areas and tribal areas: metropolitan areas (Category A); local councils (Category B); district councils (Category C); and district management areas. Metropolitan areas (Category A) stand alone and district councils (Category C) are subdivided into local councils (Category B) and district management areas (Statistics South Africa (Metadata) 2012).

In South Africa, local municipalities and district management areas have very specific functions, such as sanitation, refuse removal, water and electricity, and pertain to local towns and rural areas not covered in any other way. A local municipality of which there are 234 councils is a defined area demarcated for local administrative purposes. The local municipalities make up the larger district councils. A district municipality is a designation for a class or group of municipalities in several locations to ensure coordination with other spheres of government and planning and resource allocation across the local municipalities. There are 46 district councils, and these fulfil the functions of developing people, business and infrastructure, and of providing services such as firefighting that cannot be duplicated for every local area. District management areas are rural areas not under the jurisdiction of a local municipality and as a result need to be serviced by a district council. A metropolitan area is a large population centre consisting of a large metropolis and its adjacent zone of influence or of more than one closely adjoining neighbouring central cities and their zones of influence. South Africa has eight metropolitan areas under the jurisdiction of municipal councils similar to district councils in terms of their functions. They are listed in Table 24.1 as per province.

We calculate from this table that the total number of people living in the metropolitan areas in 2001 represents 36.1 per cent of the total population of the country. This percentage increased to 39.5 per cent in 2011 and to 39.9 per cent in 2016. While the average annual growth rate for the South African population was 1.99 per cent over the period 1996 to 2001, it decreased sharply over the first decade of the 21st century (2001–2011) and then stabilised over the next period of 2011 to 2016. The patterns of population growth for the country's metropolitan areas are different and show some variety for the three periods. The three metropoles of Gauteng showed very high growth rates in the first period but slowdowns in the second period, still with high rates. In the third period, rates for Johannesburg and Tshwane remained high, but they continued their decline in growth. In Ekurhuleni, the growth rate steadied to just over one per cent. Similar trends are seen in the Western Cape: high annual growth rates for the first period, some increase for Cape Town in the second period, and then a decrease in the third period, with a growth rate for Cape Town that is lower than the provincial rate. For KwaZulu-Natal, the initial high growth rate declined steeply in the case of the overall province, and also for eThekwini, yet with growth rates that are double or more for this metropole. The other two provinces with metropolitan areas in their midst, the Eastern Cape and the Free State, have low population growth rates that are declining and ending up in negative growth rates over the third period. To be noted, however, is that in both cases the metropolitan areas have proved increased growth in the second period, and in the case of the Eastern Cape also for the third period. In the case of the Free State, the growth in Mangaung was sustained only for the second period. Virtually no growth is recorded for the third period.

Generally, one can say that the metropolitan areas serve as magnet points that draw people to them even when the province at large does not serve as an attractive hosting area. Gauteng and the Western Cape serve as attractive areas for migrants. The Eastern Cape and the Free State (and Limpopo) are not attracting migrants; on the balance they are repelling them. Vibrant metropolitan areas or centres 'pull' people towards them, for various reasons, while poor and desolated area 'push' them away. Economic opportunities in cities are prime motivations in most reasons why people move to and from areas.

Table 24.1 Metropolitan areas in South Africa, population numbers and growth, 2001, 2011 and 2016

Province Metropolitan area	Population			Population growth (% pa)		
	2001	2011	2016	1996–2001	2001–2011	2011–2016
Eastern Cape	6 278 651	6 562 053	6 470 542	0.42	0.44	−0.28
Buffalo City	704 855	781 027	834 997	0.55	1.03	1.34
Nelson Mandela Bay	1 005 779	1 152 115	1 263 051	0.73	1.36	1.84
Free State	2 706 775	2 745 590	2 663 785	0.55	0.14	−0.60
Mangaung	645 440	775 184	787 803	1.34	1.83	0.32
Gauteng	9 388 854	12 272 263	14 039 919	3.62	2.68	2.69
Ekurhuleni	2 481 762	3 178 470	3 379 104	4.05	2.47	1.22
City of Johannesburg	3 226 055	4 434 827	4 949 347	4.02	3.18	2.20
City of Tshwane	2 142 322	2 921 488	3 275 152	3.57	3.10	2.29
KwaZulu-Natal	9 584 129	10 267 300	10 524 851	2.23	0.69	0.50
eThekwini	3 090 122	3 476 686	3 702 231	2.34	1.18	1.26
Western Cape	4 524 335	5 822 734	6 279 730	2.68	2.52	1.51
City of Cape Town	2 892 243	3 740 026	4 005 016	2.42	2.57	1.37
South Africa	44 819 777	51 770 560	55 653 654	1.99	1.44	1.45

(Sources: Compiled by author based on statistical information supplied by Statistics South Africa as in (a) Municipal Fact Sheet, 2012; (b) Community Survey 2016, Statistical Release P0301; (c) Municipalities of South Africa (https://municipalities.co.za))

Gauteng is the one province in South Africa that is nearly fully urbanised. The area (18 939 km²) carries a population of about 14 million people, which represents 741 persons per one square kilometre. Gauteng represents a conurbation, a process of lateral expansion of two or more cities toward each other to eventually form one continuous city. When this urban phenomenon approximates a population of 10 million, it becomes a megalopolis. Already before 2011, the metropolitan population of Gauteng surpassed this threshold, qualifying the province as South Africa's first megalopolis.

24.4 Urbanisation in Africa and the world

According to United Nations projections, we expect Africa's urban population to increase from 294 million to 742 million between 2000 and 2030. In 2015, 40.4 per cent of the African continent population was estimated to live in urban areas, compared with 26.7 per cent in 1980, which ranks Africa as the least urbanised continent in the world. The number of urban dwellers in Africa nearly quadrupled over the past three decades, rising from 127.8 million in 1980 to 471.6 million in 2015. Moreover, Africa is the world's fastest urbanising region. The average growth rate for the period stood at 3.7 per cent per year, with a projected decline to 3.6 per cent and 2.6 per cent for the periods 2010–2025 and 2025–2050 respectively. In addition, in absolute numbers, the urban population is expected to increase by 867 million persons over the next 35 years, rising from 471.6 million to 1.34 billion. By 2050, about 56 per cent of Africa's population is projected to be urban (UN, ECA & UNFPA 2016).

The most urbanised countries in Africa include Gabon (87.2 per cent), Libya (78.6 per cent), the Democratic Republic of the Congo (77.3 per cent), Djibouti (77.3 per cent), Algeria (70.7 per cent), Cabo Verde (65.5 per cent), Tunisia (66.8 per cent), the Congo (65.4 per cent) and South Africa (64.8 per cent) (UN, ECA & UNFPA 2016).

It is important to note that Africa's urban population tends to concentrate in the larger urban centres. Of those persons who are resident in centres of 20 000 or more, 68 per cent live in cities that are centres with a size of 100 000 or more persons. This figure is higher than the world's figure, which indicates that there are few towns of an intermediary size in Africa. Urban growth is highest in the cities. Cities grow about four and a half times faster than the general population and faster than towns of a smaller size. The larger centres were established during the colonial period. Once established, it was difficult to deploy growth to other less-prominent areas (UNFPA 2007: 8).

To put Africa within a global perspective, it should be noted that today the world's population is predominantly urban. During 2007, statistics provided by the United Nations indicate that, for the first time in human history, half the world's population is living in urban areas. The urban growth rate in the world is two per cent per year, which is nearly double that of the total world population growth rate of 1.1 per cent per year. The more developed regions are far more urbanised than the less developed ones, but the urban growth rate is far higher in the less developed regions.

In the least developed countries, the level of urbanisation is lower (below 30 per cent), but the urban growth rate is very high at a current 4 per cent. The situation in Africa is varied, but similar to the urbanisation pattern in least developed countries. Southern Africa has the highest level of urbanisation and the lowest urban growth rate, and represents the exception in these respects in Africa. Except for northern Africa, all other regions in Africa have urbanisation levels below 50 per cent but high to very high urban growth rates. This suggests that the next number of decades will see a vastly different picture of human population distribution in Africa. Rapid urbanisation is to be expected (UNFPA 2007).

It is necessary to take a broad historical overview to see the patterns and trends of urbanisation in perspective. The literature distinguishes two urbanisation waves (UNFPA 2007: 7–8). The first wave took place in North America and Europe over two centuries, from 1750 to 1950, representing an increase from 10 to 52 per cent urban and 15 to 423 million urban dwellers. The second wave of urbanisation, in the less developed regions, expects the number of urban dwellers to grow from 309 million in 1950 to 3.9 billion in 2030. In 80 years, these countries will change from 18 per cent to some 56 per cent urban. At the beginning of the 20th century, the now developed regions had more than twice as many urban dwellers as the less developed (150 million to 70 million). Despite much lower levels of urbanisation, the developing countries now have 2.6 times as many urban dwellers as the developed regions (2.3 billion to 0.9 billion). This gap will widen quickly in the next few decades.

Satterthwaite confirms this and sheds some light on current trends of urbanisation in Africa in relation to other parts of the world (Satterthwaite 2007). The world's urban population multiplied 10-fold during the 20th century, with most of this growth in less developed regions. Most of the world's growth in population between 2007 and 2020 is expected to be in these countries. How urban centres in these countries grow and develop has enormous implications for development success, including whether or not poverty is reduced, greenhouse gas emissions are decreased, and disasters linked to climate change are avoided.

According to Satterthwaite (2007) on whom we based the information in this section, many aspects of urban change over the last century are unprecedented. Most of the world's urban population is now in less developed regions. Throughout history, the richest nations had most of the world's urban population, and this is not true anymore. The rate of growth in urban populations and the size and number of very large cities in the less developed countries are also unprecedented. From the 1950s to the 1980s, the political changes associated with the ending of colonial empires and the achievement of independence underpinned rapid urbanisation in most nations in Africa and many in Asia. In recent decades, economic changes and interests have been of greater importance. The world's urban population and largest cities have shifted from Europe and North America to Africa, Latin America and Asia. Asia now has half the world's urban population, and Africa's urban population is larger than that of northern America. Europe's dominance has decreased dramatically. In 1910, the nations that now constitute Europe had more than half the world's 100 largest cities, but by 2000, they had only 10. Europe does not have any of the world's 100 fastest-growing large cities (in terms of population growth rates between 1950 and 2000), but has most of the world's slowest-growing (and declining) cities. Most of Europe's great centres of industry are no longer among the world's largest cities.

Africa, Latin America and Asia have most of the world's 100 fastest-growing large cities (in terms of population growth rates between 1950 and 2000); China alone has 15 of them and India has eight. Latin America and the Caribbean now have a declining proportion of the world's urban population, but a still-growing proportion of the world's largest cities and many of its fastest-growing large cities (especially in Brazil and Mexico).

24.5 What drives urbanisation?

What drives urbanisation? The answer to this question is not simple, although economic considerations are primary. Within an industrial context, business considerations translate into the spatial **concentration** of investment and employment opportunities, and the spaces where private enterprise chooses to establish and settle its interests. It makes economic sense to settle in a populous and dense area. The trend towards geographical concentration is often countered by government policy favouring **deconcentration** (to disperse investment and employment opportunities away from the main urban centres to rural hinterlands). Many

countries attempt to use deconcentration as an option to redirect population to settle in more dispersed centres. In South Africa, the government has policies and strategies in place for the promotion of regional industrialisation that may lead to increased human settlement outside the traditional metropoles of Gauteng, Western Cape and KwaZulu-Natal. Based on the National Spatial Development Perspective (NSDP), the Department of Trade and Industry identifies specific areas and corridors in which high economic need coincides with good economic potential. Depending on actual and potential advantages in a particular region, such as natural resources and existing institutions, development options are considered (for more information see: Republic of South Africa (NIPF) nd).

Factors that play a role in the trends towards concentration and deconcentration of human settlement include demographic realities and changes, physical infrastructure, especially transport infrastructure, and links to natural resources, markets and technology. Once an urban centre starts to take shape, these factors are then influenced by the very fact of urban settlement itself. Other factors driving urbanisation are political and social, and the competencies and accountability of metropolitan governments and their interplay with international, national and local factors. All these factors cause diversity in urbanisation patterns.

While urbanisation may be seen as the outcome of industrial capitalist entrepreneurship, where the entrepreneur as employer is driven by the profit motive and the urban area provides a convenient centre for accumulating capital, there is another side to the story. **Proletarianisation** is a social process where people move from being unemployed or self-employed within a subsistence economy to becoming employed as a wage labourer for an employer (Thompson 1963; Bundy 1979).

The process of proletarianisation is closely associated to urbanisation because it often involves the migration of people from rural areas where they were engaged in subsistence farming and sharecropping to cities and towns, in search of waged work and income in the formal economy. We find evidence of this in South Africa among rural black Africans who have moved as temporary sojourners (as migrant workers) or permanently from the deep rural areas to urban areas to work in mines or factories. This adds significantly to the level of urbanisation in the country. According to the social surveys in poor areas of South Africa, the greatest need that unemployed persons expressed to increase their livelihood is to find a regularly paid job (Republic of South Africa 2008: 19).

Explaining urbanisation in South Africa from a proletarianisation standpoint is linked to questions about land. For instance, a South African researcher, Lungisile Ntsebeza, argues that historically, white settlers in South Africa appropriated 87 per cent of the land surface under the Natives Land Act 27 of 1913, confining the indigenous people to reserves in the remaining marginal portions of land. This process forced a large number of rural residents to leave the rural areas for urban areas and farms in search of a cash income through a paid job. A significant number of rural people became fully proletarianised in this sense of the word while others became migrant workers with a tenuous link to land (Ntsebeza 2006).

Full proletarianisation, which implied permanent settlement of black people in the cities and towns, would threaten the migrant labour system upon which white profitability in the mines in South Africa had depended. This crisis coincided with rapid secondary industrialisation that occurred in the major urban centres in the form of manufacturing as a follow-up to the mining industry. A substantial, unprecedented growth of urban Africans followed in the years following World War II, as did an increase in trade union activity and rising African working-class militancy. These developments threatened not only the conditions for accumulation but white political hegemony itself. For these reasons, apartheid measures were adopted and urban influx control was implemented by the apartheid regime in South Africa (Bundy 1979; more information on the history of the rise of apartheid and urbanisation in South Africa can be found on the internet: http://www.sahistory.org.za/article/land-dispossession-1600s-1900s-5-segregation-apartheid).

Considering these arguments for explaining why urbanisation occurred at certain rates and levels, we are still not answering an interesting question – that of why an urban place developed at a certain place and in a certain way. There are many reasons why towns and cities were established in the first place. These may be regarded as the intended purpose of an urban settlement for society, its own population and immediate environment, and the economy. Such reasons include military, commercial, industrial, mining, transport (railway, harbours), fishing, recreational, educational and service functions. Many towns and cities may have started for a particular reason, but they changed their function later or added a number of additional functions (Van der Merwe & Nel 1981: 77–81).

Cape Town, for example, originally provided a settlement for the Dutch East India Company to grow fresh food for its ships and their staff en route between Europe and India. Over the years and centuries it became a military post, the capital of the Cape Colony, the legislative capital of the Union and later the Republic of South Africa, a major harbour city and commercial centre for import and export activities, a world-renowned tourist destination, a world heritage site, and many more. Additional functions to the original reason for the establishment of the settlement become forces of urbanisation in themselves.

24.6 Peri-urban areas

Many cities have seen the development of peri-urban areas, which are areas that often lack clear regulations and administrative authority over land use (UNFPA 2007: 48–50). Uncontrolled or weakly controlled peri-urban areas suffer some of the worst consequences of urban growth, including pollution, rapid social change, poverty, land use changes and the degradation of natural resources, yet they are home to a variety of economic activities, partly fuelled by land speculation. Changes in the structure and location of economic activity contribute greatly to peri-urban growth. Deconcentration and decentralisation of production are often found on the outskirts of dynamic cities where growing workplaces and workforces can no longer find space in city centres, making spill-over growth inevitable. The periphery offers cheaper infrastructure, land and labour, which encourages further peri-urbanisation. According to the United Nations, in most of sub-Saharan Africa, cities expand around a single core with restricted space for further development. Peri-urbanisation often draws a migrant workforce and abruptly changes many rural residents' economic activity from agriculture to manufacturing and services, and introduces only rudimentary urban services to the new waged workers. Environmental degradation is a significant issue in peri-urban areas. Specific health hazards arise when agricultural and industrial activities mingle with residential use. Some peri-urban areas become 'sinks' for urban-generated liquid, solid and sometimes airborne wastes.

In his study of peri-urban areas in South Africa, Barry (2003) concludes that South Africa's peri-urban areas remain economically segregated with different parts of the urban periphery occupied by affluent smallholders, growing informal settlements and traditional tenure systems. He believes that preserving peri-urban land for agriculture is critical for containing urban sprawl and for retaining valuable agricultural land for food production.

Furthermore, Barry observes that peri-urban environments are complex, and development and regularisation projects have to take account of this complexity. Market opportunities, infrastructure, health issues, administrative capacity and transportation networks are some of the factors impacting on the whole urban perimeter. In informal settlement and traditional areas, the situation is even more complex due to the nature of the tenure systems, which tend to be an adaptation of traditional and Western practices. Warlords, civics and other powerful actors play a significant role in some areas.

As we have seen, regulation of peri-urban areas seems to be a major issue in urban management and control. Since 1990, South Africa has produced policies and legislation to manage and reform land both rural and urban. All land is under some or other category of municipal control, making it possible to apply administrative regulations to peri-urban land. Barry finds that due to local-level dynamics, land tenure reform is proving very difficult to implement and that local level policy and action plans and zoning schemes are required to set the basis for strengthening peri-urban agriculture and development.

24.7   The implications of urbanisation

Our discussion of urbanisation has emphasised that this process is highly connected to other processes and trends, such as industrialisation. Another general process is **globalisation**. This is the indication that people are affected by events, decisions and activities by others, and national and international institutions elsewhere in the world. The United Nations report on the world population and urbanisation (UNFPA 2007: 8) notes that cities are the main beneficiaries of globalisation. People follow jobs, which follow investment and economic activities. Most are increasingly concentrated in and around dynamic urban areas, large and small. However, very few cities in developing countries, and even developed countries, generate enough jobs to meet the demands of their growing populations. Another point is that all segments of the population do not equally enjoy the benefits of urbanisation. In most cases, women and ethnic minorities who traditionally face social and economic exclusion are excluded from these benefits.

The steep increase in numbers of urban dwellers coupled with persistent underdevelopment and the shortage of urban jobs is responsible for conditions that outmatch the squalor of the cities of the Industrial Revolution. The speed and scale of second-wave urbanisation is far greater than in the past, which implies a variety of new problems for cities in poorer countries. There are many challenges and the resources are lacking. The list of concerns is long, but here are some of the more noteworthy issues:

- Poor quality of human settlement including housing, sanitation, water, drainage, healthcare, schools and social amenities
- Governance
- Quality of life and mental health
- Quality of the environment referring to resource use, waste and emissions.

These challenges surpass the challenges of cities during the first wave of urbanisation.

There is, however, no automatic link between rapid urban growth and urban problems. Some of the world's fastest-growing cities are also among the best governed, and have some of the best quality of life available in their countries. In addition, by concentrating people and their enterprises, cities present many opportunities for better services, environmental management and a high quality of life. There is no reason why well-governed large cities should not achieve the highest standards in terms of quality of life. Some set high environmental standards through efficient resource use, low waste outputs and low per capita emissions of greenhouse gases. In the discussion that follows, remember that it is not the level of urbanisation or the rate of urban growth that principally matters, but the ways in which urbanisation and its implications are managed and governed.

Orderly urbanisation brings improved transportation, communication and technology. Economic interaction and interdependence between urban and rural areas then takes place. In modern times, this promotes the idea that urban and rural differences can be levelled out and that the two actually can become more similar. This would happen through a process of the 'urbanisation of rural areas' and the 'ruralisation of urban areas'. We expect that such a situation will develop only in exceptional cases and only for a few. The truth is that we have experienced a far more frightening scenario. Factors creating this scenario include persistently high and rapid population growth, in some cases the depopulation of rural areas and therefore its underutilisation; in other instances, the overpopulation of rural land and its incapacity to provide for population increase, and as a result the inevitability of urbanisation. Under these conditions, urbanisation may become rampant and its potential advantages will not materialise. Such problems arise disproportionately in less developed countries, in which, in many instances, a situation of over-urbanisation develops. In the more developed countries, urban decay has become the expression of inefficiently managed urbanisation.

In understanding these issues, we need to recognise the different ways urbanisation proceeds in more and in less developed regions and countries. As we have noted, in developed regions urbanisation is both a condition for and a consequence of industrialisation. High levels of economic growth may therefore be problematic in the sense that economic development outgrows the capacity of local city administrations to provide adequate municipal services and housing. In less developed regions, urbanisation is often the result of push factors in the rural areas. These cause huge numbers of migrants moving to cities in the expectation that better livelihoods might be found. Similarly, the consequences and implications of urbanisation differ according to the levels of development of countries and their regions. When looking at South Africa, we should remember that the country represents a mixed case of and population segments from different socioeconomic politically privileged backgrounds. Accordingly, we may expect the implications of urbanisation to be of both kinds. Our discussion that follows covers economic, physical and social implications. This overview is inspired by the classic analysis of Philip Hauser (1963).

24.7.1 Economic implications and considerations

Cities generate economic advantages for urban dwellers. Local government (many times in conjunction with other government spheres and business) attempts to gain maximum benefit for citizens by providing physical and economic infrastructure that is needed and advantageous for business enterprises to start operating. This will then bring job opportunities, returns on investments and other derived benefits that affect the living standards of urban dwellers.

In South Africa, the Nelson Mandela Bay Municipality in collaboration with government structures and business interests has developed the Coega Industrial Development Zone (IDZ), including the port of Ngqura, to deliver economic benefits for the relatively poor provincial region of the Eastern Cape. The population of the metropole, 1.26 million strong, has picked up its growth rate over the last decade from 1.36 per cent to 1.84 per cent per year, outperforming the negative provincial growth of −0.28 per cent, which marked the period of the infrastructure and business development of the project.

Box 24.1 Coega IDZ

The Coega IDZ, covering 110 km² of land, is situated in the Nelson Mandela Bay municipality, in the Eastern Cape province of South Africa near Port Elizabeth. The initiative is a multibillion-dollar industrial development complex customised for heavy, medium and light industries, adjacent to a deep water port, Port of Ngqura. The Coega Development Corporation (CDC) is the developer and operator of the Coega IDZ and is responsible for the land side infrastructure, while the deep-water port facility, Port of Ngqura, is developed by the Transnet National Ports Authority.

The Coega IDZ is a phased development around industry clusters with Custom Secure Areas dedicated for export-oriented manufacturing for companies located in the zone. Coega offers a platform for global exports by attracting foreign and local investment in manufacturing industries. A strategic Development Framework Plan for the Coega IDZ has been developed, which focuses on infrastructure development and facilities for the Core Development Area, an area of 65 km². A number of multinational companies already operate from this area.

The Coega IDZ has up to 2017 signed investments worth more than R30 billion and include an oil refinery, a combined cycle gas turbine power station, a business process outsourcing park, automotive plants, and various other investments in the logistics, chemicals and food-processing sector. It is claimed that the investment projects and infrastructure development programmes created more than 100 000 jobs over 16 years. Among current contractors, 70 per cent are Nelson Mandela Bay based. Chairman Paul Jourdan claims that 'the Coega IDZ and the deep water Port of Ngqura have remained catalysts for investment and local development'.

(Sources: Adapted from http://en/wikipedia.org/wiki/Coega; Integrated Annual Report 2016/17: https://provincialgovernment.co.za/entity_annual/366/2017-eastern-cape-coega-development-corporation-(cdc)-annual-report.pdf))

The example of deliberately promoting industrial development within a metropolitan setting illustrates how the potential of an existing developed urban base is further applied and exploited. Less developed countries do not have the same potential as more developed ones to secure their urban populations. They value economic growth as a high priority, but need to address issues of poverty in a more efficient way. Owing to the already strong agricultural base of these countries, they often choose to strike a balance between the primary sector of agriculture and industrial development. Other factors also influence the choice or the nature of development projects. Governments need to choose between social investment (eg education and housing) and productive investment (industrial development). The location of industrial sites is from a regional development point of view a next choice, one between concentration and deconcentration. The choice between labour-intensive versus capital-intensive enterprises has to be made as well. Ultimately, the availability of energy and natural resources will determine many choices.

Existing and developing urban systems facilitate the transition from a subsistence economy to a money-based exchange economy. In a subsistence economy, one only possesses or accrues enough goods to be used by the household to provide for its day-to-day livelihood and to maintain its existence. Very little surplus for other investments is left and the economy does not use money to buy or exchange goods. In the money-based exchange economy, money is used by consumers for buying and selling the goods they need, which are usually produced by someone else. One needs to earn a wage for finding money. To the extent that this transition progresses, cash flow and capital formation increase due to more savings, and consumption expenditure changes and expands.

Owing to all these considerations, a critical factor for the outcome of the economic benefit of urbanisation is the type and extent of governmental intervention in industrial and urban development. The debate is whether planning, policy and development should be centralised or market regulated. We have already discussed the policy options of concentration and deconcentration, and referred to apartheid's deconcentration measures of influx control that kept black rural dwellers in the rural areas. As a motivating factor, the government of the time developed border industries to provide work opportunities for those staying in the rural 'homelands'. History has proved these developments to be dismal failures and eventually the influx control measures were scrapped, and the border industries subsided.

In post-apartheid South Africa, concentration and deconcentration policies are followed to promote developmental opportunities within and outside existing centres, but without the ideological justification of racial separation.

24.7.2 Physical problems

The maintenance and upkeep of the physical built environment and infrastructure of cities has become a problem due to population pressure and incompetent city administration. The illegal occupation of buildings and land has led to the decay of buildings and the urban environment in many cities regardless of the development status of the country. The upkeep and provision of municipal infrastructure (roads, energy, water and sanitation) has become an enormous financial liability. Substandard housing, slums and ghetto formation have become issues for these cities. City renewal programmes, also known as gentrification, have not always been successful. One particular problem is transport infrastructure and facilities for commuters.

Box 24.2 The gentrification of central cities

Gentrification refers to an inner-city process of movement and resettlement of people, changing the character of the central city from a poor sector to a place where younger and professional people find a niche. In other instances, it involves people who have been raised in the suburbs, but as young adults have moved to the city and who have chosen not to leave. In some cities, this trend has produced a central city 'revival'. This has led to the perception that gentrification may lessen the long-term physical and economic decline of cities.

Gentrification is sometimes a market-driven process and sometimes a city government-managed process. Either way, it functions to displace the urban poor in favour of professional, middle- and upper-class working people. A process of disinvestment sometimes occurs when landlords abandon rented buildings because they are no longer profitable. Such buildings then fall into disrepair, creating an opportunity for new investors to buy in cheaply and to renew them for middle- and upper-class housing.

An analysis of the plans in the early 1990s by the then Johannesburg City Council to redevelop some buildings in the central business district that had decayed after disinvestment shows that the buildings were supposed to be purchased by large corporations who aimed to restore them and then sell them to employees.

The intention was that the scheme would result in the movement of formally employed black workers mostly from Soweto into the inner city, presumably offering them a better alternative in their housing situation. ➡

However, it was felt that this would simultaneously increase the spatial marginalisation of the seasonally employed and the structurally unemployed black workers from the townships, and that this would be an unintended consequence that could intensify inequality in the city. Moreover, preference would be given to the employees of the corporations favouring them above employees of other companies.

Gentrification does not seem to be a process that can be easily engineered and is perceived as limited in its scope. It is furthermore assumed to be a process that will lure young middle-class people back to the central core and in this way counter suburbanisation and urban sprawl. In other words, it purports to contain young people in the city at a high standard of living, and yet we see new middle-class suburbs continuously being developed in all our South African cities at an unabated rate, feeding the urban sprawl.

(Sources: Steinberg, Van Zyl & Bond 1992: 274; Fick 1990: 31–35)

Physical development of cities under colonial rule maintained quite good standards, but maintenance and upkeep seemed to have become a problem due to the prioritisation of new developmental goals under the post-colonial administrations. Freedom wars and subsequent ethnic conflicts left a huge scar on the physical face of colonial cities, which will take decades to regain their erstwhile standards and architectural presentation. In addition to the decay and deterioration of buildings and infrastructure (roads, energy, water, sanitation) urban land was occupied, uncontrolled and unmanaged, resulting in substandard housing, slums, and informal structures and infrastructure.

From a government point of view, unplanned and uncontrolled occupation of urban space resulted in excessive population densities, inadequate physical infrastructure and a lack of the provision for facilities and services for social, health, economic and other similar functions. Cities or large parts of them were therefore without schools, clinics and hospitals, recreational and cultural facilities, shopping centres, and effective transportation links to such facilities. This created the need for social investment more than productive investment and large-scale building programmes for housing, educational, health and other social facilities.

Although such investments aim to benefit the poor, the poorest of the poor do not necessarily gain from the supply of sub-economic housing as they often do not have the means to provide for the daily maintenance of a formal housing structure. They often have to return to occupying substandard informal settlements, which aggravates the initial problem.

Physical urban planning becomes highly challenging and complex due to the very low (or no) income levels of the existing and new urban dwellers, rapid population growth, insufficient infrastructure and associated phenomena, each of which is becoming a competing first priority in urban development policy.

Available physical amenities in these cities are accessible only for the few wealthy industrialists, professionals, administrators and politicians. This emphasises the gap between the rich and the poor, and adds strain to intergroup relationships.

In 2004, the cabinet of the South African government adopted a Comprehensive Plan for Sustainable Human Settlements. Also known as Breaking New Ground, the plan intends to upgrade informal settlements and establish sustainable human settlements and social infrastructure. These aspects were deficient at the time due to historical conditions (Republic of South Africa 2004).

According to this plan, sustainability can be achieved when:

- there is a balance of economic growth and social development with the carrying capacity of natural systems
- there is sustainable development, wealth creation, poverty alleviation and equity
- environments are safe and secure
- there is adequate access to economic opportunities
- housing and tenure types are safe and secure
- there are reliable and affordable basic services
- educational, entertainment and cultural activities are provided for
- there are health, welfare and police services
- land utilisation is well planned, managed and monitored to ensure development of compact, mixed land use, diverse life-enhancing environments with maximum possibilities for pedestrian movement and transit via safe and efficient public transport.

Many of these requirements for human settlements in urban environments are lacking in South Africa. As a result, living conditions are harsh. Levels of frustration are growing, giving rise to public protests about the lack and quality of services provided because people were expecting a better deal and dispensation. These requirements for decent living do not only speak about the physical aspects of the urban environment but see human settlement as a holistic issue in which provision should be made for a total and all-comprehensive life situation in which people can build their quality of life and fulfil their human needs. The plan did not materialise based on its own criteria for sustainability.

Box 24.3 Service delivery protests against local government in South Africa

Municipal IQ, an independent local government data and intelligence service, provides key findings from its Municipal Hotspots Monitor in order to contribute to a better understanding of service delivery protests staged against local government. The Hotspots Monitor (see Figure 24.1), shows that service delivery protests increased since 2012 and that on average 104 service delivery protests per year were recorded. A worrying trend is the growing number of service delivery protests becoming violent in nature, especially in 2018. Municipal IQ says:

> Our uniquely SA history of anti-apartheid campaigns sought to make areas 'ungovernable'. Boycotts, stayaways and no-go zones were used as tools to assert collective disapproval of the government. Not only has the legitimacy of such techniques been eroded by democracy and participation in governance; the great tragedy is that those who are affected tend to be the very communities raising grievances.

(Sources: Municipal IQ 2013; 2018)

24.7.3 Social problems

The urban community is cosmopolitan and therefore heterogeneous with respect to its ethnic, racial, social and demographic composition. A major challenge is promoting intergroup relationships. Population growth, due to natural increase and in-migration, outgrows the tempo of the provision of urban amenities and facilities. This provision is a function of urban government and is one of the biggest challenges for the modern city. Social unrest and protest are political expressions of the social and institutional strains and personal stress characteristics of weakly managed urbanisation and often the cause of further instability in urban government. Urbanisation itself leads to rising expectations, but creates large levels of relative deprivation, and real or perceived gaps between the rich and poor, leading to even stronger forms of social unrest and protest.

In order to gain more insight into how poverty (as a social issue within urban and rural environments) is addressed and how this impacts on urbanisation, we will provide a few relevant research findings. In 2001, the government of South Africa launched its Urban Renewal Programme (URP) to focus attention on eight urban areas identified as those suffering from extreme poverty. These areas, called nodes, include Alexandra (Gauteng), Galeshewe (Northern Cape), Inanda and KwaMashu (KwaZulu-Natal), Khayelitsha and Mitchell's Plain (Western Cape), and Motherwell and Mdantsane (Eastern Cape).

Service delivery protests

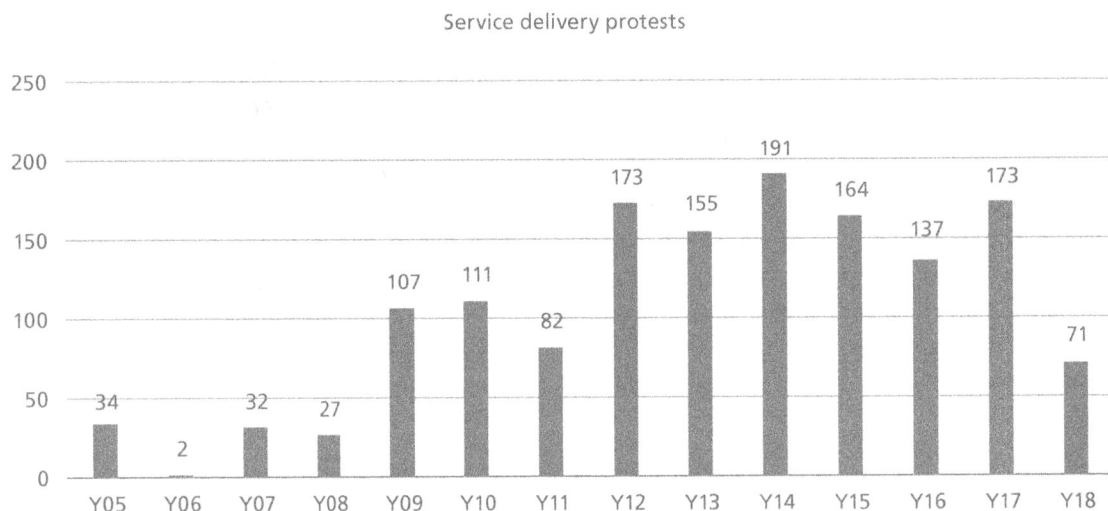

Figure 24.1 Major service delivery protests, by year, 2005 to 2018
(Source: Municipal IQ Municipal Hotspots Monitor 2019)

A similar programme launched for rural areas, under the name the Integrated Sustainable Rural Development

Programme (ISRDP), includes 13 areas for special attention. The Department of Social Development (DSD) conducts special projects in the 21 areas. During 2006 and 2008, comparative social surveys were undertaken to determine progress in socioeconomic living conditions, the poverty profile and the sustainable livelihood of the populations involved (Republic of South Africa 2008). Social surveys such as these make use of indexes to measure these aspects. An index is a research instrument that gives us a summary of the numerical value of something that we measured in a survey. This enables us to compare changes over time and from place to place, so, for instance, the poverty index for 2008 shows a substantially lower rating (numerical value) for the urban areas (18.7) in contrast to the rural areas (46.4). The higher the numerical figure, the higher the level of poverty among the population of the area. However, urban areas have experienced a slight increase in their poverty level since 2006 (18.2 to 18.7) while the rural areas have had a slight decrease over the same period (from 47.8 to 46.4) (Republic of South Africa 2008: 17).

Urban areas show more positive index figures than rural areas with respect to the proportion of female-headed households, illiteracy, unemployment, informal dwelling type, lack of refuse collection, weak sanitation service, weak water provision and weak lighting provision. On the other hand, urban dwellers have higher negative scores for overcrowding. The two area types have about the same proportions of people without a regular income.

The above patterns of urban–rural differences are in accordance to what we generally expect to be the situation. In contrast, the sustainable livelihood index scores are interesting. This index measures the things that people have access to such as land, cattle, family and friends that support them when they have to make a living on a daily basis, and is called the assets and capital index. The index also measures people's vulnerability – how and when they easily suffer from not having sufficient assets and means of life – as part of their overall or total sustainable livelihood index score (Republic of South Africa 2008: 35).

With respect to people's assets and capital, urban dwellers are worse off than their rural counterparts. This is true for *social capital* (ie family and friends that support one in time of hardship) and *natural resources* (such as land and a garden). As a result, urban dwellers' vulnerability score is actually worse than the one for rural dwellers. In the case of human resources skills (eg being trained for a job), financial resources (money) and physical infrastructure (proper roads, tap water, electricity, brick houses), urban dwellers are better off than rural ones. Overall, poor urban and rural dwellers do not differ significantly in their sustainable livelihood capacity, but rural dwellers are slightly better off. This means

that for the extreme poor – the group that was measured in this research – access to things like natural resources (land, livestock) and social capital (support among family and friends) are actually more valuable than impersonal resources such as infrastructure, finance or trained skills, which are found more in abundance among urban dwellers.

Over the period of observation (2006–2008), urban dwellers experienced a decline in water and electricity services, but gained a better ability to pay for food. Their top concerns are issues such as HIV and AIDS, alcohol abuse, crime and unemployment. Religious organisations and burial societies are their most important social networking opportunities and organisational forms. For the poor, the biggest challenge is finding a sustained income connected to a regular work opportunity, which is the main reason why rural people move to urban areas.

24.8 Rural–urban transition

It has become necessary to analyse urbanisation as a social process. Beyond the statistical, demographic and administrative meaning of urbanisation, it may be expressed as the outcome of a rural–urban transition, which is considered as a major social trend in human history signifying many elements including social significance. In this respect, a distinction is made between urbanisation before and after industrialisation. Before industrialisation, urbanisation was the result of a process of the evolutionary changes in human settlement patterns due to technological progress in agriculture-based economies. After industrialisation, it has become the result of the physical movement of people from rural areas to urban places due to a variety of reasons, but mainly because of economic considerations. The **push–pull model** is the most general and widely used framework for explaining urbanisation since industrialisation.

Let us briefly explain the concepts of industrialisation and the push-pull model. Industrialisation has become the concept to describe the profound changes and forces that the Industrial Revolution unleashed on society, first in Europe around the 1750s and afterwards in North America, and then throughout most of the world. This revolution completely transformed society and changed the way people lived. It primarily started by applying new forms of generating energy such as burning coal to use steam power to drive large machines. This enabled business entrepreneurs to increase the size of their production plants far beyond the household and community-based handcraft industries that existed until then. Production plants, or factories as we know them today, drew labourers and their families around them, creating the modern industrial city within the proximity of natural resources, harbours and railways. Mass transportation of goods and people had become possible due to the steam engine. Mine and factory work, for a wage, had become the norm and substituted largely small-scale farm production and cottage manufacturing. Industrialisation changed the social relationships between workers and the owners of production plants. It changed the character of cities as centres for government and religion to become home to the masses of people who worked in the new factories. Along with accommodation for the working people and their families located next to factories came unhygienic living conditions, ineffective or no protection against crime and fires, and weak or no sanitation, clean water and refuse services. Disease was the order of the day with cholera routinely killing thousands of people.

Regarding the push–pull model, it assumes four interactive forces or pressures that cause migrants to move between land and cities. One set of forces attracts or pulls migrants to cities, the second pushes labour off the land, the third draws migrants back to the land, and the fourth actively pushes them out of urban areas. The South African economist, Francis Wilson, has expounded and refined this model to explain what has become known as oscillating migration in South Africa (Wilson 1972).

A further explanation is the one by South African sociologist Harold Wolpe (1926–1996) (Wolpe 1972). He explains how cheap labour power came about and how it served the cause of apartheid. The racial ideology of apartheid through its policy of domination and control created and maintained a system of cheap labour among rural black Africans. As a result, they were 'pushed' out of the pre-capitalist African economy (we called it the subsistence economy earlier) in the rural areas to the industries of the towns with the promise of cash earnings but at a rate of wages below the real value of labour. This condition of cheap labour power in the urban environment acted similarly to a counter 'push' factor, compelling African workers to return to rural areas. This continuous moving from and to alternatively rural and urban areas become known as oscillating migration, and resulted in the weakening of the barriers between urban and rural areas. The apartheid regime saw this as a disadvantage for the urban industrial capitalist system that relied on cheap labour to remain profitable. The regime therefore legalised influx control and developed border industries to break the oscillating migration's effects. As we have observed, influx control became increasingly ineffective and was eventually abolished. Yet, the legacy of this system has become 'institutionalised' to such an extent

that today we still see young men (and women) from rural areas moving to urban areas, and back, in a similar manner.

From our discussions, it is clear that urbanisation is associated with deep and profound social changes. Sociologists have described such changes with the concept of the **Great Social Transformation** (Curry, Jiobu & Schwirian 1997: 42). Karl Polanyi (1886–1964) originally coined the concept (Polanyi 1944), arguing that the development of the modern state and modern market (capitalist) economy coincided historically. For the competitive market economy to develop, fundamental changes in the social structure of traditional (premodern) society were necessary. The economic transformations that happened destroyed the basic social order that had existed throughout earlier history. It is therefore a key idea for understanding the deep social and historical changes in social structure as linked to industrialisation and urbanisation. We shall inquire to what extent urbanisation in South Africa had the same effect on the rural social order.

Transformation means to change in form or appearance, condition, nature or character. In social transformation, we refer to the changes of humans in their relationships to one another, their living conditions, the way of living together in communities and lifestyle. A social transition refers to the process of changing from one form of social formation to another such as found within the social makeup of humans, their group life, community or society. The transition from rural to urban society has brought about this kind of transformation for those involved and for society at large.

Quite a number of social theorists of the 19th and 20th centuries attempted to grasp these transformations as linked to rural–urban transition. Four of them will be mentioned here, namely Max Weber (1864–1920), Ferdinand Tönnies (1855–1936), Louis Wirth (1897–1952) and Georg Simmel (1858–1918).

Max Weber suggests a major qualitative change in social relations in societies as from being predominantly communal to predominantly associational (Weber 1947/1915). **Communal societies** are characterised by features such as:
- personalised relationships
- an economy based on commodities in the nearby habitat
- a low technological level
- non-bureaucratic institutions
- limited stratification
- a rich ceremonial life (as in religious practices).

Associational societies, in contrast, have:
- a complex division of labour

- formal social units such as associations, organisations and corporations
- an economy based on manufacturing and related activities
- high levels of technology
- bureaucratic structures
- complex stratification
- strong emphasis on rationality and less on spirituality.

According to Weber's analysis, the processes that facilitate the Great Social Transformation include industrialisation, urbanisation, rationalisation, bureaucratisation and globalisation.

The work of Ferdinand Tönnies (Tönnies 1963/1887) makes a distinction between **Gemeinschaft** and **Gesellschaft**. These can literally be translated from German as 'community' and 'society' respectively. This distinction is better known than that of Weber's and forms the basis for Weber's concepts mentioned above. Together they provide a rich description of the two forms of social types. *Gemeinschaft* means that community functions very much like a big family where blood ties have a binding force on its members even when they have left home. The hometown or homeland always remains a reference point in the lives of those who have settled elsewhere. *Gesellschaft*, in contrast, represents relationships that you may enter or leave according to your own wish because they are based on free and rational choice and not on blood (family) commitment. Relationships according to *Gemeinschaft* are warm, and imply the whole personality of the participant. *Gesellschaft* relationships are cold, unattached and fragmented. They are a means to an end and not an end in itself.

The American sociologist Louis Wirth published a paper in 1938 entitled 'Urbanism as a way of life' (Wirth 1938). He was interested in how towns and cities have shaped us as social beings. He asked whether living in a town or city changes the way we think, believe, interact with friends, family and community. According to Wirth (1938), three measurements of human settlements indeed shape us as social actors:

1. *Size:* an urban place contains many thousands of people. Size criteria differ from country to country and reflect **urban hierarchy**. The point here is that an urban place has a much larger population in comparison to a rural place.
2. *Density:* density reflects the depth of urbanisation – that is, the number of people per square kilometre (or mile). Higher densities are to be found in urban places with high-rise residential and workplace buildings and

at sites for transportation (airports, railway stations, bus and taxi ranks), sports events, shopping, education, worship and others.
3. *Heterogeneity or complexity:* size and density in itself does not explain why there is a difference in experiencing urbanism as a 'way of life'. Wirth believes the difference is linked to the heterogeneity and complexity of social interactions caused by size and density. Urbanisation is experienced and internalised due to the number of social and economic interactions with others as well as the logistic and impersonal nature of these interactions and the range of opportunities for interaction and social activity.

For Wirth, then, a city is 'a relatively large, dense and permanent settlement of socially heterogeneous individuals'.

In his essay 'The metropolis and mental life', Georg Simmel (Simmel 1903) essentially asks the same question as Wirth. He is interested in the effects of the big city on the mind of the individual. Like Wirth, he identifies characteristics of the city that impact on its citizens. For instance, he sees the money economy as a feature that requires calculation in all activities. This demands the intellectual and cognitive competencies to be emphasised more than the subjective features of people. The continuous stimulation offered by the large number of people, events and happenings creates boredom and a blasé attitude. People become individualistic, indiscriminate, heartless and rational. Yet, Simmel maintains, there is always a fundamental motive at work that brings about 'a resistance of the individual to being levelled, swallowed up in the social-technological mechanism' (Simmel in Levine 1971: 324).

The social theorists referred to above provided descriptions of the way that rural and urban society are contrasting social formations. They indicate that there is a notable historical change or a transition from the one to the other. Our argument, however, is that the transition is not linear and does not need to end in a clear-cut contrast. Conceptually some of these theorists also acknowledge that there is an implicit link between urban and rural. We will show in the final section how urban society in South Africa is linked to rural society, how people interact across the rural–urban divide and how they take social values from the rural community to survive in the city.

24.9 Urban–rural linkages

We have introduced urbanisation as a multifaceted phenomenon that includes spatial, physical, demographic, economic and social aspects. One of the key social aspects of urbanisation is the process of **rural–urban transition** in social relationships affecting the whole of society. While we may speak of rural and urban spaces, social entities such as people, groups, institutions and service centres may carry urban-like profiles or identities. This is to say that localities, whether rural or urban, are affected by urbanisation as a process of social transition. We described this process as the Great Social Transformation that affects all aspects of society. One way that urbanisation impacts on rural localities is through urban–rural linkages. These personal and social linkages are beyond, but facilitated by, physical linkages such as:

- communication technology (telecommunication, mobile phones)
- media (television, print media)
- transportation links (roads, railways, air).

Personal and social linkages are those that operate through family, friends, community and nation, where an urban member of a social network or group keeps relationships with rural members alive and active. In this way, common bonds and identities between urban and rural localities are maintained yet subtly changed to manifest urban impact in rural localities, and vice versa. Many forms of keeping up the linkages between the two localities may be distinguished. Examples include:

- financial support (urban members sending money from their earnings 'home' to support the family on the rural side)
- social visits (regular visits between the family members of the two localities)
- information sharing (news about work opportunities, accommodation, health and educational facilities, disseminated by urban members to rural members)
- service utilisation (rural members making use of urban-based services, such as hospitals and shopping centres).

Research into **urban–rural linkages** confirms the observations above and adds further points. According to Tacoli (2004), urban–rural linkages include flows of agricultural and other commodities from rural-based producers to urban markets, both for local consumers and for forwarding to regional, national and international markets. They include flows in the opposite direction of manufactured and imported goods from urban centres to rural settlements. They also include flows of people moving between rural and urban settlements, either commuting on a regular basis, for occasional visits to urban-based services and administrative centres, or migrating temporarily

or permanently. Flows of information between rural and urban areas include information on market mechanisms – from price fluctuations to consumer preferences – and information on employment opportunities for potential migrants. Financial flows include, primarily, remittances from migrants to relatives and communities in sending areas, transfers such as pensions to migrants returning to their rural homes, as well as investments and credit from urban-based institutions.

In many instances, we find strong commitments and obligations between rural- and urban-based individuals and units, as is the case with '**multi-spatial households**'. In these households, reciprocal support is given across space. For example, remittances from urban-based members can be an important income source for rural-based ones, who in turn may look after their migrant relatives' children and property. These linkages can be crucial in the livelihood strategies of the poor, but are not usually taken into consideration in policymaking. According to research in Durban by Smit (1998), an urban and a rural base are maintained. The linkages between the two provide a safety net for low-income urban dwellers in times of economic hardship or political violence. However, government housing and rural development programmes do not acknowledge such multi-spatial, extended households. Eligibility for subsidies and grants is based on the size of the co-resident household (either in town or in the countryside), and the funds can only be used in one of the two locations. Since urban housing subsidies are more widely available, this may encourage urban-based members of multi-spatial households to cut their rural links. This is also an example of what has become known as the urban bias in public policy.

In Núñez's study conducted on internal and cross-border migrant households in Johannesburg in 2008, it was found that the provision of care helps to sustain links between the livelihood systems of urban and rural households. In times of sickness, many migrants choose to return to their household of origin to seek care. Female migrants play a pivotal role in the provision of care, potentially disrupting their productive livelihood roles within the city in order to return home to provide care (Núñez, Vearey & Drimie 2011).

24.10 Identity

Key social agencies facilitating these processes are community (including family and friends) and nation. In elaborating on the key concepts for this section, we rely on the work of Morris and Morton. While their concepts and definitions are used, such as locality, community, nation and identity, we apply our own interpretations (Morris &

Morton 1998). Community used to be defined according to the physical features of the environment (central business district, suburb), settlement (town, city, township) and boundaries (railway, road). It now includes reference to the local system (municipality), social interconnectivity (organisations), communion (similar beliefs, rituals and practices), bonding (friendships, family, clubs) and belonging (ethnic group and clan). All of these are considered as key issues in urban environments. Community still has a locality reference, but in many respects it transcends physical distance and boundaries. Nation appeals to collectivity (large social grouping), territory (country), borders and national governance, and an imagined community (feeling of national belonging). The rural–urban continuum may present itself within national boundaries or across national borders depending on the development status of nations. In cases where less developed nations are located next to or in close proximity to more developed nations, rural–urban linkages are affected by international variables. Such linkages within the same national territory are largely unaffected by these factors.

Nation is an important and significant factor in identity: it defines to whom you belong; where you live your life; the style of governance that you are subservient to; and the community with whom you associate yourself. It answers the questions: 'Who am I/Who are we? Where do I/we come from? Where am I/are we going?' It gives one a 'we' or 'us' association and belonging, and defines those that are outside this network or circle – the 'they' or 'them'. Under conditions of communal social relationships or Gemeinschaft (as viewed by Tönnies), one's answers to these questions are locality based – that is, restricted to time and place, and strongly linked into the local community. National identity has a strong ethnic base and appears to be homogeneous among members of the community. Nation-state is a strong social construction supporting identity that provides predetermined social formulae for life choices and behaviour.

Globalisation will potentially change this. Globalisation refers to the multiplicity of linkages and interconnections that transcend the nation-states that make up the modern world system (McGrew 1992). In a global system people are affected by events, decisions and the activities of others, and by national and transnational institutions, elsewhere in the world – regardless of where they live. Such effects invade people's private spheres and privacy, and due to communication technologies of the modern era, a diversity of images, information, knowledge and opinions present themselves indiscriminately, timely and untimely, through the all-embracing networks in which people have become involved. Globalisation may cause a kind of time–space compression that makes territorial boundaries irrelevant. Under these conditions, time and space become stretched and deepened – more things happen, more quickly and simultaneously.

This situation promotes the associational (Weber) or Gesellschaft (Tönnies) option in social relationships. Life choices and the consequent social behaviour and social outcomes are determined according to the situation at hand, which may change from one moment to the next, opening up the possibility to live a life of multiple and diverse, even contradictory, options in social relationships. The weakening of the influence of predetermined, packaged life solutions, a result of the deconstruction of the nation-state and its associated national identity, implies the possibility of multiple identities in the basic questions of life. The urban dweller who is exposed to globalisation more than the relatively isolated rural person may have different answers to the questions: 'Who am I/Where do I come from/Where am I going?' The answers may be phrased as follows: 'It depends …'. This is the condition of postmodernity.

Urban people are becoming global citizens of weakened nation-states in a world that is increasingly networked to maximise global profitability where markets and societies (not nation-states) are becoming more sensitive to each other under the jurisdiction of international codes, organisational and related forces (Held 1996). Under these conditions, identity is becoming more fragmented and less consolidated. Solidarity, which is based on the foundation of identity, is therefore no longer solidified around familial or community bonds but driven according to universal codes, human rights and values. Gender equality is a good example of how gender rights have been advanced at global forums and become written into international legal and human rights codes and not necessarily because of local employer enlightenment. Identity is temporary, movable, very personal and even fashionable. Following Hall, any one of a range of identities could be used, although usually only for a short period before a new identity becomes fashionable (Hall 1992).

24.11 The hybrid nature of South African urban life

A prominent feature of urbanisation among South Africans is the urban–rural linkages among urban people and their family and community members 'back home'. The migrant labour system that gave rise to the urban-based black industrial labour force by definition had to maintain a link between urban and rural community under the legal prescriptions of the apartheid era. Black workers were contract workers with contracts no longer than a year. Annually, workers had to return to their home base to renew the contract for another year. Those workers who renewed contracts year after year for prolonged periods developed urban identities amidst their annually reinforced rural identity. In some cases, urban families were created, while rural family ties were maintained. Over time, migrant workers developed multiple familial and communal identities, while at the same time being increasingly exposed to the urban way of life. With the abolition of influx control measures in 1986, researchers and policymakers were expecting an increased migration from rural to urban areas to 'normalise' the social and family profiles of the singular migrant workers. This did not happen to the level of expectation, perhaps because of the dual family life of many. Yet, urban and rural people maintained their interaction, sometimes over long distances, through links within multi-spatial households.

A question that begs to be answered is whether or not black African migrant workers changed according to the hypothesis of the Great Social Transformation. The answer needs to be properly researched, but one would guess that the outcome would vary:

- Some would have become globalised, world citizens.
- Others are urbanised yet driven in social choice by **ethnic identity**.
- Some are straddling across the two worlds of urban and rural realities in which they are trying to sustain a livelihood.
- Many are residing in an urban environment but longing for the phase in their life when they may 'go home'.

Our conclusion to this question would be that urban life in South Africa is a multifaceted, heterogeneous social condition that brings together in one locality the world, the nation, the ethnic, the community, the family and, sadly, the lonely, isolated and insulated individual.

Case study 24.2 *Kulture Noir* (2010)

After having produced her successful *Zandisile* (2004) and *The One Love Movement on Bantu Biko Street* (2006), Simphiwe Dana, six times SAMA award winner, presented her critically acclaimed new album *Kulture Noir* in 2010. She composes and sings peaceful yet impassioned jazz, soul, gospel, folk and traditional Xhosa. A proud ambassador for HOKISA (Homes for Kids in South Africa), this urban woman with exposure across the globe sings about her rural heritage, the new South African identity, and the transnational influences that are defining Africa at her best.

Simphiwe is from Lusikisiki on the Wild Coast of the Eastern Cape. As a child, she fetched water at the river every day and in the evenings sat by candlelight at the feet of her grandmother who told her and the other kids' stories from old Xhosa culture. Her songs are encouraging her people who are struggling to make a living in town, with this simple message:

Keep courage, we know poverty is painful, but don't let hope disappoint you. In every one of us there is light; let it shine. I love you all, because I love myself and the godliness within me. I see God in all of you. I believe that when we love, we understand the importance of justice.

She has a powerful message:

Education changes lives. I don't believe in welfare states. I am a rural girl from Transkei who through quality training at school has been saved from a life of poverty.

Our case study that opened this chapter tells the story of Adegoke Taylor who migrated to Lagos from a distant rural town. He experienced the freedom of city life as exhilarating, encouraging him to make full use of what the city had to offer. His survival was no easy task. At first, he had to use his family and friendship network to find a home. There was no sympathetic uncle or friend to give him a reference for a job, and he was exposed to ethnic riots, and yet he continued because of the promise of the city – something far beyond what was possible in his hometown. We also introduced the story of Simphiwe Dana – a talented girl from deep rural South Africa who took the world head-on and made a success with her wonderful music. Our brief comments of her philosophy of life explain some of the reasons for her success.

In her case, her rural background provided the material for her lyrics and music that brought success. Whether in Lagos or Johannesburg, survival in the city relies on rural networks and heritage. The success stories of those who have made it in city life serve as an inspiration for those back home to see urban horizons as a promise for a better life.

Summary

- Urbanisation is defined according to a number of concepts, of which the level of urbanisation and urban growth are basic. Urbanisation is brought about by the migration of people from rural to urban areas, which determines the level of urbanisation. Urban growth refers to the growth of the population already in urban areas. A third option is that urban land be classified as such and incorporated into existing urban areas, thus enlarging the urban population administratively.

- Urban areas or centres are defined differently depending on the country of study. Size of population is often a determining criterion, which leads to distinctions such as metropolitan areas, cities and towns.

- Urban centres are relatively large and permanent settlements, therefore we distinguish between different internal formations such as central business districts, suburbs and peri-urban areas. In South Africa, townships became known as suburbs for black people, particularly as a legacy from the apartheid era when different race groups were divided into separate but adjacent towns within common urban areas. Poor black people still reside in townships that were constructed under apartheid rule.

- The study of urbanisation in South Africa should take note of the processes before 1986 and since then. This date marks the abolition of influx control measures under apartheid rule and the inhibitive effect these had on the urbanisation (and migration) of black South Africans. Not only were black South Africans prohibited to settle permanently in urban areas of white South Africa, but social, economic and infrastructure development were slowed down to an insignificant level or adapted to fit the objectives of apartheid society. Not only was influx control scrapped but, since the early 1990s, all racial restrictive legislation was abolished to create a truly democratic and open society as from 1994. Urban populations have since started to show a more balanced demographic composition according to race, sex and age.

- All land in South Africa is under municipal governance. This reform was to have a developmental function regarding the area under its jurisdiction. It is therefore impossible to distinguish (on the basis of administrative and statistical reason) between urban and non-urban (rural) areas. Metropolitan areas may be used as a proxy for highly urbanised populations. It is found that populations of the metropolitan areas in South Africa are growing faster than the total and non-metropolitan populations in the country.

- More than half of the world population lives in urban areas today. Urban populations are growing faster than the total population. Developed regions are more urbanised than less developed regions, but the urban growth rate is higher for less developed regions.

- The world is now experiencing the second wave of urbanisation and we expect unprecedented numbers of people to become urban in the next two decades. More urban dwellers in less developed countries than in developed regions are currently living in urban areas, and the gap will increase.

- Africa reflects low urbanisation levels typical of least developed countries. Southern Africa is the most urbanised region, with some areas higher than 50 per cent. South Africa is said to have an urbanisation level of 60 per cent.

- Economic considerations prove to be central in the drive towards urbanisation. Varied patterns of urbanisation are observed, linked to factors such as the decision to concentrate or to deconcentrate. Business interests are primarily to invest in areas where profit-making opportunities are optimal. However, industrial investment requires the creation of job opportunities and employing waged labour – a process known as proletarianisation. Within the context of urbanisation, it provides the opportunity for subsistence workers to become involved in paid work in the urban industrial situation. From this point of view, the migratory labour system of South Africa (and elsewhere) caused the transformation of rural people to wage labourers within the industrial economy. This implication created the very seeds of destruction of the migrant labour system, which provided cheap labour to industry for a long time. Proletarianisation created a permanent labour force within a cash economy. ⇒

- A major feature of cities in less developed countries is the development of peri-urban areas, which often lack clear regulations and administrative authority over land use. This is a feature of African cities that developed around a single core and do not have sufficient space for expansion. South Africa provided for municipal control and regulation of land and land use, but has many examples of areas functioning as peri-urban to the main core. These areas have positive functions such as providing food security and agricultural development, and containing urban sprawl but are also characterised by environmental degradation, health hazards and the intermingling of residential and agricultural use.

- Urbanisation has profound social and economic implications for society. Research in this area has listed implications, consequences, issues and problems with reference to the economy, the physical environment (natural, manmade and infrastructure), social conditions and relationships, personal life, government and administration, and many more.

- The physical condition of cities is no easy challenge and sometimes city renewal programmes, also known as gentrification, are implemented. In Johannesburg, gentrification also served to deal with equity problems of society, but is not without its problems. On the social plane, intergroup relationships often are a serious challenge due to the cosmopolitan composition of the city population.

- Poverty alleviation is a major economic challenge, which results in some difficult development choices, such as the balance between industrial and agricultural development, social investment and productive investment, concentration and deconcentration, labour- and capital-intensive enterprise, and the location of industrial sites within a region. In South Africa, a Spatial Industrial Development and Industrial Infrastructure Programme assists local area development to create opportunities for industrial development and employment as a poverty alleviation measure.

- Unplanned and uncontrolled invasion of urban spaces and the informal settlement of large newly arrived or displaced populations are another challenge. The South African government adopted a Comprehensive Plan for Sustainable Human Settlements that promises to provide social infrastructure. Owing to numerous problems, it has become quite difficult to keep up with the demand in this respect and social protests against the lack of proper municipal services and urban violence have been experienced in increasing numbers.

- The social implications of urban planning and development are inextricably linked to the physical and economic challenges. Social implications are reflected on the personal level, as issues related to social cohesion, in the need for strong local government, the ability to adapt to urban life, and in the frustration of not meeting rising expectations.

- In South Africa extreme poverty is far higher in rural than in urban areas, yet it seems as if urban poverty is on the rise. Research in South Africa points to poor people's own ingenuity, the natural resources available to them, and their social networking and mutual support as significant factors in their designing of sustainable livelihood strategies.

- Sociologically, urbanisation can be seen as the expression of a global process of rural–urban transition, depicted as the Great Social Transformation. Historically, this transition received its impetus from 18th and 19th century industrialisation, in Western Europe and northern America, and later in other regions that were industrialising. The transition brought about transformative processes affecting all aspects of human life, including economic, political, social, psychological and cultural aspects. While urbanisation under the influence of industrialisation was largely engineered as an attempt to concentrate labour near factories, post-industrial urbanisation may be better explained according to the push-pull model of migration, which also considers the negative push factors present in rural areas.

- Nineteenth century social theorists conceptualised the Great Social Transformation with reference to qualitative changes in social relationships and the influence of normative forces in social life. The work of Max Weber (communal and associational society) and Ferdinand Tönnies (*Gemeinschaft* and *Gesellschaft)* provided insight into the transformations brought about by industrialisation and urbanisation. The effect of city life on urban dwellers' social and personal life has been shown by Louis Wirth (an urban way of life) and Georg Simmel (the urban personality).

- While sociologists in the past tended to focus more on the profound social impact of industrialisation particularly with reference to the new industrial working class, studies in African environments and particularly in South Africa recognised the vibrant linkages between urban and rural communities as an important mechanism to cope with city life. ➠

- Urban–rural linkages have been found to be important for facilitating the rural–urban transition and the social transformation that followed. Urban–rural linkages find expression in personal and group relationships, the use of communication technology, and transport links. Relationships are strengthened through remittances sent back home from the urban member, by social visits, sharing information, using services, etc. A special social formation – the multi-spatial household – necessitates regular and strong interrelationships. In some cases, migrant workers started multiple families that created a burden on them in managing their conflicting social obligations.

- Developing an urban identity – that is, a self-image and character needed for surviving among the many challenges that face the individual in urban society – is something that not many researchers have pursued. Sociological concepts such as community and nation are helpful in this regard. While community is the socially supportive mechanism for the individual, nation stands for the identity assumed by the person. Amidst globalisation, the urbanised individual has to work out how to form this identity and to maintain and use it for living an urban life. One of the answers to the question of identity is that multiple identities can be formed and assumed, which is typically the condition of postmodernity. The national identity, fuelled by the nation-state, is becoming weakened, and individual freedom allows the person to make free choices. The new guidelines are often universal codes, human rights and values. Identity becomes fluid and interchangeable, yet may stay moral in terms of the common heritage of humanity.

- The legacy of the migrant worker period and system, still informally in place in many cases, has had the consequence that urban–rural linkages were maintained in many instances. This created a peculiarly strong dual identity among black South Africans who have their lives straddled across the two worlds of the rural and the urban. Yet, many options are open and are indeed practised in the social makeup of urban South Africa.

ARE YOU ON TRACK?

1. What is urbanisation and what are its main concurrent processes?
2. How does urbanisation present itself today – its patterns across the world and locally?
3. What are the implications of urbanisation for society, government and the people involved?
4. What are the drivers of urbanisation?
5. How do people make sense of the world of the city when they grew up in a rural world?

More sources to consult

Satterthwaite D. 2007. 'The transition to a predominantly urban world and its underpinnings'. Human settlements discussion paper series, Urban change – 4. International Institute for Environment and Development (IIED), London. Available at: http://www.iied.org/pubs/; and accessible at www.iied.org/pubs/display.php?o= 10550IIED/

Currently David Satterthwaite is perhaps the foremost urbanisation expert in the world. In this paper he updates our comparative knowledge in a state-of-the-art presentation about urbanisation.

Satterthwaite D. 2011. 'Millennium Development Goals and Urban Areas, 2011'. Overseas Development Institute (ODI), London. 24 minutes. Presentation on video clip. Link: http://blip.tv/file/get/Odi_webmaster-DavidSatt erthwaitePresentation486.m4v; and http://www.odi. org.uk/events/documents/2616-presentation-david-satterthwaite.pdf; PDF Presentation.

David Satterthwaite discusses the promise of urban areas in achieving the MDGs. While the general indices seem promising, he points out that we need to look beyond and deeper than the general picture. (Note that the quality of the visual material is not good; hence we also provide a link to the PDF presentation.)

Swilling M, Humphries R & Shubane K (eds). 1991. *Apartheid City in Transition*. Cape Town: Oxford University Press. For those interested in the urban situation in South Africa before the era of democratisation, this compilation provides a good, honest and critical assessment.

United Nations. 2011. 'State of the World's Cities 2010/2011 – Cities for All: Bridging the Urban Divide'. Published with UN-Habitat. Available at: http://www.unhabitat. org/content.asp?cid=8051&catid=7&typeid=46&sub MenuId=0. This edition uses the framework of 'The Urban Divide' to analyse the complex social, political, economic and cultural dynamics of urban environments. It focuses on the concept of the 'right to the city' and ways in which many urban dwellers are excluded from the advantages of city life, using the framework to explore links among poverty, inequality, slum formation and economic growth.

Useful websites

Coega: http://en/wikipedia.org/wiki/Coega/; http://www.coega.co.za

South African history: http://www.sahistory.org.za/article/land-dispossession-1600s-1900s-5-segregation-apartheid

References

Anderson Literary Management Inc. 2006. 'The Megacity' – copyright 2006 © by George Packer. *The New Yorker*, 82(37): 64.

Barry M. 2003. 'Peri-urban tenure management in South Africa'. Second FIG Regional Conference, Marrakech, Morocco, 2–5 December 2003. [Online] Available at: http://www.fig.net/pub/morocco/proceedings/TS1/TS1_1_barry.pdf [Accessed 12 September 2013].

Bernstein A, McCarthy J (eds). 1990. 'Opening the cities: Comparative perspectives on desegregation'. An Indicator SA Issue Focus. Durban: Indicator South Africa. September.

Bundy C. 1979. *The Rise and Fall of the South African Peasantry*. London: Heinemann.

Cilliers SP, Groenewald CJ. 1982. 'Urban growth in South Africa 1936–2000. A demographic overview'. Occasional Paper no 5, Department of Sociology, Stellenbosch University.

Curry T, Jiobu R, Schwirian K. 1997. *Sociology for the 21st Century*. Upper Saddle River, NJ: Prentice Hall.

Eley G, Suny RG (eds). 1996. *Becoming National: A Reader*. Oxford: Oxford University Press.

Fick J. 1990. 'Cities in transition: urban renewal and suburbanisation' in *Opening the Cities: Comparative Perspectives on Desegregation. An Indicator SA Issue Focus*. Bernstein A, McCarthy J (eds). Durban: Indicator South Africa, September, 31–35.

Hall S. 1992. 'The question of cultural identity' in *Modernity and its Futures*. Hall S, Held D, McGrew A (eds). Cambridge: Polity Press.

Hall S, Held D, McGrew A (eds). 1992. *Modernity and its Futures*. Cambridge: Polity Press.

Hauser PM. 1963. 'The social, economic, and technological problems of rapid urbanisation' in *Industrialization and Society*. Hoselitz BF, Moore WE. The Hague: UNESCO-Mouton, 199–217.

Held D. 1996. 'The decline of the nation-state' in *Becoming National: A Reader*. Eley G, Suny RG (eds). Oxford: Oxford University Press.

Hoselitz BF, Moore WE (eds). 1963. *Industrialization and Society*. The Hague: UNESCO-Mouton.

Kulture Noir. 2010 by CDGURB 147, Gallo. [Online] Available at: http://www.gallo.co.za and http://www.simphiwedana.com [Accessed 1 October 2013].

Levine D (ed). 1971. *Simmel: On individuality and social forms*. Chicago University Press.

McGrew A. 1992. 'A global society' in *Modernity and its Futures*. Hall S, Held D, McGrew A (eds). Cambridge: Polity Press.

Morris A, Morton G. 1998. *Locality, Community and Nation*. London: Hodder & Stoughton.

Müller W. 2011. 'Gewilde Dana in Kaapstad' (Popular Dana in Cape Town). *Die Burger*, 26 March.

Municipal IQ: Municipal Hotspots Press Release on Major Service Delivery Protests, 16 January 2013. [Online] Available at: http://www.municipaliq.co.za/index.php?site_page=hotspots.php [Accessed 6 August 2013].

Municipal IQ: Municipal Data and Intelligence. 'Communities hurt by more frequent and more violent protests.' 18 October 2018. http://www.municipaliq.co.za/index.php?site_page=article.php&id=104 [Accessed 21 January 2020].

Ntsebeza L. 2006. 'The land and agrarian questions: What do they mean in South Africa today?' Department of Sociology, University of Cape Town. [Online] Available at: http://www.spp.org.za/publications/Seminar%20Papers/agrarianquestion.pdf [Accessed 11 October 2013].

Núñez Carrasco L, Vearey, J, Drimie, S. 2011. 'Who cares? HIV-related sickness, urban–rural linkages, and the gendered role of care in return migration in South Africa'. *Gender & Development*, 19(1):105–114. [Online] Available at: http://dx.doi.org/10.1080/13552074.2011.554028 [Accessed 9 October 2013].

Polanyi K. 1944. *The Great Transformation*. New York: Rinehart.

Republic of South Africa. nd. 'National Industrial Policy Framework (NIPF)'. Department of Trade and Industry. Pretoria. [Online] Available at: http://www.thedti.gov.za/industrial_development/docs/NIPF_r2.pdf [Accessed 13 August 2013].

Republic of South Africa. Black Labour Act 67 of 1964. Pretoria: Government Printer.

Republic of South Africa. Abolition of Influx Control Act 68 of 1986. Pretoria: Government Printer.

Republic of South Africa. 1995. Urban Development Strategy of the Government of National Unity. Ministry in the Office of the President. *Government Gazette* 365(16679): 3 November. Pretoria: Government Printer.

Republic of South Africa. 2004. *Comprehensive Plan for the Development of Sustainable Human Settlements.* Department of Housing (now Department of Human Settlements), Pretoria.

Republic of South Africa. 2008. 'Building sustainable livelihoods – an overview. Analysing a baseline (2006) and measurement (2008) survey in the 22 nodes of the URP and ISRDP; Rural synthesis report; Urban synthesis report'. Everatt D & Smith MJ. [Accessed 8 July 2013].

Satterthwaite D. 2007. 'The transition to a predominantly urban world and its underpinnings'. Human settlements discussion paper series, Urban change – 4. International Institute for Environment and Development (IIED), London. [Online] Available at: http://www.iied.org/pubs/ and at www.iied.org/pubs/display.php?o=10550IIED [Accessed 16 October 2013].

Simmel G. 1903. *Die Grosstädte und das Geistesleben* (The Metropolis and Mental Life). Dresden: Petermann. [Online] Available at: http://www.altruists.org/static/files/The%20Metropolis%20and%20Mental%20Life%20%28Georg%20Simmel%29.htm [Accessed 4 June 2013].

Simmel, G. 1971. 'The metropolis of modern life' in *Simmel: On individuality and social forms.* Levine D. Chicago University Press.

Smit W. 1998. 'The rural linkages of urban households in Durban'. 1998. *Environment and Urbanisation,* 10(1): 77–88. [Online] Available at: http://eau.sagepub.com/content/10/1/77.full.pdf [Accessed 13 June 2013].

Smith DM (ed). 1992. *The Apartheid City and Beyond: Urbanisation and Social Change in South Africa.* London: Routledge.

South Africa. Natives Land Act 27 of 1913. Pretoria: Government Printer.

South Africa. Natives (Urban Areas) Consolidation Act 25 of 1945. Pretoria: Government Printer.

South Africa. Group Areas Act 41 of 1950. Pretoria: Government Printer.

Statistics South Africa (StatsSA). 2012. *Metadata.* [Online] Available at: http://www.statssa.gov.za/Census2011/Products.asp [Accessed 10 June 2013].

Statistics South Africa (StatsSA). 2012. *Municipal Fact Sheet.* [Online] Available at: http://www.statssa.gov.za/Census2011/Products.asp [Accessed 10 June 2013].

Steinberg J, Van Zyl P, Bond P. 1992. 'Contradictions in the transition from urban apartheid: barriers to gentrification in Johannesburg' in *The Apartheid City and Beyond: Urbanisation and Social Change in South Africa.* Smith DM (ed). London: Routledge.

Swart CF, Lamont AM. 1984. *Die Stad. Sosiologie, Beplanning en Ontwikkeling.* 2nd ed. Johannesburg: McGraw-Hill.

Swilling M, Humphries R, Shubane K (eds). 1991. *Apartheid City in Transition.* Cape Town: Oxford University Press.

Tacoli C. 2004. 'Rural–urban linkages and pro-poor agricultural growth: an overview'. IIED. Prepared for OECD DAC POVNET, Agriculture and Pro-Poor Growth Task Team, Helsinki Workshop, 17–18 June 2004. [Online] Available at: http://www.oecd.org/dataoecd/25/8/36562896.pdf [Accessed 24 June 2013].

Thompson EP. 1963. *The Making of the English Working Class.* London: Victor Gollancz.

Tönnies F. 1963 (original 1887). *Community and Society.* Loomis CP (transl and ed). New York: Harper & Row.

UNFPA. 2007. 'Unleashing the potential of urban growth. State of world population'. [Online] Available at: www.unfpa.org/swp [Accessed 10 June 2013].

UN, ECA & UNFPA. 2016. United Nations Economic Commission for Africa and United Nations Population Fund. The Demographic Profile of African Countries. March 2016. https://www.uneca.org/sites/default/files/PublicationFiles/demographic_profile_rev_april_25.pdf [Accessed 23 February 2019].

Van der Merwe IJ, Nel A. 1981. *Die Stad en sy Omgewing, 'n Studie in Nedersettingsgeografie.* Stellenbosch: University Publishers and Booksellers.

Weber M. 1947 (original 1915). *The Theory of Social and Economic Organization.* Henderson AM, Parsons T (transl). New York: Free Press.

Wilson F. 1972. *Migrant Labour in South Africa. Report to the South African Council of Churches.* Johannesburg: The South African Council of Churches and SPRO-CAS.

Wirth L. 'Urbanism as a way of life'. 1938. *American Journal of Sociology,* 44: 1–24.

Wolpe H. 1972. 'Capitalism and cheap labour-power in South Africa: From segregation to apartheid'. *Economy & Society,* 1(4): 425–456.

Rurality and rural development

Paul Stewart

Three thousand years ago, in ancient Greece, the inhabitants of the rural were considered as *barbaroi* – barbarian: uncivilised, uncultured, rude and uncouth. The rural, it was thought, lacked everything the urban possessed – sophistication, art, culture and all things fine. The rural was denigrated and was consequently long defined as *non-urban*. To feel the force of this negative thinking, consider the word black to mean non-white, a distinction to which Steve Biko drew our attention. The same goes for considering the rural as *non-urban*. Such thinking about the rural must also be thrown into the dustbin of history.

Yet thinking of the rural, *positively*, has eluded the best of minds. We all have some mental picture of the rural, but as soon as we try to define what makes it *rural*, it tends to fade. The rural is hard to define. As this chapter will point out, there is no definition of the rural in our official government legislation, but then neither is there in any other. Governments have, instead, defined the rural in terms of population density, as does ours. This avoids the difficult work of conceptually capturing the occluded wealth, the unique diversity and the fabulous potential of the immensely vast natural expanses of the rural and beyond. For only between 1 and 3% of the planet's surface is urban. To define the rural in bald numbers, moreover, says nothing about what the rural is, or what it is like, or what rurality is, namely that which still bears the feint traces of natural human ways of life. Given that under half of South Africans live in areas as the previous chapter showed our mental picture tells us are rural, rethinking the rural, let us agree, might just still be important.

Around twenty years ago, a group of Dutch scholars from Wageningen University came up with a positive definition of the rural. This chapter suggests this account might still be useful for thinking about our own society. These scholars defined the rural as where *the co-production between human activity and nature* takes place. Rurality is both the result and expression of this co-production. The natural processes of life itself are *produced* and *reproduced* in the rural. The rural is hence defined in relation to the interaction between human beings and the physical, natural world.

Today, the rural remains a source of wealth. Yet what is clear is that the rural has been ignored. One piece of evidence for this is that a dedicated chapter in sociology textbooks on the countryside, or rural life or rurality are exceptionally rare. Can we, however, continue to ignore those who live beyond the city walls? Did Africa not teach us, ever since Ghana in 1957, that there is no national reconstruction without a dedicated focus on the rural? For, at the very least, the rural is to where many South Africans regularly return as this remains their real home.

Case study 25.1 Rural life

On the urban fringes of East London, Butterworth and Umtata, rural villages are quiet and deserted during the week. The only obvious evidence of productive activity is the movement of older women working at their daily chores of housekeeping, firewood collection and attending to gardens. They lament the absence of their daughters, many of whom have taken up residence in nearby towns. At midday, streams of young children criss-cross the village on their way home. Occasionally, clusters of young men are seen hanging around street corners or in the yards of houses. They come and go, but are especially evident at month-end when their mothers get pensions.

Over weekends the situation changes dramatically. The villages come alive with the return of commuters, work seekers and market women. Social activities intensify. People move freely between ritual gatherings, school meetings, credit club get-togethers and local beer drinks. By Sunday evening these activities have begun to wind down and many head for the taxi rank to get into the city for an early start on Monday. Such is the weekly cycle of the urban fringe of many Eastern Cape towns and cities.

In the deeper rural areas of the province, the weekly cycle of the urban fringe is less evident and there are more deserted homesteads and unattended fields. But even in these areas, the month-end flows back into the countryside are significant. The notable absence of especially young women has had a profound effect on the productive rural economy. Household fields are planted and harvested, but not with the same intensity as before. Ploughing teams are no longer mobilised, cattle kraals are in a state of disrepair and livestock are thin on the ground. These are facts which are lamented by local people who refer to the lost opportunities of the good rains over the past few years. At month-end, the social economy of these villages is re-invigorated with the arrival of migrants and commuters who return with remittances (Bank 1997: 24).

QUESTIONS

1. This description is dated 1997. How would you update this description of rural life?
2. Who could tell you of any changes in the past 20 years?
3. What factors explain any changes you may have identified?

Key themes

- Defining the rural
- Defining rural as co-production with nature
- The 'agrarian question' in the classical literature
- Rural transformation in South Africa

- Interrogating 'rural development'
- The trajectory of the concept of rural development
- Aspects of 'the rural' in South Africa.

25.1 Introduction

Everyone has a personalised view of rural life or **rurality** – the condition of being in the rural (Bosworth & Somerville 2014). The geographical vastness and diversity of the rural countryside has led to many meanings and functions being attributed to 'the rural'. It is consequently a 'messy and slippery idea' (Woods 2011). A leading rural sociologist has even wondered 'what we should understand as the rural' as it appears to be empty 'as a *concept*' and is consequently 'a vigorously debated empirical reality' (Van der Ploeg 1997: 39).

The lack of conceptual clarity in defining rural society became apparent in attempts to understand the long, drawn-out transition from rural to industrial society. This ongoing transition was often violent and traumatic

as feudal society based on peasant agriculturalists and **artisans** and the handicraft skills – pottery, the forging of metals, leatherwork, basket weaving, beading, bread baking, and the like – gave way to increasingly rapid industrialisation and urbanisation. In Europe, the Industrial Revolution transformed family-based smallholding farmers, other agricultural producers and artisans (peasants) into landless waged labourers (proletarians). New mechanical technologies meant new factories, which meant new goods and commodities and new markets. Traditional forms of work, ways of life and social relations were transformed as rural society became inextricably entangled with this urban-based industrial capitalist society. These changes were so extensive that Max Weber (1906) thought this was the end of rural society, whether in Europe or North America. He put it this way:

> If there is a specific rural social problem it is only this: Whether and how the rural community or society, **which no longer exists**, can arise again so as to be strong and enduring [emphasis added].

For Weber, the technological revolutions of industrialisation changed everything as capitalist social relations intruded into the rural. The landlord was no longer a farmer but leased his land; the farmer was a capitalist like any other and the workers were seasonal or wage-paid artisans like any other worker. Old social relations had ceased to exist. Rural society had become subject to the ever-complex waves of social change the industrial urban revolution left in its wake.

As we will see, however, when it comes to Africa – though not South Africa – colonial capitalism generally did *not* transform independent agricultural producers first into cash tax-paying **peasant** producers and then into waged labour in the same way as occurred in Europe (Dunaway 2010), *nor* did ancient traditional forms of society entirely disappear. The view that urbanisation brought an end to the peasantry under colonialism is 'unrealistic' at best (Bond 2007: 34).

This raises central questions for African rural sociology. Was Weber correct in thinking that rural community and society no longer existed? How is the rural to be understood? Must we agree with the 'New Ruralism' school that since the mid-20th century, the meaning of 'rural' no longer corresponds with any objective reality? (Resina 2012).

In South Africa, dispossession of the land under colonialism, entrenched under **racial segregation** and consolidated under apartheid, irrevocably transformed preconquest 'rural' society. There was a great need for labour from the earliest days of European settlement and colonial agricultural production. The imposition of colonial taxes turned independent **indigenous** agriculturalists and livestock holders into cash crop producers or wage labourers. Where preconquest societies were militarily powerful and managed to resist the new market cash economy and agricultural wage work, indentured labourers had to be introduced, as in early colonial Natal.

Labour requirements were sharply and dramatically accelerated by the mining revolution in the late 19th century. Legislative and administrative means were employed to force greater numbers of independent African peasant producers into industrial proletarian waged work. Within a few decades, large swathes of land became overpopulated **labour reserves**. The ancient traditional African mode of production was virtually entirely destroyed. Before the mid-20th century, African society had largely been reduced to bare subsistence agriculture. Such conditions fuelled uneven processes of urbanisation. A pervasive **migrant labour system** and the flow of goods and money linked the labour reserves with the burgeoning industrial mining urban centres.

Further **forced removals** initiated in the 1930s pushed previously independent African agricultural producers off the land into closer rural settlements in the name of 'betterment' schemes. It has been argued that these schemes were the 'flagship' of '**rural development**' of both the segregation and apartheid regimes (Westaway 2012: 135). In the 1980s black African people were pushed onto arid lands – the 'dumping grounds' of apartheid. Yet even now under democracy, evictions of farm workers from white farms in the two decades either side of 1994 continue to expel people from their modest footholds and homes in rural areas.

Meanwhile in Europe there is sufficient evidence, 'found everywhere', of a rediscovery of 'the local', or 'localisation', and 're-ruralisation' (a return to the countryside). Old rural-based handicrafts are re-emerging, even where they had disappeared (Van Der Ploeg 1997: 60).

Local scholars are similarly and increasingly interested in the painstaking archaeology of **indigenous knowledge systems**. These scholars recognise that in pre-conquest Africa 'communities relied on **ancestral ecological knowledge** and **earth-centred cosmologies** to sustain themselves and their environment' (McMichael 2008: 29). Scholars across southern African are unearthing evidence that, despite the massive and sustained destruction of the African countryside, rural society is resilient and that old artisanal crafts, which are re-emerging in Europe, are in our context also potentially still recoverable.

What all of this suggests is that the rural is worthy of closer investigation. It further crucially points to why **rural sociology**, globally, has always had a strong focus on poverty and rural development. In the case of the global South, Africa and South Africa, the issue is considerably more pressing.

25.2   Defining the rural

In South Africa today there is no official definition in government documentation of what the rural is and 'no clear articulation of how rural will be defined' (RHAP 2017: 22). In countries such as Britain and the US, and elsewhere, definitions of the rural are generally based on population density. Such statistical definitions are used for government and other institutional planning purposes (Bosworth & Somerville 2014; Gray 2014). Average population size, however, introduces an arbitrary element and does not capture what the rural is or what it represents, or what *rurality* means.

A significant part of the problem of definition is the *diversity* and *complexity* of rural life. It is at the receiving end of the uncertainty of natural forces on the one hand and inexorable social forces stemming from the urban on the other. Rural society has forever weathered such forces and left traces of older forms of social organisation behind. Rural sociology must consequently deal 'with extremely complicated realities' (Lefebvre 1956: 67).

25.2.1   The rural as 'backward'

The rural countryside has always stood in contrast with the town and city. The urban represented 'civilisation', while rurality represented its absence. In town and city, new forms of social organisation took shape – along with new forms of behaviour, manners and ways of being. **Urbanism** began to distinguish itself from old established, traditional styles of life. The Roman emperor Julius Caesar, for instance, consciously attracted intellectuals, lawyers and doctors to the city to develop this new **civil society**. Urbanites in the *urbs* (city), protected behind city walls in growing comfort, quickly felt superior to life closer to nature in the rus (the rural). Divided between 'us' and 'them', people in 'the rural' came to be seen as different, inferior and 'other'.

The African father of sociology, Ibn Khaldun, did not appear to hold this negative view of the rural. He admired the tough nomadic peoples of his day, hence his use of the word 'primitive' is not pejorative. The word is taken to refer to simplicity.

25.2.2   Ibn Khaldun's rural–urban typology

Writing in the Algerian countryside 600 years ago, Ibn Khaldun clearly distinguished rural society – *badwa umran* – from urban society – *hadara umran*. To explain the concept of badawa (rural), Ibn Khaldun argued that:

> *primitive people are tied to the desert because of their agricultural lifestyle. Since settled areas do not provide wide fields and pastures for animals, their social organisation is organised upon bare subsistence* (Muqaddimah 1958, cited in Soyer & Gilbert 2012).

On the other hand, *hadara umran* (urban society):

> *implies a secondary phase of social organisation ... [with] ... the economic arrangement of society centred upon commerce and crafts, in addition to* **agriculture** *and animal* **animal husbandry***. There is a higher level of life observed in terms of comfort and luxury as opposed to rural society* (Muqaddimah 1958) [emphasis added].

Aspects of this first sociological contrast between rural and urban society strike a familiar chord even today.

Box 25.1 Ibn Khaldun's rural–urban typology

Rural society	Urban society
Preceded urban society; the origin of civilisation	Indebted to rural society for its origin
Small population; low density	Large population; high density
Occupations mainly in agriculture and craft	Occupations are varied but 'secondary and animal husbandry' remain an aspect
Division of labour and specialisation are simple	Complex division of labour necessitates specialisation
Bare necessities of life; less comfortable living	Abundant and comfortable life
More 'brave'	Less 'brave'
Strong sense of social solidarity	Weak solidarity; social solidarity may vanish
Purity of lineage	Lineages are 'mixed up'
Closer to being good and as 'more remote from evil habits'	More deviance and 'blameworthy habits'
Little or no change in customs and habits	Change is inevitable and expected
Emphasis is on informal social control	Use of 'restraining laws' by 'authorities and the government'
Prevalence of illiteracy or minimal education	Learning is stressed; arts and sciences are cultivated
Generally, less 'clever'	More 'clever' – as a result of scientific and related activities

Clearly, for Ibn Khaldun life in the natural environment of the mountains, the steppes and the desert was rural. Life in the town and city was separated by protective city walls from the open spaces of the natural environment. In fact, the word 'rural' simply means 'open' (Woods 2011). Social relations between people differed in the open (rural) areas when compared to the enclosed and protected (urban) towns.

It is significant that the *key feature* of rural society was included in Ibn Khaldun's account of urban society: 'agriculture and [animal] husbandry'. This points to what is now widely recognised: we cannot talk about the rural and urban in isolation from one another, yet the stubborn *integrity* and *coherence* of rural society persists, strongly suggesting it warrants independent conceptualisation and investigation.

For despite the once primordial dominance of rural society, *it never entirely gave way* to the urban, despite the powerful forces unleashed by industrial and indeed, post-industrial nuclear society.

Box 25.2 [Exercise – consult Chapter 24 on urbanisation]

Compare and contrast Ibn Khaldun's typology with:
- Max Weber's distinction between *communal* and *associational* societies
- Ferdinand Tónnies' contrast between *Gemeinschaft* and *Gesellschaft*
- Émile Durkheim's distinction between *mechanical* and *organic* solidarity
- Georg Simmel's view of *rural* and *urban mentality* in his essay: 'The metropolis and mental life'.

25.2.3 The rural as non-urban

Since the advent of industrial society, the rural has predominantly been defined negatively – as *non*-urban. A World Development Report on agriculture defined 'rural' as those populations not defined as 'urban' (World Development Report 1981). The negative concept, *non-urban*, has consequently been subordinated to the positive concept of urban. The rural has consequently been 'a misunderstood, if not an *unknown reality*', hidden and socially invisible (Van der Ploeg 2009: 40). This even relates to the traditional core and central activity dominating rural society, namely agriculture: the ability to farm economically was, in Europe until recently, 'something of a *hidden* practice' (Van Der Ploeg 2000: 401). Outsiders have misunderstood rural communities. One scholar even claims we understand the peasants' position within capitalism no better than scholars did in the 19th century! (Dunaway 2010).

Whether elsewhere or here at home, this subordinate 'non-urban' consistently lacks what 'the urban' enjoys – advanced education, technological advancement, infrastructure and social services (Lipton 1977). A similar account is given in relation to India (Jha & Jodka 2013). Viewed with an urban bias, 'the rural' has been viewed as bereft of 'civilised' urbanity and in need of 'development' and modernisation (see Lipton 1977). An urban modernising bias has long characterised both the academic literature and socialised urban views. This has reinforced the tendency to 'render the peasants invisible' (Isaacman 1990:16). Rural society and the people who live in rural areas have consequently been widely and long ignored. This very largely continues to apply today, even though around 35 per cent of South Africa's population live in such areas. Being socially invisible and poor, rural communities are often subject to prejudice. Even rural development agencies have been found to be disparaging about the rural poor (Mpolokeng 2003).

As Case study 12.1 in Chapter 12 shows, this negative attitude towards students in universities and live in rural areas is simply not warranted. For this reason, local scholars have attempted to understand the marginalisation of the rural in South Africa (Kepe & 2012).

25.2.4 So what is rural?
A few years ago, a publication from the office of the presidency in South Africa posed the question: 'When we say rural, or rural development, what do we mean, precisely?' (Ngomane 2012). Similar questions were recently posed by scholars at a university located in a rural setting (Ntombela & Nkabinde 2018).

Defining the rural has been described as 'challenging', with 'many definitions' but 'no consensus' (Woods 2010). The inclusion of agriculture has been central to definitions of the rural as it is crucial to 'the vitality of rural areas', yet the 'increasing diversification of rural economies' has also been recognised (Siwale 2014: 165). Rural landscapes can no longer be defined solely in relation to agriculture. The rural has become considerably more complex as town and countryside become increasingly entangled.

The question 'what is rural?' is, moreover, not merely academic. A briefing issued by the Financial and Fiscal Commission (FFC), while reasserting that 'South Africa does not have a government-wide, officially agreed and accepted definition of "rural"', suggests that:

> *national government should drive efforts towards a comprehensive definition of 'rural' ... the meaning of the concept of the rural has not been adequately understood and ... the relationship between rural development and 'related aspects' such as 'land reform, food security and infrastructure' has consequently not been 'clearly defined'* (Mabugu 2017/8: 2).

Defining what 'rural' means is important. In the US it has been claimed that it is in the 'national interest' to define 'rural and urban correctly' (Isserman 2005: 465). Similarly, in South Africa, clear definition is important for policies for planning and rural development' (Hall 2014: 12).

Any definition must include a spatial dimension. This is important, otherwise allocations and investments made across government departments, for instance, miss their intended target and 'fall short of their intended aims' (Mabugu 2017/8: 2). How the spatial organisation of African rural settlements was laid out historically is further of particular relevance for understanding the land question (Beinart, Delius & Hay 2017).

The critical importance of the concept of space, and rural space in particular, becomes strikingly evident when the realisation dawns that 'the *spatial framework of apartheid* has remained intact'. The former apartheid 'tribal' **homelands** – the **Bantustan** reserves – *still persist in contemporary South Africa*' (Hendricks 2000: 291) [emphasis added].

What is important to note, then, is that, firstly, the improved delivery of social services depends on more precise definition. Secondly, any definitional exercise must incorporate a **spatial dimension**. For, as a recent interdisciplinary study concludes, 'what is *distinctive* about the rural' is that the way it is coherently structured occurs in and is related to its 'distinctive spatiality' which 'foregrounds "nature"' (Bosworth & Somerville 2014: 294) [emphasis in original text].

25.2.5 Defining rural as co-production with nature
The Wageningen School identified three spatial geographies: non-civilised areas, the rural and the urban (see Van Der Ploeg 1997; Van Der Ploeg et al 2000).

1. *Non-civilised areas* encompass the 'unspoiled', 'pure' natural environment of wilderness areas unaffected by 'man, history or society' (Van der Ploeg 2009: 41).

2. *The rural* is that which has been or is being transformed by human activity – cleared forests, ploughed fields, planted crops, grazing lands, water courses altered in their route, human dwellings and communal settlements. This also applies to nature conservation reserves, such as the Kruger National Park, in which the natural environment is *managed*. The rural, for the Wageningen scholars, is *'where the co-production of man and nature is located* … Rurality is both the result and expression of this co-production' (Van der Ploeg 2009: 41) [his emphasis]. The natural processes of life itself are *produced* and *reproduced* in the rural. *The rural is defined in relation to the interaction between human beings and the physical, natural world.*

3. The *urban*, on the other hand, signals the *absence* of co-production between human beings and the living natural environment. There is *no direct* co-production between humans and nature, nor the **reproduction** of the natural environment in the town and the city.

The urban is defined, then, as where the natural processes of life are *not produced and reproduced*. The urban *receives* or *appropriates* the results of the co-production of human activity with nature and their mutual reproduction which takes place in the rural. The urban, whether as individual or collective social human action, does *not* produce, let alone *co*-produce or *reproduce* the rhythm, shape and forms of life of the natural environment. For the city only uses 'dead' materials that have been harvested or extracted from the processes of co-production between humans and nature in the rural: gold, iron, coal, wood, maize, wool, fruit and vegetables, and the like. These 'dead' materials have been mined out of the earth, or are the produce of animal husbandry or harvested from arable soils. Neo-classical economists refer to the sectors that produce these materials as the *primary* sectors of the economy – mining, agriculture, and forestry in particular. The city consumes these raw materials of the co-production of human activity and nature for the *secondary* sector of the economy – that is, manufacturing and industry.

The spatial boundaries of the rural

To geographically trace the rural in terms of physical space there are, then, two boundaries. To understand what rural is and what *rural* space occupies is to mark 'the boundary between the urban and the rural and the boundary between the rural and the non-civilised' (Van der Ploeg 2009: 40).

What these boundaries demarcate is continually shifting. As the boundaries shift, the conceptual device of co-production permits the tracing and tracking of *actual* physical, topographical space.

Looked at from the field of any agriculturalist anywhere, this heuristic device of conceptual boundaries can be taken a step further. This further enables a drawing of a boundary between co-production and untamed land *within* the rural. The boundaries between land *actually producing*, which has the *potential to produce, has produced in the past or is purposively lying fallow,* may border either non-civilised wilderness on the one hand or non-co-producing urban areas on the other. Such boundaries can be drawn on the ground, and can, in addition, be drawn on a macro-level scale for public policy to serve the needs of rural society. Furthermore, such boundaries coincide with historical practices that define ownership of land, as the anthropologist Monica Hunter explained in 1936: '[A] woman had *exclusive right* to cultivate any area she had *once turned over, no matter how long* it was kept *lying fallow* (cited in Beinart et al 2017: 16) [emphasis added].

Even more importantly, this right was *inherited* (Beinart et al 2017: 16). This is common knowledge in rural Zululand today.

Defining rural as co-production with nature is then a meaningful, positive account of the rural appropriate for a practical rural sociology. From the perspective of the rural, *rural* is now defined *independently* of the urban. From this arguably arresting epistemic perspective, the *urban* is now defined in terms of the *rural*. This also further permits the definition of topographical space *within* the rural. The account, moreover, articulates actual historical practices that ownership rights to land, once allocated, are established by having engaged in co-production with nature. The result is a permanently identifiable, humanly produced and hence living rural productive space.

Social relations of co-production

Social relations between producers in rural and urban contexts differ as the rules shaping each environment differ:

> *Nature, especially living nature, imposes its own rules. Just as society does. It is precisely the encounter between the two, nature and mankind, that makes for co-production* (2009: 43).

The urban is organised by principles of social organisation. Co-production as the organising principle of the rural requires, 'the reproduction of *specific* social relations of production' (Van der Ploeg 2009: 43) [emphasis added]. The way in which rural society is organised, in other words, is intimately related to the natural environment and the need to be sensitive to its rules; the changing seasons and the weather, drought and dependence on rain, the kinds of crops that can be planted, and often what natural resources are available. Where modern technologies do not dominate, such as electrically or solar-powered computerised, enclosed, temperature-controlled environments in 'tunnel' agriculture – organisation will also depend on the length of the working day, which coincides with the seasons or break up the working day due to heat especially.

Forms of social organisation cannot be imposed where the rules of nature must be taken into consideration. Nature features strongly in how rural communities organise themselves and survive. Rural communities must work with and alongside nature, which is unpredictable. In the artificially constructed, more comfortable built environment of the city, this is not necessary.

As Ibn Khaldun said so long ago, urban people are 'soft' – they have no need to be 'brave'. Urbanites are protected by an artificially constructed, built environment. People in rural areas are generally closer to and must contend with nature whether they till the land, work the farms or are subsistence or capitalised commercial farmers in the global South or North.

The 'two rurals'

What is distinctive and general about rural life is difficult to define and grasp. This challenge is compounded when the differences between the rural in the developed world and Africa are viewed. These differences are so large as to make them 'almost incomparable': the differences are 'just unimaginable' (Siwale 2014: 15). In the North, the rural is perceived as idyllic and rustic and many aspire to live in the countryside. In the South, rural areas are largely neglected, and people are poorer, invisible, voiceless and excluded and hence marginalised.

Today, despite their spatial differences, there is out-migration from these 'two rurals' and they share certain features. Agriculture is a key activity in both. While the youth in the global North variously perceive rural life as 'traditional', 'dull', 'backward', 'underdeveloped', 'old fashioned' or in short, a 'dark world', in the South 'anything is better than being in a rural area' (Siwale 2014: 25).

There are likewise 'two rurals' in South Africa. These are very largely racialised: the legacy of the **colonial rural** in South Africa continues to stamp itself on the **post-colonial rural** (Siwale 2014). Well-resourced, largely white

and modern **capitalised rural** areas still stand in vivid contrast to largely black, poverty-stricken and land-hungry **communal rural** areas.

25.2.6 Henri Lefebvre's rural sociology

Thus far we have seen that a rural sociology for South Africa must take into account the rural/urban divide, the hidden character of the rural, the role of the natural environment in shaping particular sets of social relations and the contrast between 'two rurals'. The contrast exists both *between* the global South and the global North, and *within* our local South African context.

There is an additional aspect of the rural to be considered in the recently rediscovered, early rural sociology of the French thinker, Henri Lefebvre. He argues that with even only slight acquaintance of the rural, 'commonly held opinion' fails when it comes to the domain of rural sociology. As Henri Lefebvre (1956: 67) explains:

> Not only does the rural sociologist find themselves confronting [social] structures originating from different historical epochs, but they confront structures that are disintegrating and are mixed with new forms and structures.

Further, not only did agriculture come before industry in time, but an 'ocean of agriculture' surrounds 'small islands of urban life and industrial production' (Lefebvre 1956: 67). To support Lefebvre's claim, only between one and three per cent of the world's land has been urbanised (Liu et al 2014): the rest of the planet is either 'non-civilised', wilderness or has been worked on by human hand and has hence been 'civilised' and is consequently *rural*.

Such vast open **rural space**, however, does not mean, Lefebvre argues, that rural life and agricultural production are somehow more simple and easier to understand than the sophistication and technological development in towns and cities. It is, in fact, the opposite. For as rural sociology attempts to understand its varied phenomena in depth, it soon discovers 'sedimentations' of past social formations and consequently conceptual complexity. The theoretical basis of Lefebvre's rural sociology is Marx's theory of **ground rent**.

The theory of ground rent

Lefebvre is explicit that the capitalist mode of production be understood in terms of the 'constitutive trinity of capitalist society' (cited in Elden & Morton 2016: 58). This refers to the three classes Marx identified in early capitalism. These classes are best revealed in the simple formula that indicates how each class secures its income: capital – *interest*; land – *ground rent*; labour – *wages*.

The landowner contracts the capitalist farmer to rent and use the land. The farmer employs waged labour to profit from agriculture, which simultaneously improves the land and increases the value of the rented property. When the farmer's contract ends, the increased value of the land accrues to the landowner, who can then increase the ground rent. Such is the manner in which surplus profits are appropriated from agricultural wage labourers by the landowner. This is in addition to the appropriation of their surplus by the farmer, but whose business enterprise does not benefit from the increased value of the land. The independent **sharecropper**, using family labour and paying the landlord rent in kind, may be compared to the farmer (see Van Onselen1996). In South Africa, labour tenants were evicted from the land while as capitalism developed in advanced Euro-American capitalist societies, capitalist farmers absorbed the older 'third class' of landowners. As we will see, the concept of ground rent becomes useful in explaining current struggles and developments in our local communal rural area.

Rural space and the abstract space of capitalism

For Lefebvre, space is not simply empty. Space is not merely a geometrical configuration or specified by a set of coordinates on a GPS – the geographical positioning system on smartphones – to get you to a destination. Space is *socially produced*. He acknowledges that this might seem strange – 'bizarre' is the word he uses (Lefebvre 1991:15). Such social space, for example a room in a house, a street café or what Durkheim would call the 'sacred' spaces of synagogue, mosque, church or temple, 'incorporates' social actions, both individual and collective.

Over the course of time society generates – or *produces* – social space within which it represents and presents itself and its communal cultural, symbolic and political life. This is not an abstract conceptual model, but rather an active way of grasping the social reality of lived experience. Just call to mind the socially regimented space and **spatial practice** of the examination hall!

When it comes to rural space (whether of the clan or tribe or communal or feudal society), under the whip of accumulation under capitalism, opportunities open up to transform historically produced, living, socially productive space. For Lefebvre this transformation is especially apparent in the **agrarian** structures of 'underdeveloped' countries: colonial or semi-colonial ones or backward sectors in capitalist societies (Lefebvre [1953] 2003: 119, cited in Elden & Morton 2016: 60).

Capitalism has produced an *abstract* space. This is a 'world of commodities' with its own 'logic' and worldwide strategies 'founded on the vast network of banks, business centres and major productive entities' linked by 'motorways, airports and information lattices' (Lefebvre 1991: 53).

Wherever concrete buildings, tarred roads and pavements have not yet entombed nature's infinite colour of greens and browns, or has sheltered urbanites from its rain and sunshine, cold and heat, dark or light, rural spaces can be compared to Lefebvre's account of capitalism's abstract urban space. Open rural spaces must not be seen as what they *lack* – as through the prism of 'non-urban' – but how living historical rural space *might be developed* or, following Van Der Ploeg, imagined as how they *ought* to be. To do so presents the rural sociologist with a further challenge.

The rural sociologist as interdisciplinary activist

To study a village, Lefebvre suggests, the rural sociologist needs to 'double up' as historian, economist and geographer. In a literature of extraordinary wealth, historians have studied the southern African rural considerably more so than sociologists (see Beinart and Bundy (Bundy, Keegan). Lefebvre stresses that while rural sociology needs to *describe* rural phenomena, *date* the observations and then *explain* them, this cannot be done without sensitivity to historical and geographical context and economic realities.

Rural sociology must start in the present, and go back or 'regress' into the past, before 'progressing' into creating or producing a future. This 'regressive/progressive' methodology for Lefebvre's rural sociology is at once both intellectual and activist. His major work (1991) seeks to open up new possibilities of thought and action along these lines to 'detonate' that which threatens to become fixed, frozen, ossified' (Harvey 1991: 431).

Box 25.3 A revision exercise

Before proceeding, revise the following in Chapter 24 on urbanisation:

Section 24.8: Rural–urban transition
Section 24.9: Urban–rural linkages
Section 24.10: Identity
Section 24.11: The hybrid nature of South African urban life

25.3 The 'agrarian question' in the classical literature

Following Henri Lefebvre's injunction to examine rural society from a multidisciplinary perspective to find expression *within* rural sociology, it is useful to know, for instance, that the dispossession of agricultural land and the transformation of South African peasantries into wage labourers in the early 20th century mirrored the 19th century Industrial Revolution in England. It is equally important to know that this *was* not the experience of the rest of Africa where colonialism in the main resulted solely in the dispossession of land and *impoverishment without proletarianisation* (Amin 1980: 138; 151–2, cited in Dunaway 2010).

What is central to what follows has been usefully put: 'At the simplest level, *colonialism* gave rise to the *land question* and *capitalism* underlies the *agrarian question*. The two questions are *intimately connected* just as colonialism and *capitalism* are two sides of the same coin in South Africa' (Hendricks 2013: 42) [emphasis added].

25.3.1 Karl Marx: Dispossession of the land

Owing to the initiation of the Industrial Revolution in England, the model of the transition from small-scale, family-oriented, independent agricultural producer to wage labourer in the towns and cities served as the model of the transition from rural society to urban industrial society. In **feudal** England, the countryside was characterised by relatively free and independent peasant proprietors. A peasant is an agriculturalist who has access to their own parcel of land and to shared common land where cattle could be raised, wood collected for fuel, and building and general communal use. Peasant agriculturalists might sell any surplus agricultural produce or items of artisanal production in the local town.

Well before the Industrial Revolution, the feudal lords had started this process of creating a class of wage labourers. They forcibly drove the peasantry off the land and usurped the common lands. With the rise of the wool manufacturers towards the end of the 18th century, these feudal landlords turned much of the land into 'sheep walks': the transformation of arable land into grazing for sheep to supply the hungry mills of urban industrial production. They broke down the cottages and dwellings of the peasants. On losing their land and homes, the peasants cried that 'sheep eat men!' Of this rising 'new nobility' of the bourgeoisie, Marx makes it clear that what the capitalist system 'demanded was a degraded and almost servile condition of the mass of the people' (Marx 1977 [1894]: 674). The complex social and cultural formation of the making of the English working class took place over the decades from the late 18th century well into the 19th century (Thompson 1963).

Box 25.4 Applying classic concepts

Is it possible to translate the social class structure of 'kings', 'the nobles' and 'the peasants' into terms applicable to South Africa today?

25.3.2 Vladimir Lenin: the differentiation of the peasantry

As we saw in Chapter 4 on social change (section 4.1), although capitalism was well established in Russia, economic development lagged behind that of Europe. The overwhelming majority of the people were rural peasant farmers, and the minority were industrial workers. Basing himself on Karl Marx's analysis, Lenin argued that both this majority Russian **peasantry** and minority industrial working class found themselves subject to the 'contradictions' of capitalist commodity production. In different words, ordinary people, both rural and urban, found their world transformed and subject to the forces of capitalist society over which they had little or no control.

The rural peasants had become dependent on a capitalist market to sell their produce and were subject to taxes and the need to raise cash. Gradually drawn into the emergent capitalist system, peasant society underwent unprecedented change.

Box 25.5 Proposal for a research project in rural sociology

Compare the social changes identified by Lenin in Russia below to a rural village or district in South African today.
1. Competition among peasants
2. The struggle for economic independence
3. The grabbing of land
4. Concentration of production in the hands of a minority
5. Forcing the majority into the ranks of the proletariat
6. Exploitation of the majority through the medium of retail capital
7. The hiring of farm labourers.

The changed conditions of peasant life and society amounted to what the peasants themselves called '*de*-peasantising' – destroying the old independent way of life. Industrial society market relations introduced new forms of social differentiation into rural life. First, Lenin argued, a relatively small new rural bourgeoisie emerged. These were wealthier peasants aiming to become the proprietors of commercial enterprises and capitalist farmers. Second, to serve this newly emergent rural bourgeoisie, a rural proletariat started to take shape. These people lived on small allotments of land, but were increasingly subject to waged work and included farm labourers, day labourers, unskilled labourers, building workers and other allotment-holding workers.

Between these two major social classes was the middle peasantry, some of whom had managed to hold onto their parcels of land. They farmed crops when the rains and natural conditions were favourable, but struggled and relied on loans to keep going when climatic conditions were bad. This middle peasantry would, like all middle classes, fluctuate between supporting one or other of the two major political classes. Lenin adopted a conciliatory approach to the middle peasantry despite being convinced that only collective, socialised farming was the route to resolving the agrarian question in Russia (Liebman 1975).

25.3.3 Alexander Chayanov: The productivity of the rural economy

Lenin's analysis of the development of capitalism – whether conceptualised as the 'peasant question' or 'the agrarian question' – did not go unchallenged. Alexander Chayanov examined the rural economy and compared artisanal peasant economic production with that of industrialised capitalist society.

Box 25.6 'Testing' Chayanov's argument

In South Africa, can we talk about the resilience of the rural and how artisanal crafts and independent peasant agriculture were enmeshed with capitalism in complex ways?

Independent rural artisanal and farming families owned their own farming and artisanal implements. This was the key economic unit of the rural economy based on agriculture and persisted, despite massive changes occurring in the Russian countryside.

Chayanov argued that the peasant was not as market-oriented and engaged as might be understood from Lenin's analysis, nor would he have agreed with Max Weber that *capitalist* social relations entirely dominated rural society. Many peasants, instead, continued to farm their plots

of land or small farms, which remained the source of independent peasant livelihoods. Indeed, trade continued with the nobility, the market and the state – to whom they were required to pay taxes. This was the continued strength of the rural economy. The more family members engaged in rural economic production, the more developed such a family-based economic unit was. This was a cyclical development *independent* of new class formation in the countryside. While criticised for ignoring broader social and economic changes, this view had the rural economy and society as its strong focus.

Note that while some peasants did become wage earners, the majority remained semi-independent farmers as the industrial production of commodities intensified. Peasant or independent small agricultural farming communities interacted with this advancing industrial society until peasant society was utterly transformed by the liquidation of the wealthy peasant class and much of the middle peasantry by the Soviet state after 1929 as it sought to eliminate capitalist social relations in the countryside. Under changed conditions of forced collectivisation on the land, rural society was still required to feed the urban towns and cities.

By way of summary of this brief overview, it is worth noting how Marx showed that English peasants predominantly became proletarians, how Lenin analysed rural Russian peasant society as dominated by capitalist social relations and class formation, and that Chayanov pointed to the resilience of the peasantry and the rural economy. In Africa, all three of these perspectives and aspects of transformation and social transition in rural society express themselves in a highly uneven pattern of destruction, survival and development under the very different conditions of the colonial encounter.

25.4 Rural transformation in South Africa

In South Africa, the colonial, racial segregation and apartheid regimes gradually broke up indigenous African agrarian society. Dispossession of the land was a long, drawn-out, tortuous and highly uneven historical process for over a century. A previously independent African rural society characterised by a people-centred, living mode of production initially supplied capitalist society with land, labour and produce. Communal rural areas continue to supply capitalist agriculture and mining with land and labour. A much attenuated, small peasantry continues to provide society with its surplus produce.

The overall yet uneven result across countries in southern Africa, such as Kenya, Zimbabwe and South Africa, was that African society in general and black agriculture in particular were systematically destroyed in a 'planned destruction' which has left 'South African peasant agriculture in an alarming state of disrepair' (Cochet 2014: 24). This destruction of traditional African society was a precondition for the rise of capitalist development (Bundy 1979). With that condition met, post-colonial Africa has subsequently become an **'enclave economy'** of the Global North characterised by the continuation of primitive accumulation of capital and the permanence of 'accumulation by dispossession' (see Bond 2007: 29).

In much of Africa, colonising powers were more concerned with controlling or substituting the peasantry with an African agrarian bourgeoisie and proletariat (Bond 1998: 92), as opposed to destroying the African peasantry (Isaacman 1990) which occurred in South Africa and other southern African countries. Yet South Africa is *not* an exception when the form of governance by colonising powers of **'indirect rule'** comes into focus. Mamdani (1996) has argued that South Africa under democracy continues to experience 'decentralised **despotism'** via 'indirect rule', the system whereby the state rules through **traditional leaders**, but which is manipulated and was entrenched by successive white-dominated regimes. For Mamdani, this system, with traditional leaders playing a subordinate role in government, continues under democracy in the era of late post-colonial society and is represented by the 'bifurcated state' – civil rule on the one hand and traditional rule on the other.

This divided form of rule can be seen in the agricultural sector, which represents a significant footprint of rural space. This primary economic sector is bimodal: the increasing inequality, persistent poverty and landlessness of the rural poor stands in stark contrast to industrialised and capitalised commercial farming (Kariuki 2018).

Largely beyond still predominantly white-owned commercial agricultural land are the previous Bantustans or 'homeland' areas. There is no significant peasant class of smallholders in these communal areas apart from 'approximately 200 000 small- and medium-scale commercial farmers' (Hall 2009a: 3–4). While around 800 000 households owned the land they farmed, only a few people own viable farms, with 435 000 working communal land and half of those living in communal rural areas do some gardening (Magetla 2018).

In these areas, traditional authorities hold sway and have played a central, though evolving and uneven governance role under colonialism, racial segregation and apartheid, and were finally constitutionally recognised under democracy. In fact, there has been a resurgence of 'tradition' in post-colonial Africa and in this respect, South Africa has been no exception. The extent of the ambiguity of traditional governance under liberal democracy, however, is revealed by the absence of a definition of 'traditional leaders' in South Africa today (Ntsebeza 2004). In rural areas falling under traditional forms of governance, there is unrestricted building, local chiefs allocate land and road signs point the way to the location of tribal courts.

A decade ago, there were 800 ruling chiefs in rural areas and around 1 000 headmen who had authority over 18 million South Africans living in rural areas. This is roughly 40 per cent of South Africa's population (Vawda 2011: 281). Traditional forms of governance over these areas have been conceived as representing 'rural despotism'. They are destined to die out under liberal democracy, it has been argued. The traditional leaders will remain a political conveyer belt into the rural masses to garner votes, it has been suggested. Whatever the case, it is the unbroken continuity of traditional authorities that links ancient African 'rural' and the present.

25.4.1 The pre-conquest 'rural'

A look at pre-conquest African society, its main features and how it was organised sheds light on conceptions and interpretations of 'the rural'.

The historian Jeff Guy – focusing on Zululand in the early 19th century, now part of KwaZulu-Natal where one in five South Africans lives – tells us that dominated integrated African pre-conquest societies were:

> *… the accumulation of living things – human beings and their labour power – which was valued in terms of livestock and realised in the establishment of the homestead as productive unit. They can be thought of as animate modes of production: built on the production and accumulation of warm, physical, living things…* (Guy 2013: 33)

This society, mirrored across Africa and elsewhere, with the productive household as central, comprised a fluid, yet ill-defined series of chiefdoms based on kinship ties ensuring social and political cohesion (Vawda 2011: 274). In short, the central organising principle of pre-conquest African society was their independent agriculturally based and animal-stockholding character focused on nurturing the lives of people and community.

25.4.2 The rural under colonialism

Sustained European settlement and the conquest of Africa started in earnest in the late 19th century. Either through armed force and economic compulsion or a combination of these two strategies, African societies were gradually or dramatically subject to the original motivation of colonial powers to save both Africa and the European economy. The strategy adopted to achieve this was via 'Commerce, Christianity and Civilisation, a triple alliance of Mammon, God and social progress' (Packenham 1991: xxiv, xxv), effected by conquest. The justification for colonialism mirrored how the Western experience and urban mind had always viewed rural society: urban Europe was 'civilised' and rural Africa was 'backward'.

In South Africa, the two largest African societies were crushed by 100 years war against Xhosa peoples in the Eastern Cape and by more rapid military conquest of the Zulu state north of the Tugela river bordering colonial Natal. Colonial domination was achieved in Natal by maintaining the pre-conquest governance structures of traditional chieftainships. The chiefs were ultimately answerable to colonial magistrates and finally to the then Native Commissioner himself, Theophilus Shepstone (see Guy 2013). Though under different guises, the 'Shepstone system' of 'indirect rule' has remained a feature of governance of traditional communities under democracy – even in urban areas. The Cooperative Governance and Traditional Affairs (CoGTA) sub-directorate of Traditional Affairs in Gauteng, for instance, effectively continues to play this role in relation to the two traditional communities incorporated into the province in 2007 (Martins 2019). One of the criteria for the recognition of traditional leaders is that they are recognised by a community. Such communities based in communal land areas manifest deep historical continuities.

By the turn of the 20th century industrial capitalism, via the mining revolution, had asserted itself over southern African society, and its migrant labour empire had penetrated deeply into a range of societies across the region. The contrast to what overtook pre-conquest African societies, as well as the insurgent settler Boer rural republics, was stark. For indigenous African societies were 'profoundly, qualitatively different from inanimate modes [of production] such as capitalism [which were] based on the accumulation of inorganic or dead things – objects' (Guy 2013: 233).

Put in another way, rural society, the productive centre of which was a domestic economic unit of a man and his extended family, was based on livelihoods - not profits (Webster 1986). Living modes of production based on livelihoods gave way to industrial capitalist society based

on things and profit, and the 'commodification of the countryside' (Bond 1998: 92).

This shift from animate to inanimate modes of production, from the embedded to the disembedded, from embodied to disembodied, from **abantu** *[people] to* **izinto** *[things], was profound in its effects and, although still incomplete and contradictory, it was a transformation as radical and pain ridden as South African history itself* (Guy 2013: 33).

The critical point is that the momentous historical shift from a natural and living to an artificial and 'dead' form of productive life, as elsewhere in Africa, is 'still incomplete and contradictory'. Yet as we have seen, crucial aspects of traditional rural society survived, remain in evidence and were central not only to the colonial project, but continued under racial segregation with the formation of a racialised Union of South Africa in 1910.

25.4.3 The rural under racial segregation

Having accomplished the conquest of African society, the defeat of the two independent Boer rural republics of the Orange Free State and the Transvaal in the South Africa War (1899–1902), was quick to follow. A modern state administration was soon established to serve the needs of the mining revolution predicated on the largest deposits of gold ever discovered.

Urbanisation accelerated rapidly in the late 19th century. Many African migrant workers migrated to the towns, never to return to the lands and traditional societies of their ancestors, despite the policies of racial segregation and later of apartheid. Those who first did so over a century ago were known as *amakholwa* – believers or Christians. Around a century ago, many poor Afrikaner rural families, known as bywoners, likewise flocked to the towns and cities, generally due to cattle disease, poverty and being unable to compete with larger African peasant tenant families. This migration of people in the process of urbanisation from the rural to the urban has continued to increase, as it has globally.

For those who stayed behind in rural areas conditions deteriorated with changes to the shape of leadership, land and labour. Traditional leaders in rural areas were increasingly constrained and expected to be accountable to the segregationist government instead of their own people from whom many consequently became estranged. While the African National Congress (ANC) instituted a House of Chiefs at its formation in Bloemfontein in 1912, anticipating the imminent racialised land legislation, their importance in the eyes of an urban-biased leadership appeared not to have been significant. For in the 1940s, Walter Sisulu would lament that the ANC had not turned its attention to peasant struggles.

In the interests of securing a labour supply, a year later black South African society as a whole was dispossessed of its land with the promulgation of the Natives Land Act of 1913. The contemporary account of Sol Plaatje, the first general secretary of the ANC (see Plaatje [1916] 2007) remains a poignant South African literary classic. Amendments to this legislation in 1936 resulted in people crushed into increasingly overpopulated reserves in what was called a 'betterment' programme of 'enforced villagisation' (Platsky & Walker 1985: 9). Rural inhabitants were dispossessed of their land with the rigid 'spatial workings' of dividing the land into the land-use categories of residential, arable and grazing land. This reconfiguration of rural land further significantly facilitated the forced removals that would occur in the period of apartheid to follow (Westaway 2012).

Traditional agriculturally based African society was further hollowed out of the collective strength of its labour power by the migrant labour system. Rural society in the Bantustans was transformed into over-populated and land-hungry labour reserves under the 'indirect rule' of the remnants of traditional forms of preconquest African governance (Mamdani 1996).

With the bulk of rural labour power gone and land for families too small to sustain life, rural society increasingly depended on remittances by migrant workers. By this time 'the tentacles of consumerism began to reach into distant villages' (Mayer 1980: 61). The cycle of poverty in rural areas, with peasant producers transformed into poor rural consumers of the capitalist market, was immeasurably intensified by systematic forced removals, consolidating rural landlessness under apartheid after 1948.

25.4.4 The rural under apartheid

The traditional African mode of production assumed central focus in explaining the development of capitalism in South Africa. The question was why racial segregation gave way to apartheid. Much contested and argued over, it started with what became the most-ever cited journal article in the social sciences in South Africa. Harold Wolpe's 'Capitalism and cheap labour-power in South Africa: from segregation to apartheid' was published in 1972. His central argument was that *apartheid* had replaced *racial segregation* due to capitalism's need for *cheap labour*. This meant turning independent rural producers into waged labourers, achieved

through subordinating the traditional African mode of production to the emergent capitalist mode of production (Wolpe 1972; see Friedman 2015).

As conditions changed, such as the need for more labour and the flood of work seekers from rural areas into the towns and cities, the racial policy of apartheid, however, was forced to change. Apartheid was reconceptualised as 'separate development' of supposedly racially distinct peoples. It then took the form of controlled 'self-governing states' followed by the quasi 'political independence' of the Bantustan states. The attempt was consistently made to turn back the tide of African urbanisation and permanent proletarianisation. The migrant labour system was tightened up. The artificial *retribalisation* of African society was attempted. The system collapsed as the intention – that capital did not have to pay for the costs of reproduction of labour power in the Bantustans – failed as these land-hungry and over-populated labour reserves were unable to sustain life.

Meanwhile, significant subsidies were granted to white farmers who became a new racialised class of commercial farmers, the *capitalised rural* – and which continues today, the 'strongest support of all' for capitalised farming being the low cost of labour (Cochet 2015: 253). Rural areas reserved for Africans, established under colonialism and segregation, were consolidated into overcrowded, poverty-stricken labour reserves – the former homelands or Bantustans or what we have called the *communal rural*.

Central to the cleaving of rural society into the two racialised enclaves of the *communal rural* and the *capitalised rural* were the forced removals of over three and a half million people between 1960 and 1983 (Platsky & Walker 1985: 9).

Beyond the Bantustans, rural dwellers enjoyed no form of representation. In 1989, for instance, there was in 'white Natal', or elsewhere in South Africa, no form of legally recognised representation for black African rural dwellers, nor any means or mechanisms to communicate with local authorities (Ardington 1989: 32). For the 1985 National Census, 'urban' was defined as the presence of a local authority. All else – including industrial and mining towns – was defined as 'non-urban' and hence black African farm workers and their families did not officially exist.

Yet by this time local empirical research in the Bantustan of rural KwaZulu challenged the urban/rural conceptual divide and the assumption that somehow rural dwellers could get by on a smaller income than urbanites. Not only was a virtually identical income required to meet the needs of both rural and urban dwellers, but urban standards and tastes had penetrated the countryside to an 'enormous' extent (Schlemmer 1982: 7).

Meanwhile, beyond the apartheid Bantustan or 'homeland' reserves, the rural proletariat on the white-owned capitalised commercial sector of the agrarian economy was being seriously eroded. Between 1984 and the eve of democracy in 1994, 1 832 341 farmworkers had been evicted from white-owned farmlands (Nkuzi & Social Surveys 2005: 7). These forced removals, as those from the 1950s onwards, fitted the racialised Bantustan policy under apartheid. It was, however, rather the longer-term changes in farming as aggressive, profit-oriented, large-scale farming which were the key reason for the systematic eviction of farm labour (Platsky & Walker 1985: 118ff) and which was inherited in 1994 and continues today.

25.4.5 The rural under democracy

In the long decades prior to democracy, rural society in South Africa suffered from systematic de-agrarianisation in the former Bantustans. In the Eastern Cape, it has been shown, only one and four per cent of rural households derived incomes from crop production and livestock respectively (Westaway 2012: 117). Across the communal rural, of those engaged in agricultural activity, only eight per cent said it was their main source of income or food (Magetla 2018).

Despite the intentions of democracy (RDP 1994) and the pointed orientation of the new non-racial government towards the rural poor, within the first decade of democracy 2 351 086 farmworkers were evicted from white-owned farmland (Nkuzi & Social Surveys 2005). Going back decades, the advance of the structure of capitalised agriculture in an increasingly oligopolistic and concentrated capitalised rural, combined with the political fear of white farmers, has driven farm evictions. Some of this number voluntarily fled low wages and poor living and working conditions to settle around towns and cities in search of a better life. After 1994, it was in the areas of the old apartheid Bantustans that poverty reached and still manifests its highest levels. It has in fact been argued that 'bare life' characterises these rural spaces in unbroken state policy and practice since 1910 (Westaway 2012).

As elsewhere in Africa, the post-apartheid state had to respond to this contemporary version of the 'agrarian question'. It both emulated the past and broke new ground. The constitution recognised and entrenched traditional 'tribal' authorities. It consequently incorporated this age-old traditional governance system while simultaneously attempting 'to democratise rural areas' (Vawda 2011: 287) via elected councillors and community property associations (CPOs).

This has meant continuing a form of 'indirect rule' by involving these deeply rooted forms of ancient rural governance, which, like the rural society in which they are embedded, had shown remarkable resilience. Elsewhere under British 'indirect rule' chiefs had 'collapsed' traditional and modern political governance practices (Ally 2015: 981). The practical politics of incorporating traditional leaders into metropolitan governance structures usefully breaks down any monolithic conception one might have regarding these rural-based traditional leaders (Vawda 2011). The participation of traditional leaders in local (rural) governance structures, however, remains subject to the structures of (urban) civil rule.

Aimed at addressing the legacy of poverty generally and rural poverty in particular, the considerable political and practical challenge of all post-colonial African societies was 'to be resolved through "**rural development**" everywhere … [with] … the "problem" of the peasants being central to forming a new nation' (see Neocosmos 2016: 264ff). As elsewhere in Africa, the response was the South African *developmental state*. The promise of the ANC's policy regime was consequently 'an inclusive and "deracialised" rural economy' (Kariuki 2018: 220). Highly politicised, this seeks to balance 'the interests of the landowners with those of the land-deprived majority of the population within a market-oriented economic framework' (Kariuki 2004: 118). Land reform and rural development of necessity do not only go and need to go hand in hand. Of fundamental importance, land reform itself must be located *within* an overarching programme in rural development programme (Hall, Jacobs & Lahiff 2003).

25.5 Interrogating 'rural development'

The two antipodes of developed white-owned commercial farming, the *capitalised rural*, and the wasted and underdeveloped, unsustainable previous Bantustan areas, the *communal rural*, almost perfectly mirror the long-entrenched racial divide going back to colonial times.

The 'bimodal' character of agrarian society in South Africa today (Kariuki 2018) must not be understood in terms of a racially dualistic, 'two nations' model. Rather the rural must be viewed in the broader context of the spatial and geographical, economic and political, and social and cultural divides – both between and within the rural – of South African as part of the 'enclave economy' of the global South in relation to the global North. The communal rural represents the 'enclave economy' in relation to the capitalised rural *within* rural South Africa. One result is that 'underemployment in rural South Africa is one of the highest in the world' (Cochet 2014: 25).

25.5.1 Critiquing 'development'

The most superficial glance at the meaning of 'development' is sobering. Development, it has been argued, has long been imposed on developing societies (McMichael 2017), better conceived as 'late developers' (Williams 2014). McMichael argues that 'development' is a Western project and more than that, that development is 'a form of rule'.

Western 'development' was initiated in the 1940s, received its life-giving boost with political decolonisation in the 1960s, was globalised via international aid agencies to the 'less developed' or 'developing' world of Asia, Africa and Latin America by the 1970s and was central to globalisation in the final decades of the 20th century (McMichael 2017). Currently, McMichael argues, the (developmental) Globalisation Project is in crisis. '**Sustainable development**' has replaced '**integrated development**' as the latest buzzword. 'Rethinking development' and 'paradigm change' is urgently required (McMichael 2017).

Similar sentiments were expressed a decade ago locally and still apply. 'What is needed now is fresh thinking about the future of rural South Africa and a vision which confronts the still-stark divides *within* the commercial farming heartland of former "white RSA", as well as *between* it and the "Bantustans" – and aims to transform *both* of them' (Hall 2009: 5) [emphasis in original text].

What framed the development project was the belief that development, whether free-market capitalism or communist collectivism, was inevitable. There would be national development in each country. An urban-industrial society would replace agrarian civilisation. Progress towards industrialisation hence meant success. Politically decolonised governments were constrained to build *national developmental* states. Today in South Africa this is expressed in the National Development Plan (NDP), which projects a 'developmental' scenario to 2030. It is too early to say whether the NDP will be a case of the 'error of developmentalism' that has bedevilled other such efforts in the global South (Woods 2014: 138).

25.5.2 Post-colonial Africa and 'rural development'

When new post-colonial governments achieved political liberation, most of Africa had not transformed into capitalist societies via proletarianisation and urbanisation. Most rural dwellers in Africa continued to have access to land and 'few resided in households that were dependent on wages' (Rodney 1982: 53). This was not, however, the case in South Africa. For even today after political decolonisation there is unfinished business, which relates not only to the question of the land in South Africa, but also elsewhere in sub-Saharan Africa (see Chinsinga 2015). There is also, as noted above, the legacy of the 'incomplete penetration of traditional society by a weak colonial state' (Mamdani [1996] 2017: 285). The colonial project did not manage to transform the customary values and complex hierarchical, communal and participatory practices of traditional African rural society into Western civil representational politics.

For Mamdani ([1996] 2017), given the predominance of state-led social transformation in post-colonial Africa, the crucial issue for rural development in particular is that the post-colonial state has not managed to link 'the rural and the urban'. For even after political decolonisation in Africa, starting with Ghana in 1957 and ending with South Africa in 1994, the fundamental principles on which traditional African society was based stand conceptually opposed to those on which current modern liberal democratic capitalist society are based.

Box 25.7 Opposing principles to be resolved to link rural and urban in post-colonial Africa

Rural African society	Western capitalist society
Custom	Rights
Participation	Representation
Decentralisation	Centralisation
Community	Civil society

(Source: Mamdani [1996] 2017: 34)

Even after political decolonisation, the extraction of raw materials and the use of local labour continued to produce primary materials for Euro-American industrialisation and specialised economic development. The global South, on the other hand, continued to provide the basics – raw materials and labour. On a global scale, all of this simply means the perpetuation of the **colonial division of labour** with the global South, including Africa, hence *sustaining* the global North.

African liberation movements were compelled to become formal political parties in constitutional democracies and make the transition from agricultural rural to industrial urban society. To do so they had to turn to 'rural development', for the post-colonial state 'could not pretend to be national without representing the majority of its population' (Neocosmos 2016: 266).

25.5.3 Trajectory of the concept of 'rural development'

In the Western development project, from being a strategy 'to improve the economic and social life' of the rural poor in the mid-1970s, within five years the World Bank began 'popularising the *problem* of rural development and the *concept* of rural development' in the early 1980s (Lea & Chaudry 1983: 10–12) [emphasis added]. Yet, as with the absence of a definition of 'rural', 'we have no comprehensive definition of rural development' (Van Der Ploeg et al 2000: 391).

For the Wageningen School, 'rural development' means a 'multi-level, multi-actor and multi-facetted process' (Van Der Ploeg et al 2000: 391). Of even greater significance is the claim that '[r]ural development theory is not about the world as it is – it is about the way agriculture and the countryside *might* be reconfigured' (Van Der Ploeg et al 2000: 396). Yet rural development remains a disputed notion – both in practice, policy and theory' (Van Der Ploeg et al 2000: 404). There is likewise no universally accepted measure of rural development that captures its multifaceted nature (Singh 2009: 56; see also Ahmad 1996).

Locally, the multifaceted character of rural development has been taken to be 'complex and transversal' when implementing developmental initiatives, for 'different state institutions and agencies [are] assigned different aspects of rural development. National and provincial governments, rural municipalities, state-owned enterprises (SOEs) and the private sector are all involved in rural development initiatives' (Mabugu 2017/8: 1).

The spirit of what the concept of rural development aims at, however, has been formulated in different ways and hence has a number of conceptual predecessors.

Organic integration

The notion of organic integration assumed central focus in two major countries in the global South in the 20th century – China and India. Used by Mahatma Gandhi, the notion of *organic integration*, in 'a common vision' with Mao Zedong, viewed the rural villages as the main sites of rural development and national reconstruction (Lea & Chaudry 1983). In contrast to the western social scientific focus on 'the provision of inputs and infrastructure', Gandhi and Mao's view of organic integration, incorporating self-sufficiency and self-government, appears to have got lost along the way. Either Western or Soviet models of development constituted the 'conceptual basis' for developmental strategies, whether at the level of projects or programmes (see Lea & Chaudry 1983: 16ff).

'Quality of life' studies

The notion 'quality of life' provides a straightforward and simple rationale for 'engaging in improving the life of rural people' (Singh 2009: 3). Mahatma Gandhi conceived rural development in terms of the 'quality of life'. One of the earliest thinkers to spurn the rural/urban dichotomy, Gandhi held that the rural and urban have a 'complimentary relationship' (Pasricha 2000: 72). The rural and urban are not two separate domains. On the contrary, Gandhi's concept of rural development is 'so integrated' and 'so comprehensive' that 'it seems synonymous with national development' (Pasricha 2000: 78). This is not surprising given his oft-quoted statement that India lived and died in its 700 000 villages.

The basic needs approach

Development was understood a generation ago at the Rural Urban Studies Unit at the University of Natal as satisfying **basic needs**: 'nutrition, clothing, housing, domestic water, sanitation, fuel, education, health, transport, labour participation, income or material standard of living and leisure' (Ardington 1989: 7).

Within a decade, the Reconstruction and Development Programme (RDP) asserted the centrality of satisfying basic needs as fundamental to any developmental project:

The first priority is to begin to meet the basic needs of the people – jobs, land, housing, water, electricity, telecommunications, transport, a clean and healthy environment, nutrition, health care and social welfare' (ANC 1994: 7).

As explained in the chapter on the Economy, this vision was short lived.

Integrated rural development

The term *integrated* was prefaced to rural development in the mid-1970s to 'indicate a new multipurpose thrust of rural planning … [involving] … all aspects of rural land, society and economy' (Lea & Chaudry 1983: 13). While evoking the Gandhian spirit of organic integration, this notion is tautological. For 'rural development', by its very nature, must include and implicates the satisfaction of a wide range of needs provided by a diverse set of service providers over and above state-led social service provisioning.

Sustainable rural development

The 'Our Common Future' report of the World Commission on Environment and Development (WCED 1987) (see Singh 2009: 132) stressed the role of *sustainability* in agriculture as the basis of sustainable development. It was but a short step to start talking about sustainable *rural* development. The notion of 'sustainability', as noted elsewhere in this textbook, has been criticised and remains something of a buzzword (Singh 2009: 2).

The concept of 'sustainable development' must be understood in two ways. The first use, initially emerging out of ecological and biological studies, pertains to the preservation of the biosphere and has as its focus biodiversity conservation and ecological sustainability. The second use is that employed by economists regarding the preservation of the economic output, consumption, growth and dynamics of capital accumulation (see Singh 2009: 132ff). Regarding the first 'strong' sense, it might be said, this is obviously of critical importance. Of the second 'weak' sense, it is important to be critical.

The focus on livelihoods

The notion of 'livelihoods' has maintained its currency (see Carter & May 1998) and appears as a strong contemporary focus in rural studies (IIED 2017; Neves 2017) and land reform (Schoones 2015). The notion implies active agency and hence dispenses with objectivist definitions that may carry the implication that people are of a character with

things. The notion was embedded in a much-cited classic definition:

Rural development is a strategy to enable a specific group of people, poor rural men and women, to gain for themselves and their children more of what they want and need. It involves helping the poorest among those who seek a livelihood in the rural areas to demand and control more of the benefits of rural development. The group includes small scale farmers, tenants and the landless (Chambers 1983: 147).

The title of a recent report: 'Reconsidering rural development: Using livelihood analysis to examine rural development in the former homelands of South Africa' (Neves 2017) is clear. Rural development, understood as both concept and practice, needs, as the Dutch School was seen to argue, rethinking and reconceptualisation. In the European countryside, rural development was a response to a squeezed agricultural sector and contributed to the reconstruction of its erosion and that of the rural economy. It pointed towards development practices in rural work and life that became increasingly located beyond agriculture. If pluri-activity has characterised these areas, it has been multiple livelihood strategies, underpinned by social grants – received by 16 million South Africans in 2016 (Magetla 2018) – which have sustained many rural lives.

Given the preeminent role of the state in service provisioning and rural development, together with the global concern over the environment in which the rural is located, broader conceptions have asserted themselves.

The 'greening' of the state under neoliberalism

A persuasive investigation has critically interrogated what has been dubbed South Africa's 'declaratory green developmental state' (Satgar 2014: 126). The argument is that global capital has captured notions of sustainable development and ecological sustainability – and which the South African state has uncritically adopted. The rhetoric of 'sustainable development' and 'green economy' has been internalised while at the same time the state has pursued an agenda in the National Development Plan (NDP) which promotes the minerals–energy complex (MEC) (Fine 2008). This is contradictory. Such a developmental agenda is, moreover, 'an inadequate framework for agrarian transformation' particularly as it has resulted in 'new land dispossessions' of communal land (Satgar 2014: 145). This has serious implications for not only how 'rural' and rural development are understood, but also raises the question of the land and land reform.

25.5.4 Rural development and land reform

The naming of the government department of Rural Development and Land Reform signals the intimate relationship between the two terms. This renaming was controversial as the Department of Agriculture was excluded in the interests of negotiation between the state and white commercial farming. The huge question of the land is one marked by a history and practice of tortured complexity. It can only be noted in this chapter. There are three key components to land reform: redistribution (of land to the landless), restitution (of land to the dispossessed) and tenure (security of occupation on the land).

In short, under democracy land reform has been exceptionally slow. Land reforms and agrarian reforms are in a state of stagnation (Anseeuw, Liebenberg & Kirsten 2014). For instance, rural land claims have, under democracy, taken second place to urban claims and at current allocations, it has been estimated, will only be completed somewhere in the year 2190! (Du Toit 2000: 78).

Reforms focused on rural society have suffered from a lack of political will, signalled by a declining budget allocated to agrarian reform. It has been left suspended by a series of legislative promulgations resulting in policy uncertainty. There has been a failure in administrative alignment, competency and a lack of capacity regarding implementation. Much confusion and contestation has been the overall outcome. In fact, a summation of the evidence-based findings of a conference organised by three South African universities ended up not being convinced that 'government is serious about the issue' (Roodt 2019: 33). One telling piece of evidence is that, if the eviction of farmworkers from commercial farming as noted above is included, the loss of access to land by rural dwellers has *increased* since 1994.

25.6 Aspects of rurality in South Africa

Rural South Africa is marked by an extraordinary diversity of human settlements across very different landscapes and its people mirror this diversity. The rural is consequently riven with complexity as the 'sedimentations' left behind by past generations must be identified and disentangled by the rural sociologist (Lefebvre 1956). But a few aspects, some which framed the production of rural space in the past and others which represent rurality in South Africa today, provide a glimpse of the scope open to a new generation of

sociologists to develop a contemporary and enlivened rural sociology rooted in our own context.

25.6.1 Mining and community

Like agriculture, being part of the primary economic sector, mining takes place on land in rural areas. Marx's theory of ground rent has been used to explain why rural communities in South Africa have not benefited from mining on communal land (Capps 2012). In a complex story going back to segregation, rural communities clubbed together to buy land. Their names were recorded, but the title deeds were required to go in the name of the 'tribe' to whom they belonged, a tradition going back to colonial times where a black African could not own land in their own individual capacity (Manson 2013). Under apartheid this aspect of 'indirect rule' was routinely manipulated and monitored by the state when mining companies signed agreements with communities on whose land minerals had been discovered.

Under democracy, on the platinum mining belt in North West province, traditional leaders have ensured the continuation of the tradition that land is registered in the names of the *dikgosi* (traditional leaders), have appropriated significant sums of money flowing from royalty agreements signed with platinum mining companies, and have been charging community members rent. The traditional leaders in rural communities have successfully managed, in a range of instances, to transform themselves into a land-owning rent-seeking elite.

In the past elsewhere, such as in India, rural elites were often seen as benevolent. Increasingly they have become exploitative resulting from their access to state resources and their solidarity as a class (Chambers 1983: 131). This is a growing phenomenon in the communal rural locally.

In KwaZulu-Natal, for instance, a similar trend has been occurring. The Ingonyama Trust has cancelled the permission to occupy (PTO) certificates that formalised ancient African custom, whereby family units in rural communities enjoyed security of tenure on the land. The PTO system was the most common form of government over African landholding in the communal rural areas (Beinart et al 2017). The sums of money are not insignificant. Between 2016 and 2017, for instance, inhabitants in rural areas falling under the jurisdiction of the trust paid over R100 million in rentals to traditional leaders. Failure to pay results in forfeiture of the land (Harper 2019).

25.6.2 Women's agency and land tenure

Legislation relating to land tenure in the communal rural under democracy has shown greater continuity with the colonial, segregationist and apartheid past rather than a 'radical departure' from it (Ntsebeza 2013: 54ff). Not only has legislation fallen foul of the Constitution or been rigorously contested, but it has also affected women in rural areas who have been at the forefront of opposing laws which would further entrench *official* interpretations and practices of customary law. Instead, women have argued for *living* customary law which traditionally was more open to community-based decision making and the practice that it is the people who make their leaders.

The Rural Women's Movement has launched a constitutional challenge to the withdrawal of longstanding land tenure rights via PTO certificates and the charging of rentals by traditional authorities in rural areas in South Africa. With the PTO system never stable under colonialism and apartheid, since the 1990s, 'hundreds of thousands, if not millions of new land allocations' have been made as the PTO system has become more and more informal (Beinart et al 2017). This has generally strengthened the hand of traditional leaders and been a key mechanism of new class formation in the countryside. The attempt by traditional leaders to introduce ground rent under democracy occurs in their struggle for adaptation and integration into civil governance arrangements in the cities and their own economic advance in the face of a modernising urban bourgeoisie. Traditional customary rights to the land have, however, been abrogated in the process, with individual leaders standing aloof from and acting in their own interests, independently of and often without consulting the communities they represent.

It has been shown that rural women are redefining land rights in the context of **living customary law** (Claassens & Mnisi-Weeks 2009). Customary law has been manipulated by various regimes to suggest women are not able to inherit and manage land. Women in the communal rural have been contesting this manipulation since the 1930s and continue to do so today (Weinberg 2013), increasingly becoming land holders in their own right. Since 1994, access to land by women, who have either never married or have been widowed, for instance, has 'noticeably increased' across KwaZulu-Natal, North West and the Eastern Cape (Beinart, Bundy & Hay 2017: 21).

25.6.3 Rural and urban linkages

The need to conceptually link rural and urban is widely accepted: one cannot talk about the rural in isolation from the urban. This is clearly recognised in a Department of Rural Development and Land Reform (RDLR) report: 'There is recognition therefore that the rural economy space in South Africa reflects colonial patterns of economic development. The geo-spatial sources of raw materials, which are rural areas, continue to subsidise the urban economy. Put differently the *rural poor continue to subsidise the urban rich*' (RDLR 2015: 2) [emphasis added].

If the land question is 'by definition, a rural or agrarian question' and the 'struggle for the cities' must be seen in relation to the 'linkages between rural and urban areas' (Hendricks & Pithouse 2013: 103), the fate of the countryside is critical to the fortunes of the urban. These linkages are established through physical linkages such as technology, the media and transportation, and the flow of agricultural goods and commodities in one direction and manufactured and imported goods in the other. People maintain relationships and networks, and have established commitments and obligations across the rural/urban divide.

A generation ago, for instance, 70 per cent of the needs of rural households depended on the earnings of migrant workers (Nattrass 1984) who:

...are an embodiment of the urban-rural relationship that is so evident in the development of capitalism since the mineral revolution in the latter part of the nineteenth century in South Africa (Kepe & Ntsebeza 2012: 39/40).

These men, and increasingly women, straddle the two worlds of rural and urban and – as noted in Chapter 24 on urbanisation – many urbanites in South African today have family, friends and community 'back home'.

25.6.4 The rural as home

Across South Africa, black urbanites have either 'strong', 'weak' or 'no rural links' to rural areas (Smit 1998). For many, however, 'the urban area is only a temporary place to stay: the rural home is regarded as their real home and ... many urban households are only temporary urban bases ... which are part of an extended family with a permanent rural base' (Smit 1998: 77). Of a group of women who left their rural home of Phokeng, for instance, all returned after decades spent in the cities (Bozzoli 1991). The reasons in each case were rich and varied, a 'combination of circumstances and belief' – from wanting to finally build a house at a rural home, keeping alive family and kinship networks, escaping the rush and ever-increasing expense of city-life or due to 'misery and poverty' encountered there (Bozzoli 1991:212). This group of women was fortunate despite having left

Phokeng in the 1960s as the peasant economy was declining and returned in the early 1980s to one of apartheid's human 'dumping grounds'. Yet in Phokeng there was at least some work on the platinum mines owned, via complex royalty agreements with the mines, by the Bafokeng community.

While rural areas often remain poor, for many people living in the cities they are still a place of sanctuary – a place to which people can return when they are unwell or out of work, to which they can send their children in difficult times, and where they can retire to and be buried (Pithouse 2016: 166/7)

25.7 Conclusion

The longstanding definition of the rural as non-urban is negative and from this, negative implications have flowed. Understanding the rural as co-production is a practical conceptualisation. The rural as co-production, following the Wageningen scholars, not only says *what* and *where* the rural is and what happens there, but also *how* it can be mapped in a *new way*, both *on the ground* and *at a macroscopic level*, to facilitate institutional planning. This account further articulates historical experience of how rights over land were and are established in both traditional and contemporary African communal rural societies.

Defining the rural as co-production, moreover, is perhaps the logical outcome of appeals of a generation ago to take 'the part of peasants' (Williams 1982) or 'putting the last first' (Chambers 1983) in order to be 'enriched by the rural' (Ntombela & Nkabinde 2018). Understanding the rural means appreciating the viewpoint and engaging communities who are the contemporary real-life human agents in and of the rural: subsistence and garden farmers, tillers of the land, self-employed agriculturalists, small farmers, commercial farmers, businesspeople and rural townsfolk – whether previously dispossessed or of generationally established settler stock.

The question is whether and how, under democracy, the full conception of development pointed out by the dependency theorist Walter Rodney (1973) can be realised: development is that which occurs in all societies in manifold ways incorporating, but going well beyond economic development. Viewing the rural or rural space in this way would represent 'development' in a fuller, more rounded way. This has immense consequences for understanding society. Lefebvre, as we saw, stressed the need to think about creating new spaces in a non-abstract way; in other words, in ways consonant with not the urban, but co-productive rural life in natural environmental settings.

This chapter consequently presented literature which suggested land reform should be viewed in the context of a framework of rural development. This requires understanding the diverse and complex livelihoods strategies of those who live in rural areas, the diversity and manifold aspects of which need to be made a priority if an enlivened rural sociology is going to contribute to the burning issues in South Africa today.

How this should be done returns us to the beginning of the chapter, yet projects into the present and future:

Knowledgeable rural people are disregarded, despised and demoralised by urban, commercial and professional values, interests and power. For them to be better able to participate, control and benefit requires reversals. Among these, one first step is for outsider professionals, the bearers of modern scientific knowledge, to step down off their pedestals, and sit down, listen and learn (Chambers 1983: 101).

Summary

This chapter provided an interpretive outline of the neglected subdiscipline of rural sociology.

- It showed how its basic concepts, the rural and rurality, had been defined negatively as non-urban and presented the positive account of the Dutch Wageningen rural sociologists.
- The rural is where the co-production between human activity and nature takes place. This is a practical device that can be used to outline physical boundaries within rural society, can be used at a micro and macro level, and articulates historical practices of traditional rural society in South Africa.
- The rural sociology of Henri Lefebvre was introduced. The key idea is that society generates or produces spaces within which human beings represent and present their communal cultural, symbolic and political life. The living historical production of rural space produced in this way contrasts starkly with the abstract space produced in urban environments under capitalism.
- The classical literature on the 'peasant' or 'agrarian question' showed how rural society was transformed with the rise of industrial society. It was seen how aspects of this transformation occurred in ways which were both similar and different in our context of colonialism, racial segregation and apartheid.

- Rural society can be divided historically into three periods: the *preconquest rural*, the *colonial rural* and the *post-colonial rural*.
- If colonialism left society with the land question, capitalism gave rise to the *agrarian question*. Both questions represent significant challenges under democracy today.
- Rural society displays remarkable resilience despite having always been on the receiving end of interventions from external sources. In South Africa, aspects of preconquest 'rural' society survive despite the systematic historical appropriation of its land, labour and agricultural produce, and manipulation of its traditional leadership arrangements.
- The historical legacy of rural society in South Africa today is a largely racialised division between the *communal rural* (previously homeland areas) and the *capitalised rural* (white-owned commercial agricultural areas).
- Around 200 000 African farmers on small- to medium-sized plots of agricultural land today, primarily located in the *communal rural*, represent an attenuated independent peasantry and a slowly growing small black commercial farming sector.
- 'Development' and 'rural development' are contested concepts, yet are central to addressing chronic poverty and landlessness and the advancement of the livelihoods of people who live in rural areas.

The chapter concluded by briefly outlining a few aspects of rurality in South Africa today. Rural sociology awaits a new generation of academics, scholars and activists to fill in the huge gaps in describing and explaining the vast and diverse world of rural society. For rural society, long ignored, stands today at the centre of the major social questions facing South Africa, Africa, the global South and beyond. The lesson of the rural is what might society look like in the future – to be produced now in the present – or how *ought* it to be?

Are you on track?

1. Explain briefly why 'the rural' is not easy to define.
2. Outline what the Wageningen rural sociologists mean by understanding rurality as the co-production of humankind with nature.
3. Write a brief paragraph on each of the following:
   - Preconquest 'rural' society
   - Rural society under colonialism
   - Rural society under racial segregation
   - Rural society under apartheid
   - Rural society under democracy.
4. What is the problem with the concept of 'development' for post-colonial societies?
5. Explain what you understand by the notion of 'rural development'.
6. Describe the key linkages between rural and urban areas in South Africa today.

More sources to consult

Beinart W, Delius P, Hay M. 2017. *Rights to Land: A Guide to Tenure Upgrading and Restitution in South Africa.* Sunnyside, Auckland Park: Fanele, an imprint of Jacana.

Hendricks F, Ntsebeza L, Helliker K. 2013. *The Promise of Land: Undoing a Century of Dispossession in South Africa.* Jacana Media (Pty) Ltd: Auckland Park.

Harriss J (ed). *Rural Development: Theories of Peasant Economy and Agrarian Change.* Hutchinson University Library for Africa London, Melbourne, Sydney, Auckland, Johannesburg: Routledge.

Woods M. 2011. *Rural.* Abingdon: Routledge.

More advanced reading

Cochet H, Anseeuw W, Fréguin-Gresh S. 2015. *South Africa's Agrarian Question.* Cape Town: Human Sciences Research Council Press.

Kepe T, Ntsebeza L (eds). 2012. *Rural Resistance in South Africa: The Mpondo Revolts after Fifty Years.* Cape Town: UCT Press, an imprint of Juta & Co Ltd.

References

African National Congress. 1994. *The Reconstruction and Development Programme: A Policy Framework.* Johannesburg: Umanyano Publications.

Ahmad R. 1996. *Cooperatives and Integrated Rural Development.* Mittal Publications: New Delhi.

Ally S. 2015. 'Material remains: Artifice versus artefact(s) in the archive of Bantustan rule'. *Journal of Southern African Studies*, 41(5): 969–989.

Anseeuw W, Liebenberg F, Kirsten J. 2015. 'Agrarian reforms in South Africa: Objectives, evolutions and results at national level' in *South Africa's Agrarian Question.* Cochet H, Anseeuw W, Fréguin-Gresh S. Cape Town: Human Sciences Research Council Press.

Ardington ME. 1989. 'Rural towns and basic needs'. Rural Urban Studies Working Paper No 20. Centre for Social and Development Studies, University of Natal, Durban.

Bank L. 1997. Town and country: Urbanisation and migration'. *South African Labour Bulletin*, 21(4): 20–26.

Beinart W, Delius P, Hay M. 2017. *Rights to Land: A Guide to Tenure Upgrading and Restitution in South Africa.* Sunnyside, Auckland Park: Fanele, an imprint of Jacana.

Bond P. 1998. *Uneven Zimbabwe: A Study of Finance, Development and Underdevelopment.* Asmara, Eritrea: Africa World Press, Inc.

Bond P. 2007. 'Primitive accumulation, enclavity, rural marginalisation and articulation'. *Review of African Political Economy*, 34(111): 29–37.

Bosworth G, Somerville P (eds). 2014. *Interpreting Rurality: Multidisciplinary Approaches*, London and New York: Routledge.

Bozzoli B. 1991. *Women of Phokeng: Consciousness, Life Strategy, and Migrancy in South Africa.* 1900–1983. Johannesburg: Ravan Press.

Bundy C. 1972. 'The emergence and decline of a South African peasantry'. *African Affairs*, 71(285): 369–388.

Bundy C. 1979. *The Rise and Fall of the South African Peasantry.* London: Heinemann.

Capps G. 2012. 'A bourgeois reform with social justice? The contradictions of the Minerals Development Bill and black economic empowerment in the South African platinum mining industry'. *Review of African Political Economy*, 39(132): 315–333.

Carter MR, May J. 1998. 'Poverty, livelihood and class in rural South Africa'. CSDS Working Paper No 17, Centre for Social and Development Studies, University of Natal.

Chambers R. 1983. *Rural development: Putting the last first.* Harlow: Pearson Education Longman Limited.

Chinsinga B. 2015. 'An unfinished agenda in a neoliberal context: State, land and democracy in Malawi' in *State, Land and Democracy in Southern Africa.* Pallotti A, Tornimbeni C (eds). London and New York: Routledge.

Claassens A, Mnisi-Weeks S. 2009. 'Rural women re-defining land rights in the context of living customary law'. *South African Journal on Human Rights*, 25: 491–516.

Cochet H. 2015a. 'Persistent and extreme polarisation: Wide productivity and income gaps' in *South Africa's Agrarian Question.* Cochet H, Anseeuw W, Fréguin-Gresh S. Cape Town: Human Sciences Research Council Press.

Cochet H. 2015b. 'The planned destruction of "black" agriculture' in *South Africa's Agrarian Question.* Cochet H, Anseeuw W, Fréguin-Gresh S. Cape Town: Human Sciences Research Council Press.

Dunaway WA. 2010. 'Nonwaged peasants in the modern world-system: African households as dialectical units of capitalist exploitation and indigenous resistance, 1890–1930'. *The Journal of Philosophical Economics*, IV(1): 1–57.

Du Toit A. 2000. 'The end of restitution: Getting real about land claims'. *At the Crossroads: Land and Agrarian Reform in South Africa and into the 21st Century.* Programme for Land and Agrarian Studies (PLAAS) and National Land Committee (NLC), School of Government at the University of the Western Cape: Bellville and Braamfontein.

Elden S, Morton AD. 2016. 'Thinking past Henri Lefebvre: Introducing "The Theory of Ground Rent and Rural Sociology"'. *Antipode*, 48(1): 57–66.

Fine B. 2008. 'Development as zombieconomics in the age of neoliberalism'. Paper for the 35th *Anniversary Conference of the Centre for International Development Issues* (CIDIN). Radboud University, Nijmegen, Netherlands. Available at: https://eprints.soas.ac.uk/5623/1/fransrevv.pdf

Friedman S. 2015. *Race, Class and Power: Harold Wolpe and the Radical Critique of Apartheid*. Scottsville: University of KwaZulu-Natal Press.

Gee PG, Lankshear C. 1995. 'The new work order: Critical language and "fast capitalism"'. *Discourse: Studies in Cultural Politics of Education*, 16(1): 519.

Gray D. 2014. 'Economic approaches to the rural' in *Interpreting Rurality: Multidisciplinary Approaches*. Bosworth G, Somerville P (eds). London and New York: Routledge.

Guy J. 2013. *Theophilus Shepstone and the Forging of Natal*. Scottsville: University of KwaZulu-Natal Press.

Hall R, Jacobs P, Lahiff E. 2003. 'Evaluating land and agrarian reform in South Africa'. Occasional Paper Series 10, Final Report. *Programme for Land and Agrarian Studies* (PLAAS), School of Government, University of the Western Cape.

Hall R. 2009a. 'A fresh start for rural development and agrarian land reform?'. Policy Brief 29, Institute for Poverty, Land and Agrarian Studies (PLAAS), School of Government, University of the Western Cape (July).

Hall R. 2009b. 'Another Countryside? Policy Options for Land and Agrarian Reform in South Africa'. Institute for Poverty, Land and Agrarian Studies, School of Government, University of the Western Cape, Bellville, Cape Town, South Africa.

Hendricks F. 2000. 'Land policies and democracy' in *Development: Theory, Policy, and Practice*. Coetzee J, Graaff J, Hendricks F, Wood G (eds). Oxford: Oxford University Press.

Hendricks F. 2002. 'Land policies and democracy' in *Development: Theory, Policy, and Practice*. Coetzee J, Graaf J, Hendricks F, Wood G (eds). Oxford: Oxford University Press.

Hendricks F, Ntsebeza L, Helliker K. 2013. *The Promise of Land: Undoing a Century of Dispossession in South Africa*. Auckland Park: Jacana Media (Pty) Ltd.

Hendricks F, Pithouse R. 2013. 'Urban land questions in contemporary South Africa: The case of Cape Town' in *The Promise of Land: Undoing a Century of Dispossession in South Africa*. Hendricks F, Ntsebeza L, Helliker K (eds). Auckland Park, South Africa: Jacana.

International Institute for Environment and Development (IIED). 2017. 'Mobility and connectivity: Driving rural livelihood transformations in Africa'. Briefing, March. Available at: http://pubs.iied.org10814IIED

Isaacman A. 1990. 'Peasants and rural social protest in Africa'. *African Studies Review*, 33(2): 1–120.

Isserman AM. 2005. 'In the national interest: Defining rural and urban correctly in research and public policy'. *International Regional Science Review*, 28(4): 465–499.

Jha P, Jodhka SS. 2013. 'The "agrarian question" and the developmental state: India's story of rural social transformation' in *The Promise of the Land: Undoing a Century of Dispossession in South Africa*. Hendricks F, Ntsebeza L, Helliker K (eds). Sunnyside, Auckland Park: Jacana.

Kariuki S. 2004. 'Can negotiated land reforms deliver? The case of Kenya, South Africa and Zimbabwe'. *South African Journal of International Affairs*, 11(2): 117–128.

Kariuki S. 2018. 'Spatial defragmentation in rural South Africa: A prognosis of agrarian reforms'. Khadiagala GM, Mosoetsa S, Pillay D, Southall R (eds). *New South African Review 6: The Crisis of Inequality*. Johannesburg: Wits University Press.

Keegan TJ. 1986. *Rural Transformations in Industrialising South Africa: The Southern Highveld to 1914*. Johannesburg: Ravan Press.

Kepe T, Ntsebeza L (eds). 2012. *Rural Resistance in South Africa: The Mpondo Revolts after Fifty Years*. Cape Town: UCT Press, an imprint of Juta & Co.

Lefebvre H. [1953] 2003. 'Perspectives on rural sociology' in *Henri Lefebvre: Key Writings*. Elden S, Lebas E, Kofman E (eds). London: Continuum.

Lefebvre H. 1956. 'The theory of ground rent and rural sociology'. *Antipode*, 48(1): 67–73.

Lefebvre H. 1991. *The Production of Space*. Nicholson-Smith D (transl). Oxford UK and Cambridge USA: Blackwell.

Lea DAM, Chaudri DP (eds). 1983. 'The nature, problems and approaches to rural development'. *Rural Development and the State: Contradictions and Dilemmas in Developing Countries*. London and New York: Methuen.

Lipton M. 1977. *Why the Poor Stay Poor: Urban Bias in World Development*. Canberra: Australian National University Press.

Mabugu R. 2017/8. 'Responding to South Africa's rural development challenge'. Policy Brief 1, *Financial and Fiscal Commission: An Independent Constitutional Advisory Institution*. Available at: www.ffc.co.za

Magetla N. 2018. 'Inequality in South Africa' in *New South African Review 6: The Crisis of Inequality*. Khadiagala GM, Mosoetsa S, Pillay D, Southall R (eds). Johannesburg: Wits University Press.

Mamhood M. [1996] 2017. *Citizen and Subject: Contemporary Africa and the Legacy of Late Colonialism*, Johannesburg: Wits University Press and Kampala, Uganda: Makerere Institute of Social Research, Makerere University.

Manson A. 2013. 'Mining and "traditional communities" in South Africa's "platinum belt": Contestations over land, leadership and assets in North West province c 1996–2012'. *Journal of Southern African Studies*, 39(2): 409–423.

Martins M. 2019. 'Greater co-operation between CoGTA and Gauteng traditional leadership'. *Mail&Guardian*, March 15–21.

Marx K. 1977 [1894]. *Capital*, vol 3. London: Lawrence & Wishart.

Mayer P. 1980. 'The origin and decline of two rural resistance ideologies' in Mayer P (ed). *Black Villagers in an Industrial Society: Anthropological Perspectives on Labour Migration in South Africa*. Cape Town: Oxford University Press.

McMichael P. 2017 [1996]. *Development and Social Change: A Global Perspective*. 6th ed. Los Angeles, London, New Delhi, Singapore: SAGE.

Mpolokeng PG. 2003. 'People's participation in rural development: The examples from Mafikeng'. *African Journal of Political Science*, 8(2): 55–86.

Nattrass J. 1984. 'Migrant labour in KwaZulu-Natal'. Working Paper. University of Natal, Development Studies Unit.

Neves D. 2017. 'Reconsidering rural development: Using livelihood analysis to examine rural development in the former homelands of South Africa'. Research Report 54, Institute for Poverty, Land and Agrarian Studies (PLAAS), Bellville: University of the Western Cape.

Neocomos M. 2016. *Thinking Freedom: Toward a Theory of Emancipatory Politics*. Johannesburg: Wits University Press.

Ngomane T. 2012. 'Rural development in South Africa: The role of agriculture'. *The Presidency: Department of Performance Monitoring and Evaluation*, AGRISETA Annual Seminar, Kempton Park, South Africa, 21 September.

Ntombela BXS, Nkabinde WS. (Forthcoming). 'Demystifying rurality'. UNIZULU Humanities and Social Sciences Conference 2018. 17–19 October. Faculty of Arts, University of Zululand, KwaZulu-Natal, South Africa.

Ntsebeza L. 2004. 'Democratic centralisation and traditional authority: Dilemmas of land administration in rural South Africa'. *European Journal of Development Research*, March. doi:10.1080/0957881041000168874 3

Ntsebeza L. 2013. 'The more things change, the more they stay the same: Rural land tenure and democracy in former Bantustans'. Hendricks F, Helliker K (eds). *The Promise of Land: Undoing a Century of Dispossession in South Africa*. Jacana Media (Pty) Ltd: Auckland Park.

Packenham T. 1992. *The Scramble for Africa: 1876–1912*. London: Abacus.

Pasricha A. 2000. *Gandhian Approach to Integrated Rural Development*. Shakapur, Delhi: Shipra.

Pithouse R. 2016. *Writing the Decline – On the Struggle for South Africa's Democracy*. Sunnyside, Auckland Park: Jacana Media (Pty) Ltd.

Plaatje S. 2007 [1916]. *Native Life in South Africa*. Northlands: Picador Africa.

Platsky L, Walker C. 1985. *The Surplus People: Forced Removals in South Africa*. Johannesburg: Ravan Press.

Rodney W. 1983 [1973]. *How Europe Underdeveloped Africa*. Dar-es-Salaam: Bogle-L'Ouverture Publications.

Satgar V. 2014. 'South Africa's emergent green developmental state?' in *The End of the Developmental State?* Williams M (ed). Scottsville, Pietermaritzburg: UKZN Press.

Scoones I. 2015. 'Land reform, livelihoods and the politics of agrarian change in Zimbabwe' in *State, Land and Democracy in Southern Africa*. Pallotti A, Tornimbeni C (eds). London and New York: Routledge.

Siwale J. 2014. 'Challenging Western perceptions: A case study of rural Zambia' in *Interpreting Rurality: Multidisciplinary Approaches*. Bosworth G, Somerville P (eds). London and New York: Routledge.

Singh 2009.

Smit W. 1988. 'The rural linkages of urban households in Durban, South Africa'. *Environment and Urbanization*, 10(1): 77–87.

Resina JR. 2012. *The New Ruralism: An Epistemology of Transformed Space*. Vervuert: Iberoamericana.

Rural Development and Land Reform. 2015. *Framework for the Rural Economic Transformation Model: One District, One Agripark/Every Municipality a CRDP Site*. Rural Development and Land Reform, 20 March.

Roodt M. 2019. 'Search for ways to stop the land slide'. *Mail&Guardian*, 15–21 March, 33.

Schlemmer L. 1982. 'The targets and utilisation of rural development research'. Paper delivered at the Bophuthatswana Rural Development Centre Seminar, University of Bophuthatswana, 16–18 February, Centre for Applied Social Sciences, University of Natal, Durban.

Soyer M, Gilbert P. 2012. 'Debating the origins of sociology: Ibn Khaldun as a founding father of sociology'. *International Journal of Sociological Research*, 5(1–2): 13–30.

Thompson EP. 1963. *The Making of the English Working Class*, Harmondsworth: Penguin Books.

Van Der Ploeg JD. 1997. 'On rurality, rural development and rural sociology' in *Images and Realities of Rural Life: Wageningen Perspectives on Rural Transformation*. De Haan H, Long N (eds). The Netherlands: Van Gorcum.

Van Der Ploeg JD, Renting H, Brunori G, Knickel K, Mannion J, Marsden T, De Roest K, Sevilla-Guzmán E, Ventura F. 2000. 'Rural development: From practices and policies towards theory'. *Sociologia Ruralis*, 40(4): 391–408.

Van Onselen C. 1996. *The Seed is Mine: The Life of Kas Maine, A South African Sharecropper 1894–1985*. New York: Hill & Wang.

Vawda S. 2011. 'Governance policy and democracy: Reconstituting traditional authorities in the eThekwini municipality (Durban)' in *Reinventing African Chieftaincy in the Age of AIDS, Gender, Governance and Development*. Ray D, Quinlan T (eds). University of Calgary Press.

World Commission of Environment and Development (WCED). 1987. *Our Common Future. Report of World Commission on Environment and Development*. Oxford University Press: Delhi.

Weber M. 1906. 'Capitalism and rural society in Germany' in *From Max Weber: Essays in Sociology*. Gerth HH, Wright Mills C (eds). 1970. London: Routledge & Kegan Paul.

Webster D. 1986. 'The political economy of food production and nutrition in southern Africa in historical perspective'. *The Journal of Modern African Studies*, 24(3): 447–463.

Weinberg T. 2013. 'Overcoming the legacy of the Land Act requires a government that is less paternalistic, more accountable to rural people'. *Focus on Land*, 70: 28–36.

Westaway A. 2012. 'Rural poverty in the Eastern Cape province: Legacy of apartheid or consequence of contemporary segregationism?'. *Development Southern Africa*, 29(1): 115–125.

Williams G. 1982. 'Taking the part of peasants' in *Rural Development: Theories of Peasant Economy and Agrarian Change*. Harris J (ed). London, Melbourne, Sydney, Auckland, Johannesburg: Hutchinson University Library for Africa.

Williams M. 2014. 'Rethinking the developmental state in the twenty-first century' in *The End of the Developmental State?* (ed). Scottsville, Pietermaritzburg: UKZN Press.

Wolpe H. 1972. 'Capitalism and cheap labour-power in South Africa: From segregation to apartheid'. *Economy and Society*, 1(4): 425–456.

World Bank. 1975. *Rural Development: Sector Policy Paper*. Washington, DC: World Bank.

Environment

Babalwa Sishuta

The natural environment of the earth is finite, but has been exploited as if it were an infinite storehouse of resources. This fact has only too recently been appreciated. Research on the relation between human society and the natural environment is, as this chapter persuasively argues, been grossly lacking. If there is a single area and cluster of topics to which sociologists of the future must pay dedicated attention, it is to the natural environment. The focus must be on how it sustains human society and how it is being degraded by voracious forms of what goes for human development under the guise of economic growth at all costs. It is entirely misplaced to think that the human future can be sustained and earth replaced by exploring the universe beyond the atmosphere in order to colonise and inhabit spheres in outer space. Humanity has only one home and that is planet Earth. The social scientific object of this chapter is hence nothing less than the planet itself and how human intervention has interacted with and on it. One thing is frighteningly clear. Our ancient and only ancestral home is being seriously threatened and the human species is in danger of losing it.

This chapter begins by outlining the relation between sociology and the environment and stresses the point that the environment, while remaining a contested concept, is a humanly shared space. The dominant views in what has been termed the society-environment narratives, are then discussed. Around these views are a series of distinct discourses. These ways of talking about the environment are couched in terms of sustainable development and its critiques, environmental justice and environmental racism. This last term refers to the strong tendency of environmental policy to locate industrial sites and dump toxic waste in the vicinity of poor minority neighbourhoods.

The chapter goes on to define the core issue of environmentalism and recounts a brief history of environmentalism and the current state of the environment. This discussion is set in the context of global climate change and notes that South Africa, with the power stations of Medupi and Kusile coming on stream, will be one of the largest emitters of greenhouse gases on the planet. The way in which environmental management has been pursued, both during apartheid and since democracy, then again becomes the focus. There is much detail to be explored here. The salutary conclusion is that, in South Africa today, socio-economic rights and environment rights are being violated. Communities have the capacity, this chapter argues, to challenge transgressors and uphold their constitutionally defined rights.

The chapter then turns to mining – to which many references have been made, over a variety of issues, in this textbook. Ever the backbone of South Africa's still extractive-based economy, mining has, not surprisingly, been the single largest contributor to environmental degradation over the past century. With thousands of defunct, unrehabilitated and abandoned mines stretching back for over a century – which facilitates the problem and hazards associated with illegal mining – this serious environmental problem of significant proportions, has only fairly recently come under the spotlight. Despite not having adequately dealt with this historical legacy, hundreds of applications for mining licences await approval, not only locally, but across the continent of Africa. The current issue of acid mine drainage all too starkly illustrates the consequences of this legacy of this primary sector of the economy on which South Africa was built.

To end the chapter and bring this introduction on the environment up to date, the hydraulic fracturing of underground shale rock in the Karoo to release natural gas trapped in natural rock formations and the widespread social resistance with which it has been met, is briefly noted. Nuclear energy is again on the national agenda. The fundamental assumption of this chapter is a simple one. Despite the potential economic costs involved in more seriously exploring non-renewable sources of energy, the alternative might well be too ghastly to contemplate.

Case study 26.1 Environmental justice – South Africa

Zweli, a 77-year-old former mine worker living in the Eastern Cape has a debilitating life-threatening respiratory condition called mesothelioma. Mesothelioma is terminal. Zweli also suffers from recurring bouts of tuberculosis. His health has been deteriorating steadily over the past 15 years. He is hospitalised most of the time. Doctors have now given him a few months to live. Zweli started working in the gold mines when he was 20. He has never worked anywhere else except the mines. He recalls vividly the poor living and labour conditions. He blames the mines for his illness as no one in his family has a history of respiratory problems. A letter in his possession from the mining group states unequivocally that mining is a hazardous operation and miners work voluntarily. His relentless attempts to get compensation from the mines proved fruitless until September 2010. He received a once-off compensation amount of R70 000. He is grateful to the lawyers who represented him. He considers himself fortunate as most of the miners and former colleagues suffering from the same fate and other mine-related illnesses have either died or have given up any hope of ever getting any compensation.

This real-life story captures the world of an impoverished, marginalised individual and community of mine workers as well as surrounding communities. The scenario painted above repeats itself in various guises throughout the country and other developing countries.

The exploitation of local labour, the lack of social upliftment where mining operations occur, widespread occupational hazards and accidents, environmental and health risks, inequitable access and unequal ownership of mineral wealth are among a range of long-standing unresolved issues.

QUESTIONS

1. What is the impact of mining on miners, their families and the surrounding communities?
2. Can environmental justice for all citizens be achieved?
3. Is the policy framework adequate and effective?
4. How is mining as an activity contributing to the larger environmental crisis?

Case study 26.2 Environmental justice – Global

'This Is All Wrong,' Greta Thunberg Tells World Leaders At United Nations Climate Session, 23 September 2019

"My message is that we'll be watching you.

"This is all wrong. I shouldn't be up here. I should be back in school on the other side of the ocean. Yet you all come to us young people for hope. How dare you!

"You have stolen my dreams and my childhood with your empty words. And yet I'm one of the lucky ones. People are suffering. People are dying. Entire ecosystems are collapsing. We are in the beginning of a mass extinction, and all you can talk about is money and fairy tales of eternal economic growth. How dare you!

"For more than 30 years, the science has been crystal clear. How dare you continue to look away and come here saying that you're doing enough, when the politics and solutions needed are still nowhere in sight.

"You say you hear us and that you understand the urgency. But no matter how sad and angry I am, I do not want to believe that. Because if you really understood the situation and still kept on failing to act, then you would be evil. And that I refuse to believe.

"The popular idea of cutting our emissions in half in 10 years only gives us a 50% chance of staying below 1.5 degrees [Celsius], and the risk of setting off irreversible chain reactions beyond human control.

Key themes

- How the environment is defined from a social scientific perspective
- Conceptualising and defining the human-environmental interface
- Environmental activism as an important force in the society-environment debate.

26.1 Introduction

Since the 1970s sociologists have played an increasingly important role in studying the relationship between society and the environment. One of the basic premises in this debate is that in order to understand environmental problems and their solutions we need a basic understanding of the wider context within which they occur. Sociologists call for the urgent need to reconcile humanity with the natural environment. Human society has been struggling since time immemorial to exist in harmony with nature. The relationship has always been one-sided with natural resources being regarded as commodities. Overwhelming evidence suggests that human activities are causing irreparable damage to the planet's natural ecosystem processes and functioning and this is making societies more vulnerable than ever before. We now live in the age of the Anthropocene – the period in which human activity has unalterably changed the natural planetary environment. Some call it the era of the Capitalocene, the geological era in which capitalism and its insistence on the logic of growth is killing the planet.

This chapter covers a number of issues. The first part introduces a number of conceptual issues, examines the role of sociology in the society–environment debate and discusses how the environment is defined in the social sciences. The second part discusses dominant narratives in the society–environment debate and examines three main discourses of the environment, namely sustainable development, **environmental justice** and **environmental racism**. Environmentalism is discussed in part three and is an important force to be reckoned with in the society-environment debate. The fourth part begins by providing a general overview of the environmental crisis in South Africa. This is followed by a discussion of environmental management in the country from the colonial era to the current post-apartheid context. Part five provides a broad overview of the environmental issues facing South Africa using the mining industry as an example. The contemporary issues of acid mine drainage and hydraulic fracturing are used as case studies.

26.2 Environmental sociology

Environmental sociology equips us with analytical tools and skills allowing us to think critically and widely regarding the complex relationship between the natural environment and human activity. Environmental sociology allows us to 'debunk' unsubstantiated views and opinions to 'liberate our thinking' and 'move beyond the obvious', common-sense, everyday explanations about the environment – most especially those who refuse to accept the scientific evidence of how human activity has resulted in global warming and climate change (Washington & Cook 2011).

Why should we be interested in the climate and changing weather patterns you might ask? Until fairly recently, these were seen as purely natural events over which human beings had no control. The scientific evidence is now, however, overwhelming that it is human activity which has contributed to changing weather patterns and climate change. This evidence has resulted in a radically new way of understanding the relation between human beings and 'nature' (Giddens 2011). For environmental sociologists the fundamental issue is how human activity has threatened human civilisation by damaging and destroying crucial aspects of the only home we have – planet Earth. The old conceptual line between human society and the natural environment 'out there' no longer holds. Nature has been deeply implicated in the social construction of life itself via the human impact, modification and increasing destruction of the 'natural' environment. We now need to cope with what Giddens (2011:1) calls the 'nightmares' and 'catastrophes' of global warming and matters such as the distribution of environmental risks and the hyper-vulnerability of certain social groups – in the global South and sub-Saharan Africa in particular.

Only since the late 1980s and early 1990s was a concerted effort devoted to environmental issues. During the 1990s four notable local edited publications emerged:

1. *Bottom Line: Industry and the Environment in South Africa* (Bethlehem & Goldblatt 1997)
2. *Going Green: People, Politics and the Environment in South Africa* (Cock & Koch 1991)
3. *Hidden Faces: Environment, Development, Justice: South Africa and the Global Context* (Hallowes 1993)

4. *Restoring the Land: Environment and Change in Post-apartheid South Africa* (Ramphele & McDowell 1991).

These publications provided a much-needed foundational perspective, interpretation and comprehensive understanding of environmental issues within its socio-political, cultural and historical context redressing past imbalances, gaps and distortions. These sources are grounded in empirical evidence of social and environmental injustices during the apartheid years. They laid the foundational framework for the development of environmental justice scholarship.

At the turn of the century the seminal work of Jacklyn Cock, *The War Against Ourselves: Nature, Power and Justice* appeared (2007). Its first sentence explicitly advanced Environmental Sociology by presenting a sustained argument that nature itself is a site of struggle – a struggle about power and conceptions of nature and of justice. More recently, an important collection of articles in *The Climate Crisis: South African and Global Democratic Eco-Socialist Alternatives*, edited by Vishwas Satgar, has brought the local literature up to date

It is now almost a decade after South Africa hosted the 17th United Nations Conference of the Parties (COP17) to the Kyoto Protocol Climate Summit, held in Durban in 2011. The venue was appropriate as more than twenty years before a leading heterodox economist, Samir Amin, had argued that South Africa was:

> … a kind of microcosm of the world capitalist system, which brings together in a single territory a number of features peculiar to each constituent category of that system. It has a white population which, in its lifestyle and standard of living belongs to the 'first world', while the urban areas reserved for blacks and coloureds belong to the modern industrial 'third world', and the Bantustans containing the 'tribal' peasantry do not differ from peasant communities in Africa's 'fourth world' (Amin 1997, cited in Weston 2011: 141–142)

Despite significant changes in our society over the past twenty years, Amin's account of South Africa as a microcosm of the world capitalist system still holds. As environmental concerns intensify globally, new activist and popular initiatives and social movements have emerged around the global ecological crisis and its many local manifestations. Locally, new strategies and alliances, both formal and informal, are building communal solidarities as everyday issues of working people in particular, such as food and energy prices, become

focal points of organisation (Rathzel et al 2018). Given this scenario, it should not be surprising that the most recent key text adopts a radical analysis presenting an eco-socialist alternative to climate change.

Trade unions have, for instance, begun to formulate environmental programmes (Rathzel 2018). The first draft of a Climate Justice Charter dated 1 November 2019 has been formulated by the Co-Operative and Policy Alternative Centre (COPAC) and the South African Food Sovereignty Campaign (SAFSC).

These initiatives simply indicate how at this juncture in our democracy there are new opportunities for environmental sociologists to engage with the substantive issues the society-environment relation throws up. This environmental challenge needs urgently to be addressed. The volume by Satgar noted above 'treats the climate crisis as an emergency' and calls for 'civilisational transformation' (2018:2). The urgency of the current global environmental issues need to be addressed, not only by activism and social movement involvement, but need to find voice at a range of levels: policy, student training and re-orientation of the curriculum, creating local, regional and global partnerships with other scholars and disciplines, developing community environmental consciousness and contributing practical solutions to the critical environmental and developmental challenges facing our country. It is the urgent task of sociologists, for example, to conduct relevant, theoretically informed empirical research in areas such as energy and biodiversity management and tackle how climate justice, system change and what has been called the 'just transition' can be realised (see Satgar 2018: 8ff).

26.3 The environment as shared space
The first lesson to be learned is that the term environment is a highly contested concept. This demonstrates the need to broaden consensus on what the term actually stands for in order to develop a much more holistic definition which needs, in addition, to incorporate a slew of new conceptualisations emerging from within the global environmental movement. Not only do different voices within various contexts and timelines attach different interpretations, meanings and value to the term environment, there are those who deny the seriousness of the current global environmental crisis.

A second important lesson is that how the environment is defined affects how environmental problems and policy interventions are prioritised. We need to appreciate that certain groups within society have more influence and power on environmental agenda settings and which often follow trends which come and go. For example, a few years ago rhino poaching locally seemed to dominate any discussion on the environment. With climate change internationally increasingly occupying centre stage and emerging locally as a pressing concern, sociological analyses have begun to link new understandings of the environment. The causes of environmental degradation and threats to biodiversity, for instance, have been linked to unemployment in the Million Climate Jobs Campaign (Ashley 2018), with reconsiderations of *ubuntu* (Terreblanche 2018) and food sovereignty (Bennie & Satgar 2018) as the most pressing problems of our time. For it is especially poor communities who face land degradation, water, land and wood shortages and increasing poverty.

The concept environment has evolved considerably from its limited initial usage by sociologists. Briefly, sociologists have been accused of adopting a purely social dimension to the exclusion of physical and other non-social factors. The environment was defined in terms of social and/or cultural factors and not the natural environment. Since the natural environment was not the unit of analysis, the assumption was that human beings exist independently from and are separate from nature (Dunlap & Catton 1994). This view stressed the superiority and exceptional traits (eg language, social organisation) which humans possessed.

The above reflected the predominant and still ingrained dominant world view of **anthropocentrism**. Anthropocentrism basically refers to the supremacy of humans as a species and the ideology that nature exists primarily for human use. It reflects a constructed antagonistic and unecological attitude towards nature (Dunlap & Catton 1994).

The key elements include (Devall & Sessions 1985: 69; Dunlap & Catton 1994: 12–17):

- humans are distinct and exist independently of the natural world
- humans have the power to dominate, master, conquer, control, manipulate and exploit to meet their needs
- the earth is a collection and storehouse of infinite natural resources
- nature is a commodity amid excessive consumerism
- technology provides us with a world of unlimited opportunities to exploit the environment and to innovate whenever natural resource scarcity exists.

Anthropocentrism is the opposite of **biocentrism**, which emphasises the intrinsic value of all natural life forms informed by their equality where none is above the other but which is explained by their intricate network of relationships.

In South Africa definitions need to recognise and appreciate the destructive environmental legacy of colonisation and apartheid. Defined in this way, the environment is a political issue: a source of power, control and wealth. This understanding is inextricably linked to the history of accumulation, dispossession, forced removals, exploitation, social and environmental injustice, exclusion and a disproportionate access to and use of environmental resources. For the majority of the black population, the environment was used as a tool which destroyed and constrained productive opportunities and livelihoods. This had a negative impact on the interaction between people and the environment forcing the black population to live in overcrowded and degraded environments (Department of Land Affairs 1996; Khan 2000; Cock 2007; Cock & Koch 1991; McDonald 2002; Hallowes 1993). This situation still exists today.

In South Africa the natural environment remained poorly defined in official discourse for a long time. Building on the foundation laid in the South African Constitution of 1996, and the White Paper on Environmental Management Policy (1997), the National Environmental Management Act (NEMA) 107 of 1998 explicitly provides the current official definition of the **environment**. 'The surroundings within which humans exist and that are made up of:

i. *the land, water and atmosphere of the earth;*

ii. *micro-organisms, plant and animal life;*

iii. *any part or combination of (i) and (ii) and the interrelationships among and between them; and*

iv. *the physical, chemical, aesthetic and cultural properties and conditions of the foregoing that influence human health and well-being.*

Broader conceptions of the environment envisage different types of environments, ranging from the purely natural environment to the built environment and modified environments. Rather than seeing these as completely separate and isolated conceptions, it is necessary to realise their overlapping nature. In discussing the environment it is apparent that an individual approach that singles out separate components of what constitutes the environment (eg land, water, air, fauna and flora) is not helpful (Rabie 1992: 83–86). Rather, the environment needs to be understood as an integrated whole. This is clearly stated in NEMA principles that:

environmental management *must be integrated, acknowledging that all elements of the environment are linked and interrelated, and it must take into account the effects of decisions on all aspects of the environment and all people in the environment* *by pursuing the selection of the best practicable environmental option.*

Underlying current definitions is the notion of complex dynamic interaction, interdependence, interconnectedness, interrelationships and interrelatedness of humans and nature. In this sense the environment is no longer considered an 'external alien force' but rather, humans and society are considered part and parcel of the natural environment (Cock 2007: 9–13). It is exactly these interactions and interrelationships that inspired sociologists to study how human beings relate to their natural environment. It is clear that the current usage should embrace social, political, health, economic and cultural dimensions in addition to the biophysical system (Rabie 1992: 84).

It is important to distinguish between the terms *ecology*, *ecosystem* and *environment*. These terms proved useful in the early formative years of the development of the discipline of environmental sociology. The terms are often used interchangeably. **Ecology** is the scientific study of the structure, patterns and processes of interrelationships between living organisms and their natural habitat. According to the NEMA:

> an **ecosystem** *means a dynamic system of plant, animal and micro-organism communities and their non-living environment interacting as a functional unit.*

Examples of ecosystems include oceans, rivers, forests, wetlands, grasslands and deserts. Each of these ecosystems reflects a different system of internal organisation as well as the concentration of species in their respective locations. The totality of ecosystems on the planet is referred to as the **biosphere**.

The section below on dominant society-environment narratives further illustrates how different social groupings within society understand and attach meanings to the environment. South Africa is a diverse nation according to culture, religion, creed, gender, education, class, race, geographic location and age. These narratives reflect this diversity.

26.4 Dominant society–environment narratives in South Africa

At least four narratives on the relationship between society and the environment can be identified, namely the *conservation*, the *economic*, non-state actors and *local community views*. The narratives find different levels of expression in various localities and across historical time.

These narratives need not necessarily act against each other as is evident in their implementation. In practice, they show the deep social divisions and power relations that still exist in South Africa.

26.4.1 The conservation view

The environment conservation narrative is the oldest. This is an exclusive authoritarian negative perspective (Cock 2007: 150). It has always represented harsh external intervention on the local sphere, especially in the former apartheid homelands, by conservation and government agents. More importantly, the dominant narrative demonstrates how powerful and influential human agents dictate views on the interaction between society and the environment. Often these views failed to act in the interest of the majority in different localities. The focus is on protecting the environment by excluding people and removing their rights to land and other natural resources. The environment in the former homelands has always been the primary target of misdirected brutal government intervention with disastrous consequences: land dispossession and forced resettlement without compensation for loss of assets. The case of the Makuleke community who were forcefully removed from their land in 1969 to form part of the Kruger National Park is a useful example. In 1998 this 11 000-strong community, however, was restored under democracy and who now use their 22 000 hectares for hunting to develop schools and clinics in their three villages as part of the park system (Cock 2007).

Not all dispossessed communities have been as fortunate and whose interests have often been negatively portrayed in making a case for the preservation of 'wild' nature. This narrative is largely based on the **tragedy of the common** conservation thesis put forward by Gareth Harding in 1968. This basically refers to people's destructive behaviour in which a public-owned common natural resource is over-used and degraded over time because of short-term conservation gain rather than the interests of society as a whole. It advocates for the regulation of the natural resource by limiting the number of users. This narrative informed the conservation policies and practices adopted by colonial authorities and subsequent governments. This narrative continues despite the fact that it has been questioned and challenged by research.

This narrative creates alarm and panic about the state of the environment, in particular its declining quality. Its underlying assumption and rationale is the presumed destructive, ignorant attitude and practices of the local rural population. The natural environment is described as a victim that needs to be rescued from the reckless actions of those living especially in communal areas in the rural areas. The argument focuses on the over-exploitation and degradation of common natural resources because of people's over-reliance on them. Here local people are accused of mismanaging their natural resources since everyone is competing for access to and use of the resource. The narrative advances the need for the protection and conservation of the natural resources by restricting access to the resource.

At least two approaches inform this model. The first one advances complete non-human interference with the natural environment. According to this view the natural environment is sufficiently capable of regenerating and restoring itself using its own natural processes. The second strategy is the most common. It is a reactionary traditional approach which seeks to limit human interference and pressure on the natural resource base by using several measures which include fencing, fines, policing and even culling. This is sometimes referred to as the 'fences and fines' or enclosure model. In its practical implementation this is achieved by creating protected areas in the form of national parks, nature and game reserves. This approach is implemented by identifying special pieces of land, usually large tracts of land, sometimes considered ecologically sensitive and biologically diverse areas.

Several national parks were established: Pongola (1894) and Sabie (1898). The latter was incorporated in the Kruger National Park. Only the affluent and ruling class had the financial means to visit these areas (Cock 2007). For the affected communities it has a painful history of land dispossession accompanied by forced removals as occurred to the Makuleke community under apartheid.

The Cape Forest Act 28 of 1888 is an example of the first conservation statute which laid the basis for specific demarcated forest areas. The conservation drive and policies have been extended to various animal and plant species throughout South Africa. For the latter locally controlled use of certain types of vegetation was put in place. The result has been a growth of the conservation areas in various parts of the country.

The conservation model has had far-reaching consequences for the local rural population living in the former homelands. This model hides the many social injustices that have been committed in the name of conservation. The result is that the model lacked legitimacy on many levels:

- It was implemented without input from the affected populations leading to their alienation and exclusion.

- The conservation measures interfered with the freedom of movement of both people and animals.
- The model ignored how local people have traditionally interacted with natural resources. Hence their actions progressively became criminalised leading to arrests, harassment and fines for trespassing. In the most dramatic of cases the Pondo revolt in the Transkei in the 1960s led to violent uprisings with people killed and jailed.

In many instances these measures have resulted in the forcible removal and displacement of the people from their land. In the process people's welfare was compromised and livelihoods were destroyed.

26.4.2 The economic view

This narrative views the environment as a commodity (ie something to be bought and sold) not for the benefit of the locals but a select privileged few. The environment is identified as an economic asset to bring about lasting socio-economic development and transformation, not only in the specific locality, but throughout the country. This explanation is premised on the argument that the exploitation of the environment is an untapped resource that will lift people out of poverty. The model has been critiqued for its short-term commercial interests.

The Wild Coast is an ecologically rich, diverse and sensitive coastal zone. It is designated by the government as a region that requires high care from the continual exploitation of its natural resources. The region is one of the most underdeveloped areas (with high rates of illiteracy, poverty and unemployment, poor infrastructure provision, poor health and a degraded natural environment), not only in the Eastern Cape but also within the country. At some level the environment is regarded as the victim of extreme local poverty, while on the other it is seen as part of the solution to that poverty (Kepe 2001: 20). Its professed untapped economic potential has been championed as a catalyst to unlock urgently needed development in the region. The involvement of the private sector is considered important. Ecotourism, agriculture, forestry, mining and fisheries have been identified as key strategic economic sectors. The economic view, however, has not gone uncontested. The Department of Mineral Resources' (DMR) granting of a mining licence to an Australian mining company for the Xolobeni Mineral Sands Project was overturned by an important court order in February 2020 requiring the community be consulted regarding its future.

26.4.3 Non-state actor environmental views

These views normally originate from external interested parties (such as academics, scientists and non-governmental organisations (NGOs)), outside of the local community. The active participation of environmental non-governmental organisations (ENGOs), often adopting militant positions is the most visible aspect of this view. They sometimes have a close relationship with the conservation approach, identifiable mostly by a noticeable absence of local representation and or community participation. Emphasis is placed on the intrinsic value of the environment, responsible environmental stewardship, the firm belief that environmental resources are finite and the rejection of the anthropocentric attitude of humans. In addition, they question and challenge state power and decision making in promoting unrestrained economic growth. Whilst supportive of economic growth and the use of the environment by locals, the emphasis is that this should be done in a manner that does not compromise the integrity of the natural environment.

26.4.4 Local community views

These views are complex and highly differentiated according to the distribution of power, the quality of the natural environment, geographical area, class, historical period, time-related practices, gender, health, age, politics, religion, occupation, the resources involved, their usage and relevance, social institutions, conservation practices, ecological dynamics and livelihoods. It is important to note that local community views find expression in the context where people's relation to the environment has been distorted by colonisation/apartheid policies and practices as evident in the environment conservation narrative.

It is a fact that local communities derive their livelihoods from a variety of sources other than directly from the environment. However, in the context of extreme poverty in many rural areas of South Africa, the relationship between people and the environment becomes even more significant. People still do derive their livelihood from the land. Hence, the environment is widely valued as an important resource. For the local subsistence farmers, traditional healers, women and other social groups protecting the grasslands, water sources and other life forms is an important part of livelihood strategies. In this sense the environment is an important source of food, wood for fuel, construction and shelter, fodder and medicinal products.

In this section an attempt was made to demonstrate that the relationship between society and the environment is complex as reflected in the competing narratives. This does not mean that local initiatives are not taking place. A locally produced booklet, *Community Voices on Climate Change* (Buthelezi et al 2014), for instance, documents how a wide-ranging group of activists, involved in a partnership between eThekwini and the German city of Bremen, are tackling the central environmental issue of climate change. The first line of its editorial introduction notes how 'it is ironic that the contribution by Africa to climate change through carbon emissions is small, however, the impacts are postulated to be more severe on this continent than any other' (Mtapuri 2014).

The environment has been at the heart of contemporary international debates since the 1970s. It is within this context we witnessed an evolution of environmental thinking as expressed in the discourses of the environment discussed below. Combined, these discourses seek to transform and foster a new relationship between society and the environment.

26.5 Discourses of the environment

26.5.1 Sustainable development

'Our biggest challenge in this new century is to take an idea that seems abstract – sustainable development – and turn it into a reality for the entire world's people' (United Nations 2001 – Kofi Annan, former Secretary General of the UN).

The post-apartheid environmental policy framework incorporates principles of sustainable development, social and environmental justice. These signify government's attempt to redress the historical imbalances created by the apartheid system and create a new democratic and just society that respects the rule of law.

The notion of sustainable development, despite its critics, has been an important concept in the international politics of the environment since the 1980s. It came to dominate society-environment discourse. It is an appealing, compelling and multidimensional concept as many different interest groups (from ordinary people, governments, non-governmental organisations (NGOs) and multilateral institutions to the private sector) all proclaim to embrace it (Carter 2001). Sustainable development was and still is adopted by these different interest groups each with their understanding of what sustainable development means.

For multilateral agencies such as the International Monetary Fund (IMF) and the World Bank this means pursuing multiple objectives of neo-liberal policies which favour developed countries over developing countries. The private sector in pursuit of its understanding of sustainable development is interested in profit-making, investment and improving its competitiveness. The South African government believes that in order to achieve sustainable development the economy has to grow significantly. According to this reasoning it is only then that job creation, skills development, infrastructure and socio-economic development will take place. These examples illustrate clearly the fluidity of the concept of sustainable development as it is applied differently by different stakeholders.

The classic and official definition of **sustainable development** as defined in 1987 by the World Commission on Environment and Development (WCED), commonly known as the Brundtland Commission, in their report *Our Common Future*, is 'development that meets the needs of the present without compromising the ability of future generations to meet their own needs' (WCED 1987: 43). Since the inauguration of the idea we have seen a growth of the literature redefining, reinterpreting, critiquing, dismissing and even championing the notion of sustainable development (Carter 2001; Dryzek & Schlosberg 2005; Elliott 2005; Rogers, Jalal & Boyd 2008; Sachs 1999; Swanepoel & De Beer 1997).

The United Nations Conference on Environment and Development (UNCED), also known as the Rio Summit, held in 1992, was an important milestone in international environmental governance. This meant that sustainable development and its three inter-related pillars (economic development, social development and environmental protection) received formal acceptance on a global stage by world leaders.

An appraisal of sustainable development since 1992 has revealed a mixed performance record in relation to the integration of the three pillars. Hence, the call for radical reform in the build-up to the Rio+20 Earth summit, the United Nations Conference on Sustainable Development in 2010. This marked the 20th anniversary of the UNCED. Dubbed as a 'make or break summit', the Commission on Sustainable Development (CSD) referred to the summit as a 'historic opportunity to define pathways to a safer, more equitable, cleaner, greener, and more prosperous world for all' (UNCSD 2012). Just like sustainable development, contestation of what the *green economy* is dominated before and after the summit. The various understandings include economic growth, improving environmental quality, 'green' jobs, markets and investments, adapting and mitigating climate change, eco-innovation, low carbon economy, resource efficiency, infrastructure development and human development. Regardless of these controversies, the outcome document of the Rio+20 Earth summit, *The Future We Want (FWW)*, endorses the green approach to sustainable development and poverty alleviation as its key dual mandate. Thus, prioritising the green economy is a

prominent global concept for debating desirable futures (Levidow 2014: 21).

The best way to begin this discussion is to start off by looking at the 'sustainable' and 'development' components of the concept of sustainable development separately.

Sustainable

The concept of *sustainability* or what is sustainable refers to the environmental part. Implicit in the concept is the recognition that natural resources are a valuable part of human societies. Central in the debate on sustainable development is nature and the extent to which humans interact and use natural resources. The concept implies that the exploitation or the use of our natural resources occurs at a rate which ensures that they do not run out (Carley & Christie 1992). It requires prudent behaviour on our part in a manner which ensures the continued availability of the resources for current and future generations. It inculcates a mindset of care, respect and self-restraint. Implicit, therefore, is the recognition of ecological limits and disruption. Simply put, human impact on the environment must be kept to a minimum.

Sustainable development involves the integration of economic growth, social development and environmental protection into national, regional and international planning and decision making (Elliott 2005; Rogers, Jalal & Boyd 2008; Sachs 1999; Swanepoel & De Beer 1997). It requires the co-operation, commitment and co-ordination of all efforts, together with the development of partnerships, aimed at achieving sustainable development. Theoretically, sustainable development puts an emphasis on the participation of each and every citizen and or organisation in any locality. The notion of global collective effort is the cornerstone in meeting sustainable development initiatives since it is impossible for any individual, organisation and government to succeed on its own.

As a model and process of social change, sustainable development is designed to transform and foster a new relationship between society and the environment. The basic principle guiding sustainable development is that a healthy relationship between society and the environment is the only context in which any real development can take place (Carter 2001; Dryzek & Schlosberg 2005; Elliott 2005). The underlying principles informing sustainable development must at least recognise and include the following factors:

- Continued development is dependent on the protection of the environment.

- Future generations must not be disadvantaged by our current reckless and selfish actions. In other words, we need to ensure **intergenerational equity**.
- Improving the quality of life lies at the centre of sustainable development.

The argument around a sustainable environment is that unrestrained exploitation of natural resources threatens the very basis of human survival and development. The message is a clear one: if we do not *conserve*, the environment the human race faces complete *destruction*.

Along many sections of the Western Cape coastline, abalone poaching and overharvesting of other marine resources is rife. Many marine species are on the verge of extinction because of human action. There are widespread concerns about the depletion of our fisheries worldwide. Overfishing is decimating not only fish species but also impacting negatively on many other life forms. There is global concern as the amount and size of available stock continues to decline. Already the practical usage of 'sustainable' is in question.

Development

Development continues to occupy centre stage in the 21st century. Just like *sustainable* development, there is a lack of consensus on what *development* actually stands for. Traditionally, development has largely been viewed and measured simplistically in economic terms. The key focus has been on the performance of the national economy in terms of its gross domestic product (GDP) with the belief that once this is achieved the benefits will lead to the improvement in the quality of life for all.

Development as a concept finds differing levels of expression within and between countries. Defined positively, development implies progress, positive change, growth, prosperity, continuous improvement and well-being (Sen 2001; Todaro 2000). We see proponents who advocate development as a remedy for all socio-political and economic ills. Research evidence questions widespread phenomena such as hunger, homelessness, illiteracy, lack of healthcare, unemployment and social inequalities. Despite nearly four decades of 'development', we have seen growing disparities of wealth within and between countries, continued patterns of poverty and deprivation and social exclusion on a large scale, which persistently ravage the most vulnerable and marginalised.

26.5.2 Critical discussion on sustainable development

Beyond the definitional problems, the first major criticism revolves around the practical implementation of sustainable development on many levels. Lack of political will and commitment among leaders and those in positions of power and influence have been blamed for the poor progress in achieving the ideals of sustainable development.

Sustainable development has failed to live up to its stated goals of improving the standards of living of the majority of the population in developing countries. Growth in poverty, inequality and underdevelopment has increased. The number of people who have no access to basic services such as adequate shelter, health, food and nutrition, education, water and sanitation has increased, with high rates of infant mortality and maternal deaths. This has huge implications for meeting the **Sustainable Development Goals** (UN 2015) by 2030.

South Africa has achieved a poor level of economic growth since 1994. According to Statistics South Africa (2018) 'the long term economic growth under the current policy environment is estimated at 3.5 per cent. Per capita GDP growth has proven mediocre, though improving, growing by 1.6 per cent a year from 1994 to 2009 and 2.2 per cent from 2000 to 2009, compared to world growth of 3.1 per cent over the same period'. In 2018 South Africa experienced an economic recession in the first two quarters, with the economy contracting by 2.7 per cent in the first quarter and shrinking further by 0.5 per cent in the second quarter (Statistics South Africa 2018). Equally, the annual growth rate for 2018 was 0.8 per cent compared to 1.3 per cent for 2017. This has not resulted in better job opportunities especially for the majority of the youth and young graduates. Statistics show that 70 per cent of the unemployed is the youth below the age of 35. The United Nations Conference on Trade and Development (UNCTAD) report argues:

> The current pattern of Africa's economic growth is particularly worrisome given the fact the region has a young and growing population... While having a young and growing population presents opportunities in terms of having an abundant labour supply with more creative potential, it also means that African countries will need to engage in growth paths that generate jobs on a large scale to absorb the additional labour ... (UNCTAD 2012: 3)

With unemployment on the rise, basic commodities are becoming increasingly unaffordable. According to the South African Institute of Race Relations survey (2010/2011) survey the number of beneficiaries who rely on state social grants for their sustenance has increased by 300 per cent since 2000. The high rate of rural-urban migration in search of better job opportunities has put a strain on the government to provide better services. South Africa is now regarded as one of the most unequal societies in the world ahead of Brazil which has often been top of the list. If sustainable development is struggling to meet the needs of the current generation, is it possible to meet the future needs of the next generation whose needs might be completely different? We are already in debt to and borrowing from the future generations since our current exploitation of natural resources has been exceeded.

Sustainable development does not address **uneven development**, the lifestyle divide as reflected in consumption and production patterns between developed and developing countries. It is a well-known fact that developed countries consume almost 80 per cent of the world's resources, yet their population is about 20 per cent of the world's population (Sachs et al 2002). Such disproportionate consumption is not questioned by a sustainable development discourse.

The over-emphasis on economic growth, over-reliance on market forces and excessive wealth accumulation by a select few has attracted the most criticism. The quest for short-term economic growth using natural resources has by far exceeded the goals of environmental protection and social development. The proponents of sustainable development have not engaged with the fact that developing country resources have been plundered for centuries. These arguments apply equally to the green economy approach as argued by Morrow (2012: 294–297):

The conception of the green economy is pro-growth and unashamedly anthropocentric … advocates further objectification and commodification of the environment, reaffirming its subservience to human development. It relegates the environment to the status of a resource base… the green economy approach as it currently stands continues to share the (erroneous) assumption that the market can deliver sustainability.

Developing country mineral wealth is in higher demand than ever before. Exploratory mining operations are on the rise, not only in South Africa but on the rest of the continent. The UNCTAD (2012: 2) report is critical of this natural resources-led economic growth and development, cautioning that

non-renewable resources are being depleted at a very rapid rate with negative consequences for future growth and sustainability. In this sense there is less emphasis on the general and practical idea of protecting the environment, let alone restoring its integrity where it has been damaged by human action.

The debate on and appeals to sustainable development downplays the overall impact and influence of multilateral institutions such as the International Monetary Fund (IMF) and the World Bank (WB), multinational corporations and other major stakeholders pursuing a neo-liberal economic agenda. The IMF/WB have played a major role in shaping the direction of the developing countries' development through Structural Adjustment Programmes (SAPs) implemented in the developing world in the 1980s. A fundamental criticism is that SAPs worsened the continent's long-term development and environmental sustainability resulting in reduced incomes, increased poverty, deteriorating social conditions, rising prices of basic commodities, declining access to health and educational opportunities. Together with the collusion, corruption and greed of developing country elites, the funding of large-scale projects such as dams, electricity and agricultural schemes has undermined environmental sustainability. This has resulted in degraded and polluted environments with large populations forcibly removed to accommodate the new developments.

The development of strong democratic institutions at national, regional and global level is a crucial challenge. Since the global environment agenda emerged in the 1970s, institutions, policies and practices have been established at these levels. The problem revolves around strengthening, co-ordinating and building effective institutional structures. Environmental governance structures, policies and practices remain fragmented whilst at the same time lacking sufficient capacity in human and financial terms. This problem has lead to poor co-ordination, denial of responsibility, uncertainty and a delayed response in dealing with environmental matters.

Lastly, strengthening the role of civil society participation in environmental matters is urgently needed. Currently, civil society is largely viewed in a negative and antagonistic manner by powerful economic and political interests. It is hard for civil society to engage with governments, international governance institutions, multilateral organisations and multinational corporations and find common ground.

26.5.3 Environmental justice and environmental racism

Environmental justice is a rights-based and people-centred discourse focusing on the marginalised, voiceless, powerless and sometimes disenfranchised communities according to their class, gender, race, ethnicity and geographical locations. With its origins in the United States of America, environmental justice incorporated environmental racism as its departure point, adopting in large part the language of the Civil Rights Movement. Simply put, **environmental racism** describes institutionalised racial discrimination in environmental policy, regulation and practices which deliberately locates toxic waste sites and industrial facilities in poor minority neighbourhoods.

Environmental justice recognises that the people who are the least responsible for environmental risks, hazards and changes endure the greatest impact for which they are ill-equipped, ill-prepared and under-resourced to deal. The central argument is that these groups are the victims of environmental risks and hazards created by the privileged and powerful. The current economic and political system allows for such inequitable spatial distribution of environmental burdens by externalising environmental costs to society. In this sense we refer to the existence of environmental injustice. The notion of power and domination at the local, national and international levels is central to environmental justice analysis.

Environmental justice is considered both an ethical and political imperative to rid society of all forms of inequality and human rights violations, hence the call for social transformation (McDonald 2002). In this sense the fight for environmental justice is inseparable from the quest for development, 'meeting basic human needs and enhancing the quality of life' (McDonald 2002). It is this radicalism that informs the environmental justice movement in South Africa. It has become extremely difficult to divorce environmental justice from the history of exclusion and impoverishment generated and sustained by the apartheid system. Hence the environmental discourse has overtly political undertones. The concept of environmental justice as a mobilising tool critiqued the elitism of environmental discourse in the country whilst at the same time broadening its agenda to include the historically marginalised black population (Cock 2007).

26.6 Environmentalism

Environmentalism is a worldwide phenomenon found in various localities internationally, nationally, regionally and at grassroots level. The environmental activists are key actors in the international politics of the environment. They influence domestic and international environmental politics.

The environmental movement or **environmentalism** are terms usually used interchangeably to denote organised networks and collective environmental action which creates a global community of activists. Other terms include non-

state actors, environmental activists, environmental non-governmental organisations, environmental interest groups, environmental pressure groups, green lobbyists, green warriors, green movement, public interest groups and environmental justice activists. A distinction is not made in this text between these various terminologies, albeit at the risk of over-simplification. Suffice it to say, the above terms are open to diverse interpretations. The environmental movement can be seen as a distinct subset of the broader social movements not necessarily dealing directly with the environment. By drawing audiences and supporters from a variety of cross-cutting interests they are able to get support from other social constituencies creating a much broader support base. As a result, they are able to attract a large following.

It would be misleading to create an impression that environmental activists generate wide appeal and the appreciation of everyone. Often, they are met with strong opposition especially from the groups they challenge. In this sense they are often depicted as 'attention seekers' 'irrational' 'hooligans' 'arrogant' and 'extremists' who create unnecessary fear and panic in society. They have at times been jailed, kidnapped and even killed. For the environmental movement theirs is a noble cause to save the environment and humanity.

Environmentalism as used here is described as both an ideology and action-oriented political programme designed to bring about desired social change or a new social order (Harper 1996: 293). Environmentalism reflects diverse views on the society-environment interface. The environmental movement differs in terms of organisational structure, size, skills, legal status with regard to membership, focus and activity areas, the local setting, power and influence. What unites them is the rejection of anthropocentrism in all its forms.

The diversity and fragmentation in the environmental movement is considered its key strength, since this allows it to tackle a whole range of environmental issues simultaneously. At the same time fragmentation should not be interpreted as working in isolation. Environmental activists form strong working coalitions by sharing expertise which helps them to form a united front around a particular issue, as is evident in the case of hydraulic fracturing in South Africa.

As an action-oriented programme, environmental movements use a variety of strategies and tactics to convey their message. These tactics include public education, media campaigns, lobbying, direct action, advocacy research, scientific research, data collection, publications, policy making and conferences. By raising issues of public interest, they at times use highly persuasive graphic language such as 'raping our planet' and 'stop flesh eating'. No doubt environmentalism does create a climate for social dialogue no matter how the message is communicated and received. Being able to organise, mobilise and communicate unambiguously and appealing to public opinion lies at the core of environmentalism. Sometimes environmentalists enlist prominent and revered figures in society to help advance their cause.

26.6.1 The history of environmentalism in South Africa: An overview

This section provides a historical overview of the rise of environmentalism in South Africa through an appraisal of South Africa's political history within the broader context of the evolution of society-environment relations. The current environmental crisis dates back centuries ago increasing exponentially since the 1800s. South Africa's environmental history shares similarities with the rest of the African continent. Historically, South Africa lacked a cohesive environmental management system which was for the benefit of all South Africans.

Society–environment relations in South Africa have always been precarious within a highly brutal politicised climate. The country's colonial and apartheid history of unsustainable land-use practices and policies, unequal access to and ownership of natural resources, denial of citizenship rights, social and environmental injustices, unfettered wealth accumulation, politics of power, domination, control and subjugation have shaped this. Effectively, ownership of productive natural resources was a privilege rather than a right consistent with the development trajectory of the country. As such, the environment became a tool which destroyed and constrained productive opportunities and livelihoods. This had a negative impact on the interaction between people and the environment forcing the black population to live in overcrowded and degraded environments (Department of Land Affairs 1996; Khan 2001; Cock 2007; McDonald 2002; Hallowes 1993).

A prominent feature of society-environment relations is reflected in the land question. Not only were black South Africans denied the right to citizenship but inequitable access to and use of productive natural resources such as land, energy, water and mineral wealth was institutionalised.

The systematic dispossession of Africans of their land through colonisation culminated in the Native Land Act, No. 27 of 1913. This laid the basis of South Africa's distinctive pattern of racially unequal ownership which destroyed independent peasant production, turning African people into wage labourers and exporters of food. The reserves continued to slide into ever-increasing poverty and

widespread environmental degradation. Attempts to address these confronting issues through measures and policies such as Betterment Planning and Rehabilitation failed.

Historically, human beings have always relied on the natural environment to meet their basic needs. They have throughout the ages evolved with the environment. It is true that we have not always acknowledged and appreciated our 'embeddedness' with the natural environment, resulting in our 'alienation' (Cock 2007), albeit with disastrous consequences. Traditional societies such as Khoisan are an embodiment of living within nature and its limits reaching the most obtainable co-existence with nature.

The general mindset regarded Africans as enemies of nature, irrelevant, lazy, hostile and destructive (Cock 2007; Khan 2000). A growing negative perception directly linked Black South Africans to the growing problem of the destruction of wildlife and other natural habitats. The dominant perception of the environment and land was that 'of a wild and savage place, peopled by hostile tribes and overrun by beasts ... wilderness was the frightening unordered condition ... an abundance of natural resources existed in an unclaimed state' (Khan 2000: 31). Environmentalism was never designed to understand Africans' historical, cultural and social relations to land in general and to the natural environment in particular. Africans were never acknowledged, nor appreciated as having played any role in, nor considered to possess any prior knowledge of natural resources conservation and protection. This lies at the root of the (ir)relevance of indigenous (or traditional) knowledge systems (ITs) still prevalent today.

What followed the prevailing mindset and destructive practices of early settlers was the rampant use of natural resources leading to shortages, including their extinction. Van der Merwe (1962: 5) identifies three main influences, namely indiscriminate hunting, agricultural expansion with fencing and diseases. Not only wildlife was affected but the disappearance of flora and increasing soil erosion was a major concern. Remedial and protective measures were needed and instituted in the form of fines, permits, game rangers, protection of specific species and policies as early as the 1600s. The use of protected areas gained momentum in the late 1800s with 'the first game reserve, the Pongola, proclaimed on the 13th June in 1894' (Van der Merwe, 1962: 6–7). However, the decline continued.

The conservation ideology throughout the 20th century highlighted its one-dimensional, Eurocentric, authoritarian, narrow-focused preservationist image inherited from the preceding period discussed above. This artificially created binary divisions between people/society and the environment, with the marginalised African majority juxtaposed with the supposedly dynamic, environmentally friendly White minority. Equally, a disturbing uncritical dominant discourse established a direct link between Black African population growth and natural resource depletion ignoring completely South Africa's political history and development trajectory. McDonald (2002) refers to this history of environmental policy as a cruel and perverse one, whereas Cock (1991) talks about the authoritarian conservation model.

The development of mainstream environmentalism in South Africa was a slow and gradual process. Traditionally, environmentalism was mainly concerned with the conservation of threatened plants, animals and wilderness areas mirroring the orientation of colonisation/apartheid policies and practices (Cock 2007: 180). As a result, a broad-based environmental movement did not develop which would serve the needs of all South Africans. This is, also, evident in the environmental organisations formed in the 1900s, including 'the deliberate exclusion from the enjoyment of protected natural areas evident in national parks' (Khan 2000: 160).

This denied local African people any space for social engagement with environmental issues. Constrained by the prevailing political climate, minor attempts to include blacks were futile and did not yield any real benefits and outcomes. As Khan (2001: 166) argues 'it is little wonder that Black organisations established during this period were in fact established on the initiative of the White parent organisation, these were in fact creatures of apartheid'. The few established Black environmental organisations failed to attract members and were basically insignificant attempts at breaking this impasse and become part of mainstream environmentalism.

It is worth noting that the primary quest for political liberation was not met by a corresponding case for the environment. As a result, up until the late 1980s there was no clear statement on environmental matters coming from the liberation movements. During the late 1980s the environmental discourse began to emerge in the language of the liberation movement and other extra-parliamentary groups such as trade unions and civic associations. A landmark Conference for a Democratic Future (1989), with many anti-apartheid organisations in attendance, resolved that 'the right to a healthy and clean environment was fundamental for all South Africans'. There was consensus that the destruction of apartheid was a necessary precondition if environmental rights were to be realised (Khan 2000: 167).

26.6.2 The formative period and the emergence of radical environmentalism

The above developments laid the groundwork for shifting the environmental agenda with civil society in general. A new space to accommodate the majority of South Africans was opened. No longer is environmentalism seen as the preserve of the elite.

The establishment of Earthlife Africa (ELA) in 1988 was a turning point for the ENGOs of the time. Earthlife operated outside the traditional boundaries of ENGOs which were closely aligned with the apartheid state. From the beginning Earthlife Africa adopted a radical position in relation to the government and industrial pollution. Earthlife can be credited for fighting environmental and social injustices from this early formative phase.

Environmentalism in South Africa can roughly be divided into two main categories, namely, the environmental justice movement and the purely sustainable development discourse (Cock 2007). The former:

> *combines ecological and social justice issues in that it puts the rights of the poor, the excluded and the marginalised at the centre of its concern. It is located at the confluence of three greatest challenges in our society: the struggle against racism, poverty and inequality and the protection of the environment* (Cock 2007: 174–175).

This is a large network of community-based and national organisations. Today the environmental justice movement in the country can be said to have gained a level of maturity in many areas such as policy formulation, educating and organising communities and has managed to forge working coalitions locally, regionally and internationally. It has a visible presence in many forums.

The issues covered include rights of access to basic services such as sanitation, water, energy, health, food safety, natural resources, workers' health and safety, agricultural practices, industrial pollution, waste management and environmental policies. It questions state power and the regime of private capital accumulation. It emphasises public participation, transparency, right to information, accountability and informed decision-making. The prominent organisations in this group include EarthLife, Groundwork, Environmental Justice Networking Forum (EJNF), Environmental Networking Group and the Group for Environmental Monitoring.

Environmental organisations that subscribe to the sustainable development discourse are primarily concerned with the conservation of biodiversity. The Endangered

Wildlife Trust (EWT) and the Wildlife and Environment Society of Southern Africa (WESSA), and the Wilderness Foundation are examples of organisations in this group. Cock (2007: 176) describes them as 'socially shallow, with a mainly white, middle-class support base'. These organisations have launched extensive campaigns and national programmes on fauna and flora issues such as 'saving the rhino'.

Irrespective of their orientation, we have seen a growing alliance of ENGOs such as Sustaining the Wild Coast Campaign active in the Wild Coast which secured a victory against the proposed mining at Xolobeni and the N2 toll road yet with the Treasure the Karoo Action Group (TKAG) against hydraulic fracking in the Karoo with the South Durban Alliance against petrochemical multinationals continuing. The state of the environment hence depends on the existence of a vibrant broad-based environmentalism that challenges the economic and political interests.

26.6.3 Environmental management regime in democratic South Africa

The challenge for the post-apartheid government has been to develop an inclusive society and overcome the discrimination and repressive legacy of colonisation and apartheid. This meant reconstructing and reorienting the development and environmental focus of the country informed by a new value system of human and environmental rights and the rule of law. The key challenge remains the extent to which the government is committed to these values, principles and policies.

South Africa's environmental laws have been influenced to a great extent by major developments taking place at the global level.

The primary pillars of South Africa's environmental management regime are the socio-economic and environmental rights enshrined in the 1996 Constitution. In this sense the constitution provides the foundation for the legal framework for environmental protection. Theoretically, the constitution institutionalises environmental justice and the human–environment relationship through section 24 which states:

Everyone has the right:

(a) to an environment that is not harmful to their health or well-being; and

(b) to have the environment protected, for the benefit of present and future generations, through reasonable legislative and other measures that:

(i) prevent pollution and ecological degradation;

(ii) promote conservation; and

(iii) secure ecologically sustainable development and use of natural resources while promoting justifiable economic and social development.

Subsections 9(1) and (2) in the equality clause in the Bill of Rights stipulate that everyone is equal before the law and has the right to equal protection before the law; equality includes the full and equal enjoyment of all rights and freedoms. In addition, the Bill seeks to promote the achievement of equality, legislative and other measures designed to protect or advance persons, or categories of persons, disadvantaged by unfair discrimination may be taken.

The post-apartheid environmental reform agenda was initiated and negotiated in the Consultative National Environmental Policy Process (CONNEPP). CONNEPP consisted of representatives from civil society. CONNEPP gave effect to civil society's call for a new inclusive environmental policy which would be guided by the socio-economic and environmental rights. The outcome of the CONNEPP was the White Paper on Environmental Management Policy (DEAT 1997) and the National Environmental Management Act (NEMA) 107 of 1998.

The NEMA includes core environmental values: duty of care and remediation, precautionary principle, polluter-pays-principle and intergenerational equity. Combined, these principles compel the state to ensure the long-term sustainability of natural resources for both current and future generations. Moreover, the emphasis is placed on the state to ensure responsible action, accountability and prevention. In light of this Specific Environmental Management Acts (SEMAs) covering issues such as pollution and biodiversity have since been passed.

The constitution further provides for co-operation and improved relations between and among the three spheres of government from national, provincial and local government levels. The constitution states:

the environment is a functional area of concurrent national and provincial legislative competence, and all spheres of government and all organs of state must co-operate with, consult and support one another (RSA Constitution 1996).

This has resulted in the redefinition and clarification of the respective roles, responsibilities and powers of each of these levels. A major shortcoming is that 'policies and functions continue to cut concurrently across national, provincial and local government levels leading to unnecessary duplication, competition, uncertainty and confusing mandates' (Kotze 2007).

Public participation in decision-making is an important principle of environmental management policy. In addition to the constitution, the Mineral and Petroleum Resources Development Act 28 of 2002, requires that 'mineral and petroleum resources are developed in an *orderly and ecologically sustainable* manner while promoting *justifiable social and economic development*'. Similarly, Chapter 1 of NEMA states 'development must be socially, environmentally and economically sustainable'.

The ongoing Xolobeni Mineral Sands Project has illustrated the tension between ecological sustainability and economic development. From 2003 to 2008 community opposition to the proposed project grew. This revolved around five main issues:

- The government supported the mining initiative as the best route for development in the area while the community preferred the existing community-driven ecotourism business which had been operational for several years (Gqada 2011: 5; Bennie 2009). The project was poorly aligned to local concerns and needs (Bennie 2009: 106).
- The community, as interested and affected parties, had not been consulted adequately in the run-up to the government's decision to grant the mining rights (Gqada 2011: 5).
- The public consultation process was flawed. The nature of the public meetings held with the affected communities as part of the impact assessment process failed to ensure their meaningful participation in decision making (Bennie 2009: 98).
- The project favoured the local elite who managed to manipulate and influence the processes around the proposed mining including the public participation (Bennie 2009: 97).
- The community's views and concerns over the long-term impact of the proposed mining project were totally ignored and marginalised. It has the potential to cause:

severe and permanent environmental impact, land dispossession and relocation, destruction of cultural sites, which would disrupt social networks and relations as well as how people secure their livelihoods and relate to the environment (Bennie 2009: 84–89).

This shows that communities have the capacity to challenge externally imposed development strategies effectively, by making their otherwise marginalised voices heard (Gqada 2011: abstract). In pursuing this type of strategy the government goes against its own position of protecting the Wild Coast.

The conclusion reached in this section clearly shows that there is an existing gap between the stated policy *intentions* and *actual implementation*. South Africa's resistance to political reform in the pre-1994 period delayed and constrained the implementation of social and environmental transformation. Despite wide ranging environmental reforms undertaken since 1994 South Africa continues to be clouded by a deepening environmental crisis which undermines the development-environmental project. Capacity constraints – including financial, personnel, skills levels, legislative weaknesses and lack of political will – hamper effective environmental management.

The state of the environment in South Africa is also set in the context of global climate change and the energy challenge. The focus on the mining industry, further elaborates on the violation of socio-economic and environmental rights. The contemporary issues of acid mine drainage and hydraulic fracturing are used as case studies.

26.7 The state of the environment in South Africa

South Africa boasts an environmentally diverse and rich heritage. South Africa ranks third in the world (behind Brazil and Indonesia) in terms of its biodiversity (Department of Environmental Affairs and Tourism (DEAT) (2005, 2009). It is obvious that environmental quality is being threatened and undermined by reckless human action.

Two key interrelated themes currently dominate the debate on the state of the environment in South Africa, namely climate change and the energy crisis. The two constitute part of the larger environmental crisis. The debates:

- question the regime of capital accumulation based on the incessant exploitation of natural resources at all costs
- show a direct causal relationship between the exploitation and declining quality of the environment and the exploitation of human beings (Hallowes 2011; Bond, Dada & Erion 2007; Cock 2007).
- advocate an alternative development path that respects people and the environment
- focus on the relationship between inequality, poverty and energy. In addition to issues of environmental sustainability, the debate focuses on redressing past historical imbalances in energy provision.

The energy sector is crucial to the South African economy with its over-reliance on large-scale, energy-intensive mining. The main source of the current energy system is coal and will remain so for a long time. Coal constitutes around 70 per cent of South Africa's primary energy, crude oil around 23 per cent, nuclear energy around 3 per cent and renewable energy around 8 per cent (Department of Minerals and Energy 2004). Electricity generation from coal-fired power stations makes up 92 per cent (National Energy Regulator (NER) 2004). Coal-fired plants use low quality coal in the generation of final energy. This leads to the production of harmful gaseous and solid wastes with disastrous health implications such as cardiovascular problems, respiratory illness and cancer. The coal dependency of South Africa's energy system shapes the composition of its greenhouse gas emissions (Winkler & Marquand 2009: 51).

South Africa is now ranked one of the highest carbon emitters in the world. Eskom predicts that with electricity supply growing at a potential 4.4 per cent per annum CO2 emissions from electricity generation would more than double over the next twenty years (Earthlife Africa 2006: 6). In 2005, Eskom embarked on the controversial construction of two new coal power stations, Medupi and Kusile in order to boost and meet energy demand. This will place South Africa as one of the largest emitters of greenhouse gases in the world directly linked to climate change and is the reason South Africa is dubbed a carbon economy (Hallowes 2011: 7–11; Bond, Dada & Erion 2007). The Highveld has been designated a third priority area in the country in terms of the National Environment Air Quality Act 39 of 2004, due to the heavy air pollution burden experienced. The scenario painted here exists despite government's commitment to reduce greenhouse emissions by 34 per cent and 42 per cent by 2020 and 2025 respectively (Baker 2011: 10).

To address climate change, the current energy system must be overhauled (Earthlife Africa 2006: 6). Climate change requires that South Africa moves away from an energy-intensive to a low-carbon economy. The situation is tenuous as the country is hastily looking to diversify its energy mix by switching to alternative energy sources such as nuclear power, natural gas, wind, solar and other forms of renewable energy while at the same time continuing to use the old controversial sources such as cheap coal. Transition to renewable energy sources has been slow.

Industry is the largest user of energy in the country, making up to 45 per cent of total energy consumption compared to 10 per cent by households (Winkler 2006; Hallowes 2011; Baker 2011). Energy supply in the country is far from secure. This became evident in the 2006–2008 outages experienced throughout the country. Since then there have been nationwide campaigns urging all South Africans to use energy especially electricity efficiently. Currently ESKOM, the national power utility, is barely able to meet the demand for energy.

Given South Africa's history of racial discrimination and poor service delivery it is not surprising to find unevenness in the distribution, consumption, access to and use of energy, especially in low-income urban and rural areas. The National Electrification Programme (NEP) has been used to provide electricity to South Africa's poor. Despite the success of the NEP a total of 3.4 million households still do not have access to electricity (Winkler 2006). The key variables that inform energy provision by the Department of Minerals and Energy (DME) include affordability, access, availability, reliability and safety issues.

Generally, electricity consumption patterns in low-income areas are very low. The cost and availability of energy sources determine consumption patterns. Households still continue to use traditional polluting and unsafe sources such as wood, paraffin, candles, gas, methylated spirit and coal. In these areas, electricity is regarded as an expensive, unaffordable resource. It is used sparingly for limited periods in the evening for lighting and watching television. Every year many households in informal settlements lose their hard-earned possessions in wildfires especially during the cold winter months. Illegal dangerous electricity connections are a common occurrence in areas where access to electricity is minimal or non-existent, resulting in fatalities and disruption of power supply for extended periods. It is safe to conclude that 'at least a quarter of households are energy poor and these are largely black households' (COSATU nd: 40). Energy poverty means that people are denied access to electricity, due to either lack of infrastructure or to high electricity prices and an inadequate basic free allowance (COSATU nd: 40). As noted above, scientific evidence clearly states that climate change is human-induced. Climate change is worsening the environmental crisis in South Africa. Already we are witnessing extreme weather patterns in various parts of the country. Many areas suffer massive deforestation, soil erosion and loss of biodiversity. For example, we are witnessing an increasing frequency and intensity in the incidents of wildfires especially in the Western Cape. This has an impact on the regeneration of the vegetation and ultimately the loss of **biodiversity**. Other parts of the country are experiencing severe drought while others have experienced flooding in recent years.

Climate change attacks and destroys peoples' livelihoods required for daily survival. It is widely reported that climate change will affect food, income, water supply, health and biodiversity in the country. The price of basic commodities such as food is already very high with families unable to afford everyday basic necessities. The burden falls heavily on the poor, vulnerable groups such as women, children, the youth, the sick and the elderly. These are the groups who rely extensively on social grants. Climate change will further widen inequality and poverty.

26.8   Mining in South Africa: An overview

Mining remains the backbone of the South African economy contributing to job creation and economic development. While its revenues have steadily declined in terms of growth over the past decades, and there is much concern about its wasting assets, it cannot be considered weak. According to the South Africa Chamber of Mines 2008/09 annual report South Africa is the third largest mining country in the world after the United States of America and China. Not only is the mining sector a catalyst for the development of other industries such as energy, water and financial services, engineering services, geological and metallurgical services, other industries use mineral products produced by the mining sector. At the same time the mining sector uses services and inputs provided by other industries.

South Africa is well endowed with vast mineral resources. The mineral mix includes gold, diamonds, coal, titanium, manganese, iron ore, chrome, platinum group metals, oil, and gas. South Africa is believed to have the largest reserves of a number of these minerals in the world which still need to be explored and/or extracted. Coal mining was for long the second largest mining sector after gold which was recently eclipsed by platinum. The Bushveld complex stretching from Rustenburg to Burgersfort is where platinum reserves are located while the Waterberg coal reserves in Limpopo Province remain extensive and are an example of South Africa's mineral wealth.

Mining has a long history in South Africa dating as far back as the 1800s with the discovery of diamonds and gold. Since then it has spread to other provinces beyond its original home bases in Kimberley and Gauteng. Mining in South Africa is dominated by multinational corporations (MNCs) with huge assets invested not only in mining-related ventures. China, meanwhile, represents the new giant on the global block, extending its operations to the African continent at an unprecedented rate. Exploratory mining operations are on the rise, not only in South Africa but on the rest of the continent. There are hundreds of mining licence applications awaiting approval in various provinces suggesting that the exploitation of the country's mineral wealth will continue unabated. In fact, the number of mines in South Africa increased from 993 in 1994 to 1 600 in 2013 according to the Minister of Mineral Resources, Susan Shabangu (Department of Mineral Resources, Mining Indaba 2013).

The exploitation of local labour, the lack of social upliftment where mining operations occur, widespread occupational hazards and accidents, environmental and health risks and the fact that mineral wealth is characterised by inequitable access and unequal ownership are among a range of long standing unresolved thorny issues. The Mining Charter which was designed to ensure that communities around the mines benefit from productive opportunities in the mines has largely failed to ensure socio-economic development. Miners and their families often continue to live in squalor, lacking access to basic services.

A largely uneducated workforce (including their families) often live and die in abject poverty with air-borne diseases for which they have had neither legal recourse nor any form of adequate compensation, as in the case of asbestos miners and adjacent communities despite major compensation awards in the case of asbestos. While workers are the first direct victims of mining operations, communities are also not immune from the spill-over effects. It is now official that the highest prevalence of tuberculosis on mines is seven times higher compared to the general population. It was reported on World TB day on 24 March 2012 that the gold sector has the highest number of miners with tuberculosis. Miners work long hours under still unsafe and unhealthy conditions. During mining operations miners are exposed to intense heat, air pollution and are subjected to other physical pressures which exert a toll on their health.

The environmental track record of mining is far from satisfactory. The mining sector has been the single largest contributor to environmental decay for over a century affecting land, air, surface and groundwater (contamination, salinity and siltation) including the loss of biodiversity due to the transformation of natural habitats and ecosystems. Mining operations and processes, in addition to the excessive use of toxic chemicals, utilise massive amounts of water in an already water-stressed country. At the same time the mining sector produces massive amounts of solid waste, including radioactive waste, which constitutes almost two-thirds of the total waste stream (Madihlaba 2002: 158–159).

There are many defunct and unrehabilitated mines in the country, which often leads to the growing problem of illegal mining activities as poor communities settle in their vicinity. The Marathon squatter camp in Ekurhuleni municipality, with open mine pits, is a case in point. The case of abandoned coal mines with underground burning still continuing in the Witbank area, Mpumalanga Province, is a matter of increasing concern. For the poor communities living in close proximity to the mines the immediate public health, safety and security issues pose additional problems.

26.8.1 Acid mine drainage

To illustrate the impact of mining on the environment, this section of the chapter presents a broad overview focusing on **acid mine drainage (AMD)**, sometimes referred as acid rock drainage, as it relates to gold and coal mining. This mostly affects Gauteng, Limpopo, North West and Mpumalanga provinces.

Coal mining in the Witbank/Middelburg area started in 1894 supplying coal to the diamond and gold mining industries. An expansive network of coal resources is situated in the Mpumalanga Province, supplying and sustaining several large coal-fired power stations situated on the Highveld between Witbank, Standerton, Piet Retief and Carolina. Just as the geographical spread of coal mining is dispersed, so is AMD in Gauteng, covering areas such as Germiston, Johannesburg, Roodepoort, Krugersdorp, Randfontein, Westonaria and extending as far as Carletonville. Both coal and gold mining have a profound impact on surface and groundwater quality and quantity.

AMD is highly acidic and toxic underground water flowing in large quantities from derelict and or defunct mining areas usually containing high concentrations of heavy metals, salts and radioactive particles. This AMD pollutes surface water and endangers ecosystems and the health of communities. The source of AMD is both the water used during mining operations and the surrounding groundwater which has to be drained all the time to prevent any form of flooding. When a mine is closed, the water accumulates in the mine but will eventually escape, and this joins with and pollutes the water system. Other sources of AMD include a mix of industrial effluents, treated and untreated sewage and surface water run-offs.

The process of mining involves interfering with and disturbing the underground rock structure. No matter how much the rock structure is reinforced and restored, acidic water will seep through the cracks. The production and accumulation of acid starts during mining and mineral extraction which the natural processes are unable to completely neutralise. Unlike gold which generates huge amounts of solid waste, the amount of surface dumping with coal is comparatively negligible. Waste generated after the extraction of gold remains deposited in areas commonly known as mine slimes or tailing dumps found in large heaps in close proximity to many poor black communities (Madihlaba 2002). These dumps endanger the lives of residents. It is this acid that is washed out during rainfall

that ends up polluting local surface and groundwater and also eventually reaches our major rivers such as the Olifants, Crocodile, Vaal and Limpopo.

There is a level of overlap with the pollution generated by coal and gold mining such as air pollution, soil erosion, solid waste and open pits. The position with platinum mining is unclear at the moment, even though evidence suggests that they are not afflicted by the AMD problem on the same scale but problems with water quality have been identified.

In some instances, water treatment plants have failed to improve the quality of drinking water or the general condition of the polluted rivers. In the case of the eMalahleni Water Reclamation Plant, Mpumalanga Province, the improvement of drinking water quality standards means escalating costs of providing the water to the communities. At the same time there are no guarantees that the 'treated water' and 'improved water quality' pose no health risks to the communities in the long term.

The apartheid government failed dismally to assert its authority for environmental compliance and accountability by the mining industry. Denialism is prevalent in government thinking, hence, the slow response time. It is safe to conclude that the mining industry has been aware of the growing environmental and public health problems created by its mining activities. In 1996 the mining industry submitted the Strategic Water Management Report to Parliament which discussed, among other things, AMD. As early as 1976 studies warned and reported the existence of AMD in Gauteng. However, the first identified visible presence of AMD was in August 2002 in the West Rand basin. The government responded by commissioning several studies with the Finance Minister, Pravin Gordhan, announcing in February 2011 during the budget speech in parliament that an amount of R225 million had been set aside for dealing with AMD. The Inter-ministerial Committee on AMD appointed towards the end 2010 was an attempt to address the immediate problems arising from gold mining especially the defunct mines in the Western Basin (Krugersdorp area), the Central Basin (Roodepoort to Boksburg) and the Eastern Basin (Brakpan, Springs and Nigel area).

The findings of these studies were dramatic and startling (Department of Water Affairs 2010):
- As early as March 2013, AMD could flood Gauteng and its surrounding towns.
- The Johannesburg Central Business District with its enormous infrastructure network, including buildings, is under threat of total collapse and irreparable damage.
- This could adversely affect the economy of the region and the country as a whole.

- AMD threatens large-scale pollution of the water system in its entirety.
- Public health and safety are at risk.
- The growing rise of AMD above the critical limit poses significant risks of earth tremors and other seismic hazards.
- Tourist sites and protected areas are already experiencing AMD: Cradle of Humankind, Sterkfontein caves, nature reserves, bird sanctuaries and wetlands.

To address these issues the following was recommended (Department of Water Affairs, Inter-Ministerial Committee on AMD 2010):

- Upgrade the technology and existing treatment capacity
- Strengthen and co-ordinate the policy framework
- Urgent remedial measures (prevention, monitoring and the development of relevant expertise, co-operation of the various stakeholders) need to be undertaken as a matter of urgency.

Figure 26.1 Karoo targeted for hydraulic fracturing

26.8.2 Hydraulic fracturing

It is precisely due to the above concerns with AMD that the prospects of hydraulic fracturing in the Karoo have met with such widespread resistance. It is widely believed that this form of large-scale mineral exploitation will be potentially dangerous and ecologically damaging. **Hydraulic fracturing** (commonly referred to as **fracking**) as a mining process involves a high pressure deep drilling technique in order to break the shale underground rock structure using a mixture of water, sand and an elaborate mix of toxic chemicals creating wells to release and access the natural gas or oil trapped in rock formations. It is estimated that the maximum life span of a drilled well is eight years decreasing in productive capacity significantly after five years. The Karoo Basin is target for such gas exploratory activities.

The first area of contention has to do with the large quantity of water that is used in an ecologically sensitive area already facing acute water shortages. The accumulation and poor recovery of the injected corrosive chemicals underground threatens to contaminate underground water and become a human health hazard.

26.9 Conclusion

We have seen throughout this chapter that studying the societal-environment interface is complex and contested. Sociology needs to intensify research on social structure and natural environment interdependence. We need to appreciate the destructive environmental legacy of apartheid on the current and future generations. One of the lessons for us is that this has proven very difficult to erase as the environmental landscape is littered with environmental decay of a lasting magnitude. The case studies demonstrate that environmental problems have the capacity to spiral out of control beyond their immediate location and time zone. Unfortunately, South Africa has a myriad of competing and overlapping priorities and the environment needs to seen as part and parcel of this mix. In addition, the environmental challenge has the capacity to unite us beyond our sectoral interests. Lastly, environmental decline has created conditions under which environmentalism thrives. Environmental activism shows the environment as a negotiated tension-filled space with many disparate (sometimes converging interests) and actors. No doubt environmental activism demonstrates that environmental concerns are not only the government's responsibility but the civic duty of each and every citizen in the country.

Summary

- The environment performs various competing functions as a living space, supply and waste storehouse.
- The health and integrity of the environment is vital for the health and development of society.
- Man and nature should exist in a reciprocal beneficial relationship.
- The environment is a life supporting system and a public good, hence it is society's heritage.
- Good environmental stewardship does not depend on the government alone but on the participation of every citizen.
- Efforts to protect and conserve the environment fall far short of the expected outcomes.
- The anthropocentric attitude is still the prevailing mindset.
- Studying the societal-environment interface is complex and contested.
- Sociology needs to intensify research on social structure and natural environment interdependence.

- We need to appreciate the destructive environmental legacy of apartheid on the current and future generations. One of the lessons for us is that this has proven very difficult to erase as the environmental landscape is littered with environmental decay of a lasting magnitude.
- South Africa has a myriad competing and overlapping priorities and the environment needs to be seen as part and parcel of this mix. In addition, the environmental challenge has the capacity to unite us beyond our sectoral interests.
- Environmental activism shows the environment as a negotiated tension-filled space with many disparate (sometimes with converging interests) actors. No doubt environmental activism demonstrates that environmental concerns are not only the government's responsibility but the civic duty of each and every citizen in the country.

ARE YOU ON TRACK?

1. Identify at least four areas that demonstrate sociology's relevance to studying environmental issues.
2. What are the key issues involved that you should take into account in defining the environment?
3. What is the official definition of the environment in South Africa according to the National Environmental Management Act?
4. What is sustainable development according to the Brundtland Commission? What are the critical issues raised here?
5. Compare and contrast environmental justice and environmental racism?
6. List at least six factors why mining is considered an environmental and public health hazard?
7. What are the key lessons from the two discussions of acid mine drainage (Section 9.1) and hydraulic fracturing (Section 9.2)?

Websites

Earthlife Africa: www.earthlife.org.za
ELDIS: the gateway to development and environment information: www.eldis.org
Environmental Monitoring Group: www.emg.org.za
Groundwork: www.groundwork.org.za
UN Environmental Programme: www.unep.org
World Resources Institute: www.wri.org

References

Amin S. 1997. Samir Amin's 1997 Babu Memorial Lecture. https://www.pambazuka.org/governance/first-babumemorial-lecture-22-september-1997 [Accessed 27 May 2020].

Ashley B. 2018. 'Climate Jobs at Two Minutes to Midnight' in Satgar V (Ed). *The Climate Crisis: South African and Global Democratic Eco-Socialist Alternatives*. Johannesburg: Wits University Press.

Baker L. 2011. *Governing Electricity in South Africa: Wind, Coal and Power Struggles*. Norwich, UK: University of East Anglia.

Barnejee SB. 2003. 'Who sustains whose development? Sustainable development and the reinvention of nature'. *Organisation Studies*, 24(1): 143–180.

Bennie AG. 2009. 'The Relation between Environmental Protection and Development: A case study of the social dynamics in the proposed mining at eXolobeni, Wild Coast'. MA Research Report. Johannesburg: University of the Witwatersrand.

Bennie A, Satgoor A. 2018. 'Deepening the Just Transition through Food Sovereignty'. Satgar V (ed). *The Climate Crisis: South African and Global Democratic Eco-Socialist Alternatives*. Johannesburg: Wits University Press.

Bethlehem L, Goldblatt M (eds). 1997. *Bottom Line: Industry and the Environment in South Africa*. Cape Town: University of Cape Town Press.

Bond P, Dada R, Erion G (eds). 2007. *Climate Change, Carbon Trading and Civil Society: Negative Returns on South African Investments*. Durban: University of KwaZulu-Natal Press.

Buthelezi P, Carras M, Draeger J, Gwala P, Madela N, Mbele S, Mbutho A, Mdima NN, Mthombeni T, Ndlovu T, Ngema F, Nkonyeni M, Qwabe B, Rogoll J, Zondo S. 2014. *Community Voices on Climate Change*, eThekwini: eThekwini Municipality

Carley M, Christie I. 1992. *Managing Sustainable Development*. London: Earthscan.

Carter N. 2001. *The Politics of the Environment: Ideas, Activism and Policy*. Cambridge: Cambridge University Press.

Chamber of Mines. South Africa. Annual Report 2008/09. Johannesburg: Chamber of Mines.

Cock J. 1994. 'Sociology as if Survival Mattered'. *South African Sociological Review*, 6(2): 14–31.

Cock J. 2007. *The War Against Ourselves: Nature, Power and Justice*. Johannesburg: Wits University Press.

Cock J. nd. 'Green Capitalism or environmental justice?: A critique of the sustainability discourse'. Available at: https://hsf.org.za/publications/focus/focus-63/Jacklyn%20Cock.pdf (Accessed 29 March 2019).

Cock J, Koch E (eds). 1991. *Going Green: People, Politics and the Environment in South Africa*. Cape Town: Oxford University Press.

Congress of South African Trade Unions (COSATU). nd. A *Just Transition to a Low-carbon and Climate-resistant Economy: COSATU Policy on Climate Change: a call for action*. Johannesburg: COSATU.

D'Antonio WV, Sasaki M, Yonebayashi Y (eds). 1994. *Ecology, Society and the Quality of Social Life*. New Brunswick, NJ: Transaction.

Department of Environmental Affairs and Tourism (DEAT). 1997. White Paper on Environmental Management Policy. Pretoria: DEAT.

Department of Environmental Affairs and Tourism (DEAT). 2005. *South Africa Environment Outlook: a report on the state of the environment*. Pretoria: DEAT.

Department of Land Affairs. 1996. Green Paper on Land Reform. Pretoria: Government Printer.

Department of Minerals and Energy. 2004. Draft Energy Efficiency Strategy of the Republic of South Africa. Pretoria: Department of Minerals and Energy.

Department of Mineral Resources. 2013. Opening Address at the Mining Indaba by Ms Susan Shabangu, Minister of Mineral Resources of South Africa: Cape Town International Convention Centre. 5 February.

Department of Water Affairs. 2010. Report of the Inter-Ministerial Committee on Acid Mine Drainage. Pretoria: Department of Water Affairs.

Department of Water and Environmental Affairs. 2004. National Environmental Management Act: Air Quality Act 39 of 2004. Pretoria: DWEA.

Devall B, Sessions G (eds). 1985. *Deep Ecology: Living as if Nature Mattered*. Salt Lake City: G.M. City.

Drexhage J, Murphy D. 2010. *Sustainable Development: from Brundtland to Rio 2012*. New York: United Nations.

Dryzek JS, Schlosberg D. (eds). 2005. *Debating the Earth: The Environmental Politics Reader*. 2nd ed. London: Oxford University Press.

Dunlap R. Catton W. 1994. 'Struggling with Human Exemptionalism: The Rise, Decline and Revitalization of Environmental Sociology'. *The American Sociologist*, 25: 5–30.

Earthlife Africa. 2006. *Climate Change, Development and Energy Problems in South Africa: Another World is Possible*. Johannesburg: Earthlife Africa.

Elliott JA. 2005. *An Introduction to Sustainable Development*. London: Routledge.

Giddens A. 2011. *The Politics of Climate Change*. 2nd ed. Cambridge: Polity Press.

Gqada I. 2011. *Setting the Boundaries of a Social Licence for Mining in South Africa: The Xolobeni Mineral Sands Project*. Pretoria: South African Institute of International Affairs.

Hallowes D (ed). 1993. *Hidden Faces: Environment, Development, Justice – South Africa and the Global Context*. Scottsville, South Africa: Earthlife Africa.

Hallowes D. 2011. *Toxic Futures: South Africa in the Crises of Energy, Environment and Capital*. Scottsville, South Africa: University of KwaZulu-Natal Press.

Harper CL. 1996. *Environment and Society*. Upper Saddle River, NJ: Prentice Hall.

Khan F. 2000. 'Environmentalism in South Africa: A sociopolitical perspective'. *Macalester International*, 9(1): 156–181.

Khan F. 2001. 'Towards Environmentalism: A Socio-political Evaluation of Trends in South African Conservation History, 1910–1976, with a specific focus on the Role of Black Conservation Organisations'. PhD thesis. Cape Town University of Cape Town.

Kepe T. 2001. *Waking up from the Dream: The Pitfalls of 'Fast Track' Development on the Wild Coast*. Cape Town: University of the Western Cape: Programme for Land and Agrarian Studies.

Kotze LJ. 2007. 'Integrating pollution regimes: a comparative survey of the Finnish and South African legal systems'. *Obiter*, 28(3): 439–464.

Levidow L. 2014. *What Green Economy? Diverse agendas, their tensions and potential futures*. IKD: Open University.

Madihlaba T. 2002. 'The Fox in the Henhouse: the environmental impact of mining on communities in South Africa' in *Environmental Justice in South Africa*. McDonald DA (ed). Lansdowne: University of Cape Town Press.

McDonald DA (ed). 2002. *Environmental Justice in South Africa*. Cape Town: University of Cape Town Press.

Minister of Finance, Pravin Gordhan, South Africa. 2013. Budget Speech. 27 February.

Morrow K. 2012. 'Rio+20, the green economy and reorienting sustainable development'. *Env L Rev*, 14: 279–297.

Mtapuri O. 2014. 'Editorial' in *Community Voices on Climate Change*. Buthelezi P, Carras M, Draeger J, Gwala P, Madela N, Mbele S, Mbutho A, Mdima NN, Mthombeni T, Ndlovu T, Ngema F, Nkonyeni M, Qwabe B, Rogoll J, Zondo S. eThekwini: eThekwini Municipality.

National Energy Regulator. 2004. National Integrated Resource Plan 2 2003/2004. Pretoria: NER.

Nygren A. 1998. 'Environment as discourse: searching for sustainable development in Costa Rica. 1998'. *Environmental Values*, 7(2): 201–222.

Rabie MA. 1992. 'Nature and scope of environmental law' in *Environmental Management in South Africa*. Fuggle RF, Rabie MA (eds). Cape Town: Juta.

Ramphele M, McDowell C (eds). 1991. *Restoring the Land: Environment and Change in Post-apartheid South Africa*. London: Panos Publications.

Republic of South Africa. 1996. Constitution of the Republic of South Africa Act 108 of 1996. Pretoria: Government Printer.

Republic of South Africa. 1998. National Environmental Management Act (NEMA) 107 of 1998. Pretoria: Government Printer.

Republic of South Africa. 2002. Mineral and Petroleum Resources Development Act 28 of 2002. Pretoria: Government Printer.

Republic of South Africa. 2004. National Environment Air Quality Act 39 of 2004. Pretoria: Government Printer.

Rogers PP, Jalal KF, Boyd JA. 2008. *An Introduction to Sustainable Development*. London: Earthscan.

Sachs W. 1993. *Global Ecology: A New Era of Political Conflict*. London: Zed Books.

Sachs W. 1999. *Planet Dialectics: An Exploration in Environment and Development*. London: Zed Books.

Sachs et al. 2002. 'The Johannesburg Memo: Fairness in a Troubled World'. Memorandum for the World Summit on Sustainable Development. Berlin: Heinrich Boll Foundation.

Satgar V. 2018. 'The Climate Crisis and Systemic Alternatives'. Satgar V (ed). *The Climate Crisis: South African and Global Democratic Eco-Socialist Alternatives*. Johannesburg: Wits University Press.

Sen A. 2001. *Development as Freedom*. Oxford: Oxford University Press.

South Africa. 1888. Cape Forest Act 28 of 1888. Pretoria: Government Printer.

South African Institute of Race Relations (SAIRR). 2012. South Africa Survey 2010/2011. Johannesburg: South African Institute of Race Relations.

Statistics South Africa. 2018. 'Economic growth better that what many expected'. Available at: http://www.statssa.gov.za/?p=10985 [Accessed 29 March 2019].

Steyn P. 2002. 'Popular environmental struggles in South Africa, 1972–1992'. *Historia*, 47(1): 125–158.

Strydom HA, King ND. 2009. *Environmental Management in South Africa*. 2nd ed. Cape Town: Juta.

Swanepoel H, De Beer F. 1997. *Introduction to Development Studies*. Johannesburg: International Thomson.

Terreblanche C. 2018. 'The climate crisis and the struggle for African food sovereignty' in Satgar V (ed). *The Climate Crisis: South African and Global Democratic Eco-Socialist Alternatives*. Johannesburg: Wits University Press.

Todaro MP. 2000. *Economic Development*. 7th ed. Reading, MA: Addison-Wesley.

United Nations. 2001. *Statement by General-Secretary Kofi Annan*. Press Release 14 March. United Nations: Bangladesh.

United Nations. 2015. Resolution A/RES/70/1 of the United Nations General Assembly, September.

United Nations Conference on Trade and Development (UNCTAD). 2012. 'Economic Development in Africa: structural transformation and sustainable development in Africa'. *Economic development in Africa report 2012.* New York: United Nations.

United Nations Commission on Sustainable Development (UNCSD). 2012. 'Building Our Common Future'. Available at: www.unscd2012.org/rio20/content/documents/Rio20Brochure.pdf [Accessed 29 March 2019].

Van der Merwe N. 1962. *The Position of Nature Conservation in South Africa.* Pretoria: National Parks Board.

Washington H, Cook J. 2011. *Climate Change Denial: Heads in the Sand.* London, Washington DC: Earthscan.

Weston D. 2011. 'The Politics of Climate Change in South Africa' in Bond P (ed). *Durban's Climate Gamble: Trading Carbon, Betting the Earth.* Pretoria: UNISA Press.

Winkler H (ed). 2006. *Energy Policies for Sustainable Development in South Africa: Options for the Future.* Cape Town: University of Cape Town, Energy Research Centre.

Winkler H, Marquand A. 2009. 'Changing Development Paths: from an energy-intensive to carbon economy in South Africa'. *Climate and Development*, 1: 47–65.

World Commission on Environment and Development. 1987. *Our Common Future.* Oxford: Oxford University Press.

Part

5

Sociology in Context

A brief history of sociology in South Africa

Johan Zaaiman

Sociology is reflexive. Sociologists apply their theories to themselves. This is necessary as sociology becomes part of the world which it studies. Sociology must hence examine its own impact on society. This is the rationale behind the following brief history of sociology in South Africa. This overview of the discipline, covering the time from its inception around 90 years ago, shows that sociology has played a remarkably influential role in the society in which it became intimately integrated in complex ways.

Whereas sociology arose in a time of social distress in France over 160 years ago, sociology similarly arose in South Africa in response to a social need. The need, however, was very different to the European experience. In the 1930s, South Africa was an emerging society in which the need for science to address social problems was recognised. The very introduction of sociology sees it grappling with a pressing problem for a young state within the British Empire – the poor white problem. As American engineers were first employed to provide the technical advice to excavate the deep-level mines on the Witwatersrand, so were American sociologists invited to assist very early on in the establishment of sociology.

Shortly after its introduction into a number of universities over the next decade, through training and research, it became part of the way in which society examines its own shortcomings. Sociology expressed itself in different voices from the outset. It became part of the fabric of society in its role in both tertiary education and through state-sponsored research. It later expressed conflicting voices and was driven apart as it found itself in a racially divided society. Sociology consistently, however, provides a range of different analyses resulting in a series of very different, yet important social interventions in society.

This chapter traces the high and low points of a complex institutional biography. As a multidimensional discipline, sociology experiences mixed fortunes. It never seems to be far from either controversy or social acceptance, and at times assumes both roles. This applies to the discipline whether it is the founding decades of the 1930s and 1940s or the decades of the 1950s and 1960s when it established its independence and developed as an academic discipline. The chapter then devotes a section to each decade up to the present. What is noteworthy is how closely important events in society appear to be intimately related to the stresses and strains in a discipline that is divided for the bulk of its incarnation in South Africa. It is never far from influencing the exercise of institutional power on the one hand and directed to the most vulnerable members of society on the other. Sociology on occasions simultaneously played both of these roles and continues to do so, currently represented on all major university campuses and unified in a single organisation with its own academic journal.

Sociology remains deeply involved in issues affecting South African society today. Historically its role has been complex and nuanced, and is not always apparent. It informs government policy and is critical of it; it engages in institutional development and formulates its critiques; it lays down the educational basis for understanding society and yet can distance itself from the form it takes. In short, sociology does not appear, in the light of either its history or its current practice, to be far from the social action that drives society itself.

27.1 Introduction

This chapter provides an overview of the history of sociology in South Africa, briefly describing its origins and development. Different views can be held on this history. In this chapter the focus will be mainly on sociology as an institutionalised science – as it was practised within the academy. This must be distinguished from social theorising in general that also took place outside the domain of universities. There are many published works of both black and white scholars that can be viewed as exploring and theorising the South African social world. However, this was not strictly from a sociological perspective. Sociology, in contrast, entails a scientific discipline, which developed within higher education and research institutions.

27.2 First calls for sociology and its early introduction

In the late 1800s some higher-education institutions were established in South Africa, but none of them introduced sociology among their academic offerings in those early years. Shortly after the establishment of the Union of South Africa in 1910, the government created the first South African universities, of which the University of South Africa conferred degrees on behalf of a number of university colleges.

The first call for the introduction of sociology can be traced back to congresses of the Association for the Advancement of Science in South Africa (S2A3). In 1903, the first sociological contribution at such a congress was made by Prof HES Fremantle, professor of philosophy at the South African College (later the University of Cape Town). His paper read: *The sociology of Comte with special reference to the political conditions of young countries*. Although Fremantle concurred with Comte's positivistic approach, he critiqued Comte's law of three stages for its validity, abstractness and generality. Fremantle also illustrated Comte's inadequate knowledge of history and philosophy. Finally, he argued that Comte's sociology was inappropriate for young countries and that they needed to develop their own brand of sociology (Groenewald 1984: 167–176). In the following years, some more papers with sociological themes were delivered at congresses of the S2A3. These papers dealt with topics such as labour, poverty among whites, 'native issues', race relations, developmental challenges, education and crime.

The financial constraints stemming from World War I (1914–1918) made it impossible to further the ideal of establishing sociology in South Africa in those years. In 1918 the S2A3 again brought the need for sociology to the attention of the academic community and emphasised the importance of studying social problems in a scientific way. Sociology was identified as one of the important fields of study needed by the country. This need was especially motivated in view of the necessity to study social pathology in the South African society and to engage social conditions.

The first sociological themes were introduced in 1919 in first-year courses of the University of South Africa (Unisa) and the University of Pretoria (UP) (called Transvaal University College at that time). Courses in social economy already formed part of the theology programmes at Unisa and UP, and were turned into sociology courses. At Stellenbosch University (SU), sociology subjects were introduced at first- and second-year level in 1922. These courses were presented by Prof NJ Brümmer, who played a major role in social research in South Africa in the 1920s and 1930s. At the University of Witwatersrand (Wits), the first courses were presented in 1923. This was replaced by social anthropology in 1928, and the first sociology courses were again presented in 1937 by JL Gray, the focus of which was on race relations and the poverty issue.

At the University of Cape Town (UCT), the School of African Life and Languages was established in 1921. AR Radcliffe-Brown taught social anthropology and he was against the introduction of sociology courses in the university. It was only after his resignation in 1925 that UCT could begin presenting courses with sociological content in 1926. This was a parallel initiative to the introduction of social work at UCT, which was not realised until 1924. The initiative was resumed in 1930 with the introduction of a chair in social studies that came into being in 1936 with the appointment of Prof Edward Batson.

27.3 The establishment of South African sociology, 1930–1950

The establishment of an institutional presence of sociology during the 1930s was not coincidental. The 1932 Report of the Native Economic Commission indicated that the native reserves were in a state of collapse (Ally, Mooney & Stewart 2003: 75). The outcome of this condition was massive urbanisation. This resulted in serious urban problems and instances of severe social dislocation and upheaval. The related breakdown of close social networks caused strain on relationships, and therefore social institutions such as the family and religion suffered. The situation was aggravated by the Great Depression of the 1930s. This resulted in a time of acute social upheaval and profound social change for most of the South African population.

Ideologically the English-inspired ideas were gradually being phased out and replaced by an Afrikaner Nationalist ideology. Politically, the ruling classes became more unified, and economically national capital began to take over the dominance of imperial capital. The massive social changes of the time led to unregulated urbanisation and contributed to a collapse of the native reserves, which caused the segregationist social order to fall into a state of decline. These conditions created the room for the development of the idea of a new social order. Such an idea demanded an understanding of social relief and social organisation. According to Ally et al (2003: 75), the institutionalisation of sociology in the 1930s therefore came at exactly the moment in which theories of how to create social order and provide social relief in South Africa were most needed.

Two related initiatives contributed directly to the introduction of sociology as a major subject at South African universities in the 1930s. In 1928 the Dutch Reformed Church (DRC) decided to request trustees of the Carnegie Corporation for funding to do research on white poverty problems in South Africa. Stellenbosch University assisted the church in this endeavour. After the funding was obtained, the research was conducted under the chairmanship of Rev JR Albertyn, assisted by sociologists from the US namely Kenyon L Butterfield (Amherst) and Charles W Coulter (Ohio State University). The Carnegie Report followed an advanced social pathology approach. Rather than only focusing on the individual and groups as previous pathology approaches did, the Carnegie Report supported major societal reform by means of moral civil education. This included the reform of social institutions over a wide spectrum. The Carnegie research laid the basis for a multidisciplinary and methodologically pluralistic research approach which continued for a long period afterwards. In 1930 the monthly journal of the Department of Labour published two articles of Charles W Coulter that were influential: 'The need of a school of sociology' and 'Shifting the emphasis of social work'. In both articles the importance of sociological education in South Africa was stressed, which eventually contributed to sociology becoming the preferred major with social work.

The second initiative came with the South African National Council of Women in 1930 deciding to insist on the formal training of social workers. This call for the training of social workers was supported by the findings of the Carnegie Commission's research reports that were published in 1932. In view of these reports, most universities introduced sociology as a major subject after the Conference on the Training of Social Workers (CTSW) in 1936. This conference

was presented following the National Conference on Social Work presented by the National Bureau for Educational and Social Research (NBESR). At the CTSW, a serious debate took place on which subject would best support social work, namely economics, psychology or sociology. Eventually the decision was on sociology. It was decided at the conference that all universities must be informed about the decision on a common standard of training of social work students. The result was that most universities afterwards introduced departments for sociology (in combination with social work):

- The US established the Department of Social Work and Sociology in 1933. This was after Dr HF Verwoerd was appointed to teach sociology in 1932. He introduced an active research programme with postgraduate students to study poverty and social pathology.

- The UP established a Department of Social Work and Sociology in 1934 with Dr G Cronjé as the first trained sociologist appointed in South Africa who had the responsibility of teaching sociology. He focused on social pathology and had a deterministic focus. According to this, every social problem has a cause and if that cause can be addressed, then society can be improved. He strongly associated himself with the eradication of white poverty and Afrikaner empowerment. Throughout his academic term he acted as editor of *Volkswelstand* (a journal focusing on the welfare of the Afrikaner).

- At UCT a Department in Social Administration was established in 1936 with Prof E Batson as lecturer. Although he conducted sociological research, the first formal courses that were named sociology were introduced only in 1946.

- Wits launched the Department of Sociology and Social Administration in 1937 with Prof J Gray as lecturer.

- The University of Natal (UN) introduced a Department of Social Work and Sociology in 1937. HP Pollak was appointed for this purpose in 1948.

- Unisa extended its sociology course to second year in 1933 and to third year in 1939. It established a Department of Social Work and Sociology in 1939.

- The University of Potchefstroom (PU for CHE) presented its first sociology course in 1932 and established a Department of Social Work and Sociology in 1939. Dr DCS du Preez was appointed as lecturer in 1938.

- The first course in sociology at the University of Orange Free State (UFS) was presented in 1935, and the Department of Social Work and Sociology established in 1940. The first sociologist was Dr J de W Keyter, appointed in 1950.

- Rhodes University established a Department of Sociology in 1943 and appointed Dr EF Krige in 1951 as its first sociologist.

During the 1930s, sociology was therefore treated as a service discipline, only offered as part of the training programme for social workers. The discipline thus remained secondary to social work. Courses across the various universities centred on the 'problems' of alcoholism, juvenile delinquency, divorce and prostitution, while directing the training of students towards 'native administration' and social planning. Despite the social welfare orientation of early sociologists across the various universities, the discipline did not develop a coherent identity. Four distinct approaches to sociology were evident in the 1930s. They were Batson's social economics at UCT, Gray's comparative sociology at Wits, Cronjé's historical, cultural and *volk* sociology at UP, and Verwoerd's welfare or reform sociology at SU. The types of sociologies espoused by Verwoerd and Cronjé were the two dominant models of sociology in the 1930s.

Verwoerd adopted the American and British conceptions of sociology, and Cronjé's type of sociology was based on Dutch and Continental conceptions rooted in questions on *Volkskarakter*. Following an American-inspired brand of sociology, Verwoerd believed that sociology was a descriptive, empirical and applied science that could be used for welfarist and reformist politics. Sociology must assist in identifying and solving the social problems of a country. In his courses he therefore covered topics such as poverty, crime and juvenile delinquency.

In contrast, Cronjé emphasised theoretical issues in the discipline and focused on the racial question as well as the development of a cultural or national *volk*. For him the main problem of the racial question was racial mixing and racial clashing, therefore the only answer was racial separation (Ally et al 2003: 77). The purity of the white race was paramount to him and therefore he opposed racial intermarriage. Cronjé's cultural approach spread beyond UP to include Afrikaans-medium universities such as PU for CHE and UFS. Throughout the 1930s to 1950s at these universities Afrikaner intellectuals in sociology and related sciences formulated and reformulated the thought processes that legitimated the apartheid political project.

The sociologists at the English-medium universities shared the same concern as their Afrikaans counterparts for welfare, social administration and empirical research. At Wits, UCT and UN, the teaching and research focused on issues related to social welfare and the alleviation of problems associated with the economic and racial programmes and policies of the government. Gray at Wits emphasised objectivity and the scientific approach of sociology. For him, service to humanism is achieved through the thorough research of contemporary social problems. This was not agreeable to the Department of Social Welfare. In 1939 they met with the Social Studies committee of Wits and requested more attention to social work theory, social fieldwork and South African conditions. The outcome was that sociology remained concerned with especially white welfare, social problems and the racial question.

Batson at UCT separated the study of contemporary social issues from the professional training of social work. For him the social sciences implied the application of scientific methods to the investigation of social phenomena. He is known for being the first researcher to conduct a comprehensive social survey of Cape Town. In this research he used a poverty datum line and a pioneering sampling theory. This demonstrated how sociology could provide tools to identify areas in need of social relief.

A section of the higher-education system that was not reached by the implementation of sociology was the SA Native College in Fort Hare (later the University of Fort Hare or UFH). At that time, it was a constituent college of Unisa, established to meet the higher-education needs of the African population. The black intellectuals who were then most respected were those who remained moderately critical and tolerant of white rule. They were, for example, DDT Jabavu, Sol Plaatje, Selope Thema and S Morena. An independent black intelligentsia did develop from the 1930s, and UFH specifically contributed to producing such intellectuals. However, the first courses in sociology were only introduced at UFH in 1962, therefore until that time no institutional black sociological tradition existed in South Africa.

Other institutions than the universities also played an important role to establish sociological research in South Africa. In view of the dire social needs after World War I (1914–1918), the sub-secretary of education, George Hofmeyer, established the Bureau for Statistics and Information in 1928 to improve the efficiency of social research. In 1933–1934, the Carnegie Corporation of New York was asked to assist the bureau with financing. The bureau focused on research in education, the welfare of children and general welfare. This research was conducted in coordination with universities, and thereby ensured that academics of different intellectual settings converged to conduct research. The head of the bureau was Dr EG Malherbe, who was also seconded by the bureau to the Carnegie Commission and who wrote part III of the report of the commission. Research flourished under the directorship of Malherbe, but due to a lack of funding it came to a halt during World War II (1939–1945). To receive continued research support by the Carnegie Corporation, a condition was set that a body must administer the research. For this purpose, the South African Council for Educational and Social Research (SACESR) was established in 1934, which became the National Council for Social Research in 1946. In 1969, the Bureau for Statistics and Information and the National Council for Social Research was combined to form the Human Sciences Research Council (HSRC). The SACESR viewed social research as an instrument that could assist in analysing social reality and then use this information to prevent or solve social problems. For instance, HA Fagan wrote in his preface to a report of the SACESR in 1938:

The mingling of many races in South Africa and the great variety of physical and economic conditions may create many difficulties for the politician, but at the same time they provide a wonderful field for those who wish to approach our problems by the method of scientific research. It is only recently that the importance and value of this method of approach has met with fairly general recognition. I feel strongly that the more our problems are tackled in this way, the more we will find that their apparent complexity is no great cause for concern, and that they need not give rise to animosities and prejudices, but are capable of being dealt with in a practical and business-like way. Workers in social research can therefore make a great contribution to our solution of South Africa's problems and to our country's happiness and welfare (as quoted in Groenewald 1984: 358).

In 1939, the SACESR was concerned about the few applications it received for research funding. This was ascribed to:
- the universities having limited funding, equipment, time and manpower
- the universities being young and focused on teaching
- postgraduate students who were only interested in professional qualifications
- limited publication facilities (Groenewald 1984: 364).

The SACESR also identified the most urgent needs for research at that time as:
- juvenile delinquency
- the education of poor white children through farm schools
- home conditions of primary-school children

- experimental investigation into the possibility of complete rehabilitation of children of poor white parents
- the use of radio and film in furthering cultural and recreational activities in rural communities
- the use of leisure by persons of different social groups
- measurement of racial attitudes in the schools
- ideas and ideals of social significance held by primary- and high-school pupils
- the households of delinquent boys (Groenewald 1984: 365–366).

Another body that played an important role in funding early sociological research was the Research Granting Council (1918–1935) of the Department of Mines and Industry. This council assisted the Carnegie Commission with organisation and administration in its research conducted on the issue of white poverty. However, the council's funding for social research remained very limited.

A non-governmental organisation that played an important part in early social research was the South African Institute of Race Relations (SAIRR) established in 1929. The aim of the institute was 'to work for peace, goodwill and practical co-operation between the various sections of the population in South Africa and to initiate, support, assist and encourage investigations that might lead to greater knowledge and understanding of the racial groups and of the relations that subsist between them' (Groenewald 1984: 373). Hellman stated that:

The core of the Institute's work throughout its existence has been the accumulation of factual data relating to the living conditions of the African, Coloured and Asian peoples and to their legal status and civil rights. This included the regular study of reports of relevant government departments, of commissions and committees of enquiry, the analysis of legislation and ordinances bearing on race relations, and the results of various enquiries the Institute conducted itself (Groenewald 1984: 376).

Efforts were made to bring the English and Afrikaans scholars together in this endeavour. Verwoerd also supported this alliance between English and Afrikaans scholarly activities and especially those focusing on social welfare.

The SAIRR enjoyed an excellent relationship with the government until 1948 when the National Party became the governing party. In 1948 the *Suid-Afrikaanse Bond vir Rassestudies* (SABRA) was established as a counter to promote apartheid by means of social research. This was a result of English- and Afrikaans-speaking academics growing apart – with Afrikaans-speaking academics more inclined towards the apartheid ideology and English-speaking academics supporting the liberal tradition. Afrikaner intellectuals gained a voice through SABRA. The Bond became the key institution where ideas were transformed into policy and the Afrikaner's racial policy was developed.

Also significant in the 1930s was the establishment of the South African Inter-University Committee for Social Studies in 1938. This committee was the forerunner for the subject associations in the social sciences and played a functional role in the eventual establishment of the South African Sociological Association in 1967.

World War II (1939–1945) disrupted South African society, and social research was halted. During this time 'problems' such as unemployment, suicide, divorce, prostitution and alcoholism were high on the academic agenda (Ally et al 2003: 84). In 1942 the Social and Economic Planning Commission was formed as a non-statutory advisory body, which initiated research investigations into the social and economic system. The newly established Council for Research in the Social Sciences (CRSS) formulated research projects covering the national life. The CRSS had the potential to develop sociological research on a national basis but was hindered by a severe shortage of funds. Central research topics were school, family and delinquency, social pathology and race relations.

27.4 Independence and development of an academic discipline, 1950–1970

The 1950s to 1970s were characterised not only by the full implementation of the apartheid ideology but also by an upsurge of strong resistance against apartheid among blacks. For example, on 21 March 1960 black resistance was expressed in the Sharpeville campaign and on 30 March 1960 in the great march to parliament. Shortly afterwards, on 8 April 1960, the prime minister, Verwoerd, was wounded in an assassination attempt but soon returned to his office even more determined to establish apartheid. He announced a referendum to be held in October 1960 on becoming a republic, which eventually happened on 31 May 1961. Verwoerd believed that a republic would create white unity, which was a necessary prerequisite for the maintenance of apartheid.

During this period, sociology in South Africa established its own independence. In the 1960s all departments of sociology that had been conjoined to social work broke away and established the independence of the discipline.

Sociology developed the institutional capacity to produce PhDs – the first being awarded at the UN in 1965.

The UP, UOFS and PU of CHE were the key Afrikaans institutions whose sociology departments dominated the sociology discipline with their commitment to the *volk* and formulated justifications for the apartheid idea. Within the field of sociology, sophisticated theoretical justifications for apartheid were developed and debates were conducted on how the functioning of apartheid could be optimised. To support grand apartheid, these sociology departments were also involved in research related to population counting, surveillance and urban planning. According to Ally et al (2003: 87):

> during the 1950s and 1960s these universities accounted for 68.8% of all sociology graduates in the country, 40% of whom were recycled back into intellectual circles and 15% directly into government services, planning and administering the socio-economic project of Apartheid.

Many of the young Afrikaner academics were deployed to the black universities, which were established through the apartheid policy as teaching universities. In this way such universities could be described as instruments of academic colonialism. These universities could therefore not develop independent intellectual and research traditions. They were rather training institutions to produce the civil servants and administrators of the apartheid regime.

At the forefront of shaping the apartheid ideology in a sophisticated way was NJ Rhoodie at UP. His interest was in 'intergroup conflict in plural societies'. In his view, apartheid consisted of two phases, the first of which was the duty of the white man to uplift the 'undeveloped' black man. According to Rhoodie, this phase had run its course. In the second phase, the black man was in an empowered position to develop himself separately. He could do it because of his intellectual, social and economic capacity. In contrast to the other Afrikaans universities, SU was critical towards the apartheid policies of Verwoerd. The then head of sociology at SU, Prof SP Cilliers overturned Verwoerd's social engineering sociology with the Parsonian theory. Cilliers studied under Parsons and was determined to revive this theory in South African sociology.

At the English-medium universities, the American sociological imagination took root. The focus was on attitudes, social pathology, demography and criminology. Demographic techniques and related research were sought after because the apartheid state needed surveillance to track the labour population for the purposes of labour supply. Especially at UN and Wits, sociologists researched attitudes. Imitating the American psychological concern with prejudice, attitude surveys became the major research output of these sociologists. Especially sociologists such as Kuper, Dickie-Clark, Van der Berghe and several others studied group perceptions. Henry Lever, chair of the Department of Sociology at Wits, had a special interest in electoral attitudes. CW de Kiewiet, E Hellmann and M Horrell studied racial attitudes as the basis for apartheid as well as the incompatibility of apartheid and capitalism. The larger structural issues of the socio-political order were not of much interest to the English-speaking sociologists. This only changed after the 1960s with the revival of Marxist thought in view of Europe's Paris 1968 student and worker revolt.

As a research institution independent from the universities, the NBESR remained important and its name was changed in 1954 to National Council of Social Research (NCSR). The NCSR was involved in research related to social welfare, excessive drinking, single mothers, female labour, child destitution, juvenile delinquency, divorce, housing conditions, religious life and leisure activities. Afrikaans and English academics both supported the NCSR because the state financed the research projects. The link between Afrikaner sociologists and policy was strengthened with the establishment of the HSRC in 1968.

A significant disagreement that developed between sociologists came to the fore in the 1960s with the establishment of the Suid-Afrikaanse Sosiologiese Vereniging (SASOV) and the launch of its official journal, the *South African Journal of Sociology*. In 1967, Professors Cilliers of SU, Wagner of Wits and Batson of UCT drafted a constitution for SASOV which they proposed at a meeting in Stellenbosch in 1967. The constitution provided for non-racial membership, but at the meeting it was proposed that membership should be limited to whites only. This limitation on membership was adopted by 20 votes for and seven against. In view of this, Cilliers, Wagner and Batson withdrew from the organisation, and other English-speaking sociologists in the liberal tradition followed them. It was the view of CD Roode of UFS that the decision was pragmatic, because a multiracial organisation by apartheid law would only have been allowed to exist as a 'correspondence association', defeating the purpose of a professional organisation (Grundlingh 1994: 54). However, this introduced a split among sociologists that broadened in the 1970s.

27.5 South African sociology in the 1970s

For South Africa, the 1970s started with the apartheid system well established. The leaders of the ANC and the PAC were jailed or exiled. The prime minister at the time, BJ Vorster, was tough on security matters and contributed to encapsulate apartheid into a security state, which was taken further by PW Botha at the end of the decade. Structural functionalism was well established in sociology at the Afrikaans universities with Afrikaans textbooks in use. SP Cilliers, D Joubert, AF Steyn and HCJ van Rensburg contributed to this theoretical perspective, but were not necessarily supportive of the regime of that time. Nevertheless, the challenge to apartheid was growing, especially through newly formed unions and their strike actions. At the English-speaking universities Marxism grew as a theoretical perspective that could best analyse the South African society where class and not race was viewed as the basic cause of social conflict within the South African society. South African sociologists in and outside South Africa contributed to this theorising, for instance R Turner, H Wolpe, S Marks, M Leggassick, E Webster, J Rex, F Johnstone and B Magubane.

On 1 July 1 1971, in contrast to SASOV, sociologists from South Africa, Mozambique, Angola, Rhodesia (Zimbabwe) and Malawi established an open sociological association, the Association for Sociology in Southern Africa (ASSA). This stemmed from a meeting held in Maputo, Mozambique, in June 1970. Initially this association's distinctiveness sprouted more from its regionalism than its non-racialism. ASSA soon developed into an academic forum for liberal and critical social scientists. It became a very active association with its own journal, the *South African Sociological Review*. Ally et al (2003: 90) argue that the side-by-side presence of SASOV and ASSA with their respective and opposed memberships, academic focus and political commitments, inaugurated a new phase for South African sociology. This division in South African sociology also accentuated the difference in subjects studied by the groups, the contrast in theoretical frameworks, as well as the divergent methodological approaches.

Within the tension of such a division, SASOV had to reconsider its view on racial separation. The exclusively white membership became such a controversial matter within the association that eventually the racial clause was dropped in 1977. However, SASOV was already severely stigmatised in its short history, therefore it was not an attractive association anymore to progressive sociologists.

On 25 April 1974, the apartheid regime was shaken by the coup in Lisbon, Portugal, which ended Portuguese rule over Angola and Mozambique. This was followed by the Soweto uprising, which erupted on 16 June 1976. Although it started with a peaceful demonstration, the police eventually acted aggressively, which led to the death of several students, one of which Hector Pietersen. As news of the deaths filtered through, the students turned angry and two whites were beaten to death in Soweto on that day. One of them was Dr Melville Leonard Edelstein, a sociologist who worked closely with many of the youth in Soweto. Ironically, he warned that the hostility of the township youth must be taken as a serious threat to peace in Soweto. His thesis in sociology, completed in 1971 at UP, was on 'An attitude survey of urban Bantu matric pupils in Soweto, with special reference to stereotyping and social distance: a sociological study'. In July 1996, his daughter, Janet Goldblatt, testified before the Truth and Reconciliation Commission that he had told her mother a week before his death that he had a bad feeling about the mood of the students.

As was the case with Edelstein, who was a consultant for the Bantu Administration, the apartheid administration presented sociologists with many job opportunities, especially for those supportive of the system. This became even more so with the 'independence' of the 'homelands' – Transkei 1976, Bophuthatswana 1977, Ciskei 1979 and Venda 1980. But simultaneously the apartheid regime introduced reformist measures, such as granting recognition to black unions in view of the Wiehahn and Riekert reports. This challenged the Marxists to rethink their theory. Sarakinsky (1994) described their repositioning as follows:

Marxists analysts analysed this shift by arguing that while apartheid had been functional for capitalism in the past, it was now dysfunctional. Advanced industrial capitalism needed a skilled, urban workforce that could not be found in sufficient numbers among whites and, consequently, the migrant labour, influx control, job reservation, and Bantu Education systems had become a hindrance, rather than a help, to further economic growth (Sarakinsky 1994: 298).

Informed by this Marxist analysis of South African sociology, the result was that this created the opportunity for critical sociology to develop in close relationship with organised labour.

Box 27.1 The role of sociologists in South Africa

In the text above, there is a reference to Dr Melville Leonard Edelstein who performed his duties for the discredited Bantu Administration and became a casualty in the Soweto uprising.

QUESTIONS

1. What is your view on the role that sociologists should play in society and in government?
2. Natural scientists can develop an atomic bomb. Sociology can contribute to an authoritarian regime.
3. How do you think sociologists can contribute constructively to present-day South Africa?

27.6 South African sociology in the 1980s

The 1980s started with Robert Mugabe taking over the Zimbabwean government on 17 April 1980, which brought the reality of black rule replacing white rule extremely close to South African society. ANC irregular soldiers also began to strike high-profile targets: the SASOL plant in 1980, the Voortrekkerhoogte military base in Pretoria in 1981, the Koeberg nuclear reactor near Cape Town in 1982, and the air force headquarters in Church Street, Pretoria in 1983. In September 1984, urban unrest erupted with riots in the Vaal Triangle, which escalated into a widespread rebellion until the middle of 1986. The tension accompanying this conflict also affected sociologists. In 1981 the office of the head of the sociology department at Unisa, FA Maritz, was destroyed by a bomb planted by members of the Wit Kommando, an extreme right-wing group. Maritz critiqued the South African society from a phenomenological viewpoint. Against this, attempts to intimidate or assassinate left-wing sociologists by security forces also occurred in the 1980s with a number of activists indeed being killed.

The 1980s was characterised by critical sociology infusing Marxism into public debates (Burawoy 2004: 22). The United Democratic Front (UDF) was launched on 20 August 1983 and Cosatu (a union of 33 unions) in December 1985. The civic movement also became increasingly active. This presented a perfect environment for public sociology on the basis of Marxist, neo-Marxist, labour studies and liberation sociology aimed at bringing about the end of apartheid. Within such diversity, these theoretical positions displayed internal tensions. A debate also prevailed between the positions of, on the one hand, intellectual autonomy (constructive critique from outside), and on the other hand, commitment (bound to organisation) – giving voice to the oppressed or to debate the struggle strategy among the intelligentsia (Burawoy 2004: 22). Especially at the Department of Sociology at the University of Western Cape (UWC), the internal streams became clear and the positions were debated heavily among the emerging black intelligentsia, such as W James, I Evans and Y Muthien (Sitas 1997: 15).

In the 1980s the ASSA conferences were a haven for these radical debates. Against liberal claims it was argued, for instance, that industrial capitalism would not undermine apartheid. Sitas wrote that the ASSA conferences 'attracted organic intellectuals from the trade unions, the UDF, the National Forum, the civics alongside academics from disciplines beyond sociology' (Sitas 1997: 15), but it is the view of Sekgobela that '[i]t can be argued that, although Marxist sociology was critical of other theoretical traditions in South Africa, it was not very reflexive or self-critical' (Sekgobela 1994: 48). Marxist sociology experienced theoretical cul-de-sacs towards the end of the 1980s.

It is important to note regarding the 1980s that it would be an oversimplification to say that at this stage South Africa had two sociologies – one supporting the apartheid regime and the other the anti-apartheid movement. The functionalists never were a homogeneous group in their support of apartheid. However, it is also important to note the development of a humanist sociology at Unisa. This form of a more phenomenological sociology emphasised society as a human construction and the importance of society as dialogue (Alant 1990: 43–71). This sociology played an important role in especially theorising development and also had followings at other universities. Although this sociology was mainly practised at Unisa, its influence cannot be undervalued in terms of preparing the theoretical ground for the negotiations of a new South Africa. Friedrichs (1990) viewed this sociology as very relevant for South Africa: 'Ideally, a humanist sociology plays a constructive role in bringing into existence a post-apartheid society which truly exemplifies traditional humanist principles' (Friedrichs 1990: 4). The 'miracle' of the new South Africa was to a large extent an embodiment of this humanistic sociology.

At the end of the 1980s, certain events occurred that impacted heavily on the next decade. In July 1987, Afrikaner academics and journalists met with the ANC in Dakar, Senegal. One of the leaders of this grouping was a former sociologist at SU and Wits, Van Zyl Slabbert. This opened up a channel for communication between South Africans outside the struggle and the ANC. The fall of the Berlin Wall on 9 November 1989, which was a catalyst for the fall of communism, presented the ruling regime in South Africa with more space for negotiating, but presented serious challenges to critical sociology.

Nevertheless, in general it can be stated that the 1980s were the heyday of South African sociology. This period was characterised by serious internal academic debates, deep involvement in society and a peak reached in the number of publications (see Sitas 1997: 16).

27.7 South African sociology in the 1990s

On 21 March 1990, Namibia became independent, which left South Africa as the last African country ruled by whites. In South Africa, the ANC and other political organisations were unbanned on 2 February 1990. Also in 1990, Michael Burawoy (2004) attended the ASSA congress and was much impressed by what he coined as **public sociology** in South Africa, but that was the surge of the 1980s overflowing into the 1990s. However, the tide was turning.

Simons and Wolpe contributed considerably to develop an original South African Marxism in exile. Simons died in July 1995 and Wolpe in January 1996 and along with this, so did important voices in liberation sociology. In addition, the collapse of communism and dissolution of the USSR presented South African Marxism with a fundamental political and theoretical challenge (Sekgobela 1994: 49). Marxism was also challenged by post-structuralism and postmodernism as competing sociological paradigms that were appealing to young sociologists. This also relates to Sitas' view that the collapse of the left hegemony internationally has shattered the confidence of what used to constitute an 'intellectual formation' (Sitas 1997: 16). But besides this dilemma of Marxism, the incoming government presented sociologists who supported the struggle with numerous employment opportunities after the first democratic election of 26 April 1994. This drained the sociology profession of prominent Marxists, further weakening this theoretical perspective in the discipline.

In this changing environment, the leadership of both SASOV and ASSA agreed that the position of sociologists in South Africa would be strengthened in a united association, thus SASOV and ASSA amalgamated in 1993 under the chairmanship of Van Zyl Slabbert to form the South African Sociological Association (SASA). From then on, SASA held annual congresses (see Table 27.1). To promote collaboration among sociologists, thematic working groups were established that organised sessions on the themes covered at the congresses. (For a list of thematic working groups, consult the SASA website – see http://www.sociology.africa/.)

The official journal of the South African Sociological Association was called *Society in Transition*. In 1999 a report, funded by the National Research Foundation (NRF), was compiled by Wits on the state of sociology in South Africa. This report proposed the revitalisation of SASA, the establishment of the journal as a premier one, the introduction of sociology into high schools, and the commissioning of a comprehensive history of the discipline in South Africa and of its state on the continent. Furthermore, the establishment of continent-wide networks, the promotion of excellence in theory and methods, as well as the creation of strong regional networks in South Africa were proposed, but SASA never really took it upon itself to deal with these proposals.

In the meantime, outside sociology a unique and totally new voice and understanding of South African society unfolded. This came about with the establishment of the Truth and Reconciliation Commission (TRC) in 1995 and its hearings held in the following years. The commission focused on human rights violations, rehabilitation, reparation and amnesty, and thereby presenting the South African society with a very crude mirror of its functioning, especially in the 1970s, the 1980s and the beginning of the 1990s. South African sociology's engagement with the commission was minimal, largely due to a lack of the human and material means to be involved. Postgraduate studies related to the commission's work were mainly comparative studies of reconciliation. The final TRC report was presented to President Mbeki on 21 March 2003.

Another challenge for sociology was the new government's challenging views on HIV/AIDS. Mbeki and the then minister of health, Nkosazana Dlamini-Zuma, and later Manto Tshabalala-Msimang, had deviating views on HIV/AIDS. Sociologists' sentiments were largely towards that of the Treatment Action Campaign (TAC), but its involvement in this regard was limited.

Sitas sums up the dilemma of sociology in the 1990s as follows:

> At a moment when a remarkable transition is underway with its transformation processes and struggles, with competing status groups and racial tensions, when one of the world's most acute laboratories of social experience is working itself out in front of us, we have lost the capacity to respond creatively. At a moment too, when the state priorities and its research agendas are favouring meeting the majority's basic needs, we look, despite our past, conceptually threadbare (Sitas 1997: 17).

Notwithstanding this situation, sociology still delivered a strong body of research and academic output in industrial, work and labour studies during the 1990s (Jubber 2007: 538).

27.8 South African sociology in the 2000s

In the 2000s the drastic restructuring of higher education impacted on sociology. A South African Qualifications Authority (SAQA) was created to develop an educational system that was more vocationally oriented. National Standards Bodies (NSBs) and Standards Generating Bodies (SGBs) were set up to approve the outcomes of universities and for SAQA to intervene and review the academic functioning of universities (Webster 2004: 35). After SASA had spent an inordinate amount of time in setting up an SBG, the SGBs were eventually 'jettisoned in favour of the flexibility of registering entire degrees as qualifications around which programmes can be devised' (Hendricks 2006: 93). Furthermore, a reorganising of the tertiary education system to overcome a racially divided system was announced in April 2002 and implemented shortly thereafter. In addition, the NRF's new individual rating system was introduced in 2002. Owing to different reasons, sociologists did not really engage with government with regard to these transformations. This is a pity, seeing that a great number of the transformations did not make academic sense.

In the beginning of the 2000s, sociologists were perplexed. Sociology had lost its impact. In 2003, Burawoy put this notion firmly on the table by opening the debate on how South African sociology could remain engaged in public issues. Burawoy sums up the challenge facing sociology as follows:

> We are witnessing the instrumentalisation of sociology, turning it away from an interrogation of ends to an obsession with means, often means of its own survival. The post-apartheid state sees itself as representing the general interest and it, therefore, sees sociology as an instrument in plans for national reconstruction. It has little patience for public and critical sociologies that articulate the disparate interests to be found in society. The assault on sociology becomes part of a broader offensive against an active society (Burawoy 2004: 25).

On the other hand, Cock (2006) is of the view that sociology should not become so public that it bypasses the state. She argued that the state cannot be bypassed as Burawoy seems to do. 'Many of our most progressive social thinkers,' she suggested, 'do this by exaggerating the transformative capacity and emancipatory potential of "grassroots globalisation" or "globalisation-from-below". In much of this writing there is an implicit suspicion of the state as a threat, as a source of authoritarian, impersonal, bureaucratic power.' But, she argued, 'we need to leverage the state to access resources and rights as in post-apartheid South Africa only the democratic state can meet the needs of the impoverished majority' (Cock, Hassim & Webster 2004: 331). But this debate occurred against the background of the deterioration of service delivery by the state and of civil society becoming increasingly disappointed and upset. In practice, sociology's engagement with this deterioration in the 2000s was very limited.

In 2005 the official name of SASA's journal was changed to the *South African Review of Sociology*. At this time a local organising committee of SASA had the responsibility of organising the XVI ISA World Congress of Sociology 2006. The congress, presented from 23 to 29 July in Durban, was well attended. However, the greatest benefit that SASA obtained from it was the funding by the NRF of 72 South African postgraduate students in sociology to attend the congress. This was an excellent investment in the future of sociology in South Africa and the continuing interest of these young scholars in sociology became clear at the following SASA congresses. Another important initiative of 2006 was the establishment of a well-maintained SASA website. For more information visit http://www.sociology.africa/.

The NRF agreed in 2006 to fund on behalf of sociology a national workshop entitled 'SASA-NRF Workshop on Research and Teaching in Sociology'. This workshop was presented at the Birchwood Conference Centre outside Johannesburg from 14–15 October 2006. Delegates from nearly all sociology departments in the country attended. At the workshop:

The heads of department focused attention on publishing, organisational culture, the interface between academic and policy work, the role of coursework and funding in higher degrees, and the possibility of organising a winter school for doctoral students. Junior academics were concerned about work overloads and the way this inhibited development, problems of getting published and the need for mentorship, job security and incentives to stay in academia and inability to influence research foci.

Students also spoke about publishing and mentorship and they raised problems associated with accessing funding, retention of senior students, marketing, and the need for exposure to different career possibilities. The senior researchers wanted the following to be discussed: defining and defending the discipline, reproducing the next generation of sociologists, career pathing and the balance between teaching and research, restructuring of higher education, and physical space (SASA 2007: 7).

To build on the enthusiasm generated by the National Workshop, the NRF was requested to fund additional activities. The NRF agreed, and on 1 March 2007 a one-day workshop for senior sociologists was held, sharing experience with supervision and assessment of dissertations. A doctoral students' workshop was also held before the 2007 SASA congress for nine students. This became an integral part of many of the following SASA congresses.

The SASA president was also tasked to visit all sociology departments to give attention specifically to some of the matters identified in the National Workshop. Zaaiman, the then president, accepted the challenge. From 22 February to 19 June 2007 he visited 26 campuses at 18 universities. In his report covering the tour, he reported the views he found among sociologists as follows (Zaaiman 2007):

1. **Views on the body of sociological knowledge:** In general, sociologists viewed the sociological body of knowledge as excellent and comprehensive, and able to contribute directly to the intellectual development of students. It could also assist in improving society, but it seems that this body is currently out of tune with the current thinking in the state. However, sociology can be relevant and occupational through courses and postgraduate programmes in gender studies, industrial sociology, group dynamics, environmental issues, population studies, diversity studies, HIV/AIDS studies and medical sociology.

2. **Views on sociological research:** Sociology in South Africa must improve its quality of work; it must unleash a creative output and contribute to global sociology. A more local sociology must be developed without being parochial. However, the perennial problem is balancing research, teaching and administration. The NRF received a number of accusations. It was said that the NRF is race orientated, it does not have money available for universities without a research culture, that rating implies a lot of financial administration and that

the application process of the NRF is focused on risk rating rather than on the evaluation of research ability.

3. **Views on textbooks:** A general need was expressed for textbooks related to South African problems.

4. **Views on staff:** It was clear that universities in the rural areas had problems in recruiting and retaining staff. Teaching overload was also a general problem for sociologists that contributed to a low research output and to staff who struggle to attain higher degrees.

5. **Views on teaching:** Lecturers were concerned with how ignorant students were of sociology. Furthermore, lecturers were alarmed by the academic culture and ethos of students and that they viewed themselves as clients with a right to pass. Students' writing skills were also lacking.

6. **Views on SASA:** It was clear that there exists a need for SASA to do more with regard to networking and empowerment. The networking must overcome the fragmentation of sociology in South Africa, especially between weaker and stronger departments, and established and emerging sociologists. SASA must also empower the young – especially black – upcoming sociologists. SASA must also present yearly congresses of high quality to be attended by academics and sociologists in private practice. SASA must also market sociology, have more public engagement and make public statements.

7. **Views on the professionalisation of sociology:** Conflicting responses were received regarding the professionalisation of South African sociology. Those in favour of professionalisation ascribed the poor state of sociology to the fact that sociology does not have

a professional body. Against this, it seems that most sociologists were of the view that SASA ought not and cannot be professionalised. It should rather perform benchmarking among departments.

8. **Views on inequality between universities:** Challenging responses came from sociologists at the periphery/rural/teaching universities. In contrast to the city universities, they indicated that their universities were the last resort for students. They do not publish, do not have contact with practitioners on the outside, cannot attract overseas scholars and their resources are unsatisfactory.

These findings presented the subsequent SASA councils with a clear agenda to work on. With the remainder of the NRF funding, prizes were introduced for the best student papers at the 2008 congress. This became an integral part of the SASA congresses.

27.9 Current situation and conclusion

South African sociology faced serious changes and challenges since its establishment in this country. Currently, sociology is still faced with a number of challenges of which many are related to issues it had to deal with in the last decades.

With regard to the students, sociology has to deal with a great number of students who are career orientated and also with a limited number of students following postgraduate studies. However, sociology is a popular subject in programmes, which leads to substantial numbers of enrolments at first year level and to some extent at second year level.

Case study 27.1 The role of sociology in South Africa

In China the study of sociology was banned from 1952 until 1979, seeing that it was viewed as a bourgeois pseudo-science. In the Union of Soviet Socialist Republics, only Marxist sociology was allowed from the 1930s until 1966. In contrast, in South Africa the apartheid regime banned or restricted Marxist literature from the 1960s until 1990. Authoritarian governments tend to view sociological critique as dangerous or irrelevant to the state.

Sources: Wikipedia nd(a); nd(b)

QUESTION

What do you think ought to be the engagement of SASA with the current government in South Africa?

Currently, sociology in South Africa is experiencing a satisfactory level of cooperation. This stems from devoted sociologists participating in an active and vibrant society

(see, for instance, Table 27.1 listing SASA's congresses). The cooperation includes functional and dedicated councils, annual congresses, and a strong and respected journal.

From the congress papers and journal articles it is clear that sociology in South Africa is deeply involved in the issues that affect the functioning of South Africa today. Examples of these research topics are among others related to gender, migration, land, women and sexualities issues. Sociology also has a long tradition of studying labour relations. Currently sociology is a much-needed discipline in South Africa to make sense of and guide society in understanding and dealing with the current state of inequality, racism and patriarchy, as well as disillusionment and frustration with transformation. It must research the people of South Africa in such a way so as to give a voice to people by expressing their experiences and interpretations, and so contribute to self-understanding and self-recognition. Currently the debate on what the Africanisation of sociology entails is ongoing.

Table 27.1 SASA Congresses 1993–2019

1993	SASA founded through the merger of ASSA and SASOV, University of the Witwatersrand, Johannesburg, January 1993 (president elected: Johann Groenewald, University of Pretoria)
1993	First SASA congress, University of Pretoria, Pretoria, June 1993 (president elected: Johann Groenewald, University of Pretoria)
1994	The election and social transformation, University of Natal, Pietermaritzburg, 3–6 July 1994 (president elected: Johann Maree, University of Cape Town)
1995	Towards social reconstruction in a fragmented society, Rhodes University, Grahamstown, 9–13 July 1995 (president elected: Johann Maree, University of Cape Town)
1996	Southern Africa in global context, University of Natal, Durban, 7–11 July 1996 (president elected: Ari Sitas, University of Natal)
1997	Beyond Afro-pessimism: identity and development in an era of globalisation, University of Transkei, Umtata (president elected: Ari Sitas, University of Natal)
1998	Inequality and diversity: learning to change and the social sciences, Rand Afrikaans University, Johannesburg, 30 June–3 July 1998 (president elected: Dasarath Chetty, University of Durban-Westville)
1999	Securing South Africa's future, Military Academy, Saldanha, 8 July 1999 (president elected: Dasarath Chetty, University of Durban-Westville)
2000	Restructuring the institutions of South Africa for the new millennium, University of the Western Cape, Bellville, 2–5 July 2000 (president elected: Fred Hendricks, Rhodes University)
2001	Globalisation, inequality and identity, Unisa, Pretoria, 1–4 July 2001 (president elected: Fred Hendricks, Rhodes University)
2002	Citizenship, living rights and the public intellectual, Regent Hotel, East London, 30 June–3 July 2002 (president elected: Tina Uys, Rand Afrikaans University)
2003	Resistance and Reconstruction, University of Natal, Durban, 29 June–2 July 2003 (president elected: Tina Uys, Rand Afrikaans University)
2004	Ten years into democracy: challenges facing South Africa, University of Free State, Bloemfontein, 27–30 June 2004 (president elected: Jimi Adesina, Rhodes University)
2005	The renewal of sociology in South Africa, University of Limpopo, Polokwane, 26–29 June 2005 (president elected: Jimi Adesina, Rhodes University)
2006	The quality of social existence in a globalising world, SASA hosted the International Sociological Association in Durban, 23–28 July 2006 (president elected: Johan Zaaiman, North-West University)
2007	Sociology and social reconstruction in South Africa, North West University, Potchefstroom, 25–28 June 2007 (president elected: Simon Mapadimeng, University of KwaZulu-Natal)
2008	Society, power and the environment: challenges for the 21st century, Stellenbosch University, Stellenbosch, 7–10 July 2008 (president elected: Simon Mapadimeng, University of KwaZulu-Natal)

⇒

2009	Making sense of borders: identity, citizenship and power in comparative perspective. University of the Witwatersrand, Johannesburg, 28 June–2 July 2009 (president elected: Wilson Akpan, University of Fort Hare)
2010	Sport, leisure and development in the 21st century: opportunities and challenges. Fort Hare University, East London, 13–16 June 2010 (president elected: Wilson Akpan, University of Fort Hare)
2011	Gender in question: rights, representation and substantive freedom, University of Pretoria, Pretoria, 10–13 July 2011 (president elected: Freek Cronjé, North West University).
2012	Knowledge, technologies and social change, University of Cape Town, Cape Town, 1–4 July 2012 (president elected: Freek Cronjé, North West University)
2013	Doing sociology from the periphery: place, power and knowledge, Unisa, Pretoria, 30 June–3 July 2013 (president elected: Irma du Plessis, University of Pretoria)
2014	The point of critique: knowledge, society and the state in South Africa after 20 years of democracy, Nelson Mandela Metropolitan University, Port Elizabeth, 6–8 July 2014 (president elected: Irma du Plessis)
2015	Contours of violence: manifestations, interventions and social justice, University of Johannesburg, Johannesburg, 28 June–1 July 2015 (president elected: Grace Khunou)
2016	Higher education: power, practices and discourses, Rhodes University, 26–29 June 2016 (president elected: Sonwabile Mnwana)
2017	#WhatMustRise: critical sociological reflections on contemporary protest movements, North West University – Mafikeng Campus, 2–5 July 2017 (president elected: Babalwa Magoqwana)
2018	Navigating uncertainty: (re)situating and (re)imagining sociological knowledge within the context of contemporary South Africa, Africa, and the global South, University of the Western Cape, 1–4 July 2018 (president elected: Babalwa Magoqwana)
2019	Work, life & society: meanings, manifestations and trajectories of the Fourth Industrial Revolution in Africa, Pretoria, 15–17 July (president elected: Trevor Ngwane)

(Sources: SASA nd(a); nd(b))

SASA developed partnerships with the sociological associations of the other BRICS countries (Brazil, Russia, India and China). Joint projects on social themes had been identified, for example, on stratification, justice, inequality, youth and development. The aim is that this international collaboration on the sociological themes will produce publications. SASA also made a special effort to ensure participation from African sociologists at its congresses and had some success with this.

Sociology has the potential to make an important contribution to informing government policies and programmes. The sociology profession can learn from its history in South Africa that it is important to maintain a critical distance, but by doing this its recommendations can become less attractive to government. However, herein lies the continuous challenge for sociology not only in South Africa, but in all countries. In addition, it is important for sociology to be accessible to the public and supportive of social processes to ensure a vitalised civic society.

Summary

This chapter provided an overview of the successive stages in the development of sociology in South Africa, focusing on the discipline as an institutionalised science. In this chapter you dealt with the following aspects.

- The early introduction of sociology into the higher education institutions, as well as the first sociological themes to be presented
- How ideological engagement and political transition led to an institutional presence of sociology and the division between viewpoints on sociology as a service discipline and scientific analysis
- How the implementation of the apartheid ideology and black resistance to the policy contributed to sociology establishing its own independence as an academic discipline
- The divisions in institutional sociology, related to ideological positioning toward the state and capital, and based on opposing theoretical frameworks and different methods for the study of contemporary social issues
- The emergence of research institutions and NGOs, which helped to establish platforms of social research independent from the academia

- Strategic geo-political transitions in the rest of southern Africa and the spill-over of internal upheaval leading to the forming of social movements and the further strengthening of Marxist critical thought
- The new phase of South African sociology introduced by the side-by-side presence of opposing bodies of knowledge: SASOV and ASSA, accentuating the contrasting viewpoints and methodologies
- Repositioning of institutionalised sociology following the transition to a new and democratically elected government in South Africa with new challenges to sociology, leading to the unification of the two sociological associations to form SASA
- Restructuring of higher education and the reorganising of the tertiary landscape resulting in a new voicing for sociology: critically informing government on social issues without being co-opted into broader policy frameworks
- The deficiencies as well as the challenges for the institutional sociology in academia – regarding the different aspects of the discipline countrywide
- The initiatives of the national association (SASA) to engage in relevant internal social issues and the drive outward to develop new partnerships globally.

ARE YOU ON TRACK?

1. How did the initiatives of academic congresses lead to the introduction of sociology in the academia?
2. Which social and political factors led to establishing an institutional presence of sociology – and what did this 'presence' imply?
3. Sociology first dovetailed with social work to be presented as a service discipline due to the close link with government's internal policies. Do you agree? Motivate your answer.
4. In what sense did the full-scale implementation of the apartheid policy impact on sociology as institutional science? Provide two examples.
5. Would it be fair to say that South Africa had two sociologies in the 1980s: Afrikaans-speaking against English-medium sociologists? Why/why not?
6. After the transition to a new democratic dispensation, how would you describe the dualistic relationship of sociology towards government by using the terms 'critical' and 'contribute'? Provide two examples.
7. How does SASA provide a global dimension to South African institutionalised sociology?
8. Randomly choose three SASA congresses of which the theme appeals to you – and give a reason why.

References

Alant C (ed). 1990. *Sociology and Society. A Humanist Profile*. Johannesburg: Southern Book Publishers.

Alexander P, Basson L, Makhura P. 2006. 'Sociology research in contemporary South Africa'. *South African Review of Sociology*, 37(2): 218–240.

Ally S, Mooney K, Stewart P. 2003. 'The state-sponsored and centralised institutionalisation of an academic discipline: Sociology in South Africa, 1920–1970'. *Society in Transition*, 34(1): 70–103.

Botes LJS, Van Rensburg HCJ, Groenewald DC. 1991. 'Reply to Van Staden and Visser: Perhaps something more and something else happened in the SAJS of the 1980s'. *South African Journal of Sociology*, 2(22): 50–52.

Burawoy M. 2004. 'Public sociology: South African dilemmas in a global context'. *Society in Transition*, 35(1): 11–26.

Cock J. 2006. 'Public sociology and the social crisis'. *South African Review of Sociology*, 37(2): 293–307.

Cock J, Hassim S, Webster E. 2004. 'Sociological dilemmas in a local context'. *Society in Transition*, 35(2): 328–333.

Cooper D. 2006. 'International restructuring of higher education: Comments on implications of global trends, for restructuring of Sociology in South Africa'. *South African Review of Sociology*, 37(2): 260–292.

Friedrichs DO. 1990. 'A brief introduction to humanist sociology and its relevance for South Africa' in *Sociology and Society: A Humanist Profile*. Alant C (ed). Johannesburg: Southern Book Publishers.

Groenewald CJ. 1984. 'Die Institusionalisering van die Sosiologie in Suid-Afrika' (The Institutionalisation of Sociology in South Africa). Unpublished DPhil thesis, Stellenbosch.

Grundlingh A. 1994. 'Structures for sociologists: A historical perspective on the associations for sociologists in South Africa (1967–1991)' in *Social Theory*. Romm N, Sarakinsky M (eds). Johannesburg: Lexicon Publishers.

Hendricks F. 2006. 'The rise and fall of South African sociology'. *African Sociological Review*, 10(1): 86–97.

Jubber K. 1983. 'Sociology and its social context: The case of the rise of Marxist sociology in South Africa'. *Social Dynamics*, 9(2): 50–63.

Jubber K. 2007. 'Sociology in South Africa. A brief historical review of research and publishing'. *International Sociology*, 22(5): 527–546.

Maritz FA. 1984. 'Fenomenologiese sosiologie en die Suid-Afrikaanse samelewing' (Phenomenological sociology and the South African society). *South African Journal of Sociology*, 15(1): 56–59.

Oloyede O. 2006. 'Sociology cognitia: A note on recent concerns in sociology in South Africa'. *South African Review of Sociology*, 37(2): 343–355.

Rex J. 1975. 'The sociology of South Africa: A review article'. *Journal of Southern African Studies*, 1(2): 247–252.

Romm N, Sarakinsky M. 1994. *Social Theory*. Johannesburg: Lexicon Publishers.

Sarakinsky M. 1994. 'Marxist analysis of South Africa: An application of the base/superstructure model' in *Social Theory*. Romm N, Sarakinsky M (eds). Johannesburg: Lexicon Publishers.

Sekgobela E. 1994. 'A relevant sociology for South Africa' in *Social Theory*. Romm N, Sarakinsky M (eds). Johannesburg: Lexicon Publishers, 40–51.

Sitas A. 1997. 'The waning of sociology in South Africa'. *Society in Transition*, 1(4): 12–19.

SASA. 2007. 'Stimulating sociology'. Report of the task team appointed by a national workshop of sociologists. Available at: http://www.sociology.africa/.

SASA. nd(a). 'Past conferences'. [Online] Available at: http://www.sasaonline.org.za/past-conferences.html [Accessed 12 August 2013].

SASA. nd(b). 'Past councils'. [Online]. Available at: http://www.sociology.africa/ [Accessed 12 August 2013].

Uys T. 2005. 'Tradition, ambition and imagination: Challenges and choices for post-apartheid sociology'. *Society in Transition*, 36(1): 113–120.

Van Rensburg HCJ. 1989. 'Sosiologie in Suid-Afrika: Profiel van die huidige' (Sociology in South Africa: Profile of the present). *South African Journal of Sociology*, 20(2): 80–98.

Van Staden F, Visser D. 1991. '*The South African Journal of Sociology* during the eighties: An analysis of theoretical and empirical contributions'. *South African Journal of Sociology*, 2(22): 33–43.

Webster E. 2004. 'Sociology in South Africa: Its past, present and future'. *Society in Transition*, 35(1): 27–41.

Webster EC. 2001. 'Evaluating research performance: The need for a developmental approach in sociology'. SWOP, University of Witwatersrand. Unpublished report, 28–42.

Wikipedia. nd(a). 'Sociology in China'. [Online] Available at: http://en.wikipedia.org/wiki/sociology_in_China [Accessed 12 August 2013].

Wikipedia. nd(b). 'Suppressed research in the Soviet Union'. [Online] Available at: http://en.wikipedia.org/wiki/suppressed_research_in_the_Soviet_Union [Accessed 12 August 2013].

Zaaiman J. 2007. 'Report on visits to sociology departments (presidential address)'. *Congress of the South African Sociological Association*, Potchefstroom: 25–28 June.

Index

References to figures, tables, etc are in *italics*.

D

deaths *see* mortality

decolonial imaginations xxi, 41, 521, 524

decolonial theory 40, 293

decolonisation 33, 39, 41 *see also* postcolonialism

of curriculum 298–299

of knowledge 40

delinquency *see* crime

demography *see* population

dependency theory 91–94

deviance

conflict theory 552–553

definition 546–547

delinquent sub-culture 550

individuals 548

interactionist theories 553–554

social functions of 547–548

societal 554

sub-cultural theories 550–552

underclass sub-culture 551–552

working class sub-culture 551

digital technologies *see* media and technology

disabilities

and domestic violence 275–276

social model 452

discrimination, constitutional rights 181

disease *see* health and disease

division of labour 20

divorce 273

Doctors Without Borders/Médecins Sans Frontières (MSF) 452

domestic violence

child abuse 274, 276

coercion and control 274

and disabilities 275–276

economic control and material deprivation 274

elder abuse 277

gender violence 275–276

homosexual relationships 276

intimate partner violence (IPV) 275, 276

male victims 276

marital rape 274

perpetrators 275

physical violence 274

sexual violence 274

theoretical approaches 274–275, *274*

victims 275

Du Bois, WEB

double consciousness 35, 214

race 214

Durkheim, Emile xxxi, 22–27

anomie 25, 32, 84, 548, 550

collective conscience 26

collective effervescence 475, 478

cult of the individual 25

division of labour 24

education 284–285

functionalism and structuralism 24

homo duplex 25–26, 35

mechanical solidarity 24, 335

modernity 34

normative framework of society 26

norms and morality 25

order and social conflict 25, 503

organic solidarity 24, 336

pluralism 388–391, 431–432

positivism 22–23, 55

poverty 523

religion 26, 310, 319, 320

secularisation 316

social change 83–84

social cohesion xviii, 23–24, 83

social facts 22–23, 25

social stratification 503

sociology as science 12, 34

structural functionalism in media 426

structural functionalism in religion 320

suicide 23

E

economy

Accelerated and Shared Growth Initiative for South Africa (AsgiSA) 102, 538

black capitalism 365–367

black economic empowerment 102, 218, 219, 365–366, 372, 385, 512, 517, 524–525

black middle class 246, 366, 506–507, 533

capital controls 372

capital outflow 368–369, 553

commodification 337

cooperatives 363, 372

decreasing employment 370–371

de-industrialisation 361–362

deregulation 364

digital 348

domestic work 356

effects of neo-liberal policy 367–371

relationship with class and economics 216–219

relationship with class post-apartheid 218–219

relationship with identity and culture 224–227

relationship with identity in South Africa 225–226

relationship with identity post-apartheid 227

relationship with power post-apartheid 224

relationship with state and resistance 219–224

settlers and indigenous peoples 221–222

slavery and colonialism 216–217

slavery and emancipation 220

slavery as stratification system 504

and social class 216–219

social construction 207

The Spear (painting) 225

and sport 490

struggle for equality in South Africa 223

triple jeopardy/oppression with gender and class 159, 171, 266

radical elitism 391–393, 395 see also Mills, C Wright

rainbow nation xxiv, 154, 227, 312–313, 387, 432

rationalisation 30, 75

RDP see Reconstruction and Development Programme (RDP)

realist perspective 55–56

Reason xxv–xxvi, xxvii

Reconstruction and Development Programme (RDP) 101, 363, 384–385, 526

reflexivity 11, 147

religion

and capitalism 30–31

caste 308

churches 309, 324–325

civil 309–310, 312–313

conflict perspective 322–323

cults 325, 325–326

as cultural resource 315

in current society 314–315

definitions 311–314

denominations 310, 325

diversity 305, 308–310

economy of 324

elements of 326–327

and families 321

freedom of 308

as functional system 320–321

fundamentalism 314, 318–319

and globalisation 318

indigenous beliefs 308

and inequality 315–316, 327

initiation 311

interpretive perspective 323–324

introduction through immigration 308

justification for apartheid 310

marginality 315

missionary activities 308–309

and morality 314–315, 321

moral propositions 327

organisation of 324–328

participation 327

primary force of social cohesion 26

rainbow nation 312–313

and rationality 317

religiosity 327–328

resacralisation 318

rites of passage 311

rituals 305, 308

as sacred substance 312, 326–327

sects 315, 325

secularisation debate 316–318

and social change 315, 319

social location 319

and society 313–319

sociological approach to 310–314, 319–324

and stress 320

structural functionalist perspective 320

tension between different religions 309

totemism 320

research

action 52

data collection 53

descriptive and explanatory 62

design 52–53

ethics 61–62

innovative 48–49

knowledge claims 54–55

link between methodologies and problems 56–57

methodologies and data gathering methods 57–59

mixed methods 52, 59

plagiarism 62

primary and applied 62

problem statement 51

qualitative 52, 58–59

quantitative 52, 57–58

realist perspective 50

reliability 51

results 53

role of sociological theory 53–54

sampling 59–60

green economy 604, 621, 623
meaning of development 602, 622
and population 132
and rural development 604
sustainability 621–622
uneven development 623
Sustainable Development Goals 622
mortality 127, 128, 456
poverty reduction 524
symbol, definition 71
symbolic capital 515
symbolic interactionism 36
culture 70–71
education 286, 294
health and disease 458
identity 143
sexuality 199
sport 483
symbolic systems 71

T

Taylor, Frederick Winslow 341
theory
concepts 5, 6
consensus 17
criterion of simplicity 6
exploitation 18
functionalist 17
origin and meaning of 5–12
power of 8
predictions 7–8
Thompson, EP 243
Tönnies, Ferdinand, community and society 577, 579
trade unions
black 100–101, 248, 291, 343, 348, 369, 646
and class 238
environmental justice 616
flexible workers 344
Fordism 343
industrial society 336, 342
labour process 348
public sector workers 345
and race 219
role in economy 369
social movement unionism 347–348, 402
tripartite alliance 219, 359, 366, 386
use of sociologists 4
Wiehahn Commission 369
traditional healing see also health and disease

African traditional healthcare 464–466
African views on disease causation 464–465
culture-related syndromes 465
diviners 465
faith healers/prophets 466
herbalists 465–466
legitimisation and professionalisation 466
naturalistic causation of illness 464
personalistic explanations of disease 464–465
traditional treatment 465
traditional leaders
authority 81
rural areas 598, 601
Treatment Action Campaign (TAC) 416
case study 400

U

ubuntu 25, 617
Ukweshwana 69
ulwaloko see initiation
Ulyanov, Vladimir Ilyich see Lenin
unemployment see also work
causes of 361, 362
and individual identity 334
informal economy 362
neoliberal economic strategy 370
social consequence 372
and social inequality 362
and socialisation 150
urbanisation 553
in Africa 567
agricultural workers 371
during apartheid 131, 564
collapse of native reserves 640
Comprehensive Plan for Sustainable Human Settlements 573–574
concepts 563–565
conurbation 561, 564, 567
under democracy 601
economic implications 571–572
effect on families 580
factors affecting 564–565
gentrification 564, 572–573
globalisation 570
great social transformation 576–577, 578, 580
growth rate 563
historical overview 565
hybrid nature of urban life 580–581
and identity 578–579